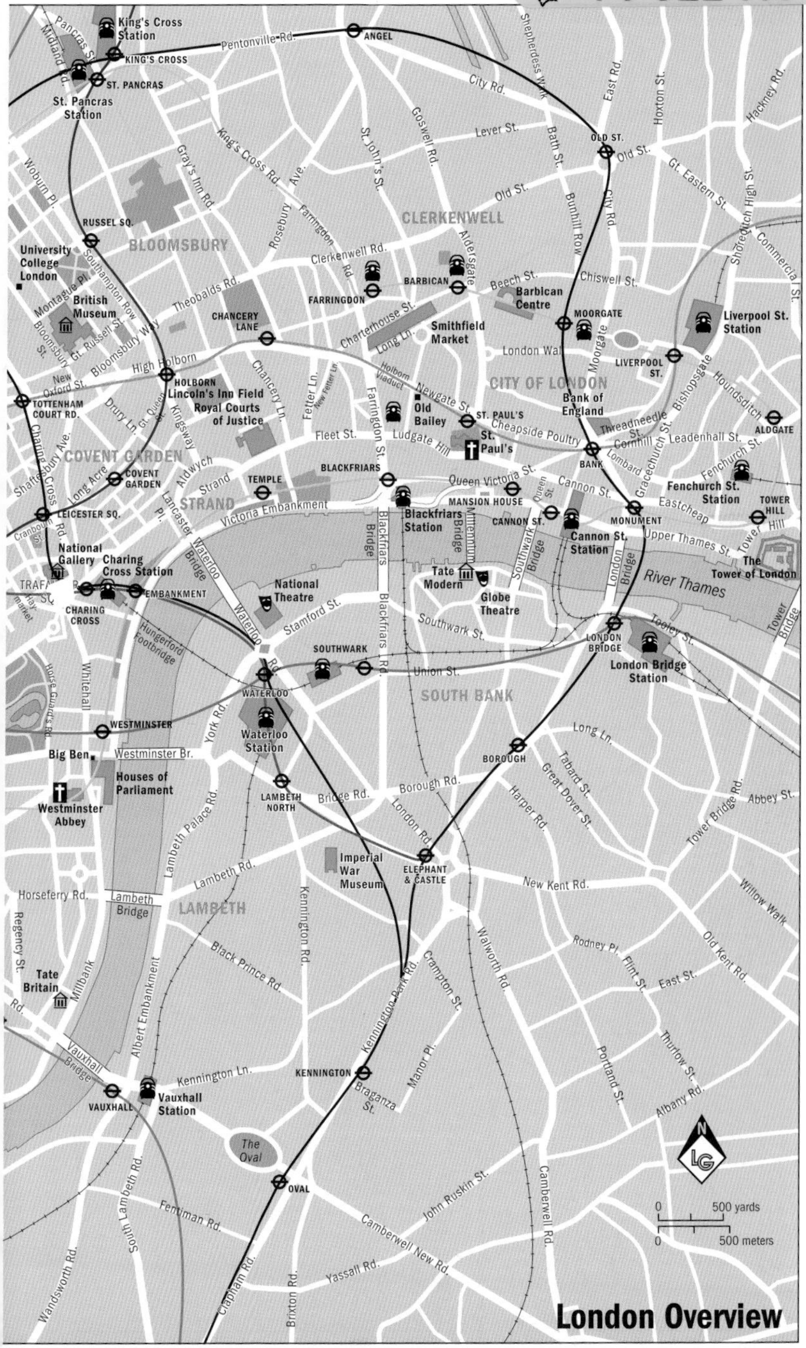

London Overview

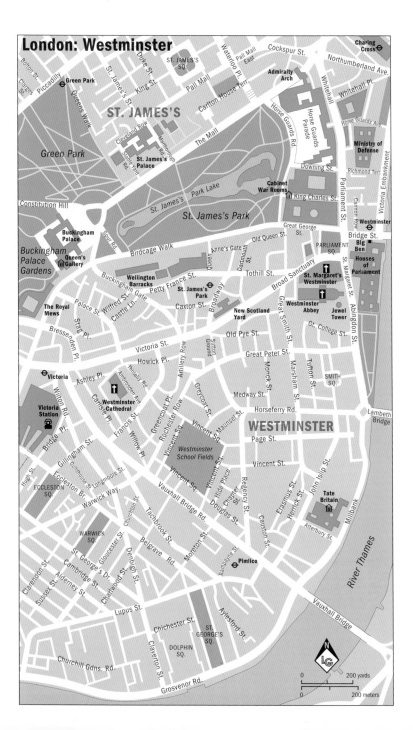

London: Westminster

Bolton St.
Clarges St.
Piccadilly
Green Park
St. James's St.
Queen's Walk
King St.
Duke St.
ST. JAMES'S SQ.
Pall Mall East
Waterloo Pl.
Cockspur St.
Charing Cross
Northumberland Ave.
Admiralty Arch
Whitehall
Whitehall Pl.
Carlton House Terr.
Pall Mall
Horse Guards Rd.
Horse Guards Parade
Horse Guards Ave.
Ministry of Defense
Richmond Terr.
ST. JAMES'S
Cleveland Row
Marlborough Rd.
Stable Yd.
St. James's Palace
The Mall
Downing St.
Green Park
St. James's Park Lake
St. James's Park
Cabinet War Rooms
King Charles St.
Parliament St.
Cannon Row
Victoria Embankment
Westminster
Constitution Hill
Buckingham Palace
Spur Rd.
Birdcage Walk
Anne's Gate
Old Queen St.
Great George St.
PARLIAMENT SQ.
Bridge St.
Big Ben
Buckingham Palace Gardens
Queen's Gallery
Buckingham Gate
Wellington Barracks
Petty France St.
St. James's Park
Dartmouth St.
Tothill St.
Queen Anne's Gate
Broad Sanctuary
St. Margaret's Westminster
St. Margaret St.
Houses of Parliament
The Royal Mews
Palace St.
Wilfred St.
Castle Ln.
Caxton St.
Broadway
New Scotland Yard
Great Smith St.
Westminster Abbey
Jewel Tower
Abingdon St.
Stag Pl.
Bressenden Pl.
Victoria St.
Old Pye St.
Gt. College St.
Howick Pl.
Artillery Row
Sutton Ground
Great Peter St.
Monck St.
Marsham St.
Tufton St.
Victoria
Ashley Pl.
Thirleby Rd.
Ambrosden Ave.
Medway St.
SMITH SQ.
Wilton Rd.
Carlisle Pl.
Westminster Cathedral
Greycoat St.
Horseferry Rd.
Lambeth Bridge
Victoria Station
Bridge Pl.
Francis St.
Willow Pl.
Greencoat Pl.
Rochester Row
Vincent Sq.
Mansel St.
WESTMINSTER
Gillingham St.
Churchwood St.
Vincent Sq.
Westminster School Fields
Vincent Sq.
Page St.
High St.
Eccleston Br.
Grundingham St.
Longmoore St.
Vauxhall Bridge Rd.
Hide Place
Regency St.
Vincent St.
Erasmus St.
Herrick St.
John Islip St.
ECCLESTON SQ.
Warwick Way
Tachbrook St.
Charter St.
Douglas St.
Causton St.
Tate Britain
WARWICK SQ.
St. George's Dr.
Gloucester St.
Denbigh St.
Belgrave Rd.
Moreton St.
Atterbury St.
Millbank
Clarendon St.
Cambridge St.
Alderney St.
Charlwood St.
Rampayne St.
Pimlico
River Thames
Sussex St.
Lupus St.
Chichester St.
Aylesford St.
Vauxhall Bridge
Churchill Gdns. Rd.
Claverton St.
DOLPHIN SQ.
ST. GEORGE'S SQ.
Grosvenor Rd.

N
LG

0   200 yards
0   200 meters

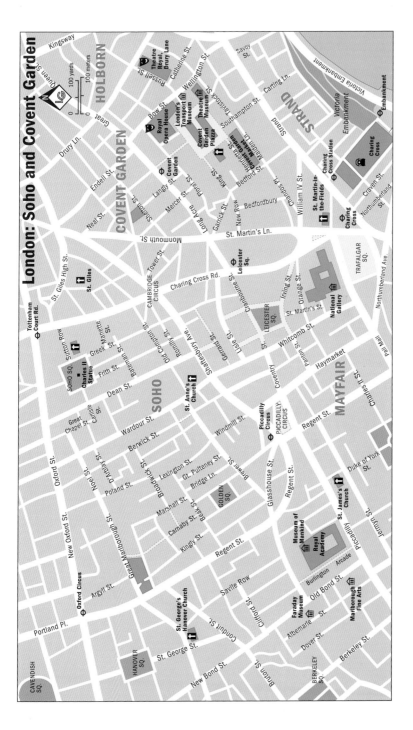

London: Soho and Covent Garden

Kingsway

HOLBORN

Queen St.

Great

0   100 yards
0   100 meters

Theatre Royal, Drury Lane

Russell St.

Catherine St.

Wellington St.

Savoy St.

Carting Ln.

Victoria Embankment

Embankment

Drury Ln.

COVENT GARDEN

Bow St.

Royal Opera House

London's Transport Museum

Theatre Museum

Covent Garden Piazza

Tavistock St.

Southampton St.

STRAND

Strand

Charing Cross Station

Charing Cross

Endell St.

Covent Garden

Langly St.

Floral St.

King St.

Henrietta St.

Jubilee Market

Maiden Ln.

Bedford St.

Bedfordbury

Chandos Pl.

William IV St.

St. Martin-in-the-Fields

Charing Cross

Craven St.

Northumberland

Neal St.

Mercer St.

Shelton St.

Long Acre

Garrick St.

New Row

St. Martin's Ln.

Monmouth St.

St. Giles High St.

St. Giles

CAMBRIDGE CIRCUS

Tower St.

Charing Cross Rd.

Leicester Sq.

Cranbourne St.

Irving St.

Orange St.

St. Martin's St.

National Gallery

TRAFALGAR SQ.

Northumberland Ave.

Tottenham Court Rd.

Sutton Row

Greek St.

Manette St.

St.

Old Compton St.

Romilly St.

Shaftesbury Ave.

Gerrard St.

Lisle St.

LEICESTER SQ.

Whitcomb St.

Panton St.

Haymarket

MAYFAIR

Charles II St.

Pall Mall

SOHO SQ.

Charles II Statue

Frith St.

Bateman St.

Dean St.

SOHO

St. Anne's Church

Coventry

Piccadilly Circus

PICCADILLY CIRCUS

Regent St.

Great Chapel St.

Carlisle St.

Wardour St.

Berwick St.

Windmill St.

Brewer St.

Glasshouse St.

Oxford St.

Noel St.

D'Arblay St.

Poland St.

Lexington St.

Gt. Pulteney St.

Bridge Ln.

Regent St.

Duke of York St.

Jermyn St.

St. James's Church

New Oxford St.

Great Marlborough St.

Broadwick St.

Marshall St.

Carnaby St.

Beak St.

Kingly St.

GOLDEN SQ.

Regent St.

Museum of Mankind

Royal Academy

Burlington Arcade

Old Bond St.

Piccadilly

Oxford Circus

Argyll St.

Savile Row

Clifford St.

Conduit St.

St. George's Hanover Church

St. George St.

Faraday Museum

Albemarle St.

Marlborough Fine Arts

Portland Pl.

CAVENDISH SQ.

HANOVER SQ.

New Bond St.

Bruton St.

Dover St.

BERKELEY SQ.

Berkeley St.

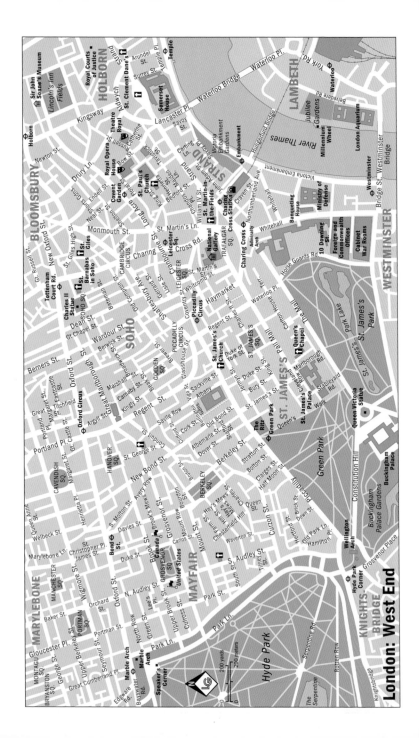

London: West End

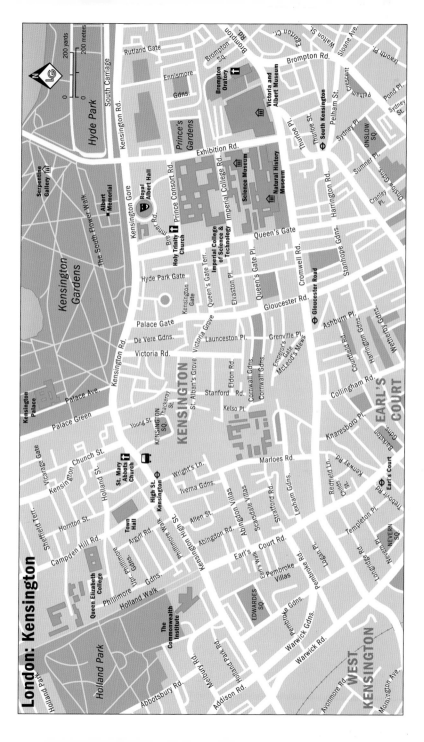

London: Kensington

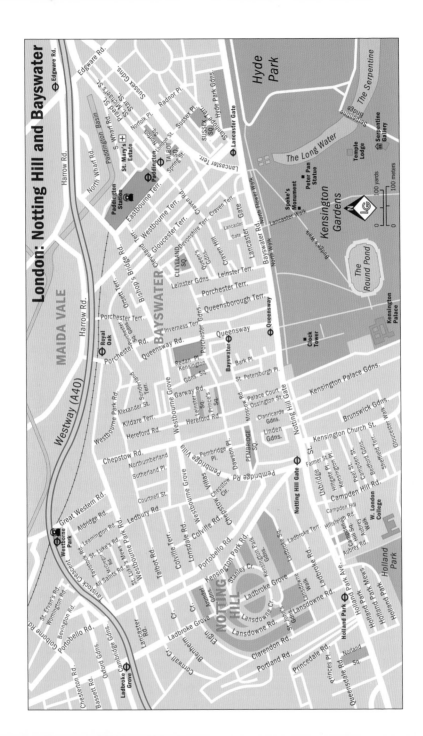

London: Notting Hill and Bayswater

LET'S GO

■ PAGES PACKED WITH ESSENTIAL INFORMATION

"Value-packed, unbeatable, accurate, and comprehensive."

—The Los Angeles Times

"The guides are aimed not only at young budget travelers but at the independent traveler; a sort of streetwise cookbook for traveling alone."

—The New York Times

"Unbeatable; good sight-seeing advice; up-to-date info on restaurants, hotels, and inns; a commitment to money-saving travel; and a wry style that brightens nearly every page."

—The Washington Post

■ THE BEST TRAVEL BARGAINS IN YOUR BUDGET

"All the dirt, dirt cheap."

—People

"Let's Go follows the creed that you don't have to toss your life's savings to the wind to travel—unless you want to."

—The Salt Lake Tribune

■ REAL ADVICE FOR REAL EXPERIENCES

"The writers seem to have experienced every rooster-packed bus and lunar-surfaced mattress about which they write."

—The New York Times

"[Let's Go's] devoted updaters really walk the walk (and thumb the ride, and trek the trail). Learn how to fish, haggle, find work—anywhere."

—Food & Wine

"A world-wise traveling companion—always ready with friendly advice and helpful hints, all sprinkled with a bit of wit."

—The Philadelphia Inquirer

■ A GUIDE WITH A SPIRIT AND A SOCIAL CONSCIENCE

"Lighthearted and sophisticated, informative and fun to read. [Let's Go] helps the novice traveler navigate like a knowledgeable old hand."

—Atlanta Journal-Constitution

"The serious mission at the book's core reveals itself in exhortations to respect the culture and the environment—and, if possible, to visit as a volunteer, a student, or a teacher rather than a tourist."

—San Francisco Chronicle

LET'S GO PUBLICATIONS

TRAVEL GUIDES

Australia 9th edition
Austria & Switzerland 12th edition
Brazil 1st edition
Britain 2008
California 10th edition
Central America 9th edition
Chile 2nd edition
China 5th edition
Costa Rica 3rd edition
Eastern Europe 13th edition
Ecuador 1st edition
Egypt 2nd edition
Europe 2008
France 2008
Germany 13th edition
Greece 9th edition
Hawaii 4th edition
India & Nepal 8th edition
Ireland 13th edition
Israel 4th edition
Italy 2008
Japan 1st edition
Mexico 22nd edition
New Zealand 8th edition
Peru 1st edition
Puerto Rico 3rd edition
Southeast Asia 9th edition
Spain & Portugal 2008
Thailand 3rd edition
USA 24th edition
Vietnam 2nd edition
Western Europe 2008

ROADTRIP GUIDE

Roadtripping USA 2nd edition

ADVENTURE GUIDES

Alaska 1st edition
Pacific Northwest 1st edition
Southwest USA 3rd edition

CITY GUIDES

Amsterdam 5th edition
Barcelona 3rd edition
Boston 4th edition
London 16th edition
New York City 16th edition
Paris 14th edition
Rome 12th edition
San Francisco 4th edition
Washington, D.C. 13th edition

POCKET CITY GUIDES

Amsterdam
Berlin
Boston
Chicago
London
New York City
Paris
San Francisco
Venice
Washington, D.C.

LET'S GO

BRITAIN
2008

PATRICK MCKIERNAN EDITOR
JENNIFER RUGANI ASSOCIATE EDITOR

RESEARCHER-WRITERS
ANNIE AUSTIN
LISA BLOOMBERG
STEVIE DEGROFF
JINU KOOLA
KATIE RIESER

DREW DAVIS MAP EDITOR
RACHEL NOLAN MANAGING EDITOR

ST. MARTIN'S PRESS ⋈ NEW YORK

HELPING LET'S GO. If you want to share your discoveries, suggestions, or corrections, please drop us a line. We read every piece of correspondence, whether a postcard, a 10-page email, or a secret message in a scone. **Address mail to:**

> **Let's Go: Britain**
> **67 Mount Auburn St.**
> **Cambridge, MA 02138**
> **USA**

Visit Let's Go at **http://www.letsgo.com,** or send email to:

> **feedback@letsgo.com**
> **Subject: "Let's Go: Britain"**

In addition to the invaluable travel advice our readers share with us, many are kind enough to offer their services as researchers or editors. Unfortunately, our charter enables us to employ only currently enrolled Harvard students.

Maps by David Lindroth copyright © 2008 by St. Martin's Press.

Distributed outside the USA and Canada by Macmillan.

Let's Go: Britain Copyright © 2008 by Let's Go, Inc. All rights reserved. Printed in the United States of America. No part of this book may be used or reproduced in any manner whatsoever without written permission except in the case of brief quotations embodied in critical articles or reviews. Let's Go is available for purchase in bulk by institutions and authorized resellers. For information, address St. Martin's Press, 175 Fifth Avenue, New York, NY 10010, USA.

ISBN-10: 0-312-37449-6
ISBN-13: 978-0-312-37449-5
First edition
10 9 8 7 6 5 4 3 2 1

Let's Go: Britain is written by Let's Go Publications, 67 Mount Auburn St., Cambridge, MA 02138, USA.

Let's Go® and the LG logo are trademarks of Let's Go, Inc.

CONTENTS

DISCOVER BRITAIN 1
When to Go 1
Things to Do 2
Suggested Itineraries 6

ESSENTIALS 10
Planning Your Trip 10
Safety and Health 20
Getting to the UK 27
Getting Around in the UK 31
Keeping in Touch 39
Accommodations 45
The Great Outdoors 49
Specific Concerns 52
Other Resources 56

BEYOND TOURISM 58
A Philosophy for Travelers 58
Volunteering 58
Studying 61
Working 63

ENGLAND 69
Life and Times 69
Culture and Customs 77

LONDON 88

SOUTH ENGLAND 145
KENT 145
Canterbury 145
Dover 152

SUSSEX 156
SOUTH DOWNS WAY 157
Brighton 161
Arundel 168
Chichester 169

HAMPSHIRE 172
Portsmouth 172
Isle of Wight 176
Winchester 179

SOUTHWEST ENGLAND 185
WILTSHIRE 187
Salisbury 187

SOMERSET AND AVON 192
Bath 192
Bristol 198
Wells 204
Glastonbury 206

THE DORSET COAST 209
Bournemouth 209
Dorchester 211

DEVON 214
Exeter 214

EXMOOR NATIONAL PARK 217

DARTMOOR NATIONAL PARK 221
Torquay 226
Plymouth 227

CORNWALL 232
BODMIN MOOR 232
Padstow 235
Newquay 237
Falmouth 240
Penzance 244
St. Ives 248
Penwith Peninsula 250

THE CHANNEL ISLANDS 252
Jersey 252
Guernsey 254

THE HEART OF ENGLAND .. 257
St. Albans 257
Oxford 262
Stratford-upon-Avon 274
Worcester 279
Cheltenham 281

THE COTSWOLDS 286
Hereford 292

THE MIDLANDS 294
Warwick 294
Birmingham 297
Ironbridge 301
Shrewsbury 303
Stamford 306
Nottingham 308
Lincoln 312

EAST ANGLIA **316**

CAMBRIDGESHIRE 317
Cambridge 317
Ely 326

NORFOLK 328
King's Lynn 328
Norwich 331

SUFFOLK AND ESSEX 337

NORTHWEST ENGLAND **339**

NORTHWEST CITIES 339
Chester 339
Liverpool 345
Manchester 353
Blackpool 359

PEAK DISTRICT NATIONAL PARK 362
Castleton 367

CUMBRIA 371
LAKE DISTRICT NATIONAL PARK 371
Carlisle 382

ISLE OF MAN 384
Douglas 386

NORTHEAST ENGLAND **392**

YORKSHIRE 392
Sheffield 392
York 395

PENNINE WAY 402

SOUTH PENNINES 403
Leeds 406

YORKSHIRE DALES NATIONAL PARK 410

NORTH YORK MOORS 416
Scarborough 420
Whitby 421

COUNTY DURHAM 425
Durham 425

TYNE AND WEAR 430
Newcastle-upon-Tyne 430

NORTHUMBERLAND 437

NORTHUMBERLAND NATIONAL PARK 437

HADRIAN'S WALL 444

WALES **448**
Transportation 448
Life and Times 450

SOUTH WALES **455**
Cardiff (Caerdydd) 455

WYE VALLEY 463
Hay-On-Wye (Y Gelli) 464

BRECON BEACONS 466
Abergavenny (Y Fenni) 470
Brecon (Aberhonddu) 471

THE GOWER PENINSULA 473
Swansea (Abertawe) 475

PEMBROKESHIRE COAST NATIONAL PARK 478
Tenby (Dinbych-y-Pysgod) 481
Pembroke (Penfro) 483
St. David's (Tyddewi) 484
Fishguard 485

NORTH WALES **487**
Aberystwyth 487
Machynlleth 491

VALE OF CONWY 493
Conwy 493
Ilandudno 496
Betws-y-Coed 498
Llangollen 499

SNOWDONIA NATIONAL PARK 501
Dolgellau 504
Harlech 505
Llanberis 507
Caernarfon 509
Bangor 511

ISLE OF ANGLESEY (YNYS MÔN) 513

LLŶN PENINSULA 516

SCOTLAND **520**
Transportation 520
Life and Times 523

SOUTHERN SCOTLAND **529**
EDINBURGH 529
THE BORDERS 548

DUMFRIES AND GALLOWAY 553
Dumfries 554
Kirkcudbright 557

AYRSHIRE 559
Ayr 559

ISLE OF ARRAN 560
GLASGOW 563

CENTRAL SCOTLAND 576
St. Andrews 576
Perth 582
Dunkeld and Birnam 584
Killin and Loch Tay 586
Pitlochry 587
Stirling 589
The Trossachs 592
Loch Lomond and Balloch 594
Oban 596
Isle of Islay 598
Isle of Jura 601
Isle of Mull 602
Iona, Staffa, and Treshnish Isles 604

**HIGHLANDS
AND ISLANDS 606**
NORTHEAST SCOTLAND 606
Aberdeen 606
Braemar 612
Cairngorm Mountains 613

THE GREAT GLEN 618
Inverness 618
Fort William and Ben Nevis 625
Glen Coe 628

ROAD TO THE ISLES 630
THE INNER HEBRIDES 632

ISLE OF SKYE 632
Kyle and Kyleakin 633
Central Skye 635
The Small Isles 638

THE OUTER HEBRIDES 640
LEWIS (LEODHAS) 641
Stornoway (Steornobhaigh) 641

HARRIS (NA HEARADH) 644
THE UISTS (UIBHIST) 646
SMALLER ISLANDS 648
BARRA (BARRAIGH) 649
NORTHWEST HIGHLANDS 651
ORKNEY ISLANDS 657
Kirkwall 658
Smaller Islands 663

SHETLAND ISLANDS 666
Lerwick and the Shetland Mainland 668
Smaller Islands 670

NORTHERN IRELAND 673
BELFAST (BÉAL FEIRSTE) 676
ANTRIM AND DERRY 687
Derry/Londonderry 688

GLENS OF ANTRIM 694
Cushendall (Bun Abhann Dalla) 694
Newtownards 697
Portaferry (Port an Pheire) 701

DUBLIN 703

APPENDIX 720

INDEX 725

MAP INDEX 736

HOW TO USE THIS BOOK

COVERAGE LAYOUT. *Let's Go: Britain* launches out of **London** and follows with a tour through **England.** From the idyllic **South,** venture to the criminally picturesque **Southwest,** through the storybook **Heart of England,** to the fens of **East Anglia** and the countryside of the **Midlands.** Cross the cities and lakes of the **Northwest** (with a quick hop to the **Isle of Man**) and the moors of the **Northeast.** Your travels restart in **Wales,** sweeping from Cardiff, through **South Wales,** into mountainous **North Wales.** In **Scotland,** wheel from Edinburgh to **Southern Scotland** to Glasgow, then trek north to the castles of **Central Scotland.** Continue to the rugged, remote **Highlands and Islands.** Next, it's across the sea to **Northern Ireland.** Begin in Belfast and then tour the Giant's Causeway. Bid farewell to the UK for a short trip and pub crawl through **Dublin.** Through it all, you will encounter extensive coverage of Britain's 14 **National Parks,** spread across the island and along the coastline.

TRANSPORTATION INFO. For connecting between destinations, info is listed under the Transportation section of the departure city. Parentheticals usually provide the trip duration, the frequency, and the price, in that order. For general information on travel, consult the **Essentials** (p. 10) section.

COVERING THE BASICS. The first chapter, **Discover Britain** (p. 1), contains highlights of Britain and **Suggested Itineraries.** The **Essentials** (p. 10) section contains practical information on planning a budget, making reservations, and staying safe. The **Life and Times** sections introduce each country (England, p. 69; Wales, p. 448; Scotland, p. 520; Northern Ireland, p. 673) and sum up its history, culture, and customs. The **Appendix** (p. 720) has climate information, a list of bank holidays, measurement conversions, and a glossary. For information on studying, volunteering, or working in Britain, consult the **Beyond Tourism** (p. 58) chapter.

SCHOLARLY ARTICLES. Two contributors with unique insight wrote articles for *Let's Go: Britain.* Columbia University professor and renowned British art historian **Simon Schama** discusses his favorite ruins (p. 391), and actor **David Ingber** sheds light on performing at the Edinburgh Fringe Festival (p. 68).

FEATURES. Britain is expensive. There's no getting around that. But *Let's Go's* features and tipboxes are meant to guide you to the very best deals, the very best sights, and the very best places to splurge. Other features give you insight into local lore, small-scale city tours, or stories from the *Let's Go* researchers.

PRICE DIVERSITY. Our researchers list establishments in order of value, from best to worst. Our absolute favorites are denoted by the *Let's Go* thumbs-up (🔧). Since the lowest price does not always mean the best value, we have incorporated a system of price ranges for food and accommodations; see p. xiii.

PHONE CODES AND TELEPHONE NUMBERS. Area codes for each city or region appear opposite the name, denoted by the ☎ icon. For more on dialing, see p. 41.

A NOTE TO OUR READERS. The information for this book was gathered by *Let's Go* researchers from May through August of 2007. Each listing is based on one researcher's opinion, formed during his or her visit at a particular time. Those traveling at other times may have different experiences since prices, dates, hours, and conditions are always subject to change. You are urged to check the facts presented in this book beforehand to avoid inconvenience and surprises.

RESEARCHER-WRITERS

Annie Austin — *N. England, Southern and Central Scotland*

Although Annie's phone calls and clever copy were always hilarious, her tireless research was no joke. Leaving no stone unturned and no distillery unsampled, she got the local story in Edinburgh and lived like a queen in a Lake District castle. With her finger on the pulse of Northeast England's live music scene, Annie rocked through her route with a little bit of cash and a whole lot of style.

Lisa Bloomberg — *Wales, Isle of Man, NW England*

"Llisa" wound her way through Wales and its tongue-twisting towns with her faithful red dragon, Llewellyn, always by her side. She overcame lost luggage, spent a sleepless night in an Isle of Man ferry terminal, and even managed to find time to blog about all her adventures. Whether she was searching for bookish bargains in Hay-on-Wye or scouring the museums in Liverpool, Lisa brought Britain's storied past to life with her enthusiasm for art and history.

Stevie DeGroff — *Midlands, Heart of England, SW and N. England*

If you're visiting a hostel in Southwest England, you're bound to meet a friend of Stevie's. In the short time she was there, she managed to meet more people than there are castles in Britain. With a discerning eye for the hottest nightlife and a love of outdoor adventure, Stevie took a pub crawl through Oxford and biked through the Cotswolds. During one of the rainiest summers in British history, Stevie still found sunny skies wherever she went. After reading her animated copy, it was clear this was no coincidence.

Jinu Koola — *S. England, Heart, Midlands, East Anglia, Yorkshire*

Britain didn't know what hit it. Jinu swept through her route in record time, conquering Britain's tricky transportation system and getting the scoop on the best punts and pints in Cambridge. From the white cliffs of Dover to Stonehenge, she beat the tourist traps to uncover the real deal on some of England's most famous sights. It's not surprising that Jinu managed to charm her way into courtside seats at Wimbledon—her upbeat enthusiasm was contagious.

Katie Rieser — *Glasgow, Central Scotland, Highlands and Islands*

Even two flat tires in one day couldn't slow Katie down. Her mission to pet a sheep (or at least to avoid running one over) brought her from Glasgow to some of the most remote places on Earth. Katie's meticulous writing was as thorough as her research, and she fit right in to tightly knit communities in the Outer Hebrides. Her knack for organization helped her to conquer the ferry timetables and visit an astounding number of islands in Orkney and Shetland.

CONTRIBUTING WRITERS

Elsa Ó Riain   *London*

Elsa took her researching experience from *Let's Go: Australia 2007* and hit the streets of London with a purpose. The Ireland native brought a worldly flavor to her London writing, boldly sampling foreign dishes and getting the low-down on uncharted clubs. Not even torrential flooding could keep her from uncovering London's best Guinness on tap. Trust us, she knows what she's talking about.

Alissa Valiante   *London*

A one-time resident of London, Alissa used her knowledge to her advantage, tracking down essential details by getting to know the Londoners who make the city tick. She shared the city with friends and other *Let's Go* researchers, enjoying the Wimbledon grounds and East London's allure. Whether it was scouring the Taste festival for the best eats or talking her way up to rooftop gardens, Alissa always brought the party.

Kyle Dalton   *Dublin*

This former team captain who appeared in the 2007 NCAA Women's Basketball tournament took her game from the hardwood to the streets of Dublin and Cork. Kyle canvassed the comedy scene in Dublin, the scuba sites of Baltimore, and everything in between. Though challenged by flat tires and the demands of researching two world-class cities, she found her groove along the coast, producing witty prose along the way and netting nothing but great copy.

Alex Ellis   *Northern Ireland*

Before beginning a graduate program in England, Alex thought he might do a little traveling. His interest in country-hopping through Europe was quickly put to the test with a diverse and challenging route in the North. While pubbing in Belfast, he received a tutorial in the city's rich social and political history. While practicing the popular sport of coasteering in Antrim, this former rugby player took on a new athletic challenge. Travelers in the North will owe a lot to this dogged researcher.

R. Derek Wetzel   *Editor,* Let's Go: London 2008

Matthew Conroy   *Editor,* Let's Go: Ireland 2008

Molly Donovan   *Associate Editor,* Let's Go: Ireland 2008

Simon Schama is an author and a professor at Columbia University. He writes for *The New Yorker* and was recently the writer and host of the BBC's *History of Britain*.

David Ingber has a degree in English and American Literature and Language from Harvard University. He is an actor and comedian living in New York City.

ACKNOWLEDGMENTS

LET'S GO

TEAM BRITAIN THANKS: Our RWs, for writing this book and keeping us on our toes. RaNo, for being an enabler. Drew, for great maps and tasty treats. Vicki and Patrick, for working miracles. Money pod, for making Grendel's Wednesdays a highlight of the week. Team GCE—it's been nice Minoan you. Nick, LON, and IRE, for completing the team. Erin O'Malley and Mix 98.5. Yolo!

PAT THANKS: Jen, for working unbelievably hard and keeping me in check. I'm sure I'll be tugging at my collar and saying, "gllllll" for years to come. Rachel, for teaching me so much and being the life of my times. Mom, Dadeo, Nicole, and Kerry, for keeping me sane. My RWs, for their marginalia and early morning phone calls. The Street Life pod, for being a well fit place to P1. Six Exeter, the Big Yellow, and the balcony in 41. Jad Bones. Sara, for ordering the coffeemaker.

JEN THANKS: Pat, for running the ship, never ending sentences with prepositions, and being so easy to talk to. You expanded my musical horizons and made every day a pleasure. My RWs, for making my job easy. Rachel, for Molly. Drew, for the daily dose of seersucker and cookies. Jake, Meghan, and Sara—you can stand under my umb-er-ella. Ella. Ella. The Ocho and the fam, of course. JD, for tolerating paper edits during TV time. Britain, for existing and for silly spellings.

DREW THANKS: The RWs, for all of their hard work. Annie, for providing me with a map done by a nine-year-old Dutch girl. Patty Mack and Jen, for being so on top of life. Mapland, for collective/obsessive calorie-counting. Kim and Judy, for being the greatest. Peace out.

Editor
Patrick McKiernan
Associate Editor
Jennifer Rugani
Managing Editor
Rachel Nolan
Map Editor
Drew Davis
Typesetter
Ankur Ghosh

Publishing Director
Jennifer Q. Wong
Editor-in-Chief
Silvia Gonzalez Killingsworth
Production Manager
Victoria Esquivel-Korsiak
Cartography Manager
Thomas MacDonald Barron
Editorial Managers
Anne Bensson, Calina Ciobanu, Rachel Nolan
Financial Manager
Sara Culver
Business and Marketing Manager
Julie Vodhanel
Personnel Manager
Victoria Norelid
Production Associate
Jansen A. S. Thurmer
Director of E-Commerce & IT
Patrick Carroll
Website Manager
Kathryne A. Bevilacqua
Office Coordinators
Juan L. Peña, Bradley J. Jones

Director of Advertising Sales
Hunter McDonald
Senior Advertising Associate
Daniel Lee

President
William Hauser
General Managers
Bob Rombauer, Jim McKellar

ABOUT LET'S GO

NOT YOUR PARENTS' TRAVEL GUIDE

At Let's Go, we see every trip as the chance of a lifetime. If your dream is to grab a machete and forge through the jungles of Costa Rica, we can take you there. If you'd rather bask in the Riviera sun at a beachside cafe, we'll set you a table. We write for readers who know that there's more to travel than sharing double deckers with tourists and who believe that travel can change both themselves and the world—whether they plan to spend six days in Mexico City or six months in Europe. We'll show you just how far your money can go, and prove that the greatest limitation on your adventures is not your wallet, but your imagination.

BEYOND THE TOURIST EXPERIENCE

To help you gain a deeper connection with the places you travel, our fearless researchers scour the globe to give you the heads-up on both world-renowned and off-the-beaten-track attractions, sights, and destinations. They engage with the local culture only to emerge with the freshest insights on everything from local festivals to regional cuisine. We've also opened our pages to respected writers and scholars to hear their takes on the countries and regions we cover, and asked travelers who have worked, studied, or volunteered abroad to contribute first-person accounts of their experiences. In addition, we increased our coverage of responsible travel and expanded each guide's Beyond Tourism chapter to share more ideas about how to give back while on the road.

FORTY-EIGHT YEARS OF WISDOM

Let's Go got its start in 1960, when a group of creative and well-traveled students compiled their experience and advice into a 20-page mimeographed pamphlet, which they gave to travelers on charter flights to Europe. Four and a half decades later, we've expanded to cover six continents and all kinds of travel—while retaining our founders' adventurous attitude toward the world. Laced with witty prose and total candor, our guides are still researched and written entirely by students on shoestring budgets, experienced travelers who know that train strikes, stolen luggage, food poisoning, and marriage proposals are all part of a day's work.

THE LET'S GO COMMUNITY

More than just a travel guide company, Let's Go is a community. Our small staff comes together because of our shared passion for travel and our desire to help other travelers see the world the way it was meant to be seen. We love it when our readers become part of the Let's Go community as well—when you travel, drop us a postcard (67 Mt. Auburn St., Cambridge, MA 02138, USA), send us an e-mail (feedback@letsgo.com), or post on our forum (http://www.letsgo.com/connect/forum) to tell us about your adventures and discoveries.

For more information, visit us online: www.letsgo.com.

PRICE RANGES ❸ ❹
BRITAIN

❷ ❶ ❺

Our researchers list establishments in order of value from best to worst; our favorites are denoted by the Let's Go thumbs-up (🖐). However, because the best value is not always the cheapest price, we have also incorporated a system of price ranges, based on a rough expectation of what you'll spend. For **accommodations,** we base our range on the cheapest price for which a single traveler can stay for one night. For **restaurants** and other dining establishments, we estimate the average amount a traveler will spend. The table tells you what you'll *typically* find in Britain at the corresponding price range. Keep in mind that no system can allow for every establishment's quirks, and you'll usually get more for your money in larger cities.

ACCOMMODATIONS	RANGE	WHAT YOU'RE LIKELY TO FIND
❶	under £13	Campgrounds, dorm rooms, or dorm-style rooms. Expect bunk beds and a communal bath; you may have to provide or rent towels and sheets.
❷	£13-20	Upper-end hostels, small hotels, and lower-end B&Bs. You may have an ensuite bath or communal facilities. Breakfast and some amenities, like TV, may be included.
❸	£21-30	Equivalent to a standard chain hotel room. Decent but basic amenities (phone and TV) and ensuite bath. Breakfast may be included.
❹	£31-59	Similar to ❸. However, expect A/C, TV, ensuite bath, refrigerator, and cleanliness. Some offer tourist services, Internet, and breakfast.
❺	above £59	Large hotels, upscale chains, nice B&Bs, even castles. If it's listed as a ❺ and doesn't have the perks you want, you've paid too much.

FOOD	RANGE	WHAT YOU'RE LIKELY TO FIND
❶	under £6	Mostly street-corner stands, food trollies, sandwiches, sha-warma, takeaway, and tea shops. Rarely a sit-down meal.
❷	£6-10	Often takeaway ethnic foods and basic sit-down options outside London.
❸	£11-15	More expensive entrees, a sit-down meal. Good pub grub, chain restaurants, and local joints.
❹	£16-24	Fancier food and better service. You're likely paying for decor and ambience. An excellent meal.
❺	above £24	Your meal might cost more than your room, but there's a reason—it's something fabulous or famous, or both, and you'll need to wear something other than sandals and a T-shirt.

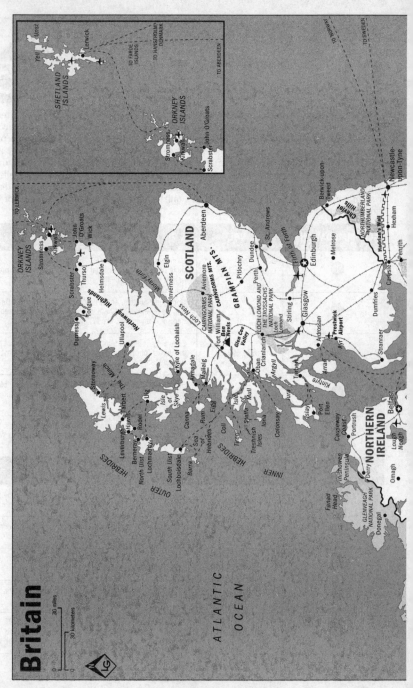

Britain

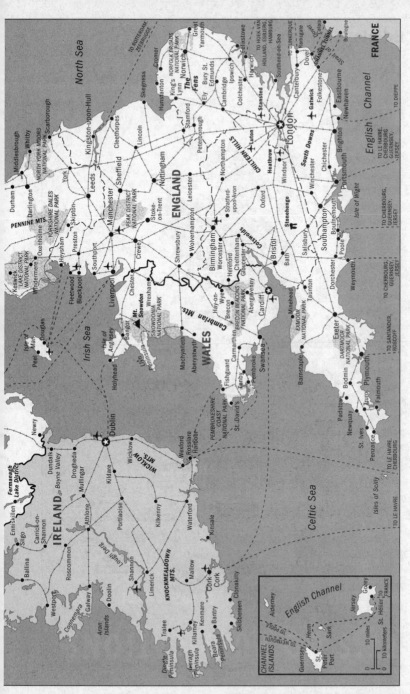

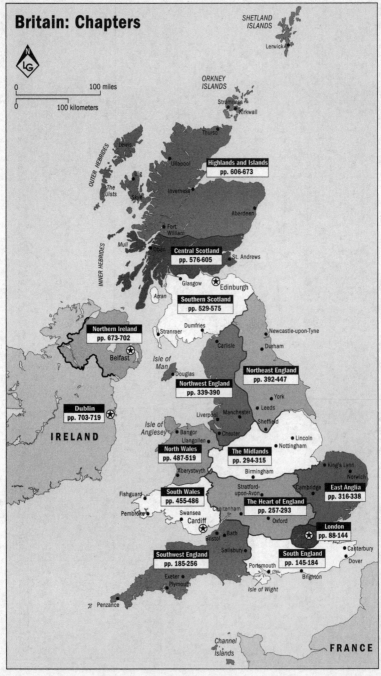

Britain: Chapters

N

0   100 miles
0   100 kilometers

SHETLAND ISLANDS
Lerwick

ORKNEY ISLANDS
Stromness
Kirkwall

Thurso

OUTER HEBRIDES
Lewis
Rùm
The Uists
Skye

Ullapool

Highlands and Islands
pp. 606-673

Inverness

Aberdeen

Mull
Fort William

INNER HEBRIDES
Oban

Central Scotland
pp. 576-605
St. Andrews

Glasgow
Edinburgh

Arran

Southern Scotland
pp. 529-575

Dumfries
Stranraer

Newcastle-upon-Tyne

Northern Ireland
pp. 673-702
Belfast

Carlisle

Durham

Isle of Man

Douglas

Northeast England
pp. 392-447

Northwest England
pp. 339-390

York
Leeds

Dublin
pp. 703-719

Liverpool   Manchester
Sheffield

IRELAND

Isle of Anglesey
Bangor
Chester
Lincoln

Llangollen

North Wales
pp. 487-519

The Midlands
pp. 294-315

Nottingham

Aberystwyth

Birmingham

King's Lynn
Norwich

Fishguard

South Wales
pp. 455-486

Stratford-upon-Avon

Cambridge

East Anglia
pp. 316-338

Pembroke
Swansea
Cardiff

Cheltenham

The Heart of England
pp. 257-293

Oxford

London
pp. 88-144

Bristol   Bath

Southwest England
pp. 185-256

Salisbury

South England
pp. 145-184

Canterbury

Portsmouth

Dover

Exeter
Plymouth

Isle of Wight

Brighton

Penzance

Channel Islands

FRANCE

DISCOVER BRITAIN

*There once was a country made up of great islands
with peat bogs and moors, great rivers and highlands.
Its people built castles and churches with spires
and started a powerful, global empire.
Meanwhile, the hills, filled with white sheep and crofters,
inspired great artists, bold monarchs, and authors.
Today, on a belly of bangers and mash,
the British continue their long, storied past
with Wimbledon, cricket, golf tourneys, and football,
festivals, dubstep, and cold pints on pub crawls.
It's time to discover and leave what you know—
boot up in your wellies, grab your pack, and let's go!*

FACTS AND FIGURES

POPULATIONS: England, 50.7 million; Wales, 3 million; Scotland, 5.1 million; Northern Ireland, 1.7 million.

PATRON SAINTS: George (England), David (Wales), Andrew (Scotland).

MONARCHS: Kings: 35. Queens: 7. Longest reign: 64 years (Victoria). Shortest reign: 9 days (Lady Jane Grey).

MOST COMMON NAMES: Jack (it's a boy!), Olivia (it's a girl!), Max (it's a dog!), The Red Lion (it's a pub!).

#1 SINGLES BY THE BEATLES: 17.

#1 SINGLES BY THE SPICE GIRLS: 9.

ANNUAL TEA CONSUMPTION PER PERSON: 860 cups.

ANNUAL BEER CONSUMPTION PER PERSON: 228 pints.

FIRST SIGHTING OF THE LOCH NESS MONSTER: 565AD. Hoaxes since then: over 1000.

HEIGHT OF A QUEEN'S GUARD BEARSKIN HAT: 18 in.

WHEN TO GO

Britain's popularity as a tourist destination makes it wise to plan around high season (June-Aug.). Spring or autumn (Apr.-May and Sept.-Oct.) are appealing alternatives, offering pleasant weather and cheaper flights. If you intend to visit the cities and spend time indoors, the low season (Nov.-Mar.) is cheapest. Keep in mind, however, that sights and accommodations often run reduced hours or close completely, especially in rural areas.

"Rain, Rain, Go Away" is less a hopeful plea than an exercise in futility. No matter when you go, it will rain. Have warm, waterproof clothing on hand at all times. Relatively speaking, April is the driest month. The mild weather has few extremes—excluding Highland altitudes, temperatures average around 15-20°C (mid-60°F) in summer and 5-7°C (low 40°F) in winter. During the winter, snow often causes roads to close in Scotland and in the northern regions of England and Wales. The British Isles are farther north than you may think: Newcastle is on the same latitude as Moscow. In Scotland, the sun shines almost all day in summer, and in winter sets as early as 3:30pm.

THINGS TO DO

With Manchester's clubs only an hour from the Lake District peaks, and Land's End only 16hr. from John O'Groats by car, Britain provides countless opportunities within an amazingly compact space. For more specific regional attractions, see the **Highlights** box at the start of each chapter.

ALL NATURAL

Britain's natural landscapes are surprisingly diverse and generally accessible via the country's **National Parks.** Discover your inner romantic (or Romantic) among the gnarled crags and crystalline waters of the peaceful **Lake District** (p. 371). The **South Downs Way** (p. 157) ambles through the hills and along the shores of Southern England. Limestone cliffs hang over the Irish Sea in **Pembrokeshire Coast National Park** (p. 478), where coasteering, cliff-diving, and death-defying water sports are popular. **Loch Lomond and the Trossachs** (p. 592), now part of Scotland's first national park, lie along the **West Highland Railway,** which travels north from Glasgow, past Loch Lomond and **Ben Nevis** (p. 625). Farther north, the misty peaks of the **Isle of Skye** (p. 632) and the **Northwest Highlands** (p. 651) lend themselves to postcard-perfect snapshots from just about any angle. Embrace the solitude of the windy **Orkney Islands** (p. 657), filled with wildlife, geological phenomena, and Iron Age monuments. Even more isolated and remote vistas characterize the **Shetland Islands** (p. 666). In Northern Ireland, the honeycomb columns of the **Giant's Causeway** (p. 692) contrast with Antrim's rocky outcrops and pristine white beaches.

EARLY RISERS

Britain was a popular destination long before the arrival of William the Conqueror and the Normans. Walk through a perfectly preserved Neolithic village at **Skara Brae** (p. 662) in the Orkneys. **Stonehenge** (p. 191) is the best-known marker of Bronze Age inhabitants and pagan revelry, while nearby **Avebury** (p. 192) is a bigger, less-touristed site. On Scotland's Isle of Lewis, the **Callanish Stones** (p. 643) reveal the ancient Celtic tribes' knowledge of astronomy, while the burial tomb of Wales's **Bryn Celli Ddu** (p. 514) rises from the middle of a modern farm. Britain's first empire (the Roman one) left its mark all over the landscape. Fabulous mosaics and a theater have been excavated at **St. Albans** (p. 257), once the capital of Roman Britannia, while **Bath** (p. 192) provided a regenerative retreat for Roman colonists. **Hadrian's Wall** (p. 444) marks an emperor's frustration with rebellious tribes to the north, and the nearby site of **Vindolanda** (p. 445) allows visitors to take part in an ongoing archaeological dig. Finding the light in the Dark Ages, early Christianity got its start in Canterbury, where the **Church of St. Martin** (p. 148) is Britain's oldest house of worship. But a new era of British history was inaugurated that fateful day in 1066 when William trounced the Saxons at **Hastings** (p. 157).

CHURCH AND STATE

Restraint was not a popular concept among Early Britons. They never held back when a fortress, castle, or cathedral could be defiantly built or defiantly razed. Edward I of England had a rough time containing the Welsh; his "iron ring" of massive fortresses—like **Caernarfon** (p. 509) or **Caerphilly** (p. 462)—mark the northwestern Welsh coast. Two castles top extinct volcanoes in Scotland, one ringed with gargoyles in **Stirling** (p. 591), the other perched high above **Edinburgh** (p. 537). **Dover Castle** (p. 154) has protected the southern coast since England ruled half of France. You can't leave Scotland without visiting **Dunnottar Castle** (p. 611); it's even more astounding on a stormy day. On your way south, stop by the ruined **St.**

Andrews Castle (p. 580) and scurry through Britain's only surviving countermine tunnel. In central England, get the full medieval experience at Warwick Castle (p. 295), complete with banquets and jousts. You can also play the lord or lady at 15th-century St. Briavel's Castle (p. 464), now a hostel near Tintern, or stay in the university dorms at Durham Castle (p. 427). The sumptuous Castle Howard (p. 401) and Alnwick Castle (p. 441) both afford a heady taste of how the other 0.001% lives.

In northeast England, York Minster (p. 399), the country's largest Gothic house of worship, competes with Durham Cathedral (p. 427) for most jaw-dropping, while Canterbury Cathedral (p. 148) has attracted pilgrims since even before the time of Geoffrey Chaucer. Salisbury Cathedral (p. 190) holds the record for England's tallest spire. In London, thousands flock to Westminster Abbey (p. 110) and St. Paul's Cathedral (p. 111), where Poets' Corner and the Whispering Gallery inspire appropriately quiet reverence. Up in Scotland, the ruined Border Abbeys—Jedburgh (p. 551), Melrose, (p. 549), Kelso (p. 552), and Dryburgh (p. 550)—draw fewer visitors but offer greater valley views.

LITERARY LANDMARKS

Even if you've never been to Britain, you've probably read about it. Unless you can't read. But then this book probably isn't very useful, is it? Jane Austen grew up in Winchester (p. 179), vacationed in Lyme Regis (p. 213), and wrote in Bath (p. 192), enabling future generations of romantic comedies and chick flicks. Farther north, the brooding Brontës—Charlotte, Emily, and Anne—lived in the parsonage at Haworth (p. 405) and captured the wildness of the Yorkshire Moors (p. 416) in their novels. Thomas Hardy was a Dorchester (p. 211) man who perfectly captured Southwest England in the imaginary county of Wessex. Sir Arthur Conan Doyle set Sherlock Holmes's house on 221b Baker St. in London (p. 88), but even super-sleuths won't find the precise address—it's fictional. Virginia Woolf often vacationed in Cornwall (p. 232) and drew inspiration for her novel *To the Lighthouse* from St. Ives (p. 248) and the Isle of Skye (p. 632). Long after shuffling off his mortal coil, William Shakespeare's legendary spirit lives on in Stratford-upon-Avon (p. 274). William Wordsworth grew up in the Lake District (p. 371) and spent much of his time roaming its surrounding mountain ridges with his poetic buddy Samuel Taylor Coleridge. J.R.R. Tolkien and C.S. Lewis crafted wizards and wardrobes over pints at The Eagle and Child in Oxford (p. 262). Welshman Dylan Thomas was born in Swansea (p. 475), moved to Laugharne (p. 483), and today enjoys a fanatical following in both

TOP TEN LIST

BRITAIN FOR UNDER £5

1. Bask in Britain's (manicured) natural beauty in London's Regent's Park (p. 119), originally designed for the wealthy but now open to the public. Free.

2. Skip the lines at the London Eye and climb the narrow staircase at the Monument (p. 116) for stunning views of the city. £2.

3. Considered the finest Norman cathedral in the world, Durham Cathedral (p. 427) houses a bishop's throne that stands 3 in. higher than the Pope's. Suggested donation £4.

4. See a world-class play as a groundling at Shakespeare's Globe theater (p. 120). £5.

5. Often billed as the eighth wonder of the world, the Giant's Causeway in Northern Ireland (p. 692) comprises 38,000 basalt columns. Free.

6. Get lost among the 50,000 items on display at London's British Museum (p. 127). Free.

7. Built in AD 122, Hadrian's Wall (p. 444) was created to protect the farthest borders of the Roman Empire. The best ruins are along the western portion. Free.

8. A daytrip from Cardiff, Caerphilly Castle (p. 462) is a masterpiece of defensive castle design, with concentric fortified walls, two parapets, and a moat. £3.50.

9. The expanses and seclusion of Gower Peninsula's Rhossili Beach (p. 473) reward visitors willing to make the trek. Free.

10. South of Aberdeen, the ruins of Dunnottar Castle (p. 611) cling to Scotland's coastline. £4.

locations. Scotland's national poet is Robert Burns, and every (really, every) town in **Dumfries and Galloway** (p. 553) pays tribute to him. **Edinburgh** (p. 529) cherishes its own favorite Scott, Sir Walter.

A SPORTS FAN'S PARADISE

Football (soccer, if you must) fanatics are everywhere: the Queen is an Arsenal fan, and the police run a National Hooligan Hotline. In **London,** become a gunner for a day at Highbury, chant for the Spurs at White Hart Lane, or don the Chelsea blue. Pay homage at **Old Trafford** (p. 358), Manchester United's hallowed turf on Sir Matt Busby Way, or move west to the stadia of bitter rivals **Everton** and **Liverpool** (p. 350). Rugby scrums are tangled in gaping Millennium Stadium, in **Cardiff** (p. 455). Discouraged by the terrace yobs and the mud? Tree-trunk throwers and kilt wearers reach their own rowdy heights annually at the Highland Games in **Braemar** (p. 612) and other Scottish towns. Cricket is more refined—the men in white play (and play, and play) their interminable games at London's Lords grounds. The world's longest cricket marathon was played by the Cheriton Fitzpaine Club in Devon for 27hr. and 34min. At the hallowed grounds of Wimbledon, huge crowds and fiercely competitive tennis are set against a garden party backdrop. The Royal Ascot horse races and the Henley regatta draw Britain's blue-bloods, but the revered coastal "links" golf courses of **St. Andrews** (p. 576) attract enthusiasts from all over. Surfers catch Atlantic waves at alternative **Newquay** (p. 237), secluded **Rhossili Beach** (p. 474), and hardcore **Lewis** (p. 641). Go canyoning or whitewater rafting at **Fort William** (p. 625), or try more tranquil punting in **Oxford** (p. 262) or **Cambridge** (p. 317). **Snowdonia National Park** (p. 501) and the **Cairngorm Mountains** (p. 613) challenge hikers and bikers. Any town will offer spontaneous kickabouts: go forth and seek your game.

FEELING FESTIVE?

Britons love to party. The concurrent **Edinburgh International** and **Fringe Festivals** (p. 546) take over Scotland's capital each summer with a head-spinning program of performances. Torch-lit Viking revelry ignites the Shetlands during **Up Helly Aa** (p. 667), and all of Scotland hits the streets to welcome the New Year for **Hogmanay.** Back in London, things turn fiery during the **Chinese New Year,** while the summer **Notting Hill Carnival** blasts the neighborhood with Caribbean color. Manchester's Gay Village hosts **Mardi Gras** (p. 359), the wildest of street parties, and the three-day **Glastonbury Festival** (p. 208) is Britain's biggest homage to rock, drawing banner names year after year. **T in the Park, Reading Festival, Leeds Festival, V Festival,** and the **Isle of Wight Festival** all bring massive musical acts and crowds; British summer music festivals sell over a million tickets annually. The **International Musical Eisteddfod** is Wales's version of the mega-fest, swelling modest **Llangollen** (p. 499) to nearly 30 times its normal size. For a celebration of all things Welsh, check out the **National Eisteddfod** (p. 454). Grab a ferry to Northern Ireland on **St. Patrick's Day** for a country-wide carnival of concerts, fireworks, street theater, and Guinness-soaked madness. More information on British festivals can be found in the sections for English (p. 87), Welsh (p. 454), and Scottish (p. 528) events.

▨ LET'S GO PICKS

BEST PLACE FOR A PINT: In Penzance, the **Admiral Benbow** (p. 247) adorns its walls with shipwreck relics. Students prowl **The Turf** (p. 271) in Oxford. Tradition mandates a pub crawl in **Edinburgh** (p. 543). Nottingham's **Ye Old Trip to Jerusalem** (p. 310), carved from rock and established in 1189, is England's oldest pub and still serves a mean pint. London brims with pubs: **Fitzroy Tavern** (p. 139) is perfect for sipping a pint on the street with your pals.

BEST LIVESTOCK: Don't pet Northumberland's psychotic **Wild Cattle,** inbred for seven centuries (p. 441). The Highlands have the harrowing **Bealach na Ba (Cattle) Pass** (p. 651), featuring plunging cliffs, hairpin turns, and daredevil cows. They aren't really livestock, but the tailless **Manx cats** on the Isle of Man (p. 384) are still pretty rad. Famous **seaweed-eating sheep** sustain themselves on North Ronaldsay's beaches (p. 665).

BEST PLACE TO FEEL LIKE ROYALTY: For the ultimate regal experience, book the Bishop's Suite in **Durham Castle** (p. 428). Fend off the ghost at **Chillingham Castle** (p. 441) during a stay in a private apartment. The hidden sea cave beneath Northern Ireland's **Dunluce Castle** (p. 692) makes for stealth escapes.

BEST NIGHTLIFE: Brighton (p. 161) does native son Fatboy Slim proud as a legendary naughty town. Hip travelers command most of **Newcastle** (p. 430), while funkier folks try Oldham St. in **Manchester** (p. 353)—home of the famous Factory Records club nights—or **Broad St.** in Birmingham (p. 297).

BEST PLACE TO BE A ROCK STAR: Rock gods like Oasis cut their teeth at The **Water Rats** in London (p. 135). Find three friends and strut the crosswalk in front of **Abbey Road Studios** (p. 125) in St. John's Wood. Alternatively, channel The Beatles in the **Cavern Club** (p. 353), Liverpool's tourist mecca. Radiohead played their debut gig in 1984 at Oxford's **Jericho Tavern** (p. 273).

BEST SUNSETS: The walled Welsh city of **Caernarfon** (p. 509) sits on the water, full on facing the western horizon. The extreme northern location of the **Shetland Islands** (p. 666) makes for breathtaking skies, while **Arthur's Seat** (p. 540) grants 360° views of the Edinburgh skyline. Get even closer to the sun on an evening hot air balloon ride in **Bristol** (p. 203).

BEST QUIRKY MUSEUMS: In Boscastle, the **Museum of Witchcraft** (p. 235) confirms the hocus pocus with biographies of living witches. The **Dog Collar Collection** in Leeds Castle (p. 151) displays medieval pooch attire. Near Shrewsbury, the **Land of Lost Content** (p. 306) salvages souvenirs of popular culture from trash cans. London's **Sir John Soane's Museum** (p. 129) contains the mummified corpse of the architect's wife's dog, among other oddities.

BEST WAY TO TEMPT FATE: According to legend, nappers on Snowdonia's **Cader Idris** (p. 505) will awake either as poets or madmen, although the two aren't mutually exclusive. Also in Snowdonia, mountaineers celebrate reaching the summit of **Tryfan** (p. 507) by jumping between its two peaks. Go coasteering in **St. David's** (p. 484), or—for the truly courageous—root for Arsenal at a **Manchester United** (p. 358) football match.

BEST OF THE MACABRE: Lay down the law at the gallows at Nottingham's **Galleries of Justice** (p. 310). Some 250,000 bodies supposedly slumber around Edinburgh's **Greyfriars Tollbooth and Highland Kirk** (p. 540), while relics of the infamous Red Barn Murder spook visitors at **Moyse's Hall Museum** (p. 337) in Bury St. Edmond's. A walk through the ruins of **Kilmainham Gaol** (p. 714) will chill you to the bone. Touch a mummy's hand in the crypt of Dublin's **St. Michan's Church** (p. 715), and watch your head at the **Tower of London** (p. 110).

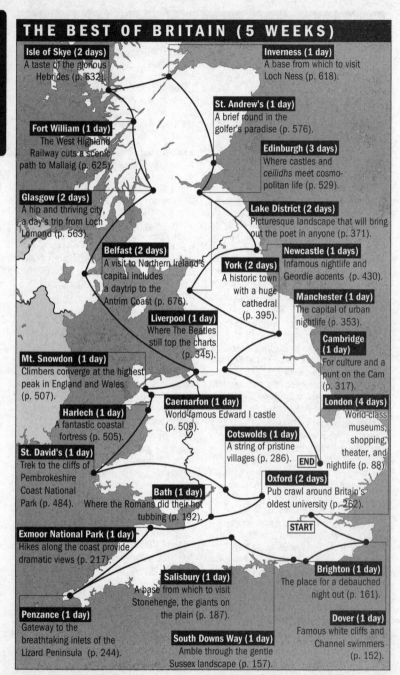

THE BEST OF BRITAIN (5 WEEKS)

Isle of Skye (2 days)
A taste of the glorious Hebrides (p. 632).

Inverness (1 day)
A base from which to visit Loch Ness (p. 618).

St. Andrew's (1 day)
A brief round in the golfer's paradise (p. 576).

Fort William (1 day)
The West Highland Railway cuts a scenic path to Mallaig (p. 625).

Edinburgh (3 days)
Where castles and *ceilidhs* meet cosmopolitan life (p. 529).

Glasgow (2 days)
A hip and thriving city, a day's trip from Loch Lomond (p. 563).

Lake District (2 days)
Picturesque landscape that will bring out the poet in anyone (p. 371).

Belfast (2 days)
A visit to Northern Ireland's capital includes a daytrip to the Antrim Coast (p. 676).

Newcastle (1 days)
Infamous nightlife and Geordie accents (p. 430).

York (2 days)
A historic town with a huge cathedral (p. 395).

Manchester (1 day)
The capital of urban nightlife (p. 353).

Liverpool (1 day)
Where The Beatles still top the charts (p. 345).

Cambridge (1 day)
For culture and a punt on the Cam (p. 317).

Mt. Snowdon (1 day)
Climbers converge at the highest peak in England and Wales (p. 507).

Caernarfon (1 day)
World-famous Edward I castle (p. 509).

London (4 days)
World-class museums, shopping, theater, and nightlife (p. 88).

Harlech (1 day)
A fantastic coastal fortress (p. 505).

Cotswolds (1 day)
A string of pristine villages (p. 286).

END

St. David's (1 day)
Trek to the cliffs of Pembrokeshire Coast National Park (p. 484).

Oxford (2 days)
Pub crawl around Britain's oldest university (p. 262).

Bath (1 day)
Where the Romans did their hot tubbing (p. 192).

START

Exmoor National Park (1 day)
Hikes along the coast provide dramatic views (p. 217).

Salisbury (1 day)
A base from which to visit Stonehenge, the giants on the plain (p. 187).

Brighton (1 day)
The place for a debauched night out (p. 161).

Penzance (1 day)
Gateway to the breathtaking inlets of the Lizard Peninsula (p. 244).

Dover (1 day)
Famous white cliffs and Channel swimmers (p. 152).

South Downs Way (1 day)
Amble through the gentle Sussex landscape (p. 157).

THE BEST OF ENGLAND (1 MONTH)

Lake District (2 days)
A peaceful, Wordsworthian landscape (p. 371).

Newcastle (1 day)
From a Roman fortification to the home of great nightlife and the famous brown ale (p. 430).

Blackpool (1 day)
Where kitsch is cool (p. 359).

END

York (2 days)
A giant cathedral in a medieval town (p. 395).

Liverpool (2 days)
Twist and shout in The Beatles's hometown (p. 345).

Manchester (1 day)
The post-industrial clubbing mecca (p. 353).

London (5 days)
The cosmopolitan center of everything English (p. 88).

Oxford (2 days)
A pint and a punt in this medieval university city (p. 262).

Cotswolds (2 days)
Rustic villages separated by short hikes (p. 286).

Dover (1 day)
A panorama of the Continent from the white cliffs (p. 152).

Exmoor National Park (1 day)
Perfect for a day of strolls through woodlands (p. 217).

START

Newquay (1 day)
An incongruous slice of surfer culture (p. 237).

Salisbury (2 days)
A base from which to explore the stone circles at Stonehenge and Avebury, with its own cathedral (p. 187).

Brighton (2 days)
The infamous "dirty week-end" on the coast (p. 161).

Penzance (2 days)
The tip of the striking Cornish coast (p. 244).

South Downs Way (1 day)
A walk in the idyllic countryside with a stop at the fairy-tale castle at Arundel (p. 157).

THE BEST OF WALES (2 WEEKS)

Caernarfon (1 day)
A Byzantine castle and Roman ruins draw visitors (p. 509).

END

Llanberis (1 day)
An idyllic point to begin an ascent of Mt. Snowdon (p. 507).

Conwy (1 day)
Curious attractions flank a turquoise harbor (p. 493).

Harlech (1 day)
Sea, sand, and summits—not to mention Wales's most dramatic fortress (p. 505).

Snowdonia (1 day)
A spectacular landscape with stops in Machynlleth and tiny Dolgellau (p. 501).

Pembrokeshire Coast National Park (1 day)
Offering scenic coastal hikes (p. 478).

Wye Valley (2 days)
Bookish Hay-on-Wye sits among the hills and dales (p. 463).

Chepstow (1 day)
From this picturesque town, it's just a quick jaunt to haunting Tintern Abbey (p. 464).

St. David's (1 day)
A tiny city with a majestic cathedral and coasteering opportunities (p. 484).

Cardiff (2 days)
The resurgent nation's young, international capital boasts a newly developed waterfront and a flourishing arts scene (p. 455).

Brecon (1 day)
Trek through the rugged Brecon Beacons (p. 471).

START

Tenby (1 day)
A beach resort town with flair (p. 481).

THE BEST OF HISTORY (4 WEEKS)

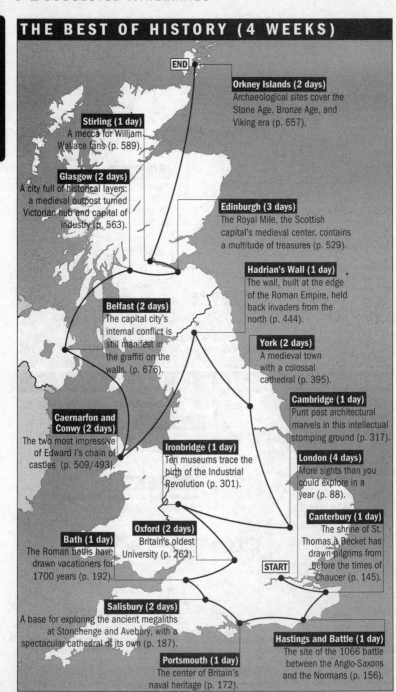

END

Orkney Islands (2 days)
Archaeological sites cover the Stone Age, Bronze Age, and Viking era (p. 657).

Stirling (1 day)
A mecca for William Wallace fans (p. 589).

Glasgow (2 days)
A city full of historical layers: a medieval outpost turned Victorian hub and capital of industry (p. 563).

Edinburgh (3 days)
The Royal Mile, the Scottish capital's medieval center, contains a multitude of treasures (p. 529).

Hadrian's Wall (1 day)
The wall, built at the edge of the Roman Empire, held back invaders from the north (p. 444).

Belfast (2 days)
The capital city's internal conflict is still manifest in the graffiti on the walls. (p. 676).

York (2 days)
A medieval town with a colossal cathedral (p. 395).

Cambridge (1 day)
Punt past architectural marvels in this intellectual stomping ground (p. 317).

Caernarfon and Conwy (2 days)
The two most impressive of Edward I's chain of castles (p. 509/493).

Ironbridge (1 day)
Ten museums trace the birth of the Industrial Revolution (p. 301).

London (4 days)
More sights than you could explore in a year (p. 88).

Canterbury (1 day)
The shrine of St. Thomas à Becket has drawn pilgrims from before the times of Chaucer (p. 145).

Bath (1 day)
The Roman baths have drawn vacationers for 1700 years (p. 192).

Oxford (2 days)
Britain's oldest University (p. 262).

START

Salisbury (2 days)
A base for exploring the ancient megaliths at Stonehenge and Avebury, with a spectacular cathedral of its own (p. 187).

Hastings and Battle (1 day)
The site of the 1066 battle between the Anglo-Saxons and the Normans (p. 156).

Portsmouth (1 day)
The center of Britain's naval heritage (p. 172).

THE BEST OF SCOTLAND (2 WEEKS)

Isle of Skye (2 days)
Offers enviable hiking and dramatic views of the Cuillin Mountains (p. 632).

Orkney Islands (2 days)
Ancient ruins on isolated islands (p. 657).

Inverness (1 day)
A good base for seeing Loch Ness and perhaps its infamous resident (p. 618).

Aberdeen (1 day)
For city life and a trip to clifftop Dunnottar Castle (p. 606).

Fort William (1 day)
For Scotland's highest peak, Ben Nevis (p. 625).

Stirling (1 day)
Home of Scottish heroes and a stunning castle (p. 589).

St. Andrews (1 day)
The golfer's paradise (p. 576).

Glasgow (2 days)
A city of art, culture, and nightlife, and base for a daytrip to the bonnie banks of Loch Lomond (p. 563).

Edinburgh (4 days)
Fantastic during festivals in August, but sparkling year-round with unbeatable pints and the historic Royal Mile (p. 529).

START
END

THE BEST OF THE OUTDOORS (VARIES)

END

Fort William and Ben Nevis
Britain's highest peak abuts a glacial valley (p. 625).

Orkney Islands
Ancient ruins and rare birds dot the remote islands (p. 657).

Cairngorm Mountains
An ideal landscape for skiing, hiking, and reindeer (p. 613).

Glen Coe
This mist-draped valley offers everything from ice climbs to lazy strolls (p. 628).

Loch Lomond and the Trossachs
Britain's largest lake and the surrounding mountains are heavily touristed and for good reason (p. 592).

North York Moors
Some of Britain's most beautiful landscape is accessible by numerous footpaths (p. 416).

Pennine Way
The 268 mi. trail leads through the valleys of the Peak District, the Yorkshire Dales, and the conifers in Northumberland National Park (p. 366).

Mt. Snowdon
Climbers converge at the highest point in Wales and Scotland (p. 507).

Exmoor National Park
Coastal paths lead past dramatic cliffs and, maybe, wild ponies (p. 217).

Pembrokeshire Coast
Coasteering draws adventurers with its combination of swimming, rock climbing, and cliff diving (p. 478).

Cotswolds
Tiny villages punctuate a leisurely bike ride through quintessentially English countryside (p. 286).

South Downs Way
Amble through the idyllic countryside and white chalk hills (p. 157).

Waterfall District
Walk behind the thundering falls at Sgwd yr Eira (p. 468).

START

Newquay
Surfers flock to this "new California" (p. 237).

Dartmoor National Park
The rugged, granite-strewn terrain challenges hikers (p. 221).

ESSENTIALS

PLANNING YOUR TRIP

 ENTRANCE REQUIREMENTS.
Passport (p. 12). Required of all foreign nationals, although they may not be checked for citizens of the EU.
Visa (p. 13). Not required of citizens of Australia, Canada, New Zealand, the US, and many other Western countries. If you are unsure, call your local embassy or complete an inquiry at www.ukvisas.gov.uk. Students planning to study in the UK for 6 months or more must obtain a student visa.
Inoculations (p. 23). No specific inoculations, vaccinations, certificates, or the International Certificate of Vaccination are required, but check to see if an ICV is required upon re-entry into your own country.
Work Permit (p. 13). Required of all foreign nationals working in the UK.

EMBASSIES AND CONSULATES

UK CONSULAR SERVICES ABROAD

For addresses of British embassies in countries not listed here, consult the **Foreign and Commonwealth Office** (☎020 7008 1500; www.fco.gov.uk). Some cities have a British consulate that can handle most of the same functions as an embassy.

Australia: Commonwealth Ave., Yarralumla, ACT 2600 (☎61 026 270 6666; bhc.britaus.net). Consular Section (UK passports and visas), Piccadilly House, 39 Brindabella Circuit, Brindabella Business Park, Canberra Airport, Canberra ACT 2609 (☎61 1902 941 555). **Consulates-General** in Brisbane, Melbourne, Perth, and Sydney; Consulate in Adelaide.

Canada: 80 Elgin St., Ottawa, ON K1P 5K7 (☎613-237-1530; www.britainincanada.org). **Consulate-General,** 777 Bay St., Ste. 2800, Toronto, ON M5G 2G2 (☎416-593-1290). Other Consulates-General in Montreal and Vancouver; Honorary Consuls in Quebec City, St. John's, and Winnipeg.

Ireland: 29 Merrion Rd., Ballsbridge, Dublin 4 (☎353 01 205 3700; www.britishembassy.ie).

New Zealand: 44 Hill St., Thorndon, Wellington 6011 (☎64 04 924 2888; www.britain.org.nz); mail to P.O. Box 1812, Wellington 6140. **Consulate-General:** 151 Queen St., Auckland (☎64 09 303 2973); mail to Private Bag 92014, Auckland.

US: 3100 Massachusetts Ave. NW, Washington, D.C. 20008 (☎202-588-7800; www.britainusa.com). **Consulate-General:** 845 Third Ave., New York, NY 10022 (☎212-745-0200). Other Consulates-General in Atlanta, Boston, Chicago, Houston, Los Angeles, and San Francisco. Consulates in Dallas, Denver, Miami, and Seattle.

IRISH CONSULAR SERVICES ABROAD

Australia: 20 Arkana St., Yarralumla, Canberra ACT 2600 (☎61 02 6273 3022).
Canada: 130 Albert St., Ste. 1105, Ottawa, K1P 5G4, Ontario (☎613-233-6281).

New Zealand: Honorary Consul General, Citibank Building, 23 Customs Street East, Level 7, Auckland (☎64 09 977 2252).

UK: 17 Grosvenor Pl., London SW1X 7HR (☎020 7235 2171). **Consulates:** 16 Randolph Crescent, Edinburgh EH3 7TT (☎0131 226 7711); Brunel House, 2 Fitzalan Rd., Cardiff CF24 0EB (☎029 2066 2000).

US: 2234 Massachusetts Ave. NW, Washington, D.C. 20008 (☎202-462-3939; www.irelandemb.org). **Consulate-General:** 345 Park Ave., 17th fl., New York, NY 10154-0037 (☎212-319-2555). Other Consulates-General in Boston, Chicago, and San Francisco.

CONSULAR SERVICES IN THE UK

Australia: Australia House, The Strand, London WC2B 4LA (☎020 7379 4334; www.australia.org.uk).

Canada: 38 Grosvenor Sq., London W1K 4AA (☎020 7258 6600; www.canada.org.uk).

Ireland: See **Irish Consular Services Abroad** (see above).

New Zealand: New Zealand House, 80 Haymarket, London SW1Y 4TQ (☎020 7930 8422).

US: 24 Grosvenor Sq., London W1A 1AE (☎020 7499 9000; www.usembassy.org.uk). Consulates in Belfast, Cardiff, and Edinburgh.

TOURIST OFFICES

VISITBRITAIN

Formerly known as the British Tourist Authority (BTA), **VisitBritain** oversees UK tourist boards and solicits tourism. The main office is located at Thames Tower, Blacks Rd., London, W6 9EL (☎020 8846 9000; www.visitbritain.com).

Australia: 15 Blue St., Level 2, North Sydney NSW 2060 (☎61 13 0085 8589; www.visitbritain.com/au). Open M-F 9am-4pm.

Canada: 5915 Airport Rd., Ste. 120, Mississauga, Ontario L4V 1T1 (☎888-847-4885; www.visitbritain.com/ca). Open M-F 9am-5pm.

Ireland: Newmount House, 22-24 Lower Mount St., Dublin 2 (☎353 01 670 8000; www.visitbritain.com/ie). Open M-F 10am-5pm.

New Zealand: IAG House, 17th fl., 151 Queen St., Auckland 1 (☎64 09 309 01899; www.visitbritain.com/nz). Open M-F 10am-6pm.

US: 551 Fifth Ave., Ste. 701, New York, NY 10176 (☎212-986-1188; www.visitbritain.com/us). Open M-F 9am-5pm. Other branches in Chicago and Los Angeles.

WITHIN THE UK AND IRELAND

Britain Visitor Centre, 1 Lower Regent St., Haymarket, London SW1Y 4XT (☎020 8846 9000). Open June-Sept. M 9:30am-6:30pm, Tu-F 9am-6:30pm, Sa 9am-5pm, Su 10am-4pm; Oct.-May M 9:30am-6:30pm, Tu-F 9am-6:30pm, Sa-Su 10am-4pm.

Irish Tourist Board (Bord Fáilte): Baggot St. Bridge, Dublin 2 (☎353 01 602 4000; www.ireland.travel.ie). Open M-F 9:30am-5:15pm.

Northern Ireland Tourist Board, 59 North St., Belfast BT1 1NB (☎028 9023 1221; www.discovernorthernireland.com). Open M-F 9am-5:15pm.

VisitScotland, Ocean Point One, 94 Ocean Dr., Leith, Edinburgh EH6 6JH (☎0131 472 2222; www.visitscotland.com). Open M-Sa 9:30am-6pm.

Welsh Tourist Board, Brunel House, 2 Fitzalan Rd., Cardiff CF24 0UY (☎08701 211 251; www.visitwales.com). Open daily 9am-5pm.

ESSENTIALS

DOCUMENTS AND FORMALITIES

PASSPORTS

REQUIREMENTS

Citizens of all countries except the Republic of Ireland need valid passports to enter Britain and to re-enter their home countries. EU citizens should carry their passports, although they may not be checked. Britain does not allow entrance if the holder's passport expires in under six months. Returning home with an expired passport is illegal and may result in a fine.

NEW PASSPORTS

Citizens of Australia, Canada, Ireland, New Zealand, the UK, and the US can apply for a passport at any passport office and many post offices and courts of law. New passport or renewal applications must be filed well in advance of departure, although most passport offices offer rush services for a steep fee.

ONE EUROPE. European unity has come a long way since 1958, when the European Economic Community (EEC) was created to promote European solidarity and cooperation. Since then, the EEC has become the European Union (EU), a mighty political, legal, and economic institution. On May 1, 2004, 10 South, Central, and Eastern European countries—Cyprus, the Czech Republic, Estonia, Hungary, Latvia, Lithuania, Malta, Poland, Slovakia, and Slovenia—were admitted to the EU, joining 15 other member states: Austria, Belgium, Denmark, Finland, France, Germany, Greece, Ireland, Italy, Luxembourg, the Netherlands, Portugal, Spain, Sweden, and the UK. On January 1, 2007, Romania and Bulgaria were also admitted to the EU.

What does this have to do with the average non-EU tourist? The EU's policy of **freedom of movement** means that border controls between the first 15 member states (minus Ireland and the UK, but plus Norway and Iceland) have been abolished, and visa policies harmonized. Under this treaty, formally known as the **Schengen Agreement,** you're still required to carry a passport (or government-issued ID card for EU citizens) when crossing an internal border, but once you've been admitted into one country, you're free to travel to other participating states. On June 5, 2005, Switzerland ratified the treaty but has yet to implement it. Eight of the newest member states of the EU are anticipated to implement the policy in October 2007. Britain and Ireland have also formed a **common travel area,** abolishing passport controls between the UK and the Republic of Ireland.

For more important consequences of the EU for travelers, and **European Customs** and **EU customs regulations** (p. 15).

PASSPORT MAINTENANCE

Photocopy the page of your passport that has your photo on it, as well as your visas, traveler's check serial numbers, and any other important documents. Carry one set of copies in a safe place and leave another set at home. Consulates also recommend that you carry an expired passport or an official copy of your birth certificate in a part of your baggage separate from other documents.

If you lose your passport, immediately notify the local police and the nearest embassy or consulate of your home government. To expedite its replacement, you must show ID and proof of citizenship; it also helps to know all information previously recorded in the passport. In some cases, a replacement may take weeks to process, and it may be valid only for a limited time. Any visas stamped in your old passport will be irretrievable. In an emergency, ask for immediate temporary traveling papers that will permit you to re-enter your home country.

VISAS AND WORK PERMITS

VISAS

EU citizens, plus citizens of Iceland, Liechtenstein, Norway, and Switzerland, do not need a visa to enter Britain. Citizens of Australia, Canada, New Zealand, and the US do not need a visa for visits shorter than six months; neither do citizens of many other Eastern European, Pacific, and South American countries. Visa requirements vary by country, and citizens of certain countries will need a visa merely to pass through Britain. Find a full list of countries whose citizens require visas online at www.ukvisas.gov.uk, or contact your embassy for more information. Tourist visas cost £63 and allow you to spend up to six months in the UK; they can be purchased from British consulates. US citizens can take advantage of the **Center for International Business and Travel** (**CIBT;** ☎1-800-929-2428; www.cibt.com), which secures visas for stays longer than six months for a variable service charge. If you need a **visa extension** while in the UK, contact the Home Office, Immigration and Nationality Directorate (☎0870 606 7766; www.ind.homeoffice.gov.uk). Double-check entrance requirements at the nearest embassy or consulate of the UK (listed under **UK Consular Services Abroad,** on p. 10) for up-to-date information before departure. US citizens can also consult http://travel.state.gov.

WORK AND STUDY PERMITS

Admission as a visitor does not include the right to work; this is authorized only by a work permit. If you plan on **working** in the UK, your employer must obtain a work visa on your behalf. Entering Britain and Ireland to **study** requires a special visa if you are planning to do so for longer than six months. Student visas cost £99. For more information, see the **Beyond Tourism** chapter (p. 58).

IDENTIFICATION

When you travel, always carry at least two forms of identification on your person, including a photo ID. A passport and a driver's license or birth certification is usually an adequate combination. Never carry all of your IDs together; split them up in case of theft or loss, and keep photocopies in your luggage and at home.

STUDENT, TEACHER, AND YOUTH IDENTIFICATION

The **International Student Identity Card (ISIC),** the most widely accepted form of student ID, provides discounts on accommodations, food, sights, and transportation; access to a toll-free 24hr. emergency helpline; and some insurance benefits for US cardholders (see **Insurance,** p. 14). In Britain, cardholders can take advantage of reduced admission to sights like the famous Madame Tussaud's Wax Museum in London (£5 off with ISIC), discounted ferry rates to Ireland, and many other travel deals. Applicants for an ISIC must be full-time secondary or post-secondary school students at least 12 years old. Because of the proliferation of fake ISICs, some services (particularly airlines) require additional proof of student identity.

The **International Teacher Identity Card (ITIC)** offers teachers the same insurance coverage as the ISIC does as well as similar but limited discounts. To qualify, teachers must be currently employed and have worked a minimum of 18hr. per week for at least one school year. For travelers who are under 26 years of age but are not students, the **International Youth Travel Card (IYTC)** offers many of the same benefits as the ISIC.

Each of these identity cards costs US$25. ISICs, ITICS, and IYTCs are valid for one year from the date of issue. To learn more about ISICs, ITICs, and IYTCs, try www.myisic.com. Many student travel agencies (p. 18) issue the cards; for a list of issuing agencies or more information, see the **International Student Travel Confederation (ISTC)** website (www.istc.org).

The **International Student Exchange Card (ISE)** is a similar identification card available to students, faculty, and youths aged 12 to 26. The card provides discounts, medical benefits, access to a 24hr. emergency helpline, and access to student airfares. An ISE card costs US$25; call ☎800-255-8000 (in North America) or ☎480-951-1177 (from all other continents) for more info, or visit www.isecard.com.

CUSTOMS

Her Majesty's Revenue and Customs (www.hmrc.gov.uk) controls customs. Travelers from outside the EU may bring up to £145 worth of non-personal goods not intended for sale (such as gifts) into the UK, with special strictures for cigarettes, alcohol, and perfume. Upon entering Britain, you must declare items beyond the £145 allowance and pay duty. Note that goods and gifts purchased at **duty-free** shops abroad are not exempt from duty or sales tax; "duty-free" merely means that you need not pay a tax in the country of purchase. Duty-free allowances were abolished for travel between EU member states on June 30, 1999, but still exist for those arriving from outside the EU. Upon returning home, you must likewise declare all articles acquired abroad and pay a duty on the value of articles in excess of your home country's allowance. In order to expedite your return, make a list of any valuables brought from home and register them with customs before traveling abroad, and be sure to keep receipts for all goods acquired abroad. If you're leaving Britain for a non-EU country, you can claim back any **Value Added Tax** paid (see **Taxes,** p. 18). For information about travelling with pets, contact the **UK Department for Environment, Food, and Rural Affairs** (www.defra.gov.uk/animalh/quarantine/index.htm) or call the **PETS helpline** (☎0870 241 1710).

> **CUSTOMS IN THE EU.** As well as freedom of movement of people within the EU (p. 12), travelers in the 15 original EU member countries (Austria, Belgium, Denmark, Finland, France, Germany, Greece, Ireland, Italy, Luxembourg, the Netherlands, Portugal, Spain, Sweden, and the UK) can also take advantage of the freedom of movement of goods. This means that there are no customs controls at internal EU borders (i.e., you can take the blue customs channel at the airport), and travelers are free to transport whatever legal substances they like as long as it is for their own personal (non-commercial) use—up to 800 cigarettes, 10L of spirits, 90L of wine (including up to 60L of sparkling wine), and 110L of beer. Duty-free allowances were abolished on June 30, 1999 for travel between the original 15 EU member states; this now also applies to Cyprus and Malta. However, travelers between the EU and the rest of the world still get a duty-free allowance when passing through customs.

MONEY

CURRENCY AND EXCHANGE

The **pound sterling** is the unit of currency in the United Kingdom. Northern Ireland and Scotland have their own bank notes; the money is of equal value but may not be accepted outside Northern Ireland and Scotland. The **Republic of Ireland** has used the **euro** since 2002. The currency chart below is based on August 2007 exchange rates between local currency and Australian dollars (AUS\$), Canadian dollars (CDN\$), European Union euro (EUR€), New Zealand dollars (NZ\$), and US dollars (US\$). Check the currency converter on websites like www.xe.com or www.bloomberg.com, or consult a large newspaper for the latest exchange rates.

POUNDS (£)		
AUS\$1 = £0.420	£1 = AUS\$2.38
CDN\$1 = £0.466	£1 = CDN\$2.15
EUR€1 = £0.674	£1 = EUR€1.48
NZ\$1 = £0.375	£1 = NZ\$2.66
US\$1 = £0.492	£1 = US\$2.03

As a general rule, it's cheaper to convert money in Britain than at home. While currency exchange will probably be available in your arrival airport, it's wise to bring enough foreign currency to last for the first 24 to 72 hours of your trip.

When changing money abroad, try to go only to banks or bureaux de change that have at most a 5% margin between their buy and sell prices. Since you lose money with every transaction, **convert large sums** (unless the currency is depreciating rapidly), but **no more than you'll need.**

If you use traveler's checks or bills, carry some in small denominations (the equivalent of US\$50 or less) for times when you are forced to exchange money at disadvantageous rates, but bring a range of denominations since charges may be levied per check cashed. Store your money in a variety of forms. Ideally, at any given time you will be carrying some cash, some traveler's checks, and an ATM and/or credit card. All travelers should also consider carrying some US dollars (about US\$50 worth), which are often preferred by local tellers.

TRAVELER'S CHECKS

Traveler's checks are one of the safest and least troublesome means of carrying funds. American Express and Visa are the most recognized brands. Many banks and agencies sell them for a small commission. Check issuers provide refunds if the checks are lost or stolen, and many provide additional services, such as toll-free refund hotlines abroad, emergency message services, and assistance with lost and stolen credit cards or passports. Traveler's checks are readily accepted in the UK. Ask about toll-free refund hotlines and the location of refund centers when purchasing checks, and always carry emergency cash.

American Express: Checks available with commission at select banks, at all AmEx offices, and online (www.americanexpress.com; US residents only). American Express cardholders can also purchase checks by phone (☎800-528-4800). Checks available in Australian, British, Canadian, European, Japanese, and US currencies, among others. American Express also offers the Travelers Cheque Card, a prepaid reloadable card. Cheques for Two can be signed by either of two people traveling together. For purchase locations or more information, contact AmEx's service centers: Australia ☎61 29 271 8666, New Zealand 649 367 4567, the UK 0127 369 6933, the US and Canada 800-221-7282; elsewhere, call the US collect at 336 393 1111.

Travelex: Visa TravelMoney prepaid cash card and Visa traveler's checks available. For information about Thomas Cook MasterCard in Canada and the US call ☎800-223-7373, the UK 0800 622 101; elsewhere call the UK collect at 017 3331 8950. For information about Interpayment Visa in the US and Canada call ☎800-732-1322, in the UK 0800 515 884; elsewhere call the UK collect at 017 3331 8949. For more information, visit www.travelex.com.

Visa: Checks available (generally with commission) at banks worldwide. For the location of the nearest office, call the Visa Travelers Cheque Global Refund and Assistance Center: in the UK ☎ 0800 895 078, in the US 800-227-6811; elsewhere, call the UK collect at 020 7937 8091. Checks available in British, Canadian, European, Japanese, and US currencies, among others. Visa also offers TravelMoney, a prepaid debit card that can be reloaded online or by phone. For more information on Visa travel services, see http://usa.visa.com/personal/using_visa/travel_with_visa.html.

CREDIT, DEBIT, AND ATM CARDS

Where they are accepted, credit cards often offer superior exchange rates—up to 5% better than the retail rate used by banks and other currency exchange establishments. Credit cards may also offer services such as insurance or emergency help, and are sometimes required to reserve hotel rooms or rental cars. **MasterCard** and **Visa** are the most frequently accepted; **American Express** cards work at some ATMs and establishments, and at AmEx offices and major airports.

The use of **ATM cards** (a.k.a. **cash cards**) is widespread in the UK. Most banks have ATMs, although they may be rare in extremely rural areas. Depending on the system that your home bank uses, you can most likely access your personal bank account from abroad. ATMs get the same wholesale exchange rate as credit cards, but there is often a limit on the amount of money you can withdraw per day (usually around US$500). Typically, there is also a surcharge of US$2-5 per withdrawal. **Barclay's** banks around the UK offer withdrawals without a surcharge.

Debit cards are as convenient as credit cards but withdraw money directly from the holder's checking account. A debit card can be used wherever its associated credit card company (usually MasterCard or Visa) is accepted. Debit cards often also function as ATM cards and can be used to withdraw cash from associated banks and ATMs throughout the UK.

The two major international money networks are **MasterCard/Maestro/Cirrus** (for ATM locations call ☎ 800-424-7787 or visit www.mastercard.com) and **Visa/PLUS** (to locate ATMs call ☎ 800-847-2911 or visit www.visa.com). The ATMs of major British and Irish banks (including Barclays, HSBC, Thomas Cook, Lloyds TSB, National Westminster, Royal Bank of Scotland, Bank of Scotland, Allied Ireland Bank, and Ulster Bank) usually accept both networks.

PINS AND ATMS. To use a cash or credit card to withdraw money from a cash machine (ATM) in Europe, you must have a four-digit **Personal Identification Number (PIN).** If your PIN is longer than four digits, ask your bank whether you can just use the first four, or whether you'll need a new one. **Credit cards** don't usually come with PINs; if you intend to use credit cards at ATMs to get cash advances, request a PIN from your credit card company before leaving. Travelers with alphabetic, rather than numerical, PINs may also be thrown off by the lack of letters on European cash machines. The following are the corresponding numbers to use: 1=QZ; 2=ABC; 3=DEF; 4=GHI; 5=JKL; 6=MNO; 7=PRS; 8=TUV; and 9=WXY. Note that if you mistakenly punch the wrong code into the machine three times, it will swallow your card for good.

GETTING MONEY FROM HOME

If you run out of money while traveling, the easiest and cheapest solution is to have someone back home make a deposit to your bank account. If this is not possible, consider one of the following options.

WIRING MONEY

It is possible to arrange a **bank money transfer,** which means asking a bank back home to wire money to a bank in Britain. This is the cheapest way to transfer cash, but it's also the slowest, usually taking several days or more. Note that some banks may only release your funds in local currency, potentially sticking you with a poor exchange rate; inquire about this in advance. Money transfer services like **Western Union** are faster and more convenient than bank transfers— but also much pricier. Western Union has many locations worldwide. To find one, visit www.westernunion.com, or call in Australia ☎1800 173 833, in Canada and the US 800-325-6000, in the UK 0800 833 833. To wire money using a credit card (Discover, MasterCard, Visa), call in Canada and the US ☎800-225-2274, the UK 0800 833 833. Money transfer services are also available to **American Express** cardholders and at selected **Thomas Cook** offices.

US STATE DEPARTMENT (US CITIZENS ONLY)

In serious emergencies only, the US State Department will forward money within hours to the nearest consular office, which will then disburse it for a US$30 fee. If you wish to use this service, you must contact the Overseas Citizens Service division of the US State Department (☎202-647-5225, toll-free 888-407-4747).

COSTS

The cost of your trip will vary considerably depending on where and when you go, how you travel, and where you stay. The most significant expenses will probably be your round-trip airfare (see **Getting to Britain and Ireland: By Plane,** p. 25) and a **railpass** or **bus pass.** Before you go, spend some time calculating a reasonable daily **budget.**

STAYING ON A BUDGET

To give you a general idea, a bare-bones day in the UK (camping or sleeping in hostels/guesthouses, buying food at supermarkets) would cost about US$60 ($30/€45); a slightly more comfortable day (sleeping in hostels/guesthouses and the occasional budget hotel, eating one meal per day at a restaurant, going out at night) would cost US$100 ($50/€74); for a luxurious day, the sky's the limit. Don't forget to factor in emergency reserve funds (at least US$200) when planning how much money you'll need.

TIPS FOR SAVING MONEY

Some simple ways include searching out opportunities for free entertainment, splitting accommodation and food costs with trustworthy fellow travelers, and buying food in supermarkets rather than eating out. Bring a **sleepsack** (p. 19) to save on sheet charges in European hostels, and do your **laundry** in the sink (unless you're explicitly prohibited from doing so). Many museums in Britain don't charge admission, and others often have certain days once a month or once a week when admission is free; plan accordingly. If you are eligible, consider getting an ISIC or an IYTC (p. 24); many sights and museums offer reduced admission to students and youths. For getting around quickly, bikes are the most economical option. Renting a bike is cheaper than renting a moped or scooter. Don't forget about walking—you can learn a lot about a city by seeing it on foot. Drinking at bars and clubs can get expensive fast. It's cheaper to buy alcohol at a supermarket before going out. That said, don't go overboard. Staying within your budget is important, but don't do so at the expense of your health or a great travel experience.

TIPPING AND BARGAINING

Tips in restaurants are often included in the bill (sometimes as a "service charge"). If gratuity is not included, you should tip your server about 12.5%. Taxi drivers should receive a 10% tip, and bellhops and chambermaids usually expect £1-3. To the great relief of many budget travelers, tipping is not expected at pubs and bars in Britain and Ireland. Bargaining is unheard of in UK shops.

TAXES

The UK has a 17.5% **value added tax (VAT),** a sales tax applied to everything but food, books, medicine, and children's clothing. The tax is **included** in the amount indicated on the price tag. The prices stated in *Let's Go* include VAT. Upon exiting Britain, non-EU citizens can reclaim VAT (minus an administrative fee) through the **Retail Export Scheme,** although the complex procedure is probably only worthwhile for large purchases. You can obtain refunds only for goods you take out of the country (not for accommodations or meals). Participating shops display a "Tax Free Shopping" sign and may have a purchase minimum of £50-100 before they offer refunds. To claim a refund, fill out the form you are given in the shop and present it with the goods and receipts at customs upon departure (look for the Tax Free Refund desk at the airport). At peak times, this process can take up to an hour. You must leave the country within three months of your purchase in order to claim a refund, and you must apply before leaving the UK.

PACKING

Pack light: Lay out only what you absolutely need, then take half the clothes and twice the money. The Travelite FAQ (www.travelite.org) is a good resource for tips on traveling light. The online **Universal Packing List** (http://upl.codeq.info) will generate a customized list of suggested items based on your trip length, the expected climate, your planned activities, and other factors. If you plan to do a lot of hiking, also consult **The Great Outdoors,** p. 49. Some frequent travelers keep a bag packed with all the essentials: passport, money belt, hat, socks, etc. Then, when they decide to leave, they know they haven't forgotten anything.

Luggage: If you plan to cover most of your itinerary by foot, a sturdy **frame backpack** is unbeatable. (For the basics on buying a pack, see p. 51.) Toting a **suitcase** or **trunk** is fine if you plan to settle down in one or two cities and explore from there, but not a great idea if you plan to move around frequently. In addition to your main piece of luggage, a **daypack** (a small backpack or courier bag) is useful.

Clothing: No matter when you're traveling, it's a good idea to bring a warm jacket or wool sweater, sturdy shoes or hiking boots, thick socks, and especially in Britain, a rain jacket (Gore-Tex® is both waterproof and breathable). A small umbrella and plastic bags to waterproof items in your pack may also be useful. Flip-flops or waterproof sandals are must-haves for grubby hostel showers, and extra socks are always a good idea. You may also want one outfit for going out, and maybe a nicer pair of shoes. If you plan to visit religious or cultural sites, remember that you will need modest, respectful dress.

Sleepsack: Some hostels require that you either provide your own linens or rent sheets from them. Save cash by making your own sleepsack: fold a full-size sheet in half the long way, then sew it closed along the long side and one of the short sides.

Converters and Adapters: In Britain and Ireland, electricity is 230 volts AC, enough to fry any 120V North American appliance. 220/240V electrical appliances won't work with a 120V current, either. Americans and Canadians should buy an adapter (which changes the shape of the plug; US$5) and a converter (which changes the voltage; US$10-30). Don't make the mistake of using only an adapter (unless appliance instructions explicitly state otherwise, like many laptops). Australians and New Zealanders (who use 230V at home) won't need a converter, but will need a set of adapters to use anything electrical. For more information, check out http://kropla.com/electric.htm.

Toiletries: Condoms, deodorant, razors, tampons, and toothbrushes are often available, but it may be difficult to find your preferred brand; bring extras. Contact lenses tend to be expensive, so bring enough extra pairs and solution for your entire trip. Also bring your glasses and a copy of your prescription in case you need emergency replacements.

If you use heat-disinfection, either switch to a chemical disinfection system (check to make sure it's safe with your brand of lenses), or buy a converter to 220/240V.

First-Aid Kit: For a basic first-aid kit, pack bandages, a pain reliever, antibiotic cream, a thermometer, a multifunction pocketknife, tweezers, moleskin, decongestant, motion-sickness remedy, diarrhea or upset-stomach medication (Pepto Bismol® or Imodium®), an antihistamine, sunscreen, insect repellent, and burn ointment.

Film: Film and developing in the UK are expensive (about US$12 per roll of 24 color exposures), so consider bringing along enough film for your entire trip and developing it when you get back home. If you don't want to bother with film, consider using a digital camera. Although it requires a steep initial investment, a digital camera means you never have to buy film again. Just be sure to bring along a large enough memory card and extra (or rechargeable) batteries. Despite disclaimers, airport security X-rays can fog film, so buy a lead-lined pouch at a camera store or ask security to hand-inspect it. Always pack film in your carry-on luggage, since higher-intensity X-rays are used on checked luggage.

Other Useful Items: For safety purposes, you should bring a **money belt** and a small **padlock.** Basic **outdoors equipment** (plastic water bottle, compass, waterproof matches, pocketknife, sunglasses, sunscreen, hat) may also prove useful. **Quick repairs** of torn garments can be done on the road with a needle and thread; also consider bringing electrical tape for patching tears. If you want to do laundry by hand, bring detergent, a small rubber ball to stop up the sink, and string for a make-shift clothes line. Other things you're liable to forget include: sealable **plastic bags** (for damp clothes, soap, food, shampoo, and other spillables), an **alarm clock,** safety pins, rubber bands, a flashlight, earplugs, garbage bags, and a small calculator. A **cell phone** can be a lifesaver (literally) on the road; see p. 43 for information on acquiring one that will work in the UK.

Important Documents: Don't forget your passport, traveler's checks, ATM and/or credit cards, adequate ID, and photocopies of all of the aforementioned in case these documents are lost or stolen (p. 12). Also check that you have any of the following that might apply to you: a hosteling membership card (p. 47); driver's license (p. 13); travel insurance forms (p. 23); ISIC (p. 13); and/or rail or bus pass (p. 32).

SAFETY AND HEALTH

GENERAL ADVICE

In any type of crisis situation, the most important thing to do is **stay calm.** Your country's embassy abroad (p. 11) is usually your best resource when things go wrong; registering with that embassy upon arrival in the country is often a good idea. The government offices listed in the **Travel Advisories** box (p. 22) can provide information on the services they offer their citizens in case of emergencies abroad.

LOCAL LAWS AND POLICE

Police presence in cities is prevalent, and most small towns have police stations. There are three types of police officers in Britain: regular officers with full police powers, special constables who work only part-time but have full police powers, and police community support officers (PCSO) who have limited police power and focus on community maintenance and safety. The national emergency numbers for both Britain and Ireland are ☎999 or ☎112. Numbers for local police stations are listed under each individual city or town.

DRUGS AND ALCOHOL

Remember that you are subject to the laws of the country in which you travel. It's your responsibility to know these laws before you go. If you carry insulin, syringes, or **prescription drugs** while you travel, it is vital to have a copy of the prescriptions and a note from your doctor. The Brits love to drink, and the pub scene is unavoidable. If you're trying to keep up with the locals, keep in mind that the **Imperial pint is 20 oz.**, as opposed to the 16 oz. US pint. The drinking age in the UK is 18 (14 to enter, 16 for beer and wine with food). As of July 1, 2007, smoking is banned in all enclosed public spaces in Britain, including pubs and restaurants.

SPECIFIC CONCERNS

DEMONSTRATIONS AND POLITICAL GATHERINGS

Sectarian violence in Northern Ireland has diminished dramatically in the past decade, but some neighborhoods and towns still experience unrest. It's best to remain alert and cautious while traveling in Northern Ireland, especially during **Marching Season** (the weeks leading up to July 12), and on August 12, when the **Apprentice Boys** march in Derry/Londonderry. The most common form of violence is property damage, and tourists are unlikely targets (but beware leaving a car unsupervised if it bears a Republic of Ireland license plate). In general, if traveling in Northern Ireland during Marching Season, prepare for transportation delays and for some shops and services to be closed. Vacation areas like the Glens and the Causeway Coast are less affected. Use common sense and, as in dealing with any issues of a different culture, be respectful of locals' religious and political perspectives.

Border checkpoints have been removed, and armed soldiers and vehicles are less visible in Belfast and Derry. Do not take **photographs** of soldiers, military installations, or vehicles; the film will be confiscated and you may be detained for questioning. Taking pictures of political murals is not a crime, although many people feel uncomfortable doing so in residential neighborhoods. Unattended luggage is always considered suspicious and is liable to confiscation.

TERRORISM

The Anti-Terrorism Crime and Security Act 2001, passed in the aftermath of the September 11, 2001 attacks, strengthens the 2000 Terrorism Act, which outlaws certain terrorist groups and gives police extended powers to investigate terrorism. Britain is committed to an extensive program of prevention and prosecution. More information is available from the Foreign and Commonwealth Office (see box on p. 22) and the Home Office (☎020 7035 4848; www.homeoffice.gov.uk). Britain raised its terrorist alert level to "elevated" after the London tube bombings of July 7, 2005, and the city stepped-up security considerably in order to deter future attacks. In August 2006, the UK raised its threat assessment level again after government authorities thwarted a potential terrorist threat on planes departing from UK airports. In the immediate aftermath, airport security was bolstered, and bottled liquids and many electronics were banned in aircraft cabins.

The US State Department website (www.state.gov) provides information on the current situation and on developing flight regulations. To have advisories emailed to you, register with your home embassy or consulate when you arrive in Britain. If you see a suspicious unattended package or bag at an airport or other crowded public place, report it immediately at ☎999 or the **Anti-Terrorism Hotline** (☎0800 789 321). The box on **travel advisories** above lists offices to contact and webpages to visit to get the most updated list of your home government's advisories about travel for its citizens.

TRAVEL ADVISORIES. The following government offices provide travel information and advisories by telephone, by fax, or via the web:

Australian Department of Foreign Affairs and Trade: ☎61 262 611 111; www.dfat.gov.au.

Canadian Department of Foreign Affairs and International Trade (DFAIT): ☎800-267-8376; www.dfait-maeci.gc.ca. Call for their free booklet, *Bon Voyage...But.*

New Zealand Ministry of Foreign Affairs: ☎64 044 398 000; www.mfat.govt.nz.

United Kingdom Foreign and Commonwealth Office: ☎020 7008 1500; www.fco.gov.uk.

US Department of State: ☎888-407-4747; http://travel.state.gov. Visit the website for the booklet *A Safe Trip Abroad.*

PERSONAL SAFETY

EXPLORING AND TRAVELING

Familiarize yourself with your surroundings before setting out, and carry yourself with confidence. Check maps in shops and restaurants rather than on the street. If you are traveling alone, be sure someone at home knows your itinerary, and never tell anyone you meet that you're by yourself. When walking at night, stick to busy, well-lit streets and avoid dark alleyways. If you ever feel uncomfortable, leave the area as quickly and directly as you can.

There is no one way to avoid all the threatening situations you might encounter while traveling, but a good **self-defense course** will give you concrete ways to react to unwanted advances. **Impact, Prepare, and Model Mugging** can refer you to local self-defense courses in Australia, Canada, Switzerland and the US. Visit the website at www.modelmugging.org for a list of nearby chapters. Workshops (2-4hr.) start at US$50; full courses (20hr.) run US$350-500.

If you are using a **car,** learn local driving signals and wear a seatbelt. Children under 40 lbs. should ride only in specially-designed carseats, available for a small fee from most car rental agencies. Study route maps before you hit the road, and if you plan on spending a lot of time driving, consider bringing spare parts. For long drives in isolated areas, invest in a cellular phone and a roadside assistance program (p. 38). Park your vehicle in a garage or well-traveled area; use a steering wheel locking device in larger cities. **Sleeping in your car** is extremely dangerous, and it's also illegal in the UK. For info on the perils of **hitchhiking,** see p. 39.

POSSESSIONS AND VALUABLES

Never leave your belongings unattended; crime occurs in even the most safe-looking hostels or hotels. Bring your own padlock for hostel lockers, and don't ever store valuables in a locker. Be particularly careful on **buses** and **trains**—horror stories abound about determined thieves who wait for travelers to fall asleep. Carry your bag or purse in front of you where you can see it. When traveling with others, sleep in alternate shifts. When alone, use good judgment in selecting a train compartment: never stay in an empty one, and use a lock to secure your pack to the luggage rack. Use extra caution if traveling at night or on overnight trains. Try to sleep on top bunks with your luggage stored above you (if not in bed with you), and keep important documents and other valuables you on at all times.

There are a few steps you can take to minimize the financial risk associated with traveling. First, **bring as little with you as possible.** Second, buy a few combination **padlocks** to secure your belongings either in your pack or in a hostel or train station locker. Third, **carry as little cash as possible.** Keep your traveler's checks and ATM/credit cards in a **money belt**—not a "fanny pack"—along with your passport and ID cards. Fourth, **keep a small cash reserve separate from your primary stash.** This should be about US$50 (pounds are best) sewn into or stored in the depths of your pack, along with your traveler's check numbers and photocopies of your passport, your birth certificate, and other important documents.

In large cities **con artists** often work in groups and may involve children. Beware of certain classics: sob stories that require money, rolls of bills "found" on the street, mustard spilled (or saliva spit) onto your shoulder to distract you while they snatch your bag. **Never let your passport and your bags out of your sight.** Hostel workers will sometimes stand at bus and train station arrival points to try to recruit tired and disoriented travelers to their hostel; never believe strangers who tell you that theirs is the only hostel open. Beware of **pickpockets** in city crowds, especially on public transportation. Also, be alert in public telephone booths: if you must say your calling card number, do so very quietly. If you punch it in, make sure no one can look over your shoulder.

If you will be traveling with electronic devices, such as a laptop computer or a PDA, check whether your homeowner's insurance covers loss, theft, or damage when you travel. If not, you can purchase a separate low-cost insurance policy. **Safeware** (☎ 800-800-1492; www.safeware.com) covers computers and charges $90 for 90-day comprehensive international travel coverage up to $4000.

PRE-DEPARTURE HEALTH

In your **passport,** write the names of any people you wish to be contacted in case of a medical emergency, and list any allergies or medical conditions. Matching a prescription to a foreign equivalent is not always easy, safe, or possible, so if you take prescription drugs, consider carrying up-to-date prescriptions or a statement from your doctor stating the medication's trade name, manufacturer, chemical name, and dosage. While traveling, be sure to keep all medication with you in your carry-on luggage. For tips on packing a **first-aid kit** and other health essentials, see p. 20.

IMMUNIZATIONS AND PRECAUTIONS

While no injections are required for entry into the UK, travelers over two years old should make sure that the following vaccines are up to date: MMR (for measles, mumps, and rubella); DTaP or Td (for diphtheria, tetanus, and pertussis); IPV (for polio); Hib (for *Haemophilus influenza* B); and HepB (for Hepatitis B). For recommendations on immunizations and prophylaxis, consult the Centers for Disease Control and Prevention (CDC; see p. 24) in the US or the equivalent in your home country, and check with a doctor for guidance.

INSURANCE

Travel insurance covers four basic areas: medical/health problems, property loss, trip cancellation/interruption, and emergency evacuation. Although regular insurance policies may extend to travel-related accidents, you may consider purchasing separate travel insurance if the cost of potential trip cancellation, interruption, or emergency medical evacuation is greater than you can absorb. Prices for travel insurance purchased separately generally run about US$50 per week for full coverage, while trip cancellation/interruption may be purchased separately at a rate of US$3-5 per day depending on length of stay.

Medical insurance (especially university policies) often covers costs incurred abroad; check with your provider. **US Medicare** does not cover foreign travel. **Canadian** provincial health insurance plans increasingly do not cover foreign travel;

check with the provincial Ministry of Health or Health Plan Headquarters for details. **Australians** traveling in the UK are entitled to many of the services that they would receive at home as part of the Reciprocal Health Care Agreement. **Homeowners' insurance** (or your family's coverage) often covers theft during travel and loss of travel documents (passport, plane ticket, railpass, etc.) up to US$500.

ISIC and **ITIC** (see p. 13) provide basic insurance benefits to US cardholders, including US$100 per day of in-hospital sickness for up to 100 days and US$10,000 of accident-related medical reimbursement (see www.isicus.com for details). Cardholders can access a toll-free 24hr. helpline for medical, legal, and financial emergencies overseas. **American Express** (☎ 800-338-1670) grants most cardholders automatic collision and theft car rental insurance on rentals made with the card.

USEFUL ORGANIZATIONS AND PUBLICATIONS

The American **Centers for Disease Control and Prevention** (**CDC;** ☎ 877-394-8747; www.cdc.gov/travel) maintains an international travelers' hotline and an informative website. Consult the appropriate government agency of your home country for consular info on health, entry requirements, and other issues for various countries (see the listings in the box on **Travel Advisories,** p. 22). For quick information on health and other travel warnings, call the **Overseas Citizens Services** (M-F 8am-8pm from US ☎ 888-407-4747, from overseas 202-501-4444), or contact a passport agency, embassy, or consulate abroad. For information on medical evacuation services and travel insurance firms, see the US government's website at http://travel.state.gov/travel/abroad_health.html or the **British Foreign and Commonwealth Office** (www.fco.gov.uk). For general health info, contact the **American Red Cross** (☎ 202-303-4498; www.redcross.org).

STAYING HEALTHY

Common sense is the simplest prescription for good health while you travel. Drink lots of fluids to prevent dehydration and constipation, and wear sturdy, broken-in shoes and clean socks. The British Isles are in the gulf stream, so temperatures are mild: around 40°F in winter and 65°F in summer. In the Scottish highlands and mountains temperatures reach greater extremes. When in areas of high altitude, be sure to dress in layers that can be peeled off as needed. Allow your body a couple of days to adjust to decreased oxygen levels before exerting yourself. Note that alcohol is more potent and UV rays are stronger at high elevations.

ONCE IN THE UK

ENVIRONMENTAL HAZARDS

Heat exhaustion and dehydration: Heat exhaustion leads to nausea, excessive thirst, headaches, and dizziness. Avoid it by drinking plenty of fluids, eating salty foods (e.g., crackers), abstaining from dehydrating beverages (e.g., alcohol and caffeinated beverages), and wearing sunscreen. Continuous heat stress can eventually lead to heatstroke, characterized by a rising temperature, severe headache, delirium, and cessation of sweating. Victims should be cooled off with wet towels and taken to a doctor.

Sunburn: Always wear sunscreen (SPF 30 or higher) when spending excessive amounts of time outdoors. If you get sunburned, drink more fluids than usual and apply an aloe-based lotion. Severe sunburns can lead to sun poisoning, a condition that can cause fever, chills, nausea, and vomiting. Sun poisoning should always be treated by a doctor.

Hyothermia and frostbite: A rapid drop in body temperature is the clearest sign of over-exposure to cold. Victims may also shiver, feel exhausted, have poor coordination or slurred speech, hallucinate, or suffer amnesia. *Do not let hypothermia victims fall asleep.* To avoid hypothermia, keep dry, wear layers, and stay out of the wind. When the temperature is below freezing, watch out for frostbite. If skin turns white or blue, waxy, and cold, do not rub the area. Drink warm beverages, stay dry, and slowly warm the area with dry fabric or steady body contact until a doctor can be found.

INSECT-BORNE DISEASES

Many diseases are transmitted by insects—mainly mosquitoes, fleas, ticks, and lice. Be aware of insects in wet or forested areas, especially while hiking and camping; wear long pants and long sleeves, tuck your pants into your socks, and use a mosquito net. Use insect repellents such as DEET and soak or spray your gear with permethrin (licensed in the US only for use on clothing). **Mosquitoes**—responsible for malaria, dengue fever, and yellow fever—can be particularly abundant in wet, swampy, or wooded areas like those in national parks. **Ticks** can carry Lyme and other diseases and can be particularly dangerous in forested regions.

Tick-borne encephalitis: A viral infection of the central nervous system transmitted during the summer by tick bites (primarily in wooded areas) or by consumption of unpasteurized dairy products. The risk of contracting the disease is relatively low, especially if precautions are taken against tick bites.

Lyme disease: A bacterial infection carried by ticks and marked by a circular bull's-eye rash of 2 in. or more. Later symptoms include fever, headache, fatigue, and aches and pains. Antibiotics are effective if administered early. Left untreated, Lyme can cause problems in joints, the heart, and the nervous system. If you find a tick attached to your skin, grasp the head with tweezers as close to your skin as possible and apply slow, steady traction. Removing a tick within 24hr. greatly reduces the risk of infection. Do not try to remove ticks with petroleum jelly, nail polish remover, or a hot match. Ticks usually inhabit moist, shaded environments and heavily wooded areas. If you are going to be hiking in these areas, wear long clothes and DEET.

Other insect-borne diseases: Lymphatic filariasis is a roundworm infestation transmitted by mosquitoes. Infection causes enlargement of extremities and has no vaccine. **Leishmaniasis,** a parasite transmitted by sand flies, can occur in Europe, usually in rural rather than urban areas. Common symptoms are fever, weakness, and swelling of the spleen, as well as skin sores. There is a treatment, but no vaccine.

FOOD- AND WATER-BORNE DISEASES

Prevention is the best cure: be sure that your food is properly cooked and the water you drink is clean. Tap water throughout Britain and Ireland is generally safe. When camping, purify your own water by **boiling** or treating it with **iodine tablets;** note that some parasites such as *giardia* have exteriors that resist iodine treatment, so boiling is more reliable. **Giardiasis** is a parasitic disease acquired by drinking untreated water from streams or lakes. Symptoms include diarrhea, cramps, bloating, fatigue, weight loss, and nausea. If untreated it can lead to severe dehydration. Giardiasis occurs worldwide, and can be treated with antibiotics. Watch out for food from markets or street vendors that may have been cooked in unhygienic conditions. Other culprits are raw shellfish, unpasteurized milk, and sauces containing raw eggs. Always wash your hands before eating or bring a quick-drying purifying liquid hand cleaner.

Two recent diseases originating in British livestock have made international headlines. Bovine spongiform encephalopathy (BSE), better known as **mad cow disease,** is a chronic degenerative disease affecting the central nervous system of cattle. The human variety is called new variant Creutzfeldt-Jakob disease (nvCJD), and both forms involve fatal brain damage. Information on nvCJD is not conclusive, but the disease is thought to be caused by consuming infected beef. The risk

ESSENTIALS

is extremely small (around 1 case per 10 billion meat servings); regardless, travelers should exercise caution when choosing to eat British beef and beef products. Milk and milk products are not believed to pose a risk.

The UK and Western Europe experienced a serious outbreak of **Foot and Mouth Disease (FMD)** in 2001. FMD is easily transmissible between cloven-hoofed animals (cows, pigs, sheep, goats, and deer), but does not pose a threat to humans, causing mild symptoms, if any. In January 2002, the UK regained **international FMD-free status.** Restrictions on rural travel have been removed. Further information on these diseases is available through the CDC (www.cdc.gov/travel) and the **British Department for Environment, Food and Rural Affairs** (www.defra.gov.uk).

OTHER INFECTIOUS DISEASES
The following diseases exist in every part of the world. Travelers should know how to recognize them and what to do if they suspect they have been infected.

Rabies: Transmitted through the saliva of infected animals; fatal if untreated. By the time symptoms (thirst and muscle spasms) appear, the disease is in its terminal stage. If you are bitten, wash the wound, seek immediate medical care, and try to have the animal located. A rabies vaccine, which consists of 3 shots given over a 21-day period, is available and recommended for developing world travel, but is only semi-effective.

AIDS and HIV: For detailed information on Acquired Immune Deficiency Syndrome (AIDS) in the UK, call the US Centers for Disease Control's 24hr. hotline at ☎800-342-2437. In the UK, call the FPA (formerly the Family Planning Association) for confidential advice (24hr. ☎0800 567 123).

Sexually transmitted infections (STIs): Gonorrhea, chlamydia, genital warts, syphilis, herpes, and other STIs can be serious and are easier to catch than HIV. Although condoms may protect you from some STIs, oral or even tactile contact can lead to transmission. If you think you may have contracted an STI, see a doctor immediately.

OTHER HEALTH CONCERNS

MEDICAL CARE ON THE ROAD
In both Britain and Ireland, medical aid is readily available and of excellent quality. For minor ailments, **chemists** (pharmacies) are plentiful. The ubiquitous **Boots** chain has a blue logo. **Late-night pharmacies** are rare even in big cities. Most major hospitals have a **24hr. emergency room** (called a "casualty department" or "A&E," short for Accident and Emergency). Call the numbers listed below for assistance.

In Britain, the state-run **National Health Service (NHS)** encompasses the majority of healthcare centers (☎020 7210 4850; www.doh.gov.uk/nhs.htm). Cities may have private hospitals, but these cater to the wealthy and are not often equipped with full surgical staff or complete casualty units. Access to free care is based on residence, not on British nationality or payment of taxes; those working legally or undertaking long-term study in the UK may also be eligible. **Health insurance** is a must for all other visitors. For more information, see **Insurance,** p. 22.

If you are concerned about obtaining medical assistance while traveling, you may wish to employ special support services. The *MedPass* from **GlobalCare, Inc.,** 6875 Shiloh Rd. East, Alpharetta, GA 30005, USA (☎800-860-1111; www.globalcare.net), provides 24hr. international medical assistance, support, and medical evacuation resources. The **International Association for Medical Assistance to Travelers** (**IAMAT;** US ☎716-754-4883, Canada 519-836-0102; www.iamat.org) has free membership, lists English-speaking doctors worldwide, and offers detailed info on immunization requirements and sanitation. If your regular **insurance** policy does not cover travel abroad, you may wish to purchase additional coverage (see p. 23).

Those with medical conditions (such as diabetes, allergies to antibiotics, epilepsy, or heart conditions) may want to obtain a **MedicAlert** membership (1st year US$35, annually thereafter US$20), which includes among other things a stainless steel ID tag and a 24hr. collect-call number. Contact the MedicAlert Foundation, 2323 Colorado Ave., Turlock, CA 95382, USA (☎ 888-633-4298, outside US 209-668-3333; www.medicalert.org).

WOMEN'S HEALTH

Women traveling are vulnerable to **urinary tract** and **bladder infections,** common and uncomfortable bacterial conditions that cause a burning sensation and painful (sometimes frequent) urination. Vaginal yeast infections are known in Britain and Ireland as **thrush** and can be treated with over-the-counter medicines like Diflucan One or Vagisil. **Tampons, pads,** and **contraceptive devices** are widely available in urban areas, although your favorite brand may not be stocked. If you are camping, remember to pack enough for your trip as pharmacies are rare in rural areas; also be prepared to pack your used feminine hygiene products to dispose outside the park. Women who need an **abortion** or **emergency contraception** while in the UK should contact the **FPA** (Family Planning Association; ☎ 0845 122 8690; www.fpa.org.uk; M-F 9am-6pm). While emergency contraception is available in the Republic of Ireland, abortions are not legal.

GETTING TO THE UK
BY PLANE

When it comes to airfare, a little effort can save you a lot of cash. If your plans are flexible enough to deal with the restrictions, courier fares are the cheapest. Tickets bought from consolidators and for standby seating are also good deals, but last-minute specials, airfare wars, and charter flights often beat these fares. The key is to hunt around, to be flexible, and to ask persistently about discounts. Students, seniors, and those under 26 should never pay full price for a ticket. Beware of the extremely exorbitant fees often tacked on to your ticket price. They can sometimes be equal to the cost of the ticket.

AIRFARES

Airfares to the UK peak between June and September; holidays are also expensive. The cheapest times to travel are November to February. Midweek (M-Th morning) round-trip flights run US$40-50 cheaper than weekend flights, but they are generally more crowded and less likely to permit frequent-flier upgrades. Not fixing a return date ("open return") or arriving in and departing from different cities ("open-jaw") can be pricier than round-trip flights. Patching one-way flights together is the most expensive way to travel. Flights between London, Dublin, and Belfast will tend to be cheaper.

If the UK is only one stop on a more extensive globe-hop, consider a round-the-world (RTW) ticket. Tickets usually include at least five stops and are valid for about a year; prices range US$1200-5000. Try **Northwest Airlines/KLM** (☎ 800-225-2525; www.nwa.com) or **Star Alliance,** a consortium of 16 airlines including United Airlines (www.staralliance.com).

Fares for round-trip flights to London from the US or Canadian east coast run US$500-1200, US$300-700 in the low season; from the US or Canadian west coast US$700-1500/US$500-900; from Australia AUS$1800 and up; from New Zealand NZ$1600 and up.

ESSENTIALS

BUDGET AND STUDENT TRAVEL AGENCIES

While knowledgeable agents specializing in flights to Britain can help you save, they may not spend the time to find you the lowest possible fare since they get paid on commission. Travelers holding **ISICs** and **IYTCs** (p. 13) qualify for big discounts from student travel agencies. Most flights from budget agencies are on major airlines, but in peak season some sell seats on less reliable chartered planes.

STA Travel, 5900 Wilshire Blvd., Ste. 900, Los Angeles, CA 90036, USA (24hr. reservations and info ☎800-781-4040; www.statravel.com). A student and youth travel organization with over 150 offices worldwide (check their website for a listing of all their offices), including US offices in Boston, Chicago, L.A., New York, Seattle, San Francisco, and Washington, D.C. Ticket booking, travel insurance, railpasses, and more. Walk-in offices are located throughout Australia (☎03 9207 5900), New Zealand (☎09 309 9723), and the UK (☎08701 630 026).

Travel CUTS (Canadian Universities Travel Services Limited), 187 College St., Toronto, ON M5T 1P7, Canada (☎888-592-2887; www.travelcuts.com). Offices across Canada and the US including Los Angeles, New York, Seattle, and San Francisco.

USIT, 19-21 Aston Quay, Dublin 2, Ireland (☎01 602 1904; www.usit.ie), Ireland's leading student/budget travel agency has 20 offices throughout Northern Ireland and the Republic of Ireland. Offers programs to work, study, and volunteer worldwide.

 FLIGHT PLANNING ON THE INTERNET. The Internet may be the budget traveler's dream when it comes to finding and booking bargain fares, but the array of options can be overwhelming. Many airline sites offer special last-minute deals on the Web. Try Virgin Atlantic (www.virgin-atlantic.com), BMI (www.flybmi.com), or British Airways (www.ba.com). **STA** (www.statravel.com) and **StudentUniverse** (www.studentuniverse.com) provide quotes on student tickets, while **Opodo** (www.opodo.com), **Expedia** (www.expedia.com), and **Travelocity** (www.travelocity.com) offer full travel services. **Priceline** (www.priceline.com) lets you specify a price and obligates you to buy any ticket that meets or beats it; **Hotwire** (www.hotwire.com) offers bargain fares, but won't reveal the airline or flight times until you buy. Other sites that compile deals include www.bestfares.com, www.flights.com, www.lowestfare.com, www.onetravel.com, and www.travelzoo.com. Increasingly, there are online tools available to help sift through multiple offers; **SideStep** (www.sidestep.com) and **Booking Buddy** (www.bookingbuddy.com) let you enter your trip information once and search multiple sites. An indispensable resource on the Internet is the **Air Traveler's Handbook** (www.faqs.org/faqs/travel/air/handbook), a comprehensive listing of links to everything you need to know before you board a plane.

COMMERCIAL AIRLINES

The commercial airlines' lowest regular offer is the **APEX** (Advance Purchase Excursion) fare, which provides confirmed reservations and allows "open-jaw" tickets. Generally, reservations must be made seven to 21 days ahead of departure, with seven- to 14-day minimum-stay and up to 90-day maximum-stay restrictions. These fares carry hefty cancellation and change penalties (fees rise in summer). Book peak-season APEX fares early. Use **Expedia** (www.expedia.com) or **Travelocity** (www.travelocity.com) to get an idea of the lowest published fares, then use the resources outlined here to try and beat those fares. Low-season fares should be appreciably cheaper than the **high-season** (June to Sept.) ones listed here.

TRAVELING FROM NORTH AMERICA

Basic round-trip fares to Britain range roughly US$350-1200. Standard commercial carriers like American and United will probably offer the most convenient flights, but they may not be the cheapest, unless you manage to grab a special promotion. You will probably find flying one of the following "discount" airlines a better deal, if any of their limited departure points is convenient for you.

Aer Lingus: (☎0870 876 2020; www.aerlingus.com.) Cheap round-trips from Boston, Chicago, Los Angeles, New York and Washington, D.C. to Birmingham, Bristol, London, Manchester, Glasgow, Dublin, and Shannon.

Finnair: (☎1-800-950-5000; www.finnair.com.) Cheap round-trips from San Francisco, New York, and Toronto to Helsinki; connections throughout Europe.

Icelandair: (☎1-800-223-5500; www.icelandair.com.) Stopovers in Iceland for no extra cost on most transatlantic flights. US$650-900; Oct.-May US$500-$700.

TRAVELING FROM AUSTRALIA AND NEW ZEALAND

Air New Zealand: (New Zealand ☎64 0800 737 000; www.airnz.co.nz.) Flights from Auckland to Dublin and London.

Qantas Air: (Australia ☎61 13 13 13, New Zealand 0800 808 767; www.qantas.com.au.) Flights from Australia and New Zealand to London for around AUS$2800.

Singapore Air: (Australia ☎61 13 10 11, New Zealand 0800 808 909; www.singaporeair.com.) Flights from Auckland, Sydney, Melbourne, and Perth to London, all through Singapore.

Thai Airways: (Australia ☎61 298 44 09 29, New Zealand 64 09 377 38 86; www.thaiair.com.) Auckland, Sydney, and Melbourne to London, all through Bangkok.

AIR COURIER FLIGHTS

Those who travel light should consider courier flights. Couriers help transport cargo on international flights by using their checked luggage space for freight. Generally, couriers must travel with carry-ons only and deal with complex flight restrictions. Most flights are round-trip only, with short fixed-length stays (usually one week) and a limit of a one ticket per issue. Most of these flights also operate only out of major gateway cities, mostly in North America.

FROM NORTH AMERICA

Round-trip courier fares from the US to Britain run about US$130-600. Most flights leave from New York, Los Angeles, San Francisco, or Miami in the US; and from Montreal, Toronto, or Vancouver in Canada. The organizations below provide members with lists of opportunities and courier brokers for an annual fee. Prices quoted below are round-trip.

Air Courier Association, 1767 A Denver West Blvd., Golden, CO 80401 (☎800-211-5119; www.aircourier.org). Ten departure cities in the US and Canada go to London and the rest of Western Europe (high-season US$150-550). 1-year membership US$39.

Courier Travel (www.couriertravel.org). Searchable online database. Multiple departure points in the US to various European destinations.

International Association of Air Travel Couriers (IAATC; www.courier.org). From 7 North American cities to Western European cities, including London, Madrid, Paris, and Rome. 1-year membership US$45.

FROM THE UK, AUSTRALIA, AND NEW ZEALAND

The **International Association of Air Travel Couriers** (www.courier.org; see above) often offers courier flights from London to Tokyo, Sydney, and Bangkok and from Auckland to Frankfurt and London. **Courier Travel** (see p. 29) also offers flights from London and Sydney.

STANDBY FLIGHTS

Traveling standby requires flexibility in arrival and departure dates and cities. Companies dealing in standby flights sell vouchers rather than tickets, along with the promise to get you to your destination (or near your destination) within a certain window of time (typically 1-5 days). You call in before your specific window of time to hear your flight options and the probability that you will be able to board each flight. You can then decide which flights you want to try to make, show up at the appropriate airport at the appropriate time, present your voucher, and board if space is available. Vouchers can usually be bought for both one-way and round-trip travel. You may receive a refund only if every available flight within your date range is full; if you opt not to take an available (but perhaps less convenient) flight, you can only get credit toward future travel. Carefully read agreements with any company offering standby flights as tricky fine print can leave you in the lurch. To check on a company's service record in the US, contact the Better Business Bureau (☎703-276-0100; www.bbb.org). Refunds are rare, and clients' vouchers will not be honored when an airline fails to receive payment in time.

TICKET CONSOLIDATORS

Ticket consolidators, or **"bucket shops,"** buy unsold tickets in bulk from commercial airlines and sell them at discounted rates. The best place to look is in the Sunday travel section of any major newspaper (such as *The New York Times*), where many bucket shops place tiny ads. Call quickly, as availability is typically extremely limited. Not all bucket shops are reliable, so insist on a receipt that gives full details of restrictions, refunds, and tickets, and pay by credit card (in spite of the 2-5% fee) so you can stop payment if you never receive your tickets. For more information, see www.travel-library.com/air-travel/consolidators.html.

TRAVELING FROM THE US AND CANADA

Some consolidators worth trying are **Rebel** (☎800-732-3588; www.rebeltours.com), **Cheap Tickets** (www.cheaptickets.com), **Flights.com** (www.flights.com), and **Travel-HUB** (www.travelhub.com). *Let's Go* does not endorse these agencies. As always, be cautious, and research companies before you give your credit card number.

CHARTER FLIGHTS

Tour operators contract charter flights with airlines in order to fly extra loads of passengers during peak season. These flights are far from hassle free. They occur less frequently than major airlines, make refunds particularly difficult, and are almost always fully booked. Their scheduled times may change and they may be cancelled at the last moment (as late as 48hr. before the trip, and without a full refund). And check-in, boarding, and baggage claim for them are often much slower. They can be, however, much cheaper.

Discount clubs and fare brokers offer members savings on last-minute charter and tour deals. Study contracts closely; you don't want to end up with an unwanted overnight layover. **Travelers Advantage** (☎800-835-8747; www.travelersadvantage.com; US$90 annual fee includes discounts and cheap flight directories) specializes in European travel and tour packages.

BY CHUNNEL

Traversing 27 mi. under the sea, the **Channel Tunnel (Chunnel)** is undoubtedly the fastest, most convenient, and least scenic route between France and England.

BY TRAIN. Eurostar, Eurostar House, Waterloo Station, London SE1 8SE (☎08705 186 186, outside the UK 0044 1233 617 575; www.eurostar.com). Runs frequent trains between London and the Continent. 10-28 trains per day run to 100 destinations including Paris (4hr., 2nd class US$90-300), Disneyland Paris, Brussels, Lille, and Calais. Book at major rail stations in the UK.

BY BUS. Eurolines and **Eurobus,** both run by National Express (UK ☎08705 808 080; www.nationalexpress.co.uk), provide bus-ferry combinations.

BY CAR. Eurotunnel, Customer Relations, P.O. Box 2000, Folkestone, Kent CT18 8XY (☎08705 35 35 35; www.eurotunnel.co.uk). Shuttles cars and passengers between Kent and Nord-Pas-de-Calais in France. Round-trip fares for vehicle and all passengers £165-400. Same-day round-trip £98. Frequent specials; highly variable prices. Book online or via phone. Travelers with cars can also use ferries (see below).

BY FERRY

A directory of UK ferries can be found at www.seaview.co.uk/ferries.html.

Brittany Ferries: ☎08703 665 333, France 0033 298 800; www.brittany-ferries.com. **Plymouth** to **Roscoff, France** and **Santander, Spain**. **Portsmouth** to **St-Malo** and **Caen, France. Poole** to **Cherbourg. Cork** to **Roscoff, France**.

DFDS Seaways: ☎08702 520 524; www.dfdsseaways.co.uk. Harwich to **Cuxhaven** (19½hr., £29-49) and **Esbjerg, Denmark** (18hr., £29-49). Newcastle to **Amsterdam** (16hr., £19-39); **Kristiansand, Norway** (18¼hr., £19-59); and **Gothenburg, Sweden** (26hr., £19-59).

Fjord Line: ☎08701 439 669; www.fjordline.no. Newcastle, England to **Stavanger** (19½hr., £30-40) and **Bergen, Norway** (26hr., £30-40).

Irish Ferries: ☎08705 171 717, France 33 1 56 93 43 40, Ireland 0818 300 400; www.irishferries.ie.) Rosslare to **Cherbourg** and **Roscoff, France,** and Pembroke, UK; and Holyhead to **Dublin, Ireland.**

P&O Ferries: ☎08705 980 333; www.poferries.com. Daily ferries from Hull to **Rotterdam, The Netherlands** and **Zeebrugge, Belgium;** Dover to **Calais, France;** Portsmouth to **LeHavre** and **Bilbao, Spain;** and several Britain to Ireland routes.

SeaFrance: France ☎08 25 08 25 05; www.seafrance.com. **Dover** to **Calais, France** (1½hr., 15 per day, £7-11).

Stena Line: ☎08705 70 70 70; www.stenaline.co.uk. Runs ferries to Ireland: Harwich to **Hook of Holland;** Fishguard to **Rosslare;** Stranraer to **Belfast;** Holyhead to **Dublin** and **Dún Laoghaire;** Fleetwood to **Larne.**

GETTING AROUND IN THE UK

Fares on all modes of transportation are referred to as **single** (one-way) or **return** (round-trip). "Period round-trips" or "open round-trips" require you to return within a specific number of days; "day round-trip" means you return on the same day. Unless stated otherwise, *Let's Go* always lists standard single fares.

BY PLANE

The recent emergence of no-frills airlines has made hopscotching around Europe (and even within the UK) by air increasingly affordable and convenient. Although these flights often feature inconvenient hours or serve less-popular regional airports, with one-way flights averaging about US$80, it's never been faster or easier to jet across the Continent. **Aer Lingus** and **British Midland Airways** fly regularly between London, Dublin, and other major cities.

If you can book in advance and/or travel at odd hours, the discount airlines listed below are a great option. A good source of offers are the travel supplements of newspapers and the airline websites. The **Air Travel Advisory Bureau** in London (☎0189 255 3500; www.atab.co.uk) provides referrals to travel agencies and consolidators that offer discounted airfares out of the UK.

AirBerlin: ☎0871 500 0737 (10p per min.); www.airberlin.com. Departures from London, Southampton, and Manchester to over 60 European cities.

Aer Lingus: ☎0870 876 5000, Ireland 353 0818 365 000; www.aerlingus.com. Services between Cork, Dublin, Galway, Kerry, Shannon, and many cities in Europe. Departures from Birmingham, Edinburgh, Glasgow, London, and Manchester in the UK.

British Midland Airways: ☎08706 070 555; www.flybmi.com. Services between Aberdeen, Belfast, Dublin, Edinburgh, Glasgow, Inverness, and London. London to Brussels, Paris, and Frankfurt.

🔳 **easyJet:** ☎0871 244 2366; www.easyjet.com. 210 routes between 63 European cities. Departures from Aberdeen, Belfast, Bristol, Edinburgh, East Midlands, Glasgow, Inverness, Liverpool, London, Newcastle. Frequent specials; online tickets.

KLM: ☎08705 074 074; www.klmuk.com. Round-trip tickets from London and other cities in the UK to Amsterdam, Brussels, Frankfurt, Düsseldorf, Milan, Paris, and Rome.

Ryanair: ☎0871 246 0000 (10p per min.); Ireland 0818 30 30 30 (national rate); www.ryanair.ie. From Dublin, London, and Glasgow to destinations in France, Ireland, Italy, Scandinavia, and elsewhere. As low as £1 on specials; book far in advance for greater savings.

The **Star Alliance European Airpass** offers economy class fares as low as US$65 for travel within Europe to more than 200 destinations in 42 countries. The pass is available to transatlantic passengers on Star Alliance carriers, including Air Canada, Austrian Airlines, BMI British Midland, Lufthansa, Scandinavian Airlines System, Thai International, United Airlines, and Varig, as well as on certain partner airlines. See www.staralliance.com for more information.

 TRAVELINE. An essential resource, Traveline (☎0871 200 2233; www.traveline.org.uk) offers comprehensive and impartial information for travel planning throughout England, Scotland, and Wales—whether by train, bus, or ferry.

BY TRAIN

Britain's train network crisscrosses the length and breadth of the island. In cities with more than one train station, the city name is given first, followed by the station name (for example, "Manchester Piccadilly" and "Manchester Victoria" are Manchester's two major stations). In general, traveling by train costs more than by bus. Railpasses covering specific regions are sometimes available from local train stations and may include bus and ferry travel. Prices and schedules often change; find up-to-date information from **National Rail Inquiries** (☎08457 484 950) or online at www.nationalrail.co.uk.

ESSENTIALS

TICKET TYPES. The array of tickets available for British trains is bewildering, and prices aren't always set logically—buying an unlimited day pass to the region may cost less than buying a one-way ticket. Prices rise on weekends and may be higher before 9:30am. Purchase tickets before boarding, except at unstaffed train stations, where tickets are bought on the train. There are several types of **discount tickets. APEX** (Advance Purchase Excursion) tickets must be bought at least seven days in advance (2 days for ScotRail); **SuperAdvance** tickets must be purchased before 6pm the day before you travel. **Saver** tickets are valid anytime with return trips within a month, but may be restricted to certain trains at peak times; **Super-Saver** tickets are similar, but are only valid at off-peak times (usually M-Th and Su and holidays). It may seem daunting, but the general rule of thumb is simple: planning a week or more in advance can make a $30-60 difference.

BRITRAIL PASSES. If you plan to travel a great deal on trains within Britain, the **BritRail Pass** can be a good buy. Eurail passes are *not* valid in Britain, but there is often a discount on Eurostar passes if you have proof of Eurail purchase at the ticket office. BritRail passes are only available outside Britain; **you must buy them before traveling to Britain.** They allow unlimited train travel in England, Wales, and Scotland, regardless of which company is operating the trains, but they do not work in Northern Ireland or on Eurostar. Unless noted, travelers under 26 should ask for a **Youth Pass** for a 25% discount on standard and first classes; **seniors** (over 60) should ask for a 15% discount on first class only. **Children** ages five to 15 can travel free with each adult pass, as long as you ask for the **Family Pass** (free). All children under 5 travel free. The **Party Discount** gets the third through ninth travelers in a party a 50% discount on their railpasses. Check with BritRail (US ☎ 1-866-2748-7245; www.britrail.com) or one of the distributors for details on other passes. Prices listed do not include shipping costs (around US$15 for delivery in 2-3 days, US$25 for priority delivery). All prices are given in US dollars.

Consecutive Pass: For consecutive days travel. 4-day standard-class $232, first-class $349; 8-day $332/499; 15-day $499/748; 22-day $631/950; 1 month $748/1124.

Flexipass: For travel within a 2-month period. Any 4 days standard-class $293, first-class $436; any 8 days $425/638; any 15 days $644/960.

England Consecutive: Travel for consecutive days, only in England. 4-day standard-class $185, first-class $279; 8-day $265/399; 15-day $399/599; 22-day $505/760; 1 month $599/898.

England Flexipass: Travel within a 2-month period, only in England. Any 4 days standard-class $235, first-class $349; any 8 days $340/510; any 15 days $515/769.

London Plus Pass: Travel between London and several popular daytrip locations, including Cambridge, Oxford, and Windsor. Travel within an 8-day period. Any 2 days standard-class $74, first-class $113; any 4 days $140/187; any 7 days within a 15 day period $187/249.

BritRail+Ireland Pass: Includes all trains in Britain, Northern Ireland, and the Republic of Ireland, plus a round-trip Stena or Irish Ferries sea crossing. No discounts apply. Travel within a 1-month period. Any 5 days standard-class $462, first-class $636; any 10 days $733/1040.

BritRail Scottish Freedom Pass: Includes all Scottish trains, the Glasgow Underground, and Caledonian MacBrayne and Strathclyde ferry services. No discounts apply. Standard-class only. Travel within a 15-day period. Any 4 days $217; any 8 days $292.

BRITRAIL DISTRIBUTORS. The distributors listed on the next page will either sell you passes directly or tell you where you can buy passes; you can also ask at travel agents for more information.

Australia: Rail Plus, 10-16 Queen St., Level 4, Melbourne, Victoria 3000 (☎61 03 9642 8644; www.railplus.com.au). **Concorde International Travel,** 403 George St., Sydney, NSW 2000 (☎61 1300 656 777; www.concorde.com.au).

Canada and US: Rail Europe, 44 South Broadway, White Plains, NY 10601 (☎800-361-7245, 877-257-2887; www.raileurope.com), is the North American distributor for Brit-Rail. Or try **Rail Pass Express** (☎877-7245-7277; www.railpass.com/new).

Ireland: USIT, 19-21 Aston Quay, O'Connell Bridge, Dublin 2 (☎353 01 602 1904; www.usit.ie).

New Zealand: Holiday Shoppe, Gullivers Holiday Rep: Holiday Shoppe, 66 Wyndham St., 5th fl., Auckland (☎64 0800 80 84 80; www.holidayshoppe.co.nz). Locations throughout New Zealand.

RAIL DISCOUNT CARDS. Unlike BritRail passes, these can be purchased in the UK. Passes are valid for one year and generally offer one-third off standard fares. They are available for young people (£20; must be 16-25 or full-time student), seniors (£20; must be over 60), families (£20), and people with disabilities (£18). Visit the **Railcards** website (www.railcard.co.uk) for details.

IN NORTHERN IRELAND. Northern Ireland Railways (☎028 9066 6630; www.nirail-ways.co.uk) is not extensive but covers the northeastern coast. The major line connects Dublin to Belfast, then splits with one branch ending at Bangor and one at Larne. There is also service from Belfast and Lisburn west to Derry and Por-trush, stopping at three towns between Antrim and the coast. BritRail passes are not valid here, but Northern Ireland Railways offers its own discounts. A valid **Translink Student Discount Card** (£7) will get you up to 33% off all trains and 15% discounts on bus fares over £1.80 within Northern Ireland. The **Freedom of Northern Ireland** ticket allows unlimited travel by train and Ulsterbus; seven consecutive days £50, three out of eight days £34, one day £14.

IN THE REPUBLIC OF IRELAND. While the **Eurailpass** is not accepted in Northern Ireland, it *is* accepted on trains in the Republic. The BritRail pass does not cover travel in Northern Ireland, but the month-long **BritRail+Ireland** works in both the North and the Republic with rail options and round-trip ferry service between Britain and Ireland (see p. 31). It's easiest to buy a Eurailpass before you arrive in Europe; contact a travel agent (p. 25) or Rail Europe (p. 31).

BY BUS AND COACH

The British distinguish between **buses** (short local routes) and **coaches** (long distances). *Let's Go* uses the term "buses" for both. Regional **passes** offer unlimited travel within a given area for a certain number of days; these are often called **Rovers, Ramblers,** or **Explorers,** and they usually offer cost-effective travel. Plan ahead and book tickets online in order to take advantage of discounts.

BUSES

In Britain, long-distance bus travel is extensive and cheap. **National Express** (☎08705 808 080; www.nationalexpress.com) is the principal operator of long-distance bus services in Britain, although **Scottish Citylink** (☎08705 505 050; www.cit-ylink.co.uk) has extensive coverage in Scotland. Discounts are available for seniors (over 50), students, and young persons (16-25). The **Brit Xplorer passes** offer unlimited travel for a set number of days (7 days £79, 14 days £139, 28 days £219; www.nationalexpress.com). For those who plan far ahead, the best option is National Express's **Fun Fares,** only available online, which offer a limited number of seats on buses from London starting at, amazingly, £1. A similar option is **Mega-**

bus (☎0900 160 0900; www.megabus.com), which also offers the one-quid price but has fewer buses. **Tourist Information Centres** carry timetables for regional buses and will help befuddled travelers decipher them.

Ulsterbus (☎028 9066 6630; www.ulsterbus.co.uk) runs extensive and reliable routes throughout Northern Ireland. Pick up a free regional timetable at any station. The **Emerald Card,** designed for travel in the Republic of Ireland as well as Northern Ireland, offers unlimited travel on Ulsterbus. The card works for eight days out of 15 (£115, under 16 £58) or 15 of 30 consecutive days (£200/50).

BUS TOURS

Staffed by young, energetic guides, these tours cater to backpackers and stop right at the doors of hostels. They are a good way to meet other independent travelers and to get to places unreachable by public transportation; most ensure a stay at certain hostels. "Hop-on, hop-off" tours allow you to stay as long as you like at each stop.

■ **HAGGIS,** 60 High St., Edinburgh EH1 1TB (☎0131 558 3738; www.haggisadventures.com). Specializes in 1-, 3-, 4-, 6-, and 8-day prearranged tours of Scotland with small groups and witty guides (from £24). Sister tours **HAGGIS Britain** (same contact info) and the **Shamrocker Ireland** (☎353 01 672 7651) run 3-8 days through England, Wales, and Ireland.

■ **MacBackpackers,** 105 High St., Edinburgh EH1 1SG (☎01315 589 900; www.macbackpackers.com). Hop-on, hop-off flexitour (£75) of Scotland and 2- to 9-day tours.

Celtic Connection, 7/6 Cadiz St., Edinburgh EH6 7BJ (☎0131 225 3330; www.thecelticconnection.co.uk). 2- to 9-day tours of Scotland, Wales, and Ireland (£25-225).

Karibuni, (☎01202 661 865; www.karibuni.co.uk). Runs daytrips, weekend trips, and adventure tours in England and Wales from London, including biking, kayaking, surfing, horseback riding, and camping (£50-225). Longer tours available for groups of 8+.

BY CAR

Cars offer speed, freedom, access to the countryside, and an escape from the town-to-town mentality of trains; but they introduce the hassle of driving, parking, traffic, and the high cost of petrol (gasoline). If you can't decide between train and car travel, you may benefit from a combination of the two; BritRail pass distributors (p. 25) sell combination rail-and-drive packages.

RENTING

Renters in Britain must be over 21; those under 23 (or even 25) may have to pay hefty additional fees. Since the public transportation system in Britain is so extensive and punctual, travelers should consider using it instead. However, for longer trips, journeys into many small, obscure destinations, or into the farthest reaches of the Highlands and Islands of the north and west, the convenience of a car can mean the difference between an amazing trip and a tiresome trek. Bear in mind that British agencies refer to rental as "car hire."

RENTAL AGENCIES. Occasionally the price and availability information agencies give doesn't match information from local offices in your country. Try checking with both numbers to make sure you get the best price and accurate information. Local desk numbers are included in town listings. At most agencies, all you need to rent a car is a driver's license; some require additional ID. Policies and prices vary from agency to agency. Be sure to ask about insurance coverage and deductibles, and always check the fine print. The following agencies rent cars in Britain:

Arnold Clark: ☎0845 607 4500; www.arnoldclarkrental.co.uk.

Auto Europe: Toll-free ☎888-223-5555, US 207-842-2000; www.autoeurope.com.

Avis: Toll-free ☎800-331-1212, Australia 136 333, 800-331-1212, New Zealand 0800 65 51 11, UK 08700 100 287; www.avis.com.

Budget: Toll-free ☎800-527-0700, Canada 800-268-8900, UK 8701 565 656; www.budgetrentacar.com.

easyCar: UK ☎09063 333 333 (60p per min.); www.easycar.co.uk.

Europe by Car: Toll-free ☎800-223-1516, US 212-581-3040; www.europebycar.com.

Europcar International: Toll-free ☎877-940-6900, UK 870 607 5000; www.europcar.com.

Hertz: Toll-free ☎800-654-3001 or 800-654-3131; www.hertz.com.

Kemwel: Toll-free ☎877-820-0668; www.kemwel.com.

LEASING. For trips longer than a few weeks, leasing can be cheaper and is often the only option for those aged 18-21. The cheapest leases are agreements to buy the car and then sell it back to the manufacturer at a prearranged price. Leases generally include insurance and are not taxed. Depending on car size, a 60-day lease starts around ₤725. Auto Europe, Europe by Car, and Kemwel handle leases.

COSTS. Rental prices vary by company, season, and pickup point; expect to pay around ₤160 per week for a small car. Prices increase for 4WD and automatic cars. If possible, reserve and pay well in advance. In many cases it is less expensive to reserve a car from the US than from Europe. Rental packages can offer unlimited miles, while others offer a set number of miles per day with a surcharge per additional mile. National chains (see Arnold Clark, above) often allow one-way rentals, picking up in one city and dropping off in another. There is usually a minimum hire period and sometimes an extra drop-off charge.

DRIVING PERMITS AND CAR INSURANCE

INTERNATIONAL DRIVING PERMIT (IDP)

To drive in Britain, you must be over 18 and have a **valid foreign driver's license.** An **International Driving Permit (IDP)** is also advisable. Your IDP, valid for one year, must be issued in your own country before you depart. An application requires one or two photos, a current local license, an additional form of identification, and a fee. To apply, contact your home country's automobile association. Be careful when purchasing online or anywhere other than your home automobile association. Many vendors sell permits of questionable legitimacy for higher prices.

CAR INSURANCE

Most credit cards cover standard insurance. If you rent, lease, or borrow a car, you will need a **Green Card,** or **International Insurance Certificate,** to certify that you have liability insurance and that it applies abroad. Green cards can be obtained at car rental agencies, car dealers (for those leasing cars), some travel agents, and some border crossings. Rental agencies may require you to purchase theft insurance in countries that they consider to have a high risk of auto theft. Be aware that cars rented on an **American Express** or **Visa/MasterCard Gold** or **Platinum** credit card in Britain might *not* carry the automatic insurance that they would in some other countries; check with your credit card company. Be sure to ask whether the price includes insurance against theft and collision. Insurance plans almost always come with an excess (or deductible) of around ₤500. The excess quote applies to collisions with other vehicles; collisions with non-vehicles, such as trees, ("single-vehicle collisions") cost more. The excess can often be reduced or waived entirely if you pay an additional charge, from £1-10 per day. If you are driving a rented vehicle on an unpaved road, you are almost never covered.

ON THE ROAD

You must be 18 to drive in Britain. Be sure you can handle **driving on the left** side of the road and driving **manual transmission** ("stick-shift" is far more common than automatic). Be particularly cautious at **roundabouts** (rotary interchanges), and remember to give way to traffic from the right. The **Association for Safe International Road Travel (ASIRT),** 11769 Gainsborough Rd., Potomac, MD 20854, USA (☎1-301-983-5542; www.asirt.org), sends travelers country-specific Road Travel Reports. Road atlases for the UK are available in travel bookshops and from many Tourist Information Centres. **Petrol** (gasoline) is sold by the liter; there are about four liters to the gallon. Prices vary, but average about 90p per liter and increase during the summer and in urban areas like London. The country is covered by a high-speed system of **motorways** ("M-roads") that connect London with major cities around the country. These are supplemented by a tight web of "A-roads" and "B-roads" that connect towns: A-roads are the main routes, while B-roads are narrower but often more scenic. **Distances** on road signs are in miles (1 mi.= 1.6km). **Speed limits** are 70mph (113km/hr.) on motorways (highways) and dual carriageways (divided highways), 60mph (97km/hr.) on single carriageways (non-divided highways), and usually 30mph (48km/hr.) in urban areas. Speed limits are marked at the beginning of town areas; upon leaving, you'll see a circular sign with a slash through it, signaling the end of the restriction. Drivers and all passengers are required to wear **seat belts.** Driving in central **London** is restricted during weekday working hours. Parking in London can be nightmarish. The **Highway Code,** which details Britain's driving regulations, is accessible online (www.highway-code.gov.uk) or can be purchased at most large bookstores or newsstands.

 DRIVING PRECAUTIONS. When traveling in the summer, bring substantial amounts of water (a suggested 5L of **water** per person per day) for drinking and for the radiator. For long drives to unpopulated areas, register with police before beginning the trek, and again upon arrival at the destination. Check with the local automobile club for details. Make sure tires are in good repair and have enough air, and get good maps. A **compass** and a **car manual** can also be very useful. You should always carry a **spare tire** and **jack, jumper cables, extra oil, flares, a flashlight (torch),** and **heavy blankets** (in case your car breaks down at night or in the winter). If you don't know how to **change a tire,** learn before heading out, especially if you are planning on traveling in deserted areas. Blowouts on dirt roads are common. If you do have a breakdown, **stay with your car;** if you wander off, there's less likelihood trackers will find you.

DANGERS

Learn local driving signals and wear a seatbelt. Carseats for infants are available at most rental agencies. Study route maps before you hit the road, and consider bringing spare parts. If your car breaks down, wait for the police to assist you. For long drives in isolated areas, consider investing in a cellular phone and a roadside assistance program (p. 38). Driving in rural areas often requires extra caution on single-lane roads. These roads feature occasional "passing places," which cars use to make way for passing vehicles. Cars **flash their lights** to signal that they will pull aside; the other car should take the right of way. Beware roaming **livestock** along remote countryside roads. Be sure to park your vehicle in a garage or well- traveled area, and use a steering wheel locking device in larger cities. **Sleeping in your car** is one of the most dangerous (and often illegal) ways to get your rest.

CAR ASSISTANCE

In the event of a breakdown, try contacting the **Automobile Association** (**AA; ☎** 0161 495 8945; emergency breakdown 08457 887 766; www.theaa.com) or the **Royal Automobile Club** (☎ 08705 722 722; www.rac.co.uk). Call ☎ **999** in an emergency.

BY FERRY

Caledonian MacBrayne, The Ferry Terminal, Gourock PA19 1QP (☎ 08705 650 000; www.calmac.co.uk). The MacDaddy of Scottish ferries, with routes in the **Hebrides** and along the west coast of Scotland. Offers various combo packages for convenient and cost-effective island hopping in the Scottish Islands.

Isle of Man Steam Packet Company serves the Isle of Man; see p. 384 for details.

P&O Ferries, Channel House, Channel View Rd., Dover CT17 9TJ (☎ 08705 980 333; www.poferries.com). Many ferries between Britain, Ireland, and the Continent.

Northlink Ferries, Stromness, Orkney, KW16 3BH (☎ 01856 885 500, reservations 0845 600 0449; www.northlinkferries.co.uk). Sails between **Aberdeen, Lerwick, Kirkwall, Stromness,** and **Scrabster.**

Norfolkline, Norfolk House, Eastern Docks, Dover, CT16 1JA (☎ 0870 870 1020; www.norfolkline-ferries.com). **Dover** to **Calais, France** and **Dunkerque, France** (equally convenient but less busy). Also travels between **Belfast, Dublin,** and **Liverpool.**

Stena Line, Stena House (☎ 08705 707 070; www.stenaline.co.uk). Ferries to Ireland: Harwich to **Hook of Holland;** Fishguard to **Rosslare;** Stranraer to **Belfast;** Holyhead to **Dublin** and **Dún Laoghaire;** Fleetwood to **Larne.**

Swansea-Cork Ferries, King's Dock, Swansea SA1 1SF (☎ 01792 456 116, Ireland 353 21 483 6000; www.swanseacorkferries.com). Swansea and Pembroke to **Cork.**

BY BICYCLE

Much of the British countryside is well-suited for cycling. Consult tourist offices for local touring routes and always bring along the appropriate **Ordnance Survey maps.** Keep safety in mind—even well-traveled routes cover uneven terrain.

GETTING OR TRANSPORTING A BIKE. Many airlines will count a bike as part of your luggage, although a few charge an extra US$60-110 each way. If you plan to explore several widely separated regions, you can combine cycling with train travel; bikes often ride free on trains and ferries. A better option for some is to buy a bike in Britain and Ireland and sell it before leaving. A bike bought new overseas is subject to customs duties if brought home. **Renting** ("hiring") a bike is often preferable to bringing your own. *Let's Go* lists bike rental stores in many towns.

BICYCLE EQUIPMENT. Riding a bike with a frame pack strapped to it or your back is extremely unsafe; **panniers** are essential. You'll also need a suitable **bike helmet** (from US$30) and a U-shaped **Citadel** or **Kryptonite lock** (from US$25). British law requires a white light at the front and a red light and red reflector at the back.

INFORMATION AND ORGANIZATIONS. The **National Cycle Network** encompasses 10,000 mi. of biking and walking trails in the UK. Information and maps are available through **Sustrans** (☎ 0845 113 0065; www.sustrans.org.uk). The **Cyclists Touring Club,** Parklands, Railton Rd., Guildford, Surrey GU2 9JX (☎ 0870 873 0060; www.ctc.org.uk), provides maps and books. Membership costs £34 (under 18 and students under 26 £12, over 65 £21) and includes a bi-monthly magazine.

TOURS. Bicycle Beano (☎ 01982 560 471; www.bicycle-beano.co.uk) offers vegetarian tours in Wales and England; **Cycle Scotland** (☎ 0131 556 5560; www.cycle-scotland.co.uk) operates "Scottish Cycle Safaris."

BY FOOT

Walking and hiking are favorite pastimes of the British. Well-marked and well-maintained long-distance paths cover Britain, from the rolling paths of the **South Downs Way** (p. 157) to the rugged mountain trails of the **Pennine Way** (p. 402). Ordnance Survey 1:25,000 maps mark almost every house, barn, standing stone, graveyard, and pub; less-ambitious hikers will want the 1:50,000 scale maps. The **Ramblers' Association,** Camelford House, 87-90 Albert Embankment, 2nd fl., London SE1 7TW (☎020 7339 8500; www.ramblers.org.uk), publishes a Walk Britain Yearbook (£6, free to members) on walking and places to stay, as well as free newsletters and magazines. Their website abounds with information. (Membership £24, concessions £14.) The **National Cycle Network** (see **By Bicycle: Information and Organizations,** p. 38) includes walking trails. **Contours Walking Holidays** (www.contours.co.uk) provides both guided and self-guided walking holidays in England, Scotland, Wales, and Ireland.

BY THUMB

Let's Go never recommends hitchhiking as a safe means of transportation, and none of the information presented here is intended to do so.

Let's Go strongly urges you to consider the risks before you choose to hitchhike. Hitching means entrusting your life to a stranger, risking theft, assault, sexual harassment, and unsafe driving. Nonetheless, hitching can get you where you're going, especially in rural parts of Scotland, Wales, and Ireland (England is tougher), where public transportation can be less than desirable. Women traveling alone should **never hitch.** A man and a woman are safer; two men will have a hard time, and three will go nowhere. Experienced hitchers pick a spot outside built-up areas, where drivers can stop, return to the road without causing an accident, and have time to look over potential passengers as they approach. Hitching or even standing on motorways (any road labeled "M") is illegal.

Safety precautions are always necessary, even for those not hitching alone. Safety-minded hitchers will not get into a car that they can't get out of again in a hurry (especially the back seat of a two-door car) and never let go of their backpacks. If they feel threatened, they insist on being let off, regardless of location. Acting as if they are going to open the car door or vomit usually gets a driver to stop. Hitching at night can be particularly dangerous; experienced hitchers stand in well-lit places and expect drivers to be leery.

KEEPING IN TOUCH

BY EMAIL AND INTERNET

Internet access is ubiquitous in big cities, common in towns, and sparse in rural areas. You can find access in the increasingly common cybercafes; in coffee shops, particularly chains such as Caffe Nero and Starbucks; and in public libraries. Sneaky travelers use computers in media shops like PC World to check email quickly.

Although in some places it's possible to forge a remote link with your home server, in most cases this is a much slower (and more expensive) than taking advantage of free **web-based email** (e.g., www.gmail.com and www.yahoo.com). **Internet cafes** and Internet terminals at public libraries or universities are listed in the **Practical Information** sections of major cities.

Increasingly, travelers find that taking their **laptop computers** on the road with them can be a convenient option for staying connected. Laptop users can call an Internet service provider via a modem using long-distance phone cards specifically intended for such calls. They may also find Internet cafes that allow them to connect their laptops to the Internet. Travelers with Wi-Fi-enabled computers may be able to take advantage of an increasing number of Internet "hotspots," where they can get online for free or for a small fee. For information on insuring your laptop while traveling, see p. 23.

BY TELEPHONE

CALLING HOME FROM BRITAIN

Using a **calling card** is often the cheapest option for travelers. You can frequently call collect without a calling card. To obtain a calling card from your national telecommunications service before leaving home, contact the appropriate company listed below. To call home with a calling card, contact the operator for your service provider in Britain by dialing their toll-free access number. Many newsstands in the UK sell **prepaid international phonecards,** such as those offered by Swiftcall; online sites such as www.nobelcom.com offer cards for a low price. Oftentimes cards are cheap but carry a minimum charge per call. Stores such as **Call Shop** offer cheap international calls from booths and can be found in large cities.

COMPANY	TO OBTAIN A CARD:	TO CALL ABROAD, DIAL:
AT&T (US)	800-364-9292; www.att.com	0800 89 0011 or 0500 89 0011
Canada Direct	800-561-8868; www.infocanadadirect.com	0800 559 3141 or 0800 096 0634
MCI (US)	800-777-5000; www.minutepass.com	0800 279 5088
Telecom New Zealand	www.telecom.co.nz	0800 890 064
Telstra Australia	1800 676 638; www.telstra.com	0800 890 061

To call home with a calling card, contact the operator for your service provider in Britain by dialing the appropriate toll-free access number (listed above in the third column). You can make direct international calls from **payphones,** but if you aren't using a calling card you may need to drop coins as quickly as your words. Occasionally major credit cards can also be used for direct international calls. In-room **hotel calls** invariably include an arbitrary, sky-high surcharge (as much as £6); the rare B&B that has in-room phones tends to as well. See the box below for directions on how to place a direct international call. Placing a **collect call** through an international operator is even more expensive. The number for the **international operator** in Britain is ☎ 155.

CALLING WITHIN BRITAIN

The simplest way to call within the country is to use a coin-operated phone, but **prepaid phone cards** (available at newspaper kiosks and other convenience stores), which carry a certain amount of phone time depending on the card's denomination, usually save time and money in the long run. The computerized phone will tell you how much time, in units, you have left on your card. Another kind of prepaid telephone card comes with a **Personal Identification Number (PIN)** and a toll-free access number. Instead of inserting the card into the phone, you call the access number and follow the directions on the card. These cards can be used to make international as well as domestic calls. Phone rates typically tend to be highest in the morning, lower in the evening, and lowest on Sunday and late at night.

PLACING INTERNATIONAL CALLS. To call Britain and Ireland from home or to call home from Britain and Ireland, dial:

1. The **international dialing prefix.** To dial *out of* Australia, dial 0011; Canada or the US, 011; the Republic of Ireland, New Zealand, or the UK, 00.

2. The **country code** of the country you want to call. To *place a call to* Australia, dial 61; Canada or the US, 1; the Republic of Ireland, 353; New Zealand, 64; the UK, 44.

3. The **city/area code.** *Let's Go* lists the city/area codes for cities and towns in Britain opposite the city or town name, next to a ☎. For international numbers, *Let's Go* writes the country code first. If the first digit of the city/area code is a zero (e.g., 020 for London), **omit the zero** when calling **from abroad** (e.g., dial 20 from Canada to reach London).

4. The **local number.**

5. **Examples:** To call the US embassy in London from New York, dial ☎011 44 20 7499 9000. To call the British embassy in Washington from London, dial ☎00 1 202 588 7800. To call the US embassy in London from London, dial ☎020 7499 9000.

To make a call within a city or town, dial the phone code and the number. For **directory inquiries,** call ☎118 500 (or any of the myriad other 118 services, such as ☎118 118 or 118 888). The services normally charge a 50p connection fee and cost 15p per min. *Let's Go* lists **phone codes** opposite the city or town name next to the ☎ symbol; all phone numbers in that town use that phone code unless specified otherwise. To call Britain from the Republic of Ireland, or vice versa, you will have to make an international call. Northern Ireland is part of the UK phone network.

PHONE CODES

Recent changes to British phone codes have produced a system in which the first three numbers of the phone code identify the type of number being called. **Premium rate calls,** costing about 50p per minute, can be identified by the 090 phone code. **Freephone** (toll-free) numbers have a 080 code. Numbers that begin with an 084 code incur the **local call rate,** while the 087 code incurs the **national call rate** (the two aren't significantly different for short calls). Calling a **mobile phone** (cell phone) is more expensive than a regular phone call. Mobile phone numbers carry 077, 078, or 079 codes, and pager numbers begin with 076.

PUBLIC PHONES

Public payphones in Britain are mostly run by **British Telecom (BT),** recognizable by the ubiquitous piper logo, although upstart competitors such as Mercury operate in larger cities. Public phones charge a minimum of 30p for calls and don't accept 1p, 2p, or 5p coins. The dial tone is a continuous purring sound; a repeated double-tone means the line is ringing. A series of harsh beeps will warn you to insert more money when your time is up. For the rest of the call, the digital display ticks off your credit. You may use any remaining credit on a second call by pressing the "follow on call" button (often marked "FC"). Otherwise, once you hang up, your remaining phonecard credit is rounded down to the nearest 10p. Pay phones do not give change, so use your smallest coins.

CELLULAR PHONES

Cell phones ("mobile phones") are everywhere in Britain. Competitive, low prices and the variety of calling plans make them accessible even for short-term, low-budget travelers. Also, Britain has developed a text-messaging culture—for every person you see talking into a mobile, another will be typing on one.

ESSENTIALS

The international standard for cell phones is **Global System for Mobile Communication (GSM).** Many cell phones today are already **GSM-compatible,** although they may not work in the UK (see box below); check your manual or contact a retailer. You'll also need a **SIM (subscriber identity module) card,** a country-specific, thumbnail-sized chip that gives you a local phone number and plugs you into the local network. Most SIM cards are **prepaid,** meaning that you need not purchase a monthly service plan. Incoming calls are usually free, and basic phones are often free with even a cheap monthly plan. When you use up the prepaid time, you can buy additional cards or vouchers at convenience stores.

 GSM PHONES. Just having a GSM phone doesn't mean you're necessarily good to go when you travel abroad. The majority of GSM phones sold in the USA operate on a different **frequency** (1900) than international phones (900/1800) and will not work abroad. Tri-band phones work on all 3 frequencies (900/1800/1900) and will operate through most of the world. Some GSM phones are **SIM-locked** and will only accept SIM cards from a single carrier. You'll need a **SIM-unlocked** phone to use a SIM card from a local carrier when you travel.

For most visitors to the UK, a **pay-as-you-go plan** is the most attractive option. Pick up an eligible mobile (from £30) and recharge, or **top-up,** with a card purchasable at a grocery store, on the Internet, or by phone. **Incoming calls and incoming text messages are always free.** Call rates listed here are by the minute.

O$_2$ (☎08705 678 678; www.o2.co.uk). Phones from £50. Calls to O$_2$ mobiles and fixed lines 25p for the first 3min., then 2-5p; to other networks 40p; text messaging 10p.

Orange (☎07973 100 450; www.orange.co.uk). Phones from £30. Calls to the US from 20p; to Orange mobiles, 20p.; to other networks 40p; text messaging 10p.

T-Mobile (☎08454 125 000; www.t-mobile.co.uk). Phones from £30; calls to US 70p flat rate; calls to any other phone from 12p; text messaging 10p.

TIME DIFFERENCES

Britain is on **Greenwich Mean Time (GMT).** Britain observes **daylight savings time** between the last Sunday of March and the last Sunday of October: in March, the clock moves 1hr. later; in October, the clock moves 1hr. earlier. The following table applies from late October to early April.

4AM	5AM	6AM	7AM	8AM	NOON	10PM
Los Angeles San Francisco Seattle Vancouver	Denver	Chicago	Boston New York Toronto	New Brunswick	**Belfast Cardiff Edinburgh London**	Canberra Melbourne Sydney

BY MAIL

SENDING MAIL HOME FROM THE UK

Airmail is the best way to send mail home from Britain. Just write "Par Avion—By Airmail" on the top left corner of your envelope, or swing by any post office and get a free Airmail label. **Aerogrammes,** printed sheets that fold into envelopes and travel via airmail, are also available at post offices. For priority shipping, ask for **Airsure;** it costs £4.20 on top of the actual postage, but your letter will get on the next available flight. If Airsure is not available to the country you wish to ship to, ask for **International Signed For** instead; for £3.50 your package will be signed for on delivery. **Surface mail** is the cheapest and slowest way to send mail from the United

Kingdom, taking one to three months to cross the Atlantic Ocean and two to four to cross the Pacific.

Royal Mail has taken great care to standardize their rates around the world. To check how much your shipment will cost, surf to the Royal Mail Postal Calculator at www.royalmail.com. From Britain, postcards cost 24p domestically, 48p to send to Europe, 54p to the rest of the world; airmail letters (up to 20g) are 24p domestically, 48p within Europe, and 78p elsewhere. These are 2nd-class mail rates, and take two to three business days to arrive. Next day delivery is also available.

International 2nd class rates are as follows: packages up to 500g cost £5.14 and take five business days to arrive; packages up to 2kg cost £18.64 and take 5 days around the world including Australia, Canada, New Zealand, and the US.

SENDING MAIL TO THE UK

To ensure timely delivery, mark envelopes "Par Avion—By Airmail." In addition to the standard postage system, **Federal Express** (Australia ☎ 13 26 10, Canada and the US 800-463-3339, Ireland 1800 535 800, New Zealand 0800 733 339, the UK 08456 070 809; www.fedex.com) handles express mail services to Britain; they can get a letter from New York to London in two days for US$50.

There are several ways to arrange pick up of letters sent to you by friends and relatives while you are abroad. Mail can be sent via **Poste Restante** (General Delivery) to almost any city or town in the United Kingdom with a post office. Address *Poste Restante* letters as follows:

William SHAKESPEARE

Poste Restante

2/3 Henley St.

Stratford-upon-Avon CV37 6PU

United Kingdom

The mail will go to a special desk in the central post office, unless you specify a post office by street address or post code. It's best to use the largest post office. Bring your passport (or other photo ID) for pick up. Have clerks check under your first name as well as your last. *Let's Go* lists post offices in the **Practical Information** section for every city and most towns.

American Express travel offices throughout the world offer a free **Client Letter Service** (mail held up to 30 days and forwarded upon request) for cardholders who contact them in advance. *Let's Go* lists AmEx office locations for most large cities in **Practical Information** sections; for a complete list, call ☎ 800-528-4800 or visit www.americanexpress.com/travel.

ACCOMMODATIONS

HOSTELS

If you want to save money, stay in a hostel. In Britain, hostels are generally clean and friendly places, and in larger cities many students even choose to live in them for extended periods of time while enrolled. They are usually dorm-style, with large single-sex rooms and bunk beds, although private rooms that sleep two to four are becoming more common. There are hostels with kitchens and utensils, bike or moped rentals, transportation to airports, breakfast and other meals, laundry facilities, and Internet access, but don't expect all of these in any one. Some close during certain daytime "lockout" hours or impose a maximum stay. Others, especially in national parks, have a curfew (usually 11pm). In Britain, a hostel bed will cost about £12-15 in rural areas, £15-20 in larger cities, and £20-35 in London.

A HOSTELER'S BILL OF RIGHTS. There are certain standard features that we do not include in our hostel listings. Unless we state otherwise, you can expect that every hostel has no lockout, no curfew, a kitchen, free hot showers, some system of secure luggage storage, and no key deposit.

HOSTELLING INTERNATIONAL

Joining a national youth hostel association (listed below) grants membership privileges in **Hostelling International (HI),** a federation of national hostelling associations. Non-HI members may be allowed to stay in some member hostels, but will have to pay an extra $3 to do so. HI hostels are prevalent throughout the UK and Ireland. They are run by the **Youth Hostels Association** (England and Wales), the **Scottish Youth Hostels Association, Hostelling International Northern Ireland (HINI),** and **An Óige** (an-OYJ) in the Republic of Ireland. HI's umbrella organization's web page (www.hihostels.com), which lists links and phone numbers of all national associations, can be a great place to begin researching hostels. Other comprehensive hostelling websites include www.hostels.com and www.hostelplanet.com.

Most student travel agencies (see p. 28) sell HI cards, as do all the organizations listed below. All prices below are for **one-year memberships** unless otherwise noted.

Australian Youth Hostels Association (AYHA), 422 Kent St., Sydney, NSW 200 (☎02 9261 1111; www.yha.com.au). AUS$52, under 18 AUS$19.

Hostelling International-Canada (HI-C), 205 Catherine St. #400, Ottawa, ON K2P 1C3 (☎613-237-7884; www.hihostels.ca). CDN$35, under 18 free.

An Óige (Irish Youth Hostel Association), 61 Mountjoy St., Dublin 7 (☎3531 830 4555; www.anoige.ie). EUR€20, under 18 EUR€10.

Hostelling International Northern Ireland (HINI), 22-32 Donegall Rd., Belfast BT12 5JN (☎02890 324 733; www.hini.org.uk). UK£15, under 25 UK£10.

Youth Hostels Association of New Zealand (YHANZ), Level 1, 166 Moorhouse Ave., P.O. Box 436, Christchurch (☎0800 278 299 (NZ only) or 03 379 9970; www.yha.org.nz). NZ$40, under 18 free.

Scottish Youth Hostels Association (SYHA), 7 Glebe Cres., Stirling FK8 2JA (☎01786 891 400; www.syha.org.uk). UK£8, under 16 free.

Youth Hostels Association (England and Wales), Trevelyan House, Dimple Rd., Matlock, Derbyshire DE4 3YH (☎08707 708 868 within Britain, 1629 592 700 outside Britain; www.yha.org.uk). £15.95, under 26 £9.95.

Hostelling International-USA, 8401 Colesville Rd., Ste. 600, Silver Spring, MD 20910 (☎301-495-1240; www.hiayh.org). US$28, under 18 free.

Independent hostels tend to attract younger crowds, be located closer to city centers, and have a more relaxed attitude about lockouts or curfews than their YHA counterparts. A useful website for hostel listings throughout the UK is Backpackers UK (www.backpackers.co.uk).

 BOOKING HOSTELS ONLINE. One of the easiest ways to ensure a bed for the night is by reserving online. Click to the **Hostelworld** booking engine through **www.letsgo.com,** and you'll have access to bargain accommodations from Argentina to Zimbabwe with no added commission.

BED & BREAKFASTS (B&BS)

For a cozy alternative to impersonal hotel rooms, B&Bs (private homes with rooms available to travelers) range from horrid to sublime. B&B owners sometimes go out of their way to be accommodating, giving personalized tours or offer-

ESSENTIALS

ing home-cooked meals. Some B&Bs, however, do not provide private bathrooms (**ensuite**) and most do not provide phones. A **double** room has one large bed for two people; a **twin** has two separate beds. *Let's Go* lists B&B prices by room type. You can book B&Bs by calling directly or asking the local **Tourist Information Centre (TIC)** to help you find accommodations; most can also book B&Bs in other towns. TICs usually charge a 10% deposit on the first night's or the entire stay's price, deductible from the amount you pay the proprietor. Occasionally a flat fee of £1-5 is added. Rooms in B&Bs generally cost £25-40 for a single and £45-60 for a double. Many websites provide B&B listings; check out InnFinder (www.inncrawler.com), InnSite (www.insite.com), or BedandBreakfast.com (www.bedandbreakfast.com). The British tourist boards operate a B&B **rating system,** using a scale of one to five diamonds (in England) or stars (in Scotland and Wales). Rated accommodations are part of the tourist board's booking system, but it costs money to be rated and some perfectly good B&Bs choose not to participate. Tourist Board approval is legally required of all Northern Ireland accommodations. Approved accommodations in the Republic of Ireland are marked with a green shamrock.

OTHER TYPES OF ACCOMMODATIONS

HOTELS AND GUESTHOUSES

Basic hotel singles in Britain cost about £70 per night, doubles £95. Some hotels offer "full pension" (all meals) and "half pension" (no lunch). Smaller guesthouses are often cheaper than hotels. If you make **reservations** in writing, indicate your night of arrival and the number of nights you plan to stay. The hotel will send you confirmation and may request payment for the first night. Not all hotels take reservations, and few accept checks in foreign currency.

UNIVERSITY DORMS

Many **colleges and universities** open their residence halls to travelers when school is not in session—some do so even during term-time. Getting a room may take a couple of phone calls and require advanced planning, but rates tend to be low and many offer free local calls and Internet access. Many dorm accommodations do not include breakfast options. Dorm information is included in the **Accommodations** section of many larger cities, and can usually be found in large university towns like Durham, Cardiff, and Glasgow.

HOME EXCHANGES AND HOSPITALITY CLUBS

Home exchange offers various types of homes (houses, apartments, condominiums, villas, even castles in some cases), plus the opportunity to live like a local and cut down on accommodation fees. For more information, contact **HomeExchange.com Inc.,** P.O. Box 787, Hermosa Beach, CA 90254, USA (☎310 798 3864 or toll free 800-877-8723; www.homeexchange.com), or **Intervac International Home Exchange** (UK ☎0845 260 5776; www.intervac.com).

Hospitality clubs link their members with individuals or families abroad who are willing to host travelers for free or for a small fee to promote cultural exchange and good karma. In exchange, members usually must be willing to host travelers in their own homes; a small membership fee may also be required. **Global Freeloaders** (www.globalfreeloaders.com) and **The Hospitality Club** (www.hospitalityclub.org) are good places to start. **Servas** (www.servas.org) is an established, more formal, peace-based organization, and requires a fee and an interview to join. An Internet search will find many similar organizations, some of which cater to special interests (e.g., women, GLBT travelers, or members of certain professions). As always, use common sense when planning to stay with or host someone you do not know.

LONG-TERM ACCOMMODATIONS

Travelers planning to stay in Britain for extended periods of time may find it most cost-effective to rent an **apartment**. Besides the rent itself, prospective tenants usually are also required to front a security deposit (frequently one month's rent) and sometimes also the last month's rent. Rent in London is usually about £400-600 per month, elsewhere in the UK about £200-400 per month. **Housepals UK** (www.housepals.co.uk) has an extensive listing of available apartments and rooms for sublet.

THE GREAT OUTDOORS

Great Britain's mild (if rainy) weather and beautiful landscape make it a wonderful place to hike and camp. Newly instituted laws, established by the Countryside and Rights of Way Act (2000), have given hikers and walkers access to open land even if privately held. Common sense restrictions remain and **camping** on common land can be frowned upon; always ask the landowner before pitching a tent, and be respectful of the grounds. Campsites are often privately owned, with basic sites costing £3 per person and posh ones costing up to £10 per person and offering basic amenities. **Camping barns,** farm buildings converted to provide basic accommodations, are owned by farmers and are usually £5-10 per person. They can be difficult to reach without a car, and campers must bring their own sleeping bag and sturdy shoes. The **Great Outdoor Recreation Pages** (www.gorp.com) provide excellent general information for travelers planning outdoor activities.

 LEAVE NO TRACE. *Let's Go* encourages travelers to embrace the "Leave No Trace" ethic, minimizing impact on natural environments and protecting them for future generations. Trekkers should camp on durable surfaces, use cookstoves instead of campfires, bury human waste away from water supplies, bag trash and carry it out with them, and respect wildlife. For more detailed information, contact the **Leave No Trace Center for Outdoor Ethics,** P.O. Box 997, Boulder, CO 80306, USA (☎800-332-4100 or 303-442-8222; www.lnt.org).

USEFUL RESOURCES

A variety of publishing companies offer hiking guidebooks to meet the needs of novice or expert hikers. For information about camping, hiking, and biking, write or call the publishers below to receive a free catalogue. Campers heading to Europe should consider buying an **International Camping Carnet.** Similar to a hostel membership card, it's required at a few campgrounds and sometimes provides discounts. It is available in North America from the **Family Campers and RVers Association** and in the UK from **The Caravan Club** (see below).

Automobile Association, Contact Centre, Lambert House, Stockport Road, Cheadle SK8 2DY, UK (☎08706 000 371; www.theAA.com). Publishes *Caravan and Camping Europe* and *Britain & Ireland* (both £10) as well as road atlases for Europe, Britain, France, Germany, Ireland, Italy, Spain, and the US (£7-11).

Association of National Park Authorities, 126 Bute St., Cardiff CF10 5LE (☎029 2049 9966; www.anpa.gov.uk). Has lists of and introductions to all British national parks, camping and hiking advice, and information on events and festivals.

The Camping and Caravanning Club, Greenfields House, Westwood Way, Coventry CV4 8JH (☎0845 130 7632; www.campingandcaravanningclub.co.uk). Offers online booking for campsites and travel and technical advice. Membership costs £39 for 1st year; £33 yearly renewal.

The Caravan Club, East Grinstead House, East Grinstead, West Sussex, RH19 1UA, (☎01342 326 944; www.caravanclub.co.uk). For £35, members receive access to sites, insurance services, equipment discounts, maps, and a monthly magazine.

The Mountaineers Books, 1001 SW Klickitat Way, Ste. 201, Seattle, WA 98134, USA (☎206-223-6303; www.mountaineersbooks.org). Over 600 titles on hiking, biking, mountaineering, natural history, and conservation.

Ordnance Survey, Customer Service Centre, Romsey Rd., Southampton SO16 4GU (☎08456 050 505; www.ordsvy.gov.uk). Britain's national mapping agency (also known as the OS) publishes excellent topographical maps, available at TICs, National Park Information Centres (NPICs), and many bookstores. Their excellent *Explorer* map series (£8) covers the whole of Britain in detailed 1:25,000 scale.

Sierra Club Books, 85 Second St., 2nd fl., San Francisco, CA 94105, USA (☎415-977-5500; www.sierraclub.org). Publishes general resource books on hiking and camping.

NATIONAL PARKS

Britain has a series of gorgeous national parks. The parks are in large part privately owned, but generally provide expansive areas for public use. There are 15 national parks in England and Wales. The Trossachs, Loch Lomond, and the Cairngorms were named Scotland's first national parks in 2002. Each park is administrated by its own National Park Authority, charged with preserving and maintaining the parks. Northern Ireland doesn't currently have any national parks designated, although a number of Areas of Outstanding Natural Beauty (AONBs) have been identified. Be sure to check out the local **National Park Information Centre (NPIC)** of the park in order to find out about various outdoor activities popular in Britain including hiking, cycling, mountaineering, coasteering, and surfing.

WILDERNESS SAFETY

TOWNS WITHIN PARKS? Unlike many countries in which government-owned parks do not include manmade settlements, the national parks in Britain often cover large tracts of privately owned land and contain many **towns** and **villages**. *Let's Go* organizes these sections by centralizing the listings of hostel accommodations at the beginning of each National Park section, and listing B&B and other budget options within descriptions of individual towns.

Staying **warm, dry,** and **well hydrated** is key to a happy and safe wilderness experience. For any hike, prepare yourself for an emergency by packing a first-aid kit, a reflector, a whistle, high-energy food, extra water, raingear, a hat, mittens, and extra socks. If possible, carry a mobile phone—while reception is spotty in rural areas, it may help in a pinch. For warmth, wear wool or insulating synthetic materials designed for the outdoors. Avoid wearing cotton, which dries slowly.

Check **weather forecasts** often and pay attention to the skies when hiking, as weather patterns can change suddenly. Always let someone—a friend, your hostel management, a park ranger, or a local hiking organization—know when and where you are going. Know your physical limits and do not attempt a hike beyond your ability. See **Safety and Health,** p. 20, for information on outdoor ailments and medical concerns. If you are in trouble and can reach a phone, **call ☎999.** If not, six blasts on a **whistle** are standard to summon help (three are the reply); a constant long blast also indicates distress. For more information, see *How to Stay Alive in the Woods,* by Bradford Angier (Fireside Books, US$10) and *Wilderness Survival,* by Greg Davenport (Stackpole Books, US$12).

CAMPING AND HIKING EQUIPMENT

WHAT TO BUY

Good camping equipment is both sturdy and light. North American suppliers tend to offer the most competitive prices.

Sleeping Bags: Most sleeping bags are rated by season; "summer" means 30-40°F (around 0°C) at night; "four-season" or "winter" often means below 0°F (-17°C). Bags are made of **down** (warm and light, but expensive, and miserable when wet) or of **synthetic** material (heavy, durable, and warm when wet). Prices range US$50-250 for a summer synthetic to US$200-300 for a good down winter bag. **Sleeping bag pads** include foam pads (US$10-30), air mattresses (US$15-50), and self-inflating mats (US$30-120). Bring a **stuff sack** to store your bag and keep it dry.

Tents: The best tents are free-standing (with their own frames and suspension systems), set up quickly, and only require staking in high winds. Low-profile dome tents are the best. Worthy 2-person tents start at US$100, 4-person tents start at US$160. Make sure your tent has a rain fly and seal its seams with waterproofer. Other useful accessories include a **battery-operated lantern,** a plastic **groundcloth,** and a nylon **tarp.**

Backpacks: Internal-frame packs mold well to your back, keep a lower center of gravity, and flex adequately to allow you to hike difficult trails, while **external-frame packs** are more comfortable for long hikes over even terrain, as they carry weight higher and distribute it more evenly. Make sure your pack has a strong, padded hip-belt to transfer weight to your legs. There are models designed specifically for women. Any serious backpacking requires a pack of at least 4000 cu. in. (16,000cc), plus 500 cu. in. for sleeping bags in internal-frame packs. Sturdy backpacks cost anywhere from US$125 to 420—your pack is an area where it doesn't pay to economize. On your hunt for the perfect pack, fill up prospective models with something heavy, strap it on correctly, and walk around the store to get a sense of how the model distributes weight. Either buy a **rain cover** (US$10-20) or store all of your belongings in plastic bags inside your pack.

Boots: Be sure to wear hiking boots with good **ankle support.** They should fit snugly and comfortably over 1-2 pairs of **wool socks** and a pair of thin **liner socks.** Break in boots over several weeks before you go to spare yourself blisters. Look into **waterproofing** your boots—you will thank yourself when it rains.

Other Necessities: Synthetic layers, like those made of polypropylene or polyester, and a pile jacket will keep you warm even when wet. A **space blanket** (US$5-15) will help you to retain body heat and doubles as a groundcloth. Plastic **water bottles** are vital; look for shatter- and leak-resistant models. Carry **water-purification tablets** for when you can't boil water. Although most campgrounds provide campfire sites, you may want to bring a small **metal grate** or **grill.** For those places (including virtually every organized campground) that forbid fires or the gathering of firewood, you'll need a **camp stove** (the classic Coleman starts at US$50) and a propane-filled **fuel bottle.** Also bring a **first-aid kit, pocketknife, insect repellent,** and **waterproof matches** or a **lighter.**

WHERE TO BUY IT

The online and mail-order companies listed below offer lower prices than many retail stores. A visit to a local camping or outdoors store will give you a good sense of the look and weight of certain items before you buy.

Blacks, Mansard Close, Westgate, Northampton, NN5 5DL (☎0800 665 410; www.blacks.co.uk).

Campmor, 400 Corporate Dr., P.O. Box 680, Mahwah, NJ 07430, USA (☎800-525-4784; www.campmor.com).

ESSENTIALS

ESSENTIALS

Eastern Mountain Sports (EMS), 1 Vose Farm Rd., Peterborough, NH 03458, USA (☎888-463-6367; www.ems.com).

Gear-Zone, 8 Burnet Rd., Sweetbriar Rd. Industrial Estate, Norwich, NR3 2BS (www.gear-zone.co.uk).

L.L. Bean, Freeport, ME 04033, USA (US and Canada ☎800-441-5713; UK 0800 962 954; www.llbean.com).

OutdoorGB, Nene House, Sopwith Way, Daventry NN11 8PB (☎8707 485 700; www.outdoorgb.com).

Recreational Equipment, Inc. (REI), Sumner, WA 98352, USA (US and Canada ☎800-426-4840, elsewhere 253-891-2500; www.rei.com).

CAMPERS AND RVS

Renting a camper van (RV in the US) costs more than tenting or hosteling but less than staying in hotels while renting a car (see **Rental Cars,** p. 35). The convenience of bringing your own bedroom, bathroom, and kitchen makes renting a camper van an attractive option, especially for older travelers and families with children.

Rental prices for a standard RV are around £450 per week; prices rise considerably during the summer. Try **Vivanti Motorhomes** (☎08707 522 225; www.vivanti.co.uk) or **Just Go** (☎0870 240 1918; www.justgo.uk.com).

ORGANIZED ADVENTURE TRIPS

Organized adventure tours offer another way of exploring the wild. Activities include hiking, biking, skiing, canoeing, kayaking, rafting, climbing, photo safaris, and archaeological digs. Tourism bureaus can suggest parks, trails, and outfitters. Organizations that specialize in camping and outdoor equipment like REI and EMS (see above) also are good sources for information. To find an organized tour, consider contacting the **Specialty Travel Index,** P.O. Box 458, San Anselmo, CA 94979, USA (US ☎888-624-4030, elsewhere 415-455-1643; www.specialtytravel.com).

SPECIFIC CONCERNS

SUSTAINABLE TRAVEL

As the number of travelers on the road continues to rise, the detrimental effect they can have on natural environments becomes an increasing concern. With this in mind, *Let's Go* promotes the philosophy of **sustainable travel.** Through a sensitivity to issues of ecology and sustainability, today's travelers can be a powerful force in preserving and restoring the places they visit.

Ecotourism, a rising trend in sustainable travel, focuses on the conservation of natural habitats and how to use them to build up the economy without exploitation or over-development. Travelers can make a difference by doing advance research and by supporting organizations and establishments that pay attention to their impact on their natural surroundings. Preserving Britain's open land is a governmental priority, passed down to the individual National Park Authorities of each National Park. For UK-specific low-impact Ecotours, visit www.earthfoot.org/uk.htm. The largest organization in Britain for environmental conservation is the **British Trust for Conservation Volunteers,** which is listed along with other conservation opportunities in the Beyond Tourism chapter (p. 58).

RESPONSIBLE TRAVEL

The impact of tourist dollars on the destinations you visit should not be underestimated. The choices you make during your trip can have powerful effects on local communities—for better or for worse. Travelers who care about the destinations and environments they explore should become aware of the social and cultural implications of the choices they make when they travel. Simple decisions such as buying local products instead of globally available ones, paying fair prices for products or services, and attempting to say a few words in the local language can have a strong positive effect on the community.

Community-based tourism aims to channel tourist dollars into the local economy by emphasizing tours and cultural programs run by members of the host community and that benefit disadvantaged groups. The *Ethical Travel Guide* (UK£13), a project of **Tourism Concern** (☎020 7133 3330; www.tourismconcern.org.uk), is an excellent resource for information on community-based travel with a directory of 300 establishments in 60 countries. The UK is filled with open-air historical sites like cathedral ruins, Bronze Age settlements, and other ancient monuments. It is rare that such testaments to the multicultural heritage of the British Isles survive today, and a greater privilege to be able to walk up, in, and among them. It is up to the tourists themselves to treat these sights respectfully and responsibly by not taking anything or leaving anything behind. For more information on how to positively interact with Britain's historical landmarks, see **Beyond Tourism**, p. 58.

TRAVELING ALONE

There are many benefits to traveling alone, including independence and a greater opportunity to connect with locals. On the other hand, solo travelers are more vulnerable to harassment and street theft. If you are traveling alone, look confident, try not to stand out as a tourist, and be especially careful in deserted or very crowded areas. Stay away from areas that are not well lit. If questioned, never admit that you are traveling alone. Maintain regular contact with someone at home who knows your itinerary, and always research your destination before traveling. For more tips, pick up *Traveling Solo* by Eleanor Berman (Globe Pequot Press, US$18), visit www.travelaloneandloveit.com, or subscribe to **Connecting: Solo Travel Network,** 689 Park Rd., Unit 6, Gibsons, BC V0N 1V7, Canada (☎604-886-9099; www.cstn.org. Membership US$30-50).

WOMEN TRAVELERS

Women on their own inevitably face some additional safety concerns, particularly in larger cities such as London, Cardiff, Glasgow, and Belfast. The following suggestions shouldn't discourage women from traveling alone—it's easy to enjoy yourself and be adventurous without taking undue risks. If you are concerned, consider staying in centrally-located hostels which offer single rooms that lock from the inside or in religious organizations with single-sex rooms. Check that your hostel offers safe communal showers.

Avoid solitary late-night walks, metro, or tube rides, and choose train or Tube compartments occupied by other women or couples. If catching a bus at night, wait at a well-populated stop. Carry extra money for a phone call, bus, or taxi. **Hitchhiking is never safe** for lone women, or even for two women traveling together. Look as if you know where you're going and approach older women or couples for directions if you're lost or uncomfortable.

Your best answer to harassment is no answer at all; feigning deafness, sitting motionless, and staring straight ahead will usually do the trick. The extremely persistent can be dissuaded by a firm, loud, and very public "Go away!" Wearing a **wedding band** may help to prevent unwanted advances. Consider carrying a whistle or rape alarm on your keychain. Mace and pepper sprays are illegal in Britain.

The national **emergency** number is ☎ 999. **Rape Crisis UK and Ireland** (a full list of helplines can be found at www.rapecrisis.org.uk; www.rapecrisisscotland.org.uk in Scotland) provides referrals to local rape crisis and sexual abuse counseling services throughout the UK. A self-defense course will prepare you for a potential attack and raise your level of awareness (see **Personal Safety**, p. 22). Be aware of the health concerns that women face when traveling (see p. 27).

GLBT TRAVELERS

Large cities, notably London, Dublin, Edinburgh, Manchester, and Brighton, are more open to GLBT culture than rural Britain, although some evidence of bigotry and violence remains. The magazine *Time Out* (p. 51) has gay and lesbian listings, and numerous periodicals make it easy to learn about the current concerns of Britain's gay community. VisitBritain publishes *Britain: Inside and Out* (www.gaybritain.org). The *Pink Paper* (free; ☎ 020 7424 7414; www.pinkpaper.com) is available from newsstands in larger cities. **Planet Out** (www.planetout.com) offers information and a comprehensive site addressing gay travel concerns.

Gay's the Word, 66 Marchmont St., London WC1N 1AB, UK (☎ 020 7278 7654; www.gaystheword.co.uk). The largest gay and lesbian bookshop in the UK, with both fiction and non-fiction titles. Mail-order service available.

International Lesbian and Gay Association (ILGA), 17 Rue de la Charité, 1210 Brussels, Belgium (☎ 32 2 502 2471; www.ilga.org). Provides political information, such as homosexuality laws of individual countries.

Outhouse, (☎ 3531 873 7932; www.outhouse.ie). Ireland's web-based GLBT resource center, including the Pink Pages online directory. Extensive urban and regional info for both the Republic and the North.

London Lesbian and Gay Switchboard, (☎ 020 7837 7324; www.llgs.org.uk). Confidential advice, information, and referrals. Open 24hr.

ADDITIONAL RESOURCES: GLBT.
Spartacus 2005-2006: International Gay Guide. Bruno Gmunder Verlag (US$33).
Damron Men's Travel Guide, Damron Accommodations Guide, Damron City Guide, and *Damron Women's Traveller.* Damron Travel Guides (US$18-24). For info, call ☎ 800-462-6654 or visit www.damron.com.
The Gay Vacation Guide: The Best Trips and How to Plan Them, Mark Chesnut. Kensington Books (US$15).

TRAVELERS WITH DISABILITIES

Traveling in Britain with a disability takes advance planning. Inform airlines and hotels of the need for special accommodations when making reservations; time may be needed to prepare special accommodations. Call ahead to restaurants, museums, and other facilities to find out if they are wheelchair-accessible.

Rail may be the most convenient form of travel for disabled travelers in Britain: many stations have ramps, and some trains have wheelchair lifts, special seating areas, and specially equipped toilets. The National Rail website (www.national-rail.co.uk) provides general information for travelers with disabilities and assistance phone numbers; it also describes the **Disabled Persons Railcard** (£18 for one year), which allows one-third off most fares as well as other benefits at participating hotels. Most **bus** companies will provide assistance if notified ahead of time. All National Express coaches entering service after 2005 must be equipped with a wheelchair lift or ramp; call the **Additional Needs Help Line** (☎0121 423 8479) for information or consult www.nationalexpress.com. The London **Underground** is slowly improving accessibility, and starting in January 2006 all of London's public buses became wheelchair-accessible; **Transport for London Access and Mobility** (☎020 7222 1234) can provide information on public transportation within the city.

Some major **car rental** agencies (Hertz, Avis, and National), as well as local agencies can provide and deliver hand-controlled cars. In addition, Lynx hand controls may be used with many rental cars; contact **Lynx,** 80 Church Ln., Aughton, Ormskirk, Lancashire L39 6SB (☎01695 422 622; www.lynxcontrols.com).

The British Tourist Boards rate accommodations and attractions using the **National Accessible Scheme (NAS),** which designates three categories of accessibility. Look for the NAS symbols in Tourist Board guidebooks, or ask a sight directly for their ranking. Many **theaters** and performance venues have space for wheelchairs; some larger theatrical performances include special facilities for the hearing-impaired. Guide dogs fall under the PETS regulations (p. 15).

USEFUL ORGANIZATIONS

Access Abroad, Disability Services, University of Minnesota, 230 Heller Hall, 271 19th Ave. S., Minneapolis, MN 55455, USA (☎612-626-7379; www.umabroad.umn.edu/access). Devoted to making study abroad available to students with disabilities.

Accessible Journeys, 35 West Sellers Ave., Ridley Park, PA 19078, USA (☎800-846-4537; www.disabilitytravel.com). Designs tours for wheelchair users and slow walkers. The site has tips and forums for all travelers.

Flying Wheels, 143 W. Bridge St., Owatonna, MN 55060, USA (☎507-451-5005; www.flyingwheelstravel.com). Specializes in escorted trips to Europe for people with physical disabilities; plans custom trips worldwide.

The Guided Tour Inc., 7900 Old York Rd., Ste. 114B, Elkins Park, PA 19027, USA (☎800-783-5841; www.guidedtour.com). Organizes travel programs for persons with developmental and physical challenges in Canada, Hawaii, Ireland, Italy, Mexico, Spain, the UK, and the US.

Mobility International USA (MIUSA), 132 E Broadway, Ste. 343 Eugene, OR 97401, USA (☎541-343-1284; www.miusa.org). Provides a variety of books and other publications containing information for travelers with disabilities.

Society for Accessible Travel and Hospitality (SATH), 347 Fifth Ave., Ste. 605, New York, NY 10016, USA (☎212-447-7284; www.sath.org). An advocacy group publishing free online travel info. Annual membership US$49, students and seniors US$29.

MINORITY TRAVELERS

Minorities make up about 10% of Britain's population and are concentrated in London. Ireland is just beginning to experience racial diversity, while rural Scotland and Wales remain predominantly white. Minority travelers should expect reduced anonymity in rural regions, but onlookers are usually motivated by curiosity rather than ill will and should not cause you to alter your travel plans. For information on measures to combat racism, contact the **Commission for Racial Equality (CRE),** St. Dunstan's House, 201-211 Borough High St., London SE1 1GZ (☎020 7939 0000; www.cre.gov.uk).

ESSENTIALS

DIETARY CONCERNS

Vegetarians should be able to find meals in Britain and Ireland. Virtually all restaurants have vegetarian selections and many cater specifically to vegetarians. *Let's Go* notes restaurants with good vegetarian selections. Good resources include: www.veggieheaven.com, for comprehensive listings and reviews of UK restaurants, and the **Vegetarian Society of the UK** (☎0161 925 2000; www.vegsoc.org). The travel section of the The Vegetarian Resource Group's website, at www.vrg.org/travel, has a comprehensive list of organizations and websites that are geared toward helping vegetarians and vegans traveling abroad. For more information, visit your local bookstore or health food store, and consult *The Vegetarian Traveler: Where to Stay if You're Vegetarian, Vegan, Environmentally Sensitive*, by Jed and Susan Civic (Larson Publications; US$16). *Vegetarian Britain 2006*, edited by Alex Bourke, lists restaurants and veggie-friendly markets throughout the UK, including Dublin (Portfolio; £10). Vegetarians will also find resources at www.vegdining.com, www.happycow.net, and www.vegetariansabroad.com.

The prevalence of South Asian and Middle Eastern communities has made **halal** restaurants, butchers, and groceries common in large cities. Your own mosque or Muslim community organization may have lists of Muslim institutions or halal eateries. Travelers looking for halal food may find the **Halal Food Authority** (www.halalfoodauthority.co.uk) and www.zabihah.com to be useful resources.

Travelers who keep **kosher** should contact synagogues in larger cities for information on kosher restaurants. Your own synagogue or college Hillel may have access to lists of Jewish institutions in Britain. Orthodox communities in North London (in neighborhoods such as **Golders Green** or **Stamford Hill**), Leeds, and Manchester provide a market for kosher restaurants and grocers. A good resource is the *Jewish Travel Guide*, edited by Michael Zaidner (Vallentine Mitchell; US$18). Both halal and kosher options decrease in rural areas, but most restaurants and B&Bs will try to accommodate your dietary restrictions.

OTHER RESOURCES

Let's Go tries to cover all aspects of budget travel, but we can't put *everything* in our guides. Listed below are books and websites that can serve as jumping-off points for your own research.

USEFUL PUBLICATIONS

Time Out, Universal House, 251 Tottenham Court Rd., London, W1T 7AB (☎020 7813 3000; www.timeout.com). The absolute best weekly guide to what's going on in London, Edinburgh, and Dublin. The magazine is sold at every newsstand in those cities, and the website is a virtual hub for the latest on dining, entertainment, and discounts.

Backpax, 14 Sevier St., St. Werburghs, Bristol BS2 9QS (☎0117 941 4555; www.backpaxmag.com). "The backpacker's mag," free at most TICs, lists up-to-date information about backpacking and working in Great Britain and Europe.

Rand McNally, P.O. Box 7600, Chicago, IL 60680, USA (☎800-777-6277; www.randmcnally.com), publishes road atlases.

WORLD WIDE WEB

Almost every aspect of budget travel is accessible via the web. In just 10 minutes online, you can make a hotel reservation, get advice on travel hot spots, and find out how much a train from London to Scarborough will cost. Because website turnover is high, use search engines (such as Google, www.google.com) to strike out on your own.

 WWW.LETSGO.COM. Our website features extensive content from our guides; a community forum where travelers can connect with each other, ask questions or advice, and share stories and tips; and expanded resources to help you plan your trip. Visit us to browse by destination and to find information about ordering our titles.

THE ART OF TRAVEL

Backpacker's Ultimate Guide: www.bugeurope.com. Tips on packing, transportation, and where to go. Also tons of country-specific travel information.

BootsnAll.com: www.bootsnall.com. Numerous resources for independent travelers, from planning your trip to reporting on it when you get back.

How to See the World: www.artoftravel.com. A compendium of great travel tips, from cheap flights to self defense to interacting with local culture.

Travel Intelligence: www.travelintelligence.net. A large collection of travel writing by distinguished travel writers.

Travel Library: www.travel-library.com. A fantastic set of links for general information and personal travelogues.

World Hum: www.worldhum.com. An independently produced collection of "travel dispatches from a shrinking planet."

INFORMATION ON BRITAIN

CIA World Factbook: www.odci.gov/cia/publications/factbook/index.html. Tons of vital statistics on British geography, government, economy, and people.

Geographia: www.geographia.com. Highlights, culture, and people of Britain.

Visit Britain: www.visitbritain.com. Exhaustive listing of British Tourist sites, from the smallest Stone Age hut to Windsor Castle.

PlanetRider: www.planetrider.com. A subjective list of links to the "best" websites covering the culture and tourist attractions of Britain.

World Travel Guide: www.travel-guides.com. Helpful practical info.

Google Maps, Multimap, and Mapquest: www.googlemaps.com, www.multimap.com, and www.mapquest.co.uk. Find addresses, directions, and aerial photos.

BEYOND TOURISM

A PHILOSOPHY FOR TRAVELERS

HIGHLIGHTS OF BEYOND TOURISM IN BRITAIN

WORK to cement peace in **Northern Ireland** (p. 59).

CARE for injured seal pups at the **National Seal Sanctuary** in Gweek, Cornwall (p. 60).

STUDY medieval history for a semester at the **University of Cambridge** (p. 63).

HARVEST gooseberries at a small farm in **Staffordshire** (p. 66).

Britain is full of opportunities to leave the tour bus behind and become a member of one of the country's varied communities. Sure, hostel-hopping and sightseeing can be great fun, but connecting with a foreign country through studying, volunteering, or working can extend your travels beyond tourist traps.

As a traveler, you don't always have to feel like a foreigner. With this Beyond Tourism chapter, *Let's Go* hopes to promote a better understanding of the United Kingdom and provide suggestions for those who want to get more than a photo album out of their travels abroad. The "Giving Back" sidebar features found throughout the text (see p. 419, p. 445, and p. 632) also highlight regional Beyond Tourism opportunities.

For those who want to try Beyond Tourism activities in the UK, opportunities for **volunteerism** abound with local and international organizations. With a long history of world-class education, Britain offers quality **study abroad** programs, through direct enrollment in local universities or independent research projects. **Working** is a way to immerse yourself in local culture while financing your travels.

As a **volunteer** in the UK, you can participate in projects from archaeological digs to advocating for continued integration in Northern Ireland. Later in this chapter, we recommend organizations that can help you find the opportunities that best suit your interests, whether you're looking to pitch in for a day or an entire year.

Opportunities for **study** are abundant in the UK. You can study everything from folklore to physics at the medieval institutions of Cambridge, Oxford, and St. Andrews. If economics is your thing, spend a summer or a year studying accounting, finance, or management at the famed London School of Economics.

Many travelers also structure their trips around the **work** that they can do along the way—either odd jobs as they go along, or full-time stints in cities where they plan to stay for some time. Whether you'd like to intern in Parliament or teach children, you can do so through a variety of organizations.

VOLUNTEERING

Volunteering can be a great way to combine the excitement of traveling in a new place with the fulfillment of helping others. Although the UK is considered wealthy by world standards, there are countless aid organizations that need volunteers. Civil strife continues to plague Northern Ireland, large urban communities throughout the region suffer from poverty and housing shortages, and the landscapes and wildlife of northern England face threats of industrialization.

Most people who volunteer in the UK do so on a short-term basis at organizations that welcome drop-in or once-a-week volunteers. The best way to find opportunities that match your interests and schedule may be to check with local or national volunteer centers. **CharitiesDirect.com** offers extensive listings and profiles on thousands of charities in the UK and can serve as an excellent tool for researching volunteering options. **Volunteering England** provides links to local charities and sponsors **Volunteer's Week**, which recognizes and recruits volunteers throughout Britain. (☎0845 305 6979; www.volunteering.org.uk.) **Northern Ireland's Volunteer Development Agency** (☎028 9023 6100; www.volunteering-ni.org) responds to inquiries concerning volunteer opportunities. Their Freephone (☎0800 052 2212) connects callers to local volunteer bureaus. The **Wales Council for Voluntary Action** (www.volunteering-wales.net) has a searchable database of opportunities organized by region and project type. **Volunteer Development Scotland** (☎01786 479 593; www.vds.org.uk) lets you connect with other volunteers in the area to share your experiences and learn about new opportunities.

Those looking for longer, more intensive volunteer opportunities usually choose to go through a parent organization that takes care of logistical details and often provides a group environment and support system—for a fee. There are two main types of organizations—religious and non-sectarian—although there are rarely restrictions on participation for either.

WHY PAY MONEY TO VOLUNTEER? Some volunteering organizations require large fees or "donations" to participate in their programs. While this may seem surprising, such fees often keep the organization afloat in addition to covering airfare, room, board, and administrative expenses for volunteers. Other organizations must rely on private donations and government subsidies. If you're concerned about how a program spends its fees, request an annual report or finance account. A reputable organization won't refuse to inform you of how their money is spent. Pay-to-volunteer programs can be a good idea for young travelers who are looking for more support and structure (such as pre-arranged transportation and housing), or for anyone wishing to avoid the uncertainty in creating a volunteer experience from scratch.

PEACE PROCESS

The conflict in Northern Ireland has dogged Britain and Ireland for centuries, resulting in violence on both sides and all over the UK. Over the past 30 years, the peace process has become an issue of increasingly international awareness and increased success. Volunteering with these organizations is a good opportunity for foreigners looking to advance political and social change.

Corrymeela Community, Corrymeela Centre, 5 Drumaroan Rd., Ballycastle BT54 6QU (☎028 2076 2626; www.corrymeela.org). A residential Christian community designed to bring Protestants and Catholics together to work for peace. Openings from 1 week to 1 year with 8-week summer programs. Ages 18-30 preferred for long-term positions.

Kilcranny House, 21 Cranagh Rd., Coleraine BT51 3NN (☎028 7032 1816; www.kilcrannyhouse.org). A residential center that provides a safe space for Protestants and Catholics to explore non-violence and conflict resolution. Volunteering opportunities from 1 month to 2 years. Food and accommodations provided. £26 per week.

Volunteers for Peace, 1034 Tiffany Rd., Belmont, VT 05730, USA (☎802-259-2759; www.vfp.org). Arranges 2- or 3-week placements in working camps. Most programs 18+. Registration fee US$250; some programs have additional costs.

Ulster Quaker Service Committee, 541 Lisburn Rd., Belfast BT9 7GQ (☎028 9020 1444; www.ulsterquakerservice.com). Runs programs for Protestant and Catholic children from inner-city Belfast. Accommodations and small allowance provided. 6- to 8-week summer posts and 1- to 2-year posts available. Short-term volunteers 17+, long-term volunteers 21+.

CONSERVATION AND ARCHAEOLOGY

The UK's national parks and natural landscapes provide scenic venues for community service opportunities, from trail maintenance to archaeological expeditions. The largest organization in Britain for environmental conservation is the **British Trust for Conservation Volunteers (BTCV)**, Sedum House, Mallard Way, Potteric Carr, Doncaster, DN4 8DB (☎01302 388 888; www2.btcv.org.uk). Their counterpart in Northern Ireland is **Conservation Volunteers Northern Ireland,** Beech House, 159 Ravenhill Rd., Belfast BT6 0BP (☎02890 645 169; www.cvni.org). Many national parks have volunteer programs—the Association of National Park Authorities can contact individual park offices (see National Parks, p. 50).

Earthwatch Europe, 267 Banbury Rd., Oxford OX2 7HT (☎01865 318 838; www.earthwatch.org/europe). Arranges 1- to 3-week programs to promote conservation of natural resources, awareness of endangered animal populations (such as the Eagles of Mull), and the study of archaeological remnants (like dinosaur footprints in Yorkshire). Fees range from US$495 to over US$3500, plus airfare.

Groundwork, 5 Scotland St., Birmingham B1 2RR (☎0121 236 8565; www.groundwork.org.uk). Local Trusts throughout England and Wales work towards green communities and sustainable development. Volunteer opportunities vary by Trust and project, but most are short-term (1 day to 1 month).

Hebridean Whale and Dolphin Trust, 28 Main St., Tobermory, Isle of Mull, PA75 6NU (☎01688 302 620; www.whaledolphintrust.co.uk). Arranges marine education courses and has 2- to 12-day opportunities for basic whale research on board their boat. 18+.

Hessilhead Wildlife Rescue Trust, Gateside, Beith, KA15 1HT (☎01505 502 415; www.hessilhead.org.uk). Volunteers rehabilitate wild birds and mammals in Scotland.

National Seal Sanctuary, Gweek, near Helston, Cornwall, TR12 6UG (☎01326 221 361; www.sealsanctuary.co.uk). Volunteers clean pools, feed pups, care for injured seals, and help with the general running of the Sanctuary, a major Cornwall sight. 18+.

The National Trust, Volunteering and Community Involvement Office, P.O. Box 39, Warrington WA5 7WD (☎08704 584 000; www.nationaltrust.org.uk/volunteering). Arranges numerous volunteer opportunities, including working holidays.

Royal Society for the Protection of Birds (RSPB), UK Headquarters, The Lodge, Sandy, Bedfordshire SG19 2DL (☎01767 680 551; www.rspb.org.uk). Volunteer opportunities throughout Britain range from a day constructing nestboxes in East Anglia to several months monitoring invertebrates in the Highlands.

Vindolanda Trust, Hexham, Northumberland NE47 7JN (☎01434 344 277; www.vindolanda.com). Work on archaeological excavation at Roman forts and settlements near Hadrian's Wall. Site open Apr. to mid-Sept. 1 week min. stay. £50 excavation fee for up to 2 weeks, additional weeks £10 each.

The Wildlife Trusts, The Kiln, Waterside, Mather Rd., Newark, Nottinghamshire NG24 1WT (☎0870 036 7711; www.wildlifetrusts.org). Includes volunteer openings in conjunction with their 47 local Wildlife Trusts. Durations vary greatly.

WWF, Panda House, Weyside Park, Godalming, Surrey GU7 1XR (☎01483 426 444; www.wwf.org.uk). World's largest independent conservation organization lists volunteer opportunities from publicity to panda-keeping.

YOUTH AND THE COMMUNITY

There are countless social service opportunities in the UK, including mentoring youths, working in homeless shelters, promoting mental health, and a number of more specific concerns.

Barnardo's, Tanner's Ln., Barkingside, Ilford, Essex IG6 1QG (☎020 855 08822; www.barnardos.co.uk). Work with abused and underprivileged children in a variety of programs.

Christian Aid: Central Office, 35 Lower Marsh, Waterloo, London SE1 7RL (☎020 7620 4444; www.christian-aid.org.uk). **Northern Ireland,** 30 Wellington Park, Belfast BT9 6DL (☎02890 381 204). **Scotland,** 41 George IV Bridge, Edinburgh EH1 1EL (☎0131 220 1254). **Wales,** 5 Station Rd., Radyr, Cardiff CF15 8AA (☎029 2084 4646). Work in various fund-raising and administrative roles, occasionally for a small stipend.

Citizens Advice Bureau, Myddelton House, 115-123 Pentonville Rd., London, N1 9LZ (☎020 7833 2181, volunteer hotline 0845 126 4264; www.citizensadvice.org.uk). Volunteers help address issues from employment to finance to personal relationships.

Community Service Volunteers, 237 Pentonville Rd., London, N1 9NJ (☎020 7278 6601; www.csv.org.uk). Part- and full-time volunteer opportunities with the homeless, the disabled, and underprivileged youth. 16+.

Habitat for Humanity Great Britain, Southwark Habitat for Humanity, 46 West Bar St., Banbury OX16 9RZ (☎01295 264 240; www.habitatforhumanity.org.uk). Volunteers build houses for low-income families. There are other offices in Liverpool, Southwark, Birmingham, Eastbourne, and Belfast.

International Voluntary Service (IVS), Old Hall, East Bergholt, Colchester CO7 6TQ (☎01206 298 215; www.ivs-gb.org.uk). Arranges placement in working camps. 18+.

SPECIAL CONCERNS

In 2002, the Disability Rights Commission launched an Educating for Equality campaign in Britain designed to ensure the equal rights of individuals with disabilities in the education system. Despite this progressive measure and increasing attitudes of acceptance and tolerance, those possessing physical and mental handicaps continue to face discrimination in the UK. Volunteers can work with one of the multiple organizations concerned with aiding the special needs of these individuals and fostering a culture of mutual respect.

Association of Camphill Communities, England and Wales Region, 55 Cainscross Rd., Stroud GL5 4EX (☎01453 753 142; www.camphill.org.uk). Christian, private communities cater to both children and adults with special needs. Volunteers generally work for at least 6mo. Food, accommodation, and stipend provided. 18+.

International Volunteer Program (IVP), 678 13th St., Ste. 100, Oakland, CA 94612, USA (☎510-433-0414; www.ivpsf.org). Lists 4- to 12-week volunteer programs working with the disabled, the elderly, and underprivileged youth. US$1550 and up, includes food, travel within country, and accommodations. 18+.

The Share Centre, Smith's Strand, Lisnaskea, Co. Fermanagh, Northern Ireland BT92 0EQ (☎028 6772 2122; www.sharevillage.org). Volunteers work as outdoors and arts activities leaders, from 1 week to 1 year. Food and accommodations provided. 16+.

Vitalise, 12 City Forum, 250 City Rd., London EC1V 8AF (☎0845 345 1972; www.vitalise.org.uk). Volunteers care for disabled people for 1-2 weeks. Food, accommodation, and travel within Britain provided. 16+.

Worcestershire Lifestyles, Woodside Lodge, Lark Hill Rd., Worcester WR5 2EF (☎01905 350 686; www.worcestershire-lifestyles.org.uk). Work one-on-one with disabled adults. 18+.

STUDYING

Study abroad programs range from basic language and culture courses to college-level classes. Research cost, duration, type of accommodation, and courseload to

VISA INFORMATION. As of November 2003, citizens of Australia, Canada, New Zealand, and the US require a visa if they plan to study in the UK for longer than 6 months. Consult www.ukvisas.gov.uk to determine if you require a visa. Immigration officials will request a letter of acceptance from your UK university and proof of funding for your first year of study, as well as a valid passport, from all people wishing to study in the UK. Student visas cost £85 and application forms can be obtained through the website listed above.

find a program that best suits your needs. The **British Council,** Bridgewater House, 58 Whitworth St., Manchester M1 6BB (☎0161 957 7755; www.britishcouncil.org), is an invaluable source of information. The **Council on International Educational Exchange** (☎888-268-6245; www.ciee.org) offers a searchable online database listing study abroad opportunities according to region. Devoted to international student mobility, the **Council for International Education,** 9-17 St. Albans Pl., London N1 ONX (☎020 7288 4330; www.ukcosa.org.uk), is another valuable resource.

Dorms provide a good opportunity to mingle with fellow students. If you live with a family, you may build lifelong friendships with locals and experience day-to-day life, but conditions can vary greatly from family to family.

UNIVERSITIES

Tens of thousands of international students study abroad in the UK every year, drawn by the prestige of some of the world's oldest, most renowned universities. Apply early, as larger institutions fill up fast.

AMERICAN PROGRAMS

For citizens of the US, studying abroad through an American program is the easiest way to arrange transfer of course credits. Non-US citizens will find the abundance of American programs helpful in finding the best fit. The following organizations place students abroad. For more, check out **www.studyabroad.com.**

American Institute for Foreign Study, College Division, River Plaza, 9 W. Broad St., Stamford, CT 06902 (☎800-727-2437; www.aifsabroad.com). Organizes programs for high school and college study in universities in the UK.

Arcadia University for Education Abroad, 450 S. Easton Rd., Glenside, PA 19038 (☎866-927-2234; www.arcadia.edu/cea). Operates programs at many universities throughout Britain. Costs and duration vary widely.

Butler University Institute for Study Abroad, 1100 W. 42nd St., ste. 305, Indianapolis, IN 46208 (☎317-940-9336 or 800-858-0229; www.ifsa-butler.org). Organizes term-time and summer study at British and Irish universities. Prices vary greatly by location.

Central College Abroad, Office of International Education, 812 University, Pella, IA, 50219 (☎800-831-3629; www.central.edu/abroad), offers internships, as well as summer (US$3625-5525), semester (US$13,785-14,875), and year-long (US$27,570-29,750) programs in Britain. Prices vary greatly by location.

Council on International Educational Exchange (CIEE), 7 Custom House St., 3rd fl., Portland, ME 04101 (☎800-407-8839; www.ciee.org/study). Sponsors work, volunteer, academic, and internship programs in the UK.

Institute for the International Education of Students (IES), 33 N. LaSalle St., 15th fl., Chicago, IL 60602 (☎800-995-2300 or 312-944-1750; www.iesabroad.org). Offers summer (US$6000), semester (US$15,700), and year-long (US$28,296) programs in London. Internship opportunities. Application fee US$50. Scholarships available.

International Partnership for Service-Learning and Leadership, 815 2nd Ave., ste. 315, New York, NY 10017 (☎212-986-0989; www.ipsl.org). Seeks to unite service and study at the University of Surrey Roehampton in London. Courses relating to volunteer work can be combined in semester (US$14,000) or full-year (US$22,700) programs.

UK PROGRAMS

Many universities accommodate international students for summer, single-term, or full-year study. Those listed below are only a few that open their gates to foreign students; the **British Council** (see p. 61) has information on additional universities. Prices listed are an estimate of fees for non-EU citizens. In most cases, room and board are not included.

London School of Economics, Undergraduate Admissions, London School of Economics, P.O. Box 13401, Houghton St., London WC2A 2AE (☎020 7955 7125; www.lse.ac.uk). Year-long courses for international students (£11,874).

Queen's University Belfast, International Office, Belfast BT7 1NN, Northern Ireland (☎028 9097 5088; www.qub.ac.uk/ilo). Study in Belfast for a semester (£3665) or a full year (£7330).

University of Cambridge, Cambridge Admissions Office (CAO), Fitzwilliam House, 32 Trumpington St., Cambridge CB2 1QY (☎01223 333 308; www.cam.ac.uk). Open to overseas applicants for summer (£515-1095) or year-long study (£3070).

University of Edinburgh, The International Office, University of Edinburgh, 57 George Sq., Edinburgh EH8 9JU (☎0131 650 4296; www.ed.ac.uk). Offers summer programs (£950-1335) and year-long courses for international students (£9400).

University of Glasgow, Student Recruitment and Admissions Service, University of Glasgow, 1 The Square, Glasgow G12 8QQ (☎0141 330 4438; www.gla.ac.uk). Offers year-long courses (£9000-16,500).

University of Leeds, Study Abroad Office, Leeds LS2 9JT (☎0113 343 7900; www.leeds.ac.uk/students/study-abroad). One of largest universities in England, Leeds offers semester (£3800) and full-year (£8600) study abroad programs.

University College London, Gower St., London WC1E 6BT (☎020 7679 2000; www.ucl.ac.uk). In the center of London. Year-long programs (£10,900-14,300).

University of Oxford, College Admissions Office, Wellington Sq., Oxford OX1 2JD (☎01865 288 000; www.ox.ac.uk). Large range of summer programs (£880-3780) through year-long courses (£8880-11,840).

University of St. Andrews, Admissions Application Centre, St. Katharine's West, 16 The Scores, St. Andrews, Fife, KY16 9AX (☎01334 462 150; www.st-andrews.ac.uk/services/admissions). Welcomes students for term-time study. Also houses the Scottish Studies Summer Program (☎01334 462 238; www.st-andrews.ac.uk/admissions/sssprog.htm). Courses in history, art history, literature, and music of the region for high-school students (£2600 all-inclusive).

University of Ulster, International Office, Shore Rd., Newtownabbey, Co. Antrim BT37 0QB, Northern Ireland (☎028 7032 4138; www.ulst.ac.uk/international), offers semester- or year-long programs for visiting international students (£3010-7090).

WORKING

LONG-TERM WORK

If you plan to spend a substantial amount of time working in the UK, search for a job well in advance. International placement agencies are often the easiest way to find employment abroad, especially for teaching. Internships, usually for college students, are a good way to segue into working abroad, although they are often unpaid or poorly paid. Be wary of advertisements or companies that offer to get you a job abroad for a fee—often the same listings are available online or in newspapers. Some reputable organizations include:

Anders Elite, 2nd fl., New London House, 6 London St., London EC3R 7LP (☎020 7680 3100; www.anderselite.com). Large job placement agency with 13 offices in Britain.

Hansard Scholar Programme, 40-43 Chancery Ln., London WC2A 1JA (☎020 7438 1223; www.hansard-society.org.uk). Combines classes at the London School of Economics with internships in British government (£6850).

IAESTE, British Council, 10 Spring Gardens, London SW1A 2BN (020 7389 4771; www.iaeste.org). Arranges paid internships in 74 countries. Visit their website for country-specific contact information.

International Cooperative Education, 15 Spiros Way, Menlo Park, CA, 94025, USA (☎650-323-4944; www.icemenlo.com). Finds summer jobs for students in England. Costs include a US$250 application fee, a US$700 fee for placement, and a US$100 fee for non-US citizens.

TEACHING

The British school system is comprised of **state** (public, government-funded), **public** (independent, privately funded), and **international** (often for children of expats) schools, as well as universities. The academic year is divided into **autumn** (September to Christmas), **spring** (early January to Easter) and **summer** (Easter to late July) terms. Applications to teach at state schools must be made through local governments, and independent and international schools must be applied to individually.

To obtain a permanent teaching position in state-maintained schools in England and Wales, you must have **Qualified Teacher Status (QTS).** To teach in Scotland, you must complete the **Initial Teacher Education (ITE)** program offered at various Scottish universities and facilitated by the General Teacher Council for Scotland (☎0131 314 6000; www.gtcs.org.uk). The government-run **Teacher Training Agency** (☎0845 600 0991; www.canteach.gov.uk) manages teacher qualification, and European Union-qualified teachers can work in the UK. The **British Council** (p. 61) has extensive information for people wishing to teach abroad. Placement agencies are useful for finding teaching jobs, although vacancies are also listed in most major newspapers across the country. The following organizations are helpful places to start your search.

Council for International Exchange of Scholars, 3007 Tilden St. NW, ste. 5L, Washington DC 20008, USA (☎202-686-4000; www.cies.org). Administers the Fulbright program for faculty and professionals.

Eteach, Academy House, 403 London Rd., Camberley, Surrey GU15 3HL (☎0845 226 1906; www.eteach.com). Online recruitment service for teachers.

European Council of International Schools, 21B Lavant St., Petersfield, Hampshire GU32 3EL (☎01730 268 244; www.ecis.org). Runs recruitments services for international schools in the UK and elsewhere.

International Schools Services (ISS), 15 Roszel Rd., P.O. Box 5910, Princeton, NJ 08543, USA (☎609-452-0990; www.iss.edu). Hires teachers for more than 200 overseas schools, including some in England; candidates should have experience teaching or with international affairs. 2-year commitment expected.

The Teacher Recruitment Company, Penbineway Offices (1), 87-89 Saffron Hill, London, EC1N 8QU (☎0845 833 1934; www.teachers.eu.com). International recruitment agency that lists positions across the country and provides info on jobs in the UK.

WORK PERMIT AND VISA INFORMATION. European Economic Area (EEA) nationals (member countries include EU member states and Iceland, Liechtenstein, and Norway) do not need a work permit to work in the UK. If you live in a Commonwealth country (including Australia, Canada, and New Zealand) and if your parents or grandparents were born in the UK, you can apply for **UK Ancestry-Employment** and work without a permit (make sure you have all the relevant birth certificates that can prove your connection to the UK). Commonwealth citizens ages 17-27 can work permit-free under a **working holiday visa.** Foreigners studying at an institution in the UK are able to work within restrictions permit-free. American citizens who are full-time students and are over 18 can apply for a special permit from the **British Universities North America Club (BUNAC),** which allows them to work for up to 6 months in the UK. Contact BUNAC at P.O. Box 430, Southbury, CT 06488, USA (☎203-264-0901) or 16 Bowling Green Ln., London EC1R 0QH (☎020 7251 3472; www.bunac.org.uk). Others will need a work permit to work in the UK. Applications must be made by the employer and can be obtained through the **Home Office,** Work Permits (UK), P.O. Box 3468, Sheffield (☎0114 207 4074; www.workpermits.gov.uk). Applications for work visas must be made through your local consulate. For more information, see www.workpermit.com/uk and **Facts for the Traveler: Embassies and Consulates** (p. 10).

AU PAIR WORK

Au pairs are typically women (although sometimes men), age 18-27, who work as live-in nannies, caring for children and doing light housework in foreign countries in exchange for room, board, and a small spending allowance or stipend. One perk of the job is that it allows you to get to know Britain without the high expenses of traveling. Drawbacks can include mediocre pay and long hours. Much of the au pair experience depends on the family with whom you are placed. The agencies below are a good starting point for an employment search.

A1 Kidscare UK, 22 Ethelbert Rd., Margate, Kent, CT9 1RY (☎01843 571 716; www.a1kidscare.com). Sets up experienced au pairs with families that provide room, board, and pocket money.

Almondbury Au Pair Agency, Napier Rd., Holland Park, London W14 8LQ (☎01803 380 795; www.aupair-agency.com). Lists job openings in the UK and Ireland.

Childcare International, Ltd., Trafalgar House, Grenville Pl., London NW7 3SA (☎020 8906 3116; www.childint.co.uk).

InterExchange, 161 Sixth Ave., New York, NY, 10013, USA (☎212-924-0446; fax 924-0575; www.interexchange.org).

SHORT-TERM WORK

Traveling for long periods of time can get expensive. Many travelers try their hand at odd jobs for a few weeks at a time to help finance another month or two of touring. Although the UK typically does not issue work permits for short-term manual or domestic labor, a popular option is to work several hours at a hostel in exchange for free or discounted room and/or board. Pub work is widely available and may not require a permit, depending on the employer. Most often, these short-term jobs are found by word of mouth. Due to the high turnover in the tourism industry, many places are eager for help. *Let's Go* lists temporary jobs like these whenever possible—look in the Practical Information sections of larger cities.

Vacation Work Publications, Westminster House, Kew Rd., Richmond, Surrey TW9 2ND (☎01865 241 978; www.vacationwork.co.uk) publishes books on working overseas and maintains an up-to-date database of seasonal jobs in many countries including the UK. **BUNAC** (p. 65) has listings for establishments that have employed short-term workers in the past. The YHA and SYHA hostel networks list openings on their websites (www.yha.org.uk, www.syha.org.uk), and independent hostels also hire short-term workers from a pool of globetrotters.

ENGLAND. Most English cities and larger towns have job spaces to fill, especially during the **high season,** and mainly in pubs or restaurants. **Brighton** (p. 161) is especially accommodating to younger people looking for temporary work. Job hunting may be harder in the northern cities, where unemployment is higher. TICs are a good place to start your search (many post listings on their bulletin boards), although you will also be advised to check newspapers or individual establishments. **Job placement organizations** arrange temporary jobs in service or office industries. They can be found in most cities, including Blue Arrow in **Cambridge** (p. 317) and throughout the southwest, the Manpower office in **Manchester** (p. 353), and JobCentres throughout England. **Bournemouth** (p. 209), **Bristol** (p. 198), **Exeter** (p. 214), **Newquay** (p. 237) and **Torquay** (p. 226) are all good places to look for work.

WALES. Many areas of Wales suffer unemployment rates higher than the British average. Picking up short-term work as a traveler may be more of a challenge here than in England. **Cardiff** (p. 455), a large, well-touristed city, is perhaps the most feasible option, especially during rugby season when smaller towns may have listings posted at TICs or outside markets.

SCOTLAND. Edinburgh (p. 529) is an excellent place to look for short-term work, especially during Festival in August. The backpacker culture fosters plenty of opportunities, and most of the larger hostels post lists of job openings. **Glasgow** (p. 563) experiences a similar boom during the summer. In both cities, low-paying domestic and food service jobs are easy to procure, and computer skills may net you higher-paying office work. **Inverness** has a JobCentre (p. 620) that can help you find temporary placements. Archaeological digs are commonplace in both **Orkney** and **Shetland,** but the application process is competitive. The fish-processing industry in Shetland (p. 668) provides hard work, good pay, and excellent scenery.

NORTHERN IRELAND. Some of the most common forms of short-term employment in Northern Ireland include **food service, domestic work,** and **farm work.** Belfast is a good place to look for work opportunities and has several placement agencies. As with other regions, word of mouth and postings in hostels are some of the best ways to find short-term employment for travelers.

FARMING IN THE UK

Working on a farm offers a chance to get away from the urban sprawl of London and other big cities and to wander among the fluffy sheep. The **Seasonal Agricultural Workers Scheme,** run by the Home Office, is a youth-oriented program that facilitates the placement of overseas nationals, especially students ages 18-25, in seasonal positions in the agricultural industry. For more information, contact the Managed Migration division of the Home Office (☎0114 259 4074; www.workpermits.gov.uk). Below are a couple of organizations that can help set up short-term exchange and work programs in the farming industry.

Fruitfuljobs.com (☎0870 727 0050; www.fruitfuljobs.com). Sets up farm work for backpackers and students all over the UK; online application.

World Wide Opportunities on Organic Farms (WWOOF), Moss Peteral, Brampton CA8 7HY (☎01273 476 286; www.wwoof.org.uk). Offers a list of organic farms in the UK that welcome volunteers. In return for 4-6hr. of work, visitors receive a bed and meals.

ADDITIONAL RESOURCES.

Alternatives to the Peace Corps: A Guide of Global Volunteer Opportunities, by Paul Backhurst. Food First Books, 2005 (US$12).

The Back Door Guide to Short-Term Job Adventures: Internships, Summer Jobs, Seasonal Work, Volunteer Vacations, and Transitions Abroad, by Michael Landes. Ten Speed Press, 2005 (US$22).

Green Volunteers: The World Guide to Voluntary Work in Nature Conservation, ed. Fabio Ausenda. Universe, 2007 (US$15).

How to Get a Job in Europe, by Cheryl Matherly and Robert Sanborn. Planning Communications, 2003 (US$23).

How to Live Your Dream of Volunteering Overseas, by Joseph Collins, Stefano DeZerega, and Zahara Heckscher. Penguin Books, 2002 (US$20).

International Job Finder: Where the Jobs Are Worldwide, by Daniel Lauber and Kraig Rice. Planning Communications, 2002 (US$20).

Live and Work Abroad: A Guide for Modern Nomads, by Huw Francis and Michelyne Callan. Vacation-Work Publications, 2001 (US$16).

Living and Working in Britain: How to Study, Work and Settle in the UK, by Christine Hall. How to Books, 2002 (US$17).

Overseas Summer Jobs 2002. Peterson's Guides and Vacation Work, 2002 (US$18).

Volunteer Vacations: Short-Term Adventures That Will Benefit You and Others, by Doug Cutchins, Anne Geissinger, and Bill McMillon. Chicago Review Press, 2006 (US$18).

Work Abroad: The Complete Guide to Finding a Job Overseas, by Clayton Hubbs. Transitions Abroad Publishing, 2002 (US$16).

Work Your Way Around the World, by Susan Griffith. Vacation-Work Publications, 2007 (US$22).

BEYOND TOURISM

fringe binge

Where art is concerned at the Edinburgh Fringe Festival, anything goes. It's one of the most supportive artistic environments a performer could want. One could sit in the same seat in the basement of C-Venues from 10am to 2am and see everything from a Spanish music tap dance show, a silly romp through the works of Shakespeare for children, a Blues Brothers cover band, and the show in which I performed, "Jihad: The Musical."

Of course, the sensationalist title of our show led to a blitz of press when we first arrived. "Aren't you worried of offending people? How do you think people will react? Isn't it in poor taste?" Even so, the interviews almost always concluded with, "Well, if there's anywhere in the world a show like yours could succeed, it's at the Edinburgh Fringe Festival."

Before I came, I did my homework on the Fringe: hundreds of venues, thousands of shows, tens of thousands performers. I wondered how a city with only 500,000 inhabitants could house something so great in scope. When I arrived, however, I realized that Edinburgh does not accommodate the Festival; Edinburgh simply becomes the Festival.

It seems that every building besides restaurants, hotels, storefronts, and Internet cafes is some sort of performance venue. There's a gigantic inflatable purple tent that holds shows during the day, and all I could think when I walked past it was, "Yeah, that makes sense."

I have not seen a single show for which I booked my ticket in advance. It doesn't seem to be the way things work here. Clearly, if a show contains a big star, a world-famous comedian, or has received an ungodly amount of media attention, it's best to purchase tickets in advance. But it is far more satisfying to stroll the Royal Mile, the main drag of the festivities, with (or without) a program, and enter whatever venue you find yourself near. I have preferred not carrying one of the many comprehensive rosters of the Festival's productions. When confronted with one of these lists, I tend to take the easy way out and attend all the shows that I think I would enjoy. But there are too many things here that I would never think I wanted to see until I was standing in front of a church-turned-theater looking at posters, thinking, "Hmm...a man standing on his head on top of another man's raised foot. I'll see that!"

Being a performer, or at least being connected with one or more productions here, is one of the best ways to experience the Fringe. It becomes very easy to make friends at one of Edinburgh's many pubs ("And why are you four ladies all painted entirely green? Oh, you're doing a show! I'm doing a show too, here's my flyer.") For a mere £5, you get a Venue pass, which allows you to see all of the shows at your venue for free. Being at C-Venues means that, for the price of a fish and chips platter, I can see more than 400 productions over the course of this month.

Register your act with the Fringe by early April. A copy of the registration form is available from Performer Services and at www.edfringe.com. It costs £150 to register for one night, and registration prices increase for

"Edinburgh doesn't accommodate the Festival; it simply becomes the Festival."

multiple nights.

Not too many shows come here with the intention of making money. Between flight costs, putting up your company in a flat or hotel, and paying the theater overhead, most would rather save their commercially viable ventures for the West End or Broadway. The Fringe is about embracing eccentricities, broadening horizons, and celebrating art.

For more information on the Fringe Festival, see p. 546.

David Ingber *has a degree in English and American Literature and Language from Harvard University. He is an actor and comedian living in New York City.*

A DIFFERENT PATH

ENGLAND

This blessed plot, this earth, this realm, this England...
—William Shakespeare, *Richard II*

The United Kingdom, Great Britain, England—the terms may seem interchangeable, but a slip of the tongue in a pub will provide travelers with a quick education. England, Scotland, and Wales constitute the island of Great Britain, the largest of the British Isles. Along with Northern Ireland (Ulster), the British countries form Her Majesty's United Kingdom of Great Britain and Northern Ireland, commonly called the **UK**. England conquered Ireland in the 12th century, Wales in the 13th, and Scotland in 1707. The Republic of Ireland won back its independence in 1921. While Wales and Scotland retain separate cultural identities marked by language and customs, the two remain part of a nation administered from London. This chapter focuses on the history, literature, and culture of England. **Wales** (p. 448), **Scotland** (p. 520), and **Northern Ireland** (p. 673) are treated separately.

LIFE AND TIMES

YE OLDE ENGLAND

THE ANCIENT ISLE. Britain's residents first developed a distinct culture when the land bridge between the European continent and Britain eroded (c. 6000-5000 BC). Little is known about the island's prehistoric inhabitants, but the massive, astronomically precise stone circles left behind at **Stonehenge** (p. 191) and **Avebury** (p. 192) testify to their scientific and technological prowess. The **Celts** and **Druids** emigrated from the Continent in the first millennium BC, but were eradicated by the blood-thirsty armies of the Roman Emperor Claudius in AD 43. The Roman conquerors established "Britannia" (England and Wales) as the northernmost border of the empire by the end of the first century, building **Londinium** (London), **Verulamium** (St. Albans, p. 257), and a resort spa at **Bath** (p. 192). Further expansion proved difficult as the Romans faced marauders from the northwest. In defense, the Emperor Hadrian constructed his extensive wall in the 2nd century AD. By the 4th century, the Roman empire waned and the Angles and the Saxons—tribes from Denmark and northern Germany—established settlements and kingdoms in the south. The name "England" derives from "Anglaland," land of the Angles.

THE CONQUERORS. The Britons became Christian when the famed missionary **Augustine** converted King Æthelbert in AD 597 and founded England's first Catholic church at **Canterbury** (p. 145). From the 8th to the 10th centuries, the Norse sacked Scotland and Ireland, and Danish Vikings raided England's east coast. In AD 878, legendary **Alfred the Great** defeated the Danes, curtailing their rapidly expanding influence. The birth of Britain and the death of the Anglo-Saxon dynasty was assured when, allegedly, **Edward the Confessor** promised the throne to a Norman named William. Better known as **The Conqueror**, William I invaded the

2500-2000 BC
An ancient tribe—likely the Druids but likelier a troupe of Martians—constructs the Neolithic stone circle at Stonehenge.

AD 43
Emperor Claudius invades Britain and founds Londinium.

AD 597
Saint Augustine converts King Æthelbert (and all Britons) to Christianity.

ENGLAND

1066
At the epic Battle of Hastings, the Norman William I, the Conqueror, defeats the Anglo-Saxon Harold II.

1209
Migrant scholars found a university at Cambridge. Learning ensues.

1270
The enclosure of Chillingham Park isolates the majestic Wild Cattle of Chillingham—the only cattle in the world to remain free of breeding management.

1307
Robert Hood of Wakefield, the real-life Robin Hood, is fined for refusing to invade Scotland.

1327
King Edward II is murdered with a red-hot rod iron through the bowels at Berkeley Castle.

1348-1361
"Bring out chyer dead!" The Black Death kills one-third of Britain's population.

1534
In between wives, Henry VIII founds the Church of England (the Anglican Church).

island after Edward's death in 1066, won the pivotal **Battle of Hastings** (p. 157), slaughtered his rival Harold II (and Harold's two brothers, for good measure), and established the House of Norman. He then set about cataloguing his new English acquisitions—each peasant, cow, and bale of hay—in the epic **Domesday Book** (p. 179). William introduced **feudalism** to Britain, and under the "Norman yoke," he doled out vast tracts of land to his cronies and subjugated English tenants to French lords.

BLOOD AND DEMOCRACY. With conquest, infighting, and plague as reoccurring themes, the Middle Ages were a mess. In 1154, Henry Plantagenet ascended the throne as **Henry II,** armed with a healthy inheritance and a marital dowry from his wife that entitled him to most of France. He quelled internal uprisings and spread his influence across the Isles, claiming Ireland in 1171. Henry's son, **Richard the Lionheart,** was more interested in the Crusades than in domestic insurgents and spent only six months of his 10-year reign on the island. In 1215, tired of such royal pains, noblemen forced his hapless brother and successor, King John, to sign the **Magna Carta,** the precursor to the United States' Bill of Rights and a keystone of modern democracy. The first **Parliament** convened 50 years later. Defying this move toward egalitarian rule, **Edward I** absorbed Wales under the English crown in 1284 and waged war against the Scots, establishing some of Britain's greatest castles along the way (see **Caernarfon,** p. 509). While English kings expanded the nation's boundaries, the **Black Death** ravaged its population; between 1348 and 1361, it killed one-third of the population. Many more fell in the **Hundred Years' War** (or the 116 Years' War, to be precise), a costly conflict over the French throne.

In 1399, Henry Bolingbroke usurped the throne from his cousin, Richard II, placing the House of Lancaster in control. In 1415, Bolingbroke's son, **Henry V,** and his band of brothers won a legendary upset victory over the French in the Battle of Agincourt. But **Henry VI's** failure to stave off revived French resistance under Joan of Arc resulted in the loss of almost all of Britain's holdings in France. The **Wars of the Roses** (1455-85)—a crisis of royal succession between the houses of Lancaster and York (whose respective emblems were a red and a white rose)—ended when Richard of York sent his nephew, the boy-king Edward V, to the Tower of London for safekeeping. When Edward conveniently disappeared, Richard ascended.

REFORMATION, RENAISSANCE, AND REVOLUTION. The **House of Tudor** replaced the House of Lancaster in 1485, when Henry VII defeated Richard III at the Battle of Bosworth Field. England's most infamous king, **Henry VIII,** reinforced England's control over the Irish and struggled with the more intimate concern of producing a male heir. Henry's domestic troubles led him to marry six women (two of whom he executed) and establish the **Anglican Church** when the Pope refused his request for a divorce. Henry's only son, Edward VI, was overshadowed by his staunchly Catholic half-sister, nicknamed **Bloody Mary** for ordering mass burnings of Protestants. Henry's daughter, **Elizabeth I,** inherited control after Mary's death. Elizabeth reversed the religious persecution enforced by her sister and cemented the success of the **Protestant Reformation.** Under her extraordinary guidance, Britain became the leading Protestant power in Europe: the English defeated the **Spanish Armada** in 1588, **William Shakespeare** dipped his quill in the inkpot, and **Sir Francis Drake** circumnavigated the globe. Henry VII's great-granddaughter, the Catholic **Mary, Queen of Scots,** briefly threatened the stability of the throne, but her implication in a plot against Queen Elizabeth's life backfired, leading to her 20-year imprisonment and execution.

The first union of England, Wales, and Scotland as Great Britain took place in 1603, when the philosopher prince James VI of Scotland ascended the throne as **James I.** But James's—and his successor, **Charles I's**—Catholic sympathies, extravagant spending, and insistence on divine right of kings aroused suspicion in the largely Puritan parliament. After their refusal to fund his desired wars, Charles suspended Parliament for 11 years, spurring the **English Civil War** (1642-51). The monarchy came to a violent end with the execution of Charles I and the founding of the first **British Commonwealth** in 1649.

REPUBLICANISM AND RESTORATION. The fanatically puritanical **Oliver Cromwell** emerged as the charismatic but despotic leader of the new Commonwealth. Cromwell led a bloody conquest of Ireland, ordering the execution of all Catholic priests and every 10th Irish common soldier. He also enforced oppressive measures in Britain, outlawing swearing and the theater. To the relief of many, the Republic collapsed under the lackluster leadership of Cromwell's son Richard. The 1660 **Restoration** of **Charles II** to the throne did not cure Britain's troubles. Debate raged over the exclusion of Charles's Catholic brother **James II** from the succession. Amid the politicking, England's first political parties arose: the **Whigs** opposed the kings and supported reform; the **Tories** supported hereditary succession.

LAWS AND LOGIC. James II took the throne in 1685, but was deposed three years later by his son-in-law **William of Orange.** In the **Glorious Revolution of 1688,** the Dutch Protestant William and his wife Mary forced James to France and implemented a **Bill of Rights,** ensuring the Protestantism of future monarchs. Supporters of James II (called **Jacobites**) remained a threat until 1745, when James II's grandson Charles, commonly known as **Bonnie Prince Charlie** and immortalized in Scottish song, failed in his attempt to recapture the throne (p. 524). Britain accumulated wealth and continental political clout under the rule of William and Mary, marking the end of a century of upheaval and a rise in liberalism and tolerance. By the end of the **Seven Years' War** (1756-63), Britain controlled Canada, 13 unruly colonies to the west, and much of the Caribbean. Parliament prospered thanks to the ineffectual leadership of the Hanoverian kings, **George I, II,** and **III,** and the position of Prime Minister eclipsed the monarchy as the seat of power. Britain's uppity cross-Atlantic colonial holding declared, fought for, and won its independence between 1776 and 1783. Meanwhile, **Sir Isaac Newton** theorized the laws of gravity and invented calculus on the side, and Enlightenment figures **John Locke, Francis Bacon, David Hume,** and **Adam Smith** revolutionized political and philo-

1599
The Burbage brothers construct Shakespeare's Globe Theatre out of wood and thatch. Flammable.

1603
James I (James VI of Scotland) becomes the first British monarch to rule England, Scotland, and Ireland.

1649
Oliver Cromwell takes control of the short-lived British Commonwealth. Three years after his death from malaria, he is exhumed, drawn, quartered, and beheaded.

1657
Thomas Garway begins selling tea to the public in London.

1687
Sir Isaac Newton publishes *Principia Mathematica.* High school becomes exponentially more difficult.

1688
Dutch William of Orange and his wife Mary ascend the English throne, ending the wars of succession.

1776
The colonies in America declare independence. King George III loses his sanity.

sophical thought. Religious fervor occasionally returned, with Bible-thumping **Methodists** preaching to outdoor crowds in the middle of the century.

MODERN ENGLAND

EMPIRE AND INDUSTRY. During the 18th and 19th centuries, Britain seized rule of more than one quarter of the world's population and more than two-fifths of its land, styling itself as "the empire on which the sun never sets." By 1858, Britain controlled India, the "jewel in the imperial crown." Control of the Cape of Good Hope secured shipping routes to the Far East, and plantations in the New World produced staples like sugar and rum. Many British considered it a moral duty to "civilize" the non-Christians in their imperial domain. This method of control replaced a system of slavery, abolished in 1833.

The **Industrial Revolution**—spurred by the mechanization of the textile industry and the perfection of the steam engine by **James Watt** in 1765—bankrolled Britain's colonizing. Massive portions of the populace migrated to towns like **Manchester** (p. 353) and **Leeds** (p. 406), and a wide economic gap between factory owners and laborers replaced the age-old gap between landowners and tenant farmers. The **gold standard,** adopted in 1821, stimulated trade and ensured the pound's value.

VICTORIA AND COMPANY. The reign of **Queen Victoria** (1837-1901) marked a period of foreign and domestic stability and peace. A series of **Factory** and **Reform Acts** limited child labor, capped the average workday, and made sweeping changes in (male) voting rights. Prince Albert's 1851 **Great Exhibition** in London's newly built **Crystal Palace** displayed over 13,000 consumer goods from Britain's territories. The rich, bohemian upper-crust embraced *fin de siècle* decadence with ornate art and clothing and even more ornate social rituals. While commercial self-interest defined 19th-century British society, proto-socialists like **John Stuart Mill** and the members of the **Fabian Society**—including **George Bernard Shaw** and **H.G. Wells**—made the case against bourgeois values. Trade unions strengthened and found a political voice in the **Labour Party,** founded in 1906. The Ireland question became increasingly pressing when Prime Minister **William Gladstone** failed to pass his **Home Rule Bill,** a proposal for partial Irish political autonomy. The **Suffragettes,** led by **Emmeline Pankhurst,** fought for enfranchisement for women by disrupting Parliament and staging hunger strikes. Women won the right to vote after **World War I.**

A LOST GENERATION. The **Great War** (1914-1918), as WWI was known until 1939, left two million British injured and one million dead. Technological advances of the 19th century begot powerful weaponry such as the machine gun, poison gas, and the tank. Combined with the European militaries' outmoded strategies (predominantly, a stubborn insistence on trench warfare), these advances contributed to the enormous human cost of the war. The war destroyed the Victorian dream of a peaceful, progressive society and left Europe scarred by thousands of deaths and thousands of miles of trenches.

1812-1815
The phrase *Pax Britannica* comes into use, referring to the "civilizing" style of British Imperialism.

1833
Parliament passes the Slavery Abolition Act, banning slavery in the British empire.

1856
Thomas Burberry, age 21, opens a small outfitters shop in Basingstoke.

1874
Samuel Bath Thomas leaves England for New York, where he perfects the nooks and crannies of English Muffins.

1880
J. Rand Capron documents his discovery of crop circles in Surrey.

1916
French and British forces engage the Germans in the Battle of the Somme during WWI. July 1 becomes the bloodiest day in British history, with over 55,000 casualties.

ENGLAND

The 1930s brought economic depression and unemployment. A representative for the British Treasury, **John Maynard Keynes,** argued against German war reparations and for interventionism. In 1936, King Edward VIII created controversy by abdicating to marry twice-divorced American socialite Wallis Simpson. After Germany reoccupied the Rhineland, Prime Minister **Neville Chamberlain** pushed through a notorious appeasement agreement with Hitler in Munich, naïvely promising "peace in our time." Following Hitler's invasion of Poland in 1939, however, Britain declared war. Even the Great War failed to prepare Britain for the horrors of the **Holocaust** and the utter devastation of **World War II.** During the prolonged **Battle of Britain** in the summer of 1940, London, Coventry, and other English cities suffered extensive damage from thunderous **"blitzkriegs"**—which left scores of British citizens dead or homeless. The fall of France in 1940 precipitated the creation of a war cabinet, led by the determined and eloquent Prime Minister **Winston Churchill.** In June 1944, Britain and the Allied Forces launched the Battle of Normandy, commonly known as the **D-Day Invasion.** The move changed the tide of the war, leading to the liberation of Paris and eventually peace in May 1945.

ENGLAND'S EVOLUTION. Following the wars, Britain suffered continued economic hardship as its infrastructure and workforce lay in ruins. India declared independence from the British empire in 1947, marking a step in decolonization and the decline of the empire. War rationing didn't end until 1954, and the government owed an huge war debt to the United States. At the same time, immigration from former British colonies increased. In response, Britain adopted socialist economic policies. In 1946, left-wing politicians established the **National Health Service,** which provides free medical care to all British citizens. In the 1960s, Labour relaxed laws against divorce and homosexuality and abolished capital punishment. Despite new policies, Britain could not replace the economic boon of a colonial empire. Unemployment and economic unrest culminated in public service strikes during 1979's **"Winter of Discontent."**

In May 1979, conservative Tory **Margaret Thatcher** became Britain's first female Prime Minister. She espoused reduced government spending, denationalization, and lower taxes. She was unpopular until the **Falkland Islands War** against Argentina in 1982 elicited a surge of patriotism. Thatcher privatized nearly every industry that the Labour government had brought under public control, dismantling vast segments of the welfare state. Her policies brought prosperity to many but sharpened the divide between the rich and the poor. Aggravated by her support of the **poll tax** and resistance to the EEC, the Conservative Party presided over a vote of no confidence that led to Thatcher's 1990 resignation and the election of **John Major.** In 1995, Major forced an election by stepping down and re-running; he won, but the Conservatives lost parliamentary seats.

Under the leadership of the charismatic, youthful **Tony Blair,** the Labour Party refashioned itself into the alternative for discontented middle-class voters. "New Labour" won decisively under Blair in 1997 and garnered a second landslide victory in

1922
The BBC begins broadcasting live from London.

1940
A month after France's surrender to the Germans, the Battle of Britain commences. The Germans bomb London and Royal Air Force sites for nearly a year.

1945
WWII ends. Britain, the United States, and the Soviet Republic craft the Marshall Plan, the United Nations, and a precursor to the EU.

1966
England defeats Germany 4-2 to win its first and only FIFA World Cup.

1969
The Beatles record and release their last album, *Abbey Road,* and disband one year later.

1978
The world's first test-tube baby is born in Oldham.

2001
Reality-TV singing competition *Pop Idol* premiers on ITV1, beginning a franchise of international spinoffs.

ENGLAND

ASHES TO ASHES

The law has been passed, the signs have been made, and the ashtrays have been ceremoniously crushed. On July 1st, 2007, England went where it had never gone before: smoke-free. England joined already smoke-free Northern Ireland, Scotland, and Wales when Parliament passed the 2006 Health Act, which bans smoking in all enclosed public spaces and workplaces. For some, the ban is a long-overdue step toward promoting public health in Britain. For others, it's a total drag.

Britain isn't the first European country to go smoke-free. In 2004, Ireland became the first country in the world to ban smoking in the workplace, and several other countries, including Italy, Norway, and Spain, have since followed suit. Despite the wave of clean air sweeping the Continent, it remains to be seen whether the citizens of England will really breathe easier.

Health officials hope that the smoking ban will prompt more smokers to kick the habit. The National Health Service has implemented new programs aimed at helping smokers use the ban to quit, and quit smoking help lines have already seen increased traffic since the ban too effect. Officials are most optimistic about the long-term benefits of the ban and expect that its major payoff will be seen in future generations.

June 2001. Blair nurtured relations with the EU and maintained inclusive, moderate economic and social positions. Britain's stance on the Kosovo crisis gained Blair the moniker of "Little Clinton."

Blair's Labour government also tackled various constitutional reforms, beginning with domestic **devolution** in Scotland and Wales and a movement toward local governance. The Scottish Parliament (p. 525) and Welsh National Assembly both opened in 1999. Progress has been more halting in attempts at **Northern Irish autonomy.** The **Good Friday Agreement** (p. 675) of 1998 began the disarmament process and created a Northern Ireland Assembly with limited powers, but the British government suspended Belfast's **Stormont Assembly** in 2000, hoping to instigate the decommissioning of arms by the IRA and the Unionists; a lack of progress led to a spate of terrorist attacks. In July 2005, Sinn Fein, the political party associated with the IRA, announced the complete disarmament of the IRA. In May 2007, the loyalist Ulster Volunteer Force signaled the end of the conflict when it renounced violence and placed weapons out of the hands of its soldiers. Britain has yet to cede full parliamentary control back to Stormont.

TODAY

BRITAIN RULES. Britain has become one of the world's most stable constitutional monarchies without the aid of a written constitution. A combination of parliamentary legislation, common law, and convention composes the flexible system of British government. Since the 1700s the monarch has played a largely symbolic role. Real political power resides with **Parliament,** consisting of the **House of Commons,** with its elected Members of Parliament (MPs), and the **House of Lords.** Over time, power has shifted from the Lords to the Commons. Reforms in 1999 removed the majority of hereditary peers from the House of Lords, replacing them with Life Peers, appointed by prime ministers to serve for life. Parliament holds supreme legislative power and may change and even directly contradict its previous laws. All members of the executive branch, which includes the **Prime Minister** and the **Cabinet,** are also MPs. This fusing of legislative and executive functions, called the "efficient secret" of the British government, ensures the quick passage of the majority party's programs into bills. The Prime Minister is appointed by the Sovereign, who typically chooses the leader of the party with the majority in the House of Commons. From an elegant roost on **10 Downing Street,** the Prime Minister chooses a Cabinet, whose members head the government's departments and present a cohesive platform to the public. Political parties keep their MPs in line on most votes in Parliament and provide a pool of talent and support for the smooth functioning of the executive. Roughly, the **Labour** party is center-left; the **Conservatives,** or Tories, are center-right; and the smaller **Liberal Democrat** party is left. Labour supported the war in Iraq, which the Conservatives opposed. Gay marriage and abortion are legal in the UK, but the death penalty is not.

BLAIR'S BRITAIN. In the May 2005 general election, Labour won bragging rights when Tony Blair became the only post-war Prime Minister other than Thatcher to win a third term. However, the victory came in spite of his dwindling popularity. Although his domestic and welfare policies had been generally well-received, Blair's continued support of US foreign policy and his political alliance with President George W. Bush incited resistance in Britain. In February 2003, an estimated one million people gathered in London to protest military intervention in Iraq. Blair's detractors also pointed to the Prime Minister's stance on the **euro;** his long-time insistence that Britain would convert to the currency "when the economy is ready" was seen as a side-stepping political strategy. British public opinion remains ambivalent regarding integration with Europe, but many think that Blair pulled too close to the US, separating himself too far from the Continent.

Horrific **terrorist attacks** shook the country in July 2005. Four suicide bombs detonated on public transportation in London on the morning of July 7, killing 52. A failed second attack occurred two weeks later. The bombings were the deadliest attack in London since WWII. London received international attention again in August 2006, when government officials thwarted a potential terrorist attack on planes traveling through Heathrow airport, resulting in a ban on bottled liquids in aircraft cabins. Blair's popularity continued to decline in the events following the 2005 election, and he announced his resignation in May 2007. Gordon Brown, Chancellor of the Exchequer under Blair, was appointed Prime Minister in June 2007.

A ROYAL MESS? Although largely political figureheads, the royals have long been a juicy subject of gossip among the British public. Matronly **Queen Elizabeth II** won kudos when she began paying income tax in 1993 and threw a year-long Golden Jubilee for the 50th year of her reign in 2002. The world mourned the untimely death of the "People's Princess," **Diana,** following a Paris car crash in 1997. Her widower **Prince Charles** and his paramour **Camilla Parker-Bowles** married in April 2005 after a clandes-

Looking to Scotland, though, where the smoking ban has been in place since March 2006, it appears that these healthful hopes may go up in smoke. Shooed from their pubs, Scottish locals line the sidewalks and create outdoor smoking lounges out of busy pedestrian areas. As one smoker outside a pub in Glasgow remarked, "They can stop us from doing it inside, but they'll never stop the smoking altogether!"

The English are taking more concrete steps to ensure that the smoking ban doesn't change their lifestyles. Hundreds of pubs planned a "day of defiance" on July 1 and allowed patrons to smoke despite the implementation of the ban. Many vow to continue allowing their patrons to smoke if the demand remains high—a calculated risk considering the hefty £2500 fine slapped down on owners who break the law. Fines for individuals caught smoking in public buildings by officials is £50.

Still, some have accepted the ban with a sorrowful goodbye. At midnight on June 30th, the Naval and Military Club in London's St. James's Square had a solemn "extinguishing of the cigars." The farewell was a popular idea; many people planned gatherings with friends for one last public puff. Only time will tell how English culture will evolve around the smoking ban, but for now, it's lights out.

tine 30-year romance, although the Queen did not attend the service. A quick stop at a drug rehab clinic in 2002 heralded the onset of adult celebrity (and tabloid notoriety) for **Prince Harry,** the younger of Charles and Diana's sons. The elder **Prince William,** "his royal sighness," claimed headlines in 2007 after his public breakup with longtime sweetheart **Kate Middleton.**

ENGLISH CULTURE

FOOD AND DRINK

English cooking, like the English climate, is a training for life's unavoidable hardships.
—Historian R.P. Lister

Historically, England has been derided for its awful cuisine. But do not fear the bland, boiled, fried, and gravy-laden traditional nosh, hungry travelers! Britain's cuisine might leave something to be desired, but food in Britain can be excellent. In the spring of 2007, a panel of chefs, food critics, and restaurateurs cast more than 3,000 ballots and voted 7 British restaurants into the world's top 50; the Fat Duck in Berkshire was named Chef's Choice. Popular television chef Jamie Oliver led a well-publicized, successful campaign to increase the British government's spending on school lunches—and travelers on a budget can eat the benefits, too.

The best way to eat in Britain is to avoid British food. Thankfully, ethnic cuisine has rapidly spread from the cities to the smallest of towns, so that most any village with a pub (and you'd be hard-pressed to find one without) will have an Indian takeaway, an Asian noodle shop, or late-night Shawarma stand to feed stumbling patrons after closing. **Vegetarianism** and organic foods are also popular in Britain. Even the most traditional pubs and local markets, let alone the trendy cafe-bars and gastropubs, offer at least one meatless option.

All visitors to Britain should try the famed, cholesterol-filled **full English breakfast,** which generally includes fried eggs, bacon, baked beans, sauteed mushrooms, grilled tomato, and black pudding (sausage made with pork blood), smothered in HP sauce (a vinegar base mixed with fruit and spices). The full brekky is served in B&Bs, pubs, and cafes across the country. Toast smothered in jam or Marmite (the most acquired of tastes—a salty, brown spread made from yeast) is a breakfast staple. The best dishes for lunch or dinner are **roasts**—beef, lamb, and Wiltshire hams—and **Yorkshire pudding,** a type of popover drizzled with meat juices. **Bangers and mash** and **bubble and squeak,** despite their intriguing names, are simply sausages and potatoes and cabbage and potatoes, respectively. Vegetables, often boiled into a flavorless mush, are typically the weakest part of a meal. Beware the British salad, which is often just a plate of lettuce and sweetened mayonnaise called "salad cream." Be careful, too, of sandwiches with hidden mayonnaise (frequently called "club sauce") and butter. The Brits make their **desserts** ("puddings" or "afters") exceedingly sweet and gloopy. Sponges, trifles, tarts, and the ill-named **spotted dick** (spongy currant cake) will satiate the sweetest tooth.

Pub grub is fast, filling, and a fine option for budget travelers. Try savory pies like **Cornish pasties** (PASS-tees), **shepherd's pie,** and **steak and kidney pie.** For those on a serious budget, the **ploughman's lunch** (bread, cheese, and pickles) is a staple in country pubs and can be divine. The local "chippy," or chip shop, sells deep-fried **fish and chips** dripping with grease, salt, and vinegar, in a paper cone. Seek out **outdoor markets** for fresh bread and dairy—try Stilton cheese and biscuits or baps. **Boots, Benjys, Marks & Spencer,** and **Prêt à Manger** sell an impressive array of readymade sandwiches. **Crisps,** or potato chips, come in astonishing variety, with flavors like prawn cocktail. Try Chinese, Turkish, Lebanese, and especially Indian cuisines—Britain offers some of the best **tandoori** and **curry** outside India.

British **"tea"** refers both to a drink and a social ceremony. The ritual refreshment, accompanying almost every meal, is served strong with milk. The standard tea, colloquially known as a **cuppa**, is PG Tips or Tetley. More refined cups specify particular blends such as **Earl Grey** and **Darjeeling.** The oft-stereotyped ritual of afternoon **high tea** includes cooked meats, salad, sandwiches, and pastries. **Cream tea,** a specialty of Cornwall and Devon, includes toast, shortbread, crumpets, scones, and jam, accompanied by **clotted cream** (a cross between whipped cream and butter). The summer teatime potion **Pimm's** is a sangria-esque punch of fruit juices and gin (the recipe is a well-guarded secret). On the softer side, super-sweet fizzy drinks **Lilt** and **Tango** as well as the popular juice **Ribena** keep whistles wet.

PUBS AND BITTER. Sir William Harcourt believed that English history was made in pubs as much as in the Houses of Parliament. After all, stopping in at lunchtime and after work is not an uncommon daily routine. Brits rapidly develop loyalty for neighborhood establishments, or "local," and pubs in turn tend to cater to their regulars and develop a particular character. Pubs are everywhere—even the smallest village can support a decent pub crawl. The drinking age is an inconsistently enforced 18, and you need only be 14 to enter a pub.

Bitter, named for its sharp, hoppy aftertaste, is a standard pub drink. It should be hand-pumped or pulled from the tap at cellar temperature into government-stamped pint glasses (20oz.) or the more modest half-pint glass. Real ale retains a diehard cult of connoisseurs in the shadow of giant corporate breweries. Visit www.camra.org.uk to find out more about the Campaign for Real Ale. Brown, pale, and India pale ales—less common varieties—all have a relatively heavy flavor with noticeable hop. Stout, the distinctive subspecies of ale, is rich, dark, and creamy. Try Irish Guinness (p. 713), with its silky foam head. Most draught ales and stouts are served at room temperature, but if you can't stand the heat, try a lager, a precursor of American beer typically served cold. Cider is a tasty fermented apple juice served sweet or dry. Variations on the standard pint include black velvet, which is stout and champagne; black and tan, layers of stout and ale; and snakebite, lager and cider with a dash of black currant syrup or Ribena.

Since WWI, government-imposed closing times have restricted pub hours. In England and Wales, drinks are usually served 11am-11pm Monday to Saturday, and noon-3pm and 7-10:30pm Sunday; more flexible hours are in place in Scotland. A bell approximately 10 minutes before closing time signifies last call. Controversial legislation passed in 2003 allows pubs, clubs, and supermarkets in England and Wales to obtain special licenses and increasingly flexible opening hours—creating the 24hr. pub. Pubs without special licenses sometimes circumvent closing times by serving food or having an entertainment license.

CULTURE AND CUSTOMS

The United Kingdom, roughly the size of the state of Oregon, is home to over 60 million people from diverse and dynamic local subcultures. Jane Austen, Sid Vicious, and Winston Churchill are all quintessentially "English," and stiff-upper-lipped public schoolboys and post-punk Hoxton rockers sit next to Burberry-clad football hooligans on the Tube.

There is little that a traveler can do that will inadvertently cause offense while traveling in England. However, the English do place weight on proper decorum, including **politeness** ("thanks" comes in many varieties, including "cheers"), **queueing** (that is, lining up—never disrupt the queue), and keeping a certain **respectful distance.** You'll find, however, that the British **sense of humor**—dark, wry, explicit, even raunchy—is somewhat at odds with any notion you may have of their coldness or reserve.

THE ARTS

LANGUAGE AND LITERATURE

Eclipsed only by Mandarin Chinese in sheer number of speakers, the history of the English language reflects the diversity of the hundreds of millions who use it today. Once a minor Germanic dialect, English incorporated words and phrases from Danish, French, and Latin, providing even its earliest wordsmiths with a vast vocabulary rivaled by few world languages. Throughout centuries of British colonialism, the language continued to borrow from other tongues and supplied a literary and popular voice for people far removed from the British Isles. Welsh (p. 452) and Scottish (p. 526) languages and literatures are treated separately.

BARDS AND BIBLES. Britain is undeniably the birthplace of much of the world's best literature. A strong oral tradition informed most of the earliest poetry in English, little of which survives. The best-known piece of Anglo-Saxon (Old English) poetry is *Beowulf* (c. 700-1000), a tale of an egoistic prince, his heroic deeds, and his ultimate defeat in a battle by a dragon. The unknown author of *Sir Gawain and the Green Knight* (c. 1375) narrates a romance of Arthurian chivalry in which the bedroom becomes a battlefield and a young knight journeys on a mysterious quest. **Geoffrey Chaucer** tapped into the more spirited side of Middle English: his *Canterbury Tales* (c. 1387) remain some of the sauciest, most incisive stories in the English canon and poke fun at all stations of English life. **John Wycliffe** made the Bible accessible to the masses, translating it from Latin to English in the 1380s. **William Tyndale** followed suit in 1525, and his work became the model for the popular **King James** version (completed in 1611 under James I).

THE ENGLISH RENAISSANCE. English literature flourished under the reign of Elizabeth I (1559-1603). **Sir Philip Sidney's** sonnet sequences and **Edmund Spenser's** moral allegories like *The Faerie Queene* earned favor at court, while **John Donne** and **George Herbert** crafted metaphysical poetry. Playwright **Christopher Marlowe** lost his life in a pub brawl, but not before he produced popular plays of temptation and damnation such as *Dr. Faustus* (c. 1588). **Ben Jonson**, when he wasn't languishing in jail, redefined satiric comedy in works like *Volpone* (1606). The son of a glove-maker from Stratford-upon-Avon (p. 274), Shakespeare's influence and brilliance would be difficult to overstate. His success as a writer and linguistic innovator—he created the words "scuffle," "lonely," "arouse," and "skim milk," among others—helped make him, in the words of literary critic Harold Bloom, the "inventor of the human." (OK, so maybe his brilliance *is* possible to overstate.)

HOW NOVEL! Britain's civil and religious turmoil in the late 16th and early 17th centuries spurred a huge volume of obsessive and brilliant literature, like **John Milton's** epic *Paradise Lost* (1667) and **John Bunyan's** allegorical *Pilgrim's Progress* (1678). In the 18th century, **John Dryden** penned neoclassical poetry, **Alexander Pope** satires, and **Dr. Samuel Johnson** his idiosyncratic dictionary. In 1719, **Daniel Defoe** inaugurated the era of the English **novel** with his swashbuckling *Robinson Crusoe*. Authors like **Samuel Richardson** (*Clarissa*, 1749) and **Fanny Burney** (*Evelina*, 1778) perfected the form, while **Henry Fielding's** wacky *Tom Jones* (1749) and **Laurence Sterne's** experimental *Tristram Shandy* (1759-67) pushed its limits. **Jane Austen's** intricate narratives portrayed the modes and manners of the early 19th century. In the Victorian period, poverty and social change spawned the sentimental novels of **Charles Dickens**. *Oliver Twist* (1837-39) and *David Copperfield* (1849-50) draw on the bleakness of his childhood in Portsmouth (p. 172) and portray the harsh living conditions of working-class Londoners. Secluded in the wild Yorkshire moors (see Haworth, p. 405), the **Brontë sisters** staved off tuberculosis and crafted the tumultuous romances *Wuthering Heights* (Emily; 1847),

Jane Eyre, and *Villette* (Charlotte; 1847 and 1853). **George Eliot** (Mary Ann Evans) wrote her intricately detailed "Study of Provincial Life," *Middlemarch* (1871). *Tess of the d'Urbervilles* (1891) and *Jude the Obscure* (1895) by **Thomas Hardy** mark a sombre end to the Victorian age.

ROMANTICISM AND RESPONSE. Partly in reaction to the rationalism of the preceding century, the **Romantic** movement garnered turbulent verse that celebrated the transcendent beauty of nature, the power of imagination, and the profound influence of childhood experiences. Reclusive painter-poet **William Blake** printed *The Marriage of Heaven and Hell* from brilliantly painted etched plates in 1790. **William Wordsworth** and **Samuel Taylor Coleridge** wrote the watershed collection *Lyrical Ballads,* which included "Tintern Abbey" (p. 463) and "The Rime of the Ancient Mariner," in the late 1790s. Wordsworth's poetry reflects on a long, full life—he drew inspiration from the Lakes (p. 371) and Snowdonia (p. 501)—but many of his colleagues died tragically young. The astonishing prodigy **John Keats,** who concocted the Romantic maxim "beauty is truth, truth beauty," succumbed to tuberculosis at 26. Lyric poet and advocate of vegetarianism **Percy Bysshe Shelley** drowned off the Tuscan coast at 29. The pansexual heartthrob **Lord Byron** defined the heroic archetype in *Don Juan* (1819-24) and died fighting in the Greek War of Independence at the age of 36.

The poetry of the Victorian age struggled with the impact of societal changes and religious skepticism. **Alfred, Lord Tennyson** spun verse about faith and doubt for over a half-century and inspired a medievalist revival with Arthurian idylls like "The Lady of Shalott" (1842). Celebrating the grotesque, **Robert Browning** composed piercing dramatic monologues, and his wife **Elizabeth Barrett** counted the ways she loved him in *Sonnets from the Portuguese* (1850). Meanwhile, fellow female poet **Christina Rossetti** envisioned the fantastical world of "Goblin Market" (1862). **Matthew Arnold** abandoned poetry in 1867 to become the greatest cultural critic of the day, and Jesuit priest **Gerard Manley Hopkins** penned tortuous verse with a unique "sprung rhythm" that makes him the chief forerunner of poetic modernism.

THE MODERN AGE. "On or about December 1910," wrote **Virginia Woolf,** "human nature changed." Woolf, a key member of London's bohemian intellectual **Bloomsbury Group,** captured the spirit of the time and the real life of the mind in her novels. She and Irish expatriate **James Joyce** (p. 714) were among the groundbreaking practitioners of **Modernism** (c. 1910-1930). **T.S. Eliot's** *The Waste Land* (1922), a schizophrenic poem journeying through diverse cultural influences, is one of the 20th century's most important works. Reacting to the Great War, Eliot portrays London as a fragmented and barren desert in his difficult, highly allusive verse. **D.H. Lawrence** explored tensions in the British working-class family and challenged sexual convention in *Sons and Lovers* (1913). Although he spoke only a few words of English when he arrived in Britain at 21, **Joseph Conrad** demonstrated his mastery of the language in *Heart of Darkness* (1902). Disillusionment with imperialism surfaces in **E.M. Forster's** half-Modernist, half-Romantic novels, particularly *A Passage to India* (1924). Authors of the 1930s captured the tumult and depression of the decade: **Evelyn Waugh** turned a ruthlessly satirical eye on society and **Graham Greene** explored moral ambiguity. The sardonic poet **W.H. Auden,** disturbed by the violence of the world, wrote in 1939: "We must love one another or die."

LATER TWENTIETH-CENTURY. Fascism and the horrors of WWII motivated musings on the nature of evil, while **George Orwell's** dystopic *1984* (1949) strove to strip the world of memory and words of meaning. **Anthony Burgess's** *A Clockwork Orange* (1962) imagines the violence and anarchy of a not-so-distant future. The end of Empire, rising affluence, and the growing gap between classes splintered British literature. Nostalgia pervades the poetry of **Philip Larkin** and **John Betjeman,** and an angry working class found voices in **Allan Sillitoe** and **Kingsley Amis.** Post-

ENGLAND

colonial voices like Indian expatriate **Salman Rushdie** and 2002 Nobel laureate **V.S. Naipaul** have found a place in British literary tradition. Today, Britain's hip literary circle includes working writers **A.S. Byatt, Martin Amis, Kazuo Ishiguro, Zadie Smith,** and the masterful neo-realist **Ian McEwan.** British playwrights continue to innovate: **Harold Pinter** infuses living rooms with horrifying silences, **Tom Stoppard** challenges theatrical convention in plays like *Rosencrantz and Guildenstern are Dead* (1967), and **Caryl Churchill** provides blistering commentary on "the state of Britain" in plays like *Cloud Nine* (1988).

OUTSIDE THE CLASSROOM. English literature thrives away from the ivory tower. The mysteries of **Dorothy L. Sayers** and **Agatha Christie** are read worldwide, while the espionage novels of **John le Carré** and **Ian Fleming,** inventor of James Bond, provide more in-your-face thrills. **P.G. Wodehouse,** creator of Jeeves, the consummate butler, adeptly satirizes the idle aristocrat. **James Herriot** (Alf Wight), beloved author of *All Creatures Great and Small* (1972), chronicled his work as a young veterinarian. **Douglas Adams** parodied sci-fi in his humorous series *Hitchhiker's Guide to the Galaxy,* and **Helen Fielding's** hapless *Bridget Jones* speaks on behalf of singletons everywhere. British children's literature delights all ages: **Lewis Carroll's** *Alice's Adventures in Wonderland* (1865), **C.S. Lewis's** *Chronicles of Narnia* (1950-56), **Roald Dahl's** stories, like *Charlie and the Chocolate Factory* (1964), *The Witches* (1983), *Matilda* (1988), and **Brian Jacques's** *Redwall* series (1986-2005) enjoy continued popularity. A linguist named **J.R.R. Tolkien,** Lewis's companion in letters and Oxford pub-readings (p. 271), wrote tales of elves and wizards, including *The Hobbit* (1934) and *Lord of the Rings* (1954-56). **Nick Hornby** writes witty novels, like *High Fidelity* and *About a Boy.* Earning herself a fortune greater than that of the Queen, **J.K. Rowling** has enchanted the world with her saga of juvenile wizardry in the *Harry Potter* series. The last installment hit shelves in July 2007, bringing readers one final, page-turning adventure.

ART AND ARCHITECTURE

LEARN A NEW LANGUAGE. The sheer number of castles and cathedrals in England should be sufficient motivation to learn the words associated with their architecture. A castle's **keep** is the main tower and residence hall. Some early keeps sit atop a steep mound called a **motte.** The slender external wall supports that hold up the tallest castles and the loftiest cathedrals are **buttresses.** A **vault** is a stone ceiling, a ribbed vault is held up by spidery stone arcs or **ribs,** and the **webs** are the spaces in between ribs. Most churches are **cruciform,** or cross-shaped. The head of the cross is the **choir,** the arms are the **transepts,** and support of the cross is the **nave.** Medieval churches usually have a three-tiered nave: the ground level is the **arcade,** the middle level (where monks would walk and ponder scripture) is the **triforium,** and the highest level (where the light comes in) is the **clerestory.** The beautifully detailed stained glass is outlined by **tracery,** the lacy stonework that holds it in place.

HOUSES OF GODS AND MEN. Early English architects often borrowed styles from mainland Europe, although some are particular to Britain. The Normans introduced **Romanesque** architecture (round arches and thick walls) in the eleventh century, and the British adopted the fashion in the imposing Durham cathedral (p. 427). The **Gothic** style, originating in France (12th-15th century), ushered in intricate, haunting buildings like the cathedrals of Wells (p. 205) and Salisbury (p. 190). By the 14th century, the English had developed the unique **perpendicular style** of window tracery, apparent at King's College Chapel in Cambridge (p. 321). Sadly, the **Suppression of Monasteries** in 1536 under Henry VIII spurred the wanton smashing of stained glass and even of entire churches, leaving picturesque **ruins** scattered along the countryside (like **Rievaulx,** p. 424; or **Glastonbury,** p. 207). After the **Renaissance,** architects used new engineering methods—evident in **Christopher Wren's** fantastic dome on **St. Paul's Cathedral** (p. 111), built in 1666.

Early domestic architecture in Britain progressed from the **stone dwellings** of pre-Christian folk (see **Skara Brae,** p. 662) to the Romans' **forts and villas** (see **Hadrian's Wall,** p. 444) to the famed medieval castles. The earliest of these, the hilltop **motte-and-bailey** forts, arrived with William the Conqueror in 1066 (see **Round Tower of Windsor,** p. 261, or **Carisbrooke,** p. 179) and progressed into tall, square **Norman keeps** like the **Tower of London** (p. 110). Warmongering Edward I constructed a string of astonishing **concentric castles** along the Welsh coast (Harlech, p. 505; Caernarfon, p. 509; Beaumaris, p. 515; Caerphilly, p. 462). By the 14th century, the advent of the cannon made castles obsolete, yet they lived on as **palaces** for the oligarchy (see the breathtaking **Warwick,** p. 295). During the Renaissance, the wealthy built sumptuous **Tudor homes,** like Henry VIII's Hampton Court (p. 144). In the 18th century, both the heady **baroque** style of Castle Howard (p. 401) and the severe **Palladian** symmetry of Houghton Hall (p. 330) were in vogue. **Stately homes** like Howard and Houghton were furnished with **Chippendale** furniture and surrounded by equally stately **gardens** (see **Blenheim Palace,** p. 274). The Victorians built in the ornate **neo-Gothic revival (Houses of Parliament,** p. 114) and **neo-Classical** (British Museum, p. 127) styles. Today, hotshots (and colleagues) **Richard Rogers** and **Norman Foster** vie for bragging rights as England's most influential architect, littering London with avant-garde additions like the **Lloyd's Building** (p. 117), City Hall, and a host of Millennium constructions.

ON THE CANVAS. Britain's early religious art, including **illuminated manuscripts,** gave way to secular patronage and the institution of court painters. Renaissance art in England was largely dominated by foreign portraitists such as **Hans Holbein the Younger** (1497-1543) and Flemish masters **Peter Paul Reubens** (1577-1640) and **Anthony Van Dyck** (1599-1641). **Nicholas Hilliard** (1547-1619) was the first English-born success of the period. Vanity, and thus portraiture, continued to flourish into the 18th century, with the satirical London scenes of **William Hogarth** (1697-1764), classically-inspired poses of **Joshua Reynolds** (1723-1792), and provincial backdrops of **Thomas Gainsborough** (1727-1788). Encouraged by a nation-wide interest in gardening, **landscape painting** peaked during the 19th century. Beyond the literary realm, Romanticism inspired the vibrant rustic scenes of **John Constable** and the violent sense of the sublime depicted in **J.M.W. Turner's** stunning seascapes. The Victorian fascination with reviving old art forms sparked movements like the Italian-inspired, damsel-laden Pre-Raphaelite school, propagated by **John Everett Millais** (1829-1896) and **Dante Gabriel Rossetti** (1828-82). Victorians also dabbled in new art forms like photography and took advantage of early mass media with engravings and cartoons. Modernist trends from the Continent such as Cubism and Expressionism were picked up by **Wyndham Lewis** (1882-1957) and sculptor **Henry Moore** (1898-1986). WWII broke art wide open yielding experimental, edgy works by **Francis Bacon** (1909-1992) and **Lucian Freud,** whose controversial portrait of the Queen was unveiled in 2002. **David Hockney** (b. 1937) and **Bridget Riley** (b. 1931) gave American pop art a dose of British wit. The monolithic, market-controlling collector **Charles Saatchi,** the success of the new Tate Modern (p. 128), the infamy of the Turner Prize, and the rise of the conceptual and sensationalist **Young British Artists (YBAs)** have invigorated Britain's contemporary art scene. The multi-media artists **Damien Hirst** (b. 1965) and **Tracey Emin** (b. 1963) have become the media-savvy *enfants terribles* of modern art. Other talented YBAs include painter **Bridget Riley** (b. 1931) and sculptor **Sarah Lucas** (b. 1962). Art galleries in London (Tate Britain, p. 128; the British Museum, p. 127; the National Gallery, p. 126; White Cube, p. 131; the Serpentine) are among the world's best. Beyond the museums,

ENGLAND

Bristol-based graffiti artist **Banksy** creates phenomenal and thought-provoking masterpieces for the public with the simple tools of a street artist.

FASHION. First introduced as a trench coat lining, the **Burberry** Check, a trade-marked design, has become synonymous with English style. Inspired by the hip street energy of London in the 1960s and movements like Op and Pop Art, England's fashion designers achieved notoriety, although not the fame of continental designers. **Mary Quant** (b. 1934) sparked a fashion revolution by popularizing the mini-skirt in 1966. **Vivienne Westwood** (b. 1941) is credited with originating punk fashion in the early 1970s. Young British designers have made their mark at prestigious fashion houses, such as **John Galliano** (b. 1960) at Dior. In recent years, several designers have formed independent houses, as did ex-Givenchy star **Alexander McQueen** (b. 1970) and Sir Paul's daughter, ex-Chloé designer **Stella McCartney** (b. 1972). As British style tends to predict fashions in America, look for euromullets and tights to become all the rage across the pond.

MUSIC

CLASSICAL. In the middle ages, traveling **minstrels** sang narrative folk **ballads** and **Arthurian romances** in the courts of the rich. During the Renaissance, English ears were tuned to cathedral anthems, psalms, and madrigals, along with the occasional lute performance. **Henry Purcell** (1659-1695) crafted anthems, instrumental music for Shakespeare's plays, and the opera *Dido and Aeneas*. In the 18th century, regarded as England's musical Dark Age, Britain welcomed visits of the foreign geniuses Mozart, Haydn, and **George Frideric Handel,** a German composer who wrote operas in the Italian style but spent most of his life in Britain. Thanks to Handel's influence, England experienced a wave of **operamania** in the early 1700s. Enthusiasm waned when listeners realized they couldn't understand what the performers were saying. **John Gay** satirized the opera house in *The Beggar's Opera* (1727), a low-brow comedy in which Italian arias were set to English folk tunes. Today's audiences are familiar with the operettas of **W.S. Gilbert** (1836-1911) and **Arthur Sullivan** (1842-1900). Although the pair were rumored to hate each other, they managed to produce successes like *The Pirates of Penzance*. A second renaissance of more serious music began under **Edward Elgar** (1857-1934), whose *Pomp and Circumstance* is a staple of graduation ceremonies.

Also borrowing from folk melodies, **Ralph Vaughan Williams** (1872-1958) and **John Ireland** (1879-1962) brought musical modernism to the Isles. The world wars provided adequate inspiration for this continued musical resurgence, provoking **Benjamin Britten's** (1913-76) heartbreaking *War Requiem* and **Michael Tippett's** (1905-98) humanitarian oratorio, *A Child of Our Time*. The popular **Proms** (short for "promenades") at Royal Albert Hall celebrate classical music with an eight-week festival of whistle-blowing and flag-waving. Commercially lucrative music—like **Oliver Knussen's** one-act opera of Maurice Sendak's *Where the Wild Things Are* and **Andrew Lloyd Webber's** blend of opera, pop, and falling chandeliers—became popular in the 1980s and 90s.

THE BRITISH ARE COMING. Invaded by American blues and rock 'n' roll following WWII, Britain staged a musical offensive unprecedented in history. The **British Invasion** groups of the 60s infiltrated the world with a daring, inventive, and controversial sound. Out of Liverpool, **The Beatles** became gods with their moppy 'dos and maddeningly catchy hooks. The edgier lyrics and grittier sound of the **Rolling Stones** shifted teens' thoughts from "I Wanna Hold Your Hand" to "Let's Spend the Night Together." Over the next 20 years, England exported the hard-driving **Kinks,** the Urban "mod" sound of **The Who,** the psychedelia-meets-Motown **Yardbirds,** and guitar gurus Eric Clapton of **Cream** and Jimmy Page of **Led Zeppelin.**

ANARCHY IN THE UK. Despite (or perhaps because of) England's conservative national character, homosexuality became central to the flamboyant scene of the mid-70s. British rock schismed as the theatrical excesses of **glam rock** performers like **Queen, Elton John,** and **David Bowie** contrasted with the conceptual, album-oriented **art rock** emanating from **Pink Floyd** and **Yes.** Dissonant **punk rock** bands like **Stiff Little Fingers** and **The Clash** emerged from Britain's ailing industrial centers, especially Manchester. London's **The Sex Pistols** stormed the scene with profane and wildly successful antics—their angry 1977 single "God Save the Queen" topped the charts despite being banned. Sharing punk's anti-establishment impulses, the metal music of **Ozzy Osbourne** and **Iron Maiden** still attracts a cult following. Sheffield's **Def Leppard** carried the hard-rock-big-hair ethic through the 80s, while punk offshoots like **The Cure** and **goth** bands rebelled during the era of conservative Thatcherism.

I WANT MY MTV. Buoyed by a booming economy, British bands achieved popularity on both sides of the Atlantic thanks to the advent of MTV. **Dire Straits** introduced the first computer-animated music video, while **Duran Duran,** the **Eurythmics, Tears for Fears,** and the **Police** enjoyed Top-10 hits. England also produced some of the giants of the lipstick-and-synthesizer age, including **George Michael, the Pet Shop Boys, Bananarama,** and **Boy George.** The music scene splintered along regional and musical lines into countless fragments of electronica, punk, and rock. Modern balladists **The Smiths** developed a cult following. At the end of the decade, a crop of bands from Manchester, spearheaded by **New Order,** galvanized post-punk and the early **rave** movement. Any clubber worth her tube top ("boob tube" in Britain) can tell you about England's influence on dance music, from the **Chemical Brothers** and Brighton-bred **Fatboy Slim** to the house, trip-hop, and ska sounds of **Basement Jaxx, Massive Attack,** and **Jamiroquai.** Britpop resurged in the 1990s: **Blur** and **Oasis** left trashed hotel rooms and screaming fans in their wake. The tremendous popularity of American **grunge rock** inspired a host of poseurs in the UK, including **Radiohead,** who have since become arguably the most influential British rock band since The Beatles. The UK also produced some brilliant, awful pop, including **Robbie Williams** (survivor of the bubblegummy **Take That**), who continues to be a stadium-filling force. Tragically, the **Spice Girls** have not enjoyed the same longevity.

These days, socially conscious **Coldplay** is still one of the UK's best-selling rock exports (thanks in large part to soccer moms and dentist offices). Modern post-punk and New Wave bands like **Bloc Party** and **Franz Ferdinand** enjoy indie cred and impressive fan bases. A product of instant Internet success, **Lily Allen** has established herself as a major player in the world of commercial pop, winning audiences with an upbeat sound and sassy attitude. Meanwhile, **Amy Winehouse** smooths over her rough-and-tumble personality with deep, soulful jazz vocals. Formed in 2005, ⧉**The Kooks** have exploded out of Brighton to climb the charts with catchy pop rock tunes, and postmodern hipsters **The Rakes** and **The Pigeon Detectives** are drawing attention from young fans of guitar rock revival.

UK GARAGE. Stumble into any nightclub in Britain and feel the two-step sub-bass bypass your ears and get straight to shaking your body. Dance music of the mid-90s got lame, but instead of drying up in the hands of a few glowstick-waving pill-poppers, an amalgamation of drum and bass and jungle music became **UK Garage (UKG)**—electronica produced in basements and bedrooms around South London and made popular through repeated play on pirate radio stations. Characterized by island rhythms and dark-sounding bass lines that skip every other beat, UKG eventually split into two sub-genres: **dubstep** (slow and minimalist), and **grime** (sounding like sped-up reggae instrumentals with rap-like vocals). **Skream** and **Benga** are exemplars of dubstep, and the popularity of **Wiley** and Mike Skinner's ⧉**The Streets** stands testament to grime's relative accessibility.

ENGLAND

FILM

British film has endured an uneven history, alternating between relative independence from Hollywood and emigration of talent to America. **Charlie Chaplin** and Archibald Alec Leach (a.k.a. **Cary Grant**) were both British-born but made their names in US films. The **Royal Shakespeare Company** has seen heavyweight alumni **Dame Judi Dench, Dame Maggie Smith, Sir Ian McKellen,** and **Jeremy Irons** make the transition to cinema. Master of suspense **Alfred Hitchcock** snared audiences with films produced on both sides of the Atlantic, terrifying shower-takers everywhere. The 60s phenomenon of "swingin' London" created new momentum for the film industry and jump-started international interest in British culture. American Richard Lester made **The Beatles'** *A Hard Day's Night* in 1963, and a year later Scottish **Sean Connery** downed the first of many martinis as **James Bond** in *Dr. No*.

Elaborate costume drama and offbeat independent films characterized British film in the 80s and 90s. The sagas *Chariots of Fire* (1981) and *Gandhi* (1982) swept the Oscars in successive years. Director-producer team **Merchant-Ivory** led the way in adaptations of British novels like Forster's *A Room with a View* (1986). **Kenneth Branagh** focused his talents on adapting Shakespeare for the screen, with glossy, well-received works such as *Hamlet* (1996). **Nick Park** took claymation and British quirkiness to a new level with his *Wallace and Gromit* shorts and the blockbuster feature film *Chicken Run* (2000). The dashing **Guy Ritchie** (Mr. Madonna) tapped into Tarantino-esque conventions with his dizzying *Lock, Stock and Two Smoking Barrels* (1998), followed by the trans-Atlantic smash *Snatch* (2000), although the film's success may or may not have had something to do with American stud Brad Pitt.

Recent British films have garnered a fair number of international awards; the working-class feel-goods *The Full Monty* (1997) and *Billy Elliot* (2000); **Mike Leigh's** affecting *Secrets and Lies* (1996) and costume extravaganza *Topsy-Turvy* (1999); and the endearing comedies *Bend it Like Beckham* (2002) and *Love, Actually* (2003) have all taken home awards from sources like the Academy, Cannes, and the Golden Globes. Then of course, there is the *Harry Potter* franchise, which kicked off in 2001 and continues to break box office records. It has been filmed at gorgeous Alnwick Castle, Christ Church College, Oxford (p. 268), and in Fort William of the Scottish Highlands (p. 628).

MEDIA

ALL THAT'S FIT TO PRINT. In a culture with a rich print-media history, the influence of newspapers remains enormous. The UK's plethora of national newspapers yields a wide range of political viewpoints. *The Times*, long a model of thoughtful discretion, has turned Tory under the ownership of Rupert Murdoch. *The Daily Telegraph*, dubbed "Torygraph," is fairly conservative and old-fashioned. *The Guardian* (often known as "The Guarniad" after its infamous typos) leans left, while *The Independent* stays true to its name. Of the tabloids, *The Sun*, Murdoch-owned and better known for its Page Three topless pin-up than for its reporting, is the most influential. Among the others, *The Daily Mail, The Daily Express*, and *The London Evening Standard* (the only evening paper) make serious attempts at popular journalism, although the first two tend to position themselves as the conservative voice of Middle England. *The Daily Mirror, The News of the World*, and *The Star* are as shrill and lewd as *The Sun*. *The Financial Times*, on pleasing pink paper, distributes the news of the City of London. Although closely associated with their sister dailies, Sunday newspapers are actually separate entities. *The Sunday Times, The Sunday Telegraph, The Independent on Sunday*, and the highly polished *Observer*—the world's oldest paper and now part of *The Guardian*—offer detailed arts, sports, and news coverage, together with more "soft bits" than the dailies.

A quick glance around any High St. newsstand will prove that Britain has no shortage of magazines. World affairs are covered with candor and wit by *The Economist*. *The New Statesman* on the left and *The Spectator* on the right cover politics and the arts with verve. The satirical *Private Eye* is subversive, witty, and overtly political. Some of the best music mags in the world—the Strokes-discovering, highly biased but indispensable *New Musical Express* (*NME*), the more intellectual *Q*, and *Gramophone*—are UK-based. Movie and other entertainment news comes in the over-sized *Empire*. The indispensable London journal *Time Out* has an exhaustive listings guide to the city; its website (www.timeout.com) also keeps tabs on events in Dublin and Edinburgh. Recent years have seen the explosion of "lads' mags" such as *FHM* and *Loaded*, which feature scantily clad women and articles on beer, "shagging," and "pulling." London-born *Maxim* offers similar content for a marginally more mature crowd. Britain has excellent fashion glossies—there are British versions of *Vogue*, *Mademoiselle*, and *Elle*, which often come in a handy smaller size. *Tatler*, a W-made-*Vanity Fair*, is witty, pretty, and snobby. *Hello*, *OK*, and a bevy of imitators feed the insatiable appetites of royal-watchers and B-list aficionados.

ON THE AIRWAVES. The **BBC** (British Broadcasting Corporation, known as "the Beeb") established its reputation with radio services. The World Service provides countries around the world with a glimpse into British life. Within the UK, the BBC has **Radios 1-7,** covering news (4), sports (5), and a spectrum of music from pop (1) to classical and jazz (3) to catch-all (2 and 6)—and recently, for kids (7).

Aside from the daytime suds, British television has brought the world such mighty comic wonders as *Monty Python's Flying Circus, Mr. Bean, Da Ali G. Show* (booyakasha!), and the across-the-pond hit *The Office*. The BBC has produced some stellar adapted miniseries; 1996's *Pride and Prejudice* sparked an international "Darcy-fever" for **Colin Firth** and is widely considered one of the best film versions of Austen's work. Britain currently suffers from an obsession with home-improvement shows, cooking programs, and voyeur TV (they invented *Big Brother* and *Pop Idol*). A commercial-free repository of wit and innovation, the BBC broadcasts on two national channels. **BBC1** carries news and Britcoms, while **BBC2** telecasts cultural programs and fledgling sitcoms (like *AbFab*, *Blackadder*, *Coupling*, and *Little Britain*). **ITV,** Britain's first and most established commercial network, carries drama, comedy, and news. **Channel 4** has morning shows, highly respected arts programming, and imported American shows. **Channel 5** features late-night sports shows and action movies. Rupert Murdoch's satellite **Sky TV** shows football, fútbol, soccer, and other incarnations of the global game on its Sky Sports channel, while its Sky One channel broadcasts mostly American shows.

SPORTS

There is a great noise in the city caused by hustling over large balls, from which many evils arise which God forbid.
  —King Edward II, banning football in 1314

FOOTBALL. It's the "beautiful game," the world's most popular sport, and a British national obsession. The top 20 English football (soccer) **clubs** (teams) occupy the **Premier League,** populated with world-class players. The powerful Football Association (F.A.) regulates the British leagues and sponsors the contentious **F.A. Cup,** held every May in **Wembley,** where a new **National Stadium** opened in March 2007 with the second largest capacity in Europe. The ultimate achievement for an English football club is to win the treble—the Premier League, the F.A. Cup, and the Champion's League (a competition between the top teams in several European countries). Clubs like Arsenal, Liverpool, and Everton dominate the Premier

League perennially, but **Manchester United** (p. 358) is the red victory machine that many Brits loves to hate. Even many Mancunians support the city's other club, Manchester City. Fans and paparazzi alike mourned the team's loss of celebrity star **David Beckham** to Real Madrid in 2003, and Beckham made even more fans weep when he signed with the US based L.A. Galaxy in January 2007.

Unfortunately, the four British international teams (England, Scotland, Wales, and Northern Ireland compete as separate countries) have not performed well in the **World Cup** or in the **European Championships**—England's 1966 World Cup victory being the glorious exception. The next World Cup will be in South Africa in 2010.

Over half a million fans attend professional matches in Britain every matchday weekend from mid-August to May, and they spend the few barren weeks of summer waiting for the publication of the coming season's **fixtures** (match schedules). The lower Division fans are often crazier than those in the Premiership. It's almost like worship at postmodern cathedrals—grand, storied stadiums full of painted faces and team colors, resounding with rowdy choruses of uncannily synchronized (usually rude) songs. Intracity rivalries (London's Chelsea-Tottenham or Glasgow's "Auld Firm") have been known to divide families. Violence and vandalism used to dog the sport, but matches have become safer now that clubs offer seating-only tickets, rather than standing spaces in the terraces, and clubs generally no longer allow drinking in the stands. **Hooligans** ("yobs" or "chavs") are usually on their worst behavior when the England national team plays abroad, while home games are a bit tamer.

OTHER GAMES. According to legend, **rugby** was born one glorious day in 1823 when William Webb Ellis, an inspired (or perhaps slightly confused) Rugby School student, picked up a soccer ball and ran it into the goal. Since then, rugby has evolved into a complex, subtle, and thoroughly lunatic game. The amateur **Rugby Union** and professional **Rugby League**, both 19th-century creations, have slightly different rules and different numbers of players (15 and 13). In Britain, the former is associated with Scotland, Wales, and the Midlands, and the latter with northwest England. With little stoppage of play, no non-injury substitutions, and scanty protective gear, rugby is a melée of blood, mud, and drinking songs. An oval-shaped ball is carried or passed backward until the team can touch the ball down past the goal line (a "try" and worth five points) or kick it through the uprights (three points). Club season runs from September to May. The culmination of international rugby is the **Rugby World Cup,** hosted by Australia in the fall of 2009.

Although fanatically followed in the Commonwealth, **cricket** remains a spectacle confusing to the uninitiated. The game is played by two 11-player teams on a green, marked by two **wickets**, three sticks with two bails (dowels) balancing on the top (see www.cricket.org for explanations and diagrams of these mysterious contraptions). In an inning, one team acts as **batsmen** and the other as **fielders.** The batting team sends up two batsmen, and a **bowler** from the fielding side throws the ball so that it bounces toward the wickets. The fielders try to get the batsmen out by **taking** the wickets (hitting the wickets so that the bails fall) or by catching the ball. The batsmen attempt to make as many runs as possible while protecting their wickets, scoring each time they switch places. The teams switch positions once 10 batsmen are out, and both sides usually bat twice. Matches last one to five days. We don't really get it either. International games are known as **Test** matches; the **Ashes,** named for the remains of a cricket bail, are the prize in England's Test series with Australia. Cricket has its own **World Cup,** set for February and March of 2011. London's **Lords** cricket ground is regarded as the spiritual home of the game.

Tennis became the game of the upper class in the 15th century, when Henry VII played in slimming black velvet. As the game developed, white became the traditional color, while today almost any garb goes—that is, except at **Wimbledon,** the über-traditional grass-court Grand Slam event held in late June and early July.

SNITCHED. Sadly, scientists and engineers have not yet developed magical broomsticks to play **Quidditch,** the imaginary sport of flying wizards popularized by the *Harry Potter* series. For now, at least, hopeful Chasers and Seekers are stuck firmly on the ground.

HORSES AND COURSES. The Brits have a special affinity for their horses, demonstrated in the tallyhooing of fox-killing excursions and Princess Anne's competition in **equestrian** during the 1976 Olympics. In late June, **polo** devotees flock to the **Royal Windsor Cup.** The Royal Gold Cup Meeting at **Ascot** has occurred in the second half of June every summer since 1711, although some see it as an excuse for Brits of all strata to indulge in drinking and gambling while wearing over-the-top hats. Top hats also distinguish the famed **Derby** (DAR-bee), which has been run since 1780 on Epsom Racecourse, Surrey, on the first Saturday of June.

Britain remains a force in rowing, and the annual **Henley Royal Regatta,** on the Thames in Oxfordshire, is the most famous series of rowing races in the world. The five-day regatta ends on the first Sunday of July. While Saturday is the most popular day, the Sunday finals provide some of the most exciting races. The **Boat Race** (also on the Thames, but in London), between Oxford and Cambridge, enacts the traditional rivalry between the schools. Britain is the center of Formula One racecar design, and the **British Grand Prix** is held every July at Silverstone racecourse in Northamptonshire. Meanwhile, the **TT Races** bring hordes of screeching motorcycles to the Isle of Man during the early days of June (p. 386).

HOLIDAYS AND FESTIVALS

It's difficult to travel anywhere in Britain without bumping into some kind of festival. Below is a list of major festivals in England. The local Tourist Information Centre for any town can point you toward the nearest scene of revelry and merry-making, and *Let's Go* lists individual events in the appropriate towns. The chart below also includes some large nationwide festivals and **public holidays.** See the corresponding sections of Scotland (p. 528), Wales (p. 454) for more country-specific festivals. **Bank holidays** are listed in the **Appendix,** see p. 720.

DATE IN 2008	NAME AND LOCATION	DESCRIPTION
February 7	Chinese New Year, London	Fireworks! Lots of fireworks!
April 23	St. George's Day	Honoring England's dragon-slaying patron saint.
May 3-25	Brighton Festival	Largest mixed-arts festival in England.
May 20-24	Chelsea Flower Show	The world's premier garden event.
May 24-June 6	TT Races, Isle of Man	101st Anniversary of this annual road racing celebration.
June 7	The Derby, Surrey	Horses and hats!
June 27-29	Glastonbury Festival	Britain's gigantic three-day homage to rock music.
June 17-21	Royal Ascot, York	Hats and horses!
June 23-July 6	Wimbledon	A lot of racquet and a big silver dish.
July 2-6	Henley Royal Regatta	The world's premier boat race.
August 15-25	Manchester Pride	A wild street party in Manchester's Gay Village.

ENGLAND

LONDON

When a man is tired of London, he is tired of life; for there is in London all that life can afford.
      —Samuel Johnson, 1777

 Beyond the blinding lights of Oxford and Piccadilly Circuses, London is just as much a working and living city as it is a tourist destination. Comprised of 32 boroughs along with the City, London is better described as a conglomeration of villages than as a homogenous city. While this understates the pride Londoners take in their city as a whole, it is true that locals are strongly attached to their neighborhoods. Each area's heritage and traditions are alive and evolving, from the City of London's 2000-year-old association with trade to the West End's ever-changing theater scene. The London "buzz" is continually on the move—every few years, a previously disregarded neighborhood explodes into cultural prominence. Most recently, South London has thrived with the cultural rebirth of the South Bank and the thumping nightlife of Brixton. No matter where you start your journey, Londoners from all neighborhoods invite visitors to take part. If you're spending a significant amount of time in London, you'll find more extensive coverage in ▓*Let's Go: London.*

LONDON	❶	❷	❸	❹	❺
ACCOMMODATIONS	under £25	£25-40	£41-55	£56-75	over £75
FOOD	under £6	£6-10	£11-15	£16-20	over £20

LONDON HIGHLIGHTS

GO ROYAL in stately Westminster at **Westminster Abbey** (p. 110) and at the **Houses of Parliament** (p. 114); take tea with the queen at **Buckingham Palace** (p. 114); gaze up at the dome of **St. Paul's Cathedral** (p. 111) and the pigeons that nest there; and watch your head at the imposing **Tower of London** (p. 110). To cover the highlights of the South Bank, follow our **"Millennium Mile" Walking Tour** (p. 112).

LOSE YOURSELF in the galleries of London's museums, some of the best in the world; most of the big names are free. The **British Museum** (p. 127) and the **Victoria and Albert Museum** (p. 127) recap the glory days of the British Empire, while the **National Portrait Gallery** (p. 121) chronicles the life and times of those who ran it. The **National Gallery** (p. 126) holds the first half of the national collection, and the **Tate Modern** (p. 126) holds, well, everything modern. For a string of up-and-comers, head to galleries in the East End, including **Whitechapel** (p. 131) and **White Cube** (p. 131). The **Courtauld Galleries** (p. 129) at Somerset House are worth the admission fee.

INDULGE IN world-renowned drama at **Shakespeare's Globe Theatre** (p. 136), an open-air venue where you can stand right in front of the stage as a "groundling," or take a seat in the **National Theatre** (p. 136) or **Royal Court Theatre** (p. 136). Head to a stage-play in the **West End** (p. 135), which boasts the best of mega-musicals and Andrew Lloyd Webber classics. Fringe theater is alive and well at the **Almeida** (p. 136) and **Donmar Warehouse** (p. 136).

RELAX for an afternoon in one of London's many parks, such as **Hyde Park** and **Kensington Gardens** (p. 118), the perfect escape from the summer heat or the urban crowd.

◼ INTERCITY TRANSPORTATION

BY PLANE

HEATHROW

Heathrow (☎08700 000 123; www.baa.co.uk/main/airports/heathrow), 15min. by train from central London, is just what you'd expect from one of the world's busiest international airports. It has four terminals.

> **Underground:** ☎7222 1234, toll-free 08453 309 880; www.thetube.com. Heathrow's 2 Tube stations form a loop on the end of the Piccadilly Line—trains stop at **Heathrow Terminal 4** and then at **Heathrow Terminals 1, 2, 3** (both Zone 6) before heading back to central London (from central London 50min.-1¼hr., every 4-5min., £4-10). Stairs are an integral part of most Tube stations.
>
> **Heathrow Express:** ☎08456 001 515; www.heathrowexpress.com. A speedy, expensive train connection from Heathrow to Paddington (15min. daily every 15min. 5:10am-11:40pm; £14.50, round-trip £27; £2 extra if bought on train; AmEx/MC/V). Railpasses and Travelcards not valid. Discounts for day returns, students, and groups. Paddington has check-in facilities. Ticket counters at Heathrow accept foreign currency.
>
> **Heathrow Connect:** ☎08456 786 975; www.heathrowconnect.com. A cheaper alternative to the Express, with direct routes from Paddington, Ealing Broadway, West Ealing, Hanwell, Southall, and Hayes to Terminals 1, 2, and 3 (from Paddington; 20min.; daily every 30min. 4:45am-11:30pm; £9.50 to Paddington). Railcards accepted. For Terminal 4, take the first Heathrow Express train.
>
> **National Express:** ☎08705 808 080; www.nationalexpress.com. Runs between Heathrow and Victoria Coach (40min.-1½hr.; about every 20min. daily Heathrow-Victoria 5:35am-9:35pm, Victoria-Heathrow 7:15am-11:30pm; from £8; AmEx/MC/V). Railpasses and Travelcards not valid.
>
> **Taxis:** Licensed (black) cabs cost at least £50 and take 1-1¾hr.

GATWICK

Thirty miles south of the city, Gatwick (☎0870 0002 468; www.baa.co.uk) looks distant, but two train services make transportation a breeze. The **train station** is in the **South Terminal.** Gatwick Express (☎08456 001 515; www.gatwickexpress.com) offers service to **Victoria Station** (30-35min.; departs Gatwick every 15min. 5am-11:45pm; £13, round-trip £24). Thameslink (☎08457 484 950; www.thameslink.co.uk) also heads regularly to **King's Cross Station,** stopping at **London Bridge** and **Blackfriars** (50min., every 30min., £10). Gatwick's distance from London makes **road services** slow and unpredictable. National Express's **Airbus A5** (contact info same as Heathrow) goes to **Victoria Coach Station** (1½hr., at least every hr. 4:50am-10:15pm, from £6.60). Never take a **taxi** from Gatwick to London; the trip will take over an hour and cost at least £95.

STANSTED AND LUTON

Many discount airlines (see **By Plane,** p. 32) operate from secondary airports. **Stansted Airport** (☎08700 000 303; www.stanstedairport.com) is 30 mi. north. Stansted Express (☎08457 484 950; www.stanstedexpress.co.uk) **trains** run to **Liverpool St. Station** (45min.; every 15-30min.; £14.50, round-trip £24). National Express's **Airbus A6** runs to **Victoria Station** (1¼-1¾hr., every 15min., £10). From **Luton Airport** (☎0158 240 5100; www.londonluton.co.uk), Thameslink **trains** head to **King's Cross, Blackfriars,** and **London Bridge** (30-40min.; every 30min. M-Sa 3:20am-1am, Su less frequent 6am-11:15pm; £10.40). Green Line (☎08706 087 261; www.greenline.co.uk) **buses** serve **West End** and **Victoria Station** (1-1¾hr.; 3 per hr. 8am-6pm, £9, round-trip £12.50; ages 5-15 £5.50/8).

LONDON

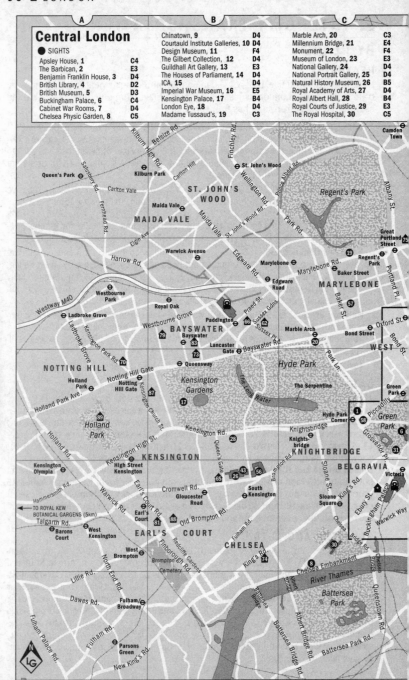

Central London

Central London

● SIGHTS

Apsley House, **1**	C4
The Barbican, **2**	E3
Benjamin Franklin House, **3**	D4
British Library, **4**	D2
British Museum, **5**	D3
Buckingham Palace, **6**	C4
Cabinet War Rooms, **7**	D4
Chelsea Physic Garden, **8**	C5

Chinatown, **9**	D4
Courtauld Institute Galleries, **10**	D4
Design Museum, **11**	F4
The Gilbert Collection, **12**	D4
Guildhall Art Gallery, **13**	E3
The Houses of Parliament, **14**	D4
ICA, **15**	D4
Imperial War Museum, **16**	E5
Kensington Palace, **17**	B4
London Eye, **18**	D4
Madame Tussaud's, **19**	C3

Marble Arch, **20**	C3
Millennium Bridge, **21**	E4
Monument, **22**	F4
Museum of London, **23**	E3
National Gallery, **24**	D4
National Portrait Gallery, **25**	D4
Natural History Museum, **26**	B5
Royal Academy of Arts, **27**	D4
Royal Albert Hall, **28**	B4
Royal Courts of Justice, **29**	E3
The Royal Hospital, **30**	C5

LONDON

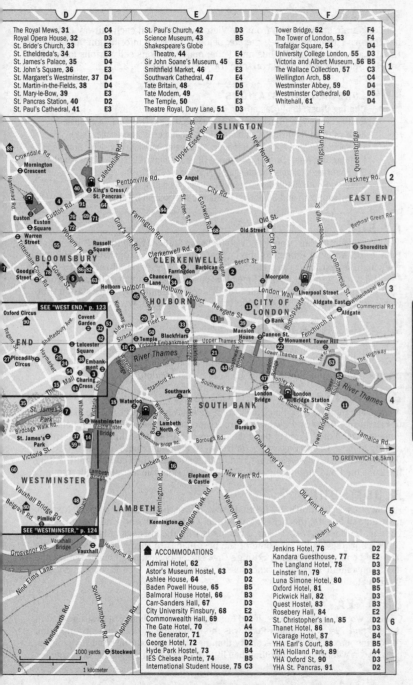

The Royal Mews, 31 — C4
Royal Opera House, 32 — D3
St. Bride's Church, 33 — E3
St. Etheldreda's, 34 — E3
St. James's Palace, 35 — D4
St. John's Square, 36 — E3
St. Margaret's Westminster, 37 — D4
St. Martin-in-the-Fields, 38 — D4
St. Mary-le-Bow, 39 — E3
St. Pancras Station, 40 — D2
St. Paul's Cathedral, 41 — E3

St. Paul's Church, 42 — D3
Science Museum, 43 — B5
Shakespeare's Globe
 Theatre, 44 — E4
Sir John Soane's Museum, 45 — E3
Smithfield Market, 46 — E3
Southwark Cathedral, 47 — E4
Tate Britain, 48 — D5
Tate Modern, 49 — E4
The Temple, 50 — E3
Theatre Royal, Dury Lane, 51 — D3

Tower Bridge, 52 — F4
The Tower of London, 53 — F4
Trafalgar Square, 54 — D4
University College London, 55 — D3
Victoria and Albert Museum, 56 — B5
The Wallace Collection, 57 — C3
Wellington Arch, 58 — C4
Westminster Abbey, 59 — D4
Westminster Cathedral, 60 — D5
Whitehall, 61 — D4

SEE "WEST END," p. 123

SEE "WESTMINSTER," p. 124

TO GREENWICH (6.5km)

LONDON

⌂ ACCOMMODATIONS

Admiral Hotel, 62 — B3
Astor's Museum Hostel, 63 — D3
Ashlee House, 64 — D2
Baden Powell House, 65 — B5
Balmoral House Hotel, 66 — B3
Carr-Sanders Hall, 67 — D3
City University Finsbury, 68 — E2
Commonwealth Hall, 69 — D2
The Gate Hotel, 70 — A4
The Generator, 71 — D2
George Hotel, 72 — D2
Hyde Park Hostel, 73 — B4
IES Chelsea Pointe, 74 — B5
International Student House, 75 — C3

Jenkins Hotel, 76 — D2
Kandara Guesthouse, 77 — E2
The Langland Hotel, 78 — D3
Leinster Inn, 79 — B3
Luna Simone Hotel, 80 — D5
Oxford Hotel, 81 — B5
Pickwick Hall, 82 — D3
Quest Hostel, 83 — B3
Rosebery Hall, 84 — D3
St. Christopher's Inn, 85 — D3
Thanet Hotel, 86 — D3
Vicarage Hotel, 87 — B4
YHA Earl's Court, 88 — B5
YHA Holland Park, 89 — A4
YHA Oxford St, 90 — D3
YHA St. Pancras, 91 — D2

0   1000 yards
0   1 kilometer

BY TRAIN

London's train stations date from the Victorian era, when each railway company had its own city terminus; see the box below for service information. All London termini are well-served by bus and Tube; major stations sell various **Railcards,** which offer regular discounts on train travel (see **By Train,** p. 32).

LONDON TRAIN STATIONS
Charing Cross: Kent (Canterbury, Dover)
Euston: Northwest (Birmingham, Glasgow, Holyhead, Liverpool, Manchester)
King's Cross: Northeast (Cambridge, Edinburgh, Leeds, Newcastle, York)
Liverpool St.: East Anglia (Cambridge, Colchester, Ipswich, Norwich), Stansted
Paddington: West (Oxford), Southwest (Bristol, Cornwall), South Wales (Cardiff)
St. Pancras: Midlands (Nottingham), Northwest (Sheffield)
Victoria: South (Brighton, Canterbury, Dover, Hastings), Gatwick
Waterloo: South and Southwest (Portsmouth, Salisbury), Paris, Brussels

BY BUS

Most long-distance buses arrive at **Victoria Coach Station** (⊖Victoria), Buckingham Palace Rd. **National Express** is the largest intercity operator (☎08705 808 080; www.nationalexpress.com). **Eurolines** dominates international service (☎08705 143 219; www.eurolines.co.uk). **Green Line** coaches serve much of the area around London and leave from the Eccleston Bridge mall behind Victoria station. Purchase tickets from the driver. (⊖Victoria. ☎0870 608 7261; www.greenline.co.uk.)

■ ORIENTATION

While Greater London consists of 32 boroughs, the City of Westminster, and the City of London, *Let's Go* focuses on central London and divides this area into 12 neighborhoods, plus North, South, East, and West London.

BAYSWATER

Aside from being a cheap place to sleep, Bayswater is nondescript. The main drags of **Westbourne Grove** and **Queensway** are frequented by teenage mall hoppers. The longest stretch of walking is along the fringes of the beautiful Kensington Gardens and Hyde Park. Use ⊖Bayswater for the west; Paddington and Lancaster Gate for the east. There are two separate Paddington stations: the Hammersmith & City line runs the Paddington train station; the others run from a station underground.

BLOOMSBURY

Bloomsbury is London's intellectual powerhouse, home to the British Museum, near **Russell Square;** the British Library, on **Euston Road;** and University College London, on **Gower Street.** The area resounds with the musings of the Bloomsbury Group, but its squares are some of the best places to throw books aside in the name of picnics and suntans. ⊖King's Cross is the biggest interchange but not the most convenient. Goodge St. and Russell Sq. are central; Euston, Euston Sq., and Warren St. hit the north border.

CHELSEA

Chelsea would like to be considered London's artistic bohemia, a desire rooted in the 60s and 70s, when **King's Road** was the birthplace of the miniskirt and punk rock. This makes Chelsea less stuffy than nearby Knightsbridge and Kensington, but today's wealthy neighborhood has little stomach for radicalism. ⊖Sloane Sq.

to the east and South Kensington to the north will put you close to most attractions. Taking a bus is critical during bad weather; most run from **Sloane Square** down King's Rd. on their way from Knightsbridge or Victoria.

THE CITY OF LONDON

The City is where London began—indeed, for most of its history, the City *was* London. Even though urban sprawl has pushed the border of London out, the City remains as tightly knit as ever, with its own mayor, separate jurisdiction, and sway over even the Queen, who must ask permission of the Lord Mayor before entering. Upper and Lower Thames Streets run along the Thames to the Tower of London; Aldersgate Street passes by the Barbican Centre on its way to Clerkenwell; Ludgate Hill extends from Fleet St. to St. Paul's Cathedral. ⊖Bank and St. Paul's are within easy reach of most sights; use Tower Hill for eastern destinations.

HOLBORN AND CLERKENWELL

London's second-oldest area, Holborn was the first part of the city settled by Saxons—**Aldwych,** on the western edge, is Anglo-Saxon for "old port." **Fleet Street** remains synonymous with the British press although the newspapers have moved on. Traveling north to Clerkenwell, **Farringdon Street** intersects **High Holborn** and **Clerkenwell Road** before becoming **King's Cross Road.** A monastic center until Henry VIII closed the priory of St. John, Clerkenwell became home to London's top artisans. During Victoria's reign, it devolved into slums, famously described by Dickens. With renewed energy, the area has recently come storming back onto the London dining and nightlife scene. Holborn is served by ⊖Holborn, Farringdon, Chancery Ln., and Temple. In Clerkenwell, everything is near ⊖Farringdon; southern and eastern parts can be reached from Barbican, western parts can be reached by Chancery Ln., and northern parts can be reached by Angel.

KENSINGTON AND EARL'S COURT

The former stomping ground of Princess Di, Kensington is divided into two distinct areas. To the west is the posh shopper's dream, **Kensington High Street,** while to the east are the museums and colleges of **South Kensington's** "Albertopolis." In the 1960s and 70s, **Earl's Court** was mainly the destination of Aussie backpackers and home to London's gay population, but today others have caught on to its combination of cheap accommodations and transportation links, and Soho has taken up the rainbow flag. As one of central London's larger neighborhoods, public transportation is necessary to get around. Tube stations are helpfully named: ⊖High St. Kensington for High St., South Kensington for the South Kensington museums, and Earl's Court for Earl's Court.

KNIGHTSBRIDGE AND BELGRAVIA

Knightsbridge and Belgravia are smug and expensive. The primary tourist draw is window-shopping on **Sloane Street** and **Brompton Road** at shopping's biggest names: Harrods and Harvey Nichols. **Belgravia** occupies the region east of Sloane St., sporting an expanse of 19th-century mansions occupied by millionaires and embassies. ⊖Knightsbridge is near the shops; most hotels in Belgravia are close to Victoria, but the north end of the neighborhood is closest to Hyde Park Corner.

MARYLEBONE AND REGENT'S PARK

Marylebone is defined by its eclectic borders. Adjacent to academic Bloomsbury in the east, beautiful **Portland Place** stands as an architectural wonder. To the west, **Edgware Road** houses London's largest Lebanese population and boasts many Middle Eastern eateries, shops, and markets. **Marylebone Road** traps tourists with Madame Tussaud's wax museum and chain stores, but also acts as the gateway to

LONDON

Regent's Park. ⊖Baker St. is convenient for northern sights; Bond St. covers the south. There are two separate Edgware Rd. stations, but they aren't far apart.

NOTTING HILL

Once the stopping point for those traveling between London and Uxbridge, Notting Hill has retained its appeal as an offshoot of central London; running from Oxford St., **Notting Hill Gate** actually had a gate out of (or into) the city. Its appeal has much to do with its mix of mansions, ethnic cultures, and artsy vibe. **Portobello Road** is best known for its market. ⊖Notting Hill Gate serves the south, while Ladbroke Grove deposits you near Portobello Rd.

THE SOUTH BANK

Just across the river from the City, the South Bank has long been the center of London's entertainment industry. Cross the Thames on **Waterloo Road, Blackfriars Road, Borough High Street,** or **Tower Bridge Road.** Dominated by wharves and warehouses in the 19th and early 20th centuries, the South Bank was rebuilt after its destruction in WWII. Now, the "Millennium Mile" stretches from the London Eye in the west to Butlers Wharf in the east. ⊖Waterloo for inland attractions, Southwark for Bankside, and London Bridge for Borough and Butlers Wharf. See the **"Millennium Mile" Walking Tour** (p. 112) of the South Bank.

THE WEST END

If Westminster is the heart of historical London, then the West End is at the center of just about everything else. The biggest, brightest, and boldest (although not always best) of London nightlife, theater, shopping, and eating can all be found within this tough-to-define district, wedged between royal regalia to the south and financial powerhouses to the northeast.

See a world-renowned musical at one of over 30 major theaters in the area, head to **Chinatown** for some dim sum, and window-shop on **Oxford Street.** If it's nightlife you're craving, the awe-inspiring collection of bars and clubs in **Soho** will keep you busy through the wee hours of morning. Stroll around the gay nightlife nexus of **Old Compton Street** or mingle with street performers in **Covent Garden.**

And if none of this sounds like your cup of tea, you can always cruise the posh streets of **Mayfair** and **St. James's,** which offer a more distinct flavor than the West End's more touristed areas do. Spend a little time in central **Trafalgar Square** to bask in the glory of Britain's greatest days. The Tube is best for getting in and out of the West End. Use ⊖Charing Cross for Trafalgar Sq.; the stops are often only a few blocks apart. Once you've made it, buses are the best way to get around; stops can be found along any major thoroughfare.

WESTMINSTER

Westminster, with its spires and parks, feels like the heart of the old British Empire. It is, after all, home to the Houses of Parliament and the Queen—convenient for die-hard tourists who want to cram London's biggest sights into one day. Apart from the bureaucracy of **Whitehall** and the grandeur of the Abbey, Westminster is a down-to-earth district—thousands of commuting workers make **Victoria** the busiest Tube station in the city. South of Victoria, **Pimlico** is residential, with row after row of B&Bs. ⊖Westminster is near most sights; use St. James's Park for Buckingham Palace; use Pimlico for accommodations and for the Tate Britain.

NORTH LONDON

What we call "North London" is actually a group of distinct neighborhoods, all of which lie to the north of central London. Once the center of London's counterculture movement, **Camden Town** and **Islington** now offer more posh restaurants and funky pubs than punk rockers. **Hampstead** and **Highgate** still feel like small villages. **St. John's Wood** and **Maida Vale** are wealthy, residential extensions of Marylebone and Bayswater. Most individual neighborhoods are walkable. Tube stops are ⊖Camden Town for (surprise) Camden Town; Kentish Town for Camden; Angel for Islington; and Kilburn and Swiss Cottage for St. John's Wood and Maida Vale.

SOUTH LONDON

Historically maligned for being "dodgy," areas of South London are now hot spots for hipsters looking for upscale dining and all-night parties. Some areas still feel slightly unsafe; keep an eye on your purse at all times. Once a swanky suburb, **Brixton** has been thoroughly urbanized, showcasing the charm of its Afro-Caribbean market. **Stockwell** and **Vauxhall** offer pubs galore, while **Dulwich** and **Forest Hill** have quiet streets and off-beat museums. **Clapham** is experiencing a boom in nightlife and culture. ⊖Stockwell, Brixton and Clapham serve the area. For access to some areas, overland rail service from Victoria, Waterloo, and London Bridge is necessary. From Brixton, the P4 bus will take you to all the Dulwich sites.

EAST LONDON

At Aldgate, the wealth of the City of London gives way to the historically impoverished **East End,** the heart of East London. Cheap land and nearby docks made this area a natural gathering point for immigrants, including waves of Huguenots, Jews, and, more recently, Bangladeshis. The East End remains one of the last affordable areas in central London and was the inspiration behind the famous British television show, *The EastEnders*. Today, it's famous for Spitalfields Market, a funky indoor market bursting with cheap silver jewelry, crafts, food, and antiques. There's no reason to get off the elevated Docklands Light Railway (DLR) trains in **Docklands** until they reach **Greenwich,** home to sights documenting its maritime past. ⊖Old St. and Liverpool St. are best for the East End. Farther east, Tube lines serve Canary Wharf and Wapping. The DLR will take you to Greenwich.

WEST LONDON

West London stretches for miles along the Thames before petering out in the valley's hills. The river changes track so often and so sharply that it is difficult to distinguish between the north and south banks, and communities have developed almost in isolation from their neighbors. **Shepherd's Bush,** one of these relatively autonomous districts, distinguishes itself with a number of well-known concert and theatre venues. **Hammersmith** bridges the gap between the shopping malls around the Tube station and the pleasant parks and pubs along the Thames. To the north, **White City** is home to the world-famous BBC. Historically, the western reaches of the Thames were fashionable spots for country retreats, and the river still winds through the grounds of stately homes and former palaces. The District Line on the Underground goes to most sights.

▛ LOCAL TRANSPORTATION

Local gripes aside, London's public transportation system is remarkably efficient. (☎7222 1234, 24hr.; www.tfl.gov.uk.) The network is divided into a series of concentric zones; ticket prices depend on the number of zones you cross. To make matters even more confusing, there are two different zoning systems. The **Tube, rail,** and **Docklands Light Railway (DLR)** network operates on six zones, with zone 1 being the most central. **Buses** reduce this to four zones. Bus zones 1, 2, and 3 are the same as the Tube zones, and bus zone 4 comprises Tube zones 4, 5, and 6.

OYSTER CARDS AND TRAVEL PASSES

You'll save money by investing in an **Oyster card.** Oyster cards work on the zone system and can be purchased at major Tube, DLR, and rail stations. Buying one requires some paperwork and a £3 deposit, renewable upon return, after which all transactions work via a pay-as-you-go scheme. You can add money to your Oyster card at designated kiosks within major Tube stations. Using an Oyster card is extremely convenient: simply touch it on a card reader at the beginning and end of a Tube journey, and use it on buses, rails, and trams for a substantial discount off normal fares. Although they are less flexible than Oyster cards, **Travelcards** offer similar discounts. **One-Day Travelcards** are valid for bus, Tube, DLR, and commuter rail services. There are two types of One-Day Travelcards: **Peak** cards (valid all day) and **Off-Peak** cards (M-F after 9:30am, Sa-Su all day). **Three-Day Travelcards** are also available. **Family Travelcards** and discounts for children are available. **Weekend** or **Weekly Travelcards** are valid two consecutive days on weekends and public holidays or seven consecutive days, respectively. See www.tfl.gov.uk for Travelcard rates. Although they are not a very good deal, you can also buy individual passes for single rides on the Tube. Beware of people trying to sell you second-hand passes—there's no guarantee the ticket will work, and it's illegal (penalties are stiff). Passes expire at 4:30am the morning after the expiration date.

THE UNDERGROUND

The **Tube** is best suited to longer trips; within Zone 1, adjacent stations are so close that you might as well walk, and buses are cheaper and often get you closer to your destination. The **Docklands Light Railway (DLR)** is a driverless, overland version of the Tube running in East London; the ticketing structure is the same. If you'll be traveling by Tube a lot, you'll save money with an **Oyster card** or a **Travelcard.** If you choose to buy single-ride paper tickets, you must buy them at the start of your journey; they are valid only for the day of purchase. **Keep your ticket** for the entire journey, since you'll need it to exit the station. Regular ticket prices depend on two factors: number of zones traveled and whether you traveled through zone 1. Prices increase if you are traveling in or through zones higher than zone 4. With an **Oyster card,** these fares drop significantly. The Tube runs daily approximately **5:30am to midnight.** The time of the first and last train is posted in each station; check if you plan to take the Tube after 11:30pm. Trains run less frequently early in the morning, late at night, and on Sundays.

BUSES

Only tourists use the Tube for short trips in central London—if it's only a couple of stops or if it involves more than one change, a bus will likely get there faster. Excellent signposts make the bus system easy to use; most stops display a map of local routes and nearby stops, along with a key to help you find your bus and stop. Normal buses run approximately **5:30am to midnight.** During the day, double-deckers run every 10-15min.; single-deckers arrive every 5-8min. A reduced network of **Night Buses** fills in the gap. Night Bus route numbers are prefixed with an N; they typically operate the same routes as their daytime equivalents but occasionally start and finish at different points. Buses that run 24hr. have no N Bus and Night Bus fares are the same: £1.20, ages 11-15 40p, under 11 free. All tickets are good for traveling across the network and can be purchased at roadside machines or on the bus. **Keep your ticket** until you get off the bus to avoid a £20 on-the-spot fine.

TAXIS

Taxis in London come in two forms: licensed taxis **(black cabs)** and **minicabs.** Fares for black cabs are regulated by the Transport for London. Taxis must take passengers anywhere in central London up to 12 mi., even just one block. Longer journeys are at their discretion—negotiate a fare in advance if you're going outside the city. A **10% tip** is expected. **Taxi One-Number** (☎ 08718 718 710) connects to six radio taxi circuits, allowing you many booking options.

Anyone with a car and a drivers license can be a minicab company. As a result, competition is fierce and prices are lower than licensed cabs. **Minicabs are not always safe** for those traveling alone; there have been many reports of sexual assault. Call one of the following reputable companies ahead or take a black cab: **London Radio Cars** (☎ 8905 0000); **Liberty Cars** (☎ 0800 600 006; www.liberty-cars.com), which caters to GLBT passengers; or **Lady Cabs** (☎ 7254 3501), which caters to female drivers.

▼ PRACTICAL INFORMATION

TOURIST AND FINANCIAL SERVICES

Tourist Information Centre: Britain Visitor Centre, 1 Regent St. (www.visitbritain.com), ⊖Piccadilly Circus. Open M 9:30am-6:30pm, Tu-F 9am-6:30pm, Sa-Su 10am-4pm. **London Information Centre,** 1 Leicester Pl. (☎ 7930 6769; www.londoninformation-centre.com), ⊖Leicester Sq. Open M-F 8am-midnight, Sa-Su 9am-6pm.

Tours: The **Big Bus Company,** 35-37 Grosvenor Gardens (☎ 7233 7797; www.big-bus.co.uk), ⊖Victoria. Multiple routes and buses every 5-15min. 1hr. walking tours and mini Thames cruise. Buses start at central office and at hubs throughout the city. £20. £2 discount for online purchase. AmEx/MC/V. **Original London Walks** (☎ 7624 3978, recorded info 7624 9255; www.walks.com) runs themed walks, from "Haunted London" to "Slice of India." Most 2hr. £6, concessions £5, under 16 free.

Financial Services: American Express, 84 Kensington High St. (☎ 7795 6703; www.americanexpress.com), ⊖High St. Kensington. Open M-Sa 9am-5:30pm. Branch at 30-31 Haymarket (☎ 7484 9610), ⊖Piccadilly Circus. Open M-F 9am-7pm, Sa 9am-6pm, Su 10am-5pm.

LOCAL SERVICES

Transport for London: Access and Mobility (☎ 7222 1234; www.tfl.gov.uk/tfl/ph_accessibility.shtml) provides info on public transportation accessibility.

GLBT Resources: Gay London (www.gaylondon.co.uk) is an online community for gays and lesbians. A web portal for lesbian and bisexual women, **Gingerbeer** (www.ginger-beer.co.uk), lists clubs, bars, restaurants, and community resources.

EMERGENCY AND COMMUNICATIONS

 London's phone code is **020.**

Emergency: ☎ 999 from any land line or 122 from a mobile phone.

Police: London is covered by 2 police forces: the **City of London Police** (☎ 7601 2222) for the City and the **Metropolitan Police** (☎ 7230 1212) for the rest. At least 1 station in each of the 32 boroughs is open 24hr. Call ☎ 7230 1212 to find the nearest station.

Hospitals: Charing Cross, Fulham Palace Rd. (☎ 8846 1234), entrance on St. Dunstan's Rd., ⊖Hammersmith. **Royal Free,** Pond St. (☎ 7794 0500), ⊖Belsize Park. **St. Thomas's,** Lambeth Palace Rd. (☎ 7188 7188), ⊖Waterloo. **University College London Hospital,** Grafton Way (☎ 0845 1555 000), ⊖Warren St.

Pharmacies: Most pharmacies open M-Sa 9:30am-5:30pm; a "duty" chemist in each neighborhood opens Su, although hours may be limited. Late-night chemists are rare.

One 24hr. option is **Zafash Pharmacy,** 233 Old Brompton Rd. (☎ 7373 2798), ⊖Earl's Ct. **Bliss,** 5-6 Marble Arch (☎ 7723 6116), ⊖Marble Arch. Open daily 9am-midnight.

Internet Access: If you're paying more than £2 per hr., you're paying too much. Try the ubiquitous **easyEverything** (☎ 7241 9000; www.easyeverything.com). Locations include 9-16 Tottenham Ct. Rd. (⊖Tottenham Ct. Rd.); 456-459 Strand (⊖Charing Cross); 358 Oxford St. (⊖Bond St.); 160-166 Kensington High St. (⊖High St. Kensington). Prices vary with demand, from £1 per 15min. during busy times; usually around £1.60 per hr. Min. 50p-£1. Generally open until 11pm.

Post Office: Post offices are on almost every major road. When sending mail to London, include the full post code. The largest office is the **Trafalgar Square Post Office,** 24-28 William IV St. ⊖Charing Cross. Open M and W-F 8:30am-6:30pm, Tu 9:15am-6:30pm, Sa 9am-5:30pm.

⚑ ACCOMMODATIONS

Accommodations in London cost a good deal more than anywhere else in the UK. The area near **Victoria Station** (Westminster) is convenient for major sights and transportation, but is expensive. **Bloomsbury** is by far the budget traveler's best option. Competing for second place, **Kensington** and **Earl's Court** have a number of mid-range, high-quality digs, while **Bayswater** has less expensive ones that are also a step down in quality. Book well in advance, especially in summer. (Book YHAs online at www.yha.org.) Check out university dorms for good summer deals.

BY PRICE

UNDER £25 (PRICE ICON ❶)	
Ashlee House	BLOOM
Astor's Museum Hostel	BLOOM
▨The Generator	BLOOM
Hyde Park Hostel	BAY
International Student House	M/RP
Quest Hostel	BAY
St. Christopher's Inn	NL
YHA Earl's Court	KEN/EC
▨YHA Holland House	KEN/EC
▨YHA Oxford Street	WEND

£25-40 (PRICE ICON ❷)	
Carr-Saunders Hall	BLOOM
City University Finsbury	CLERK
Commonwealth Hall	BLOOM
Pickwick Hall	BLOOM
Rosebery Hall	CLERK
YHA St. Pancras International	BLOOM

£41-55 (PRICE ICON ❸)	
Admiral Hotel	BAY
Balmoral House Hotel	BAY
George Hotel	BLOOM
IES Chelsea Pointe	CHEL
The Langland Hotel	BLOOM
Kandara Guesthouse	NL
▨Luna Simone Hotel	WESTMIN
Morgan House	K/B
Oxford Hotel	KEN/EC
▨Vicarage Hotel	KEN/EC

£56-75 (PRICE ICON ❹)	
The Gate Hotel	NH
▨Jenkins Hotel	BLOOM
Thanet Hotel	BLOOM

BY NEIGHBORHOOD
BAYSWATER

Quest Hostel, 45 Queensborough Terr. (☎ 7229 7782; www.astorhostels.com). ⊖Queensway. Night Bus #N15, 94, 148. A chummy staff operates this simple backpacker hostel with a whiteboard welcoming new check-ins by name. Mostly mixed-sex dorms (1 female-only room); nearly all have bath. Otherwise, facilities on every other fl. Kitchen available. Continental breakfast, lockers, and linen included. Laundry, luggage storage, free Wi-Fi. 4- to 9-person dorms £18-23; doubles £30. MC/V. ❶

Hyde Park Hostel, 2-6 Inverness Terr. (☎7229 5101; www.astorhostels.com). ⊖Queens-
way. Night Bus #N15, 94, 148. 260 tightly bunked beds and a veritable theme park
of diversions. Jungle-themed basement bar and dance space hosts DJs and parties
(open W-Su 8pm-3am). Kitchen, laundry, TV lounge, secure luggage room. Continental
breakfast and linens included. Internet access 50p per 30min. Reception 24hr. Reserve
2 weeks in advance for summer. 24hr. cancellation policy. Online booking with 10%
non-refundable deposit. 4- to 18-bed dorms £11-18; twins £25; weekly rates available
from £81-95 per person. Ages 16-35 only. MC/V. ❶

Admiral Hotel, 143 Sussex Gardens (☎7723 7309; www.admiral-hotel.com). ⊖Pad-
dington. Night Bus #N15, 94, 148. Beautifully kept B&B with a sleek bar. Rooms with
bath, hair dryer, satellite TV, and kettle. No smoking. English breakfast included. Free
Wi-Fi. 4-day cancellation policy. Singles £40-50; doubles £58-75; triples £75-90;
quads £88-110; quints £100-130. Ask about winter and long-stay discounts. MC/V. ❸

Balmoral House Hotel, 156 Sussex Gardens (☎7723 7445; www.balmoralhouseho-
tel.co.uk). ⊖Paddington. Night Bus #N15, 94, 148. Convenient location close to the
Tube station. Well-kept rooms have smallish bathroom, satellite TV, kettle, and hair-
dryer. English breakfast included. Singles £50; doubles £75; triples £90; quads £104;
family suites for 5 £120. MC/V with 5% surcharge. ❸

BLOOMSBURY

🏠**The Generator,** Compton Pl. (☎7388 7666; www.generatorhostels.com), off 37 Tavistock Pl. ⊖Russell Sq. or King's Cross St. Pancras. Night Bus #N19, N35, N38, N41,
N55, N91, N243. Mixed-sex dorms (all-female available), a hopping bar (6pm-2am),
cheap pints (6-9pm, £1), dinner specials, nightly entertainment, and well-equipped
common rooms. You might be greeted with a complimentary beer. All rooms have sink;
private doubles have tables and chairs. Continental breakfast included. Lockers (bring
your own lock), laundry, kitchen, ATM, and a shop that sells Tube and train tickets.
Internet 50p per 7min. Reception 24hr. Reserve 1 week in advance for Sa-Su. Credit
card required with reservation. 12- to 14-bed dorms M-W and Su £12.50, Th-Sa
£17.50; singles £30/35; doubles with 2 twin beds £40/44; triples £54/60; quads
£60/68. Discounts for long stays. 18+ unless part of a family group. MC/V. ❶

🏠**Jenkins Hotel,** 45 Cartwright Gardens (☎7387 2067; www.jenkinshotel.demon.co.uk),
entry on Barton Pl. ⊖Euston or King's Cross St. Pancras. Night Bus #N10, N73, N91,
390. A small hotel with plenty of fun. Taller folks should avoid the low-ceilinged basement (although it boasts the nicest bathroom). Rooms have TV, kettle, phone, fridge,
hair dryer, and safe. Access to tennis courts in Cartwright Gardens. English breakfast
included. Reserve 1-2 months in advance for summer. Singles £52, with bath £72; doubles with bath (some with tub) £89; triples with bath £105. MC/V. ❹

Ashlee House, 261-265 Gray's Inn Rd. (☎7833 9400; www.ashleehouse.co.uk).
⊖King's Cross St. Pancras. Night Bus #N10, N63, N73, N91, 390. A "designer" budget accommodation fit for the most discerning of backpackers. Retro-themed rooms
and common areas. Mixed-sex (all-female available) dorms are small but bright, while
private rooms include table, sink, and kettle. Luggage room, safe, laundry, and kitchen.
Small elevator and TV room. Continental breakfast included. Linens included; towels
£1. Internet £1 per hr. 2-week max. stay. Reception 24hr. 16-bed dorms £9-18; 8- to
10-bed £11-20; 4- to 6-bed £13-22; singles £37; doubles £50. MC/V. ❶

George Hotel, 58-60 Cartwright Gardens (☎7387 8777; www.georgehotel.com). ⊖Rus-
sell Sq. Night Bus #N10, N73, N91, 390. Rooms with satellite TV, radio, kettle, phone,
alarm clock, and sink. Hair dryer and iron on request. The forward-facing rooms on the
1st fl. are the best, with high ceilings and tall windows. English breakfast included. Free
Internet. Reserve 3 weeks in advance for summer; 48hr. cancellation policy. Singles
£50, with shower £75; doubles £68.50/75, with bath £89; triples £79/89/99; basic
quad £89. Discount for stays over 4 days. MC/V. ❸

Astor's Museum Hostel, 27 Montague St. (☎ 7580 5360; www.astorhotels.com). ⊖Tottenham Court Rd., Russell Sq., or Goodge St. Night Bus #N19, N35, N38, N41, N55, N91, N243. This backpackers' hostel is bare-bones but friendly. High-maintenance types and anyone over 35 need not apply—you'll be asked for proof of age. Communal kitchen and free DVDs available to watch in downstairs lounge. English breakfast and linens included. Towels £5. Reservations recommended. 12-bed dorms £19; 10-bed £20; 8-bed £21; 6-bed £23; private double £66. AmEx/MC/V. ❶

YHA St. Pancras International, 79-81 Euston Rd. (☎ 0870 770 6044; stpancras@yha.org.uk). ⊖King's Cross St. Pancras. Night Bus #N10, N73, N91, 390. Opposite the British Library. Caters to families and older adults. Family bunk rooms, single-sex dorms, basic doubles, and premium doubles with bath and TV. Breakfast included. Lockers (bring your own lock). Internet £1 per 15min. 10-day max. stay. Reserve 1 week in advance for Sa-Su or summer, 2 weeks for doubles. Dorms £26.50, under 18 £22.50; doubles £60, with bath £65. £3 discount with ISIC or NUS card. MC/V. ❷

Thanet Hotel, 8 Bedford Pl., Russell Sq. (☎ 7636 2869; www.thanethotel.co.uk). ⊖Russell Sq. or Holborn. Night Bus #N19, N35, N38, N41, N55, N91, N243. A homey B&B. Some rooms have been recently refurbished with fireplaces and big mirrors, but even the old rooms are bright and comfortable. Request a room with a view of the garden. All rooms with bath, TV, hair dryer, kettle, and phone. Breakfast included. Reserve 1 month in advance. Singles £76; doubles £100; triples £112; quads £120. AmEx/MC/V. ❹

The Langland Hotel, 29-31 Gower St. (☎ 7636 5801; www.langlandhotel.com). ⊖Goodge St. Night Bus #N5, N10, N20, 24, N29, N73, 134, N253, N279, 390. A comfortable B&B with lower rates. Staff keeps the large rooms spotless. Lounge with satellite TV. Recently refurbished rooms have TV, kettle, and fan. English breakfast included. 48hr. cancellation policy. Singles from £45; doubles from £55, with bath £65; triples from £60/75; quads from £75. Discounts in winter and for longer stays, students, and advance booking. AmEx/MC/V. ❸

Pickwick Hall International Backpackers, 7 Bedford Pl. (☎ 7323 4958; www.pickwickhall.co.uk). ⊖Russell Sq. or Holborn. Night Bus #N7, N91. Small, clean rooms include mini-fridge and microwave. Continental breakfast included. Lockers (bring your own lock). Coin laundry, kitchen, TV lounge, and Internet available. Reception approx. 8am-10pm. Book 2-3 days in advance, 3 weeks in advance for July-Aug. Singles £35, with bath £55; doubles £46/62; triples £63/69; quads £84/92. MC/V. ❷

Commonwealth Hall, 1-11 Cartwright Gardens (☎ 7121 7000; www.lon.ac.uk/services/students/halls1/halls2/vacrates.asp). ⊖Russell Sq. Night Bus #N10, N73, N91, 390. Post-WWII block residential hall. 425 recently refurbished student singles. English breakfast included. Fridge and microwave on each floor. Elevators and cafeteria. Access to tennis and squash courts for a fee. Dinner included. Open from mid-Mar. to late Apr. and from mid-June to mid-Sept. Reserve at least 3 months in advance for July-Aug. Walk-ins only accommodated M-F 9am-5pm. Singles from £28. AmEx/MC/V. ❷

Carr-Saunders Hall, 18-24 Fitzroy St. (☎ 7955 7575; www.lse.ac.uk/vacations). ⊖Warren St. Night Bus #N7, N8, N10, 25, N55, N73, N98, 176, N207, 390. Old student residential hall. Rooms are large and include sink and phone. TV lounge, game room, and elevator to all floors, including roof terrace. English breakfast included. Internet access. Reserve 6-8 weeks in advance for July-Aug., but check for openings any time. Open late Mar.-late Apr. and late June-late Sept. 30% deposit required. Singles from £30; doubles from £48, with bath from £52. Discounts for stays over 5 weeks. MC/V. ❷

CLERKENWELL

City University Finsbury Residences, 15 Bastwick St. (☎ 7040 8811; www.city.ac.uk/ems/accomm/fins.html). ⊖Barbican. Night Bus #N35 and N55 stop at the corner of Old St. and Goswell Rd. A 1970s tower block is simple but sufficient for a budget stay in central London. The rooms are within walking distance of City sights, Islington restaurants, and Clerkenwell nightlife. Singles in the main building have shared shower, toilet, kitchen access, and a laundry room. Early reservations recommended. Open from early June to early Sept. Wheelchair-accessible. Singles £21. MC/V. ❷

Rosebery Hall, 90 Rosebery Ave. (☎ 7955 7575; www.lse.ac.uk/collections/vacations). ⊖Angel. Night Bus #N19, N38, 341. Exit left from the Tube, cross the road, and take the 2nd right on Rosebery Ave. Ring bell to enter. A quick walk from Exmouth Market, the 2 LSE student residence buildings surround a garden. Rooms in the newer block are more spacious, with wheelchair-accessible baths. Pool tables, TV lounge, laundry, and bar. Open from mid-Aug. to Sept. and from mid-Dec. to early Jan. Singles from £31; doubles £50, with bath £60; triples £62. ❷

KENSINGTON AND EARL'S COURT

YHA Holland House, Holland Walk (☎ 7937 0748; www.yha.org.uk). ⊖High St. Kensington or Holland Park. Night Bus #27, 94, 148. One of the better hostels in the city. In the middle of Holland Park, half the rooms are in a 17th-century mansion overlooking a large courtyard. Standard 12- to 20-bed single-sex dorms are less alluring (some bunks are 3-tiered), but a cleaner facility would be hard to find. Caters mostly to student groups. Internet access (50p per 7min.), TV room, laundry, kitchen. Full English breakfast included; 3-course set dinners £5.50. Reception 24hr. Book 2-3 weeks in advance for summer, although there are frequent last-minute vacancies. Dorms £21.50, under 18 £16.50. £3 discount with student ID. AmEx/MC/V. ❶

Vicarage Hotel, 10 Vicarage Gate (☎ 7229 4030; www.londonvicaragehotel.com). ⊖High St. Kensington. Night Bus #27, N28, N31, N52. Walking on Kensington Church St. from Kensington High St., there are 2 streets marked Vicarage Gate; take the 2nd on your right. Victorian house with ornate hallways, TV lounge, and bedrooms; all rooms have solid wood furnishings, kettle, and hair dryer. Ensuite rooms with TV. Full English breakfast included. Reserve 2 months in advance with 1 night's deposit; personal checks accepted for deposit with at least 2 months notice. Singles £50, with private bathroom £85; doubles £85/110; triples £105/140; quads £112/155. MC/V. ❸

Oxford Hotel, 24 Penywern Rd. (☎ 7370 1161; www.the-oxford-hotel.com). ⊖Earl's Court. Night Bus #N31, N74, N97. Sir William Ramsey, the physicist who discovered helium, once lived in this hotel—guests would often hear high-pitched voices coming from his room. Mid-sized, bright rooms, all with shower and some with full bath. Minimal, high-quality furnishings: comfortable beds, TV, kettle, and safe. Rooms in annex down the road of comparable quality. Continental breakfast included. Reception 24hr. Reserve 2-3 weeks in advance for June. Singles with shower £45, with bath £58; doubles £65/75; triples with bath £83; quads £92/100; quints £120. MC/V. ❸

YHA Earl's Court, 38 Bolton Gdns. (☎ 7373 7083; www.yha.org.uk). ⊖Earl's Court. Night Bus #N31, N74, N97. Victorian townhouse better-equipped than most YHAs. Single-sex dorms (4-10 people) have wooden bunks, lockers (bring your own lock), and sink. Small garden, spacious kitchen, 2 TV lounges, and luggage storage. Breakfast included only for private rooms; otherwise £4. Laundry and Internet access. 2-week max stay. 24hr. cancellation policy; £5 cancellation charge. Book private rooms a day in advance. Dorms £19.50, under 18 £17.20; doubles £60; quads £82. MC/V. ❶

OTHER NEIGHBORHOODS

YHA Oxford Street (HI), 14 Noel St. (☎ 7734 1618; www.yha.org.uk). ⊖Oxford Cir. Night Bus: More than 10 Night Buses run along Oxford St., including #N7, N8, and N207. Small, clean, sunny rooms with limited facilities but an unbeatable location for nightlife. Some double rooms have bunk beds, sink, mirror, and wardrobe; others have single beds and wardrobes. Toilets and showers off the hallways. Spacious, comfy TV and smoking lounge. Towels £3.50. Internet terminal and Wi-Fi available. Travelcards sold at reception. Reserve at least 2 weeks in advance. May-Sept. 3- to 4-person dorms £25, under 18 £20.50; 2-bed dorms £27. Oct.-Mar. £23.50/19/25.50. MC/V. ❶

■ **Luna Simone Hotel,** 47-49 Belgrave Rd. (☎7834 5897; www.lunasimonehotel.com). ⊖Victoria or Pimlico. Night Bus #N2, 24, N36. Sparkling, spacious showers, modern decor, and a staff that takes a keen interest in its guests. Singles without bath are cramped. Full English breakfast included. Free Internet access. Reserve at least 2 weeks in advance. 48hr. cancellation policy £10; 1 night's charge if less than 48hr. notice. Singles £40, with bath £60; doubles with bath £90; triples with bath £110; quads with bath £130. 10-20% discount in low season. MC/V. ❸

IES Chelsea Pointe (☎7808 9200; www.iesreshall.com), corner of Manresa Rd. and King's Rd., entrance on Manresa Rd. ⊖Sloane Sq., then Bus #11, 19, 22, 319; ⊖South Kensington, then Bus #49. Night Bus #N11, N19, N22. Brand-new university residence hall offers clean, spacious dorm rooms year-round. In the heart of trendy Chelsea, these prices are unheard of. All rooms have bath and data ports (free Internet), access to laundry services, and 5 TV lounges. Reservations recommended. 72hr. cancellation policy. Wheelchair-accessible. More availability during summer and winter school breaks. Singles £285 per week; doubles £375 per week. AmEx/MC/V. ❸

Morgan House, 120 Ebury St. (☎7730 2384; www.morganhouse.co.uk). ⊖Victoria. Mid-sized, stylish rooms, many with fireplaces, all with TV, kettle, and phone for incoming calls. English breakfast included. Reserve 2-3 months in advance. 48hr. cancellation policy. Singles with sink £52; doubles with sink £72, with bath £92; triples £92/112; quads (1 double bed and 1 set of bunk beds) with bath £132. MC/V. ❸

International Student House, 229 Great Portland St. (☎7631 8310; www.ish.org.uk). ⊖Great Portland St. Night Bus #N18. Large, institutional dorm. Good selection of rooms during summer, limited options during school year. Most rooms have desk, sink, phone, and fridge; some have ensuite bath. Bar, nightclub, cafeteria, fitness center (£6 per day), and cinema (Su only). Continental breakfast included except for dorms (£2.30); English breakfast £3. Laundry. Internet £2 per hr. £20 key deposit. Some rooms wheelchair-accessible. 3-week max. stay. Advance booking recommended. Dorms £12; singles £34; doubles £52; triples £62; quads £76. 10% discount on singles, doubles, and triples with ISIC. MC/V. ❶

The Gate Hotel, 6 Portobello Rd. (☎7221 0707; www.gatehotel.co.uk). ⊖Notting Hill Gate. Night Bus #N52. A great base for Notting Hill and West End excursions. Clean, relatively spacious, and a good deal for the area. Rooms have bath, TV/DVD, desk, mini-fridge, and phone. Continental breakfast included, served in-room. 48hr. cancellation policy. Singles £55-70; doubles £75-90; triples £90-110. AmEx/MC/V. ❹

Kandara Guesthouse, 68 Ockendon Rd. (☎7226 5721; www.kandara.co.uk). From ⊖Angel, take Bus #38, 56, 73, 341 to the Ockendon Rd. stop. Night Bus #N38, N73, 341. Far from the Tube but with ample access to downtown. Bustling atmosphere and clean rooms that offer plenty of privacy. 11 rooms with 5 communal baths. Hair dryer and iron on request. Breakfast included. Reserve well in advance; call for family quad. 1-night deposit required with reservation; 1-week cancellation notice or loss of deposit. Singles £44-54; doubles £59-71; triples £69-82. MC/V. ❸

St. Christopher's Inn, 48-50 Camden High St. (☎7388 1012; www.st-christophers.co.uk). ⊖Mornington Crescent. Night Bus #N5, N20, N253. Reception in Belushi's Bar downstairs is a fitting entrance to this party-friendly backpacker hostel. Nicknamed the "hostel with attitude," St. Christopher's gets you started right with 10% off all food and drinks at the bar. Near Camden Town bars and Clerkenwell clubs. Most rooms ensuite. Continental breakfast included. Luggage room, safety deposit boxes, lockers, laundry, and common rooms. Internet access. Reception 24hr. 10-bed dorms from £9.50; 8-bed £17; 6-bed £18; doubles £24. Discount with online booking. ❶

◘ FOOD

While insiders have known London as a hot spot for internationally influenced cuisine for years, it has taken a little while to spread the word that Great Britain is
more than just bangers and mash. London's food scene is fueled by its growing
ethnic communities, many of which use their culinary traditions to maintain ties to
their own culture while introducing others to their cuisine. Head to Whitechapel
for the region's best Baltic food, to Chinatown for traditional dim sum, to South
Kensington for French pastries, and to Edgware Rd. for a stunning assortment of
Lebanese Shawarma. Still, it would be a shame to come to the home of afternoon
tea and fish and chips and deny yourself these delicious British traditions.

BAYSWATER

▨ **Levantine,** 26 London St. (☎7262 1111; www.levant.co.uk). ⊖Paddington. A Lebanese restaurant with the faint aroma of incense and rose petals. Indulge in Mezze offerings like falafel and homemade hummus (£4.75). Loads of vegetarian options. Belly-
dancing and *shisha* (water pipe) nights. Open daily noon-12:30am. MC/V. ❷

▨ **La Bottega del Gelato,** 127 Bayswater Rd. (☎7243 2443). ⊖Queensway. The creamy
gelato is ideal after a hard day of sightseeing. Perfect to take on a stroll in the Kensington Gardens across the street. 1-3 scoops £2-4. Open daily 11am-10pm. ❶

Aphrodite Taverna, 15 Hereford Rd. (☎7229 2206). ⊖Bayswater. Fabulous menu is a
grab bag of polysyllabic treats, like *dolmedes* (stuffed grape leaves; £8.50) or *keftedes*
(Greek meatballs; £8.50). £1 cover is amply rewarded with baskets of fresh pita bread
and other appetizers. **Cafe Aphrodite** next door offers some of Taverna's specialties at
lower prices as well as a full sandwich menu (from £2.60). Restaurant open M-Sa noon-
midnight. Cafe open daily 8am-5pm. AmEx/MC/V. Restaurant ❷, Cafe ❶

Durbar Tandoori, 24 Hereford St. (☎7727 1947; www.durbartandoori.co.uk). ⊖Bay-
swater. One of London's more famous Indian restaurants. Simple dining room and low
prices. Large portions and dishes from several regions throughout India. Veggie and
meat entrees from £5.25. Bargain take-away lunchbox £4. Chef's special dinner £23
for 2. Open M-Th and Sa-Su noon-2:30pm and daily 5:30-11:30pm. AmEx/MC/V. ❷

Khan's Restaurant, 13-15 Westbourne Grove (☎7727 5420; www.khanrestau-
rant.com). ⊖Bayswater. This family-run restaurant, with landscape murals and faux-
palm tree pillars, dishes out hearty portions of Indian favorites. Chicken tikka (£5) and
fish curry (£5.55) are favorites from the extensive menu. Takeaway available. Open M-
Th and Sa-Su noon-3pm and 6pm-midnight, F 6pm-midnight. AmEx/MC/V. ❷

BLOOMSBURY

▨ **ICCo (Italiano Coffee Company),** 46 Goodge St. (☎7580 9688). ⊖Goodge St. A
young student crowd usually fills the steel-tabled dining area. Delicious 11 in. pizzas
made to order from £3. Pre-packaged sandwiches and baguettes on fresh bread start at
£1.50 (rolls 50p). Pasta from £2. Buy any hot drink before noon and get a free freshly
baked croissant. Sandwiches and baguettes half-price after 4pm. Takeaway available.
Pizzas available after noon. Open daily 7am-11pm. AmEx/MC/V. ❶

▨ **Navarro's Tapas Bar,** 67 Charlotte St. (☎7637 7713; www.navarros.co.uk). ⊖Goodge
St. Colorful, bustling tapas restaurant with tiled walls and flamenco music. The authenticity carries over to the excellent food—try the spicy *patatas bravas* (fried potatoes; £3.55).
Tapas £3.50-11; 2-3 per person is plenty. £7.50 min. purchase. Open M-F noon-3pm
and 6-10pm, Sa 6-10pm. AmEx/MC/V. ❸

Newman Arms, 23 Rathbone St., (☎7636 1127). ⊖Tottenham Court Rd. or Goodge St.
A pub with a famous upstairs pie room and restaurant. Connoisseurs at 10 sought-after
tables dig into homemade meat pies. Seasonal game fillings most popular; vegetarian

CORNISH PASTIES

Cornish pasties are everywhere in London. They line the shelves of supermarkets, make guest appearances in the hot food sections of delis, and are sold to intoxicated clubbers from late-night street stalls and takeaway joints. While convenient, the ubiquity of these tasty treats does not do justice to their importance in British history.

The story of the pasty begins in the Cornish tin mines of the 19th century. Miners' wives engineered the pasty as a food durable enough for long hours in the mines. Unlike today's potato-heavy imitations, the original Cornish pasty contained skirt steak, potato, Swede turnip, onion salt, and pepper—all enclosed by a protective chunky crust. By holding the pasty by its folded edge, miners were able to eat their lunch without ingesting the grime and arsenic of their surroundings. Legend also has it that the miners threw the crusts down the mineshafts to appease the "knockers," mischievous goblins who lived deep below the surface.

When mining ended in Cornwall, the miners scattered, bringing their pasties with them. As a result, people all over the country enjoy these versatile meals. Travelers should beware, however, that the presence of carrots in store-bought pasties is a sign of inferior quality. Those seeking genuine pasties should stick to bakeries or venture to Cornwall (p. 232) for the real deal.

and fish options available. Pie with potatoes and veggies on the side £9. Pints start at £3. Book in advance or be faced with a hungry wait. Pub open M-F 11am-11pm. Restaurant open M-Th noon-3pm and 6-9pm, F noon-3pm. ❷

Savoir Faire, 42 New Oxford St. (☎7436 0707). ⊖Tottenham Court Rd. or Holborn. Cherubic murals and handwritten quotations cover the walls of this bistro. Sit at wooden tables and enjoy excellent seafood and continental standards like steak frites and salad (£12). 2-course vegetarian dinner £9. Popular brunch spot serving eggs Benedict and florentine (£7). Open M-Sa noon-4pm and 5-11:30pm, Su noon-10:30pm. AmEx/MC/V. ❷

Diwana Bhel Poori House, 121-123 Drummond St. (☎7387 5556; www.diwanarestaurant.com). ⊖Euston or Euston Sq. No frills here—just great, cheap South Indian vegetarian food and efficient service. Try the all-you-can-eat lunch buffet (£6.50, served daily noon-2:30pm) or enjoy ample portions on the regular menu. Outside buffet hours, *thali* set menu is a good deal (£6-9). Open daily noon-11:30pm. AmEx/MC/V. ❷

North Sea Fish Restaurant, 7-8 Leigh St. (☎7387 5892). ⊖Russell Sq. or King's Cross St. Pancras. Fish and chips done right. The classy little restaurant, heavily populated by retired Brits, offers a boatload of fresh seafood dishes (£9-19) in a warm setting. For lower prices, order from the takeaway shop next door (cod fillets £4.30-6). Restaurant open M-Sa noon-2:30pm and 5:30-10:30pm. Takeaway M-Sa noon-2:30pm and 5-11pm. AmEx/MC/V. ❸

CHELSEA

🏛 **Buona Sera, at the Jam,** 289a King's Rd. (☎7352 8827). ØSloane Sq., then Bus #19 or 319. With patented "bunk" tables stacked high into the air, the treetop-esque dining experience alone justifies a visit. Waiters climb small wooden ladders to deliver sizeable pasta plates (£7.20-8.50) along with fish and steak dishes (£8-12). Don't drop your fork. Alcohol only served with food. Open M 6pm-midnight, Tu-F noon-3pm and 6pm-midnight, Sa-Su noon-midnight. Reservations recommended F-Sa. AmEx/MC/V. ❸

Chelsea Bun, 9a Limerston St. (☎7352 3635). ⊖Sloane Sq., then Bus #11 or 22. Spirited, casual Anglo-American diner that serves heaping portions of everything from the "Ultimate Breakfast" (eggs, pancakes, sausages, and french toast; £10.30) to Tijuana Benedict (eggs with chorizo sausage; £8). Sandwiches, pasta, and burgers £2.80-8. No need to set the alarm clock: early-bird specials available M--F 7am-noon (£2.20-3.20) and breakfast (from £4) served until 6pm. £3.50 min. per person lunch, £5.50 dinner. Open M-Sa 7am-midnight, Su 9am-7pm. MC/V. ❸

Phât Phúc, The Courtyard at 250 King's Rd. (☎07832 199 738), entrance on Sydney St. ⊖Sloane Sq., then Bus #11, 19, 22, 319. Most are drawn by the witty name, but the heaping portions of Vietnamese soup are no joke. Choose from a selection of soups (£6) along with the dessert of the day. Open daily noon-4pm. Cash only. ❷

My Old Dutch, 221 King's Rd. (☎7376 5650; www.myolddutch.com). ⊖Sloane Sq. One of 3 locations in London. Quiet place for lunch, dinner, and, most importantly, dessert. Dutch food has never tasted better, with scrumptious offerings like the Amsterdammer (savory pancake with apple and smoked bacon; £8) and sweet pancakes with fruit and ice cream (£6-7.25). Open M-Sa 11am-11pm, Su 11am-10pm. MC/V. ❷

THE CITY OF LONDON

🔲 **Cafe Spice Namaste,** 16 Prescot St. (☎7488 9242; www.cafespice.co.uk). ⊖Tower Hill or DLR: Tower Gateway. While somewhat out of the way, Spice is well worth the trek. Bright, festive decoration brings an exotic feel to this old Victorian warehouse, and the outdoor courtyard seating is a plus. The extensive menu of Goan and Parsi specialties explains each dish. Meat mains are on the pricey side (from £14.25), but vegetarian dishes (from £4.75) are affordable. A varied wine list and excellent, expensive desserts. Open M-F noon-3pm and 6:15-10:30pm, Sa 6:30-10:30pm. AmEx/MC/V. ❸

Futures, 8 Botolph Alley (☎7623 4529; www.futures-vta.net), between Botolph Ln. and Lovat Ln. ⊖Monument. London's workforce besieges this tiny takeaway joint during lunch; come before noon. Variety of vegetarian soups (from £2.50), salads (from £2.20), and hot dishes (from £5.20) all change weekly. For breakfast, you'll find a wide variety of pastries (from 85p) Open M-F 8-10am and 11:30am-2:30pm. ❶

The Place Below (☎7329 0789; www.theplacebelow.co.uk), on Cheapside, in the basement of St. Mary-le-Bow Church. ⊖St. Paul's or Mansion House. Be prepared to wait at lunchtime. Fresh sandwiches (from £4.50), yummy porridge (£1.70), and a changing menu of tasty mains (from £6). Also pastries (from £1.35) and the daily health bowl, a concoction of various healthful foods (from £4.50). Open M-F 7:30am-3pm. ❶

Spianata & Co., 73a Watling St. (☎7236 3666; www.spianata.com). ⊖Mansion House. The name comes from the wide, flat sandwiches (from £2.50) served on Italian *spianata* bread and made on the premises. Daily offerings include classic mozzarella and tomato or slightly more elaborate shrimp and roasted pepper. Wheelchair-accessible. Open M-F 7:30am-3:30pm. ❶

CLERKENWELL AND HOLBORN

🔲 **Anexo,** 61 Turnmill St. (☎7250 3401; www.anexo.co.uk). ⊖Farringdon. This Spanish restaurant and bar serves Iberian dishes in a colorful tiled interior. The large menu has authentic paella (£7.50-9), fajitas (£7.50-11.50), and tapas (from £3.50). Takeaway available. Wheelchair-accessible. Happy hour M-Sa 5-7pm. Open M-F 10am-11pm, Sa 6-11pm, Su 4:30-11pm. Bar open 11am-2am. AmEx/MC/V. ❷

Bleeding Heart Tavern, corner of Greville St. and Bleeding Heart Yard (☎7404 0333). ⊖Farringdon. Highlights include the roast suckling pig with spiced apple slices (£12), classic beer-battered fish (£10), and chocolate honey pot dessert (£4.50). Good service and fine ale round out your dining experience. Open M-F 7-10:30am, noon-2:30pm and 6-10:30pm. Upstairs pub open M-F 11:30am-11pm. AmEx/MC/V. ❸

St. John, 26 St. John St. (☎7251 0848; www.stjohnrestaurant.com). ⊖Farringdon. Unusual dishes here reward the adventurous eater. Menu changes daily; meals include veal heart and celeriac (£6.80) and roast bone marrow (£7). Bakery at the back of the bar churns out delicious loaves of bread (£2.50). Drinks £8-12. Open M-F noon-3pm and 6-11pm, Sa 6-11pm. Bar open M-F 11am-11pm, Sa 6-11pm. AmEx/MC/V. ❸

The Greenery, 5 Cowcross St. (☎7490 4870). ⊖Farringdon. For the vegetarian or health fanatic this tiny restaurant is a bit of leafy heaven. Salads starting at £2, savories (lasagna, pizza, quiche) from £2.10, and jacket potatoes from £1.50 make for delicious, cheap lunches. Packed sandwiches from £2. Vitamin-enriched smoothies from £2.30. Expect long queues during lunch. There are only a few tables in this busy shop; takeaway your organic goodies. Open M-F 7am-5pm. ●

Al's Bar/Cafe, 11-13 Exmouth Market (☎7837 4821). ⊖Angel or Farringdon. A favorite hangout for journalists from nearby *Guardian, Face,* and *Arena* newspapers. Red-lit with a basement club. With comfortable leather lounge chairs and windows all around, Al's is a prime spot to relax with coffee (£1.20-2) and people-watch. Outdoor seating. Sandwiches and salads from £1.50. Daily pasta specials £7. All-day weekend breakfast (from £3.75). DJs visit W-Su. Open M 8am-11pm, Tu-F 8am-2am, Sa 9am-2am, Su 9am-11pm. Kitchen closes at 10pm. AmEx/MC/V. ●

Woolley's, 33 Theobald's Rd. (☎7405 3028; www.woolleys.co.uk). Rear entrance on Lamb's Conduit Passage. ⊖Holborn. Narrow takeaway joint in 2 parts: salads (£2-4), savories (£2-4), and jacket potatoes (£2.50-3.50) dished out from the Theobald's Rd. side while the Lamb's Conduit side supplies fresh sandwiches (£2-3). Daily specials like lentil coconut curry (£6) and duck and orange pate (£5). You can walk through to the Lamb's Conduit side and eat in the charming passage, which makes for great rush-hour people-watching. Open M-F 7:30am-3:30pm. MC/V. ●

Chutney Raj, 137 Gray's Inn Rd. (☎7831 1149). ⊖Chancery Ln. The smaller size of this Indian and Bangladeshi restaurant belies the enormous menu. Traditional tandoori and Balti dishes from £6. Lunch special includes papadams, a starter, and a main course (daily noon-2:30pm; £6), and the similar "student offer" is a great deal (daily noon-2pm and 5:30-11:30pm; £5). Takeaway and delivery also available. Open M-Sa noon-2:30pm and 5:30-11:30pm, Su noon-2pm and 5:30-11pm. MC/V. ❷

Cafe 180, 118 Gray's Inn Rd. (☎7916 1279). ⊖Chancery Ln. Spacious, with more sitting room than nearby cafes. 180's high ceilings, crown moldings, and tiny tables are reminiscent of an old-fashioned ice cream parlor. Pop in for a filled bagel or croissant (£1.60) or a large cup of soup with a baguette (£1.50). Sandwiches and salads £1.20-£3.80. Takeaway also available. Open M-F 6:30am-4pm. MC/V. ●

Aki, 182 Gray's Inn Rd. (☎7837 9281). ⊖ Chancery Ln. The bambooed warmth of this cozy Japanese restaurant is an appropriate setting for its traditional menu and dishes. Noodle dishes (from £5), meat dishes (£7-12), and sushi meals (from £5) are bargains. *Bento* box lunch from £5.20. Wheelchair-accessible. Open M-F noon-2:30pm and 6-11pm, Sa 6-10:30pm. AmEx/MC/V. ❸

MARYLEBONE AND REGENT'S PARK

▩ Mandalay, 444 Edgware Rd. (☎7258 3696; www.mandalayway.com). ⊖Edgware Rd. 5min. walk north from the Tube. Looks ordinary, tastes extraordinary—one of the best deals around. With huge portions of wildly inexpensive food, this Burmese restaurant is justly plastered with awards. Lunch specials offer great value (curry and rice £4; 3 courses £6). Entrees, including sizeable vegetarian selection, £4-8. Open M-Sa noon-2:30pm and 6-10:30pm. Dinner reservations recommended. MC/V. ●

▩ Patogh, 8 Crawford Pl. (☎7262 4015). ⊖Edgware Rd. With just 10 tables (5 upstairs and 5 downstairs) and a cave-like interior, this tiny, charming Persian restaurant gives new meaning to "hole in the wall." Generous portions of sesame-seed flatbread (£2) and freshly prepared starters (£2.50-6) will whet your appetite; flame-grilled entrees like *kebab koobideh* (minced lamb kebab) with bread, rice, or salad (£6-11) will feed you for days. Takeaway available. Open daily noon-midnight. ❷

The Golden Hind, 73 Marylebone Ln. (☎7486 3644). ⊖Baker St. or Bond St. Short of serving food on newspaper, this fish and chips joint is as authentic as they come in London. Open since 1914, the no-nonsense "chippie" serves up fried cod and haddock (£3.40-£5.70) to a local clientele and savvy travelers. Takeaway available.

Open M-F noon-3pm and 6-10pm, Sa 6-10pm. Reservations strongly recommended after 7pm. AmEx/MC/V. ❷

Spighetta, 43 Blanford St. (☎7486 7340). ⊖Baker St. While not for pepperoni-and-sausage purists, this 2-story Sardinian restaurant offers creative wood-fired pizzas (£7-11), pastas (£7-14), and seafood dishes (£12-13). Try the couscous soup with baby clams (£6.50) as a starter. Takeaway available. Lunch daily noon-3pm. Dinner M-Sa 6:30-11pm, Su 6:30-10:30pm. AmEx/MC/V. ❸

Royal China, 24-26 Baker St. (☎7487 4688; www.royalchinagroup.co.uk). ⊖Baker St. This upscale branch of the micro-chain straddles the line between faux and real elegance. Service is variable, but food is reliable. Keep your eyes open—this restaurant is crawling with minor celebs. Try the 5-course seafood menu (£38) or the standard and vegetarian versions (£30). Most entrees £8-18. Open M-Th noon-11pm, F-Sa noon-11:30pm, Su 11am-10pm; dim sum served until 5pm. AmEx/MC/V. ❸

THE WEST END

▥ **Masala Zone,** 9 Marshall St. (☎7287 9966; www.realindianfood.com). ⊖Oxford Circus. Also in Islington at 80 Upper St. (☎7359 3399). Masala Zone oozes hipness with its softly lit interior and sunken dining room. The menu has typical favorites (£6-8), as well as "street food," which is served in small bowls (£3.40-5.50). The speciality is *thalis,* platters with samples of a variety of dishes (£7.50-11.50). Open M-F noon-2:45pm and 5:30-11pm, Sa 12:30-11pm, Su 12:30-3:30pm and 6-10:30pm. MC/V. ❷

▥ **Rock and Sole Plaice,** 47 Endell St. (☎7836 3785). ⊖Covent Garden. One of London's most picturesque fish and chips joints. A self-proclaimed "master fryer" (qualifications unclear) turns out tasty haddock, cod, halibut, and sole filets (all with chips) for £9-11. Specialties change daily but range from £4 to 6. Packed during mealtime rushes. Open M-Sa 11:30am-11:30pm, Su 11:30am-10pm. MC/V. ❷

Busaba Eathai, 106-110 Wardour St. (☎7255 8686). ⊖Tottenham Court Rd., Leicester Sq., or Piccadilly Circus. Large, tightly packed communal tables ensure a lively wait for the affordable, filling dishes. Students and locals line up for pad thai, curries, and wok creations (£6-8). Plenty of vegetarian options. No reservations. Open M-Th noon-11pm, F-Sa noon-11:30pm, Su noon-10pm. AmEx/MC/V. ❷

Golden Dragon, 28-29 Gerrard St. (☎1705 2503). ⊖Leicester Sq. The ritziest and best-known dim sum joint in Chinatown. 2 red-and-gold rooms pack on weekends. Entrees £6-20. Dim sum £12.50-22.50. Open M-Th noon-11:30pm, F-Sa noon-midnight, Su 11am-11pm. Dim sum served M-Sa noon-5pm, Su 11am-5pm. AmEx/MC/V. ❸

Cafe in the Crypt, Duncannon St. (☎7839 4342). ⊖Embankment or Charing Cross. In the basement of St.-Martins-in-the-Fields Church, this exposed-brick cellar is a monastery gone modern. An excellent fresh salad bar (£6.75), freshly made sandwiches (£4), and hearty warm puddings (£3) served cafeteria-style. Linger with a glass of wine (from £3) or stay for afternoon tea (£5). Jazz some W nights. Open M-W 8am-8pm, Th-Sa 8am-10:30pm, Su noon-6:30pm. £5 min. for AmEx/MC/V. ❶

Scoop, 40 Shorts Gardens (☎7240 7086; www.scoopgelato.com). ⊖Covent Garden. Bright orange storefront attracts passersby, but the creamy gelato and sorbet keeps them coming back. Uses only fresh ingredients—many imported from the owner's Tuscan homeland. Flavors range from *pompelmo* (grapefruit) to *cioccolato al latte* (milk chocolate). Cups and cones start at £2. Open daily 8am-11:30pm. MC/V. ❶

Carluccio's, St. Christopher's Pl. (☎7935 5927; www.carluccios.com). ⊖Bond St. Short menu stocks many variations on pasta as well as a few meat dishes. Choose from shared tables on the ground floor, more formal indoor seating, or the open patio. *Antipasti* from £4.50, mains from £8.75. Carluccio's also has an on-site deli. Branches in Islington and the City, and delis all over London. Wheelchair-accessible patio. Open M-F 8am-11pm, Sa 9am-11pm, Su 9am-10:30pm. AmEx/MC/V. ❷

NORTH LONDON

Gallipoli, 102 Upper St. (☎7359 0630), **Gallipoli Again,** 120 Upper St. (☎7359 1578), and **Gallipoli Bazaar,** 107 Upper St. (☎7226 5333). ⊖Angel. Dark walls and patterned tiles provide the background to Lebanese, North African, and Turkish delights like *iskender kebab* (grilled lamb with yogurt and marinated pita bread in secret sauce; £8.75) and the 2-course lunch (£7). Gallipoli Bazaar sits between the other 2 and serves up food, cocktails, and sheesha pipes. Open M-Th 10:30am-11pm, F-Sa 10:30am-midnight, Su 10:30am-11pm. Reservations recommended F-Sa. MC/V. ❷

Le Crêperie de Hampstead, 77 Hampstead High St. (www.hampsteadcreperie.com), the metal stand on the side of the King William IV statue. ⊖Hampstead. Don't let the slow-moving line deter you; these phenomenal crepes are worth the wait. Among many other varieties, try the favorite ham, egg, and cheese (£3.70) or the maple, walnut, and cream (£3). Open M-Th 11:45am-11pm, F-Su 11:45am-11:30pm. ❶

Mango Room, 10-12 Kentish Town Rd. (☎7482 5065; www.mangoroom.co.uk). ⊖Camden Town. Decor includes funky paintings and orange walls. The small Caribbean menu features fish complemented with plenty of mango, avocado, and coconut sauces. Entrees from £10. Lunch from £6. Wheelchair-accessible. Open daily noon-midnight. Reservations recommended Sa-Su. MC/V. ❷

New Culture Revolution, 42 Duncan St. (☎7833 9083; www.newculturerevolution.co.uk). ⊖Angel. The revolution refers to the wealth of healthful menu options. Huge portions of noodles and soups can be ordered from a menu that includes dumplings (£5), vegetable chow mein (£5.20), and chili and lemongrass seafood lo mein (from £6). Open daily noon-11pm. AmEx/MC/V. ❶

Bloom's, 130 Golders Green Rd. (☎8455 1338). ⊖Golders Green (Zone 3). The takeaway shop in the front serves freshly made dishes like potato salad and sandwich fillers (from £4.50), and the sleek restaurant in back has traditional dishes like chopped liver sandwiches (£8.50). Jewish favorites like *gefilte* fish (£4.50) and *latkes* (£2) served as sides. Kosher. Wheelchair-accessible. Open M-Th and Su noon-11pm, F 11am-3pm. ❷

EAST LONDON

Café 1001, 91 Brick Lane, Dray Walk (☎7247 9679; www.cafe1001.co.uk), in an alley just off Brick Ln. ⊖Aldgate East. Bring your sketch pad to this artists' den. Spacious upstairs and outdoor seating. Freshly baked cakes (£2 per slice), premade salads (£3), and sandwiches (£2.50). Nightly DJs 7pm-close, W live jazz. Open M-W and Su 7am-11:30pm, Th-Sa 7pm-midnight. ❶

Yelo, 8-9 Hoxton Sq. (☎7729 4626; www.yelothai.com). ⊖Old St. Pad thai, curry, and stir-fry (£5) make for familiar fare, but the industrial lighting, exposed brick, and house music shake things up. Outdoor seating available. For a more formal affair, call to book a "proper" table downstairs. Wheelchair-accessible. Takeaway and delivery available. Open daily noon-3pm and 6-11pm. ❶

Aladin, 132 Brick Ln. (☎7247 8210). ⊖Aldgate East. Serving up Pakistani, Bangladeshi, and Indian food. BYO wine and beer. Mains £4-8.50; 3-course lunch menu £6. Lunch special noon-4:30pm. Open M-Th and Su noon-11:30pm, F-Sa noon-midnight. ❷

The Real Greek, 14-15 Hoxton Market (☎7739 8212; www.therealgreek.com). ⊖Old St. Somewhat hidden except for its cobalt blue doors, this Mediterranean restaurant serves a large variety of hot and cold *mezze* dishes such as grilled octopus and stuffed grape leaves (£3.25-5.75). Several dining rooms with large windows facing onto the square accommodate a large crowd. Open M-Sa noon-11pm, closed Su. ❷

The Drunken Monkey, 222 Shoreditch High St. (☎7392 9606; www.thedrunkenmonkey.co.uk). ⊖Liverpool St. This dim sum restaurant-bar is hipper than most Shanghai nightclubs. Spacious wooden tables. and DJs Tu-Su. Large lounge area in the front with smaller, dining rooms in the back. Rice and noodle dishes £3-6; small dim sum plates £2.50-4.50. Takeaway available. Happy hour drinks from £4.50; M-F 5-7pm, Sa 6-8pm, Su noon-11pm. Open M-F noon-midnight, Sa 6pm-midnight, Su noon-11pm. AmEx/MC/V. ❷

OTHER NEIGHBORHOODS

🏶 **George's Portobello Fish Bar,** 329 Portobello Rd. (☎8969 7895). ⊖Ladbroke Grove. George opened up here in 1961, and although the little space has lived through various incarnations, the fish and chips are still as good as ever: cod, rockfish, plaice, and skate come with a huge serving of chunky chips (from £7). Open M-F 11am-midnight, Sa 11am-9pm, Su noon-9:30pm. ❷

🏶 **Jenny Lo's Teahouse,** 14 Eccleston St. (☎7259 0399). ⊖Victoria. Around the corner from Jenny's father's high-end restaurant (Ken Lo is one of the most famous chefs in the UK). The delicious *cha shao* (pork noodle soup; £6.50) and the broad selection of Asian noodles (£6.50-8) make eating here worth the wait. Takeaway and delivery available (min. £5 per person). Open M-F noon-3pm and 6-10pm, Sa 6-10pm. Cash only. ❷

Cantina del Ponte, 36c Shad Thames, Butlers Wharf (☎7403 5403). ⊖Tower Hill or London Bridge. The busy Mediterranean mural can't hold a candle to the views of the Thames, but given the quality of the classic Italian food, it's okay if you can't get a riverside seat. *Prix-fixe* lunch menu is a bargain at 2 courses for £10, 3 for £13.50 (available M-F noon-3pm). Pizzas from £5. Entrees from £8.50. Wheelchair-accessible. Open M-Sa noon-3pm and 6-10:45pm, Su noon-3pm and 6-9:45pm. AmEx/MC/V. ❸

Lazy Daisy Cafe, 59a Portobello Rd. (☎7221 8417). ⊖Notting Hill Gate. Tucked into an alleyway, alongside a church. A healthful selection of salads and pastries. All-day breakfast, including a lazy fry-up (£6) and eggs florentine (£5). Lunches include quiche (£5) and a make-your-own panini option (£4.75). Outdoor patio in summer. Wheelchair-accessible. Open M-Sa 9am-5pm, Su noon-2:30pm. 70p surcharge with MC/V. ❶

Tas, 33 The Cut (☎7928 1444; www.tasrestaurant.com). ⊖Southwark. Also at 72 Borough High St.; **Tas Cafe,** 76 Borough High; **Tas Pide,** 20-22 New Globe Walk (☎7928 3300). ⊖London Bridge. A group of affordable Turkish restaurants. Soups and baked dishes outshine the respectable kebabs. Mains from £7.35, 2-course *prix-fixe* menus from £8.75. Live music daily from 7:30pm. Open M-Sa noon-11:30pm, Su noon-10:30pm. Dinner reservations recommended at Tas and Tas Pide. AmEx/MC/V. ❷

Goya, 34 Lupus St. (☎7976 5309; www.goyarestaurant.co.uk). ⊖Pimlico. Join the local clientele for a post-siesta meal. Mirrors, large windows, and bright wood. Generous, diverse tapas (mostly £4-7), including plenty of vegetarian options; 2-3 per person is more than enough. Special sangria £3; alcohol served only with food. Wheelchair-accessible. Open daily 11:30am-11:30pm. £10 min. for AmEx/MC/V. ❸

Newens Maids of Honor, 288 Kew Rd. (☎8940 2752). ⊖Kew Gardens. Facing Kew Rd. from the Victoria Gate of Kew Gardens, cross the street and walk left for 5min. Sip tea with an extended pinky finger at this historical tea house. Best for set tea (2:30-5:30pm, £7) served with traditional fixtures. Open M 9:30am-1pm, Tu-F 9:30am-5:30pm, Sa 9am-5:30pm. MC/V. ❶

⊙ SIGHTS

To walk from east to west is to watch the city unfold through time: from Christopher Wren's playground in the 2000-year-old City of London down to Westminster to hold court with the regents, royals, and ruffians who run this capital, and then up to Bloomsbury to mingle with students and other partying youngsters. Unlike London's many free museums, sights tend to empty a budget traveler's pocket. From avant-garde architecture in Islington to the urban wilderness of Hampstead Heath, the best of London's sights are often those seen on foot.

QUEEN'S GUARD

Let's Go got the scoop on a London icon. Corporal of Horse Simon Knowles is an 19-year veteran of the Queen's Guard.

LG: What sort of training did you undergo?

A: In addition to a year of basic military camp, which involves mainly training on tanks and armored cars, I was also trained as a gunner and radio operator. When I joined the service regiment at 18 years of age.

LG: So it's not all glamor?

A: Not at all. That's a common misconception. After armored training, we go through mounted training on horseback in Windsor for six months where we learn the tools of horseback riding, beginning with bareback training. The final month is spent in London training in full state uniform.

LG: Do the horses ever act up?

A: Yes, but it's natural. During the Queen's Jubilee Parade, with three million people lining the Mall, to expect any animal to be fully relaxed is absurd. The horses rely on the rider to give them confidence. If the guard is riding the horses confidently and strongly, the horse will settle down.

LG: Your uniforms look pretty heavy. Are they comfortable?

A: They're not comfortable at all. They were designed way back in Queen Victoria's time, and the

MAJOR SIGHTS

■ **WESTMINSTER ABBEY.** Founded as a Benedictine monastery, Westminster Abbey has become a house of kings and queens living and dead. Almost nothing remains of St. Edward's Abbey; Henry III's 13th-century Gothic reworking created most of the current grand structure. Britons buried or commemorated inside the Abbey include: **Henry VII, Mary, Queen of Scots, Elizabeth I** and the scholars and artists honored in the **"Poet's Corner"** (Chaucer, Dylan Thomas, the Brontë sisters, Jane Austen, Handel, and Shakespeare). A door off the east cloister leads to the octagonal **Chapter House,** the original meeting place of the House of Commons with a 13th-century tiled floor. Next to the Abbey (through the cloisters), the lackluster **Abbey Museum** is housed in the Norman undercroft. The highlights of the collection are medieval royal **funeral effigies,** undergarments and all.

St. Margaret's Church, just north of the Abbey, enjoys a strange status: as a part of the Royal Peculiar it is not under the jurisdiction of the diocese of England or the archbishop of Canterbury. It was built for local residents by Abbey monks and has been beautifully restored in the past few years. Since 1614, it's been the official worshipping place of the House of Commons—the first few pews are cordoned off for the Speaker, Black Rod (an official of Parliament), and other dignitaries. *(Parliament Sq. Access Old Monastery, Cloister, and Garden from Dean's Yard, behind the Abbey. ⊖Westminster. Abbey ☎7654 4900, Chapter House 7222 5152; www.westminster-abbey.org. No photography. Abbey open M-Tu and Th-F 9:30am-3:45pm, W 9:30am-7pm, Sa 9:30am-1:45pm, Su open for services only. Museum open daily 10:30am-4pm. Partially wheelchair-accessible. Abbey and Museum £10, students and children 11-17 £7, families of 4 £24. Services free. 1½hr. tours £5 Apr.-Oct. M-F 10, 10:30, 11am, 2, 2:30pm, Sa 10, 10:30, 11am; Oct.-Mar. M-F 10:30, 11am, 2, 2:30pm, Sa 10:30, 11am. Audio tours £4 available M-F 9:30am-3pm, Sa 9:30am-1pm. AmEx/MC/V.)*

THE TOWER OF LONDON. The turrets of this multifunctional block—serving as palace, prison, royal mint, and museum over the past 900 years—are impressive not only for their appearance but also for their integral role in England's history. A popular way to get a feel for the Tower is to join one of the theatrical ■**Yeoman Warders' Tours.** Queen Anne Boleyn passed through **Traitor's Gate** just before her death, but entering the Tower is no longer as perilous as it used to be. St. Thomas's Tower begins the self-guided tour of the **Medieval Palace.** At the end of the **Wall Walk**—a series of eight towers—is **Martin Tower,** which houses an exhibit that traces the history of the

British Crown and is now home to a fascinating collection of retired crowns (without the gemstones that have been recycled into the current models); informative plaques are much better here than in the **Jewel House,** where the crown jewels are held. With the exception of the Coronation Spoon, everything dates from after 1660, since Cromwell melted down the original booty. The centerpiece of the fortress is **White Tower,** which begins with the first-floor **Chapel of St. John the Evangelist.** Outside, **Tower Green** is a lovely grassy area—not so lovely, though, for those once executed there. *(Tower Hill, next to Tower Bridge, within easy reach of the South Bank and the East End. ⊖Tower Hill or DLR: Tower Gateway. ☎0870 751 5175, ticket sales 0870 756 6060; www.hrp.org.uk. Open Mar.-Oct. M 10am-6pm, Tu-Sa 9am-6pm, Su 10am-6pm; buildings close at 5:30pm, last entry 5pm; Nov.-Feb. all closing times 1hr. earlier. Tower Green open only by Yeoman tours, after 4:30pm, or for daily services. Admission £16, concessions £13, children 5-15 £9.50, children under 5 free, families of 5 £45. Tickets also sold at Tube stations; buy them in advance to avoid long queues at the door. Tours: "Yeoman Warders' Tours" meet near entrance; 1hr., every 30min. M and Su 10am-3:30pm, Tu-Sa 9:30am-3:30pm. Audio tours £3.50, concessions £2.50.)*

▧ ST. PAUL'S CATHEDRAL. Majestic St. Paul's is a cornerstone of London's architectural and historical legacy and an obvious tourist magnet. Architect Christopher Wren's masterpiece is the 5th cathedral to occupy the site; the original was built in AD 604. In 1668, after Old St. Paul's had been swept away in the Great Fire, construction began on the current cathedral. Inside, the **nave** leads to the second-tallest free-standing dome in Europe (after St. Peter's in the Vatican), its height accentuated by the tricky perspective of the paintings on the inner surface. The first stop to scaling the heights yourself is the narrow **Whispering Gallery,** reachable by 259 shallow wooden steps. None of the galleries are wheelchair-accessible, and the first climb is the only one that isn't steep, narrow, or slightly strenuous. Climbing the stairs is exhausting, but the views from the top of the dome are incredible and well worth the effort. Circling the base of the inner dome, the Whispering Gallery is a perfect resounding chamber: whisper into the wall, and your friend on the other side will hear you—or, theoretically, they could if everyone else weren't trying the same thing. Far, far below the lofty dome, the **crypt** is packed wall-to-wall with plaques and tombs of great Britons and, of course, the ubiquitous gift shop. Nelson commands a prime location, with radiating galleries of gravestones and tributes honoring other military heroes, from Epstein's bust of T.E.

leather trousers and boots are very solid. The uniform weighs about 3 stone [about 45 lb.].

LG: How do you overcome the itches, sneezes, and bees?

A: Discipline is instilled in every British soldier during training. We know not to move a muscle while on parade no matter what the provocation or distraction— unless, of course, it is a security matter. But our helmets are akin to wearing a boiling kettle on your head; to relieve the pressure, sometimes we use the back of our sword blade to ease the back of the helmet forward.

LG: How do you make the time pass while on duty?

A: The days are long. At Whitehall the shift system is derived upon inspection in Barracks. Smarter men work on horseback in the boxes in shifts from 10am-4pm; less smart men work on foot from 7am-8pm. Some guys count the number of buses that drive past. Unofficially, there are lots of pretty girls around here, and we *are* allowed to move our eyeballs.

LG: What has been your funniest distraction attempt?

A: One day a taxi pulled up, and out hopped four Playboy bunnies, who then posed for a photo shoot right in front of us. You could call that a distraction if you like.

Time: 8-9hr.

Distance: 2.5 mi. (4km)

When To Go: Begin at 8am.

Start: ⊖Tower Hill

Finish: ⊖Westminster

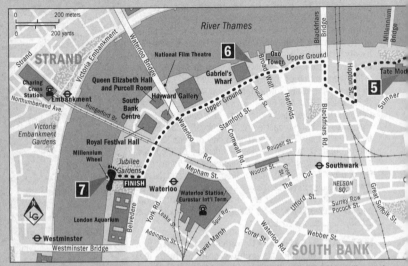

THE MILLENNIUM MILE

A stroll along the South Bank is a trip through history and back again. Across the river you will pass the timeless monuments of London's past, like the Tower of London and St. Paul's Cathedral, while next to you the round glass sphere of City Hall and the converted power facility of the Tate provide a stark, modern contrast. Whether it's a search for Shakespeare and Picasso that brings you to the South Bank, or just a hankering for a nice walk, you will find yourself rewarded.

1. TOWER OF LONDON. Begin your trek to the Tower **early** to avoid the crowds. Tours given by the Yeomen Warders meet every 1½hr. near the entrance. Listen as they expertly recount tales of royal conspiracy, treason, and murder. See the **White Tower,** once a fortress and residence of kings. Shiver at the executioner's stone on the tower green and pay your respects at the Chapel of St. Peter ad Vinculum, holding the remains of three queens. First, get the dirt on the gemstones at **Martin Tower,** then wait in line to see the **Crown Jewels.** The jewels include such glittering lovelies as the First Star of Africa, the largest cut diamond in the world (p. 110). Time: 2hr.

2. TOWER BRIDGE. An engineering wonder that puts its plainer sibling, the London Bridge, to shame. Marvel at its beauty, but skip the Tower Bridge Experience. Better yet, call in advance to inquire what times the Tower drawbridge is lifted (p. 116). Time: no need to stop walking; take in the mechanics as you head to the next sight.

3. DESIGN MUSEUM. On Butler's Wharf, let the Design Museum introduce you to the latest innovations in contemporary design. See what's to come in the forward-looking Review Gallery or hone in on individual designers and products in the Temporary Gallery (p. 129). From the museum, walk along the **Queen's Walk.** To your left you will find the **HMS Belfast,** which was launched in 1938 and led the landing for D-Day, 1944. Time: 1hr.

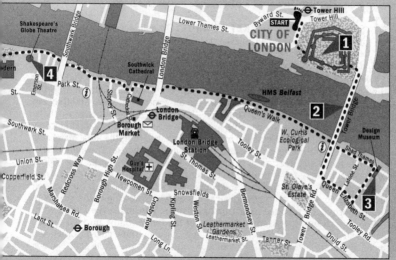

4. SHAKESPEARE'S GLOBE THEATRE. "I hope to see London once ere I die," says Shakespeare's Davy in *Henry IV*. In time, he may see it from the beautiful recreation of The Bard's most famous theater. Excellent exhibits demonstrate how Shakespearean actors dressed and the secrets of stage effects, and tell of the painstaking process of rebuilding of the theater almost 400 years after the original burned down (p. 120). You might be able to catch a matinee performance if you time your visit right. Call in advance for tour and show times. Time: 1hr. for tour; 3hr. for performance.

5. TATE MODERN. It's hard to imagine anything casting a shadow over the Globe Theatre, but the massive former Bankside Power Station does just that. One of the world's premier Modern art museums, the Tate promises a new spin on well-known favorites and works by emerging British artists. Be sure to catch one of the informative docent tours and don't forget to check out the rotating installation in the Turbine Room (p. 126). Time: 2hr.

6. GABRIEL'S WHARF. Check out the cafes, bars, and boutiques of colorful **Gabriel's Wharf.** If you missed the top floor of the Tate Modern, go to the public viewing gallery on the 8th fl. of the **OXO Tower Wharf.** On your way to the London Eye, stop by the **South Bank Centre.** Established as a primary cultural center in 1951, it now exhibits a range of music from Philharmonic extravaganzas to low-key jazz. You may even catch one of the free lunchtime or afternoon events. Call in advance for dates and times. Time: 1½hr. for schmoozing and dinner.

7. LONDON EYE. The London Eye has firmly established itself as one of London's top attractions, popular with locals and tourists alike. The Eye offers amazing 360° views from its glass pods; you may be able to see all of London lit up at sunset. Book in advance to minimize queue time (p. 121). Time: 1hr.

Lawrence (of Arabia) to a plaque commemorating the casualties of the Gulf War. *(St. Paul's Churchyard. ⊖St. Paul's. ☎ 7246 8350; www.stpauls.co.uk. Open M-Sa 8:30am-4pm; last admission 3:45pm. Dome and galleries open M-Sa 9:30am-4pm. Open for worship daily 7:15am-6pm. Partially wheelchair-accessible. Admission £9.50, concessions £8.50, children 7-16 £3.50; worshippers free. Group of 10 or more 50p discount per ticket. "Supertour" M-F 11, 11:30am, 1:30, 2pm; £3, concessions £2.50, children 7-16 £1; English only. Audio tour available in many languages daily 9am-3:30pm; £3.50, concessions £3.)*

ST. PAUL'S FOR POCKET CHANGE. To gain access to the Cathedral's nave for free, attend an Evensong service (M-Sa 5pm, 45min.). Arrive at 4:50pm to be admitted to seats in the quire.

BUCKINGHAM PALACE. The Palace is open to visitors from the very end of July to the end of September every year. Don't expect to find any insights into the Queen's personal life—the **State Rooms** are the only rooms on view, and they are used only for formal occasions. "God Save the Queen" is the rallying cry at the **Queens Gallery,** dedicated to changing exhibits of jaw-droppingly valuable items from the Royal Collection. Detached from the palace and tour, the **Royal Mews** acts as a museum, stable, riding school, and working carriage house. The main attraction is the Queen's collection of coaches, including the Cinderella-like "Glass Coach" used to carry royal brides, including Diana, to their weddings, and the State Coaches of Australia, Ireland, and Scotland. Another highlight is the four-ton **Gold State Coach,** which can occasionally be seen wheeling around the streets in the early morning on practice runs for major events. To witness the Palace without the cost, attend a session of **Changing of the Guard.** Show up well before 11:30am and stand in front of the Palace in view of the morning guards, or use the steps of the Victoria Memorial as a vantage point. *(At the end of the Mall, between Westminster, Belgravia, and Mayfair. ⊖St. James's Park, Victoria, Green Park, or Hyde Park Corner. ☎ 7766 7324; www.the-royal-collection.com. Palace open from late July to late Sept. daily 9:30am-6:30pm, last admission 4:15pm. £15, students £13.50, children 6-17 £8.50, under 5 free, families of 5 £69.50. Advance booking is recommended; required for disabled visitors. Queens Gallery open daily 10am-5:30pm, last admission 4:30pm. Wheelchair-accessible. £8, concessions £7, families £22. Royal Mews open from late July to late Sept. daily 10am-5pm, last admission 4:15pm; Mar.-July and from late Sept. to late Oct. M-Th and Sa-Su 11am–4pm, last admission 3:15pm. Wheelchair-accessible. £7, seniors £6, children under 17 £4.50, families £18.50. Changing of the Guard from Apr. to late July daily, Aug.-Mar. every other day, excepting the Queen's absence, inclement weather, or pressing state functions. Free.)*

THE HOUSES OF PARLIAMENT. The Palace of Westminster has been home to both the House of Lords and the House of Commons (together known as Parliament) since the 11th century, when Edward the Confessor established his court here. Standing guard on the northern side of the building, the **Clock Tower** is famously nicknamed **Big Ben,** after the robustly proportioned Benjamin Hall, a former Commissioner of Works. "Big Ben" actually refers only to the 14-ton bell that hangs inside the tower. **Victoria Tower,** at the south end of the palace building, contains copies of every Act of Parliament since 1497. Sir Charles Barry rebuilt the tower in the 1850s after it burned down in 1834; his design won an anonymous competition, and his symbol, the portcullis, still remains the official symbol of the Houses of Parliament. A flag flying from the top indicates that Parliament is in session. When the Queen is in the building, a special royal banner is flown instead of the Union flag. Visitors with enough patience or luck to make it inside the chambers can hear the occasional debates between members of both the House of Lords and the House of Commons. *(Parliament Sq., in Westminster. Queue for both Houses forms at St. Stephen's entrance, between Old and New Palace Yards. ⊖Westminster.*

☎ 08709 063 773; www.parliament.uk/visiting/visiting.cfm. "Line of Route" Tour: includes both Houses. UK residents can contact their MPs for tours year-round, generally M-W mornings and F. Foreign visitors may tour Aug.-Sept. Book online, by phone, or in person at Abingdon Green ticket office (open mid-July) across from Palace of Westminster. Open Aug. M-Tu and F-Sa 9:15am-4:30pm, W-Th 1:15-4:30pm; Sept. M and F-Sa 9:15am-4:30pm, Tu-Th 1:15-4:30pm. 75min. tours depart every few min. £12, students £8, families of 4 £30. MC/V.)

 PARLIAMENTARY PROCEDURE. Arrive early in the afternoon to minimize the wait, which often exceeds 2hr. Keep in mind that the wait for Lords is generally shorter than the wait for Commons. To sit in on Parliament's "question time" (40min.; M-W 2:30pm, Th-F 11am), apply for tickets several weeks in advance through your embassy in London.

BY NEIGHBORHOOD

BLOOMSBURY

BRITISH LIBRARY. Castigated during its long construction by traditionalists for being too modern and by modernists for being too traditional, the new British Library building (opened in 1998) now impresses haters with its stunning interior. Most of the library is underground, with 12 million books on 200 mi. of shelving; the above-ground brick building is home to cavernous reading rooms and an engrossing museum. Displayed in a glass cube toward the rear of the building, the 65,000 volumes of the King's Library were collected by George III and bequeathed to the nation in 1823 by his less bookish son, George IV. The plaza out front offers a series of free concerts and events, although the integrated restaurant, cafes, and coffee bars are overpriced. (96 Euston Rd. ➔ Euston Sq. or King's Cross St. Pancras. ☎ 7412 7332; www.bl.uk. Open M 9:30am-6pm, Tu 9:30am-8pm, W-F 9:30am-6pm, Sa 9:30am-5pm, Su 11am-5pm. Tours of public areas M, W, F 3pm; Sa 10:30am and 3pm. Tours including one of the reading rooms Su and bank holidays 11:30am and 3pm. Reservations recommended. Wheelchair-accessible. To use reading rooms, bring 2 forms of ID—1 with a signature and 1 with a home address. Free. Tours £8, concessions £6.50. Audio tours £3.50, concessions £2.50.)

OTHER BLOOMSBURY SIGHTS. A co-founder and key advisor of **University College London**—the first in Britain to ignore race, creed, and politics in admissions and, later, the first to allow women to sit for degrees—social philosopher Jeremy Bentham still watches over his old haunts; his body has sat on display in the South Cloister since 1850, wax head and all. (Main entrance on Gower St. South Cloister entrance through the courtyard. ➔ Euston. ☎ 7679 2000; www.ucl.ac.uk. Quadrangle gates close at midnight; access to Jeremy Bentham ends at 6pm. Wheelchair-accessible. Free.) Next to the British Library are the soaring Gothic spires of **St. Pancras Chambers.** Formerly housing the Midland Grand Hotel, today the gorgeous red brick building is a hollow shell being developed as apartments and a five-star hotel. (Euston Rd. just west of the King's Cross St. Pancras Tube station. ➔ King's Cross St. Pancras.)

CHELSEA

ROYAL HOSPITAL. The environs of the Royal Hospital—including a chapel, a small museum detailing the history of the hospital, and a retirement home—house the Chelsea Pensioners, who totter around the grounds as they have done since 1692. The main draw is the once ritzy **Ranelagh Gardens.** They're a quiet oasis for picnics and park-playing—except during the **Chelsea Flower Show** in late May, when the braying masses of the Royal Horticultural Society descend en masse. (2 entrance gates on Royal Hospital Rd. ➔ Sloane Sq., then bus #137. ☎ 7881 5200; www.chelsea-pensioners.co.uk. Museum, Great Hall, and chapel open daily 10am-noon and 2-

4pm; museum closed Su Oct.-Mar. Grounds open Nov.-Mar. M-Sa 10am-4:30pm, Su 2-4:30pm.; Apr. daily 10am-7:30pm, May-Aug. daily 10am-8:30pm, Sept. daily 10am-7pm, Oct. daily 10am-5pm. Wheelchair-accessible. Flower show www.rhs.org.uk; tickets must be purchased well in advance. Admission to Royal Hospital free.)

CHELSEA PHYSIC GARDEN. Founded in 1673 to provide medicinal herbs to locals, the Physic Garden remains a carefully ordered living repository of useful, rare, or just plain interesting plants. It has also played an important historic role, serving as the staging post from which tea was introduced to India and cotton to America. Today, the garden is a quiet place for picnics, teas, and scenic walks. You can purchase flora on display. *(66 Royal Hospital Rd.; entrance on Swan Walk. ⊖Sloane Sq., then bus #137. ☎7352 5646; www.chelseaphysicgarden.co.uk. Open early Apr.-Oct. W noon-9pm, Th-F noon-6pm, Su noon-6pm; during Chelsea Flower Show in late May and Chelsea Festival in mid-June M-F noon-5pm. Tea served daily from 12:30pm, Su from noon. Call in advance for wheelchair access. £7, students and children under 16 £4.)*

THE CITY OF LONDON

GUILDHALL. This used to be the administrative center of the Corporation of London, but the Lord Mayor and his associates have since moved to more modern digs in the surrounding area in the City and on the South Bank. Before heading into the building itself, take a moment in the open stone **Guildhall Yard,** which is usually empty. The towering Gothic building dates from 1440, although after repeated remodeling in the 17th and 18th centuries—not to mention almost complete reconstruction following the Great Fire and the Blitz—little of the original remains. Still, the hall maintains its style and skeleton; there are statues and gargoyles inside to preserve the Gothic image. The stained-glass windows bear the names of all Mayors and Lord Mayors of the Corporation, past and present—the builders must have foreseen the City's longevity, since there is still room for about 700 more. The downstairs crypt is only open by guided tour. Guildhall is more often than not closed for events, but arrive early and you might be able to pop in for a look. The **Guildhall Library,** in the 1970s annex and accessed via Aldermanbury or the Yard, specializes in the history of London. Its unparalleled collection of microfilm and books is a must for any serious history scholar. It houses the **Guildhall Clockmaker's Museum** as well. *(Off Gresham St. Enter the Guildhall through the low, modern annex; entrance for library on Aldermanbury. ⊖St. Paul's, Moorgate, or Bank. Guildhall: ☎7606 3030, for occasional tour information 7606 3030, ext. 1463. Open May-Sept. daily 10am-5pm; Sept. weekends are open-house; Oct.-Apr. M-Sa 10am-5pm. Last admission 4:30pm. Free. Library ☎7332 1862. Open M-Sa 9:30am-5pm. Free.)*

MONUMENT. The only non-ecclesiastical Wren building in the City, the Monument was built to commemorate the devastating Great Fire of 1666. Finished in 1677, the 202 ft. column stands 202 ft. from the bakery on Pudding Ln. where the fire first broke out. The colossal monument can only be scaled by climbing the very narrow spiral staircase inside. The climb brings you close to the copper urn of flames that caps the pillar, a mythic reminder of the fire. The enclosed platform at the top, however, offers one of the best views of London, especially of the Tower Bridge. The brave who make the steep climb are rewarded with a certificate of completion on the way out—the best souvenir. *(Monument St. ⊖Monument. ☎7626 2717. Open daily 9:30am-5pm; last admission 4:40pm. £2.50, children £1. The Monument and the Tower Bridge Exhibition (p. 116) offer joint admission £7, concessions £5, children £3.50.*

TOWER BRIDGE. Not to be mistaken for its plainer sibling, London Bridge, Tower Bridge is the one you know from all the London-based movies. A relatively new construction—built in 1894—its impressive stature and bright blue suspension cables connect the banks of the Thames and rise above the many other bridges in the area. A marvel of engineering, the steam-powered lifting mechanism remained in use until 1973, when electric motors took over. Although clippers no longer sail into London very often, there's still enough large river traffic for the bridge to be lifted around 1000 times per year and five or six times per day in the summer. Call for the schedule or check the signs posted at each entrance. Historians and technophiles will appreciate the **Tower Bridge Exhibition,** which combines scenic 140 ft. glass-enclosed walkways with videos presenting a history of the bridge. *(Entrance to the Tower Bridge Exhibition is through the west side upriver of the North Tower. ⊖Tower Hill or London Bridge. ☎7403 3761, for lifting schedule 7940 3984; www.towerbridge.org.uk. Open daily Apr.-Sept. 10am-6:30pm, last entry 5:30pm; Oct.-Mar. 9:30am-6pm, last entry 5pm. Wheelchair-accessible. £6, concessions £4.50, children 5-16 £3.)*

ALL HALLOWS-BY-THE-TOWER. Nearly hidden by redevelopment projects and nearby office buildings, All Hallows bears its longevity with pride. Just inside the entrance on the left stands the oldest part of the church, a Saxon arch dating from AD 675. The main chapel has three parts: the right and left transepts date from the 13th and 14th centuries, respectively, and the central ceiling from the 20th. The undercroft museum is home to a diverse collection of Roman and Saxon artifacts, medieval art, and church record books from the time of the plague, all well worth a look. The spectacular Lady Chapel is home to a magnificent altarpiece dating from the 15th century and has been restored to look like it did when it was built in 1489. The stark cement arches and barred windows of the nave, rebuilt after the Blitz, give this church a mysterious and impressive dignity. *(Byward St. ⊖Tower Hill. ☎7481 2928; www.allhallowsbythetower.org.uk. Church open M-F 8:30am-5:45pm, Su 9:30am-5pm; crypt and museum open daily 10:30am-4pm. Free.)*

OTHER CITY OF LONDON SIGHTS. The most famous modern structure in the City is **Lloyd's of London.** What looks like a towering postmodern factory is actually the home of the world's largest insurance market, built in 1986. With raw metal ducts, lifts, and chutes on the outside, it wears its heart (or at least its internal organs) on its sleeve. *(Leadenhall St. ⊖Bank. Wheelchair-accessible.)* Only the tower and outer walls remain of Wren's **St. Dunstan-in-the-East.** The blitzed, mossy ruins have been converted into a stunning garden and peaceful picnic spot. Vines cover the Gothic-style walls, and a bubbling fountain surrounded by benches makes it an oasis in the City. *(St. Dunstan's Hill. ⊖Monument or Tower Hill. Wheelchair-accessible.)*

CLERKENWELL AND HOLBORN

Clerkenwell buildings are beautiful from the outside but inaccessible to tourists; walk the **Clerkenwell Historic Trail.** (Free maps available at the 3 Things Coffee Room, 53 Clerkenwell Close. ☎7125 37438. ⊖Farringdon. Open daily 8am-8pm.)

▨**THE TEMPLE.** The Temple is a complex of buildings that derives its name from the crusading Order of the Knights Templar, which embraced this site as its English seat in 1185. Today the Temple houses legal and parliamentary offices, but its charming network of gardens and its medieval church remain open to the enterprising visitor. Make sure to check out the **Inner Temple Gateway,** between 16 and 17 Fleet St., the 1681 fountain of **Fountain Court** (featured in Dickens's *Martin Chizzlewit*) and **Elm Court,** tucked behind the church, a tiny yet exquisite garden ringed by massive stone structures. *(Between Essex St. and Temple Ave.; church courtyard off Middle Temple Ln. ⊖Temple or Blackfriars. Free.)*

  Temple Church is one of the finest surviving medieval round churches and London's first Gothic church, completed in 1185 on the model of Jerusalem's Church of the Holy Sepulchre. Intricately crafted stained-glass windows, towering ceilings, an original Norman doorway, and 10 armored effigies complete the impressive interior, although much of it was rebuilt after WWII bombings. Adjoining the round church is a rectangular Gothic choir, built in 1240, with 1682 altar screen by Christopher Wren. The church hosts frequent recitals and musical services, including weekly organ recitals. *(☎ 7353 3470. Hours vary depending on the week's services and are posted outside the door of the church for the coming week. Organ recitals W 1:15-1:45pm; no services Aug.-Sept.)*

The Middle Temple escaped the destruction of WWII and retains fine examples of 16th- and 17th-century architecture. In Middle Temple Hall (closed to the public), Elizabeth I saw Shakespeare act in the premiere of *Twelfth Night*, and his *Henry VI* points to Middle Temple Garden as the origin of the red and white flowers that served as emblems in the War of the Roses. *(Open May-Sept. M-F noon-3pm.)*

ROYAL COURTS OF JUSTICE. This massive Neo-Gothic structure, designed in 1874 by G.E. Street, holds its own among the distinguished facades of Fleet St. Inside are 88 courtrooms, chambers for judges and court staff, and cells for defendants. The architecture is impressive, more akin to a castle than a courthouse. Exterior views from Carey St. are also quite amazing, and the Great Hall features Europe's largest mosaic floor. Skip the uninspired display of legal costume at the rear of the Great Hall and instead watch the real thing. The back bench of every courtroom is open to the public during trials unless the courtroom door says "In Chambers." The notice boards beside the Enquiry Desk in the Great Hall display a list of cases being tried. *(Where the Strand becomes Fleet St.; rear entrance on Carey St. ⊖Temple or Chancery Ln. ☎ 7947 6000, tours 7947 7684. Open M-F 9am-4:30pm; cases are heard 10:30am-1pm and 2-4pm. Wheelchair-accessible. Be prepared to go through a security checkpoint with metal detector. Free. Tours £6.)*

OTHER CLERKENWELL AND HOLBORN SIGHTS. The mid-13th-century **Church of St. Etheldreda** is the last remaining vestige of the Bishop of Ely's palace and the only pre-Reformation Catholic church in the city. *(In Ely Place. ☎ 7405 1061. Church open daily 7:30am-7pm. Free.)* The unusual spire of Wren's 1675 **St. Bride's Church** is one of the most imitated pieces of architecture in the world: a local baker used it as the model for the first-ever multi-tiered wedding cake. *(St. Bride's Ave., just off Fleet St. ⊖Blackfriars. ☎ 7427 0133; www.stbrides.com. Open daily 8am-4:45pm. Lunchtime concerts and nighttime classical music; call for details. Free.)* Legend places **St. Clement Danes Church** over the tomb of Harold Harefoot, a Danish warlord who settled here in the 9th century. Its fame with Londoners derives from its opening role in the famous nursery rhyme—"Oranges and Lemons Say the Bells of St. Clement's," and they still do, daily, at 9am, noon, 3, and 6pm. *(186a Fleet St. ⊖Temple or ⊖Chancery Ln. ☎ 7405 1929; www.stdunstaninthewest.org. Open Tu 11am-3pm. Free.)*

KENSINGTON AND EARL'S COURT

■**HYDE PARK AND KENSINGTON GARDENS.** Surrounded by London's wealthiest neighborhoods, Hyde Park has served as the model for city parks around the world, including Central Park in New York and Paris's Bois de Boulogne. **Kensington Gardens,** contiguous with Hyde Park and originally part of it, was created in the late 17th century when William and Mary set up house in Kensington Palace. *(Framed by Kensington Rd., Knightsbridge, Park Ln., and Bayswater Rd. ⊖Queensway, Lancaster Gate, Marble Arch, Hyde Park Corner, or High St. Kensington. ☎ 7298 2100; www.royalparks.org.uk. Open daily 6am-dusk. Admission free. "Liberty Drive" rides available Tu-F 10am-5pm for seniors and the disabled; call ☎ 077 6749 8096. A full program of music, performance, and children's activities takes place during the summer; see park notice boards for details.)* In the middle of the park is the **Serpentine,** officially known as the "Long Water West of the Serpentine Bridge." Dog-paddling tourists and boaters have made it London's busiest swimming hole. Nowhere near the water, the **Serpentine Gallery** holds contemporary art and is free and open to the public daily from 10am-6pm. *(⊖Hyde Park Corner. Boating: ☎ 7262 1330. Open daily Apr.-Sept. 10am-5pm 6pm or later in fine weather. £4 per person for 30min., £6 per hr.; children £1.50/2.50. Swimming at the Lido, south shore; ☎ 7706 3422. Open daily from June to early Sept. 10am-5:30pm. Lockers and sun lounges avail-*

able. £3.50, £2.80 after 4pm, students £2.50/1.60, children 80p/60p, families £8. Gallery open daily 10am-5pm. Free.) At the northeast corner of the park, near **Marble Arch,** you can see free speech in action as proselytizers, politicos, and flat-out crazies dispense wisdom to bemused tourists at **Speaker's Corner** on Sundays, the only place in London where demonstrators can assemble without a permit.

KENSINGTON PALACE. In 1689, William and Mary commissioned Christopher Wren to remodel Nottingham House into a palace. Kensington remained the principal royal residence until George III decamped to Kew in 1760, but it is still in use—Princess Diana was the most famous recent inhabitant. Royalty fanatics can tour the rather underwhelming Hanoverian **State Apartments,** with *trompe l'œil* paintings by William Kent. More impressive is the **Royal Ceremonial Dress Collection,** a magnificent spread of tailored and embroidered garments. *(Western edge of Kensington Gardens; enter through the park. ⊖High St. Kensington, Notting Hill Gate, or Queensway. ☎ 7937 9561; www.royalresidences.com. Open daily 10am-6pm, last admission 1hr. before closing. Wheelchair-accessible. £12, students £10, children 5-15 £6, families of 5 (no more than 2 people over 15) £33. Combo passes with Tower of London or Hampton Court available. MC/V.)*

HOLLAND PARK. Smaller and less touristed than Kensington Gardens, Holland Park probably makes for a better picnic spot or quiet stroll than Hyde Park. Off Kensington High St. and full of shady paths, the grounds also offer open fields, popular soccer pitches, a golf bunker, cricket nets, tennis courts, and Japanese gardens. *(Bordered by Kensington High St., Holland Walk, and Abbotsbury Rd. Enter at Commonwealth Institute. ⊖High St. Kensington. ☎ 7471 9813, police 7441 9811, sport league and recreation info 7602 2226; Open daily 7:30am-dusk. Free.)*

KNIGHTSBRIDGE AND BELGRAVIA

▨**APSLEY HOUSE.** Named for Baron Apsley, the house later known as "No. 1, London" was bought in 1817 by the Duke of Wellington, whose heirs still occupy a modest suite on the top floor. Most visitors come for Wellington's fine art collection, much of which was given to him by the crowned heads of Europe following the Battle of Waterloo. Most of the old masters hang in the Waterloo Gallery, where the duke held his annual Waterloo banquet around the stupendous silver centerpiece, which is now displayed in the dining room. *(Hyde Park Corner. ⊖Hyde Park Corner. ☎ 7499 5676; www.english-heritage.org.uk/london. Open Apr.-Oct. Tu-Su 10am-5pm; Nov.-Mar. Tu-Su 10am-4pm. Wheelchair-accessible. £5.30, students £4, children 5-18 £2.70. Joint ticket with Wellington Arch £7/5.20/3.50. Audio tour free. MC/V.)*

WELLINGTON ARCH. Standing at the center of London's most infamous intersection, the Wellington Arch was ignored by tourists and Londoners alike until April 2001, when the completion of a restoration project revealed the interior to the public for the first time. Exhibits on the building's history and the changing nature of war memorials play second fiddle to the two observation platforms which provide nice views of Buckingham Palace gardens, Green Park, and Hyde Park. *(Hyde Park Corner. ⊖Hyde Park Corner. ☎ 7930 2726; www.english-heritage.org.uk/london. Open W-Su Apr.-Oct. 10am-5pm, Nov.-Mar. 10am-4pm. Wheelchair-accessible. £3.20, students with ISIC £2.40, children 5-16 £1.60. Joint tickets with Apsley House available. MC/V.)*

MARYLEBONE AND REGENT'S PARK

▨**REGENT'S PARK.** When Crown Architect John Nash designed Regent's Park, he envisioned a residential development for the "wealthy and good." Fortunately for us commonfolk, Parliament opened the space to all in 1811, creating London's most popular and attractive recreation area. Most of the park's top attractions and activities lie near the **Inner Circle,** a road that separates the regal, meticulously maintained ▨**Queen Mary's Gardens** from the rest of the grounds. While the few villas in the park—**The Holme** and **St. John's Lodge**—are private residences for the unimaginably rich and are not available for public viewing, the formal **Gardens of St. John's Lodge** ("The Secret Garden"), on the northern edge of the Inner Circle, provide a peek into the backyard of one such mansion. The climb up **Primrose Hill**, just north of Regent's Park proper, offers an impressive view of central London. The famous **Open Air Theatre**, which began in 1932, is now Britain's premier outdoor Shakespeare theater and stages performances from May to Sept. (⊖*Baker St., Regent's Park, Great Portland St., or Camden Town. ☎7486 7905, police 7706 7272; www.royalparks.org. Open daily 5am-dusk. Free.*)

LONDON ZOO. First opened in 1826, the London Zoo has a range of expansive and completely modern exhibits along with a few less-current bars-and-cement enclosures. The very oldest buildings are now considered too small to house animals and instead test parents with an array of stuffed toys at exorbitant prices. Perennial zoo favorites include the itch-inducing **BUGS!** (complete with American cockroaches devouring a messy kitchen), the jungle-like **primate** house, and the **komodo dragon** exhibit. For up-close-and-personal interaction, head to the **Meet the Monkeys** exhibit, an enclosed area where guests and playful squirrel monkeys can mingle. Pick up a Daily Event Planner leaflet to catch all the free special displays and keeper talks. (*Main gate on Outer Circle, Regent's Park.* ⊖*Camden Town plus a 10-15min. walk guided by signs or a short ride on bus #274. ☎7722 3333; www.zsl.org. Open daily Apr.-Oct. 10am-5:30pm; Nov.-Mar. 10am-4pm. Last admission 1hr. before closing. Wheelchair-accessible. Admission £14.50, children 3-15 £11, family of 4 £48.50, concessions £13. AmEx/MC/V.*)

MADAME TUSSAUD'S. It may be one of London's top tourist attractions, but Madame Tussaud's is the most expensive round-the-block queue in the entire city. For those unwilling to pass up a photo-op with wax models of everyone from Pope John Paul II to Tom Cruise, it is at least an indisputably unique 1½hr. experience. The Spirit of London ride inside brings back memories of old-fashioned carnivals. (*Marylebone Rd.* ⊖*Baker St. ☎0870 999 0293; www.madame-tussauds.com. Open Jan.-June and Sept.-Dec. M-F 9:30am-5:30pm, Sa-Su 9am-6pm; Jul.-Aug. daily 9am-6pm. Wheelchair-accessible. Prices depend on day of the week, entrance time, and season. Admission £14-23, under 16 £7-17. "Chamber Live" exhibit adds £2. Advance booking by phone or online £2 extra; groups of 10+ approx. £1.50 less per person. Call in advance to ensure. AmEx/MC/V.*)

THE SOUTH BANK

■ **SHAKESPEARE'S GLOBE THEATRE.** This incarnation of the Globe is faithful to the original, thatch roof and all. The original burned down in 1613 after a 14-year run as the Bard's preferred playhouse. Today's reconstruction had its first full season in 1997 and now stands as the cornerstone of the International Shakespeare Globe Centre. The informative exhibit inside covers the theatre's history and includes displays on costumes and customs of the theatre, as well as information on other prominent playwrights of Shakespeare's era. There's also an interactive display where you get to trade lines with recorded Globe actors. Try to arrive in time for a tour of the theatre itself. Tours that run during a matinee skip the Globe but are the only way to gain admission to the neighboring **Rose Theatre**, where both Shakespeare and Christopher Marlowe performed. For info on performances, see p. 136. (*Bankside, close to Bankside pier.* ⊖*Southwark or London Bridge. ☎7902 1400; www.shakespeares-globe.org. Open daily Apr.-Sept. 9am-noon exhibit and tours and 12:30-5pm exhibit only; Oct.-Apr. 10am-5pm exhibit and tours. Wheelchair-accessible. £9, concessions £7.50, children 5-15 £6.50, families of 5 £20.*)

SOUTHWARK CATHEDRAL. A site of worship since AD 606, the cathedral has undergone numerous transformations in the last 1400 years; it was a convent in 606, a priory in 1106, a parish church in 1540, and finally, a cathedral since 1905.

Shakespeare's brother Edmund is buried here. In the rear of the nave, there are four smaller chapels; the northernmost Chapel of St. Andrew is dedicated to victims of HIV and AIDS. Near the center, the **archaeological gallery** is actually a small excavation by the cathedral wall, revealing a first-century Roman road. *(Montague Close. ⊖London Bridge. ☎7367 6700; www.southwark.anglican.org/cathedral. Open M-F 8am-6pm, Sa-Su 9am-6pm. Wheelchair-accessible. Admission free, suggested donation £4. Groups should book in advance; group rates available. Audio tours £5; concessions £4, children 5-15 £2.50. Camera permit £2; video permit £5.)*

LONDON EYE. Also known as the Millennium Wheel, at 135m (430 ft.) the British Airways London Eye is the biggest observational wheel in the world. The ellipsoidal glass "pods" give uninterrupted views from the top during each 30min. revolution. *(Jubilee Gardens, between County Hall and the Festival Hall. ⊖Waterloo. ☎087 990 8883; www.ba-londoneye.com. Open daily Oct.-May 10am-8pm, June-Sept. 10am-9pm. Wheelchair-accessible. Buy tickets from box office at the corner of County Hall. Advance booking recommended, but check the weather. £14.50, concessions £11, children under 16 £7.25.)*

THE REAL DEAL. While the **London Eye** does offer magnificent views (particularly at night), the queues are long, and it's expensive. For equally impressive sights in a quieter atmosphere, head to the **Monument** (p. 116), **Primrose Hill** (p. 119), or **Hampstead Heath** (p. 124). If you have the cash to spare, do take a 30min. "flight" on the Eye; seeing the city lit up at night is a treat.

THE WEST END

▓**TRAFALGAR SQUARE.** John Nash first suggested laying out this square in 1820, but it took almost 50 years for London's largest traffic roundabout to take on its current appearance. The square is named in commemoration of the defeat of Napoleon's navy at Trafalgar, considered England's greatest naval victory. It has traditionally been a site for public rallies and protest movements, but it is packed with tourists, pigeons, and the ever-ubiquitous black taxis on a daily basis. Towering over the square is the 170 ft. granite **Nelson's Column,** which until recently was one of the world's tallest displays of decades-old pigeon droppings. Now, thanks to a deep-clean sponsored by the Mayor, this monument to naval hero Lord Nelson sparkles once again. *(⊖Charing Cross.)*

ST. MARTIN-IN-THE-FIELDS. The 4th church to stand here, James Gibbs's 1726 creation is instantly recognizable: the rectangular portico building supporting a soaring steeple made it the model for countless Georgian churches in Ireland and America. Handel and Mozart both performed here, and the church hosts frequent concerts. In order to support the cost of keeping the church open, a delicious cafe (p. 107), book shop, and art gallery dwell in the Crypt. *(St. Martin's Ln., northeast corner of Trafalgar Sq.; crypt entrance on Duncannon St. ⊖Leicester Sq. or Charing Cross. ☎7766 1100; www.smitf.org. Call or visit website for hours and further information.)*

ST. PAUL'S CHURCH. Not to be confused with St. Paul's Cathedral, this 1633 Inigo Jones church is now one of the last remnants of the original square, and is the only Inigo Jones church in London. It follows a double cube design, standing 80 ft. long and 40 ft. high. St. Paul's was part of the introduction of classicism to England. Known as "the actors' church" for its long association with nearby theaters, the interior is festooned with plaques detailing the achievements of Boris Karloff, Vivien Leigh, and Charlie Chaplin. *(On Covent Garden Piazza; enter via the Piazza, King St., Henrietta St., or Bedford St. ⊖Covent Garden. ☎7836 5221; www.actorschurch.org. Open M-F 8:30am-5:30pm. Morning services Su 11am. Evensong 2nd Su of month 4pm. Free.)*

ST. JAMES'S PALACE. Built in 1536 over the remains of a leper hospital, St. James's is London's only remaining palace built as such (Buckingham Palace was a rough-and-ready conversion of a Duke's house). As the official home of the Crown, royal proclamations are issued after the death of a monarch from the balcony in the interior Friary Court. Unless your name starts with "His Royal Highness," the only part you'll get into is the **Chapel Royal,** open for Sunday services from October to Easter at 8:30 and 11:30am. From Easter to July, services are held in Inigo Jones's **Queen's Chapel,** across Marlborough Rd. from the Palace, which was built in the 17th century for the marriage of Prince Charles I. (⊖*Green Park.*)

SOHO. A conglomeration of squares and tourist capitalists, Soho is at least one of the most diverse areas in central London. Old Compton Street is the center of London's GLBT culture. In the 1950s, immigrants from Hong Kong started moving en masse to the few blocks just north of Leicester Sq., around Gerrard St. and grittier Lisle St., which now form Chinatown. Gaudy, brash, and world-famous, Piccadilly Circus is made up of four of the West End's major arteries (Piccadilly, Regent St., Shaftesbury Ave., and the Haymarket). In the middle of all the glitz and neon stands the Gilbert's famous Statue of Eros. (⊖*Piccadilly Circus.*) Lined with tour buses, overpriced clubs, and generic cafes, Leicester Sq. is one destination that Londoners go out of their way to avoid but that attracts sneaker-and-shorts-clad tourists like a magnet. (⊖*Piccadilly Circus or Leicester Sq.*) A calm in the midst of the storm, Soho Square is a rather scruffy patch of green space popular with picnickers. Its removed location makes the square more hospitable and less trafficked than Leicester. (⊖*Tottenham Ct. Rd. Park open daily 10am-dusk.*)

WESTMINSTER

▨**ST. JAMES'S PARK AND GREEN PARK.** The streets leading up to Buckingham Palace are flanked by two expanses of greenery: St. James's Park and Green Park. In the middle of St. James's Park is the placid St. James's Park Lake, where you can catch glimpses of the pelicans that call it home—the lake and the grassy area surrounding it comprise an official waterfowl preserve. In the back corner, closest to the palace, is a children's playground in memory of Princess Diana. Across the Mall, the lush Green Park is the creation of Charles II; it connects Westminster and St. James's. "Constitution Hill" refers not to the King's interest in political theory but to his daily exercises. If you sit on one of the lawn chairs scattered enticingly around both parks, an attendant will magically materialize and demand money. Alternatively, bring a blanket for a picnic at no charge. (*The Mall.* ⊖*St. James's Park or Green Park. Open daily 5am-midnight. Lawn chairs available, weather permitting, June-Aug. 10am-10pm; Mar.-May and Sept.-Oct. 10am-6pm. £2 for 2hr., student deal £30 for the season. Last rental 2hr. before close. Summer walks in the park some M 1-2pm, including tour of Guard's Palace and Victoria Tower Gardens. Book in advance by calling ☎7930 1793.*)

WESTMINSTER CATHEDRAL. Following Henry VIII's divorce from the Catholic Church, London's Catholic community remained without a cathedral until 1884, when the Church purchased a derelict prison on what used to be a monastery site. The Neo-Byzantine church looks somewhat like a fortress and is now one of London's great religious landmarks. An elevator, well worth the minimal fee, carries visitors up the striped 273 ft. bell tower for an all-encompassing view of Westminster, the river, and Kensington. (*Cathedral Piazza, off Victoria St.* ⊖*Victoria.* ☎7798 9055; www.westminstercathedral.org.uk. Open daily 8am-7pm. Free; suggested donation £2. Bell tower open daily 9:30am-12:30pm and 1-5pm. Organ recitals Su 4:45pm.*)

WHITEHALL. Whitehall refers to the stretch of road connecting Trafalgar Sq. with Parliament Sq. and is synonymous with the British civil service. From 1532 until a devastating fire in 1698, it was the home of the monarchy and one of the grandest palaces in Europe, of which very little remains. Toward the north end of Whitehall, Great Scotland Yard marks the former headquarters of the Metropolitan Police.

West End

ACCOMMODATIONS
YHA Oxford Street, 6

FOOD
Busaba Eathai, 11
Cafe in the Crypt, 26
Golden Dragon, 20
Masala Zone, 10
Rock and Sole Plaice, 4

PUBS/BARS
Comptons of Soho, 17
Dog and Duck, 12
Escape, 18
Lab, 13
The Langley, 16

ENTERTAINMENT
Comedy Store, 22
Donmar Warehouse, 14
English National Opera, 24
London Astoria (LA1), 1
Royal Opera House, 15
tkts, 23

SHOPPING
Fortnum & Mason, 25
Liberty, 9
Selfridges, 8

CLUBS
Bar Rumba, 21
Ghetto, 2
Ku Bar, 19

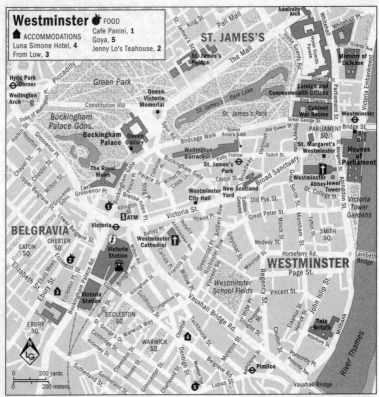

Westminster ● FOOD
▲ ACCOMMODATIONS
Luna Simone Hotel, **4**
From Low, **3**

Cafe Panini, **1**
Goya, **5**
Jenny Lo's Teahouse, **2**

Nearer Parliament Sq., heavily guarded steel gates mark the entrance to **Downing Street.** In 1735, No. 10 was made the official residence of the First Lord of the Treasury, a position that became permanently identified with the Prime Minister. The Chancellor of the Exchequer traditionally resides at No. 11 and the Parliamentary Chief Whip at No. 12. When Tony Blair's family was too big for No. 10, he switched with Gordon Brown, a move that proved convenient when Brown was appointed Prime Minister in 2007. The street is closed to visitors, but if you wait long enough, you might see the PM. South of Downing St., in the middle of Whitehall, Edward Lutyen's **Cenotaph** (1919) stands, a proud tribute to WWI's dead. Many of the islands in the middle of the road hold statues honoring monarchs and military heroes, a testament to the avenue's identity as the center of civil service. *(Between Trafalgar Sq. and Parliament Sq. ❸Westminster, Embankment, or Charing Cross.)*

NORTH LONDON

▧**HAMPSTEAD HEATH.** Unlike so many other London parks, the Heath does not comprise manicured gardens and paths, but wild, spontaneous growth tumbling over rolling pastures and forested groves. Dirt paths through the Heath are not well marked and are as random as the surrounding vegetation; travel in groups and bring a map to avoid getting lost. In the midst of the Heath is ▧**Hill Garden**—unless you're specifically on the lookout for this lovely secret garden, you're unlikely to find it. The flower-encrusted walkway passes over the former kitchen gardens of Lord Leverhulme's (founder of Lever Soap) mansion. (❷Hampstead. Train: Hampstead Heath. Bus #210. Wheelchair-accessible. Open 24hr. Hill Garden: take North End Way to Inverforth Close. Open daily from 8:30am to 1hr. before sunset.)

LORD'S CRICKET GROUND. The most famous cricket ground in England, Lord's is home to the local Marylebone Cricket Club (MCC) and hosts most of London's international matches. Cricket itself is the second-most popular team sport in the world. To see the **Lord's Museum,** home to the **Ashes Urn** and all the cricket-related memorabilia you could ever want to see, attend a match or take a 1¾hr. tour led by a senior club member. On game days, tours after 10am skip the Long Room and media center (no tours during major international test matches). Games take place on most summer days. MCC games are around £10, but tickets to the rare international test matches are £45-60 and difficult to get. Test matches at the Lord's Cricket Ground sell out immediately. Book tickets as far in advance as possible. (10min. walk from ❷St. John's Wood. Enter at Grace Gate, on St. John's Wood Rd. ☎7432 1000; www.lords.org.uk. Tours daily Oct.-Mar. noon and 2pm; Apr.-Sept. 10am, noon, 2pm. Wheelchair-accessible. Tours £10, concessions £7, children under 16 £6, families £27.)

ABBEY ROAD. Abbey Rd. is a long, residential thoroughfare stretching from St. John's Wood to Kilburn. Most people are only interested in the famous **zebra crossing** at its start, where it merges with Grove End Rd. The best way to stop traffic: a photo-op crossing the street a la John, Paul, George, and Ringo. (❷St. John's Wood.)

EAST LONDON

ROYAL OBSERVATORY GREENWICH. The climb to the peak of Greenwich Park is not for the lazy, but the view is worth the trek; you can see all of the Docklands and Westminster on a clear day. The peak is home to the Royal Observatory, founded by Charles II in 1675 to accelerate the task of "finding the longitude" after one too many shipwrecks led to public outcry. The **Prime Meridian,** marked by a constantly photographed red LED strip in the courtyard, is the axis along which the astronomers' telescopes swung. Stand with one foot in each hemisphere before ducking into **Flamsteed House,** a Christopher Wren creation originally designed as a living space for the Astronomer Royal and now home to famous clocks and old astronomical equipment. Next to the Meridian Building's telescope display you can climb the **Observatory Dome,** cunningly disguised as a freakishly large rust-colored onion, to see the cleverly named 28 in. Telescope, constructed in 1893. It's still the seventh-largest refracting lens in the world, and, although it was officially retired in 1971, it is still fully functional. (At the top of Greenwich Park, a short but fairly steep climb from the National Maritime Museum; for an easier walk, take the Avenue from St. Mary's Gate at the top of King William Walk. Tram leaves from the back of the Museum every 30min. on the ½hr. ☎8858 4422; www.nmm.ac.uk. Open daily 10am-5pm; last admission 4:30pm. Open in summer 10am-6pm; call to confirm. Daily guided tour leaves at 2:30pm in front of the Flamsteed House; free.)

CUTTY SARK. The *Cutty Sark* was the fastest of the British tea-liners. Built in 1869, she made the round-trip voyage from China in only 120 days, carrying over a million pounds of tea. Retired from the sea in the 1930s, the deck and cabins have been partially restored to their 19th-century prime (complete with animatronic sailors). The hold houses an exhibit on the ship's history and a fascinating collection of figureheads. The upper deck has the officer's quarters—a far cry, comfort-wise, from those of the crew. Due to a large-scale conservation project that began in 2006 and was set back by a large fire in the spring of 2007, the ship is closed to visitors until early 2009. A small shop is open but not worth the trip unless already in the area. (King William Walk, by Greenwich Pier. ☎8858 3445; www.cuttysark.org.uk. Open daily 10am-5pm. Call for opening updates and details.)

OTHER EAST LONDON SIGHTS. The **Thames Barrier** is the world's largest movable flood barrier. When raised, the main gates stand as high as a five-story building—you can see it from the Thames Barrier Information Centre. Call to verify times (*Information Centre: 1 Unity Way. ☎8305 4188. Center open M-Sa Apr.-Sept. 10:30am-4pm; Oct.-Mar. 11am-3:30pm. Admission £2, concessions £1.50, children £1.*) The newly renovated **O₂ Dome** is a modern entertainment venue that hosts everything from concerts to museum exhibits. (*Drawdock Rd., ⊖Greenwich. www.millennium-dome.com*)

WEST LONDON

WIMBLEDON LAWN TENNIS MUSEUM. The All England Lawn Tennis and Croquet Club—the proper name for the arena that hosts the Wimbledon tennis championships every summer—includes a brand new museum dedicated to the history of tennis. Visitors can peruse memorabilia displays and interactive video exhibits. Tours (2hr.) of the grounds are led by certified Blue Badge Guides and include stops in the Millennium Building and the iconic Centre Court. (*Church Rd. ⊖Southfields. From Tube station, take Bus #493, or cross street and walk south on Wimbledon Park Road. Visitors to the museum should enter through Gate 3. ☎8946 6131; www.wimbledon.org/museum. Museum open daily 10:30am-5pm, guided tours at noon, 1:30, and 2:30pm. Museum £8.50, students £7.50, children £4.75; museum and guided tour £14.50/13/11.*)

🏛 MUSEUMS AND GALLERIES

For centuries, rich Londoners have exhibited a penchant for collecting. On top of private collections, London also has a substantial national collection, helped in large part by its position in the 18th and 19th centuries as the capital of an empire. In the 2002 celebration of the Queen's Golden Jubilee, the City made admission to all major collections free indefinitely.

MAJOR COLLECTIONS

▉TATE MODERN. Sir Giles Gilbert Scott's mammoth building, formerly the Bankside power station, houses the second half of the national collection (the earlier set is held in the National Gallery). The Tate Modern is probably the most popular museum in London, as well as one of the most famous modern art museums in the world. The public galleries on the third and fifth floors are divided into four themes. The collection is enormous while gallery space is limited—works rotate frequently. If you are dying to see a particular piece, head to the museum's computer station on the fifth floor to browse the entire collection. The seventh floor has unblemished views of the Thames and north and south of London. (*Main entrance on Bankside, on the South Bank; 2nd entrance on Queen's Walk. ⊖Southwark or Blackfriars. From the Southwark tube, turn left up Union, then left on Great Suffolk, then left on Holland. ☎7887 8000; www.tate.org.uk. Open M-Th and Su 10am-6pm, F-Sa 10am-10pm. Wheelchair-accessible on Holland St. Free tours meet on the gallery concourses: Level 3 11am and noon, Level 5 2 and 3pm. 5 types of audio tours include highlights, collection tour, architecture tour, children's tour, and the visually impaired tour; £2. Free; special exhibits up to £10. Free talks M-F 1pm; meet at the concourse on the appropriate level.*)

▉NATIONAL GALLERY. The National Gallery was founded by an Act of Parliament in 1824, with 38 pictures displayed in a townhouse; over the years its grown to hold an enormous collection of Western European paintings, ranging from the 1200s to the 1900s. Numerous additions have been made, the most recent (and controversial) being the massive modern Sainsbury Wing—Prince Charles described it as "a monstrous carbuncle on the face of a much-loved and elegant friend." The Sainsbury Wing holds almost all of the museum's large exhibitions as well as restaurants and lecture halls. If pressed for time, head to **Art Start** in the

Sainsbury Wing, where you can design and print out a personalized tour of the paintings you want to see. Themed audio tours and family routes also available from the information desk. *(Main Portico entrance on north side of Trafalgar Sq. ⊖Charing Cross or Leicester Sq. ☎7747 2885; www.nationalgallery.org.uk. Open M-Tu and Th-Su 10am-6pm, W 10am-9pm. Special exhibitions in the Sainsbury Wing occasionally open until 10pm. 1hr. tours start at Sainsbury Wing information desk. Tours M-F and Su 11:30am and 2:30pm, Sa 11:30am, 12:30, 2:30, and 3:30pm. Wheelchair-accessible at Sainsbury Wing on Pall Mall East, Orange St., and Getty Entrance. Free; some temporary exhibitions £5-10, seniors £4-8, students and children ages 12-18 £2-5. Audio tours free, suggested donation £4. AmEx/MC/V for ticketed events.)*

■ **NATIONAL PORTRAIT GALLERY.** The Who's Who of Britain began in 1856 and has grown to be the place to see Britain's freshest new artwork as well as centuries-old portraiture. It was recently bolstered by the addition of the sleek Ondaatje Wing. New facilities include an IT Gallery, with computers to search for pictures and print out a personalized tour, and a third-floor restaurant offering an aerial view of London—although the inflated prices (meals around £15) will limit most visitors to coffee. To see the paintings in historical order, take the escalator in the Ondaatje Wing to the top floor. The Tudor Gallery is especially impressive. *(St. Martin's Pl., at the start of Charing Cross Rd., Trafalgar Sq. ⊖Leicester Sq. or Charing Cross. ☎7312 2463; www.npg.org.uk. Open M-W and Sa-Su 10am-6pm, Th-F 10am-9pm. Wheelchair-accessible on Orange St. Lectures Tu 3pm free, but popular events require tickets, available from the information desk. Some evening talks Th 7pm free, others up to £3. Live music F 6:30pm free. Free; some special exhibitions free, others up to £6. Audio tours £2.)*

BRITISH MUSEUM. With 50,000 items from all corners of the globe, the magnificent collection is expansive and, although a bit difficult to navigate, definitely worth seeing. Most people don't even make it past the main floor, but they should—the galleries upstairs and downstairs are some of the best. Must-sees include the Rosetta stone, which was the key in deciphering ancient Egyptian hieroglyphs, and the ancient mummies. *(Great Russell St. ⊖Tottenham Court Rd., Russell Sq., or Holborn. ☎7323 8299; www.thebritishmuseum.ac.uk. Great Court open M-W and Su 9am-6pm, Th-Sa 9am-11pm, 9pm in winter; galleries open daily 10am-5:30pm, selected galleries open Th-F 10am-8:30pm. Free 30-40min. tours daily starting at 11am from the Enlightenment Desk. "Highlights Tour" daily 10:30am, 1, and 3pm; advance booking recommended. Wheelchair-accessible. Free; £3 suggested donation. Temporary exhibitions around £5, concessions £3.50. "Highlights Tour" £8, concessions £5. Audio tours £3.50, family audio tours for 2 adults and up to 3 children £10. MC/V.)*

VICTORIA AND ALBERT MUSEUM. As the largest museum of decorative (and not-so-decorative) art and design in the world, the V&A has over 9½ mi. of corridors open to the public, and is twice the size of the British Museum. It displays "the fine and applied arts of all countries, all styles, all periods." Unlike the British Museum, the V&A's documentation is consistently excellent and thorough. Interactive displays, hi-tech touch points, and engaging activities ensure that the goodies won't become boring. Some of the most interesting areas of the museum are the Glass Gallery, the Japanese and Korean areas with suits of armor and kimonos, and the Indian Gallery. Themed itineraries (£5) available at the desk can help streamline your visit, and **Family Trail** cards suggest kid-friendly routes. *(Main entrance on Cromwell Rd., wheelchair-accessible entrance on Exhibition Rd. ⊖South Kensington. ☎7942 2000; www.vam.ac.uk. Open M-Th and Sa-Su 10am-5:45pm, F 10am-10pm. Free tours meet at rear of main entrance. Introductory tours daily 10:30, 11:30am, 1:30, and 3:30pm, plus W 4:30pm. British gallery tours daily 12:30 and 2:30pm. Talks and events meet at rear of main entrance. Free gallery talks Th 1pm and Su 3pm, 45min.-1hr. Wheelchair-accessible. Admission free; additional charge for some special exhibits.)*

TATE BRITAIN. Tate Britain is the foremost collection on British art from 1500 to the present, including pieces from foreign artists working in Britain and Brits working abroad. There are four Tate Galleries in England; this is the original Tate, opened in 1897 to house Sir Henry Tate's collection of "modern" British art and later expanded to include a gift from famed British painter J.M.W. Turner. Turner's modest donation of 282 oils and 19,000 watercolors can make the museum feel like one big tribute to the man. The annual and always controversial **Turner Prize** for contemporary visual art is still given here. Four contemporary British artists are nominated for the £40,000 prize; their short-listed works go on show from late October through late January. In 2008, the exhibition moves temporarily to the Liverpool branch of the Tate (p. 349). The Modern British Art Gallery, featuring works by Vanessa Bell and Francis Bacon, is also worth a look. *(Millbank, near Vauxhall Bridge, in Westminster. ⊖Pimlico. Information ☎ 7887 8008, M-F exhibition booking 7887 8888; www.tate.org.uk. Open daily 10am-5:50pm, last admission 5pm. Wheelchair-accessible via Clore Wing. Regular events include "Painting of the Month Lectures." 15min. M 1:15pm and Sa 2:30pm; occasional "Friday Lectures" F 1pm. Free; special exhibitions £7-11. Audio tours free. Free tours: "Art from 1500-1800" 11am, "1800-1900" M-F noon; "Turner" M-F 2pm; "1900-2005" M-F 3pm; "1500-2005" Sa-Su noon, 3pm.)*

BY NEIGHBORHOOD

THE CITY OF LONDON

■ **MUSEUM OF LONDON.** Located in the southwest corner of the Barbican complex, the gray and brown Museum of London resembles an industrial fortress from the outside. Once inside, the collection traces the history of London from its Roman foundations to the present day, incorporating architectural history. You can view the ruins of the ancient **London Wall** from the museum walkway. *(London Wall. Enter through the Barbican or from Aldersgate. ⊖St. Paul's or Barbican. ☎08704 444 3851; www.museumoflondon.org.uk. Open M-Sa 10am-5:50pm, Su noon-5:50pm; last admission 5:30pm. Wheelchair-accessible via the elevator at Aldersgate entrance. Free. Audio tour £2. Frequent demonstrations, talks, and guided walks; some free, others up to £10.)*

■ **BANK OF ENGLAND MUSEUM.** The Bank is open only to those on business; for the museum, you will be shuttled by security. The museum traces the history of the Bank from its foundation (1694) to the present day. Mini-displays showcase items like the Bank's official silver and German firebomb casings. *(Threadneedle St. ⊖Bank. ☎7601 5545; www.bankofengland.co.uk. Open M-F 10am-5pm. Wheelchair-accessible. Free.)*

GUILDHALL ART GALLERY. Devoted to displaying the City's art collection, the walls are home to portraits of former Lord Mayors. Downstairs is a fine collection of Victorian and pre-Raphaelite art that includes works by Stevens, Poynter, Rossetti, and Millais. John Singleton Copley's gigantic *Defeat of the Floating Batteries at Gibraltar* is also on display. *(Guildhall Yard, off Gresham St. ⊖Moorgate or Bank. ☎7332 3700; www.guildhall-art-gallery.org.uk. Open M-Sa 10am-5pm, last admission 4:30pm; Su noon-4pm, last admission 3:30pm. Wheelchair-accessible. Free M-Th and Sa-Su 3:30-5pm, F 10am-5pm; M-Th and Sa-Su 10am-3:30pm £2.50, concessions £1, children under 16 free.)*

CLERKENWELL AND HOLBORN

■ **THE GILBERT COLLECTION.** The Gilbert Collection of Decorative Arts houses some of the more exquisite objects in any London museum. Its 800 pieces fall into three categories: mosaics, gold- and silver-work, and snuffboxes. Pick up a complimentary magnifying glass at the front desk, where you can also get a free audio tour. *(In Somerset House, on the Embankment side. Strand, just east of Waterloo Bridge. ⊖Temple. ☎7420 9400; www.gilbert-collection.org.uk. 1hr. tours Sa 2:30pm. Wheelchair-accessible. Tours £6.50, concessions £6.)*

THE COURTAULD INSTITUTE GALLERIES. The Courtauld's small, outstanding collection ranges from 14th-century Italian icons to 20th-century abstractions. Works are arranged by collector, not chronologically, so don't fret if you think you skipped a few hundred years. The undisputed gems of the collection are from the Impressionist and Postimpressionist periods: Manet's *A Bar at the Follies Bergères*, Van Gogh's *Self-Portrait with Bandaged Ear*, and a room devoted to Degas bronzes. *(In Somerset House. Strand, just east of Waterloo Bridge. ⊖Charing Cross or Temple. ☎ 7420 9400; www.courtauld.ac.uk. 1hr. tours held Sa 2:30pm. Wheelchair-accessible. Tours £6.50, concessions £6; M 10am-2pm free. Lunchtime talks free.)*

SIR JOHN SOANE'S MUSEUM. Eccentric architect John Soane let his imagination run free when designing this intriguing museum for his own collection of art and antiquities. Framed by narrow hallways and oddly shaped nooks and crannies, its items range from the mummified corpse of his wife's dog to an extraordinary sarcophagus of Seti I, for which Soane personally outbid the British Museum when it wasn't willing to pay £2000 for it. *(13 Lincoln's Inn Fields. ⊖Holborn. ☎ 1405 2107. Open Tu-Sa 10am-5pm, 1st Tu of month also 6-9pm. Tours Sa. Tours £5, students free. Tickets sold from 11am. Free; £3 donation requested.)*

KENSINGTON AND EARL'S COURT

SCIENCE MUSEUM. Dedicated to the Victorian ideal of Progress, the Science Museum focuses on the transformative power of technology in all its guises. It is also home to an IMAX theater, which shows 45min. scientific documentaries. Breeze through the entrance hall on your way to the **Welcome Wing.** Highlights include **Who am I?,** the **Flight Lab,** and the **Science of Art and Medicine.** *(Exhibition Rd. ⊖South Kensington. ☎08708 704 868, IMAX 08708 704 771; www.sciencemuseum.org.uk. Open daily 10am-6pm, except Dec. 24-26. Wheelchair-accessible. Admission free. Audio tours: "Soundbytes" cover Power, Space, and Making the Modern World; £3.50 each. IMAX: Shows usually every 1¼hr., 10:45am-5pm daily; £7.50, concessions £6. Call to confirm showtimes and for bookings. Online booking available. Daily demonstrations and workshops in the basement galleries and theatre. SimEx £3.75, concessions £2.75. MC/V.)*

NATURAL HISTORY MUSEUM. Architecturally the most impressive of the South Kensington trio, this cathedral-like museum has been a favorite with Londoners since 1880. Shudder from **Creepy Crawlies** into the **Dinosaur** galleries, making sure to swing by the **blue whale.** *(Cromwell Rd. ⊖South Kensington. ☎ 7942 5000; www.nhm.ac.uk. Open M-Sa 10am-5:50pm, Su 11am-5:50pm; last admission 5:30pm. Closed Dec. 24-Dec. 30. Wheelchair-accessible. Admission free; special exhibits usually £5, concessions £3. MC/V.)*

THE SOUTH BANK

IMPERIAL WAR MUSEUM. Naval guns guard the entrance to the building, formerly the infamous asylum known as Bedlam. The best and most publicized display is on the third floor: the **Holocaust Exhibition** provides an honest, poignant look at all the events surrounding the tragedy. (Not recommended for children under 14.) On the 4th floor, **Crimes Against Humanity** is a sobering interactive display with a 30min. film. *(Lambeth Rd., Lambeth. ⊖Lambeth North or Elephant & Castle. ☎7416 5320; www.iwm.org.uk. Open daily 10am-6pm. Admission free. Audio tour £3.50, concessions £3.)*

DESIGN MUSEUM. Housed in a white Art Deco riverfront building, this contemporary museum's installations fit right into the cool surroundings. You might find anything from avant-garde furniture to galleries on big-name graphic designers, depending on when you visit; all exhibitions are temporary. *(28 Shad Thames, Butlers Wharf. ⊖Tower Hill or London Bridge. ☎0870 833 9955; www.designmuseum.org. Open daily 10am-5:45pm, last entry 5:15pm. Wheelchair-accessible. £7, concessions £4.)*

THE WEST END

■**ROYAL ACADEMY OF ARTS.** Founded in 1768 with King George III's patronage, the Academy was designed to cultivate sculpture, painting, and architecture. Today the Academy shares courtyard space with the Royal Societies of Geology, Chemistry, Antiquaries, and Astronomy. The academics in charge are all accomplished artists or architects. The Summer Exhibition (June-Aug.), held every year since 1769, is open to any artist for submissions, providing an unparalleled range of contemporary art in every medium, much of which is available for purchase. On Friday nights, the museum stays open late with free jazz in the Friends Room after 6:30pm and candlelit suppers in the cafe. *(Burlington House, Piccadilly. ⊖Piccadilly Cir. or Green Park. ☎7300 8000; www.royalacademy.org.uk. Open M-Th and Sa-Su 10am-6pm, F 10am-10pm. Wheelchair-accessible. Free. Exhibits in the Main Galleries £7, students £5.)*

■**THE PHOTOGRAPHERS' GALLERY.** This is one of London's only public galleries devoted entirely to photography. A few exhibits run concurrently at the larger location (No. 5), which also boasts a cafe. Displays usually feature a single artist's work, ranging from classic landscape to socially conscious photography. The gallery and small bookshop at No. 8 house an equally exemplary show and also have a good selection of photographic monologues. Frequent gallery talks, book readings, and film screenings are free; occasional photographers' talks may charge admission. *(5 and 8 Great Newport St. ⊖Leicester Sq. or Covent Garden. ☎7831 1772; www.photonet.org.uk. Open M-W and F-Sa 11am-6pm, Th 11am-8pm, Su noon-6pm. Free.)*

BENJAMIN FRANKLIN HOUSE. Minutes away from the Charing Cross Tube station lies the world's only remaining Franklin residence. Franklin lived in the house from 1757-1775, and not much has changed since then; the tilted floors and ceilings are evidence that the original interior has been well-preserved. This living history museum combines history with theater; costumed guides lead visitors around the house, conveying a sense of Franklin's life and inventions. *(36 Craven St. ⊖Charing Cross or Embankment. ☎7839 2006; www.benjaminfranklinhouse.org. Open W-Su noon-5pm with tours at noon, 1, 2, 3:15, and 4:15pm. £7.)*

INSTITUTE OF CONTEMPORARY ARTS (ICA). A minute's walk out of Trafalgar Sq. through the Admiralty Arch, the ICA is London's center for avant-garde art and contemporary artists. Films, talks, performances, and club nights can all be found here. *(The Mall. ⊖Charing Cross or Piccadilly Cir. ☎7930 0493; www.ica.org.uk. Galleries open M-W and F-Su noon-7:30pm, Th noon-9pm. Cafe and bar open M noon-11pm, Tu-Sa noon-1am, Su noon-10:30pm. "Day membership," giving access to galleries, cafe, and bar M-F £2, concessions £1.50, Sa-Su £3, concessions £2. Cinema £8, M-F before 5pm £7; concessions £7/6.)*

CHRISTIE'S. Like a museum but more crowded and all for sale, Christie's is the best of the auction houses. The public can enter on days before an auction to peruse what's up for grabs. Lots range from busts of Greek gods to Monets to sports memorabilia. *(8 King St. ⊖Green Park. There is a smaller branch at 85 Old Brompton St. in Kensington. ☎7839 9060; www.christies.com. Open M-F 9am-5pm; call in advance for exact timings. Public viewings can close early for evening auctions. Wheelchair-accessible. Free.)*

SOTHEBY'S. Before each auction, the items to be sold are displayed for viewing in the many interlocking galleries. Aristocratic Sotheby's is a busy place; auctions occur within days of each other. Each sale is accompanied by a glossy catalog (from £10). *(34-35 New Bond St. ⊖Bond St. ☎7293 5000; www.sothebys.com. Open for viewing M-F 9am-4:30pm, Sa and occasional Su noon-4pm, call in advance for exact hours. Public viewings can close early for evening auctions. Wheelchair-accessible. Free.)*

EAST LONDON

■ **WHITECHAPEL ART GALLERY.** Long the only artistic beacon in a culturally impoverished area, Whitechapel is now at the forefront of a buzzing art scene, featuring international and contemporary artists. Thursday nights bring music, poetry readings, and film screenings, in addition to regular events and talks during the week. *(Whitechapel High St. ⊖Aldgate East. ☎7522 7888; www.whitechapel.org. Open Tu-W and F-Su 11am-6pm, Th 11am-9pm. Call for opening details. Wheelchair-accessible. Free.)*

■ **WHITE CUBE.** This stark white building has showcased some of the biggest names in contemporary art. White Cube has an impressive list of alums and featured exhibits, including heavyweights Chuck Close and Damien Hirst. *(48 Hoxton Sq. ⊖Old St. ☎7930 5373; www.whitecube.com. Open Tu-Sa 10am-6pm. Sometimes closes for exhibit installation; call in advance. Wheelchair-accessible. Free.)*

OTHER NEIGHBORHOODS

■ **CABINET WAR ROOMS.** From 1939 to 1945, what started as a government coal storage basement quickly became the bomb-proof nerve center of a nation at war. Winston Churchill stood in the Cabinet Room and declared, "This is the room from which I will direct the war." The day after WWII ended in August 1945, the Cabinet War Rooms were abandoned, closed off, and left undisturbed for decades until their re-opening in 1984 by Margaret Thatcher. The display includes the ■**Churchill Museum,** with all sorts of Churchill's WWII artifacts. A giant interactive timeline produces sound effects and visuals in the center of the exhibit. *(Clive Steps, far end of King Charles St. ⊖Westminster. ☎7930 6961; www.iwm.org.uk. Open daily 9:30am-6pm; last admission 5pm. £10, students £8, children under 16 free. MC/V.)*

■ **BRITISH LIBRARY GALLERIES.** Housed within the British Library (p. 115) is an appropriately stunning display of books, manuscripts, and related artifacts from around the world and throughout the ages. Displays are arranged by theme, and a rundown of highlights reads like some fantastic list of the most precious pages imaginable. Grab a free map at the main info desk. Highlights include the 2nd-century *Unknown Gospel*, The Beatles' hand-scrawled lyrics, a Gutenberg Bible, Joyce's handwritten draft of *Finnegan's Wake*, and pages from da Vinci's notebooks. *(96 Euston Rd. ⊖King's Cross St. Pancras. ☎7412 7332; www.bl.uk. Grab a free map at the main info desk. Open M and W-F 9:30am-6pm, Tu 9:30am-8pm, Sa 9:30am-5pm, Su 11am-5pm. Wheelchair-accessible. Free. Audio tours £3.50, concessions £2.50.)*

THE WALLACE COLLECTION. Housed in palatial Hertford House, this stunning array of paintings, porcelain, and armor was bequeathed to the nation by the widow of Sir Richard Wallace in 1897. Excellent daily gallery tours will ensure that you see a good overview of the collection. *(Hertford House, Manchester Sq. ⊖Bond St. or Marble Arch. ☎7563 9500; www.wallacecollection.org. Open daily 9am-5pm. 1hr. tours M-Tu and Th-F 1pm; W and Sa 11:30am, 1, 3pm; Su 1, 3pm; free. Talks M-F 1pm and occasional Sa 11:30am; free. Wheelchair-accessible. Admission free; £2 suggested donation. Audio tour £3. Cafe: mains £12.50-18; call for reservations ☎7563 9505.)*

THE IVEAGH BEQUEST. The Iveagh collection in Kenwood House was given to the nation by the Earl of Iveagh, who purchased the estate in 1922. Highlights include *The Guitar Player*—one of 35 Vermeers in the world—and Rembrandt's compelling self-portraits. *(Kenwood House. Road access from Hampstead Ln. Walk or take bus #210 from North End Way or Spaniards Rd. or from ⊖Archway or Golders Green. ☎8348 1286. Open daily Apr.-Oct. 11am-5pm.; Nov.-Mar. 11am-4pm. Wheelchair-accessible. Free.)*

ENTERTAINMENT

Although West End ticket prices are through the roof and the quality of some shows is highly questionable, the city that brought the world Shakespeare, the Sex Pistols, and even Andrew Lloyd Webber still retains originality and its theatrical edge. London is a city of immense talent, full of student up-and-comers, experimental writers, and undergrounders who don't care about the neon lights. Experiencing the world-class drama is a must.

CINEMA

The heart of the celluloid monster is **Leicester Square,** where new releases premiere a day before hitting the city's chains. The dominant cinema chain is **Odeon** (☎08712 241 999; www.odeon.co.uk). Tickets to West End cinemas cost £9-12.50; weekday matinees are cheaper. For less mainstream offerings, try the ▇**Electric Cinema,** 191 Portobello Rd., for the combination of baroque stage splendor and the big screen. For a special experience, choose a luxury armchair or two-seat sofa. (◒Ladbroke Grove. ☎7908 9696; www.the-electric.co.uk. Box office open M-Sa 9am-8:30pm, Su 10am-8:30pm. Front 3 rows M £5, Tu-Su £10; regular tickets M £7.50, Tu-Su £12.50; 2-seat sofa M £20, Tu-Su £30. Double bills Su 2pm £5-20. Wheelchair-accessible. MC/V.) **Riverside Studios,** Crisp Rd., shows a variety of excellent foreign and classic films. (◒Hammersmith. ☎8237 1111; www.riverside-studios.co.uk. £6.50, concessions £5.50.) The **National Film Theatre (NFT)** screens a mind-boggling array of films—six movies hit the three screens every evening, starting around 6pm (South Bank, under Waterloo Bridge. ◒Waterloo, Embankment, or Temple. ☎7928 3232; www.bfi.org.uk/nft. £7.50, concessions £5.70.)

COMEDY

On any given night, you'll find at least ten comedy clubs in operation: check listings in *Time Out* or in a newspaper. London empties of comedians in August, when most head to Edinburgh to take part in the annual festivals (p. 545); consequently, July provides plenty of comedians trying out material.

▇ **Comedy Store,** 1a Oxendon St. (club inquiries ☎7839 6642, tickets 08700 602 340; www.thecomedystore.biz), in **Soho.** ◒Piccadilly Circus. The UK's top comedy club (founded in a former strip club) sowed the seeds that gave rise to *Absolutely Fabulous* and *Whose Line is it Anyway?* All 400 seats have decent views of stage. Grab food at the bar before the show and during intermission (burgers £6). Tu Cutting Edge (contemporary news-based satire); W and Su London's well-reviewed ▇ **Comedy Store Players improv;** Th-Sa standup. Shows Tu-Th and Su 8pm; F-Sa 8pm and midnight. Book in advance. 18+. Tu-W and F midnight shows and all Su shows £16; concessions £8; Th-F early show and all Sa shows £15. Happy hour 6:30-7:30pm. Box office open M-Th and Su 6:30-9:30pm, F-Sa 6:30pm-1:15am. AmEx/MC/V.

▇ **Canal Cafe Theatre,** Delamere Terr. (☎7289 6054; www.canalcafetheatre.com), above the Bridge House pub; in **North London.** ◒Warwick Ave. One of the few comedy venues to specialize in sketch comedy. Cozy red velvet chairs and a raised rear balcony means that everyone gets a good view. Grab dinner below and enjoy your drinks around the small tables. Box office opens 30min. before performance. Weekly changing shows W-Sa 7:30 and 9:30pm (£5, concessions £4). "Newsrevue," Th-Sa 9:30pm and Su 9pm, is London's longest-running comedy sketch show, a satire of weekly current events (£9, concessions £7). £1.50 membership included in ticket price.

DANCE

The **Barbican Theatre** at Barbican Hall hosts touring contemporary companies. The **Peacock Theatre,** Portugal St., off of Kingsway and a 5min. walk from Holburn station, has a program that leans toward contemporary dance, ballet, popular dance-troupe shows, and family-geared productions. (⊖Holborn. ☎0894 412 4322; www.sadlerswells.com. Some wheelchair-accessible seats can be booked in advance. Box office open M-F 10am-6:30pm, performance days 10am-8:30pm. £10-35. Standby concession tickets 1hr. before show £15, cash only. Cheapest tickets at box office; fees for telephone and online booking. AmEx/MC/V.) Dancing in the Royal Opera House, the **Royal Ballet** is one of the world's premiere companies. (See Royal Opera, p. 134.) Recently rebuilt, historic **Sadler's Wells**, Rosebery Ave., in Islington (right next to Clerkenwell), remains London's premier dance theater, with many contemporary shows and the occasional ballet. Recent performances have included Matthew Bourne's *Swan Lake*, which premiered at Sadler's Wells in 1995. (⊖Angel. Exit left from the Tube, cross the road, and take the 2nd right on Rosebery Ave. Sadler's Wells Express (SWX) bus to Waterloo via Farringdon and Victoria leaves 8min. after the end of each mainstage evening show; £1.50, with period Travelcard £1. ☎7863 8000; www.sadlerswells.com. Box office open M-Sa 9am-8:30pm. £10-50; students and seniors £15; under-16 standbys £15 1hr. before curtain, cash only. Wheelchair-accessible. AmEx/MC/V.)

MUSIC

CLASSICAL

▨ **Barbican Hall,** Silk St. (☎7638 4141; www.barbican.org.uk), in the **City of London.** ⊖Barbican or Moorgate. Recently refurbished, Barbican Hall is one of Europe's leading concert halls, with excellent acoustics and a nightly performance program. The resident **London Symphony Orchestra** plays here frequently. The hall also hosts concerts by international orchestras, jazz artists, and world musicians. Barbican is also the place to go for information on **festivals** and **season-specific events.** As many summer events sell out, it's worth checking what's going on early. Call in advance for tickets, especially for popular events. Otherwise, the online and phone box offices sometimes have good last-minute options. £10-35. Also includes the 2 venues below:

Barbican Centre. Famous for the quality of its diverse offerings and its mildly confusing layout, the Barbican is a 1-stop cultural powerhouse. The main **Theatre** is a futuristic auditorium that hosts touring companies and short-run shows as well as frequent short-run multicultural and contemporary dance performances. Prices vary considerably by seat, day, and production: £10-35, cheapest M-F evening and Sa matinee; student and senior standbys from 9am day of performance. **The Pit** is a smaller, intimate theatre used primarily for new and experimental productions. £10-15.

Barbican Cinema. Part of the Barbican Centre conglomerate. 2 smallish screens offering a rotation of the latest blockbusters with art-house, international, and classic movies. £8.50, seniors and students £6, under 15 £4.50.

English National Opera, London Coliseum, St. Martin's Ln. (☎7632 8300; www.eno.org), in **Covent Garden.** ⊖Charing Cross or Leicester Sq. The Coliseum is staggering—huge, ornate, and complete with 500 balcony seats (£15-18) for sale every performance—and the ENO has proven it can fill the venue with its innovative, updated productions of classics as well as contemporary work. Purchase best-available, standby student tickets (£12.50) and balcony tickets (£10) at box office 3hr. before show. Call to verify availability. ½-price tickets for children under 17. Box office open M-Sa 10am-8pm. Wheelchair-accessible. AmEx/MC/V.

Holland Park Theatre, Holland Park (box office ☎08452 309 769; www.rbkc.gov.uk/hollandpark), in **Kensington and Earl's Court.** ⊖High St. Kensington or Holland Park. Open-air performance space in the atmospheric ruins of Holland House, grounds of a Jacobean mansion. Sitting outside is generally the most adventurous part of the program. No need to fear the rain—everything is held under a huge white canopy. Performances June to early Aug. Tu-Sa 7:30pm, occasional matinees Sa 2:30pm. Box office in the Old Stable Block just to the west of the opera; open from late Mar. M-Sa 10am-

6pm or 30min. after curtain. Tickets £21, £38 (£35 for students during select performances), and £43. Special allocation of tickets for wheelchair users. AmEx/MC/V.

Royal Opera, Bow St. (☎ 7304 4000; www.royaloperahouse.org), in **Covent Garden.** ⊖Covent Garden. Productions in this recently refurbished venue tend to be conservative but lavish, although recent experiments with contemporary works have proven successful as well. Prices for the best seats (orchestra stalls) regularly top £100, but standing room and restricted-view seating in the upper balconies (if you're not afraid of heights) runs for as little as £5. For some performances, 100 of the very best seats available for £10; apply a minimum of 2 weeks in advance at www.travelex.royaloperahouse.org.uk. 67 seats available from 10am on day of performance, limit 1 per person. Box office open M-Sa 10am-8pm. AmEx/MC/V.

JAZZ

▧ **Jazz Café,** 5 Parkway (☎ 7534 6955; www.jazzcafe.co.uk), in **North London.** ⊖Camden Town. Famous and popular. Crowded front bar and balcony restaurant overlook the dance floor and stage, both of which are just the right size. Shows can be pricey at this nightspot, but the top roster of jazz, hip-hop, funk, and Latin performers (£10-30) explains Jazz Café's popularity. Jazzy DJs spin F-Sa following the show. Partially wheelchair-accessible. Cover £5-10. Open daily 7pm-2am. MC/V.

▧ **Spitz,** 109 Commercial St. (☎ 7392 9032; www.spitz.co.uk), in **East London.** ⊖Liverpool St. Features an upstairs bar and a bistro downstairs. Crowds spill onto the Spitalfields market area during busy hours. Fresh range of live music including klezmer, jazz, world music, indie, pop, and rap. All profits support worthy causes through the Dandelion Trust, including global refugee health. Free music in the bistro 4 nights per week. For ticketed shows, book online at www.wegottickets.com. A small art gallery holds free exhibits from local artists. Occasional cover up to £15. Upstairs opens at 7pm most nights, when evening acts usually begin. Open M-W 10:30am-midnight, Th-Sa 10:30am-1am, Su 4-10:30pm. MC/V.

Ronnie Scott's, 47 Frith St. (☎ 7439 0747; www.ronniescotts.co.uk), in **Soho.** ⊖Tottenham Court Rd. or Leicester Sq. London's oldest, most famous jazz club, having hosted everyone from Dizzy Gillespie to Jimi Hendrix. A recent change in ownership means the club isn't pulling in the legends it used to, but in-the-know folks are expecting a comeback. Support and main acts switch back and forth throughout the night. Table reservations essential for big-name acts, although there's limited unreserved standing room at the bar; if it's sold out, try coming back at the end of the main act's 1st set, around midnight. Chicken, pasta, and traditional English dishes £7-28; mixed drinks £7-9. Box office open M-F 11am-6pm, Sa noon-6pm. Club open M-Sa 6pm-3am, Su 6pm-midnight. Tickets generally £26. AmEx/MC/V.

100 Club, 100 Oxford St. (☎ 7636 0933; www.the100club.co.uk), in **Soho.** ⊖Tottenham Court Rd. Stage, audience, and bar are all bathed in sallow orange light in this jazz venue that makes frequent excursions into indie rock. Weekdays offer serious indie and jazz, while weekends tend to become more "date friendly" and mellow. Punk burst on the scene at a legendary gig here in 1976, when the Sex Pistols, the Clash, and Siouxsie and the Banshees shared the stage. Featured nights: M "Stompin'" (swing and big band), Sa swing. Open F-Su 7:30pm, closing time varies; other nights vary. Cover £7-15, students with ID £5-10. AmEx/MC/V.

606 Club, 90 Lots Rd. (☎ 7352 5953; www.606club.co.uk), in **Chelsea.** ⊖Sloane Sq., then Bus #11 or 22. Look for the brick arch labeled 606 opposite the "Fire Access" garage; ring the doorbell to be let in downstairs. The intrepid will be rewarded with live jazz music in a candlelit basement venue. Entrance F-Su is with a meal only; M-Th you can choose to order just soft drinks. Mains £9-16. Cover (added to the bill): M-Th £8, F-Sa £12, Su £10. M-W doors open 7:30pm, 1st band 8-10:30pm, 2nd 10:45pm-1am;

Th-Sa doors open 8pm, music 9:30pm-1:30am; Su doors open 8pm, music 9pm-midnight. Reservations recommended F-Su. MC/V.

ROCK AND POP

▨ **The Water Rats,** 328 Grays Inn Rd. (☎7813 1079; www.themonto.com), in **Bloomsbury.** ⊖King's Cross St. Pancras. A hip pub-cafe by day, a stomping venue for top new talent by night—this is where young indie rock bands come in search of a record deal. Oasis was signed here after their first London gig, although the place has been spiffed up since. Cover from £4. Open for coffee M-F 8:30am-midnight. Excellent, generous gastro-pub lunches (fish and chips and baguettes £5-6) M-F noon-3pm. Music M-Sa 8pm-late (headliner 9:45pm). MC/V.

Carling Academy, Brixton, 211 Stockwell Rd. (☎7771 3000; www.brixton-academy.co.uk), in **South London.** ⊖Brixton. Art Deco ex-cinema with a sloping floor ensures a good view of the band. Named *Time Out*'s "Live Venue of the Year" in 2004 and *New Music Express*'s "Best Live Venue" in 2007. Recent performers include Lenny Kravitz, Pink, and Basement Jaxx. Box office open only on performance evenings; order online, by telephone, or at Carling Academy, Islington box office (16 Parkfield Street, Islington. Box office open M-Sa noon-4pm). Tickets £20-40.

London Astoria (LA1), 157 Charing Cross Rd. (info ☎8963 0940, 24hr. ticket line ☎08701 500 044), in **Soho.** ⊖Tottenham Court Rd. Formerly a pickle factory, strip club, and music hall before becoming a full-time rock venue in the late 1980s. Now basking in an air of somewhat faded glory, the 2000-person venue occasionally hosts big names (recently, the Red Hot Chili Peppers and Blink 182). The venue is more famous for the popular "G-A-Y" M and Th-Sa club night (see p. 143). Box office open M-F 10am-6pm, Sa 10am-5pm. AmEx/MC/V.

THEATER

LONG-RUNNING SHOWS (WEST END)

London's West End is dominated by musicals and plays that run for years—if not decades. For discounted tickets on the day of a performance, head to the **tkts** booth in Leicester Sq. (⊖Leicester Sq. www.tkts.co.uk. Most musicals around £23, plays £20-22; up to £2.50 booking fee per ticket. Open M-Sa 10am-7pm, Su noon-3:30pm. MC/V.) It's nearly always cheaper to go to the theater itself, especially for less popular shows; you are likely to get a better seat and pay less for same-day, rush, or concession tickets. However, you can try www.londontheatrebookings.com (☎7851 0300), or one of the discount shops that line Leicester Sq. if you really are looking for a cheap deal. **Billy Elliot: The Musical** is based on the movie, with music by Elton John. (Victoria Palace Theatre, Victoria St. ⊖Victoria. ☎08708 955 577. Shows M-W and F 7:30pm; Th and Sa 2:30, 7:30pm. £17.50-50. Call about limited day-of student standby tickets. AmEx/MC/V.) **The Lion King** is the same old script, with gorgeous new puppets. (Lyceum Theatre, Wellington St. ⊖Covent Garden. ☎08702 439 000; www.thelionking.co.uk. Shows Tu and Th-F 7:30pm; W and Sa 2, 7:30pm; Su 3pm. £20-50. Limited day-of seats and standing-room tickets released at noon. Ask about student discounts. Purchase 2 tickets max. in person at box office. AmEx/MC/V.) **Mamma Mia!** is one of the best of the "pop's greatest hits"-style megashows—it is so popular that it is nearly always sold out. (Prince of Wales Theatre, Coventry St. ⊖Leicester Sq. Box office ☎0870 950 0902, agents 0870 264 3333; www.mamma-mia.com. Shows M-Th 7:30pm; F 5, 8:30pm; Sa 3, 7:30pm. £25-49. Check the box office daily for returns. AmEx/MC/V.) Ideal for kids and families, **Mary Poppins** has gotten rave reviews. (Prince Edward Theatre, Old Compton St. ⊖Leicester Sq. ☎08708 509 191; www.marypoppinsthemusical.co.uk. Shows M-W and F 7:30pm; Th and Sa 2:30, 7:30pm. £15-55. Same-day tickets released at noon; limit 2 per person. AmEx/MC/V.)

REPERTORY

■ **Shakespeare's Globe Theatre,** 21 New Globe Walk (☎7401 9919; www.shakespeares-globe.org), in the **South Bank.** ✆Southwark or London Bridge. Innovative, top-notch performances at this faithful reproduction of Shakespeare's original 16th-century playhouse. Choose among 3 covered tiers of hard, backless wooden benches (cushions £1 extra) or stand through a performance as a "groundling"; come 30min. before the show to get as close as you can. Should it rain, the show must go on, and umbrellas are prohibited. For tours of the Globe, see p. 120. Wheelchair-accessible. Performances from mid-May to late Sept. Tu-Sa 7:30pm, Su 6:30pm; June-Sept. also Tu-Sa 2pm, Su 1pm. Box office open M-Sa 10am-6pm, 8pm on performance days. Seats from £12, concessions from £10, yard (i.e., standing) £5. Raingear £2.50.

■ **Royal Court Theatre,** Sloane Sq. (☎7565 5000; www.royalcourttheatre.com), in **Chelsea.** ✆Sloane Sq. Recognized by *The New York Times* as a standout theatre in Europe, the Court is dedicated to challenging new writing and innovative interpretations of classics. Their 1956 production of John Osborne's *Look Back in Anger* is universally acknowledged as the starting point of modern British drama. Tackles politically thorny issues like AIDS and the Middle East. Main auditorium £10-25, concessions £10, standing room 10p 1hr. before curtain. 2nd venue upstairs £15, concessions £10. M all seats £10, with some advance tickets and some released 10am on day of performance. Wheelchair-accessible. Box office open M-Sa 10am-7:45pm, closes 6pm non-performance weeks. AmEx/MC/V.

National Theatre, South Bank (info ☎7452 3400, box office 7452 3000; www.nationaltheatre.org.uk), in the **South Bank.** ✆Waterloo or Embankment. Founded by Laurence Olivier, the National Theatre opened in 1976 and has been at the forefront of British theatre ever since. The schedule often includes Shakespearian classics and hard-hitting new works from Britain's brightest playwrights. Bigger shows are mostly staged on the **Olivier,** seating 1160. The 890-seat **Lyttleton** is a proscenium theatre, while the **Cottesloe** offers flexible staging for new works. Tickets typically start at £10. Complicated pricing scheme, which is liable to change from show to show; contact box office for details. Wheelchair-accessible. Box office open M-Sa 9:30am-8pm. MC/V.

 NATIONAL THEATRE FOR POCKET CHANGE. Almost every day in the summer, the courtyard at the National Theatre holds a free concert, film, or performance art exhibition. From magic shows to physical comedy, the Theatre will satisfy anyone looking for live entertainment.

"OFF-WEST END"

■ **The Almeida,** Almeida St. (☎7359 4404; www.almeida.co.uk), in **North London.** ✆Angel or Highbury and Islington. The top fringe theatre in London, if not the world. Always comes up with novel scripts and quality shows, both dramatic and opera; also puts on classics from the likes of Shakespeare and Moliere. Hollywood stars, including Kevin Spacey and Nicole Kidman, have both performed here. The metallic bar and foyer areas were part of the expensive 2003 renovations. Shows M-Sa 7:30pm, Sa matinees 3pm. Tickets from £10. Wheelchair-accessible. MC/V.

Donmar Warehouse, 41 Earlham St. (☎08700 606 624; www.donmarwarehouse.com), in **Covent Garden.** ✆Covent Garden. In the mid-90s, artistic director Sam Mendes (later of *American Beauty* fame) transformed this gritty space into one of the most excellent theatres in the country, featuring highly regarded contemporary shows with an edge. This is the infamous stage where Nicole Kidman bared all in *The Blue Room* in 1998, so it's not surprising that this nondescript warehouse rarely has difficulty filling its 251 seats. Tickets £13-29; under 18 and students standby 30min. before curtain £12; £7.50 standing room tickets available once performance sells out. 10 tickets available on the day of a performance from 10:30am, limit 2 per person. Wheelchair-accessible. Box office open M-Sa 10am-7:30pm. AmEx/MC/V.

Royal Academy of Dramatic Arts (RADA), 62-64 Gower St. (☎ 7636 7076; www.rada.org), entrance on Malet St., in **Bloomsbury.** ⊖Goodge St. A cheaper alternative to the West End, Britain's most famous drama school has 3 on-site theaters. Call in advance for event details. Wheelchair-accessible. £3-10, concessions £2-7.50. Regular Foyer events during the school year, including plays, music, and readings M-Th 7 or 7:30pm (up to £4). Box office open M-F 10am-6pm, on performance nights 10am-7:30pm. AmEx/MC/V.

Old Vic, Waterloo Rd. (☎ 7369 1722; www.oldvictheatre.com), in the **South Bank.** ⊖Waterloo. Still in its original 1818 hall (the oldest theatre in London), the Old Vic is one of London's most historic theatres. These days, it hosts touring companies like the Royal Shakespeare Company, which set their own prices and schedules. Contact box office or check website for listings. Box office M-Sa 10am-7:30pm. MC/V.

◻ SHOPPING

London has long been considered one of the fashion capitals of the world. Unfortunately, the city that was at the forefront of the historical development of shopping malls features as many underwhelming chain stores as it does one-of-a-kind boutiques, such as those on **Oxford Street.** The truly budget-conscious should forget buying altogether and stick to window-shopping for ideas in **Knightsbridge** and **Regent Street.** Vintage shopping in **Notting Hill** is a viable alternative; however, steer clear, once again, of Oxford St., where so-called "vintage" clothing was probably made in 2002 and sells for twice as much as the regular line.

MAJOR CHAINS

Like any large city, London retail is dominated by chains. Fortunately, local shoppers are picky enough that buying from a chain doesn't mean abandoning the style for which Londoners are famed. Most chains have a flagship on or near Oxford Street, a second branch in Covent Garden, and another on King's Road or Kensington High St. Branches keep different hours, but usually stores are open 10am-7pm on weekdays and noon-5pm on weekends. Popular chains include Jigsaw, Karen Millen, Monsoon, Topshop/Topman, and Zara. For books, head to Waterstone's.

Harrods, 87-135 Brompton Rd. (☎ 7730 1234; www.harrods.com). ⊖Knightsbridge. In the Victorian era, this was the place for the wealthy to shop. Over a century later, it is a tourist extravaganza. Given the sky-high prices, it's no wonder that only tourists and oil sheiks actually shop here. Do go, though; it's an iconic bit of London that even the cynical tourist shouldn't miss. If nothing else, ride the Egyptian escalator in the middle, which leads down to the eerie "Diana and Dodi" memorial, with Diana's engagement ring and a wine glass she drank out of on her last night alive. Open M-Sa 10am-8pm, Su noon-6pm. Wheelchair-accessible. AmEx/MC/V.

Harvey Nichols, 109-125 Knightsbridge (☎ 7235 5000; www.harveynichols.com). ⊖Knightsbridge. Imagine Bond St., Rue St. Honoré, and 5th Ave. all rolled up into one store. 5 of its 7 fl. are devoted to the sleekest, sharpest fashion, from the biggest names to the hippest unknowns. Food hall on the 5th fl. has a swanky restaurant, a YO!Sushi, and the chic 5th Floor Cafe; there's a juice bar on the main fl. and a Wagamama in the basement. Sales late June-late July and late Dec.-late Jan. Open M-F 10am-8pm, Sa 10am-8pm, Su noon-6pm. Wheelchair-accessible. AmEx/MC/V.

Selfridges, 400 Oxford St. (☎ 0870 837 7377; www.selfridges.com). ⊖Bond St. Tourists may flock to Harrods, but Londoners head to Selfridges. Fashion departments run the gamut from traditional tweeds to space-age clubwear. They also include small selections from many chain stores, such as Oasis and Topshop. With 18 cafes and restaurants, a hair salon, a bureau de change, and even a hotel, shopaholics need never leave. Massive Jan. and July sales. Open M-F 10am-8pm, Sa 9:30am-8pm, Su noon-6pm. Wheelchair-accessible. AmEx/MC/V.

Liberty, 210-220 Regent St. (☎7734 1234; www.liberty.co.uk), entrance on Marlborough St. ⊖Oxford Circus. Liberty's timbered, Tudor chalet (built in 1922) sets the regal tone for this department store. The focus on top-quality design and handcrafts makes the store more like one giant boutique. Liberty is famous for custom fabric prints—with 10,000 Liberty prints now archived—which appear sewn into everything from shirts to pillows. Open M-W and F-Sa 10am-7pm, Th 10am-8pm, Su noon-6pm. Wheelchair-accessible. AmEx/MC/V.

Fortnum & Mason, 181 Piccadilly (☎7734 8040; www.fortnumandmason.co.uk). ⊖Green Park or Piccadilly Circus. As the official grocer of the royal family, this gourmet department store provides quality foodstuffs fit for a queen. Don't come here to do your weekly shopping—prices aside, the focus is very much on gifts and luxury items. A complete renovation in 2007 added a basement wine bar to the existing 3 restaurants. The fancy St. James Restaurant serves a lovely formal afternoon tea M-Sa 3-7:30pm. Classic set tea £24, rare set tea £27. Fountain Restaurant open M-Sa 8:30am-8pm. Fortnum & Mason open M-Sa 10am-6:30pm, Su noon-6pm (food hall and patio restaurant only). Wheelchair-accessible. AmEx/MC/V.

STREET MARKETS

Better for people-watching than hardcore shopping, street markets may not bring you the big goods but are a much better alternative to a day on Oxford St. **Portobello Road Markets** includes foods, antiques, secondhand clothing, and jewelry. In order to see it all, come Friday or Saturday when everything is sure to be open. (⊖Notting Hill Gate; also Westbourne Park and Ladroke Grove. Stalls set their own times. General hours Th 8am-1pm, F 9am-5pm, and Sa 6:30am-5pm.) **Camden Passage Market** is more for looking than for buying—London's premier antique shops line these charming alleyways. (Islington High St., in North London. ⊖Angel. Turn right from the Tube; it's the alleyway that starts behind "The Mall" antiques gallery on Upper St. Stalls open W 7:30am-6pm and Sa 9am-6pm; some stores open daily, but W is the best day to go.) Its overrun sibling **Camden Markets** (☎7969 1500) mostly includes cheap clubbing gear and tourist trinkets; avoid the canal areas. The best bet is to stick with the **Stables Market,** farthest north from the Tube station. (Make a sharp right out of the Tube station to reach Camden High St., where most of the markets start. All stores are accessible from ⊖Camden Town. Many stores open daily 9:30am-6pm; Stables open F-Su.) **Brixton Market** has London's best selection of Afro-Caribbean fruits, vegetables, spices, and fish. It is unforgettably colorful, noisy, and fun. (Along Electric Ave., Pope's Rd., and Brixton Station Rd., and inside markets in Granville Arcade and Market Row; in South London. ⊖Brixton. Open M-Tu and Th-Sa 7am-7pm, W 7am-3:30pm.) Formerly a wholesale vegetable market, **⊠Spitalfields** has become the best of the East End markets. On Sundays, food shares space with rows of clothing by 25-30 independent local designers. (Commercial St., in East London. ⊖Shoreditch (during rush hour), Liverpool St., or Aldgate East. Crafts market open M-F 11am-3:30pm, Su 10am-5pm. Antiques market open Th 9am-5pm. Organic market open F and Su 10am-5pm.) **Petticoat Lane Market** is Spitalfield's little sister market, on Petticoat Ln., off of Commercial St. It sells everything from clothes to crafts, and is open M 8am-2pm and Tu-F 9am-4pm. Crowds at this market can be overwhelming at times; head to the **Sunday (Up) Market** for similar items in a calmer environment. (☎7770 6100; www.bricklanemarket.com. Housed in a portion of the old Truman Brewery just off Hanbury St., in East London. ⊖Shoreditch or Aldgate East. Open Su 10am-5pm.)

◙ NIGHTLIFE

From pubs to taverns to bars to clubs, London has all the nightlife that a person could want. First-time visitors may initially head to the **West End,** drawn by the flashy lights and pumping music of Leicester Sq. For a more authentic experience, head to the **East End** or **Brixton.** Soho's **Old Compton Street** is still the center of GLBT nightlife. Before heading out for the evening, make sure to plan out **Night Bus** travel. Listings open past 11pm include local Night Bus routes. Night Buses in the West End are ubiquitous—head to Trafalgar Sq., Oxford St., or Piccadilly Circus to catch buses to all destinations.

PUBS

◙ Fitzroy Tavern, 16 Charlotte St. (☎ 7580 3714). ⊖Goodge St. Popular with artists and writers (Dylan Thomas was known to frequent Fitzroy), this pub now oozes with students. Overflows with crowds on summer evenings. The center of Bloomsbury's "Fitzrovia" neighborhood (guess where the area's name came from). Umbrella-covered outdoor seating in summer. W 8:30pm comedy night (£5). Open M-Sa 11am-11pm, Su noon-10:30pm. MC/V.

◙ The Golden Eagle, 59 Marylebone Ln. (☎ 7935 3228). ⊖Bond St. The quintessence of "olde worlde"—both in clientele and in charm. Sidle up to this local-filled bar and enjoy authentic pub sing-alongs (Tu 8:30-10:30pm, Th-F 8:30-11pm) around the piano in the corner. Limited menu—sausage rolls (£1.50) and pasties (£2.20). Sandwiches (£3.50) available M-F noon-3pm. Open M-Sa 11am-11pm, Su noon-7pm. MC/V.

◙ The Jerusalem Tavern, 55 Britton St. (☎ 7490 4281; www.stpetersbrewery.co.uk). ⊖Farringdon. Showcase pub for St. Peter's Brewery with many nooks and crannies. The availability of brews changes with the seasons and is advertised on a chalkboard outside. Specialty ales (£2.40) like grapefruit or cinnamon, several organic ales, Honey Porter, Summer Ale, and Suffolk Gold are available in season. Bring home a case of their speciality beer (£26). Popular with locals. Pub grub £6.50-8.50. Open M-F 11am-11pm. Lunch served daily noon-3pm, dinner served Tu-Th 5-9:30pm. MC/V.

French House, 49 Dean St. (☎ 7437 2799). ⊖Leicester Sq. or Piccadilly Cir. This small Soho landmark used to be frequented by personalities such as Maurice Chevalier, Charlie Chaplin, Salvador Dali, and Dylan Thomas before it became the unofficial gathering place of the French Resistance during World War II. It's said that Charles de Gaulle wrote his "Appeal of 18 June," a speech to the French people, in this very pub. Enjoy the extensive wine selection and hob-nob with some of the most interesting characters in Soho. Wheelchair-accessible. Open M-W noon-11pm, Th-Sa noon-midnight, Su noon-11pm. Restaurant open daily noon-3pm and 5:30-11pm. AmEx/MC/V.

Ye Olde Cheshire Cheese, Wine Office Court. (☎ 7353 6170; www.yeoldecheshire-cheese.com). By 145 Fleet St., not to be confused with The Cheshire Cheese on the other side of Fleet St. Entrance in alleyway. ⊖Blackfriars or St. Paul's. Dating from 1667, the Cheese was once a haunt of Samuel Johnson, Charles Dickens, Mark Twain, and Theodore Roosevelt. A dark labyrinth of oak-paneled, low-ceilinged rooms on 3 fl. Enjoy salads or sandwiches (£3-4) in the Cheshire, meaty traditional dishes in the Chop Room (entrees from £10), daily hot specials (£5) in the downstairs Cellar; or fancier cuisine upstairs in the Johnson Room (£7-13). Front open M-Sa 11am-11pm, Su noon-6pm. Cellar Bar open M-Th noon-2:30pm and 5:30-11pm, F noon-2:30pm. Chop Room open M-F noon-9:30pm, Sa noon-2:30pm and 6-9:30pm, Su noon-5pm. Johnson Room open M-F noon-2:30pm and 7-9:30pm. AmEx/MC/V.

Ye Olde Mitre Tavern, 1 Ely Court (☎ 7405 4751), off #8 Hatton Garden. ⊖Chancery Ln. To find the alley where this pub hides, look for the street lamp on Hatton Garden bearing a sign of a mitre. This classic pub fully merits the "ye olde"—it was built in 1546 by the Bishop of Ely. With oak beams and spun glass, the 2 rooms are perfect for nestling up to a bitter, and the winding courtyard outside is ideal in nice weather. Hot meals subject to availability (about £4), with bar snacks and superior sandwiches (£1.50) served until 9:30pm. Open M-F 11am-11pm. AmEx/MC/V.

The Troubadour, 265 Old Brompton Rd. (☎ 7370 1434; www.troubadour.co.uk). ⊖Earl's Court. A combination pub/cafe/deli. Once upon a time, the likes of Bob Dylan, Joni Mitchell, and Paul Simon played in the intimate basement club. The quirky decor is equally suited for morning espresso shots and evening vodka shots. Live music or poetry readings most nights. Breakfast 9am-3pm £3-9, meals £5.50-10. 2-for-1 mixed drinks in the cafe weekdays 4:30-7:30pm. Open daily 9am-midnight. MC/V.

Dog and Duck, 18 Bateman St. (☎ 7494 0697). ⊖Tottenham Court Rd. This historic establishment sits on the past site of the Duke of Monmouth's Soho house, and is the smallest and oldest pub in Soho. The name refers to Soho's previous role as royal hunting grounds. This was a regular haunt of George Orwell's; the bar on the 1st fl. is named in his honor. Standing room is available near the bar or outside on the sidewalk when the weather is nice. Wheelchair-accessible. Open M-Sa noon-11pm, Su noon-10:30pm. Kitchen open daily noon-3pm and 5-9pm. MC/V.

The George Inn, 77 Borough High St. (☎ 7407 2056). ⊖London Bridge. With a mention in Dickens's *Little Dorritt* and the honor of being the only remaining galleried inn in London, the George takes great pride in its tradition. A deceptively tiny interior leads out into a popular patio. The ale (from £2.50) is excellent. Open M-Sa 11am-11pm, Su noon-10:30pm. Wheelchair-accessible patio. AmEx/MC/V.

BARS

▨ **Absolut Icebar,** 31-33 Heddon St. (☎ 7894 208 848; www.belowzerolondon.com). ⊖Oxford Circus. Because it's everyone's dream to see what it's like to get tipsy in the Arctic. Absolut Icebar is kept just below freezing year-round, and guests are escorted in wearing silver capes and hoods for their pre-booked 40min. time slot. The entire bar is constructed completely of Swedish-imported ice and undergoes a complete renovation every 6 months. Entrance includes use of cape and hood, an ice mug, and vodka cocktail; M-W and Su £12, Th-Sa £15. Open M-W 3:30-11pm, Th 3:30-11:45pm, F 3:30pm-12:30am, Sa 12:30pm-12:30am, Su 3:30-10:15pm.

▨ **Lab,** 12 Old Compton St. (☎ 7437 7820; www.lab-townhouse.com). ⊖Leicester Sq. or Tottenham Court Rd. With restroom signs for "bitches" and "bastards," the only thing this funky cocktail bar takes seriously is its stellar drink menu. Licensed mixologists serve up their own award-winning concoctions (£6-7). DJs spin house and funk nightly from 8pm. Open M-Sa 4pm-midnight, Su 4pm-10:30pm. AmEx/MC/V.

Bar Kick, 127 Shoreditch High St. (☎ 7739 8700). ⊖Old St. World flags and football paraphernalia adorn the beamed ceiling and walls while upbeat music and 4 foosball tables keep crowds happy and wrists sore. More bar than pub, despite sports influence. Tasty mixed drinks (mojitos and martinis £6.50). Food such as nachos and burgers (£4-5) served M-F noon-3:30pm and 6-10pm, Sa-Su all day. Open M-W 10am-11pm, Th-F 10am-midnight, Sa noon-midnight, Su noon-10:30pm. AmEx/MC/V.

Filthy MacNasty's Whiskey Café, 68 Amwell St. (☎ 7837 6067; www.filthymacnastys.com). ⊖Angel or King's Cross. Night Bus #N10, N63, N73, N91, 390. Shane MacGowan, U2, and the Libertines have all played in this laid-back Irish pub. Recently renovated, it has become a trendy neighborhood destination. Outside, red picnic benches support the rowdy overflow. It's actually 2 spaces with separate entrances, linked by the passage marked "toilets." Live music and occasional literary readings add to the hipster-intellectual atmosphere. 14 varieties of whiskey from £2. Pub grub £5-6. Open M-Sa noon-11pm, Su noon-10:30pm.

Vibe Bar, 91-95 Brick Ln. (☎ 7426 0491; www.vibe-bar.co.uk). ⊖Aldgate East. Once the home of the Truman Brewery, this funky bar is loaded with style and is light on pretension. Vibe prides itself on promoting new artists. Relax on a sofa in the all-red lounge or arrive early for an outside table. Free Internet access. Groove to hip-hop, garage, techno, and more. DJs spin M-Sa 7:30-11:30pm, Su 7-11:30pm. Cover F-Sa after 8pm £4. Open M-Th and Su 11am-11:30pm, F-Sa 11am-1am, Su 11:30am-11:30pm.

Big Chill Bar, Dray Walk (☎7392 9180; www.bigchill.net), off Brick Ln. ⊖Liverpool St. or Aldgate East. Despite its lack of address, no one seems to have trouble finding this watering hole off Brick Ln. DJs spin nightly while famously friendly crowds chat it up on big leather couches and on the patio. Stay all day during popular "Big Chill Sundae," with board games, brunch, and prime people-watching with the surrounding market crowds. Mixed drinks from £4. Menu of shareable foods like pizza (£7-9). Su brunch noon-9pm. Open M-Th noon-midnight, F-Sa noon-1am, Su 11am-midnight. MC/V.

The Langley, 5 Langley St. (☎7836 5005). ⊖Covent Garden. This all-purpose basement party bar draws the crowds in early and keeps them there. Happy hour deals (daily 5-7pm; mixed drinks £3.25, margaritas and martinis £4.25). Head to the Geneva Bar, a cavernous dance floor and bar out back with DJs playing old-school dance and pop music. Exposed brick and piping and chain-link chairs make for a sleek, casual experience. Bar food served until midnight. DJs Th-Sa from 9pm. Cover Th after 10pm £3, F-Sa after 10pm £7. Open M-Sa 4:30pm-1am, Su 4-10:30pm. AmEx/MC/V.

NIGHTCLUBS

▩ Fabric, 77a Charterhouse St. (☎7336 8898; www.fabriclondon.com). ⊖Farringdon. Night Bus #242. One of London's most-hyped clubbing venues; expect lines. Europe's first vibrating "bodysonic" dance floor that is actually 1 giant speaker. Beds (for *relaxing*), multiple bars, and 3 dance floors crammed with 2000 Londoners and tourists. The young crowd is generally dressed down. F "Fabric Live" (hip hop, breakbeat, drum and bass); Sa DJs and live acts; Su "DTPM Polysexual Night" (☎7749 1199; www.bluecube.net). Wheelchair-accessible. Cover F £12; Sa in advance £12, at the door £15. Open F 9:30pm-5am, Sa 10pm-7am, Su 10pm-5am. MC/V.

▩ Notting Hill Arts Club, 21 Notting Hill Gate (☎7598 5226; www.nottinghillartsclub.com). ⊖Notting Hill Gate. Night Bus #N94, 148, 207, 390. Turntables, a dance floor, and minimal decoration make the club very chill. A casual venue to sip mixed drinks (from £5) and move to a range of music. House beer and wine (£2.10) until 9pm. Capacity is 218 people, strictly enforced with a 1-in, 1-out policy. Cover Th-Sa after 8pm £5-7. Open M-F 6pm-2am, Sa 4pm-2am, Su 4pm-1am. MC/V.

Ministry of Sound, 103 Gaunt St. (☎7378 6528; www.ministryofsound.co.uk). ⊖Elephant and Castle; take the exit for South Bank University. Night Bus #N35, N133, N343. Mecca for serious clubbers worldwide—arrive before it opens or queue all night. Massive main room, smaller 2nd dance floor, and perpetually packed overhead balcony bar. Dress code generally casual, but famously unsmiling door staff make it sensible to err on the side of smartness: no tracksuits or sneakers, especially on weekends. F "Smoove" R&B; 10:30pm-5am; Sa vocal house 11pm-7am. Cover F £12, Sa £15.

Tongue & Groove, 50 Atlantic Rd. (☎7274 8600; www.tongueandgroove.org). ⊖Brixton. Humbly trendy club and bar so popular and narrow that people dance on the speakers. Arrive early to claim a seat. Relax on huge black leather sofas lining 1 wall. Don't underestimate the mixed drinks (doubles £5). Cover Th after 11pm £2; F-Sa after 10:30pm £3. Open M-W and Su 7pm-3am, Th-Sa 7pm-5am. MC/V.

Aquarium, 256 Old St. (☎7253 3558; www.clubaquarium.co.uk). ⊖Old St.; Exit 3. The only club in London where bringing your bathing suit is par for the course, this club boasts a huge pool and hot tub open to revelers. The 4 bars and 2 sofa-laden chill out rooms keep the dry occupied. F "Creme de la Kremlin" (Russian pop and funky house; dress is smart casual; 10pm-4am). Sa "Carwash" (funky/retro-glam-funk fashion fest)—one of the most awe-inspiring clubbing experiences in London; join stiltwalkers, performers, and dancers in your finest

70s, 80s, and 90s gear (tickets ☎08702 461 966; www.carwash.co.uk; 10pm-3:30am). Cover F men £15, women £10; Sa online £12, at door £15.

The End, 16a West Central St. (☎7419 9199; www.endclub.com), next to AKA. ⊖Tottenham Court Rd. or Holborn. With speaker walls capable of earth-shaking bass, a huge dance floor, and a lounge bar. M "Trash" (glam rock to disco); Th "Discotec" (mixed/gay clubbing with cosmopolitan crowd). Cover M £6; W before 11:30pm £5, after 11:30pm £6; Th before midnight £8, after midnight £9; F £10-15; Sa £15. Open M 10pm-3am, W 10:30pm-3am, Th-F 10pm-4am, Sa 6pm-7am. AmEx/MC/V with £10 min.

Ghetto, Falconberg Court (☎7287 3726; www.ghetto-london.co.uk). ⊖Tottenham Court Rd. Behind the Astoria. Crusading against "lack of originality," Ghetto squeezes alternative nightlife into Soho. Mixed crowd. M Rockstarz (rock, indie); Tu "Don't Call Me Babe" (bubblegum pop); W "NagNagNag" (alternative pop and rock); Th "Miss Shapes" (pop and indie); F "The Cock" (gay night); Sa "Top Secret" (kitsch and trashy tunes); Su "Detox" (funky house). Cover M £3; Tu after 11:30pm £3; W after 11:30pm £5; Th £2, after 11:40pm £4; F £7, students £5; Sa £7 students before 11:30pm £5; Su £6, with flyer £5. Open M-W 10:30pm-3am, Th-Sa 10:30pm-5am, Su 10pm-3am.

Bar Rumba, 36 Shaftesbury Ave. (☎7287 6933; www.barrumba.co.uk). ⊖Piccadilly Circus. Draws a young crowd and has an industrial interior. Many of the best DJs spin here. M Leaders of the True Skool (hip hop, reggae, house); Tu "Barrio Latino" (salsa-rap and techno-merengue; salsa dance class 7:30-9pm; club and class £7); W Flavaz (hip-hop, R&B, reggaeton); Th "Movement" (drum and bass); F "GetDown" (hip hop, 21+); Sa "Flip'd" (urban eclectic; no sportswear); Su "Bubbling Over" (street soul and R&B). Cover M after 10pm £5, students £3; Tu 9-11pm £4, 11pm-3am £5, students £3 all night; W £7; Th before 10pm £4, after 10pm £7, students £6, women free before 11pm; F 9-11pm £8, after 11pm £10, students £6; Sa 10-11pm £5, after 11pm £10; Su £5, women free before 10pm. Open M 9pm-3am, Tu 6pm-3am, W hours vary, Th 8pm-3:30am, F 6pm-3:30am, Sa 9pm-4am, Su 9pm-2am. MC/V.

GLBT NIGHTLIFE

Many venues have Gay and Lesbian nights on a rotating basis. Check *Time Out* and look for flyers and magazines floating around Soho. *The Pink Paper* (free; available from newsstands) and *Boyz* (www.boyz.co.uk) are the main gay listings magazines for London. In addition to the listings below, try "The Cock" at **Ghetto,** "Polysexual Night" at **Fabric,** or ▇**Discotec** at **The End.**

▇ **The Edge,** 11 Soho Sq. (☎7439 1313; www.edge.uk.com). ⊖Oxford Circus or Tottenham Court Rd. A friendly gay and lesbian drinking spot off Soho Sq. offers several venues, complete with Häagen Dazs ice cream and £14 bottles of wine. 4 fl. of brick, silver, and hot pink interior feature a lounge bar on the 1st fl., a piano bar on the 2nd, and a newly refurbished disco dance bar on the top fl. Piano bar Tu-Sa, DJs and dancing Th-Sa. Cover Th-Sa after 10pm £2. Open M-Sa noon-1am, Su noon-11pm. MC/V.

▇ **The Black Cap,** 171 Camden High St. (☎7428 2721; www.theblackcap.com). ⊖Camden Town. North London's most popular gay bar and cabaret is always buzzing and tends to draw an eclectic male and female crowd. The rooftop patio is the highlight of the place. Live shows and club scene downstairs F-Su nights and some weeknights (times vary; call for details). Partially wheelchair-accessible. Cover for downstairs M-Th and Su before 11pm £2, 11pm-close £3; F-Sa before 11pm £3, 11pm-close £4. Open M-Th noon-2am, F-Sa noon-3am, Su noon-1am. Kitchen open noon-10pm.

Escape Dance Bar, 10a Brewer St. (☎7731 2626; www.kudosgroup.com). ⊖Leicester Sq. A small gay and lesbian dance bar with something for everyone—including those with a fetish for scantily clad, costumed doormen. Dance with young, friendly folks to the latest pop hits in an enjoyably cramped, sweaty space. A video DJ plays tunes with big, bright screens from 8pm to 3am daily. Open Tu-Sa 4pm-3am. AmEx/MC/V.

Candy Bar, 4 Carlisle St. (☎7494 4041; www.thecandybar.co.uk). ⊖Tottenham Court Rd. or Oxford Circus. This estrogen-packed, pink-hued drinking spot is a one-stop shop for lesbian entertainment. Karaoke, striptease performances, DJs, and popular dance nights. Pool bar on the 1st fl. and dance bar in the basement. Guys allowed in only with a female escort. M "Set it Off" (alternative); Tu "Indie Girl" (indie); W "Opportunity Knockers" (karaoke); Th "First Class" professional pole-dancing (house and R&B); F "Grind" (house, urban); Sa funky house and R&B; Su funk, soul, and R&B. Cover F-Sa after 9pm £5. Open M-Th 5-10:30pm, F-Sa 3pm-2am, Su 3-10:30pm. MC/V.

G-A-Y, 157 Charing Cross Rd. (☎7434 9592; www.g-a-y.co.uk). ⊖Tottenham Court Rd. Madonna previewed 6 songs from her newest album here. G-A-Y (you spell it out when you say it) has become a Soho institution. M "Pink Pounder" (90s classics with 70s and 80s faves in the bar); Th "Music Factory" (house, dance, and a little pop); F "Camp Attack" (attitude-free 70s and 80s cheese with a 2nd room devoted to 90s music); Sa G-A-Y big night out, rocking the capacity crowd with commercial-dance DJs and live pop performances. Wheelchair-accessible. Cover M and Th with flyer or ad (available at most gay bars) £1, students 50p; F with flyer or ad £2, after midnight £3; Sa depending on performer £8-15. Open M and Th-F 11pm-4am, Sa 10:30pm-5am. Cash only.

Comptons of Soho, 53 Old Compton St. (☎7479 7961). ⊖Leicester Sq. or Piccadilly Circus. Soho's oldest gay pub. Fills up early with a friendly, predominantly older male crowd. Horseshoe-shaped bar is open all the time, while upstairs, the Soho Club Lounge (opens 6:30pm) has a more mellow scene and a break from the noise. Open M-Sa noon-11pm, Su noon-10:30pm. MC/V.

Ku Bar, 30 Lisle St. (☎7600 4353; www.ku-bar.co.uk). ⊖Leicester Sq. Dance space in the basement, a bar on the ground fl. and a lounge on the top fl. It attracts a mixed crowd, with the ages of the clientele generally increasing with the fl. number. Drink specials M-Th and Su. M "Karaoke" (a live band followed by open mic); Tu "Ruby Tuesdays" (for girls and their guy friends); W "Cabaret"; Th "Silk" (screenings of gay films from around the world); Su "Gay Tea Dance" (dance party). Main bar open M-Sa noon-11pm, Su 1-10:30pm. Downstairs Dance Bar open M-Sa 8pm-3am. AmEx/MC/V.

Heaven, The Arches, Craven Terr. (☎7930 2020; www.heaven-london.com). ⊖Charing Cross or Embankment. Self-proclaimed "most famous gay nightclub in the world." Intricate interior and fantastically lit main fl., 5 bars, and a coffee bar. M "Popcorn" (mixed crowd; chart-toppers, 70s-80s disco hits, and commercial house; £2 drinks); F "Bang" (pop; drinks from £3). Cover M before midnight £5, after midnight £8; W before 11:30pm £2, after 11:30pm £4; F before midnight £5, after midnight £7; Sa £12, with flyer £10. Open M 10pm-5am, W 10:30pm-3:30am, F varies, Sa 10:30pm-5am.

◪ DAYTRIPS FROM LONDON

▓ **ROYAL BOTANICAL GARDENS, KEW.** In the summer of 2003, UNESCO named the Royal Botanical Gardens a World Heritage site. The 250-year-old Royal Botanical Gardens, about an hour's Tube ride outside of central London, extend with a green English placidity in a 300-acre swath along the Thames. The three conservatories are at the center of the collection. The steamy Victorian Palm House boasts *Encephalartos Altensteinii,* "The Oldest Pot Plant In The World"; while the Princess of Wales Conservatory houses 10 different climate zones, from rainforest to desert, including two devoted entirely to orchids. Low-season visitors will not be disappointed—the Woodland Glade is renowned for displays of autumn color. Close to the Thames in the northern part of the gardens, newly renovated Kew Palace is a modest red-brick affair used by royalty on garden visits, and which is now open to the public for the first time in 200 years. On the hill behind and to the right of the palace, 17th-century medicinal plants flourish in the Queen's Garden. *(Kew, on the south bank. Main entrance and Visitors Center are at Victoria Gate, nearest the Tube. Go* up the white stairs that go above the station tracks, and walk straight down the road. ⊖Kew Gardens. Zone 3. ☎8332 5000; www.kew.org. Open Apr.-Aug. M-F 9:30am-6:30pm, Sa-Su 9:30am-7:30pm; Sept.-Oct. daily 9:30am-6pm; Nov.-Jan. daily 9:30am-4:15pm. Last admission 30min. before close. Glasshouses close Apr.-Oct. 5:30pm; Nov.-Feb. 3:45pm. Free 1hr. walking tours daily 11am and 2pm start at Victoria Gate Visitors Center. £12.25, concessions £10.25, children under 17 free; 45min. before close £10.25. "Explorer" hop-on, hop-off shuttle makes 40min. rounds of the gardens; 1st shuttle daily 11am, last 4pm; £3.50, children under 17 £1. Free 1hr. "Discovery Bus" tours for mobility-impaired daily 11am and 2pm; booking required; free.)

■**HAMPTON COURT PALACE.** Although a monarch hasn't lived here for 250 years, Hampton Court still exudes regal charm. Cardinal Wolsey built the first palace here in 1514, showing the young Henry VIII how to act the part of a powerful ruler. Henry learned the lesson all too well, confiscating Hampton in 1528 (because Wolsey's palace was nicer than his) and embarking on a major building program. In 1689, William and Mary employed Christopher Wren to bring the Court up to date, but less than 50 years later George II abandoned it for good. The **palace** is divided into six 20min.-1hr. tour routes, all starting at **Clock Court,** where you can pick up a program of the day's events and an audio tour. In ▓**Henry VIII's State Apartments,** only the massive Great Hall and exquisite Chapel Royal hint at past magnificence. A costumed guide leads the Henry VIII tour. Below, the **Tudor Kitchens** offer insight into how Henry ate himself to a 54 in. waist. Predating Henry's additions, the 16th-century **Wolsey Rooms** are complemented by Renaissance masterpieces. Wren's **King's Apartments** were restored to their original appearance after a 1986 fire. The **Queen's Apartments** weren't completed until 1734, postponed by Mary II's death. The **Georgian Rooms** were created by William Kent for George II's family. No less impressive are the **gardens,** with Mantegna's *Triumphs of Caesar* paintings secreted away in the Lower Orangery. North of the palace, the **Wilderness,** a pseudo-natural area earmarked for picnickers, holds the ever-popular **maze,** planted in 1714. Its small size belies a devilish design. (45min. from Waterloo by train; round-trip £5.60. 3-4hr. by boat; daily 10:30, 11am, noon, and 2pm; £13.50, round-trip £19.50; concessions £9/13; children £6.75/9.75. Westminster Passenger Cruises ☎7930 4721; www.thamesriverboats.co.uk. Palace ☎08707 527 777; www.hamptoncourtpalace.org.uk. Open daily from late Mar. to late Oct. 10am-6pm; from late Oct. to late Mar. 10am-4:30pm. Last admission 45min. before close. Palace and gardens £13, concessions £10.50, children 5-15 free. Audio and guided tours included. Admission free for worshippers at Chapel Royal; services Su 11am and 3:30pm.)

SOUTH ENGLAND

 Visitors to South England never seem to want to leave. Early Britons who crossed the Channel settled the counties of Kent, Sussex, and Hampshire, and William the Conqueror left his mark in the form of castles and cathedrals, many built around former Roman settlements. Today, Victorian mansions balance atop seaside cliffs, and the masts of ships grace the skyline. An easy escape from London, the region offers seaside relaxation, while the cobbled streets of Canterbury draw pilgrims.

HIGHLIGHTS OF SOUTH ENGLAND

SHIMMY until the break of dawn at the nightclubs in **Brighton** (p. 161) to burn off those margaritas on the pebbly beach.

CAPTURE a photograph of the famous chalk-white cliffs of **Dover** (p. 152)—and look across to France.

CATCH YOUR BREATH while walking the **South Downs Way** (p. 157), strewn with Bronze Age burial mounds.

KENT

CANTERBURY ☎ 01227

And specially from every shires ende
Of Engelond to Caunterbury they wende.
—Geoffrey Chaucer, *The Canterbury Tales*

In 1170, four knights left Henry II's court in France and traveled to Canterbury to murder Archbishop Thomas à Becket beneath the massive columns of his own cathedral. Three centuries of innumerable pilgrims in search of miracles flowed to St. Thomas's shrine, creating a great medieval road between London and Canterbury. Chaucer caricatured the pilgrimage in *The Canterbury Tales*, which have done more to enshrine the cathedral than the saint's now-vanished bones. In summer, hordes of tourists descend upon the cobbled city center, while for the rest of the year, Canterbury remains a lively college town.

▐ TRANSPORTATION

Trains: Canterbury has 2 central stations.

East Station, Station Rd. E, off Castle St. Open M-Sa 6:15am-8pm, Su 6:30am-9pm. South Eastern trains to **London Victoria** (1¾hr., 2 per hr., before 10am £19.50, after 10am £15.40), **Cambridge** (3hr., 2 per hr., £32.40), and **Dover** (20min., 3 per hr., round-trip £5.60).

West Station, Station Rd. W, off St. Dunstan's St. Open M-Sa 6:15am-7:30pm, Su 9am-4:30pm. Trains to **Central London** (1½hr., every hr., £16.10) and **Brighton** (3hr., 3 per hr., £15.50).

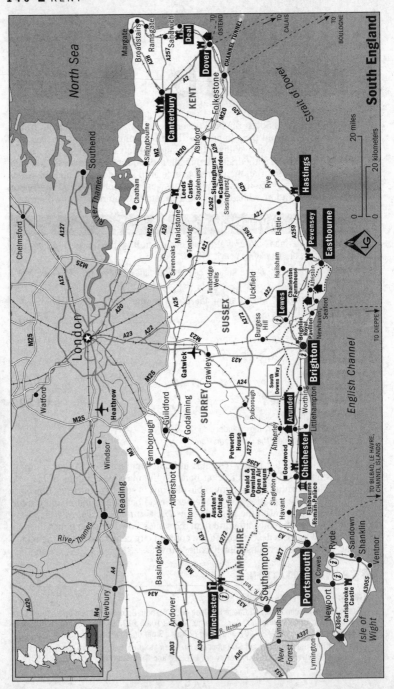

SOUTH ENGLAND

South England

Buses: Bus station, St. George's Ln. (☎472 082). Open M-Sa 8am-5pm. **National Express** (☎08705 808 080) to **London** (2hr., 2 per hr., £13.10). **Explorer** tickets allow 1-day unlimited bus travel in Kent (£8, concessions £6).

Taxis: Longport Cars Ltd. (☎458 885). 24hr.

Bike Rental: Downland Cycle Hire, West Station (☎479 643; www.downlandcycles.co.uk). £10 per day. Bike trailers £7 per day; £25 deposit. Open Tu-Sa 10am-6pm, Su 11am-5pm.

✦☷ ORIENTATION AND PRACTICAL INFORMATION

Canterbury's center is roughly circular, defined by the eroding medieval city wall. The main street crosses the city northwest to southeast, changing names from **Saint Peter's Street** to **High Street** to **The Parade** to **Saint George's Street.** Butchery Ln. and Mercery Ln., each only a block long, run north to the **Cathedral Gates,** while numerous other side streets lead to hidden pubs and chocolatiers.

Tourist Information Centre: The Buttermarket, 12-13 Sun St. (☎378 100, www.visit-canterbury.co.uk). Books beds for £2.50 plus a 10% deposit. Open Easter-Christmas M-Sa 9:30am-5pm, Su 10am-4pm; Christmas-Easter M-Sa 10am-4pm.

Tours: 1½hr. guided tours of the city leave from the TIC. Apr.-Oct. daily 2pm; July-Sept. M-Sa 11:30am and 2pm. £4.25, concessions £3.75, families £12.50.

Financial Services: Banks and **ATMs** are on High St. **Thomas Cook,** 9 High St. (☎597 800). Open M-W and F-Sa 9am-5:30pm, Th 10am-5:30pm, Su 11am-4pm.

Launderette: Canterbury Clothes Care Company, 4 Nunnery Fields (☎452 211). Open M-F 9am-6pm, Sa 9am-4pm, Su 9am-3pm. Last wash 30min. before close. £3.

Police: Old Dover Rd. (☎762 055), outside the eastern city wall.

Hospital: Kent and Canterbury Hospital, 28 Ethelbert Rd. (☎766 877).

Internet Access: Dot Cafe (☎478 778; www.ukdotcafe.com), at the corner of St. Dunstan's St. and Station Rd. £3 per hr. Wi-Fi £2 per hr. Open daily 9am-9pm. Canterbury **Library,** in the Beaney Institute on High St. (☎463 608). Free. Open M-W and Sa 9am-6pm, Th 9am-8pm, Sa 9am-5pm.

Pharmacy: Boots, 12 Gravel Walk. (☎470 944). Open M-W and F 9am-6pm, Th and Sa 8am-7pm, Su 11am-5pm.

Post Office: 29 High St. (☎473 810). **Bureau de change.** Open M and W-Sa 9am-9:30pm, Tu 9:30am-5:30pm. **Post Code:** CT1 2BA.

▮ ACCOMMODATIONS

Canterbury attracts visitors throughout the year, and single rooms are scarce; always reserve ahead. **B&Bs** cluster around High St. and near West Station. The less-expensive options ($18-20) on **New Dover Road,** ½ mi. from East Station, fill fast; turn right from the station and continue to Upper Bridge St. At the second roundabout, turn right onto St. George's Pl., which becomes New Dover Rd.

Kipps Independent Hostel, 40 Nunnery Fields (☎786 121), 10min. from the city center. Century-old townhouse with modern amenities. Self-catering kitchen and TV lounge. Laundry £3. Internet access £1 per 30min. If there are no vacancies, ask to set up a tent in the garden. Key deposit £10. Dorms £14. Singles £19; doubles £33. MC/V. ❷

YHA Canterbury, 54 New Dover Rd. (☎462 911), located 1 mi. from East Station and town center. The trek through town is rewarded by quiet rooms and an all-you-can-eat breakfast buffet. Game room, TV lounge, and self-catering kitchen. Lockers £1. Laundry £1.50. Internet 7p per min. Reception 7:30-10am and 3-11pm. Book ahead in summer. Dorms £17.50, under 18 £13.50. MC/V. ❷

Castle Court Guest House, 8 Castle St. (☎463 441). Adequate, quiet B&B a few minutes from the cathedral and East Station. Breakfast vouchers for cafe next door, vegetarian breakfast available. Singles £25; doubles £45; ensuite £50. Cash only. ❸

Camping: Camping & Caravanning Club Site, Bekesbourne Ln. (☎463 216), off the A257, 1½ mi. east of the city center on a large plot of land near the golf course. Hot showers, laundry (£3), and facilities for the disabled. £5 per person. MC/V. ❶

▶ FOOD

The Safeway **supermarket,** St. George's Center, St. George's Pl., is a 4min. walk from the town center. (☎769 335. Open M-F 8am-9pm, Sa 8am-8pm, Su 11am-5pm.) A **farmers' market** fills the streets near the cathedral on Wednesday afternoons.

Cafe des Amis du Mexique, St. Dunstan's St. (☎464 390; www.cafedez.co.uk), just outside the West Gate. Share a plate of the sizzling steak fajitas (£22) and grab your own margarita (£6). Inspired Mexican dishes in a funky cantina setting. Open M-Sa noon-10:30pm, Su noon-9:30pm. AmEx/MC/V. ❷

Marlowe's, 55 St. Peter's St. (☎462 194; www.marlowesrestaurant.co.uk). The walls, covered with black-and-white photos from New York's Broadway, are as busy as the restaurant. Manages to add some pizzazz to traditional English food. Choose from 7 toppings for 8 oz. burgers (£7). Open M-Sa 9am-10:30pm, Su 10am-10:30pm. MC/V. ❷

Azouma, 4 Church St. (☎760 076; www.azouma.co.uk). Arabic music, pillow seating, and belly dancers every Th night. The Morrocan and Lebanese lunch buffet (£7) is a great deal, and dinner brings generous portions of Middle Eastern and Mediterranean cuisine (£11-14). Open M-Sa noon-midnight, Su noon-11pm. AmEx/MC/V. ❸

C'est la Vie, 17b Burgate (☎457 525). Grab an inventive takeaway sandwich and head to the nearby cathedral. Fill a chicken (£2.50) or fish (£3.20) baguette with any of the 30+ fillings. 10% student discount. Open M-Sa 9:30am-3:30pm. Cash only. ❶

◉ SIGHTS

▓CANTERBURY CATHEDRAL. The massive gate and stony facade of Canterbury cathedral command attention and advertise opulence. Pilgrims' contributions funded most of the cathedral's architectural wonders, including the early Gothic **nave,** constructed mostly between the 13th and 15th centuries on a site allegedly consecrated by St. Augustine 700 years earlier. The shrine to **Saint Thomas à Becket,** destroyed by Henry VIII in 1538, is marked by a single candle. The **Martyrdom** stands where Becket fell—the fatal strike was supposedly so forceful that the blade's tip shattered as it sliced Becket's skull. Henry IV, possibly uneasy after having usurped the throne, had his body entombed near Becket's sacred shrine instead of in Westminster Abbey. Across from Henry lies Edward, the Black Prince, and the decorative armor he wore at his funeral adorns the wall. The **treasury** houses a 1200-year-old saxon pocket sundial among other excavated objects. The **Corona Tower** rises above the eastern apse but is closed to visitors. Stand under the **Bell Harry Tower,** at the crossing of the nave and transepts, to see the perpendicular arches supporting the 15th-century fan vaulting. (☎762 862; www.canterbury-cathedral.org. Cathedral open Easter-Sept. M-Sa 9am-6:30pm, Su 12:30-2:30pm and 4:30-5:30pm; Oct.-Easter M-Sa 9am-5pm, Su 12:30-2:30pm and 4:30-5:30pm. 1¼hr. tours available, 3 per day M-Sa; check nave for times. Evensong M-F 5:30pm, Sa-Su 3:15pm. £6.50, concessions £5. Tours £4, concessions £3. Audio tour £3.50, concessions £2.50.)

SAINT AUGUSTINE'S ABBEY. The skeletons of once-magnificent arches and walls are all that remain of one of the most significant abbeys in Europe, built in AD 598 to house Augustine and 40 monks sent to convert England. Indoor exhibits

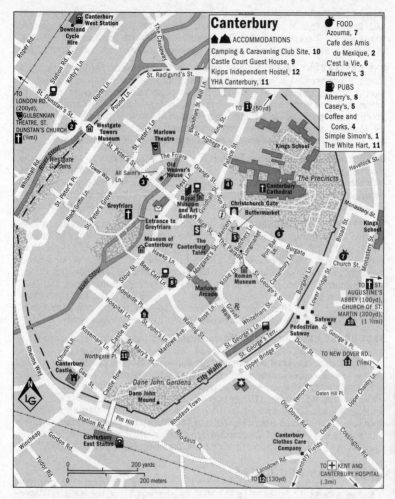

Canterbury

⛺ ACCOMMODATIONS
Camping & Caravaning Club Site, **10**
Castle Court Guest House, **9**
Kipps Independent Hostel, **12**
YHA Canterbury, **11**

🍎 FOOD
Azouma, **7**
Cafe des Amis
du Mexique, **2**
C'est la Vie, **6**
Marlowe's, **3**

🍺 PUBS
Alberry's, **8**
Casey's, **5**
Coffee and
Corks, **4**
Simple Simon's, **1**
The White Hart, **11**

and a free audio tour reveal the abbey's history as a burial place, royal palace, and pleasure garden. Don't miss St. Augustine's humble tomb under a pile of rocks. *(Outside the city wall near the cathedral. ☎ 767 345. Open Apr.-Sept. daily 10am-6pm; Oct.-Mar. W-Su 10am-4pm. £4, concessions £3.)* Just beyond the abbey, the **Church of Saint Martin,** the oldest parish church in England, witnessed the marriage of pagan King Æthelbert and the French Christian Princess Bertha in AD 562, which paved the way for England's conversion to Christianity. The church also holds the final resting place of author Joseph Conrad. *(North Holmes St. ☎ 463 469. Open July-Aug. daily 10am-6pm; Apr.-Jun. W-Su 10am-5pm; Sept.-March Su 11am-5pm. £4, concession £2.)*

MUSEUM OF CANTERBURY. Housed in the medieval Poor Priests' Hospital, the museum spans Canterbury's history from St. Thomas to WWII bombings to children's book character Rupert the Bear. Browse through displays to learn about

Roman foundations and Becket's unsanitary undergarments. *(20 Stour St. ☎475 202. Open June-Sept. M-Sa 10:30am-5pm, Su 1:30-5pm; Nov.-May M-Sa 10:30am-5pm; last entry 4pm. £3.30, concessions £2.20. The Museum Passport grants admission to the Museum of Canterbury, the Westgate Museum, and the nearby Roman Museum. £6, concessions £3.60.)*

THE CANTERBURY TALES. Interested in literature but not in reading? Chaucer's England is recreated in scenes complete with moving wax characters. The smell isn't the guy standing next you—the facility pipes in the "authentic" stench of sweat, hay, and grime to help bring you back in time. Headphone narrations take you through the scenes in a 45min. abbreviation of Chaucer's bawdy masterpiece. *(St. Margaret's St. ☎479 227; www.canterburytales.org.uk. Open daily July-Aug. 9:30am-5pm; Mar.-June and Sept.-Oct. 10am-5pm; Nov.-Feb. 10am-4:30pm. £7.50, students £6.50.)*

GREYFRIARS. England's first Franciscan friary, Greyfriars was built over the River Stour in 1267. It was used as a prison in the 19th century, and prisoners' etchings still mark the cell walls. Now the building has a museum about the local order and a chapel. For a quiet break, walk through the **riverside gardens.** *(6a Stour St. ☎462 395. Gardens open daily 10am-5pm. Chapel open Easter-Sept. M-Sa 2-4pm. Free.)*

WESTGATE TOWERS MUSEUM. The Westgate Towers have guarded the road to London for centuries and are one of the few medieval fortifications to survive wartime blitzing. Built in 1380 as an English defense against France in the Hundred Years War, the structure was a town prison before it was converted into a museum for armor and old weapons. Up a steep, winding staircase sits James, the perennially incarcerated wax figure, enjoying commanding views and plotting his escape from his cell atop the gates. *(☎789 576; www.canterburymuseum.co.uk. Open M-Sa 11am-12:30pm and 1:30-3:30pm. Last admission 15min. before close. £1.25, concessions 70p, families £2.70. Westgate gardens free.)*

BEST OF THE REST. Canterbury Historic River Tours runs 30min. cruises several times per day. *(1 St. Peter's St. ☎07790 534 744; www.canterburyrivertours.co.uk. £6.)* In the city library, the **Royal Museum and Art Gallery** showcases paintings by locally born artists of earlier centuries and recounts the history of the "Buffs," one of the oldest regiments of the British Army. Don't miss the newly acquired Van Dyck and collections by T.S. Cooper. *(18 High St. ☎475 221. Open M-Sa 10am-4:45pm. Free.)* Near the city walls to the southwest lie the remnants of **Canterbury Castle.** *(☎378 100. Open daily 8:30am to dusk. Free.)* The vaults of **Saint Dunstan's Church** contain a buried relic said to be the head of Thomas More; legend says that his daughter bribed the executioner for it. *(St. Dunstan's St. ☎ 463 654. Open daily 8am-4pm; call to confirm. Free.)*

◢◣ ◗ PUBS AND CLUBS

Coffee & Corks, 13 Palace St. (☎457 707). Cafe-bar with a cool, bohemian feel. Mixed drinks (£4), wines by the bottle (£10), and a wide selection of teas (£1.50). Scrabble, occasional live music, and Wi-Fi. Open daily noon-midnight. MC/V.

Alberry's, 38 St. Margaret's St. (☎452 378). Cuddle on leather couches in the corners of this stylish wine bar that pours late into the evenings. Free Wi-Fi. M live music, Tu-Th DJ. Happy hour 5:30-7pm. Open M 11am-1am, Tu-Sa 11am-2am.

Simple Simon's, 3-9 Radigunds Ln. (☎762 355). Any local can direct you to this 14th-century alehouse. Settle down with a hand-pulled Kent brew on the terraced garden for live jazz, folk, and blues music. The restaurant upstairs serves entrees (£8-11) daily 6-9pm. Open M-Sa 11am-11pm, Su noon-10:30pm. AmEx/MC/V, £10 min.

Casey's, Butchery Ln. (☎463 252). Centrally located near the cathedral, Casey's offers quasi-Irish ambience and traditional food (£6), all in the company of Harry the cat. Schedule of live Irish music (Th-Sa) posted outside. Open M-Th noon-11pm, F-Sa 11am-midnight, Su noon-10:30pm. Food served daily until 4pm.

The White Hart, Worthgate Pl. (☎765 091), near East Station. Walk off the train and into this congenial pub. Lunches (£6-8), sweets (£3.50), and some of Canterbury's best bitters (£2.30-2.80). Home of the city's largest beer garden. Open M-Sa noon-11pm, Su noon-4pm. Food served W-F noon-2:30pm, Sa noon-11pm, Su noon-4pm.

♫ 🌿 ENTERTAINMENT AND FESTIVALS

The TIC distributes brochures on up-to-date entertainment listings. **Buskers,** especially along St. Peter's St. and High St., play streetside Vivaldi while bands of impromptu players ramble from corner to corner, acting out the more absurd of Chaucer's scenes. **Marlowe Theatre,** The Friars, across from the Pilgrim Hotel, puts on touring productions in the largest theater in Kent. (☎787 787; www.marloweatheatre.com. Box office open M and Sa 10am-9pm, Tu 10:30am-9pm, Su 2hr. before performances. Tickets £10-35, concessions available. £5 student standbys available from 30min. before most performances.) The **Gulbenkian Theatre,** at the University of Kent, University Rd., west of town on St. Dunstan's St., shows films in Cinema 3 and stages dance, drama, music, and comedy performances. (☎769 075; www.gulbenkiantheatre.co.uk. Box office open M-F 11am-5pm, Sa-Su 5:30-9pm. Tickets £7-25, £7 rush available from 7pm on performance nights.)

In the fall, the **Canterbury Festival** fills two weeks in October with drama, music, dance, walks, and exhibitions. (☎452 853, box office 378 188; www.canterburyfestival.co.uk.) In Ashford, 5 mi. southwest of Canterbury, the **Stour Music Festival** celebrates Renaissance music for seven days in mid-June. The festival takes place at All Saint's Boughton Aluph Church, on the A28 and accessible by rail from West Station. Call the bookings office a month in advance. (☎812 740. Tickets £5-14.)

▣ DAYTRIPS FROM CANTERBURY

▨ SISSINGHURST CASTLE GARDEN

Trains run from Canterbury West to Staplehurst (50min., round-trip £9.10), where buses #4 and 5 run to Sissinghurst (M-Sa every hr., round-trip £3.50). Shuttle runs from Staplehurst station to Sissinghurst gardens (15min., round-trip £4). The garden is 1 mi. from the bus stop; turn back on The Street and walk ¼ mi. before turning left onto the footpath. ☎01580 710 700; www.nationaltrust.org.uk/sissinghurst. Open from mid-Mar. to Oct. M-Tu and F 11am-6:30pm, Sa-Su 10am-6:30pm. Last entry 1hr. before close. £7.80, children £3.50.

A masterpiece of floral design by Bloomsbury Group stalwarts Vita Sackville-West and her husband, Harold Nicolson, Sissinghurst is one of the most popular gardens in a garden-obsessed nation. Eight gardeners maintain the original design, a varied array of carved hedges and flower beds. After touring the White Garden or the Cottage Garden, visitors may visit the property's large Elizabethan mansion or stroll along the moat to forested lakes. The library and tower are also open to the public and chronicle the garden's development. The staff encourages visitors to come after 4pm, when the afternoon sunlight enhances the garden's beauty.

LEEDS CASTLE

Near Maidstone, 23 mi. west of Canterbury on the A20. Trains run from Canterbury West to Bearsted (every hr., £11.50); a shuttle goes from the station to the castle (£4). Shuttles leave the train station M-Sa 10:35am-2:35pm every hr., Su 10:55am-2:55pm every hr.; return shuttles leave the castle M-Sa 2-6pm on the hour, Su 2:15-6:15pm on the quarter hour. ☎01622 765 400 or 0870 600 8880; www.leeds-castle.com. Castle open daily Apr.-Sept. 10:30am-7pm, Oct.-Mar. 10:30am-5pm. Last admission to castle 1½hr. before close. Grounds open daily Apr.-Sept. 10am-7pm; Oct.-Mar 10am-5pm. Last admission to grounds 2hr. before close. Castle and grounds £14, concessions £11. Call for combined transportation and admission tickets, available at train and bus stations.

Sitting amid 500 acres of parkland and 1000 years of history, Leeds Castle was built immediately after the Norman Conquest and remained a favorite royal playground until Edward VI, Henry VIII's son, sold it for a song. The Tudor-style ground floor contrasts sharply with the modern second floor, which was impeccably outfitted by the same interior decorator responsible for Jackie Kennedy's White House overhaul. One wing displays an alarming collection of medieval dog collars. The grounds host a jousting tournament at the beginning of June and summer concerts during July (consult TIC for exact dates). Outdoors, wind through a maze of 2400 yew trees, practice your swing on the 9-hole golf course, or take one of the woodland walks, which cross paths with black swans and other unusual waterfowl. Come back often—a ticket is good for one year from the date of purchase.

DOVER   ☎ 01304

From the days of Celtic invaders to the age of the Chunnel, the white chalk cliffs of Dover have been many a traveler's first glimpse of England. In July and August, adventurous swimmers make the 21 mi. doggy-paddle across the Channel to France. On land, walk along the cliffs or through the formidable castle.

▐ TRANSPORTATION

Trains: Priory Station, Station Approach Rd. Ticket office open M-Sa 4:15am-11:20pm, Su 6:15am-11:20pm. Trains (☎08457 484 950) to **Canterbury** (20min., 2 per hr., round-trip £5.60) and **London** (2hr., 4 per hr., £22).

Buses: Pencester Road Station between York St. and Maison Dieu Rd. Office open M-Tu and Th-F 8:45am-5:15pm, W 8:45am-4pm, Sa 8:30am-noon. The TIC sells National Express (☎08705 808 080) tickets. Buses run to **London,** continuing to the **Eastern Docks** (2½hr., every hr., £11.80). Stagecoach (☎08702 433 711) to **Canterbury** (30min., every hr., £4.40) and **Deal** (45min., every hr., £3.10). A bus runs to **Folkestone,** a stop for Chunnel trains (30min., every hr., £3.40). A **Day Explorer** ticket (£4.50) gives 1 day of unlimited travel on Stagecoach buses in East Kent.

Ferries: Eastern Docks sails to **Calais, France** and **Oostend, Belgium;** the TIC offers a booking service. P&O Stena (☎08705 980 333; www.posl.com) sails to **Calais** (40 per day, £18); as does SeaFrance (☎0870 443 1653; www.seafrance.com. 15 per day, £6). The Seacat leaves the Hoverport at **Prince of Wales Pier** for Calais (£25). Bus service (£1) leaves Priory Station for the docks 45-60min. before sailing. (See **By Ferry,** p. 31.) The **Channel Tunnel** offers passenger service on Eurostar and car transportation on Le Shuttle to and from the continent. (See **By Chunnel,** p. 31.)

Taxis: Central Taxi Service (☎240 0441). 24hr.

▐ PRACTICAL INFORMATION

Tourist Information Centre: The Old Town Gaol (☎205 108; www.whitecliffscountry.org.uk), off High St. where it divides into Priory Rd. and Biggin St. Helpful staff sells ferry, bus, and hoverspeed tickets and books accommodations for 10% deposit; after hours call ☎01271 336 093 for accommodations list. Open June-Aug. daily 9am-5:30pm; Apr.-May and Sept. M-F 9am-5:30pm, Sa-Su 10am-4pm; Oct.-Mar. M-F 9am-5:30pm, Sa 10am-4pm.

Tours: White Cliffs Boat Tours at the Marina (☎01303 271 388; www.whitecliffsboattours.co.uk). 4 per day. £5.

Financial Services: Several **banks** and **ATMs** are in Market Sq., including **Barclays** in the northwest corner. Open M-F 9:30am-4:30pm.

Launderette: Cherry Tree Launderette, 2 Cherry Tree Ave. (☎242 822), off London Rd. Wash and dry £3. Full service available. Open daily 8am-8pm. Last wash 7:15pm.

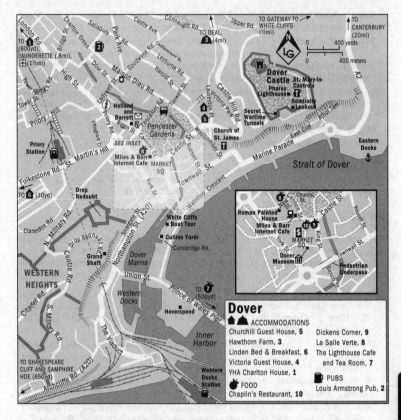

Dover

🏠🏠 ACCOMMODATIONS

Churchill Guest House, **5**
Hawthorn Farm, **3**
Linden Bed & Breakfast, **6**
Victoria Guest House, **4**
YHA Charlton House, **1**

Dickens Corner, **9**
La Salle Verte, **8**
The Lighthouse Cafe
  and Tea Room, **7**

🍴 FOOD
Chaplin's Restaurant, **10**

🍺 PUBS
Louis Armstrong Pub, **2**

Police: Ladywell St. (☎ 240 055), off High St.

Pharmacy: Superdrug, 33-34 Biggin St. (☎ 211 477). Open M-Sa 8:30am-5:30pm, Su 10am-4pm.

Internet: Miles & Barr Coffee Barr, 7 Canon St. (☎ 202 111). £2 per hr., Wi-Fi £1.50 per hr. Open Tu-F 9:30am-5:30pm, Sa 9:30am-5pm.

Hospital: Buckland Hospital, Coomb Valley Rd. (☎ 201 624), northwest of town. Take bus #67 or 67A from the post office.

Post Office: 68-72 Pencester Rd. (☎ 241 747). Open M-F 8:30am-5:30pm, Sa 8:30am-2pm. **Post Code:** CT16 1PW.

🏠 ACCOMMODATIONS

Rooms are scarce in summer; book well ahead. July and August are especially busy due to the influx of distance swimmers eager to try the Channel. Cheaper **B&Bs** gather on **Folkestone Road,** a hike past the train station. Pricier B&Bs lie near the city center on **Castle Street,** and more can be found on **Maison Dieu Road.**

Churchill Guest House, 6 Castle Hill Rd. (☎ 208 365). Enormous, tidy rooms near the castle base. Breakfast included. Singles £35; doubles £55-70. Cash only. ❹

Victoria Guest House, 1 Laureston Pl. (☎205 140). Cheerful ensuite rooms and talkative owners in a large mansion with views of Dover. Doubles £48-58. AmEx/MC/V. ❸

YHA Charlton House, 306 London Rd. (☎201 314), ½ mi. from Priory station; turn left on Folkestone Rd. then left at the roundabout on High St., which becomes London Rd. Lounge, pool table, kitchen, lockers, and Internet access. Sells ferry tickets. Breakfast included. Lockout 10am-1pm. Curfew 11pm. Dorms £17.50, under 18 £14. MC/V. ❷

Linden Bed & Breakfast, 231 Folkestone Rd. (☎205 449). A bit far from the town center, but this plush B&B makes every effort to accommodate—ask about pickup from the train station or docks and breakfasts for special diets. Discount vouchers for local sights. Satellite TV. Singles £30; doubles and twins £45-60. MC/V. ❸

Camping: Hawthorn Farm (☎852 658), at Martin Mill Station off the A258 between Dover and Deal. 2min. walk from the train station; follow the signs. Set among 28 acres of gardens. Hot showers and laundry facilities available. Closed Nov.-Feb. June-Aug. 2-person tent and car £14, with electricity £17; Mar.-May and Sept.-Oct. £12/14. Hikers and bikers £4; Mar.-May and Sept.-Oct. £3.50. Cash only. ❶

◼ FOOD AND PUBS

Despite Dover's proximity to the Continent, its cuisine remains staunchly English. Most of the restaurants in the city are unimpressive, but diligent travelers will find a few worthwhile options. Chip shops line **London Road** and **Biggin Street.** Visit Holland & Barrett, 35 Biggin St., for **groceries.** (☎241 426. Open M-Sa 9am-5:30pm.)

La Salle Verte, 14-15 Cannon St. (☎201 547). A relative newcomer to the city center, this modern cafe has old-fashioned charm. Specialty coffees (£1.50-2) and a selection of pastries (£2-4) served on a garden patio or comfy leather love seats. Wi-Fi £1.50 per hr. Open M-Su 9am-5pm. Cash only. ❶

Dickens Corner, 7 Market Sq. (☎206 692). The ground floor bustles with channelers downing baguettes and cakes (£2-3.50) or hot lunches (£4-5.50) in a sun-filled room. Upstairs, avoid the wait and have a more leisurely meal. Additional outdoor seating faces the water fountain in Market Sq. Open M-Sa 9am-4:30pm. MC/V. ❶

Chaplins, 2 Church St., off Market Sq. (☎204 870). Huge portions of traditional English food. Sandwiches (£2.75), savory pies (£6), and heavenly apple pie with cinnamon cream (£2.75). Su roast served noon-3pm. Open daily 8am-5pm. MC/V. ❷

Louis Armstrong Pub, 58 Maison Dieu Rd. (☎204 759), on the outskirts of town, marked by a picture of Satchmo himself. Live music with Su jazz nights. Excellent selection of ales. Open M-Sa 11am-11pm, Su noon-2pm and 7-11pm. Cash only. ❶

The Lighthouse Cafe and Tea Room, at the end of Prince of Wales Pier. View emerald waters and chalky cliffs from ½ mi. offshore in the closest cafe to France. Mediocre food, but worth it for the view. Open in summer daily 10am-5:30pm. Cash only. ❶

◉ SIGHTS

◼**DOVER CASTLE.** More fortress than fairytale, Dover Castle, Castle Hill Rd. on the east side of town, is imposing and magnificent. The safeguard of England since Roman times, the castle was a focus of conflict from the Hundred Years' War to WWII, during which its guns were pointed toward German-occupied France. Watch the introductory video in the **Keep** before entering simulations of the castle under siege and in preparation for a king's visit. Hitler's missiles destroyed the **Church of St. James,** leaving the ruins crumbling at the base of the hill. The **Pharos lighthouse**—the only extant Roman lighthouse and the tallest remaining Roman edifice in Britain—towers over **St. Mary-in-Castro,** a tiled Saxon church. Climb to

SOUTH ENGLAND

the platform of the **Admiralty Lookout** for views of the cliffs and harbor. For 20p, you can spy on France through binoculars. The (not so) ■**Secret Wartime Tunnels,** a 3½ mi. labyrinth deep within the white rock, were only recently declassified. Begun in 1803, when Britain was under the threat of attack by Napoleon, the underground burrows doubled as the base for the WWII evacuation of Allied troops from Dunkirk and a shelter for Dover citizens during air raids. The lowest of the five levels, not open to the public, was intended to house the government should the Cuban Missile Crisis have gone sour. Tours fill quickly, and there is often a long wait; check in at the tunnels first. Give yourself at least three hours to tour the entire castle and grounds. *(Buses from the town center run daily Apr.-Sept. (every hr., 55p). Otherwise, scale Castle Hill using the pedestrian ramp and stairs to the left of Castle St. Open Apr., June-July, and Sept. daily 10am-6pm; Aug. daily 9:30am-6pm; Oct. daily 10am-5pm; Nov.- Jan. M and Th-Su 10am-4pm; Feb.-Mar. daily 10am-4pm. £9.80, concessions £7.40.)*

THE WHITE CLIFFS. Lining the most famous strip of England's coastline, the white cliffs are a beautiful backdrop for a stroll along the pebbly beach. A few miles west of Dover, the whitest, steepest, and most famous of them all is **Shakespeare Cliff,** traditionally identified as the site of blind Gloucester's battle with the brink in *King Lear. (25min. by foot along Snargate St. and Archcliffe Rd.)* To the east of Dover, past Dover Castle, the **Gateway to the White Cliffs** overlooks the Strait of Dover and is an informative starting point. *(Buses go from the town center to Langdon Cliff at least once per hr. ☎202 756. Open daily Mar.-Oct. 10am-5pm; Nov.-Feb. 11am-4pm.)* Dozens of **cliff walks** lie a short distance from Dover; consult the TIC or the visitor center at the Gateway to the White Cliffs for trail information. Dover White Cliffs Boat tours, at the Clock Tower in Dover Marina, offers 40min. trips around the coastline. *(☎01303 271 388; www.whitecliffsboattours.co.uk. £6, children £3, families £16.)* **The Grand Shaft,** a 140 ft. triple-spiral staircase, was shot through the rock in Napoleonic times to link the army on the Western Heights with the city center. *(Snargate St. ☎201 066. Open select days throughout year; call for dates. The cliffs to the east and west of Dover can be viewed and photographed at a distance from the tip of Prince of Wales Pier.)*

DOVER MUSEUM. This museum depicts Dover's Roman days as the colonial outpost Dubras. The **Bronze Age Boat Gallery** houses the remnants of the oldest ship yet discovered—it's 3550 years old. *(Market Sq. ☎201 066. Open Apr.-Sept. M-Sa 10am-5:30pm, Su noon-5pm; Oct.-Mar. M-Sa 10am-5:30pm. £2.50, concessions £1.50, families £6.)*

OTHER SIGHTS. Recent excavations unearthed a remarkably well-preserved **Roman painted house.** It's the oldest Roman house in Britain, with central heating and indoor plumbing. It also holds the best-preserved Roman wall painting in Britain, more than 1800 years old. *(New St., off York St. and Cannon near Market Sq. ☎203 279. Open Apr.-Sept. Tu-Su 10am-5pm. Last admission 4:30pm. £2, concessions 80p.)* For striking views, take the A20 toward Folkestone to **Samphire Hoe,** a park planted in the summer of 1997 with material dug from the Channel Tunnel. The D2 bus to Aycliffe (£1) stops about a 10min. walk from the park, or follow the North Downs Way along the clifftop. *(Open daily 7am-dusk.)* Climb the 73 steps of the **South Foreland Lighthouse** for 360° views of Kent and the channel. *(2 mi. from the Gateway to the White Cliffs Visitor Centre. Open daily 11am-5:30pm. Visits by guided tours only. £4.)*

■ **DAYTRIP FROM DOVER**

DEAL
Trains from Dover Priory arrive in Deal Station (15min., every hr., £3.40). The TIC, in the Landmark Centre on corner of Union Rd. and High St., books beds for a 10% deposit. ☎369 576. Open M-F 10am-4pm, Sa 10am-2pm.

Julius Caesar landed here in 55 BC, and Deal's castles represent Henry VIII's 16th-century attempt to prevent similar invasions. **Deal Castle,** south of town at the corner of Victoria and Deal Castle Rd., is one of Henry's largest Cinque Ports (antipirate establishments) and has an impressive artillery collection in a symmetrical maze of dark cells and corridors. (☎01304 372 762. Open Apr.-Sept. daily 10am-6pm. Last admission 5:30pm. £4.) **Walmer Castle,** ½ mi. south of Deal via the beach-front pedestrian path or the A258 (and 1 mi. from the Walmer train station), is the best-preserved and most elegant of Henry VIII's citadels. Walmer has been transformed into a country estate, which has been the official residence of the Lords Warden of the Cinque Ports since the 1700s. Notable Wardens past include the Duke of Wellington, William Pitt, Winston Churchill, and, most recently, the Queen Mother. The gardens were planted with her favorite flowers for her 95th birthday. (☎01304 364 288. Open Apr.-Sept. M-F and Su 10am-6pm, Sa 10am-4pm; Mar. daily 10am-4pm; Oct. W-Su 10am-4pm. Last admission 30min. before close. Closed when the Lord Warden is in residence. £6.20. Free 30min. audio tour.) Stay the night at **Sondes Lodge Guest House** ❸, 14 Sondes Rd., which offers three ensuite rooms close to the beach and town center. (☎368 741. Breakfast included. £28-40.) Residents from all over the region dine on local fish dishes (£15-25) at **Dunkerley's Restaurant Bistro** ❹, 19 Beach St., overlooking the sea. (☎375 016. Open M 7-9:30pm, Tu-F noon-2:30pm and 7-9:30pm, Sa noon-2:30pm and 6-10pm, Su noon-3pm and 7-9:30pm. AmEx/MC/V.)

SUSSEX

HASTINGS   ☎01424

Huddled between sandstone cliffs and the emerald channel, Hastings has been claimed by Romans, Normans, and Victorians throughout its turbulent history. Having finally surrendered its name and identity to a decisive battle (p. 69), the seaside resort town of Hastings still revels in its 1000-year-old claim to fame. Looming above the carousel and mini-golf-strewn promenade, the remains of **Hastings Castle,** built by William the Conqueror, mark the spot where the Norman duke's troops camped before confronting Harold II and the Saxons. The castle met its demise in the 13th century, when part of the cliff collapsed and took half the fortifications with it. During WWII, homeward-bound Germans finished the job by dropping excess explosives on Hastings. Catch the **1066 Story,** a 20min. film on the famous tussle, and visit the castle's moldy dungeons. The castle offers some of the region's best views. (☎781 111; www.discoverhastings.co.uk. Take the West Hill Railway from George St. to the top of the hill. Round-trip £1.50, concessions 90p. Open daily from mid-Sept. to mid-Mar. 11am-4pm, from mid-Mar to mid-Sept. 10am-5pm. £3.65, concessions £3.) Before heading back to sea level, duck into St. Clements Caves for the **Smugglers Adventure.** Now more like a theme park with games and smuggling simulations, these miles of caves and tunnels were once the center of the Sussex smuggling ring. (☎422 964; www.smugglersadventure.co.uk. Open daily Mar.-Sept. 10am-5:30pm, Oct.-Feb. 11am-4:30pm. £6.40.) Exhibits about the area's nautical past reside in several charity-run museums on the seafront. The **Shipwreck Heritage Centre,** Rock-a-Nore Rd. at the end of Marine Parade, is the largest, featuring the complete hull of a Victorian river barge. (☎437 452. Open daily Mar.-Sept. 10am-5pm; Nov.-Feb. 11am-4pm. Free.)

　　B&Bs crowd around Cambridge Gardens, by the train station. A 5min. walk from the town center, **Apollo Guest House** ❸, 25 Cambridge Gardens, is trimmed in pink and offers nine rooms with large beds complete with TV and full breakfast. They also rent a self-catering apartment for longer stays. (☎444 394. Singles £23-

33; doubles £46-66. Apartment £350 per week.) For **groceries**, visit Morrison's, Supermarkets Pl. behind the train station. (☎720 833. Open M-W and Sa 8am-8pm, Th-F 8am-10pm, Su 10am-4pm.) Restaurants and takeaways are ubiquitous. Try **Frenz Grill Bar ❶**, 46 Robertson Rd. for their delicious assortment of sandwiches (£3), "wrapz" (£2.75), and £1 pizza slices. (☎426 832. Open M-W and Su 11am-11pm, Th-Sa 11am-3am). Around the corner, **Bor Thong Thai Restaurant ❷**, 6 Claremont, serves sizzling courses (£5-10) and veggie options. (☎429 629. Open daily noon-3pm and 6-11pm.) For an affordable vegetarian feast, try **Heaven and Earth ❷**, 37E Robertson St. (☎712 206. Open T-Su 10am-5pm.)

Hastings is a good base for exploring its historic neighbors. **Trains** (☎08457 484 950) go from Hastings Station to: Dover (2hr., every hr., £13.40); Eastbourne (40min., every hr., £5.20); Brighton (1½hr., every hr., £10); London Victoria (2hr., every hr.). The helpful staff at the **Tourist Information Centre**, in Queens Sq., signposted from the train station, books accommodations for £2. (☎08452 741 001; www.hastings.gov.uk. Open M-F 8:30am-6:15pm, Sa 9am-5pm, Su 10:30am-4:30pm.) **Internet** access is available at Mahaul's Internet Cafe, 1 York Building. (☎434 885. £1.60 per hr. Open daily 9am-10pm.) The **post office** is at 10 Cambridge Rd. (Open M and W-Sa 9am-5:30pm, Tu 9:30am-5:30pm.) **Post Code**: TN34 1AA.

DAYTRIP FROM HASTINGS

BATTLE

Trains run from Hastings (15min., 2 per hr., round-trip £2.80). Battle Abbey is in the center of town; turn left out of the train station and walk to the signposts at the end of the road. The Battle Abbey TIC books accommodations for a 10% deposit. ☎01424 773 721; www.battletown.co.uk. Open Apr.-Sept. daily 10am-5pm; Oct.-Mar. M-Sa 10am-4pm.

The small town of Battle was named after the famous 1066 clash between the Normans and Anglo-Saxons that occurred here. To commemorate his victory in the Battle of Hastings, William the Conqueror built **Battle Abbey** in 1094, spitefully positioning its altar upon the spot where Harold fell (p. 69). Little remains of the abbey apart from the gate and a series of 13th-century monks' quarters. A free audio tour narrates the story of the battle from both Saxon and Norman perspectives. (Open daily Apr.-Sept. 10am-6pm; Oct.-Mar. 10am-4pm. £5.50, concessions £4.10.) Retrace the action as you walk the 1½ mi. trail around the now-peaceful **battlefield.**

SOUTH DOWNS WAY

The South Downs Way stretches 99 mi. from Eastbourne west toward Portsmouth and Winchester. The paths meander through chalk hills and livestock-laden meadows, never far from coastal towns, yet rarely crossing into civilization. The Downs were initially cultivated by prehistoric peoples, whose settlements still mark the countryside. The Way is marked from start to finish, but a detailed guide is obtainable at any local TIC. The walking is moderate, wooing novice hikers and making the South Downs one of the most accessible outdoor experiences in England.

TRANSPORTATION

Trains (☎08457 484 950) run from Eastbourne to London Victoria (1½hr., 2 per hr., £19) and from Petersfield to London Waterloo (1hr., 3 per hr., £16.20). Eastbourne's helpful **Bus Stop Shop**, Arndale Centre, dispenses info on **buses.** From the train station, turn left onto Terminus Rd.; Arndale Centre is on the left. (☎01323 416 416. Open M-Sa 9am-5pm.) Walking the path takes about 10 days, but public transportation

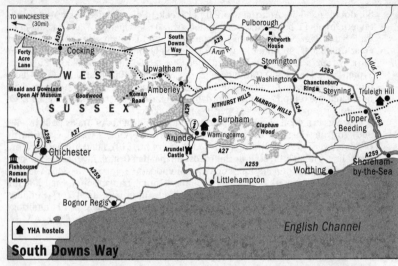

TO WINCHESTER (30mi.)

Forty Acre Lane

Cocking

WEST

Weald and Downland Open Air Museum

Goodwood

Roman Road

SUSSEX

A286

A27

Chichester

A286

Fishbourne Roman Palace

A259

Bognor Regis

Upwaltham

Amberley

A29

Arundel

Arundel Castle

Warningcamp

A27

Littlehampton

South Downs Way

Pulborough

Petworth House

A29

Arun R.

Storrington

A283

Washington

Chanctonbury Ring

Steyning

Truleigh Hill

KITHURST HILLS

HARROW HILLS

A24

Burpham

Clapham Wood

Upper Beeding

A283

Adur R.

A259

A259

Worthing

Shoreham-by-the-Sea

YHA hostels

English Channel

South Downs Way

allows you to take it in segments. **Trains** connect Lewes to Southease (6min., 2 per hr., £2), County **Buses** #143 and 21 connect Eastbourne to Lewes (20min., 2 per day, £2), and #126 connects Eastbourne with Alfriston (40min., 5 per day, round-trip £5). For details, call Eastbourne Buses (☎01323 416 416) or Traveline (☎870 608 2608).

Cycling has long been a popular means of seeing the Downs. D.H. Lawrence cycled the Way in 1909 to visit his friend Rudyard Kipling. Cyclists and **horses** have access to most of the trail, but in a number of places their routes diverge from those of the walkers. Cycling the Way takes 2-3 days. The Harvey map (£10 at the TIC or bookstores) shows all of the cycling paths in detail. If you're starting from Eastbourne, try Nevada Bikes, 324 Seaside (☎01323 411 549) for **bike rental.** At the other end of the trail, in Winchester, is Halford's, Moorside Rd. (☎01962 853 549). The **Cyclists Touring Club** (☎0870 873 0060; www.ctc.org.uk) answers questions. Audiburn Riding Stables, Ashcombe Ln., Kingston, conducts guided 1hr. **horseback tours.** (☎01273 474 398. £20, under 16 £17.)

■ ORIENTATION

Serious hikers begin their trek in **Eastbourne,** the official start of the Way. Eastbourne's **Beachy Head** cliff (p. 160) is accessible by the 12A bus to Brighton and is marked from the train station. From **Winchester** town center (p. 179), at the other end of the Way, head east on Bridge St., turn right on Chesil St., then left on East Hill. When East Hill splits, take the right fork onto Petersfield Rd. and head for the car park, where signs for the Way will appear. From the village of **Amberley,** just north of Arundel (p. 168), the Way runs north, parallel to the main road (B2139).

ⓘ PRACTICAL INFORMATION

Eastbourne is the most convenient location to arrange accommodations and find local services. Any of the following TICs can provide information, maps, and book accommodations for the Way.

Tourist Information Centres:

Eastbourne: Cornfield Rd. (☎09067 112 212; www.visiteastbourne.com). Provides basic free maps and sells guides. Open Mar.-Oct. M-F 9:30am-5:30pm, Sa 9:30am-5pm; Nov.-Feb. M-F 9:30am-4pm, Sa 9:30am-1pm.

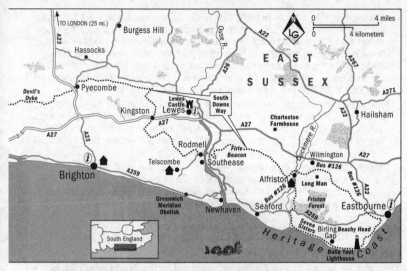

Brighton: Royal Pavilion Shop, 4-5 Pavilion Building. See p. 162.

Lewes: 187 High St. (☎01273 483 448). Books rooms and sells Ordnance Survey maps and guides. Open Apr.-Sept. M-F 9am-5pm, Sa 10am-5pm, Su 10am-2pm; Oct.-Mar. M-F 9am-5pm, Sa 10am-2pm.

Winchester: The Guildhall; see p. 180.

Guidebooks:

In Print: *Harvey's South Downs Way* (£10) is the Bible of the Downs, available at all local TICs. It includes a waterproof map. The Eastbourne and Lewes TICs sell *50 Walks in Sussex* (£8). The South Downs Way accommodation guide (£3.50) is helpful for finding places to stay, as is the free *Caravan and Camping Sites in Sussex* brochure, available at local TICs.

Online: Find more info at the South Downs Way Virtual Information Centre (www.vic.org.uk) and the Rural Walks site (www.ruralways.org.uk). YHA listings are available at www.yha.org.uk.

Camping Supplies: Millets, The Outdoors Store, 146-148 Terminus Rd., Eastbourne (☎01323 728 340). Stocks camping supplies and Ordnance Survey maps. Open M-Sa 9am-5pm, Su 10:30am-4pm. Brighton also has many outdoors shops.

Financial Services: Banks with **ATMs** are located in **Eastbourne** town center and in bigger cities on the Way. Pick up cash before hitting the trail. **Lloyd's TSB,** 104 Terminus Rd. (☎08453 000 000). Open M-Tu and Th-F 9am-5pm, W 10am-5pm, Sa 9am-2pm.

ACCOMMODATIONS

There are few towns along the Way, and **B&Bs** fill quickly. **Brighton** (p. 161) makes a good base, as do **Lewes** (p. 167), **Arundel** (p. 168), **Alfriston,** and Southcliff Ave. in **Eastbourne.** For a relaxing night on the seafront, take a room at **Alexandra Hotel ❸,** King Edward's Parade, in Eastbourne. (☎1323 720131. Breakfast included. June-Sept. from £32 per person; Mar.-May and Oct.-Dec. from £30 per person. MC/V.) The **Atlanta Guest House ❸,** 10 Royal Parade, offers comfortable ensuite rooms with seaside views. (☎730 486. Singles £30; doubles £27 per person.) **Camping** on the Way is permitted with the landowner's permission. A guide to camping sites along the Way can also be obtained in the Eastbourne TIC.

The following **YHA hostels** lie along or near the Way, each within a day's walk of the next, and each with an 11am-8pm lockout and 11pm curfew. For other hostels, check the accommodations sections in Brighton (p. 162) or Arundel (p. 168).

Alfriston, Frog Firle, Alfriston (☎0870 770 5666). 1½ mi. from the Way and from Alfriston, 8 mi. from Eastbourne. Bus #126 from Seaford to Eastbourne passes the hostel. By foot from Alfriston, turn left from the market cross and pass the village green, then follow the overgrown riverside trail to Litlington footbridge and turn right along the path; the hostel is at the end in a stone house with bovine neighbors. 16th-century house with spacious rooms. Full breakfast £4. Internet access. Open July-Aug. daily; Feb.-June and Sept.-Oct. M-Sa; Nov.-Dec. F-Sa. Dorms £13.75, under 18 £11. MC/V. ❷

Telscombe, Bank Cottages, Telscombe Village (☎0870 770 6062). 2 mi. south of Rodmell, 2 mi. from the Way, 12 mi. west of Alfriston. From Rodmell (p. 160), follow signs directly to the hostel or take bus #123 or 14A and ask to be let off. A short walk from Virginia Woolf's house. 18th-century house with cottages and a cheery staff. Open daily Apr.-Aug. Dorms £12, under 18 £9. MC/V. ❷

Truleigh Hill, Tottington Barn, Truleigh Hill, Shoreham-by-Sea (☎01903 813 419). 10 mi. from Brighton, 4 mi. from Shoreham station. Converted 1930s house serves mostly hikers and cyclists. Meals £3.75. Open daily July-Aug.; Mar.-June and Sept.-Oct. call in advance. Dorms £14, under 18 £10. MC/V. ❷

⛰ HIKING THE SOUTH DOWNS WAY

EASTBOURNE TO ALFRISTON

The Victorian seaside city of **Eastbourne,** sheltered by the **Beachy Head** cliff, is the path's official starting point. The 12A bus toward Brighton makes a stop at Beachy Head (10min., every 20min., £1.20). Otherwise, walk west along the promenade following the signs until you reach the bottom of the cliffs, then make the strenuous ascent and follow the fields upward past wind-bent trees. The entire 4 mi. journey from the town center to the top of Beachy Head takes about 1½hr. Beware that at a sheer 543 ft. above the sea, Beachy Head can induce vertigo. Because the chalky cliffs are eroding, it is wise to stay far from the edge. From the top you can view the **Seven Sisters,** 4½ mi. away. The Sisters are a series of white chalk ridges carved by centuries of receding waters. Far below, the 19th-century red-and-white-striped lighthouse **Belle Tout** threatens to fall into the turquoise sea.

From Beachy Head, the path winds past a number of **tumuli,** Bronze Age burial mounds dating to 1500 BC. The Way continues west to **Birling Gap,** the last undeveloped stretch of coast in South England. To reach **Alfriston,** a sleepy one-road village called "the last of the old towns," follow the Way 4 mi. inland over a path once used by smugglers between the Cinque Ports. Another option is the shorter **bridleway path** to Alfriston (8 mi.), which joins a trail just below East Dean Rd. The path passes through **Wilmington** and its famous **Long Man,** a 260 ft. earth sculpture variously attributed to prehistoric peoples, Romans, monks, and aliens. The Long Man is unmarked by signs and is best viewed from a distance.

The **Giant's Rest ❷,** on The Street in Wilmington, serves home-cooked meals (£5-12) and has a number of table games to keep people amused as they wait for their food. It is also a great starting point for walks. (☎01323 870 207. Open M-F 11am-3pm and 6-11pm, Sa 11:30am-11pm, Su noon-10:30pm. Food served noon-2pm and 7-9pm. Cash only.) Fuel up at **The Singing Kettle ❷,** Waterloo Sq., at the end of High St. in Alfriston. Specials are £4-7, including the delicious ham and pineapple melt on organic bread for £5.75. (☎01323 870 723. Open daily 10am-5pm. Cash only.) To continue from Wilmington to Alfriston, go back through Long Man's gate and over Windover Hill to the South Downs Way.

ALFRISTON TO FORTY ACRE LANE

From Alfriston, join the Way behind the Star Inn, on High St. (the only street), and continue 7 mi. down gentle slopes to **Southease.** The Way crosses Firle Beacon, which has a mound at the top said to contain a giant's silver coffin. From Southease, proceed north ¾ mi. to **Rodmell.** Rodmell's single street contains **Monk's House,** home of Leonard and Virginia Woolf from 1919 until their deaths. The faithful can retrace the writer's last steps to the River Ouse (1 mi. away), where she committed "the one experience I shall never describe;" her ashes nourish a fig tree in the garden. (☎01892 890 651. Open Apr.-Oct. W and Sa 2-5:30pm. £3.10.) Good ale and English homecooking await at the **Abergavenny Arms ❷,** Newhaven Rd. (☎01273 472 416. Food served M-Sa 11am-2:30pm and 6-9pm, Su noon-3:30pm.)

The closest that the Way comes to **Lewes** (LEW-is) is the village of **Kingston,** where hikers from **Brighton** should pick up the trail. Fortifying pub grub (£7-10) is available at **Juggs Inn ❷,** Juggs St. in Kingston. (☎01273 472 523. Open M-Sa 11am-11pm, Su noon-10:30pm. Food served noon-2:30pm and 6-9pm.) A stone at the parish boundary, called **Nan Kemp's Corner,** represents a gruesome Downs legend: Nan, jealous of her husband's affection for their newborn, roasted it for him to eat and then killed herself here. Continue from Kingston for 8 mi. to **Pyecombe,** which brings you to **Ditchling Beacon,** the highest point in East Sussex Downs.

The path from Pyecombe to **Upper Beeding** (8 mi.) goes to **Devil's Dyke,** a chalk cliff supposedly built by Lucifer himself in an attempt to let the sea into the Weald and wash away all the churches. Climb through fields overrun with poppies to reach the **YHA Truleigh Hill** (p. 160), just 1½ mi. east of Upper Beeding. On the path from Upper Beeding to **Washington** (6¾ mi.) lies the grove of **Chanctonbury Ring**—trees planted in the 18th century around a 3rd-century Roman template.

The 6½ mi. trek from Washington to **Amberley** brings you to a path leading to **Burpham,** 3 mi. from the **YHA Warningcamp ❷** (p. 168). The 19 mi. of orchids and spiked rampion fields from Amberley to **Buriton,** passing through **Cocking,** complete the Way to the northwest. Southward, across the River Arun to **Littleton Down,** are views of the Weald and the North Downs. The spire of Chichester Cathedral marks the beginning of **Forty Acre Lane,** the Way's final arm.

BRIGHTON ☎01273

Brighton (pop. 250,000) is one of Britain's largest seaside resorts. King George IV came to Brighton in 1783, and enjoyed the anything-goes atmosphere so much that he transformed a farmhouse into his headquarters for debauchery (the Royal Pavilion). A regal rumpus ensued. Since then, Brighton continues to turn a blind eye to some of the more scandalous activities that occur along its shores, as holiday-goers and locals alike peel it off—all off—at England's first bathing beach. Kemp Town (also known as Camp Town), has a thriving gay and lesbian population. The huge student crowd, flocks of foreign youth, and frequent hen and stag partiers feed the notorious clubbing scene of this "London-by-the-Sea."

▓ TRANSPORTATION

Trains: Brighton Station, uphill at the northern end of Queen's Rd. Ticket office open 24hr. Travel center open M-Sa 8:15am-6pm. Trains (☎08457 484 950) to: **Arundel** (1¼hr., every hr., £7.30); **London Victoria** (1hr., 2 per hr., £18.40); **Portsmouth** (1½hr., 2 per hr., £13.80); **Rye** (1¾hr., every hr., £13.50).

Buses: Tickets and info at **One Stop Travel,** 16 Old Steine (☎700 406). Open June-Sept. M-Tu and Th-F 8:30am-5:45pm, W 9am-5:45pm, Sa 9am-5pm, Su 9:30am-3pm; Oct.-May M-Tu and Th-F 8:30am-5:45pm, W 9am-5:45pm, Sa 9am-5pm. National Express (☎08705 808 080) leave from Preston Park to **London Victoria** (2-2½hr., every hr., £10.30). Tickets available on board or online.

Public Transportation: Local buses operated by **Brighton** and **Hove** (☎886 200; www.buses.co.uk) congregate around Old Steine. The TIC can give route and price information for most buses; all carriers charge £1.50 in the central area. Frequent local buses serve Brighton's town center and Marina. **Daysaver** tickets available for £3.

Taxis: **Brighton Taxis** (☎202 020). 24hr.

✦ 🛈 ORIENTATION AND PRACTICAL INFORMATION

Brighton is easily explored on foot. **Queen's Road** connects the train station to the English Channel, becoming **West Street** halfway down the slope at the intersection with Western Rd. Funky stores and restaurants cluster around **Trafalgar Street,** which runs east from the train station. From Queen's Rd., head east onto North St. to reach the narrow streets of the **Lanes,** a pedestrian shopping area by day and nightlife center after dark. **Old Steine,** a road and a square, runs in front of the **Royal Pavilion,** while **King's Road** parallels the waterfront.

Tourist Information Centre: Royal Pavilion Shop, 4-5 Pavilion Buildings (☎09067 112 255; www.visitbrighton.com). Staff sells guides and maps, books National Express tickets, and reserves rooms for £1.50 plus a 10% deposit. Open June-Sept. M-F 9:30am-5pm, Sa 10am-5pm, Su 10am-4pm; Oct.-May M-F 9:30am-5pm, Sa 10am-5pm.

Tours: CitySightseeing (☎01708 866000; www.city-sightseeing.com). 50min. bus tours leave from Brighton pier every 30min. Apr.-Oct., with stops at Royal Pavilion, the railway station, and Brighton Marina. £6.50, students £5.50, families £15.50.

Financial Services: Banks line North St., near Castle Sq. **ATMs** outside **Lloyds,** at the corner of North St. and East St. (☎08453 000 000. Open M-Tu and Th-F 9am-5pm, W 10am-5pm, Sa 9:30am-1pm.)

Special Concerns: Disability Advice Centre, 6 Hove Manor, Hove St., Hove (☎203 016). Open M and F 10am-4pm, Tu-Th 10am-1pm.

GLBT Resources: Lesbian and Gay Switchboard (☎204 050). Open daily 5pm-11pm. The **TIC** also offers an extensive list of gay-friendly accommodations, clubs, and shops.

Launderette: Preston St. Launderette, 75 Preston St. (☎738 556). Open M-Sa 8am-9pm, Su 9am-7pm. Last wash 1½hr. before close. Wash and dry £4.

Police: John St. (☎0845 607 0999).

Hospital: Royal Sussex County, Eastern Rd. (☎696 955).

Pharmacy: Boots, 129 North St. (☎207 461). Open M-Sa 8am-7pm, Su 11am-5pm.

Internet Access: Internet cafes cluster in the town center, especially along West St. and St. James St. Try **Starnet,** 94 St. James St. (80p per 30min., £1.20 per hr.). **Riki-Tik,** 18a Bond St. (☎ 683 844) has free Wi-Fi. Open daily 10am-2am.

Post Office: 51 Ship St. (☎08457 223 344). **Bureau de change.** Open M and W-Sa 9am-5:30pm, Tu 9:30am-5:30pm. **Post Code:** BN1 1BA.

🏠 ACCOMMODATIONS

On weekdays, accommodations in Brighton go for about half the price of their weekend mark-ups. Brighton's best budget beds are in its **hostels;** the TIC has a complete list. The city's **B&Bs** and **hotels** begin at £25-30 and skyrocket from there. Many mid-range (£35-50) B&Bs line **Madeira Place;** cheaper establishments abound west of **West Pier** and east of **Palace Pier.** To the east, perpendicular to the shoreline, **Kemp Town** has a huge number of B&Bs. Frequent conventions and weekenders, especially in summer, make rooms scarce—book early or consult the TIC.

🎒 **Baggies Backpackers,** 33 Oriental Pl. (☎733 740). Join in the fun at this super-social hostel, where spontaneous parties on "Baggies Beach" are common. Racecar sheets and welcoming staff. Book ahead, especially on weekends. Coed bathrooms. Kitchen. Laundry £1.40. Key deposit £5. Dorms £13; one double £35. Cash only. ❷

Brighton

ACCOMMODATIONS
Baggies Backpackers, 5
Christina Guest House, 20
Dorset Guest House, 8
Hotel Pelirocco, 6

FOOD
Deli India Restaurant, 1
Food for Friends, 10
The Hop Poles, 9
The Mock Turtle, 14
Nia Restaurant and Cafe, 2
Queen Adelaide
Tea Room, 7

PUBS
The FishBowl, 13
Fortune of War, 16
The Mash Tun, 4
Three and Ten, 18
Ye Olde King and Queen, 3

CLUBS
Audio, 15
The Beach, 17
Candy Bar, 12
Casablanca Jazz Club, 11
Charles St., 19

SOUTH ENGLAND

English Channel

▨ **Hotel Pelirocco,** 10 Regency Sq. (☎327 055; www.hotelpelirocco.co.uk). Wannabe rock stars will revel in the over-the-top, hip-to-be-different atmosphere of Pelirocco. Each of 19 individually themed rooms (try leopard-print "Betty's Boudoir," or Jamie Reid's "Magic Room," decorated by the Sex Pistols artist himself) has video games and a private bath. Singles £50-65; doubles £100-145. AmEx/MC/V. ❹

Christina Guest House, 20 St. George's Terr. (☎690 862; www.christinaguesthouse-brighton.co.uk). Family-run house a short walk from the seafront, with ensuite rooms. Full breakfast with vegetarian options included. £25-35 per person. MC/V. ❸

Dorset Guest House, 17 Dorset Gardens (☎571 750). On the lively streets of Kemp Town, this B&B offers small, pleasant rooms with all the amenities of home. Convenient location near the Lanes. Breakfast included. Singles £25, doubles £35. MC/V. ❸

▶ FOOD

Over 400 restaurants in the city satisfy almost any craving. **Queen's Road** is lined with chain restaurants and fast food. Cheap ethnic eateries from Indian to Mediterranean to Morrocan can be found along **Preston Street. The Lanes** are full of trendy patisseries and cafes that offer over-priced but memorable meals and great people-watching. Get **groceries** at Somerfield, 6 St. James St. (☎570 363. Open M-Sa 8am-10pm, Su 11am-5pm.) Brighton's history as a health resort has not been forgotten—vegetarian options pervade the city. Satisfy sugar cravings with **Brighton rock candy** from any of the many shops claiming to have invented it.

▨ **Food for Friends,** 17a-18a Prince Albert St. (☎202 310). This bright corner restaurant offers inventive vegetarian dishes and a decadent afternoon tea (£5.50). Elegant entrees (£8-11) draw on Indian and East Asian cuisines. Open M-Th and Su noon-10pm, F-Sa noon-10:30pm. AmEx/MC/V. ❷

Nia Restaurant and Cafe, 87 Trafalgar St. (☎671 371), east of the train station. Delicious dishes (£11-15) in a romantic cafe near the North Laine. Unique menu offers international flavors, drawing from Japanese, French, and Mediterranean cuisine. Open M-Sa 9am-11pm, Su 9am-6pm. MC/V. ❸

Deli India, 81 Trafalgar St. (☎ 699 985). A stand-out among the many Indian restaurants in Brighton. Delicatessen and tea shop with mouth-watering vegetarian and meat *thalis* (£6.50-7.50). Open M-F 10am-7:30pm, Sa 10am-6pm, Su noon-3pm. MC/V. ❷

The Mock Turtle, 4 Pool Valley (☎327 380). With homemade pastries and lace decor, this tucked-away cafe is the perfect stop for afternoon tea with scones and a generous helping of clotted cream (£5.50). Open T-Su 9:30am-6:30pm. Cash only. ❶

The Hop Poles, 13 Middle St. (☎710 444). This popular hangout is also a bar with a heated garden. Unique entrees, like Thai vegetable green curry. Vegan options. Entrees £7. Food served M-Th and Su noon-9pm, F-Sa noon-7pm. MC/V. ❷

◉ ◗ SIGHTS AND BEACHES

In 1752, Dr. Richard Russell's treatise on the merits of drinking and bathing in seawater to treat glandular disease was published in English. Thus began the transformation of the sleepy village of Brighthelmstone into a free-spirited beach town.

▨ **ROYAL PAVILION.** A touch of the Far East in the heart of England. Much of Brighton's present extravagance can be traced to the construction of the unabashedly gaudy Royal Pavilion. In 1815, George IV enlisted architect John Nash to turn an ordinary farm villa into an ornate fantasy palace, with Taj Mahal-style architecture offset by Chinese interiors. After living there for several months, Queen Victoria was going to have it demolished until the town bought the royal playground and opened it to the public. The **Banquet Room** centers around a 30 ft. chandelier held by the claws of a dragon. Smaller dragons hold lotus lamps that, when lit, give the impression of breathing. After your tour, find a seat on the balcony of the **Queen Adelaide Tea Room ❶** for tea and scones. *(☎ 292 880. Open daily Apr.-Sept. 9:30am-5:45pm; Oct.-Mar. 10am-5:15pm. Last admission 45min. before close. £7.50. Tours daily 11:30am and 2:30pm; £2. Free audio tour. Queen Adelaide Tea Room open daily Apr.-Sept. 10am-5pm; Oct.-Mar. 10:30am-4:30pm. Admission to the Pavilion required for Tea Room.)*

▨DOWN BY THE SEA. Brighton's original attraction is, of course, the beach, but the closest things to sand are fist-sized rocks. Turquoise waters, bikini-clad beach bums, live bands, and umbrella-adorned drinks make the seaside a must-visit. A debaucherous Brighton weekend would not be complete without a visit to the **nude beach,** 20min. east of Brighton Pier, marked by green signs.

THE PIERS. The bright lights of the **Brighton Pier** give the oceanfront some kitsch and character. The pier houses slot machines, video games, and candy-colored condom dispensers, with a roller coaster and other mildly dizzying rides thrown in for good measure. Give weary legs a rest on **Volk's Railway,** the oldest electric railway in the world, which shuttles along the waterfront from the pier to the marina. *(☎ 292 718. Open Apr.-Sept. M-F 11am-5pm, Sa-Su 11am-6pm. Round-trip £2.50.)* The **Grand Hotel,** King's Rd., has been rebuilt since a 1984 IRA bombing that killed five but left target Margaret Thatcher unscathed. A short walk along the coast past the ruins of West Pier leads to the smaller residential community of **Hove.**

BRIGHTON MUSEUM AND ART GALLERY. Adding a touch of class to the town's attractions, this recently renovated gallery features English and international paintings, pottery, and Art Deco collections, and an extensive Brighton historical exhibit that fully explicates the phrase "dirty weekend." The fine **Willett Collection of Pottery** has postmodern porcelains and Neolithic relics. *(Church St., around the corner from the Pavilion. ☎ 292 882. Open Tu 10am-7pm, W-Sa 10am-5pm, Su 2-5pm. Free.)*

LANES AND LAINES. Small fishermen's cottages once thrived in the **Lanes,** an intricate maze of 17th-century streets (some no wider than 3 ft.) south of North St. in the heart of Old Brighton. Replace those cottages with overpriced, touristy boutiques and a plethora of chic restaurants, and you have the Lanes today. For a less commercialized foray into shopping, head to **North Laines,** off Trafalgar St., where a variety of novelty shops crowd around colorful cafes and impromptu markets.

ON THE MENU

BATTER UP!

Aside from a good pint, there are few culinary creations more British than fish and chips. Numerous chippies, chippers, and chip shops line the streets, but before you chow down on the greasy nosh, it's important to know the particulars of proper fish and chips.

The Fish: The cornerstone of the dish, cod is the fish of choice to fry and serve wrapped in newspaper. Haddock is another popular option, and other white fish like pollock and skate are occasionally used. The fish is deep fried until golden brown and flaky.

The Chips: It must be noted that the fish is served with chips—not french fries. While both are fried potato slices, chips are thicker and more potato-like than their slim counterpart. You should always get a heaping portion, and by the end of the meal they'll have soaked up a hearty amount of grease.

The Fixings: What would be an otherwise bland dish of fried matter is spiced up with salt and vinegar—and loads of it. If you want less, more, or (gasp) ketchup, make sure to tell your chef before he chucks all the ingredients and condiments into one giant bag for your eating pleasure.

🔊 🎵 NIGHTLIFE AND ENTERTAINMENT

For info on happening nightspots, check *Latest 7* or *The Source*, free at pubs, newsagents, and record stores, or *What's On*, a poster-sized flyer found at record stores and pubs. **GLBT-friendly** venues can be found in the free monthly issues of *G Scene* and *3Sixty*, available at newsstands; *What's On* also highlights gay-friendly events. The City Council spent £5 million installing surveillance equipment on the seafront and major streets to ensure safety during late-night partying, but still exercise caution. The Lanes, in particular, can be too deserted for comfort, and don't be surprised to stumble across a drunk (or 20) along the beach. **Night buses** N69, 85, and 98-99 run infrequently but reliably in the early morning, picking up at Old Steine, West St., Clock Tower, North St., the train station, and in front of many clubs, usually hitting each spot twice between 1 and 2:30am (£1-4).

PUBS

J.B. Priestley once noted that Brighton was "a fine place either to restore your health…or to ruin it again." The waterfront between West Pier and Brighton Pier is a good party spot, and there is a pub or bar on practically every corner of the city center. Many pubs also offer specials and long Happy hours during the week.

■ **The Fish Bowl,** 73 East St. (☎ 777 505). Crowded by hip twentysomethings and students, this bar is a chilled-out hot spot that's cool without trying to be. You can't miss the bright turquoise exterior. Open M-Sa 11am-11pm, Su noon-10:30pm.

■ **Fortune of War,** 157 King's Road Arches (☎ 205 065), beneath King's Rd. Popular beachfront bar shaped like the hull of a 19th-century ship. Patrons sip their beverage of choice (pints £3.10) and watch the sun set over the Channel, and night owls keep the place packed until it rises again. Open daily from noon until they feel like closing.

The Mash Tun, 1 Church St. (☎ 684 951). Lounging in plush leather sofas and on wooden church pews, a laid-back student crowd parties until the wee hours. Good food, graffiti-adorned walls, and music ranging from hip-hop to rock to country keep the scene lively. Happy hour M-Th and Su 3-9pm; £4 for a "double spirit and splash." Open M-Th noon-midnight, F noon-1am, Sa 11am-1am. Food served daily noon-7pm.

Three and Ten, 10 Steine St. (☎ 609 777). Fills early and stays busy with a mellow crowd of locals and tourists in the know. Cheap beer (£2) and mixed drinks (£3). Open M-Th and Su noon-1am, F-Sa noon-3am.

Ye Olde King and Queen, Marlborough Pl. (☎ 607 207). This 1779 farmhouse offers TV, a beer garden, and multiple bars. Packed during football matches. Open M-Th noon-11pm, F-Sa noon-midnight, Su noon-10:30pm. Food served noon-6pm, Su noon-5pm.

CLUBS

The clubbing capital of the South, Brighton is also the hometown of Fatboy Slim and major dance label Skint Records—it's no surprise that Brightonians know their dance music. Most clubs are open Monday through Saturday 10pm-2am; after 2am the party moves to bonfires and revelry on the waterfront. Many clubs have student discounts on weeknights and higher covers (£5-10) on weekends.

Audio, 10 Marine Parade (☎ 606 906; www.audiobrighton.com). This nightlife fixture is the place to be in Brighton. 2 fl. of debauchery and a mix of music. Always packed to the brim. Cover M-Th £3-4, F £5, Sa £7. Open M-Sa 10pm-2am.

The Beach, 171-181 King's Road Arches (☎ 722 272). Big beats right on the shore. Packed with weekenders dancing to an eclectic mix of hits. Snacks served noon-2pm. Cover £10, students £8. Open M and W-Th 10pm-2am, F-Sa 10pm-3am.

Charles St., 8-9 Marine Parade (☎ 624 091). Gay-friendly party with DJs spinning dance tracks. Anything-goes atmosphere breeds anything-goes dancing. Cover M £1.50, Th £3, F no cover, Sa £5-8. Open M 10:30pm-2am, Th-Sa 10:30pm-3am.

Casablanca Jazz Club, 3 Middle St. (☎321 817; www.casablancajazzclub.com). One of few clubs in Brighton that regularly offers live bands playing jazz, funk, disco, and Latin tunes for a mix of students and 20-somethings. Dance floor, DJ, and bar upstairs. Bands in the basement. Cover W after 11pm £2, F-Sa £5-7. Student discount £1. Open M and Th-Sa 9:30pm-3am, Tu-W 9:30pm-2am.

Candy Bar, 129 St. James St. (☎622 424; www.thecandybar.co.uk). This venue caters mainly to lesbian clubbers with always entertaining, often risque theme nights. Check signs outside for the week's events. Tu karaoke nights. Cover M £3, F-Sa free before 10pm, £4 from 10-11pm, £5 from 11pm-midnight, £6 after midnight. Open M-Th 9pm-2am, F-Su 9pm-until manager's discretion.

MUSIC, THEATER, AND FESTIVALS

Pick up free *Events Guide* and *Theatre Royal Brighton* brochures at the TIC for the latest info on dates and locations. **Brighton Centre,** King's Rd. (☎0870 900 9100; www.brightoncentre.co.uk; box office open M-Sa 10am-5:30pm), and **The Dome,** 29 New Rd. (☎709 709; www.brighton-dome.org.uk; box office open 10am-6pm), host Brighton's biggest events, from Chippendales shows to concerts. Local plays and London productions take the stage at the **Theatre Royal** on New Rd., a Victorian beauty with a plush interior. (☎328 488; www.theatreroyalbrighton.co.uk. Tickets £10-25. Open M-Sa 10am-8pm.) **Komedia,** on Gardner St., houses a cafe with Wi-Fi, bar, comedy club, and cabaret. (☎647 100; www.komedia.co.uk. Tickets £5-12; discounts available. Standby tickets 15min. before curtain. Box office open M-F 10am-10pm, Sa 10am-10:30pm, Su 1-10pm.) The **Brighton Festival** (box office ☎709 709), held each May, is one of the largest arts festivals in England, celebrating music, film, and other art forms. The **Brighton Pride Festival** in early August is the largest Pride Festival in the UK (☎730 562; www.brightonpride.org).

◪ DAYTRIPS FROM BRIGHTON

LEWES. The hilltop city of Lewes (LEW-is) has an appealing location in the Sussex chalklands and is a gateway to **South Downs Way** trails (p. 157). *(Trains from Brighton's Queen's Rd. station leave for Lewes every 15min., £3.50.)* Consult the Lewes TIC (p. 159), right out of the train station and uphill on Station Rd., which becomes Station St. The views of the countryside from the ruins of the Norman **Lewes Castle**, High St., 5min. walk uphill from the TIC, and the small collections of the **Museum of Sussex Archaeology** at the castle's base merit a quick visit. The museum's 30min. film on the history of Lewes can further enlighten your visit. *(☎486 290. Open M and Su 11am-5:30pm; Tu-Sa 10am-5:30pm or dusk. Last admission 5pm. £4.50, students £4. Admission to the museum comes with a castle ticket.)* The 15th-century **Anne of Cleves House Museum,** Southover High St., 15min. from the castle, celebrates Henry VIII's fourth wife, the clever woman who managed to keep her head and her house. *(☎474 610. Open Mar.-Oct. M and Su 11am-5pm, Tu-Sa 10am-5pm; Nov.-Feb. Tu-Sa 10am-5pm. £3.10, concessions £2.80. Castle and museum combination ticket £6.40/5.50.)* Past Anne of Cleves's House down Cockshut Rd. lie the ruins of **Lewes Priory,** where Henry III, after his loss at the battle of Lewes in 1264, signed the treaty that ended the struggle with his barons and the nation's first representative parliament. ▨**Bill's Produce Store ❷,** 56 Cliffe High St., offers piping hot pizzas, salads, and entrees (£9) packed with fresh produce. (☎476 918; www.billsproducestore.co.uk. Open daily 8am-6pm.)

THE CHARLESTON FARMHOUSE. Artist Vanessa Bell and her husband Duncan Grant moved here in 1916, turning the house into the retreat of the Bloomsbury group. Frescoes and post-Impressionist paintings decorate the walls. Virginia Woolf was a frequent guest at the house. On Fridays, visitors can take **A Day in the Life of Charleston** tours. *(East of Lewes, off the A27. Take bus #125 from the Lewes station (6* *per day).* ☎ *01323 811 265; www.charleston.org.uk. Open July-Aug. W-Sa 11:30am-6pm, Su 2-6pm; Apr.-June and Sept.-Oct. W and Sa 11:30am-6pm, Th-F and Su 2-6pm. Last admission 5pm. W and Sa entrance by guided tour only. £6.50; F £7.50. Garden only £2.50.)*

ARUNDEL ☎ 01903

Arundel sits in the shadow of towers and spires. The town center is plagued by antique shops and other small-town staples, but the magnificent fairytale castle gives the sleepy town an enchanting quality. The River Arun runs through the west of the city. Arundel provides an ideal base from which to explore the surrounding countryside and the **South Downs Way** (p. 157).

▣ ⁊ TRANSPORTATION AND PRACTICAL INFORMATION

Trains (☎ 08457 484 950) run to: Brighton (1hr., every hr., £7.10); Chichester (20 min., 2 per hr., £4); London Victoria (1½hr., 2 per hr., £18.50); Portsmouth (1hr., every hr., £8.70). Many routes connect at Littlehampton to the south or Barnham to the west. Stagecoach Coastline **buses** (☎ 0845 121 0170) stop on High St. and just on the town's side of the river, and leave for Littlehampton (#702; 1-2 per hr.). South Downs Cycle Hire rents **bikes** 3 mi. east of Arundel on Blakehurst Farm. (☎ 889 562. £16 per day.) Call Castle Cars (☎ 884 444; 24hr.) for a **taxi.**

The **Tourist Information Centre,** 61 High St., dispenses the free *Town Guide* and information on the South Downs Way. (☎ 882 268. Open M-Sa 10am-5pm, Su 10am-4pm.) Other services include: a Lloyds **bank** with **ATM,** 14 High St. (☎ 717 221; open M-Tu and Th-F 9:30am-4pm, W 10am-4pm); **police,** on the Causeway (☎ 0845 607 0999; open M-F 10am-8pm, Sa 10am-6pm); and the **post office,** 2-4 High St. (☎ 882 113; open M-F 9am-5:30pm, Sa 9am-12:30pm). **Post Code:** BN18 9AA.

▮ ACCOMMODATIONS

The elegant **B&Bs** (£30-40) in the town center can be pricey. Reserve ahead in summer and ask the TIC for an up-to-date list of vacancies.

YHA Warningcamp (☎ 0870 770 5676), 1½ mi. out of town. Turn right out of the train station, cross the railroad tracks, turn left on the next road, and follow the signs. Family- and group-oriented accommodations near the River Arun with 2 kitchens, laundry facilities, and Internet access. Breakfast included. Lockout 10am-5pm. Curfew 11pm. Open July-Aug. daily; Apr.-June M-Sa; Sept.-Oct. Tu-Sa; Nov.-Dec. F-Sa. Dorms £15, under 18 £11. Camping £8 per person. MC/V. ❷

Arden House, 4 Queens Ln. (☎ 882 544). 8 immaculate, centrally located rooms. Full breakfast included. Singles £34; doubles £54, ensuite £58. Cash only. ❹

Camping: Ship and Anchor Marina, Ford Rd. (☎ 01243 551 262), 2 mi. from Arundel beside the River Arun. 12 acres of countryside with pub and shops nearby. Apr.-Sept. £7 per person; Mar. and Oct. £5 per person. £1.50 per vehicle. Showers 50p. ❶

◖ FOOD

Arundel's pubs and tea shops are expensive and unremarkable. For produce, a **farmers' market** convenes on the morning of the 3rd Saturday of each month. The Co-op, 17 Queen St., sells **groceries.** (Open M-Sa 6:30am-10pm, Su 7:30am-10pm.)

Belinda's, 13 Tarrant St. (☎ 882 977). Once a 16th-century barn, this tearoom is a local favorite for its large selection of traditional English fare. Linger over cream teas (tea and 2 scones; £4.80) and Belinda's famous homemade jam in the cheerful outdoor tea garden. Open daily 9:30am-4:45pm. MC/V, £10 min. ❶

White Hart, 12 Queen St. (☎882 374). Enjoy pub grub and local ales in a garden by the bridge. Homemade meals (£6-10) and veggie options. Open M-Sa noon-11pm, food served until 8:30pm; Su noon-10:30pm, food served until 7:30pm. ❷

Castle Tandoori, 3 Mill Ln. (☎884 224). Spicy and delicious, the buffet lunch (£9) and dinner (£13) will leave you full and happy. Traditional entrees £8-13. Open daily noon-2:30pm and 6-11:30pm. MC/V. ❸

🌀 🏵 SIGHTS AND FESTIVALS

Poised high above the town, ⬛**Arundel Castle** looks like the backdrop of a Disney movie. A privately owned castle, it has been the seat of the Duke of Norfolk for over nine centuries. Winding passages and 131 steps lead to the Norman **keep**, which contains scenes of 12th century life using models, music, and stories. The top of the keep also offers great views of the surrounding countryside. Enjoy cream tea (£4) and gaze at the grounds' three manicured gardens from the **tea terrace,** near the car park. (☎882 173. Entrances at the top of High St. or on Mill Rd. Open Apr.-Oct. M-F and Su 11am-5pm. Last entry 4pm. £12. Grounds only £6.50.)

Along the river across from the castle, a placard describes the monks of **Blackfriars,** the Dominican priory whose ruins are nearby. Atop the same hill as Arundel Castle, the **Cathedral of Our Lady and St. Philip Howard** is more impressive for its French Gothic exterior than its standard interior. Sixty days after Easter, the Cathedral celebrates **Corpus Christi**—or Carpet of Flowers—by laying thousands of flowers in a pattern stretching 93 ft. down the aisle. The tradition dates from 1877. (☎882 297; www.arundelcathedral.org. Open daily in summer 9am-6pm; in winter 9am-dusk. Free.) At the **Wildfowl and Wetlands Trust Centre,** on Mill Rd., paths through over 60 acres of wetlands let visitors watch rare birds in a natural habitat. Many of them will feed right from your hands. (☎883 355. Open daily in summer 9:30am-5:30pm; in winter 9:30am-4:30pm. Last admission 30min. before close. £7.)

At the end of August, the castle is the centerpiece of the **Arundel Festival,** 10 days of theatrical performances. The **Festival Fringe** simultaneously offers inexpensive events. Tickets for both go on sale six to eight weeks beforehand and must be purchased in advance. (☎889 821; www.arundelfestival.org.uk. Tickets up to £30.)

🔒 DAYTRIP FROM ARUNDEL

PETWORTH HOUSE. Situated among 700 acres of sculpted lawns, gardens, and fallow deer, Petworth's 17th-century mansion is home to one of the UK's finest art collections. J.M.W. Turner often painted the house and landscape, and many of his works hang beside canvases by masters like Van Dyck, Blake, Bosch, Dahl, and Reynolds. Petworth is also famous for the Petworth Chaucer, an early 15th-century manuscript of *The Canterbury Tales,* and the intricate carvings in the legendary Carving Room. (*Take the train 10min. to Pulborough and catch bus #1 to Petworth.* ☎*01798 342 207. House open Apr.-Oct. M-W and Sa-Su 11am-5pm. Last entry 4:30pm. Park open daily 8am-dusk. Tours of house 11am-1pm. House and grounds £8. Park only £3.)*

CHICHESTER   ☎01243

Confined for centuries within Roman walls, Chichester remains insular: it thrives off its own markets, and all roads lead to the 16th-century Market Cross. However, Chichester's tourist appeal relies on modern attractions. The town has excellent theater, an arts festival from May to September, gallery exhibits, and racing spectacles (both motor and horse) in nearby Goodwood. Chichester's cathedral and the Fishbourne Roman Palace provide permanent entertainment.

⌇ TRANSPORTATION. Chichester is 45 mi. southwest of London and 15 mi. east of Portsmouth. **Trains** (☎08457 484 950) leave Southgate station for Brighton (45min., 3 per hr., £9), London Victoria via Horsham (1¾hr., 2 per hr., £18), and Portsmouth (30min., 3 per hr., £5.70). The **bus station** (☎01903 237 661) is opposite the train station. National Express (☎08705 808 080) buses go to London Victoria (3¾hr., 2 per day, £16). Stagecoach Coastline buses connect Chichester with Brighton (#700; 3hr., 2 per hr.) and Portsmouth (#700; 1hr., 2 per hr.). For **taxis,** call Central Cars (☎0800 789 432; 24hr.), outside the train station.

◪◪ ORIENTATION AND PRACTICAL INFORMATION. Four Roman streets named for their compass directions converge at **Market Cross** and divide Chichester into quadrants. The **Tourist Information Centre,** 29a South St., books rooms for £2 plus a 10% deposit. Walk along Southgate from the train station until it becomes South St. (☎775 888; www.visitsussex.org. Open Apr.-Sept. M 10:15am-5:15pm, Tu-Sa 9:15am-5:15pm, Su 11am-3:30pm; Oct.-Mar. M 10:30am-5:15pm, Tu-Sa 9:15am-5:15pm.) **Guided tours** depart from the TIC. (May-Sept. Tu 11am, Sa 2:30pm; Oct.-Apr. Sa 2:30pm. £3.50.) Other services include: HSBC **bank** with **ATM,** Market Cross at the corner of South and East St. (open M and W-F 9am-5pm, Tu 9:30am-5pm, Sa 9:30am-12:30pm); **police,** Kingsham Rd. (☎0845 607 0999); **Internet** access at **Internet Junction,** 2 Southgate (☎776 644; www.internetjunction.co.uk; £1 per 20min.; open M-Tu 9am-9pm, W-Sa 9am-8pm, Su 11am-8pm), and free at the public **library,** Tower St. off West St. (☎777 351; open M-F 9am-7:30pm, Sa 9am-5pm); and the **post office,** 10 West St., with a **bureau de change** (☎08457 223 344; open M and W-F 9am-5:30pm, Tu 9:30am-5:30pm, Sa 9am-3pm). **Post Code:** PO19 1AB.

⌂⌂ ACCOMMODATIONS AND FOOD. **B&Bs** abound, but cheap rooms are rare, especially during July's theater festival or on big race weekends in **Goodwood** (p. 172). Plan on paying at least £30 and expect a 15min. walk from the town center. **Bayleaf ❸,** 16 Whyke Rd., offers spacious rooms and full English breakfast. (☎774 330. No smoking. Singles £27; doubles and twins £54. Cash only.) **University College Chichester ❸,** College Ln., a 30min. walk from the train station, rents out singles in student housing as a B&B from June to August. (☎816 070. Singles £27, ensuite £33.) **Camp** at **Southern Leisure Centre ❷,** Vinnetrow Rd., 2 mi. southeast of town. (☎787 715. Facilities include showers, heated outdoor swimming pool, and laundry. Open Apr.-Oct. £15.50, with electricity £17.50.)

A **market** of miscellany convenes in the car park at Market Ave. and East St. on Wednesdays. Fresh produce can be found at the **farmers' market** in Cattle Market car park from 8:30am-1:30pm on the first and third Friday of each month. Bakeries line North St. Stock up on **groceries** at Iceland, 55 South St. (Open M-Sa 9am-6pm, Su 10am-4pm.) The Francophile staff at ◪**Maison Blanc Boulangerie and Patisserie ❶,** 56 South St., makes sandwiches (£4-5) and an assortment of desserts (£4-6) for dining in the rear cafe or as takeaway. Other specialties include personal-sized pizzas with unusual toppings for £2-3. (☎539 292. Open M-F 8:45am-5:30pm, Sa 8:45am-6pm, Su 9:30am-4pm. MC/V.) **Casson's Restaurant and Bar ❸,** Arundel Rd., has a fancy menu of English and French specialties (entrees £8-15). Weekday lunch specials include an entree and a glass of wine or a pint for £10. (☎773 294. Open Tu 7-10pm, W-Sa noon-3pm and 7-10pm, Su noon-3pm. MC/V.) The **Pasta Factory ❷,** 5 South St., rolls out fresh pasta daily with a selection of toppings. (☎785 764. Entrees £7-10. Open M-F noon-3pm and 5-11pm, Sa noon-11pm, Su noon-9pm. Cash only.) A hungry pre-theater crowd flocks to the dim interior of **Woodies Wine Bar and Brasserie ❸,** 10 St. Pancras, the oldest wine bar in Sussex. Innovative meals, like crayfish and avocado salad (£6), are served in a sophisticated, informal atmosphere. (☎779 895. Entrees £10-16. Open M-F noon-2:30pm and 5:45-10:30pm, Sa noon-2:30pm and 5:45-11pm, Su noon-4pm and 5:45-11pm. MC/V.)

◙ **SIGHTS.** Begun in 1076, **Chichester Cathedral,** just west of the Market Cross, links medieval Christianity to modern Anglicanism. Norman arches frame Reformation stained glass, Queen Elizabeth II and Prince Philip peer from the recently renovated West Front, and Chagall's stained-glass window depicts Psalm 150 with intense colors and detailed symbolism. Older items include two Romanesque sculptures and a Roman mosaic. The tomb of Joan de Vere depicts one of the first English examples of "weepers" on its side, while the 14th-century tomb of Earl Fitzalan and his wife scandalously displays a rare image of medieval hand-holding. (☎782 595; www.chichestercathedral.org.uk. Open daily in summer 7:15am-7pm; in winter 7:15am-6pm. Tours Apr.-Oct. M-Sa 11am and 2:15pm. Evensong M-Sa 5:30pm, Su 3:30pm. Free.) Chichester's other attractions include the **Pallants,** a quiet area with 18th- and 19th-century houses in the southeast quadrant. The **Pallant House,** 9 North Pallant, is a restored Queen Anne building attributed to Christopher Wren. Both the cathedral and the Pallant house hold collections of 20th-century British modern art. (☎774 557; www.pallant.org.uk. Open Tu-Sa 10am-5pm. Last admission 4pm. £6.50, students £3.50. Tu ½-price admission.)

🎭 **ENTERTAINMENT AND FESTIVALS.** Just north of town, the **Chichester Festival Theatre,** in Oaklands Park, is the cultural center of Chichester. Founded by Sir Laurence Olivier, the venue has attracted such artists as Maggie Smith, Peter Ustinov, and Julie Christie. The theater is complemented by the **Minerva Studio Theatre,** a new addition used for more intimate productions. A guide to each year's program is available at the TIC and online at www.cft.org.uk. Booking in advance reduces regular ticket prices (£10-35) for students. For more budget entertainment, attend a Saturday Short at 11am, which has shows for £4. Close by, the **Theatre Restaurant and Cafe** caters to theater-goers from noon on matinee days, and from 5:30pm for evening shows. (☎781 312. Box office open M-Sa 10am-6pm; until 8pm on performance days. Rush seats £6-8, available at 10am day of show.) During the first two weeks in July, artists and musicians collaborate for the **Chichester Festivities.** (Box office in the Cathedral Bell Tower. ☎780 192; www.chifest.co.uk. Talks £2-10; concerts £8-35. Open from June to festival's end M-Sa 10am-5pm.)

▌▌ **DAYTRIPS FROM CHICHESTER**

WEALD AND DOWNLAND OPEN AIR MUSEUM. The museum showcases 45 historical buildings that were saved from destruction when they were transplanted from the southeastern countryside to this parkland in the South Downs. The mostly medieval structures contain exhibits on husbandry, forestry, and culture. A fully functioning Tudor kitchen churns out samples from morning to early afternoon, including frumenty and elderflower fritters. The main houses—Bayleaf farmstead, Whittaker's cottage, and the Mill—host demonstrations on the purpose, structure, and decor of Tudor homes. (*7 mi. north of Chichester off the A286; take bus #60 to Singleton Horse and Groom (round-trip £6), then head back up the road and take the 1st left at the brown sign; ask the driver for a combination bus and admission ticket £8.50. ☎01243 811 363. Open Mar.-Oct. daily 10:30am-6pm; Nov.-Feb. W and Sa-Su 10:30am-4pm. Last admission 1hr. before close. £8, seniors £6.70, children and students £4.25.*)

FISHBOURNE ROMAN PALACE. Built c. AD 80, possibly by local ruler Togidubnus, the Fishbourne Palace is the largest extant domestic Roman building in Britain. Today, the most beautiful part of the ruined mansion is the floor, covered in tile mosaics. Don't miss the largely intact Cupid on a Dolphin mosaic from the mid-2nd century. Outside, a formal garden was replanted according to the original excavated Roman layout. (*About 2 mi. west of the town center; follow the signs from the end of Westgate Street or take bus #700 to Salthill Rd. and follow the brown signs; round-trip £2.40.*)

☎ 785 859. *Open Aug. daily 10am-6pm; Mar.-July and Sept.-Oct. daily 10am-5pm; Feb. and Nov.- Dec. daily 10am-4pm; Jan. Sa-Su 10am-4pm. Last admission 20min. before close. £6.50, students £5.50.)*

GOODWOOD. Three miles northeast of Chichester, works by Canaletto, Reynolds, and Stubbs vie for attention with a world-famous sculpture collection in **Goodwood House,** the seat of the Duke of Richmond for over 300 years. *(☎ 755 040; www.goodwood.co.uk. Open Aug. M-Th and Su 1-5pm; Apr.-July and Sept.-Oct. M and Su 1-5pm. 5 tours per day. Last admission 4pm. The schedule is irregular; call ahead. £8.)* Goodwood also has some of England's best horse and motor **racing.** From May to September, the rich and famous come to watch the "Glorious Goodwood" horse race, a 200-year-old tradition. *(☎ 755 022. Runs from May-Sept.)* In early July and September, the motor racing extravaganzas **Festival of Speed** and **Goodwood Revival** take center stage.

HAMPSHIRE

PORTSMOUTH   ☎ 023

Sailing enthusiasts and history buffs will wet themselves at this waterfront destination, a famous naval port since Henry V set sail for France in 1415. Portsmouth's Victorian seaside setting and its 900-year history of prostitutes, drunkards, and cursing sailors give the city a compelling, gritty history. Despite modern attempts to build up the waterfront, the pride of Portsmouth is still its harbor, whose waters teem with ferries, barges, and pleasure boats. Unfortunately, the city's naval prominence caused its devastation during WWII, and today many of its buildings are examples of 1950s utilitarian (read: ugly) architecture.

◫ TRANSPORTATION

Trains: Portsmouth and Southsea Station, Commercial Rd., in the city center. Ticket office open M-Sa 5:40am-8:30pm, Su 6:40am-8:40pm. Travel center open M-F 8:40am-6pm, Sa 8:40am-4:30pm. **Portsmouth Harbour Station,** The Hard, also sends ferries to the **Isle of Wight.** Office open M-Sa 6am-7:15pm, Su 6:40am-7:45pm. **Fratton Station,** Selbourne Terr., is closest to Southsea. Ticketing office open M-Sa 6am-7pm, Su 7am-11pm. Trains (☎08457 484 950) go to **Chichester** (30min., 2 per hr., £5.70), **London Waterloo** (1¾hr., 4 per hr., £23), and **Salisbury** (1hr., every hr., £13).

Buses: The Hard Interchange, The Hard, next to Harbour Station. National Express (☎08705 808 080) buses go to **London Victoria** (2½hr., every hr., £20.60) and **Salisbury** (1½hr., 1 per day, £8.30).

Ferries: Frequent Wightlink (☎08705 827 744; www.wightlink.co.uk) **ferries** run from **Portsmouth Harbour** to **Fishbourne** (35min.; round-trip £10.40, children 5.20) and from **Portsmouth Harbour** to **Ryde** (15min., round-trip £12.40, children £6.20, ½-day £10 round-trip). **Hovertravel** (☎811 000; www.hovertravel.co.uk) sails from Clarence Esplanade in **Southsea** to **Ryde** (9min.; 2 per hr.; round-trip £10.40, children £5.20).

Public Transportation: A reliable, comprehensive bus system connects the city. **Local bus** companies First (☎08700 106 022) and Stagecoach (☎01903 237 661) run throughout. Daily pass £4, weekly pass £13.

Taxis: Aqua Cars (☎0800 666 666). 24hr.

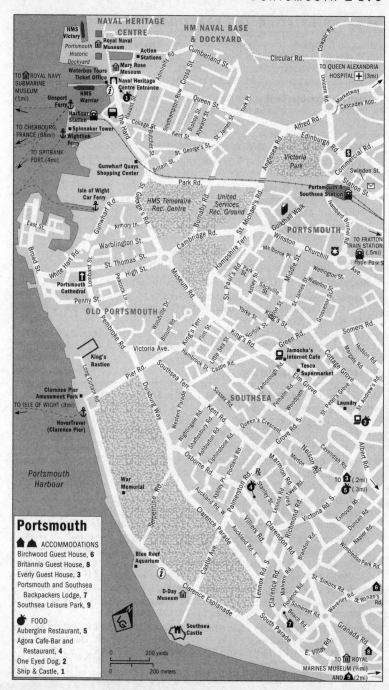

SOUTH ENGLAND

HMS Victory

NAVAL HERITAGE CENTRE

Portsmouth Historic Dockyard

HM NAVAL BASE & DOCKYARD

Royal Naval Museum

Action Stations

Mary Rose Museum

Waterbus Tours Ticket Office

Naval Heritage Centre Entrance

TO ROYAL NAVY SUBMARINE MUSEUM (1mi)

Gosport Ferry

HMS Warrior

Harbour Station

Spinnaker Tower

Wightlink Ferry

TO CHERBOURG, FRANCE (88mi)

TO SPITBANK FORT (4mi)

Cumberland St.

Cross St.

Admiralty Rd.

Southampton Row

Queen St.

Bishop St.

Aylward St.

St. James St.

York Pl.

Circular Rd.

Cowper Rd.

TO QUEEN ALEXANDRIA HOSPITAL (3mi)

Unicorn Rd.

Marketway

Cascades App.

Alfred Rd.

Edinburgh Rd.

Anglesea Rd.

Commercial Rd.

Swindon St.

Station St.

College St.

Kent St.

St. George's St.

Britain St.

The Hard

Butcher St.

Gunwharf Quays Shopping Center

Park Rd.

Victoria Park

Portsmouth & Southsea Station

Isle of Wight Car Ferry

HMS Temeraire Rec. Centre

United Services Rec. Ground

Guildhall Walk

PORTSMOUTH

TO FRATTON TRAIN STATION (.5mi)

Hyde Park S.

East St.

Armory Ln.

Gunwharf Rd.

St. George's Rd.

Burnaby Rd.

Cambridge Rd.

St. Michael's Rd.

Winston Churchill Ave.

Melbone Pl.

Broad St.

Warblington St.

St. Thomas' St.

High St.

Museum Rd.

Hampshire Terr.

St. Paul's Rd.

Park Rd.

Middle St.

Wellington St.

Waterloo St.

St. James St.

Grosvenor St.

White Hart Rd.

Lombard St.

Peacock Ln.

Penny St.

Portsmouth Cathedral

OLD PORTSMOUTH

Woodville Dr.

Blount Rd.

King's Terr.

Flint St.

King's Rd.

Astley St.

Sackville St.

Yorke St.

Norfolk St.

King's St.

Green Rd.

Somers Rd.

Pembroke Rd.

Victoria Ave.

Hambrook St.

Castle Rd.

Little Sea Rd.

Yarborough Rd.

Jamocha's Internet Cafe

Tesco Supermarket

Cottage Grove

Hudson Rd.

Margate Rd.

King's Bastion

Pier Rd.

Southsea Terr.

Sussex Rd.

SOUTHSEA

Elm Grove

Pelham Rd.

Woodpath

Laundry

St. Peter's Grove

St. Andrew's Rd.

Clarence Pier Amusement Park

TO ISLE OF WIGHT (8mi)

HoverTravel (Clarence Pier)

Duisburg Way

Western Parade

Kent Rd.

Nightingale Rd.

Shaftesbury Rd.

Ashburton Rd.

Elphinstone Rd.

Queen's Crescent

Grove Rd. S.

Nelson Rd.

Cavendish Rd.

Albert Rd.

Portsmouth Harbour

War Memorial

Serpentine Rd.

Osborne Rd.

Auckland Rd. W.

Astley Pl.

Portland Rd.

Stanley St.

Marmion Rd.

Lennox Rd.

Foot Twell Rd.

Merton

Victoria Rd. S.

Exmouth Rd.

Duncan Rd.

Napier Rd.

(.2mi)

(.3mi)

Blue Reef Aquarium

Villiers Rd.

Clarence Parade

Auckland Rd. E.

Clarendon Rd.

Richmond Rd.

Brandon Rd.

Wimbledon Park Rd.

Castle Ave.

Lennox Rd. S.

Clarence Rd. S.

Malvern Rd.

Florence Rd.

St. Simons Rd.

Waverley Rd.

St. Ronan's Rd.

D-Day Museum

Clarence Esplanade

Southsea Castle

Somerset Rd.

Beach Rd.

Granada Rd.

South Parade

E. Villas Rd.

TO ROYAL MARINES MUSEUM (½mi) AND (2mi)

0   200 yards

0   200 meters

Portsmouth

🏠🏠 ACCOMMODATIONS

Birchwood Guest House, **6**

Britannia Guest House, **8**

Everly Guest House, **3**

Portsmouth and Southsea Backpackers Lodge, **7**

Southsea Leisure Park, **9**

🍎 FOOD

Aubergine Restaurant, **5**

Agora Cafe-Bar and Restaurant, **4**

One Eyed Dog, **2**

Ship & Castle, **1**

■ ⚡ 🄻 ORIENTATION AND PRACTICAL INFORMATION

Portsmouth sprawls along the coast for miles—**Portsmouth, Old Portsmouth** (near the Portsmouth and Southsea train station and Commercial Rd.), and the resort community of **Southsea** (stretching to the east) can seem like entirely different cities. Major sights cluster at Old Portsmouth, **The Hard,** and Southsea's **Esplanade.**

Tourist Information Centre: The Hard (☎826 722; www.visitportsmouth.co.uk), by the historic ships. Bursting with brochures and maps (£1.50). Books accommodations for £2 plus a 10% deposit. Discounts available for museum and attractions. Open daily Apr.-Sept. 9:30am-5:45pm, Oct.-Mar. 9:30am-5:15pm. **Southsea offices,** in front of the Blue Reef Aquarium, also has info. Open daily 9:30am-5:15pm.

Tours: Waterbus (☎07889 408 137) offers 1hr. guided rides in Portsmouth Harbour, leaving from The Hard. Open daily 10:20am-4:30pm. £5.50.

Financial Services: Banks cluster around the Commercial Rd. shopping precinct, north of Portsmouth and Southsea Station. **Barclays** (☎305 858), at the corner of Commercial and Edinburgh Rd. Open M-F 9am-5pm, Sa 9:30am-4pm.

Launderette: Laundrycare, 121 Elm Grove (☎826 245). Wash £2.50, dry £2. Open daily 8am-6pm. Last wash 4:45pm.

Police: Winston Churchill Ave. (☎0845 454 545).

Hospital: Queen Alexandra Hospital, Southwick Hill Rd. (☎286 000).

Pharmacy: Boots, 31-33 Palmerston Rd. (☎821 046). Open M-Sa 9am-5:30pm.

Internet Access: Online Cafe, 163 Elm Grove (☎831 106). 50p per 10min. Open daily 9am-10pm. **Jamochas Internet Cafe,** 99 Elm Grove (☎ 875 000) has free Wi-Fi. Open M-F 9am-8pm, Sa 9am-5:30pm.

Post Office: Swindon St. (☎08457 223 344), opposite the train station. Open M and W-Sa 9am-5:30pm, Tu 9:30am-5:30pm. **Post Code:** PO1 1AA.

🅁 ACCOMMODATIONS

Moderately priced **B&Bs** ($35-40) can be found in **Southsea.** Many are located along Waverley, Clarendon, Festings and Granada Rd., and South Parade. If you're arriving via the Portsmouth and Southsea Station, catch one of the frequent buses on Commercial Rd. (#1 and 40). From Portsmouth Harbour, hop aboard one of the buses (#5 and 6) that make the trek from The Hard to South Parade.

Britannia Guest House, 48 Granada Rd., Southsea (☎814 234). Colorful, spotless rooms decorated with the owner's modern artwork. Full English breakfast included. Singles £25; doubles £45-50. MC/V. ❸

Everly Guest House, 33 Festings Rd. (☎731 001). Comfortable ensuite rooms on a quiet street near the Southsea Esplanade. Swap tips with world-traveling owners. Full English and vegetarian breakfast included. Singles £25; doubles £35. MC/V. ❸

Portsmouth and Southsea Backpackers Lodge, 4 Florence Rd. (☎832 495). Take #5 or 6 to The Strand and walk back up to the 2nd road on the left. Pan-European crowd and accommodating owners. Lounge, satellite TV, kitchen, and grocery counter. Laundry £2. Internet access £1 per 30min. Dorms £13; doubles £30, ensuite £34. Cash only. ❷

Birchwood Guest House, 44 Waverley Rd. (☎811 337). 7 bright, spacious rooms have Wi-Fi, TV, coffee, hair dryer, and alarm clock. Personable hosts make sure your stay is comfortable. Singles £27-35; doubles £60-65. MC/V. ❹

Camping: Southsea Leisure Park, Melville Rd., Southsea (☎735 070). At the eastern end of the seafront, 5-6 mi. from The Hard. Site has toilets, showers, laundry, shop, restaurant-bar, and pool. 1-person tent £10; 2-person tent £18. Electricity £2. ❶

FOOD AND PUBS

Chain restaurants line the waterfront, between the shopping districts in Southsea, and on Commercial Rd. There is no shortage of pubs in Portsmouth, especially near The Hard. Ethnic eateries are clustered along Albert Rd. near the University of Portsmouth's student housing. Tesco **supermarket** is at 56-61 Elm Grove. (☎08456 269 090. Open daily 6am-midnight.)

Agora Cafe-Bar and Restaurant, 9 Clarendon Rd. (☎822 617). Serves English breakfasts (£3-5), light fare by day, and Turkish and Greek cuisine (£7-10) by night. Open daily 9am-4pm and 5:30-11:30pm. Student discount. MC/V, £10 min. ❷

One Eyed Dog (☎827 188), corner of Elm Grove and Victoria Rd. South. Trendy pub draws a steady flow of students in the afternoon and evening. Sate your thirst (mixed drinks £2-3) but not your hunger (bar snacks only). M nights cheap beer. Open M-Th 4-11pm, F-Sa 1-11pm, Su 5-10:30pm. Cash only. ❶

Aubergine, 93 Albert Rd. (☎ 820 116). Among the many options for Indian takeaway, this small eatery is one of the best. Entrees like tasty chicken tikka from £5-7. M special 4-course meal for £8. Open M and Su 6pm-1:30am, Tu-Sa 6pm-3am. MC/V. ❷

Ship & Castle, 1-2 The Hard (☎832 009). The oldest pub and restaurant in Portsmouth, Ship & Castle is a good stop after a day of sightseeing by the harbor. Stretching down the block, it offers ample space including a play-barn for children and a hip bar for adults. Food served daily 11:30am-7:30pm. Entrees £7-10. MC/V. ❷

◉ SIGHTS

Portsmouth is a seafarer's paradise, overflowing with ships and sea-weary relics. Most of the naval attractions are in the historic harbor near The Hard. The sail-shaped **Spinnaker Tower,** with three observation decks high above the harbor, offers panoramic views of the city. To satisfy a less nautical fancy, **Gunwharf Quays** has shopping, while **Clarence Pier** is full of traditional amusement park fare.

■ PORTSMOUTH HISTORIC DOCKYARD

Historians and armchair admirals can plunge head-first into the **Historic Dockyard,** which brings together a trio of Britain's most storied ships and nautical artifacts. The *Mary Rose*, HMS *Victory*, and HMS *Warrior* were launched in 1512, 1765, and 1860, respectively. These floating monuments chronicle Britain's mastery of the seas. The five galleries of the **Royal Naval Museum** fill in the temporal gaps between the three ships. *(In the Naval Yard. Entrance next to the TIC; follow the signs. ☎861 512. Ships open daily Apr.-Oct. 10am-5:30pm; Nov.-Mar. 10am-5pm. Last entry 1hr. before close. Each sight £10. All-inclusive ticket £16, allows 1-time entrance to each sight, valid for 1yr.)*

MARY ROSE. Henry VIII's *Mary Rose* is one of England's earliest warships and the only 16th-century ship of its kind on display in the world. Henry was particularly fond of her, but, like many of his women, she died before her time. Sunk by the French after setting sail from Portsmouth in July 1545, it wasn't until 1982 that Henry's flagship rose from her watery grave. The hull can be seen behind a glass display. It will be sprayed with a preservative until 2009, a 15-year process that should make *Mary* immortal. The **Mary Rose Museum** displays over 19,000 artifacts discovered with the ship, including a collection of 168 longbows.

HMS VICTORY. Napoleon must be rolling over in his spacious tomb knowing that Nelson's Trafalgar flagship is still afloat. The vessel holds artifacts of British nationalism, from the plaque on the spot where Nelson fell to the flag code display of his statement, "England expects that every man will do his duty." The *Victory* is still a commissioned warship, the oldest in the world, so espionage laws prohibit taking photographs on board. Visitors can take a tour of the ship through five levels of compartments, including the sickberth and the captain's quarters.

HMS WARRIOR. The fast, furious HMS *Warrior* was the pride of Queen Victoria's navy and the first iron-hulled warship in the world. Its revolutionary design led to its downfall, as it paved the way for the even faster, larger, and more powerful warships that replaced it. After some hard times as an oil jetty and depot ship, the *Warrior* returned once again to the limelight as one of the few surviving Victorian battleships. Today, visitors can explore the gun decks, living quarters, and engine room of the most expensive ship restoration ever completed.

ACTION STATIONS. After you see the Navy, you can pretend to be the Navy at the Action Stations. High-tech simulations let you pilot a helicopter, or you can test your prowess on the climbing wall. The short Omni film shows a day aboard a Type 23 frigate: missiles fly as the ship engages in a war with modern-day pirates (June-Sept. every 30min.; Oct.-May every hr.).

THE BEST OF THE REST

OTHER NAVAL SIGHTS. The **Royal Navy Submarine Museum** surfaces in Britain's only walk-on submarine, the HMS *Alliance*. It also displays the Royal Navy's first submarine, *Holland I*. The control room trainer lets visitors play captain. The Gosport ferry crosses from the Harbour train station (£2); follow the signs or take bus #9 to Haslar Hospital. (☎529 217; www.rnsubmus.co.uk. Open daily Apr.-Oct. 10am-5:30pm; Nov.-Mar. 10am-4:30pm. Last admission 1hr. before close. £6.50.) **Spitbank Fort,** a peculiar manmade island, protected Portsmouth through two World Wars. It is a tour site by day and, oddly, a swinging party venue by night. (☎504 207; www.spitbankfort.co.uk. 25min. crossing from the Dockyard. Tours June-Aug. Su 2:45pm; call Solent Cruises ☎01983 564 602. Tours £8, children £5. Party Nights with dinner and disco F-Sa 8pm-midnight, £22.50. Book in advance ☎01329 242 077.) The **Royal Marines Museum** chronicles the British empire through its four-century trajectory of triumph and failure. (In Southsea down the Esplanade. ☎819 385; www.royalmarinesmuseum.co.uk. Open daily June-Aug. 10am-5pm; Sept.-May 10am-4:30pm. £4.75, students £2.25.)

SOUTHSEA. The ■**D-Day Museum,** Clarence Esplanade, leads visitors through life-size dioramas of the June 6, 1944 invasion. Recreations of life at home and in the tunnels share perspectives from soldiers and the families they left behind. It also houses the **Overlord Embroidery,** a 272 ft. tapestry that provides an overview of events from the war surrounding the Overlord operation. (☎827 261. Open daily Apr.-Sept. 10am-5:30pm; Oct.-Mar. 10am-5pm. Last admission 30min. before close. £6, students £3.60. Embroidery audio tour 50p.) **Southsea Castle,** built by Henry VIII at the point of the Esplanade, was an active fortress until 1960. The underground **Time Tunnels** are not to be missed. (Clarence Esplanade. Open daily Apr.-Sept. 10am-5:30pm; Oct. 10am-5pm. Last admission 30min. before close. £3, students £1.80.) The **Blue Reef Aquarium** features sting rays, sharks, exotic coral, anacondas, and poison dart frogs. The adorable otters make the rest of the sea life jealous for attention. (☎9287 5222. Towan Promenade. Open daily Mar.-Oct. 10am-5pm; Nov.-Feb. 10am-4pm. £7.50, students £6.50.)

ISLE OF WIGHT ☎01983

More tranquil and sun-splashed than its mother island to the north, the Isle of Wight's stunning countryside and sandy beaches are the perfect backdrop to a leisurely weekend or daytrip. The Isle has softened the hardest of hearts, from Queen Victoria, who found the island a perfect setting for her lavish country house, to Karl Marx, who proclaimed the island "a little paradise." Follow in the footsteps of these famous fans along the Isle's 67 miles of romantic coastline.

⌐ TRANSPORTATION

Ferries: Wightlink (☎08705 827 744; www.wightlink.co.uk) ferries frequently from: **Lymington** to **Yarmouth** (30min.; 2 per hr.; round-trip £10.40, children £5.20); **Portsmouth Harbour** to **Fishbourne** (35min.; round-trip £10.40, children 5.20); **Portsmouth Harbour** to **Ryde** (15min.; round-trip £12.40, children £6.20, ½-day noon-4:30pm round-trip £10). Red Funnel ferries (☎08704 448 898; www.redfunnel.co.uk) run from **Southampton** to **East Cowes** (every hr., round-trip £14.30). Hovertravel (☎811 000; www.hovertravel.co.uk) sails from **Southsea** to **Ryde** (9min.; 2 per hr.; round-trip £10.40, children 5.20).

Public Transportation: Train service on the Island Line (☎08457 484 950; www.island-line.com) is limited to the eastern end of the island, including Ryde, Brading, Sandown, Shanklin, and a few points between. Trains 2 per hr. 1st train 6am, last train midnight. Southern Vectis **buses** (☎827 000; www.svoc.co.uk) cover the entire island; TICs and travel centers (☎827 005) in Cowes, Shanklin, Ryde, and Newport sell the complete timetable (50p). Buses meet ferries at Yarmouth and Ryde. Buy tickets on board. The **Island Day Rover** ticket gives you unlimited bus travel (1-day £9, children £4.50).

Car Rental: South Wight Rentals, 10 Osborne Rd. (☎864 263), in Shanklin. Offers free pickup and drop-off. From £23 per day. Open daily 8:30am-5:30pm. **Solent Self Drive,** 32 High St. (☎282 050), in Cowes. From £25 per day, £150 per week. All-Island **parking permits** are available at any TIC for 2-4, 7, and 14 days in any city council car park.

Bike Rental: Tav Cycles, 140 High St. (☎812 989; www.tavcycles.co.uk), in Ryde. £12 per day. Longer rentals available. £25 deposit per bike. MC/V.

◢◪ ORIENTATION AND PRACTICAL INFORMATION

The Isle of Wight is 23 mi. by 13 mi. and shaped like a diamond. Most of the towns are clustered along the coasts: **Ryde** and **Cowes** are to the north; **Sandown, Shanklin,** and **Ventnor** lie along the east coast heading south; and **Yarmouth** is on the west coast. The capital, **Newport,** sits in the center, at the source of the River Medina.

Tourist Information Centres: Located close to the bus station or ferry port in most of the major cities. Each center supplies individual town maps and information along with travel and attraction guides for the entire island. The free, thorough *Isle of Wight Official Pocket Guide* is chock full of what to do and where to do it. A general inquiry service (☎813 818; www.islandbreaks.co.uk) directs questions to one of the 7 regional offices listed below. For accommodations, call the central booking line (☎813 813) or book online. Books rooms for a 10% deposit. In winter, TICs have reduced hours.

> **Ryde:** Western Esplanade, at the corner of Union St., opposite Ryde Pier and the bus station. Open M-Sa 9:30am-5pm, Su 10am-4pm.
>
> **Cowes:** Fountain Quay, in the alley next to the RedJet ferry terminal. Open M-Sa 9:30am-5:30pm, Su 10am-4pm; during Cowes Week (1st week in Aug.) daily 8am-8pm.
>
> **Newport:** The Guildhall, High St.; signposted from the bus station. Open M-Sa 9:30am-5pm, Su 10am-4pm.
>
> **Sandown:** 8 High St., across from Boots Pharmacy. Open July-Aug. M-Sa 9:30am-5:30pm, Su 9:30am-4:30pm; Apr.-June and Sept.-Oct. M-Sa 9:30am-5:30pm, Su 10am-4pm.
>
> **Shanklin:** 67 High St. Open Apr.-Oct. M-Sa 9:30am-5:30pm, Su 10am-4pm.
>
> **Ventnor:** The Coastal Visitor's Centre, Salisbury Gardens, Dudley Rd. Open Apr.-Oct. M-Sa 9:30am-4:30pm.
>
> **Yarmouth:** The Quay; signs posted from ferry. Open Apr.-Oct. M-Sa 9:30am-5:30pm, Su 10am-4pm.

Financial Services: Banks and **ATMs** can be found in all major town centers. ATMs are rare in smaller towns.

Police: Isle of Wight Police (☎0845 454 545).

Medical Services: St. Mary's Hospital, Parkhurst Rd. (☎524 081), in Newport. **Ryde Medical Center,** George St. (☎615 555).

Disabled Concerns: Disabled travelers can find help from **Dial Office** (☎522 823).

Internet Access: Ask the local TIC for the nearest location. **Internet Cafe,** 16-18 Melville St. (☎408 294), off High St. by the pier in Sandown. £1.50 per 15min. Open Tu-Sa 11am-6pm. **Ryde Library,** 101 George St. (☎562 170). Free with membership. **Lord Louis Library,** Orchard St. (☎823 800), behind the bus station in Newport. Free.

Post Office: Post offices are in every town center. **Post Code:** PO30 1AB (Newport).

⚑ ACCOMMODATIONS

Accommodation prices on Wight range from decent to absurd, often depending on proximity to the shore. Budget travelers should try one of the YHA hostels at either end of the island, look in less-visited areas, or try their luck with the **Accommodation Booking Service** (☎813 813). Campsites are plentiful; check the free *Isle of Wight Camping and Touring Guide,* available at all TICs.

YHA Totland Bay, Hurst Hill, Totland Bay (☎752 165), on the west end of Wight. Take Southern Vectis bus #7 or 7A to Totland War Memorial; turn left up Weston Rd., and walk 10min. to the fork in the road. Hostel is on the top of Hurst Hill on the left fork. Brown signs guide you from the bus station. Clean, spacious lodgings near the Needles and Alum Bay. Kitchen. Breakfast £4. Lockout 10am-5pm. Curfew 11pm. Open May-Aug. daily; Mar.-Apr. and Sept.-Oct. Tu-Sa. Dorms £17, under 18 £10. AmEx/MC/V. ❷

Claverton House, 12 The Strand, Ryde (☎613 015). Lavish bedrooms and flower-scented bathrooms could tempt even ardent sightseers to spend the day in the tub. Singles £40; doubles £50. Self-catering apartment £200-350 per week. Cash only. ❹

Seaward Guest House, 14-16 George St., Ryde (☎563 168). Near the hovercraft, bus, and train stations. 7 airy rooms with TV and coffee-maker. Hearty breakfast with vegetarian options included. Singles £22-30; doubles £36-52. MC/V. ❸

Camping: Beaper Farm Camping Site (☎615 210), between Ryde and Sandown. Take bus #3. Family-run park welcomes guests near the beach. Showers and laundry. July-Aug. 2 people £10; May-June and Sept. 2 people £7. Electricity £2. ❶

◖ FOOD

Wanderers on Wight can find food on the local High St. or Esplanade. Local fish is a specialty. The *Official Eating Out Guide,* free and distributed by TICs, offers additional dining options. Most larger cities have supermarkets, and the island has nearly one pub per sq. mi. **S. Fowler & Co. ❶,** 41-43 Union St., Ryde, buzzes with hungry tourists and locals. Plenty of pub meals are under £6, including several vegetarian options. (☎812 112. Open daily 10am-midnight. Food served until 10pm. AmEx/MC/V.) In Ryde, feast on gourmet pastries and baguettes stuffed to the brim (£1.40-4.70) from the **Baguette Factory ❶,** 24 Cross St. (☎611 115. Open M-Sa 8:30am-4pm.) Drop into **Liberty's Cafe-Bar ❷,** 12 Union St., Ryde (☎811 007), for a specialty coffee or tasty lunch (£7-12) in a stylish atmosphere. (Open M-Th 10am-11pm, F-Sa 10am-midnight, Su 11am-11:30pm. MC/V.) In Newport, **God's Providence House ❶,** is a block from the bus station at the intersection of Town Ln. and Pyle St., offering sandwiches for £3-6. (☎522 085. Open M-Sa 9am-5pm. MC/V.)

◉ ✿ SIGHTS AND FESTIVALS

Wight's natural sights are especially beautiful in the west, with hillsides, multicolored **beaches,** and the famous **Needles** overlooking the sea. Keep your camera nearby on the ride along cliff roads on buses #7, 7A, and 7B to **Alum Bay.** Sandier beaches next to shopping areas are on the eastern coast in Ventnor, Shanklin, Sandown, and Ryde. Ryde is a convenient hub, but is less scenic than the western side of the island. The **Isle of Wight Zoo** in Sandown is home to the UK's largest collection of tigers. (☎403 883; www.isleofwightzoo.com. Open daily 10am-6pm. £6, children £5.) The **Isle of Wight Summer Festival** has hosted bands like REM, Coldplay, The Who, and David Bowie; ticketing information and dates are available at TICs.

■**ALUM BAY AND THE NEEDLES.** On the western tip of the island lie three white peaks jutting from the water. The **Needles** are actually made of chalk—break out a sheet of paper to see for yourself. A **chairlift** runs down the cliffs to the colored beaches. The **Needles Pleasure Park** on the cliff offers activities and street performers. In August, stay for a dazzling display of fireworks on Thursdays at 9:30pm at Tennyson Downs, a short walk from the Park. *(Take bus #7, 7A, 7B, or 42 to Alum Bay. Needles Park ☎0870 458 0022; www.theneedles.co.uk. Open daily Easter-Oct. 10am-5pm; later hours in Aug. Free. Tours July-Aug. F 2:30pm. Parking £3. Chairlift round-trip £4.)*

CARISBROOKE CASTLE. Carisbrooke includes one of England's most complete Norman shell-keeps, an interior wall that has been sitting atop its moat for 900 years. A walk along its ramparts offers unbeatable views of the Isle. Visitors can see where Charles I, a prisoner at Carisbrooke in 1647, got stuck in a window during his first (obviously unsuccessful) attempt to escape from the castle. The museum details the structure's history and includes the **Tennyson Room,** with the Victorian poet laureate's desk, cloak, and funeral pall. *(From Newport, follow Upper St. to James St., turn right on Trafalgar St., and bear left on Castle Rd., which becomes Castle Hill. The 30min. walk from the bus station can be shortened by taking bus #7 to Carisbrooke, at the beginning of Castle Rd. ☎522 107. Open daily Apr.-Sept. 10am-5pm; Oct.-Mar. 10am-4pm. £5.50, concessions £4.20)*

OSBORNE HOUSE. Despite its extravagance—with halls full of paintings and statues of Victoria, Albert, and family—this former royal residence reveals a peek into Queen Victoria's private life. Victoria and Prince Albert commissioned it as a "modest" country home and refuge. After Albert died in 1861, it became Victoria's retreat, decorated with mementos and family photographs. The India Exhibit is a sumptuous display of Indian decor. In the **Horn Room,** nearly all of the furniture is made from antlers. **Horse-and-carriage rides** (£2.50) through the grounds pass the royal children's Swiss Cottage; free minibuses follow the same route. *(Take Southern Vectis bus #4 or 5 from Ryde or Newport, respectively. ☎200 022. Open Apr.-Sept. daily 10am-5pm, last entry 4:30pm; Oct. M-Th and Su 10am-4pm; Nov.-Mar. by tour only. House and grounds £10, concessions £7.40. Grounds only £6, concessions £4, under 16 £2.70.)*

WALKING, CYCLING, AND FESTIVALS. Walkers and cyclists enjoy 500 mi. of footpaths and 60 mi. of coastal paths stretching from **Totland,** past lighthouses both modern and medieval at **St. Catherine's Point,** to **St. Lawrence** at the southern end of the island. Explore the island footpaths during the annual **Walking Festival** (☎813 800), the UK's largest, in mid-May and the **Cycling Festival** (☎823 347) in late September. More information can be obtained at any of the TICs.

WINCHESTER ☎01962

This ancient capital of medieval England is now a modern hot spot best known for its massive cathedral. Home to Jane Austen and John Keats, Winchester was the center of the kingdoms of both Alfred the Great and William the Conqueror. During the Great Plague of 1665, the town was also a temporary court for Charles II. Winchester's royal history continues to draw visitors, particularly during the floral summer season.

SOUTH ENGLAND

TRANSPORTATION

North of Southampton, Winchester makes an excellent daytrip from **Salisbury** (p. 187), 25 mi. west, or **Portsmouth** (p. 172), 27 mi. south.

> **TIP** **TXT 4 TIMES.** Public transportation got you flustered? Bus stands all over England have a bus stop code posted on their flag. Text the code to 84268 (25p), and you'll get a text back with the full bus timetable for that stop.

Trains: Winchester Station, Station Hill, northwest of the city center. Ticket counter open M-F 6am-8:30pm, Sa 6am-7:30pm, Su 7am-8:30pm. Trains (☎08457 484 950; www.visitwinchester.co.uk) to: **Brighton** (1½hr., every hr., £20); **London Waterloo** (1hr., 3-4 per hr., £22); **Portsmouth** (1hr., every hr., £9); **Salisbury** (1hr., 2 per hr., £12). Be prepared to change trains at Basingstoke or Fareham.

Buses: Buses stop outside on Broadway near Alfred's statue, or inside the **bus station** on Broadway. Open M-F 8:30am-5pm, Sa 8:30am-noon. National Express (☎08705 808 080) runs to: **London** via **Heathrow** (1½hr., 7 per day, £13.50) or **Victoria Station** (2hr., 12 per day, £13); **Oxford** (2½hr., 2 per day, £10); **Southampton** (30min., 12 per day, £3). Wilts and Dorset (☎01722 336 855) runs to **Salisbury** (#68; 1¼hr., 6 per day, £5). **Explorer** tickets are available for buses in Hampshire and Wiltshire (£6.50, children and seniors £5, families £13). **Local buses** (☎01256 464 501) stop by the bus and train stations. Day pass £2.60. Ask for a bus timetable at the TIC.

Taxis: Francis Taxis (☎884 343), by the market. **WinTaxi** (☎866 208) and **Wessex Cars** (☎877 749) are also available.

■ ☷ **ORIENTATION AND PRACTICAL INFORMATION**

Winchester's main commercial axis, **High Street,** stretches from the statue of Alfred the Great at its east end to the arch of **Westgate** opposite. The city's bigger roads stem off High St., which becomes **Broadway** as you approach Alfred.

Tourist Information Centre: The Guildhall, Broadway (☎840 500; www.visitwinchester.co.uk), across from the bus station. Stocks free maps, helpful brochures, seasonal *What's On* guides, and other city guides. **Walking tours** £3, children free. Books accommodations for £3 plus 10% deposit. Open May-Sept. M-Sa 9:30am-5pm, Su 11am-3:30pm; Oct.-Apr. M-Sa 10am-4:30pm.

Financial Services: Major **banks** and **ATMs** cluster at the junction of Jewry St. and High St. Farther down is the **Royal Bank of Scotland,** 67-68 High St. (☎863 322). Open M-Tu and Th-F 9:15am-4:45pm, W 10am-4:45pm.

Launderette: 27 Garbett Rd., Winnall (☎840 658). Climb Magdalen Hill, turn left on Winnall Manor Rd., and follow until Garbett Rd. is on your left. £2.50. Open M-F 8am-8pm, Sa 8am-6pm, Su 10am-6pm. Last wash 1hr. before close.

Police: North Walls (☎08450 454 545), near the intersection with Middle Brook St.

Hospital: Royal Hampshire County, Romsey Rd. (☎863 535), at St. James Ln.

Pharmacy: Boots, 35-39 High St. (☎852 2020). Open M-Sa 8:30am-6pm, Su 10:30am-4:30pm.

Internet Access: Winchester Library, Jewry St. (☎853 909). Open M-Tu and F 9:30am-7pm, W-Th and Sa 9:30am-5pm.

Post Office: Middlebrook St. Open M and W-Sa 9am-5:30pm, Tu 9:30am-5:30pm. **Post Code:** SO23 8UT.

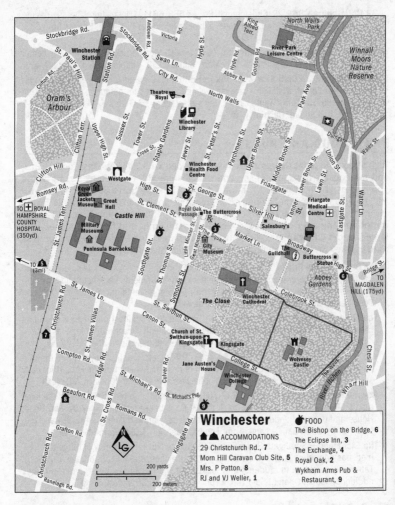

Winchester

🏠▲ ACCOMMODATIONS
29 Christchurch Rd., **7**
Morn Hill Caravan Club Site, **5**
Mrs. P Patton, **8**
RJ and VJ Weller, **1**

🍴 FOOD
The Bishop on the Bridge, **6**
The Eclipse Inn, **3**
The Exchange, **4**
Royal Oak, **2**
Wykham Arms Pub &
Restaurant, **9**

🏠 ACCOMMODATIONS

B&Bs are the best option in Winchester but are often difficult to find and book. For last-minute bookings, the TIC is your best bet. Buses #29 and 47 (2 per hr.) make the journey from the town center to the corner of **Ranelagh** and **Christchurch Roads**, where many of the B&Bs are located. Many pubs also offer accommodations.

Mrs. P. Patton, 12 Christchurch Rd. (☎854 272), down the road from the train station. Elegant Victorian mansion on beautifully landscaped property. Homemade bread and preserves with breakfast. Singles £35-40; doubles £45-50. Cash only. ❸

29 Christchurch Rd., 29 Christchurch Rd. (☎868 661), 10min. from the city center. Well-kept rooms with TV and soft beds. 2 blocks from Mrs. P. Patton. Singles from £35; doubles from £65. Cash only. ❸

RJ and VJ Weller, 63 Upper Brook St. (☎416 560) Victorian cottage in the city center with big rooms and large English breakfast. Singles £30; doubles £55. Cash only. ❸

Morn Hill Caravan Club Site, Morn Hill (☎869 877), 3 mi. east of Winchester off A31, toward New Forest. Mainly for caravans. Limited facilities for campers. Open Mar.-Oct. Caravans £8.50-20.60. Tents (at warden's discretion) £3-6 plus £3-4 per adult, £1-2 per child; call ahead. Cash only. ❶

🍴🍺 FOOD AND PUBS

High Street and **Saint George's Street** are crowded with markets, fast-food chains, and tea houses. Restaurants serve more substantial fare on **Jewry Street,** where you'll find Winchester Health Food Centre, 41 Jewry St. (☎851 113. Open M-F 9:30am-5:45pm, Sa 9am-5:30pm.) For **groceries,** go to Sainsbury's, Middle Brook St., off High St. (☎861 792; open M-Sa 7am-8pm, Su 11am-5pm). For a fresher option, try the open-air **market** (open W-Sa 8am-6pm) and **farmers' market**—the largest in the UK with everything from ostrich meat to locally grown watercress (2nd and last Su of every month; open early morning until 3pm).

The Bishop on the Bridge, 1 High St. (☎855 111), on the river. Enjoy a leisurely meal on the heated terrace or lounge inside on leather chairs. Students flock here and stay late. Most entrees £7-9. Open M-Th noon-11pm, F-Sa noon-midnight, Su noon-10:30pm. Food served M-Sa noon-9pm, Su noon-8pm. MC/V. ❷

The Eclipse Inn, The Square (☎865 676). Winchester's smallest pub is also one of its most popular. 16th-century rectory attracts regulars and, according to legend, ghosts. Open M-Sa 11am-11pm, Su noon-11pm. Food served daily noon-3pm. MC/V. ❶

Wykham Arms, 175 Kingsgate St. (☎854 411). A Winchester institution, this pub draws a large crowd day and night. Sit in an old school desk and check the blackboard for daily specials. Try the Wyke cottage pie (£6) or bangers at the bar for 40p each. MC/V. ❷

Royal Oak, Royal Oak Passage (☎842 701). Yet another pub that claims to be the kingdom's oldest, tracing its origins back to 1390. Squeeze into the alley by God Begot House and descend underground to enjoy the locally brewed cask ale (£2.35) and pub food (£4-7). Open daily 11am-11pm. Food served daily 11am-9pm. MC/V. ❶

The Exchange, 9 Southgate St. (☎854 718). Sports pub with a variety of burgers ("gourmet" has goat cheese and red onion jam), sandwiches, and jacket potatoes (all £2-5). Tables fill quickly with students and locals, but the multi-level beer garden provides additional space. Open M-Sa 11am-11pm, Su noon-10:30pm. MC/V. ❷

🔍 SIGHTS

WINCHESTER CATHEDRAL. Winchester and Canterbury, housing the respective shrines of St. Swithun and St. Thomas à Becket, were the two spiritual capitals of medieval England. Winchester Cathedral's placement atop peat bogs has forced several reconstructions, rendering the modern structure a stylistic hybrid. The Norman transept, crypt, and tower are juxtaposed with the Gothic nave—the longest medieval nave in Europe at 556 ft. The oddly Cubist stained-glass, replaced after Cromwell's window-shattering soldiers, offset the older architecture. Jane Austen is entombed beneath a humble stone slab in the northern aisle in the company of several former English kings. (5 The Close. ☎857 200; www.winchester-cathedral.org.uk. Free 1hr. tours depart from the west end of the nave daily 10am-3pm on the hr. 1¼hr.

tower tours also available W 2:15pm, Sa 11:30am and 2:15pm; £3. Open M-Sa 8:30am-6pm, Su 8:30am-5:30pm. East End closes at 5pm. £4, concessions £3.50, students £2. Photography permit £2.) At the south transept, the illuminated 12th-century Winchester Bible resides in the **Library**, and the **Triforium Gallery** contains several relics, including a Saxon bowl said to have held King Canute's heart. *(Open in summer M 2-4:30pm, Tu-F 11am-4:30pm, Sa 10:30am-4:30pm; in winter W and Sa 11am-3:30pm. £1.)* Outside, to the south of the cathedral, tiny **St. Swithun's Chapel** sits above **Kingsgate.** *(Free.)*

GREAT HALL. William the Conquerer built Winchester Castle in 1067, but unyielding forces (time and Cromwell) have all but destroyed the fortress. The Great Hall remains, a gloriously intact medieval structure containing an imitation (or, according to locals, legendary) Arthurian Round Table. Henry VIII tried to pass the table off as authentic to Holy Roman Emperor Charles V, but the repainted "Arthur," resembling Henry himself, fooled no one. *(At the end of High St. atop Castle Hill. Open daily Mar.-Oct. 10am-5pm; Nov.-Feb. 10am-4pm. Free.)*

MILITARY MUSEUMS. From the Great Hall, cut through Queen Eleanor's Garden to the Peninsula Barracks. Five military museums (the **Royal Hampshire Regiment Museum,** the **Light Infantry Museum,** the **Royal Greenjackets Museum,** the **Royal Hussars Museum,** and the **Gurkha Museum**) celebrate the city's military might. The Royal Greenjackets Museum is the best of the bunch. The highlight is a 276 sq. ft. diorama of the Battle of Waterloo containing 21,500 tiny soldiers and 9600 tiny steeds. Arrive at noon at the **Royal Armouries,** near Fort Nelson, for the firing of the guns. *(Between St. James Terr. and Southgate St. ☎828 549. Open M-Sa 10am-1pm and 2-5pm, Su noon-4pm. £2, concessions £1, families £6. Hours for the other 4 museums are similar. The Gurkha Museum is the only other to charge admission; £1.50, concessions 75p.)*

CITY MUSEUM. The city's history is displayed through archaeological finds, photographs, and interactive exhibits. The Roman gallery includes a complete floor mosaic from the local ruins of a Roman villa, and the Anglo-Saxon room holds a 10th-century tomb. *(At Great Minster St. and The Square. ☎848 269. Open Apr.-Oct. M-Sa 10am-5pm, Su noon-5pm; Nov.-Mar. Tu-Sa 10am-4pm, Su noon-4pm. Free. Audio tour £2.)*

WOLVESEY CASTLE. Some may find the walk along the River Itchen to Wolvesey Castle, a previous home to the Norman bishop, more enjoyable than the site itself. Only the walls of the once magnificent castle remain. Check out the mansion next door, where the current bishop resides. *(The Close. Walk down The Weir on the river or to the end of College St. ☎252 000. Open Apr.-Sept. daily 9am-5pm. Free.)*

WALKS. The Buttercross, at 12 High St., is a good starting point for several walking routes through town. This statue, portraying St. John, William of Wykeham, and King Alfred, derives its name from the shadow it cast over the 15th-century market, keeping the butter cool. A beautiful walk runs along the **River Itchen,** the same route taken by poet John Keats. Directions and his "Ode To Autumn" are available at the TIC (50p). For a panoramic view of the city, including the Wolvesey ruins, climb to **Saint Giles's Hill Viewpoint** at sunset. Pass the mill and take Bridge St. to the gate marked Magdalen Hill; follow the paths from there. *The Winchester Walk,* detailing various walking tours of Winchester, is available at the TIC.

♫ ▨ ENTERTAINMENT AND FESTIVALS

Weekends attract revelers to bars along **Broadway** and **High Street.** The **Theatre Royal,** Jewry St., hosts regional companies and concerts. (☎840 440; www.theatre-royal-winchester.co.uk. Box office open M-F 10am-6pm, Sa 10am-5pm.) The **Homelands Music Festival** takes place the last weekend of May, drawing big names in rock every year. (Buy tickets from the TIC.) In early July, Winchester plays host to the **Hat Fair** (☎849 841; www.hatfair.co.uk), the longest-running street theater festival in all of Britain. The event fills a weekend with free theater performances and peculiar headgear.

 DAYTRIPS FROM WINCHESTER

AUSTEN'S COTTAGE

Take Hampshire bus X64 (40min., M-Sa 11 per day, round-trip £5.70) or London and Country bus #65 on Su, from Winchester. Ask to be let off at the Chawton roundabout and follow the brown signs. ☎01420 83262. Open daily Mar.-May 11am-4:30pm; June-Sept. 10am-5pm; Oct.-Feb. 11am-4:30pm. £5, students £3.50, children £1.

From 1809 to 1817, Jane Austen lived in the village of **Chawton**. It was in this ivy-covered cottage at a tiny wooden table in the dining room that Elizabeth Bennet, Emma Woodhouse, and their respective suitors were brought to life. Personal letters, belongings, and a copy of her will fill the house (although visitors should be warned that many of the documents are not originals).

THE NEW FOREST

20 mi. southwest of Winchester. Take bus #46 to Southampton (round-trip £5) and transfer to bus #56 or 56A to Lyndhurst (round-trip £5.40), or catch a train to Southampton and then a bus to Lyndhurst. Museum open daily 10am-5pm. ☎02380 283 444; www.newforestmuseum.org.uk. £3, concessions £2.50, families £9.

England's newest National Park was once William the Conqueror's 145 sq. mi. personal hunting ground. It remains, 1000 years later, a model of rural England. Wild ponies, donkeys, and deer wander freely along winding roads. As you explore the park, stop by the historic villages in the countryside. The **Rufus Stone** (near Brook and Cadnam) marks the spot where William's son was accidentally slain. For the young, pony rides are popular; the young at heart can play cowboy at **Burley Villa Riding School** (☎01425 610 278) in New Milton, which offers 2hr. "western riding" tours for £47. The **Museum and Visitor Centre,** at High St. and Gosport Ln., has a list of accommodations. (☎02380 282 269. Open daily 10am-5pm.)

SOUTHWEST ENGLAND

In a country with an incredibly rich history, no other region is as steeped in legend, mystery, and monument as England's southwest. King Arthur is said to have been born at Tintagel on Cornwall's northern coast. One village purports to be the site of Camelot, another the resting place of the Holy Grail, and no fewer than three small lakes are identified as the grave of Arthur's sword, Excalibur. Cornwall was the last stronghold of the Celts in England, and evidence of even older Neolithic communities remains, most famously at Stonehenge. Other eras have left their monuments as well, from Salisbury's medieval cathedral and Bath's Roman spas to the fossils on Dorset's Jurassic Coast.

HIGHLIGHTS OF SOUTHWEST ENGLAND

COMMUNICATE with Martians at **Stonehenge,** one of history's most mysterious engineering feats (p. 191).

DALLY in the world of 18th-century pleasure-seekers in **Bath,** a Roman spa town with a history of improper behavior (p. 192).

DIG for fossils along the shore of **Lyme Regis** (p. 213).

▐ TRANSPORTATION IN SOUTHWEST ENGLAND

It is generally easier to get to Somerset, Avon, and Wiltshire than regions farther southwest. **Trains** (☎08457 484 950) offer service from London and the north. The region's primary east-west line from London passes through Taunton, Exeter, and Plymouth before ending at Penzance. Trains from London Waterloo connect to Bath, Bristol, and Salisbury. Branch lines connect St. Ives, Newquay, Falmouth, and Barnstaple to the network. A variety of Rail Rover passes can be used in the region: the **Freedom of the Southwest Rover** covers Cornwall, Devon, Somerset, and parts of Avon and Dorset (8 days out of 15, £61). The **Devon Rail Rover** includes the Taunton-Exmouth line on the east and the Gunnislake-Plymouth line in the west (3 days out of 7, £24; 8 out of 15, £39.50). The **Cornish Rail Rover** runs on the Gunnislake-Plymouth line (£18/33). The **Cornwall Explorer** pass allows one day of travel on all trains and buses in Cornwall (£12).

Buses are a cheaper option, but mastering the complicated regional companies and schedules can be a pain. **National Express** (☎08705 808 080) runs to major points along the north coast via Bristol and to points along the south coast (including Penzance) via Exeter and Plymouth. For journeys within the region, local buses are usually less expensive and farther-reaching than trains. First (☎01752 402 060) is the largest bus company in the area. The comprehensive Traveline service (☎0870 608 2608; open daily 7am-10pm) can help plan travel to any destination. **Explorer** and **Day Rambler** tickets (£5-6, concessions £4.25, families £12.50) allow unlimited travel on all buses within one region, while the **DaySouthwest** ticket allows travel on all First buses in the southwest area (£6). Many tourist destinations are only served by trains and buses seasonally. For transportation from October to May, call Traveline to check routes and schedules.

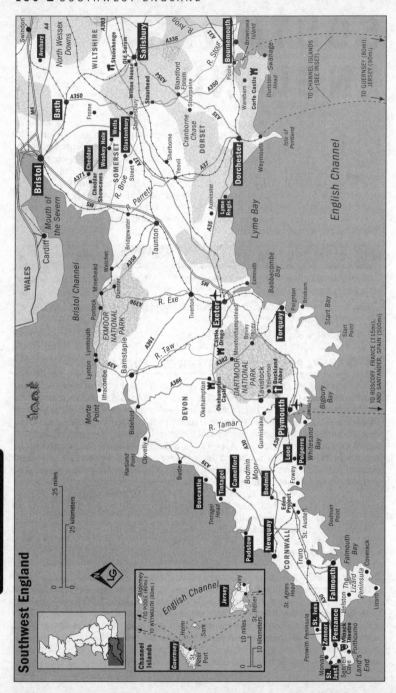

SOUTHWEST ENGLAND

Southwest England

🅑 🅝 HIKING AND OUTDOORS

Distances between towns in southwest England are so short that you can travel through the region on your own steam. The narrow roads and hilly landscapes can make biking difficult, but hardy cyclists will find the quiet lanes rewarding. Bring along a large-scale Ordnance Survey map (£7; available at TICs).

The region's most popular walk is the 630 mi. **South West Coast Path,** England's longest coastal path, which originates in Somerset (at Minehead, in Exmoor National Park) and passes through North Devon, Cornwall, and South Devon, ending in Dorset (Poole). It takes several weeks to walk the whole path. However, it is accessible by bus and features B&Bs and hostels at manageable intervals. Many rivers intersect the path, some requiring ferries—check times carefully to avoid being stranded. Most TICs sell guides and Ordnance Survey maps covering sections of the path, which is generally smooth enough to cover by **bike;** rental shops can often suggest three- to seven-day cycling routes. The path is divided into four parts. The **Somerset and North Devon Coastal Path** extends from Minehead through Exmoor National Park to Bude, and features the highest cliffs in southwest England. The **Cornwall Coast Path,** with some of the most rugged stretches, starts in Bude, where Cornish cliffs harbor a vast range of birds and marine life. It then rounds the southwest tip of Britain and continues along the coast to Plymouth. The **South Devon Coast Path** runs from Plymouth to Paignton, tracing cliffs, estuaries, and remote bays set off by wildflowers. The final section, the **Dorset Coast Path,** picks up in Lyme Regis and runs to Poole Harbor. For more information, contact the **South West Coast Path Association** (☎01752 896 237) or any local TIC.

WILTSHIRE

SALISBURY   ☎01722

Salisbury's winding alleyways and old-fashioned cinema are a step back in time. Despite its popularity among tourists, Salisbury retains its small-town charm. Town life spirals outward from the market, overlooked by the towering cathedral spire. On a windy plain nearby, awe-inspiring Stonehenge stands on a lonely plain.

▐ TRANSPORTATION

Trains: Station on S. Western Rd., west of town across the River Avon. Ticket office open M-Sa 5:30am-8pm, Su 7:30am-8:45pm. Trains (☎08457 484 950) to: **London Waterloo** (1½hr., 2 per hr., £26.30); **Portsmouth** and **Southsea** (1½hr., 2 per hr., £13.50); **Southampton** (40min., every hr., £7); **Winchester** (1hr., 2 per hr., £12).

Buses: Station at 8 Endless St. (☎336 855). Open M-F 8:15am-5:30pm, Sa 8:15am-5pm. National Express (☎08705 808 080) runs to **London** (3hr., 3 per day, £13.50). Buy tickets at the bus station. Wilts and Dorset (☎336 855) runs to **Bath** (X4; M-Sa every hr. 8am-4pm, £4.20) and **Winchester** (#68; 1¾hr., 8 per day, £4.50). An **Explorer** ticket is good for 1 day of travel on Wilts and Dorset buses and some Hampshire, Provincial, Solent Blue, and Brighton & Hove buses (£6.50).

Taxis: Cabs cruise by the train station. **505050 Value Cars** (☎505 050) runs 24hr.

Bike Rental: Hayball Cycles Sport, 26-30 Winchester St. (☎07909 883 006), across from Coaches and Horses. £10 per day, £5 overnight, £65 per week; deposit £25 per bike. Open M-Sa 9am-5pm; bikes due back at 5pm. TIC has suggested routes.

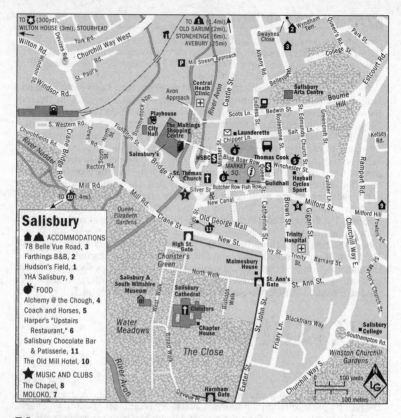

Salisbury

🏠🏠 **ACCOMMODATIONS**
78 Belle Vue Road, **3**
Farthings B&B, **2**
Hudson's Field, **1**
YHA Salisbury, **9**

🍎 **FOOD**
Alchemy @ the Chough, **4**
Coach and Horses, **5**
Harper's "Upstairs
    Restaurant," **6**
Salisbury Chocolate Bar
    & Patisserie, **11**
The Old Mill Hotel, **10**

★ **MUSIC AND CLUBS**
The Chapel, **8**
MOLOKO, **7**

▌ PRACTICAL INFORMATION

Tourist Information Centre: Fish Row (☎334 956, accommodations booking 01271
336 066; www.visitsalisbury.com), the Guildhall, in Market Sq. Free maps. Books
rooms for a 10% deposit. Open June-Sept. M-Sa 9:30am-6pm, Su 10:30am-4:30pm;
Oct.-May M-Sa 9:30am-5pm. 1½hr. **guided walks** leave Apr.-Oct. daily 11am and F
8pm; Nov.-Mar. weekends only 11am. £3.50-4, children £1.50-2.

Financial Services: Banks are everywhere. **Thomas Cook,** 18-19 Queen St. (☎08701
111 111). Open M-W and F-Sa 9am-5:30pm, Th 10am-5:30pm. **HSBC,** corner of Market Pl. and Minster St., has a 24hr. **ATM.**

Launderette: Washing Well, 28 Chipper Ln. (☎421 874). Open daily 8am-9pm. Wash
£3.40, dry £1.40.

Hospital: Central Health Clinic, Avon Approach (☎328 595).

Police: Wilton Rd. (☎411 444).

Pharmacy: Boots, 51 Silver St. (☎333 233). Open M-Tu and Th-Sa 8:30am-5:30pm, W
9am-5:30pm, Su 10:30am-4:30pm.

Internet Access: Salisbury Library, Market Pl. (☎324 145). Open M 10am-7pm, Tu-W
and F 9am-7pm, Th and Sa 9am-5pm. 30min. free with photo ID. **Internet Cafe,** 14
Endless St. (☎421 328). Open M-Sa 10am-7pm.

Post Office: 24 Castle St. (☎ 08457 223 344), at Chipper Ln. **Bureau de change.** Open M-F 8:30am-5:30pm. **Post Code:** SP1 1AB.

ACCOMMODATIONS

Salisbury's proximity to a certain stone circle breeds numerous guest houses and B&Bs, most of them starting at around $35 per person—ask for an accommodations guide or free booking assistance from the TIC. Be sure to book ahead in the busy summer season.

Farthings B&B, 9 Swaynes Close (☎ 330 749; www.farthingsbandb.co.uk), 10min. from the city center. Comfortable retreat with large, floral rooms and subtle touches of home. Smaller rooms share a bath. Continental breakfast included. May-Sept. singles £32; doubles £56. Oct.-Apr. £25/46. Cash only. ❸

YHA Salisbury, Milford Hill House, Milford Hill (☎ 327 572), on the edge of town. 70 beds. Kitchen and TV lounge. Breakfast included. Laundry £3. Internet access 7p per min. Book in advance, especially Easter-Oct. Dorms £17.50, under 18 £14. MC/V. ❷

78 Belle Vue Rd. (☎ 329 477), on a residential road near the cathedral. Victorian terrace house offers 2 rooms with shared bath. Single £23; double £45. Cash only. ❷

Camping: Hudson's Field, Castle Rd. (☎ 320 713). Between Salisbury and Stonehenge, 30min. from city center. Clean, modern facilities. Vehicle curfew 11pm. Electricity £2.60. Open Mar.-Oct. Tents £5.40, adults £5.30, children £2.50. MC/V. ❶

FOOD AND PUBS

Even jaded pub-dwellers can find a pleasant surprise among Salisbury's 60-odd watering holes. **Market Square,** in the town center, fills from May to December on Tuesdays and Saturdays for the **market** and on Wednesdays for the **farmers' market** (open 7am-4pm). The TIC has the summer market schedule. A Sainsbury's **supermarket** is at The Maltings. (☎ 332 282. Open M-Sa 7am-10pm, Su 10am-4pm.)

Harper's "Upstairs Restaurant," 6-7 Ox Rd., Market Sq. (☎ 333 118). Specializes in inventive English and international dishes (£7-10). 2-course early-bird dinner before 8pm £7.50. Open June-Sept. M-F noon-2pm and 6-9:30pm, Sa noon-2pm and 6-10pm, Su 6-9pm; Oct.-May M-F noon-2pm and 6-9:30pm, Sa noon-2pm and 6-10pm. AmEx/MC/V. ❷

Alchemy @ the Chough, Blue Boar Row (☎ 330 032). Find a couch in one of Alchemy's many nooks and crannies. Original art and signs still hang on the walls. The Alchemy mix (£10) is a platter of finger foods. Entrees £8-10. Open M and W noon-11pm, Tu 11am-11pm, Th-F noon-midnight, Sa 11am-midnight, Su noon-10:30pm. MC/V. ❷

Coach and Horses, 39 Winchester St. (☎ 414 319). Traditional pub food (£8-14) and generously poured drinks (pints £2.70) flow nonstop. Salisbury's oldest pub, open since 1382. Check out the beer garden in the back. Open M-Sa 11:30am-11pm, Su noon-10:30pm. Food served M-Sa 11:30am-9:30pm, Su noon-9pm. MC/V. ❶

Salisbury Chocolate Bar & Patisserie, 33 High St. (☎ 327 422). Indulge your sweet tooth with luscious hot chocolates (£2) or scrumptious pastries (£3-4), like the decadent ganache-filled Fudgey cake. Open daily 9:30am-5pm. MC/V. ❶

The Old Mill Hotel, Town Path (☎ 327 517). At the end of a 10min. walk along Town Path through the Harnem Water Meadow, in a 12th-century mill. Entrees can be pricey (£13-17), but the pub food is cheaper (£6-8) and just as delicious. Open M-Sa 11am-11pm, Su noon-10:30pm. Food served M-Th noon-2pm and 7-9pm, F-Sa 11am-11pm, Su noon-10:30pm. AmEx/MC/V. ❸

HERE COMES THE SUN

Perhaps no manmade structure evokes more mystical associations than Stonehenge. Ties to Arthurian legend, Celts, druids, aliens, giants, and witches bring tourists to the mysterious stones year-round. For 364 days of the year they are roped off—almost regal in their standoffishness. But every June, the summer solstice arrives, the ropes are pulled back, admission is free, and visitors enter the circle to worship as they like.

In droves they come: Druids with staffs waiting for the sun, hippies carrying magical plants and caressing the stones, and curious bystanders unsure of what will happen next. In a matter of hours, the vacant field is transformed into a drum-filled festival complete with glow sticks and champagne.

As the crowd swells to an impenetrable mob, the drumming thunders and the sun finally rises, casting a shadow perfectly across the center of the stones. Suddenly, cheering erupts from the milling masses—an unforgettable energy that validates the mystical qualities of Stonehenge.

The 2008 summer solstice occurs on June 21. There is no admission fee the night before or morning of the solstice, but make plans to get a bus early as crowds form quickly.

SIGHTS

SALISBURY CATHEDRAL. Salisbury Cathedral, built between 1220 and 1258, rises to a neck-breaking 404 ft., making it medieval England's highest spire and one of Britain's most impressive displays of Gothic architecture. The bases of the marble pillars bend inward under the strain of 6400 tons of limestone. Nearly 700 years have left the building in need of repair, and scaffolding shrouds parts of the outer walls that are under extensive renovation, expected to be completed by 2015. A tiny stone figure rests in the nave—legend has it that either a boy bishop is entombed on the spot or that it covers the heart of the cathedral's founder. The **Chapter House** holds the best preserved of the four surviving copies of the Magna Carta. The text is still legible, great for those who can read medieval Latin. Spot the punctures at the bottom of the vellum where King John's seal was once attached—the priceless artifact was inadvertently chucked with the weekly trash. (☎555 120. *Cathedral open daily 7:15am-6:15pm. More limited hours in winter. Free tours every 30min.: May-Oct. M-Sa 9:30am-4:45pm, Su 4-6:15pm; Nov.-Feb. M-Sa 10am-4pm. 1½hr. roof and tower tours: May-Sept. M-Sa 11:15am, 2:15, 3:15, and 5pm; Su 4:30pm. June-Aug. M-Sa 11am, 2, 3, and 6:30pm; Su 4:30pm. Requested donation £4, concessions £3.50. Roof and tower tour £4.50, concessions £3.50.*)

SALISBURY AND SOUTH WILTSHIRE MUSEUM. The museum, in the Cathedral's close, has artwork ranging from Turner's watercolors to period clothing and dollhouses. The Stonehenge exhibit gives extensive history, and displays the bones of an archer buried at Stonehenge around the time the first stones were raised. (*65 The Close, along the West Walk.* ☎332 151. *Open July-Aug. M-Sa 10am-5pm, Su 2-5pm; Sept.-June M-Sa 10am-5pm. £5, concessions £3.50, families £9.50.*)

NIGHTLIFE AND FESTIVALS

Read the sign outside **The Chapel,** 30 Milford St., carefully before trying to enter. It states, in mathematical terms: "no effort=no entry." Loosely translated—dress to impress. This club advertises itself as one of the UK's best. Without much competition in Salisbury, it can surely claim to be the best in town. (☎504 255; www.thechapelnightclub.co.uk. Cover W £2; Th £4, ladies free until 11:30pm; F £8; Sa £10. Open W-Th 10:30pm-2:30am, F-Sa 10:30pm-3am.) **MOLOKO,** 5 Bridge St., is a chain bar, but still one of the most popular hangouts in town. There's an endless list of vodkas (£2.50-4.50) and a stylish crowd. (☎507 050. Special £1 house vodkas F 7-9pm. Open M-Th noon-midnight, F-Sa noon-2am, Su 3-10:30pm.)

Salisbury's repertory theater company puts on shows at the **Playhouse,** Malthouse Ln., over the bridge off Fisherton St. (☎320 333; www.salisburyplayhouse.com. Box office open M-Sa 10am-6pm, until 8pm on performance days. Tickets £8.50-17. ½-price tickets available same day.) During summer, enjoy free Sunday **concerts** in various parks; call the TIC for info. The **Salisbury International Arts Festival** features dance exhibitions, music, and wine-tasting for two weeks in late May and early June. Contact the Festival Box Office at the Playhouse or the TIC for a program. (☎320 333; www.salisburyfestival.co.uk. Tickets from £2.50.)

⚡ DAYTRIPS FROM SALISBURY

🗿 STONEHENGE

Wilts and Dorset (☎336 855) runs daily service from the Salisbury train station and bus station (#3, 40min., round-trip £7.50). The 1st bus leaves Salisbury at 9:45am, and the last leaves Stonehenge at 4:05pm. Check a schedule before you leave; intervals between drop-offs and pickups are at least 1hr. An Explorer ticket (£6.50) allows travel all day on any bus, including those to Avebury, Stonehenge's less-crowded cousin (p. 192), and Old Sarum (p. 192). Wilts and Dorset runs a tour bus from Salisbury (3 per day, £7.50-15). ☎01980 624 715. Open daily June-Aug. 9am-7pm; from mid-Mar. to May and from Sept. to mid-Oct. 9:30am-6pm; from mid-Oct. to mid-Mar. 9:30am-4pm. £6, concession £4.40.

A half-ruined ring of colossal stones amid swaying grass and indifferent sheep has become a world-famous attraction. Tourists visit Stonehenge in droves to see the 22 ft. high stones, pockmarked by the wind that whips across the flat Salisbury plains. The current ring is actually the fifth temple constructed on the site—Stonehenge was already ancient in ancient times. The first arrangement probably consisted of an arch and circular earthwork furrowed in 3050 BC. Its relics are the **Aubrey Holes** (white patches in the earth) and the **Heel Stone** (the rough block standing outside the circle). The present shape, once a complete circle, dates from about 1500 BC. The tremendous workforce—estimated at tens of millions of man-hours—and innovation required to transport and erect the 45-ton stones make Stonehenge an impressive monument to human (alien?) effort. Sensationalized religious and scientific explanations for Stonehenge's purpose add to its intrigue. Some believe the stones are oriented as a calendar, with the position of the sun on the stones indicating the time of year. Celtic druids, whose ceremonies took place in forests, did not actually worship here, but modern druids are permitted to enter Stonehenge on the summer solstice to perform ceremonial exercises. Admission to Stonehenge includes a 30min. audio tour. The tour is helpful, including legends about the stones and the surrounding landscape. English Heritage also offers free guided tours (30min.). From the roadside or from Amesbury Hill, 1½ mi. up the A303, you can get a free, if distant, view of the stones. There are also many walks and trails that pass by; ask at the Salisbury TIC.

 RUIN YOUR DAY. Early risers can see Stonehenge, Avebury (p. 192), and Old Sarum (p. 192) in 1 day. Head out to Stonehenge on the 8:45 or 9:45am bus (buy the Explorer ticket), then catch the 11:10am or 12:20pm bus to Amesbury and transfer to an Avebury bus. Take the 2 or 3pm bus back from Avebury and stop off in Old Sarum before you reach Salisbury.

OTHER DAYTRIPS FROM SALISBURY

STOURHEAD. Once the home of a wealthy English banking family, this 18th-century estate is a classical marriage of architecture and landscape. The Palladian mansion is surrounded by endless gardens, lakes, and waterfalls. The miniature reproductions of Greek temples are visited by colorful peacocks. *(Transportation dif-*

ficult without a car. Trains run to Gillingham station from Salisbury. 25min., W and F every hr., £4. Bus #58A runs infrequently between Gillingham station and Stourhead. Bus #25 runs from Salisbury Bus Station to Hindon Sq. 45min., Tu-F 11:40am. Then take the Wigglybus from Hindon Sq. to Stourton. £1. For the return journey, catch the 4:50pm bus #25 from Hindon Sq. back to Salisbury. ☎01747 841 152. Open from late Mar. to late Oct. M-Tu and F-Su 11:30am-4:30pm. Last admission 30min. before close. Garden and house £11, children £5.50.)

WILTON HOUSE. Declared by James I to be "the finest house in the land," the home of the Earls of Pembroke is the quintessential aristocratic country home and the setting for films like *Sense and Sensibility* (1995) and *Pride and Prejudice* (2005). The house served as an allied headquarters on D-Day. The art collection includes the largest assortment of Van Dycks in the world. Rembrandt's portrait of his mother was stolen in 1994 and discovered two years later in the trunk of a car in London. *(3 mi. west of Salisbury on the A30; take bus #60 or 61. M-Sa every 15min., Su every hr.; round-trip £3. ☎746 720; www.wiltonhouse.com. Open daily late Mar.-Oct. 10:30am-5:30pm; last admission 4:30pm. House and grounds £12. Grounds only £4.50.)*

OLD SARUM. This unassuming grassy mound evolved from a Bronze Age gathering place into a Celtic fortress, which was won by the Romans, taken by the Anglo-Saxons, seized by the Normans, and eventually fell into the hands of the British Heritage Society. Civilization left Old Sarum in the 1300s when a new cathedral was built nearby, leaving stone ruins of the earlier castle strewn across the hill. *(Off the A345, 2 mi. north of town. Buses #3 and 6-9 run every 15min. from Salisbury. ☎335 398. Open daily Apr.-June 10am-5pm; July-Aug. 9am-6pm; Sept.-Oct. 10am-5pm; Nov.-Feb. 11am-3pm; Mar. 10am-4pm. £3, concessions £2.20.)*

AVEBURY. A wonder for the world: why is Avebury's stone circle, larger and older than its cousin Stonehenge, often so lonely during the day? Avebury gives an up-close and largely untouristed view of its 98 stones, standing in a stone circle with an 1000 ft. diameter. Visitors can amble among the megaliths and have a beer in the **Red Lion Pub,** which sits in the center of the circle. Dating from 2500 BC, Avebury was built over the course of centuries but has remained steadfast in its original form. Outside the ring, mysterious Silbury Hill rises from the ground; its date of origin, 2660 BC, was only determined by the serendipitous excavation of an ant. Due to previous excavations, the top of the hill has collapsed and visitors are no longer allowed to reach the top. The **Alexander Keiller Museum** details the history of the stone circle. *(☎539 250. Open daily Apr.-Oct. 10am-6pm; Nov.-Mar. 10am-4pm. £4.20, children £2.10, families £7.50.)* Locate the Avebury **Tourist Information Centre,** in the Avebury Chapel Center, next to the bus stop. *(☎539 425. Open Apr.-Oct. Tu-Su 9:30am-5pm; Nov.-Mar. W-Su 9:30am-5pm. Buses #5 and 6 from Salisbury (2hr., 5 per day, round-trip £6.50) stop in front of the Red Lion.)*

SOMERSET AND AVON

BATH ☎01225

Perhaps the world's first tourist town, Bath has been a must-see since AD 43, when the Romans built an elaborate complex of baths to house the curative waters of the town they called *Aquae Sulis*. In the 18th and 19th centuries, Bath became a social capital second only to London, immortalized by Jane Austen and others. Today, hordes of tourists and backpackers admire the nationally recognized Georgian architecture by day and continue to create scandal by night.

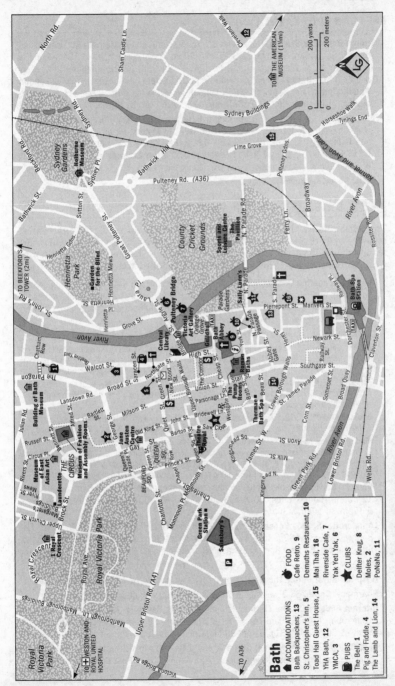

Bath

▲ ACCOMMODATIONS
Bath Backpackers, **13**
St. Christopher's Inn, **5**
Toad Hall Guest House, **15**
YHA Bath, **12**
YMCA, **3**

🍺 PUBS
The Bell, **1**
Pig and Fiddle, **4**
The Lamb and Lion, **14**

🍴 FOOD
Cafe Retro, **9**
Demuths Restaurant, **10**
Mai Thai, **16**
Riverside Cafe, **7**
Yak Yeti Yak, **6**

★ CLUBS
Delfter Krug, **8**
Moles, **2**
PoNaNa, **11**

SOUTHWEST ENGLAND.

▐ TRANSPORTATION

Trains: Bath Spa Station, Dorchester St., at the south end of Manvers St. Ticket office open M-Sa 5:45am-8:30pm, Su 8:45am-8:30pm. Travel center open M-F 8am-7pm, Sa 9am-6pm, Su 9:30am-6pm. Trains (☎08457 484 950) to: **Birmingham** (2hr., every hr., £32.50); **Bristol** (15min., 3 per hr., £5.60); **Exeter** (1¼hr., every hr., £25); **London Paddington** (1½hr., 2 per hr., £46); **London Waterloo** (2-2½hr., 2 per day, £34); **Plymouth** (2¼hr., every hr., £40); **Salisbury** (1hr., every hr., £12.20).

Buses: All buses depart from the **Green Park Station.** Ticket office open M-Sa 8am-5:30pm. National Express (☎08705 808 080) to **London** (3½hr., every 1½hr., £17) and **Oxford** (2¼hr., 1 per day, £9.20). First (☎0871 200 2233) bus X39 runs to **Bristol** M-Sa 6am-7pm every 12min. Badgerline sells a **Day Explorer** ticket, good for 1 day of unlimited bus travel in the region (£7, concessions £5).

Taxis: Abbey Radio (☎444 444).

▐▐ ORIENTATION AND PRACTICAL INFORMATION

The **Roman Baths,** the **Pump Room,** and **Bath Abbey** cluster in the city center, bounded by York and Cheap St. The River Avon flows just east of them and wraps around the south part of town near the train and bus stations. Uphill to the northwest, historical buildings lie on **Royal Crescent** and **The Circus.**

Tourist Information Centre: Abbey Chambers (☎08704 446 442; www.visitbath.co.uk). Town map and mini-guide £1. The free *This Month in Bath* lists events. Books rooms for £5 plus a 10% deposit. Open May-Sept. M-Sa 9:30am-6pm, Su 10am-4pm; Oct.-Apr. M-Sa 9:30am-5pm, Su 10am-4pm.

Tours: Several companies run tours of the city and surrounding sights.

Bizarre Bath (☎335 124; www.bizarrebath.co.uk). The guides impart few historical facts on this comedic walk, but their tricks (including a bunny escape) prove entertaining. 1½hr. tours begin at the Huntsman Inn at N. Parade Passage. Daily tours Apr.-Sept. 8pm. £7, concessions £5.

The Great Bath Pub Crawl (☎310 364; www.greatbathpubcrawl.com). Meets at Lambretta's Bar on N. Parade Passage, delves into Bath's illicit past, and stops for a few rounds. Tours Apr.-Sept. M-W and Su 8pm. £5.

Ghost Walk (☎350 512; www.ghostwalksofbath.co.uk). Tours leave from the Nash Bar of Garrick's Head, near Theatre Royal. 2hr. tours Apr.-Oct. M-Sa 8pm; Nov.-Mar. F 8pm. £6, concessions £5.

Mad Max Tours (☎464 323; www.madmaxtours.com). Tours begin at the Abbey and go to Stonehenge, Avebury, Castle Combe in the Cotswolds, and Lacock National Trust Village (where classroom scenes in *Harry Potter* films were shot). Full-day tours depart daily 8:45am, ½-day tours depart daily 1:30pm. ½-day £12.50, full-day £22.50. Entrance to Stonehenge not included.

Financial Services: Banks are ubiquitous; most are open M-F 9:30am-5pm, Sa 9:30am-12:30pm. **Thomas Cook,** 20 New Bond St. (☎492 000). Open M-W and F-Sa 9am-5:30pm, Th 10am-5:30pm.

Launderette: Spruce Goose, Margaret's Buildings, off Brock St. (☎483 309). Wash £2-3, dry £1.20, soap 60p. Bring £1 coins for washers, 20p coins for dryers. Open M-F and Su 8am-9pm, Sa 8am-8pm. Last wash 1hr. before close.

Police: Manvers St. (☎01275 818 181), near the train and bus stations.

Hospital: Royal United Hospital, Coombe Park, in Weston (☎428 331). Take bus #14.

Pharmacy: Boots, 33-35 Westgate St. (☎482 069.) Open daily 10am-6pm.

Internet Access: Central Library, Podium Shopping Centre (☎394 041). Free. Open M 10am-6pm, Tu-Th 9:30am-7pm, F-Sa 9:30am-5pm, Su 1-4pm. **Ret@iler Internet,** 12 Manvers St. (☎443 181). £1 per 20min. Open M-Sa 9am-9pm, Su 10am-9pm.

Post Office: 21-25 New Bond St. (☎08457 740 740), across from the Podium Shopping Centre. **Bureau de change.** Open M-Sa 9am-5:30pm. **Post Code:** BA1 1AJ.

ACCOMMODATIONS

Well-to-do visitors drive up prices in Bath, but the city's location and popular sights bring in enough backpackers and passing travelers to sustain several budget accommodations. **B&Bs** cluster on **Pulteney Road** and **Pulteney Gardens. Marlborough Lane** and **Upper Bristol Road,** west of the city center, also offer options.

Bath Backpackers, 13 Pierrepont St. (☎446 787; www.hostels.co.uk/bath). Laid-back backpacker's lair with music-themed dorms. Hang out in the lounge with a big-screen TV or have a drink in the "Dungeon." Kitchen. Luggage storage £2 per bag. Internet access £2 per hr., free Wi-Fi. Reception 8am-11pm. Checkout 10:30am. Dorms £15; doubles £35; triples £52.50. Book ahead in summer. MC/V. ❷

YMCA, International House, Broad St. Pl. (☎325 900; www.bathymca.co.uk). Up the stairs from High and Walcot St. Spacious rooms overlooking a courtyard garden. Continental breakfast and access to the rec room included. Internet access. Dorms £13-15; singles £24-28; doubles £36-44; triples £48-54; quads £60-68. MC/V. ❷

YHA Bath, Bathwick Hill (☎465 674). From N. Parade Rd., turn left on Pulteney Rd., right on Bathwick Hill, and climb the hill (40min.), or take bus #18 or 418 (every 20min., 80p). Secluded Italianate mansion is far away but beautiful. Frequented mostly by families and school groups. Kitchen. Reception 7am-11pm. Dorms £12.50, under 18 £9; doubles £32, ensuite £36. MC/V. ❷

St. Christopher's Inn, 16 Green St. (☎481 444; www.st-christophers.co.uk). Downstairs bar offers an ideal hangout area for young crowd. Simple and clean bunks, but not a lot of space to do much else but sleep. Free luggage storage. Internet access £1 per 20min. Dorms £14-22; 1 double £40-48. Online booking discounts. MC/V. ❷

Toad Hall Guest House, 6 Lime Grove (☎423 254). Make a left off Pulteney Rd. after passing under the overpass. 3 spacious rooms and hearty breakfasts. Singles £25; doubles £48. Cash only. ❸

FOOD

Although the restaurants in Bath tend to be expensive, reasonably priced eateries can be found throughout the city. For fruits and vegetables, visit the **Bath Guildhall Market.** (☎477 945. Open M-Sa 9am-5:30pm.) Next door to Green Park Station, a Sainsbury's **supermarket** will satisfy. (☎444 737. Open M-F 8am-10pm, Sa 7am-10pm, Su 10am-4pm.)

Cafe Retro, 18 York St. (☎339 347). Mismatched chairs and wooden floors give this cafe-bar a simultaneously hip and old-world feel. 2 floors and plenty of space to enjoy your sandwich (£4) or entree (£6). Open M-W and Su 9am-5pm, Th-Sa 9am-11pm. Breakfast served all day. MC/V. ❶

Riverside Cafe, below Pulteney Bridge (☎480 532). Serves up light dishes and coffee in a sheltered enclave overlooking the River Avon. If you can't get a table outside, take your food to the nearby park. Sandwiches and soups £3-8. Open daily in summer 9am-9:30pm; winter 9am-4:30pm. MC/V. ❶

Mai Thai, 6 Pierrepont St. (☎445 557). Huge portions of Thai food at affordable prices. Ornate tables and authentic decorations make the atmosphere as rich as the food. Entrees £6.50-11. Open daily noon-2pm and 6-10:30pm. 10% discount on takeaway orders of £10 or more. Reserve ahead on weekends. AmEx/MC/V. ❷

Yak Yeti Yak, 12 Argyle St. (☎442 299), 2nd entrance under the arch of Pulteney Bridge. Dine on traditional floor cushions at this colorful Nepalese restaurant. Spices ground in-house create unique and delicious dishes. Entrees from £7. Set menu £11.50. Open M-Th and Su noon-2pm and 6-10pm, F-Sa noon-2pm and 6-10:30pm. MC/V. ❸

Demuths Restaurant, 2 N. Parade Passage (☎446 059; www.demuths.co.uk), off Abbey Green. Exotic vegetarian and vegan dishes (£11-16) served in a small, purple-tinted dining room. Superb chocolate fudge cake £5.25. *Prix-fixe* lunch £8. Open M-F and Su 10am-5pm and 6-10pm, Sa 9:30am-5:30pm and 6-11pm. Reservations recommended in summer. MC/V. ❷

👁 SIGHTS

THE ROMAN BATHS. In 1880, sewer diggers uncovered an extravagant feat of Roman engineering. For 400 years, the Romans harnessed Bath's bubbling springs, which spew 264,000 gallons of 115°F (47°C) water every day. The city became a mecca for Britain's elite. The 🔎**museum** has displays on excavated Roman artifacts and building design. It's also the only way to get up close and personal with the ancient baths. Make sure to see the Roman curses (politely referred to as offerings to Minerva), wishing eternal damnation upon naughty neighbors. Audio tours are a must. *(Stall St. ☎477 785; www.romanbaths.co.uk. Open daily July-Aug. 9am-9pm; Sept.-Oct. and Mar.-June 9am-6pm; Jan.-Feb. and Nov.-Dec. 9:30am-5:30pm. Last admission 1hr. before close. £10-11, concessions £8.75. Joint ticket with Museum of Costume £13.50/11.50.)*

BATH ABBEY. Occupying the site where King Edgar was crowned the first king of England in AD 973, the 140 ft. Abbey stands in the city center. Bishop Oliver King commissioned the abbey to replace a Norman cathedral, and the crowned olive tree on the ceiling symbolizes the message he heard from God: "let an Olive establish the Crown and a King restore the Church." A stunning stained-glass window contains 56 scenes from the life of Christ. Also note the church's extraordinarily high number of memorial plaques (including one for William Bingham, a 19th-century US Senator). The underlying **Heritage Vaults** contain an exhibit on the abbey's uses through the ages. *(Next to the Baths. ☎422 462; www.bathabbey.org. Open Apr.-Oct. M-Sa 9am-6:30pm, Su 8am-6pm; Nov.-Mar. M-Sa 9am-4pm, Su between services. Requested donation £2.50. Heritage Vaults open M-Sa 10am-4pm. Last admission 3:30pm. £1 donation.)*

MUSEUM OF FASHION AND ASSEMBLY ROOMS. The museum hosts a dazzling parade of 400 years of catwalk fashions, from 17th-century silver tissue garments to Jennifer Lopez's racy Versace jungle-print ensemble. Thematic displays show how fashion has changed through the years in everything from pockets to gloves, and interactive displays let visitors try on a corset and hoop skirt. *(Bennett St. ☎477 785; www.museumofcostume.co.uk. Open daily Mar.-Oct. 11am-6pm; Nov.-Feb. 11am-5pm. Last admission 1hr. before close. £6.50, concessions £5.50.)* The museum is in the basement of the **Assembly Rooms,** which once held *fin de siècle* balls and concerts. Bombing during WWII ravaged the rooms, but a renovation has duplicated the originals. *(☎477 785. Open daily 11am-5pm. Free. Rooms are sometimes booked for private functions.)*

OTHER MUSEUMS AND GALLERIES. Next to Pulteney Bridge, the **Victoria Art Gallery,** Bridge St., holds a diverse collection of paintings from the mid-18th century to today. It houses Thomas Barker's "The Bride of Death"—Victorian melodrama at its sappiest. Rotating exhibits take place on the ground floor. *(☎477 233; www.victoriagal.org.uk. Open Tu-F 10am-5:30pm, Sa 10am-5pm, Su 2-5pm. Free.)* The **Jane Austen Centre** depicts Austen's time in Bath, where she visited her family and lived briefly. Ironically, she disliked living in Bath and wrote nothing while living here, but she frequently wrote about the city in her novels—most notably in *Persuasion* and *Northanger Abbey.* Tours of Bath sights mentioned in Austen's books and her family's homes are also available. *(40 Gay St. ☎443 000; www.janeausten.co.uk. Open daily in summer 10am-5:30pm, in winter 11am-4:30pm. Last entrance 1hr. before close. £6, students £4.50. Tours Oct.-Sept. Sa-Su 11am. £4.50, concessions £3.50.)* Architecture buffs will enjoy the **Building of Bath Museum,** which explains the extensive planning and building of Bath as well as the history of the city's famous Gregorian buildings. Check out the model of the city—it took 10,000 hours to perfect its 1:500 scale layout. *(Countess of Huntingdon's Chapel, the Paragon. ☎ 338 727; www.bath-preservation-trust.org.uk. Open Tu-Su 10:30am-5pm. £4, concessions £3.50.)* The **American Museum,** Claverton Manor, has enough colonial relics to make any Yank feel at home. *(☎ 460 503; www.americanmuseum.org. Open Mar.-Oct. Tu-Su 2-5:30pm. Last admission 5pm. Gardens and tea room open Tu-Su noon-5:30pm. £6.35, concessions £3.50. Grounds admission £4/2.50.)*

HISTORIC BUILDINGS. The city's oldest house in Bath is **Sally Lunn's,** 4 North Passage Parade. Built on the sight of an old monastery, you can check out the ancient "faggot" oven used to bake her world-famous buns and buy a giant bun to take home. *(Museum free, hot buns £1.54. Open daily from 10am.)* In the city's residential northwest corner are the **Georgian rowhouses,** built by famed architects John Wood the elder and John Wood the younger. **The Circus,** which has the same circumference as Stonehenge, has attracted illustrious inhabitants for two centuries; former residents include Thomas Gainsborough and William Pitt. Proceed up Brock St. to the **Royal Crescent,** a half-moon of 18th-century townhouses. The interior of **1 Royal Crescent** has been restored to the way it was in 1770, down to the last butter knife. *(☎ 428 126. Open from mid-Feb. to Oct. Tu-Su 10:30am-5pm; Nov. Tu-Su 10:30am-4pm. Last admission 30min. before close. £5, concessions £3.50.)* For stupendous views, climb the 154 steps of **Beckford's Tower,** Lansdown Rd., 2 mi. north of town. Take bus #2 or 702 to Ensleigh; otherwise, it's a 45min. walk. *(☎ 460 705. Open Easter-Oct. Sa-Su 10:30am-5pm. £3, concessions £2, families £7.)*

GARDENS AND PARKS. Consult a map or the TIC's *Borders, Beds, and Shrubberies* brochure to find the city's many stretches of cultivated green. Next to the Royal Crescent, **Royal Victoria Park** contains rare trees and an aviary. *(Always open. Free.)* **Henrietta Park,** laid in 1897 to celebrate Queen Victoria's Diamond Jubilee, was redesigned as a garden for the blind—only the most fragrant plants were chosen for its grounds. The **Parade Gardens,** at the base of N. Parade Bridge, won the Britain in Bloom competition so often that they were asked not to enter again. *(☎ 391 041. Open daily June-Aug. 10am-8pm; Apr. and Sept. 10am-7pm; Nov.-Mar. 10am-4pm. Apr.-Sept. £1; Oct.-Mar. Free.)*

🎭 🍺 PUBS AND CLUBS

Tourists and two universities keep this small town full of nightlife. Most pubs close around 11pm, and late-night clubs almost always charge a cover.

THE BIG SPLURGE

SO FRESH AND SO CLEAN

The waters that have drawn people to Bath since ancient times have once again opened their warm arms to the public. Ironically, for over 30 years, the spa town of Bath had no public baths to call their own. Thermae Bath Spa has corrected this egregious crime—channeling the natural, thermal spas into three glorious pools and a one-of-a-kind bathhouse worth every penny.

The £20-50 admission grants access to the peaceful pools and the four intoxicating aroma steam rooms, waterfall showers, and foot baths that occupy the Georgian buildings. The *pièce de résistance* is the open-air rooftop pool, where bathers relax in natural spring water and enjoy beautiful views of the city and surrounding hills. For a smaller splurge, try the smaller Cross Bath, a secluded, oval pool where waters cascade from a fountain.

Whatever you choose, bathing in the waters of Thermae Bath Spa is guaranteed to leave you feeling relaxed and rejuvenated, like the Roman royalty who took to the waters before you.

The Hetling Pump Room, Hot Bath St. ☎ 335 678; www.thermaebathspa.com. Open daily 9am-10pm. 2hr. £20, 4hr. £30, full day £50; 1½hr. in Cross Bath £12. No reservations required.

Pig and Fiddle, 2 Saracen St. (☎460 868), off Broad St. The 1st stop for many pub crawlers. The cozy interior and huge heated patio are always full of backpackers enjoying cider and local ales. Can't get enough of the pig? Join their facebook.com group for updates on live music. Open M-Sa 11am-11pm, Su noon-10:30pm.

The Lamb and Lion, 15 Lower Borough Walls (☎474 931). Cheap pints make this a popular pre-club pub with students and locals on the weekends. Beer garden out back is fabulous in the summer, as is the perfectly crafted fruit-filled Pimm's. Open M-Sa 11am-11pm, Su noon-10:30pm. MC/V.

Moles, 14 George St. (☎404 445; www.moles.co.uk). Pounds out soul, funk, and house with frequent live acts in an underground setting. M and Th up-and-coming live bands. Tu and F-Sa dance club night. Cover £3-5. Open M-Th 9pm-2am, F-Sa 9pm-4am.

The Bell, 103 Walcot St. (☎460 426), challenges its clientele to talk over (or sing along with) the live folk, jazz, blues, funk, salsa, and reggae playing most nights. Pizza served in the garden on weekend evenings. Live music M and W evenings, Su lunch. Free Wi-Fi. Open M-Sa 11:30am-midnight, Su noon-10:30pm.

Delfter Krug, Saw Close (☎443 352; www.delfterkrug.com). Draws a large weekend crowd with its outdoor seating and lively 2-story club. Comfy couches offer a break from the crowded dance floor. Jams hip hop and pop with drink specials almost every night. Cover £2-5. Open M-Sa noon-2am, Su noon-10:30pm.

PoNaNa, North Parade & Pierrepont St. (☎401 115; www.barclub.com/ponana). Descend the staircase into a subterranean lair to find tons of beats and sweaty dancers. W drum and bass. F "Squeeze the Cheese." Cover £3-5. Open M and W 9:30pm-2am, Tu and Th 10pm-2am, F-Sa 10:30pm-2:30am.

ENTERTAINMENT AND FESTIVALS

In summer, buskers (street musicians) fill the streets with music, and a brass band often graces the Parade Gardens. The magnificent **Theatre Royal,** Saw Close, at the south end of Barton St., showcases opera and theater. (☎448 844. Box office open M-Sa 10am-8pm, Su noon-8pm. Tickets £5-27.) The **Little Theatre Cinema,** St. Michael's Place, Bath St., is Bath's local arthouse cinema. (☎330 817. Box office open daily 1-8pm. Tickets £6, concessions £4-5.) Bath hosts several festivals; for information or reservations, call the Bath Festivals Box Office, 2 Church St., Abbey Green. (☎463 362; www.bathfestivals.org.uk. Open M-Sa 9:30am-5:30pm.) The **Bath International Music Festival** (typically May-June, check www.bathmusicfest.org.uk for updates) features world-class symphony orchestras, choruses, and jazz bands. The overlapping **Fringe Festival** (☎480 079; www.bathfringearts.co.uk) celebrates the arts with over 200 live performances (May-June annually). The **Jane Austen Festival,** at the end of September, features Austen-themed walks, meals, and movies (contact the Jane Austen Centre). The **Literature Festival** is held in March, the **Balloon Fiesta** in mid-May, and the **Film Festival** in late October. Pick up the weekly *Venue* (£1.30), available at bookstores.

BRISTOL
☎0117

Well-cultured and hip, Bristol is Britain's latest urban renewal success story. Ten years ago, you'd have been hard-pressed to find someone who wanted to visit Bristol—let alone live there. But today, the southwest's largest city (pop. 410,000) is one of England's fastest growing communities, with expansive docks and a famed annual hot-air balloon festival. A growing population of students and young professionals has reinvigorated the city and made its nightlife one of Britain's best-kept secrets.

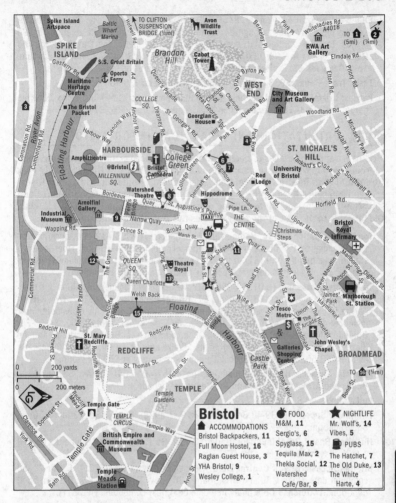

Bristol

🏠 ACCOMMODATIONS
Bristol Backpackers, 11
Full Moon Hostel, 16
Raglan Guest House, 3
YHA Bristol, 9
Wesley College, 1

🍴 FOOD
M&M, 11
Sergio's, 6
Spyglass, 15
Tequila Max, 2
Thekla Social, 12
Watershed
Cafe/Bar, 8

⭐ NIGHTLIFE
Mr. Wolf's, 14
Vibes, 5

🍺 PUBS
The Hatchet, 7
The Old Duke, 13
The White
Harte, 4

⎘ TRANSPORTATION

Trains: Temple Meads Station. Ticket office open M-Sa 5:30am-9:30pm, Su 6:45am-9:30pm. Trains (☎08457 484 950) to: **Bath** (15min., 4 per hr., £5.20); **Cardiff** (50min., 2 per hr., £11); **London Paddington** (1¾hr., 2 per hr., £48); **Manchester** (3½hr., 2 per hr., £48). Another station, **Bristol Parkway,** is far, far away—make sure to get off at Temple Meads.

Buses: Marlborough Street Bus Station. Ticket office open M-F 7:30am-6pm, Sa 10am-5:30pm. National Express (☎08705 808 080) buses to **London** (2½hr., every hr., £17) and **Manchester** (5¾hr., 5-7 per day, £31.50) via **Birmingham** (2½hr., £17). National Express info shop open M-Sa 7:20am-6pm, Su 9am-6pm.

Public Transportation: First (☎08456 020 156) **buses** run in the city. Buses #8 and 9 are the primary routes through city center, making a circular route through Temple Meads, Broadmead, Redland, and Clifton Downs. Get info at the **Travel Bristol Info Centre,** Colston Ave. (☎08706 082 608). Open M-F 8:30am-5:30pm, Sa 8:30am-1pm. **Day pass** £3. **Explorer** ticket, for 1-day unlimited travel in the southwest, £7.

Taxis: Trans Cabs (☎953 8638) or 24hr. **Streamline** (☎926 4001).

Ferries: Bristol Ferry Boat Co. brings commuters and tourists to various stops along the harbor. (☎927 3416; www.bristolferryboat.co.uk). £1, round-trip £1.70.

⚑ 🛈 ORIENTATION AND PRACTICAL INFORMATION

Bristol is a sprawling mass of neighborhoods. **Broadmead** is the shopping and commercial center, while restaurants and clubs fill the heart of the city along **Park Street** and **Park Row** in the **West End.** The student population in the northwest makes **Whiteladies Road** (follow Queen's Rd. north) another option for cafes and hip shopping. Upriver, **Clifton Village** offers elegant Georgian architecture, while **Old City,** just to the east of the quay, houses the area's oldest pubs and shops.

Tourist Information Centre: Harbourside (information ☎09067 112 191, accommodations booking 0845 408 0474; www.visitbristol.co.uk), inside @Bristol. From the train station, take bus #8 or 9 (£1) to the city center. Follow signs to Millennium Sq. Books beds for £3 plus a 10% deposit. Open M-F 10am-5pm, Sa-Su 10am-6pm.

Tours: CitySightseeing (☎01934 830 050; www.city-sightseeing.com). Runs bus tours every hr. 10am-4:30pm. £8, students £7. **Bristol Packet** (☎926 8157; www.bristol-packet.co.uk). Begins at Wapping Wharf near the SS *Great Britain.* Also runs boat tours, including daytrips to Avon Gorge and Bath. Aug. daily; Apr.-Sept. Sa-Su. £4.25-20. **Guided Walks of Bristol** (☎968 4638). Offers tours such as "Bristol Merchants and the Slave Trade" and "Historic Wine Merchants." Walks start at the TIC. Tours Mar.-Sept. Sa at 11am £3.50, children free. Special group tours starting at £50 per group.

Financial Services: HSBC, 11 Broadmead (☎08457 404 404). Open M-Sa 9am-5pm. **Banks** and **ATMs** on Corn St. and The Centre Promenade.

Police: Bridewell St. (☎927 7777).

Pharmacy: Superdrug, 39-43 Broadmead (☎927 9928). Open M-Sa 8:30am-5:30pm, Su 11am-5pm.

Hospital: Bristol Royal Infirmary, Upper Maudlin St. (☎923 0000). Frenchay (☎970 1212), in North Bristol near the M32.

Internet Access: Bristol Central Library, College Green (☎903 7200). £3 for ID and computer time. Open M-Tu and Th 9:30am-7:30pm, W 10am-5pm, F-Sa 9:30am-5pm, Su 1-5pm. **Watershed Cafe** offers free time on 4 busy computers. Free Wi-Fi.

Post Office: Mall Galleries, Union St. (☎08457 223 344), on the top floor of the shopping center. Open M-Sa 9am-5:30pm. Smaller location at the corner of Baldwin and Marsh St. (☎722 3344). Open M-F 9am-5pm. **Post Code:** BS1 3XX.

⌂ ACCOMMODATIONS

A few cheap, comfortable **B&Bs** lie south of the harbor on **Coronation Road.** Walk west along Cumberland Rd. for 15min., cross the red footbridge, turn right on Coronation Rd., and walk a few blocks past Deans Ln.

Bristol Backpackers, 17 St. Stephen's St. (☎925 7900; www.bristolbackpackers.co.uk). This former newspaper building in the heart of Bristol is more like a youth apartment building than a hostel. Great facilities and location mean that many residents stay for months. Well-stocked bar, huge kitchen, and common spaces. Laundry

£2. Internet access £1 per hr., Wi-Fi free. Reception 9am-11:30pm. Photo ID required. Dorms £14. Book at least a week in advance for the summer months. MC/V. ❷

YHA Bristol, Hayman House, 14 Narrow Quay (☎08707 705 726). From the city center, cross Pero's Bridge. Spacious rooms and cafe-bar in a central location overlooking the water. Breakfast included. Free luggage storage. Laundry £4.50. Internet £5 per hr. Reception 24hr. Dorms £18.50, under 18 £14.50. Book ahead. AmEx/MC/V. ❷

Full Moon Hostel, 1 North St. (☎07989 974 736). Brand new, eco-friendly hostel with organic sheets and tons of room in the courtyard. 2 bars, plasma TVs, and massive parties on full moon nights. Internet available. Dorms £15. Singles £36. MC/V. ❷

Raglan Guest House, 132 Coronation Rd. (☎966 2129). Budget lodgings with comfy beds a short walk from town. Full English breakfast included. Singles £25; doubles £40; triples £60. Cash only. ❸

Wesley College, 5 mi. outside the city center (☎958 1127). Take bus #1 north to the Henbury Rd. stop and walk up Henbury Rd. The college is signposted at the top of the hill. Offers the area's cheapest single rooms and a self-catering kitchen. Laundry £2 wash, £1.50 dry. Reception M-F 9am-5pm. Singles £20, ensuite £27. MC/V. ❷

◪ FOOD

Restaurants line **Park Street,** with trendier options on **Whiteladies Road.** On Wednesdays, a **farmers' market** takes over Corn St. (open 9:30am- 2:30pm). Get **groceries** at Tesco Metro, on Broadmead. (☎948 7400. Open M-F 7am-10pm, Sa 7am-8pm, Su 11am-5pm.)

Watershed Cafe/Bar, 1 Canons Rd. (☎927 5101). You could spend all day chatting with friends in the seating area overlooking the quay. Filling sandwiches and entrees £5-8. Free Internet and Wi-Fi. Open M 11am-11pm, Tu-F 9:30am-11pm, Sa 10am-11pm, Su 10am-10:30pm. Food served M-Sa noon-9pm, Su noon-10pm. AmEx/MC/V. ❷

Thekla Social, The Grove, East Mud Dock (☎293 301), on a boat. Long tables and large booths make this the perfect boat for a bite with friends. Sandwiches (£5), steaks and burgers (£7), and a scrumptious Su roast served inside the boat or on the outdoor deck overlooking the quay. Stick around at night for live music. Open daily noon-late. Food served until 9pm. MC/V. ❷

M&M, 1 Marsh St. (☎291 906). You can't beat £2 burgers or £3 kebabs, especially when they're served until 3am. Whatever your shallow pockets or late-night munchies demand, M&M will satisfy. If you're nice to the owner, he'll pull out the special pita bread his mom bakes. Open daily 11am-late. ❶

Spyglass, Welsh Back (☎927 2800), in the Old City. If you're looking for unique food on a classy boat (and who isn't?), this is the place. Heaping portions of Mediterranean food with a large vegetarian selection served on the quay. Entrees start at £7. Open daily 11am-11pm. MC/V. ❸

Sergio's, 1-3 Frogmore St. (☎929 1413; www.sergios.co.uk), right before the underpass. This Italian eatery serves up delicious dishes in a cozy atmosphere. Entrees £7-14. Open M-F noon-2:30pm and 5:30pm-late, Sa 5:30pm-late. AmEx/MC/V. ❷

Tequila Max, 109 Whiteladies Rd. (☎466 144). Mexican restaurant by day, tequila bar by night. Enchiladas £10. Select entrees 2-for-1 for students on W. Open M-Th and Su noon-2:30pm and 5-11:30pm, F-Sa noon-12:30am. AmEx/MC/V. ❸

◉ SIGHTS

■▨ **@BRISTOL.** Get ready for sensory overload at this interactive science center. **Explore** features hands-on exhibits in physics and biology with simulations of spaceflight, what it's like to be an embryo in the womb (cozy), and a catchy rap

THE LOCAL STORY

BANKSY'S BRISTOL

n most cities, graffiti is an eye-
sore. In Bristol, pseudo-anony-
mous street artist Banksy is tak-
ng graffiti from vandalism to
modern art. His distinctive stencil-
ng techniques have become
conic, and his satirical masterpieces are now cropping up on
streets and buildings worldwide.
n his hometown of Bristol, a high
concentration of Banksy creations
makes it easy to catch a glimpse
of this guerrilla Van Gogh.

On the side of the Sexual
Health Clinic on Frogmore St.,
down the steps from Park St., a
naked man dangles from a sten-
ciled window while a couple peers
out from inside. Bristolians have
voted to preserve this piece as
public art.

From Cheltenham Rd., look for
"The Mild, Mild West," which features a white bear tossing a Molo-
tov cocktail at a group of police
with the Banksy tag below. This
work is in the running for Britain's
alternative landmark of the year.

A ghost sailor rows a boat
tagged onto the side of the Thekla
Social boat, moored in the harbor. For the best view, cross the
Prince St. bridge from the city
center and turn left along the
quayside.

A 25 ft. Banksy mural adorns
the side of a house at 21 Milvart
St. The owners have decided to
sell the mural with their five-bed-
room house included "for free" in
the £160,000 price tag.

about the brain. You can also play memory games
and learn how many pints are too many—and how
many are just right. *(Anchor Rd., Harbourside. ☎08453
451 235; www.at-bristol.org.uk. Open M-F 10am-5pm, Sa-Su
10am-6pm. £7-9, concessions £5.50-6.50.)*

■ **BRITISH EMPIRE AND COMMONWEALTH
MUSEUM.** Britain may be small, but no other
nation since Rome has had as expansive an empire.
Nation- and time-specific exhibits bring museum-
goers back to when "the sun never set on the British
empire," offering even-handed perspectives on the
development of imperialism and the effects of colonialism on native populations. "Breaking the Chains,"
a special exhibit celebrating the 200th anniversary of
the abolition of the British slave trade, is an audio/
visual display documenting the history of slavery.
*(Station Approach, Temple Meads, in a former rail station.
☎925 4980; www.empiremuseum.co.uk. Open daily 10am-
5pm. £8, concessions £7.)*

CLIFTON SUSPENSION BRIDGE. The unofficial
symbol of Bristol, this sight is a must-see. Isambard
Kingdom Brunel, famed engineer of London's Paddington Station, built this masterpiece spanning the
Avon Gorge, which looks like a scientific impossibil-
ity. The visitors center explains just how Brunel did
it. Check it out at night, when the lights over the
water add a little something extra. *(Take bus #8 or 9.
☎974 4664; www.clifton-suspension-bridge.org.uk. Bridge
always open, visitors center open 10am-5pm. Free guided
tours daily June-Sept. 3pm. Free.)*

SS GREAT BRITAIN. The *Great Britain* was the
largest ship in the world when it was launched in
1843. The "world's first great ocean liner" traveled a
million miles and now depicts realities of 19th-cen-
tury boating, from the elegant lodging of first-class
passengers to the grit of the ship's engine room.
Beware of creepy life-like wax figures that hide on
the boat. *(☎926 0680; www.ss-great-britain.com. Open daily
Apr.-Oct. 10am-6pm; Nov.-Mar. 10am-4:30pm. Audio tour
included. £9, students £5.)*

OTHER MUSEUMS. The **City Museum and Art Gallery,**
Queen's Rd., has an extensive and eclectic collection
of everything from minerals to mummies, including a
handsome collection of British ceramics. The Bristol
dinosaur and gypsy car are highlights of the collection. *(☎922 3571; www.bristol-city.gov.uk/museums. Open
daily 10am-5pm. Free.)* From April to October, you can
also visit the **Georgian House,** 7 Great George St., built
in 1791, and the **Red Lodge,** Park Row, an Elizabethan
home. *(Georgian House ☎921 1326, Red Lodge 921 1360.
Both open M-W and Sa-Su 10am-5pm. Free.)* The **Arnolfini
Gallery,** 16 Narrow Quay, houses contemporary

works and hosts events in a sleek setting. *(☎917 2300; www.arnolfini.org.uk. Open M-W and F-Su 10am-8pm, Th 10am-6pm. Free.)*

CHURCHES. John Wesley's Chapel, 36 The Horsefair, Broadmead, which sits incongruously in the middle of Bristol's shopping district, is the world's oldest Methodist building. Note the chair fashioned from an inverted elm trunk. *(☎926 4740. Open M-Sa 10am-4pm. Free.)* Founded in 1140, the **Bristol Cathedral** is known as a "hall church" because the nave, quire, and aisles are of equal height. The beautiful **Norman Chapter House** housed the monks' many books. *(☎926 4879. Open daily 8am-6pm. Evensong M-F 5:15pm, Sa 3:30pm. Free guided tour Sa 11am.)* The father of Sir William Penn (of Pennsylvania fame) is buried in **St. Mary Redcliffe,** a classic Gothic church. *(☎953 7260; www.stmaryredcliffe.co.uk. Open May-Oct. M-Sa 8:30am-5pm, Su 8am-7:30pm; Nov.-Apr. M-Sa 9am-4pm, Su 8am-7:30pm. Free.)*

BRANDON HILL. Just west of Park St. lies one of the most peaceful and secluded sights in Bristol. Pathways snake through flower beds to **Cabot Tower,** a monument commemorating the 400th anniversary of explorer John Cabot's arrival in North America. Ascend the 108 steps for a stunning panoramic view. *(☎922 3719. Open daily until dusk. Free.)*

⬛⬛ PUBS AND NIGHTLIFE

On weekend nights, the entire city turns out in clubwear. Bars and clubs cluster around Park St. and Park Row in the West End, and Baldwin and St. Nicholas St. in the Old City. A handful of gay clubs line Frogmore St. If you're looking for a late-night dance club, popular chains like Revolution and Walk-A-Bout run up and down Corn and Baldwin St., near St. Nicholas Markets.

The White Harte, 54-58 Park Row (☎456 060). Collegiate crowd packs in for cheap pints. A good place to start a pub crawl up Park St. Beer and curry £3 until 3pm. Mondays £1 per pint. Open M-Th and Su noon-midnight, F-Sa noon-2am.

The Old Duke, King St. (☎277 137). The energy is always high in Dukes, with live jazz music nightly and crowds spilling outside. It tends to get packed (and loud) inside, so enjoy your cider or ale on the outdoor patio connected with 4 other bars—you can still hear the music, try out other bars, and keep your table. Open daily noon-midnight.

Mr. Wolf's, 33 St. Stephen's St. (☎927 3221). A late-night cafe and excellent live music forum make Mr. Wolf's a great place to start or end your night. DJs on nights without live music. Open M-Tu 6pm-2am, W-Sa 6pm-4am, Su 6pm-12:30am.

The Hatchet, 27 Frogmore St. (☎929 4118). The fact that this may be the oldest pub in Bristol is overshadowed by the rumor that the door was originally made of human flesh. Either way, you'll have a great story to tell after you have a pint in this classic pub. F-Sa DJ. Open M-Sa 11am-11pm, Su 11am-10pm.

Vibes, 3 Frog Ln., (☎934 9076) off Frogmore St. A neon-lit gay venue. Different rooms play different music, from pop to hard house. Cover £1.50-4. Open M-Th 11:30pm-2am, last entry 1:30am; F-Sa 10pm-3:30am, last entry 2:30am.

🎵🎭 ENTERTAINMENT AND FESTIVALS

Britain's oldest theater, the **Theatre Royal,** King St., was rebuked for debauchery until George III approved the actors' antics. (☎987 7877. Box office open M-Sa 10am-6pm. Tickets £7-20, £2 student discount.) The **Hippodrome,** St. Augustine's Parade, presents the latest touring productions. (Box office open M-Sa 10am-6pm, 8pm on evenings with performances. Tickets £5-40.) The popular **Watershed,** 1 Canon's Rd. (☎927 5100; www.watershed.co.uk), an arthouse cinema on the quay, holds discussions on independent and foreign films and has a lively cafe. (Box office open daily 10am until 15min. after the start of the day's final film.) **Bristol**

Harbour Festival (☎903 1484) explodes with fireworks, raft races, street performances, live music, boats, and a French market at the end of July. During the **Bristol International Balloon Fiesta** (☎966 8716) in early August, hot-air balloons fill the
sky while acrobats and motorcycle teams perform at ground level. **Bailey Balloons**
takes visitors high above the gorge to sightsee. (☎01275 375 300; www.baileybal-
loons.co.uk. £145 per hr., includes champagne). **GWR FM Big Balloon,** Castle Park,
Castle St., offers a more affordable balloon-riding opportunity. (www.gwrfmbig-
balloon.co.uk. £10, students £8. Open daily 10am to dusk, weather permitting.)

WELLS   ☎01749

Named for the natural springs at its center, Wells's (pop. 10,000) main feature is
undoubtedly its magnificent cathedral. Charming and self-consciously classy, this
little town is lined with petite Tudor buildings and golden sandstone shops.

▐ TRANSPORTATION. Wells has no train station. **Buses** stop at the **Princes Road
Bus Park.** (☎673 084. Ticket office open M-F 9am-4:45pm, Sa 9am-12:45pm.)
National Express (☎08705 808 080) buses go to London (3½hr., 1 per day, £19).
First runs to: Bath (#173; 1¼hr.; M-Sa every hr., Su 7 per day; £4.50); Bridgewater
(#375; 1½hr., every hr., £4) via Glastonbury; Bristol (#375 or 376; 1½hr., every
30min., £4.50); Taunton (#29; 1hr., every 3hr.) **Day Explorer Passes** (£7, concessions
£5), grant unlimited transportation on all First buses. For a taxi, call Wookey Taxis
(☎678 039; 24hr.). Rent **bicycles** at Bike City, 31 Broad St. (☎671 711. £15 per day.
Open M-Th 9am-5:30pm, F-Su 9am-5pm.)

▐ PRACTICAL INFORMATION AND ORIENTATION. Navigation in Wells is
easy. The town's spring runs in a paved channel through the main streets. Follow
the water upstream to the cathedral and the TIC, and downstream to the bus station. The **Tourist Information Centre,** Market Pl., at the end of High St., books rooms
for £3 plus a 10% deposit and has bus timetables. Exit left from the bus station and
turn left onto Priory Rd., which becomes Broad St. and merges with High St. (☎672
552. Open Apr.-Oct. M-Sa 10am-5pm, Su 10am-4pm; Nov.-Mar. M-Sa 10am-4pm.)
Other services include: Barclays **bank,** 9 Market Pl. (☎313 907; open M-F 9:30am-
4:30pm) and Thomas Cook, 8 High St. (☎313 000; open M-W and F-Sa 9am-5:30pm,
Th 10am-5:30pm); **work opportunities** at JobCentre, 46 Chamberlain St. (☎313 200;
open M-Tu and Th-F 9am-5pm, W 10am-5pm); **police,** 18 Glastonbury Rd. (☎01275
818 181); a Boots **pharmacy,** 19-21 High St. (☎01749 673 138; open M-Sa 9am-
5:30pm); free **Internet** access with ID at the **library** (open M-Th 9:30am-5:30pm, F
9:30am-7pm, Sa 9:30am-4pm); and the **post office,** Market Pl. (☎08457 223 344; open
M-F 9am-5:30pm, Sa 9am-12:30pm), with a **bureau de change. Post Code:** BA5 2RA.

▐ ACCOMMODATIONS. Most **B&Bs** only offer doubles, so making Wells a daytrip from Bristol or Bath may be a better option for solo travelers. At **17 Priory Road
❸,** across from the bus station, Mrs. Winter offers warm, spacious rooms with
books lining the walls. (☎677 300; www.smoothhound.co.uk/hotels/brian.html.
Singles £25; doubles £50; family rooms £25 per person. Cash only.) **Canon Grange
❹,** Cathedral Green, Sadler St., with the cathedral in its backyard, features rustic
decor and a glass of sherry for each guest. Follow the directions to the TIC, but
from High St., turn left on Sadler. (☎671 800; www.canongrange.co.uk. Doubles
£50, ensuite £60-65. MC/V.)

▐ FOOD. Wells is not exactly a wellspring of culinary talent. While food options
tend more toward takeaway and ice cream shops, a handful of quality restaurants
can be found along Sadler St. near Cathedral Green. Assemble a picnic at the **mar-**

ket on High St., in front of the Bishop's Palace (open W and Sa), or purchase **groceries** at Tesco, across from the bus station on Tucker St. (☎08456 779 710. Open M 8am-10pm, Tu-Sa 6am-10pm, Su 10am-4pm.) At **Good Earth ❶,** 4 Priory Rd., get vegetarian soups (£2.65-3.25), quiches (£2.70), and homemade pizza (£2.50 per slice) for takeaway or enjoy them on the backyard patio. (☎678 600. Open M-Sa 9am-5:30pm. MC/V with £10 min.) **Goodfellows ❸,** 5 Sadler St., is a delicious patisserie and fish delicatessen. The lunch special (£10) includes any dish on the menu, a glass of wine, and a piece of cake. (☎673 8666. Patisserie open daily 8:30am-5pm; restaurant open Tu-Sa noon-2pm, dinner Th-Sa 6:30pm onward. MC/V.) A city jail opened in the 16th century, the **City Arms ❸,** 69 High St., serves delicious meals, including a number of vegetarian options (entrees £7-16). At night, this is the town's most popular pub. (☎673 916. Restaurant open M-Sa 9am-10pm, Su 9am-9pm. Bar open M-Sa 10am-11pm, Su noon-10:30pm. AmEx/MC/V with a £10 min.)

SIGHTS

WELLS CATHEDRAL. The 12th-century church at the center of town is also the center of a preserved cathedral complex, with a bishop's palace, vicar's close, and cavernous octagonal chapter house. The facade is one of England's best collections of medieval statues (293 figures in all). The grandeur and precision of medieval architecture is displayed in the 14th-century **scissor arches,** which prevent the tower from sinking. The church's **astronomical clock** (c. 1390) is the second-oldest working clock in the world. Watch a pair of jousting mechanical knights duke it out every 15min. and pity the knight who has lost for 600 years. The **Wells Cathedral School Choir,** an institution as old as the building itself, sings services from September to April. *(☎674 483. Open daily Mar.-Sept. 7am-7pm; Oct.-Feb. 7am-6pm. Free tours 10, 11am, 1, 2, and 3pm. Evensong M-Sa 5:15pm, Su 3pm. Suggested donation £5, students £2.)* Beside the Cathedral, **Vicar's Close,** constructed to house the choir members, is Europe's oldest continuously inhabited street. Most of its houses date to 1363.

BISHOP'S PALACE. This palace has been the residence of the Bishop of Bath and Wells for 800 years. The medieval buildings are situated on perfectly manicured gardens and lawns, including one reserved for summer croquet matches. Wood sculptures sit on the grounds, including "Adam and Eve," which took 200 hours to create. **St. Andrew's Well** offers beautiful views of the Cathedral and benches for picnicking. The mute swans in the moat pull a bell-rope when they want to be fed—the first swans to learn lived here 150 years ago, and their descendants have continued to teach their young. Visitors can feed them brown bread—white makes them sick. *(Near the cathedral. ☎678 691; www.bishopspalacewells.co.uk. Open Apr.-Oct. M-F 10:30am-6pm, Su noon-6pm; often open Sa, call ahead. Last admission 5pm. £5, students £2.)*

WELLS AND MENDIP MUSEUM. This tiny museum contains archaeological finds of the Mendip area and remnants of the cathedral's decor, including several statues found during renovations. Also on display are the milking pot, crystal ball, and bones of the "Witch of Wookey Hole," a woman who, after mysteriously losing her beauty, retreated to a cave and occasionally spooked the locals. *(8 Cathedral Green. ☎673 477. Open daily Easter-Oct. 10am-5:30pm; Nov.-Easter 11am-4pm. £3, students £1.)*

DAYTRIPS FROM WELLS

CHEDDAR

From Wells, take bus #126 or 826 (25min.; M-Sa every hr. at 40min. past the hr., Su 7 per day; round-trip £4.35). Purchase tickets at the base of the hill near the bus stop or at Gough's Cave. ☎01934 742 343; www.cheddarcaves.co.uk. Open daily from May to mid-Sept. 10am-5pm; from mid-Sept. to Apr. 10:30am-4:30pm. Caves, Jacob's Ladder, and open-top bus

£14, students £9 (unpublished rate, be sure to ask). "Gorge Outdoors" ticket £4. Discount tickets available from the Wells TIC. Cheddar's TIC is at the base of the hill. ☎01934 744 071. Open Mar.-Oct. daily 10am-5pm; Dec.-Easter M-Sa 10am-5pm, Su 11am-4pm.

A short journey from Wells, the town of Cheddar is laden with dairy products, cheesy attractions, and Neolithic goats. **Cheddar Gorge and Caves** is both a miracle of nature as well as a kitsch attraction. Carved by the River Yeo (YO), the gorge is perforated by the **Cheddar Showcaves,** limestone hollows extending deep into the earth. Colored lights and an audio tour narrated by the "Cheddar Man" himself guide you through **Gough's Cave.** Gough's Cave also houses a replica of **Cheddar Man,** a 9000-year-old skeleton (the original is now in the British Museum in London). More info on Cheddar Man can be found at the **Museum of Prehistory,** at the base of the Gorge across from the TIC. Parental supervision is required for this over-the-top museum that explains everything from theories of evolution and our cannibalistic human ancestors to prehistoric sex and religion. If 🔲**caveman kamasutra** isn't your thing, **Cox's Cave** provides a more subdued experience. Admission to the caves includes a ride on an **open-top bus** that travels through the gorge and to the cave entrances in summer, and access to **Jacob's Ladder,** a 274-step climb to a lookout. At the top, a 3 mi. **clifftop gorge walk** has views that outstrip the sights below. No trip to a town called Cheddar would be complete without a taste of the good stuff. The **Cheddar Gorge Cheese Company,** at the hill's base, features cheese-making and tasting. (☎742 810. Open daily 10am-5:30pm. Free.)

WOOKEY HOLE. Two miles west of Cheddar, the **Wookey Hole Caves** are as beautiful as their neighbor's. A 35min. tour takes visitors into the caves, which legend holds once contained the Holy Grail as well as druid witches and their dogs. The caves have also inspired Coleridge, Wordsworth, and Pope, who stole stalactites that are now on display in his London home. The faint smell of cheese is, in fact, local cheddar aging in the caves. After the caves, visitors must slog through a bevy of smaller attractions—including a **dinosaur park,** a working **paper mill,** a **penny arcade,** and a **hall of mirrors**—to get back to the car park. *(From Wells, take bus #670 (15min., M-Sa 8 per day, round-trip £2). Caves ☎01749 672 243; www.wookey.co.uk. Caves and paper mill open daily Apr.-Oct. 10am-5pm; Nov.-Mar. 10am-4pm. £12.50, children £9.50.)*

GLASTONBURY   ☎01458

The reputed birthplace of Christianity in England and an Arthurian hotspot, Glastonbury is a quirky intersection of mysticism and pop culture. According to legend, King Arthur, Jesus, Joseph of Arimathea, and St. Augustine all came here. The town's appeal continues today as huge crowds return every year for England's biggest music festival. Glastonbury's shops do their part to perpetuate a mystical vibe, peddling trinkets and "healing" crystals.

⌐ TRANSPORTATION. Glastonbury has no train station; **buses** stop at the town hall in the town center. Consult the Public Transport Timetable for the Mendip Area, free at TICs, for schedules. First Badgerline (☎08706 082 608, fare info 08456 064 446) buses run to Bristol (#375 or 376; 1hr., £5.10) via Wells. Travel to Yeovil (#376; 1hr.; M-Sa every hr., Su every 2hr.) to connect to destinations in the south, including Lyme Regis and Dorchester. Travel a full day on all buses with the **Explorer Pass** (£6, concessions £5, families £15).

◼🄵 ORIENTATION AND PRACTICAL INFORMATION. Glastonbury is 6 mi. southwest of Wells on the A39 and 22 mi. northeast of Taunton on the A361. The town is bounded by **High Street** in the north, **Bere Lane** in the south, **Magdalene Street** in the west, and **Wells Road/Chilkwell Street** in the east. Most shops line High St. and Magdelene St. The **Tourist Information Centre,** The Tribunal, 9 High St., books rooms for £3 plus a 10% deposit and has a book of accommodation listings (£1); after hours, find the B&B list behind the building in St. John's car park. (☎832 954; www.glastonburytic.co.uk. Open Apr.-Sept. M-Th and Su 10am-5pm, F-Sa 10am-5:30pm; Oct.-Mar. M-Th and Su 10am-4pm, F-Sa 10am-4:30pm.)

Other services include: Barclays **bank,** 21-23 High St. (☎241 381; open M-F 9:30am-4:30pm) and Thomas Cook, 42 High St. (☎831 809; open M-Sa 9am-5:30pm); **police,** 1 West End (☎01823 337 911); Moss **pharmacy,** 39 High St. (☎831 211; open M-F 9am-6pm, Sa 9am-5:30pm); **Internet** access at the **library,** 1 Orchard Ct., The Archer's Way, left off of High St. when heading up the hill (☎832 148; free for 1hr.; photo ID required; open M and Th-F 10am-5pm, Tu 10am-7pm, Sa 10am-4pm); and the **post office,** 35 High St. (☎831 536. Open M-F 9am-5:30pm, Sa 9am-1pm.) **Post Code:** BA6 9HG.

ꕯ ACCOMMODATIONS. Glastonbury offers expensive, luxurious **B&Bs**—don't be surprised if your accommodation also offers "healing treatments" and meditation. Buses stop by **Glastonbury Backpackers ❷,** 4 Market Pl., at the corner of Magdalene and High St. The bright blue building houses a popular pub and a small cafe with terrific coffee. (☎833 353; www.glastonburybackpackers.com. Kitchen. Internet access until 6pm. Check-in 4pm, check-out 11:30am. Reception open until 11pm. Dorms £14; doubles £34. MC/V.) Off Chickwell on the way to the Tor, **Shekinashram ❷,** Dod Ln., is a serene B&B. A wide range of accommodations, from a secluded yurt to a king-sized suite all include an organic breakfast and morning meditation. (☎832 300; www.shekinashram.org. Kitchen available. Single in cabin £19, single in yurt £27, single in house £29, double £39. MC/V.) The nearest YHA hostel is the **YHA Street ❶,** Higher Brooks Rd., off the B3151 in the town of Street. On public transportation, take bus #376, 375, or 29 to Street, turn onto Gooselade Rd., then follow the footpath on the right side; the hostel will be signposted at the end of the path. A small facility (28 beds) overlooking the Tor. (☎442 961. Kitchen. Reception 8:30-10am and 5-10pm. Lockout 10am-5pm. Open July-Aug. daily; May-June Tu-Su; Sept.-Apr. call 48hr. in advance.)

🏠🍴 FOOD AND PUBS. A **farmers' market** takes place behind the TIC on the last Saturday of the month. Heritage Fine Foods, 32-34 High St., stocks **groceries** and discounted beer. (☎831 003. Open M-W 7am-9pm, Th-Sa 9am-10pm, Su 8am-9pm.) Find yummy muffins and sandwiches (£1-5) at **Burns the Bread ❶,** 14 High St. (☎831 532. Open M-Sa 6am-5pm, Su 11am-4pm. Cash only.) The vegetarian and whole-food menu at **Rainbow's End ❶,** 17a High St., changes with the chef's whims, with dishes such as Greek cheese pie with salad and garlic potatoes (£6). Soups, salads, and quiches run £3-7. (☎833 896. Open M-Sa 10am-5pm, Su 11am-4pm. Cash only.) Carnivores should head to **Gigi's ❸,** 2-4 Magdalene St. for authentic Italian dishes and sizable portions. (☎834 612. Entrees £11.50-15. Open Tu-Th 6-10:45pm, F 6-11pm, Sa-Su noon-2:30pm and 6-11pm. MC/V.) Try a pint at **Ye Queens Head,** Skittle Alley, off High St., which shows local sports on a flat-screen TV in a classic pub atmosphere. Frequent live music brings in a younger crowd on performance nights. (☎832 745. Open M-Sa 11am-11pm, Su noon-10:30pm.)

📷🎉 SIGHTS AND FESTIVALS. Legend holds that Joseph of Arimathea, the Virgin Mary's uncle, traveled with the young Jesus to do business in modern-day Somerset. Joseph later returned in AD 63 and founded a simple church that would later become the massive **⛪Glastonbury Abbey,** on Magdelene St. Although the abbey was destroyed during the English Reformation, the colossal pile of ruins that remains still evokes the grandeur of the original church. After a fire damaged the abbey in 1184, the monks needed to raise some cash. Fortunately, they "found" Arthur's grave on the south side of Lady Chapel in AD 1191 and reburied the bones

DIRTY DANCING

The Glastonbury Festival is an experience: hippies craft pyramid-shaped hats and discuss time travel, families visit the circus and theater, grail hunters search for King Arthur's remains. At the center of it all, rock and roll legends perform on stages set across 900 acres of parkland at the Vale of Avalon.

The first Festival was held in September of 1970, the day after Jimi Hendrix passed away in London. In its first year, 1500 people bought £1 tickets that granted entrance and milk from the local farm. By the end of the 80s, nearly 65,000 people were pitching a tent to see their favorite bands. Van Morrison took the stage with the Pixies and Suzanna Vega. At the end of the millennium, 100,000 fans saw Moby and David Bowie for £87.

Now, weekend tickets, which go for about £145, sell out faster than you can say "I hope I still get free milk with my ticket." You don't. However, it's well worth the price. Performers are a mix of old and new, from Modest Mouse and Björk to The Who and Elvis Costello.

Tickets for Glastonbury go on sale on the 1st Su in Apr. at www.SeeT-ickets.com or by phone at ☎0870 165 2007. The 2008 festival is June 27-29. For more information, visit www.glastonburyfestivals.co.uk.

here, inviting the King and Queen—and the royal treasurer—to attend the ceremony. A metal chain surrounds the anticlimactic **Tomb of Arthur and Guinevere,** in the center of the pillars. Near the entrance to the abbey, the **Holy Glastonbury Thorn** blooms every Christmas and Easter. The original thorn, on **Wearyall Hill** southeast of town, is said to have miraculously sprouted when Joseph of Arimathea drove his staff into the ground. The **Lady Chapel, Abbot's Kitchen,** and **museum** recreate the history of the sacred ground. (☎832 267; www.glastonburyabbey.com. Open daily June-Aug. 9am-6pm; Sept.-Nov. and Mar.-May 9:30am-dusk; Dec.-Feb. 10am-dusk. £5.50.)

Long lines of weary tourists converge at the top of the 526 ft. **Glastonbury Tor.** A steep 15min. hike yields 360° views as far as Bristol—a reward worth the climb. To reach the Tor, turn right at the top of High St. on Lambrook, which becomes Chilkwell St.; turn left at Wellhouse Ln. and follow the footpath uphill. Excavations have revealed a pre-Christian settlement on the hill, thought to have been an Arthurian fort. The Tor's crowning feature is a 14th-century bell tower, guarded by cows who have deftly marked their territory—keep one eye on the ground. In summer, the **Glastonbury Tor Bus** takes weary pilgrims from the city center (St. Dunstan's car park, next to the abbey) to a shorter climb on the far side of the Tor, returning to town via Chalice Well and the Rural Life Museum. (Always open; free. Hop-on, hop-off bus Apr.-Oct. every 30min. 9:30am-1pm and 2-5pm; £2.)

At the base of the Tor on Chilkwell St., **Chalice Well** is said to be where Joseph of Arimathea washed the holy grail, the cup from which Jesus drank at the Last Supper. Legend once held that the well ran with Christ's blood. The red tint actually comes from rust deposits in the stream, but the revelation has not stopped modern-day mystics from making pilgrimages to wade in the waters. Ancient believers interpreted the iron-red water's mingling with clear water from nearby **White Well** (which runs from a tap across the street) as a symbol of balance between the divine feminine and divine masculine. (☎831 154. Open daily Apr.-Oct. 10am-5:30pm; Feb.-Mar. and Nov. 11am-5pm; Dec.-Jan. 10am-4pm. £3, concessions £1.50.)

One of Glastonbury's biggest celebrations occurs in early November during the **Guy Fawks Night Carnival.** The city lights up with elaborate floats and parades for a whole day of Mardi Gras-like festivities. (First Saturday after November 5th.) Glastonbury's greatest attraction is 5 mi. away in Pilton, the site of the annual ■**Glastonbury Festival,** undoubtedly the biggest and best of Britain's multitude of summer music festivals. Recent headliners include The Killers, The Who, The White Stripes, David Bowie, Coldplay, Oasis, and Radiohead. The festival takes place at the end of June for three mud-covered and music-filled days. The festival office is at 28 Northload St. (☎834 596; www.glastonburyfestivals.co.uk.)

THE DORSET COAST

BOURNEMOUTH   ☎01202

Unassuming tourists may be pleasantly surprised by Bournemouth's cosmopolitan seaside manner. The town's Victorian buildings, lavish gardens, and expansive beach are colonized by swimsuit-toting daytrippers in summer. Unpretentious and student-friendly, Bournemouth houses some of southern England's best nightlife, ensuring that the fun doesn't stop when the sun dips below the gentle waves.

TRANSPORTATION. The **train station** lies on Holdenhurst Rd., 15min. east of the town center. (Travel center open M-F 9am-7pm, Sa 9am-6pm, Su 9am-5pm. Ticket office open M-Sa 5:40am-9pm, Su 6:40am-9pm.) **Trains** (☎08457 484 950) depart to: Birmingham (3hr., every hr., £55); Dorchester (40min., every hr., £8.60); London Waterloo (2hr., 2 per hr., £36); Poole (10min., 2 per hr., £2.80). National Express (☎08705 808 080) **buses** queue in front of the train station (ticket office open M-Sa 7:30am-6pm, Su 9am-6pm) and serve: Birmingham (5-6hr., 3 per day, £36.50); Bristol (3½hr., 1 per day, £15); London (3hr., every hr., £18); Poole (20min., 2-3 per hr., £1.50). Tickets are also sold at the TIC. Wilts and Dorset (☎673 555) runs local buses, including services to Poole and Southampton. An **Explorer** ticket (£6.50) provides unlimited travel. United **Taxi** (☎556 677) runs 24hr.

ORIENTATION AND PRACTICAL INFORMATION. The downtown centers around **The Square,** which is flanked by the **Central Gardens** to the northwest and the **Lower Gardens** toward the beach. The **Tourist Information Centre,** Westover Rd., sells a map (£1.50) and guide (£1), and books rooms for a 10% deposit. From the train station, turn left on Holdenhurst Rd. onto Bath Rd. and follow the signs. (☎0845 051 1701; www.bournemouth.co.uk. Open from mid-July to Aug. M-Sa 9:30am-7pm, Su 10:30am-5pm; from Sept. to mid-July M-Sa 9:30am-5:30pm.) Other services include: **American Express,** 95a Old Christchurch Rd. (☎780 752; open M-Tu and Th-F 9am-5pm, W 9:30am-5pm, Su 9:30am-3pm); **work opportunities** at JobCentre, 181-187 Old Christchurch Rd. (☎08456 060 234 or 276 000; open M-Tu and Th-F 9am-5pm, W 10am-5pm); a **launderette,** 172 Commercial Rd. (☎551 850; wash £2.70, dry £1.50; open M-F 8am-9pm, Sa-Su 8am-8pm; last wash 1hr. before close); **police,** Madeira Rd. (☎552 099); Boots **pharmacy,** 18-20 Commercial Rd. (☎551 713; open M-Sa 9am-6pm, Su 10:30am-4:30pm); **Bournemouth Hospital,** Castle Land East, Littledown (☎303 626); **Internet** access at the **Cyber Place,** 25 St. Peter's Rd. (☎290 099; £1 per 30min., £1 per hr. for students; open daily 9:30am-midnight) and at the **library,** 22 The Triangle, uphill from City Square (☎454 848; free for up to 1hr. per day; reservations requested; open M 10am-7pm, Tu and Th-F 9:30am-7pm, W 9:30am-5pm, Sa 10am-4pm); and the **post office,** 292 Holdenhurst Rd. (☎395 840; open daily 9am-5:30pm). **Post Code:** BH8 8BB.

ACCOMMODATIONS AND FOOD. The **East Cliff** neighborhood, 5min. from the train station, bristles with **B&Bs.** Exit left from the station, cross Holdenhurst Rd. to St. Swithuns, and turn left on Frances Rd.; the route is signposted. **Bournemouth Backpackers ❷,** 3 Frances Rd., is a small hostel with comfy lounges and a barbecue pit. (☎299 491; www.bournemouthbackpackers.co.uk. Kitchen. Reception M-F 5-6pm. Luggage storage £1 at the Travel Interchange. Reservations taken for 2 or more nights; call ahead for 1-night stays. Dorms £11-17; doubles £36-40. Rates highest on Sa; discounts for longer stays. Cash only.) **Kantara ❸**, 8 Gardens View, has bright rooms a short walk from the train and bus stations. It frequently houses stag and hen parties in the summer, so call ahead. (☎557 260; www.kantaraguesthouse.co.uk. £18-32 per person, weekly rates available. MC/V.)

Christchurch Road has diverse eateries; **Charminster Road** is a center of Asian cuisine. Get **groceries** at ASDA, St. Paul's Rd. across from the train station. (☎298 900. Open 24hr. M 8am to Sa 8pm and Su 10am-4pm.) **Eye of the Tiger ❷**, 207 Old Christchurch Rd., serves Bengali curries for £6-10 and other Tandoori specialties for £6.75-11. (☎780 900. Vegetarian options available. Open daily noon-2pm and 6pm-midnight. 10% takeaway discount. MC/V.) **Shake Away ❶**, 7 Post Office Rd., provides 150 flavors of milkshakes (£2.25-3.25), from marshmallow to rhubarb. (☎310 105. Open M-F 9am-5:30pm, Sa 9am-5pm, Su 10am-4:30pm. Student discount. Cash only.) For coffee and people-watching, stop at **Obscura Cafe ❶**, The Square. The upper level has a camera obscura (£2), which projects a panorama of the town on a 6 ft. screen. (☎314 231. Baguettes £4-5. Open daily 9am-dusk. MC/V.)

◐◖ SIGHTS AND BEACHES. The city center holds few interesting attractions. The **Russell-Cotes Art Gallery and Museum,** Russell-Cotes Rd., East Cliff, houses a collection of Victorian art in a lavish turn-of-the-century seaside house. (☎451 858. Open Tu-Su 10am-5pm. Free.) On the corner of Hilton and St. Peter's Rd., **St. Peter's** parish church holds the remains of Mary Shelley, author of *Frankenstein*. (☎290 986. Open M-F 9am-5pm, Sa 10am-4pm, Su services.) From the church to the waves, you can't miss the **Bournemouth Eye,** a helium-filled balloon that gives visitors a bird's-eye view of the boardwalk. (☎314 539; www.bournemouthballoon.com. Open daily 10am-11pm, hours vary with weather conditions. £10, students £7.50.) Most visitors come for **Bournemouth Beach** (☎451 781), a 7 mi. sliver of shoreline packed with sun worshippers on hot summer days. Amusements and a theater can be found at **Bournemouth Pier** (open July-Aug. 9am-11pm; Apr.-June and Sept.-Oct. 9am-5:30pm; 50p); a short walk leads to quieter spots.

A 95 mi. stretch of the Dorset and East Devon coast, dubbed the **Jurassic Coast,** was recently named a World Heritage site for its famous fossils and unique geology (www.jurassiccoast.com; see also **Lyme Regis,** p. 213). Beautiful **Studland Beach** sits across the harbor, reachable by Wilts and Dorset bus #150 (50min., every hr., round-trip £3). Take bus #150 or 151 (25min., 2 per hr., £3) to reach the themed landscapes of **Compton Acres,** featuring an Italian garden with Roman statues and a sensory garden designed for the blind. (☎700 110. Open daily Mar.-Oct. 9am-6pm, last entrance 1hr. before close. £6, concessions £5.25.) The 1000-year-old **Corfe Castle** is no gently weathered pile of ruins: Parliamentarian engineers were ordered to destroy the castle during the English Civil War. Travel to Poole (bus #151) or Swanage (#150) to catch bus #142 (every hr., round-trip £5.75) to the castle. (☎01929 481 294. Open daily Apr.-Sept. 10am-6pm; Mar. and Oct. 10am-5pm; Nov.-Feb. 10am-4pm. £5.30, children £2.70. Discount for those arriving by public transportation.)

♫❋ ENTERTAINMENT AND FESTIVALS. Students and vacationers fuel Bournemouth's nightlife. Check www.bournemouthbynight.com to make plans for the evening's festivities. Most start at the roundabout up the hill from **Fir Vale Road,** working downhill through the numerous bars on **Christchurch Road.** Gay-friendly nightlife options cluster where Commercial St. meets The Triangle. Just next door, **Toko** is a sleek, sophisticated bar with fish tanks, flat-screen TVs, and free Wi-Fi. Thursday is student night; "retox" with £1.50 drinks. (☎315 821. Open M and Su 6pm-2am, W 6pm-3am, Th 6pm-4am, F-Sa 6pm-6am.) **Bliss,** 1-15 St. Peter's Rd., offers an upscale night out with mood lighting and a sleek bar. (☎297 149. Free Wi-Fi. Open M-Th noon-2am, F-Sa noon-4am, Su 9am-2am. MC/V.) The biggest club in Bournemouth, **Elements** attracts hordes of vacationing students from London. (☎311 178. W student night. Cover £3-8; often free before 10pm. Open M and Su 9pm-2am, W-Sa 9pm-3am.) A mile east of The Square, the **Opera House,** 570 Christchurch Rd., a former theater renovated into two dance floors, is one of the wildest (and cheapest) clubs in town. Take bus #22 from The Square. (☎399 922; www.operahouse.co.uk. Most drinks £1-2. F "Slinky" with dance and trance music. Cover £1-15. Open F-Sa 9pm-5am, Su 9pm-3am.) In a tradition dating from 1896, 15,000 candles light up the Lower Gardens every Wednesday in summer during the **Flowers by Candlelight Festival.** In late June, Bournemouth's **Live! Music Festival** (☎451 702; www.bournemouth.co.uk) hosts free concerts.

DORCHESTER ☎01305

Stratford has Shakespeare, Swansea has Thomas, Haworth has the Brontës, and Dorchester has Thomas Hardy. Locals invoke his spirit to no end, from pub regulars sharing time-worn stories about the author to the somber statue towering over the town's main street. In addition to being the inspiration for the fictional Casterbridge, the sleepy town has a rich history that extends back into the Iron Age and serves as a convenient base for exploring the fossil-laden Jurassic coast.

■ TRANSPORTATION

Most **trains** (☎08457 484 950) leave from **Dorchester South,** off Weymouth Ave., south of the town center. (Ticket office open M-F 6am-8pm, Sa 6:40am-8pm, Su 8:40am-7pm.) Trains run to Bournemouth (40min., every hr., £8.60) and London Waterloo (2½hr., every hr., £37-46). Some trains leave the unmanned station, **Dorchester West,** also off Weymouth Ave., including those to Weymouth (15min., 8 per day, £3). Dorchester has no bus station, but **buses** stop at Dorchester South train station and on Trinity St. National Express (☎08705 808 080) runs buses to Exeter (2hr., 1 per day, £10) and London (5hr., 3 per day, £18). Tickets are sold at the TIC. Wilts and Dorset (☎673 555) bus #184 goes to Salisbury via Blandford (2hr., 6 per day, £4.50). First bus #212 goes to Yeovil (1½hr., every hr., £3.50), with connections south. Coach House Travel (☎267 644) provides local service. **Taxis** are available from Bob's Cars (☎269 500; 24hr.) and Dorset Cars (☎250 666). **Bike rental** is available from Dorchester Cycles, 31 Great Western Rd. (☎268 787. £10 per day. ID required. Open M-Sa 9am-5:30pm.)

■ ORIENTATION AND PRACTICAL INFORMATION

The intersection of **High West** and **South Streets** (which eventually becomes **Cornhill Street**) is the unofficial center of town. The main **shopping district** extends along South St. and runs parallel to Trinity St. The **Tourist Information Centre,** 11 Antelope Walk, off Trinity St., stocks free town maps and books accommodations for a 10% deposit. (☎267 992; www.westdorset.com. Open Apr.-Oct. M-Sa 9am-5pm; Nov.-Mar. M-Sa 9am-4pm.) Other services include: Barclays **bank,** 10 South St. (☎326 730; open M-Tu and Th-F 9:30am-4:30pm, W 10am-4:30pm); a **launderette,** 16c High East St. (wash £2.60-3, dry 20p per 4min.; open daily 8am-8pm); **police,** Weymouth Ave. (☎251 212); Dorset County **Hospital,** Williams Ave. (☎251 150); Boots **pharmacy,** 12-13 Cornhill St. (☎264 340; open Aug. M-Sa 8:30am-5:30pm, Su 10am-4pm; Sept.-July M-Sa 8:30am-5:30pm); free **Internet** access at the **library,** Colliton Park, off The Grove (☎224 448; open M 10am-7pm, Tu-W and F 9:30am-7pm, Th 9:30am-5pm, Sa 9am-4pm) and at **Amici,** 7a Tudor Arcade, off South St. (☎261 700; £1 per 20min., free Wi-Fi; open daily 8am-6pm); and the **post office,** 43 South St., with a **bureau de change** (☎08457 223 344; open M-Sa 9am-5:30pm). **Post Code:** DT1 1DH.

ACCOMMODATIONS

The White House ❸, 9 Queens Ave., off Weymouth Ave., offers two gorgeous rooms in a residential neighborhood. From the train station, exit left onto Station Approach and turn left onto Weymouth Ave.; Queen's Ave. is a few blocks up, past Lime Close. (☎266 714. Breakfast included. Singles £27; doubles £44. Cash only.) **Tolpuddle Hall ❷,** Tolpuddle, was once home to the vicars of Tolpuddle parish. (☎848 986. From £20. Cash only.) **The King's Arms ❺,** 30 High East St., is a splurge near the center of town and was featured in Hardy's *Mayor of Casterbridge*. (☎265 353; www.kingsarmsdorchester.com. Full English breakfast £6, continental £4. Rooms £79. MC/V.) Self-catering **YHA Litton Cheney ❷** is 10 mi. west of the city. Take bus #31 to Whiteway and follow the signs for 1½ mi. (☎01308 482 340. Reception 8-10am and 5-10pm. Lockout 10am-5pm. Curfew 11pm. Open Apr.-Aug. Dorms £13, under 18 £10. MC/V.) For camping, try **Giant's Head Caravan and Camping Park ❶,** Old Sherborne Rd., in Cerne Abbas, 8 mi. north of Dorchester. If you're driving, head out of town on The Grove and bear right onto Old Sherborne Rd. For bus travel, take the #216 from Dorchester to Cerne Village and take the road to Buckland Newton. (☎01300 341 242; www.giantshead.co.uk. Showers, laundry, and electricity available. Open Apr.-Sept. Tent, car, and 2 adults £7-11. Cash only.)

FOOD AND PUBS

The eateries along **High West Street** and **High East Street** provide a range of options. Get your **groceries** at the weekly Dorchester Market, in the car park near South Station (open W 8am-3pm), or at Waitrose, in the Tudor Arcade, off South St. (☎268 420. Open M-W and Sa 8:30am-7pm, Th-F 8:30am-8pm, Su 10am-4pm.) **6 North Square ❸** serves fresh Dorset seafood off High St. near the town hall. (☎267 679. Dinner entrees £12.50. Open M-Sa 10:30am-2:30pm and 6:30-9:30pm. MC/V.) **The Celtic Kitchen ❶,** 17 Antelope Walk, near the TIC, serves delicious Cornish pasties for £1.70-2.10. (☎269 377. Open M-Sa 9am-4pm. Cash only.) The **Potters Cafe Bistro ❷,** 19 Durngate St. off South St., offers delicious dishes made with local and organic products. (☎260 312. Lunch dishes £5-8. Open M-W 10am-5pm, Th-Sa 10am-9pm, Su 6pm-10pm. Cash only.) **The Spice Centre ❸,** 37-38 High West St., has an extensive menu including curries for £5-8. (☎267 850. Open M-Th and Su noon-2:30pm and 6-11:30pm, F-Sa noon-2:30pm and 6pm-midnight. MC/V.)

Dorchester barely dabbles in nightlife, but you can find a good pint at **Old George,** at the bottom of Trinity St. (☎263 534. DJs and live bands F-Sa. Open M-Th 11am-11pm, F-Sa 11am-midnight, Su noon-10:30pm.) **Bojangles,** 33 Trinity St., has flat-screen TVs and £2.50 drink specials. (☎263 404. Open M-W 11am-11pm, Th 11am-midnight, F 11am-1am, Sa 11am-2am, Su noon-midnight.) **Klimax,** 37-38 High West St., is the only club in town, offering £1 drinks and Dorchester's latest hours. Party on Thursday night to collect a £9 drink voucher for Friday or Saturday. (☎269 151. Open Th-F 10pm-2am, Sa 7pm-3am.)

SIGHTS

Dorchester is quaint, but its attractions can fill a day. East of town, Hardy-related sites hint at the poet-novelist's inspiration for Wessex, a fictional region centered around Dorset. West of town, remnants of Iron Age and Roman Britain appear.

Here's the **Thomas Hardy** breakdown: he designed **Max Gate,** 1 mi. southwest of town off Arlington Rd., and lived there from 1885 until his death in 1928, penning *Tess of the D'Urbervilles* and *Jude the Obscure*. (☎262 538. Open Apr.-Sept. M, W, and Su 2-5pm. £2.75.) He was christened in **Stinsford Church,** 2 mi. northeast of town in Stinsford Village, and the yard holds the family plot where his first and second wives are buried, although only his heart is buried here—his ashes lie in Westminster Abbey (p. 110). Take bus #184 from Trinity St. toward Puddletown; ask to be dropped off near the church (admission free). Finally, he was born in **Hardy's Cottage,** Bockhampton Ln., deep in the woods 3 mi. northeast of Dorchester. Take bus #184 or 185 and ask to be let off at the cottage. (☎262 366. Open Apr.-Oct. M and Th-Su 11am-5pm or until dusk. £3.) Finish your literary tour at the Hardy memorial **statue,** located at the "Top o' Town."

The **Dorset County Museum,** 66 High West St., has a replica of Hardy's study and relics of the city's other keepers—Druids, Romans, and Saxons. (☎262 735. Open July-Sept. daily 10am-5pm; Oct.-June M-Sa 10am-5pm. £6, concessions £5. Audio tour free.) On the other side of town is **Maiden Castle,** the largest Iron Age fortification in Europe, dating to 3000 BC. Modern visitors can scale what little is left of the ramparts, today patrolled by sheep. Take shuttle #2 (M-Sa 5 per day, £1) to Maiden Castle Rd., ¾ mi. from the hill. If weather permits, opt to hike the scenic 2 mi. from the town center down Maiden Castle Rd. Closer to town is the first-century **Roman Town House,** at the back of the County Hall complex. Glass walls complete the remains of the house and allow visitors to view the mosaic floors inside. Just past the South Station entrance sprawls the **Maumbury Rings,** a monument dating from the Bronze Age.

🔖 DAYTRIP FROM DORCHESTER

LYME REGIS

From Dorchester, take First (☎01305 783 645) bus #31 from South Station (1¼hr., every hr., £4). The TIC, Guildhall Cottage, Church St., downhill from the bus stop, locates lodgings and stocks walking guides. ☎01297 442 138; www.lymeregistourism.com. Open Apr.-Oct. M-Sa 10am-5pm, Su 10am-4pm; Nov.-Mar. M-Sa 10am-4pm, Su 10am-2pm.

Known as the "Pearl of Dorset," Lyme Regis (pop. 3500) surveys a majestic coastline. In 1811, a resident shopkeeper named Mary Anning discovered the first Ichthyosaurus fossil 1 mi. west of Lyme Regis. Since then, the town has thrived on its prehistoric past, even forming the streetlights into a spiral shell shape. Paleontologist Steve Davies (see **Jurassic Park,** p. 213) has amassed an immense collection of local fossils, artfully displayed in the **Dinosaurland Fossil Museum,** Coombe St. (☎01297 443 541; www.dinosaurland.co.uk. Open daily 10am-5pm. £4, students £3.) The museum has 200-million-year-old shells and a 100-million-year-old lobster fossil. Davies leads a 2hr. **dinosaur hunting walk** (£6); contact Dinosaurland for

THE HIDDEN DEAL

JURASSIC PARK

Antiques can cost a pretty penny, but one British collectible can be absolutely free: fossils. The beaches surrounding Lyme Regis are littered with specimens from 65 to 200 million years ago. How can Wedgwood china compete with a perfectly preserved prehistoric fish?

The best way to make a fossil find is to join an expert-led tour. Steve Davies, owner of **Dinosaurland Fossil Museum,** has decades of experience, degrees in geology and micro-paleontology, and the fossils to prove it. Steve conducts 2hr. fossil-hunting excursions at Black Ven, the mudflow 1 mi. east of Lyme in which Mary Anning discovered her famous ichthyosaurus in 1811. Due to the erosion of the cliffs, a new crop of fossils arises every day, virtually guaranteeing a geological discovery.

The most common fossil-finds are belemnites (squid-like mollusks) and ammonites (beautiful spiral-shelled cephalopods). The fossils often striate the soft, sandy rock into interesting shapes. Some fossils are preserved in iron pyrite, or fool's gold, which gives them a lustrous appearance. Other common fossils include oysters, snails, fish, and even ichthyosauri.

For tour times, contact Dinosaurland Fossil Museum, Coombe St., Lyme Regis, ☎01297 443 541; or consult the chalk board outside the museum doors. £4, children £3.

times, which depend on the tides. Lyme Regis is also renowned for the **Cobb**, a 10-20 ft. manmade seawall that cradles the harbor. The **Marine Aquarium** on the Cobb exhibits a small collection of local sea creatures, including a 5 ft. conger eel. (☎01297 444 230. Open daily Mar.-Oct. 10am-5pm. £3, concessions £2.50.) The **Lyme Regis Museum,** Bridge St., chronicles Lyme's history. (☎01297 443 370; www.lymeregismuseum.co.uk. Open Apr.-Oct. M-Sa 10am-5pm, Su 11am-5pm; Nov.-Apr. Sa 10am-5pm, Su 11am-5pm. £2.50, concessions £2.)

DEVON

EXETER   ☎01392

Legend holds that in 1068, the inhabitants of Exeter earned the respect of William the Conqueror by holding their defenses against his army for 18 days. When the city's wells ran dry, the Exonians used wine for cooking, bathing, and drinking—which might help to explain the city's eventual fall. Today, restaurants, shops, and wine-bars surround the magnificent cathedral, which miraculously avoided bombardment during WWII. The rest of the city was far less fortunate: High St. and the city center were quickly rebuilt in the 1950s. Rapid growth and a desire for a more modern aesthetic led to a massive makeover in 2007.

▐ TRANSPORTATION

Trains: Exeter has 2 stations.

St. David's Station, St. David's Hill, 1 mi. from town. Ticket office open M-F 5:45am-8:40pm, Sa 6:15am-8pm, Su 7:30am-8:40pm. Trains (☎08457 484 950) to **Bristol** (1hr., every hr., £19), **London Paddington** (2½hr., every hr., £58), and **Salisbury** (2hr., every 2hr., £24.50).

Central Station, Queen St. Ticket office open M-Sa 7:50am-6pm. To **London Waterloo** (3hr., 12 per day, £47.40).

Buses: Bus station, Paris St. (☎427 711). Ticket office open M-F 8:45am-5:30pm, Sa 8:45am-1pm. **National Express** (☎08705 808 080) sends buses to **Bristol** (2hr., 5 per day, £12), **Dorchester** (1hr., 1 per day, £10), and **London** (4-5hr., 9 per day, £22). **First** (☎01752 402 060) handles most travel throughout Devon and Dorset, including to **Bude** (X9; 1¼hr., every 2hr., £4.80) via **Okehampton** (45min., every 2hr., £3.70), and **Weymouth** (X53; 3hr., every 2hr., £5.50). The X53 Coast Link runs along the Jurassic Coast between Exeter and Bournemouth. Bus tickets on this service include discounted admission at sights along the coast. (Day Pass £5.50.)

Public Transportation: An **Exeter Freedom Ticket** (£3.50 per day, £9 per week) allows unlimited travel on city **minibuses.** The **Explorer Ticket** (£5.50 per day, £17 per week) allows unlimited travel on **Stagecoach** (☎427 711) buses.

Taxis: Capital (☎433 433). **Club Cars** (☎213 030).

▐ PRACTICAL INFORMATION

Tourist Information Centre: Dix's Field (☎265 700). Books accommodations for £3 plus a 10% deposit and sells National Express tickets. Open July-Aug. M-Sa 9am-5pm, Su 10am-4pm; Sept.-June M-Sa 9am-5pm.

Tours: The best way to explore is with the City Council's free 1½hr. **themed walking tours** (☎265 700), including "Murder and Mayhem," "Ghosts and Legends," and "Medieval Exeter." Most leave from the Royal Clarence Hotel off High St.; some depart from the Quay House Visitor Centre. Apr.-Oct. 4-5 per day; Nov.-Mar. 11am and 2pm.

Financial Services: Thomas Cook, 177 Sidwell St. (☎601 400). Open M-Sa 9am-5:30pm.

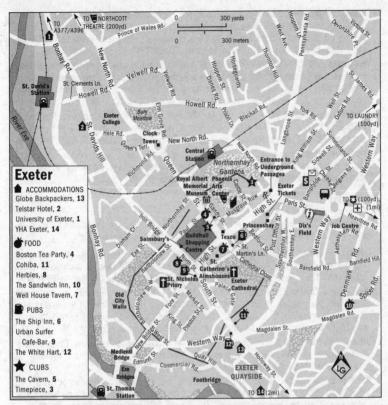

Exeter

🏠 **ACCOMMODATIONS**
Globe Backpackers, **13**
Telstar Hotel, **2**
University of Exeter, **1**
YHA Exeter, **14**

🍴 **FOOD**
Boston Tea Party, **4**
Cohiba, **11**
Herbies, **8**
The Sandwich Inn, **10**
Well House Tavern, **7**

🍺 **PUBS**
The Ship Inn, **6**
Urban Surfer
    Cafe-Bar, **9**
The White Hart, **12**

⭐ **CLUBS**
The Cavern, **5**
Timepiece, **3**

Work Opportunities: JobCentre, Clarendon House, Western Way (☎ 474 700), on the roundabout near the TIC. Open M-Tu and Th-F 9am-5pm, W 10am-5pm.

Launderette: Silverspin Cleaning Centre, 12 Blackboy Rd. (☎ 270 067). Wash small £2.60, large £5; dry 50p per 8min. Open daily 8am-10pm.

Police: Heavitree Rd. (☎ 08705 777 444).

Hospital: Royal Devon and Exeter, Barrack Rd. (☎ 411 611).

Pharmacy: Boots, 251 High St. (☎ 432 244). Open M-W and F-Sa 8:15am-6pm, Th 8:15am-7pm, Su 10am-4:30pm.

Internet Access: Central Library, Castle St. (☎ 384 206). Free for the first 30min., £1.50 per 30min. thereafter. Free Wi-Fi. Open M-Tu and Th-F 9:30am-7pm, W 10am-5pm, Sa 9:30am-4pm, Su 11am-2:30pm.

Post Office: Sidwell St. (☎ 08457 223 344). **Bureau de change.** Open M-Sa 9am-5:30pm. **Post Code:** EX1 1AH.

🏠 ACCOMMODATIONS

There are a large number of **B&Bs** near the **Clock Tower** roundabout just north of Queen St., especially on **St. David's Hill,** between St. David's Station and the center of town.

☒ **Globe Backpackers,** 71 Holloway St. (☎215 521; www.exeterbackpackers.co.uk). Spacious common rooms full of social backpackers. Luggage storage £1 per bag. Laundry service £3. Internet access 5p per min. Key deposit £5. Reception 8am-11pm. Checkout 11am. Book ahead. Dorms £14; doubles £32. MC/V with 50p surcharge. ❷

YHA Exeter, 47 Countess Wear Rd. (☎873 329), 2 mi. southeast of city center. Take minibus K or T from High St. to the Countess Wear post office; follow signs 10min. to the spacious, cheery hostel. Internet access 50p per 7min. Reception daily 8-10am and 5-10pm. Dorms £15.50, students and under 18 £11. MC/V. ❷

Telstar Hotel, 75-77 St. David's Hill (☎272 466; www.telstar-hotel.co.uk). Family-run B&B with comfortable, floral-themed rooms, many newly renovated. Full breakfast included. Book 2 weeks ahead in summer. Singles £30-35; doubles £55-65. MC/V. ❸

The University of Exeter (☎215 566). Offers a range of accommodations throughout the city when the students are off campus. Open Apr. and July-Sept. Book ahead. B&B singles, ensuite £45; 4 people for 1 room for 1 week £400. ❸

◨ FOOD

Get **groceries** at Sainsbury's, in the Guildhall Shopping Centre. (☎432 741. Open M-W 8am-6:30pm, Th-F 8am-7pm, Sa 7:30am-6:30pm, Su 10:30am-4:30pm.)

Cohiba, 36 South St. (☎678 445). Let the suede couches engulf you at this delicious tapas bar. Latin tunes complement the decor and flavorful food. 2 tapas and drink lunch special £7. Tapas £4.50; entrees £9-15. Open M-Sa noon-midnight. MC/V. ❸

Well House Tavern, Cathedral Close (☎233 611). Good pub grub with a view of the cathedral in an annex of the beautiful Royal Clarence Hotel. Check out the skeleton in the crypt downstairs. Entrees £8.50-13. Open M-Sa 11am-11pm, Su noon-10:30pm. Food served noon-2:30pm, bar menu served 2:30-5:30pm. AmEx/MC/V. ❷

Boston Tea Party, 84 Queen St. (☎201 181; www.bostonteaparty.co.uk). Cheap prices and delicious sandwiches. Enjoy freshly prepared meals on the 2nd fl. cafe overlooking the city. Open M-Sa 7am-6pm, Su 8am-6pm. MC/V. ❷

The Sandwich Inn, 36 Magdalen St. The singing chef/owner/sandwich god whips up food to go (from £2.70) and full English breakfast (£3.75). The dining area is tiny, but grab a sandwich to enjoy on the quay. Open daily 8:30am-3:30pm. Cash only. ❶

Herbies, 15 North St. (☎258 473). A casual venue for vegetarian delights. Fair trade wines and local ingredients. Entrees £6.25-8.25. Open M 11am-2:30pm, Tu-F 11am-2:30pm and 6-9:30pm, Sa 10:30am-4pm and 6-9:30pm. MC/V. ❷

◉ SIGHTS

EXETER CATHEDRAL. Largely spared from the WWII bombings in Exeter, this cathedral is one of England's finest. Two massive Norman towers preside over the West Front, decorated with kings, saints, and a sculpture of St. Peter as a nude fisherman. The 16th-century astronomical clock is reputed to be the source of the nursery rhyme "Hickory Dickory Dock" and shows the Earth as the center of the universe. The cathedral is home to the 60 ft. **Bishop's Throne** (made without nails), disassembled and taken to the countryside in 1640 and again during WWII. The Bishop's Palace library is home to the **Exeter Book,** the world's richest treasury of early Anglo-Saxon poetry. (☎255 573. Cathedral open M-F and Su 7:30am-6:30pm, Sa 7:30am-5pm. Library open M-F 2-5pm. Evensong M-F 5:30pm, Sa-Su 3pm. Free guided tours Apr.-Oct. M-F 11am and 2:30pm, Sa 11am, Su 4pm. Requested donation £3.50.)

UNDERGROUND PASSAGES. The ancient underground passages in Exeter are the only of their kind that can be explored in England. Originally built to protect the city's lead water pipes, the tunnels are full of mysterious stories of rogue nuns and priests, buried treasure, and ghosts. The museum and information center contain everything you could ever hope to learn about subterranean history. *(Entrance near Boots, info center next to TIC in Princesshay. ☎665 887. Open daily, call for tour times.)*

THE ROYAL ALBERT MEMORIAL MUSEUM. This museum has 16 galleries of fascinating hodgepodge, including a clock room and a massive collection of starfish. The world culture galleries, amassed largely by local explorers (including Captain Cook), feature everything from totem poles to Egyptian tombs. The museum is set for renovation in fall 2007. *(Queen St. ☎665 858. Open M-Sa 10am-5pm. Free.)*

ST. CATHERINE'S ALMSHOUSES. Hidden among the cafes and shops near the cathedral, these sobering red ruins were originally 15th-century housing for the poor. After WWII, they were preserved and dedicated to those who lost their lives in battle. Inscriptions surround the ruins, and a Roman mosaic found after the bombing is in the center. *(Bedford St., near Princesshay. Open daily. Free.)*

NIGHTLIFE AND ENTERTAINMENT

Exeter boasts growing nightlife, with bars and clubs in the alleyways off **High Street,** near **Exeter Cathedral,** and on **Gandy Street.** Young party-goers enjoy the slightly rustic atmosphere and beer garden at **Timepiece,** Little Castle St. (☎493 096; www.timepiecenightclub.co.uk. Cover £2-5. Open M-W and Su 7pm-1am, Th 7pm-1:30am, F-Sa 7pm-2am.) **The Cavern,** 83-84 Queen St., just off Gandy St., is a tiny joint that and hosts live bands. (☎495 370; www.cavernclub.co.uk. Cover after 10pm £2-5. Open M-Th 8:30pm-1am, F-Sa 9pm-2am, Su 8pm-midnight. Cafe open M-Sa 11am-4pm.) **Urban Surfer Cafe-Bar,** 2 South St., serves drinks in a surf shack. (☎411 700. Open daily 9am-11pm, food served until 7pm.) The **White Hart,** 66 South St., a 14th-century house, has a "secret garden" and a tap room. (Open M-Sa noon-11pm, Su noon-10:30pm.) Over 700 years old, **The Ship Inn,** 1-3 St. Martin's Ln., was a favorite of Sir Francis Drake, who wrote, "next to mine own shippe I do love that Shippe in Exon." (☎272 040. Open M-Th noon-11:30pm, F-Sa noon-midnight.)

The professional company at the **Northcott Theatre,** Stoker Rd., performs throughout the year. (☎493 493. Box office open M-Sa 10am-6pm, until 8pm on performance nights. Tickets £11-18; student standby tickets £6.) In July and August, the Northcott company performs Shakespeare in the park. Tickets can be booked at **Exeter Tickets,** High St., which supplies monthly listings of cultural events in the city. (☎211 080. Open M-Sa 9:30am-5:30pm.) The **Exeter Festival,** in late June and early July, features concerts, opera, dance lessons, stand-up comedy, and theater. For tickets, contact the **Festival Box Office,** Paris St. in the Civic Center. (☎213 161; www.exeter.gov.uk/festival. Open M-Sa 10am-5pm. Tickets £8-20.) The **Exeter Phoenix Arts Center,** Gandy St. (☎667 080; www.exeterphoenix.org.uk), offers everything from dance classes to gallery talks and free summer public movie screenings in Northernhay Gardens.

EXMOOR NATIONAL PARK

Once a royal hunting preserve, Exmoor is among the smallest and most picturesque of Britain's national parks, covering 265 sq. mi. on the north coast of the island's southwestern peninsula. The park's lush woods grow up to the shoreline, offering spectacular hiking ground. Wild ponies still roam the area, and England's last herds of Red Deer graze in the woodlands. Although over 80% of Exmoor is privately owned, the territory is accommodating to respectful hikers and bikers.

▐ TRANSPORTATION

Exmoor's western gateway is **Barnstaple**; its eastern gateway is **Minehead**. Most transportation into and within the park runs through one of these towns—often connecting in **Taunton**. Bus service within the park is poor; some small villages are served only once per day, and many services operate only in a 9am-6pm window. Western Exmoor lies in Devon, and bus routes are detailed in *North Devon Bus Times*. Eastern Exmoor occupies the western part of Somerset and is covered by the *Public Transport Timetable for the Exmoor and West Somerset Area*. Both are free at TICs. *Accessible Exmoor*, free from National Park Information Centres (NPICs), provides a guide for disabled visitors. Since single bus fares in the park are £3-4, it's wise to purchase **First Day Explorer** (£7) or **First Week Explorer** (£22) tickets, which allow unlimited travel on all First buses. Call to check times. Traveline (☎0870 608 2608) is the most helpful resource for planning public transportation in the park.

Trains: From Barnstaple, trains travel to **Bristol** (2½hr., 12 per day, £25.50), **Exeter Central** and **St. David's** (1¼hr.; M-Sa 12 per day, Su 5 per day; £11.60), and **London Paddington** (4hr., 12 per day, £63). Trains from Minehead go to **Exeter St. David's** (25min., every hr., £13.60).

Buses: From Barnstaple, National Express (☎08705 808 080) buses travel to **Bristol** (3hr., 1 per day, £18.40) and **London Victoria** (5½hr., 3-4 per day, £28). First Devon (☎01752 402 060; open M-F 9am-4pm) buses #86 and X85 to **Plymouth** (3¼hr.; M-Sa 6 per day, Su 2 per day; £4), #337 to **Taunton** (2hr., M-Sa 9am, £5.50), #319 to **Bude** (2hr., 3 per day, £5.50) via **Hartland**. Minehead Station serves National Express buses to **Exeter St. David's** (25min., every hr., £12). First #28/X28 to **Taunton** (1¼hr.; M-Sa every ½hr., Su 9 per day; £4). Drivers sell combined bus and train tickets (£12). No buses directly connect Minehead to Barnstaple.

Local Transportation: Listed prices are for off-peak hours (purchased after 8:45am). First Somerset bus #300 runs along the coast, from Minehead to **Lynmouth** (M-Sa every hr., 1hr., £2.40) connecting to **Ilfracombe** (daily 11am, 2, and 5pm). **Barnstaple** serves Devon buses (☎01752 402 060) to **Ilfracombe** (#103; 40min.; M-Sa 4 per hr., Su every hr.; £2), **Lynmouth** (#309-310; 1hr., M-Sa 3 per day, £2.20), and **Lynton** (#309-310; 1hr., M-Sa every hr., £2.20). **Minehead** sends Somerset (☎01823 272 033) buses to: **Dunster** (#28, 39, 300, and 398; 10min., 1-2 per hr., £1.25); **Ilfracombe** (#300; 2hr., 3 per day, £4.50); **Lynton** (#300; 1hr., 3 per day, £2.80); **Porlock** (#38 or 300; 15min.; M-Sa 9 per day, Su 3 per day; £2). West Somerset Railway offers steam and diesel trains (5 per day) from **Minehead** to **Dunster** (6min., £2.40) on its way to **Bishops Lydeard** (45min., £12.40).

▐▐ ▐ ORIENTATION AND PRACTICAL INFORMATION

Exmoor lies on 23 mi. of the Bristol Channel coastline, between Barnstaple and Minehead. The park spans Somerset and Devon counties and sits north of Dartmoor National Park. Both TICs and NPICs stock Ordnance Survey maps (£7.50), transportation timetables, and the invaluable *Exmoor Visitor* newspaper, which lists events, accommodations, and walks, and has a useful map and articles on the park. This information can also be found at www.exmoor-nationalpark.gov.uk.

National Park Information Centres: The best places for updated trail information and advice. Dulverton is open year-round and stocks information for the entire park.

Blackmoor Gate: South Moulton Junction (☎01598 763 466), on the A399/A39. Open Apr.-Oct. daily 10:30am-5pm; limited winter hours.

Combe Martin: Seacot, 13 Cross St. (☎01271 883 319), 3 mi. east of Ilfracombe. Open daily Apr.-Sept. 10am-5pm.

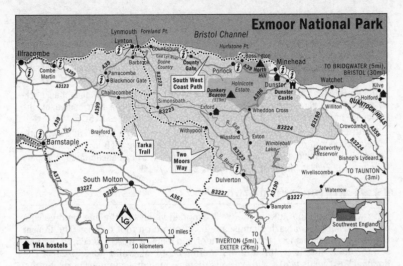

Dulverton: Dulverton Heritage Centre, The Guildhall, Fore St. (☎01398 323 841). Open daily Apr.-Oct. 10am-5pm.

Dunster: Dunster Steep Car Park (☎01643 821 835), 2 mi. east of Minehead. Open daily Apr.-Oct. 10am-5pm; limited winter hours.

Tourist Information Centres: All TICs book accommodations for a 10% deposit.

Ilfracombe: The Landmark Seafront (☎01271 863 001). Shares a building with the Landmark Theatre. Open Easter-Oct. daily 10am-5pm; Nov.-Easter M-Sa 10am-4pm.

Lynton: Town Hall, Lee Rd. (☎0845 660 3232 or 01598 752 225; www.lyntourism.co.uk). Open M-F 9:30am-5pm, Su 10am-4pm.

Minehead: 17 Friday St. (☎01643 702 624). Open July-Aug. M-Sa 9:30am-12:30pm and 1:30-5pm.

Porlock: West End High St. (☎01643 863 150; www.porlock.co.uk). Open Easter-Oct. M-F 10am-1pm and 2-5pm, Sa 10am-5pm, Su 10am-1pm; Nov.-Easter Tu-F 10am-1pm, Sa 10am-2pm.

ACCOMMODATIONS

Hostels and **B&Bs** (£20-25) fill up quickly; check listings and the *Exmoor Visitor* at the TIC. At busy times, **camping** may be the easiest way to see the park. Most land is private; before pitching a tent, get consent from the owner (p. 49). There are three YHA hostels in the area. All have a 10am-5pm lockout.

YHA Elmscott (☎01237 441 367). Buses #319 and X19 from Barnstaple go to Hartland; from the west end of Fore St., a footpath leads 2½ mi. through the Vale to the hostel. Kitchen. Laundry £3. Open Easter-Sept. Frequently closed on Su; call ahead. Dorms £16, under 18 £12.50. MC/V. ❶

YHA Exford, Withypoole Rd. (☎01643 831 288), next to the River Exe bridge in the center of the village. Take bus #178 (F), 285 (Su), or Red Bus #295 from Minehead (June-Sept.; 1 per day). Victorian house in the middle of Exmoor. Kitchen and laundry. Curfew 11pm. Open July-Aug. daily; Sept.-June M-Sa. Dorms £15, under 18 £9.50. MC/V. ❷

YHA Minehead, Alcombe Combe (☎01643 702 595). Between the town center and Dunster (2 mi. from either). A 20min. walk from town, or take bus #28 toward Dunster and ask the driver to stop near the YHA (5min. walk from the main road). Beautiful location in the forest with easy access to 2 short walks in the park. Large rooms and a cozy lounge area. Organic meals served by request. Laundry £1.50. Open daily July-Aug.; call 48hr. in advance. Dorms £13, under 18 £9; doubles £29. MC/V. ❷

Base Lodge, 16 the Parks, Minehead (☎01643 703 520). Excellent location in the center of Minehead with easy access to Exmoor's trails. Owners Graham and Wendy are full of hiking advice. Bike and gear storage. Reception 9am-7pm. Call ahead in summer, especially for private rooms. Dorms £13.50; singles £15; doubles £20. MC/V. ❶

Ocean Backpackers, 29 St. James Pl. (☎01271 867 835; www.oceanbackpackers.co.uk). Surfer-centric hostel on Ilfrecombe's main drag. Rooms are cramped, but the lounge has a pool table and video games. Dorms £9-12; doubles £15-16. MC/V. ❶

South Leigh Hotel, Runnacleave Rd., Ilfracombe (☎01271 863 976; www.south-leigh.co.uk), next to the Tunnel Beaches. Least expensive B&B in town, with huge ensuite rooms and a bar. Typically full of tour groups, so call ahead to book a spare room. Full English breakfast £5. All rooms £15. MC/V. ❶

HIKING AND OUTDOORS

With wide-open moorland in the west, wooded valleys in the east, and coastal paths, Exmoor has a varied landscape best toured on foot or bike. The **Exmoor National Park Rangers** lead nature and moorland **tours** (☎01398 323 665; £3 per person for up to 4hr., over 4hr. £5). NPICs offer 1½-10 mi. walks (£3-5, p. 218). The **National Trust** leads walks with various themes, including summer birds, butterflies, deer, and archaeology. (☎01643 862 452. £1-8 per person.) More walks are listed in the *Exmoor Visitor*, free at NPICs and TICs.

Barnstaple isn't a particularly suitable hiking base, but it is the largest town in the region, a transportation center, and the best place to get gear. Since getting to Barnstaple can be a logistical nightmare, consider continuing on to Exford or Dulverton to be a bit closer to the hiking action. Two good points to start woodland treks are **Blackmoor Gate,** 11 mi. northwest of Barnstaple, and **Parracombe,** 2 mi. farther northwest. Both are on the Barnstaple-Lynton bus route (#309). The **Tarka Trail** starts in Barnstaple and traces a 180 mi. figure-eight, 31 mi. of which are bicycle-friendly. **Tarka Trail Cycle Hire,** at the Barnstaple train station, is located at the trailhead. (☎01271 324 202. £10 per day. Open daily Apr.-Oct. 9:25am-5pm.) The *Coast Path* booklet (£2.75), available at any Exmoor TIC, details three walks from Minehead to Combe Martin, with color-coded paths and marked stops. Only 1 mi. from the park's eastern boundary, **Minehead** is a fantastic place to start hiking. The busy seaside resort provides plenty of lodging and a **nature trail,** beginning on Parkhouse Rd. The 630 mi. **South West Coast Path** (p. 187) starts in Minehead and ends in Poole. Contact the South West Coast Path Association for more information (☎01752 896 237; www.swcp.org.uk). The trailhead is on Quay St.—follow signs for "Somerset and North Devon Coastal Path." The **YHA Minehead** (p. 219) sits within the Quantock Hills, England's first designated "Area of Outstanding Beauty." Ordnance Survey Map Explorer 140 marks all the walking paths through Quantock (☎01278 732 845).

Set in wooded valleys 9 mi. along the South West Coast Path from Minehead, **Porlock** offers good hiking and horseback riding. The TIC sells *13 Narrated Walks around Porlock* (£2), which includes a 2 mi. hike to **Weir-Culborne Church,** England's smallest church, and an 8 mi. trek to Exmoor's highest point, **Dunkery Beacon** (1721 ft.). The TIC also has a list of local stables, including **Burrowhayes Farm Riding Stables,** West Luccombe, 1 mi. east of Porlock off the A39. (☎01643 862 463. Open Easter-Oct. M-F and Su. Last ride 3:30pm. Pony rides £14 per hr.)

England's "Little Switzerland," the upper village of **Lynton** sits overlooking its twin village, the lower, waterfront **Lynmouth.** The **Cliff Railway,** a Victorian-era water-powered lift, shuttles visitors between the two villages—otherwise it's a steep walk between them. (☎01598 753 486. Open daily late July-Aug. 10am-9pm; June and Sept. 10am-7pm; Oct.-May call ahead. £2, bikes £3.) **Exmoor Coast Boat Trips,** at the Lynmouth Quay, leads drift-fishing trips and runs to Lee Bay and the Valley of Rocks. (☎01598 753 207. 1 trip per day, inquire before 11am. Both trips 1hr. £10.) A short walk from the harbor, **Glen Lyn Gorge,** at the Lynmouth Cross-roads, showcases hydroelectric power on its ravine walk. (☎01598 753 207. Open Easter-Oct. 10:30am-5:30pm. £4.) **Dunster** is a tiny village of cobblestone sidewalks 2½ mi. east of Minehead. Set above the town on a tor, the **Dunster Castle** houses England's only leather tapestries and what's rumored to be the oldest bathroom in Somerset. (☎01643 821 004. Open Mar.-Oct. M-W and Sa-Su 11am-5pm. Last admission 4:30pm. Gardens open daily 11am-4pm. £7.80. Gardens only £4.30.)

White-washed **Ilfrecombe** sits between Lynton and Woolacombe on the coastal path. With sandy beaches, hidden coves, and active surf, the small town makes a great seaside alternative to explore Exmoor. The **Tunnel Beaches** were built by Victorians as saltwater bathing pools in the 1820s. Hand-carved tunnels open onto secluded beaches, with one pool still open and plenty of salty water to dive into. **Kayak** from the beaches for £10 per hr. (☎01271 879 882; www.tunnels-beaches.co.uk. Open daily Easter-July and Sept. 10am-6pm; July-Aug. 9am-7pm; Oct. 10am-5pm. £2, concessions £1.75.)

DARTMOOR NATIONAL PARK

Although it is just a few miles from Plymouth and the crowded streets of Exeter, Dartmoor National Park seems a world away. Hikers fill the park each summer, and small villages greet travelers with local brews and Devon cream tea.

▐ TRANSPORTATION

Public transportation in Dartmoor can be scarce. The invaluable *Discovery Guide to Dartmoor by Bus and Train* (free at TICs) has a map and timetables. The bus stations and TICs also carry booklets of bus schedules for the four areas of Dartmoor. **Disabled visitors** should also look for the *Access Guide to Dartmoor Towns and Villages*, available at TICs. Travelers planning to use public transportation in Dartmoor should consider purchasing **Explorer** tickets, which allow unlimited travel on services like Stagecoach (one-day £6) and First (one-day £5.50). **Sunday Rover** tickets allow unlimited travel on all buses and local trains on Sundays in summer (£5). The Rover Helpline (☎01837 54545) is open from 9am to 6pm on Sundays and bank holidays. For updated timetables, contact Traveline (☎08706 082 608). Only one **train** services the park. The Dartmoor Line (☎01837 55637) runs from Okehampton to Exeter Central and Exeter St. David's from late May to mid-September (45min.; Su 5 per day; single day return £3.50, day rover £6).

Bus service is more extensive. Prices change often—some travelers report that sometimes bus drivers don't even charge. Make sure to pick up a free local bus guide from the TIC for the most up-to-date information. First DevonBus (☎0845 600 1420, fare inquiries 01752 402 060) #82, a.k.a. the "Transmoor Link," connects **Plymouth** to **Exeter** (late July and Aug. M-F 2 per day; from late May to late Sept. Sa 2 per day, Su 5 per day), via **Yelverton, Princetown, Postbridge, Moretonhampstead,** and **Steps Bridge.** Bus #359 also connects Exeter to Moretonhampstead (50min., M-Sa 7 per day). For the northwestern parts of the park, take a bus from Plymouth to **Tavistock** and **Yelverton** in the west (#83 or 86; 1hr., 3 per hr.) or Okehampton in the north (#86 or 118; 1½-2hr.; M-Sa 9 per day, Su 3 per day). To reach **Okehampton** from Exeter, take X9/10/11 (1hr.; M-Sa every hr., Su 2 per day). Connect to smaller towns via local buses in Tavistock (#86 or 118; 1hr.; M-Sa every hr., Su 7 per day).

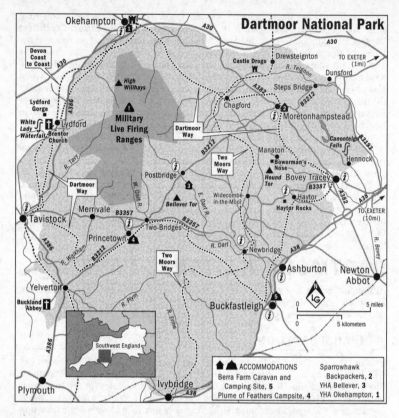

Dartmoor National Park

ACCOMMODATIONS
Berra Farm Caravan and Camping Site, **5**
Plume of Feathers Campsite, **4**
Sparrowhawk Backpackers, **2**
YHA Bellever, **3**
YHA Okehampton, **1**

To reach the park's southern towns, try Stagecoach Devon (☎ 01392 427 711). Bus X38 runs from Plymouth to Exeter (M-Su every hr.). First X80/81 runs to **Ivybridge** (45min.; M-Sa at least 1 per hr., Su 8 per day) and **Torquay** (1-1¼hr.).

✸ 🛈 ORIENTATION AND PRACTICAL INFORMATION

Dartmoor National Park sits in Dartmoor county, 7 mi. inland from the southern coast. Roughly diamond shaped, the park lies between the towns of Okehampton in the north, Tavistock in the west, Ivybridge in the south, and Bovey Tracey and Ashburton in the east. Rivers and hiking paths crisscross the park. A Range Danger Area (used by the military) occupies its northwest corner—keep out of this area. The city of Exeter is 10 mi. east of the park; Plymouth is 5 mi. south. All NPICs and TICs stock the indispensable, free *Dartmoor Visitor*, which has a map and listings of events, accommodations, and guided walks. As signs in TICs will often tell you, you can "learn moor" at www.dartmoor-npa.gov.uk.

National Park Information Centres: The NPICs are staffed by park officials and often house small park exhibits.

Haytor: (☎ 01364 661 520), on the B3387, midway between Bovey Tracey and Whitticombe. Open Easter-Oct. daily 10am-5pm; Nov.-Dec. Sa-Su 10am-4pm.

Newbridge: (☎01364 631 303), in the Riverside car park. Open Easter-Oct. daily 10am-5pm; Nov.-Dec. Sa-Su 10am-4pm.

Postbridge: Yelverton Rd., Moretonhampstead (☎01822 880 272), in a car park off the B3212. Open Easter-Oct. daily 10am-5pm; Nov.-Dec. Sa-Su 10am-4pm.

Princetown (High Moorland Visitor Centre): The Square, Tavistock Rd. (☎01822 890 414), in the former Duchy Hotel. The main visitors center for the park, with an exhibit on the area. Sells hiking supplies like walking sticks and waterproof map cases. Open Easter-Oct. M-Sa 10am-6pm, Su 10am-5pm; Nov.-Dec. daily 10am-4pm.

Tourist Information Centres: The following TICs offer in-town and regional advice as well as information about Dartmoor.

Ashburton: Town Hall, North St. (☎01364 653 426). Open M-Sa 9am-4:30pm.

Bovey Tracey: Lower Car Park, Station Rd. (☎01626 832 047). Open Easter-Oct. M-F 10am-4pm, Sa 9:30am-3:30pm.

Buckfastleigh: The Valiant Soldier (☎01364 644 522). Open Easter-Oct. M-Sa 12:30-4:30pm.

Moretonhampstead: 11 The Square (☎01647 440 043). Books accommodations. Donations requested. Internet access. Open Apr.-Oct. daily 9:30am-5pm; Nov.-Mar. F-Su 10am-5pm.

Okehampton: 3 West St. (☎01837 53020), in the courtyard adjacent to the White Hart Hotel. Books accommodations with a 10% deposit. Open Easter-Oct. M-Sa 10am-5pm; Nov.-Easter M and F-Sa 10am-4:30pm.

Tavistock: Town Hall Building, Bedford Sq. (☎01822 612 938). Books accommodations for a 10% deposit. Open Apr.-Oct. M-Sa 9:30am-5pm; Nov.-Mar. M-Tu and F-Sa 10am-4:30pm.

ACCOMMODATIONS

B&B signs often appear on pubs and farmhouses along the roads. It's wise to stick to those listed at the TIC and to book ahead. Try www.dartmooraccommodation.co.uk for more options. In **Okehampton,** a few B&Bs are on **Station Road** between the train station and the town center. **Tavistock,** the largest town in the area, has more expensive options near the bus station, but single rooms are scarce. Tavistock is best for stocking up on supplies and is a transportation hub for the park. **Moretonhampstead** ("Moreton" to the locals) and **Princetown** are the two largest villages in the park and can serve as good hiking bases.

HOSTELS

YHA Bellever (☎01822 880 227), 1 mi. southeast of Postbridge village. Bus #98 from Tavistock stops in front. #82 from Exeter or Plymouth (Oct.-Easter Sa-Su; late July-Aug. M-F) stops in Postbridge; from there, walk west on the B3212 and turn left on Bellever (20-25min. walk). In the heart of the park, popular with adventure-bound school groups. Reception 7-10am and 5-10:30pm. Dorms £15.50, under 18 £10. MC/V. ❷

YHA Okehampton, Klondyke Rd. (☎01837 539 16)., a 15min. walk from the town center. From the TIC, bang a right on George St., right onto Station Rd., and continue under the bridge. Converted railroad warehouse. Game room and kitchen. Mountain bike rental £10 per day. Reception 8-10am and 5-10pm. Open Feb.-Nov. Dorms £15.50, under 18 £11. Camping Feb.-Nov. £5, under 18 £4. MC/V. ❷

Sparrowhawk Backpackers, 45 Ford St., Moretonhampstead (☎01647 440 318; www.sparrowhawkbackpackers.co.uk). From the bus car park, turn left toward the church; take the left fork and turn left onto Ford St. Sky-lit bunkhouse and courtyard with chickens. Vegetarian kitchen and comfortable beds. Dorms £14. Cash only. ❷

CAMPING

Although official **campsites** and **camping barns** exist, many camp on the open moor. Most of Dartmoor is privately owned, but permission of the owner is required only in certain areas; consult a park map or NPIC for information on land access.

SOUTHWEST ENGLAND

Camping is allowed on non-enclosed moor land more than ¾ mi. from the road or out of sight of inhabited areas; camping is prohibited within sight of any paved road, in common areas used for recreation, or on archaeological sites. Campers may stay only 2 nights in a single spot and must not build fires.

Check www.dartmoor-npa.gov.uk or www.discoverdartmoor.com before heading out, or consult *Camping and Backpacking on Dartmoor* (free at NPICs). When using official campsites, call ahead for reservations, especially in summer. **YHA Okehampton ❶** also offers camping (p. 223).

> **Buckfastleigh: Berra Farm Caravan and Camping Site,** Colston Rd. (☎01364 642 234), 1½ mi. from town center. Follow the signs for the Otter Park, continue 200 yd. past the entrance, and walk 1 mi. down Old Totnes Rd. 2-person tent £8. ❶

> **Princetown: Plume of Feathers Campsite and Camping Barn** (☎01822 890 240; www.plumeoffeathers-dartmoor.co.uk), behind the Plume of Feathers Inn, opposite the NPIC. Solid bunks with showers and access to TV. Book 2-3 months in advance. The "new bunk" has an indoor bathroom; the "old bunk" bathroom is outdoors. Bunks £10. Campsites £5.50. Showers included. MC/V. ❶

⚑ ⚑ HIKING AND OUTDOORS

The Dartmoor Commons Act of 1985 gives visitors free reign to trek the registered common land in Dartmoor, but access may be restricted in other areas; consult the free pamphlet *Walking on Dartmoor* or www.openaccess.gov.uk for specifics. Ordnance Survey Explorer Map #28 (1:25,000; £7.45) is essential. The **Dartmoor Rescue Group** is on call at ☎999. The Devon Air Ambulance, for medical emergencies only, can be reached directly at ☎466 666 (see **Wilderness Safety,** p. 50).

The rugged terrain of Dartmoor offers unparalleled **hiking.** The **National Park Authority** conducts guided walks (1-6hr.; £3.50-6, free if arriving at starting point by public transportation), which are listed in the *Dartmoor Visitor* and by the events hotline (☎01822 890 414). The free *Dartmoor Walks* compiles eight of the most popular routes. **Dartmoor Way** is a 90 mi. circular route that hits the park's main towns. The 180 mi. **Tarka Trail** runs from Okehampton to Exmoor National Park in the north (p. 220). The trail recently went digital with audio tours marking the way. You can download the audio clips at www.northdevonbiosphere.co.uk, put them on your mp3 player, and listen when you come to markers. The 102 mi. **Two Moors Way** also connects the two parks, running from Lynmouth to Ivybridge.

The area is crowned by several peaks, the highest of which is **High Willhays** (2038 ft.). The peak, a hilly 4 mi. from Okehampton, is accessible only by foot. A mile from Lydford, the 1½ mi. **Lydford Gorge** has a lush forest and a whirlpool known as the **Devil's Cauldron.** Walk along the top of the gorge to reach the fantastic 90 ft. **White Lady Waterfall.** A circular walk of the gorge takes about two hours, but you can also start at one entrance and walk to the other. The latter option lets you see both the cauldron and the waterfall, and buses pick up and drop off at both entrances. (☎01822 820 320. Open daily Apr.-Sept. 10am-5pm; Oct. 10am-4pm. Oct.-Mar. 10:30am-3pm. Last admission 30min. before close. £5.20.)

A wealth of **Bronze Age structures,** the remains of a Neolithic civilization, cluster near Merrivale. Merrivale is on the #98 and 172 (summer only) bus routes. Haytor, near Bovey Tracey, features numerous tors, including the massive **Haytor Rocks** and the ruins at **Hound Tor,** where excavations unearthed the remains of 13th-century huts and longhouses. Venture 1 mi. north from Manaton to discover the 40 ft. **Bowerman's Nose,** named after the man who first recognized the rock's resemblance to the human organ. Also near Bovey Tracey is the 220 ft. **Canonteign Falls,**

England's highest waterfall; leave plenty of travel time. (☎01647 252 434. Open daily 10am-6pm or dusk. Last admission 1hr. before close. £5.75.)

Dartmoor's roads are good for **cycling.** Bookended by Ilfracombe and Plymouth, the 102 mi. **Devon Coast to Coast** route winds along rivers and rural countryside. The 11 mi. portion between Okehampton and Lydford is known as the **Granite Way** and offers traffic-free biking along a former railway line. **Okehampton Cycle Hire** rents bikes. From Fore St., go uphill on North St., then bear left off the main road, continuing downhill to the T-junction; follow signs for Garden Centre. (☎01837 532 48. Open M-Sa 9am-5pm, Su 10am-4pm. £9.50 per day.) For **horseback riding,** NPICs can refer you to stables (rides £8-16 per hr.). **Dartmoor Safaris** operates **tours** through the moors in SUVs. Most tours leave from Plymouth Bus Station. Thursday tours leave from The Strand, Torquay. (☎01752 500 567; www.dartmoorsafaris.co.uk. 8hr. tours depart Apr.-Sept. 9-9:30am £20.)

WARNING. The Ministry of Defense uses parts of the northern moor for target practice and has done so since the 1880s. Consult the *Dartmoor Visitor* or a current Ordnance Survey map for the boundaries of the danger area, which changes yearly. Weekly firing schedules are available in NPICs, post offices, police stations, hostels, campsites, and pubs; by military freephone (☎0800 458 4868); and online at www.dartmoor-ranges.co.uk. Boundaries are marked by red and white posts, and live firing areas are designated by red flags by day and red lamps by night. Do not handle military debris.

◉ SIGHTS

The Dartmoor landscape stretches across 368 sq. mi. of moorland, with Bronze Age burial mounds and stone circles scattered throughout. Also prevalent are **tors,** granite towers that resulted from thousands of years of geological activity.

CASTLE DROGO. The "last castle in England" was built from 1910 to 1930 for tea baron Julius Drewe, who believed he was a descendant of a 10th-century Norman and wanted to live accordingly. Ancient tapestries surround "modern" conveniences and 20th-century furniture, including a pre-WWII foosball table. From the castle, easy 3-4 mi. hikes go to the **River Teign** and its **Fingle Bridge,** where there are croquet lawns open all summer with equipment for rent. *(Take bus #173 from Moretonhampstead or Exeter, 174 or 179 from Okehampton. ☎01647 433 306. Open Mar.-Oct. M and W-Su 11am-5pm. Last admission 4:30pm. Grounds open daily 10:30am-5:30pm. £7.)*

PRINCETOWN PRISON. Dartmoor's maximum-security prison in Princetown, the highest town in England, is still in use today and has a museum to showcase its history. The surrounding moorland is the setting for Sherlock Holmes's famed escapade, *The Hound of the Baskervilles,* which emerged from a Dartmoor legend of a black dog that stalked a not-so-nice aristocrat. The **Dartmoor Prison Heritage Centre,** a 10-15min. walk up Tavistock Rd. from the TIC, features a gallery of weapons made by inmates, including a knife made of matchsticks. *(☎01822 892 130. Open daily 9:30am-12:30pm and 1:30-5pm. £2, concessions £1.)*

BUCKLAND ABBEY. A few miles south of Yelverton, the abbey was built by Cistercian monks in 1273 and was later bought by Sir Francis Drake, who was born on a nearby farm. The abbey houses Drake's drum, and it is said that when England is in grave danger, the drum will sound to defend the mother country. *(Citybus #55 or 48 from Yelverton or 48 from Plymouth to the Milton Combe stop. ☎01822 853 607. Open from mid-Mar. to Nov. M-W and F-Su 10:30am-5:30pm; from Dec. to mid-Mar. Sa-Su and sometimes F 10:30am-5:30pm. Last admission 45min. before close. £7.40, grounds only £4.)*

TORQUAY
☎ 01803

The largest city in the Torbay resort region and the self-proclaimed "English Riviera," Torquay (Tor-KEY) isn't quite as glamorous as the French original. However, the town Agatha Christie called home and in which the fictional Basil Fawlty ran his madcap hotel does have plenty of beaches, palm trees, and stimulating nightlife. A popular resort area for British city-dwellers, Torquay is a good base for exploring the sunnier parts of the southwestern English coast.

📟 TRANSPORTATION AND PRACTICAL INFORMATION. Torquay's **train station** (open M-F 7am-5:45pm, Sa 7am-4:45pm, Su 9:40am-5:10pm) is off Rathmore Rd., near the Torre Abbey gardens. To get to town, take a left and walk along the shoreline. **Trains** (☎08457 484 950) go to: Bristol (2hr., 6 per day, £23); Exeter (45min., every hr., £7.50); London Paddington (3½hr., 1 per day, £48); London Waterloo (4hr., 1 per day, £48); Plymouth (1½hr., every hr., £10). **Buses** depart from The Pavilion, the roundabout where Torbay Rd. meets The Strand. The Stagecoach office, 15 Victoria Parade, has information on its buses. (☎664 500. Open M-F 9am-5pm, Sa 9am-1pm.) Bus #85 runs to Exeter (1½hr.; May-Sept. M-Sa 2 per hr., Su 3 per day; Oct.-Apr. M-Sa 2 per hr.; £5.20), as does the more direct X46 (1hr.; M-Sa every hr., Su 7 per day; £5.20). First buses X80 and X81 run to Plymouth (1¾hr., every hr., £6). Torbay Cab Co. **taxis** (☎292 292) are on call 24hr.

The **Tourist Information Centre,** Vaughan Parade, past the Pavilion shopping center, arranges theater bookings, offers discounted tickets for attractions, and books accommodations for a 10% deposit. The TIC also sells tickets for the **Eden Project** (p. 243). (☎08707 070 010; www.englishriviera.co.uk. Open June-Sept. M-F 9:30am-5:30pm, Su 10am-4:30pm; Oct.-May M-Sa 9:30am-5pm.) Cruise Tours offers **tours** (1hr.; £6) from Princess Pier to Brixham (Western Lady Ferry Service) and Paignton (Paignton Pleasure Cruises ☎529 147). Buy tickets for both at the booth on Victoria Parade (open daily 9am-5pm). Other services include: **banks** on Fleet St.; Thomas Cook **bureau de change,** 54 Union St. (☎352 100; open M and W-Sa 9am-5:30pm, Tu 10am-5:30pm); **Sparkle Launderette,** 63 Princes Rd., off Market St. (☎293 217; wash £3-3.50, dry £2-3; open M-F 9am-7pm, Sa 9am-6pm, Su 10am-4pm; last wash 2hr. before close); **police,** South St. (☎08705 777 444); a **pharmacy,** 2 Tor Hill Rd. (☎213 075; open M-F 9am-6pm, Sa 9am-5pm); **Torbay Hospital,** Newton Rd. (☎614 567); free **Internet** access at the **library,** Lymington Rd., beside the Town Hall (☎208 300; open M, W, F 9:30am-7pm, Tu 9:30am-5pm, Th 9:30am-1pm, Sa 9:30am-4pm) and at **PC Bits,** Market Shopping Court, Market St. (☎299 550; £1 per 20min.; open M-Sa 9:30am-4:30pm); and the **post office,** 25 Fleet St., with a **bureau de change** (☎0845 722 3344; open M-Sa 9am-5:30pm). **Post Code:** TQ1 1DB.

🏠 ACCOMMODATIONS AND FOOD. Torquay's hotels and B&Bs are busy during summer, especially in August; book rooms in advance. Find less expensive beach hotels on Babbacombe Road, including **Torwood Gardens Hotel ❸,** 531 Babbacombe Rd., where rooms provide respite 5min. from the surf. (☎298 408. Breakfast included. Apr.-Oct. singles £25; doubles £50. Nov.-Mar. singles £28; doubles and twins £45. MC/V.) Cheaper B&Bs line Scarborough Road and Morgan Avenue. Flower boxes and walls covered in chalk-scrawled poems foster a warm atmosphere at **Torquay Backpackers ❷,** 119 Abbey Rd. Ask if one of the ensuite rooms is available when you book—they're the same price. (☎299 924; www.torquaybackpackers.co.uk. Laundry £3.50. Internet access £1 per 20min. Reception 9am-10pm. June-Sept. dorms £13; doubles £30. Oct.-May dorms £10; doubles £24. MC/V.)

Buy **groceries** at Tesco, 25-26 Fleet St. (☎351 400. Open M-Sa 7am-10pm, Su 11am-5pm.) **No. 7 Fish Bistro ❸,** Inner Harbor, Beacon Terr., across from Living Coasts, is the place to splurge for superb seafood (£11-17) in a cozy setting. (☎295

055; www.no7-fish.com. Open M-Tu 7-9pm, W 12:15-1:45pm and 6-9:45pm, Th-Sa 12:15-1:45pm and 6-9:45pm, Su 7-9pm. Reservations recommended. AmEx/MC/V.) Locals flock to **Hanbury's** ❷, Princes St., 2 mi. up Babbacombe Rd., for sit-down fish and chips (₤7-11) and takeaway. Take bus #32 or 85 (8min., every 10-30min., ₤1.20) from The Strand to the Babbacombe stop. Hanbury's is up the road on the right. (☎314 616. Open M-Sa noon-1:45pm and 5:30-9:30pm; takeaway open 4:30-9:30pm. MC/V.) Push aside the bead curtains at **Richmonds** ❷, 59 Abbey Rd. for Mediterranean-inspired seafood and vegetarian dishes. Be sure to save room for a delicious mango smoothie. (☎296 081. Takeaway available. Open daily 11am-2pm and 6-9pm.)

🔲🔲 **SIGHTS AND BEACHES.** Opened in 2003 with a spectacular view of the bay, **Living Coasts**, Beacon Quay, is an aviary that recreates nearly all of the world's major coastal environments, from Africa to the Antarctic. (☎202 470; www.living-coasts.org.uk. Open daily Easter-Sept. 10am-6pm; Oct.-Easter 10am-dusk. Last admission 1hr. before close. ₤6.75, students ₤5.25.) To get out of the sun, head for the **Torquay Museum,** 529 Babbacombe Rd., which features an exhibition of Agatha Christie's time in Torquay. (☎293 975; www.torquaymuseum.org. Open from mid-July to Sept. M-Sa 9:30am-5pm, Su 1:30-5pm; from Oct. to mid-July M-Sa 9:30am-5pm. ₤3, students ₤1.50.) Mystery enthusiasts can also walk the **Agatha Christie Mile,** which starts at the Grand Hotel and visits places in Torquay that inspired the author. Pick up a free map from the TIC. **Princess Theatre,** Torbay Rd., offers a weatherproof option, presenting live entertainment throughout the year. (☎08702 414 120. Tickets ₤10-30. Box office open M-Sa 10am-6pm, until 8pm on performance nights.)

The weather in the "English Riviera" is not quite as ideal as in its more established French cousin, yet on the precious sunny days, locals flock to the beaches. **Torre Abbey Sands** draws hordes, but visitors can reach better beaches by bus. Just southeast of Torquay, **Meadfoot** (bus #200) features beach huts and pebbly shores. Take bus #200 north to rockier **Oddicombe,** hidden under a cove (every 10min.) and **Babbacombe,** where water sports await. Bus #34 heads farther north to peaceful **Watcombe** (15min., every 30min.) and nearly deserted **Maidencombe** (20min.).

🔲🔲 **NIGHTLIFE AND FESTIVALS.** When the sun dips and beaches empty, nightlife options come alive. **Mojo,** Palm Court Hotel, Torbay Rd., is a seaside hangout with Torquay's latest bar hours and dancing. Look for the huge murals as you head into town. (☎294 882. Live bands Sa. Open M-Th 11am-11pm, F-Sa 11am-1am, Su 11am-12:30am.) **Mambo,** 7 The Strand, changes from a spicy Thai restaurant to a saucy club at night. Enjoy two-for-one drinks daily 7pm-midnight. (☎291 112. Open M-Sa 11am-3am, Su 11am-2am.) During the last week of August, Torquay lives the high life during its annual **Regatta;** call the TIC for details.

PLYMOUTH   ☎01752

Plymouth is best-known not as a destination, but as a point of departure—Sir Francis Drake, Captain Cook, Lord Nelson, and the pilgrims all left from the city's harbor. Heavily bombed during WWII, much of Plymouth was rebuilt in an unfortunate industrial style. Now, modern shopping centers stand alongside the ancient pubs and cobblestone streets of the harborside Barbican district.

🔲 **TRANSPORTATION**

Plymouth lies on the southern coast between Dartmoor National Park and the Cornwall peninsula.

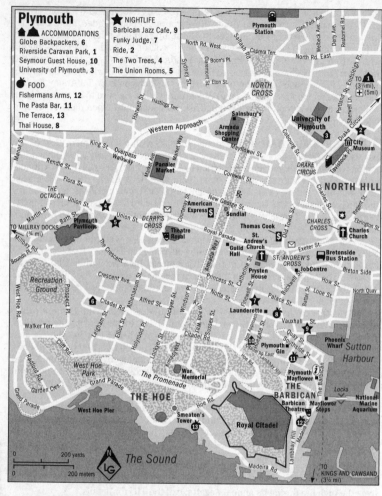

Plymouth

🏠🏠 ACCOMMODATIONS
Globe Backpackers, **6**
Riverside Caravan Park, **1**
Seymour Guest House, **10**
University of Plymouth, **3**

🍎 FOOD
Fishermans Arms, **12**
The Pasta Bar, **11**
The Terrace, **13**
Thai House, **8**

★ NIGHTLIFE
Barbican Jazz Cafe, **9**
Funky Judge, **7**
Ride, **2**
The Two Trees, **4**
The Union Rooms, **5**

Trains: Plymouth Station, North Rd. Ticket office open M-F 5:20am-8:30pm, Sa 5:30am-7pm, Su 8am-8:30pm. Buses #5 and 6 run to the city center (35p). Trains (☎08457 484 950) to **Bristol** (2hr., every 30min., £42), **London Paddington** (3½hr., every hr., £65), and **Penzance** (2hr., every 30min., £12.60).

Buses: Bretonside Station (☎254 542). Ticket office open M-Sa 9am-5:30pm, Su 9:30am-3:30pm. National Express (☎08705 808 080) to **Bristol** (3hr., 4 per day, £25) and **London** (5-6hr., 8 per day, £28). Stagecoach bus X38 runs to **Exeter** (1¼-1¾hr., 12-13 per day, £6).

Ferries: Brittany Ferries (☎08703 665 333; www.brittanyferries.com), at Millbay Docks. Follow signs to "Continental Ferries," 15min. from the town center. Taxi to the terminal £4. Buy tickets 24hr. ahead, although foot passengers may be able to purchase tickets upon arrival. Check in well before departure. To **Roscoff, France** (4-6hr., 12 per week, £58-65) and **Santander, Spain** (18hr., W and Su, £168).

Public Transportation: Citybus (☎222 221, line open M-F 8am-5:30pm, Sa 9am-5:30pm) **buses** from Royal Parade (from £1.10 round-trip; DayRover £3).

Taxis: Plymouth Taxis (☎606 060).

🌠 🚺 ORIENTATION AND PRACTICAL INFORMATION

The commercial district formed by **Royal Parade, Armada Way,** and **New George Street** is Plymouth's city center. Directly south, the **Hoe** (or "High Place") is a large, seaside park. The **Royal Citadel** is flanked by the Hoe to the west and, **The Barbican,** Plymouth's historic harbor, to the east.

Tourist Information Centre: 3-5 The Barbican (☎306 330; www.visitplymouth.co.uk), shares a building with the Mayflower Museum. Books accommodations for 10% deposit. Open Apr.-Oct. M-Sa 9am-5pm, Su 10am-4pm; Nov.-Mar. M-Sa 9am-5pm.

Tours: Plymouth Boat Cruises (☎822 797) leave from Phoenix Wharf for short trips around Plymouth Sound (1½hr., £5.50).

Financial Services: Banks line Old Town St., Royal Parade, and Armada Way. **Thomas Cook,** 9 Old Town St. (☎612 600). Open M-Sa 9am-5:30pm, Su 10:30am-4:30pm.

Work Opportunities: JobCentre, Buckwell and Hoegate St. (both ☎616 100). Open M-Tu and Th-F 9am-5pm, W 10am-5pm.

Launderette: Hoegate Laundromat, 55 Notte St. (☎223 031). Service wash only. £6.50 per load. Open M-F 8am-6pm, Sa 9am-1pm.

Police: Charles Cross (☎08705 777 444), near the bus station.

Hospital: Derriford Hospital (☎777 111). In Derriford, about 5 mi. north of the city center. Take bus #42 or 50 from Royal Parade.

Pharmacy: Kings Street Pharmacy, 140 King St. (☎662 712).

Internet Access: Library (☎305 907), Northhill. Free. ID required. Open M and F 9am-7pm, Tu-Th 9am-5:30pm, Sa 9am-4pm. Computers close 30min. before library close.

Post Office: 5 St. Andrew's Cross (☎08457 740 740). **Bureau de change.** Open M-Sa 9am-5:30pm. **Post Code:** PL1 1AB.

🚩 ACCOMMODATIONS

B&Bs (£18-35) line **Citadel Road;** rooms tend to be small and have a shared bath.

Globe Backpackers, 172 Citadel Rd. (☎225 158). Minutes from the Hoe, Globe has comfortable beds and spacious rooms. Kitchen, patio, and cozy TV room. Laundry £3. Reception 8am-11pm. Dorms £12; doubles £32. MC/V, with 50p service charge. ❶

Seymour Guest House, 211 Citadel Rd. East (☎667 002), where Hoegate St. meets Lambhay Hill. Recently renovated lodgings with a great location between The Barbican and The Hoe. Singles £25-36; doubles £40-45, ensuite £50-60. AmEx/D/MC/V. ❸

University of Plymouth, Gibbon St. (☎232 061; www.plymouth.ac.uk/holidayaccommodation). Dorm rooms in self-catering units. All dorms in city center. Book ahead. Singles £18 per night, £112 per week, ensuite £25/160; double ensuite £40/252. MC/V. ❷

Camping: Riverside Caravan Park, Longbridge Rd., Marsh Mills (☎344 122; www.riversidecaravanpark.com). Follow Longbridge Rd. 3½ mi. toward Plympton or catch the #50 bus. £8.25-12. MC/V. ❶

🌃 🍻 FOOD AND PUBS

Tesco Metro, on the corner of New George St., sells **groceries.** (☎617 400. Open M-Sa 7am-8pm, Su 11am-5pm.) **Pannier Market,** an indoor bazaar at the west end of

New George St., has fruit and vegetable stands and knick-knacks. (☎304 904. Open M-Tu and Th-Sa 8am-5:30pm, W 8am-4:30pm.)

Thai House, 63 Notte St. (☎661 600; www.thethaihouse.com). A black and white facade hides a brightly colored, tasty restaurant at the heart of Plymouth. Delicious pad thai. Entrees £6-18. Open Tu-Su 6-10:30pm. 15% takeaway discount. AmEx/MC/V. ❸

Fishermans Arms, 31 Lambhay St. (☎661 457). Plymouth's 2nd-oldest pub. Darts and pool table help pass time while you wait for food. Open M-Th noon-11 pm, F-Sa 11am-11pm, Su noon-10:30pm. Food served daily noon-3pm and F-Sa 6-9pm. MC/V. ❶

The Pasta Bar, 40 Southside St. (☎671 299), near the intersection with The Barbican. Heaping bowls of creative pasta dishes (£7-10) and a large vegetarian selection. Open M-Sa 11:30am-11:30pm, Su 11:30am-10:30pm. MC/V. ❷

The Terrace, Madeira Rd. (☎603 533). A self-service cafe with reasonably priced light meals (salads and sandwiches £6.25-7). Practically on the water, with views of docking boats. Open daily 8am-8pm. MC/V. ❶

👁 ⚓ SIGHTS AND BEACHES

THE HOE. Legend has it that Sir Francis Drake was playing bowls on the Hoe in 1588 when he heard that the Armada had entered the Channel. Finger in the air, he tested the wind and said "there is time still for me to win this game and defeat the Spanish." He did both. Today, the soft grass, sound of the ocean, and passing ice cream trucks make the Hoe a perfect place to spend the afternoon. Climb spiral steps and leaning ladders to the balcony of **Smeaton's Tower** for magnificent views of Plymouth and the Royal Citadel. (☎603 300; www.plymouthdome.info. Tower open Apr.-Oct. daily 10am-4pm; Nov.-Mar. Tu-Sa 10am-3pm. £2.50.)

PLYMOUTH GIN. The oldest working gin distillery in England, Plymouth has produced refreshing gin here since 1793. A tour of the factory includes an introduction to the ingredients specific to Plymouth gin, a tasting, and a free gin and tonic at the bar downstairs. Keep your eyes open for monk figurines, harkening back to the building's days as an abbey. (60 Southside St. ☎665 292; www.plymouthgin.com. 35min. tours. Open Mar.-Dec. M-Sa 10:30am-4:30pm, Su 11:30am-4:30pm. £6.)

PLYMOUTH MAYFLOWER. The small museum tells the tale of the Mayflower and everything you could possibly want to know about pilgrims. (3-5 The Barbican, above the TIC. ☎306 330. Open May-Oct. daily 10am-4pm; Nov.-Apr. M-Sa 10am-4pm. £2.)

ST. ANDREW'S CHURCH. St. Andrew's has been a site of Christian meetings since 1087. Three days of bombing in 1941 left it gutted. The building's brilliant stained glass and arching rafters are the products of postwar restoration. (Royal Parade. ☎661 414. Open M-F 9am-4pm, Sa 9am-1pm, Su for services only.)

NATIONAL MARINE AQUARIUM. Britain's largest and Europe's deepest tank is home to six sharks as well as Britain's only giant squid. The aquarium also has several interactive displays, including one on water energy. (The Barbican. ☎600 301; www.national-aquarium.co.uk. Open daily Apr.-Oct. 10am-6pm; Nov.-Mar. 10am-5pm. Last admission 1hr. before close. £9.50, students £8.)

OTHER SIGHTS. The still-in-use **Royal Citadel,** built 300 years ago by Charles II, may be seen only via a guided tour. (Tours May-Sept. Tu and Th 2:30pm; £3.50.) At the **Mayflower Steps,** on The Barbican, a balcony monument and American flag mark the spot from which the pilgrims set off in 1620. The actual steps are across the street, but the marked ones make for better pictures. The blackened shell of **Charles Church,** destroyed by a bomb in 1941, now stands in the middle of the Charles Cross roundabout as a memorial for victims of the Blitz.

BEACHES. Plymouth's shores are ideal for ships, but the beaches are just OK. Take a ferry to **Kingsand** and **Cawsand,** villages with small, pretty slips of sand. **Cawsand Ferry** leaves from the Mayflower Steps but sometimes cancels trips due to unfavorable winds. (☎ *07833 936 863. 30min., 4 per day, £3.)*

🅡 🌿 NIGHTLIFE AND FESTIVALS

Both young and old enjoy the traditional pubs along The Barbican. **Barbican Jazz Cafe,** 11 The Parade, strikes the right chord with daily live jazz. (☎ 672 127; www.barbicanjazzcafe.com. 15% student discount. Open M-Sa 8pm-2am, Su 8pm-midnight.) Next to St. Andrew's, ☒**Funky Judge,** 2 St. Andrews St., has the perfect mix of soul and style. Enjoy drinks in a leather booth or under the stars in the outdoor garden. (☎ 295 240. Open daily 11am-11pm). Farther inland, Union St. offers a string of bars and clubs. **The Union Rooms,** 19 Union St., is a popular early-evening bar; selected pints and wines are £1.50-2.50. (☎ 254 520. Open M-W and Su 10am-midnight, Th-Sa 10am-2am.) **Ride,** 2 Sherwell Arcade, North Hill, beyond the City Museum, draws a rowdy crowd of University of Plymouth students. (☎ 669 749. Tu live music. Su "Cheese and Wine"; cheese free, bottle of wine £5. Happy hour daily 4:30-9pm. Open M-Th 4:30pm-2am, F-Sa 4:30pm-3am, Su 4:30pm-1:30am.) **Two Trees,** 30 Union St., has late bar hours and a small venue. (☎ 561 189. Karaoke Tu and Su 10pm. Open M-Th 8pm-4am, F-Sa 8pm-4am, Su 7pm-2am.)

The **Theatre Royal,** on Royal Parade, has one of the West Country's best stages, featuring ballet, opera, and West End touring companies, including the Royal National Theatre. (☎ 267 222. Box office open M-Sa 10am-8pm; on non-performance days until 6pm. Tickets £16-44. Concessions available.) On the August Bank Holiday in even-numbered years, the public can explore the ships and submarines in the city's maximum-security naval base during **Plymouth Navy Days.** (☎ 553 941. Tickets on sale in late June.) The British **National Fireworks Championship** explodes in mid-August, while **Powerboat Championships** take place in mid-July.

🅡 DAYTRIPS FROM PLYMOUTH

LOOE. Picturesque **Looe** is split in half by a wide estuary. Far from the sandy shores and into the sea lies mile-wide **Looe Island,** until recently the only privately owned island in the UK, now under the care of the Cornish Wildlife Trust. **Boat tours** run around the coast and the bay; check for information at the quay. For hiking, the **Discovery Centre,** Millpool, on Looe's west side, stocks the free *Looe Valley Line Trails from the Track.* The **Tourist Information Centre,** Fore St., East Looe, books rooms for £2 plus a 10% deposit. *(Reach Looe by train from Plymouth via Liskeard (1hr., £5.80). Discovery Centre ☎ 01503 262 777. Open daily Feb.-June and Oct. 10am-4pm; July-Sept. 10am-6pm; Nov.-Dec. 10am-3pm. TIC ☎ 01503 262 072; www.southeastcornwall.co.uk. Open Apr.-Oct. daily 10am-5pm, unstaffed Nov.-Mar. M-F 10am-noon.)*

POLPERRO. Polperro was once England's most notorious smuggling bay—its proximity to the Channel Islands made it perfect for illegal alcohol and tobacco transportation. The **Polperro Heritage Museum of Smuggling and Fishing** displays photos of smugglers, a smuggler's sword, and stories about smugglers. This place loves its smugglers. The **Visitors Information Centre,** Talland St., is at end of New St. *(From Looe, take Hamblys Coaches ☎ 01503 220 660 or First buses #80A and 81A all 3 per day, £4.80. Heritage Museum ☎ 01503 273 005. Open daily Easter-Oct. 10am-6pm. Last admission 5:15pm. £1.60, children £1. Visitors Centre ☎ 01503 272 320. Open M-Sa 9:30am-5pm.)*

CLOVELLY. Clovelly's steep main street has 170 treacherous cobbled steps. The Rous family has owned the entire town for 700 years, but time-capsule upkeep isn't cheap—visitors pay a town admission fee, after which most sights are free. Choose between the restored 1930s **Fisherman's Cottage** *(open 9am-4:45pm)* or making your own pottery at **Clovelly Pottery.** *(☎01237 431 042. £1.50 per pot. Open M-Sa 10am-6pm, Su 10am-5pm.)* In winter, a short walk east along the shore brings trekkers to a surging waterfall, which slows to a stream in warmer months. **Boat trips** from the harbor run to **Lundy Island,** a nature reserve. *(☎01237 431 042; www.lundyisland.co.uk. 2-4 per week. 1-day round-trip £29; concessions available.)* Visitors pay admission to the village at the **Clovelly Visitor Centre,** in the car park. *(First bus #319 connects Clovelly to Bideford 40min.; M-Sa 6 per day, Su 2 per day; £2.20 and Barnstaple 1hr., £2.10. Town admission £4.75, children £3.25. Visitors Centre ☎01237 431 781. Open daily July-Aug. 9am-5:30pm, Sept.-June 9am-6:30pm.)*

CORNWALL

A rugged landscape of cliffs and sandy beaches, it's no wonder the Celts chose to flee to Cornwall in the face of Saxon conquest. Today, the westward movement continues with surfers, artists, and vacationers. Ports like Falmouth and Penzance celebrate England's maritime heritage, while beach-laden St. Ives and Newquay fulfill many a surfer's fantasies.

▐ TRANSPORTATION

Penzance is the southwestern terminus of Britain's **trains** (☎08457 484 950) and the best base from which to explore the region. The main rail line from **Plymouth** to **Penzance** bypasses coastal towns, but connecting rail service reaches **Newquay, Falmouth,** and **St. Ives.** A **Rail Rover** ticket may come in handy (3 days out of 7 £25.50, 8 of 15 £40.50). A **Cornish Railcard** costs £10 per year and saves a third off most fares.

The **First bus** network is thorough, although the interior of Cornwall is more often served by smaller companies. *The Public Transport Guide*, free at bus stations and TICs, compiles every route in the region. Buses run from **Penzance** to **Land's End** and **St. Ives** and from St. Ives to **Newquay,** stopping in the smaller towns along these routes. Many buses don't run on Sundays, and often only operate from May to September. A **First Day South West Explorer** offers unlimited travel on First buses (£7.50), while a **First Week Explorer** offers a week's unlimited travel anywhere in Cornwall (£28). The cliff paths, with their evenly spaced hostels, make for easy **hiking.** Serious trekkers can try the famous **Land's End** to **John O'Groats** route, running from the tip of Cornwall to the top of Scotland.

BODMIN MOOR

Bodmin Moor is high country, containing Cornwall's highest points: **Rough Tor** (1312 ft.) and **Brown Willy** (1378 ft.). The region is rich with ancient remains, like the stone circles that crowd Rough Tor. Legend has it that Camelford, at the moor's north edge, is the site of King Arthur's Camelot, and that Arthur and his illegitimate son Mordred fought each other at Slaughter Bridge, a mile north of Bodmin.

▐ TRANSPORTATION. The town of Bodmin is at the southern edge of Bodmin Moor, which spreads north to coastal (but not beachfront) Tintagel and Camelford. **Trains** (☎08457 484 950) travel from **Bodmin Parkway** (station open M-F 6:10am-8pm, Sa 6:30am-8pm, Su 10:35am-7:40pm) to London Paddington (4hr., every hr., £68), Penzance (1¼hr., 15 per day, £7.50), and Plymouth (40min., every

hr., £6). National Express **buses** (☎ 08705 808 080) go to Plymouth (1hr., 2 per day, £4.60). Western Greyhound (☎ 01637 871 871) #593 runs buses to Newquay (1hr., M-Sa 5 per day, £2.70). Access Camelford by first hopping the #555 to Wadebridge (30min., every hr., £2.20); from Wadebridge, take the #594 to Camelford (30min., M-Sa 5 per day, £2). To get to Camelford on weekends, or to reach Tintagel and Boscastle, take the #555 to Wadebridge (30min., every hr., £2.20) and transfer to #524 (M-Sa 4 per day, Su 3 per day, £2.40). **Hiking** is convenient from Camelford, and is the only way to reach the tors. **Bikes** can be hired in surrounding towns. **Hitchhiking** in this area is dangerous. *Let's Go* does not recommend hitchhiking.

■ **ORIENTATION.** Bodmin Moor, in central Cornwall, sits directly west of Dartmoor National Park. Its main city and transportation hub is Bodmin, 10 mi. inland from the Channel. The moor stretches across 30 mi.

■ **ACCOMMODATIONS. B&Bs** can be booked through the Bodmin TIC (p. 233). **Jamaica Inn ❶**, Bolventor, Launceston, is an 18th-century inn that inspired the novel of the same name by Daphne du Maurier. Take First bus X10 (M-Sa 6 per day) from Wadebridge. (☎ 01566 86250. Singles £65-80; doubles £90-100. AmEx/MC/V.) The nearest **YHA hostels** are in Boscastle (p. 235) and Tintagel (p. 234).

■ **HIKING AND OUTDOORS.** Most of the Moor is privately owned, but as of 2005, **hikers** can use the areas of the moor that are mapped as "Access Land" on local maps. **Camping** and **fires** are not allowed here. **Dogs** should be kept on a leash around livestock and always between March 1 and July 31, the breeding time for groundnesting birds. The moor was originally used to mine copper and quarry granite. Stay aware of your footing, as **mineshafts and abandoned buildings** remain.

The **River Fowley** divides the moor in half, running from the slopes of **Brown Willy** to end at **Golitha Falls** just outside Common Moor. The 60 mi. **Copper Trail** circumnavigates the moor, while the 17 mi. **Camel Trail** starts in Padstow and passes through Bodmin on the way to Poley's Bridge. A former railway track, the trail is mostly smooth and level, providing excellent biking. Numerous trails lead to the area's curious rock structures, including the **Cheesewring,** a precariously balanced set of rocks near the town of Minions. **Cardinham Woods,** to the east of Bodmin, is a dense forest which was originally planted for timber production but now offers shaded hiking and cycling paths. **Colliford Lake,** south of Bolventor, is the region's largest body of water, and nearby **Dozmary Pool** is rumored (among other places) to be the resting place for Excalibur. Ordnance Survey Explorer Map 109 (£8) covers Bodmin Moor and is available for purchase at most local TICs. Rent **bikes** at Bodmin Bikes & Cycle Hire, 3 Hamley Court, across the street from where the Camel Trail hits Bodmin. (☎ 01208 731 92. £10 per day. Open daily 9am-5pm.)

Guided walks are offered by locals through the Coast and Countryside Service. A schedule of these walks is available in *Coast Lines and Countryside News*, a guide distributed by the North Cornwall District Council (☎ 01208 265 644).

BODMIN   ☎ 01208

The town of Bodmin is at the heart of northern Cornwall. The historic capital of the region, Bodmin now caters to hikers, who pass through on their way to the Arthurian stomping grounds of Bodmin Moor. In town, only a few sights are of interest. The **Military Museum,** off St. Nicholas St., behind Bodmin General Station, displays several artifacts related to Tommy Atkins, the heroically ordinary soldier, as well as George Washington's Bible and account book (which reveals a missing US$3000). (☎ 728 10. Open M-F 9am-5pm; July-Aug. also Su 10am-5pm. £2.50.) The **Bodmin Jail,** Berrycombe Rd., was the safekeep for the crown jewels and Domesday Book during WWI. The museum's eerie exhibits on 18th-century jail life (and death) are complemented by a plethora of ghost stories. The jail is also near the Camel Trail and offers discounted bike rental with admission price. (☎762 92; www.bodminjail.org. Open daily 10am-dusk. £5.) Hidden in Bodmin's forests, the stately 17th-century mansion **Lanhydrock** was gutted by a fire in 1881 and is now encompassed by gardens. Inside, plaster ceilings portraying scenes from the Old Testament hang over Victorian furnishings. From Bodmin, take Western Greyhound bus #555 (round-trip £2.70), or travel 2½ mi. southeast on the A38. (☎265 950. House open from mid-Mar. to late Sept. Tu-Su 11am-5:30pm. Gardens open daily 10am-6pm. £9.40.) Outside Bodmin, **Camel Valley Vineyards** sit in the moors from which they create their award-winning wine. A full tour and wine tasting is a steal at £6.50 (Apr.-Oct. W at 5pm), while a shorter tour and glass of wine on the terrace is £4.50 (Apr.-Oct. W at 2:30pm). Follow the signs on the A389 from Bodmin toward Wadebridge or follow the Camel Trail out of Bodmin for about 3 mi. (☎779 59. Open Easter-Sept. M-Sa 10am-5pm; Oct.-Easter M-F 10am-5pm. MC/V.)

The **Bodmin General Station,** St. Nicholas St. (☎736 66), serves Bodmin & Wenford Railway's trains, which run to Bodmin Parkway and Boscarne Junction, 6 mi. toward Wadebridge. Look for Thomas and other childhood favorites to pull into the station. (☎0845 125 9678. Apr.-Sept. 4-7 per day. £10, children £6, family £28; Bodmin General to Boscarne Junction or Bodmin Parkway £7.50/4/21.50.)

While the building dates back to the 16th century, **Milobel House ❸,** 20 Lower Bore St., near the town center, provides modern rooms and a convenient location. (☎269 818. £30-35 per person. Cash only.) A mile north of town, camp at the **Camping and Caravanning Club ❶,** Old Callywith Rd., with laundry and showers. Head north of town on Castle St., which becomes Old Callywith Rd. (☎738 34. Open Apr.-Oct. £6.60 per person. Electricity available. Cash only.) To reach town from the **Bodmin Parkway Station,** 3 mi. away on the A38, take Western Greyhound **bus** #555 (every hr.; £2.20, day pass £6) or call Parnell's **Taxis** (☎750 00; £5 between station and town). For **car rental,** contact Bluebird Car Hire (☎07764 154 768), near St. Austell. The **Tourist Information Centre,** Shire Hall, Mount Folly, sells Ordnance Survey maps (£7.50). (☎766 16; www.bodminlive.com. Open Apr.-Oct. M-Sa 10am-5pm; Nov.-Apr. M-F 10am-5pm.) Other services include: **banks** on Fore St.; **police** (☎08705 777 444), up Priory Rd.; a Boots **pharmacy,** 34 Fore St. (☎728 36; open M-Sa 9am-5:30pm); and the **post office,** 40 Fore St. (☎08457 740 740; open M-F 9am-5:30pm, Sa 9am-12:30pm), behind Cost Cutters. **Post Code:** PL31 2HL.

TINTAGEL   ☎01840

Tintagel is a tiny seaside village proud of its connection to Arthurian lore. Its star attraction is the sprawling ruin of ◧**Tintagel Castle,** rumored to be the site of King Arthur's birth. Even if you don't buy into the lore, the views are worth the admission price. Be sure to see the rocky **Merlin's Cave,** beneath the castle ruins, at low tide, when you can climb through the caves to the other side of the island. Find the remains of a latrine that juts out from the cliffs so that the toilet's contents land in the churning sea below. (☎770 328. Open daily Apr.-Sept. 10am-6pm; Oct. 10am-5pm; Nov.-Mar. 10am-4pm. £4.50, concessions £3.40. Merlin's Cave free.)

 A NIGHT AT THE ROUND TABLE. Access to the castle ruins and cliffs is free at night, but be careful: slippery rocks and steps can be treacherous when trying to channel the spirit of King Arthur in the dark.

Inland, **King Arthur's Great Halls of Chivalry,** Fore St., allegedly held the round table of King Arthur. Millionaire Frederick Thomas Glasscock founded an Arthurian order of knights following WWI, hoping to spread chivalry and virtue. In its heydey, the order boasted 17,000 supporters, and visitors today can still put in an application to join. The Great Hall has two rooms: an antechamber with a light show telling the legend of King Arthur, and a hall with three round tables. The hall also contains 73 stained-glass windows portraying the virtues of a good knight as well as the shields of Arthur and his comrades. (☎770 526. Open daily summer 10am-5pm; winter 10am-dusk. £3.50, concessions £2.50.) Escape homages to Arthur on a 1½ mi. walk through **St. Nectan's Glen** to a 60 ft. waterfall, historically a spiritual healing center. From the Visitor Centre, head toward Bossiney for about 1 mi., then follow signs along the footpath to your right. (☎770 760. Open Easter-Oct. daily 10:30am-6:30pm; Nov.-Easter M, W, and F-Su 10:30am-6:30pm. £3.)

The **Tintagel Visitor Centre,** Bossiney Rd., has an exhibit separating Arthurian fact from fiction. (☎779 084. Open daily Mar.-Oct. 10am-5pm; Nov.-Feb. 10:30am-4pm.) Western Greyhound **buses** #594 (M-Sa) and 524 (Su) go to Wadebridge (40min., M-Sa 5 per day, £5) via Camelford (20min.; M-Sa 5 per day, Su 3 per day; £1.20). The **YHA Tintagel ❷,** at Dunderhole Point, is ¾ mi. from Tintagel and has views of the coast. The facilities are a bit cramped, but eating dinner on the patio overlooking the water more than makes up for it. Basic food is sold on site. Head out of town past St. Materiana's Church, then follow the footpath along the shore. The hostel is set in the side of the cliff and is nearly invisible from this approach; you'll be on top of it after about ¼ mi. (☎770 6068. Kitchen. Laundry £2.50. Lockout 10am-5pm. Open Easter-Oct. Dorms £13, under 18 £10. MC/V.)

BOSCASTLE ☎01840

Flanked by two grassy hills, tiny Boscastle is a scenic Cornish village divided by a sparkling river. This enviable valley location proved destructive in August 2004, when a flash flood swept through the village and destroyed the town center. The community recovered quickly, and visitors will find that the village's charm remains. The **National Trust Information Centre,** The Old Forge, Boscastle Harbour, offers hiking suggestions and sells maps. (☎250 353. Open Apr.-Oct. 10:30am-5pm.) The new **Boscastle Visitor Centre,** The Harbour, shows a video about the flood and has a small exhibit about the history of the town. Pick up the *Boscastle Village Trail Guide* (40p), which outlines walks through the area and points out the village's quaint sights. The visitors center is also the only place in the area to get **Internet** access. (☎250 010. Internet £1 per 15min. Open daily Easter-July 10am-5pm; July-Aug. 10am-7pm; Nov.-Mar. 10:30am-4:30pm.) Before he picked up his pen, Thomas Hardy was an architect and designed the church. In town, the **Museum of Witchcraft** is the largest of its kind. Its quirky collection of artifacts, trinkets, and newspaper articles explain and defend the occult. Look for the weighing chair used by witch hunters as well as audio stations containing spells from modern witches. (☎250 111. Open Easter-Halloween M-Sa 10:30am-6pm, Su 11:30am-6pm. Last admission 30min. before close. £3, "naughty little monsters" £16.)

Western Greyhound **buses** #524 and 594 leave from Boscastle to **Wadebridge** (1-1½hr.; M-Sa 9 per day, Su 3 per day; £2.40) via **Tintagel** (10min., £1), and to **Bude** (40min., £2.20). The self-catering **YHA Boscastle Harbour ❷** has an incredible location on the water. Reconstructed after the flood, the stables now boast four-star accommodations. (☎0870 770 5710. Dorms £15, under 18 £10. MC/V.) Five minutes from the coast, **The Old Coach House ❸,** on Tintagel Rd. at the top of the village, has ensuite rooms and English breakfast. (☎250 398. Open Mar.-Oct. £27-30. MC/V.)

PADSTOW ☎01841

Padstow's harbor is filled with the requisite sailboats, and its nearby beaches with lounging sunbathers. Near the more heavily touristed Newquay and St. Ives, Padstow has become a quiet alternative for a seaside holiday. The small town has

SOUTHWEST ENGLAND

drawn Rick Stein, the famous British seafood chef, and four of his restaurants to the streets of Padstow. Gourmet food and quaint culture come with a high price tag, so those not intent on blowing their budget on bite-sized portions and expensive B&Bs may choose to make this scenic town a daytrip.

▐ 🛈 TRANSPORTATION AND PRACTICAL INFORMATION. Western Greyhound **buses** #555 and 556 go to Bodmin from Padstow (45min., every hr., £4 round-trip) via Wadebridge and between Newquay and Padstow (2hr., 4-5 daily, round-trip £5). Buses arrive on the far side of the South Quay, a few minutes from the center of town and the TIC. The **TIC**, Red Brick Building, North Quay, books rooms for a 10% deposit. (☎533 449. Internet access £1 per 15min. Open Apr.-Oct. M-F 9:30am-5pm, Sa 10am-4pm; Nov.-Mar. M-F 9:30am-4:30pm.) **Rent bikes** at Padstow Cycle Hire, South Quay, in the car park. (☎533 533. Open daily from mid-July to Aug. 9am-9pm; from Sept. to mid-July 9am-5pm. £10 per day. Helmets £1.) **Fishing** and **boating trips** depart from the harbor. Sport&Leisure, North Quay, books and operates mackerel and reef fishing trips (2-8hr.) on the *Celtic Warrior;* anything you catch is yours. Call on the morning of your trip to confirm the launch time. (☎532 639. Trips daily Easter-Oct. 9am-5pm. £12 for 2hr., £30 for 4hr.) **Banks** cluster on Market Pl. and Duke St. Fill your prescriptions at Moss **pharmacy**, 8-10 Market St. (☎532 327. Open M-F 9am-5:30pm, Sa 9am-5pm.) There is a **post office** on Duke St. (Open M-F 9am-5:30pm, Sa 9am-1pm.) **Post Code:** PL28 8AA.

▐ 🛏 ACCOMMODATIONS AND FOOD. Lodgings in Padstow are pleasant but pricey (from £30). **Ms. Anne Humphrey ❸**, 1 Caswarth Terr., offers cozy rooms. By foot, follow New St. uphill from the harbor. (☎532 025. Singles £25; doubles £45. Cash only.) Find a wealth of knowledge at the home of **Peter and Jane Cullinan ❹**, 4 Riverside, along the harbor. The top-floor double has a balcony overlooking the bay, but the small room in the back is the cheapest. (☎532 383. Doubles £27-37. Cash only.) The nearest hostel, the **YHA Treyarnon Bay ❷**, is 4½ mi. from Padstow, on Tregonnan in Treyarnon. It's off the B3276; take bus #56. (☎0870 770 6076. Open Apr.-Feb. Dorms £15.50, under 18 £11. MC/V.) **Padstow Touring Park ❶**, a mile south of town on B3274/A389, offers camping and caravanning. (☎532 061. Laundry and camp shop. Open Apr.-Oct. Sites £9.50-13. Electricity £12.25-16. MC/V.)

With fresh fish and an almost unavoidable Rick Stein influence in the restaurant scene, you're pretty much guaranteed quality, expensive food. Splurge at **St. Petrocs Bistro ❹**, New St., a Rick Stein creation, offering mouth-watering seafood for £14-20. (☎532 700; www.rickstein.com. Open daily noon-2pm and 7-9:30pm. MC/V.) Take afternoon tea on 19th-century china at the intimate **Victorian Tea Room ❷**, 22 Duke St. (☎533 161. All-day breakfast £5. Open daily Apr.-Oct. 9am-7:30pm. Cash only.) Grab a plate of fish and chips (£8) at **Stein's Fish & Chips ❷**, South Quay, the most affordable of Rick Stein's many eateries. (☎532 700. Open M-Sa 11:30am-2:30pm and 5-9pm, Su noon-6pm. MC/V.)

◉ 🎵 SIGHTS AND ENTERTAINMENT. Beyond the ferry point near the TIC, an easy **coastal walk** ascends the cliffs for ocean views—follow the path past the war memorial to reach expansive sands and an island-studded bay. Cyclists converge in Padstow for the start of the **Camel Trail** and the 26 mi. **Saints' Way,** which follows the route of the Celtic saints who landed here from Ireland and Wales. The **National Lobster Hatchery,** South Quay, across from the bus stop, was built to save the ailing lobster industry from overfishing. Expectant lobster moms are brought here to lay their eggs, and visitors can see the insect-like babies in various stages of development. (☎533 877; www.nationallobsterhatchery.com. Open from May to mid-Sept. daily 10am-6pm; from mid-Sept. to Apr. M-Sa 10am-4pm. £3, concessions £2.) Numerous nearby beaches are perfect for exploring, surfing, and sunbathing.

SOUTHWEST ENGLAND

Cave-pocked **Trevone Beach** can be reached via bus #556 (5min.; M-Sa 7 per day, Su 5 per day). Bus #556 continues to remote **Constantine Bay** (15min.), with great surfing, and **Porthcothan Beach** (30min.), a good spot for tanning. The professionals at **Harlyn Surf School,** 23 Grenville Rd. in Padstow, teach to all levels at nearby Harlyn Bay. (☎533 076; www.harlynsurfschool.co.uk. Book in advance and meet at the school's trailer on Harlyn Beach. Open May-Oct. £30 per ½-day, £60 per day.) Black Tor **ferries** chug from Padstow Harbor across the bay to nearby **Rock,** where visitors will find sailing, waterskiing, windsurfing, and golfing. (☎532 239. 10-15min. Easter-Oct. daily 8am-8pm; Nov.-Easter M-Sa 8am-5pm. £2.)

NEWQUAY   ☎01637

Known to the hordes of teenage travelers who crowd the streets as "the new California," Newquay (NEW-key; pop. 20,000) is an incongruous slice of surfer culture in the middle of Cornwall. The town has long attracted riders for its superior waves (by England's standards), and a steady stream of partiers has transformed the once-quiet seaside resort into an English Ibiza, with wet T-shirt contests and dance parties that rage late into the night.

▆ TRANSPORTATION

Transportation info is available at the **train station** on Cliff Rd. (Ticket office open M-F 9am-4pm, Sa 9am-1pm.) **Trains** (☎08457 484 950) to Newquay all pass through Par (50min.; in summer M-F 8 per day, Sa-Su 5 per day; £4.50), where they connect to Bodmin (1hr.; 8 per day, Sa-Su 5 per day; £4), Penzance (1½hr., 12 per day, £11), and Plymouth (50min., 15 per day, £7). National Express (☎08705 808 080) **buses** depart to London (7hr., 4-7 per day, £36). Western Greyhound buses travel from Manor Rd. to Padstow (#556; 1½ hr., 1 per hr., £5), St. Austell (#521; 1hr., every hr., round-trip £3.60) and St. Ives (#501; 2¼hr., 2 per day, round-trip £5.50). Buses #89 and 90 go to Falmouth (1½hr., M-Sa every hr., round-trip £5). Get a 24hr. **taxi** from Fleet Cabs (☎875 000).

▐ PRACTICAL INFORMATION

A few blocks toward the city center from the train station, the **Tourist Information Centre,** Marcus Hill, has free maps and books accommodations for £2.50 in the office (£4 by phone) plus a 20% deposit. The TIC also handles all Western Union money transfers. A 24hr. computer information system is open to the public. (☎854 020; www.newquay.co.uk. Open June-Sept. M-Sa 9:30am-5:30pm, Su 9:30am-3:30pm; Oct.-May M-F 9:30am-4:30pm, Sa 9:30am-12:30pm.) Western Greyhound, 14 East St., runs **bus tours** to the Eden Project (p. 243) and nearby coastal towns. (☎871 871. 5-8hr. daily tours. £8-15.) Book tickets at the TIC.

Other services include: **banks** on Bank St. (most open M-Tu and Th-F 9am-4:30pm, W 10am-4:30pm); **work opportunities** at a very busy JobCentre, 32 East St. (☎894 900; open M-Tu and Th 9am-5pm, W 10am-5pm); **luggage storage** at Station Cafe (£2 per item; no overnight storage; open Apr.-Oct. daily 7am-3pm); a **launderette,** 1 Beach Parade, off Beach Rd. (☎875 901; wash £2.30-3, dry 20p per 4min., soap 45p; open M-F 10am-4pm, Sa 10am-3pm; last wash 1hr. before close); **police,** Tolcarne Rd. (☎08452 777 444); **Newquay Hospital,** St. Thomas Rd. (☎893 623); a Boots **pharmacy,** 15 Bank St. (☎872 014; open in summer M-F 8:30am-8:30pm, Sa 8:30am-7pm, Su 10:30am-4pm; in winter M-Sa 9am-5:30pm); **Internet** access at Cyber Surf @ Newquay, 2 Broad St., across from Somerfield (☎875 497; 9p per min.; open in summer M-Sa 10am-10pm, Su noon-8pm; in winter M-Sa 11am-6pm, Su noon-5pm) or at Quintdown Web, the giant yellow building across the street

(☎875 132; 5p per min.; open M-F 9am-5pm, Sa 9:30am-4:30pm.); and the **post office,** 31-33 East St. (☎08457 223 344; open M 8:45am-5:30pm, Tu-F 9am-5:30pm, Sa 9am-12:30pm). **Post Code:** TR7 1BU.

ACCOMMODATIONS

B&Bs (£18-30) are near the TIC; numerous **hostels** and surf lodges (£12-16) gather on **Headland Road** and **Tower Road,** near Fistral Beach. Accommodations fill up weeks in advance during surfing competitions, so call ahead in summer.

Fistral Backpackers, 18 Headland Rd. (☎873 146; www.fistralbackpackers.co.uk). Seconds from Fistral Beach, this surf lodge has everything you could need, from satellite TV to great advice and a warm bed. Lounge and patio are the perfect places to recover from a night out. Reception 24hr. Dorms £10-19. ❷

Matt's Surf Lodge, 110 Mount Wise (☎874 651; www.surflodge.co.uk). Between Fistral Beach and the town. You can't get much more laid-back than this. Hundreds of DVDs and a bar keep visitors happy when they're not hanging ten. Toast and all-day coffee and tea. High season £15, ensuite £17; low season £8/10. ❷

Newquay International Backpackers, 69-73 Tower Rd. (☎879 366; www.backpackers.co.uk). Friendly and funky, with a dining area that looks like the tube of a wave. The cozy common room is great for making friends. Rooms and showers are co-ed. Dorms £10-17; twins £11-17. July-Aug. 7-night min. MC/V. ❷

Original Backpackers, 16 Beachfield Ave. (☎874 668), off Bank St. Steps from the beach and nightlife. Kitchen. Laundry £3. Dorms £12-17; winter £8-10. MC/V. ❷

Camping: Trenance Chalet and Caravan Park, Edgcumbe Ave. (☎873 447). A campsite miraculously located in town. From the train station, turn right on Cliff Rd., then right on Edgcumbe Ave., and follow it for 15min. Laundry, restaurant, and cafe. Open Easter-Oct. £5-6.50 per person. Electricity 50p. AmEx/MC/V. ❶

FOOD AND PUBS

Sit-down restaurants in Newquay tend to be costly. Pizza and kebab shops, catering to late-night stumblers, fill the town center. Most takeaway is relatively cheap. For other options, head to pubs or Somerfield **supermarket,** at the end of Fore St. (☎876 006. Open July-Aug. M-Th and Sa 8am-9pm, F 8am-10pm, Su 11am-4pm; Sept.-June M-Th and Sa 8am-8pm, F 8am-9pm, Su 11am-4pm.)

Cafe Irie, 38 Fore St. (☎859 200). Cafe and coffee bar serving creative dishes and all-day breakfast options (full English £5, pancakes and bacon £3.75). Waitstaff plops down on sofas next to you to take your order while you groove to the music. Open July-Aug. daily 10am-midnight; Sept.-Nov. M-F 10am-5pm. Cash only. ❶

Ye Olde Dolphin, 39-47 Fore St. (☎874 262). Laden with old-world decor, combining kitsch and class to create a quality seafood restaurant. Meals are expensive, but take advantage of specials (6-8pm), including a 3-course meal for £12.45. Reservations recommended. Open M-Sa 6-11:30pm, Su noon-2pm and 6-10:30pm. MC/V. ❸

The Shack, 52 Bank St. (☎875 675). Sit-down restaurant with a beach theme and tasty dishes (£4-11), from vegetarian and Caribbean plates to the lunchtime Shack Wraps (£3.75-4.75). Open in summer daily 10am-11pm; in winter hours limited. MC/V. ❷

The Chy Bar and Kitchen, 12 Beach Rd. (☎873 415). Enjoy one of the best views in Newquay in this chic upstairs eatery on the beach. Lunch from £6.25, dinner entrees £11-18. Trendy bar crowd takes over after 7pm. Open daily 10am-2am. Food served until 11pm. Reservations for upstairs kitchen recommended. MC/V. ❷

BEACHES

Atlantic winds descend on **Fistral Beach** with a vengeance, creating what most consider to be the best surfing in Europe. The shores are less cluttered than the sea, where throngs of wetsuited surfers paddle out between the crests. Local surfers say that ominous skies often forecast the liveliest surf, but as always, use caution. Lifeguards roam the sands from May to September from 10am to 6pm.

 SOARING SYMBOLS. Avoid getting into trouble by paying close attention to safety flags. The space between checkered flags is designated for water craft, while swimming is permissible between red-and-yellow striped flags. Inflatables are forbidden when an orange flag is flying, and no swimming at all is allowed when the red flag flaps over the beach.

On the bay side, the sands are divided into four beaches: tamer waters at **Towan Beach** and **Great Western Beach,** smack dab in the middle of town, lure throngs of sunbathers and novice surfers. **Tolcarne Beach** and **Lusty Glaze Beach** are privately owned, with spotless sand and dry day facilities. Cross the Trethellan footbridge and head toward the sea to reach **Crantock Beach** and its sandy shores. **Sunset Surf Shop,** 106 Fore St., rents out surf paraphernalia. (☎877 624. Boards £5-10 per day, £12-25 per 3 days, £25-40 per week. Wetsuits or bodyboards £4-5/10-12/20. Open Apr.-Oct. daily 9am-6pm.) The professionals at **O'Neill Surf Academy** teach intro, one-day, and two-day courses for both amateur and advanced surfers. (☎01637 876 083. Book online at www.oneillsurfacademy.co.uk. Courses Mar.-Dec. Intro £30, 1-day £40, 2-day £75.)

NIGHTLIFE

Newquay teems with large groups of sun-kissed surfers and visitors ready to drink, dance, and drink some more. Watch out for ubiquitous stag and hen parties, and head toward the shore for more relaxed nightlife venues. The trail of surfer bars begins on **North Quay Hill,** at the corner of Tower Rd. and Fore St.

Central Inn, 11 Central Sq. (☎873 810), in the town center. A great place to grab early drinks. Watch the bustle from the crowded outdoor seating. Open M-Th 11am-11pm, F-Sa 11am-midnight, Su 11am-10:30pm.

On The Rocks, 14 The Crescent (☎872 897; www.ontherocksbar.co.uk). Eclectic live music, pool tables, and big-screen TVs playing surfing footage. A good time for everyone, from the posh to flip-flop devotees. £1 bottles on W. Open daily 10:30am-2am.

Belushi's, 35 Fore St. (☎859 111). Popular bar beneath St. Christophers is a great place to meet fellow travelers. Live music most nights, but if nothing's on, enjoy the billiards and loyal patrons. Open M-W and Su 11am-midnight, Th-Sa 11am-2am.

Sailors, 15 Fore St. (☎872 838). Elaborate lighting enhances the vibrant dance scene. Crowded downstairs pub. Tu "Unzipped" theme. W beach party. Open June-Sept. M-Sa 10pm-2am, Su 10pm-12:30am; Oct.-May Th-Sa 10pm-2am, Su 10pm-12:30am.

The Koola, 8-10 Beach Rd. (☎873 415). A relaxed crowd, with barefoot surfers fresh from the waves and dolled-up locals out on the town. Less hectic than other clubs in the area. 3 levels of dancing. Popular M drum and bass night. Open daily 9pm-2am.

Buzios, Cliff Rd. (☎870 300). Contemporary decor gives a Miami-like feel to this ultra-chic bar and pool hall. Dance the night away, cavort in leather booths, or stumble upstairs away from canoodling couples for a few games of pool. Open daily 11am-1am.

🎵 🌿 ENTERTAINMENT AND FESTIVALS

Everyone knows that there's great surfing and partying in Newquay, but on the off chance that bad weather or a hangover prevents one or the other, Newquay also provides other diversions. Head to the Rowing Club at the Harbour for **gig racing**, a traditional form of Cornish rowing. Refreshments follow at the clubhouse. (☎876 810. Races M at 7pm.) **Pitch & Putt**, where you hit a golf ball as hard as possible then tap, tap, tap it home, is popular. The most central course is located off Narcliff Rd. between Tolcarne and Lusty Glaze beaches. Enjoy the coastline on a stallion from the **Newquay Riding Centre,** Trenance Stables, Trenance Ln. Ride length varies based on experience. (☎872 699; www.newquayridingstables.co.uk. Open M-Sa. Call for tour times, prices vary depending on horse and length of ride.)

Several festivals and concerts coincide with local surf competitions. May is a busy month, with the **English Surf Championships** during the first week and the **Red Stripe British Longboard Championships** at the end. Souped-up VWs come to Newquay for the **Run to the Sun** festival, also at the end of May. In early August, the **RipCurl Boardmasters Championships** bring six days of surfing, music, and mayhem to Fistral's shoreline. (☎0208 789 6655. Tickets £29 per day, £50 for the weekend.) Check with the TIC events hotline (☎854 040) for the most up-to-date information, as weather can affect dates, especially of surfing competitions.

FALMOUTH   ☎01326

The historic port of Falmouth offers five sandy beaches, a busy city center with one-of-a-kind shops, and a harbor full of sailboats from around the world. Get a taste of history at the 450-year-old twin fortresses of Pendennis and St. Mawes, built by Henry VIII to protect England from Spanish and French invasion, or live the local life in the town's thriving restaurant and pub scene.

▶ TRANSPORTATION

Trains: Falmouth has 3 unmanned **train stations. Penmere Halt** is near Melvill Rd. and Killigrew St.; **Falmouth Town** is near the town center; and **Falmouth Docks** is near Pendennis Castle. Buy tickets M-F 9am-5pm by calling Lynne at ☎0870 224 9545. Debit or credit card only. Trains (☎08457 484 950) to: **Exeter** (3½hr., 8 per day, £15-30); **London Paddington** (5½hr., 5 per day, £69); **Plymouth** (2hr.; M-Sa 12 per day, Su 7 per day; £11.80); **Truro** (20min., every hr., £3).

Buses: All buses stop at the **Moor station,** directly off the main road next to the large traffic circle. National Express (☎08705 808 080) to **London** (8hr., 2 per day, £36) and **Plymouth** (2½hr., 2 per day, £6.10). Pick up schedules and tickets at the TIC. First bus #2 runs to **Penzance** (2hr., 6 per day, round-trip £5) via **Helston** (50min., 2 per hr., £3.50), while #89 and 90 go to **Newquay** (1½hr., M-Sa every 2hr., £5.70) via **Truro** (30min., £2.70) First #88 runs to Truro more frequently. Truronian (☎01872 273 453) sends buses to the **Lizard Peninsula** (p. 244).

Ferries: Ferries leave from Prince of Wales Pier and Custom House Quay. St. Mawes Ferry Company (☎313 201; www.stmawesferry.co.uk) sails to **St. Mawes** (25min., 2 per hr., £4). Runs July-Aug. 8:30am-11pm; Sept.-June 8:30am-5:15pm. Newman's Cruises (☎01872 580 309) runs to **Smuggler's Cottage,** up the River Fal (45min.; M-Sa 2 per day; round-trip £6.50). Enterprise (☎374 241; www.enterprise-boats.co.uk) makes the idyllic trip to **Truro** (1hr.; May-Sept. M-Sa 5 per day, Oct.-Apr. call ahead; £6).

Taxis: Checkers (☎212 127; 24hr.); **Radio Taxis** (☎315 194).

Falmouth

▲▲ ACCOMMODATIONS
Castleton Guest House, **6**
Eagleton Guest House, **4**
Falmouth Lodge
Backpackers, **12**

■★ PUBS/NIGHTLIFE
Blue South, **10**
Grapes Inn, **2**
M.I. Bar, **3**
Remedies, **1**
The Shed, **11**

🍴 FOOD
Citrus Cafe, **5**
Cribbs, **8**
Harbour Lights, **9**
Pipeline, **7**

✳ 🔋 ORIENTATION AND PRACTICAL INFORMATION

The rail line runs along the highest parts of Falmouth; streets to the sea and to B&Bs are steep in areas. **The Moor** is Falmouth's main square. The main street extends from there, changing names from **High Street** to **Market Street, Church Street, Arwenack Street,** and finally **Grove Place**, which leads to **Discovery Quay**, the dockside area home to the Maritime Museum and a number of shops and cafes.

The **Tourist Information Centre**, 11 Market Strand, Prince of Wales Pier, books beds for a 10% deposit. (☎312 300; www.go-cornwall.com. Open Apr.-June and Sept. M-Sa 9:30am-5:15pm; July-Aug. M-Sa 9:30am-5:15pm, Su 10:15am-4:15pm; Oct.-Mar. M-F 9:30am-5:15pm.) Many companies run **cruises** (1-2hr., £5-7) on River Fal to the north and Helford River to the southwest. K&S Cruises (☎211 056) offers fishing trips (2½ or 4hr.; M-F and Su 11am, 1, and 2:35pm; £8/16); book trips at the yellow kiosk on the Prince of Wales Pier. Other services include: **banks** on Market St.; Bubbles **launderette**, 99 Killigrew St. (☎311 291; open M-F 8am-7pm, Sa 9am-7pm, Su 10am-3pm); **police**, Dracaena Ave. (☎08452 777 444); **Falmouth Hospital,** Trescobeas Rd. (☎434 700); Boots **pharmacy**, 47 Market St. (☎312 373; open M-Sa 9am-5:30pm, Su 10:30am-4:30pm); **Internet** access at the Falmouth **Library**, The Moor (☎314 901; 75p per 15min.; open M-Tu and Th-F 9:30am-6pm, Sa 9:30am-4pm) or at Q Bar, a few doors from the TIC (☎210 634; 50p per 15min.; open M-W 9am-6:30pm, Th-Sa 9am-11pm, Su 10:30am-4:30pm); and the **post office** with a **bureau de change**, The Moor (☎08457 740 740; open M-Tu 8:45am-5:30pm, W-F 9am-5:30pm, Sa 9am-12:30pm). **Post Code:** TR11 3RB.

🏠 ACCOMMODATIONS

Western Terrace has a wealth of B&Bs (£20-45 per person) a 15min. walk from town. **Avenue** and **Melvill Roads** sport additional lodgings. Most fill up in summer, so book ahead. ▓**Falmouth Lodge Backpackers ❷**, 9 Gyllyngvase Terr., is run by the knowledgeable Charlotte, who has been around the world to Timbuktu and back. She provides a self-catering kitchen and Internet access. (☎319 996. Check-in before 10am or after 5pm. Dorms £16. Cash only.) The plethora of B&Bs on Western Terr. vary in price and style, but they all provide the same basic services. The proprietors at **Castleton Guest House ❸**, 68 Killigrew St., are happy to meet requests, from veggie breakfasts to a spare umbrella. (☎311 072. Singles £25; doubles £44; families £60. Cash only.) **Eagleton Guest House ❸**, 67 Killigrew St., next door to the Castleton Guest House, also offers clean rooms and personalized service for a reasonable price. (☎372 644. £25 per person. MC/V.)

█ FOOD

Pick up **groceries** at Tesco, The Moor (☎0845 677 9267; open M-Sa 7am-8pm, Su 10am-4pm), at the foot of Killigrew St. Falmouth has many options for quality eats, from cheap pasties to outrageously priced (but oh, so fresh and tasty) lobsters. **Citrus Cafe ❷**, 6 Arwenack St., creates delicious Indian and Mediterranean fusion dishes, served among bright yellow walls and bamboo seats. Extensive takeaway menu includes baguettes and smoothies at discounted prices. (☎318 383. Restaurant open 11am-2pm and 5-9pm. MC/V.) The blue interior of **Cribbs ❷**, 33 Arwenack St., embraces the sea. During the day, enjoy sandwiches and coffee on the couches. Early evenings bring an assortment of dinner entrees, and late at night, the bar fills up for good drinks and music. (☎210 000. Free Wi-Fi. Open 11am-12:30pm, food served until 9pm. MC/V.) **Pipeline ❸**, 21 Church St., serves Mediterranean and Cajun fusion (£8.50-17) amid playful decor. (☎312 774. Open July-Sept. Tu-Su noon-2pm and 6:30-10:30pm; Oct.-June W-Sa noon-2pm and 7-9:30pm, Su breakfast 10am-2pm. MC/V.) You've got your pick of seafood options around the pier, but **Harbour Lights ❶**, Arwenack St., offers award-wining fish and chips and other battered treats. The price jumps dramatically in the restaurant, so take your fish and chips to the pier and have a picnic—just watch for crazy seagulls dive-bombing for fries. (☎316 934. Takeaway open daily 11:30am-2pm, 5-10pm; restaurant open daily 11:30am-2pm, 5-9pm. Takeaway cash only; restaurant MC/V.)

◐ ◑ SIGHTS AND BEACHES

Opened in 2003, the **National Maritime Museum Cornwall,** Discovery Quay, houses a remarkable collection of boats, suspended mid-air in a state-of-the-art gallery. The museum covers all aspects of the sea, from interactive exhibits on navigation and weather patterns to boat-building to search and rescue. (☎313 388; www.nmmc.co.uk. Open daily 10am-5pm. £7.50, concessions £5, families £20.) Experience modern history at **Pendennis Castle,** a Tudor castle built by Henry VIII to guard the harbor at Pendennis Point. The sight features a walk-through diorama with waxen gunners and battle re-enactments in summer. The grounds also contain massive WWII "disappearing" guns and a strategic half-moon battery. Walking to the castle is a bit of a hike from town, but the First bus #41 and Truronian #400 ("Falmouth Explorer") drop you off nearby. (☎316 594. Open daily Apr.-June and Sept. 10am-5pm; July-Aug. 10am-6pm; Oct.-Mar. 10am-4pm. £5.40, concessions £4.10.) A 25min. ferry across the channel (p. 240) ends among thatched roofs and aspiring tropical gardens in St. Mawes village. **St. Mawes Castle,** 10min. uphill from the ferry drop-off point, is actually a circular battlement built by Henry to blow holes through any ship spared by Pendennis's gunners. (☎270 526. Open Apr.-June daily 10am-5pm; July-Sept. M-F and Su 10am-6pm; Oct. daily 10am-4pm; Nov.-March M and F-Su 10am-4pm. £4, concessions £3. Free 1hr. audio tour.)

Falmouth has five beaches, four of which are within a 15min. walk of the town center. If you're not up for walking, #400 "Falmouth Explorer" bus runs a route along all the beaches. **Castle Beach,** on Pendennis Head, may be too pebbly for sunbathing, but it's great for snorkeling. At low tide, **Tunnel Beach** connects Castle Beach with **Gyllyngvase Beach.** Gyllyngvase, the town's main beach, has pristine sand and a cafe that rents chairs for sunbathing. **Swanpool Beach** also has sandy shores, and both Gyllyngvase and Swanpool offer windsurfing. **Maenporth Beach,** about 2 mi. south of town, makes up for the distance with soft sand and views of Pendennis Castle and the St. Anthony Lighthouse.

🅿 🎵 NIGHTLIFE AND ENTERTAINMENT

For a small town, Falmouth has a surprisingly vibrant social scene. At night, tourists and locals head to the main street, where many of the cafes turn into pubs. At any time of day, enjoy a harbor view with your pint at the **Grapes Inn,** 64 Church St. (☎314 704. Open M-Sa 10:30am-11pm, Su 11am-10:30pm.) The mixed drinks (£4) are worth your money at **Blue South,** 35-37 Arwenack St., a freewheeling surf bar. (☎212 122. Happy hour 5-6pm; 2 mixed drinks £5. Open M-Sa 11am-11pm, Su 11am-10:30pm.) The town's hottest club, **Remedies,** The Moor, is best on weekends, when young crowds groove to Top 40 hits on two floors. (☎314 454. Cover F-Sa £5 after 10pm. Open daily noon-2am.) Cafe-bar **The Shed,** Discovery Quay, is the perfect place to start a night, with wine, coffee, and hot pink 50s decor. (☎318 502. Wi-Fi available. Open M-Sa 10am-11pm, Su 10am-10pm.) **M.I. Bar,** Church St., across from the Grapes Inn, has large leather couches and a sleek, modern look. (☎316 909. F live music. Open M-F 5pm-2am, Sa noon-2am, Su noon-1am.)

The popular **Falmouth Arts Centre,** 24 Church St., hosts exhibitions, concerts, theater, and films. (☎212 300; www.falmoutharts.com. Box office open M-Sa 10am-2pm. Exhibitions free. Theater and concert tickets £5-10.) The **Princess Pavilion,** Melvill Rd., hosts live music in an outdoor venue. (Box office ☎211 222; www.princesspavilion.co.uk. Gardens, patio, and bandstand with free shows £10-20.) **Regatta Week,** the second week of August, is Falmouth's main sailing event, with boat shows and music performances. The mid-October **Oyster Festival** features oyster tasting, craft fairs, and a parade. Contact the TIC for details.

🏃 DAYTRIP FROM FALMOUTH

▨ THE EDEN PROJECT

Bodelva, St. Austell. The St. Austell railway station is located on the Plymouth-Penzance line. From the station, Truronian (☎01872 273 453; www.truronian.com) bus T9 runs daily (20min., 1 per hr., £2.70). Bus T10 runs from Newquay in summer (50min., 2 per day, £4); bus T11 runs from Falmouth in summer (1½hr., 1 per day, £5.) Combined bus and Eden Project ticket £16.50, students £12, available from any Truronian bus line running to the project. Western Greyhound bus #527 also runs from Newquay year-round, via the St. Austell Railway station (2hr., M-Sa every hr., £5). Signposted from the A390, A30, and A391. ☎01726 811 972; www.edenproject.com. Open daily Apr.-Oct. 9am-6pm; Nov.-Mar. 10am-4:30pm. Last admission 1½hr. before close. Buy advance tickets at any TIC or online. £14, students £10; £4 discount for those who arrive on foot or by bicycle.

A "living theatre of plants and people," the Eden Project is one of England's most unique and fascinating sights. Nestled into hills on the site of a former clay quarry, space-age biomes and awe-inspiring gardens recreate the most beautiful ecosystems on Earth. Enter the Mediterranean villas of the **Warm Temperate Biome** and breathe in the scent of olive groves and citrus trees. Keep your eyes open for the steel sculptures that recreate the Rites of Bacchus. Brave the heat and humidity to enjoy the palm-tree-laden **Humid Tropics Biome,** the world's largest greenhouse, which houses a rainforest of over 1000 plants. The 30-acre **Roofless Biome** features hemp, sunflowers, tea, and a host of public art displays. The Alchemy Centre shows how to recycle trash into art, while the Plant Takeaway display is a representation of what would befall humans if all plants vanished. The stage acts as a major concert venue, bringing the likes of Amy Winehouse and Rufus Wainwright to the gardens for evening concerts. Check the website for details. Plans are in the works for a fourth biome, dedicated to the world's deserts, which would contain a gigantic oasis. It takes at least 3hr. to walk through the grounds.

THE LIZARD PENINSULA   ☎01326

The beautiful, remote Lizard Peninsula is one of England's least touristed corners. Although its name has nothing to do with reptiles—"Lizard" is a corruption of Old Cornish "Lys ardh," meaning "the high place"—the peninsula does possess a significant outcrop of serpentine rock, so described because of its uncanny resemblance to snake skin. **South West Coastal Path** (p. 187) traces the Lizard around Britain's southernmost point, through dramatic seascapes and lonely fishing villages. The tiny village of **Lizard** receives more attention thanks to **Lizard Point,** the southernmost tip of Britain. A short, signposted walk from the village, this outcrop houses a few "most southerly" shops and the **National Trust Information Centre** but is largely undeveloped. (☎290 604. Open daily Apr.-Oct. 10am-4pm; from mid-June to mid-Sept. until 5pm.) **Kynance Cove,** 3 mi. northwest of Lizard Point along the coast, is a sandy beach studded by masses of rock that create lively surf.

Escape the summer crowds by trekking 3hr. farther northwest to rocky **Mullion Cove,** where steep but climbable cliffs await. **Mullion Island,** 250 yd. off the cove, is home to more seabirds than officials can count. The cove is also accessible from Mullion village, 1½ mi. inland. Seven miles from Helston in the middle of the peninsula, over 60 satellite dishes make up **Goonhilly Satellite Earth Station Experience,** the world's largest satellite station. The site covers an area equivalent to 160 soccer fields. Visitors can take a 40min. bus tour through the facility and use what might be the fastest Internet connection on earth. (☎0800 679 593; www.goonhilly.bt.com. Open daily June-Sept. 10am-6pm. Last admission 5pm. Call ahead in winter. £6.50, concessions £5.) The **National Seal Sanctuary,** Europe's leading marine mammal rescue center and home to sea lions, otters, and seal pups is 6 mi. from Helston, in the town of Gweek. The animals are most entertaining during their daily feedings at 12:30pm for the otters and 3:30pm for the seals. (☎221 361; www.sealsanctuary.co.uk. Open daily 10am-4pm. £11, concessions £10.) Truronian **buses** run from Helston to Goonhilly (T2; 20min., M-Sa every 2hr.; T3; 20min., Su 2 per day, round-trip £2.50) and Gweek (T2; 30min., 2 per day, round-trip £2.30). The **YHA Lizard ❷,** a refurbished Victorian villa, boasts clean facilities and stunning views of the Lizard Point waters. (☎291 145. Kitchen and laundry. Reception 8:30-10am and 5-10pm. Open Apr.-Oct. Dorms £15, under 18 £11. MC/V.)

There is no longer a tourist information center in the Lizard Peninsula, so get brochures and information from the TICs in Falmouth and Penzance. Lizard is home to its fair share of gimmicky attractions; most aren't worth the admission. Stock up on cash and supplies in Helston—elsewhere, **banks** and **ATMs** are rare. The easiest way to reach Lizard's coasts is in a car. If you're taking the bus, you'll need to connect to Truronian buses in Helston. The T34 runs a direct route between Helston and Lizard, while the T3 "Lizard Rambler" takes the scenic route along the coast. Both buses are covered by the Truronian day pass (£6).

PENZANCE   ☎01736

Although Penzance was formerly an ancient English pirate town, it appears Disney has moved all the pirates to the Caribbean, because you won't find too many here that aren't wax figures or in murals. What Penzance lacks in swashbucklers it makes up for in galleries and stores. The city's armada of antique shops and flea markets lures tourists with troves of trinkets. Sights are few, but with glorious sunsets and bawdy pubs, it's difficult not to enjoy such an irreverent town.

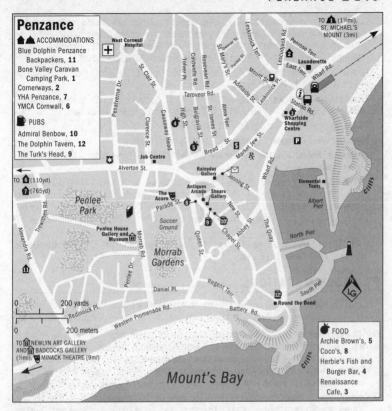

Penzance

▲▲ ACCOMMODATIONS
Blue Dolphin Penzance
   Backpackers, **11**
Bone Valley Caravan
   Camping Park, **1**
Cornerways, **2**
YHA Penzance, **7**
YMCA Cornwall, **6**

PUBS
Admiral Benbow, **10**
The Dolphin Tavern, **12**
The Turk's Head, **9**

TO **6** (110yd)
7 (765yd)

Penlee Park

Penlee House
Gallery and
Museum

*Morrab
Gardens*

Daniel Pl.

0   200 yards

0   200 meters

Redinnick Pl.

Western Promenade Rd.

TO NEWLYN ART GALLERY
AND BADCOCKS GALLERY
(½mi), MINACK THEATRE (9mi)

West Cornwall
Hospital

St. Clair St.
Penalverne Dr.
Clarence St.
Causeway Head
High St.
Belgravia St.
Taroveor Rd.
Caldwells Rd.
Tolver Pl.
Rosevean Rd.
St. Mary's St.
St. James St.
Alma Terr.
Bread
Alverton St.
Job Centre

Trewithen Rd.
Alexandra Rd.
Parade St.
The Acorn
Antiques
Arcade
Shears
Gallery
New St.
Morrab Rd.
Penlee Dr.
Queen St.
Chapel St.
Abbey St.
Regent Terr.
Soccer
Ground

Rainyday
Gallery
Jenning St.
Market Jew St.
The Quay

Leskinnick Terr.
St. Clare St.
Mount St.
Adelaide St.
Leskinnick Pl.
Penrose Terr.
Lescudjack Rd.
East Terr.
Station Rd.
Wharf Rd.

TO **1** (1½mi),
ST. MICHAEL'S
MOUNT (3mi)

2
Launderette
Wharf Rd.
Wharfside
Shopping
Centre

Elemental
Tours
Albert
Pier
North Pier
South Pier
Round the Bend

Battery Rd.

Mount's Bay

Cliffs

FOOD
Archie Brown's, **5**
Coco's, **8**
Herbie's Fish and
   Burger Bar, **4**
Renaissance
   Cafe, **3**

TRANSPORTATION

Trains: Station on Wharf Rd., at Albert Pier. Ticket office open M-F 6:05am-8:10pm, Sa 6am-6:10pm, Su 8:15am-5:30pm. Trains (☎08457 484 950) to: **Exeter** (3¼hr., every hr., £15); **London** (5½hr., 7 per day, £69); **Newquay** (3hr., 8 per day, £7); **Plymouth** (2hr., every hr., £9); **St. Ives** via **St. Erth** (40min.-1hr., every hr., £4.80).

Buses: Station on Wharf Rd. (☎0845 600 1420), at the head of Albert Pier. Ticket office open M-F 8:30am-4:45pm, Sa 8:30am-3pm. National Express (☎08705 808 080) to **London** (8½hr., 7 per day, £36) and **Plymouth** (3hr., 7 per day, £6.70).

Taxis: Nippy Cabs (☎366 666) and **A Cars** (☎333 222).

ORIENTATION AND PRACTICAL INFORMATION

Penzance's train station, bus station, and TIC cluster on **Wharf Road. Market Jew Street** (a corruption of the Cornish "Marghas Yow," meaning "Market Thursday") is laden with pasty shops and bargain stores. It becomes **Alverton Street,** then **Alverton Road,** before turning into the **A30,** the road to Land's End.

Tourist Information Centre: Station Rd. (☎362 207; www.penwith.gov.uk), between the train and bus stations. Books beds for £3 plus 10% deposit. Open May-Sept. M-F 9am-5pm, Sa 10am-4pm, Su 9am-2pm; Oct.-Apr. M-F 9am-5pm, Sa 10am-1pm.

Tours: Anyone interested in riotous jokes about Neolithic man should try **Harry Safari** (☎08456 445 940; www.harrysafari.co.uk), a trip through the Cornish wilds, with stops at all of Cornwall's hidden attractions. Call Harry to book, and he'll pick you up on the morning of the tour. 4hr. M-F and Su leaves Penzance at 9:30am. £20.

Financial Services: Barclays, 8-9 Market Jew St. Open M-Tu and Th-F 9am-4:30pm, W 10am-4:30pm, Sa 9am-1:30pm.

Launderette: Polyclean, 4 East Terr. (☎364 815), opposite the train station. Wash £3-4.50, dry 20p per 3min., soap 20p. Open daily 9am-8pm; last wash 7pm.

Police: Penalverne Dr. (☎08705 777 444), off Alverton St.

Hospital: West Cornwall Hospital, St. Clare St. (☎874 000).

Pharmacy: Boots, 100-102 Market Jew St. (☎362 135). Open M-Sa 9am-5:30pm, Su 10am-4pm.

Internet Access: Penzance Public Library, Morrab Rd. (☎363 954). First 30min. free, then 75p per 15min. Open M-F 9:30am-6pm, Sa 9:30am-4pm. Also at **Penzance Computers,** 36b Market Jew St. (☎333 391), opposite the Wharfside Centre. 90p per 15min., 6p per min. Open May-Oct. M-Sa 9am-8pm, Su 9am-6pm; Nov.-Apr. M-Sa noon-4pm, Su noon-2pm.

Post Office: 113 Market Jew St. Open M-F 9am-5:30pm, Sa 9am-12:30pm. **Bureau de change. Post Code:** TR18 2LB.

ACCOMMODATIONS

Penzance's **B&Bs** (£20-30) gather mostly on **Alexandra Road,** a 10min. walk from the town center. Buses #1, 1A, 5A, and 6A run from the station to Alexandra Rd. (50p).

YHA Penzance, Castle Horneck (☎362 666). Walk 20min. from town or take First bus #5 or 6 to the Pirate Pub, and walk up Castle Horneck Rd. Greyhound runs 2 buses per day directly between town and the hostel. 18th-century mansion with spacious dorms. Tickets reserved for Minack Theatre shows (p. 248). Internet access. Lockout 10am-noon. Dorms £16, under 18 £13; twins £18.70 per person. Camping £7. MC/V. ❷

Cornerways, 5 Leskinnick St. (☎364 645; www.penzance.co.uk/cornerways), across Market Jew St. from the train station. Backpacker-friendly owner manages cozy, ensuite single, double, and triple rooms. Veggie breakfasts available. 10% *Let's Go* discount. Book months ahead in summer. £25 per person. AmEx/MC/V. ❸

Blue Dolphin Penzance Backpackers, Alexandra Rd. (☎363 836; www.pzbackpack.com), close to town. Relaxed ensuite dorms in a residential neighborhood. Dorms £14; doubles and twins £28. Reception 8am-2pm and 5-10pm. MC/V. ❷

YMCA Cornwall, The Orchard, Alverton (☎334 820, ext. 20; www.cornwall.ymca.org.uk). Spacious hostel with cafe and large lounge with a pool table and Sky TV. Breakfast £4. Internet access £1.20 per 30min. Reception M-F 10am-8:30pm. Dorms from £15.75; singles £21; twins £18.70 per person. Cash only. ❷

Bone Valley Caravan Camping Park, Heamoor (☎360 313). Take bus #11 or 17, disembark at the Sportsman's Arms pub, and walk ¼ mi. Family-run site, 1½ mi. from the city center. Kitchen and laundry. Call ahead in July and Aug. Open Mar.-Dec. From £6.50 per pitch. AmEx/MC/V. ❶

FOOD

Expect to pay around £10-15 to dine at one of Penzance's excellent seafood spots along The Quay. The best buys are in coffee shops and local eateries on smaller streets and alleyways near Market Jew St. **Groceries** can be purchased at Iceland, on the lower floor of the shopping center. (☎361 130. Open M-W 8:30am-6:30pm, Th-F 8:30am-8pm, Sa 8am-6:30pm, Su 10am-4pm.)

Renaissance Cafe, Wharfside Shopping Centre (☎366 277). Ultra-modern coffee bar and restaurant overlooking the harbor. Brilliant views are accompanied by an extensive, moderately priced seafood and vegetarian menu. Try the prawn, mango, and avocado salad (£6). Breakfast 9am-noon, lunch noon-3:30pm, dinner 5:30pm-9pm. MC/V. ❷

Coco's, 12-13 Chapel St. (☎350 222). Relaxed tapas with Matissean decor. Tapas £5-9; entrees £9.50-13. Open M-Sa 9:30am-11pm, Su 10:30am-9:30pm. Food served M-Sa 10:30am-2:30pm and 6:30-10pm, Su 10:30am-2:30pm and 6:30-9pm. MC/V. ❷

Herbie's Fish and Burger Bar, 56 Causeway Head (☎362 850). Ample, delicious burgers and fish made to order at superbly cheap prices. Pile on the burger toppings at no extra charge. Open in summer M-Sa 11:30am-2:30pm and 4:15-7pm. Cash only. ❶

Archie Brown's, Bread St. (☎362 828), above Richard's Health Food Store. Sunny and artsy, this vegetarian cafe features a changing menu of creative dishes. Open M-Sa 9am-5pm. Kitchen closes around 3:30pm. MC/V. ❷

◉ SIGHTS

St. Michael the Archangel is said to have appeared to some fishermen on Marazion, just offshore from Penzance, in AD 495—reason enough to build a Benedictine monastery on the spot. Today, **St. Michael's Mount** has an active church and castle at its 30-story peak. At low tide, visitors can stroll there via a cobblestone causeway, but at high tide, the small ferries (£1.50) are the only way to go. Keep your eyes open for the ghost of the infamous fifth baron of the castle, who had 15 illegitimate children. A model of the castle made by a butler from the corks of champagne bottles is in the map room. Walk 3 mi. from the TIC to Marazion Sq. or take the £2 round-trip bus ride on #2, 2A, 2B, 7, 16B, 17B, or 301. (☎710 507, ferry and tide info 710 265. Open Apr.-Oct. M-F and Su 10:30am-5:30pm; Nov.-Mar. by tour only, appointment necessary. Last admission 4:45pm. £6.40; with private garden £9.40.)

Penzance features an impressive number of **art galleries,** which crop up every other block. **Chapel Street** is particularly full of display rooms. The *Cornwall Gallery Guide* booklet (£1), available at galleries and the TIC, lists the best galleries in Penzance and nearby cities. The **Penlee House Gallery and Museum,** Morrab Rd., is internationally known for its impressive collection of Newlyn School art, while the museum upstairs has an eclectic collection of historical artifacts. Look for the 18th-century Scold's Bridle, a menacing warning against loose lips. (☎363 625; www.penleehouse.org.uk. Open May-Sept. M-Sa 10am-5pm; Oct.-Apr. 10:30am-4:30pm. £3, concessions £2, children free. Sa free.) The curator of the **Rainyday Gallery,** 116 Market Jew St., compiles the *Cornwall Gallery Guide.* (☎366 077. Open M-Sa 10am-5pm.) **Round the Bend,** The Barbican, Battery Rd., is England's only permanent exhibition of contemporary automata. These quirky machines range from the daring to the droll, and most are for sale. (☎332 211. Open daily Easter-Sept. 11am-5pm. £2.50, children £1.50.) The brand-new **Elemental Tours,** Albert Pier, provide marine wildlife tours in Cornish waters. (☎811 200; www.elementaltours.co.uk. Tours held year-round; times depend upon weather. Call ahead.)

🍺 🎵 PUBS AND ENTERTAINMENT

The true characters of Penzance emerge in its excellent pubs, most of which line Chapel St. ◪**Admiral Benbow,** 46 Chapel St., has the town's liveliest scene and is decorated with paraphernalia culled from local shipwrecks. Postings list frequent live folk music. (☎363 448. Pints £2.20. Open M-Sa 11am-11pm, Su noon-10:30pm.)

SOUTHWEST ENGLAND

▨**The Turk's Head,** 49 Chapel St., dating from the 13th century, is Penzance's oldest pub and was sacked by Spanish pirates in 1595. (☎363 093. Open M-Sa 11am-3pm and 5:30-11pm, Su noon-3pm and 5:30-10:30pm.) **The Dolphin Tavern,** The Quay, has the dubious distinction of the being the first place tobacco was smoked in Britain upon Sir Walter Raleigh's return from Virginia. The pub is said to be haunted by at least three ghosts, although you're more likely to find a different kind of spirit. (☎364 106. Pint £2-2.80. Open M-Sa 11am-11pm, Su noon-10pm.) **The Acorn,** Parade St., hosts jazz bands, comedy clubs, and productions of the **Kneehigh Theatre.** (☎365 520. Box office open Tu-Sa 11am-3pm. Tickets £5-20.) The week of June 26 brings the **Golowan Festival,** featuring the election of the mock Mayor of the Quay.

▶ DAYTRIP FROM PENZANCE

▨ MINACK THEATRE

9 mi. southwest of Penzance, in the town of Porthcurno. Take First bus #1A from the bus station (30min.; M-Sa 6-9 per day, Su 2 per day; round-trip £4), or Western Greyhound #345 or 346 from YHA Penzance or the TIC (1hr.; M-F 2 per day, Sa 1 per day). Car access via the B3283. ☎810 181; www.minack.com. Open Apr.-May daily 9:30am-5:30pm; from June to mid-Sept. M, Tu, Th, and Sa-Su 9:30am-5:30pm, W and F 9:30am-noon; from mid-Sept. to Mar. daily 10am-5pm. £3.50, under 16 £1.40. Performances M-F 8pm, also W and F 2pm. Tickets £7-8.50, children £3.40-4.50. £2 surcharge for phone booking. MC/V.

In summer, patrons flock to the open-air ▨**Minack Theatre,** hacked into a cliffside at Porthcurno, Minack. The theater hosts performances of everything from classic Shakespearean drama to modern comedies to ballet. As legend has it, a woman named Rowena Cade constructed the amphitheater by hand. The theater's 750 stone seats have afforded patrons views of the surrounding waters since 1932. Dolphins frequently put on their own show behind the stage. On a clear day, visitors can see the Lizard Peninsula, 20 mi. to the southeast. During intermission, patrons break out wine and picnic baskets.

ST. IVES   ☎01736

St. Ives (pop. 11,400), bordered by pastel beaches and azure waters, has attracted visitors for centuries. The cobbled alleyways, colored by flowerpots, drew a colony of painters and sculptors in the 1920s; today, their legacy fills the windows of local art galleries, including a branch of the Tate. Virginia Woolf's *To the Lighthouse* is thought to refer to St. Ives's Godrevy Lighthouse.

▤ ▨ TRANSPORTATION AND PRACTICAL INFORMATION. Trains (☎08457 484 950) to St. Ives pass through or change at St. Erth (15min., every hr., £1.70), although direct service is sometimes available. National Express (☎08705 808 080) **buses** stop in St. Ives (4 per day) between Plymouth (3hr., £6.70) and Penzance (25min., £3.10). First buses also head to Penzance (#16, 16B, 17B; 40min., 2 per hr., round-trip £3). Bus #301 runs in July and August to Newquay (1¾hr., 4 per day, £4.70). First **DayRover** tickets allow unlimited travel on First buses for £5.50.

St. Ives is a jumble of alleyways and tiny streets. Wharf St. runs along the harbor to the north, while Fore St. runs parallel to it. The town is roughly triangular, with beaches to the north and south. The **Tourist Information Centre,** in the Guildhall, books accommodations for £3 plus a 10% deposit and sells maps (20p). From the bus or train station, walk to the foot of Tregenna Hill and turn right on Street-an-Pol. Pick up the free *A Walk Around the Historic Town of St. Ives.* (☎796 297. Open May-Sept. M-F 9am-5pm, Sa 10am-4pm; July-Sept. also Su 10am-2pm; Oct.-Easter M-F 9am-5pm, Sa 10am-1pm.) **Columbus Walks** leads 4-8 mi. hikes through the area. (☎07980 149 243. M-Th £3-7.50, F-Sa walks available with 2 days notice.)

Other services include: **banks** along High St., including Barclays (☎08457 555 555; open M-Tu and Th-F 9:30am-4:30pm, W 10am-4:30pm); **work opportunities** at JobCentre, Royal Sq. (☎575 200; open M 9am-12:30pm and 1:30-4pm, Tu 10am-12:30pm and 1:30-4pm), across from International Backpackers; Boots **pharmacy,** High St. (☎795 072; open M-Sa 8:30am-8:30pm, Su 9am-4:30pm); **Internet** access at the **library,** Andrews St., near the TIC (☎795 377; first 30min. free, then £3 per hr.; open Tu 9:30am-9:30pm, W-F 9:30am-6pm, Sa 9:30am-12:30pm); and the **post office,** Tregenna Pl. (☎795 004; open M-F 9am-5:30pm, Sa 9am-12:30pm), with a **bureau de change. Post Code:** TR26 1AA.

⌂ ACCOMMODATIONS. Expensive **B&Bs** (£25-35) are near the town center on **Parc Avenue** and **Tregenna Terrace.** Walk uphill on West Pl., which becomes **Clodgy View** and **Belmont Terrace** (10min.), where cheaper B&Bs offer fine sea views. **St. Ives International Backpackers ❶,** The Stennack, a few blocks uphill from the library, is covered with bright murals and has a huge lounge area. (☎799 444; www.backpackers.co.uk. Internet access £1 per 15min. Dorms £11-16; twins £13-18 per person; July-Aug. 7-night min. for advance bookings. MC/V.) **Hobblers House ❸,** on the corner of The Wharf and Court Cocking, near Dive St. Ives, has harbor-view rooms at the heart of the town's wharf area. (☎796 439. Open Mar.-Sept. No singles. Doubles £60. MC/V.) **Making Waves ❸,** 3 Richmond Pl., has gorgeous, eco-friendly rooms and organic breakfasts. The second-floor double has a brilliant view of the town. (☎793 895; www.veganholiday.co.uk. £24 per person, second-floor double £33 per person. Cash only.) For camping or caravanning, **Ayr Holiday Park ❶** is the closest site. Make the 10min. walk to Bullan's Ln. (off The Stennack), then turn right on Bullan Hill and left on Ayr Terr. at the top of the road. (☎795 855; www.ayrholidaypark.co.uk. Laundry £5. £9 per person. MC/V.)

⚎⌘ FOOD AND PUBS. Get **groceries** at the Co-op, Royal Sq., two blocks uphill from the TIC. (☎796 494. Open M-Sa 8am-11pm, Su 8am-10:30pm.) For local sea-food at reasonable prices, the trendy **Seafood Cafe ❸,** 45 Fore St., can't be beat. Choose your fish raw from the display area (£8.50-17) and select garnishes. (☎794 004. Open daily noon-3pm and 5:30-11pm. MC/V.) The **Porthminster Cafe ❸,** at the end of Porthminster Beach, offers a relaxed atmosphere overlooking the surf. Most sandwiches are available for takeaway. (☎796 791. Entrees £4.50-16. Open daily 8:30am-3pm and 6-9:30pm. MC/V.) **The Dolphin ❷,** 57 Fore St., has quick take-away and views of the sea if you dine in. Bring your own wine or beer and take advantage of dinner specials, like two meals for £7. (☎795 701. Open daily 11am-9pm. Takeaway until around 5pm. MC/V.) Perhaps the best view in Cornwall is from the **Tate Cafe ❷,** on the roof of the Tate, overlooking the beach. Enjoy modern cuisine in a postmodern atmosphere. (☎791 122. Sandwiches £5-7. Open daily 10am-4:50pm.) At **Something Tasty ❶,** 52 Fore St., the jolly staff makes everything from traditional Cornish pasties to yummy apple pies. (☎797 369; Pasties run out around 2pm. Open daily 11am-4pm. Cash only.)

▥ GALLERIES AND MUSEUMS. Renowned for its superb light, St. Ives was once an artists' pilgrimage site, and the town's art community is still strong. *Cornwall Galleries Guide* (£1) navigates the dozens of galleries littered throughout St. Ives's maze-like alleys. A special ticket offers same-day admission to the Tate and the Barbara Hepworth Museum (£8.70, concessions £4.50). Like its sister, the Tate Modern in London (p. 126), the **Tate Gallery,** on Porthmeor Beach, focuses on mod-ern and abstract art. The whitewashed building is a piece of art itself, with rounded corridors and gradual lines mimicking the ocean. (☎796 226; www.tate.org.uk. Open Mar.-Oct. daily 10am-5:30pm, last admission 5pm; Nov.-Feb. Tu-Su 10am-4:30pm. Free 1hr. tours M-Sa 2:30pm. £5.75.) Associated with the

Tate, the **Barbara Hepworth Museum and Sculpture Garden,** on nearby Ayr Ln., allows visitors to view the famed 20th-century sculptor's former home, studio, and garden. (Open Mar.-Oct. daily 10am-5:30pm, last admission 5pm; Nov.-Feb. Tu-Su 10am-4:30pm. £4.75, students £2.75.) To view works in the St. Ives School style, try the **Belgrave Gallery,** 22 Fore St., associated with the Belgrave Gallery London (☎794 888; open M-Sa 10am-1pm and 2-6pm), or **Wills Lane Gallery,** Wills Ln. (☎795 723. Open 11am-1pm and 2-5pm. Call ahead.)

┌───┐
│ ▟TIP◣ **DRAWING THE LINE.** In summer, both the Tate and the Barbara Hep- │
│   worth Museum are full of art students sketching and taking notes. Visit early in │
│   the day to avoid stepping over busy artists and their hovering instructors. │
└───┘

🄲 **BEACHES.** St. Ives's **beaches** are among England's finest. Follow the hill down from the train station to **Porthminster Beach,** a magnificent stretch of golden sand and tame waves. To escape the sunbathing crowds, head for quieter **Porthgwidden Beach. Porthmeor Beach,** below the Tate, attracts surfers. Farther east, **Carbis Bay,** 1¼ mi. from Porthminster, is less crowded and easily accessible. Take the train one stop toward St. Erth or bus #17 (M-Sa) or 17B (Su).

Beach activities in St. Ives are numerous. Rent surf boards from shops on Fore St., like **Wind An' Sea Surf Shop,** 25 Fore St. (☎794 830. £5 per day, £25 per week. £5 deposit. Wetsuit £5. Open daily Easter-Oct. 10am-10pm; Nov.-Easter 10am-6pm.) Beginners can start with a lesson at **St. Ives Surf School,** on Porthmeor Beach. (☎07792 261 278. £25 per 2hr., £100 for 5 days. Price includes equipment. Open daily May-Sept. 9am-6pm.) The less athletically inclined may prefer **boat trips,** which leave from the harbor. **Pleasure Boat Trips** travels around the bay and to **Seal Island,** a permanent seal colony. (☎797 328. 1¼-2hr. £8.) Many boat companies head to the famous **Godrevy Lighthouse** (£7). Rent a motor boat from **Mercury Self-Drive** at the harbor. (☎07830 173 878. £8 per 15min., £12 per 30min., £18 per hr. All for 5-6 people. Open daily Easter-Sept. 9am-dusk.)

🄽 **NIGHTLIFE.** St. Ives caters to an older crowd than other resort towns, and the nightlife tends to wrap up at 11pm, when the pubs close. Beer has flowed at **The Sloop,** Fish St. and The Wharf, since 1312. (☎796 584. Open M-Sa 9am-midnight, Su 9am-11pm.) Nearby, the **Lifeboat Inn,** Wharf Rd., hosts live music on Fridays. (☎794 123. Open M-Th 11am-11pm, F-Sa 11am-midnight, Su noon-10:30pm.) The Irish **Craic Bar,** The Stennack, inside the Western Hotel, offers live music. (☎795 227. Craic Bar open M-Sa 6-11pm.) The adjoining **Kettle 'n' Wink** got its name from the old practice of hiding smuggled brandy in a kettle. Customers placed their order by looking at the kettle and winking. (☎01736 795 277. Open M-Th and Su 11am-11pm, F-Sa 11am-midnight.) **Isobar,** at the corner of Street-an-Pol and Tregenna Pl., is St. Ives's busiest club. On Wednesdays, all drinks are £1. (☎796 042. Cover W and Sa up to £5. Open M-Th noon-1am, F-Sa noon-2am, Su 8pm-12:30am.)

PENWITH PENINSULA   ☎01736

A largely untouched region of cliffs and sandy shores, Penwith was once the center of Cornwall's mining industry. Today, the views over the jagged shores from green pastures attract mostly beach-goers and hikers. From June to September, the Penwith Circular bus, on a loop from Penzance, passes through Land's End, Sennen, St. Just, Pendeen, Zennor, and St. Ives (5 per day, day pass £5.50).

ZENNOR. Legend holds that a mermaid drawn by the singing of a young man in this tiny village returned to the sea with the man in tow. On misty evenings, locals claim to see and hear the pair. The immaculate **Old Chapel Backpackers Hostel ❷** is close to gorgeous hiking and 4 mi. from the beaches at St. Ives. (☎798 307; www.backpackers.co.uk/zennor. Cafe. Continental breakfast £3, English £4.50. Showers 20p. Laundry wash £1.50, dry £1. 2-night max. stay. Dorms £12-15; family rooms £50; camping £4.50. MC/V.) Western Greyhound **bus** #343 comes from St. Ives en route to Penzance (20min., M-Sa 6 per day); First bus #201 runs between St. Ives and Land's End, stopping in Zennor (from mid to May-Sept., 3 per day).

LAND'S END. A small complex of tacky tourist attractions capitalize on England's westernmost point, but none merits the admission fee. Grab some delicious Cornish ice cream and take in the beautiful views. They're free—unless you want your picture taken in front of the famous sign. That will cost you £15 plus shipping. On Tuesdays and Thursdays in August, there are fireworks over the water. First **buses** #1 and 1A go to Land's End from Penzance (1hr., every hr., £4) and #201 comes from St. Ives (35min., 5 per day, £4.30 round-trip). The **Visitor Centre** sells tickets to local attractions and dispenses local history. (☎08704 580 044. Open daily July-Aug. 10am-6pm; Sept.-June 10am-5pm.)

ST. JUST. On Cape Cornwall, 4 mi. north of Land's End, the coast of St. Just (pop. 4000) remains untainted by tourism. One mile from the TIC, **Cape Cornwall** was thought to mark the intersection of the Atlantic Ocean and the English Channel. From the cape, Land's End is a tough 6 mi. walk south along the **South West Coastal Path.** Three miles northeast of St. Just in Pendeen, **Geevor Tin Mine** functioned until 1990, and now has a museum dedicated to mining. (☎788 662; www.geevor.com. Open Easter-Oct. M-F and Su 10am-5pm; Nov.-Easter M-F and Su 10am-4pm. Last admission 1hr. before close. £6.50. 50% discount with bus ticket.)

The **YHA Land's End ❷,** Letcha Vean, in Cot Valley, occupies three pristine acres. From the bus station car park, turn left, keeping the primary school on your right, and follow the road as it becomes a footpath leading to the hostel (25min. walk). A map is posted at the St. Just library. (☎788 437. Breakfast £3.80. Reception 8:30-10am and 5-10pm. Open May-Sept. daily; from mid-Feb. to Apr. and Oct. Tu-Sa. Dorms £15, under 18 £11. MC/V.) Most routes to Land's End pass through Pendeen and St. Just. **Buses** #17, 17A, and 17B go to Penzance (45min., every hr., round-trip £3). Bus #201 (whose open upper deck offers fantastic views) runs from St. Ives (1hr., 5 per day, £3.50). The **Tourist Information Centre,** at the library opposite the bus park, books rooms and carries *Ancient Sites in West Penwith* (£4). (☎788 669. Open June-Sept. M-W 10am-1pm and 2-5pm, F 10am-1pm and 2-6pm, Sa 10am-1pm. **Internet** access available, first 30min. free, 75p per 15min. thereafter.)

▨SENNEN COVE. Just 2 mi. from Land's End along the coast, Sennen Cove is a gorgeous mile-long beach, bordered on the north by a small village. A variety of lodgings and restaurants are available in the cove, but many are pricey. First **buses** #1, 101, and 201 and Western Greyhound Coach #345 come from Penzance (45min.; M-Sa 7 per day, Su 5 per day; £3.50).

ANCIENT MONUMENTS. Inland on the Penwith Peninsula, some of the least-spoiled Stone and Iron Age monuments in England lie on the Land's End-St. Ives bus route. Once covered by mounds of dirt, the quoits (also called cromlechs, dolmens, and old rocks in the middle of nowhere) are thought to be burial chambers from 2500 BC. The **Zennor Quoit** is named for the village. The **Lanyon Quoit,** off the Morvah-Penzance road about 3 mi. from each town, is one of the most impressive megaliths. The famous stone near Morvah, on the Land's End-St. Ives bus route, has the Cornish name **Mên-an-Tol,** or "stone with a hole through the middle." The doughnut allegedly has curative powers. The best-preserved Iron Age village in Britain is at **Chysauster,** about 4 mi. from both Penzance and Zennor; there's a 2½ mi. footpath off the B3311 near Gulval.

THE CHANNEL ISLANDS

Situated in the waters between England and France, tiny Jersey and Guernsey (and even tinier Alderney, Sark, and Herm) form the Anglo-French holiday spot that is the Channel Islands. Eighty miles south of England and 30 mi. west of France, the Islands provide a fusion of cultures and a touch of elegance for those willing to foot the bill. The Channel Islands declared their loyalty to the British Crown in 1204, but Jersey and Guernsey still consider themselves autonomous, as displayed by their high-flying flags and unique currency. Among the rocky coves lie fortifications built during the islands' occupation by the Germans during WWII, a wealth of cafes, shops, and tourists make the islands a perpetual holiday.

✈ GETTING THERE

From England, **ferries** are your best bet for getting to the islands. Condor Ferries (☎01202 207 216; www.condorferries.com) run one early and one late high-speed ferry per day to St. Helier, Jersey (3½-3¾hr.) and Saint Peter Port, Guernsey (2hr.) from the mainland cities of Weymouth, Poole, and Portsmouth (£45-67, round-trip £56-109). Condor also runs a return daytrip to Jersey or Guernsey for £24.50. Departing from Portsmouth is cheapest, but the ferries are slower (10½hr. to Jersey, 7hr. to Guernsey). The tides and the season affect frequency and ticket prices. Check the website for schedules or call the reservation hotline (☎0845 124 2003). Arrive 45min. prior to departure. ISIC holders (p. 13) receive a 20% discount.

> **TIP** **A WHOLE NEW WORLD.** Although part of the UK, Jersey and Guernsey are self-governing—in some senses, you're in foreign territory. ATMs dish out Jersey or Guernsey pounds. They are equal in value to British pounds, but are not accepted outside the islands. Change your money as few times as possible to avoid exchange commissions. Toward the end of your stay, ask merchants to give you your change in British pounds. Also, your mobile phone may think you're in France, affecting your rate. Some mobiles may not work at all, and pay-as-you-go phones from the mainland usually can't be topped up here. Purchase an international "Speedial" phone card from a post office or newsstand.

JERSEY   ☎01534

Jersey, the largest Channel Island, is notorious for both its landscape-altering tides and its budget-altering high prices. You can avoid the latter by breaking free from the pull of trendy shops and eateries in the port of St. Helier and escaping to the island's countryside, where you'll truly experience the region's beguiling blend of British sensibility and French *joie de vivre*.

🚌 TRANSPORTATION. An efficient, color-coded system of **buses** makes local travel on the 45 sq. mi. island relatively painless. The public buses, Connex (☎877 772; www.mybus.je), are based at the station on Weighbridge in St. Helier and travel all over the island. Look for the conspicuous "Out of the Blue" signs. (Office open M-F 8am-6pm, Sa-Su 9am-5pm. Many auxiliary routes stop service around 7pm. Timetables 50p. Tickets 90p-£1.60, all fares £1 after 7pm. Unlimited travel passes 1-day £6, 3-day £15.30, 5-day £22.50, 7-day £31.50.) Private competitor Island Explore offers a hop-on, hop-off **tour** service. (☎876 418. M-F and Su from Weighbridge Terminal. Office open 9am-5:30pm.) **Explorer** tickets are best if your plans take you all over the island (1-day £7.50, 3-day £17.50, 5-day £22.50, 1 additional person under 16 free with every ticket). Call the island's **taxi** hotline (☎0871 855 0933) to hail a cab 24hr. Rent **bicycles** at Zebra Car and Cycle Hire, 9 The Esplanade. (☎736 556; www.zebrahire.com. Bicycles £10 per day. Open daily 8am-5pm.)

⊞ ⁊ ORIENTATION AND PRACTICAL INFORMATION. The ferry drops travelers at **Elizabeth Harbor,** which lies at the southwest corner of **St. Helier,** the hub of the island's nightlife and shopping. From the harbor, follow the pedestrian pathway signs along the pier toward Liberation Sq. and the **Tourist Information Centre.** (☎448 800; www.jersey.com. Open M-Sa 8:30am-5:30pm, Su 8:30am-2:15pm. Hours vary in winter.) The TIC maintains an accommodations list (posted outside off-hours) and stocks a variety of maps. Les Petits Trains runs 40min. **tours** through St. Helier or to St. Aubin village with English or French commentary from the TIC (Train-Hopper pass for both routes £8.50). Also try Tantivy Blue Coach Tours, which takes bookings over the phone. (☎706 706; www.jerseycoaches.com. All-day island tour £16.) **Luggage storage** is available at Ace Travel, 5 Esplanade, Liberation Sq. (☎488 488. £3 ½-day, £5 full day.) Other services include: **banks** at the intersection of Conway, New, and Broad St., and a Thomas Cook, 14 Charing Cross (☎506 900; open M-Tu and Th-Sa 9am-5:30pm, W 10am-5:30pm); **police,** Rougebouillon St. (☎612 612); Jersey General **Hospital,** Gloucester St. (☎622 000) and a **visitors' doctor** (☎616 833); Roseville **pharmacy,** 7 Roseville St. (☎734 698; open daily 9am-9:30pm); **Internet** access at Jersey **Library,** Halkett Pl. (☎759 991; £1 per 15min.; open M and W-F 9:30am-5:30pm, Tu 9:30am-7:30pm, Sa 9:30am-4pm); and the **post office,** Broad St. (☎616 616; open M-F 8:30am-5pm, Sa 8:30am-5pm) with a **bureau de change. Post Code:** JE1 1AA.

⁊ ⌂ ACCOMMODATIONS AND FOOD. With tourism as their biggest industry, the islands are teeming with accommodation options. Pick up *Out of the Blue,* an accommodations guide (free at the TIC) or contact the **Jersey Hospitality Association** (☎721 421; www.jerseyhols.com). Book ahead, as accommodations fill quickly in summer. In St. Helier, pretty—and pricey—**B&Bs** line the Havre des Pas, south of the town center by the beach. Expect to pay at least £30-45 for a single in summer. Travelers looking for a cheaper night's rest should head east to the coastal St. Martin area. The only hostel on the island is the new, beautiful, 105-bed **YHA Jersey ❸,** Haut de la Garenne, La Rue de la Pouclée et des Quatre Chemins, St. Martin. Take bus #3a from St. Helier (20min., every hr.), get off before Ransoms Garden Centre, and walk 200 yd. to the hostel; after 5:45pm take bus #1 to Gorey (last bus 11pm) and walk ½ mi. up the hill behind the row of restaurants on the pier, turn left, and walk up the hill. (☎0870 770 6130. Breakfast included. Reception 7-10am and 5-11pm. Open Feb.-Nov. daily; Dec.-Jan. F-Sa. Dorms £21.50, under 18 £14.50. MC/V.) Located along the Havre des Pas, the **Havelock Inn ❸** offers a convenient location and an elegant English breakfast. (☎730 663; www.havelockguesthouse.com. High season £21-39, low season £13-28 per person. MC/V.) **Rozel Camping Park ❶,** St. Martin, offers a view of the French coast and has showers, pool, laundry, and toilet access. Take bus #3 and ask to be let off at the camping park. (☎855 200; www.rozelcamping.co.uk. Tents only. £7.50-9 per person. MC/V.)

Jersey offers a range of excellent restaurants. St. Helier has numerous Chinese and ethnic takeaway eateries that offer filling, low-priced entrees. Chic furnishings and ample people-watching await at the **Beach House ❷,** Gorey Pier. Enjoy an extensive menu, from tortilla wraps (£6) to salmon (£9). Call ahead to reserve an outdoor table. (☎859 902. Open M 11am-6pm, Tu-Su 12:30-3:30pm and 6:30-9:30pm. Food served until 30min. before close. MC/V.) Pass through the bright red door of **Rojo ❷,** 10 Bond St., for filling tapas. (☎729 904. Tapas £3. Express lunch discount noon-2pm. Open noon-3pm and 6pm-10pm. MC/V.) **City Bar and Brasserie ❷,** 75-77

Halkett Pl., offers sizable portions and free Internet access in a sleek coffee shop. (☎510 096; www.cityjersey.com. Sandwiches £4.50-6.25; entrees £7-14.50. Open M-Sa 10am-11pm. AmEx/MC/V.) Grab coffee, a milkshake, or cake at the **Curiosity Coffee Shop ❷**, 14 Sand St. Shelves of novels and board games prompt patrons to linger. (☎510 075. Free Wi-Fi with purchase. Open in summer M-F 7am-7pm, Sa 7am-6pm, Su 11am-7pm; other seasons M-F 7am-7pm, Sa 7am-6pm.)

◩ **SIGHTS.** Jersey's sights celebrate the island's ever-changing role in the world beyond its waters. The **Jersey Heritage Trust** oversees many of the museums; check out www.jerseyheritagetrust.org. The newly renovated ◪**Mont Orgueil Castle,** on Gorey Pier, was built in the 13th century to protect the island from the French. Most of the rooms are open for exploring. (☎853 292. Open daily Apr.-Oct. 10am-6pm; Nov.-Mar. 10am-dusk. Last admission 1hr. before close. £9, concessions £8.20.) Across from Liberation Sq. by the St. Helier marina, the **Maritime Museum and Occupation Tapestry Gallery** contains a nautical hodgepodge. You'll find everything from ships in bottles to hands-on exhibits on tides, sailing, and seascape painting. Open the boxes throughout the museum to see ancient weapons and documents, including a letter from George III, legalizing piracy in times of war. (☎811 043. Open daily Apr.-Oct. 10am-5pm; Nov.-Mar. 10am-4pm. £6.50, concessions £5.70.) The **Jersey War Tunnels,** Les Charrieres Malorey, St. Lawrence, provide a somber history lesson about life in Jersey under Nazi occupation. Exhibits are housed in a former German military hospital. (☎860 808; www.jerseywartunnels.com. Open from mid-Feb. to mid-Dec. daily 10am-6pm. Last admission 4:30pm. £9.30, students £6.30.) **Durrell Wildlife** (formerly the Jersey Zoo), in Trinity Parish, is run by a conservation trust and features endangered species on its 31 acres of land. The zoo has an organic garden where it grows food for the animals. Take bus #3a, 3b, or 23. (☎860 000. Open daily July-Aug. 9am-6pm; Sept.-June 10am-dusk. £11.50, students £8.50.)

♫❇ **ENTERTAINMENT AND FESTIVALS.** The **Opera House,** Gloucester St., features both West End hits and local productions. (☎511 115; www.jerseyoperahouse.co.uk. Open M-Sa 10am-6pm; open until 8pm on performance nights and from 1hr. before performances on Su.) Various pubs and clubs offer nightlife options. The popular **Liquid and Envy Club,** at the Waterfront Centre, underwent renovations in summer 2006 and has reopened in all its former glory. Tourists in posh fashions fill the dance floors until the early morning. Envy has a 25+ age requirement. (☎789 356. F-Sa dance music, Su alternative. Open daily 10pm-2am.) **The Cosmopolitan,** on The Esplanade just north of Gloucester St., features drag musical revues. (☎720 289. Performances W 9:15pm (summer only), Th-Sa 10pm, Su 6pm. Nightclub cover £6. Open F-Sa 11:30pm-2:30am.) Escape the ruckus of St. Helier's pubs and head to the **Buddha Bar,** 10 Wharf St., off Conway St. Patrons curl up with their drinks in lounge chairs or munch on entrees, which often run against the bar's theme and cater to British tastes for meat and gravy. (☎729 111. £10 for appetizer and entree M-Th evenings and Su afternoons. Open daily noon-1am. MC/V.) In October, take a bite of **Tennerfest,** which challenges local restaurants to come up with the best £10 menu. Check out www.jersey.com for more on all festivals.

GUERNSEY ☎01481

Guernsey, 25 mi. west of Jersey, is quieter than its sister island but harbors the bustling town of St. Peter Port. With a carefree island spirit and an expansive seascape view that inspired Victor Hugo during his exile from France, the island draws well-heeled travelers seeking both surf and serenity.

TRANSPORTATION. Island Coachways **buses** (☎720 210; www.buses.gg) operate island-wide, with frequent service to tourist favorites. The bus terminal is on the waterfront, where Quay and South Esplanade converge. Buses #7 and 7a (every hr., 60p) circle the coast. "Wave and Save" cards (£4.50 for 10 rides) offer discounts on multiple fares. Island Coachways also offers themed **tours** ("Guernsey in a Day" and "Fairy Princesses of Pleinmony," £10) from May to September. Tours begin at 10am and typically end at the bus terminal. Call for information. For a **taxi,** call Island Taxis (☎07781 129 090; 24hr.) or PTR Taxis (☎07781 133 233).

⚂⚁ ORIENTATION AND PRACTICAL INFORMATION. Ferries land at St. Julian's Pier in St. Peter Port. To reach the **Tourist Information Centre** on North Esplanade, take a left at the end of the pier. The TIC has maps and the helpful *Naturally Guernsey,* which provides information on the attractions of the island as well as nearby Herm, Sark, and Alderney. The center also books accommodations for a £2 charge plus a 10% deposit, and maintains a small accommodation information booth at the ferry terminal. (☎723 552; www.visitguernsey.com. Open in summer M-Sa 9am-6pm, Su 9am-1pm; in winter M-F 9am-5pm, Sa 9am-4pm.) St. Martin, southwest of St. Peter's Port, has a number of necessities. Other services include: **banks** on High St.; **Thomas Cook,** 22 Le Pollet (☎724 111; open M-Sa 9am-5:30pm); **police,** Hospital Ln. (☎725 111); Princess Elizabeth **Hospital,** Le Vauquiedor, St. Martin (☎725 241); Boots **pharmacy,** 26-27 High St. (☎726 565; open M-Sa 8:30am-5:30pm); **Internet** access at Guille-Alles **Library,** The Market, St. Peter Port (☎720 392; £1 per 30min.; open M and Th-Sa 9:15am-4:45pm, Tu 10am-4:45pm, W 9:15am-7:45pm; reservations required); and the **post office,** Smith St. (☎711 720; open M-F 8:30am-5pm, Sa 8:30am-noon). **Post Code:** GY1 2JG.

⚃⚄ ACCOMMODATIONS AND FOOD. With more reasonable prices than Jersey, hotels fill quickly. The TIC posts vacancies in front of the building. For lodgings near town with views of Sark and Herm, try **St. George's Guest House ❹,** St. George's Esplanade, St. Peter Port. (☎721 027. Breakfast included. Aug. £35 per person; Sept.-July £33 per person. MC/V.) A 20min. uphill walk from the pier, the **Grisnoir Guest House ❸,** Les Gravees at the top of Grange Rd., has friendly keepers and a great price. (☎727 267; www.grisnoir.co.uk. Breakfast included. Shared bathrooms. Reservations recommended. £24-28 per person. MC/V with surcharge.)

It seems almost mandatory for Guernsey restaurants to serve fresh seafood. Takeaway places line the street behind the TIC and are the best bet for cheap eats. Get fresh fruit and veggies at the **market,** appropriately located on Market St. (open M-Sa 7:30am-5pm). The **Terrace Bar ❷,** on Corner St., offers sandwiches (£2.50-4) and Thai dishes (£3-8) under a vine-laced terrace overlooking the harbor. (☎724 478. Open 9am-dusk, weather permitting. MC/V.) **La Cucina ❷,** North Plantation, above Yugo's Take-Out, serves sandwiches (£5) with a Mediterranean influence. (☎715 166. Tapas special £16. Open Tu-F noon-2pm and 5:30-10pm, Sa 2-10pm, Su 1-5pm. Cash only.) **Christie's ❸,** Le Pollet, has a bistro facing the street and a more expensive restaurant overlooking the harbor. (☎726 624. Lunch entrees £4.50-15. Open daily noon-2:30pm and 6-10:30pm. MC/V.)

◈ SIGHTS. Pull yourself away from Guernsey's wildflowers and beaches long enough to tour **◈Hauteville House,** St. Peter Port. Victor Hugo's home during his exile from France remains virtually unaltered since the days when he wrote *Les Misérables* here. The house is full of hidden inscriptions and mantles constructed by Hugo from recycled furniture. (☎721 911. Open from May to early Oct. M-Sa 10am-4pm; Apr. M-Sa noon-4pm. £4, concessions £2, under 20 free.) The **Castle Cornet,** on the marina in St. Peter Port, has unbeatable views. Built in 1204, the castle has changed hands often, most recently when Britain gave it back to Guernsey in 1947 in recognition of the island's loyalty during WWII. Time your visit with the noon gun salute. (☎ 721 657. Open daily Apr.-Oct. 10am-5pm. Last admission 4:15pm. £6.50, students free.) A "Venue" ticket (£10) may be purchased for entrance into the castle, the **Fort Grey Shipwreck Museum** (☎ 265 036; open daily Easter-Oct. 10am-5pm), the **Telephone Museum** (open M-Sa 2pm-5pm), and the **Guernsey Museum and Art Gallery,** (☎ 726 518; www.museums.gov.gg; open daily 10am-5pm).

Island RIB Voyages takes visitors on a 34 ft. commercial boat to see puffins, seals, and other wildlife in their natural habitats while learning about their environment from the on-board marine zoologist. (☎ 713 031; www.islandribvoyages.com. Open Apr.-Oct. daily 10am-dusk. 1hr. tour £23.50, children £16.) Nearby **Herm** (www.herm-island.com) and **Sark** (www.sark.info) are worthwhile daytrips. Pristine beaches await travelers at Herm, and Sark is untouched by cars—transportation on the island is left to foot, bicycle, and horse-drawn carriage. In July, be sure to check out the annual **Sheep Racing** competition.

🎭 🎪 **ENTERTAINMENT AND FESTIVALS.** Shopping in Guernsey is particularly popular due to the absence of Britain's staggering 17.5% value added tax (VAT; p. 19). After collecting your bargains, plop down for a pint at one of the bars that line the waterfront. **Ship & Crown**, North Esplanade, is a local favorite with frequent live music (☎ 721 368; pints £2-2.50; open M-Sa 10am-midnight, Su noon-midnight), and the **Albion House Tavern,** Church Sq., is a historic experience in its own right—it's the tavern closest to a church in the British Isles, thanks to a gargoyle that almost bridges the alleyway (☎ 723 518; pints £1.75-2.50; open daily 10:30am-midnight). Along with **Tennerfest** in October (p. 254), Guernsey hosts many other competitions and celebrations year-round. Don't miss the **Battle of Flowers** (☎ 254 473) in August, when locals duke it out for the honor of best floral float.

THE HEART
OF ENGLAND

The pastures and half-timbered houses that characterize the country-side west of London are the stuff of stereotype. Traveling through the Heart of England, however, you'll be hard-pressed to find a field, dale, or town that isn't picturesque. The Heart has England's most famous attractions: Oxford, Britain's oldest university town; Stratford-upon-Avon, Shakespeare's home; and the gorgeous villages of the Cotswolds. The region's touring hordes can be difficult to avoid, but resourceful travelers will find an abundance of untrod adventures around every corner.

HIGHLIGHTS OF THE HEART OF ENGLAND

ADMIRE the gargoyles in Oxford, a stunning university town, rich in architecture and bizarre student traditions (p. 262).

PLAY PRINCESS at Windsor, one of the world's most sumptuous royal residences, which has housed 40 reigning monarchs (p. 261).

SHAKE IT UP in Stratford-upon-Avon, where tourist trails honor the Bard's footsteps and the Royal Shakespeare Company venerates his every syllable (p. 274).

ST. ALBANS   ☎01727

From the Roman legion to Norman conquerors to warring houses, each new ruling class has wanted either to set St. Albans on fire or to make it a capital. In the 3rd century, the Roman soldier Alban was beheaded here, making him England's first Christian martyr. Because of the town's traditional architecture, it is frequented by film crews as a substitute for Westminster Abbey and Oxford University.

▐ TRANSPORTATION. St. Albans has two **train stations:** City Station, the main one, and Abbey Station, which runs local services. **Trains** (☎08457 484 950) to London's King's Cross Thameslink leave City Station (25min., 4 per hr., round-trip £8). To get to the town center, turn right out of the station onto Victoria Rd., follow the road back over the train tracks, and continue uphill for about 10min. Avoid the hike by hopping any "Into Town" bus (65p). Sovereign (☎854 732) **buses** stop at City Station and along St. Peter's St. To Heathrow, take bus #724 from St. Peter's St. in front of the post office (2hr., every hr., £6.70).

▐ ORIENTATION AND PRACTICAL INFORMATION. Leaving City Station, **Hatfield Road** to the left and **Victoria Street** to the right both lead uphill to town; at the town center, they are intersected by the main drag. To get to the main attractions, turn left onto this street, which changes from **St. Peter's Street** to **Chequer Street** to **Holywell Hill.** The **Tourist Information Centre,** at the intersection of Victoria and St. Peter's St., has a free map and a sight-filled miniguide, and books accommodations for £3 plus a 10% deposit. (☎864 511; www.stalbans.gov.uk. Open Easter-Oct. M-Sa 10am-5pm; Nov.-Easter M-Sa 10am-4pm.) Other services include: **banks** with **ATMs** at the beginning of Chequer St.; **police,** on Victoria St. (☎08453 300

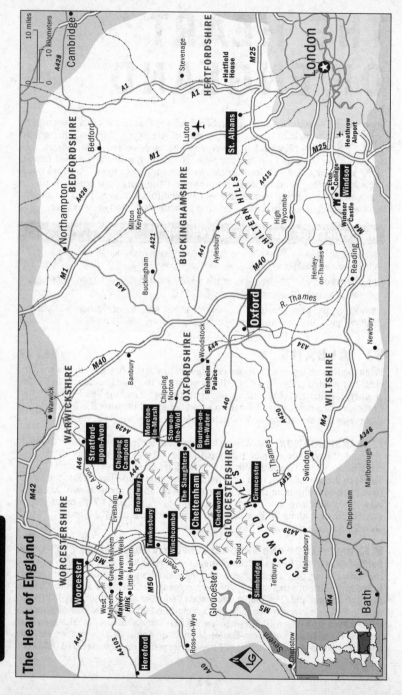

HEART OF ENGLAND

The Heart of England

222); Maltings **pharmacy,** 6 Victoria St. (☎839 335; open M-F 9am-6:30pm, Sa 9am-5pm); **Internet** at the **library** in The Maltings shopping center, across from the TIC (☎01438 737 333; £1.25 per 30min., open M-Th 9am-8pm, F 10:30am-6pm, Sa 9am-4pm); and the **post office,** 2 Beaconsfield Rd. (☎860 110). **Post Code:** AL1 3RA.

🏠🛏 ACCOMMODATiONS AND FOOD. Reasonably priced **B&Bs** (£20-40) are scattered and many times unmarked. The best way to secure a room is through the TIC. Near City Station, the host at **Mrs. Murphy ❸,** 478 Hatfield Rd., offers a tidy rooms at reasonable prices. (☎842 216. Singles £25-35; doubles, twins, and family rooms £40-60. Cash only.) **Mrs. Norton ❸,** 16 York Rd., near the town center, has comfortable rooms with shared bath. Breakfast comes with homemade preserves. (☎853 647. Singles £25; doubles £50. Cash only.) At **178 London Rd. ❹,** Mrs. Nicol opens her beautiful home to guests. (☎846 726; www.178londonroad.co.uk. Satellite TV in all rooms. Singles £35; doubles £50; family rooms £50-80. Cash only.)

Buy veggies at the **market** (W and Sa by the TIC) and Iceland **grocery,** 144 Victoria St. (☎833 908. Open M-F 9am-8pm, Sa 9am-7pm, Su 11am-5pm.) For lunch, visit **🍺Ye Olde Fighting Cocks ❶,** Abbey Mill Ln., between the cathedral and Verulamium park. Once a 16th-century public house, this octagonal building may be the oldest pub in England. Tunnels, used by monks to see cockfights and later to flee Henry VIII's cronies, run from the cathedral to the pub. (☎865 830. Open Th 11am-11pm, F-Sa 11am-midnight, Su noon-11pm. Food served daily noon-9pm. MC/V.) Ducks waddle from the River Ver near the **Waffle House ❷,** St. Michael's St., toward the Roman quarter. Choose from many toppings (£2.40-7), ranging from bananas to hummus. (☎853 502. Open daily Apr.-Oct. 10am-6pm; Nov.-Mar. 10am-5pm. MC/V.) For a delicious Moroccan meal in a cozy cafe, try **Little Marrakech ❷,** 31 Market St., with sandwiches (£3.50-5) on Moroccan bread or a set lunch for £6.50. (☎853 569. Open daily 9am-4pm and 6:30pm-11pm. MC/V.)

◘ SIGHTS. Built on the foundations of a Saxon church, the **🏛Cathedral of St. Alban** is defined by its 1077 Norman design. At 227 ft., the medieval nave is the longest in Britain, and the wooden roof is one of the largest. Painted while the outcome of the Wars of the Roses was uncertain, the ceiling features the white and red roses of York and Lancaster. (☎860 780. Open M-F and Su 8:30am-5:45pm, Sa 8:30am-9pm. Suggested donation £2.50. Guided tours available for £1.) From the cathedral, walk 10min. down Fishpool St., over the river, and uphill as it becomes St. Michael's St. to visit the **🏛Verulamium Museum.** Homes of the rich and poor of Roman Britain have been recreated with mosaics, painted wall plasters, and artifacts discovered in the area. (☎751 810. Open M-Sa 10am-5:30pm, Su 2-5:30pm. Last admission 5pm. £3.30, concessions £2, families £8.) A block away, the remains of one of five **Roman theaters** built in England huddle against a backdrop of English countryside. Archaeologists still scour the site. (☎835 035. Open daily 10am-5pm. £2, concessions £1, children 50p.) Two miles south of St. Albans, the **Gardens of the Rose** in Chiswell Green are the "flagship gardens" of the Royal National Rose Society. Over 30,000 roses scale buildings. (☎850 461. Open June-Sept. M-Sa 9am-5pm, Su 10am-6pm. £4, children £1.50, seniors £3.50, families £10.)

▶ DAYTRIP FROM ST. ALBANS

HATFIELD HOUSE
Buses #300 and 301 link St. Albans and Hatfield House (20min., 1-3 per hr., round-trip £3.60). The Hatfield train station, across from the main gate, makes the house easily accessible from other towns. ☎01707 287 000. House open daily Easter-Sept. noon-4pm. Th 1hr. guided tours. House, park, and gardens £9, children £4.50. Park and gardens £4.50/3.50. Park only £2/1.

Stately 225-room Hatfield House is best-known as Queen Elizabeth I's childhood home. Elizabeth was placed under house arrest here for suspected treason by her sister, Mary, Queen of Scots (p. 70), and ascended the throne to hold her first Council of State after Mary's death. Hatfield holds two famous portraits of Elizabeth, and, although the stockings attributed to her are fakes, the gloves are real. Keep an eye out for the Queen's 22 ft. family tree, tracing her lineage to Adam and Eve via Noah, Julius Caesar, King Arthur, and King Lear. All that remains of her original palace is the Great Hall; the rest was razed to make way for the mansion that dominates the estate today.

WINDSOR AND ETON   ☎ 01753

The town of Windsor and the attached village of Eton center entirely on Windsor Castle and Eton College, two famed symbols of the British upper crust. Windsor is thick with specialty shops, tea houses, and pubs, which cater mostly to the throngs of daytrippers from nearby London.

▉ TRANSPORTATION

Two train stations lie near the castle. **Trains** (☎ 08457 484 950) pull out of Windsor and Eton **Royal Station** to London Paddington via Slough (40min., 2 per hr., round-trip £7.40). Trains leave Windsor and Eton **Riverside** to London Waterloo (40min., 4 per hr., round-trip £8). Green Line **bus** #702 goes to London Victoria (1¼hr., every hr., round-trip £5-10) from High St. opposite Parish Church. Bus #77 to London Heathrow (45min., every hr., round-trip 4.20) leaves from St. Leonard Rd.

✴▉ ORIENTATION AND PRACTICAL INFORMATION

Windsor village slopes from the foot of the castle. **High Street** spans the hilltop, then becomes **Thames Street** at the statue of Queen Victoria and continues to the river, at which point it reverts to High St. as it enters Eton. The main shopping area, **Peascod Street,** meets High St. at the statue. The **Tourist Information Centre,** Old Booking Hall, Windsor Royal Shopping Center, has free brochures, great maps, and an accommodations guide. (☎ 743 900; www.windsor.gov.uk. Open Apr.-June daily 10am-5pm; July-Aug. M-Sa 10am-5:30pm, Su 10am-5pm; Sept.-Mar. M-Sa 10am-5pm, Su 10am-4pm.) Other services include: **police,** on the corner of St. Mark's Rd. and Alma Rd. (☎ 08458 505 505; M-Sa 8am-10pm, Su 9am-5pm); **Internet** at the **library** on Bachelors Acre (☎ 743 940; guest pass for 30min. free; open M and Th 9:30am-5pm, Tu 9:30am-8pm, W 2-5pm, F 9:30am-7pm, Sa 9:30am-3pm) or **McDonald's,** 13-14 Thames St. (£2 per hr.; open daily 6:30am-10pm); **banks** with **ATMs** along Peascod St.; Boots **pharmacy,** 113 Peascod St. (☎ 863 595; open M-Sa 8:20am-6pm, Su 10:30am-4:30pm); and the **post office,** 38-39 Peascod St. (open M and W-F 9am-5:30pm, Tu 9:30am-5:30pm, Sa 9am-4pm). **Post Code:** SL4 1LH.

⌂▉ ACCOMMODATIONS AND FOOD

Windsor lacks budget accommodations. You can avoid the high prices by making it a daytrip from London. If you decide to stay, the TIC booking service (☎ 743 907; windsor.accommodation@rbwm.gov.uk) will book **B&Bs** for £5 plus a 10% deposit. **Rutlands ❸,** 102 St. Leonard's Rd., is a centrally located Victorian guest house with two ensuite rooms. (☎ 859 533. Single £35-40; double £60-65.) The **Clarence Hotel ❹,** 9 Clarence Rd., offers spacious rooms and includes a lounge with cable TV. (☎ 864 436; www.clarence-hotel.co.uk. Breakfast included. Singles £45-66; doubles £55-77; family rooms £60-93.) **Alma House ❹,** 56 Alma Rd., is in a quiet neighborhood a few minutes from town. (☎862 983; www.almahouse.co.uk. Free Wi-Fi. Singles £50; doubles £70-75; family rooms £85-95.)

Chain restaurants dominate Thames St. **Waterman's Arms ❶**, Brocas St., is the first left after crossing the bridge to Eton. Founded in 1542, it's still a local favorite, offering pub classics for £5-8. (☎861 001. Food served M-F noon-3pm and 6-9pm, Sa noon-9pm, Su noon-4:30pm.) **Gran Panini ❶**, 49 Thames St., has sandwiches (£3.50-4.30) and pasties for £2.50. (☎853 991. Open daily 8am-6pm. Cash only.)

👁 SIGHTS

WINDSOR CASTLE

The largest and oldest continuously inhabited castle in the world, Windsor features some of the most sumptuous rooms in Europe and some of the rarest artwork in the Western tradition. Windsor Castle was built high above the Thames by William the Conqueror as a fortress rather than as a residence, and 40 reigning monarchs have since left their marks. In 1992, a fire devastated over 100 rooms, including nine state rooms, but a massive project has restored the apartments to their original glory. Windsor is the official residence of the Queen, who spends the month of April and many of her private weekends here. During royal stays, large areas of the castle are unavailable to visitors. The admission prices are lowered on these occasions, but it is wise to call ahead or check out the flag pole—when the Queen is in residence, the castle flies the light blue flag of the monarchy. Visitors can watch the **Changing of the Guard** in front of the Guard Room at 11am (Apr.-July M-Sa; Aug.-Mar. alternate days M-Sa). The Guards can also be seen at 10:50 and 11:30am as they march to and from the ceremony. (☎831 118. Open daily Mar.-Oct. 9:45am-5:15pm; Nov.-Feb. 9:45am-4:15pm. Last admission 1¼hr. before close. £13.50, students £12, under 17 £7.50. Tours free.)

UPPER WARD. Reach the upper ward through the Norman tower and gate. Stand in the far left line to enter 📷**Queen Mary's Doll House**, a replica of a home on a 1:12 scale, with tiny, handwritten classics in its library, miniature crown jewels, and functional plumbing and electrical systems. Velvet ropes lead to the **state apartments**, used for ceremonial events and entertainment for world leaders and heads of state. The rooms are ornamented with art from the **Royal Collection**, including works by Reubens, Rembrandt, Van Dyck, and Queen Victoria herself. The **Queen's Drawing Room** features portraits of Henry VIII, Elizabeth I, and Mary I, but don't miss smaller touches, like the silver dragon doorknobs. The fully restored **Lantern Room**, the **Grand Reception Room**, and **St. George's Hall** are stunning.

MIDDLE AND LOWER WARD. The **Round Tower** dominates the middle ward. A stroll downhill to the lower ward brings you to **St. George's Chapel**, a 15th-century structure with delicate vaulting and a wall of stained glass dedicated to the Order of the Garter, England's most elite knighthood. Used for the marriage of Sophie and Prince Edward, the chapel also holds the tombs of the Queen Mother, George III, and Queen Mary. Ask a guide to explain how the bones of Charles I and Henry VIII were accidentally placed under the same stone.

OTHER SIGHTS

ETON COLLEGE. Eton College is best known as one of England's most elite public—which is to say, private—schools. Ironically, it was founded by Henry VI in 1440 as a college for paupers. Despite its position at the apex of the British class system, Eton has shaped some notable dissident thinkers, including Aldous Huxley, George Orwell, and former Liberal Party leader Jeremy Thorpe. The male students still stay true to many of the old traditions, including wearing tailcoats to

ETON-SPEAK

The elite prep school Eton College has educated philosophers, princes, and Prime Ministers. Eton has a vernacular to describe the school's many ranks, quirks, and rituals. Common words (with example sentences) include:

1. Stick-ups: collars worn with the school's black morning suit. "Tom's had a pink **stick-up** because he washed a red sock with his white laundry."

2. Beak: a schoolmaster. "Barnaby passed a note to Allister while the **beak** wasn't looking."

3. Absence: roll call. "Jacob ran into the classroom just on time for **absence.**"

4. Wet bob: a boy who rows crew in summer. "David, a **wet bob,** suffered from bad tan lines."

5. Dry bob: a boy who plays cricket in summer. "Daniel, a **dry bob,** suffered from shin splints."

6. Half: a school term. "At Eton, three **halves** make a year."

7. Tap: the school's bar. "Jeremy counted down the days until his birthday celebration at the **tap.**"

8. Division: a class, or grade. "Tipsy Tim spent too much time at the tap and failed sixth **division.**"

9. The Block: a stool where students were flogged. "Michael, and his buttocks, quivered as he passed **The Block.**"

10. Pop, popper: one of the 25 self-elected student prefects. "Peter Piper picked a peck of pickled **poppers.**"

class. The 25 houses that surround the quad act as residences for the approximately 1250 students. The **Museum of Eton Life** displays relics and stories of the school's extensive past. *(A 10-15min. walk down Thames St., across Windsor Bridge, and along Eton High St.* ☎671 177. *Open daily from late Mar. to mid-Apr. and July-Aug. 10:30am-4:30pm; Sept.-June 2-4:30pm; schedule depends on academic calendar. Tours daily 2:15 and 3:15pm. £4, under 16 and seniors £3.25. Tours £5, under 16 £4.20.)*

LEGOLAND WINDSOR. A whimsical addition to the town, this amusement park has 50 rides, playgrounds, and circuses. Its Miniland took 100 workers, three years, and 25 million Lego bricks to craft. The replica of the City of London includes a 6 ft. St. Paul's Cathedral. *(Tickets available at the Windsor TIC.* ☎08705 040 404; www.legoland.co.uk. *Open daily Apr.-June and Sept.-Oct. 10am-5pm or 6pm; from mid-July to Aug. 10am-7pm. £30, children and seniors £23. Shuttle from town center £3, children £1.50.)*

OXFORD   ☎01865

Oxford has been home to nearly a millennium of scholarship—25 British prime ministers and numerous other world leaders have been educated here. In 1167, Henry II founded Britain's first university, and its distinguished spires have since captured the imaginations of luminaries such as Lewis Carroll and C.S. Lewis. The city's legendary scholarship and enthralling architecture also make Oxford a must-see for tourists and a popular place to study abroad. For a true sense of this enclave of academia, avoid the hordes choking Broad St. and roam the alleyways to find ancient bookshops, serene college quads, and, of course, history-laden pubs inviting you to sample their brew.

◧ TRANSPORTATION

Trains: Station on Botley Rd., down Park End. Ticket office open M-F 5:45am-8pm, Sa 6:15am-8pm, Su 7:10am-8pm. Trains (☎08457 484 950) to: **Birmingham** (1¼hr., 2 per hr., £20); **Glasgow** (5-7hr., every hr., £65-75); **London Paddington** (1hr., 2-4 per hr., £9.50-18.10); **Manchester** (3hr., 1-2 per hr., £21-42).

Buses: Station on Gloucester Green. **Stagecoach** (☎772 250; www.stagecoachbus.com) runs to **Cambridge** (3hr., 2 per hr., £6) and operates the **Oxford Tube** (☎772 250) to **London** (1¾hr.; 3-5 per hr.; £12, students £10). **National Express** (☎08705 808 080) runs to **Birmingham** (1½hr., 5 per day, £15), **Cambridge** (3hr., 2 per hr., £9), and **Stratford-upon-Avon** (1hr.; 2 per day; £8.50). The **Oxford Bus Company**

(☎785 400; www.oxfordbus.co.uk) runs to **London** (1¾hr.; 3-5 per hr.; £12, students £10), **Gatwick** (2hr.; every hr. 8am-9pm; £20, concessions £10), and **Heathrow** (1¼hr.; 3 per hr.; £15, concessions £7.50).

Public Transportation: The **Oxford Bus Company Cityline** (☎785 400) and **Stagecoach Oxford** (☎772 250) offer swift and frequent service to: **Iffley Road** (Stagecoach #3, Oxford Bus #4, 4A, 4B, 4C); **Banbury Road** (Stagecoach #2, 2A, 2B, 2D); **Abingdon Road** (Stagecoach #32, 33; Oxford Bus X3, X4); **Cowley Road** (Stagecoach #1, 5A, 5B, 10; Oxford Bus #5). Fares are low (most 60p-£1.40). Stagecoach offers a **Day-Rider ticket** and the Oxford Bus Company a **Freedom ticket,** which give unlimited travel on the respective company's local routes (£3.30-5.50 for 24hr., £10-17 for 5 days). A **Plus Pass** grants unlimited travel on all Oxford Bus Company, Stagecoach, and Thames Travel buses and can be purchased onboard any of these companies' buses (☎785 410; 1 day £5, 1 week £14).

Taxis: Radio Taxis (☎242 424). **ABC** (☎770 077). **City Taxis** (☎201 201). All 24hr.

■ 🛈 ORIENTATION AND PRACTICAL INFORMATION

Oxford's colleges gather around **St. Mary's Church,** which is the spiritual heart of both the university and the greater city. The city's center is bounded by **George Street** and connecting **Broad Street** to the north, and **Cornmarket** and **High Street** in the center. To the northwest, the district of **Jericho** is less touristed and is the unoffical hub of student life.

Tourist Information Centre: 15-16 Broad St. (☎726 871; www.visitoxford.org). The busy staff books rooms for £4 plus a 10% deposit. Unless you're dutifully toting your copy of *Let's Go,* expect to pay for information: visitors guide and map £1.25, accommodations list £1. Look for the free restaurant list and *In Oxford* monthly guide. Job listings, long-term accommodations listings, and entertainment news posted daily at the TIC and at www.dailyinfo.co.uk. Open M-Sa 9:30am-5pm; Easter-June and Aug.-Oct. also Su 10am-3:30pm; June-July also Su 10am-4pm. Last room booking 4:30pm.

Tours: The 2hr. official Oxford University **walking tour** (☎726 871) leaves from the TIC and provides access to some colleges otherwise closed to visitors. Tours only allow up to 19 people and are booked on a first come, first served basis, so get tickets early in the day. Daily 11am and 2pm; in summer also 10:30am and 1pm. £6.50, children £3. **Blackwell's** (☎333 606) walking tours leave from Canterbury Gate at Christ Church. General tours Tu 2pm, Th 11am, Sa noon. £6, concessions £5.50. Literary tour of Oxford Tu 2pm, Th 11am; "Inklings" tours about C.S. Lewis, J.R.R. Tolkien, and their circle of friends W 11:45am; Historic Oxford Tour F 2pm. All tours 1½hr. £6, concessions £5. **Guided Tours** (☎07810 402 757), 1½hr., depart from outside Trinity College on Broad St. and offer access to some colleges and other university buildings. Daily every hr. 11am-4pm. £6, children £3. The same company runs evening **Ghost Tours.** 1¼hr. In summer daily 8pm. £5, children £3. **City Sightseeing** (☎790 522) offers hop-on, hop-off bus tours of the city with over 20 stops. Every 10-15min. from bay 14 of the bus station. Pick up tickets from bus drivers or stands around the city. £9.50, students £8.50.

Budget Travel: STA Travel, 36 George St. (☎792 800). Open M, W, F 9:30am-6pm, Th 10am-6pm, Sa 10am-5pm, Su 11am-4pm.

Financial Services: Banks line Cornmarket St. **Marks & Spencer,** 13-18 Queen St. (☎248 075), has a **bureau de change** with no commission. Open M-W and F 8:30am-6:30pm, Th 8:30am-7:30pm, Sa 8:30am-6:30pm, Su 11am-4:30pm. **Thomas Cook,** 5 Queen St. (☎447 000). Open M-Sa 9am-5:30pm. The **TIC** also has a **bureau de change** with no commission.

Work Opportunities: JobCentre, 7 Worcester St. (☎445 000). Open M-Tu and Th 9am-4:30pm, W 10am-4:30pm, F 9am-4pm.

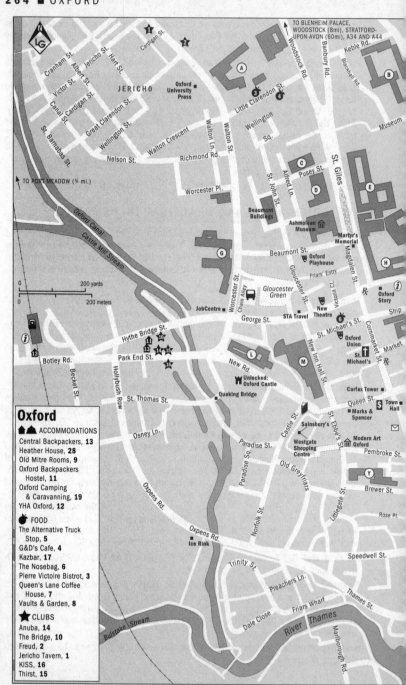

TO BLENHEIM PALACE,
WOODSTOCK (8mi), STRATFORD-
UPON-AVON (60mi), A34 AND A44

TO PORT MEADOW (¾ mi.)

JERICHO

Oxford
University
Press

Cardigan St.

Cranham St.
Jericho St.
Hart St.
Albert St.
Victor St.
Canal Cardigan St.
Great Clarendon St.
Wellington St.
Nelson St.
St. Barnabas St.

Little Clarendon St.
Walton St.
Walton Ln.
Walton Crescent
Richmond Rd.
Worcester Pl.

Wellington
Sq.

St. John St.
Alfred Ln.
Pusey St.
St. Giles

Keble Rd.
Blackhall Rd.
Banbury Rd.

Museum

Beaumont
Buildings

Ashmolean
Museum

Martyr's
Memorial

Oxford Canal
Castle Mill Stream

Worcester St.
Beaumont St.
Oxford
Playhouse
Gloucester St.
Friars' Entry
Magdalen St.
Victoria Rd.

Oxford
Story

Gloucester
Green

JobCentre

Chain Alley

George St.
STA Travel
New
Theatre

St. Michael's St.
Cornmarket St.

Ship

Oxford
Union

St.
Michael's

Market

0   200 yards
0   200 meters

Hythe Bridge St.
Park End St.
Botley Rd.
Becket St.
Hollybush Row

New Rd.

New Inn Hall St.

Carfax Tower

Queen St.
Marks &
Spencer

Town
Hall

St. Thomas St.
Quaking Bridge
Unlocked:
Oxford Castle

Osney Ln.

Castle St.

Sainsbury's

St. Ebbe's St.

Modern Art
Oxford

Paradise St.

Westgate
Shopping
Centre

Pembroke St.

Oxpens Rd.
Paradise Sq.
Old Greyfriars
Littlegate St.

Brewer St.

Rose Pl.

Oxpens Rd.
Ice Rink
Norfolk St.

Speedwell St.

Trinity St.
Preachers Ln.
Thames St.

Dale Close
Friars Wharf

River Thames

Bulstake Stream

Marlborough Rd.

Oxford

▲▲ ACCOMMODATIONS
Central Backpackers, **13**
Heather House, **28**
Old Mitre Rooms, **9**
Oxford Backpackers
  Hostel, **11**
Oxford Camping
  & Caravanning, **19**
YHA Oxford, **12**

🍴 FOOD
The Alternative Truck
  Stop, **5**
G&D's Cafe, **4**
Kazbar, **17**
The Nosebag, **6**
Pierre Victoire Bistrot, **3**
Queen's Lane Coffee
  House, **7**
Vaults & Garden, **8**

★ CLUBS
Anuba, **14**
The Bridge, **10**
Freud, **2**
Jericho Tavern, **1**
KISS, **16**
Thirst, **15**

HEART OF ENGLAND

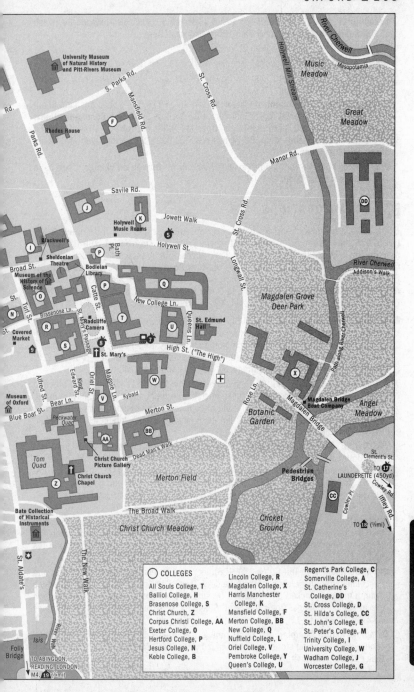

University Museum of Natural History and Pitt-Rivers Museum

S. Parks Rd.

Parks Rd.

Rd.

Mansfield Rd.

St. Cross Rd.

River Cherwell

Music Meadow

Mesopotamia

Great Meadow

Rhodes House

F

Manor Rd.

Savile Rd.

J

Holywell Music Rooms

K

Jowett Walk

5

Holywell St.

St. Cross Rd.

DD

Blackwell's

I

Sheldonian Theatre

P

Bath Pl.

Bodleian Library

Broad St.

Museum of the History of Science

O

Catte St.

P

Q

New College Ln.

River Cherwell
Addison's Walk

Magdalen Grove Deer Park

St.

N

Tun St.

Brasenose Ln.

R

St. Mary's Passage

Radcliffe Camera

T

U

St. Edmund Hall

Queen's Ln.

Longwall St.

Covered Market

9

S

8

7

St. Mary's

High St. ("The High")

Path along River Cherwell

Alfred St.

Museum of Oxford

Blue Boat St.

Bear Ln.

King Edward St.

V

Oriel St.

Magpie Ln.

Kybald

W

Merton St.

Rose Ln.

Magdalen Bridge

X

Magdalen Bridge Boat Company

Angel Meadow

Peckwater Quad

AA

BB

Dead Man's Walk

Botanic Garden

St. Clement's St.

TO **17**

Christ Church Picture Gallery

Christ Church Chapel

Tom Quad

Z

Merton Field

Pedestrian Bridges

LAUNDERETTE (450yd)

Cowley Pl.

Cowley Rd.

Iffley Rd.

Bate Collection of Historical Instruments

The Broad Walk

Christ Church Meadow

Cricket Ground

CC

TO **18** (½mi)

St. Aldate's

The New Walk

The New Walk

Isis

River Walk

Folly Bridge

TO ABINGDON, READING, LONDON, M4, **19** (½mi)

○ **COLLEGES**

All Souls College, **T**
Balliol College, **H**
Brasenose College, **S**
Christ Church, **Z**
Corpus Christi College, **AA**
Exeter College, **O**
Hertford College, **P**
Jesus College, **N**
Keble College, **B**

Lincoln College, **R**
Magdalen College, **X**
Harris Manchester College, **K**
Mansfield College, **F**
Merton College, **BB**
New College, **Q**
Nuffield College, **L**
Oriel College, **V**
Pembroke College, **Y**
Queen's College, **U**

Regent's Park College, **C**
Somerville College, **A**
St. Catherine's College, **DD**
St. Cross College, **D**
St. Hilda's College, **CC**
St. John's College, **E**
St. Peter's College, **M**
Trinity College, **I**
University College, **W**
Wadham College, **J**
Worcester College, **G**

HEART OF ENGLAND

Launderette: 127 Cowley Rd. Wash £2.60-4, dry £2.60. Also 66 Abingdon Rd. Wash £2-3. Soap 70p-£1. Open daily 7am-10pm; last wash 9pm.

Police: St. Aldates and Speedwell St. (☎505 505).

Hospital: John Radcliffe Hospital, Headley Way (☎741 166). Take bus #13 or 14.

Pharmacy: Boswell's, 1-4 Broad St. (☎241 244). Open M-F 9:30am-6pm, Sa 9am-6pm, Su 11am-5pm.

Internet Access: Oxford Central Library, Queen St. (☎815 549), near Westgate Shopping Centre. Free. Open M-Th 9:15am-7pm, F-Sa 9:15am-5pm. **Link Communications,** 33 High St. (☎204 207). £1 per 45min. Open M-F 9:30am-10pm, Sa 10am-10pm, Su 11am-8pm. **The Letting Shop,** 60 High St. (☎790 609). £1 per hr. Open M-F 10am-8pm, Sa 10am-5pm.

Post Office: 102-104 St. Aldates (☎08457 223 344). **Bureau de change.** Open M-Sa 9am-5:30pm. **Post Code:** OX1 1ZZ.

⛏ ACCOMMODATIONS

Book at least a week ahead from June to September, especially for singles. **B&Bs** (from £25) line the main roads out of town. Try www.stayoxford.com for affordable options. The 300s on **Banbury Road** are accessible by buses #2, 2A, 2B, and 2D. Cheaper B&Bs lie in the 200s and 300s on **Iffley Road** (bus #4, 4A, 4B, 4C, and 16B to Rose Hill) and on **Abingdon Road** in South Oxford (bus #16 and 16A). If it's late, call the **Oxford Association of Hotels and Guest Houses** (East Oxford ☎721 561, West Oxford ☎862 138, North Oxford ☎244 691, South Oxford ☎244 268).

▨ **Central Backpackers,** 13 Park End St. (☎242 288). Located above Thirst Bar. Newest hostel in Oxford. Spacious rooms. Have a few drinks with the Aussie owners on the rooftop terrace—a frequent spot for summertime barbecues. Reception 8am-11pm. Checkout 11am. Free luggage storage. Free Internet. Self-service kitchen. 4-bed dorms £18; 6-bed female or 8-bed mixed dorms £16; 12-bed dorms £14. MC/V. ❷

Oxford Backpackers Hostel, 9a Hythe Bridge St. (☎721 761), between the bus and train stations. A self-proclaimed "funky hostel" with murals and music playing in the hallway. Inexpensive bar and pool table in common area. Passport required. Female dorm available. Luggage storage £2 per item. Laundry £2.50. Internet £1 per 30min. Dorms £14; quads £16 per person. MC/V. ❷

YHA Oxford, 2a Botley Rd. (☎727 275). To get there from the train station, turn right onto Botley Rd. Photos of famous Oxfordians line the walls. The quietest of Oxford's 3 hostels. TV room, library, and ensuite bathrooms. Full English breakfast included. Lockers £1. Towels 50p. Laundry £3. Internet access 7p per min. 4- and 6-bed dorms £21 per person, under 18 £16; twins £46. Add £3 for non-members. £3 student discount. MC/V. ❷

Heather House, 192 Iffley Rd. (☎249 757). A 5-10min. walk from Magdalen Bridge, or take the bus marked Rose Hill from the bus or train station or from Carfax Tower. The charming proprietor keeps spotless ensuite rooms complete with small flat-screen TVs and Wi-Fi. Soft carpet. Singles £35-45; doubles £65-75. MC/V. ❹

Old Mitre Rooms, 4b Turl St. (☎279 976), located between Mahogany Hair Salon and Past Times Stationery. Look for the blue door. Owned by Lincoln College and used as a dorm term-time. Packed on weekends; be sure to book ahead. Bookings and check-in are at Lincoln College. Open July-Sept. Singles £30; twins £55, ensuite £60; triples £72. MC/V. ❸

Camping: Oxford Camping and Caravanning, 426 Abingdon Rd. (☎244 088), behind Touchwoods camping store. Toilet and laundry facilities. £4.10-5.80 per person. Electricity £2.30. MC/V. ❶

◖ FOOD

A bevy of budget options seduce tourists and students fed up with standard college food. ▨**Gloucester Green Market,** behind the bus station, abounds with tasty treats (open W 8am-3:30pm). The **Covered Market,** between Market St. and Carfax, has produce and deli goods (open M-Sa 8am-5pm). Get **groceries** at the Sainsbury's inside the Westgate Shopping Centre (open M-Sa 7am-8pm, Su 11am-5pm). Across Magdalen Bridge, you'll find cheap restaurants on **Cowley Road** that serve international food in addition to the standard fish and chips. For an on-the-go meal, try a sandwich from the **kebab vans,** usually found on Broad St., High St., Queen St., and St. Aldates.

▨ **The Alternative Tuck Shop,** 24 Holywell St. (☎792 054). Behind an unassuming veneer lies Oxford's most popular sandwich shop. Students and residents alike line up for any number of delicious made-to-order sandwiches (under £3) and panini (£2.80). There will more than likely be a line, but the staff moves quickly. Open daily 8:30am-6pm. Cash only. ❶

▨ **Vaults & Garden,** Radcliffe Sq., under St. Mary's Church (☎279 112; www.vaultsandgarden.co.uk). Follow your nose to the delectable homemade soups and organic entrees (£6). Cozy booths inside and outdoor tables in the garden overlooking the iconic Radcliffe Camera. Open daily 9am-5:30pm. Cash only. ❷

Kazbar, 25-27 Cowley Rd. (☎202 920). Mediterranean tapas bar near town. Spanish-style decor and sexy lighting. Tasty tapas (£2.20-4.75) like *patatas con chorizo.* Free tapas with drink M-F 4-7pm. Open M-F 4-11pm, Sa-Su noon-midnight. AmEx/MC/V. ❶

G&D's Cafe, 55 Little Clarendon St. (☎516 652). Superb homemade ice cream (£1.75-4), pizza bagels (£3.45-4.15), and a boisterous student atmosphere. The great food and outdoor patio make it a favorite in the Jericho area. Branch on St. Aldates. Open daily 8am-midnight. Cash only. ❶

The Nosebag, 6-8 St. Michael's St. (☎721 033). Cafeteria-style service on the 2nd fl. of a 15th-century stone building. Eclectic menu includes great vegan and vegetarian options and tasty homemade soups for under £8. Indulge in a scrumptious dessert such as double fudge cake (£1.35-2.75). Lunch specials under £3. Open M-Th 9:30am-10pm, F-Sa 9:30am-10:30pm, Su 9:30am-9pm. AmEx/MC/V. ❷

Pierre Victoire Bistrot, 9 Little Clarendon St. (☎316 616). French cuisine with daily specials. Lunch £5-7; dinner £9-14. Pre-theater menu of 2 courses and coffee £10 M-Th and Su 7-9pm. 3 courses, wine, and coffee £17.50 M-Th and Su. Open M-Sa noon-2:30pm and 7-11pm, Su noon-3:30pm and 6-10pm. MC/V. ❸

Queen's Lane Coffee House, 40 High St. (☎240 082). Opened in 1654, the Queen's Lane is supposedly the first place where coffee was sold in all of Europe. You can still get a good cup of java here, as well as a selection of delicious sandwiches and desserts (£3-6). Half-price sandwiches after 5:30pm on busy nights. Open daily 7:30am-8pm. Cash only. ❶

◐ SIGHTS

The TIC sells a map (£1.25) and the *Welcome to Oxford* guide (£1), which lists the visiting hours for all of the college. Hours can also be accessed online at www.ox.ac.uk/visitors/colls.shtml. Note that those hours can be changed without explanation or notice, so confirm in advance. Some colleges charge admission, while others are only accessible through blue badge tours, booked at the TIC. Don't bother trying to sneak into Christ Church outside open hours—bouncers, affectionately known as "bulldogs," in bowler hats and stationed 50 ft. apart, will squint their eyes and kick you out.

CHRIST CHURCH

THE COLLEGE. "The House" has Oxford's grandest quad and its most distinguished students, counting 13 past Prime Ministers among its alumni. Charles I made Christ Church his headquarters for three and a half years during the Civil Wars and escaped dressed as a servant when the city was besieged. Lewis Carroll first met Alice, the dean's daughter, here. The dining hall and Tom Quad serve as shooting locations for *Harry Potter* films. In June, be respectful of irritable undergrads prepping for exams as you navigate the narrow strip open to tourists.

Through an archway, to your left as you face the cathedral, lie **Peckwater Quad** and the most elegant Palladian building in Oxford. Look for rowing standings chalked on the walls and for the beautiful exterior of Christ Church's library. Spreading east and south from the main entrance, **Christ Church Meadow** compensates for Oxford's lack of "backs" (the riverside gardens in Cambridge). The meadows themselves are beautiful and offer great views of Christ Church College if you don't want to pay to go inside. *Down St. Aldates from Carfax. ☎ 286 573; www.chch.ox.ac.uk. Open M-Sa 9am-5:30pm, Su 1-5:30pm; last admission 4pm. Chapel services M-F 6pm; Su 8, 10, 11:15am, and 6pm. £4.70, concessions £3.70, families £9.40.*

CHRIST CHURCH CHAPEL. The only church in England to serve as both a cathedral and college chapel, it was founded in AD 730 by Oxford's patron saint, St. Fridesweide, who built a nunnery here in honor of two miracles: the blinding of her persistent suitor and his subsequent recovery. A stained-glass window (c. 1320) depicts Thomas à Becket kneeling moments before his death in Canterbury Cathedral. Look for the floating toilet in the bottom right of a window showing St. Fridesweide's death and the White Rabbit fretting in the windows in the hall.

TOM QUAD. The site of undergraduate lily-pond dunking, Tom Quad adjoins the chapel grounds. The quad takes its name from Great Tom, the seven-ton bell that has rung 101 (the original number of students) times at 9:05pm (the original undergraduate curfew) every evening since 1682. The bell rings at 9:05pm because, technically, Oxford should be 5min. past Greenwich Mean Time. Christ Church keeps this time within its gates. Nearby, the college hall displays portraits of some of Christ Church's famous alums—Sir Philip Sidney, William Penn, John Ruskin, John Locke, and a bored-looking W.H. Auden in a corner by the kitchen.

CHRIST CHURCH PICTURE GALLERY. Generous alumni gifts have established a small but noteworthy collection of works by Tintoretto, Vermeer, and da Vinci, among others. *(In the Canterbury quad. Entrances on Oriel Sq. and at Canterbury Gate; visitors to the gallery should enter through Canterbury Gate. ☎ 276 172. Open Apr.-Sept. M-Sa 10:30am-1pm and 2-5:30pm, Su 2-5pm; Oct.-Mar. closes at 4:30pm. £2, concessions £1.)*

OTHER COLLEGES

Oxford's extensive college system (totalling 39 official Colleges of the University) means that there are plenty of beautiful grounds to stroll year-round. The following is a selection of the most popular colleges. For information on others, check one of the many guides found at the TIC.

ALL SOULS COLLEGE. Candidates who survive the admission exams to All Souls are invited to a dinner, where the dons confirm that they are "well-born, well-bred, and only moderately learned." All Souls is also reported to have the most heavenly wine cellar in the city. The Great Quad may be Oxford's most serene, as hardly a living soul passes over it. *(Corner of High and Catte St. ☎ 279 379; www.all-souls.ox.ac.uk. Open Sept.-July M-F 2-4pm. Free.)*

BALLIOL COLLEGE. Students at Balliol preserve tradition by hurling abuse over the wall at their Trinity College rivals. Matthew Arnold, Gerard Manley Hopkins,

Aldous Huxley, and Adam Smith were all sons of Balliol's mismatched spires. The interior gates of the college bear lingering scorch marks from the executions of 16th-century Protestants, and a mulberry tree planted by Elizabeth I still shades slumbering students. *(Broad St. ☎ 277 777; www.balliol.ox.ac.uk. Open daily 2-5pm. £1, students and children free.)*

MAGDALEN COLLEGE. With extensive grounds and flower-laced quads, Magdalen (MAUD-lin) is considered Oxford's handsomest college. The college has a deer park flanked by the river Cherwell and Addison's Walk, a circular path that touches the river's opposite bank. The college's most brilliant wit is alumnus Oscar Wilde. *(On High St., near the Cherwell. ☎ 276 000; www.magd.ox.ac.uk. Open daily Oct.-Mar. 1pm-dusk; Apr.-June 1-6pm; July-Sept. noon-6pm. £3, concessions £2.)*

MERTON COLLEGE. Merton's library houses the first printed Welsh Bible. Tolkien lectured here, inventing the Elven language in his spare time. The college's 14th-century **Mob Quad** is Oxford's oldest and least impressive, but nearby **St. Alban's Quad** has some of the university's best gargoyles. Japanese Crown Prince Narahito lived here during his university days. *(Merton St. ☎ 276 310; www.merton.ox.ac.uk. Open M-F 2-4pm, Sa-Su 10am-4pm. Free, library tours £2.)*

NEW COLLEGE. This is the self-proclaimed first real college of Oxford. It was here, in 1379, that William of Wykeham dreamed up an institution that would offer a comprehensive undergraduate education under one roof. The bell tower has gargoyles of the Seven Deadly Sins on one side and the Seven Virtues on the other—all equally grotesque. New College claims Kate Beckinsale and Hugh Grant as two attractive alums. *(New College Ln. Use the Holywell St. Gate. ☎ 279 555; www.new.ox.ac.uk. Open daily from Easter to mid-Oct. 11am-5pm; Nov.-Easter 2-4pm. £2, students and children £1.)*

QUEEN'S COLLEGE. Although the college dates back to 1341, Queen's was rebuilt by Wren and Hawksmoor in the 17th and 18th centuries in the distinctive Queen Anne style. A trumpet call summons students to dinner, where a boar's head graces the table at Christmas. That tradition supposedly commemorates a student who, attacked by a boar on the outskirts of Oxford, choked the animal to death with a volume of Aristotle—probably the nerdiest slaughter ever. *(High St. ☎ 279 120; www.queens.ox.ac.uk. Open to blue-badge tours only.)*

TRINITY COLLEGE. Founded in 1555, Trinity has a Baroque chapel with a limewood altarpiece, cedar latticework, and cherubim-spotted pediments. The college's series of eccentric presidents includes Ralph Kettell, who would come to dinner with a pair of scissors to chop anyone's hair that he deemed too long. *(Broad St. ☎ 279 900; www.trinity.ox.ac.uk. Open M-F 10am-noon and 2-4pm, Sa-Su 2-4pm; during vacations also Sa-Su 10am-noon. £1.50, concessions 75p.)*

UNIVERSITY COLLEGE. Built in 1249, this soot-blackened college vies with Merton for the title of oldest, claiming Alfred the Great as its founder. Percy Bysshe Shelley was expelled for writing the pamphlet *The Necessity of Atheism* but was later immortalized in a monument, on the right as you enter. Bill Clinton spent his Rhodes days here. *(High St. ☎ 276 602; www.univ.ox.ac.uk. Open to blue badge tours only.)*

OTHER SIGHTS

ASHMOLEAN MUSEUM. The grand Ashmolean—Britain's finest collection of arts and antiquities outside London and the country's oldest public museum—opened in 1683. The museum is undergoing extensive renovations until 2009 but continues to show an exhibit of "treasures"—more than 200 artifacts from its galleries—including the lantern carried by Guy Fawkes in the Gunpowder Plot of 1605 and the deerskin mantle of Powhatan, father of Pocahontas. *(Beaumont St. ☎ 278 000. Open Tu-Sa 10am-5pm, Su noon-5pm; in summer open Th until 7pm. Free. Tours £2.)*

BODLEIAN LIBRARY. Oxford's principal reading and research library has over five million books and 50,000 manuscripts. It receives a copy of every book printed in Great Britain. Sir Thomas Bodley endowed the library's first wing in 1602—the institution has since grown to fill the immense **Old Library** complex, the **Radcliffe Camera** next door, and two newer buildings on Broad St. Admission to the reading rooms is by ticket only. The Admissions Office will issue you a two-day pass (£3) if you are able to prove your research requires the use of the library's books and present a letter of recommendation and ID. No one has ever been permitted to take out a book, not even Cromwell. Well, especially not Cromwell. *(Broad St. ☎277 000. Library open M-F 9am-10pm, Sa 9am-1pm; in summer M-F 9am-7pm, Sa 9am-1pm. Tours leave from the Divinity School in the main quad; in summer M-Sa 4 per day, in winter 2 per day, in the afternoon. Tours £4, audio tour £2.)*

BOTANIC GARDEN. Green things have flourished for three centuries in the oldest botanic garden in the British Isles, owned and used by Oxford University. The path connecting the garden to Christ Church Meadow provides a view of the Thames and the cricket grounds on the opposite bank. *(From Carfax, head down High St.; at the intersection of High St. and Rose Ln. ☎286 690. Open daily May-Sept. 9am-6pm, last admission 5:15pm; Mar.-Apr. and Oct. 9am-5pm, last admission 4:15pm; Nov.-Feb. 9am-4:30pm, last admission 4:15pm. Glass houses open daily 10am-4pm. Throwing stones in glass houses is not advised. £2.70, concessions £2, children free; by donation Nov.-Feb.)*

CARFAX TOWER. The tower marks the center of the pre-modern city. A climb up its 99 (very narrow) spiral stairs affords a superb view from the only remnant of medieval St. Martin's Church. "Carfax" gets its name from the French *carrefour* (crossroads), referring to the intersection of the North, South, East, and West Gates. *(Corner of Queen St. and Cornmarket St. ☎792 653. Open daily Apr.-Oct. 10am-5pm; Oct.-Mar. 10am-3:30pm, weather permitting. £1.90, under 16 90p.)*

MUSEUM OF OXFORD. From hands-on exhibits to a murderer's skeleton, the museum provides an in-depth look at Oxford's 800-year history. *(St. Aldates. Enter at corner of St. Aldates and Blue Boar St. ☎252 761. Open Tu-F 10am-4:30pm, Sa 10am-5pm, Su noon-4pm. Last admission 30min. before close. £2, concessions £1.50, children 50p, under 5 free, families £4.)*

OXFORD CASTLE. Oxford's newest attraction, the castle has been an Anglo-Saxon church, a Norman castle commissioned by William the Conqueror, a courthouse, and (until 1996) a prison. Now the complex houses restaurants, an open-air theater, and a luxury hotel. Visitors are issued personal video-guides outlining life as an inmate and the gory details of 17th-century executions, and can climb to the top of St. George's tower for a view of the city formerly enjoyed only by prison guards. *(44-46 Oxford Castle on New Rd. ☎293 679, tour bookings 411 414. Open daily 10am-5pm, last tour at 4:20pm. £7.25, concessions £5.95, children £5.25.)*

SHELDONIAN THEATRE. This Roman-style auditorium was designed by a teenage Christopher Wren. Graduation ceremonies, conducted in Latin, take place in the Sheldonian, as do everything from student recitals to world-class opera performances. *The Red Violin* and *Quills*, as well as numerous other movies, were filmed here. Climb up to the cupola for views of Oxford's quads. The ivy-crowned stone heads on the fence behind the Sheldonian are a 20th-century study in beards. *(Broad St. ☎277 299. Open M-Sa 10am-12:30pm and 2-4:30pm; in winter until 3:30pm; July-Aug. also Su 11am-4pm. Occasionally closed for university ceremonies. £2, concessions £1. Purchase tickets for shows from Oxford Playhouse, ☎305 305. Box office open M-Tu and Th-Sa 9:30am-6:30pm or until 30min. before last showing, W 10am-6:30pm. Shows £15.)*

BEST OF THE REST. At **The Oxford Story,** 6 Broad St., a slow-moving but informative ride hauls visitors through dioramas that chronicle Oxford's past. *(☎728 822.*

Open July-Aug. daily 9:30am-5pm; Sept.-June M-Sa 10am-4:30pm, Su 11am-4:30pm. 45min. ride. £7.25, students and seniors £6, children £5.25.) Oxford's oldest building, a Saxon tower built in 1040, stands as part of **St. Michael at the North Gate.** Climb the steps for a brief history of the tower and the church as well as a birds-eye view of the city. *(☎240 940. Open daily Apr.-Oct. 10:30am-5pm; Nov.-Mar. 10:30am-4pm. £1.80, concessions £1.20.)* With six miles of bookshelves, **Blackwell's bookstore,** 53 Broad St., is by far the largest bookshop in Oxford and is famous for letting patrons read undisturbed. *(☎792 792. Open M and W-Sa 9am-6pm, Tu 9:30am-6pm, Su 11am-5pm.)*

Behind the **University Museum of Natural History,** Parks Rd., the **Pitt-Rivers Museum** has an archaeological and anthropological collection, including shrunken heads and magical amulets. *(Natural History Museum ☎272 950. Open daily noon-5pm. Free. Pitt-Rivers Museum ☎270 927; www.prm.ox.ac.uk. Open daily noon-4:30pm. Free.)* The **Museum of the History of Science,** Broad St., features clocks, astrolabes, and Einstein's blackboard, preserved as he left it after an Oxford lecture in the 1930s. *(☎277 280. Open Tu-Sa noon-4pm, Su 2-5pm. Free. Tours £1.50.)* The **Modern Art Oxford,** 30 Pembroke St., hosts international shows. *(☎722 733. Open Tu-Sa 10am-5pm, Su noon-5pm. Free.)*

PUBS

In Oxford, pubs far outnumber colleges—some even consider them the city's prime attraction. Most open by noon, begin to fill around 5pm, and close at 11pm (10:30pm on Su). Recent legislation has allowed pubs to stay open later, but there may be conditions, including an earlier door-closing time or a small cover charge. Be ready to pub crawl—many pubs are so small that a single band of celebrating students will squeeze out other patrons, while just around the corner others will have several spacious rooms.

▨ The Turf Tavern, 4 Bath Pl. (☎243 235), hidden off Holywell St. Arguably the most popular student bar in Oxford, this 13th-century pub is tucked in an alley off an alley, but that doesn't stop just about everybody in Oxford from partaking in its 11 different ales. Bob Hawke, former prime minister of Australia, downed a yard of ale (over 2½ pints) in a record 11 seconds here while at the university. Open M-Sa 11am-11pm, Su noon-10:30pm. Hot food served in back room and beer garden daily noon-7:30pm.

The King's Arms, 40 Holywell St. (☎242 369). Oxford's unofficial student union (locally known as "the KA"). Lots of space and large tables make getting a seat possible even when it's busy. Merry masses head to the back rooms, and locals sip tea and coffee in the bright tea room. Open M-Sa 10:30am-11pm, Su 10:30am-10:30pm.

The Bear, 6 Alfred St. (☎728 164). Patrons once exchanged their club neckties for a free pint at this oldest and tiniest of Oxford's many pubs. Now over 4500, adorn the walls and ceiling of the pub, established in 1242. Unfortunately, the deal no longer applies. During the day, clients are older than the neckwear, and the young sit out back with pitchers of Pimm's (£9). Open M-Sa noon-11pm, Su noon-10:30pm.

The White Horse, 52 Broad St. (☎722 393), between the 2 entrances of Blackwell's. Tiny pub favored by locals. Relatively late closing time means students head here at the end of the night. Open daily noon-midnight. Food served noon-7pm.

The Jolly Farmers, 20 Paradise St. (☎793 759; www.jollyfarmers.com). One of Oxfordshire's first gay and lesbian pubs. Recent renovations make this pub popular with students and twenty-somethings, especially on weekends. More sedate in summer. Get there early for a seat in the garden. Open M-Sa noon-11pm, Su noon-10:30pm.

The Eagle and Child, 49 St. Giles (☎302 925). A historic pub, the dark-paneled back (now middle) room hosted "The Inklings," a group of 20th-century writers including C.S. Lewis and J.R.R. Tolkien, who referred to it as the "Bird and Baby." *The Chronicles of Narnia* and *The Hobbit* were first read aloud here. Open M-Sa 11am-11pm, Su noon-10:30pm. Food served M-F noon-10pm, Sa-Su noon-9pm.

Oxford Pub Crawl

🍺 PUBS

All Bar One, **6**
The Bear, **8**
Chequers Inn, **7**
The Eagle and Child, **1**
The Grapes, **5**
The Head of the River, **11**
The Jolly Farmers, **10**
The King's Arms, **2**
St. Aldates Tavern, **9**
Turf's Tavern, **4**
The White Horse, **3**

The Head of the River, Folly Bridge, St. Aldates (☎ 721 600). This aptly named pub has the best location in all of Oxford to view the Thames, known locally as the Isis. Much bigger than the pubs situated closer to the town center, this is the place where at least you can be sure you'll find a seat. The large beer garden fills up quickly in the early evening hours. Open M-Sa 11:30am-1pm, Su noon-10:30pm. Food served daily noon-2:30pm and 5-9pm.

St. Aldates Tavern, 108 St. Aldates (☎ 250 201). Local charm and regional ales make this a classic Oxford pub. Student discounts keep the crowds coming back for more. Open M-Sa 11am-11pm, Su noon-10:30pm.

Chequers Inn, 131 High St. (☎ 727 463). Numerous pool tables and a heated beer garden make this a great place to kick off a pub crawl. Rustic decor and energetic atmosphere. Open M-Th and Su 11am-11:30pm, F-Sa 11am-midnight.

The Grapes, 7 George St. (☎ 793 380). This Victorian pub hasn't changed much since the 19th century. A veritable Oxford institution frequented by professors and students alike. Open M-W and Su 11am-11pm, Th-Sa 11am-midnight.

All Bar One, 124 High St. (☎ 258 991). Part of a national chain, the Oxford branch of All Bar One steps up to the challenge posed by smaller local pubs with affordable beers and a very extensive wine list. Open M-F 11:30am-11pm, Sa 11am-11pm, Su 11:30am-10:30pm.

CLUBS

After Happy hour at the pubs, head up **Walton Street** or down **Cowley Road** for clubs.

Jericho Tavern, 56 Walton St. (☎311 775). Recently renovated, this pub has an upstairs venue where Radiohead had their debut gig in 1984 and Britpop group Supergrass was discovered. Downstairs, patrons enjoy the sleek new decor and specialty draft beer. Open M-Sa noon-midnight, Su noon-11pm.

Thirst, 7-8 Park End St. (☎242 044). Lounge bar with a DJ and back-door garden. Across from KISS, Thirst serves up cheap mixed drinks (from £1.50) until 1am M-W. Budget drinks served during "happy hour" (8-10pm) and "stupid hour" (5-8pm). Open M-Sa 5pm-2am, Su 6pm-12:30am.

Freud, 119 Walton St. (☎311 171). Formerly St. Paul's Church. Bizarre decoration: part cathedral, part circus, part modern art installation gone wrong. Cafe by day, cocktail bar by night. Open M-Tu and Su 11am-midnight, W 11am-1am, Th-Sa 11am-2am.

The Bridge, 6-9 Hythe Bridge St. (☎242 526; www.bridgeoxford.co.uk). Dance to R&B, hip hop, dance, and pop on 2 floors. Erratically frequented by big student crowds. Cover £3-7. Open M-Sa 9pm-2am.

Anuba, 11-13 Park End St. (☎242 526; www.bridgeoxford.co.uk). Sister club to The Bridge. Intimate pre-club atmosphere. Small dance floor is a nice alternative to the huge clubs throughout the city. Open M-Sa 6:30pm-11pm, Su 6:30pm-12:30am.

KISS, 36-39 Park End St. (☎200 555; www.kissbar.co.uk). Intimate bar conveniently located near several clubs for some pre-dancing drinks. Specializes in vodka drinks with 40 flavors of vodka and a special vodka cocktail menu. 2-for-1 drink specials during daily happy hour (7-9:30pm). No cover. Open M-Sa 7:30pm-2am.

♫ ENTERTAINMENT

Check *This Month in Oxford*, free at the TIC, or *Daily Information*, posted all over town and online (www.dailyinfo.co.uk), for event listings.

MUSIC. Centuries of tradition give Oxford a solid music scene. Colleges offer concerts and Evensong services; **New College** has an excellent boys' choir. Performances at the **Holywell Music Rooms,** on Holywell St., are worth checking out; **Oxford Coffee Concerts** feature famous musicians and ensembles every Sunday at 11:15am. (☎305 305. Tickets £9.) The **City of Oxford Orchestra,** a professional symphony orchestra, plays a subscription series at the Sheldonian and in college chapels during the summer. (☎744 457. Tickets £16-18.) The **New Theatre,** George St., features performances from jazz to musicals to the Welsh National Opera. (☎320 760. Tickets £10-50. Student, senior, and child discounts available.) With a large student population and its proximity to Manchester and London, Oxford is on an excellent circuit for smaller bands at clubs and large venues like South Park.

THEATER. The **Oxford Playhouse,** 11-12 Beaumont St., hosts amateur and professional musicians and dance performances. The playhouse also sells discounted tickets for venues city-wide. (☎305 305; www.oxfordplayhouse.com, www.ticketsoxford.com. Box office open M-Tu and Th-F 9:30am-6:30pm, W 10am-6:30pm.) College theater groups often stage productions in gardens or cloisters.

FESTIVALS. The university celebrates **Eights Week** at the end of May, when the colleges enter crews in bumping races and beautiful people sip Pimm's on the banks. In early September, **St. Giles Fair** invades one of Oxford's main streets with an old-fashioned English fun fair. Daybreak on **May Day** (May 1) cues one of Oxford's most inspiring moments: the Magdalen College Choir sings madrigals from the top of the tower beginning at 6am, and the town indulges in Morris dancing, beating the bounds, and other age-old rituals of merry men. Pubs open at 7am.

⚡ DAYTRIP FROM OXFORD

BLENHEIM PALACE

In the town of Woodstock, 8 mi. north of Oxford. Stagecoach (☎ 772 250) bus #20 runs to Blenheim Palace from Gloucester Green bus station (30-40min., every hr. 8am-5pm, round-trip £4.50). ☎ 01993 811 091. House open daily from mid-Feb. to mid-Dec. 10:30am-5:30pm. Last admission 4:45pm. Grounds open daily 9am-9pm. £14, concessions £10.50, children £8.50. Grounds only £9/7/4.50. Free tours every 5-10min.

The largest private home in England, Blenheim Palace (BLEN-em) was built in honor of the Duke of Marlborough's victory over Louis XIV at the 1704 Battle of Blenheim. The 11th Duke of Marlborough now calls the palace home. His rent is a flag from the estate, payable each year to the Crown—not a bad deal for 187 furnished rooms. Archways and marble floors accentuate the artwork inside, including wall-size tapestries of 17th- and 18th-century battle scenes. Winston Churchill, a member of the Marlborough family, spent some years here before he was shipped off to boarding school (the palace still houses his baby clothes). He proposed to his wife here, and now rests with her in a nearby churchyard. The vast grounds consist of 2100 acres, all designed by good old "Capability" Brown.

STRATFORD-UPON-AVON ☎ 01789

Shakespeare was born here. This fluke of fate has made Stratford-upon-Avon a major stop on the tourist superhighway. Proprietors tout the dozen-odd properties linked, however remotely, to the Bard and his extended family: shops and restaurants devotedly stencil his prose and poetry on their windows and walls. Beyond the sound and fury of rumbling tour buses and chaotic swarms of daytrippers, there lies a town worth seeing for the beauty of the river Avon and for the riveting performances in the Royal Shakespeare Theatre.

◖ HENCE, AWAY!

Trains: Station Rd., off Alcester Rd. Office open M-Sa 6:20am-8:20pm, Su 9:45am-6:30pm. Trains (☎ 08457 484 950) to **Birmingham** (50min., 2 per hr., £5.60); **London Paddington** (2¼hr., 2 per hr., £41.50); and **Warwick** (25min., 9 per day, £3.70).

Buses: Riverside Coach Park, off Bridgeway Rd. near the Leisure Centre. National Express (☎ 08705 808 080) to **London** (3hr., 5 per day, £17) and **Oxford** (1hr., 2 per day, £9.50). Stagecoach (☎ 08456 001 314) to **Birmingham** (1hr., 1 per hr., £6), **Chipping Norton** (45min., 2 per day, £3.25), and **Oxford** (1½hr., 3 per Su, £6).

Public Transportation: Stagecoach #1618 services **Coventry** (2hr., every hr., £3.50) via **Warwick** (20-40min., every hr., £3).

Taxis: Taxi Line (☎ 266 100). **Shakespeare Tours** (☎ 204 083).

Bike Rental: Stratford Bike Hire, Guild St. (☎ 177 634). Mountain bikes £10 per day, £5 per half-day. Open Tu-F 9am-5pm, Sa 10am-4pm.

Boat Rental: Avon Boating, Swan's Nest Ln. (☎ 01789 267 073), by Clopton Bridge. Rents rowboats (£2.50 per hr., children £1.50) and motorboats (£10 per 30min., £16 per hr.). 30min. river trips £3.50, concessions £3, children £2. Open daily Apr.-Oct. 9am-dusk, weather permitting.

⚡ WHO IS'T THAT CAN INFORM ME?

Tourist Information Centre: Bridgefoot (☎ 0870 160 7930). Provides maps (£1.20), guidebooks, tickets, and accommodations lists. Books rooms for £3 and a 10% deposit. Open Apr.-Oct. M-Sa 9am-5:30pm, Su 10am-4pm; Nov.-Mar. M-Sa 9am-5pm.

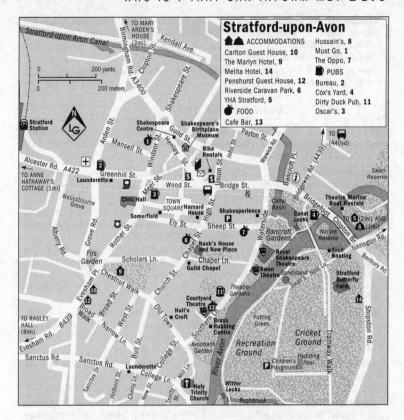

Stratford-upon-Avon

🏠🏠 ACCOMMODATIONS
Carlton Guest House, **10**
The Marlyn Hotel, **9**
Melita Hotel, **14**
Penshurst Guest House, **12**
Riverside Caravan Park, **6**
YHA Stratford, **5**
🍴 FOOD
Cafe Bar, **13**

Hussain's, **8**
Must Go, **1**
The Oppo, **7**
🍺 PUBS
Bureau, **2**
Cox's Yard, **4**
Dirty Duck Pub, **11**
Oscar's, **3**

Tours: 2hr. **walking tours** led by Shakespearean actors start at the Royal Shakespeare Theatre (☎412 617). Sa 10:30am. £8, concessions £6. **City Sightseeing Bus Tours,** Civic Hall, 14 Rother St. (☎412 680; www.stagecoachbus.com/warwickshire), heads to Bard-related houses every 15-20min. from the front of the Pen and Parchment next to the TIC. £10, concessions £8, children £5. Office open daily 9am-5:30pm. **Stratford Town Walk** (☎292 478) arranges various walking tours throughout the city, including the popular **Ghost Walks.** All walks depart from the Swan fountain, near the Royal Shakespeare Theatre, Th 7:30pm. £5. Normal town walk M-W 11am, Th-Su 2pm. Advanced booking required for Ghost Walk.

Financial Services: Barclays, (☎08457 555 555), at the intersection of Henley and Wood St. Open M-Tu and Th-F 9am-5pm, W 10am-4:30pm. **Thomas Cook,** 37 Wood St. (☎293 582). Open M and W-Sa 9am-5:30pm, Tu 10am-5:30pm.

Launderette: Greenhill, 34 Greenhill St. Wash £3-5.60; dry 20p per 4 min.; soap £1. Bring change. Open daily 8am-8pm, last wash 7pm.

Police: Rother St. (☎414 111).

Hospital: Stratford-upon-Avon Hospital, Arden St. (☎205 831), off Alcester Rd.

Pharmacy: Boots, 11 Bridge St. (☎292 173). Open M-Sa 8:30am-5:30pm, Su 10:30am-4:30pm.

Internet Access: Central Library, 12 Henley St. (☎292 209). Free. Open M and W-F 9am-5:30pm, Tu 10am-5:30pm, Sa 9:30am-5pm, Su noon-4pm. **Cyber Junction,** 28 Greenhill St. (☎263 400). £2.50 per 30min., £4 per hr.; concessions £2-3.50. Open M-F 10am-6pm, Sa 10:30am-5:30pm.

Post Office: 2-3 Henley St. (☎08457 223 344). **Bureau de change.** Open M-Sa 8:30am-6pm. **Post Code:** CV37 6PU.

⚡ TO SLEEP, PERCHANCE TO DREAM

B&Bs abound, but singles are rare. Accommodations in the £25-35 range line **Evesham Place, Evesham Road,** and **Grove Road.** Try **Shipston Road** across the river, a 15-20min. walk from the station.

▨ **Carlton Guest House,** 22 Evesham Pl. (☎293 548). Spacious rooms and spectacular service make this B&B a great value. Book early; the B&B hosts groups in the summer. Singles £20-26; doubles and twins £40-52; triples £60-78. Cash only. ❸

The Marlyn Hotel, 3 Chestnut Walk, (☎293 752). New B&B near the RSC theater. Pristine white linens and pastel walls will make you feel like you're by the sea. Full English breakfast included. Singles £30; doubles £45. AmEx/MC/V. ❸

YHA Stratford, Wellesbourne Rd., Alveston (☎297 093), 2 mi. from Clopton Bridge. Follow B4086 from town center (35min.), or take bus X18 or 77 from Bridge St. (10min., every hr., £2). Isolated hostel catering mostly to school groups and families. A solid, inexpensive option for longer stays. Breakfast included. Internet 7p per min. Dorms £21, under 18 £14.50. Add £3 for non-members. MC/V. ❷

Melita Hotel, 37 Shipston Rd. (☎292 432). Upscale B&B with gorgeous garden, retreat-like atmosphere, and excellent breakfasts. Guests relax on the sunny patio with less-than-intimidating guard dog Harvey and his accomplice, Daisy. Singles from £52; doubles £79; triples £106; quads £125. AmEx/MC/V. ❹

Penshurst Guest House, 34 Evesham Pl. (☎205 259; www.penshurst.net). Four distinctly decorated rooms. Access to a large self-catering kitchen. Ensuite double and triple £30-45; ensuite family room £40-57. Prices vary; call ahead. Cash only. ❸

Camping: Riverside Caravan Park, Tiddington Rd. (☎292 312), 30min. east of town on the B4086. Sunset views on the Avon, but often crowded. A 3-4min. walk to the village pub. Showers. Open Easter-Oct. Tent sites for up to 4 people £11. AmEx/MC/V. ❶

◖ IN THE CAULDRON BOIL AND BAKE

Baguette stores and bakeries are scattered throughout the town center; a Somerfield **supermarket** is in Town Sq. (☎292 604. Open M-W 8am-7pm, Th-Sa 8am-8pm, Su 10am-4pm.) The first and third Saturdays of every month, the River Avon's banks welcome a **farmers' market.**

The Oppo, 13 Sheep St. (☎269 980). Receives rave reviews from locals. Low 16th-century-style ceilings and candles. Try the grilled goat cheese and tomato salad (£10). Open daily noon-2pm, M-Th 5:30-9:30pm, F-Sa 5-11pm, Su 6-9:30pm. MC/V. ❸

Hussain's, 6a Chapel St. (☎267 506). Stratford's best Indian menu and a favorite of Ben Kingsley. Tandoori prepared with homemade spices and served in an elegant red dining room. 3-course lunch £6. Entrees from £6.75, but they don't include rice or naan, so be prepared to shell out an extra £2 for sides. 10% discount for takeaway and pre-theater dining. Open daily 12:30-2:30pm and 5pm-midnight. AmEx/MC/V. ❷

Cafe Bar, inside the Courtyard Theatre (☎403 415). Serves homemade sandwiches and pastries by the river. A perfect spot for a drink during matinee intermission. Summer specials £3.50-8.50 Open M-Sa 10:30am-8:30pm. ❷

Must Go, 21 Windsor St. (☎293 679). This Asian restaurant is unabashedly straightforward. After perusing the 4 ft. long menu outside, enter the "Out" doorway for takeaway or the "In" door for a meal in surprisingly comfortable quarters. "Meal deals" £5-7. Open Apr.-Oct. M-Th and Su noon-midnight, F-Sa noon-12:30am; Sept.-Mar. M-Th and Su noon-2pm and 5pm-midnight, F-Sa noon-12:30am. MC/V. ❷

◪ DRINK DEEP ERE YOU DEPART

Oscar's, 14 Meer St. (☎292 202). Cafe by day, bar by night. Feels like a treehouse for adults. Red walls, bubble machine, and seats by upstairs windows. Themed nights every day of the week, including live music on Tu, "International Wednesdays," and DJs Th-Sa. Try the 10-shot "Bullseye" (£20) if you dare. Open M-Sa 8pm-3am.

Bureau, 1 Arden St. (☎297 641). Silver staircase leading to a huge dance area. Various promotions, like M "£1-ish drinks" and Th 2-for-1 drink specials. Heats up late. Cover M and W-Sa £2-5. Open M and Th-F 9pm-2am, Tu-W 8pm-midnight, Su 11pm-2am.

Dirty Duck Pub, 66 Waterside (☎297 312). Originally called "The Black Swan" and rechristened by alliterative Americans during WWII. Huge bust of Shakespeare inside. Actors make entrances almost nightly. Dame Judy Dench got engaged here and has her own table in the back room. Open M-Sa 11am-11pm, Su noon-10:30pm.

Cox's Yard, Bridgefoot (☎404 600; www.coxsyard.co.uk), next to Bancroft Gardens. Have an outdoor pint in this massive complex on the banks of the Avon. Upstairs bar with tribute bands. Call for performance times and tickets. Pub and beer garden open in summer M-Tu and Su noon-11pm, W-Th noon-12:30am, F-Sa noon-1:30am.

◉ THE GILDED MONUMENTS

TO BARD...

Stratford's Will-centered sights are best seen before 11am, when the daytrippers arrive, or after 4pm, when the crowds disperse. The five official **Shakespeare properties** are Shakespeare's Birthplace, Mary Arden's House, Nash's House and New Place, Hall's Croft, and Anne Hathaway's Cottage. Opening hours are listed by season: summer (June-Aug.); mid-season (Apr.-May and Sept.-Oct.); and winter (Nov.-Mar.). Diehards should get the **All Five Houses** ticket, which also includes entrance to Harvard House. (☎204 016. £14, concessions £12, children £6.50, families £29.) Those who don't want to visit every shrine can get a **Three In-Town Houses** pass, covering the Birthplace, Hall's Croft, and Nash's House and New Place (£11/9/5.50/23).

SHAKESPEARE'S BIRTHPLACE. The only in-town sight directly associated with Him includes an exhibit on his father's glove-making business, a peaceful garden, and the requisite walkthrough on the Bard's documented life, including a First Folio and records of his father's illegal refuse dumping. Join such distinguished pilgrims as Charles Dickens in signing the guestbook. *(Henley St. ☎201 822. Open in summer M-Sa 9am-5pm, Su 9:30am-5pm; mid-season daily 10am-5pm; winter M-Sa 10am-4pm, Su 10:30am-4pm. £7, concessions £5.50, children £2.75, families £17.)*

SHAKESPEARE'S GRAVE. The least-crowded and most authentic way to pay homage to the Bard is to visit his grave inside the quiet Holy Trinity Church— although groups pack the arched door at peak hours. Rumor has it that Shakespeare was buried 17 ft. underground by request, so that he would sleep undisturbed. To the left is a large bust of Shakespeare and his birth and death records. The church also harbors the graves of wife Anne and daughter Susanna. *(Trinity St. ☎266 316. Entrance to church free; almost forced donation to see grave £1, students and children 50p. Open Apr.-Sept. M-Sa 8:30am-6pm, Su noon-5pm; Mar. and Oct. M-Sa 9am-5pm, Su noon-5pm; Nov.-Feb. M-Sa 9am-4pm, Su noon-5pm. Last admission 20min. before close.)*

HEART OF ENGLAND

NASH'S HOUSE AND NEW PLACE. Tourists flock to the home of the first husband of Shakespeare's granddaughter Elizabeth, his last descendant. **Nash's House** has been restored to its Elizabethan grandeur and holds temporary exhibits on the Bard, but most want to see **New Place,** Shakespeare's retirement home and, at the time, Stratford's finest house. Today, only the foundations and a garden remain due to a disgruntled 19th-century owner named Gastrell who razed the building and cut down Shakespeare's mulberry tree in order to spite Bard tourists (jealous much?). Gastrell was run out of town, and to this day Gastrells are not allowed in Stratford. Knowledgeable guides hang out to answer questions. *(Chapel St. ☎ 292 325. Open in summer M-Sa 9:30am-5pm, Su 10am-5pm; mid-season daily 11am-5pm; winter M-Sa 11am-4pm. £3.75, concessions £3, children £1.75, families £9.)* Down Chapel St. from Nash's House, the sculpted hedges, manicured lawn, and abundant flowers of the **Great Garden of New Place** offer a respite from the mobbed streets and hold a mulberry tree said to be grown from the one Gastrell chopped down. The garden also holds surrealist sculptures depicting famous scenes from Shakespeare's plays. *(Open M-Sa 9am-dusk, Su 10am-5pm. Free.)*

MARY ARDEN'S HOUSE. This farmhouse in Wilmcote, a village 3 mi. from Stratford, was only recently determined to be the childhood home of Mary Arden (Shakespeare's mother). Historians thought she grew up in the stately building next door. She didn't. Cattle roam the farm, and a history recounts how Mary fell in love with Shakespeare, Sr. *(Connected by footpath to Anne Hathaway's Cottage, or take the train from Stratford 1 stop north to Wilmcote. ☎ 293 455. Open in summer M-Sa 9:30am-5pm, Su 10am-5pm; mid-season daily 10am-5pm; winter daily 10am-4pm. £6, concessions £5, children £2.50.)*

ANNE HATHAWAY'S COTTAGE. The birthplace of Shakespeare's wife, about a mile from Stratford in **Shottery,** is a fairy-tale, thatched-roof cottage. It boasts (very old) original Hathaway furniture and a hedge maze. Entrance entitles you to sit on a bench He may or may not also have sat on. *(Take the hop-on, hop-off Guide Friday tour bus or brave the poorly marked footpaths north. ☎ 292 100. Open in summer M-Sa 9am-5pm, Su 9:30am-5pm; mid-season M-Sa 9:30am-5pm, Su 10am-5pm; winter daily 10am-4pm. £5.50, concessions £4.50, children £2, families £13.)*

SHAKESPEARIENCE. A Shakespearian extravaganza, if you will, and the most unique exhibit in town. A two-act show starting with a visual tour of Shakespeare's life and times and featuring a holographic summary of his most famous works. The blasting winds and surround sound may seem a bit over the top, but it's definitely a fun way to chill with Will. Have a drink at the bar upstairs after the show to help wash down the cheese. *(Waterside, across from the Bancroft gardens and carousel. ☎ 293 678. Shows daily every hr. from 10am-5pm. £7.95, concession £6.95.)*

...OR NOT TO BARD

Believe it or not, non-Shakespearean sights are available.

STRATFORD BUTTERFLY FARM. Europe's largest collection of butterflies flutters through tropical surroundings. Less appealing creepy-crawlies—like the Goliath Bird-Eating Spider—dwell in glass boxes nearby. *(Off Swan's Nest Ln. at Tramway Walk, across the river from the TIC. ☎ 299 288. Open daily in summer 10am-6pm; in winter 10am-5pm. Last admission 30min. before close. £5.25, concessions £4.75, children £4.25.)*

HARVARD HOUSE. Once inhabited by the mother of the founder of that university in Cambridge (across the pond), the house is now owned by the Shakespeare Birthright Trust. It houses more pewter than crimson, but Johnny gets a small exhibit on the second floor. *(High St. ☎ 204 507. Open May-July and Sept.-Oct. F-Su noon-5pm; July-Sept. W-Su noon-5pm. £2.75, children free.)*

RAGLEY HALL. Eight miles from Stratford on Evesham Rd. (A435), Ragley Hall houses the Earl and Countess of Yarmouth. Set in a stunning 400-acre park, the estate has an art collection and a sculpture park. *(Bus #246 (M-Sa 5 per day) runs to Alcester Police Station. Walk 1 mi. to the gates, then ½ mi. up the drive. ☎ 762 090. House open Apr.-Sept. M-Th and Su 10am-6pm; last entry 4:30pm. £8, concessions £6.50.)*

🎭 ALL THE WORLD'S A STAGE

THE ROYAL SHAKESPEARE COMPANY

The box office in the Courtyard Theatre handles the ticketing for all theaters. Ticket hotline ☎ 0844 800 1110; www.rsc.org.uk. Open M and W-Sa 9:30am-8pm, Tu 10am-8pm. Tickets £5-40. Students and those under 25 receive advance half-price tickets for M-W evening performances, otherwise by availability on performance days. Standby tickets in summer £15; winter £12. Disabled travelers should call in advance to advise the box office of their needs; some performances feature sign language interpretation or audio description.

One of the world's most acclaimed repertories, the Royal Shakespeare Company (RSC) sells well over one million tickets each year and claims Kenneth Branagh and Ralph Fiennes as recent members. The Royal Shakespeare Theatre is currently undergoing a £100 million renovation and will re-open in 2010 with a 1000-seat thrust stage, bringing the whole audience within 50 ft. of the action. The construction will also close the Swan Theatre, the RSC's more intimate neighbor, until 2010. The company will continue to perform shows down the road at The Courtyard Theatre. Visitors can get backstage tours and a glimpse at the high-tech stage to be installed at the Royal Shakespeare Theatre. The RSC has also planned an extensive touring campaign throughout England and the US while the theaters are renovated; inquire at the box office for details.

🌿 OUR RUSTIC REVELRY

A **traditional town market** is held on Rother St. in Market Pl. on the second and fourth Saturdays of every month. On Sundays from June to August, a **craft market** takes place along the river. (☎ 267 000. Both open daily 9am-5pm.) Stratford's biggest festival begins on the weekend nearest April 23, **Shakespeare's birthday.** The modern, well-respected **Shakespeare Birthplace Trust,** Henley St., hosts a **Poetry Festival** every Sunday evening in July and August. Past participants include Seamus Heaney, Ted Hughes, and Derek Walcott. (☎ 292 176. Tickets £7-10.)

WORCESTER   ☎ 01905

Worcester (WUH-ster) sits between Cheltenham and Birmingham, along the Severn. A small city, Worcester has certain quirky claims to fame—Edward Elgar, Worcestershire sauce, and Royal Worcester Porcelain among them. Visitors might find the city's cathedral vaguely familiar: it's on the 20-pound note.

📠 **TRANSPORTATION. Foregate St. Station,** at the edge of the town center on Foregate St., is the main train station. (Ticket window open M-Sa 6:10am-7pm, Su 9:10am-4:30pm. Travel center open M-Sa 9:30am-4pm.) **Shrub Hill Station,** just outside of town, serves Cheltenham and has less frequent service to London and Birmingham. (Ticket window open M-Sa 5:10am-9pm, Su 7:10am-9:30pm.) **Trains** (☎ 08457 484 950) travel from Worcester to Birmingham (1hr., 2 per hr., £6.70), Cheltenham (30min., every 2hr., £5.80), and London Paddington (2½hr., every 1½hr., £40). The **bus station** is at Angel Pl., near the Crowngate Shopping Centre. National Express buses (☎ 08705 808 080) run to: Birmingham (1½hr., 2 per day,

£5); Bristol (5½hr., 1 per day, £10); Cheltenham (1hr., 2 per day, £5.20); London (4hr., 4 per day, £18.80). First (☎359 393) is the regional bus company, and its **First-Worcester City** ticket allows for one day of travel within Worcester (£2.50). Associated Radio **taxis** (☎763 939) run 24hr. **Bike rental** is available at Peddlers, 46-48 Barbourne Rd. (☎24 238. £8 per day, £30 per week. Deposit £50. Open M-Sa 9:30am-5:30pm.) "Free ride" bikes can be found throughout the city.

■ ⚡ **ORIENTATION AND PRACTICAL INFORMATION.** The city center is bounded by Foregate St. Station to the north and the cathedral to the south. The main street runs between the two, switching names from Barbourne Rd. to The Tything to Foregate St. to The Foregate to The Cross to High St. (Got all that?)

The **Tourist Information Centre,** The Guildhall, High St., sells the *Worcester Visitor Guide* (75p) and books beds for a 10% deposit. From Foregate St. Station, turn left on Foregate St. and walk 15min. The TIC is on the ground floor of The Guildhall, on High St. (☎726 311. Open M-Sa 9:30am-5pm.) "Worcester Walks" **tours** leave from the TIC. Purchase National Express tickets here. (☎222 117; www.worcesterwalks.co.uk. 1½hr. M-F 11am. Ghost tours also available.) Other services include: a Barclays **bank,** 54 High St. (☎08457 555 555; open M-F 9am-5pm, Sa 9am-3pm); a **bureau de change** at Barclays (open M-F 9am-3pm); Severn Laun-Dri **launderette,** 22 Barbourne Rd. (wash £4.20, dry £1, soap 70p; open daily 9am-7pm; last wash 6pm); **police,** Castle St. (☎08457 444 888), off Foregate St.; a Boots **pharmacy,** 72-74 High St. (☎726 868; open M-F 8:30am-5:30pm, Sa 8:30am-6pm, Su 10:30am-4:30pm); **Worcestershire Royal Hospital,** Newtown Rd., Charles Hastings Way (☎763 333; bus #31); free **Internet** access at the **library,** in the City Museum (☎765 312; open M and F 9:30am-7pm, Tu-Th 9:30am-5:30pm, Sa 9:30am-4pm) and at **Coffee Republic,** 31 High St. (£1 per 20min., £3 per hr.; open M-F 7am-6pm, Sa 8:30am-6pm, Su 9am-6pm); and the **post office,** 8 Foregate St., with a **bureau de change** (☎08457 223 344; open M-Sa 9am-5:30pm). **Post Code:** WR1 1XX.

🏠 **ACCOMMODATIONS. B&B** prices in Worcester are high—proprietors cater to businesspeople and Londoners weekending in the country. Surrounding suburbs offer lower rates, or try your luck with the rowhouses on **Barbourne Road,** a 15-20min. walk north on Foregate St. from the city center or a short ride on buses #144 and 303. Book a few weeks ahead in the summer. The comfortable **Osborne House ❸,** 17 Chestnut Walk, has a TV in every ensuite room. (☎22 296. Book in advance. Singles £30-40; doubles £55. MC/V.) At **The Barbourne ❸,** 42 Barbourne Rd., many of the pink rooms are ensuite. Some have bathtubs. (☎27 507. Singles £30; twins and doubles £50; families £60. AmEx/MC/V.) Its blue counterpart, the nearby **City Guest House ❸,** 36 Barbourne Rd., features comfy beds and great service. (☎24 695. Singles £20, ensuite £25. MC/V.) Riverside **Ketch Caravan Park ❶,** Bath Rd., has camping with toilets and showers. Take the A38 2 mi. south of Worcester or take local bus #32, which stops across the road. Walk across the street from the Harvester Pub. (☎820 430. Open Apr.-Oct. £9 per tent or caravan. Electricity £1.75. Showers 20p. Cash only.)

🍴🍺 **FOOD AND PUBS.** A Sainsbury's **supermarket** is tucked into the Lynchgate Shopping Centre, 26-27 Cathedral Plaza. (☎21 731. Open M-Sa 8am-6pm, Su 10:30am-4pm.) Look for Indian restaurants and cheap sandwich shops near **The Tything,** at the north end of the city center. At ⚫**Chesters ❷,** 51 New St., you'll find outstanding service and quality food to match. An eclectic menu of whatever the chef feels like whipping up features several vegetarian and vegan specialties. (☎611 638. Entrees from £7. Open M-Tu noon-3pm and 6-10pm, W-Th noon-3pm and 6-10:30pm, F noon-3pm and 6-11pm, Sa noon-11pm. MC/V.) **Monsoon ❷,** 35 Foregate St., delivers well-priced Asian entrees (£6-10) and excellent service.

(☎726 333. Takeaway discount 20%. Open M-Th and Su 6pm-midnight, F-Sa 6pm-1am. AmEx/MC/V.) At **Clockwatchers ❶**, 20 Mealcheapen St., sandwiches and homemade soups are available mostly for takeaway, but you can stay and eat under the closed patio. (☎611 662. Open M-F 8:30am-5pm, Sa 8:30am-4pm. AmEx/MC/V.) For pint-sized entertainment, the pub scene on **Friar Street** is popular. **The Conservatory**, 34 Friar St., has bright decor and ales from £2. (☎26 929. Open M-Sa 11am-11pm.) Later in the night, check out **RSVP**, The Cross, a church-turned-bar filled with students. (☎729 211. Live DJ Th-Sa 8pm. Open M-W 11am-midnight, Th 11am-2am, F-Sa 11am-3am, Su noon-2am.)

◪ **SIGHTS. Worcester Cathedral,** founded in AD 680, towers over the River Severn at the south end of High St. Over the years, the buttresses supporting the nave have deteriorated, and the central tower is in danger of collapsing. Renovation attempts are perpetual, but even steel rods set in the tower's base don't detract from the building's beautiful Norman details. The **choir** contains intricate 14th-century misericords and King John's tomb. To the right of the choir lie the remains of Henry VIII's older brother **Arthur, prince of Wales. Wulston's Crypt** is the oldest part of the cathedral, an underground chapel dating back to the 11th century with a display of the boot remnants from a skeleton found during construction. Ask about the lunchtime concerts featuring free performances by musicians and choirs. (☎28 854; www.worcestercathedral.org.uk. Open daily 7:30am-6pm. Evensong M-Th and Sa 5:30pm, Su 4pm. Tours late July M-F and Sa; from Jan. to mid-July and Aug.-Dec. Sa only. Suggested donation £3. Guided tours £5; book ahead.)

The recently renovated ▨**Commandery Museum**, Sidbury Rd., offers a one-of-a-kind trip through history. An audio tour takes you through the six "layers" of time, describing the various uses of the house from the 16th century, which include a monastery, a hospital, Civil War headquarters, and a school for the blind. (☎25 371; www.worcestercitymuseums.org.uk. Open M-Sa 10am-5pm, Su 1:30-5pm. £5.25, concessions £3.50.) The **Royal Worcester Porcelain Company**, Severn St., makes the bone china on which the royal family has been served since the reign of George III. Factory tours show how the dishware goes from the work room to the dining room. (☎21 247. Book ahead. £5, concessions £4.25; family £10.) Crockery junkies can visit the adjacent **Worcester Museum of Porcelain**, which holds England's largest collection. (☎746 000; www.worcesterporcelainmuseum.org. Open M-Sa 9am-5:30pm, Su 11am-5pm. £5, concessions £4.25, families £10.) The highlight of the **Worcester City Museum and Art Gallery**, Foregate St., near the post office, is Hitler's clock, found in his office in 1945 by the Worcester Regiment. While the selection of art is less than impressive, the exhibit chronicling the 29th Regiment from Worcester (involved in the Boston Massacre and every major British and world war) is worth a stop. (☎25 371. Open M, W, F 9:30am-8pm; Tu, Th, and Sa 9:30am-5:30pm. Free.) Three miles south of the train station, **Elgar's Birthplace Museum**, Lower Broadheath, is filled with the manuscripts and memorabilia belonging to Sir Edward Elgar, the composer responsible for the *Pomp and Circumstance March No. 1* (of graduation-ceremony fame). Midland Red West bus #419/420 stops 1 mi. away at Crown East Church. Or, walk 6 mi. along the Elgar trail. (☎333 224; www.elgarmuseum.org. Open from Feb. to late Dec. daily 11am-5pm. Last admission 4:15pm. £5, seniors £4.50, students £3, children £2.)

CHELTENHAM ☎01242

Cheltenham (pop. 110,000), also known as Cheltenham Spa, is a small but well-to-do city. Ever since George III sampled its waters in 1788, the town has flourished. Cheltenham's reputation as a fashionable place of leisure is evident in its upscale restaurants, spacious gardens, and trendy boutiques. On weekends, students from

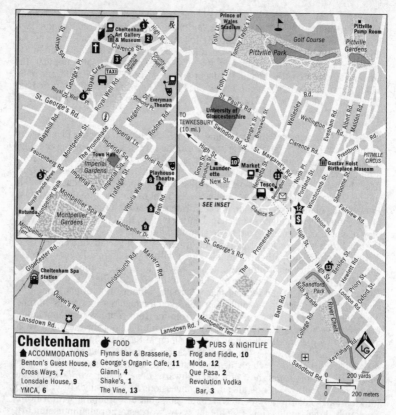

Cheltenham

▲ ACCOMMODATIONS
Benton's Guest House, 8
Cross Ways, 7
Lonsdale House, 9
YMCA, 6

🍎 FOOD
Flynns Bar & Brasserie, 5
George's Organic Cafe, 11
Gianni, 4
Shake's, 1
The Vine, 13

🍺★ PUBS & NIGHTLIFE
Frog and Fiddle, 10
Moda, 12
Que Pasa, 2
Revolution Vodka
Bar, 3

the University of Gloucestershire pack the pubs and clubs, energizing the city center. Although it has few important sights, Cheltenham continues to draw visitors as the most convenient base for exploring the Cotswolds.

▐ TRANSPORTATION

Cheltenham is 43 mi. south of Birmingham. *Getting There* (free from the TIC) details bus services.

Trains: Cheltenham Spa Station, Queen's Rd., at Gloucester Rd. Ticket office open M-F 5:45am-8:15pm, Sa 5:45am-7pm, Su 8:15am-8:15pm. Trains (☎08457 484 950) to: **Bath** (1½hr., 2 per hr., £12); **Birmingham** (45min., 2 per hr., £11); **London** (2½hr., every hr., £33-56.50); **Worcester** (25min., every 2hr., £5.40).

Buses: Royal Well Coach Station, Royal Well Rd. National Express office on Clarence Parade open M-Sa 9am-4:45pm. Stagecoach Office, 229 High St. (☎0871 200 2233) open M-Sa 9am-5pm. National Express (☎08705 808 080) to: **Birmingham** (1½hr., 3 per day, £6); **Bristol** (1¼hr., 3 per day, £6.10); **London** (3hr., every hr., £15.50); **Manchester** (4hr., 3 per day, £20.50). Stagecoach (☎0871 200 2233) serves **Gloucester** (40min., every 10min., £1.70). Swanbrook Coaches (☎01452 712 386) runs to **Oxford** (1½hr., 3 per day, £6.50).

Taxis: Taxi stands by the Royal Well Coach Station and on the Promenade. Free phone in train station. Try **Central Taxis** (☎228 877), **Starline Taxi** (☎250 250), **Handycars** (☎262 611; 24hr.), or **A to B** (☎580 580; 24hr.).

🔎 ORIENTATION AND PRACTICAL INFORMATION

The heart of Cheltenham is the intersection of **High Street** and the **Promenade,** the town's central boulevard. The train station is at the western edge of town; to get there, walk 30min. on a signposted path or catch local bus D or E (5min., every 10min., £1.25).

Tourist Information Centre: Municipal Offices, 77 The Promenade (☎522 878, accommodations booking 517 110; www.visitcheltenham.info). Books accommodations with a 10% deposit and posts B&B vacancies. Open M and W-Sa 9:30am-5:15pm.

Financial Services: Banks are along High St. Most are open M-F 9am-4:30pm, W 10am-4:30pm, Sa 9am-12:30pm. **Thomas Cook,** 159 High St. (☎847 900). Open M-Tu and Th-Sa 9am-5:30pm, W 10am-5:30pm, Su 11am-5pm.

Library: Central Library, Clarence St. (☎532 685). Open M, W, F 9am-7pm, Tu and Th 9am-5:30pm, Sa 9am-4pm.

Launderette: Soap-n-Suds, 312 High St. (☎512 107). Wash £2-3, dry 20p per 3min. Open daily 7:30am-8pm. Last wash 7pm.

Police: Holland House, 840 Lansdown Rd. (☎08450 901 234).

Hospital: Cheltenham General, Sandford Rd. (☎08454 222 222). Follow Bath Rd. southwest from town and turn left onto Sandford Rd.

Internet Access: Smart Space, Regent St. (☎063 7177), upstairs from the Everyman Theatre. Free with purchase from the cafe. Open M-Sa 9:30am-late. The **Library** has free computer access in 15min. time slots, 2hr. free with a guest ticket from the front desk. **The Loft Internet Cafe,** 8-9 Henrietta St. (☎539 573), upstairs from Moss Books. £1 per 20min., before noon £1 per hr. Open M-Th 10am-7pm, F-Sa 10am-6pm.

Post Office: 225-227 High St. (☎08457 223 344). **Bureau de change.** Open M-Sa 9am-5:30pm. **Post Code:** GL50 1AA.

🏠 ACCOMMODATIONS

Standards and prices tend to be high (£30-40) at Cheltenham's **B&Bs.** Most establishments cluster in the **Montpellier** area and along **Bath Road,** a 5min. walk from the town center.

Benton's Guest House, 71 Bath Rd. (☎517 417). English countryside decor with hair dryers and towel warmers. The owner is always up for a chat. £30 per person. ❸

YMCA, 6 Vittoria Walk (☎524 024; www.cheltenhamymca.com). Large facilities frequented by a mix of travelers and locals. One 4-bed male bunkroom, one 4-bed female bunkroom. If the bunks are full, inquire about single rooms, which cannot be booked in advance. Adjacent gym. Showers feel slightly prison-like, but the water is always warm. Breakfast included. Kitchen available. Laundry (wash and dry) £1.90. Reception M-F 7am-10pm, Sa-Su 9am-10pm. Dorms £16.50; singles £25. Book ahead. MC/V. ❷

Cross Ways, 57 Bath Rd. (☎527 683). The proprietor's experience as an interior designer is apparent in this Regency home's furnishings. Rooms as comfortable as they are lavish. £40 per person. Book a few weeks in advance. AmEx/MC/V. ❹

Lonsdale House, 16 Montpellier Dr. (☎232 379). Large bedrooms and an elegant dining room. Top-floor rooms are smaller; ask for the ground or 1st fl. Singles £30, ensuite £42; doubles £55/62. AmEx/MC/V. ❸

HEART OF ENGLAND

🗘 FOOD

Fruit stands, butchers, and bakeries dot **High Street,** while posh restaurants and cafe-bars line **Montpellier Street** across from Montpellier Gardens. A Tesco Metro **supermarket** is at 233 High St. (☎847 400. Open M-F 7am-11pm, Sa 7am-10pm, Su 11am-5pm.) A **farmers' market** is held the second and last Friday of the month outside the TIC (9am-3pm). A Thursday morning **market,** in the car park near Henrietta St., sells fruits, meats, and other wares.

Gianni, 1 Royal Well Pl. (☎221 101), just south of the bus stop on Royal Well Rd. Huge portions of modern Italian food served in a homey dining room. Enthusiastic waiters (some who sing while serving) make dining here a delight. Appetizers £1.50-7. Pastas £6-8. Entrees £10-14. Open M-Th and Su noon-3pm and 6:30-10:30pm, F-Sa noon-3pm and 6:30-11pm. AmEx/MC/V. ❸

George's Organic Cafe, 10 Bennington St. (☎238 733). Fresh flowers and checkered floor create a classic-diner feel. Huge sandwiches served on fresh bread (£2.45). Daily specials with organic salad (from £5.20). Open M-F 9:30am-3:30pm. Cash only. ❶

The Vine, 47 High St. (☎220 170). Rich colors and old world, wax-covered candle holders. Thai-inspired meals are cheap and filling (£5-6). The bar fills up quickly, so get in early if you want a table at dinner. Open daily noon-midnight. MC/V. ❶

Flynn's Bar and Brasserie, 16-17 The Courtyard, Montpellier St. (☎252 752). Walk down the stairs and look left to find Flynn's. Locals swear by it. Appetizers, like the delicious deep-fried goat cheese in phyllo dough (£5), are small—entrees (£9-13) are not. Outdoor seating. Open M-Sa noon-3pm and 6-9pm. AmEx/D/MC/V. ❷

Shake's, 216 High St. Look for the bright pink sign and the cartoon cow. Over 100 flavors of ice cream and freshly blended yogurt smoothies, the perfect morning cure for a night on the town. Open M-F 11am-6pm, Sa 10am-6pm, Su 11am-5pm. Cash only. ❶

👁 🌺 SIGHTS AND FESTIVALS

Cheltenham possesses the only naturally **alkaline water** in Britain. You can enjoy its diuretic and laxative effects—if "enjoy" is the right word—at the town hall, Imperial Sq. (☎521 621. Open M-Sa 9:30am-5:30pm.) The **Pittville Pump Room,** 10min. north of High St., presides over a park designed in its honor. Opened in 1830, the former spa is Cheltenham's finest Regency building. (☎523 852. Open M and W-Su 10am-4pm.) Treatment of the well system periodically interrupts free tastings. On your way back to town, stop by the **Gustav Holst Birthplace Museum,** 4 Clarence Rd., to relive the composer's early life in his impeccably restored home. (☎524 846; www.holstmuseum.org.uk. Open Feb.-Dec. Tu-Sa 10am-4pm. £2.50, children and concessions £2, families £7.) The **Cheltenham Art Gallery and Museum,** Clarence St., showcases a horde of English miscellany from the Arts and Crafts movement. Items include stuffed pheasants and Victorian tiaras. (☎237 431; www.artsandcraftsmuseum.org.uk. Open M-Sa 10am-5:20pm. Free.) Down the Promenade, locals sunbathe at the **Imperial Gardens.**

The indispensable *What's On* poster, displayed on kiosks and at the TIC, lists concerts, plays, tours, sporting events, and hot spots. The **Cheltenham International Festival of Music** celebrates modern classical works for three weeks in July. The concurrent **Fringe Festival** organizes jazz, big band, and rock performances. The **International Jazz Festival** takes place at the end of April and the beginning of May, while October heralds the **Cheltenham Festival of Literature.** Full details on these festivals are available from the box office. (Town Hall, Imperial Sq. ☎227 979; www.cheltenhamfestivals.co.uk.) The **Cheltenham Cricket Festival,** the oldest in the country, starts in August. Inquire about match times at the TIC, or call ☎0117 910 8000. Purchase tickets (£12-15) at the gate.

◨◪ PUBS AND NIGHTLIFE

Nightlife is dead during the week, but Cheltenham springs to life on the weekends as students and twenty-somethings invade. Numerous pubs, bars, and clubs line **High Street** east of the Promenade. Popular venues also cluster around **Clarence Street** and at the top of **Bath Road**. Many offer drink specials and reduced covers for students.

Frog and Fiddle, 315 High St. (☎701 156). Leather couches and outdoor seating. Pool and arcade games upstairs. Students make for a laid-back scene. Tu curry and a pint £5. F live music and open mic 9pm. Open M-Sa noon-11pm, Su noon-10:30pm.

Que Pasa, 15-21 Clarence St. (☎230 099; www.quepasa.co.uk). A regular student stop for weekend pub crawls. The *fiesta* is best on Sa nights. Nightly promotions. Open M-Th 11am-midnight, F-Sa 11am-1am, Su noon-10:30pm.

Revolution Vodka Bar, Clarence Parade (☎234 045). Newly opened. Huge converted church fills with a younger crowd on weekends and has a lounge feel during the day. Hidden booths in the back. Open daily 11:30am-midnight.

Moda, 33-35 Albion St. (☎570 583; www.clubmoda.co.uk). Enter from High St. A stylish place full of equally stylish students. 3 fl. of house, R&B, 70s, and 80s music. Cover £3-5. Open M and W-Sa 9pm-3am.

◪ DAYTRIP FROM CHELTENHAM

TEWKESBURY

Stagecoach (☎01242 575 606) bus #41 departs from High St., across from the Tesco Metro, in Cheltenham (25min.; M-Sa every 20-30min., Su every 2hr.; round-trip £3.40). The Tourist Information Centre (☎01684 295 027) is moving to a new location on Church St. within the year and sells pamphlets (20p) highlighting the town's rich history. Open Easter-Oct. M-Sa 9:30am-5pm, Su 10am-4pm; Nov.-Easter M-Sa 9:30am-5pm.

Ten miles northwest of Cheltenham, Tewkesbury (TOOKS-bury) is a quiet medieval town with a trove of half-timbered houses. Its most celebrated structure is **Tewkesbury Abbey,** whose Norman tower is the largest such structure in all of England. Massive pillars support the vaulted nave and panels of 14th-century stained glass. First consecrated in 1121, the abbey was reconsecrated after the 1471 Battle of Tewkesbury, when Yorks killed the abbey's monks for attempting to protect refuge-seeking Lancastrians in the Wars of the Roses. The townspeople later bought the cathedral from Henry VIII. The cathedral houses three organs, including the recently rebuilt "Milton Organ," rumored to have been played by John Milton himself. (☎01684 850 959; www.tewkesburyabbey.org.uk. Open Apr.-Oct. M-Sa 7:30am-6pm, Su 7:30am-7pm; Nov.-Mar. M-Sa 7:30am-5:30pm, Su 7:30am-7pm. Services Su 8, 9:15, 11am, and 6pm. Requested donation £3.) Beside the abbey, the **John Moore Countryside Museum,** 45 Church St., is in a merchant's cottage built in 1450. The museum displays exhibits of native 15th-century wildlife and live animal shows. (☎01684 297 174; www.gloster.demon.co.uk/jmcm. Open Apr.-Oct. Tu-Sa 10am-1pm and 2-5pm; Nov.-Mar. Sa and bank holidays 10am-1pm and 2-5pm. £1.25, concessions £1.) The small **Tewkesbury Borough Museum,** 64 Barton St., contains an exhibit on the 1471 battle that ended the Wars of the Roses. (☎01684 292 901. Open W-Sa, hours vary due to volunteer staff. £1, concessions 75p, children 50p, families £2.50.) The battle is recreated at the annual **Tewkesbury Medieval Festival.** (1st weekend in July 11am-5pm. Free.) **Kingfisher Ferries** runs boats down the Avon to Twyning. Boats depart at the pier behind the Sainsbury. (☎01684 294 088. 4-5 per day. £3.50.)

HEART OF ENGLAND

THE COTSWOLDS

The Cotswolds have deviated little from their etymological roots: "Cotswolds" means "sheep enclosures in rolling hillsides." Despite the rather sleepy moniker, the Cotswolds are filled with rich history and traditions (like cheese-rolling) that date back to Roman and Saxon times. While it may seem that the classic English hedgerows outnumber the people, the more urban towns of Gloucester, Cirencester, and Cheltenham supply both shoppers and hikers in the Cotswolds.

TRANSPORTATION

Public transportation to and within the Cotswolds is scarce; planning ahead is a must. The villages of the "Northern" Cotswolds (Stow-on-the-Wold, Bourton-on-the-Water, Moreton-in-Marsh) are easily reached via Cheltenham, while Gloucester serves the remote "Southern" Cotswolds (Slimbridge, Stroud, and Painswick).

Train stations in the Cotswolds are few and far between. **Trains** to London (1½hr., every 1-2hr., $30) via Oxford (30min., $9.50) from **Moreton-in-Marsh Station** (open M-Sa 5:45am-7:15pm, Su 5:45am-12:30pm). In the Southern Cotswolds, trains run from **Cam and Dursley Station** (3 mi. from Slimbridge, unstaffed) to Gloucester (15min., every hr., $4) and London Paddington (2½hr., every hr., $20). It's easier to reach the Cotswolds by **bus.** The Cheltenham TIC's free *Getting There* details service between the town and 27 destinations. The free *Explore the Cotswolds by Public Transport*, available at most TICs, lists routes for major services between villages. Consult the TIC for departure times, and note that schedules vary depending on the day. Pulham's Coaches #801 (☎01451 820 369) runs from Cheltenham to Moreton-in-Marsh (1hr., M-Sa 7 per day, $1.75) via Bourton-on-the-Water (35min., $1.65) and Stow-on-the-Wold (50min., $1.70). For Lower and Upper Slaughter, ask to stop at Slaughter Pike, between Bourton-on-the-Water and Stow-on-the-Wold; the villages are ½ mi. from the road. Castleways Ltd. #606 (☎01242 602 949) goes from Cheltenham to Broadway (50min., M-Sa 4 per day, $2.10) via Winchcombe (20min., $2). Johnsons buses #21, 22, and 522 (☎01564 797 000) run to Chipping Campden from Moreton-in-Marsh (20min., M-Sa 9 per day, $1.60) via Broadway (5min., M-Sa 5 per day) before ending in Stratford (1hr., M-Sa 8 per day, $2.60).

In the Southern Cotswolds, Stagecoach bus #51 runs from Cheltenham to Cirencester (40min., M-Sa every hr., $2.25). Beaumont Travel (☎01452 309 770) bus #855 Fosse Link runs to Cirencester from Moreton-in-Marsh (1hr., M-Sa 8 per day, $1.50) via Stow-on-the-Wold (40min., $1.30) and Bourton-on-the-Water (20min., $1.20). Both buses are covered by a **Cotswold Rover ticket,** which may be purchased from the driver ($4, children $2). Service from Cheltenham to Gloucester is frequent on Stagecoach bus #94 (30min.; M-F every 10min., Su every 20min.; $2.10). From Gloucester bus station, Stagecoach bus #91 runs to Slimbridge Crossroads (35min.; M-Sa every hr., Su 4 per day continuing to Wetlands Trust; $2.50). As always, Traveline (☎0870 608 2608) is a true lifeline for those traveling by public transportation, especially in the Cotswolds, where a journey from one small village to another may require a few transfers.

The easiest way to explore is by car, but the best way to experience the Cotswolds is on foot or by bike. The Toy Shop, on High St. in Moreton-in-Marsh, offers **bike rentals** with a lock, map, and route suggestions. (☎01608 650 756. $12

TIP **GOOD MORNING SUNSHINE.** It is possible to see 3 or even 4 small villages in 1 day by public transportation, but travelers should be mindful that many buses run on a 9am-6pm schedule. To avoid getting stuck, make the 1st morning bus out to your destination (typically between 8:45 and 9:30am).

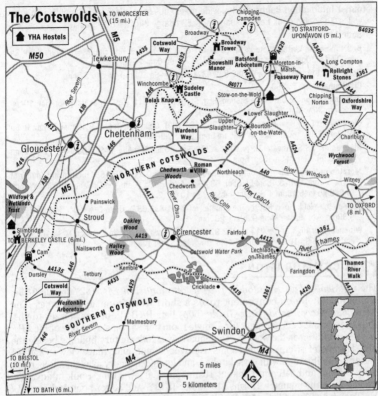

The Cotswolds

▲ YHA Hostels

TO WORCESTER (15 mi.)

M50

M5

Tewkesbury

A435

A38

River Severn

River Severn

Cotswold Way

B4632

Broadway

Broadway Tower

Snowshill Manor

Batsford Arboretum

Chipping Campden

TO STRATFORD-UPON-AVON (5 mi.)

B4035

A429

A3400

A44

A361

Long Compton

Rollright Stones

Winchcombe

A46

Sudeley Castle

Belas Knap ■

B4077

Stow-on-the-Wold

Moreton-in-Marsh

Fosseway Farm

Chipping Norton

Oxfordshire Way

A44

Cheltenham

Wardens Way

B4632

Lower Slaughter

Upper Slaughter

Bourton-on-the-Water

A436

A424

A361

A424

Charlbury

Wychwood Forest

Gloucester

A46

A48

A46

A417

NORTHERN COTSWOLDS

Chedworth Woods

Roman Villa

Northleach

Chedworth

A429

A40

River Windrush

Witney

River Leach

River Coln

River Chun

TO OXFORD (8 mi.)

M5

Painswick

Wildfowl & Wetlands Trust

Slimbridge

TO BERKELEY CASTLE (6 mi.)

Cam

Dursley

A4135

A46

Stroud

A417

A419

Oakley Wood

Hailey Wood

Cirencester

Fairford

Cotswold Water Park

Lechlade-on-Thames

A417

A361

River Thames

Faringdon

Thames River Walk

Nailsworth

Tetbury

A433

A429

Kemble

Cricklade ●

A419

A361

A420

A417

Cotswold Way

Westonbirt Arboretum

River Severn

Malmesbury

SOUTHERN COTSWOLDS

Swindon

M4

A46

TO BRISTOL (10 mi.)

M4

TO BATH (6 mi.)

0   5 miles
0   5 kilometers

N

LG

per half-day, £14 per day. Credit card deposit. Open M and W-Sa 9am-1pm and 2-5pm.) The **YHA** in Stow-on-the-Wold (p. 288) also rents bikes with a lock and helmet. (☎01451 830 497. Open daily 8-10am and 5-10pm. £6 per ½-day, £9.50 per full day.) **Taxis** are a convenient, if expensive, way of getting to areas inaccessible by public transportation. TICs have lists of companies serving their area: "K" Cars (☎01451 822 578 or 07929 360 712) is based in Bourton-on-the-Water, and Cotswold Taxis (☎07710 117 471) operates from Moreton-in-Marsh. **Coach tours** cover the Cotswolds from Cheltenham, Gloucester, Oxford, Stratford-upon-Avon, Tewkesbury, and other cities. Try the **Cotswold Discovery Tour,** a full-day bus tour that starts in Bath and visits five of the most scenic villages. (☎09067 112 000; www.madmax.abel.co.uk. Tours Apr.-Oct. Tu, Th, and Su 9am-5:15pm. £25.)

■✈🚲 ORIENTATION AND PRACTICAL INFORMATION

The Cotswolds lie mostly in Gloucestershire, bounded by Stratford-upon-Avon in the north, Oxford in the east, Cheltenham in the west, and Bath in the south. The northern Cotswolds house more postcard-worthy villages and hills, hence more visitors and higher B&B prices. The range hardly towers—the average hill reaches only 600 ft.—but the rolling hills make hiking and biking tough. The best bases, transportation- and provision-wise, from which to explore are Cheltenham, Cirencester, Gloucester, Moreton-in-Marsh, and Stow-on-the-Wold.

Tourist Information Centres: All provide maps, bus schedules, and pamphlets on area walks. They also book beds, usually for a £2 charge plus a 10% deposit.

Bath: See p. 194.

Bourton-on-the-Water: Victoria St. (☎01451 820 211). Open Apr.-Oct. M-F 9:30am-5pm, Sa 9:30am-5:30pm; Nov.-Mar. M-F 9:30am-4pm, Sa 9:30am-4:30pm.

Broadway: 1 Cotswold Ct. (☎01386 852 937). Open M-Sa 10am-1pm and 2-5pm.

Cheltenham: See p. 283.

Chipping Campden: Old Police Station, High St. (☎01386 841 206). Open daily Apr.-Oct. 10am-5:30pm; Nov.-Mar. 10am-5pm.

Cirencester: Corn Hall, Market Pl. (☎01285 654 180). Open Apr.-Dec. M 9:45am-5:30pm, Tu-Sa 9:30am-5:30pm; Jan.-Mar. M 9:45am-5pm, Tu-Sa 9:30am-5pm.

Gloucester: 28 Southgate St. (☎01452 396 572). Open July-Aug. M-Sa 10am-5pm, Su 11am-3pm; Sept.-June M-Sa 10am-5pm.

Moreton-in-Marsh: District Council Building, High St. (☎01608 650 881). Open in summer M 8:45am-4pm, Tu-Th 8:45am-5:15pm, F 8:45am-4:45pm, Sa 10am-1pm; in winter M 8:45am-4pm, Tu-Th 8:45am-5:15pm, F 8:45am-4:45pm, Sa 10am-12:30pm.

Stow-on-the-Wold: Hollis House, The Square (☎01451 831 082). Open Easter-Oct. M-Sa 9:30am-5:30pm; Nov.-Easter M-Sa 9:30am-4:30pm.

Winchcombe: High St. (☎01242 602 925), next to Town Hall. Open Apr.-Oct. M-Sa 10am-1pm and 2-5pm, Su 10am-1pm and 2-4pm; Nov.-Mar. Sa-Su 10am-4pm.

ACCOMMODATIONS

The *Cotswold Way Handbook and Accommodation List* (£2) details **B&Bs,** which usually lie on convenient roads a short walk from small villages. The *Cotswolds Accommodation Guide* (50p) lists B&Bs in or near larger towns. Expect to pay £30-55 per night for a single room unless you stay at one of the YHA hostels. **YHA Stow-on-the-Wold ❷,** The Square, is a 16th-century building beside the TIC. The hostel offers ensuite rooms with wood bunks and village views. (☎01451 830 497. Family room with toys, kitchen, and lounge. Laundry available. Reception daily 8-10am and 5-10pm. Lockout 10am-5pm. Curfew 11pm. Book in advance, especially in the summer. Dorms £15, under 18 £12. Add £3 for nonmembers. MC/V.) The 56-bed **YHA Slimbridge ❶,** Shepherd's Patch, off the A38 and the M5, has spacious common areas and a large duck pond behind the building. The nearest train station (Cam and Dursley) is 3 mi. away. It's easier to take bus #91 from Gloucester to the Slimbridge Crossroads roundabout and walk 2 mi. (☎08707 706 036. Laundry £2.60. Reception daily 7:15-10am and 5-11pm. Curfew 11pm. Open from mid-July to early Sept. daily; Oct.-Nov. and from Jan. to mid-July F-Sa. Dorms £11, under 18 £8; twins £26; families £38-69. MC/V.) There are several **campsites** close to Cheltenham, but there are also convenient places to rough it within the Cotswolds. Try **Fosseway Farm ❶** (p. 290). *Camping and Caravanning in Gloucestershire and the Cotswolds,* free at local TICs, lists more options.

HIKING AND BIKING

For centuries, travelers have walked the well-worn Cotswolds footpaths from village to village. Tranquil hillsides and the allure of pubs with local brews make moving at a pace beyond three or four villages per day inadvisable. The free *Cotswold Events* booklet, available at TICs, lists music festivals, antique markets, woolsack races, and cheese-rolling events.

The TIC stocks a variety of **walking** and **cycling guides.** The *Cotswold Map and Guidebook in One* (£5) is good for planning bike routes and short hikes. Hikers planning more than a short stroll should use the Ordnance Survey Outdoor Leisure Map #45 (1:25,000; £7), which provides topographic information and highlights nearly all public footpaths. The Cotswolds Voluntary Warden Service (☎01451 862 000) leads free **guided walks**, some with themes (1½-7½hr.). All walks are listed on its website (www.cotswoldsaonb.com) and in the Programme Guide section of the biannual *Cotswold LION* (free at the TIC).

Long-distance hikers can choose from a handful of trails. The extensive **Cotswold Way** spans just over 100 mi. from Bath to Chipping Campden, has few steep climbs, and can be done in a week. The trail passes through pastures and the remains of ancient settlements. Pockmarks and gravel make certain sections unsuitable for biking or horseback riding. Consult the **Cotswold Way National Trail Office** (☎01453 827 004) for details. The **Oxfordshire Way** (65 mi.) runs between the popular (hyphen-havens) Bourton-on-the-Water and Henley-on-Thames, site of the famed regatta. Amble through pastures on your way from Bourton-on-the-Water to Lower and Upper Slaughter along the **Warden's Way,** a half-day hike. Adventurous souls can continue to Winchcombe. The **Thames Path Walk** starts on the western edge of the Cotswolds in Lechlade and follows the Thames 184 mi. to Kingston, near London. The section from the Cotswolds to Oxford is low-impact and particularly peaceful. The **Severn Way** runs for 210 mi. from Plynlimon in Wales to Bristol along the River Severn and runs along the western border of the Cotswolds. Contact the **National Trails Office** (☎01865 810 224) for details. Local roads are perfect for **biking**—rolling hills welcome both casual and hardy cyclers. Parts of the Oxfordshire Way are hospitable to cyclists, if slightly rut-riddled. TICs in all towns have a Cotswolds cycling route packet (£3) that outlines five different routes between villages. They also have free cycling guides detailing trails from 16-30 mi.

WINCHCOMBE. A tiny village 7 mi. north of Cheltenham, Winchcombe is home to the secluded **Sudeley Castle,** a 10min. walk from the town center. Lord and Lady Ashcombe have filled the castle with Tudor memorabilia. The castle also has 14 acres of prize-winning gardens, all of which offer stunning views of the surrounding hills. The chapel contains the tomb of Henry VIII's Queen number six, Katherine Parr. In summer, Sudeley also holds jousting tournaments and Shakespeare under the stars. (☎01242 602 308; www.sudeleycastle.co.uk. Castle open daily Mar.-Oct. 11am-5pm. Last admission 4:30pm. Gardens open daily Mar.-Oct. 10:30am-5:30pm. Castle and gardens £7.20, concessions £6.20, children £4.20. Gardens only £5.50/4.50/3.25. £1 surcharge Su May-Aug.) **Belas Knap,** a 4000-year-old burial mound, stands 1½ mi. southwest of Sudeley Castle. It is accessible from the Cotswold Way or via a scenic 2½hr. walk from Winchcombe. The Winchcombe TIC has a free pamphlet with directions.

BOURTON-ON-THE-WATER. Known as the most beautiful village in the Cotswolds, Bourton-on-the-Water feels like an old-fashioned town. The footbridge-straddled River Windrush runs along the main street, giving Bourton the moniker "Venice of the Cotswolds." The beauty and location of Bourton has made it a popular destination, so expect more tourist traps here than in other villages. The Oxford Way trailhead is here, as is a confluence of other trails, including the Warden's, Heart of England, Windrush, and Gloucestershire Ways. For a taste of life as a giant, follow signs to **The Model Village,** a scale model of Bourton built in 1937. (Open daily in summer 10am-5:45pm; in winter 10am-4pm. £2.75, concessions £2.25-2.50.) **Birdland,** on Rissington Rd., has a motley crew of winged creatures from neon pink flamingos to penguins. (☎820 480; www.birdland.co.uk. Open daily Apr.-Oct. 10am-6pm; Nov.-Mar. 10am-4pm. Last admission 1hr. before close. £5.20, seniors £4.20, children £3, families £15.) Next door, the **Dragonfly** maze is the best place to get lost in the Cotswolds. An intricate hedge maze contains a hidden chamber where you must solve a puzzle. *Let's Go* could tell you the answer, but then we'd have to kill you. (Open daily 10am-5:30pm, weather permitting. £2.50.) Between rose-laden gates and cobbled streets, the **Cotswold Perfumery,** on Victoria St., offers a factory tour, but a mere visit to the shop is an olfactory adventure. You can purchase one of the nine fragrances made in the shop or splurge and make your own in a day-long perfumery course. (☎01451 820 698; www.cotswold-perfumery.co.uk. Call to book a tour in advance; usually 1-2 per day. Open M-Sa 9:30am-5pm, Su 10:30am-5pm. £5, concessions £3.50.)

STOW-ON-THE-WOLD. Inns and taverns crowd the Market Sq. of this self-proclaimed "Heart of the Cotswolds." Despite chain stores, like the **Tesco** supermarket on Fosse Way (☎01451 807 400; open M-F 6am-midnight, Sa 6am-10pm, Su 10am-4pm), Stow still exudes Cotswold quaintness. A traditional **farmers' market** takes place on the second Thursday of every month in the Market Square. (☎01453 758 060. Open 9am-2pm.) Three miles downhill, off the A424, **Donnington Trout Farm** lets visitors fish, feed, and eat the trout. The staff can smoke just about anything—even pigeons. (☎01451 830 873. Open Apr.-Oct. daily 10am-5:30pm; Nov.-Mar. Tu-Su 10am-5pm.) The **YHA hostel ❷** (p. 288) is in the center of town. (☎0870 770 6050. £15.50, under 18 £11.) Ensuite rooms are a perk at the **Pear Tree Cottage ❹,** a stone house on High St. (☎01451 831 210. Singles £32-35; doubles £45-50. Cash only.)

THE SLAUGHTERS. No need to fear—the Slaughters got their names from the Old English word slough, meaning "stream." The towns, complete with bubbling brooks, are a few miles southwest of Stow. The less touristed and more charming Lower Slaughter is connected to its sister village, Upper Slaughter, by the Warden's Way. In Lower Slaughter, the **Old Mill,** on Mill Ln., scoops water from the river that flows past. A mill has stood on this spot for 1000 years. (☎01451 820 052. Open daily in summer 10am-6pm; in winter 10am-dusk. £1.25, children 50p.)

MORETON-IN-MARSH. With a train station, frequent bus service, and a bike shop, Moreton is a convenient base from which to explore the north. The village has typical Cotswolds charm, but holds few attractions. Two miles west on A44 is **Batsford Arboretum,** with 56 acres of waterfalls, a Japanese rest house, and more than 1600 species of trees. (☎01386 701 441; www.batsarb.co.uk. Open from Feb. to mid-Nov. daily 10am-5pm; from mid-Nov. to Jan. Sa-Su 10am-4pm. £6, concessions £5, children £2.) A Tesco Express **market** is on High St. in the center of town, next to the bus stop. (☎01608 652 287. Open M-Sa 6am-11pm, Su 7am-11pm.) Every Tuesday, High St. plays host to the largest **open-air market** in the region. **Warwick House B&B ❸,** London Rd., has an energetic owner and a bevy of perks, including four-poster beds, Wi-Fi, and an ample breakfast. Follow A44 east out of town toward Oxford for 10min.; the hostel is on the left. (☎01608 650 773; www.snooze-andsizzle.com. Free pickup from station. £30-35 per person. Cash only.) **Blue Cedar House ❸,** Stow Rd., a 5min. walk on High St. toward Stow Rd., has welcoming rooms and an airy breakfast area. (☎01608 650 299. Book ahead. From £26 per person. Cash only.) Try **Fosseway Farm ❶,** Stow Rd., 5min. out of Moreton-in-Marsh toward Stow-on-the-Wold. (☎01608 650 503. Campers' breakfast £3.50. Caravans and tents £12. Electricity available. MC/V.) Enjoy tea and lunch at **Tilly's Tea Room ❶,** High St., which has a host of homemade cakes and jams to enjoy in their garden. (☎01608 650 000. Tea and scone £4.35. Cash only.)

BROADWAY. Broadway lives up to its name, with a long, wide High St. bordered by pubs and specialty shops. **Broadway Tower,** a 30-40min. uphill hike, inspired the likes of poet Dante Gabriel Rossetti and affords an excellent view of 12 counties. Take Johnson bus #21/22 from the High St. to Broadway Tower Park (M-Sa 4 per day, 10min.). Alternatively, from High St., follow the Cotswold Way uphill out of town. (☎01386 852 390. Open Apr.-Oct. daily 10:30am-5pm; Nov.-Mar. Sa-Su 11am-

3pm, may be closed in poor weather. £3.80, concessions £3, children £2.50, families £10.) **Snowshill Manor,** 2½ mi. southwest of Broadway, was once home to a collector of everything and anything. It now houses about 20,000 knick-knacks. (☎01386 852 410. Open late Mar.-Apr. M-Th and Su noon-5pm; May-Oct. M-W and Su noon-5pm. £7.30, children £3.65.) Past Snowshill Manor, **Snowshill Lavender Farm** lets you wander through the sweet-smelling lavender fields and watch the distillation process. (☎01386 854 821; www.snowshill-lavender.co.uk. Open from Good Friday through summer W-Su 11am-5pm. £2.50.)

CHIPPING CAMPDEN. Years ago, quiet Chipping Campden was the capital of the Cotswolds' wool trade ("chipping" means "market"). Market Hall, in the middle of the main street, attests to 400 years of commerce. The gothic **St. James Church,** a 5min. walk from High St., houses England's only full set of 15th-century altar hangings. From the TIC entrance, turn right onto High St. and take the right fork up the hill to the church. (☎01386 840 671; www.stjameschurchcampden.co.uk. Open Mar.-Oct. M-Sa 10am-5pm, Su 2-6pm; Nov. and Feb. M-Sa 11am-4pm, Su 2-4pm; Dec.-Jan. M-Sa 11am-5pm. Suggested donation £1.) Currently, the town is famous for its **Cotswold Olympic Games,** held in the first week of June. The games take place on Dovers Hill. From St. Catherine's on High St., turn right onto West End Terr., take the first left, and follow the public footpath 1 mi. uphill. The 2012 Olympic Games in London will coincide with the 400th anniversary of the Cotswold Games. The town has scheduled a massive celebration.

CIRENCESTER. One of the larger towns in the Cotswolds and regarded as the capital of the region, Cirencester (SI-ruhn-ses-ter) is the site of Corinium, a Roman town founded in AD 49. Although only scraps of the amphitheater remain, the **Corinium Museum,** Park St., has a formidable collection of Roman mosaics and relics from the town's past as well as exhibits on the region's Anglo-Saxon and wool-producing history. (☎01285 655 611. Open M-Sa 10am-5pm, Su 2-5pm. £4, concessions £2-3.) Cirencester's **Parish Church of St. John the Baptist** is Gloucestershire's largest "wool church." The church is home to a cup made for Anne Boleyn in 1535. (☎01285 659 317. Open M-Sa 9:30am-5pm, Su 2:15-5pm. 3 services per day. Grounds close 9pm. Donation requested.) The world's highest yew hedge bounds Lord Bathurst's mansion at the top of Park St. Bear right and make a left on Cecily Hill to enter the 3000-acre **Cirencester Park,** whose stately central aisle was designed by Alexander Pope. Alexcars (☎01285 653 985) bus A1 runs to the arboretum from Cirencester on Saturdays in summer (40min., Apr.-Sept. Sa 2 per day, £3 round-trip). Otherwise, take the A1 to Tetbury (45min., M-F 7 per day, £1.70) and transfer to Stagecoach bus #620 or 628 (7min., M-Sa 5 per day, £1.30). An **antique market** occurs on Fridays in Corn Hall, near the TIC. (☎0171 263 6010. Open 10am-4:30pm.) A **cattle market** takes place every Tuesday on Tetbury Rd., and a **country market** every Friday at Brewery Arts, off Castle St. (Open 8:30-11:30am.) A short walk south of town center, **Apsley Villa Guest House ❸,** 16 Victoria Rd., offers affordable rooms and elegance. (☎01285 653 489. Singles £30; doubles and twins £45. Cash only.)

CHEDWORTH. Tucked in the hills southeast of Cheltenham, Chedworth contains a well-preserved **Roman villa,** halfway between Cirencester and Northleach off A429. The villa's famed mosaics were found in 1864 when a gamekeeper noticed tile fragments revealed by busy rabbits. (☎01242 890 256. Open Tu-Su 10am-5pm. £5.) From Cirencester, Ebly Bus/Pulman Coach #864 reaches the villa on weekends and some weekdays, but service is infrequent; leave enough time to avoid being stranded. The #855 Fosse Link passes by the town between Bourton-on-the-Water and Cirencester; ask the driver to drop you off.

SLIMBRIDGE. Slimbridge, 12½ mi. southwest of Gloucester off the A38, is a dull village with two draws: a pleasant hostel (**YHA Slimbridge,** p. 288) and the largest of seven **Wildfowl & Wetlands Trust** centers in Britain. Sir Peter Scott has developed the world's biggest collection of wildfowl here, with over 180 different species, including all six varieties of flamingos. To avoid a 3½ mi. walk from Slimbridge Crossroads, take the First bus service from Gloucester on Sundays, which goes directly to the Trust. (☎01453 891 900; www.wwt.org.uk. Open M-Tu and Th-Su 9:30am-5:30pm, W 9am-5pm. Last admission 30min. before close. £6.75, concessions £5.50, children £4, families £19.) Six miles southwest of Slimbridge, off the A38 between Bristol and Gloucester, lies massive **Berkeley Castle** (BARK-lay). The stone fortress boasts impressive towers, a dungeon, the cell where King Edward II was murdered, Queen Elizabeth I's bowling green, and a Great Hall where West Country barons met before forcing King John to sign the Magna Carta. (☎01453 810 332. Open Apr.-Sept. Tu-Sa 11am-4pm, Su 2-5pm; Oct. Su 2-5pm. £7.50, seniors £6, children £3.50, families £18.50. Gardens only £4, children £2. Tours free and frequent.)

HEREFORD
☎01432

Near the Welsh border and the scenic River Wye, Hereford (HAIR-eh-fuhd; pop. 60,000) boasts a centuries-long history as the agricultural hub of the Wye Valley. Once known for its "whiteface" cattle and still known for its cathedral, Hereford now attracts shoppers to the upscale stores of High Town, a pedestrian area that hosts farmers' markets and local entertainment. Good bus and rail connections provide a springboard for travel to the Wye Valley.

▐ **TRANSPORTATION.** The **train** and **bus stations** are on Commercial Rd. **Trains** (☎08457 484 950; www.nationalrail.com) depart to: Abergavenny (25min., 2 per hr., £6.50); Cardiff (1¼hr., every hr., £13.70); Chepstow via Newport (1½hr., every hr., £15.40); London Paddington via Evesham (3hr., every hr., £35.50); Shrewsbury (1hr., 2 per hr., £13.20). National Express (☎08705 808 080) runs **buses** to Birmingham (2hr., 1 per day, £7.50) and London (4¼hr., 3 per day, £19). A bus stop is on Broad St., past the TIC. Stagecoach Red and White buses go to Cardiff via Abergavenny (X4, 2½hr., every 2hr.) and Brecon via Hay-on-Wye (#39; 1¾hr., M-Sa 6 per day). On Sundays, Yeoman's bus #40 takes over the Brecon route (4 per day). For bus info, pick up the *Herefordshire Public Transport Map and Guide* (40p) or the free *Monmouthshire County Council Local Transport Guide* at the TIC.

▐ **PRACTICAL INFORMATION.** The **Tourist Information Centre,** 1 King St., books beds for £1.50 plus a 10% deposit. (☎268 430. Open M-Sa 9am-5pm.) **Walking tours** leave from the TIC. (1½hr. From mid-May to mid-Sept. M-Sa 11am, Su 2:30pm. £3.) Other services include: **banks** with **ATMs** along Broad St.; a **launderette,** Coin-Op Launder Centre, 136 Eign St. (☎269 610; wash £2.50, soap 30p, dry 20p per 5min.; open M-Sa 8am-8:30pm, Su 8:30am-5pm; last wash 1hr. before close); **police** on Bath St. (☎08457 444 888); free **Internet** at the **library,** Broad St. (open Tu-W and F 9am-7:30pm, Th 9am-5:30pm, Sa 9:30am-4pm); and the **post office,** 14-15 St. Peter's St. (☎275 221. Open M-F 9am-5:30pm, Sa 9am-4pm.) **Post Code:** HR1 2LE.

▐▐ **ACCOMMODATIONS AND FOOD.** Cheap lodgings in the center of Hereford are scarce; your best bet is to walk to the **B&Bs** (from £25) near the end of **Bodenham Road.** Five-star quality at three-star prices await visitors at the newly renovated **Somerville Guest House ❸.** The Victorian house is run by the former accommodations quality inspector for the British government. (☎273 991; www.somervilleguesthouse.com. Free Wi-Fi. Singles £38; doubles £79.50.) The **Holly Tree Guest House ❸,** 19-21 Barton Rd., has clean, comfortable rooms. (☎357

845. No smoking. Singles £25; doubles £50. Cash only.) **Westfields ❷**, 235 White-cross Rd., has low prices a 10-15min. walk from town. Rooms are clean and bathrooms are spacious. (☎267 712. £20-25 per person. Cash only.)

Quiche with salad, takeaway lunch specials (each £3), and local artwork await at **Andy's Kitchen ❶**, King St., down the road from the TIC (☎272 001. Open M-Sa 8:30am-4pm.) At **Cafe@All Saints ❶**, in All Saints Church on High St., try the open-face foccaccia sandwich special (£4.65) and gaze out of stained-glass windows. (☎370 415. Open M-Sa 8:30am-5:30pm. MC/V.) Locals and tourists relax on couches at the **Antique Teashop ❶**, 5a St. Peter's St. Pastries (from 90p) and teas (£1.30) allow for dignified nibbling and sipping. (☎342 172. Open M-Sa 9:45am-5pm, Su 10:15am-5pm. Cash only.) Sweet and savor pork (£6) complements sweet and sudsy ale at the **Black Lion Inn ❷**, 31 Bridge St. (☎343 535. Open M-Th and Su noon-midnight, F-Sa noon-2am, last entry 11pm. Food served M-F noon-3pm, Sa-Su noon-4pm. MC/V.) A Tesco **supermarket,** Newmarket St., has your picnic needs covered (open M 8am-midnight, Tu-F 6am-midnight, Sa 6am-10pm, Su 10am-4pm). Stop by the **Market Hall Buttermarket** for produce (open M-Sa 8am-5:30pm).

 HEREFORD FOR POCKET CHANGE. Instead of having a pricey (and run-of-the-mill) pub lunch, grab a sandwich from Andy's Kitchen (p. 293) and head to the cathedral grounds for a picnic in the shadow of the oaks.

◙◱ **SIGHTS AND SHOPPING.** The massive **Hereford Cathedral** may surprise visitors—there are few Romanesque basilicas in Britain, and Hereford's is particularly monumental. The cathedral hosts monthly organ concerts in the summer (£6) and offers garden tours, which include tea and cake at the Cloister Cafe, for £4. (☎374 253; www.herefordcathedral.org. Garden tours run June-Aug. W and Sa at 3pm.) The cathedral holds the 13th-century **Mappa Mundi** ("cloth of the world"), a map that dates from back when the earth was flat and shows little-known regions of the world full of unicorns and headless men. In the **Chained Library,** 1500 volumes are linked to the shelf by slender chains; the practice was common in the 17th century, when books were as valuable as small parcels of land. (☎374 200. Cathedral open daily 7:30am until Evensong at 5:30pm. Mappa Mundi and library open May-Sept. M-Sa 10am-4:30pm, Su 11am-3:30pm; Oct.-Apr. M-Sa 11am-3:30pm. Cathedral free. Mappa Mundi and library £4.50, concessions £3.50, families £10.) A slew of cider facts and vats are inside the **Cider Museum,** off Pomona Pl. Don't let their "What Went Wrong with the Brew" display deter you from the free brandy-tasting at the on-site King Offa's Distillery. (☎354 207; www.cidermuseum.co.uk. Open Tu-Sa Apr.-Sept. 10am-5pm; Oct.-Mar. 11am-3pm. £3, students £2.)

Hereford's **High Town** area is a network of shop-lined walkways featuring a generic parade of chain stores. Thrifty shoppers might prefer ◪**The Dinosaw Market,** 16-17 Bastion Mews, off Union St., which promises "things that are not normal" and delivers. An array of vintage garb, wooden turtles, pink boas, and assorted bric-a-brac fills the store. (☎353 655. Open M-Sa 10am-5:30pm.) **Chapters,** 17 Union St., sells used books. (☎352 149. Open M-Sa 9:30am-4:30pm.)

◪ **NIGHTLIFE.** Old and young come out to play on weekends in Hereford, but options are few and crowded. **Play,** 51-55 Blueschool St., is a fabric-draped haunt of avid clubbers. Ladies drink free on Monday nights. (☎270 009. Cover £3-5. Open M 9:30pm-2am, Th-Su 9:30pm-3am.) **Booth Hall,** East St., is a popular pub that cranks up its music during evening hours, although in summer most patrons crowd in the courtyard beer garden. (☎344 487. Open M-Sa 11am-11pm, Su 7:30-10:30pm. Food served M-Sa noon-3pm.)

THE MIDLANDS

Mention "the Midlands," and you'll evoke grim, urban, and decidedly sunless images. But go to the Midlands and you'll be surprised by the quiet grandeur of the smoke-stacked center of England. Warwick's castle and Lincoln's breathtaking cathedral are two of Britain's standout attractions, Shrewsbury and Stamford are architectural wonders, and even Birmingham, the region's oft-maligned center, has its saving graces, among them lively nightlife and the Cadbury chocolate empire. Deep in the Severn Valley, gorgeous Ironbridge is a World Heritage Site.

HIGHLIGHTS OF THE MIDLANDS

ADMIRE the world's first cast-iron bridge in **Ironbridge** and explore museums at this monument to Britain's Industrial Revolution (p. 301).

CLIMB your way to **Lincoln Cathedral,** once Europe's tallest building and now the stunning centerpiece of this city-on-a-hill (p. 312).

STROLL past the stone buildings of Stamford on your way to **Burghley House,** one of Britain's most lavish homes (p. 306).

WARWICK   ☎01926

Otherwise modest Warwick (WAR-ick) is justified in its fierce pried in its famous castle. Reputedly the UK's biggest attraction, the turreted fortification has brought the town more than its fair share of tea shops and bewildered tourists. Those who wish to explore the surrounding countryside may find accommodation-rich Warwick a good base camp, but with its limited budget options, most will want to make it a daytrip from Birmingham or Stratford-Upon-Avon.

⛿ 🛈 TRANSPORTATION AND PRACTICAL INFORMATION. The Warwick **train station** is off Coventry Rd. To reach town from the station, take a right and follow Coventry Rd. south to Smith Rd., which turns into Jury St., High St., and Friars St. (Ticket office open M-Sa 5:50am-7:50pm, Su 9:30am-5:40pm.) **Trains** (☎08457 484 950) run to Birmingham (40min., 2 per hr., £5.20), London Marylebone (2hr., 3 per hr., £15-41), and Stratford-Upon-Avon (25min., every 1½hr., £3.40). National Express (☎08705 808 080) **buses** depart from Puckerings Ln. to Birmingham (2½hr., 5 per day, £6.70), London (3hr., 4 per day, £15.40), and Heathrow Airport (4½hr., 4 per day, £19.40). Buy tickets at **Co-op Travel,** 15 Market St. (☎410 709. Open M and W-F 9am-5:30pm, Tu 9:30am-5:30pm, Sa 9am-5pm.) **Local buses** #17 and 18 (3-4 per hr., £2.55-2.85) leave Market Pl. and stop at Coventry (55min.) and Stratford (20min.). **Warwickshire Traveline** (☎414 140) has local bus info. **Taxis** at **B&R Cars** (☎771 771).

The **Tourist Information Centre,** Court House, Jury St., books rooms for £2.50 plus a 10% deposit and stocks a free town map. (☎492 212; www.warwick-uk.co.uk. Open daily 9:30am-4:30pm.) **Tours** leave from the TIC (Su 11am, £3). Other services include: Barclays **bank,** 5 High St. (☎303 000; open M-Tu and Th-F 9:30am-4:30pm, W 10am-4:30pm); a Boots **pharmacy,** 6-8 Cornmarket St. (☎247 461; open M-Th and Sa 8:45am-5:30pm, F 9am-5:30pm); Warwick **Hospital,** Lakin Rd. (☎495 321); the **police,** Priory Rd. (☎410 111); and the **post office,** Westgate House, 45 Brook St. (☎491 061; open M-F 9am-5:30pm, Sa 9am-4pm). **Post Code:** CV34 4BL.

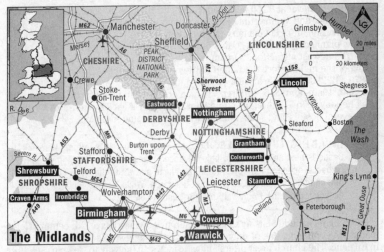

The Midlands

▛▜ ACCOMMODATIONS AND FOOD. A stay near the castle can be pricey, but **Emscote Road** has quality, affordable options. From the train station, turn right on Coventry Rd. and left at the Crown and Castle Inn on Coten End, which becomes Emscote Rd. (Bus X17 runs from Market St. to Emscote frequently.) A nice young couple runs the bright **Avon Guest House ❸**, 7 Emscote Rd. Guests can stay in the elegant, well-decorated main house or the coach house, which caters to backpackers and long-term guests. (☎491 367; www.avonguesthouse.co.uk. Singles £22.50-35; doubles and twins £45-60; family rooms £20 per person. Cash only.) Find **Chesterfields ❸**, 84 Emscote Rd., by looking for the sign with the pajama-clad elephant. Cozy floral rooms make this a great place to doze. (☎774 864. Singles from £22; doubles and twins from £44, ensuite from £46; family rooms from £45. Cash only.) **Park House ❸**, 17 Emscote Rd., has a castle-like facade. The cozy rooms may look like they were decorated by your grandmother, but the included full English breakfast makes up for any aesthetic problem. (☎464 359. Singles £25; double £44. All rooms ensuite. Cash only.)

For **groceries,** try Tesco on Emscote Rd. (☎307 600. Open 24hr. M 8am-Sa 10pm, Su 10am-4pm. AmEx/MC/V.) Find traditional pub fare at the **Tilted Wig ❷**, 11 Market Pl. On warm days, most patrons forego the dark wood interior and dine al fresco on the square. (☎411 534. Entrees £5-12. Live music Th. Open M-Sa 11am-11pm, Su 11am-10:30pm. Food served M-Sa noon-2:45pm and 6-8:45pm, Su noon-3:45pm. MC/V.) Behind the Castle, **Catalan ❷**, 6 Jury St., takes you off the streets of medieval England and into a Spanish villa. Soft music and beautiful, modern decor perfectly complement the delicious tapas. (☎498 390; www.cafecatalan.com. M 2-course rustica menu £10. W £7.50 per person for paella night. Open M and W-F noon-3pm and 6-9pm, Tu noon-3pm, Sa noon-10pm. MC/V.)

◙ SIGHTS. Many medievalists and architects regard 14th-century ◙**Warwick Castle** as England's finest. Today, it exists as a study in marketing by the people who brought you Madame Tussaud's. The dungeons are manned by life-size wax soldiers preparing for battle, and the castle's main chambers contain rooms with Tudor and Victorian trimmings, complete with royal residents posed in amusing vignettes. The grounds host archery demonstrations and carnival games (prices are hardly medieval at £2.50 per play). Highlights include the launching of a massive trebuchet and summertime jousting. Climb to the top of the towers and see the countryside unfold like a fairy-tale kingdom, or stroll through one of the many gardens planned by Lancelot "Capability" Brown, including a peacock-populated park. The newest attraction, "Dream of Battle," is a fully interactive holographic telling of the night before the famed Battle of Barnet. (☎495 421, 24hr. recording ☎0870 442 2000; www.warwick-castle.co.uk. Open daily Apr.-Sept. 10am-6pm; Oct.-Mar. 10am-5pm. £16, children £10, seniors £12, families £45; weekends and bank holidays 50p-£1 more; from mid-Sept. to Apr. £1-2 less. Audio tours £3.) The TIC, several hostels, and some tour groups offer discounted tickets.

 INVADING THE CASTLE. Consistently crowded in summer, Warwick Castle is best enjoyed with a little advanced planning. If you can, arrive early (expect a queue to form by 9:45am) and head straight to the dungeon and torture chamber on the left as you enter the castle. While it may sound masochistic, you'll avoid the 1½hr. wait that most encounter.

Other sights include **St. Mary's Church,** Church St., which has a 12th-century Norman crypt containing one of only two surviving ducking stools (used on witches) in England. The church **tower** offers fantastic views all the way to Coventry. (☎403 940. Open daily summer 10am-6pm; winter 10am-4:30pm. Requested donation £1. Tower £1.50, children 50p, families £3.50.) In 1571, Elizabeth I gave Lord Leycester the **Lord Leycester Hospital,** 60 High St., to house 12 old soldiers who had fought with him in the Netherlands. Today, veterans still live inside. Visitors can view the Brethren's chapel (still used every morning for prayers), the 16th-century great hall, and the small, memorabilia-filled **Regimental Museum.** (☎491 422. Open Easter-Oct. Tu-Su 10am-5pm; Nov.-Easter 10am-4pm. £5, concessions £4.40, children £3.40. Includes entrance to the Master's Garden in the summer.)

▣ DAYTRIP FROM WARWICK

COVENTRY
12 mi. northeast of Warwick. Take X17 Stagecoach bus from Market St. and Elmscote Rd. (1hr., 4 per hr., £3.75) to the train station on Trinity St. in Coventry.

Coventry deserves a visit if only for its magnificent **twin cathedrals.** The juxtaposition of the old and new, destroyed and resurrected cathedrals, is breathtaking. The modern cathedral towers over the stained-glass and stone skeleton of the old. (☎024 7652 1200. Open daily 9am-5pm. Donation £3.50. Camera charge £3.) Behind the cathedrals, **St. Mary's Guildhall,** Bayley Ln., has stood in Coventry for over 650 years. Surviving election riots and the Blitz, the guildhall displays stunning stained glass and the 16th-century Tournai tapestry. The room where Mary, Queen of Scots was imprisoned is on the top floor. (☎024 7683 2381. Open daily in summer 10am-4pm; winter M-Th and Su 10am-4pm. Free.) The underground ruins of the 11th-century **Priory Cathedral** were recently opened for display after a massive archaeological project. Henry VIII destroyed the monastery, but today you can view what's left: a garden and an underground museum complete with wax monks. (☎024 7655 2242. Open M-Sa 10am-5pm, Su noon-4pm. Entrance to gardens free, Priory tour £1. Tours daily at 12:30pm.)

The tourist season commences the first weekend of June during the **Lady Godiva Festival,** which honors Countess Godgifu (but who would buy chocolates with that name?) of Coventry. Lady Godiva's renowned nude ride through the town on horseback is celebrated in an annual parade. A statue of the lady lies near the cathedrals. For less scandalous modes of travel, try the **Coventry Transport Museum,** Hales St. The museum displays the largest collection of British cars in the world. (☎024 7683 4270. Open daily 10am-5pm; last admission 4:30pm. Free.) The **Tourist Information Centre** is on 4 Priory Row. (☎024 7622 7264. Open M-F 9:30am-5pm, Sa 10am-4:30pm, Su 10am-12:30pm and 1:30-4:30pm.)

BIRMINGHAM ☎0121

Birmingham, second in Britain only to London in population, has a long-standing reputation as a grim, industrial metropolis. To counter this bleak stereotype, the city has revitalized itself with a sure-fire visitor magnet: shopping—and lots of it. The massive Bullring, Europe's largest retail establishment, is the foundation of Birmingham's material-world makeover. The new construction creates a disconnected feeling throughout the city: gothic churches stand next to ultra-modern buildings, and beautiful gardens border night clubs. Awkward design aside, the city is the hub of Midlands nightlife, and offers a thriving arts scene. It is steadfastly defended by fun-loving "Brummies" as one of the UK's most lively cities.

▊ TRANSPORTATION

Birmingham is situated along train and bus lines running between London, central Wales, southwest England, and points north.

Flights: Birmingham International Airport (☎08707 335 511). Free transfer to the Birmingham International railway station for connections to New St. Station and London.

Trains: New Street Station serves trains (☎08457 484 950) to: **Liverpool Lime Street** (1½hr., every hr., £19.80); **London Euston** (1½hr., every 30min., £27.40); **Manchester Piccadilly** (2hr., 2 per hr., £19); **Oxford** (1¼hr., at least 1 per hr., £19); **Sheffield** (1¼hr., 1 per hr., £19). Others pull out of **Moor Street, Jewellery Quarter,** and **Snow Hill** stations. Follow signs to get from New St. to Moor St. Station (10min. walk). The Birmingham Stationlink bus provides connections between train stations.

Buses: Digbeth Station, High St., Digbeth. National Express (☎08705 808 080; office open M-Sa 7:15am-7pm, Su 8:15am-7pm) to: **Cardiff** (1½hr., 4 per day, £19.40); **Liverpool** (1hr., 5 per day, £13); **London Heathrow** (2½hr., 1 per hr., £14); **Manchester** (2½hr., 1 per 2hr., £10.50); **Oxford** (2¼hr., 5 per day., £10).

Public Transportation: Information at **Centro** (☎200 2700 or 200 2787; www.centro.org.uk), in New St. Station. Stocks transit maps and bus schedules. Call ahead. Bus and train daypass £5; bus £2.80, children £1.70. Open M-Tu and F 8:30am-5:30pm, W-Th and Sa 9am-5pm.

Taxis: Blue Arrow (☎0121 622 1000), **A2B** (☎733 3000), **TOA** (☎427 8888), **Go 2 Cars** (☎705 2222), **M&M** (☎242 1222), **Ambassador Cars** (☎444 1000).

▊ PRACTICAL INFORMATION

Tourist Information Centre: The Rotunda, 150 New St. (☎202 5099 or 202 5116; www.beinbirmingham.com). Books rooms for a 10% deposit and sells theater and National Express tickets. Open M and W-Sa 9:30am-5:30pm, Tu 10am-5:30pm, Su 10:30am-4:30pm. Also a small information center at the junction with New and Corporation St. Open M-Sa 9am-5pm, Su 10am-4pm.

Financial Services: American Express, Bank House, 8 Cherry St. (☎644 5533). Open M-Tu and Th-F 8:30am-5:30pm, W 9:30am-5:30pm, Sa 9am-5pm. **Thomas Cook,** 99 New St. (☎255 2600). Open M-W and F-Sa 9am-5:30pm, Th 10am-5:30pm.

Police: Steelhouse Ln. (☎0845 113 5000).

Birmingham

🏠 ACCOMMODATIONS
Bailey Hotel, **14**
Birmingham Central
  Backpackers, **9**
Merry Maid, **13**
Nitenite, **6**

🍴 FOOD
Cafe Villaggio, **8**
Canalside Cafe, **5**

Mr. Egg, **12**
Thai Edge, **4**
Warehouse Cafe, **3**

⭐ NIGHTLIFE
Barfly, **11**
Nightingale, **15**
Sunflower Lounge, **10**
Rococo Lounge, **7**
The Yard Bird, **1**

Pharmacy: Boots, The Bullring (☎632 6418), across from New St. station. Open M-F 8am-8pm, Sa 9am-8pm, Su 11am-5pm.

Internet Access: Central Library, Chamberlain Sq. (☎303 4511), has free access on its 100 computers, but there's usually a wait. Call ahead to book a 1hr. slot. Open M-F 9am-8pm, Sa 9am-5pm. **Ready to Surf,** Corporation St. (☎236 2523). £1 per hr. Open M-Sa 9am-6pm, Su 11-5pm.

Post Office: Big Top, 19 Union Passage (☎643 7051). **Bureau de change.** Open M-Sa 9am-1pm. **Post Code:** B2 4TU.

🏠 ACCOMMODATIONS

The TIC holds listings and flyers for budget accommodations in the city. **Hagley Road** houses several B&B budget options—the farther away from the city center you travel, the lower the price (and the standard). Take bus #9, 109, 126, or 139 from Colomore Row to Hagley Rd.

Birmingham Central Backpackers, 58 Coventry St. (☎643 0033; www.birminghamcentralbackpackers.com). Recently renovated pub now sporting cotton candy colored walls, tidy ensuite rooms, and huge TV in common area. Full bar also stocks plenty of snacks and simple items for dinner. Laundry and unlimited Internet available for a small donation to Oxfam. Light breakfast included. Beds from £16. AmEx/MC/V. ❷

The Merry Maid, 263 Moseley Rd. (☎440 6126). Located above a pub of the same name, the Merry Maid offers standard dorm-style rooms and a staff full of city knowledge. Complimentary tea and coffee served at breakfast. Beds from £16. MC/V. ❷

Bailey Hotel, 21 Sandon Rd. (☎434 5700; www.baileyhotel.org). Located in the B&B-rich Hagley Rd. area, Bailey's rooms are clean, bright, and recently renovated. Buses #120 and 126 stop outside at the Sanderson stop, and bus #9 takes you to the heart of Broad St. nightlife. Standard single £22, ensuite £26; double £32/36. MC/V. ❸

Nitenite, 18 Holliday St. (☎0845 890 9099; www.nitenite.com). A 5min. walk from New St. Station. Like something from another planet—seriously. 104 "city boutique" (read: tiny, spaceship-like) rooms with comfy double bed and ensuite shower. In place of windows, a flat-screen TV loops live video of the city. From £40. MC/V. ❹

 FOOD

Birmingham is most proud of **balti,** a Kashmiri-Pakistani cuisine invented by immigrants and cooked in a special pan. Brochures at the TIC map outline the city's *balti* restaurants; the best are southeast of the city center in the "Balti Triangle." **Groceries** can be purchased from Sainsbury's, Martineau Pl., 17 Union St. (☎236 6496. Open M-Sa 7am-8pm, Su 11am-5pm.) An indoor **market** on Edgbaston St. offers fresh produce. (☎622 5449. Open M-Sa 9am-5:30pm.)

Canalside Cafe, 35 Worcester Bar (☎441 9862). Baguettes and hearty specials like homemade chili served in an 18th-century canalside house. Outdoor seating along the canal offers good people-watching. Most sandwiches £3-5. Open daily 9am-5pm with occasional evening openings. Cash only. ❶

Mr. Egg, 22 Hurst St. (☎622 4344), corner of Ladywell. Favorite student spot for late-night (or early-morning) grub. Cramped, campy interior features a giant inflatable egg on the ceiling. Food is quick, cheap, and filling. Egg and chips £1.50; chicken burger £2.20. Open M-Sa 7am-5am, Su 8am-5pm. Cash only. ❶

Thai Edge, 7 Oozells Sq. (☎643 3993; www.thaiedge.com), off Broad St., next to Ikon Gallery. Bamboo poles and stark white walls give this popular Thai restaurant a seriously slick look. Enjoy the £8 lunch special on the patio. Entrees £8-15. Open M-Th noon-2:30pm and 5:30-11:30pm, F-Sa noon-2:30pm and 5:30pm-midnight, Su noon-3pm and 5:30-11pm. AmEx/MC/V. ❸

Warehouse Cafe, 54-57 Allison St. (☎633 0261; www.thewarehousecafe.com), off Digbeth. Look for the brick building with the mural on the side. Chill vegetarian restaurant with a homey feel. A creative organic menu with daily specials made to order. Delicious pastries £2-3. Entrees £7-8. Open M-Sa noon-10pm, Su 11am-6pm Cash only. ❷

Cafe Villaggio, 245 Broad St. (☎643 4224). Budget sibling to adjacent Del Villaggio. Italian cafe serving hearty portions of pizza and pasta. Music and photos pay homage to Italy and famous Italians. Heavenly gelati. Open daily noon-10pm. AmEx/MC/V. ❷

 SIGHTS

Birmingham's most significant attraction may be its regenerated shopping districts. **The Mailbox,** Wharfside St., is home to upscale designers like Emporio Armani, and has three floors of terraced cafe-bars overlooking the city's canals. Look for the giant red building, which used to be a mail-sorting factory. (☎632 1123; www.mailboxlife.com. Open M-W 10am-6pm, Th-Sa 10am-7pm, Su noon-6pm. Restaurants operate on different hours.) The sprawling **Bullring,** The Bullring, recognizable by the wavy, blue-scaled Selfridges department store, has over 140 retail shops plus restaurants and cafes. (☎632 1500; www.bullring.co.uk. Open M-F 9:30am-8pm, Sa 9am-8pm, Su 11am-5pm.) **Brindleyplace,** 2 Brunswick St., along the

MIDLANDS

canals, has more restaurants than shops, but it's still worth a look. (☎ 643 6866; www.brindleyplace.com.) **The Custard Factory,** Digbeth and Heath Mill Ln., houses small vintage shops and cafes. (☎ 224 7777. Most open M-Sa 10am-5pm, Su noon-4pm.)

Despite the size of the city, the art collections can be hit or miss. **Ikon Gallery,** 1 Oozells Sq., in Brindleyplace, shows cutting-edge multimedia art and Turner Prize-winning exhibitions. The beautiful Neo-gothic 1877 building hides a post-postmodern white cube interior. (☎ 248 0708; www.ikon-gallery.co.uk. Open Tu-Su 11am-6pm. Free.) The massive **Birmingham Museum and Art Gallery,** Chamberlain Sq. off Colmore Row, holds costumes, pre-Raphaelite paintings, William Blake's illustrations of Dante's "Inferno," and a new gallery for modern art. Many of the collections, like Blake's, are in storage, and you'll need to call ahead to see them. (☎ 303 2834; www.bmag.org.uk. Open M-Th and Sa 10am-5pm, F 10:30am-5pm, Su 12:30-5pm. Free.) The **Barber Institute of Fine Arts,** in the University of Birmingham on Edgbaston Park Rd., displays works by Degas, Gauguin, Matisse, Renoir, and Rubens. (Bus #61, 62, or 63 from the city center. ☎ 414 7333. Open M-Sa 10am-5pm, Su noon-5pm. Free.) Hop onto **The Wheel of Birmingham,** Centenary Sq., to see Birmingham's latest architecture from high above Symphony Hall, the International Convention Center, and the Birmingham Repertory Theatre. (☎ 236 2952. Open M-Th and Su 11am-9pm, F-Sa 11am-11pm. £6, children £4.) **St. Martin's in the Bullring,** the site of Birmingham's first parish church, has assumed its role as a place of peace in a sea of commercialism. The church is the city's unofficial icon and is worth a visit. (☎ 643 5428. Open Tu-Su noon-6pm.)

The **National Sea Life Centre,** The Water's Edge, Brindleyplace, is home to over 3000 creatures and has the world's first fully transparent 360° underwater tunnel. The Atlantis Hall of Mirrors is a blast to get lost in. Watch for (and laugh at) hordes of wandering school children walking into the glass. (☎ 643 6777. Open daily 10am-5pm. £13, students £8.50, seniors £9, children £7.) **Thinktank at Millennium Point,** Curzon St., Digbeth, offers an interactive science experience geared primarily toward the 12-and-under set. An IMAX theater is in the same complex. (☎ 202 2222. Open daily 10am-5pm. £7, concessions and children £5, families £20. Special exhibits add £3-4.) Signs point northwest to over 100 shops lining the **Jewellery Quarter,** which hammers out almost all the jewelry in Britain. **Birmingham City Walks** offers private and public tours along the canals and through The Bullring and the city center to view the Victorian and modern architecture. (☎ 427 2555 or through the TIC; www.birmingham-tours.co.uk. Public tours £3-6, private tours vary.)

Twelve minutes south of town by rail or bus lies ◨**Cadbury World,** a cavity-inducing celebration of the chocolate empire. Sniff your way through the story of chocolate's birth in the Mayan rainforests, watch the factory at work, indulge in free samples, and take a trippy train ride through a land of animatronic cacao beans. Be prepared to fight through crowds of sugar-high schoolchildren. Get there by train from New St. to Bournville (every 10min.) or by bus #84 from the city center. (☎ 451 4159; www.cadburyworld.co.uk. Open Mar.-Oct. daily 10am-3pm; Nov.-Feb. Tu-Th and Sa-Su 10am-3pm. Pre-booking highly recommended. Pre-booking ☎ 0845 450 3599. £12.50, concessions £10, children £9.50. Oompa-Loompas free.)

▣♫ NIGHTLIFE AND ENTERTAINMENT

Birmingham's student population fuels its excellent nightlife venues. Streets beyond the central district can be unsafe, and weekend nights are rowdy on Broad St. Take care at night, stay in well-lit areas, and be aware of your surroundings.

BARS, PUBS, AND CLUBS

Broad Street teems with trendy cafe-bars and clubs. A thriving gay-friendly scene centers on **Lower Essex** and **Hurst Streets** southwest of The Bullring. Pick up the bimonthly *What's On* for the latest hotspots. Clubbers on a budget should grab a guide to public transportation's Night Network from the Centro office in New St. Station; **night buses** generally run every hour until 3:30am on Friday and Saturday.

The Yardbird, Paradise Pl. (☎212 2524). This new, super-chill jazz club might be the coolest place in Birmingham. No dress code, no cover, no pretense. Arrive early for a spot on the patio. F DJs spin drum and bass, prompting street dancers to break it down in the middle of the bar. Sa live music. Open M-W and Su 11am-midnight, Th-Sa 11am-2am.

Sunflower Lounge, 76 Smallbrook Queensway (☎632 6756). Nice alternative to the Broad St. scene. Indie bar and live music venue; check postings at the door for dates. Dress up for mod night on M. Open M-W 4pm-1am, Th-Sa 4pm-2am.

Rococo Lounge, 260 Broad St. (☎207 0283). Popular bar at the heart of Brum nightlife. Classic example of student clubbing. Near similar venues if you get bored with or kicked out of another one. Outdoor patio and retro-modern furnishings. Open M-W and Su 9am-1am, Th-Sa 9am-2am.

Barfly, 78 Digbeth High St., (☎633 8311; www.barflyclub.com). Hidden behind an unassuming pub, Barfly is one of the most lively spots in Birmingham. Live music nightly. F features indie and alternative bands until 4am, Tu is 90s night, with your favorite middle school hits until 3:30am. Other nights vary depending on the show.

Nightingale, Essex House, Kent St. (☎622 1718; www.nightingaleclub.co.uk). 2 frenzied dance floors, 5 bars, jazz lounge, and billiard room attract a mostly gay and lesbian crowd from all over. Cover (around £3) varies. Dress smart casual. Open Tu-Th 9pm-2am, F 7pm-4am, Sa 7pm-6am, Su 7pm-2am.

MUSIC AND THEATER

Birmingham Academy, (officially **Carling Academy Birmingham**), 52-54 Dale End (☎262 3000; www.birmingham-academy.co.uk). Birmingham offshoot of monolithic Brixton music venue. Most popular live venue in Birmingham. Previous performers include Dave Matthews and the Goo Goo Dolls. Hours and ticket prices vary; events nearly every night in summer. Box office open M-F 11am-5pm, Sa 11am-3:30pm.

Birmingham International Jazz Festival, (☎454 7020; www.birminghamjazzfestival.com). Brings over 200 jazz bands, singers, and instrumentalists to town during the first 2 weeks of July. Most events are free; check the website or TIC for specific listings.

City of Birmingham Symphony Orchestra, CBSO Centre, Berkley St. (☎616 6500; www.cbso.co.uk). Plays in the glass Symphony Hall, opened by the Queen in 1991. Box office open M-Sa 10am-8pm, 10am-6pm if no performance. Su hours depend on concert times. Tickets £5-80, concessions and group discounts available, student standby tickets 1hr. before concerts £3-5.

Birmingham Hippodrome, Hurst St. (☎0870 730 1234; www.birminghamhippodrome.com). Once featuring vaudeville artists, the theater now hosts West End musicals and ballet. Box office open M-Sa 10am-8pm. Tickets £8.50-75, concessions available.

Birmingham Repertory Theatre, Centenary Sq. (☎236 4455), on Broad St. A less grandiose but still celebrated theater hosting dramas, comedies, and new plays. Box office open M-Sa 10am-8pm on performance days, 10am-6pm on non-performance days. Tickets £10-21, discount standby tickets for students and seniors.

IRONBRIDGE ☎01952

Pretty towns shouldn't have ugly names. Luckily, Ironbridge rises above its moniker and charms visitors with its local character and rugged beauty. The center of the city is (surprise!) a grand 18th-century iron bridge arching 55 ft. above the Severn. The self-proclaimed birthplace of the Industrial Revolution, Ironbridge combines rough industrial facades with quaint riverside slopes.

☐ TRANSPORTATION. The nearest **train station** is at Telford, 20min. from Shrewsbury on the Birmingham-Shrewsbury-Chester line (M-Sa 1-4 per hr., Su every hr.). The only way to reach Ironbridge directly is by **bus.** Call ahead, as the patchy timetables available at TICs don't always agree with posted schedules. For bus information, call the TIC, Telford Travelink (☎ 200 005), or use Traveline (☎ 0870 608 2608; www.traveline.org.uk). Arriva Midlands North (☎ 08457 056 005) #96 goes to Telford (15min., M-Sa 6 per day) and Shrewsbury (40min., M-Sa 6 per day). Most buses to and from Ironbridge do not run past 5 or 6pm, and don't run at all on Sunday. Arriva (☎ 08456 015 395) runs #99 on the Wellington-Bridgnorth route, stopping at Ironbridge and sometimes Coalbrookdale from Telford (25min., M-Sa 10 per day). Arriva #76 and #77 (20min., 6 per day) provide service between Coalbrookdale and Coalport (both home to YHA hostels), stopping at the Iron-bridge Museum of the Gorge en route. On weekends and bank holidays, two Gorge Connect services (WH1 and WH2, both 1-2 per hr.) shuttle between the Ironbridge museums at 50p per ride, continuing on to Telford before noon and after 3pm. **Day-Rover** (£2.50, children £1.50) tickets are good for all-day travel.

◪ ⁊ ORIENTATION AND PRACTICAL INFORMATION. Ironbridge is the name of both the river gorge and the village at the gorge's center. The 10 **Ironbridge Gorge Museums** huddle on the banks of the Severn Valley in an area of 6 sq. mi. Some are difficult to reach without a car—buses run infrequently and stop only at selected points, and bike rental is hard to find. Everything is walkable (if lengthy), and scenic paths connect most of the sites. The **Tourist Information Centre,** on the ground floor of the Tollhouse across the Iron Bridge, provides the free *Ironbridge Gorge Visitor Guide* and books rooms for a 10% deposit. (☎ 884 391; www.iron-bridge.org.uk. Open M-F 9am-5pm, Sa-Su 10am-5pm.) The only **ATM** in town is in Walker's Newsstand on Tontine Hill. (£1.85 surcharge. Open daily 7:30am-5:30pm.) Lloyd's **pharmacy** is located on The Square (open M-F 9am-6pm, Sa 9am-1pm) near the **post office.** (☎ 433 201. Open M-Tu and Th-F 9am-1pm and 2-5:30pm, W 9am-1pm, Sa 9am-12:30pm.) **Post Code:** TF8 7AQ.

⁊ ☐ ACCOMMODATIONS AND FOOD. The two buildings of the **YHA Ironbridge Gorge** grace the valley's opposite ends, 3 mi. apart. One resides in a renovated china factory in **Coalport ❷,** next to the Coalport China Museum. (☎ 588 755. Break-fast £4. Laundry. Reception closes 11pm. Open Easter-Oct. daily; Nov.-Easter F-Sa. Dorms £16, under 18 £11; ensuite doubles £36. MC/V.) The more basic hostel in **Coalbrookdale ❷** inhabits a remodeled schoolhouse on a hill, 1 mi. from the bridge and TIC. Walk past the Museum of the Gorge and turn right at the roundabout in Coalbrookdale, heading up the road to the museums. (☎ 0870 770 5882. Game room, kitchen, laundry. Reception closes 10:30pm. Lockout 10am-5pm. Open Eas-ter-Oct. daily; in winter Sa-Su. Dorms £16, under 18 £11. MC/V.) Both hostels are rarely available in July and August since they host children's camps. Arriva bus #76 reaches both; Coalbrookdale is also a stop on #77. From Shrewsbury or Tel-ford, #96 passes within ½ mi. of each; the Madeley stop is closer than Ironbridge to Coalport. Built in the center of Ironbridge village in 1784, **The Tontine Hotel ❸,** The Square, was constructed by the same men responsible for the bridge and is possi-bly the nicest hotel ever to be named after an investment plan. Rooms have TV, telephone, and view of the bridge. (☎ 432 127; www.tontine-hotel.com. Singles £25, ensuite £40; doubles £40/56. MC/V.) Area **B&Bs** charge from £30 per person; expect to pay at least £35 for a single. The nearest campsite to Ironbridge is the **Severn Gorge Caravan Park ❶,** Bridgnorth Rd., in Tweedale, roughly 3 mi. from Ironbridge and 1 mi. north of Blists Hill. (☎ 684 789. 2-person tent sites £10-12. Electricity £4. Showers free. MC/V.)

Try the warm sausage rolls ($1.10) or the world-famous pork pies at **Eley's ❶**, on Tontine Hill. They've been around for so long that the shop is recreated in the Victorian village of Blists Hill. (☎ 432 030; www.eleys-ironbridge.co.uk. Open daily 8am-5:30pm. Cash only.) Walk 5-10min. uphill on Madeley Rd. for the famed steak and kidney pie ($6.50) at the **Horse and Jockey ❶**, 15 Jockey Bank. (☎ 433 798. Open daily noon-2pm and 6:30-9:30pm. MC/V.)

🏛 **MUSEUMS.** The Ironbridge Gorge Museums are the area's pride and joy, and with good reason: you'd be hard pressed to find a better portrayal of Britain's unique industrial heritage. You'll need at least two days to cover them well. If visiting all 10 (or even a significant fraction), buy an **Ironbridge Passport** from any of them. It allows you unlimited visits to all museums for a year. ($14, seniors $12.50, students and children $9.50, families $46.) All of the museums are open daily 10am-5pm, except the Broseley Pipeworks (open daily 1-5pm) and Blists Hill (open daily 10am-4pm). The Pipeworks and the Tar Tunnel are closed in winter. The famous **Iron Bridge** was built in 1779 by Abraham Darby III, who went into debt to create a monument to the new iron industry. The result of his efforts spans the River Severn with eye-catching black trusses. A small sign posted on the side of the **Tollhouse** at its southern end lists the fares for every carriage, mule, or child that crosses—even royalty isn't exempt. The TIC occupies the ground floor while the second level houses an exhibit about the bridge's history. It includes a brief biography of one of its more eccentric funders, John "Iron Mad" Wilkinson, who minted iron coins stamped with his own image. (☎ 884 391. Open Easter-Oct. M-F 9am-5pm, Sa-Su 10am-5pm. Free.) A 10min. walk from Ironbridge, the **Museum of the Gorge** provides an introduction to the area's history and is a good place to begin a day's exploration. (☎ 884 391. $2.75, children and students $1.75.)

In Coalbrookdale to the northwest, the 🗹**Coalbrookdale Museum of Iron** traces the history of the Darby family iron saga and gives a helpful crash course on the Industrial Revolution. The massive furnace where Abraham Darby first smelted iron with coke (a type of coal, not cola) is also on-site. (☎ 435 960. $6.50, concessions $4.50.) Just up the hill, the **Darby Houses** model the quarters of the multiple generations of ironmasters who lived there. (☎ 432 551. Free with admission to Museum of Iron.) **Enginuity,** across the courtyard from the Museum of Iron, houses child-friendly, hands-on displays. (☎ 435 905. $5.75, concessions $4.25.)

In Coalport to the west, the **Coalport China Museum** and the recently re-opened **Jackfield Tile Museum** display the products of their industries. Both also offer demonstrations and workshops. At the China Museum, climb inside the huge kilns that were used to create the factory's intricate ware. (Both museums ☎ 580 650. $5.25, seniors $4.80, students and children $3.75.) Don a hard hat in the eerie **Tar Tunnel,** where workers first discovered smudgy natural bitumen dripping from the walls and at one time collected 1000 gallons per week. (☎ 580 827. Adults $1.75, seniors $1.50, students and children $1.25.) Across the river from the village are the **Broseley Pipeworks.** Here, clay pipe-making workrooms have been preserved in a state of decrepit authenticity. This is the farthest museum (about 30min. by foot), but worth visiting nonetheless. (☎ 884 391. Open daily June-Sept. 1-5pm. $3.75, students and children $2.25.) At the **Blists Hill Victorian Town,** a ½ mi. uphill from Coalport, over 40 recreated buildings deliver kitschy antiquity through local craft. (☎ 582 050. $9.50, seniors $8.50, students $6.50.)

SHREWSBURY ☎ 01743

Bright hatters' windows, hole-in-the-wall boutiques, and a crooked network of ancient roads make Shrewsbury suit those with a weakness for stereotypically English streetscapes. Roger de Montegomery, second-in-command to William the

Conqueror, claimed the area during the 11th century. Shrewsbury's favorite son, however, is Charles Darwin—he and his (r)evolutionary ideas are memorialized all over town in the names of streets and shopping centers.

▐ TRANSPORTATION. The **train station** is at the end of Castle St. (ticket office open M-Sa 5:30am-10pm). **Trains** (☎ 08457 484 950) run to: **Aberystwyth** (1¾hr.; M-Sa 7 per day, Su 5 per day; £16.60); **London** (3hr., 1-2 per hr., £50.70); **Swansea** (3½-4hr.; M-Sa 1-2 per hr., Su about 1 per hr.; £18); **Wolverhampton** (40min., 2-3 per hr., £7-8); and most of North Wales via **Wrexham General** and **Chester** (1hr.; M-Sa every hr., Su 6 per day; £7). The **bus station** is on Raven Meadows, which runs parallel to Pride Hill. (☎ 231 010. Ticket office open M-F 8:30am-5:30pm, Sa 8:30am-4pm.) National Express (☎ 08705 808 080) goes to **Birmingham** (1½hr., 2 per day, £5.20), **Llangollen** (1hr., 1 per day, £4), and **London** (4½hr., 2 per day, £17). Arriva Midlands #96 runs to **Telford** via **Ironbridge** (1hr., M-Sa 6 per day). **Taxis** queue in front of the train station, or call Access Taxis. (☎ 360 606. 24hr.)

▐ ORIENTATION. The **River Severn,** Britain's longest river, circles Shrewsbury's town center in a horseshoe shape, with the curve dipping southward. The town's central axis runs from the train station in the northeast to Quarry Park in the southwest. Beginning as **Castle Gates,** the main road becomes **Castle Street,** then pedestrian-only **Pride Hill,** then **Shoplatch, Mardol Head,** and **St. John's Hill. St. Mary's Street** and **High Street** branch off from either end of Pride Hill at the center of town, converging to become **Wyle Cop.** This road turns into the **English Bridge,** crosses the river, and leads to the Abbey. The accessible A5 nearly circles the city at a distance of 10 mi.

▐ PRACTICAL INFORMATION. The **Tourist Information Centre,** Music Hall, The Square, across from the Market Building, books accommodations for £1.50 (£2 over the phone) plus a 10% deposit. (☎ 281 200; www.shropshiretourism.info. Open May-Sept. M-Sa 9:30am-5:30pm, Su 10am-4pm; Oct.-Apr. M-Sa 10am-5pm.) Historic 1½hr. **walking tours** from the TIC pass through Shrewsbury's medieval "shutts" (closeable alleys). Special Wednesday summer tours feature tea with the mayor at no extra cost. (☎ 281 200. May-Sept. M-Sa 2:30pm, Su 11am; Oct. M-Sa 2:30pm; Nov.-Apr. Sa 2:30pm. £3.50, children £2.) Other services include: Barclays **bank,** 44-46 Castle St., off St. Mary's St. (open M-F 9am-5pm and Sa 9:30pm-3:30pm); a **launderette,** Stidger's Wishy Washy, 55 Monkmoor Rd., off Abbey Foregate (☎ 355 151; wash £3, dry £2, service £9 per load; open M-F 9am-5pm, Sa 10am-4pm, and Su 10am-2pm; last wash 1hr. before close); **police,** Clive Rd. in Monkmoor (☎ 08457 444 888); Royal Shrewsbury **hospital,** Mytton Oak Rd. (☎ 261 000); free **Internet** access and Wi-Fi at the **reference library,** 1A Castle Gates, just downhill from the main library (☎ 255 380; open M, W, F 9:30am-5pm; Tu and Th 9:30am-8pm, Sa 9am-5pm, Su 1-4pm; photo ID required); Boots **pharmacy,** 9-11 Pride Hill (☎ 351 111; open M-Sa 9am-5:30pm and Su 10:30am-4:30pm); and a **post office,** in WHSmith, where Castle St. turns into Pride Hill, with a **bureau de change** (☎ 08457 740 740; open M-Sa 9am-5:30pm). **Post Code:** SY1 1DE.

▐ ACCOMMODATIONS AND FOOD. Singles are hard to find, so reserve several weeks ahead in summer. Several **B&Bs** (£20-30) lie between **Abbey Foregate** and **Monkmoor Road.** A charming brick townhouse, **Allandale ❸** is behind the abbey on Abbey Foregate and has hanging flower baskets on its porch. (☎ 240 173. £25 per person; £20 without breakfast, all rooms ensuite. Cash only.) **Glyndene ❷,** nearby on Abbey Forgate, has an elaborate bell-pull and tasteful rooms with TVs. From the bridge, follow the road left of the abbey. One single room, none ensuite. (☎ 352 488; www.glyndene.co.uk. £18 per person. Cash only.) The quirky **Trevellion**

POTATO, POTAHTO. Shrewsbury has 2 pronunciations, even among locals. "SHROWS-bree" is more posh and is usually spoken by people living inside the river's horseshoe. "SHREWS-bree" is more working-class, used primarily by residents on the outskirts of town. Posh or not? The choice is yours.

House ❸, 1 Bradford St., off Monkmoor Rd. (look for signs) features ensuite rooms with wrought-iron beds and packed with knick-knacks. The lively host fosters a warm atmosphere inside and maintains a tidy garden out back. (☎ 249 582. Singles £30; doubles £50. Cash only.)

Shrewsbury hosts an indoor "Market under the Clock" at the corner of Shoplatch and Bellstone. (☎ 351 067. Open Tu-Sa, roughly 7:30am-4pm.) Somerfield **market** is at the Riverside Mall, on Raven Meadows near the bus station. (Open M-W and Sa 8am-6pm, Th-F 8am-7pm, Su 10:30am-4:30pm.) Tucked in St. Alkmund's Sq., by Butcher Row, the **⊠Bear Steps Coffee House ❶** has patio seating next to a shaded park and warns its taller guests to watch their heads when dining indoors, as timbers are lower than 6 ft. The delicious quiche with bread and butter goes for £5. (☎ 244 355. Open daily 10am-4pm, M-Sa 10am-4pm in winter. Cash only.) A stylish grill with Tudor architecture and decidedly modern accents, **The Peach Tree ❷,** 18-21 Abbey Foregate, has excellent fare at good prices and a colossal drinks list. Try one of the huge starter platters or lavish sandwich offerings (£4-6). Finish with the Kaffir lime and dark chocolate tart (£5). (☎ 355 055; www.thepeachtree.co.uk. Open daily 9am-late. Lunch and sandwiches served M-Th noon-3pm, F-Sa noon-6pm. AmEx/MC/V.) **The Good Life Wholefood Restaurant ❶,** Barracks Passage, off Wyle Cop, serves cheap vegetarian cuisine. The nut loaves (£2.70) are wonderful. Takeaway only. (☎ 350 455. Open Tu-F 9:30am-3pm and Sa 9am-4pm.)

◪ SIGHTS. Aside from its annual flower show, Shrewsbury's biggest attraction is its architecture. Tudoresque houses dot the shopping district and rally in full force at the **Bear Steps,** which start in the alley on High St. across from The Square and emerge in a lovely little park. **Churches,** many on Saxon foundations, cluster in the town center. Don't miss the circular design of St. Chad's near the park. At the end of Castle St., the riverside acres of **Quarry Park** are filled with expansive grassy lawns along the oft-flooded Severn. At the center of the park, **Dingle Garden** explodes with bright flowers. A **statue of Darwin** presides opposite the castle, the colossal **Lord Hill Column** at the end of Abbey Foregate is the tallest Doric column in Europe, and a stone likeness of MP **Robert Clive of India** stands stoically outside Market Sq.

Vivid red sandstone makes **Shrewsbury Castle,** near the train station, stand out. Built out of wood in AD 1083 and more recently repaired after an IRA bombing, the castle now consists of the Great Hall, which holds the **Shropshire Regimental Museum** and displays arms from as early as the 18th century. The Shropshire regiment guarded Napoleon on the island of St. Helena and saw massive losses in WWI's Battle of the Somme. The exhibit features a roll of actual footage from the battle. For great views, climb to nearby **Laura's Tower,** a summer garden house built in the 1780s. (☎ 358 516; www.shrewsburymuseums.gov.uk. Museum and tower open from mid-Feb. to May and from mid-Sept. to Dec. Tu-Sa 10am-4pm; from June to mid-Sept. M-Sa 10am-5pm, Su 10am-4pm. Grounds open Easter-Sept. daily 9am-5pm; Oct.-Easter M-Sa 9am-5pm. Museum £2.50, seniors £1.30, students and children free. Grounds and Tower free.) The **Shrewsbury Museum and Art Gallery** displays items from Shrewsbury's extensive history. It re-opens in 2008 in the TIC building in Music Hall; call the TIC for more information.

Beyond the English Bridge stands **Shrewsbury Abbey,** a Benedictine abbey founded in 1083, dissolved by Henry VIII in 1540, and later reformulated as part of the Church of England. The abbey holds the remains of a shrine to St. Winefride, a 7th-century princess who was beheaded and then miraculously re-capitated to become an abbess and patron of North Wales and Shrewsbury. A memorial to local WWI poet Wilfred Owen stands in the garden. (☎232 723. Open Easter-Oct. M-Sa 10am-4:45pm, Su between services, about 11am-2:30pm; Nov.-Easter M-Sa 10:30am-3pm. Free.) Shrewsbury hosts an annual **Art Festival** (☎07817 167 772) during July, but the mid-August **Flower Show** sees Shrewsbury's population blossom to 100,000 over two days for the world's longest-running horticultural show. (☎234 050; www.shrewsburyflowershow.org.uk. £14.)

■ DAYTRIP FROM SHREWSBURY

CRAVEN ARMS

Craven Arms is located 20 mi. south of Shrewsbury on the A49. Easiest access is by bus #435 from Shrewsbury (1hr., 7 per day).

Twenty miles south of Shrewsbury in Craven Arms, the ■**Land of Lost Content,** at the corner of Dale and Market St., offers a fascinating collection of nostalgic Britpop cultural relics and an entertaining walk down memory lane. Named after A.E. Housman's "A Shropshire Lad," the museum holds over 30 displays, including a clip-on "Roy Rogers" tie, lace-trimmed diapers, cod liver oil, and favorite childhood memorabilia. (☎01588 676 176; www.lolc.org.uk. Open Feb.-Nov. daily 11am-5pm; Dec.-Jan. by appointment. Last admission 4:15pm. £5, children £2.50.) A few blocks away at the **Secret Hills Shropshire Discovery Centre,** on the corner of School Rd. and the A49, visitors explore exhibits on local history, including a replica of the local mammoth skeleton. (☎01588 676 000; www.shropshire.gov.uk/discover.nsf. Open daily Apr.-Oct. 10am-5:30pm; Nov.-Mar. 10am-4:30pm. Last admission 1hr. before close. £4.50, concessions £4, children £3.)

STAMFORD ☎01780

Limestone architecture holds centuries of history in the city of Stamford, a longtime playground for royalty en route from London to Scotland. Although William the Conqueror's castle here has been destroyed and is now the site of a bus station, the city continues to lure visitors with its high spires and crooked alleyways.

■ **TRANSPORTATION AND PRACTICAL INFORMATION.** Stamford sits at the edge of Lincolnshire, with Cambridgeshire to the south. **Trains** (☎08457 484 950) leave **Stamford Station,** south of town, to: Cambridge (1hr., every hr., £15); Lincoln (2hr., 2 per hr., £20.70); Nottingham (1½hr., every hr., £15.60); London King's Cross (1hr., every hr., £28.50). **Buses** are much less frequent but pass through Sheepmarket, off All Saints' St. National Express (☎08705 808 080) makes the trip to London (3hr., 1 per day, £12.80) and Nottingham (1½hr, one bus at 9:30am, £15). To reach the **Tourist Information Centre,** in the Stamford Arts Centre on St. Mary's St., walk straight out of the train station and follow the road as it curves to the right. Take a left on High Street St. Martin's, cross the River Welland, and take a right on St. Mary's St. The TIC gives away a town map, sells the *Town Trail* guide (£1), and books beds for free. (☎755 611. Open Apr.-Sept. M-Sa 9:30am-5pm, Su 10:30am-3:30pm; Oct.-Mar. M-Sa 9:30am-5pm.) Other services include: **banks** with **ATMs** along High St., like **Lloyd's TSB,** 65 High St. (☎0845 072 3333; open M-Tu and Th-F 9am-5pm, W 10am-5pm, Sa 9am-12:30pm); **police,** North St. (☎752 222; open daily 8:30am-6:30pm); free **Internet** at the **library,** on High St. (☎763 442; book in advance; open M and W 9am-8pm, Tu and Th-F 9am-5:30pm, Sa 9am-1pm); and the **post office,** 9 All Saints' Pl. (☎08457 223 344; open M and W-F 9am-5:30pm, Tu 9:30am-5:30pm, Sa 9am-12:30pm). **Post Code:** PE9 2EY.

▐▌▐▌ ACCOMMODATIONS AND FOOD. The limited number of budget accommodations in town fill quickly; book well in advance during the summer or consider daytripping from Cambridge, Lincoln, or Nottingham. **B&Bs** are located mostly on the outskirts. Call ahead to get a lift or check for frequent local buses. Try **Gwynne House** ❹, 13 King's Rd., a large Victorian townhouse with a pool and three large ensuite rooms. Conveniently located a 5min. walk from the town center. (☎762 210; www.gwynnehouse.co.uk. Full English breakfast included. Singles £35; doubles and twins £55; family room £75. Cash only.) A welcoming couple runs **Sandon Barn** ❹, Casterton Rd., a modern home with beautiful views a 25min. walk from town or short ride on bus #9. (☎757 784. Homemade breakfast included. Singles £40; doubles and twins £60-£80. Cash only.) For **groceries**, stop at Tesco, 46-51 High St. (☎683 000. Open M-F 7:30am-7:30pm, Sa 7:30am-6pm, Su 10am-4pm.) Scrumptious desserts (£1.50), hot lunches (£6.75-7.25), and a wide array of sandwiches (£5.50) await at **Central Kitchen** ❷, 7 Red Lion Sq. (☎763 217. Open M-Th 9am-4:45pm, F-Sa 8am-4:45pm. AmEx/MC/V with £5 min.) Once the Midlands' premier coaching inn, where horses were changed on the long route between London and Edinburgh, the **George Hotel** ❸, High Street St. Martin's, now caters to a high-rolling crowd. This upscale hotel and restaurant near the River Welland serves traditional afternoon tea in the garden at 3:30pm and continental fare around the clock. (☎750 750. Entrees £10-15. Food served noon-10:30pm. AmEx/MC/V.) Savor a pot of tea (£1.20) and warm your stomach with omelettes and jacket potatoes (£3-6) at **Paddington** ❶, 12a Ironmonger St. (☎751 110. Open M-Th and Sa 9:15am-5pm, F 9:15am-4:30pm. Cash only.)

◉▐▌ SIGHTS AND ENTERTAINMENT. Stamford's main attraction is **Burghley House**, England's largest Elizabethan mansion. A 1 mi. jaunt from Stamford's town center leads to **Burghley Park**, and the house is marked by frequent signposts from High Street St. Martin's. Ringed with gardens designed by "Capability" Brown, the house was the prized creation of William Cecil, Queen Elizabeth I's High Treasurer from 1555 to 1587, and is still occupied by his descendants today. The famous **Heaven Room** and infamous **Hell Staircase** display fantastic works by Antonio Verrio—look for where he painted himself into the scene. Don't miss Burghley's newest addition, a 12-acre **Sculpture Garden** showcasing rare flowers and modern sculpture. (☎752 451; www.burghley.co.uk. House open Apr.-Oct. M-Th and Sa-Su 11am-5pm. Last admission 4:30pm. £10.40, concessions £9, children £5. Sculpture garden open Apr.-Oct. £3.20, children £1. Park open daily 10am-5pm. Free.) The **Stamford Arts Centre**, 27 St. Mary's St., hosts local productions and national tours. (☎763 203; www.stamfordartscentre.com. Box office open M-Sa 9:30am-8pm.) Begun in 1968, the **Stamford Shakespeare Festival** is based at Elizabethan **Tolethorpe Hall** and attracts over 35,000 visitors each year. The open-air amphitheater lies on gentle slopes—try a sunset picnic before the performance. (☎756 133; www.stamfordshakespeare.co.uk. June-Aug. Tickets £11-15, concessions £7-14.)

▶ DAYTRIPS FROM STAMFORD

GRANTHAM. Some of England's finest attended school in Grantham at the **King's School**, including young Sir Isaac Newton and William Cecil, the first Lord Burghley. Newton carved his name into a windowsill. (*Brook St.* ☎*01476 563 180. School library open to visitors M-F 9am-3:30pm. Free; donations accepted.*) The **Grantham Museum** has exhibits on Newton and another of Grantham's own, Margaret Thatcher. (*Kimes Coaches #4; 50min., 1 per hr., £13.80. Museum on St. Peter's Hill, by the TIC.* ☎*01476 568 783. Open M-Sa 10am-5pm. Last admission 4:30pm. Free.*)

COLSTERWORTH. Seven miles from Grantham stands Woolsthorpe Manor, Newton's birthplace. A young Isaac scribbled his early musings on the farmhouse wall where present-day visitors can still see his graffiti. Find the apple tree that supposedly bonked his famous "what goes up, must come down" ideas into existence. The barn contains the **Sir Isaac Newton Science Discovery Centre,** 23 Newton Way, a fantastic exhibit especially for children (or the mathematically disinclined) that clarifies Newtonian ideas. *(Lincolnshire Roadcar (☎522 255) runs from Grantham (20min., every 2-3hr., round-trip £3). ☎01476 860 338. Open Apr.-Aug. W-Su 1-5pm; Mar. and Sept.-Oct. Sa-Su 1-5pm. Last admission 4:30pm. Manor £3.60, children £1.80. Discovery Centre free.)*

NOTTINGHAM ☎0115

Nottingham uses its favorite rogue to lure tourists to its attractions: everything, from streets to buses to Indian restaurants, manages to exploit Robin Hood's legendary name. Designer boutiques and huge malls perpetuate the town's tradition of robbing from the rich. Despite all this, Nottingham is a center of commerce and non-fictional history. Victorian architecture mingles with modern shopping centers, while streets crowd with merry men and women at trendy bar-cafes.

┌ TRANSPORTATION

Trains: Nottingham Station, Carrington St., south of the city, across the canal. Trains (☎08457 484 950) to **Lincoln** (1hr., 1 per hr., £7.10), **London St. Pancras** (1¾hr., 2 per hr., £44.70), and **Sheffield** (1hr., 2 per hr., £8.20).

Buses: Broad Marsh Bus Station (☎950 3665), between Collin and Canal St. Ticket and info booth open M-F 9am-5:30pm. **National Express** (☎08705 808 080) to **London** (3hr., 10 per day, £16) and **Sheffield** (1½hr., 10 per day, £6.40). **Victoria Bus Station** is at the corner of York and Cairn St. and provides more local services. **Nottinghamshire County Council Buses** link points throughout the county.

Public Transportation: The best way to see the main attractions in Nottingham is on foot. For short urban journeys, hop on a **Nottingham City Transport** bus (50p-£1.30). All-day local bus pass £2.50. For public transit info, call the **Nottinghamshire Buses Hotline** (☎0870 608 2608; www.nctx.co.uk). Open daily 7am-8pm. The city also has a **tram** system (☎942 7777; www.thetram.net; prices depend on route) which connects Nottingham to various points in Nottinghamshire.

■✷ 🛈 ORIENTATION AND PRACTICAL INFORMATION

Nottingham is a busy city with confusing and often poorly labeled streets. Its hub is **Old Market Square,** the plaza that spreads before the domed Council House. Nottingham Canal cuts across the south of the city.

Tourist Information Centre: 1-4 Smithy Row (☎915 5330; www.experiencenottinghamshire.com), off Old Market Sq. Many reference guides, tour and **job listings,** a free city map, and free entertainment listings. Books rooms (before 4:30pm) for a 10% deposit. Open M-F 9am-5:30pm, Sa 9am-5pm, Su 10am-4pm.

Financial Services: Banks and **ATMs** line Long Row and Old Market Sq. **American Express,** 2 Victoria St. (☎924 7705). Open M-Tu and Th-F 9am-5:30pm, W 9:30am-5:30pm, Sa 9am-5pm.

Launderette: Brights, 150 Mansfield Rd. (☎948 3670), near the Igloo hostel. Wash £2.40, dry £1.20-1.60. Open M-Sa 9:30am-7pm, Su 9:30am-5pm; last wash 1hr. before close on weekdays, 1½hr. before close on weekends.

Police: North Church St. (☎967 0999).

Hospital: Queen's Medical Centre, Derby Rd. (☎924 9924).

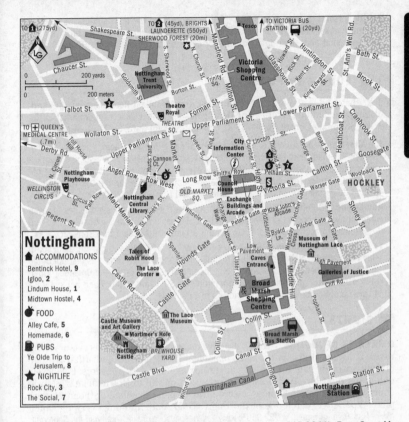

Nottingham

ACCOMMODATIONS
Bentinck Hotel, **9**
Igloo, **2**
Lindum House, **1**
Midtown Hostel, **4**

FOOD
Alley Cafe, **5**
Homemade, **6**

PUBS
Ye Olde Trip to
Jerusalem, **8**

NIGHTLIFE
Rock City, **3**
The Social, **7**

Internet Access: Nottingham Central Library, Angel Row (☎915 2841). Free. Open M-F 9:30am-7pm, Sa 9am-1pm. **TIC** for £2 per hr.

Post Office: Queen St. Open M-Sa 10am-5:30pm. **Post Code:** NG1 2BN.

ACCOMMODATIONS

Moderately priced **guest houses** ($30-35) cluster on **Goldsmith Street,** near Nottingham Trent University north of the city center.

Midtown Hostel, 5A Thurland St. (☎941 0150; www.midtownhostel.co.uk). Great budget option centrally located near Pelham St. nightlife and bus stations. Comfortable and clean bunk beds in mixed-sex rooms. Lounge with TV and videos. Free Internet access. Laundry £3. Luggage storage £1. Dorms £16. MC/V with 50p surcharge. ❷

Lindum House, 1 Burns St. (☎847 1089). Take the tram to the High School station, near the Arboretum, to this Victorian guest house. Wooden stairs lead to 3 well-kept rooms. Breakfast included. No smoking. Singles £40; doubles and twins £50-60. Cash only. ❹

Igloo, 110 Mansfield Rd. (☎947 5250), on the north side of town, across from Golden Fleece. Affordable hostel with 36 bunk beds, recently renovated with new TV lounge, game room, and kitchen. Single sex rooms available. Curfew 3am. Dorms £14.50. After one week, longterm residents pay £58 per week. MC/V with 50p surcharge. ❷

MIDLANDS

Bentinck Hotel, Station St. (☎958 0285), across from the train station. Convenient location makes up for lackluster rooms with TV. Rooms are clean but hallways have cracked paint and water damage. The bar downstairs is open until 11:30pm. Singles £24, ensuite £29.50. MC/V. ❸

FOOD AND PUBS

Quick, cheap bites abound on **Milton Street** and **Mansfield Road.** Gaggles of sandwich shops and ethnic eateries line **Goosegate.** There is a Tesco **supermarket** in the Victoria Shopping Centre. (☎980 7500. Open M-Sa 8am-8pm, Su 11am-5pm.)

The Alley Cafe, 1a Cannon Ct. (☎955 1013), off Long Row West across from the library. Seating is limited, but the vibe is cool and the music is mellow. Refreshing smoothies and vegetarian sandwiches are affordable (everything under £5). Discounts during off-peak meal times. The bar is a hotspot after 9pm. Schedule for live DJs Th-Sa nights posted downstairs. Open M-Tu 11am-6pm, W-Sa 11am-11pm. MC/V. ❶

Homemade, 20 Pelham St. (☎924 3030). Tiny cafe serving tasty sandwiches for even more appetizing prices (all selections under £3). Pass time W playing board games and Th listening to acoustic music. Open M-Sa 8:30am-4:30pm, Su 11am-3pm. MC/V. ❶

Ye Olde Trip to Jerusalem, 1 Brewhouse Yard (☎947 3171; www.triptojerusalem.com). This popular pub, claiming the title of "Oldest Inn in England," served its first pot of ale in AD 1189, when it was a staging point for soldiers setting off on the Crusades. Open M-W 10:30am-11pm, Th-Sa 10:30am-midnight, Su 11am-11pm. Food served M-Sa 11am-6pm, Su noon-6pm. MC/V with £5 minimum. ❶

SIGHTS

GALLERIES OF JUSTICE. This interactive museum comes to life as visitors experience a taste of British crime and punishment through actors and artifacts. Role-playing prisoners wait for unsuspecting tourists in the dark corridors. Five levels below the old Shire Hall present information on life in Nottingham's historic county gaol and the sometimes absurd array of punishments. For the most complete experience, catch one of the 1¼hr. group tours, running every 15-30min. (Shire Hall, High Pavement. ☎952 0555; www.galleriesofjustice.org.uk. Open mid-July-Sept. daily 10am-5pm; from Sept. to mid-July Tu-Su 10am-3pm. Last admission 1hr. before close. £8, concessions and children £6, families £23. Joint ticket with City of Caves £9.50/7.50/30.)

CITY OF CAVES. Nottingham is riddled with hundreds of caves. As early as the 10th century, Anglo-Saxon dwellers dug homes out of the soft, porous "Sherwood sandstones" on which the city rests. Tours take visitors through the cave complexes with stops at the only known underground tannery in Britain and a mock WWII air-raid shelter. The caves are, strangely enough, situated beneath (and accessed through) the second floor of Broad Marsh Shopping Centre. (☎952 0555; www.cityofcaves.com. Open daily 10:30am-4:30pm. 40min. guided tours M-F every 30min., Sa-Su every 15min. Last tour 4pm. £5, concessions £4, families £15.)

NOTTINGHAM CASTLE. William the Conqueror put up the original timber structure in 1068, and Henry III had the whole thing redone in stylish gray stone. The ruins of the castle now top a sandstone rise south of the city center. In 1642, Charles I raised his standard against Parliament here, kicking off the Civil War. For its part in the affair, the castle was destroyed by Parliamentarians. What's left now houses the **Castle Museum and Art Gallery,** a collection of historical exhibits on Nottinghamshire's past, Victorian art, and regimental memorabilia of the Sherwood Foresters, the regional militia. (☎915 3700. Friar Ln. Open daily Apr.-Nov. 10am-5pm; Dec.-Mar. 10am-4pm. Last entry 30min. before close. £3, concessions £1.50, families £7.)

While you're there, check out **Mortimer's Hole**, the underground passageway leading from the base of the cliff to the castle. (☎915 3700. *50min. tours leave from the museum entrance M-Sa 11am, 2, and 3pm. £2, concessions £1.*)

TALES OF ROBIN HOOD. Cable cars and audio tours transport visitors through an amusement-park version of Sherwood Forest. Robin Hood and his merry men await you after the child-friendly 45min. ride, and evenings bring the **medieval banquet**: for £40 per person you get a costume, four courses, and lots of beer. (*30-38 Maid Marian Way.* ☎948 3284. *Open daily 10am-5pm. Last admission 4:30pm. £9, concessions £8, children £7, families £27.*)

🎭🎵 NIGHTLIFE AND ENTERTAINMENT

Students crowd the city's 30+ clubs and pubs. For weekend festivities, try Pelham St. or the outdoor patios along Forman St. Indie and alternative fans will appreciate the live bands (recent acts include Coldplay and the White Stripes) that play to a young crowd at **The Social**, 23 Pelham St. (☎950 5078; www.thesocial.com. Open M-Sa noon-3am, Su 5pm-3am.) **Rock City**, 8 Talbot St., has hosted 25 years of hip hop, heavy metal, and everything in between. Past performers include Nirvana, a naked Robbie Williams, Marilyn Manson, and Guns N' Roses—Axl Rose was almost refused entry because of his bath towel garb. "Loveshack" Fridays bop to three decades of pop, while Saturdays feature alternative music. (☎941 2544; www.rock-city.co.uk. Cover £5-25. Open F-Sa 10pm-2am, and whenever bands are playing during the week. Check online for billing.)

Traditional theater, musicals, and the largest pantomime show in the Midlands can be found at the **Theatre Royal**, Theatre Sq. (☎989 5555; www.royalcentre-nottingham.co.uk. Box office open M-Sa 8:30am-8:30pm.) The **Nottingham Playhouse**, Wellington Circus, features more offbeat productions, although it offers its share of Shakespeare as well. (☎941 9419; www.nottinghhamplayhouse.co.uk. Box office open M-Sa 10am-8pm. Tickets £7-35.) Pick up a *Late Night Public Transport Guide* available at the TIC and bus stations for a complete schedule of trams running until midnight and buses running until 4am.

🔁 DAYTRIPS FROM NOTTINGHAM

NEWSTEAD ABBEY. The ancestral estate of poet **Lord Byron** stands in the village of Linby north of Nottingham. The sprawling, stately home is built around the remnants of the 1274 Newstead Priory church. Many

LOCAL LEGEND

MAN IN TIGHTS

You've probably heard of him and his questionable taste in fashion. But who was the real Robin Hood? Stories vary, but one of the likeliest theories is that the bandit was actually Robert Hodde, a 13th-century Saxon farmer who was declared an outlaw when he resisted taxation. He and his wife, Miriam (Maid Marian) fled to Sherwood Forest in Nottinghamshire to escape arrest.

What about his merry men? Robin Hood has been associated with upwards of 100 followers, but only a few are repeatedly mentioned in historical records. Little John was probably John Little, a King's soldier who supposedly met Hodde in the forest on a march to Yorkshire. Guillarme Scarletti of Italy, perhaps Hodde's first cousin, became Will Scarlet, completing the merry band.

Whether Robin Hood was a generous champion of the poor or simply a thieving knave remains a mystery, but the city of Nottingham has adopted Robin as a local hero nonetheless. Exhibits and attractions all over explore the legends and history of everyone's favorite stockinged crusader. Still can't get enough of the Hood? The University of Nottingham began a Master's degree program in Robin Hood studies beginning in Fall 2007.

personal effects remain, including Byron's original writing table and a replica of Byron's "skull cup"—an ancient human cranium the poet coated with silver, inscribed with verse, and filled with wine. The original was reinterred in 1863. Frisky peacocks hold court in the gardens—signs warn that shiny cars are vulnerable in mating season. *(Pronto buses run from Nottingham Victoria Station to the gates. 25min., 3 per hr., round-trip £4. 1 mi. from the grounds. ☎01623 455 900; www.newsteadabbey.org.uk. House open Apr.-Sept. daily noon-5pm. Last entry 4pm. Grounds open 9am-6pm; last admission 5pm. House and grounds £6, concessions £4. Grounds only £3, concessions £2.50.)*

SHERWOOD FOREST. For the "real" Robin Hood experience, travel to the famed 450-acre Sherwood Forest north of Nottingham. The **Sherwood Forest Visitor Centre,** near the entrance, has a small museum. Beware of children armed with mini-archery sets. To escape the crowds, take the signposted 3½ mi. walk, stopping at the "Major Oak," which, at 33 ft. in girth, allegedly served as Robin Hood's hideout. In early August, the medieval **Robin Hood Festival** includes a jousting tournament. Check with the TIC for exact dates. *(Bus #33 leaves Nottingham Victoria Station 1hr., M-Sa 4 per day, Su 2 per day. Sherwood Dart Rover Ticket, £4.50, gives unlimited travel for a day. Visitor Centre ☎01623 823 202. Forest and visitor center open daily 10:30am-5pm. Free.)*

EASTWOOD. Eastwood native and author of *Lady Chatterley's Lover,* D. H. Lawrence (1885-1930) wrote novels that were banned from bookstores. Now, he rests honorably in Westminster Abbey. The **D.H. Lawrence Birthplace Museum** is in the house where he spent his first two years—look for his original watercolors. *(8a Victoria St., near Mansfield Rd. ☎01773 717 353. Open daily Apr.-Oct. 10am-5pm; Nov.-Mar. 10am-4pm. M-F free; Sa-Su £2, concessions £1.20, families £5.80.)* Ask the staff about walking brochures for Eastwood. The Blue Line Trail is a self-guided tour that links the museum with numerous other Lawrence heritage sites, including three more homes in Eastwood where the family lived. *(Eastwood is 6 mi. west of Nottingham. Rainbow bus #1 (40min., 6 per hr., £4.20) leaves often from Nottingham Victoria Station.)*

LINCOLN ☎01522

Cobbled streets climb past half-timbered homes to Lincoln's dominating 12th-century cathedral, a relative newcomer in a town built for retired Roman legionnaires in the first century AD. Visitors will find a bustling marketplace and, after a steep uphill climb to the city's peak, sweeping views of the dusky Lincolnshire Wolds. Lincoln is also renowned for its sausage, a staple of the local market.

▐ TRANSPORTATION

Lincoln's **Central Station** is on St. Mary's St. (Office open M-F 5:15am-7:30pm, Sa 5:45am-7:30pm, Su 10:30am-9:15pm. Travel center open M-Sa 9am-5pm.) **Trains** run to: Sheffield (50min., every hr., £12.90); Leeds (2hr., 2 per hr., £24.50); London King's Cross (2hr., every hr., £51.70); and Nottingham (1hr.; M-Sa 1 per hr., Su 7 per day; £7.50). Opposite Central Station is **City Bus Station,** Melville St. (Open M-F 8:30am-5pm, Sa 9am-1:45pm.) National Express **buses** go to London (4½hr., 1 per day, £20) and Birmingham (3hr., 1 per day, £13.40). There is no National Express office in Lincoln; buy tickets online or on the bus. For info on Lincolnshire bus services, contact the Lincolnshire Roadcar station on Deacon Rd. (☎522 255; www.roadcar.co.uk. Open M-F 8:30am-5pm.)

▓ ? ORIENTATION AND PRACTICAL INFORMATION

Lincoln has an affluent acropolis on **Castle Hill** and a cottage-filled lower town near the tracks. The TIC and major sights lie at the junction of **Steep Hill** and Castle Hill near the cathedral.

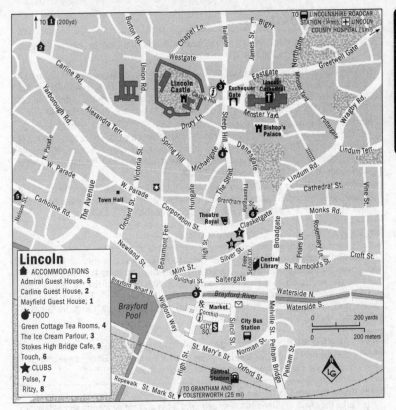

Lincoln

🏠 ACCOMMODATIONS
Admiral Guest House, **5**
Carline Guest House, **2**
Mayfield Guest House, **1**

🍴 FOOD
Green Cottage Tea Rooms, **4**
The Ice Cream Parlour, **3**
Stokes High Bridge Cafe, **9**
Touch, **6**

★ CLUBS
Pulse, **7**
Ritzy, **8**

Tourist Information Centre: 9 Castle Hill (☎873 213; www.lincoln.gov.uk). Books rooms for £3 plus a 10% deposit. Pick up a mini-guide with map (50p). Open M-Th 9:30am-5:30pm, F 9:30am-5pm, Sa-Su 10am-5pm. Branch at The Cornhill (☎873 256). Open M-Th 9:30am-5:30pm, F 9am-5pm, Sa 10am-5pm.

Tours: 1hr. Cathedral Quarter walking tours depart from the Castle Hill TIC July-Aug. daily 11am and 2:15pm; Sept.-Oct. and Apr.-June Sa-Su only. £4.

Financial Services: Major **banks** with **ATMs** line High St. and Cornhill Pavement. **Thomas Cook,** 4 Cornhill Pavement (☎346 400). Open M-Tu and Th-Sa 9am-5:30pm, W 10am-5:30pm.

Pharmacy: Boots, 311-312 High St. (☎524 303). Open M-Sa 8:30am-6pm, Su 10:15am-4:45pm.

Police: West Parade (☎882 222), near the town hall.

Hospital: Lincoln County Hospital, Greetwell Rd. (☎512 512), off Greetwell Gate.

Internet Access: Central Library, Free School Ln. (☎510 800). Free. Open M-F 9:30am-7pm, Sa 9:30am-4pm. Also at **Sun Cafe,** 36 Portland St. (☎569 292). Free. Open M-Su 11am-9pm.

Post Office: City Sq. Centre, Sincil St. (☎513 004). **Bureau de change.** Open M-Tu and Th 8:30am-5:30pm, W and F 9am-5:30pm, Sa 9am-5pm. **Post Code:** LN5 7XX.

ACCOMMODATIONS

B&Bs (most £25-35) dot **Carline** and **Yarborough Roads,** west of the castle. Consult the accommodations list at the TIC on Cornhill.

Carline Guest House, 1-3 Carline Rd. (☎530 422; www.carlineguesthouse.co.uk). 15min. walk northwest of the train station, or take bus #7 or 8 to Yarborough Rd. Immaculate house with big beds, big rooms, and a big breakfast in the historic heart of Lincoln. Singles £35-40; doubles £55. Book ahead in summer. AmEx/MC/V. ❸

Mayfield Guest House, 213 Yarborough Rd. (☎533 732). Entrance behind house on Mill Rd., off Long Leys Rd., a 20min. walk northwest from the station (or take bus #7 or 8 to Yarborough Rd.). Victorian mansion near a windmill offering bright, mostly ensuite rooms. Mind the enthusiastic cockatiel. No smoking. Singles £30; doubles £54; twins £56. Book ahead in summer. AmEx/MC/V. ❸

Admiral Guest House, Nelson Yard (☎544 467), take Bayford Wharf N. to Nelson St. A 10min. walk from the station. Small, basic rooms. Wharfside location gives a nautical feel. Full English breakfast included. Singles £25; doubles £50. MC/V. ❸

FOOD

The Cornhill **market,** on Sincil St., sells local food and oddities such as household appliances and infants' clothing. (Open M-F 9am-4pm, Sa 9am-4:30pm.) Farmers' markets grace City Sq. (1st F of the month), High St. (2nd W of the month), Castle Hill (3rd Sa of the month), and St. Benedict's Sq. (every Sa). Restaurants, tea rooms, and takeaways are all along **High Street** and **Steep Hill,** while pubs line **Bailgate Street,** on the other side of the hill.

 POUND FOR £1. At the farmers' markets in Lincoln, load up on 1lb. of fresh fruit for only £1. Many other British towns offer the same or similar deals, which are makes market shopping more cost effective than at grocers.

The Green Cottage Tea Rooms, 18 Steep Hill (☎537 909). Reward yourself with cream tea after the climb up Steep Hill. Tiny cafe with 3 tea and coffee menus and a delicious selection of baguettes (£4.80) and pastries (£2-3). Open M-Tu and F 10:30am-4:30pm; Sa 9:30am-5pm; Su 11am-4pm. Lunch served noon-3pm. Cash only. ❶

Touch, 43-47 Clasketgate (☎522 221; www.touchrestaurantbar.com). The European cuisine is as sleek and modern as the interior. Bargain buffet lunch noon-2pm £4.25. For dinner, try entrees like lime-scented tuna (£12.75). F and Sa live piano bar and Su is jazz night (£8.50 for a table). £1 discounts 5:30-7pm and 9:30-10:30pm. Open daily 11am-3pm and 5:30-10:30pm. MC/V. ❸

The Ice Cream Parlour, 3 Bailgate. Tiny shop with homemade ice cream, frozen yogurt, and sorbet. A single scoop (£1) of orange brandy or passion fruit sorbet may only whet the appetite for a double (£1.90). Downstairs find affordable afternoon high tea and snacks (everything under £1.60). Open daily 10am-dusk. Cash only. ❶

Stokes High Bridge Cafe, 207 High St. (☎513 825; www.stokes-coffee.co.uk). Enjoy afternoon high tea and excellent people-watching in this century-old, Tudor-style house on High Bridge. Watch swans float on the canal while nibbling on cheap sandwiches and snacks. 2-course lunch special (£4.50) served 11:45am-2pm. Open M-Sa 9am-5pm; stops serving at 4:30pm. Tea 2-5pm. MC/V with £10 minimum. ❶

⊙ SIGHTS

A **Time Travel Pass,** available at the TIC, works at Lincoln Cathedral, Lincoln Castle, Museum of Lincolnshire Life, Medieval Bishop's Palace, and Ellis Mill for £10.

■ LINCOLN CATHEDRAL. While the rest of Lincoln endured a millennium of the rise and fall of Roman barricades, bishops' palaces, and conquerors' castles, the magnificent cathedral remained king of the hill. Begun in 1072 but not completed for three centuries, it was the continent's tallest building until the spire toppled. The shimmering Lincolnshire limestone and broad front overwhelm even Lincoln Castle across the street. Its many endearing features include the Lincoln imp in the **Angel Choir,** who supposedly turned to stone while trying to chat with seraphim. A treasury room displays sacred silver and a shrine to child martyr Sir Hugh. Rotating exhibits reside in the first library designed by **Christopher Wren.** In the summer, Peregrine falcons fly overhead and nest in the facade. (☎ 544 544; www.lincolncathedral.com. Open June-Aug. M-Sa 7:15am-8pm, Su 7:15am-6pm; Sept.-May M-Sa 7:15am-6pm, Su 7:15am-5pm. Evensong M-Sa 5:30pm, Su 3:45pm. Tours M-Sa 11am, 1, 3pm; free roof tours M, W, F 2pm; Tu, Th, and Sa 11am and 2pm. Tour required to enter tower. Library open daily Apr.-Oct. 2-4pm. Cathedral £4, concessions £3. Audio tour £1.)

LINCOLN CASTLE. Home to one of four surviving copies of the Magna Carta, this castle, built by William the Conqueror in 1068, was also the house of pain and solitude for inmates of the Victorian Castle Prison. A wall-walk and visit to the observatory tower offer rewarding panoramic views of Lincolnshire and the Trent Valley. In the dungeon in Cobb Hall, shackles still protrude from the stone walls. (☎ 511 068. Open Apr.-Oct. M-Sa 9:30am-5:30pm, Su 11am-5:30pm; Nov.-Mar. M-Sa 9:30am-4:30pm, Su 11am-4:30pm. Last admission 1hr. before close. Guided tours daily Sa-Su 11am and 2pm. £4, concessions £2.50, families £10.)

BISHOP'S PALACE. Resting in the shadow of the Cathedral, the Bishop's Palace has a vaulted undercroft and formidable entrance tower. It was the seat of England's largest diocese in the 12th century and is now peacefully ruined, surrounded by vineyards and views. (☎ 527 468. Open Apr.-June and Sept.-Oct. daily 10am-5pm; July-Aug. daily 10am-6pm; Nov.-Mar. M and Th-Su 10am-4pm. £4, concessions £3, children £2, families £9.30. Audio tour free.)

■ ☀ NIGHTLIFE AND FESTIVALS

The monthly *What's On,* at the TIC, has the latest nightlife listings. On the corner of Silver St. and Flaxengate, **Ritzy** (☎ 522 314) draws young people, while upstairs, **Pulse** (☎ 522 314; www.pulselincoln.co.uk) has three rooms blaring chart-topping hits and a range of theme nights including weekly student nights. (Both clubs open M-W 10pm-2am, Th 10pm-2:30am, F-Sa 10pm-3am, Su 9:30pm-2am. Last admission 1hr. before close. Cover £5. Casual on weekdays and smart dress on weekends.) The **Theatre Royal,** Clasketgate, near the corner of High St., stages concerts and musicals. (☎ 525 555; www.theatreroyallincoln.com. Box office open M-F 10am-2pm and 3-6pm, Sa 10am-2pm and 5-6pm. Tickets £7-22, concessions available M-Th.) In early December, Europe's largest **Christmas Market** takes over Cathedral Quarter when 150,000 people come to peruse 300 stalls. Late July brings the **Waterfront Festival,** with street theater, acrobats, and jet ski displays. The **Lincoln Early Music Festival,** with workshops and street-dancing lessons, is in August.

EAST ANGLIA

The swampy fens in East Anglia were drained in the 1820s, yielding fertile farmland. The water that drenched enormous medieval peat bogs was channeled into a maze of waterways known as the Norfolk Broads, now a popular national park. Norman invaders brought stone over the flooded fens to build the Ely Cathedral, which still dominates the landscape. In a village to the south, renegade scholars from Oxford set up a rival institution along the River Cam in the 15th century.

HIGHLIGHTS OF EAST ANGLIA

PUNT along the river Cam in the university town of **Cambridge,** one of the world's oldest centers of scholarship (p. 317).

GAZE skyward at **Ely Cathedral,** a medieval masterwork towering over fenland (p. 326).

CELEBRATE in **Norwich,** once the largest town in Anglo-Saxon England, where wool markets and festivals have endured for centuries (p. 331).

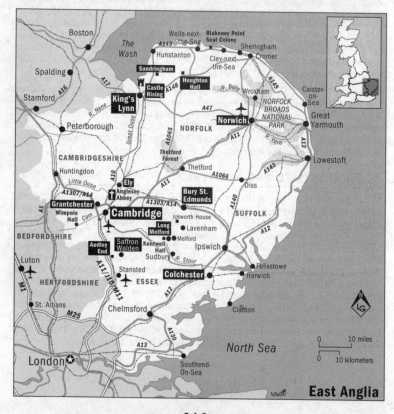

East Anglia

⊏ TRANSPORTATION IN EAST ANGLIA

The major rail operator is **One Railway** (☎0845 600 7245; www.onerailway.com). An Anglia **Plus Pass** (£11), available at stations within East Anglia, grants you a day's unlimited travel on all **train** and local **bus** routes in the region. An Anglia **Plus Three Day Pass** allows three days of unlimited travel (£22). Cyclists and hikers appreciate East Anglia's flat terrain and relatively dry climate, although bike rental shops are rare outside of Cambridge and Norwich. The area's most popular walking trail is **Peddar's Way**, which runs from Knettishall Heath to Holme and includes the **Norfolk Coast Path** and **Weaver's Way**. TICs in Norwich, Bury St. Edmunds, and several Suffolk villages issue *Peddar's Way and Norfolk Coast Path* guides.

Harwich (HAR-idge) is a ferry depot for Holland, Germany, and Scandinavia. **Felixstowe** has ferries to Belgium. (See **By Ferry**, p. 31). Call the Harwich **Tourist Information Centre,** Iconfield Park, Parkeston, for details. (☎01255 506 139. Open Apr.-Sept. M-F 9am-5pm, Sa-Su 9am-4pm; Oct.-Mar. M-F 9am-5pm, Sa 9am-4pm.) The Felixstowe TIC is on the seafront. (☎01394 276 770. Open daily 9am-5:30pm.)

CAMBRIDGESHIRE

CAMBRIDGE ☎01223

Unlike museum-oriented, metropolitan Oxford, Cambridge is a town for students before tourists. It was here that Newton's gravity, Watson and Crick's model of DNA, the poetry of Byron and Milton, and Winnie the Pooh were born. No longer the exclusive academy of upper-class sons, the university feeds the minds of women, international, and state-school pupils alike. At exams' end, Cambridge explodes in Pimm's-soaked glee, and May Week is a swirl of parties and balls.

⊏ TRANSPORTATION

Bicycles are the primary mode of transportation in Cambridge, a city which claims more bikes per person than any other place in Britain. If you are prepared to face the maze of one-way streets by driving to Cambridge, take advantage of its efficient park-and-ride system.

Trains: Station on Station Rd. Ticket office open daily 5am-11pm. Trains (☎08457 484 950) run to **London King's Cross** (45min., 3 per hr., £18) and **Ely** (20min., 3 per hr., round-trip £3.50).

Buses: Drummer St. Station. Ticket booth open daily 8:45am-5:30pm; tickets often available onboard. National Express (☎08705 808 080) buses and airport shuttles pick up at stands on Parkside St. along Parker's Piece park. Buses to: **London Victoria** (3hr., every hr., £10); **Gatwick** (4hr., every hr., £29.50); **Heathrow** (2½hr., 2 per hr., £25); **Stansted** (1hr., every hr., £10). Stagecoach Express (☎01604 676 060) runs to **Oxford** (3hr., every hr., from £6.50).

Public Transportation: Stagecoach (☎423 578) runs CitiBus from the train station to the city center and around town (£1-2).

Taxis: Cabco (☎312 444) and **Camtax** (☎313 131). Both 24hr.

Luggage Storage: Cambridge Station Cycles, outside the train station. (☎307 125). £3-4 per item. Open M-F 8am-7pm, Sa 9am-5pm, Su 10am-5pm.

Bike Rental: Mike's Bikes, 28 Mill Rd. (☎312 591). £10 per day. £35 deposit. Lock and light included. Open M-Sa 9am-6pm, Su 10am-4pm. MC/V.

✈ ? ORIENTATION AND PRACTICAL INFORMATION

Cambridge has two main avenues; the main shopping street starts at **Magdalene Bridge** and becomes **Bridge Street, Sidney Street, Saint Andrew's Street, Regent Street,** and **Hills Road.** The other main thoroughfare starts as **Saint John's Street,** becoming **Trinity Street, King's Parade,** and **Trumpington Street.** From the **Drummer Street** bus station, **Emmanuel Street** leads to the shopping district near the TIC. To get to the center from the train station, turn right onto Hills Rd. and follow it for ¾ mi.

Tourist Information Centre: Wheeler St. (☎09065 862 526; www.visitcambridge.org), 1 block south of Market Sq. Books rooms for £3 plus a 10% deposit. Cambridge Visitors Card gives city-wide discounts (£2.50). Sells National Express tickets. Open Easter-Oct. M-F 10am-5:30pm, Sa 10am-5pm, Su 11am-4pm; Nov.-Easter M-F 10am-5:30pm, Sa 10am-5pm.

Tours: 2hr. walking tours leave from the TIC daily (July-Aug. 4 per day). Tours including King's College £9, children £4.50; St. John's College £7, children £4.50. Call for times and tickets (☎457 574). **City Sightseeing** (☎01353 663 659) runs 1hr. hop-on, hop-off bus tours every 15-30min. Apr.-Oct. £9, concessions £7, children £3.50.

Budget Travel: STA Travel, 38 Sidney St. (☎366 966; www.statravel.co.uk). Open M-Th 9:30am-6:30pm, F 10am-5:30pm, Sa 11am-5pm.

Financial Services: Banks and **ATMs** on Market Sq. **Thomas Cook,** 8 St. Andrew's St. (☎543 100). Open M-Tu and Th-Sa 9am-5pm, W 10am-5pm. **American Express,** 25 Sidney St. (☎08706 001 060). Open M-F 9am-5:30pm, Sa 9am-5pm.

Work Opportunities: Blue Arrow, 40 St. Andrews St. (☎323 272; www.bluearrow.co.uk). Year-round temp work. Arrange early for summer. Open M-F 8am-5:30pm.

Pharmacy: Boots, 65-67 Sidney St. (☎350 213). Open M 9am-6pm, Tu 8:30am-6pm, W 8:30am-7pm, Th-Sa 8:30am-6pm, Su 11am-5pm.

Launderette: Clean Machine, 22 Burleigh St. (☎566 677). £3 per small load. Open M-F 9am-8:30pm, Sa-Su 9am-4pm. Last wash 1hr. before close.

Police: Parkside (☎358 966).

Hospital: Addenbrookes, Long Rd. (☎245 151). Take Cambus C1 or C2 from Emmanuel St. (£1), and get off where Hills Rd. intersects Long Rd.

Internet Access: Jaffa Net Cafe, 22 Mill Rd. (☎308 380). From £1 per hr. 10% student discount. Open daily 10am-10pm. **Budget Internet Cafe,** 30 Hills Rd. (☎464 625). 3p per min. Open daily 9am-11pm.

Post Office: 9-11 St. Andrew's St. (☎08457 223 344). **Bureau de change.** Open M and W-Sa 9am-5:30pm, Tu 9:30am-5:30pm. **Post Code:** CB2 3AA.

⌂ ACCOMMODATIONS

Demand for accommodations in Cambridge is always high, and rooms are scarce. John Maynard Keynes, who studied and taught at Cambridge, tells us that low supply and high demand usually means one thing: high prices. **B&Bs** gather around **Portugal Street** and **Tenison Road** outside the city center. Book ahead in summer.

Tenison Towers Guest House, 148 Tenison Rd. (☎363 924; www.cambridgecitytenisontowers.com), 2 blocks from the train station. Freshly baked muffins and impeccable rooms in a Victorian house. No smoking. Singles £35; doubles £55. Cash only. ❹

YHA Cambridge, 97 Tenison Rd. (☎354 601), close to the train station. Relaxed, welcoming atmosphere draws a diverse clientele. Always crowded. 103 beds. Well-equipped kitchen, laundry, luggage storage (£1-2), 2 TV lounges, and bureau de change. English breakfast included; other meals available. Lockers £1. Internet 50p per 7min. Reception 24hr. Dorms £18.50, under 18 £14.50. MC/V. ❷

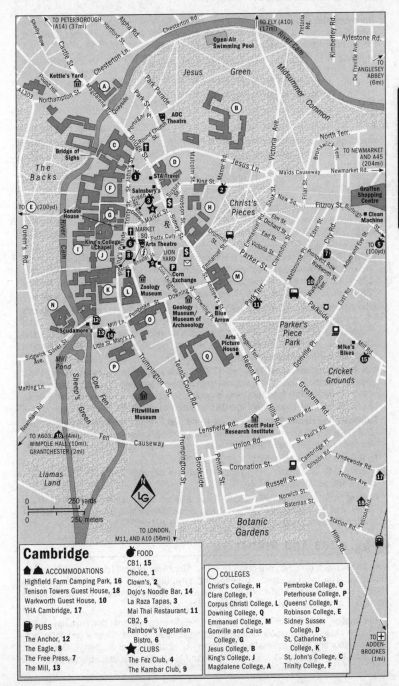

Cambridge

🏠🏠 ACCOMMODATIONS
Highfield Farm Camping Park, **16**
Tenison Towers Guest House, **18**
Warkworth Guest House, **10**
YHA Cambridge, **17**

🍺 PUBS
The Anchor, **12**
The Eagle, **8**
The Free Press, **7**
The Mill, **13**

🍎 FOOD
CB1, **15**
Choice, **1**
Clown's, **2**
Dojo's Noodle Bar, **14**
La Raza Tapas, **3**
Mai Thai Restaurant, **11**
CB2, **5**
Rainbow's Vegetarian
  Bistro, **6**

★ CLUBS
The Fez Club, **4**
The Kambar Club, **9**

○ COLLEGES
Christ's College, **H**
Clare College, **I**
Corpus Christi College, **L**
Downing College, **Q**
Emmanuel College, **M**
Gonville and Caius
  College, **G**
Jesus College, **B**
King's College, **J**
Magdalene College, **A**

Pembroke College, **O**
Peterhouse College, **P**
Queens' College, **N**
Robinson College, **E**
Sidney Sussex
  College, **D**
St. Catharine's
  College, **K**
St. John's College, **C**
Trinity College, **F**

Warkworth Guest House, Warkworth Terr. (☎363 682). Sunny, spacious ensuite rooms near the bus station in a family-run Victorian mansion. Free Wi-Fi in lounge. Breakfast included. Singles £50; twins and doubles £70, families £90. MC/V. ❹

Highfield Farm Camping Park, Long Rd., Comberton (☎262 308; www.highfieldfarm-touringpark.co.uk). Take Cambus #18 to Comberton (every 45min.) from Drummer St. Showers and laundry. July-Aug. £9.50; May-June and Sept. £10.75; Apr. and Oct. £7.25-8.50. Electricity £2. Cash only. ❶

🍴 FOOD

Market Square has bright pyramids of cheap fruit and vegetables (open M-Sa 9:30am-4:30pm). Get **groceries** at Sainsbury's, 44 Sidney St. (☎366 891. Open M-Sa 8am-10pm, Su 11am-5pm.) Cheap Indian and Mediterranean fare on the edges of the city center satisfies hearty appetites. South of town, **Hills Road** and **Mill Road** are full of budget restaurants popular with the college crowd.

■ **Clown's,** 54 King St. (☎355 711). The staff at this cozy Italian eatery will remember your name if you come more than once. Children's artwork plasters the orange walls. Huge portions of pasta and dessert (£2.50-6.50). Set menu includes a drink, salad, small pasta, and cake (£6.50). Open M-Sa 8am-midnight, Su 8am-11pm. Cash only. ❶

■ **CB1,** 32 Mill Rd. (☎576 306). A student hangout coffee shop with piping hot drinks (£1-1.50) and walls crammed with books. Enjoy free Wi-Fi and the decidedly chill atmosphere while lounging on couches. Open M-F 8am-8pm, Sa-Su 10am-8pm. Also try **CB2,** 5-7 Norfolks St. (☎508 503. Both open daily noon-midnight.) Cash only. ❶

Dojo's Noodle Bar, 1-2 Mill Ln. (☎363 471; www.dojonoodlebar.co.uk). Rave reviews bring long lines, but the enormous plates of wok-fried, soup-based, and sauce-based noodles are served quickly from the counter. Wide selection of vegetarian options and rice dishes. Everything under £7. Open M-Th noon-2:30pm and 5:30-11pm, F noon-4pm and 5:30-11pm, Sa-Su noon-11pm. MC/V. ❶

Mai Thai Restaurant, Park Terr. (☎367 480; www.mai-thai-restaurant.com). Location, location, location. This stylish, colorful restaurant with great views across Parker's Piece serves authentic Thai food with fresh ingredients. Popular set lunch menu £10. Entrees £7-16. Open daily noon-3pm and 6-11pm. AmEx/MC/V. ❸

Rainbow's Vegetarian Bistro, 9a King's Parade (☎321 551; www.rainbowcafe.co.uk). Even carnivores enjoy this tiny basement spot in the city center. Asian-inspired vegetarian fare, all for £8. Open Tu-Sa 10am-10pm. Food served until 9:30pm. Cash only. ❷

La Raza, 4 Rose Crescent (☎464 550). Live music every night and an affordable tapas menu (£3-8). Stays busy with a bar crowd well into the night. Open M-Th 9am-1am F-Sa 9am-2am, Su 9am-midnight. MC/V. ❷

Choice, 11 St. John's St. (☎568 336). A quick, cheap stop popular with students. Make a picnic of the flapjacks (£1.20 each) and ample sandwiches (£2-2.60). 20% student discount. Open daily 8am-5pm. Cash only. Branch at 16 Silver St. ❶

🍺 PUBS AND NIGHTLIFE

King Street has a diverse collection of pubs. Most stay open 11am-11pm (Su noon-10:30pm). The local brewery, **Greene King,** supplies many of them. Pubs are the core of Cambridge nightlife, but clubs are also in the curriculum. The city is small enough that a quick stroll will reveal popular venues.

The Anchor, Silver St. (☎353 554). Have a beer in the same spot that Pink Floyd's Syd Barrett drew his inspiration. Crowded undergrad watering hole. Savor a pint on an outdoor table and scoff at amateur punters colliding under Silver St. Bridge. Open M-Sa 10am-11pm, Su 11am-10:30pm. Food served M-Sa noon-9:30pm, Su noon-9pm.

The Mill, 14 Mill Ln. (☎357 026), off Silver St. Bridge. Low ceilings, wood interior, and great beer. Patrons relax outside for punt- and people-watching. Features a rotating selection of ales. Open M-Th noon-11pm, F noon-midnight, Sa 11am-midnight, Su 11am-11pm. Food served M-Th noon-3pm and 5-9pm, F-Sa noon-7pm, Su noon-9pm.

The Free Press, Prospect Row (☎368 337), behind the police station. Named after an abolitionist rag and popular with locals. No pool table, no cell phones, no overwhelming music. Just good beer and entertaining conversation. Open M-F noon-2:30pm and 6-11pm, Sa noon-3pm and 6-11pm, Su noon-3pm and 7-10:30pm.

The Eagle, 8 Benet St. (☎505 020). Cambridge's oldest pub located in the heart of town. Packed with boisterous tourists. When Watson and Crick rushed in to announce their discovery of DNA, the barmaid insisted they settle their 4-shilling tab before she'd serve them. Check out the RAF room, where WWII pilots stood on each other's shoulders to burn their initials into the ceiling. Open M-Sa 11am-11pm, Su noon-10:30pm.

The Fez Club, 15 Market Passage (☎519 224). Moroccan setting complete with floor cushions. Students dance to everything from Latin to trance. Show up early to avoid the cover. Cover M-Th £2-5, F-Sa £6-8; M and W students ½-price. Open daily 9pm-3am.

The Kambar Club, 1 Wheeler St. (☎842 725), opposite the Corn Exchange box office. Small and dim, with a mix of indie and electronica tunes. Drinks can be expensive, but the energy is great on weekends. Cover £5, students £3. Open M-Sa 10pm-2:30am.

◉ SIGHTS

Cambridge is an architect's utopia, packing some of England's most impressive monuments into less than a single square mile. The soaring **King's College Chapel** and St. John's postcard-familiar **Bridge of Sighs** are sightseeing staples, while more obscure college quads open onto ornate courtyards and gardens. Most historic buildings are on the **east bank** of the Cam between Magdalene Bridge and Silver St. The gardens, meadows, and cows of the **Backs** lend a pastoral air to the **west bank.** The **University of Cambridge** has three eight-week terms: Michaelmas (Oct.-Dec.), Lent (Jan.-Mar.), and Easter (Apr.-June). Visitors can access most of the 31 colleges daily, although times vary; call the TIC for hours. Many are closed to sightseers during Easter term, virtually all are closed during exams (from mid-May to mid-June), and visiting hours are limited during May Week festivities. A visit to **King's, Trinity,** and **Saint John's Colleges** should top your to-do list, as should a stroll or punt along the Cam. Porters (bowler-wearing ex-servicemen) maintain security. The fastest way to blow your tourist cover is to trample the **grass** of the courtyards, a privilege reserved for the elite. In July and August, most undergrads skip town, leaving it to PhD students, international students, and mobs of tourists.

COLLEGES

KING'S COLLEGE. King's College was founded by Henry VI in 1441 as a partner school to Eton: it was not until 1873 that students from schools other than Eton were admitted. King's is now the most socially liberal of the Cambridge colleges, drawing more of its students from state schools than any other. Its most stunning attraction is the gothic **King's College Chapel.** From the southwest corner of the courtyard, you can see where Henry's master mason left off and the Tudors began work—the earlier stone is off-white. The wall that separates the college grounds from King's Parade was a 19th-century addition; the chapel and grounds were originally hidden behind a row of shops and houses. Inside, painted angels hover against the world's largest fan-vaulted ceiling. Behind the altar hangs Rubens's *Adoration of the Magi* (1639). John Maynard Keynes, E. M. Forster, and Salman Rushdie lived in King's College. In mid-June, university degree ceremonies are held in the Georgian Senate House. *(King's Parade.* ☎ *331 100. Chapel and grounds open M-Sa 9:30am-5pm, Su 10am-5pm. Last admission 4:30pm. Contact TIC for tours. Listing of services and musical events available at porter's lodge. Choral services 10:30am and 5:30pm most nights. £4.50, students £3; with audio tour £7, students £5.50.)*

TRINITY COLLEGE. Henry VIII intended the College of the Holy and Undivided Trinity (founded 1546) to be the largest and richest in Cambridge. Currently Britain's third largest landowner (after the Queen and the Church of England), the college has amply fulfilled his wish. The alma mater of Sir Isaac Newton, who lived in E staircase for 30 years, the college has many illustrious alumni: literati Dryden, Byron, Tennyson, and Nabokov; atom-splitter Ernest Rutherford; philosopher Ludwig Wittgenstein; and Indian statesman Jawaharlal Nehru. The **Great Court**, the world's largest enclosed courtyard, is reached from Trinity St. through **Great Gate.** The castle-like gateway is fronted by a statue of Henry VIII grasping a wooden chair leg—the original scepter was stolen so frequently that the college administration removed it. The apple tree near the gate supposedly descended from the tree that inspired Newton's theory of gravity, while in the north cloister of **Nevile's Court,** Newton calculated the speed of sound by stamping his foot and timing the echo. On the west side of the court stand the dour **chapel** and the **King's Gate tower.** Lord Byron used to bathe nude in the **fountain,** the only one in Cambridge. The poet also kept a bear as a pet (college rules only forbade cats and dogs). The south side of the court is home to the **Master's Lodge** and the **Great Hall.** The building houses alumnus **A. A. Milne's** handwritten copies of *Winnie the Pooh* and Newton's personal copy of his *Principia.* Pass through the drab **New Court** (Prince Charles's former residence), adjacent to Neville's Court, to get to the Backs, where you can enjoy the view from **Trinity Bridge.** *(Trinity St.* ☎ *338 400. Chapel and courtyard open daily 10am-5pm. Easter-Oct. £2.20, concessions £1.30, families £4.40; Nov.-Easter free.)*

SAINT JOHN'S COLLEGE. Established in 1511 by Lady Margaret Beaufort, mother of Henry VIII, St. John's centers around a paved plaza rather than a grassy courtyard. The **Bridge of Sighs,** named after the Venetian original, connects the older part of the college with the towering neo-Gothic extravagance of **New Court.** The **School of Pythagoras,** a 12th-century pile of wood and stone thought to be the oldest complete building in Cambridge, hides in St. John's Gardens. The college also boasts the longest room in the city—the **Fellows' Room** in Second Court spans 93 ft. and was the site of D-Day planning. *(St. John's St.* ☎ *338 600. Open daily 10am-5:30pm. Evensong Tu-Su 6:30pm. £2.50, concessions £1.50, families £5.)*

QUEENS' COLLEGE. Aptly named Queens' College was founded by two queens: Queen Margaret of Anjou in 1448 and Elizabeth Woodville in 1465. Queens' College has the only unaltered Tudor courtyard in Cambridge, but the main attraction is the **Mathematical Bridge.** The structure is rumored to be built on geometric principles alone, which is perhaps why the 1749 original no longer stands. *(Silver St.* ☎ *335 511. Open Mar-Oct. M-F 10am-5pm, Sa-Su 9:30am-5pm. £1.30.)*

CLARE COLLEGE. Clare's coat of arms—golden teardrops ringing a black border—recalls the college's founding in 1326 by thrice-widowed, 29-year-old Lady Elizabeth de Clare. The college has some of the most cheerful **gardens** in Cambridge, and elegant **Clare Bridge,** dating from 1638, is the oldest surviving college bridge. Walk through Wren's **Old Court** for a view of the University Library, where 82 mi. of shelves hold books arranged by size rather than subject. *(Trinity Ln.* ☎ *333 200. Open daily 10am-4:30pm. £3, under 10 free.)*

CHRIST'S COLLEGE. Founded as "God's house" in 1448 and renamed in 1505, Christ's has since won fame for its **gardens** and its association with John Milton and Charles Darwin. Darwin's rooms (unmarked and closed to visitors) were on G staircase in First Court. **New Court,** on King St., is one of Cambridge's most modern structures, with symmetrical concrete walls and dark windows. Bowing to pressure from aesthetically offended Cantabrigians, the college built a wall to block the view of the building from all sides except the inner courtyard. *(St. Andrews St.* ☎ *334 900. Gardens open term-time daily 9am-4:30pm; in summer 9:30am-noon. Fellows' garden open term-time M-F 9:30am-noon and 2-4pm; in summer M-F 9:30am-noon. Free.)*

JESUS COLLEGE. Jesus College has preserved an enormous amount of medieval work on its grounds. Beyond the walled walk called the "Chimney" lies a three-sided courtyard fringed with flowers. Through the arch on the right sit the remains of a gloomy medieval nunnery. *(Jesus Ln.* ☎ *339 339. Courtyard open daily 9am-8pm.)*

MAGDALENE COLLEGE. Located within a 15th-century Benedictine hostel, Magdalene (MAUD-lin), was the occasional home of Christian allegorist and Oxford man C.S. Lewis. **Pepys Library,** in the second court, displays the noted statesman and prolific diarist's collections. The college did not accept women until 1988. *(Magdalene St.* ☎ *332 100. Library open Easter-Aug. M-Sa 11:30am-12:30pm and 2:30-3:30pm; Sept.- Easter M-Sa 2:30-3:30pm. Free.)*

SMALLER COLLEGES. Thomas Gray wrote his *Elegy in a Country Churchyard* while staying in **Peterhouse College,** the smallest college, founded in 1294. *(Trumpington St.* ☎ *338 200.)* The modern brick pastiche of **Robinson College** is the newest. In 1977, local self-made man David Robinson founded it for the bargain price of £17 million, the largest single gift ever received by the university. *(Across the river on Grange Rd.* ☎ *339 100.)* **Corpus Christi College,** founded in 1352 by the townspeople, contains the oldest courtyard in Cambridge, aptly named Old Court and unaltered since its enclosure. The library has a huge collection of Anglo-Saxon manuscripts. Alums include Sir Francis Drake and Christopher Marlowe. *(Trumpington St.* ☎ *338 000.)* The 1347 **Pembroke College** holds the earliest work of Sir Christopher Wren and counts Edmund Spenser, Ted Hughes, and Eric Idle among its grads. *(Next to Corpus Christi.* ☎ *338 100.)* A chapel designed by Wren dominates the front court of **Emmanuel College,** known as "Emma." John Harvard, benefactor of a different university, studied here and is commemorated in a stained-glass window in the chapel. *(St. Andrews St.* ☎ *334 200.)* **Gonville and Caius** (KEYS) **College** was founded twice, once in 1348 by Edmund Gonville and again in 1557 by John Keys, who chose to use the Latin form of his name. *(Trinity St.* ☎ *332 400.)*

MUSEUMS AND CHURCHES

▨**FITZWILLIAM MUSEUM.** The museum fills an immense Neoclassical building, built in 1875 to house Viscount Fitzwilliam's impressive collections. Egyptian, Chinese, Japanese, Middle Eastern, and Greek antiquities downstairs are joined by 16th-century German armor. Upstairs, galleries feature works by Reubens, Monet, Van Gogh, and Picasso. *(Trumpington St.* ☎ *332 900. Open Tu-Sa 10am-5pm, Su noon-5pm. Call about lunchtime and evening concerts. Suggested donation £3.)*

OTHER MUSEUMS. For those with a green thumb, the Botanic Garden displays over 8000 plant species and was opened in 1846 by John Henslow, Darwin's mentor. *(*☎ *336 265. Open daily Apr.-Sept. 10am-6pm, Feb.-Mar. and Oct. 10am-5pm, Jan. and Nov.-Dec. 10am-4pm. £3, concession £2.50.)* **Kettle's Yard,** at the corner of Castle and Northampton St., was founded by former Tate curator Jim Ede and displays extensive early 20th-century art. *(*☎ *352 124; www.kettlesyard.org.uk. House open Apr.-Sept. Tu-Su 1:30-4:30pm; Oct.-Mar. Tu-Su 2-4pm. Gallery open Tu-Su 11:30am-5pm. Free.)* The **Scott Polar Research Institute,** Lensfield Rd., commemorates arctic expeditions with photos and memorabilia. *(*☎ *336 540; www.spri.cam.ac.uk. Open Tu-Sa 2:30-4pm. Free.)*

CHURCHES. The **Round Church (Holy Sepulchre),** where Bridge St. meets St. John's St., is one of five surviving circular churches in England and the second oldest building in Cambridge, predating even the university. Built in 1130, it is based on the pattern of the Holy Sepulchre in Jerusalem. *(☎311 602. Open M and Su 1-5pm, Tu-Sa 10am-5pm. £1.50, students and children free. Tours W 11am, Su 2:30pm. £3.50.)* The only older building is **St. Benet's,** a rough Saxon church on Benet St., built in 1025. *(☎353 903. Open daily 8am-6pm. Free.)* The tower of **Great St. Mary's Church,** off King's Parade, gives views of the broad greens and the colleges. Pray that the 12 bells don't ring while you're ascending the 123 tightly packed spiral steps. *(Tower open M-Sa 9:30am-5:30pm, Su 12:30-5pm. £2.30, children £1, families £5. Church free.)*

🎵 🎭 ENTERTAINMENT AND FESTIVALS

🚣 PUNTING

Punting on the Cam is as traditional and obligatory as afternoon tea. Touristy and overrated? Maybe, but it's a still a blast. Punters take two routes—from Magdalene Bridge to Silver St. or from Silver St. to Grantchester. The shorter, busier, and more interesting first route passes the colleges and the Backs. To propel your boat, thrust the pole behind the boat into the riverbed and rotate the pole in your hands as you push forward. Punt-bombing—jumping from bridges into the river alongside a punt to tip it—is an art form. Some more ambitious punters climb out midstream, scale a bridge while their boat passes underneath, and jump back down from the other side. Be careful of bridge-top pole-stealers. You can rent at **Scudamore's,** Silver St. Bridge (☎359 750; www.scudamores.com; M-F £14 per hr. plus a £70 deposit, Sa-Su £16 per hr. plus a £70 deposit. MC/V). Student-punted tours (about £12) are another option.

THEATER & CINEMA

The **Arts Box Office** (☎503 333; open M-Sa noon-8pm), around the corner from the TIC on Pea's Hill, handles ticket sales for the **Arts Theatre,** which shows musicals, dramas, and pantomime. The **ADC Theatre** (Amateur Dramatic Club), Park St. (☎359 547), offers student-produced plays, term-time movies, and a folk festival during the summer months. The **Corn Exchange,** at the corner of Wheeler St. and Corn Exchange St. across from the TIC, is a popular venue for concerts. (☎357 851. Box office open M-Sa 10am-6pm, until 9pm on performance days; Su 6-9pm on performance days only. £10-30, concessions available.) The **Cambridge Shakespeare Festival** (www.cambridgeshakespeare.com), in association with the festival at Oxford, features plays throughout July and August. Tickets (£12, concessions £9) are available at the door and from the City Centre Box Office at the Corn Exchange. Independent and foreign-language films play at the **Arts Picture House,** 38-39 St. Andrews St. (☎551 242; www.picturehouse.co.uk. £6, students £5.)

MAY WEEK

May Week is actually in June—you would think that all those bright Cambridge students would understand a calendar. A celebration of the end of the term, the week is crammed with concerts, plays, and balls followed by recuperative riverside breakfasts and 5am punting. The boat clubs compete in races known as the **bumps.** Crews attempt to ram the boat in front before being bumped from behind. The celebration includes **Footlights Revue,** a series of comedy skits by current undergrads. Past performers have included future *Monty Python* stars John Cleese and Eric Idle. Guests can partake in the festivities for a mere £250.

FESTIVALS

Midsummer Fair, dating from the 16th century, fills the Midsummer Common with carnival rides and wholesome fun for five days during the 3rd week of June (call

☎457 555 for specific dates and hours; www.cambridge-summer.co.uk). The free **Strawberry Fair** (www.strawberry-fair.org), on the first Saturday in June, attracts a crowd with food, music, and body piercing. **Summer in the City** (www.cambridge-summer.co.uk) keeps Cambridge buzzing with a series of concerts and special exhibits culminating in a huge weekend celebration, the **Cambridge Folk Festival** (☎357 851; www.cambridgefolkfestival.co.uk) on the last weekend of July. World renowned musicians—with past performers such as James Taylor and Elvis Costello—gather for folk, jazz, and blues in Cherry Hinton Hall. Book tickets (about £43) well in advance; camping on the grounds is an additional £5-18.

DAYTRIPS FROM CAMBRIDGE

GRANTCHESTER

To reach Grantchester Meadows from Cambridge, take the marked path following the river. Grantchester village lies 1 mi. from the meadows; ask the way or follow the blue bike path signs (1½hr. by foot from Cambridge). If you have the energy to paddle your way, rent a punt or canoe. You can also hop on Stagecoach #18 or 18A (9-11 per day, round-trip £2.70).

In 1912, poet Rupert Brooke wrote, "Grantchester! Ah Grantchester! There's peace and holy quiet there." His words hold true today, as Grantchester is still a mecca for Cambridge literary types. The peaceful walk along the Cam is a refreshing break from the university's intensity. Brooke's home at the Old Vicarage is now owned by bad-boy novelist Lord Jeffrey Archer and is closed to the public. The 14th-century **Parish Church of St. Andrew and St. Mary,** on Millway, is weathered and intimate. (☎01223 840 460. Free.) Head to the idyllic ⚑**Orchard Tea Gardens ❶**, 45 Millway, once a haunt of the "neo-Pagans," a Grantchester offshoot of the famous Bloomsbury Group, and still a popular breakfast stop for students. Start your morning with scones (£2) and end your day with one of the occasional summer plays (☎01223 845 788; event schedule available at www.orchard-grantchester.com. Open daily 9:30am-5:30pm). The main village pub, the **Rupert Brooke ❷**, 2 Broadway, is striving to improve the reputation of British cuisine. It also has a large beer garden overlooking Grantchester meadows. (☎840 295; www.therupertbrooke.com. Open M-F 11:30am-2:30pm, Sa 11:30am-11pm, Su noon-10:30pm.)

ANGLESEY ABBEY

6 mi. northeast of Cambridge on the B1102 (signposted from A14). Bus #10 runs from Drummer St. (30min., 2 per hr.); ask to be let off at Lode Crossroads. ☎810 080. House open Apr.-Oct. W-Su and bank holidays 1-5pm. Gardens open Apr.-Oct. W-Su and bank holidays 10:30am-5:30pm; last admission 4:30pm. £9. Garden and mill only £5.

Northeast of Cambridge, 12th-century Anglesey Abbey has been remodeled to house the priceless exotica of the first Lord Fairhaven. The abbey has a collection of over 50 clocks, including the mesmerizing Congreve rolling ball clock in the library. If you have the time (or really need to find some), make your own scavenger hunt and try to find them all. After contemplating the 7000 volumes on the bookshelves, stroll through the 98 acres of gardens, where trees punctuate lines of clipped hedges and manicured lawns.

AUDLEY END AND SAFFRON WALDEN

Trains leave Cambridge for Audley End (15min., 3 per hr., round-trip £5). ☎01799 522 399. House open Apr.-Sept. W-F and Su 11am-5pm; Sa 11am-3pm. Grounds open Apr.-Sept. W-Su 10am-6pm; Mar. and Oct. W-Su 10am-5pm. Last admission 1hr. before close. £9.20, concessions £7. Grounds only £5/4. Free 1hr. guided tours, 10 per day. TIC ☎01799 510 444. Open Easter-Aug. M-Sa 9:30am-5:30pm, Su 10:30am-1pm; Sept.-Oct. M-Sa 9:30am-5:30pm; Nov.-Mar. M-Sa 10am-5pm.

LOCAL LEGEND

DON'T SNICKER, IT'S SNOOKER

Admit it—you thought that snooker was just another kind of billiards. Well, you were right. But the popular pub and parlor game is also much more. Here are some basic facts and phrases that will have you sounding like a pro in no time:

The object of the game is to pot 15 **red balls** and six **colored balls.** Each ball has a point value, and the team or person who pots the most points wins. The green fuzzy stuff covering the table is called **baize.** If a ball enters a pocket it is **potted.** The white cue ball is **snookered** if a direct shot to all of the balls on the table is obstructed.

The game was popular with British colonists in India in the late 19th century. When an early player missed a shot, his opponent called him a snooker, a military term for a rookie cadet. The name stuck and traveled back to Britain with the game.

Today, nearly all snooker world champions come from Britain and Ireland. Most sport clever nicknames, like Beckham of the Baize or ☒ **The Sheriff of Pottingham.**

The 2008 Snooker World Champion-ships will be held in Sheffield from April 19 to May 5 at the Crucible Theatre. For more info, visit www.worldsnooker.com.

The magnificent Jacobean hall is only a quarter of Audley End's former size—it once extended down to the river, where part of the Cam was rerouted into an artificial lake. The grand halls display cases of stuffed critters, including some extinct species, amid paintings by Holbein and Canaletto. One mile east of Audley End is the town of **Saffron Walden,** best known for the "pargetting" (plaster molding) of its Tudor buildings. The town holds a Victorian hedge maze as well as England's largest turf maze, located on the town common. The **Tourist Information Centre** is on Market Sq. Rest at the **YHA hostel ❶,** 1 Myddylton Pl. (☎0870 770 6014. Lockout 10am-5pm. Curfew 11pm. Open July-Aug. daily; Apr.-June and Sept.-Oct. Tu-Sa; Mar. F-Sa. £12, under 18 £9. MC/V.)

ELY
☎01353

The prosperous town of Ely (EEL-ee) was an island until steam power drained the surrounding fenlands in the early 1800s, creating a flat, reed-covered region of rich farmland. Legend has it that the city got its name when St. Dunstan transformed local monks into eels for their lack of piety. A more likely story is that "Elig" (Isle of Eels) was named for the bountiful slitherers that infested the surrounding waters—they were once so numerous that taxes were payable in eels. Today, Ely remains proud of its eel-inspired heritage: local restaurants offer the delicacy straight from the Great River Ouse, Eel Day celebrates the city's history, and the "Eel Heritage Walk" snakes through all of the city's major sights.

🖳🚊 TRANSPORTATION AND PRACTICAL INFORMATION. Ely is the junction for **trains** (☎08457 484 950) between London (1¼hr., 2 per hr., £20.20) and various points in East Anglia, including Cambridge (15min., 3 per hr., round-trip £3.50) and Norwich (1hr., 2 per hr., £10.80). Cambus **buses** (☎01223 423 554) #9, X9, and 12 leave from Market St. to Cambridge (50min., 1 per hr., £3.70). **Walking** from Cambridge to Ely is also possible, offering a beautiful 17 mi. trek through the flat fens. Ask at the TIC in Cambridge or Ely for a copy of *The Fen Rivers Way* (£2).

Ely's two major streets—**High Street** and **Market Street**—run parallel to the length of the cathedral. To reach the cathedral from the train station, walk up Station Rd. which changes to Back Hill and then to The Gallery. Oliver Cromwell's house is the current home of the **Tourist Information Centre,** 29 St. Mary's St., which books rooms for £2 plus a 10% deposit; call at least two days ahead. (☎662 062. Open Apr.-Oct. daily 10am-5:30pm; Nov.-Mar. M-F and Su 11am-4pm,

Sa 10am-5pm). Other services include: **police,** Nutholt Ln. (☎ 01223 358 966); Prince of Wales **Hospital,** Lynn Rd. (☎ 652 000); **Internet** access at the **library,** 6 The Cloisters, just off Market Pl. (☎ 616 158; Internet 50p per 10min.; open Tu-W and F 10am-5pm, Th 9:30am-8pm, Sa 9:30am-4pm); and the **post office,** 19-21 High St. (☎ 669 946; open M-F 9am-5:30pm, Sa 9am-1pm). **Post Code:** CB7 4LQ.

▎▎◖◗ ACCOMMODATIONS AND FOOD. Ely has few single rooms—your best bet is the TIC accommodations booking service. **The Post House ❸,** 12a Egremont St., is a family home close to the city center with two singles and two doubles. (☎ 667 184; www.posthouse-ely.co.uk. Singles £25; doubles £50, ensuite £55. Cash only.) Find spacious, ensuite rooms in an Edwardian house at **57 Lynn Road ❸,** just steps away from the cathedral. (☎ 744 662. Doubles and twins £28.50 per person.)

Many shops close on Tuesday afternoons, as they have for centuries. Stock up on provisions at the **market** in Market Pl. (Open Th and Sa 8am-3pm.) Tesco **supermarket,** Angel Drove, is located right next to the train station and has **ATMs** outside. (☎ 08456 779 256. Open 24hr. M 8am-Sa 10pm, Su 10am-9pm. AmEx/MC/V.) Don't miss the Tea Guild's "Top Tearoom of 2007," ▨**Peacocks Tearoom ❶,** 65 Waterside, near the Babylon Gallery on the River Ouse. The small shop has over 50 varieties of teas (£2) and sweet and savory snacks for £4-7. (☎ 661 100; www.peacockstearoom.co.uk. Open W-Su 10:30am-5pm.) Although the River no longer oozes eels, the **Old Fire Engine House ❸,** 25 St. Mary's St., often features the local delicacy on their constantly changing menu. Appropriately enough, smoking is not allowed. (☎ 662 582. Entrees £15.50. Lighter fare £6-10. Open M-Sa 10:30-11:30am, 12:30-2pm, 3:30-5:30pm, and 7:30-9pm; Su 12:30-2pm and 4-5:30pm. MC/V.) The **Steeplegate ❶,** 16-18 High St., serves snacks, light meals, and tea (£2-5) in two rooms built over a medieval undercroft next to the cathedral. (☎ 664 731. Open June-Oct. M-Sa 10am-5pm; Nov.-May M-F 10am-4:30pm and Sa 10am-5pm. MC/V.) Affordable Indian restaurants line Backhill St.

◖◗ SIGHTS. Let the tower of ▨**Ely Cathedral** guide you to the city center. When lit, it can be seen for miles. The Saxon princess St. Etheldreda founded a monastery on the site in AD 673, early Norman masons took a century to construct the nave, and Victorian artists painted the ceiling and completed the stained glass. The **Octagon,** an altar topped by the lantern tower, replaced the original tower, which collapsed in 1322. The eight-sided cupola shoots up vertically from the domed ceiling's center, supported by eight stone pillars. Don't overlook the 215 ft. tiled **floor maze.** (☎ 667 735. Open Apr.-Sept. daily 7am-7pm; Oct.-Mar. M-F 7:30am-6pm, Su 7:30am-5pm. Cathedral £5.20, concessions £4.50. Evensong M-Sa 5:30pm, Su 3:45pm. Free guided tours. Octagon tours Apr.-Oct. 3 per day, Nov.-Mar. weekends only, call ahead. £5, concessions £3.50; with cathedral entry £3.20/2.50. West Tower tours Apr.-Oct. subject to guide availability £3.50/2.50; call ahead. Book tower tours in advance.) In the brilliant ▨**Stained Glass Museum,** in the Cathedral, visitors take a closer look at eight centuries of kaleidoscopic glass art. One hundred exquisite pieces detail the history of the art form. (☎ 660 347; www.stainedglassmuseum.com. Open Easter-Oct. M-F 10:30am-5pm, Sa 10:30am-5:30pm, Su noon-6pm; Nov.-Easter M-Sa 10:30am-5pm, Su noon-4:30pm. Last admission 30min. before close. £3.50, concessions £2.50, families £7. Museum and cathedral £8, concessions £7.30. Audio tour £1.) At the **brass rubbing center** in the cathedral, visitors can use chalk and paper to rub copies of brass engravings. (☎ 660 345. Materials £2-6.50. Open M-Sa 10:30am-4pm, Su noon-3pm.)

For an architectural tour of Ely, follow the path outlined in the TIC's free *Eel Trail* pamphlet, which also notes artwork related to the eel. **Oliver Cromwell's House,** 29 St. Mary's St., holds wax figures, 17th-century decor, and Cromwell's "haunted" bedroom. Fish and chips will look positively gourmet after a perusal of

Lady Cromwell's recipe for eel pie with oysters. (☎662 062. Open Apr.-Oct. daily 10am-5:30pm; Nov.-Mar. M-Sa 10am-5pm, Su 11am-4pm. £4, concessions £3.45, children £2.70.) **Ely Museum,** at the Bishop's Gaol on the corner of Market St. and Lynn Rd., gives the history of the fenland city. (☎666 655. Open in summer M-Sa 10:30am-5pm, Su 1-5pm; in winter M and W-Sa 10:30am-4pm, Su 1-4pm. Last admission 30min. before close. £3, concessions £2.50.)

NORFOLK

KING'S LYNN   ☎01553

King's Lynn was one of England's foremost 16th-century ports. Five hundred years later, the once-mighty current of the Great Ouse (OOZE) River has slowed considerably, reflecting the pace of the sleepy town. The dockside city's Germanic look is inspired by former trading partners such as Hamburg and Bremen. Although the sights are underwhelming, the town makes a perfect stopover for hikers and tourists exploring the region.

TRANSPORTATION AND PRACTICAL INFORMATION. King's Lynn's two main streets are **High Street** and **Broad Street** (which becomes Tower St.). These two roads are parallel, intersected perpendicularly by **New Conduit,** and are pedestrian only, as is much of the city center. The bus and train stations are near High St. **Trains** (☎08457 484 950) leave from the station on Blackfriars Rd. to: Norwich (2 hrs. via Ely, every hr., £15.10), Cambridge (50min., every hr., £8.20), London King's Cross (1½hr., every hr., £28.20), and Peterborough (1½hr., every hr., £9.70). **Buses** arrive at the Vancouver Centre in front of Pedlar's Hall (office open M-F 9am-5pm). First Eastern Counties (☎01603 660 553) bus X1 travels from Vancouver Centre to Norwich (1½hr., 2 per hr., £4), and Peterborough (1¼hr., 2 per hr., round-trip £7). National Express (☎08705 808 080) runs to London (4hr., 1 per day, £14.20). For daytrips from King's Lynn to Hunstanton, Sandringham, or Castle Rising take local buses #40, 41, or 41A, which leave regularly from Vancouver Station.

The **Tourist Information Centre,** in the Custom House on the corner of King St. and Purfleet Quay, 10min. from the train station, books rooms for a 10% deposit and supplies bus timetables and free maps. Take a left out of the station and a right onto Blackfriars St., which becomes New Conduit St. and then Purfleet St. (☎763 044. Open Apr.-Sept. M-Sa 10am-5pm, Su noon-5pm; Oct.-Mar. M-Sa 10:30am-4pm, Su noon-4pm.) Buy National Express tickets at the station or from **West Norfolk Travel,** 2 King St. (☎772 910. Open M-F 8am-5:30pm; Sa 8am-4pm. AmEx/MC/V.) Other services include: **police,** at the corner of St. James and London Rd. (☎691 211); the **hospital,** on Gayton Rd. (☎613 613); **banks** on High St., including Lloyds, 23 High St., with 24hr. **ATMs** outside (☎0845 300 0000; open M-Tu and Th-F 9am-5pm, W 10am-5pm, Sa 9am-1pm); Boots **pharmacy** on High St. (open M-Sa 8:30am-5:30pm, Su 10am-4pm); **laundry** at 20 St. James St. (☎767 164; wash £2, dry £1; open M-Su 7am-9:30pm); free **Internet** access at the **library,** London Rd. across from The Walks (☎772 568; open M, W, F 9am-8pm; Tu, Th, Sa 9am-5pm); and the **post office** at Baxter's Plain on the corner of Broad and New Conduit St. (☎08457 223 344; open M-F 9am-5:30pm, Sa 9am-12:30pm). **Post Code:** PE30HB.

ACCOMMODATIONS AND FOOD. Budget accommodations in King's Lynn are scarce. The quayside **HI/YHA King's Lynn ❶,** College Ln., a 10min. walk from the train and bus stations in King's Lynn, occupies part of 16th-century

Thoresby College. The rooms are small and basic, but this is the best budget option in town. (☎0870 770 5902. Breakfast buffet £4.20. Open July-Aug. daily; Easter-June M-Tu and F-Su; Sept. M-Tu and Su. Reception open from 5pm. Call ahead for availability. Dorms and singles £13, under 18 £9. MC/V.) Most **B&Bs** are a 10min. walk east of the train station, away from the River Ouse. Several options line Gaywood Rd. and Tennyson Ave. Eight dainty rooms stocked with homemade biscuits await at the Victorian **Fairlight Lodge ❸**, 79 Goodwins Rd. (☎762 234; www.fairlightlodge-online.co.uk. Full breakfast included. Singles £27-32; doubles and twins £43-49. Discount for 2 nights or more. Cash only.) The **Maranatha Guest House ❸**, 115-117 Gaywood Rd. has large, sun-lit rooms near many pubs and eateries. (☎774 596. Most rooms ensuite. Singles £25; twin £40; ensuite £44. MC/V.) Many King's Lynn restaurants close in the middle of the day; even more take Sundays off. Supermarkets congregate around the Vancouver Centre. For fresh fruit, visit the large **Tuesday Market Place,** on the north end of High St., or try the **Saturday Market Place** on the south end. For sandwiches (£4) and creamy smoothies like mango-orange or passionfruit (£2), try **Norbury's Deli ❷**, 21 Tower St. (☎762 804. Open M-Sa 9:30am-5pm. MC/V.) Pancetta and pasta await at **Antonio's Wine Bar ❷**, an inexpensive Italian bistro at Baxter's Plain, on the corner of Tower St. and Blackfriars St. (☎772 324. 2-course lunch £5. Entrees £5-7.50. Open Tu-Sa noon-3pm and 6:30-11pm. Food served until 9:30pm. MC/V.) The **Thai Orchid ❷**, 33-39 St. James St., offers authentic Thai dishes for £6-9. Try their bargain "quick lunch" specials starting from £4. (☎767 013. Open T-Th noon-2pm and 6-11:30pm, F noon-2pm and 5:30pm-midnight, Sa noon-2pm and 6pm-midnight, Su noon-2pm and 6-10:30pm. MC/V.)

◖◗ **SIGHTS AND ENTERTAINMENT.** A leisurely walk through the streets lets you see all of King Lynn's main attractions in a day. Take the *King's Lynn Town Walk* booklet (50p at the TIC) with you or head to the **Old Gaol House,** the starting point for 1½hr. guided tours of the town (June-Sept. Tu and F-Sa 2pm; Oct. Sa 2pm; £3, concessions £2.50, children £1). Start your walk at the **Tales of the Old Gaol House,** Saturday Market Pl., the former King's Lynn police station. The 200-year-old cells hold role-playing "criminals," and the Regalia Room displays treasures in the undercroft. Take home souvenir fingerprints or try out the stocks for a taste of 17th-century justice. (☎774 297. Open Apr.-Oct. M-Sa 10am-5pm; Nov.-Mar. Tu-Sa 10am-4pm. Last admission 1hr. before close. £2.80, concessions £2.45, children £2.) Steps away is **St. Margaret's Church,** also on Saturday Market Pl., built in 1101. (☎772 858; www.stmargaretkingslynn.org.uk. Free.) **Greyfriars Tower** sits in the center of town, surrounded by the **Tower Gardens** and marked paths through the greenery. Walk up Market St. to the recently reopened **Lynn Museum,** which displays all you'd ever want to know (and more) about King's Lynn history. (☎775 001. Open Tu-Sa 10am-5pm. Free.) The **Town House Museum of Lynn Life,** 46 Queen St., showcases doll-sized reconstructions of rooms from medieval kitchens to 1950s living rooms. (☎773 450. Open May-Sept. M-Sa 10am-5pm; Oct.-Apr. M-Sa 10am-4pm. £3, concessions £2.40, children £1.60, families £8.) The **Corn Exchange** at Tuesday Market Pl. sells tickets for music, dance, and theater events. (☎764 864. Open M-Sa 10am-6pm; performance nights and Su 1hr. prior to show. Shows usually 7:30 or 8pm.) Near Tuesday Market Pl., the 15th-century **Guildhall of St. George,** 27-29 King St., is said to be the last surviving building where Shakespeare appeared in one of his own plays. Inside, find the auditorium and the **King's Lynn Arts Centre.** (☎764 864. Open M-F 10am-2pm. Free.) King's Lynn comes alive during the last two weeks of July, when the Guildhall brings the **King's Lynn Festival** to town. The festival presents international talent from musicians, operas, ballets, puppet shows, and films. Get schedules at the TIC or the Festival Office, 5 Thoresby College, Queen St. (Info ☎767 557, tickets 764 864; www.kingslynnfestival.org.uk. Box

EAST ANGLIA

office open M-Sa 10am-6pm. Tickets £3-32. Standby tickets available 30min. prior to performance for £5. MC/V, plus £1 surcharge.) During the second week of July, the streets of Tuesday Market Pl. are overtaken by live entertainment and fireworks during free **Festival Too.** (☎09067 362 557, calls £1 per min.; www.festival-too.co.uk). Find further information at the TIC or the Corn Exchange.

▌ DAYTRIPS FROM KING'S LYNN

SANDRINGHAM. Get a taste of royal living at the 60-acre Sandringham estate. The house has been a royal country retreat since 1862; the final version was built in 1870 by the Prince and Princess of Wales and has since been home to four generations of monarchs. The main rooms feature delicate tapestries and King Edward II's collection of weaponry. Highlights include cars owned by Edward VII in 1900, Prince Charles in 1990, and Princes William and Harry today. Sandringham closes for one week in July; ask the King's Lynn TIC or call for exact dates. *(10 mi. north of King's Lynn. First Eastern Counties bus #411 arrives from King's Lynn. 25 min.; M-Sa 9 per day, Su every hr.; round-trip £3.80. ☎01553 612 908; www.sandringhamestate.co.uk. Open daily Apr.-Sept. 11am-4:45pm, Oct. 11am-3pm; museum and gardens open daily Apr.-Sept. 11am-5pm; Oct. 11am-4pm. £9, concessions £7, children £5, families £23. Museum and gardens only £5.50/4.50/3.50/14.50. Guided garden tours F and Sa 11am and 2pm; £2.)*

CASTLE RISING. Queen Isabella, the "She-Wolf of France," was imprisoned here after she plotted the murder of her husband, Edward II. It remains one of the largest, most intact castles in the country, with several levels of steep, narrow passageways. An informative audio tour details tidbits of history along the way, and the castle's defensive earthworks (up to 120 ft. high) provide beautiful views. *(First Eastern Counties buses #41 and 41A run from King's Lynn. 15min.; M-Sa 17 per day, Su 8 per day; round-trip £3.40. ☎01553 631 330; www.castlerising.com. Open Apr.-Sept. daily 10am-6pm; Oct. daily 10am-6pm or dusk; Nov.-Mar. W-Su 10am-4pm. Admission and audio tour £3.85, concessions £3.10, children £2.20.)*

HOUGHTON HALL. Built in the 1720s for Robert Walpole, England's first prime minister, Houghton Hall is a magnificent example of Palladian architecture. A museum displaying 20,000 model soldiers in battle formations will make any war fanatic or seven-year-old boy's day. Five acres of gardens are only the beginning—the hall rests on 4500 acres of estate with over 600 deer. *(13 mi. northeast of King's Lynn and 10 mi. southwest of Fakenham, off the A148 toward Cromer. Easily reached by car; otherwise, take the X8 bus and ask the driver to stop at Houghton Hall, then follow signs for 1 mi. (40min., 6 per day, round-trip £3.70). ☎01485 528 569; www.houghtonhall.com. Grounds and museum open Easter-Sept. W-Th and Su 11am-5:30pm; house open Easter-Sept. W-Th and Su 1:30-5pm. Last entry 4:30pm. £8, children £3, families £20. Grounds only £5.)*

THE NORTHERN NORFOLK COAST

The northern Norfolk Coast is a tranquil expanse of British shoreline full of untamed beaches, salt marshes, and boggy bays punctuated only by the occasional windmill or mansion. Those with a week to spare can traverse the linked 93 mi. of the **Norfolk Coast Path** and **Peddar's Way** (p. 317), two relatively easy treks. The Peddar's Way, an old Roman road to the coast, begins in **Knettishall Heath Country Park,** extending through **Little Cressingham, North Peckenham,** and the medieval ruins of **Castle Acre,** meeting the Norfolk Coast Path between Hunstanton and Brancaster. The Norfolk Coast Path begins 16 mi. north of King's Lynn at Hunstanton, stretches east to **Wells-next-the-Sea, Sheringham,** and the **Norfolk Broads** (p. 336) before finishing in **Cromer.** The trail and its villages are also fine daytrips from both Norwich and King's Lynn. The **Norfolk Coast Hopper** (☎0870 608 2608) follows the coastline and makes numerous stops between Hunstanton and Sheringham (1½hr.; in summer every 2hr., in winter less frequent; all-day ticket £5). **Searles** runs sea tours from Hunstanton Central Promenade (☎01485 534 444, www.sea-tours.co.uk; £7-12, children £3.50-6; book in advance) and **Skyride Balloons** at Clarkes Lane in King's Lynn (☎07000 110 210; 4hr., £169 per person) offers unbeatable aerial views. The highlight of the coast is ☒**Blakeney Point Seal Colony.** Although the colony is accessible by a 4 mi. footpath from Cley-next-the-Sea, the seals would rather their admirers visit by boat. **Bishop's Boats** runs trips from March to October from Blakeney Quay. (☎01263 740 753; www.bishopsboats.co.uk. 1-3 trips per day. £7, children £4. Book in advance at ☎08000 740 754.) More boat trips to Blakeney run from Morston Quay. In Hunstanton, on the Southern Promenade, the **Hunstanton Sea Life Sanctuary and Aquarium** rehabilitates injured and abandoned seals. (☎01485 533 576; www.sealsanctuary.co.uk. Open daily July-Aug. 10am-5pm; Apr.-June and Sept.-Oct. 10am-4pm; Jan.-Mar. and Nov.-Dec. 10am-3pm. £9.50, concessions £6.50.) For a taste of luxury, visit 18th-century **Holkham Hall,** 2 mi. west of Wells-next-the-Sea, the present-day home of the Earl of Leicester. The **Bygones Museum** has over 4000 knick-knacks from the family's past. (☎01328 710 227. Open June-Sept. M and Th-Su 1-5pm. Hall and museum £10, children £5, families £25. Hall only £6.50, children £3.25. Museum only £5/2.50.)

The Norfolk Coast is an easy daytrip from King's Lynn and Norwich. Hunstanton, at the western edge, is the best base. **Buses** #40, 41, and 41A run from Vancouver Centre in King's Lynn to Hunstanton (45min.; M-Sa 2 per hr., Su every hr.; single £3). For details on the Northern Norfolk Coast, maps, and bus schedules, consult the Hunstanton **Tourist Information Centre,** Town Hall, The Green. (☎01485 532 610. Open daily Apr.-Sept. 10am-5pm; Oct.-Mar. 10:30am-4pm.) *Walking the Peddar's Way* and *Norfolk Coast Path with Weavers Way* (£2.70) are available at the TIC and include accommodations listings. On the coast, Hunstanton's **YHA hostel ❷,** 15 Avenue Rd., is a 5min. walk from the bus station. Take Sandringham Rd. uphill, then turn right on Avenue Rd. (☎01485 532 061. TV lounge. Breakfast £4. Open Apr.-Oct. W-Sa. Dorms £14, under 18 £10. MC/V.) For a picnic by the beach, grab takeaway toasties (£3) at **Tina's Sandwich Bar,** Le Strange Ct. Unit 2, The Green. (☎535 298. Open M-F 9am-4:30pm, Sa-Su 10am-5:30pm. Cash only.)

NORWICH   ☎01603

The dizzying streets of Norwich (NOR-idge) wind outward from the Norman castle, past the cathedral, and to the scattered fragments of the 14th-century city wall. Although Norwich retains the hallmarks of an ancient city, a university and active art community give it a modern feel. The hum of "England's city in the country" is still going strong, with a daily market almost a millennium old thriving alongside busy art galleries, roadside cafes, and nightlife.

▐ TRANSPORTATION

Easily accessible by bus, coach, or train, Norwich makes a logical base for touring both urban and rural East Anglia, particularly the Norfolk Broads.

Trains: Station at the corner of Riverside and Thorpe Rd., 15min. from the city center (bus 90p). Ticket window open M-Sa 4:45am-8:45pm, Su 6:45am-8:30pm. Trains to: **Bury St. Edmunds** (2hr., every hr., £10.50); **Great Yarmouth** (30min., every hr., £5); **London Liverpool Street** (2½hr., 2 per hr., £37); **Peterborough** (1½hr., every hr., £18.50).

Buses: Station (☎660 553) on Surrey St., off St. Stephens St. Open M-F 8am-6pm, Sa 9am-5:15pm. National Express (☎08705 808 080) runs to **London** (3hr., 5 per day,

£14.60). First Eastern Counties (☎08456 020 121) X1 travels to **King's Lynn** (2hr., every 30min., £4) and **Peterborough** (3hr., £9). **Network tickets** give 1 day of unlimited travel on First Eastern Counties (£10, children £6.50, seniors £5, families £20).

Taxis: Five Star (☎0800 575 575). 24hr.

✦🔋 ORIENTATION AND PRACTICAL INFORMATION

Although the sights are fairly close together, Norwich's twisting streets can cause confusion. Keep a map handy and be wary of deceptive side alleyways that are often hard to spot.

Tourist Information Centre: The Forum, Millennium Plain, Bethel St. (☎727 927; www.visitnorwich.co.uk). Sells mini-guides (50p), gives away the essential Norwich visitor map, and books rooms for a 10% deposit. Open Apr.-Oct. M-Sa 10am-6pm, Su 10:30am-4:30pm; Nov.-Mar. M-Sa 10am-5:30pm. Offers 1½hr. **walking tours** Apr.-Oct. £3, children £1.50.

Financial Services: Thomas Cook, 14 London St. (☎241 100). Open M-Sa 9am-5:30pm.

Launderette: Wash-In, 31b Thorpe Rd. (☎762 602), just after Stracey Rd. Wash £3, dry £2. Detergent 20p. Open M-F 9am-8pm, Sa 9am-7pm, Su 9am-6pm. Last wash 1hr. before close.

Pharmacy: Boots, Riverside Retail Park (☎662 894). Open M-F 9am-9pm, Sa 9am-6pm, Su 10:30am-4:30pm.

Police: Bethel St. (☎0845 456 4567). Open daily 8am-midnight.

Hospital: Norfolk and Norwich University Hospital, Colney Ln. (☎286 286), at the corner of Brunswick Rd. and St. Stephens Rd.

Internet Access: The city center has free Wi-Fi, with signal in most of the area surrounding the Forum. Check www.norfolkopenlink.com for a map. **No. 33 Cafe,** 33 Exchange St. (☎626 097). Free Wi-Fi. Open daily 8:30-6pm. At the **library** (☎774 774), next to Origins in the Forum, register for a simple "Internet only" user card and get free access on 20+ computers upstairs or at 6 "Express Terminals" downstairs. Open M and W-F 9am-9:30pm, Tu 10am-9:30pm, Sa 9am-10:30pm, Su 10:30am-4:30pm.

Post Office: Castle Mall (☎08457 223 344). **Bureau de change.** Open M and W-Sa 9am-5:30pm, Tu 9:30am-5:30pm. **Post Code:** NR1 3DD.

🔖 ACCOMMODATIONS

Several **B&Bs** (from £22) are located on **Stracey Road,** a 5min. walk from the train station. Turn right onto Thorpe Rd., walk two blocks from the bridge, and go right onto Stracey Rd. B&Bs also line **Earlham** and **Unthank Roads,** but they're at least 20min. west of downtown and farther from the train station (or take the #26 or 27 bus to Earlham Rd.). Also worth a try is **Dereham Road;** follow St. Benedict's St., which becomes Dereham.

▧ **The Abbey Hotel,** 16 Stracey Rd. (☎612 915), 5min. from the train station up Thorpe Rd. Free hot cocoa and chocolates in floral rooms. Owners make you feel right at home. Full breakfast included. Singles £29; ensuite doubles and twins £65. MC/V. ❸

Stracey Hotel, 2 Stracey Rd. (☎628 093). Sunny rooms in a large Victorian mansion. Super-soft beds and soothing tea. Conveniently located near the train station. Bar, snooker room, and TV lounge. Full English breakfast included. Singles £22, ensuite £28; twins £40; doubles £50. Cash only. ❷

Earlham Guest House, 147 Earlham Rd. (☎454 169; www.earlhamguesthouse.co.uk). Take bus #26 or 27 from city center to The Mitre bus stop or walk 15min. across town to a residential neighborhood near the University of East Anglia. Rooms with TV. Full breakfast included. Singles £25-28; doubles £46. AmEx/MC/V. ❸

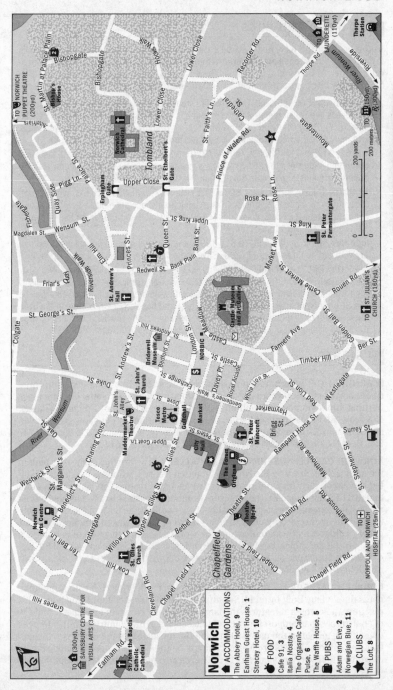

EAST ANGLIA

Norwich

▲ ACCOMMODATIONS
The Abbey Hotel, **9**
Eartham Guest House, **1**
Stracey Hotel, **10**

◆ FOOD
Cafe 91, **3**
Italia Nostra, **4**
The Orgasmic Cafe, **7**
Pulse, **6**
The Waffle House, **5**

● PUBS
Adam and Eve, **2**
Norwegian Blue, **11**

★ CLUBS
The Loft, **8**

TO NORWICH PUPPET THEATRE (200yd)

St. Martin at Palace Plain
Bishopgate

Bishop's House

Bishopgate

Hooks Walk

Lower Close

Recorder Rd.

Thorpe Rd.

LAUNDERETTE (110yd)

Thorpe Station

Lower Close

River Wensum

Riverside

(150yd; R 300yd)

Mountergate

Whitefriars

Quay Side

Pigg Ln.

Palace St.

Erpingham Gate

Upper Close

Norwich Cathedral

Tombland

St. Ethelbert's Gate

St. Faith's Ln.

Cathedral St.

Prince of Wales Rd.

Rose St.

Rose Ln.

King St.

St. Peter Parmentergate

Magdalen St.

Wensum St.

Elm Hill

Riverside Walk

Friar's Quay

Princes St.

Queen St.

Upper King St.

Bank St.

Market Ave.

St. Andrew's Hall

Redwell St.

Bank Plain

Cattle Market St.

Rouen Rd.

St. George's St.

Colgate

Duke St.

St. Andrew's St.

St. Andrews Hill

Bedford St.

Bridewell Museum

NORBIC

London St.

Castle Meadow

Castle St.

Castle Museum and Art Gallery

Royal Arcade

Farmers Ave.

Timber Hill

Ber St.

Golden Ball St.

TO ST. JULIAN'S CHURCH (160yd)

River Wensum

Oak St.

St. John's Alley

St. John's Church

Maddermarket Theatre

Tesco Metro

Dove St.

Guildhall

Exchange St.

Gentleman's Walk

Davey Pl.

White Lion St.

Market

St. Peter's St.

Red Lion St.

Westlegate

Surrey St.

St. Margaret's St.

Charing Cross

Upper Goat Ln.

City Hall

St. Giles St.

St. Peter Mancroft

The Forum

Brigg St.

Rampant Horse St.

Haymarket

Malthouse Rd.

Westwick St.

St. Benedict's St.

Pottergate

Willow Ln.

Upper St. Giles St.

Bethel St.

Theatre St.

Theatre Royal

Chantry Rd.

St. Stephens St.

Malthouse Rd.

TO NORFOLK AND NORWICH HOSPITAL (25mi)

Norwich Arts Centre

Ten Bell Ln.

Cow Hill

St. Giles Church

Chapel Field N.

Chapelfield Gardens

Chapel Field E.

Chapel Field Rd.

Grapes Hill

Cleveland Rd.

Chapel Field Rd.

Cleveland Rd.

St. John the Baptist Catholic Cathedral

Eartham Rd.

TO SAINSBURY CENTRE FOR VISUAL ARTS (3mi)

(300yd)

0   200 meters
0   200 yards

🍴🍺 FOOD AND PUBS

In the heart of the city, just a stone's throw from the castle, is one of England's largest and oldest **open-air markets,** with a wide variety of fresh and organic produce. (Open M-Sa roughly 8:30am-4:30pm.) Tesco Metro **supermarket,** on St. Giles St., is in the city center. (Open M-Sa 7:30am-8pm, Su 11am-5pm.)

Pulse, Guildhall (☎765 562), in the old fire station stables. Deliciously creative vegetarian dishes like Welsh rarebit with portabella and watercress (£5-6) or spicy bean enchiladas (£7). Busy courtyard and upstairs seating overflows at lunch and on weekends. Live music once a week. Open M-Sa 10am-11pm, Su 11:30am-5pm. MC/V. ❷

Cafe 91, 91 Upper St. Giles St. (☎627 4229). A typical French patisserie with tasty butternut and stilton risotto (£6.45). Cakes and pastries displayed in the window (£2.50) entice customers. Open M-Sa 8am-10pm, Su 10am-4pm. MC/V. ❷

The Waffle House, 39 St. Giles St. (☎612 790; www.wafflehouse.co.uk). Waffles, waffles, and more waffles. Smothered in everything from chocolate mousse to hummus and avocado. Sweets (£2-5) and savories (£4-8) are available, with vegan options. Open M-Sa 10am-10pm, Su 11am-10pm. MC/V. ❷

Italia Nostra, 52 St. Giles St. (☎617 199; www.italianostra.co.uk). Sicilian-owned eatery with authentic entrees (£7-14). Save room for the tiramisu (£4.50). Open M-Th noon-2pm and 6-10pm; F noon-2pm and 6-10:30pm; Sa 6-10:30pm. MC/V. ❷

The Orgasmic Cafe, 6 Queen St. (☎760 650; www.orgasmic-cafe.com). Gasp stylishly after a meal of freshly baked bread stuffed with salmon, spinach, and *crème fraiche* (£5.50) or one of many inventive pizzas (£5-8) and bagels (£7-8). Lounge in the oversized leather chairs. Crowd gets busy in the evening. Open M-Tu 10:30am-11pm, W-Sa 10:30am-midnight, Su 11am-10:30pm. Food served until 10:30pm. MC/V. ❷

👁 SIGHTS

ORIGINS. Get your hands on history in this interactive complex, with three floors displaying 2000 years of Norfolk history in over 60 exhibits. Visitors press buttons, flip switches, and pull on levers to make exhibits of Romans, Vikings, Normans, and American soldiers come to life. An 18min. film shows the hidden sights of Norfolk on a dizzying panoramic screen. *(In the Forum, next to the TIC. ☎727 922. Open M-Sa 10am-5:15pm, Su 11am-4:45pm. £6, concessions £4.)*

NORWICH CASTLE MUSEUM AND ART GALLERY. The original castle was built in the early 12th century by the Norman monarch Henry I, who was intent on subduing the Saxon city. Its exterior dates from an 1830s restoration, although a more recent £12 million facelift, the largest restoration in castle history, has also left its mark. The **Norman Keep** has multimedia displays about the lives of medieval nobility, and the archaeology gallery displays relics of Celtic Queen Boudicca. The art gallery holds tons of watercolors and the world's largest collection of ceramic tea pots. *(☎493 645. Open July-Aug. M-Sa 10am-5:30pm, Su 1-5pm; Sept.-June M-F 10am-4:30pm, Sa 10am-5pm, Su 1-5pm. Last admission 30min. before close. £6.50, concessions £5.50, children £4.60; 1hr. before close £1.)*

NORWICH CATHEDRAL. Along with the Norman castle, Norwich cathedral dominates the skyline. Built by an 11th-century bishop as penance for having bought his position, the cathedral features the largest monastic cloisters in England and flying buttresses that support the second-tallest spire in the country (315 ft.). Use the magnifying mirror in the nave to examine the intricate carving overhead. In summer, the cathedral hosts orchestral concerts on the Close, 44 acres of land sloping down to the River Wensum. *(☎218 300. Open daily from mid-May to mid-Sept. 7:30am-*

7pm; from mid-Sept. to mid-May 7:30am-6pm. Evensong M-F 5:15pm, Sa-Su 3:30pm. Suggested donation £4. Tours M-Sa 10:45am, noon, and 2:15pm; £2.50.)

BRIDEWELL MUSEUM. This museum once served as a merchant's house, mayor's mansion, factory, and prison for women and beggars. Now, it displays the history of local industry. Linger over mysterious bottles in the recreated 19th-century pharmacy or check out the exhibit on the Canaries, Norwich's favored football team. *(Bridewell Alley, off St. Andrew's St. ☎615 975. Open July-Aug. M-Sa 10am-5pm; Apr.-June and Sept.-Oct. Tu-F 10am-4:30pm, Sa 10am-5pm. £3.10, concessions £2.60, children £1.70, families £8.50.)*

ST. JULIAN'S CHURCH. Julian of Norwich, a 14th-century nun, was walled into a cell behind the altar during a mass for the dead. She stayed there for years and had intense visions, which she wrote down in *Revelations of Divine Love*, the book that made her the first-known woman to pen a book in English. The church, first erected in Saxon times, was bombed during WWII and later rebuilt. *(St. Julian's Alley off Rouen Rd. ☎767 380. Open daily May-Sept. 7:30am-5:30pm; Oct.-Apr. 7:30am-4pm. Free.)*

SAINSBURY CENTRE FOR VISUAL ARTS. Located at the University of East Anglia, 3 mi. west of town on Earlham Rd., this center was destroyed during the English Reformation and restored after WWII. Sir Sainsbury, of supermarket fame, donated his small, world-class modern art collection, including works by Picasso and Bacon, to the university in 1973. The building, designed by Sir Norman Foster, is itself a work of art. *(Take buses #22, 25, 26, or 27, and ask for the Sainsbury Centre stop. ☎593 199; www.scva.org.uk. Open Tu and Th-Su 10am-5pm, W 10am-8pm. Free, with separate charges for special exhibitions.)*

🔊 NIGHTLIFE

Many Norwichian pubs and clubs offer live music. On **Prince of Wales Road,** near the city center, five clubs within two blocks jockey for social position. **Tombland,** the area just below the cathedral near the cemetery, serves as a somewhat macabre nightlife center. **The Loft,** on Rose Ln., is a relaxed, gay-friendly club with live music and two dance floors. Fridays feature local radio DJs while Th and Sa have R&B and techno beats. Frequent theme nights include wild foam parties. (☎623 559; www.loftnightclub.co.uk. Cover Th £3 after 11:30pm, F £5, Sa free before 11pm and £5 after 11pm, students £3. Open Th 10pm-2am, F 10:30pm-3am, Sa 10pm-4am.) The Riverside has several popular clubs and bars. **Norwegian Blue,** a trendy newcomer in the Riverside Leisure complex, has decor inspired by fjords and IKEA minimalists. A 30 ft. waterfall behind the bar splashes over 27 different vodkas. (☎618 082. Open M-Sa noon-11pm, Su noon-10:30pm. Food served until 10pm.) Pints of dark ale and walls of dark wood greet patrons at **Adam and Eve,** Bishopgate, at the end of Riverside Walk behind the cathedral. Norwich's first pub (est. 1249) is now its most tranquil, hugging the wall around the cathedral yard. (☎667 423. Open M-Sa 11am-11pm, Su noon-10pm.)

🎵 🎌 ENTERTAINMENT AND FESTIVALS

The TIC, cafes, and B&Bs have information on all things entertaining. Next to the Assembly House on Theatre St., the Art Deco **Theatre Royal** hosts opera and ballet companies and London-based theater troupes such as the Royal Shakespeare Company and Royal National Theatre. (☎630 000; www.theatreroyalenorwich.co.uk. Box office open M-Sa 9:30am-8pm, non-performance days 9:30am-6pm. Tickets £4-45, concessions available.) The home of the Norwich Players, **Maddermarket Theatre,** St. John's Alley, stages drama in an Elizabethan-style theater. Adhering to tradition, all actors remain anonymous. (☎620 917; www.mad-dermarket.co.uk. Box office open M-Sa 10am-9pm. Non-performance days M-F 10am-5pm, Sa 10am-1pm. Tickets £7-9.) The **Norwich Arts Centre,** Reeves Yard, St. Benedicts St., hosts international music, ballet, and comedy. (☎660 352; www.nor-wichartscentre.co.uk. Box office open M-Sa 10am-10pm; non-performance days 10am-5:30pm. Tickets £3-18.) The **Norwich Puppet Theatre,** St. James, Whitefriars, is one of two in the country and presents shows for all ages. (☎629 921. Box office open M-F 9:30am-5pm, Sa 1hr. prior to show. Tickets £6, concessions £4.20, children £3.75.) Ask the TIC about free summer **Theatre in the Park** (☎212 137).

The **Norfolk and Norwich Festival** explodes with music and theater for 10 days every May. **Open Studios,** held in late May, offers two weeks of open artists' studios around the county. July welcomes the **Lord Mayor's Celebration** with a raucous parade. Check the TIC and the free *Norwich City Council Events 2007* for festival details.

▶ DAYTRIP FROM NORWICH

NORFOLK BROADS NATIONAL PARK

Trains from Norwich, Lowestoft, or Great Yarmouth to Beccles, Cantley, Lingwood, Oulton Broad, Salhouse, or Wroxham. From Norwich, First Eastern Counties buses go to: Brundell (#17, 17a; 30min., 2 per hr., round-trip £3); Horning (#54; 30min., every hr., round-trip £4.40); Strumpshaw (#17a; 30min., every hr., round-trip £3); Wroxham (#54; 40min., every hr., round-trip £3.60); other Broads towns (#705; M-F every hr.).

Birds and bird-watchers flock to the Norfolk Broads, a soggy maze of marshlands. The landscape was formed in medieval times when peat was dug out to use for fuel. Over the centuries, water levels rose, and the shallow lakes, or "broads," were born. Traffic in hidden waterways conjures the surreal image of sailboats floating through fields. Travel with care, as floods are frequent. Among the many **nature trails** that pass through the Broads, **Cockshoot Broad** lets you birdwatch, a circular walk around **Ranworth** passes various flora, and **Upton Fen** is, amazingly enough, popular for its bugs. Hikers can challenge themselves with the 56 mi. **Weaver's Way** between Cromer and Great Yarmouth. The village of **Strumpshaw** has a popular bird reserve. (☎715 191. Open daily dawn-dusk. £2.50, concessions £1.50, families £5.) The best way to see the Broads is by boat—the 200km of navigable waters are perfect for a nautical jaunt. Many companies in Wroxham rent day launches (£10-17 per hr.). Numerous companies also offer **cruises** around the Broads. **Broads Tours** of Wroxham, on the right before the town bridge, runs river trips and rents day boats. (☎782 207. Boat rentals £12-14 per hr. Open daily 9am-5:30pm. 1-2½hr. tours July-Aug. 7 per day; June and Sept. 4-5 per day, less frequent on weekends; Apr.-May and Oct. 11:30am and 2pm. £6-8, children £4.50-6.50.) Certain areas of the Broads are accessible only by car or bike; the pamphlet *Broads Bike Hire*, available at the Wroxham TIC, lists rental shops. A convenient place to rent **bikes** is Broadland Cycle Hire in Wroxham. Follow Station Rd. to the river and take a left onto The Rhond. (☎783 096; www.broadlandcyclehire.co.uk. Book in advance. £7 per ½-day, £10 per day. Open daily 9:30am-4:30pm.)

Wroxham, 15min. from Norwich by train (every hr., £3.10), is the best base for information-gathering and preliminary exploration of some of the area's wetlands. To reach the **Wroxham and Hoveton Broads Information Centre** from the train station and bus stop, turn right on Station Rd. and walk about 90 yd. Knowledgeable Broads rangers supply guides and maps for walking and cycling routes. The office also lists boat rental companies and campsites throughout the area and books rooms around the park. (☎782 281. Open Easter-Oct. M-Sa 9am-1pm and 2-5pm.)

SUFFOLK AND ESSEX

BURY ST. EDMUNDS
☎ 01284

In AD 869, Viking invaders tied the Saxon monarch King Edmund to a tree, used him for target practice, and then beheaded him. Approximately 350 years later, 25 barons met in the Abbey of St. Edmund to swear to force King John to sign the Magna Carta, sowing the seeds of democracy in Western Europe. From these two defining moments comes Bury's motto: "sacrarium regis, cunabula legis" ("shrine of the king, cradle of the law"). Bury St. Edmunds is now a vigorous market town. Any time of year is a good time to visit: November promises fireworks, December hosts the Christmas Fayre, and May brings in the Bury Festival.

Along Crown St. lie the ▓**Abbey Gardens,** a peaceful park with award-winning flower beds. The Gardens also contain the ruins of the 11th-century **Abbey of St. Edmund,** where the barons met in 1214 to put a check on royal power. Next door, the 16th-century **St. Edmundsbury Cathedral** stands out with its Millenium tower and strikingly colorful interior. Painted wooden ceilings and the shields of the Magna Carta barons hang above the High Altar. (☎ 754 933. Open daily June-Aug. 8:30am-8pm; Sept.-May 8:30am-6pm. Evensong W-Sa 5:30pm, Su 3:30pm. Suggested donation £3. 1hr. guided tours M-Sa 11:30am, donations appreciated.) **Moyse's Hall Museum,** Corn Hill in the marketplace, is rumored to be one of the oldest townhouses in East Anglia. Since 1899, however, it has been devoted to town history, man-traps, and mummified cats. (☎ 706 183. Open daily 10am-5pm. £2.60, concessions £2.10.) In late May, the two-week **Bury Festival** (www.buryfestival.co.uk) brings music, street entertainment, and fireworks to the town center.

Most budget accommodations are in the residential outskirts of the historical town center. The TIC books **B&Bs** in town or on nearby farms (£20-30). For spotless rooms, try **Westland Park ❷,** 116a Westley Rd., a 20min. walk from the train station. (☎ 753 874; www.westbank-house.co.uk. Singles £28.) **Dunston Guest House ❷,** 8 Springfield Rd., has 17 bedrooms in a Victorian mansion only 5min from the town center. Full breakfast included. (☎ 767 981; www.dunstonguesthouse.co.uk. Singles £25-40; doubles and twins £30-33 per person.) Pamper yourself at the luxurious **Clarice House ❸,** Horringer Ct., Horringer Rd., a mansion with a health club and 20 acres of parkland. (☎ 705 550; www.claricehouse.co.uk. Ensuite singles and doubles start at £27.50 per person). Bury bustles on **market** days (W and Sa 9am-4pm), when the town center fills with fresh food and flowers. At the **Tickety Boo Cupcake Room ❶,** 6-7 St. Johns St., the cupcake (£2-4) is king—sweet, frosting-covered king. (☎ 747 111. Free Wi-Fi. Open M-Sa 9:30am-5pm. Cash only.) For huge sandwiches and salads (£5-7), visit the always busy **Lacey's Bistro ❷,** Brentgovel St. (☎ 763 293. Cash only.) The pint-sized **Nutshell,** Abbeygate at the Traverse, claims to be Britain's smallest pub—ask about its entry in the *Guinness Book of World Records.* (☎ 764 867. Open M-Sa noon-11pm, Su noon-10:30pm. Cash only.)

Bury makes a good daytrip from Norwich or Cambridge, especially if you include a jaunt to Lavenham, Sudbury, or Long Melford. **Trains** (☎ 08457 484 950) to Cambridge (40min., every hr., £7.50), Felixstowe (1½hr., every hr., £7), and London (2¼hr., 2 per hr., £33). A National Express **bus** (☎ 08705 808 080) comes from London (2¼hr., 3 per day, £12.20) and continues on to Cambridge (1hr., £3.20). Cambus #11 (☎ 0870 608 2608) runs to Drummer St. in Cambridge (1hr., M-Sa every hr., round-trip £4.40). The **Tourist Information Centre** is on 6 Angel Hill opposite Abbey Gate. (☎ 764 667. Open Easter-Oct. M-Sa 9:30am-5:30pm, Su 10am-3pm; Nov.-Easter M-Sa 10am-4pm.) Other services include: free **Internet** access at the public **library** on St. Andrews St.; **banks** with **ATMs** on Abbeygate St.; Boots **Phar-**

macy, 11-13 Cornhill (☎ 701 516; open M, W-Sa 8:30am-5:30pm, Tu 9am-5:30pm, Su 10am-4pm); 24hr. **taxi** (☎ 753 836); **police,** Raingate St. (☎ 774 100); West Suffolk **Hospital** (☎ 713 000); and the **post office,** 17-18 Cornhill St. with a **bureau de change** (☎ 08457 223 344; open M and W-F 9am-5:30pm, Tu 9:30am-5:30pm, Sa 9am-12:30pm). **Post Code:** IP33 1AA.

☒ DAYTRIPS FROM BURY ST. EDMUNDS

COLCHESTER. As Britain's oldest town on record, Colchester has seen its share of violence. The first Roman capital in Britain, it was burned to a crisp during Celtic Queen Boudicca's revolt in AD 60. Romans recaptured the place and built what is now the oldest surviving city wall in Britain. It is the site of one of William the Conqueror's first castles, which King John successfully besieged in 1216. Colchester's half-timber buildings now make up a pedestrian-friendly town center. Completed in 1125, **Colchester Castle** houses the morbid **Castle Museum,** with extensive hands-on displays of Roman artifacts found in the area, including skeletons, coffins, and weapons from the period of the Boudiccan revolt. A tour takes you from the depths of the Roman foundations to the heights of the Norman towers. (☎ 282 939. Open M-Sa 10am-5pm, Su 11am-5pm. Last admission 4:30pm. Guided tours of the Roman vaults and castle roof noon-4pm on the hr. Castle £5, concessions £3. Tours £2, children £1.) View the fine collection of 18th-century Colchester grandfather clocks in **Tymperleys Clock Museum,** off Trinity St. (☎ 282 939. Open Apr.-Oct. Tu-Sa 10am-1pm and 2-5pm. Free.) Colchester also has several small, free museums devoted to tea, jam, and art; visit www.colchestermuseums.org.uk.

If planning to stay overnight, budget travelers can reserve in advance one of the few rooms in **Apple Blossom House ❸,** 8 Guildford Road, close to the town center. (☎ 512 303. Full English breakfast included. Singles £26; doubles £46. Cash only.) At the **Thai Dragon ❷,** 35 East Hill, costumed waitresses serve a three-course lunch for £8. (☎ 863 414. Open M-Sa noon-2:30pm and 6-11pm, Su noon-2:30pm and 6-10:30pm. MC/V.)

Trains (☎ 08457 484 950) pull into North Station from Bury St. Edmunds (1hr., every hr., £15.30 return) and London Liverpool St. (1hr., 12 per hr., £18.50). Regional trains arrive at North Station; take a connecting train to Colchester Town Station or follow the signs 1½ mi. into town. The **Tourist Information Centre,** 1 Queen St., across from the castle, leads 2hr. city tours. (☎ 282 920; www.visitcolchester.com. Open Easter-Oct. M-Tu and Th-Sa 9:30am-6pm, W 10am-6pm, Su 11am-4pm; Oct.-Easter M-Sa 10am-5pm. Tours Mar.-Oct.; call ahead for dates. £3, children £2.)

LONG MELFORD. Two Tudor mansions, complete with turrets and moats, grace the village of Long Melford. **Melford Hall,** the more impressive, has retained much of its original Elizabethan exterior and its paneled banquet hall. Still the home of the Hyde Parker family, the mansion displays exquisite vases, china, and ivory figures from a Spanish treasure ship captured by Captain Hyde Parker I. (☎ 01787 379 228. Open May-Sept. M, W-Su, and bank holidays 1:30-5pm; Apr. and Oct. Sa-Su 1:30-5pm; last admission 4:30pm. £5, children £2.50.) More entertaining than stately, 500-year-old **Kentwell Hall** is filled with authentically costumed guides. The mansion also hosts the occasional WWII recreation and open-air theater in the summer, featuring opera, Shakespeare, and bands. (☎ 01787 310 207; www.longmelford.com. Open July-Aug. daily noon-5pm; Mar.-May and Sept.-Oct. Su noon-5pm. £7.50, children £4.75. Gardens and farm only £5.30/3.50.) Stop by the **Long Melford Church,** built in 1484 with funding from rich wool merchants. (14 mi. from Bury, accessible by H.C. Chambers bus #753 (50min., M-Sa 11 per day, round-trip £4.70). ☎ 01787 310 845; www.longmelfordchurch.com. Open daily Apr.-Sept. 10am-5pm, Oct. and Mar. 10am-4pm, Nov.-Feb. 11am-3pm. Free.)

NORTHWEST ENGLAND

Once upon a time, Northwest England was a land of sleepy villages and lots of sheep. Then the Industrial Revolution came along and turned the once quiet cities into some of the richest and most cosmopolitan in the world. The decline of industry hit the region hard, but the cities of the Northwest bounced back by embracing their quirky history and avant-garde hipness. Today, their innovative music and art scenes are world-famous—Liverpool and Manchester alone produced four of *Q* magazine's 10 biggest rock stars of the century—and a large student population feeds through-the-roof nightlife. Travelers can find respite from the frenetic urbanity in the rolling hills and pastures of the Peak District to the east or Cumbria to the north, where the stunning crags and waters of the Lake District have sent poets into pensive meditation for centuries.

HIGHLIGHTS OF NORTHWEST ENGLAND

WORSHIP the Beatles: virtually every pub, restaurant, and corner in **Liverpool** claims some connection to the Fab Four (p. 345).

REVEL in **Manchester's** nightlife, where trendy cafe-bars morph into late-night venues for dancing and drinking (p. 358).

ROAM the hills, caverns, and moors of the **Peak District** (p. 362), then explore the mountains and sparkling waters of the **Lake District** (p. 371).

NORTHWEST CITIES

CHESTER   ☎ 01244

With fashionable stores behind mock-medieval facades, tour guides in Roman armor, and a town crier, Chester is a proud purveyor of the quintessentially English. The city was a base for Plantagenet campaigns against the Welsh—old town law stated that Welshmen in the streets after sunset could be beheaded. Thankfully, today the city is less bloodthirsty. Its Roman ruins and quiet location on the River Dee make Chester a relaxing, historic entry point to the Northwest.

◧ TRANSPORTATION

Chester serves as a rail gateway to Wales via the North Wales line. The train stops 10min. northeast of the city proper, off Hoole Rd., but showing your ticket gets a free bus ride downtown. Buses converge between Northgate St. and Inner Ring Rd. near Town Hall.

Trains: Station on City Rd. (☎08457 484 950; www.nationalrail.co.uk). Ticket office open M-Sa 5:30am-12:30am, Su 8am-midnight. Trains to: **Birmingham** (1¾hr.; 1-2 per hr., most indirect; £13); **Holyhead** (2hr., 1-2 per hr., £13.50); **London Euston**

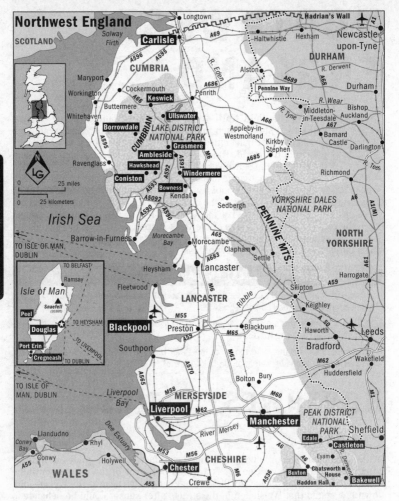

(2½hr., 1-2 per hr., £58.70); **Manchester Piccadilly** (1hr., 3 per hr., £10.70). Frequent **Merseyrail** service makes Chester an easy daytrip from **Liverpool** (45min., 2 per hr., £4.30).

Buses: The station is near Town Hall off Northgate St. An information kiosk helps travelers during the day. **National Express** (☎08705 808 080; www.nationalexpress.co.uk) to: **Birmingham** (3hr., 6 per day, £10.60); **Blackpool** (3-5hr., 4 per day, £9.20); **London** (6-8hr., 7 per day, £21); **Manchester** (1½-2hr., 5 per day, £6). **Huxley Coaches** (☎01948 770 661; www.huxleycoachholidays.co.uk) bus C56 runs from Foregate St. to **Wrexham** (1hr., M-Sa every hr.). **First** buses connect to **Liverpool** (1½hr., every 20min., £2.50).

Public Transportation: Call for local bus info (☎0870 608 2608 daily 8am-8pm). Routes can be found in the 15 *Bus Times* booklets, available free at the TIC.

Taxis: Radio Taxis (☎372 372), **Abbey Taxis** (☎318 318), and **King Cabs** (☎343 343). All 24hr.

✴ ❼ ORIENTATION AND PRACTICAL INFORMATION

Chester's center is surrounded by a **city wall** with seven gates. **Chester Cross** is at the intersection of **Eastgate, Northgate, Watergate,** and **Bridge Streets,** which comprise the heart of the downtown commercial and pedestrian district. Outside the southern walls, a tree-lined path, **The Groves,** runs along a mile of the River Dee. North of the walled city, **Liverpool Road** heads toward the hospital as well as the zoo. The train station is on the northeastern edge of town, the bus station is off Northgate St. near the town hall, and the **Roodee** (Chester Racecourse) is on the southwest edge.

Tourist Information Centre: Town Hall, Northgate St. (☎402 385; www.chestertourism.com), at the corner of Princess St. **Bureau de change** inside. Branch at the **Chester Visitor Centre,** Vicar's Ln. (☎402 111; www.visitchester.com), opposite the Roman amphitheater. Both book accommodations for a 10% deposit, book National Express tickets and city tours, and sell city maps and a guide with accommodation listings. Pick up *What's On in Chester and Cheshire* (free) for information on upcoming events. Both open May-Oct. M-Sa 9:30am-5:30pm, Su 10am-4pm; Nov.-Apr. M-Sa 9:30am-5pm, Su 10am-4pm. On Su in winter, only the visitor center is open.

Tours: A legionnaire in full armor leads the **Roman Soldier Wall Patrol.** June-Aug. Th-Sa 1:45pm from the visitor center, 2pm from the TIC. Ghouls lurk along the **Ghost Hunter Trail.** After 5:30pm, buy tickets at the Shropshire Arms pub. June-Oct. Th-Sa 7:30pm from the TIC; Nov.-May Sa only. A similar self-guided tour is detailed in *Haunted Chester,* a £1.50 pamphlet sold in bookstores and the TIC. For Chester's local story, try the **History Hunter.** May-Oct. daily 10:30am from the visitor center; Nov.-Apr. Sa-Su only. The **Secret Chester** tour, which also departs from the visitor center (Tu, Th, Su 2pm; Sa 10am and 2pm), reveals the secrets of Chester's past by granting special access to historic buildings. All guided tours £5, children and concessions £4. Inquiries for all tours ☎351 609; www.chestertourism.com.

Financial Services: NatWest is on the corner of Eastgate and Werburgh St. Open M-Tu and Th-F 9am-5pm, W 9:30am-5pm, Sa 9:30am-3:30pm. **Thomas Cook** (☎583 500) has a commission-free **bureau de change** near Chester Cross on Bridge St. Open M-Tu and Th-Sa 9am-5:30pm, W 10am-5:30pm, Su 11am-4pm. **ATMs** are plentiful in the town center, especially along Eastgate and Bridge St.

Launderette: Garden Lane Launderette, 56 Garden Ln. (☎382 694). Wash £2.50, dry £1 per 20min., soap 50p, required service charge 50p. Open M-F 8:30am-6pm, Sa 8:30am-5pm, Su 11:30am-5pm.

Police: In the Town Hall (☎350 000).

Pharmacy: Boots, adjacent to the TIC in the Forum Center (☎342 852). Open M-F 8am-6pm, Sa 9am-6pm. The Foregate St. branch is open Su 11am-5pm.

Hospital: Countess of Chester (West Chester) Hospital, Liverpool Rd. (☎365 000). Take bus #40A from the station or #3 from the Bus Exchange.

Internet Access: Library, Northgate St. (☎312 935), beside the Town Hall. Free. Open M and Th 9:30am-7pm, Tu-W and F 9:30am-5pm, Sa 9:30am-4pm. **CafenetUK,** 63 Watergate St. (☎401 116). £3 per hr. Open M-Th 8:30am-8:30pm, F 8:30am-7pm, Sa 9am-6pm, Su 10am-6pm.

Post Office: 2 St. John St. (☎348 315), off Foregate St. **Bureau de change.** Open M and W-Sa 9am-5:30pm, Tu 9:30am-5:30pm. Branch at 122 Northgate St. (☎326 754). Open M-F 9am-5:30pm, Sa 9am-12:30pm. **Post Code:** CH1 2HT.

NORTHWEST ENGLAND

ACCOMMODATIONS

B&Bs (from $25) are concentrated on **Hoole Road,** a 5min. walk from the train station. Turn right from the exit, climb the steps to Hoole Rd., and turn right over the train tracks. **Brook Street** also has budget options. Turn right from the train station, then take the first left). Bus #53 (6 per hr.) runs to the area from the city center.

Chester Backpackers, 67 Boughton St. (☎400 185; www.chesterbackpackers.co.uk). Convenient location within a 5-10min. walk from both the train station and the city center. Laid-back and comfortable, including a lounge with video and book collections. The patio on the 2nd fl. is a perfect for an afternoon chat. Kitchen, free luggage storage, laundry, and free Wi-Fi. Dorms £15; singles £18.50; doubles £32. MC/V. ❷

YHA Chester, 40 Hough Green (☎680 056), 1½ mi. from the city center. Cross the river on Grosvenor Rd. and turn right off the roundabout onto Hough Green. Buses #7 and 16 arrive from the bus station, #4 from the train station. Breakfast included. YHA membership required. Laundry £2, dry 20p per 10min. Reception 7am-10:30pm. Open from mid-Jan. to mid-Dec. Dorms £17.50, under 18 £14. MC/V. ❷

Laburnum Guest House, 2 St. Anne St. (☎380 313; www.laburnumhousechester.co.uk). 4 large, ensuite rooms close to town. Breakfast included. Singles £28; doubles £50. Cash only. ❸

FOOD

A Tesco **supermarket** is at the end of an alley off Frodsham St. (open M-Sa 7am-9pm, Su 11am-5pm). The **market,** 6 Princess St., in Market Hall, has cheap fruits and vegetables. (☎402 340. Open M-Sa 9am-5:30pm, Su 11am-5pm) On Sundays the town hosts an outdoor **Farmers' Market** (open 9:30am-4pm).

Philpott's, 2 Goss St. (☎345 123), off Watergate St. Pristine counter and fabulous made-to-order sandwiches (from £2.10). Takeaway only. Open M-Sa 7:30am-2:30pm. Cash only. ❶

Chez Jules, 71 Northgate St. (☎400 014; www.chezjules.com). Popular gourmet French bistro. Holds splurge-worthy "Gastronomique" evenings every month with 5 award-winning courses of French cuisine (£21.50). Every M features a student special (2 courses and a bottle of wine, £15); Tu is the same deal for everyone. Also hosts French movie nights. Call or check the website for dates. 2-course lunches are £7; dinner entrees start at £7.50. Open M-Sa noon-3pm and 6-10:30pm; Su noon-4pm. AmEx/MC/V. ❸

La Tasca, 6/12 Cuppin St. (☎400 887; www.latasca.co.uk). Lively atmosphere and delicious food make this tapas bar and restaurant a great weekend spot. A variety of meat and vegetarian tapas available, as well as plenty of sangria. Tapas £2.85-4.55. Open daily 11am-10pm. AmEx/MC/V. ❷

Hattie's Tea Shop, 5 Rufus Ct. (☎345 173), off Northgate St. A bustling teashop with great fresh-baked cakes (£1.80) and a homey feel. Open M-Sa 9am-5pm, Su 11am-4pm. Cash only. ❷

SIGHTS

ARCHITECTURE. Chester's architecture is the most prominent feature of its city center. Although many of the buildings are faux-historic and house chain stores and fast-food cafes, some actually do date from medieval times. The 13th-century **Three Old Arches** on Bridge St. are believed to make up the oldest storefront in England. Black-and-white painted facades usually signify Victorian imitations of traditional Tudor style—most of the originals were destroyed by fire or invasion. Occasional street performers grace this much-trafficked area, and the costumed

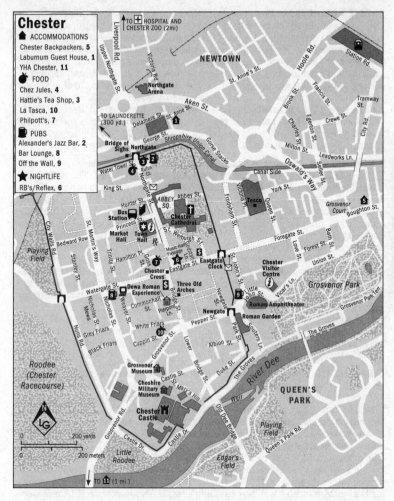

Chester

🏠 ACCOMMODATIONS
Chester Backpackers, **5**
Laburnum Guest House, **1**
YHA Chester, **11**

🍴 FOOD
Chez Jules, **4**
Hattie's Tea Shop, **3**
La Tasca, **10**
Philpott's, **7**

🍺 PUBS
Alexander's Jazz Bar, **2**
Bar Lounge, **8**
Off the Wall, **9**

⭐ NIGHTLIFE
RB's/Reflex, **6**

TO ✚ HOSPITAL AND
CHESTER ZOO (2mi)

NEWTOWN

Liverpool Rd.
Upper Northgate St.
Victoria Rd.
Station Rd.
Hoole Rd.
St. Anne's St.
Brook St.
Francis St.
Tramway St.
Crewe St.
City Rd.
Egerton St.
Charles St.
Milton St.
Leadworks Ln.
Oswald's Way
Canal Side
Seller St.
Grosvenor Court
Boughton St.

Aken St.
Gorse Stacks
Shropshire Union Canal
George St.
Delamere St.
St. Anne St.
Northgate Arena
TO LAUNDERETTE (300 yd.)
Bridge of Sighs
Northgate
Water Tower
Rufus Ct.
King St.
Northgate St.
Abbey St.
ABBEY SQ.
Hunter St.
Bus Station
Princess St.
Market Hall
Town Hall
St. Martin's Way
Bedward Row
Stanley St.
City Walls Rd.
Playing Field
Nicholas St. Mews
Watergate St.
Nicholas St.
Weaver St.
Trinity St.
Hamilton St.
Grey Friars
Black Friars
Nuns Rd.
White Friars
Commonhall St.
Cuppin St.
Grosvenor St.
Lower Bridge St.
Pepper St.
Albion St.
Duke St.
St. Mary's Hill
Castle St.
Grosvenor Rd.
Castle Dr.
Little Roodee
Chester Castle
Grosvenor Museum
Cheshire Military Museum
Dewa Roman Experience
Chester Cross
Three Old Arches
Bridge Pl.
Pierpont Ln.
Newgate
Roman Garden
Abbey St.
Frodsham St.
Victoria Pl.
Tesco
York St.
Queen St.
Canal Side
Foregate St.
Love St.
Forest St.
Bath St.
Union St.
Eastgate
Eastgate Clock
Chester Cathedral
St. John's St.
Music Hall Passage
Werburgh St.
Chester Visitor Centre
Little John St.
St. John St.
Vicar's Ln.
Grosvenor Park
Newgate St.
Park St.
Souters Ln.
Roman Amphitheater
Grosvenor Park Terr.
The Groves
River Dee
QUEEN'S PARK
Weir
The Groves
Old Dee Bridge
Playing Field
Queen's Park Rd.
Edgar's Field

Roodee (Chester Racecourse)

N
0   200 yards
0   200 meters

TO 🏛 (1 mi.)

town crier delivers the shocking news of the American colonies' secession. The crier will also announce birthdays and other special occasions; inquire at the TIC to embarrass a friend. (Crier performs May-Aug. Tu-Sa at noon.) Climb the famous **city walls** or the 13th-century **rows** of Bridge, Watergate, and Eastgate St., where walkways provide access to a second tier of storefronts. **Northgate,** which offers a fine view of the Welsh hills, was rebuilt in 1808 to house the city's jail. The **Bridge of Sighs,** which carried doomed convicts from jail to chapel for their last mass, is outside the gate. A good number attempted escape by jumping into the canal before railings were installed. Shutterbugs flock to **Eastgate Clock,** the second-most-photographed timepiece in the world behind London's Big Ben. **Chester Castle,** completed in 1237, is mostly inaccessible to visitors, but the climb up Agricola tower offers views of the River Dee as it winds through town. *(Tower open M-Sa 10am-4pm and Su 1-4pm. Free.)*

CHESTER CATHEDRAL. Begun in the 11th century, the construction of Chester Cathedral continued for more than 500 years. Traces of this schizophrenic past appear in the current building's mix of Norman arches, Gothic carvings, and 14th-century shrine to St. Werburgh. One-of-a-kind intersecting stone arches known as **"the crown of stone"** support its main tower, and a choir at the front showcases intricate and magnificently preserved woodwork full of strange beasts and battle scenes. More elaborate carvings can be found on the **misericords** ("mercy seats") where monks would rest during lengthy worship sessions. A northern niche holds a 19th-century **Cobweb painting**, a short-lived art form that used silk instead of canvas. Construction hasn't stopped yet—the most recent addition is the stunning "Creation Window" installed in the refectory in 2001. *(Off Northgate St. ☎324 756. Open daily 8am-6pm. £4, children £1.50, concessions £3. Audio tour included.)*

ROMAN SIGHTS. The Romans had conquered most of Britannia by AD 43, and Dewa (modern-day Chester) was an important strategic outpost. The walled city housed the soldiers' barracks and military headquarters, while the *canabae* (civilian towns) outside were set up for wicked indulgences like prostitutes and gambling. The **Grosvenor Museum** houses a display of artifacts and models that illustrate a day in the life of a Roman soldier-in-residence. The rest of the museum is devoted to Chester's later history with rooms and figures in period adornment. *(27 Grosvenor St. ☎402 008; www.grosvenormuseum.co.uk. Open M-Sa 10:30am-5pm, Su 1-4pm. Free.)* At the edge of Grosvenor Park, just outside the city wall, specialists are unearthing the largest **Roman amphitheater** in Britain. In its heyday, it featured animal fights, executions, and bloody gladiatorial bouts. *(Open 24hr. Free.)* Nearby, the **Roman Garden** provides picnic space on shaded grass lined with stunted Roman columns. Off Bridge St., the **Dewa Roman Experience**, Pierpoint Ln., is a full-immersion encounter with Chester's classical past. Visitors board a galley vessel bound for a recreated version of old Britannia. The museum chronicles the archaeological exploration of the town with a walk through an actual dig. *(☎343 407. Open Feb.-Nov. M-Sa 9am-5pm, Su 10am-5pm; Dec.-Jan. daily 10am-4pm. £4.25, concessions £3.75.)*

OTHER SIGHTS. Chester Zoo, one of Europe's largest, houses everything from elephants to lions, as well as human-sized prairie dog tunnels and a "monkey kitchen." Watch out for the free-roaming peacocks as you make your way to the "Twilight Zone," Europe's largest free-flight bat cave. Check the posted signs to witness action-packed animal feedings. *(Take First bus #1 from the Bus Exchange (every 20min., round-trip £2). On Su, catch Arriva #411 or 412. ☎380 280; www.chesterzoo.org. Open daily in summer 10am-6pm; otherwise, 10am-4:30pm. Last admission 1-1½hr. before close. £15, concessions £13.50, families £49.50.)* The **Cheshire Military Museum,** in the castle complex, traces Chester's armed forces from medieval archers to contemporary special forces. Learn how 18th-century recruiting sergeants "enlisted" unsuspecting beer-guzzlers with a well-placed shilling. *(☎327 617; www.chester.ac.uk/militarymuseum. Open daily 10am-5pm. Last admission 4pm. £3, concessions £2.)*

🎭🎵 NIGHTLIFE AND ENTERTAINMENT

Many of the city's 30-odd pubs mimic Olde English decor, and most are open Monday through Saturday noon-11pm and Sunday noon-10:30pm. Watering holes cluster on **Eastgate** and **Foregate Streets** and the town center. Jazz and blues melodies waft into the outdoor courtyard of **Alexander's Jazz Bar,** Rufus Ct., Wednesdays and Thursdays in summer. *(☎340 005; www.alexandersjazz.com. Tu acoustic; F soul and funk; Sa live comedy. Cover £2-10 after 7pm, free jazz Su 2-5pm. Open M-Sa 11am-2am, Su noon-12:30am.)* On a former Roman defense ditch, **Off the Wall,** 12 St. John's St., draws rowdy crowds during football matches. M beer £1, W mixed drinks £1. An adjoining coffee bar is open M-Th 7am-10pm; F-Sa 7am-1am, Su 10am-8pm (☎348 964. Food served daily noon-7pm, snacks until 11pm. Open M-Th and Su noon-1am, F-Sa noon-3am.) Put on your dancing shoes and head to **RB's/ Reflex,** 12-16 Northgate St., Chester's only traditional nightclub. Booty shakers come here to explore the club's three floors, each with different music. (☎327 141. Cover £2-7. Open M-Th and Su 10pm-3am, F-Sa 8pm-4am.) Winner of the Best Bar Award in Chester for the last few years, **Bar Lounge,** 75 Watergate St., has something for everyone. The bar caters to a champagne-cocktail crowd, while the spacious beer garden is more low-key. (☎327 394. Open daily 11:30am-midnight.)

On some spring and summer weekends, England's oldest **horse races** are held on the **Roodee,** attracting huge, boisterous crowds. If you plan to visit over a race weekend, book far in advance. (☎304 600. Tickets from £6, average £20.) The **Chester Summer Music Festival** draws classical musicians to the cathedral in July. (☎320 722. Ticket prices vary starting at £7.) Check the TIC's free *What's On in Chester* for other events.

LIVERPOOL
☎0151

Brits can be quick to belittle once-industrial Liverpool, but Scousers—as Liverpudlians are colloquially known—don't seem to mind. Their good humor has stood the tests of time and hard knocks after significant bombings during WWII. With over 65,000 students in residence and the ongoing construction of museums and public projects, the energetic city is in the midst of a major cultural face-lift. All that development pays off: Liverpool has been named the 2008 European Commission's European Capital of Culture, and will host innumerable exhibitions, performances, and events throughout the year to celebrate. Scousers pack the streets to enjoy the raucous nightlife and to show their devotion to the area's two near-deified football squads. Oh, yeah—and some fuss is made over The Beatles.

NORTHWEST ENGLAND

▐ TICKET TO RIDE

Trains: Lime Street Station, Lime St. and St. John's Ln. Ticket office open M-Sa 5:15am-11:35pm, Su 7:15am-10:30pm. Trains (☎08457 484 950) to **Birmingham** (1¾hr.; M-Sa every hr., Su 6 per day; £27.60), **London Euston** (3hr., every hr., £59.70), and **Manchester Piccadilly** (1hr., 2-4 per hr., £8.50). **The Moorfields, James Street,** and **Central** stations serve mainly as transfer points to local Merseyrail trains, and to **Chester** (45min., 2 per hr., £4.35).

Buses: Norton Street Station sends National Express (☎08705 808 080) to **Birmingham** (3hr., 4 per day, £14), **London** (4½-5½hr., 2 per hr., £22), and **Manchester** (1hr., 1 per hr., £6). Other buses stop at **Queen Square** and **Paradise Street** stations. The 1-day **Mersey Saveaway** (£2.40-4.30, children £1.80-2.20) works on area buses and is unrestricted during off-peak hours. Also valid on ferry and rail.

Ferries: Liverpool Sea Terminal, Pier Head, north of Albert Dock. Open daily 9am-5pm. The Isle of Man Steam Packet Company (☎08705 523 523; www.steam-packet.com) runs ferries from Princess Dock to the **Isle of Man.** The P&O Irish Ferry service (☎08702 424 777; www.poirishsea.com) runs to **Dublin** from North Quay (see **By Ferry,** p. 31).

Local Transportation: Private buses cover the city and the Merseyside area. Consult the experts at **Mersey Travel** (☎08706 082 608; www.merseytravel.gov.uk) in their information center in Williamson Sq. Open M and W-Sa 9am-5:30pm, Tu 10am-5:30pm, Su 10:30am-4:30pm.

Taxis: Mersey Cabs (☎207 2222). 24hr.

HELP!

Liverpool's central district is pedestrian-friendly. There are two clusters of museums: on **William Brown Street,** near Lime St. Station and the urban oasis of St. John's Garden, and at **Albert Dock,** on the river. These flank the central shopping district, which is located around **Bold, Church,** and **Lord Streets** and is largely composed of pedestrian-only walkways and plazas. The area of shops and pubs between Bold and Duke St. is called the **Ropewalks.** To the south, a glittering arch over Nelson St.—imported from Shanghai as a recent gift from the People's Republic—marks the entrance to the oldest **Chinatown** in the world. Watch out for construction near Hanover and Paradise St. that can make it difficult to traverse the city.

> **THE BIG DIG.** Liverpool is undergoing a structural facelift that will fill the city with construction until 2010. Most road closures still offer pedestrian access, but those traveling by car should check out www.liverpol.gov.uk/bigdig for updated maps of closures and projects.

Tourist Information Centre: 08 Place, Whitechapel (☎233 2008; www.visitliverpool.com). Gives away the handy *Visitor Guide to Liverpool, Merseyside, and England's Northwest,* as well as a huge stock of pamphlets and local events schedules. Books beds for a 10% deposit. Free email kiosks. Open M and W-Sa 9am-6pm, Tu 10am-6pm, Su 11am-4pm.

Tours: In addition to those listed below, numerous **bus tours** (from £5) and **walking tours** (£4, concessions £3) run in summer; ask the TIC. The TIC also offers guided 2hr. expeditions around and inside **John and Paul's Liverpool homes** through the National Trust. Apr.-Oct. W-Sa. Book in advance. £13, children £2.

Phil Hughes (☎228 4565, mobile 07961 511 223). Phil will treat you to the most comprehensive Beatles tour in Liverpool. This expert guide runs personalized 3-4hr. tours with Liverpool highlights, including Strawberry Fields and Eleanor Rigby's grave. 1 per day. Book in advance. Refreshments included. £13; private tours £65.

Magical Mystery Tour (☎709 3285; www.cavern-liverpool.co.uk/mmt). A yellow-and-blue bus takes 40 fans to Fab Four sights, leaving from the Queens Sq. TIC. The 2hr. tour is fancier but less personal than Phil Hughes. Purchase tickets in advance at either of the TICs or at the Beatles Story. M-F 2:10pm, Sa-Su 11:40am and 2:10pm. £13, small souvenir included.

Financial Services: Banks are everywhere in the shopping districts, and **ATMs** seem to sprout from every alleyway. **Lloyd's TSB,** 53 Great Charlotte St. (open M-W and F 9am-5pm, Th 10am-5pm), and **HSBC,** 4 Dale St. (open M-F 9:30am-5pm), are 2 options.

Work Opportunities: JobCentrePlus, 20 Williamson Sq. (☎801 5700; www.jobcentreplus.gov.uk.). Open M-Tu and Th-F 9am-5pm, W 10am-5pm.

Volunteer Opportunities: The Volunteer Centre, on the 7th fl. of the Goston Building, 32-36 Hanover St. (☎707 1113; www.volunteercentreliverpool.org.uk). Open M-F 9am-5pm. The Liverpool Millennium Volunteers, which runs out of the same office, is targeted at ages 16-25.

Launderette: The **YHA Liverpool** (p. 348) allows non-residents to use its facilities. Wash £1.20, dryer 20p per 10min.

Police: Canning Pl. and 70 Church St. (both branches ☎709 6010).

Hospital: Royal Liverpool University Hospital, Prescot St. (☎706 2000).

Pharmacy: Boots, 18-20 Great Charlotte St. (☎709 4711). Open M-Tu and F-Sa 8:15am-6:15pm, W 8:30am-6:15pm, Th 8:15am-8pm, Su 10:30am-4:30pm.

Internet Access: Central Library, William Brown St. (☎233 5817). Free access on the 2nd fl. Open M-F 9am-6pm, Sa 9am-5pm, Su noon-4pm. Free access for 11- to 25-year-olds at the Door Cafe in the **Merseyside Youth Association Ltd.,** 65-67 Hanover St. (☎702 0700). Open M 10am-5pm, Tu-Th 9:30am-5pm, F 9:30am-4pm.

Liverpool

▲ ACCOMMODATIONS
Embassie Backpackers, 19
International Inn, 13
University of Liverpool, 8
YHA Liverpool, 18

● FOOD
Granary Sandwich Bar, 1
Everyman Bistro, 19
Hole in the Wall, 3
Kimos, 4
Tabac, 10
TeaGather Cafe, 19

■ PUBS
Bar Hannah, 12
Korova, 7
Modo, 5
The Philharmonic, 14
The Pilgrim Pub, 16
Slaters Bar, 6

CLUBS
BaaBar, 8
The Blue Angel, 15
The Cavern Club, 2
Society, 11

Post Office: 42-44 Houghton Way (☎08457 223 344), in St. John's Shopping Centre below the Radio City Tower. **ATM** and **bureau de change.** Open M and W-Sa 9am-5:30pm, Tu 9:30am-5:30pm. **Post Code:** L1 1AA.

🎸 A HARD DAY'S NIGHT

Cheap accommodations lie east of the city center. **Lord Nelson Street** is lined with modest hotels, as is **Mount Pleasant,** one block from Brownlow Hill and Central Station. Stay only at places approved by the TIC, and if you need a good night's sleep, consider springing for a single—some hostels host herds of clubbing teens on weekend nights. Demand for beds is highest in early April for the Grand National Race and during the Beatles Convention at the end of August.

🏆 **Embassie Backpackers,** 1 Falkner Sq. (☎707 1089; www.embassie.com). A comfy remodeled Georgian house with an enjoyable family atmosphere. Evenings often bring free barbecues or karaoke. Embassie has a couple of connections to the Beatles: one of the owners faced (and beat) John Lennon's band in a 1957 competition, and the hostel now arranges for the Phil Hughes tour to pick up from its door. Laundry. Free Wi-Fi. Reception 24hr. Dorms £14.50 for the 1st night, £13.50 each additional night. Cash only. ❷

🏆 **International Inn,** 4 S. Hunter St. (☎709 8135; www.internationalinn.co.uk), off Hardman St. Clean and energetic, this hostel welcomes visitors from all over the world with style and 2-, 4-, 6-, 8-, and 10-person ensuite rooms. Pool table, huge lounge, and kitchen. Bedding is provided as well as coffee, tea, and toast. Internet access £1.50 per 30min. in the adjoining **Cafe Latténet,** which doubles as a live music venue in the evenings. Cafe open M-F 8am-7pm, Sa-Su 9am-5:30pm. Dorms M-Th and Su £15, F-Sa £20; twins £36/45. AmEx/MC/V. ❷

YHA Liverpool, 25 Tabley St. (☎0870 770 5924). Pristine, upscale digs on 3 Beatles-themed floors (hallways are called "Penny Lane" and "Mathew Street") near Albert Dock. Suitable rooms for families. Kitchen, currency exchange, and Big Apple Diner. Breakfast included. Laundry. Internet access £1 per 15min. Dorms £18, under 18 £16; ensuite M-Th and Su £21, F-Sa £22.50. YHA membership required. MC/V. ❷

University of Liverpool. The conference office (☎794 6453) has information for travelers; for booking call ☎794 6243. Breakfast £2. Dorms available from mid-June to mid-Sept. Singles £18. Cash only. ❷

🍫 SAVOY TRUFFLE

Cafes and budget-friendly kebab stands line **Bold, Hardman,** and **Leece Streets,** while takeaways crowd near late-night venues and around **Berry Street.** Cheap all-you-can-eat deals can be found in both posh and dodgy neighborhoods. **Chinatown** abounds with inexpensive buffets. Upscale restaurants cluster around **Queen Square** and downtown. A Tesco Metro **supermarket** with great sandwiches is in Clayton Sq., across from St. John's Shopping Centre. (Open M-F 6am-midnight, Sa 6am-10pm, Su 11am-5pm.)

🏆 **Tabac,** 126 Bold St. (☎709 9502). Sleek, trendy decor and an aquarium in the counter. Sandwiches on freshly baked foccacia bread (melted brie and bacon £4.55) are served all day. Dinner specials £5.50-8. Breakfast from £2. Wine bar opens early. Open M-F 9am-11pm, Sa 9am-midnight, Su 10am-11pm. MC/V with 75p charge. ❷

The Granary Sandwich Bar, 7 Drury Ln. (☎236 0509), between Brunswick and Water St. Breakfast, lunch, and snack foods line the walls. Low prices advertised on brightly colored posters. Try the toasties (from £1) or lunchtime roasts (£3). Open M-F 7:30am-3:30pm. Cash only. ❶

Hole in the Wall, 37 School Ln. (☎709 7733). Considerably larger and brighter than its name would suggest, with 2 fl. of dining area. Serves a huge variety of barms (sandwiches) from £3.50 and quiches (from £4; takeaway £2.50). Takeaway discounts. Open M-Sa 10am-4:30pm. Cash only. ❶

Kimos, 38-44 Mt. Pleasant (☎707 8288). A large menu of Mediterranean and North African cuisine with lots of vegetarian options. All tapas, salads, burgers, pizzas, soups, and sandwiches are under £5, and dinner specials like lamb couscous (£7.70) are delicious. Breakfast (£3.30) served until 6pm. Order and pay at the counter. Open daily 10am-11pm. Cash only. ❷

Everyman Bistro, 5-9 Hope St. (☎708 9545) in the basement. Generous portions of tasty dishes. The menu changes twice a day and is never the same, but always features several vegetarian and gluten-free options from about £6. Leave room for the famed desserts. Open M-W noon-midnight, Th-F noon-2am, Sa 11am-2am. MC/V. ❷

TeaGather Cafe, 12 Myrtle St. (☎703 0222) offers a spread of English and Chinese cuisine, plus kebabs, sandwiches, pizza, and burgers. Its 12 varieties of Chinese teas like refreshing honey-ginger (£1-1.50), cheerful staff, and squeaky-clean premises set it apart from other nearby cafes and takeaway joints. Open M-F 8am-10pm, Sa 10am-10pm. Cash only. ❶

◉ MAGICAL MYSTERY TOUR

With first-rate museums, two dazzling cathedrals, and the twin religions of football and The Beatles, Liverpool's attractions are filled with spirited heritage and modern vitality. The city center is packed with theaters and cultural centers, while **Hope Street** to the southeast connects Liverpool's two 20th-century cathedrals. Most other sights are located on or near **Albert Dock,** an open rectangle of Victorian warehouses now stocked with offices, restaurants, and museums. In 2010, the Museum of Liverpool will become the waterfront's newest landmark.

▩ THE BEATLES STORY. Recreations of Hamburg, the Cavern Club, and a shiny Yellow Submarine trace the rise and fall of the Fab Four from their humble beginnings to Beatlemania to shag haircuts and to solo careers. The audio tour (included with admission) is narrated by Paul McCartney, Alan Williams (The Beatles' first manager), and numerous family members and friends. Audio-taped screeches of fans and recordings of the bands #1s accompany the tour. Lines form early on weekends. *(Albert Dock.* ☎*709 1963; www.beatlesstory.com. Open daily 10am-6pm. Last admission 1hr. before close. £10, concessions £7, children £5, families £25.)*

WALKER ART GALLERY. The massive collection in this stately gallery centers on British art from the 18th and 19th centuries, including a particularly impressive set of Victorian narrative paintings. It also features a collection of British art from the last several decades, much of it culled from its own biennial painting competition. *(William Brown St.* ☎*478 4199; www.thewalker.org.uk. Open daily 10am-5pm. Free.)*

TATE GALLERY. The Liverpool branch of this legendary institution boasts a collection of favorites (Warhol, Pollock, Picasso) and lesser-knowns from the 19th and 20th centuries. Contemporary international art dominates the ground floor, the next level shows a rotating collection from the gallery's archives, and the top floor is reserved for special exhibitions, including the UK's first major Klimt exhibit in 2008. *(Albert Dock.* ☎*702 7400; www.tate.org.uk/liverpool. Open Tu-Su 10am-5:50pm. Suggested donation £2. Special exhibits £5, concessions £4.)*

LIVERPOOL CATHEDRAL. Begun in 1904 and completed in 1978, this Anglican cathedral makes up for what it lacks in age with sheer size. It claims a number of superlatives: the highest Gothic-style arches ever built (107 ft.), the highest and heaviest (31 tons) bells in existence, and an organ with 9765 pipes second in size only to the one in Royal Albert Hall in London. Take two elevators and climb 108 stairs for awe-inspiring views from the tower. *(Upper Duke St. ☎ 709 6271; www.liverpoolcathedral.org.uk. Cathedral open daily 8am-6pm. Tower open daily Mar.-Sept. 11am-5pm; Oct.-Feb. 11am-4pm. Tower £4.25, children free. Cathedral free.)*

MORE BEATLES. For other Beatles-themed locales, get the **Beatles Map** (£3) at the TIC or the free but less detailed "How to Get to The Beatles Attractions in Merseyside" map from Merseytravel. To reach **Penny Lane,** take bus #86A, 76, or 77 from Paradise St.; for **Strawberry Fields,** take #76 or 77 from Paradise St. Souvenir hunters can raid the **Beatles Shop,** 31 Mathew St., canopied with shirts and the best Beatles posters in town. Doors are open "8 Days a Week." *(☎ 236 8066; www.thebeatlesshop.co.uk. Open M-F 9:30am-5:30pm, Sa 9:30am-5:45pm, Su 10:30am-4:30pm.)*

FACT. Housed in a shimmering metallic building, FACT stands for Film, Art, and Creative Technology. Built to showcase the digital arts, most of the exhibits revolve around film and video—some in the free galleries and some in more traditional theaters. Films shown are a mix of standard Hollywood fare, experimental, and foreign films. A new special exhibition opens every six weeks and is usually a demonstration of new media. *(88 Wood St. ☎ 707 4450; www.fact.co.uk. Open M-Sa 11am-11pm, Su 11am-10:30pm. Free Wi-Fi throughout the building. Entrance and all exhibits free; suggested donation £2. Film screenings about £6, W £3.50. Students pay £3.50 for weekday showings before 6pm.)*

METROPOLITAN CATHEDRAL OF CHRIST THE KING. Controversially "modern," some would sooner call this oddity of the skyline "ugly." A crown of crosses tops its reinforced-concrete Lantern Tower, which resembles an upside-down funnel. The payoff is inside: the cavernous main chapel is stunning, with slivers of stained glass sending jewel-toned light glittering across the floor. Dramatic bronze Stations of the Cross by sculptor Sean Rice circle the edge, and the several smaller chapels are also worth a look. Call ahead for information about tours of the Edwardian-era Lutyen's Crypt that lurks underneath. *(Mt. Pleasant. ☎ 709 9222. Open in summer M-Sa 8am-6pm, Su 8am-5pm; in winter closes earlier. Free.)*

MERSEYSIDE MARITIME MUSEUM. Liverpool's heyday as a major port has passed, but the six floors of this museum allow you to explore the nautical side of Scouser history. On the bottom floor is the **H.M. Customs and Excise Museum** (part is being remodeled in time for the 2008 Capital of Culture festivities), with an intriguing array of confiscated goods from smugglers including a tortoise-turned-mandolin, a cane that hides a knife, and a teddy bear full of cocaine. In the basement, the **Transatlantic Slavery Gallery** lets visitors traverse the hull of a recreated slave ship and learn how many of Liverpool's street names are connected to the slave trade (answer: a lot). A larger **International Slavery Museum** opens on the third floor in late 2007. Across from the Slavery Gallery, the **Immigrant Story** tells of happier Atlantic crossings, celebrating Liverpool's heritage as an embarkation point. *(Albert Dock. ☎ 478 4499; www.merseymaritimemuseum.org.uk. Open daily 10am-5pm. Free.)*

LIVERPOOL AND EVERTON FOOTBALL CLUBS. If you're not here for The Beatles, you're probably here for football. The rivalry between the city's two main teams, **Liverpool** and **Everton,** is deep and passionate. Both offer tours of their grounds—Anfield and Goodison Park, respectively—which may be booked in advance. *(Bus #26 from the city center to Anfield. Bus #19 from the city center to Goodison Park. Liverpool ☎ 260 6677; www.liverpoolfc.tv. Everton ☎ 330 2277; www.evertonfc.com. Liverpool tour, including entrance to their museum £10, concessions £6. Everton tour £8.50/5. Match tickets usually £29-32 and sell out well in advance.)*

WILLIAMSON TUNNELS HERITAGE CENTRE. Called "The King of Edge Hill" by some (and "The Mole of Edge Hill" by skeptics), William Josephson kept hundreds of local laborers employed during a 19th-century depression by building huge, multilevel tunnels to nowhere. What little has been excavated can now be explored by visitors in a 40min. guided tour. *(The Old Stableyard, Smithdown Ln. ☎ 709 6868; www.williamsontunnels.co.uk. Open in summer Tu-Su 10am-6pm; in winter Th-Su 10am-5pm. Last admission 1hr. before close. £4, concessions £3.50, children £2.50, families £10.)*

🎵 AND YOUR BIRD CAN SING

Liverpool is gearing up for its reign as the European Capital of Culture 2008 with countless one-time festivals and events in the coming year, from outdoor concerts to scientific exhibitions. Check www.liverpool08.com or contact the TIC for schedules. The **International Street Theatre Festival** (☎ 709 3798; www.brouhaha.uk.com) brings international performances to the city annually from late June to early August. At the end of August, a week-long **Beatles Convention** draws Fab Four devotees. (☎ 236 9091; www.cavern-liverpool.co.uk/beatleweek.) The TIC stocks a comprehensive festival list.

Philharmonic Hall, Hope St. (☎ 709 3789; www.liverpoolphil.com). Home of the **Royal Liverpool Philharmonic,** one of England's best orchestras. The hall also hosts jazz and funk bands. Office open for telephone bookings M-Sa 10am-5:30pm, Su noon-5pm; on concert nights, box office open from 5pm until 15min. after the performance begins. Tickets average £20, same-day concessions £5. Classic film nights £4-6.

Liverpool Empire Theatre, Lime St. (☎ 0870 607 7575; www.livenation.co.uk/liverpool). Focuses primarily on touring musicals, as well as comedy and music shows. Box office open M-Sa 10am-6pm, 30min. after curtain on performance days, Su from 2hr. prior to performances. Tickets £6-50, student standby tickets sometimes available.

Liverpool Playhouse, in Williamson Sq. (☎ 709 4776; www.everymanplayhouse.com). Presents classic works, literary adaptations, and productions from other regional theaters. Box office open M-Sa 10am-6pm, 7:30pm performance nights. Tickets £7.50-19.50, concessions and £5 student standby tickets available.

Everyman Theatre, 13 Hope St. (☎ 709 4776; www.everymanplayhouse.com). The non-traditional counterpart to Liverpool Playhouse, the Everyman focuses on new and experimental works. Box office open M-Sa 10am-6pm, 8pm on performance nights. Tickets £8-12.50, student standby tickets available.

CAPITAL OF CULTURE

In 2003, a plane circled Liverpool pulling a banner that read, "We won it!" The city had been named the European Capital of Culture, and plans for the celebration began immediately. In 2008, the party is finally here. Here's a rundown of the highlights:

All year long, the city's parks and streets are home to theater and dance events during the **Brouhaha International Festival,** the **Mathew Street Music Festival,** and **Africa Oyé,** a free African music festival.

The **Tate Liverpool** shows the first major UK exhibition of work by Viennese icon **Gustav Klimt.** The museum also hosts the exhibition of **Turner Prize** finalists, the first time the painting award has been presented outside London.

Chinatown's **Festival of Light,** the **Liverpool Irish Festival,** the **Liverpool Arabic Arts Festival,** and the **Jamaica Street Carnival** celebrate the city's cultures.

The avant-garde finds an outlet in FACT's **Crossing Screens** film and video exhibit, **LEAP 08,** a contemporary dance festival, and the **Liverpool Fringe Festival.**

It's not all about art: the Merseyside Maritime Museum hosts the **"Magical History Tour,"** the **Festival of Science** takes over the university, and, in another first away from London, the **Tour of Britain** cycling race finishes in Liverpool.

For more info, visit the festival website at www.liverpool08.com.

Unity Theatre, 1 Hope Pl. (☎709 4988; www.unitytheatreliverpool.co.uk). Established in 1937 to support Spanish citizens fighting Franco. Today it produces work by new and little-known playwrights. Box office open M 1-6pm, Tu-Sa 10:30am-6pm, 8:30pm on performance nights. Tickets £6-9, concessions available.

🏴 COME TOGETHER

Two of Liverpool's most notable creations—football fans and rock musicians—were bred in pub culture, and the city has continued to incorporate both traditions into its nightlife. There's not a spot in Liverpool that's far from a good selection of watering holes; the younger set clusters between **Slater** and **Berry Streets,** where cheap drink specials are in plentiful supply. Several pubs and clubs have a 21+ policy posted, but travelers over 18 often find this loosely enforced.

The Philharmonic, 36 Hope St. (☎707 2837). John Lennon once said the worst thing about being famous was "not being able to get a quiet pint at the Phil." Non-celebrities can still enjoy a beer in this gorgeous turn-of-the-century lounge, where wood-panelled rooms have names like "Liszt" and "Brahms." Don't miss the famous mosaic tiling in the men's bathroom (women should ask at the bar first). Food served daily noon-9pm upstairs; at bar noon-5pm. Open daily noon-midnight. MC/V.

Bar Hannah, 2 Leece St. (☎708 5959). Offers great live music on weekdays (Tu and Su acoustic open-mic; W jazz) and a DJ on weekends for a laid-back student crowd. The huge beer garden adjacent to the downstairs bar bustles with activity in nice weather. 2-for-1 mixed drinks M-Th and Su noon-8pm. Open M-Sa 11:30am-2am, Su noon-12:30am. Cash only.

Modo, 23-25 Fleet St. (☎709 8832). Bubbling with eager young professionals. Lounge blasts techno nightly. Couches hidden in candlelit nooks provide ample space to hang out. The expansive urban beer garden fills quickly and makes Modo exceedingly popular. M-Th 11:30am-2am, F-Sa 11:30am-3am, Su noon-1am.

Korova, 39-41 Fleet St. (☎706 7770; www.korova-liverpool.com). With a sleek, loungy bar upstairs and daily live music downstairs, Korova is a magnet for local musicians, students, and scenesters. Cover can reach up to £10 for better-known groups; Tu "Underdog Jukebox" features several local groups with no cover. Most nights fall somewhere in between—call or check posters. Open daily 11am-2am.

The Pilgrim Pub, 34 Pilgrim St. (☎709 2302), tucked behind an archway under "Welcome to the Pilgrim" sign. Frequented by students and drama types, the Pilgrim provides a relaxed atmosphere in its 2 bars and beer garden. Cheap drinks and occasional live music. Food served M-F 10am-4pm. Open M-Sa 10am-11pm, Su 10am-10:30pm.

Slaters Bar, 26 Slater St. (☎708 6990). Well known for its cheap drinks. Pints from £1.10. Gets busy later in the evening. Open M-Th 11am-midnight, F-Sa 11am-1am, Su 11am-10:30pm.

📣 TWIST AND SHOUT

The *Liverpool Echo* (35p), sold daily by street vendors, has up-to-date information, especially in the *What's On* section of Friday editions. *Itchy Liverpool* (£3 at TICs or www.itchyliverpool.co.uk) is another useful guide to the nightlife scene. Generally, however, you need only wander near the Ropewalks to find something that suits your style. For information on gay and lesbian events, check out posted bills and pick up the free *Out Northwest* magazine at **News From Nowhere,** 96 Bold St., a "radical and community bookstore" run by a women's cooperative. (☎708 7270; www.newsfromnowhere.org.uk. Open Jan.-Nov. M-Sa 10am-5:45pm; Dec. daily 10am-5:45pm.)

On weekend nights, the downtown area overflows with young pubbers and club-bers, especially **Mathew Street** (www.mathewstreet.st), **Church Street,** and the area known as the **Ropewalks,** bounded by Hanover, Bold, Duke, and Berry St. Dress smartly (no sneakers) to avoid provoking an army of bouncers. The pricier bars and clubs clustered around **Albert Dock** draw well-groomed twenty-somethings.

Society, 64 Duke St. (☎707 3575; www.societyuk.com). With a plush Temple Room and VIP lounge above a steamy dance floor, this is Liverpool's sexiest club. Theme nights are notorious, and Tu student nights are known as "Mischief." Cover F and Su £5, Sa £10. Open F 10:30pm-2am, Sa 10:30pm-4am, Su 10:30pm-1am.

The Cavern Club, 10 Mathew St. (☎236 1965, tickets 236 4041; www.cavern-liver-pool.co.uk/cavernclub). The restored incarnation of this legendary underground Beatles venue still has many of the original brick archways in place. Talented up-and-comers play here, hoping that history will repeat itself. Th features first-rate Beatles tribute bands. Live music W-Su; DJ F-Sa after concerts finish. To buy tickets in advance, head across the street to the Cavern Pub. Cover £2 after 11pm to dance, varies for concerts. Pub open M-Sa from 11am, Su noon-11:30pm. Club open M-Tu 11am-6pm, W-Sa 11am-2am, Su noon-12:30am.

BaaBar, 43-45 Fleet St. (☎708 8673). Admire the scrolling marquee advertising drink specials behind the bar while deciding among 35 varieties of shooters (£1). Student-oriented, and, as its slogan proclaims, "late, cheap, unisex." M-Th 5pm-2am, F-Sa 5pm-3am, Su 5pm-1am. MC/V.

The Blue Angel, 108 Seel St. (☎709 1535). This local dive, better known as the Raz, has an appeal that's less about style and more about good times. Frequent drink spe-cials. Cover £1-1.50. Open Tu-Sa 10pm-2am.

MANCHESTER ☎0161

The Industrial Revolution transformed the unremarkable village of Manchester into Britain's second-largest urban area. A center of manufacturing in the 19th cen-tury, the city became a hotbed of liberal politics and deplorable working-class con-ditions. For years it was thought of as just another dirty post-industrial city, but an IRA bomb in the city center in 1996 injured over 200 people and sparked a wave of urban renewal, which has given Manchester a sleek, modern look. With a bee as its unofficial mascot, Manchester is a hive of activity, from its thriving shopping dis-tricts and museums to its wild nightlife and preeminent football team.

▐ TRANSPORTATION

Flights: Manchester International Airport (☎489 3000, arrival information 090 1010 1000, 50p per call). Trains (15-20min., 4-6 per hr., £3) and buses #44 and 105 run to Piccadilly Station.

Trains: 2 main stations, connected by Metrolink, serve Manchester. Additional service to local areas available at the **Deansgate** and **Oxford Road** stations.

Manchester Piccadilly, London Rd. Station reception open M-F 7am-5pm. Trains (☎08457 484 950) to: **Birmingham** (1¾hr., every hr., £23); **Chester** (1hr., every hr., £10.70); **Edinburgh** (4hr., 5 per day, £45); **London Euston** (2½-3hr., every hr., £58.50); **York** (40min., 2 per hr., £17.70).

Manchester Victoria, Victoria St., serves trains mostly from the north. Ticket office open M-Sa 6:30am-10pm, Su 8am-10:15pm. Trains to **Liverpool** (50min., 2 per hr., £9).

Buses: Chorlton Street Coach Station, Chorlton St. Office open M-Th and Sa 7:30am-7pm, F and Su 7:30am-8pm. National Express (☎08705 808 080) to: **Birmingham** (2½hr., every hr., £13.50); **Leeds** (1¼hr., every hr., £7.80); **Liverpool** (1hr., every hr.,

£6); **London** (4-6hr., every hr., £21.50); **Sheffield** (1-3hr., every hr., £7).

Public Transportation: Piccadilly Gardens is home to about 50 bus stops, and the new **Shudehill** station to the north houses even more. Get a free route map from the TIC. Buses generally run until 11:30pm, some until 2:30am on weekends. Office open M-Sa 7am-6pm, Su 10am-6pm. Fares 80p-£2.20. All-day ticket £3.30.

Metrolink: Trams (☎205 2000, service information 08706 082 608; www.gmpte.com) link 8 stops in the city center with **Altrincham** in the southwest, **Bury** in the northeast, and **Eccles** in the west (4 per hr., 60p-£4.60). Combined bus and tram ticket £4.60. **Metroshuttle** bus service runs from the city center to main attractions and shopping areas. Buses every 10min., M-Sa 7am-7pm, Su 10am-6pm. Free.

Taxis: Mantax (☎230 3333), **Radio Cars** (☎236 8033), **Hastings** (☎226 1066), **Taxiphone** (☎236 2322).

Manchester		Trof, **1**
⌂ ACCOMMODATIONS		The Ox Pub, **19**
Hilton Chambers, **6**		★ NIGHTLIFE
New Union Hotel, **15**		Cord, **2**
The Hatters Hostel, **9**		Cruz 101, **14**
The Millstone Hotel, **3**		Dry Bar, **5**
University of Manchester, **22**		Essential, **11**
YHA Manchester, **20**		The New Union Showbar, **16**
🍎 FOOD		Night and Day Cafe, **7**
Barburrito, **10**		Queer, **13**
Eden, **17**		Simple Bar & Restaurant, **4**
Soup Kitchen, **8**		Thirsty Scholar, **21**
Tampopo Noodle House, **12**		The Temple, **18**

⊞🛈 ORIENTATION AND PRACTICAL INFORMATION

The city center is an odd polygon formed by **Victoria Station** to the north, **Piccadilly Station** to the east, the canals to the south, and the **River Irwell** to the west. The many byways can be tricky to navigate, but the area is fairly compact, and Mancunians are generally helpful.

Tourist Information Centre: Manchester Visitor Centre, Town Hall Extension, Lloyd St. (☎234 3157; www.visitmanchester.com). Books accommodations for £2.50 plus a 10% deposit. Distributes the *Manchester Pocket Guide* and the *Greater Manchester Network Map.* Open M-Sa 10am-5:30pm, Su 10:30am-4:30pm. Guided walks and private **tours** available from the TIC.

Tours: City Sightseeing (☎0871 666 0000; www.city-sightseeing.com). Runs hop-on, hop-off bus tours, departing from St. Peter's Sq. Tours May-Sept. daily 10am-4:30pm, every 30min.-1hr. **Urbis** (☎605 8205; www.urbis.org.uk) runs a series of themed walking tours departing from Cathedral Gardens including the free "Introduction to Manchester" (daily 1pm). Other tours leave daily at 11pm. £3.

Budget Travel: STA Travel, 75 Deansgate (☎839 3253). Open M-F 10am-6pm, Sa 10am-5pm.

Financial Services: There are many banks in city center. **Thomas Cook,** 23 Market St. (☎910 8787). Branch at 22 Cross St. Both open M-F 10am-6pm, Sa 9am-5:30pm, Su 11am-5pm. **American Express,** 10-12 St. Mary's Gate (☎833 7303). Open M-Tu and Th-F 9am-5:30pm, W 9:30am-5:30pm, Sa 9am-4pm.

Work Opportunities: Visa holders can contact **Manpower,** 87-89 Mosley St. (☎236 8891), for work placement.

Police: Bootle St. (☎872 5050).

Crisis Line: Samaritans, 72-74 Oxford St. (☎236 8000, 24hr. 08457 909 090).

Pharmacy: Boots, 32 Market St. (☎832 6533). Open M-W 8am-6pm, Th 8am-8pm, F 8am-6:30pm, Sa 9am-6:30pm, Su 11am-5pm. Many branches, including 116 Portland St. and 20 St. Ann St.

Hospital: Manchester Royal Infirmary, Oxford Rd. (☎276 1234).

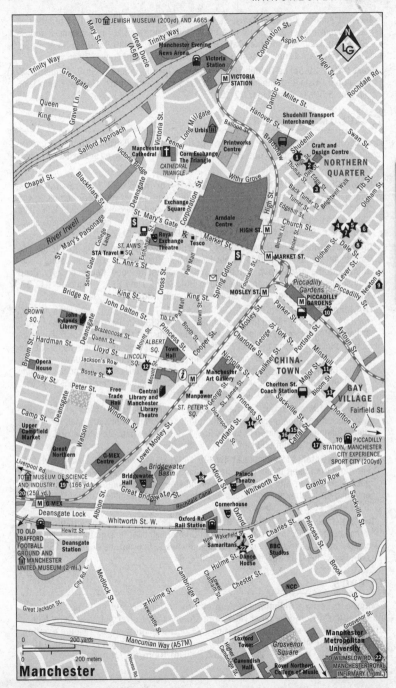

TO JEWISH MUSEUM (200yd) AND A665

Trinity Way

Great Ducie (A56)

Manchester Evening News Arena

Victoria Station

VICTORIA STATION

Corporation St.

Aspin Ln.

Angel St.

Rochdale Rd.

Mary St.

Trinity Way

Greengate

Queen

King

Gravel Ln.

Salford Approach

Victoria St.

Victoria Bridge

Chapel St.

Blackfriars St.

River Irwell

St. Mary's Parsonage

Manchester Cathedral

Long Mill gate

Urbis

Fennel

CATHEDRAL TRIANGLE

Corn Exchange/The Triangle

Exchange Square

St. Mary's Gate

Royal Exchange Theatre

ST. ANN'S SQ.

STA Travel

St. Ann's St.

Balloon St.

Hanover St.

Dantzic St.

Miller St.

Shudehill Transport Interchange

Printworks Centre

Withy Grove

Arndale Centre

HIGH ST.

Shudehill

Thomas St.

Oak St.

Craft and Design Centre

NORTHERN QUARTER

Swan St.

Tib St.

Oldham St.

Back turner St.

Turner St.

Edgehill St.

Bradshaw

Church St.

Birdin Ln.

Joiner St.

Dale St.

Lever St.

Newton St.

Bridge St.

College Land

South Gate

King St.

John Dalton St.

Cross St.

King St.

Spring Gdns.

Fountain St.

MOSLEY ST.

MARKET ST.

Tesco

Market St.

Pall Mall

Piccadilly Gardens

PICCADILLY GARDENS

Piccadilly

Parker St.

CROWN SQ.

John Rylands Library

Brazennose St.

Queen St.

Mount St.

ALBERT SQ.

LINCOLN SQ.

Tib Lane

Booth St.

Princess St.

Cooper St.

Town Hall

Charlotte St.

George St.

York St.

Mosley St.

Portland St.

Minshull

CHINA-TOWN

Aytoun St.

Hardman St.

Deansgate

Byrom St.

Opera House

Quay St.

Jackson's Row

Bootle St.

Peter St.

Free Trade Hall

Central Library and Manchester Library Theatre

Manchester Art Gallery

Manpower

ST. PETER'S SQ.

Nicholas St.

Faulkner St.

St. James St.

Princess St.

Dickinson St.

Portland St.

Chorlton St. Coach Station

Major St.

Bloom St.

GAY VILLAGE

Chorlton St.

Fairfield St.

Camp St.

Upper Campfield Market

Great Northern

Watson

Windmill St.

Lower Mosley St.

Oxford St.

Canal

TO PICCADILLY STATION, MANCHESTER CITY EXPERIENCE, SPORT CITY (200yd)

Liverpool Rd.

TO MUSEUM OF SCIENCE AND INDUSTRY, (166 yd.), (250 yd.)

G-MEX Centre

Bridgewater Hall

Bridgewater Basin

Great Bridgewater St.

Rochdale Canal

Palace Theatre

Whitworth St.

Granby Row

Sackville St.

G-MEX

Deansgate Lock

Whitworth St. W.

Oxford Rd. Rail Station

Cornerhouse

Oxford Rd.

Charles St.

Princess St.

Brook

TO OLD TRAFFORD FOOTBALL GROUND AND MANCHESTER UNITED MUSEUM (2 mi.)

Hewitt St.

Deansgate Station

Albion St.

City Rd. E.

Medlock St.

New Wakefield St.

Samaritans

Dance House

Hulme St.

BBC Studios

Cambridge St.

Lower Chatham St.

Chester St.

NCP

Sackville St.

Great Jackson St.

Hulme St.

Newcastle St.

Mancunian Way (A57M)

Princess Rd.

Upper Cambridge St.

Higher Cambridge St.

Loxford Tower

Cavendish Hall

Grosvenor Square

Royal Northern College of Music

Manchester Metropolitan University

TO WILMSLOW RD., MANCHESTER ROYAL INFIRMARY (½ mi.)

Grosvenor St.

0   200 yards

0   200 meters

Manchester

Internet Access: Central Library, St. Peter's Sq. (☎234 1900). Library card required. Call ahead to book a 2hr. slot or expect a long wait. Open M-Th 9am-8pm, F and Sa 9am-5pm. Free. **easyInternet Cafe,** 8-10 Exchange St. (☎839 3500), in St. Ann's Sq. Open M-Sa 7am-11pm, Su 9am-11pm. £2.50 per hr., £3 per day, £7 per wk.

Post Office: 26 Spring Gardens (☎839 0687). Open M-Tu and Th-Sa 8:30am-6pm, W 9am-6pm. Poste Restante (☎834 8605) has a separate entrance. Open M-F 6am-1pm, Sa 6am-8:50am. **Post Code:** M2 1BB.

ACCOMMODATIONS

Hostels fill up quickly in the summer, but decently priced student housing can be available when school lets out. Browse the free *Where to Stay* (at the TIC) for listings. Book ahead to be safe.

Hilton Chambers, 15 Hilton St. (☎236 4414 or 0800 083 3848; www.hattersgroup.com). Large ensuite rooms cleaned daily and a killer roof deck complete with grill. Conveniently located in the Northern Quarter. Self-service kitchen, free Wi-Fi, and 24hr. coffee and tea. Private rooms available. Reception 24hr. Laundry washed, dried, and ironed £5. Dorms from £15; singles from £40. MC/V. ❷

The Hatters Hostel, 50 Newton St. (☎236 9500; www.hattersgroup.com). Clean beds and bright dorms in a renovated hat factory near the Northern Quarter. Young attendants with the inside scoop on the city. Light breakfast included. Reception 24hr. Coed and single-sex dorms. 12- or 16-bed dorm £14; 8- or 10-bed £15; 4-bed dorm £17.50; triples £20 per person; twins or doubles £45. AmEx/MC/V. ❷

YHA Manchester, Potato Wharf, Castlefield (☎08707 705 950; www.yhamanchester.org.uk). Take the metro to G-Mex Station or bus #33 from Piccadilly Gardens toward Wigan to Deansgate and follow the signs to the Industrial Museum. The beautiful canal surroundings are worth the walk. Slightly cramped showers and rooms feel a bit like summer camp, but there is plenty of room to stretch out in the common area and library. Breakfast included. Lockers £1-2; free lockable cupboards in rooms. Laundry £1.50. Internet access 7p per min. Hair dryers, irons, and towels free with £2-5 deposit. Reception 24hr. Dorms £21; doubles £45. MC/V. ❷

University of Manchester: Call the **University Accommodation Office** (☎275 2888; www.accommodation.manchester.ac.uk) to find out which dorms are open for lodging during summer (from mid-June to mid-Sept.). 3- to 7-day min. stay. Reserve 1 week or more in advance. From £60 per wk. MC/V. ❶

New Union Hotel, 111 Princess St. (☎228 1492; www.newunionhotel.com/hotel.asp). Located in the heart of the Gay Village within walking distance of all the dancing and glitz. Spacious ensuite rooms with beautiful views of the canal. Guests receive free entrance to the showbar downstairs. Breakfast in bed £3. Double £35; twin £45; triple £55; quad £65. MC/V. ❹

The Millstone Hotel, 67 Thomas St. (☎839 0213). Simple but comfortable ensuite rooms conveniently located near Northern Quarter nightlife. Be sure to say hello to the colorful bar regulars at the pub downstairs. Singles £35; twins and doubles £45; triples £60. Book ahead on weekdays. AmEx/MC/V. ❹

FOOD

Conquer the pricey **Chinatown** restaurants by eating the multi-course "Businessman's Lunch" offered by most (M-F noon-2pm; £4-8). Better yet, visit **Curry Mile,** a stretch of Asian restaurants on Wilmslow Rd., for quality cuisine. Come evening, hip youths wine and dine in the cafe-bars. A Tesco **supermarket** is at 58-66 Market St. (☎911 9400. Open M-F 6am-midnight, Sa 6am-10pm, Su 11am-5pm.)

■ **Trof,** 2a Landcross Rd. (☎224 0476; www.trof.co.uk). A self-proclaimed "eating and drinking palace." The three-story bohemian cafe/bar/restaurant offers delicious food in an ever-changing atmosphere. Wash down a bacon and brie sandwich (£4.25) or roast pepper penne pasta (£7) with one of the 45 international beers from the bar. Check out the Trof times on the table for upcoming live shows. Food served noon-midnight. Open daily 9am-midnight. MC/V. ❷

▨ **Soup Kitchen,** 31-33 Spear St. (☎236 5100; www.soup-kitchen.co.uk). Communal tables and delicious homemade soups and pies make this a perfect place for a stop while exploring the Northern Quarter. Arrive early—the soups of the day are generally gone by 2pm. Open M-F 9am-4pm. £4 lunch special. Cash only. ❶

Tampopo Noodle House, 16 Albert Sq. (☎819 1966; www.tampopo.co.uk). This spartan basement noodle house is one of Manchester's favorites. Noodles (£6-11) with ingredients from Thailand, Malaysia, Indonesia, Vietnam, and Japan are quick and delicious. Open daily noon-11pm. AmEx/MC/V. ❷

The Ox Pub, 71 Liverpool Rd., Castlefield (☎839 7740; www.theox.co.uk). Gourmet pub food may seem like an oxymoron, but that's exactly what you get at this cozy, traditional pub on the canal. Light meals from £3.50, 2-course set dinner £12. Food served M-Sa noon-3pm and 5:30-9:30pm, Su noon-7pm. MC/V. ❸

Barburrito, 1 Piccadilly Gardens (☎228 6479; www.barburrito.co.uk). Serves up authentic Mexican dishes with fresh ingredients. Even more delicious? Just about everything on the menu is under £5. Open M-Sa 11am-8pm, Su noon-6pm. MC/V. ❶

Eden, 3 Brazil St. (☎237 9852). Adams and Eves enjoy Italian and continental dishes and drinks at this canal-side restaurant in the Gay Village. Dine on "the barge" (a boat-shaped deck on the water) and enjoy the pizza special (2 pizzas and 2 bottles of beer £12, M-Sa noon-5pm). Open M-F 11am-11pm, Sa-Su 11am-2am. ❸

◎ SIGHTS

The ▨**Manchester Art Gallery,** on Nicholas St., features an interactive exhibit (try to make one of the paintings burp) and a gallery where you can watch art restoration. In addition, the famous Pre-Raphaelite collection is impressive. (☎235 8888; www.manchestergalleries.org. Guided tours every Su at 2pm. Open Tu-Su and bank holidays 10am-5pm. Free; admission for special exhibitions varies.) In the **Museum of Science and Industry,** Liverpool Rd., in Castlefield, a large complex of buildings shows working looms and steam engines in a dramatic illustration of Britain's industrialization. (☎832 2244. Open daily 10am-5pm. Free. Special exhibits £3-5.) The fantastic **Urbis** museum, Cathedral Gardens, between Victoria Station and Exchange Sq., explores modern urban culture and art. The awe-inspiring museum is a sculpture itself, clad in 2200 handmade plates of glass with a "ski-slope" copper roof. High-tech interactive exhibits provide insights into city life in Manchester and beyond. (☎605 8205; www.urbis.org.uk. Open Tu-Su 10am-6pm. Free.) The **Manchester Craft and Design Centre,** 17 Oak St., showcases crafts, from specialty stationary to handmade jewelry, in a glass-roofed atrium that was a Victorian fish market. (☎832 4274; www.craftanddesign.com. Open M-Sa 10am-5:30pm. Free.) For a stunning panoramic view of the city, head to the top of the Shudehill Interchange parking garage. This little-known spot offers an aerial view of the whole city and beyond. (Always open. Free if you walk in.)

Tucked behind the Town Hall, the **Central Library** is the city's masterpiece. One of the largest municipal libraries in Europe, the domed building has a music and theater library, a literature library, and the UK's second-largest Judaica collection. The **Library Theatre Company** (☎236 7110; www.librarytheatre.com), located in the basement of Central Library, puts on top-shelf productions of modern plays. The **John Rylands Library,** 150 Deansgate, is a stunning Gothic building that collects rare books. Its most famous holding is the St. John Fragment, a piece of New Testament writing from the 2nd century. (☎275 3764; www.library.manchester.ac.uk. Open M and W-Sa 10am-5pm, Tu and Su noon-5pm. Free.)

Loved, reviled, and always sung about in the streets, **Manchester United** is England's reigning football team. The **Manchester United Museum and Tour Centre,** Sir Matt Busby Way, at the Old Trafford football stadium, displays memorabilia dating from the club's inception in 1878 to its recent successes. Follow signs from the Old Trafford Metrolink stop. (☎08704 421 994. Open daily 9:30am-5pm. Tours every 10min., 9:40am-4:30pm. Pre-booking encouraged. No tours on match days. £9, seniors £6, children free, families £25. Special rates available for groups.) Manchester's less-infamous team, **Manchester City,** offers the **Manchester City Experience,** with a tour of the new museum and stadium. Sport City, in the ReebokCity Building, is a 20min. walk from Piccadilly Station to Ashton New Rd. (☎062 1894. Open M-Sa 9:30am-4pm, Su 10:30am-2:30pm. £8.75, concessions £4.75, families £25.) For tickets to a match (£10-25), visit www.manutd.com or call the ticket order line at ☎0870 442 1999.

 NIGHTLIFE

CAFE-BARS AND CLUBS

Many of Manchester's excellent lunchtime spots morph into pre-club drinking venues or become clubs themselves. Manchester's clubbing and live music scenes remain national trendsetters. Centered on **Oldham Street,** the **Northern Quarter** is the city's youthful outlet for live music, with its alternative vibe and underground shops attracting a hip crowd. Partiers flock to **Oxford Street** for late-night clubbing and reveling. Don't forget to collect fliers—they'll often score you a discount. **Afflecks Palace,** 52 Church St., supplies paraphernalia from punk to funk—the walls of the stairway are postered with event notices. (☎839 6392. Open M-F 10am-5:30pm, Sa 10am-6pm.) **Fat City,** 20 Oldham St., sells hip hop, reggae, funk, and jazz records as well as passes to clubbing events. (☎237 1181. Open M-Sa 10am-6pm, Su noon-5pm.) If you're feeling unsafe crossing from Piccadilly to Swan St. or Great Ancoats St., use **Oldham Street,** where the neon-lit clubs (and their supersized bouncers) provide reassurance.

Cord, 8 Dorsey St. (☎832 9494). Where corduroy meets chic. No, really. Cozy home to bohemian intellectuals playing mellow tunes. Giant booths for gathering with friends. Su nights feature "Out of the Gloom" DJ sets with eclectic feel-good music spinning until 11pm. Open M-Th and Su noon-10:30pm, F-Sa noon-1am.

Dry Bar, 28-30 Oldham St. (☎236 9840). Used to be called Dry 201, in reference to the Factory Records catalogue system. Cavorting clubbers fill this sultry spot, known as the longest bar in Manchester. Live bands in the front room and DJs in the back. Open M-Th 11am-midnight, F 11am-1am, Sa 11am-2am.

Night and Day Cafe, 26 Oldham St. (☎236 1822; www.nightandday.org). Mild-mannered cafe by day, live entertainment venue (featuring punk, jazz, folk, and alternative music) by night. Open daily 10am-2am, with music starting at 8pm most nights.

The Temple, 100 Great Bridgewater (☎278 1610). Literally a hole-in-the-street bar, this tiny pub was built in an old Victorian public toilet. Frequented by local artists and students. The much-praised German beer selection and intimate setting make it worth a stop. Open daily 2pm-1am.

Simple Bar and Restaurant, 44 Tib St. (☎0870 757 1996). Fuel up before heading out to the clubs. 2-course lunch £6.50. Open M-Th 12:30-11pm, F-Sa 12:30pm-midnight, Su 10am-10pm.

Thirsty Scholar, off Oxford St. (☎236 6071). Students packs into this small bar underneath a railroad bridge. At night, the rumble of overhead trains is drowned out by the thudding beats of local DJs. M and Th acoustic nights. F-Su DJs. Open daily noon-2am.

THE GAY VILLAGE

The **Gay Village** developed along **Canal Street,** once a run-down part of the city, in the 1990s and has since become one of the premier "going-out" neighborhoods. Northeast of Princess St., the Gay Village fills with mixed crowds that dance by night and mingle by day. When the weather cooperates, patrons can be found flooding the many sidewalk tables lining the canal.

Essential, Bloom St. (☎236 0077; www.essentialmanchester.com), at the corner of Bloom St., off Portland St. One of the Gay Village's more popular clubs. Dress smart casual. Cover £3-8. Open F 10:30pm-5am, Sa 10:30pm-6am, Su 10:30pm-3am.

Cruz 101, 101 Princess St. (☎950 0101, info line 237 1554; www.cruz101.com). Fun and sexy cruisers teach lessons in attitude. 2 fl. with 6 bars. Dress smart casual. Cover £2-5. Students discounts available. Open M and W-Su 11pm-5am.

Queer, 4 Canal St. (☎228 1360; www.queer-manchester.com). Huge booths and flatscreen TVs create a great atmosphere at this new bar midway down Canal St. DJs spin excellent music that will keep you cutting rugs all night long. Open M-Sa 11pm-2am, Su 11pm-12:30am.

The New Union Showbar, 111 Princess St. (☎228 1492; www.newunionhotel.com/hotel.asp). Lively show bar and club featuring live entertainment and music. Tu night karaoke and Su night drag show. Open M-Sa 11am-2am, Su noon-12:30am.

🎵 🎋 ENTERTAINMENT AND FESTIVALS

Manchester's many entertainment venues accommodate diverse interests. The **Manchester Evening News (MEN) Arena** (☎930 8000; www.men-arena.com), behind Victoria Station, hosts concerts and sporting events. The **Manchester Festival** (☎234 3157; www.the-manchester-festival.org.uk) runs dramatic and musical events all summer. The Gay Village hosts a number of festivals, most notably late August's **Mardi Gras** (☎238 4548), which raises money for AIDS relief. **Manchester Pride** (☎230 2624; www.manchesterpride.com), held on the August bank holiday weekend, has live entertainment, sporting events, and a parade.

Royal Exchange Theatre (☎833 9833; www.royalexchange.co.uk) has returned to St. Ann's Sq. after a 1996 IRA bomb destroyed the original building. The theater stages traditional and Shakespearean plays and premiers original works. Box office open M-Sa 9:30am-7:30pm. Tickets £7.25-25.50. Concessions available.

Bridgewater Hall, Lower Mosley St. (☎907 9000; www.bridgewater-hall.co.uk). Manchester's foremost venue for orchestral concerts and home of Manchester's own Hallé Orchestra. Open M-Sa 10am-8pm, Su noon-6pm. Tickets £5-30.

Palace Theatre, Oxford St. (☎245 6600). Caters to classical tastes in theater, opera, and ballet. Box office open M-Sa 10am-6pm and before performances.

Cornerhouse, Oxford St. (☎200 1500; www.cornerhouse.org). Screens indie films and art events. Bar and cafe on-site. M night "Reel Deal" includes movie ticket, a pizza, and a glass of wine or pint for £10. Th-Sa DJ nights from 8pm. Box office open daily noon-8pm.

BLACKPOOL   ☎01253

Blackpool has something for everybody—except, perhaps, lovers of peace and quiet. Arcade games jostle for space with slot machines, liquor stores are outnumbered only by stalls selling "Blackpool Rock" hard candy, ferris wheel lights cast their neon glow on entrances to strip clubs, and a bustling Promenade stands over the crowded beach. Its posh 19th-century resort status has long been lost, but Blackpool's spirit of gaudy hedonism still attracts children, stag parties, grandparents, and everyone in between.

▐ TRANSPORTATION

Buses and trains are regular, but drivers be warned: it's not uncommon to see two or more traffic cops on a single street dispensing fines.

Trains: Blackpool North Station (☎620 385), 4 blocks down Talbot Rd. from North Pier. Booking office open M-Sa 5:30am-9pm, Su 8am-9pm. Trains (☎08457 484 950) to: **Birmingham** via **Preston** (2½hr., 1-2 per hr., £34); **Leeds** (2hr., every hr., £15.50); **Liverpool** (1½hr., every 2hr., £12.35); **London Euston** via **Preston** (3hr., every hr., £94); **Manchester** (1¼hr., 2 per hr., £12.40).

Bus Station: On Talbot Rd. Ticket office open M-Sa 9:30am-5pm. National Express (☎08705 808 080) buses to **Birmingham** (3-4hr., 5 per day, £18); **London** (6½-8hr., 4 per day, £25.50); **Manchester** (2hr., 5 per day, £6.40).

Public Transportation: Local trains use Blackpool South and Pleasure Beach stations. **Local bus** info is available at the transportation center at 22-24 Market St. (☎473 302). Open M-Sa 8:15am-5:30pm and Su 10:15am-3pm. Bus #1 runs from North Pier to Pleasure Beach every 20min.; on weekends, **vintage trams** run this route more frequently. A 1-day **Travelcard** (£5.75, concessions £5.25) buys unlimited travel on trams and local buses; otherwise, 1 ride costs about £1.30, 3-day pass £14.

Taxi: C Cabs (☎292 929)

▐ PRACTICAL INFORMATION

Tourist Information Centre: 1 Clifton St. (☎478 222). Arranges accommodations for a 10% deposit, books local shows for £1.50, and sells maps (50p) that are extremely useful for navigating Blackpool's maze of truncated streets. Open May-Oct. M-Sa 9am-5pm, Su 10am-4pm; Nov.-Apr. M-Sa 9am-5pm. Branch (☎478 222) on the Promenade. Open M-Sa 9:30am-5pm, Su 10am-4:30pm.

Financial Services: Banks are easy to find, especially along Corporation and Birley St. Most are open M-F 9am-4:30pm. **ATMs** are ubiquitous, often sharing space with phone booths or just inside arcades.

Launderette: Albert Road Launderette, Regent Rd. Open M-F 9am-6pm, Sa 9am-4pm, Su 9am-2pm. Last wash 30min. before close. Wash £2.40, dry 20p per 5min.

Police: Bonny St. (☎293 933).

Hospital: Victoria Hospitals, Whinney Heys Rd. (☎300 000).

Pharmacy: Boots (☎622 276), at Bank Hey and Victoria St. Open M-F 9am-5:30pm, Sa 8:30am-6pm, Su 10am-4pm.

Internet Access: Blackpool Public **Library,** Queen St. (☎478 111). Free, but limited to 15min. slots. Open M and F 9am-5pm, Tu and Th 9am-7pm, W and Sa 10am-5pm. **Cafe@Claremont,** Dickson Rd. (☎299 306). 50p per 10min. Open M-F 9am-4pm.

Post Office: 26-30 Abingdon St. (☎08457 223 344). **Bureau de change.** Open M-Sa 9am-5:30pm. **Post Code:** FY1 1AA.

▐ ACCOMMODATIONS

With over 2600 guest houses holding 96,000 beds, you won't have trouble finding a room, except on weekends during the Illuminations (p. 362), when prices skyrocket. Budget-friendly **B&Bs** dominate the blocks behind the Promenade between the North and Central Piers (£15-30). Pick up the free *Visit Blackpool* guide at the TIC for an impressive list.

Silver Birch Hotel, 39 Hull Rd. (☎622 125). From either station, head down Talbot Rd. to the ocean, take a left on Market St., pass the Tower, and turn left onto Hull Rd. The Irish proprietor provides pleasant, if basic, rooms and warm hospitality. Most rooms are ensuite with TVs. Breakfast £3. £17 per person. Cash only. ❷

Summerville Guest House, corner of S. King St. and Albert Rd. (☎621 300; www.avrilanddavid.supanet.com). Follow the directions to Raffles (below), but turn onto S. King St. after the left on Church St. The radiantly-colored rooms all have TVs. Breakfast included. £16-20 per person. MC/V. ❷

Manor Grove Hotel, 24 Leopold Grove (☎625 577; www.manorgrovehotel.com). Follow the Raffles directions, but turn right at Church St., left onto Leopold Grove, and walk 1 block. Spacious ensuite rooms with TV, phone, and bath. Hearty English breakfast included. Singles from £28; doubles £44-52. MC/V. ❸

Raffles Hotel, 73-77 Hornby Rd. (☎294 713; www.raffleshotelblackpool.co.uk). From the train or bus station, head toward the ocean along Talbot Rd., turn left on Topping St., left on Church St., right on Regent Rd., and right onto Hornby Rd. Large, comfortable rooms. Breakfast included. Twins, doubles, and family rooms £26-32 per person. Single occupancy 20% discount. MC/V. ❸

☐ FOOD

Because waterfront cuisine consists mostly of candy floss (cotton candy) and fish and chips, heading off the Promenade should yield some more appetizing alternatives. The Iceland **supermarket,** 8-10 Topping St., is on the same block as the bus station. (☎751 575. Open M-Sa 8:30am-8pm, Su 10am-4pm.) **Henry's Bistro and Wine Bar ❸,** Queen St., offers a three-course dinner (including steak) for £14. Sip your wine in this former theater, with curtains still intact and chandeliers draped in lights. (☎752 977. Open M and W-Th 6:30pm-10:30pm, F-Sa 6pm-10:30pm, Su 6:30pm-9:30pm. MC/V.) The cozy **Coffee Pot ❶,** 12 Birley St., serves big portions of hearty fare. Try the roast beef dinner (£5.75), which comes with Yorkshire pudding and two vegetables. (☎751 610. Open daily 7:30am-5:30pm. Cash only.)

☐ ☐ SIGHTS AND ENTERTAINMENT

Thirty-six nightclubs, 38,000 theater seats, several circuses, and a tangle of roller coasters line the **Promenade,** which is traversed by Britain's first electric tram line. Even the three 19th-century piers are stacked with ferris wheels and chip shops. Blackpool quiets down during the week, but when the town packs with crowds of weekenders from the South, attractions run in full force.

▓**BLACKPOOL TOWER.** A London businessman returned from the 1890 Paris World Exposition determined to erect Eiffel Tower imitations throughout Britain. Only Blackpool embraced his enthusiasm, and by 1894 the 560 ft. tower graced the city's skyline. It never quite reached international icon status, but the tower retains a kitschy charm all its own. **Towerworld,** the entertainment center surrounding its base, features exhibits on the tower, an elevator to the top, and the more eclectic arcade games, jungle gym, casino, and aquarium. An ornate Victorian-revival ballroom hosts senior citizens dancing sedately to the sounds of an electric organ by day and live swing band performances by night (8pm). Towerworld's **circus,** named the UK's best, runs up to four shows per day and features mesmerizing dance, tightrope, and stunt acts in a performance arena that converts to a pool in

NORTHWEST ENGLAND

the show's perplexing grand finale. Mooky the Clown was voted Britain's best. Admission covers all activities. (☎ 292 029; www.theblackpooltower.co.uk. Open daily May-Oct. 10am-11pm; Nov.-Apr. 10am-6pm. £16, concessions £10, children £11. Tickets are all-day.)

PLEASURE BEACH. Around 6.8 million people visit this sprawling amusement park each year, second in Europe only to EuroDisney. Pleasure Beach is known for its wooden roller coasters—the twin-track **Grand National** (c. 1935) is a mecca for coaster enthusiasts. Thrill-seekers line up for the aptly named **Big One** and aren't disappointed as the 235 ft. steel behemoth sends them down a heartstopping 65° slope at 87 mph. Admission to the park is free, and the pay-as-you-ride system keeps queues fairly short. By night, Pleasure Beach features illusion shows. (Across from South Pier. ☎ 0870 444 5566; www.blackpoolpleasurebeach.com. Opening times vary–call to verify–but are generally daily 10:30am-9:30pm in summer months. £2-7 per ride. 1-day pass varies depending on season, starting at £25, junior £15; 2-day £45.)

THE ILLUMINATIONS. Blackpool, the first town in Britain with electricity, consummates its love affair with bright lights in the Illuminations. The annual display takes place over 5 mi. of the Promenade from September to early November, running from dusk until about midnight. In a colossal waste of electricity, 72 mi. of cables light up the tower, the Promenade, star-encased faces of Hollywood actors, and LED displays. (More information at www.visitblackpool.com)

THE GRUNDY ART GALLERY. If you've had enough of the dizzying Promenade, head to the Grundy, which showcases up-and-coming artists and displays the original collection of its 19th-century founder. The special galleries on the first floor rotate exhibits, while the second floor has Viking artifacts from around Blackpool's beaches. (Queen St. ☎ 478 170; www.blackpool.gov.uk/grundyartgallery. Open M-Sa 10am-5pm. Free.)

⬛ NIGHTLIFE

Between North and Central Piers, Blackpool's famous **Golden Mile** shines with more neon than gold, hosting scores of sultry theaters, cabaret bars, and bingo halls. Clubs fall into two categories: the cool modern and the cheerfully cheesy. Rowdy **Syndicate,** self-advertised as "the biggest club in the UK," brings droves to Church St. (☎ 753 222; www.thesyndicate.com. Th £3 cover and £1.50 drinks; F £3 cover before 11:30pm, £5 after; Sa £10 cover. Open Th-F 10pm-3am, Sa 10pm-4am.) Blackpool's most frequented clubs are on the Promenade. **Sanuk,** 167-170 Promenade, is farther north at the corner of Springfield Rd. Fill out the online form to get on the guest list and enter for free before 11:30pm. (☎ 292 900; www.sanukblackpool.co.uk. Smart casual. Cover £2-5. Open Tu, Th, and Su 10:30pm-3am, F-Sa 10:30pm-4am.) Most clubs have a £2-5 cover and are open 10pm-2am.

PEAK DISTRICT NATIONAL PARK

The Peak District's landscape is beautiful regardless of its lack of any actual mountains or peaks. In the more touristed southern region, known as the White Peak, green hills hold idyllic country villages and miles of gentle walks. The more rugged northern region, the Dark Peak, is a playground for hikers seeking moors, cliffs, and peat bottoms. Located between industrial leviathans Manchester, Nottingham, and Sheffield, the Peak District is one of the most visited National Parks in the world—over 20 million visit each year. It's only been popular since 1951, when it was made Britain's first national park. Before that, the entire area was fenced off as a royal hunting ground. Transportation is best in the south and near outlying cities, but travelers can veer north for a more isolated escape.

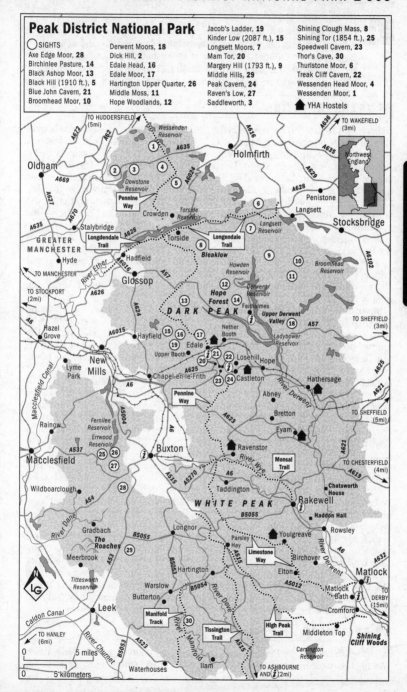

Peak District National Park

○ SIGHTS

Axe Edge Moor, **28**
Birchinlee Pasture, **14**
Black Ashop Moor, **13**
Black Hill (1910 ft.), **5**
Blue John Cavern, **21**
Broomhead Moor, **10**

Derwent Moors, **18**
Dick Hill, **2**
Edale Head, **16**
Edale Moor, **17**
Hartington Upper Quarter, **26**
Middle Moss, **11**
Hope Woodlands, **12**

Jacob's Ladder, **19**
Kinder Low (2087 ft.), **15**
Longsett Moors, **7**
Mam Tor, **20**
Margery Hill (1793 ft.), **9**
Middle Hills, **29**
Peak Cavern, **24**
Raven's Low, **27**
Saddleworth, **3**

Shining Clough Mass, **8**
Shining Tor (1854 ft.), **25**
Speedwell Cavern, **23**
Thor's Cave, **30**
Thurlstone Moor, **6**
Treak Cliff Cavern, **22**
Wessenden Head Moor, **4**
Wessenden Moor, **1**

▲ YHA Hostels

NORTHWEST ENGLAND

NATIONAL PARK COVERAGE. *Let's Go's* coverage of the Peak District National Park includes the towns of **Castleton, Edale, Buxton,** and **Bakewell.** The first section provides an overview of transportation, practical information, and accommodations (such as **YHA hostels**) for the entire park. Local services, B&Bs, and activities are listed within coverage for the individual towns.

▶ TRANSPORTATION

Trains (☎ 08457 484 950) are scarce in the Peak District: three lines enter its boundaries, but only one crosses the park itself. One line travels from Derby to Matlock on the park's southeast edge (30min.; M-Sa 13-14 per day, Su 9 per day; £4). Another runs from Manchester to Buxton (1hr., every hr., £6.70). The **Hope Valley line** (M-F 12 per day, Sa 18 per day, Su 12 per day) goes from Manchester across the park via Edale (45min., £7.70), Hope (50min., £7.85), and Hathersage (55min., £7.85), ending in Sheffield (1¼hr., £12.90). Both lines from Manchester enter the park at New Mills—the Buxton line at Newtown Station and the Hope Valley line at Central Station. A 20min. signposted walk separates the stations.

Inter-village travel is possible with determination and a sturdy pair of legs. For the less hiking-inclined, the Derbyshire County Council's *Peak District Timetables* (80p) is invaluable. The booklet includes all bus routes as well as a map and info on day-long bus tickets, cycle hire, hostels, TICs, campgrounds, market days, and hospitals. The website www.derbysbus.net is a helpful resource for planning regional travel.

Buses make a noble effort to connect the scattered Peak towns, and Traveline (☎ 0870 608 2608) is a comprehensive and centralized resource. Coverage of many routes improves on Sundays, especially in summer. The "Transpeak" makes the journey between Manchester and Nottingham (3½hr., 15 per day), stopping at Buxton, Bakewell, Matlock, Derby, and other towns in between, although some buses only cover part of the route—pick up a free timetable at any TIC. Bus #218 (M-Sa 4 per day, Su 3 per day) runs from Sheffield to Bakewell (45min.) and Buxton (1¼hr.), connecting with #118 to Leek (1¾hr.) en route to Hanley (2¼hr.). Buses #272, 273, and 274 reach Castleton from Sheffield (50min-1¼ hr.; M-F 21 per day, Sa 19 per day, Su 15 per day). Bus #65 runs between Sheffield and Buxton via Eyam (1¼hr.; M-Sa 6 per day, Su 3 per day) and bus #173 runs from Bakewell to Castleton (50min.; M-Sa 4 per day, Su 3 per day). Bus #200 runs from Castleton to Edale (20min., M-F 3 per day), sometimes continuing to Chapel-en-le-Frith. On weekends it runs as bus #260 and stops at the Castleton caverns (6 per day). Ride is free with proof of railway transportation.

National Express buses run once per day to London from Buxton (5hr., £20), Bakewell (4¾hr., £20), and Matlock (4½hr., £20) with changes in Nottingham, Leicester, and Derby. Bus #218 (4 per day, Su 3 per day) runs from Buxton to Bakewell (30min.) and on to Sheffield (1¼hr.).

Pick up one of the half-dozen bargain day tickets outlined in the *Timetables* booklet—several have their own brochures at the TIC. The best deal is the **Derbyshire Wayfarer** (£8.30, concessions £4.15, families £13.10), which allows one day of train and bus travel throughout the Peak District and surrounding area north to Sheffield and south to Derby. It also provides a variety of discounts at local attractions and shops. Day passes are sold at the Manchester train stations, National Park Information Centres (NPICs), local rail stations, and on most buses.

▶ PRACTICAL INFORMATION

Daytime facilities in the Peak District generally stay open all winter. Some B&Bs and hostels welcome travelers until December. **YHA Edale** is open year-round, although it hosts camps in July and August. Most TICs book accommodations for a 10% deposit or £2. The **Peak District National Park Office,** Aldern House, Baslow Rd., Bakewell, Derbyshire, (☎01629 816 200; www.peakdistrict-npa.gov.uk) provides useful information and fun facts about the park.

National Park Information Centres: All NPICs carry detailed walking guides.

Bakewell: Old Market Hall (☎0870 444 7275), at Bridge St. From the bus stop, walk a block down Bridge St. with Bath Gardens on your left. Also a TIC, with accommodations booking. Upstairs exhibit on the town's history. Open daily Easter-Oct. 9:30am-5:30pm; Nov.-Easter 10am-5pm.

Castleton: Buxton Rd. (☎01629 816 558). From the bus stop, follow the road past the post office into town and head right; the NPIC is along the road that leads to the caverns. Great geological and cultural display in annex. Open daily Easter-Oct. 9:30am-5:30pm; Nov.-Easter 10am-5pm.

Edale: Fieldhead (☎01433 670 207), between the rail station and village; signs point the way from both directions. Open Easter-Oct. M-F 9am-5pm, Sa-Su 9am-5:30pm; Nov.-Easter M-F 10:30am-3:30pm, Sa-Su 9:30am-4:30pm.

Fairholmes: Upper Derwent Valley (☎01433 650 953), near Derwent Dam. Open Easter-Oct. M-F 9:30am-5pm, Sa-Su 9:30am-5pm; Nov.-Jan. 2 M-F 10am-3:30pm, Sa-Su 9:30am-4:30pm; Jan. 3-Feb. 11 Sa-Su 9:30am-4:30pm; Feb. 12-Easter M-F 10am-3:30pm, Sa-Su 9:30am-4:30.

Tourist Information Centres:

Ashbourne: 13 Market Pl. (☎01335 343 666). Open Mar.-Oct. M-Sa 9:30am-5pm, Su 10am-4pm; Nov.-Feb. M-Sa 10am-4pm. Off-season hours subject to change. Call for more information.

Buxton: The Crescent (☎0129 825 106; www.visitbuxton.com). Open daily Mar.-Oct. 9:30am-5pm; Nov.-Feb.10am-4pm.

Matlock: Crown Sq. (☎01629 583 388), in the town center. Open daily Mar.-Oct. 9:30am-5pm; Nov.-Feb. 10am-4pm.

Matlock Bath: The Pavilion (☎01629 55082), along the main road. Open Mar.-Oct. daily 9:30am-5pm; Nov.-Feb. Sa-Su 10am-4pm. Hours vary.

ACCOMMODATIONS

NPICs and TICs both distribute the park-wide *Peak District Camping and Caravanning Guide*, which lists all campsites and caravanning (RV) sites. The *Peak District Visitor Guide* lists accommodations and attractions and is free from TICs and NPICs. **B&Bs** are plentiful and moderately priced in the countryside (singles £20-25) and more expensive in towns (£30-35), although single rooms can be in short supply. Check the Visitor Guide for room information. YHA hostels (£13-15) usually fill far in advance. Note that many hostels are not open every day—most are closed on Sunday nights. Expect to pay higher rates in more tourist-oriented towns. **Buxton, Bakewell,** and **Matlock Bath** are well-stocked with B&Bs.

The nine YHA-operated, farmer-owned **camping barns ❶** are simple shelters, providing a sleeping platform, water tap, and toilet. Visitors should bring a sleeping bag and camping equipment. Lucky travelers will find a shower and/or hot water. Book and pay ahead through the **YHA Camping Barns Department,** Trevelyan House, Dimple Rd., Matlock, Derbyshire, DE4 3YH (☎0870 770 8868). You can pay over the phone with a credit card, or they'll hold your reservation for five days while you mail a booking form, available in camping barn booklets and distributed at NPICs and TICs. Barns can be found in: **Abney,** between Eyam and Castleton; **Alstonefield,** between Dovedale and Manifold Valley; **Birchover,** near Matlock off the B5056; **Butterton,** near the southern end of the park, along the Manifold track; **Edale** village; **Middleton-by-Youlgreave; Nab End,** in Hollinsclough; **Taddington,** Main Rd.; and **Underbank,** in Wildboarclough.

The Peak District has about a dozen **YHA hostels,** some of which are listed below. Don't let numbers fool you—most fill quickly with school groups, so call ahead to reserve a space. The hostels generally lie within a day's hike of one another and sell maps detailing routes to neighboring hostels. Alternatively, *Peak District*

Timetables (80p at TICs) lists both YHAs and the bus services to them. Most hostels serve meals and are phasing out 10am-5pm lockouts, but 11pm curfews are still generally in place. Many offer a £1 student discount. Two of the smaller hostels (Bretton and Langsett) book through the central **YHA Diary** office (☎0870 770 8868). Only call these hostels directly for general information or for lodging within the following week, and remember that most require booking 48hr. in advance.

Castleton: Castleton Hall (☎0870 770 5758). Pretty country house and attached vicarage in the heart of town. The vicarage has nicer rooms with baths and no curfew or lockout. Free coffee and tea. Spacious self-catering kitchen, several lounges, and small bar with excellent beer. Book at least 2-3 weeks ahead. Hosts camps from mid-July to Aug. Curfew in country house 11pm. Dorms £14, under 18 £10. MC/V. ❷

Edale: Rowland Cote (☎0870 770 5808), Nether Booth, 2 mi. east of Edale village. From the train station, turn right and then left onto the main road; follow it to Nether Booth, where a sign points the way. Buses also stop within ½ mi. of the hostel. Includes a climbing tower for supervised groups. Closed from mid-July to the end of Aug. for children's camps. Doors locked at 11pm, but keypad allows 24hr. access. Dorms £13.50, under 18 £10. MC/V. ❷

Eyam: Hawkhill Rd. (☎0870 770 5830). Walk down the main road from the square, pass the church, and look right for the sign. With a turret and an oaken door, it's more castle than hostel. Lockout 10am-3pm. Curfew 11pm. Open Feb.-Oct. M-Sa; late Oct. to Nov. F-Sa; call otherwise. Dorms £15, under 18 £11. MC/V. ❷

Hathersage: Castleton Rd. (☎0870 770 5852). Stone building with white-framed windows and creeping ivy. Lockout noon-5pm. Curfew 11pm. Open Apr.-Aug. M-Sa; Sept.-Oct. Tu-Sa. Dorms £13, under 18 £9.50. MC/V. ❶

Ravenstor: (☎0870 770 6008), ½ mi. from Millers Dale. Buses #65 and 66 will stop here (both M-Sa 10 per day, Su 7 per day). Bar, TV, and game room. Open Feb.-Oct. Sa-Su. Dorms £14, under 18 £10. MC/V. ❷

Youlgreave: Fountain Sq. (☎0870 770 6104). Take bus #171 or 172 from the nearby Bakewell stop. The building was once used as a village co-operative department store, and the windows still advertise "Groceries and Provisions." Reception closed 10am-5pm, but key allows 24hr. access. Curfew 11pm. Open Feb.-Mar. F-Sa; Apr.-Oct. M-Sa; Nov.-Dec. F-Sa. Dorms £14, under 18 £10. MC/V. ❷

■ ▲ HIKING AND OUTDOORS

With over 5000 mi. of public footpaths, the central Peak District is marvelous territory for rambling. Settlement is sparser and buses are fewer north of Edale near the **Kinder Scout Plateau,** the great **Derwent Reservoirs,** and the gritty cliffs and peat moorlands. From Edale, the **Pennine Way** (p. 402) runs north to Kirk Yetholm in Scotland. Local hikers prefer the trails near the Derwent Reservoirs, the paths to Kinder Scout from Edale, and the route from Dovedale to Tissington. Ask at NPICs for details and further recommendations. Be advised that hikers should bring warm clothing and the customary supplies (see **Wilderness Safety,** p. 50). Be respectful of the many acres of private land close to (and sometimes on) the trails. Guidebooks and a variety of walking and hiking maps (some free, others from £2) are available at TICs and NPICs (p. 365). The park authority offers guided walks most weekends and some weekdays. Enquire at any NPIC for a schedule.

The park authority offers **bike rentals** at four Cycle Hire Centres, all of which are listed in the *Peak District Timetables.* They can be found in Ashbourne (☎01335 343 156), on Mapleton Ln.; Derwent (☎01433 651 261), near the Fairholmes NPIC; Middleton Top (☎01629 823 204), at the visitors center; and Parsley Hay (☎01298 84493), in Buxton (Bikes £11 per 4hr., £14 per day; children £8/10; £20 deposit. Tandem bikes £25 per 4hr., £32 per day, £50 deposit). Privately run bike rentals are at Waterhouses (☎ 01538 308 609), in the Old Station Car Park between Ashbourne and Leek on the A523; and Carsington Water (☎ 01629 540 478), near Matlock off Ashbourne-Wirksworth Rd. Call for rates. (Most open Apr.-Sept. daily 9:30am-6pm; Oct.-Mar. call for hours.) *Cycle Derbyshire*, available at NPICs, includes opening hours, locations, and trail info.

CASTLETON ☎ 01433

The small town of Castleton (pop. 1200) has tremendous natural beauty and the busy tourist traffic to match. Rolling pastures and low stone walls conceal caves full of the colorful mineral Blue John (from the French "bleu et jaune," or blue and yellow), found only in the local bedrock and in gift shops. With its postcard-perfect streets lined with ivy-covered stone buildings and hedged gardens, Castleton is a lovely base from which to explore the rest of the Peak District.

TRANSPORTATION AND PRACTICAL INFORMATION. Castleton lies 2 mi. west of the **Hope** train station (avoid Castleton Station or you'll end up in a suburb of Manchester). Bus #272 runs from Hope to Castleton. **Buses** run to Sheffield, Buxton, and Bakewell (p. 364), and the bus station has a useful town map. Hikers looking for a challenge can set off southward from town on the 26 mi. **Limestone Way Trail** to Miller's Dale and Matlock Bath. Castleton's **NPIC** (p. 365) stocks maps and brochures (many under £1) on local walks. Particularly useful is *Walks around Castleton* (£1.40), which outlines 2½-9½ mi. hikes. Hikers can visit the **Adventure UIP,** in the center of town off the marketplace by the hostel, for supplies and information. (☎ 620 320; www.adventureuip.co.uk. Open M-F 9:30am-5pm, Sa-Su 9:30am-5:30pm. MC/V.) The nearest **bank** is 6 mi. east in Hathersage; the Cheshire Cheese Inn, How Ln., and the Peaks Inn, How Ln., both have **ATMs**. The **post office,** How Ln., is in a convenience store close to the bus stop. (☎ 620 241. Open M-Tu and Th-F 9am-1pm and 2- 5pm, W and Sa 9am-12:30pm.) **Post Code:** S33 8WJ.

🛏 🍴 ACCOMMODATIONS AND FOOD. Castleton is home to several B&Bs, but expect to pay at least £35 for a single. The **YHA Castleton ❶,** Castle St., with a cluster of old stone buildings around a quiet courtyard, looks and feels like home. It sits in the center of town, next to the castle entrance (p. 366). Those seeking the luxury of a B&B can try ivy-walled **Cryer House ❸,** Castle St., where the proprietors keep two double rooms and treat guests to breakfast in a skylit conservatory. (☎ 620 244. Doubles £50. Cash only.) **Ye Olde Cheshire Cheese Inn ❸,** How Ln. above a pub, has one of the few single rooms in town. (☎ 620 330. Singles £35; doubles £65. Min. 2 night stay on weekends. MC/V). Attractive patios and traditional pubs line Castle St. "Families, ramblers, and pets all welcome...apart from goldfish, elephants, and goats" reads a sign at **The George ❷,** Castle St. The warm staff whips up excellent pub fare (dinner from £7.65) and bedecks the beer garden with flowers. (☎ 620 238. Open daily noon-11pm. Food served noon-3pm and 6-8pm. MC/V.)

🗻 SIGHTS. Buses don't serve the caves on weekdays, but on weekends #260 makes a loop between Edale and Castleton (Sa-Su and bank holidays 6 per day), stopping at Blue John, Speedwell, and Treak Cliff caverns. The lack of weekday buses should not discourage visitors since all caves are within walking distance of town. Peak Cavern is 5min. from town, both Speedwell and Treak Cliff caverns are about 20min. outside the city, and Blue John Cavern is within a 45min. walk. All caves are in the same direction; as you leave Castleton on Cross St. (which becomes Buxton Rd.), formerly the A625, pass a large sign for Peak Cavern. Road signs for the others appear within 10min. Peak Cavern is also accessible by a footpath starting in the middle of town near Peveril Castle. Follow the posted signs.

Although it's not the first cave on the road out of Castleton, ⬛**Treak Cliff Cavern** is the one most worth visiting. The engaging 40min. tours accentuate the amazing natural features of its interiors—deep purple seams of Blue John, frozen cascades of rigid flowstone, and "sculpted" mineral stalactites and stalagmites. Highlights include a view of the huge Dream Cave by candlelight, as miners from a century ago would have seen it. (☎620 571; www.bluejohnstone.com. Open Mar.-Oct. daily 10am-4:20pm; Nov.-Feb. 10am-3:20pm. Tours every 15-30min. £6.80, student or YHA members £5.80, children £3.50, families £18.50. MC/V, min. £10.) Just outside Castleton, in the gorge beneath the castle ruins, **Peak Cavern** features the largest aperture in Britain. Known in the 18th century as the "Devil's Arse," the cavern is known more for its history—highlighted on high-spirited (and occasionally overdramatic) 1hr. tours—than for its natural features. Christmastime brings mincemeat pies and live brass bands for subterranean merrymaking. (☎620 285; www.devilsarse.com. Open Easter-Oct. daily 10am-5pm; Nov.-Easter Sa-Su 10am-5pm. 2 to 3 tours per weekday; call for times. Last tour 4pm. £6.75, concessions £5.75, children £4.75.) A **joint pass** (£11.50, concessions £10, children £8) is sold for Peak Cavern and **Speedwell Cavern.** The latter has boat tours through the underground canals of an old lead mine that end at "The Bottomless Pit," a huge subterranean lake. (☎620 512; www.speedwellcavern.co.uk. Tours daily in summer 9:30am-5pm; in winter 10am-3:30pm. £7.25, concessions £6.25, children £5.25.) **Blue John Cavern** is the only cave besides Treak Cliff Cavern to offer views of the mineral veins from which it takes its name. (☎620 638. Open daily in summer 9:30am-5:30pm; in winter 9:30am-dusk. Last tour at about 4:30pm. £7.50, children £4, concessions £5.50, families £21.) The caverns are all cold, so dress warmly. Screeching school groups often convene midday—arrive early.

William Peveril, a baron of William the Conqueror, built 11th-century **Peveril Castle** atop a hill with far-reaching views so that he could survey possible threats to his lead mines and keep the local peasantry in check. After changing hands several times, it was eventually used as a jail before falling into disrepair in the 1500s. The climb may be daunting, but the view of Hope Valley is worth the effort. (☎620 613; www.english-heritage.co.uk. Open May-Aug. daily 10am-6pm; late Mar.-Apr. daily 10am-5pm; Sept.-Oct. daily 10am-5pm; Nov.-late Mar. M and Th-Su 10am-4pm. £3.50, concessions £2.60, children £1.80, families £8.80. Guidebooks £3.50.)

BUXTON   ☎01298

A bustling spa town and excellent transportation hub, Buxton emerged from a recent cleanup as a picture of Georgian elegance. Visitors lounge on the steep lawns of **The Slopes** (above **The Crescent**). The "spas" are still open for use, and **Pavilion Gardens,** St. John's Rd., offers a calming stream, expanses of grass, and several man-made pools that are a welcome treat for weary hikers. (☎265 48. Hours vary, call for times. £2.70, children £2.) Nearby **St. Anne's Well** provides a source of cool mineral water at the foot of The Slopes, close to the TIC. Entrepreneurs bottle and sell this "Buxton water," but it's free for the taking. Up the hill on Terrace Rd., the **Buxton Museum and Art Gallery** showcases and sells work by local artists in its two rotating exhibits and explains the geology of the Peaks in a permanent one. (☎246 58. Open Tu-F 9:30am-5:30pm, Sa 9:30am-5pm, Su in summer 10:30am-5pm. Free.) Just outside of town is the spectacular **Poole's Cavern,** within **Buxton Country Park.** Legend has it that Mary, Queen of Scots visited the caves in 1580, and a large rock formation inside is named in her honor. (☎269 78; www.poolescavern.co.uk. Open daily Mar.-Oct. 10am-5pm. 45 min. tours leave every 30min.; the last tour departs at 4:20pm. £6.75, concessions £5.50, children £4.) The surrounding park is a destination in its own right, with scenic walking trails and Solomon's Temple, a Victorian folly (faux castle). The best deal in town is the elegant **Roseleigh Hotel ❸**, 19 Broad Walk, facing the Pavilion Gardens and only 5min. from the TIC. The hosts are both former adventure guides and give guests free run of their large reading parlor. (☎249 04; www.roseleighhotel.co.uk. Singles with private baths £31-33; ensuite doubles £66, more for lake view. MC/V.) A Co-op on Spring Gardens (☎278 44; open M-Sa 8am-11pm, Su 8am-10:30pm) sells **groceries**, while **The Slopes Bar ❶** (in the Grove Hotel off Spring Gardens, near the TIC) offers a menu of light meals and cafe fare, such as panini (£3.75) and homemade pizza (£1.50 per slice) in a swank bistro setting. (☎238 04. Open 9:30am-midnight; hot food served noon-5pm. MC/V.)

Trains run from Buxton to: London (3hr., 1 per hr., £58.70), Liverpool (2hr., 1-2 per hr., £15.10), and Manchester (1hr., 1-2 per hr., £6.70). National Express **buses** depart for London (5hr., 1 per day, £20) and Manchester (1hr., 1 per day, £6.40). The well-stocked **TIC** (p. 365) is in the Crescent, near Market Sq. Other services include: Barclays **bank**, The Quadrant (☎0870 241 2381; open M-F 9:30am-4:30pm); **camping supplies** at Yeoman's, 41 Spring Gardens (☎743 30; open M-Sa 9am-5:30pm and in summer Su 10am-5pm); **police**, Silverlands (☎0845 123 3333); free **Internet** access at Buxton Public **Library**, Kents Bank Rd. (☎253 31; open M and W-F 9am-7pm, Tu 9am-5:30pm, Sa 9am-4pm); and a **post office**, in the Co-op on Spring Gardens (☎230 01; open M-F 8:30am-6pm, Sa 8:30am-3pm). **Post Code:** SK17 6AA.

BAKEWELL   ☎01629

Light-hued stone homes and a gentle river make Bakewell the quintessential country getaway. Located near several scenic walks through the **White Peaks**, the town is best known as the birthplace of **Bakewell pudding**, a sweet dessert tart. Bakewell's stone buildings line a network of crooked streets and hidden courtyards that converge on a park at central **Rutland Square**. Spanned by the five graceful arches of a **medieval bridge** (c. 1300), the River Wye curls around the town, edging the tiny **Bakewell Sensory Gardens** (open 24hr.). On the hill above town, **All Saints Church** (open to visitors daily until 5pm) is surrounded by weathered gravestones. Nearby on Cunningham Pl., a 16th-century timber-frame house shelters the **Old House Museum**, which displays regional heritage in the form of a Tudor lavatory, blueprints for a house made of cow dung, and other less excrementitious items. (☎813 642; www.oldhousemuseum.org.uk. Open Apr.-Oct. daily 11am-4pm. £3, children £1, under 5 free. Guidebooks £1.50.)

Accommodations in Bakewell are expensive. The *Peak District Visitor Guide*, free at the TIC, lists **B&Bs** in the area, but expect to pay at least £40 for a single. Truly elegant stays await at the **Rutland Arms Hotel ❹**, The Square, which has lodged famous Peak-country pilgrims like Byron, Coleridge, Wordsworth, and Turner. Individually decorated rooms feature luxurious beds and satellite TVs. (☎812 812; www.bakewell.demon.co.uk. Full breakfast included. June-Oct. singles £59-65; doubles £99-120. Nov.-May £55-65/89-101. 20% discount during the week. AmEx/MC/V.) **The Garden Room ❹**, 1 Park Rd., is a 5min. walk from the town center; head out of town on Marlock St. and turn right on Holywell, which becomes Park Rd. The tasty Bakewell Breakfast will keep you running all day. (☎814 299. Singles £45. Cash only.) Locals pour into Bakewell's **market**, held since 1330, off Bridge St. (open M 9am-4pm). The Midlands Co-op peddles **groceries** at the corner of Granby Rd. and Market St. (open M-Sa 8am-10pm, Su 10am-4pm). **JC's ❷**, Kings Ct., delivers superior bistro fare in its cozy upstairs dining room and adjoining courtyard. Indulgences include smoked salmon and black pepper panini (£5) and French lemon tarts with raspberry *coulis* (£3). Take advantage of the significant takeaway discounts (about £2) on sandwiches and panini. (☎810 022. Open M-Th and Su 10:30am-5pm, F 10:30am-7pm, Sa 10am-5:30pm. MC/V.) Located in a courtyard off Water St. in the center of town, **The Treeline Cafe ❷**, Diamond Ct., has an outside courtyard draped with vines and serves light lunch fare starting at £4. (☎813 749. Open Easter-Oct. M-F 10am-4:30pm, Sa 10am-5pm, Su 11am-4:30pm; Nov.-Easter M-W and F-Su 10am-5pm. Last orders 30min. before close. MC/V.)

From Bakewell, buses depart to: Manchester (6 per day, 2 hr.); Sheffield (1 hr.; M-Sa 14 per day, Su 12 per day); Matlock (Transpeak #172, 20-50min., about 2 per hr.). Bakewell's **NPIC**, at the intersection of Bridge and Market St., doubles as a **TIC** (<u>p. 365</u>). Other services include: an HSBC **bank**, Rutland Sq. (open M-F 9:30am-4:30pm); **camping supplies** at Yeoman's, 1 Royal Oak Pl., off Matlock St. (☎815 371; open M-Sa 9am-5:30pm, Su 10am-5pm); **police**, Granby Rd. (☎812 504); free **Internet** access at Bakewell Public **Library**, Orme Ct. (☎812 267; open M-Tu and Th 9:30am-5pm, W and F 9:30am-7pm, Sa 9:30am-4pm); and a **post office**, in the Spar on Granby Rd. (☎815 112; open M 8:30am-5:30pm, Tu-F 9am-5:30pm, Sa 9am-1pm). **Post Code:** DE45 1ET.

🔃 DAYTRIPS FROM BAKEWELL

🏛 CHATSWORTH HOUSE

Take bus #58 (2 per day) directly to the house or ask the TIC about other buses that stop nearby. ☎01246 582 204; www.chatsworth.org. 1½hr. audio tour £2.50. Guidebooks for house and garden £3.50 each. Open daily from mid-Mar. to late Dec. 11am-5pm; last admission 4:30pm. Gardens open daily June-Aug. 10:30am-5pm; Sept.-May 11am-5pm. Mar.-Oct. £10.50, concessions £8.50, children £4, families £27.50; Nov.-Dec. £10.50/10/4.50/28. Gardens only £6.75/5.25/3.25/15. Special exhibition £1.75, concessions £1. Grounds free.

When the sixth Duke of Devonshire ordered a new set of marble carvings for the fireplaces of his (third) dining room at Chatsworth, he was a bit disappointed with the results; he had wanted "more abandon and joyous expression." Only in a house as magnificent as this could his complaint seem anything but ridiculous. Once called "the National Gallery of the North," the manor house is a jumble of architectural and artistic treasures ranging from antiquity to the present day: a 2006 Frank Gehry vase sits alongside delicate eighteenth-century porcelain dishes. Scenes from the 2005 adaptation of *Pride and Prejudice* were filmed on the impressive grounds, which feature several elaborate fountains and a dizzying hedge maze. The unstructured beauty of the rock garden stands in sharp contrast to the neatly groomed lawns.

HADDON HALL

Haddon Hall is 2 mi. from Bakewell. From town, walk down Matlock St. as it becomes Haddon Rd. and then the A6. A nicer path along the river covers half the distance. Several buses, including #171-172 and TP, stop outside the gate. ☎812 855; www.haddonhall.co.uk. Open May-Sept. daily noon-5pm; Apr. M and Sa-Su noon-5pm, Oct. M and Sa-Su noon-5pm. £8.50, concessions £7.50, children £4.50, families £22. Audio tour £2.50. Guidebook £5.

One of the best-preserved English houses from the Middle Ages, Haddon was spared from the Victorian renovations that altered so many other estates. The house isn't as opulent as Chatsworth, but it retains an Elizabethan ambience and authenticity that make it worth visiting. Its stone walls, covered with climbing roses, seem perfectly at home in the sheep-studded countryside, and visitors can admire the Wye River from Haddon's award-winning gardens. Many filmmakers have been charmed by the building. Visitors may recognize it as the setting for *The Princess Bride*, Franco Zefferelli's *Jane Eyre*, and *Elizabeth*. The house museum includes numerous artifacts, some dating back to the 16th century, found during the renovation of the house in the 1920s.

CUMBRIA

LAKE DISTRICT NATIONAL PARK

Blessed with some of the most stunning scenery in England, the Lake District owes its beauty to a thorough glacier-gouging during the Ice Age. The district's jagged peaks and glassy lakes are paradise for countless hikers, bikers, and boaters, who nearly outnumber sheep in the summer. However, visitors needn't be hardened explorers to enjoy the region—tranquil valleys and coves are within a short walk of even the busiest towns and roads.

NATIONAL PARK COVERAGE. *Let's Go*'s coverage of the Lake District National Park includes the towns of **Windermere, Bowness, Ambleside, Coniston, Hawkshead, Grasmere, Keswick, Borrowdale,** and **Ullswater.** The first section provides an overview of transportation, practical information, and general accommodations (such as **YHA hostels**) for the entire park. Local services, B&Bs, and activities are listed within the coverage for individual towns.

⬛ TRANSPORTATION

Trains: By train, **Oxenholme,** on the West Coast Mainline, is the primary gateway to the lakes. Trains (☎08457 484 950) leave from Oxenholme to: **Birmingham** (2hr., every hr., £46.30); **Edinburgh** (2hr.; M-F 10 per day, Sa-Su 5 per day; £33.20); **London Euston** (3½hr.; M-Sa 9 per day, Su 7 per day; £108); **Manchester Piccadilly** (1½hr.; M-Sa 10 per day, Su 4 per day; £20.40). A branch line covers the 10 mi. to **Windermere** from Oxenholme (20min., every hr., £3.50). Direct service runs to Windermere from **Manchester Piccadilly** (1¾hr.; M-Sa 5 per day, Su 1 per day; £13.25).

Buses: National Express (☎08705 808 080) goes from **Windermere** to **Birmingham** (4½hr., 1 per day, £31) and **London** (8hr., 1 per day, £29), continuing through **Ambleside** and **Grasmere** to **Keswick.** Stagecoach connects **Keswick** with **Carlisle** (1¼hr., 3 per day). Stagecoach in Cumbria is the primary operator in the region. *The Lakesrider*, a complete timetable, is available free from TICs and on board each bus. Major routes include: Lakeslink bus #555 from **Lancaster** to **Carlisle,** stopping at **Kendal, Windermere, Ambleside, Grasmere,** and **Keswick** (M-Sa 14 per day, Su 10 per day), and the open-top #599 between **Bowness** and **Grasmere** (50min., Apr.-Aug. 2-3 per hr.). An **Explorer Ticket,** available on buses and at TICs, offers unlimited travel on area Stagecoach buses. The 4- and 7-day passes save money, even for shorter stays. 1-day £9, children £6; 4-day £19/13; 7-day £28/19.

YHA Shuttle: The **YHA Ambleside** provides a minibus service (☎01539 432 304) that meets the train at Windermere station and ferries hikers (or just their packs) to **Windermere** and **Ambleside** hostels (7 per day; 1st trip from station free, additional trips £2; bags only £1.50). It also completes a circular route of hostels in **Coniston Holly How, Coniston Coppermines, Elterwater, Grasmere, Helvellyn, Hawkshead,** and **Langdale** (2 per day, £2.50, schedules available at hostels), plus a daily service by request to **Patterdale.** Runs Easter-Oct. for £4.

Tours: Mountain Goat (☎01539 445 161), downhill from the TIC in Windermere, has off-the-beaten-track, ½- and full-day themed bus tours, like the Beatrix Potter tour (£21-30). Across the street, **Lakes Supertours,** 1 High St. (☎01539 442 751), in the Lakes Hotel, runs similar ½- and full-day tours (£17-27.50).

■ 🔋 ORIENTATION AND PRACTICAL INFORMATION

The Lake District National Park occupies the heart of Cumbria. The A591 runs along the north-south axis of the park, joining the towns of **Windermere, Bowness, Ambleside, Grasmere,** and **Keswick.** From these towns, paths snake out into the rest of the park. The major lakes surround Grasmere, at the park's center. **Derwentwater** is one of the most beautiful lakes, Windermere is the largest and most developed, and western lakes like **Buttermere** and **Crummock Water** are more natural.

National Park Information Centres: Dispense maps, fishing licenses, book accommodations (local accommodations 10% deposit, non-local accommodations £3 plus 10% deposit), and offer guided walks. More information at www.lake-district.gov.uk.

Bowness Bay: (☎015394 42895), on the steamer pier in Bowness-on-Windermere. Open daily Apr.-Oct. 9:30am-5:30pm; Nov.-Mar. 10am-4pm.

Brockhole: (☎01539 446 601), between Windermere and Ambleside. Most buses stop here. Exhibits, talks, films, and special events. Open Apr.-Oct. daily 10am-5pm.

Keswick: (☎017687 72645), in the Moot Hall in Market Pl. Open daily Apr.-Oct. 9:30am-5:30pm; Nov.-Mar. 10am-4pm.

Ullswater: Main Car Park (☎01768 482 414). Open daily Easter-Oct. 9:30am-5:30pm; Nov.-Easter 9:30am-3:30pm.

🛏 ACCOMMODATIONS

Despite **B&Bs** lining every street in many towns and **hostels** around nearly every bend, lodgings in the Lake District fill up quickly in summer. Reserve well in advance, especially for weekend stays. Many B&Bs will refuse to take reservations for less than two nights in summer. The Lake District is home to the widest selection of youth hostels in Britain: 24 **YHA hostels** provide accommodations in the park but can differ substantially in facilities and style. *Let's Go* only lists YHA hostels that are located in or near the major Lake District towns. Information regarding YHA hostels in more remote areas of the Lake District is available at www.yha.org.uk, or by calling the Lake District Reservations Service (☎015394 31117). At all YHA hostels, reception is often closed 10am-5pm, although public areas and restrooms are usually accessible throughout the day. Many of the larger hostels rent mountain bikes (£1.50 per hr., ½-day £6, full-day £8.50), which can be ridden from hostel to hostel by arrangement. The **YHA shuttle** travels between the bigger hostels (p. 371). YHA also operates 14 wilderness **camping barns** in the Lakes; for information or reservations call the Keswick NPIC (☎01768 772 645). **Campgrounds** are scattered throughout the park; use the convenient YHA **reservation service** (☎01539 431 117). The YHA hostels below are listed alphabetically.

Ambleside: Waterhead, Ambleside (☎01539 432 304), 1 mi. south of Ambleside on Windermere Rd. (A591), 3 mi. north of Windermere. Buses #505, 554, 555, 556, 599, and 618 stop in front of this mother of all hostels. 257 beds right on the lake. Hosts hordes of loud schoolchildren. Books tours, rents canoes, and serves great meals. Bar available. Breakfast included. Wi-Fi £2.50 per 30min. at coin-operated kiosk. Dorms £20, under 18 £14.50. MC/V. ❷

Borrowdale: Longthwaite, Borrowdale (☎01768 777 257). Take bus #79 from Keswick and then follow signs from Rosthwaite Village. Riverside hostel with 88 beds and a laid-back atmosphere. Internet £2.50 per 30min. Reception 7:30am-noon and 1-11pm. Curfew 11pm. Open Mar.-Dec. Dorms £15.50, under 18 £11. MC/V. ❷

Buttermere: Buttermere, Cockermouth (☎0870 770 5736). Quiet hostel near Crummock Water is a respite from the hustle of larger, more touristed Lake District hostels. Enjoy views of Red Pike from the lounge, and ask reception about great walks that start

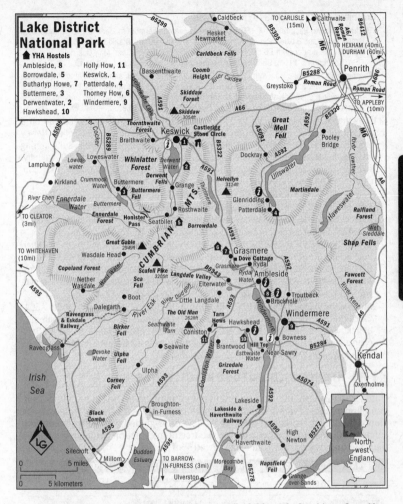

Lake District National Park

♠ YHA Hostels

Ambleside, **8**
Borrowdale, **5**
Butharlyp Howe, **7**
Buttermere, **3**
Derwentwater, **2**
Hawkshead, **10**
Holly How, **11**
Keswick, **1**
Patterdale, **4**
Thorney How, **6**
Windermere, **9**

NORTHWEST ENGLAND

right from the hostel. Reception 8:30-10am and 5-10:30pm. Curfew 11am. Open Mar.-Oct. daily; Nov.-Feb. Sa-Su. Dorms £17.50, under 18 £14. ❷

Coniston Holly How: Far End, Coniston (☎01539 441 323), just north of the village at the junction of Hawkshead and Ambleside Rd. Modernized country house with many walks that leave right from the hostel's doorstep. 61 beds. Breakfast £4; packed lunch £3.50-4.50. Free laundry. Curfew 11pm. Open Jan.-Sept.; call ahead. Dorms £14, under 18 £10. MC/V. ❷

▨ **Derwentwater:** Barrow House, Borrowdale (☎01768 777 246), 2 mi. south of Keswick on the B5289. Take bus #79, also a Keswick Launch stop. 88-bed, 200-year-old house with its own waterfall and playground. Self-catering kitchen. Breakfast £3.80, packed lunch £3.40-4.30, dinner from £7.50. Internet access £2.50 per 30min. Curfew 11:30pm. Open Mar.-Oct. daily; Nov.-Feb. F-Sa. Dorms £14, under 18 £10. MC/V. ❷

Grasmere (☎01539 435 316) has 2 hostels.

Butharlyp Howe: Easedale Rd., 150 yd. from town center. The more modern, conveniently located Grasmere hostel. 81-bed Victorian house with 2- to 9-bed dorms. Breakfast £3.80, packed lunch £3.40-4.30, dinner from £6.50. Internet access 50p per 15min. Open Mar.-Oct. daily; Nov.-Feb. F-Sa. Reception 5-11pm. Curfew 11pm. Dorms £15.50, under 18 £11. MC/V. ❷

Thorney How: Easedale Rd. From Butharlyp Howe walk another ½ mi. and turn right at the fork; the hostel is ¼ mi. down on the left. 51-bed, 350-year-old farmhouse whose lounge still makes use of the original open fire, although all the rest of the facilities have been updated and modernized. A popular stop for Coast-to-Coast walkers. Dorms £13, under 18 £9.50. MC/V. ❷

🏠 **Hawkshead:** Esthwaite Lodge (☎01539 436 293), 1 mi. south of Hawkshead on a posted route. Bus #505 from Ambleside stops at the village center. Follow Newby Bridge Rd. to this mansion overlooking Esthwaite Water. 109 beds. Self-catering kitchen. Breakfast £3.80, packed lunch £3.40-4.30, 3-course dinner £7.50. Laundry. Internet £2.50 per 30min. Reception 7:30-10am and 1-10:30pm. Curfew 11:30pm. Open Feb.-Oct. daily; Nov.-Dec. F-Sa. Dorms £14-22, under 18 £10. MC/V. ❷

🏠 **Keswick:** Station Rd. (☎0870 770 5894). From the TIC, bear left down Station Rd.; YHA sign on the left. Newly renovated with modern facilities in a riverside location near Keswick's bustling town center. Breakfast included. Packed meals and Internet access available. Curfew 11:30pm. Call ahead. Dorms £20, under 18 £14.50. MC/V. ❷

Patterdale: (☎01768 482 394), on the A592 to Kirkstone Pass ¼ mi. south of Patterdale village. Scandinavian-style, grass-roofed building with great access to Ullswater. 82 beds. Remedial massage clinic. Reception 8:30am-noon and 1-10pm. Curfew 11pm. Open Apr.-Aug. daily; Sept.-Oct. and Feb.-Mar. M and Th-Su; from Nov. to mid-Feb. F-Sa. Dorms £14, under 18 £10; doubles £32/20-26. MC/V. ❷

Windermere: Bridge Ln. (☎01539 443 543), 2 mi. north of Windermere off the A591. Catch the YHA shuttle from the train station. Small rooms in 70-bed house with panoramic views of the lake. Rents bikes. Breakfast £4, packed lunch £3.50-4.50, 3-course dinner £7.50. Laundry available. Internet access £2.50 per 30min. Open Feb.-Nov. daily; early Dec. F-Sa. Dorms £12.50-15.50, under 18 £9-10.50. MC/V. ❷

🥾 🏔 HIKING AND OUTDOOR ACTIVITIES

Outdoor enthusiasts run (and walk and climb) rampant in the Lakes. NPICs have guidebooks and advice for mountain-bike trails, pleasant family walks, tough climbs, and hikes ending at pubs. Most also offer guided walks throughout the summer. Hostels are another excellent source of information, with large maps on the walls and free advice from experienced staff.

HIKE NAME	LENGTH	LEVEL	HIKE NAME	LENGTH	LEVEL
Orrest Head (p. 376)	1½ mi. round-trip	Moderate	Wordsworth Walk (p. 379)	6 mi. circular	Easy
Stockghyll Force (p. 376)	1 mi. one way	Easy	Castlerigg Stone Cir. (p. 380)	4 mi. circular	Easy
Coppermines (p. 377)	4½ mi. round-trip	Easy	Catbells/Newlands (p. 380)	8½ mi. circular	Difficult
Old Man (p. 377)	5 mi. one way	Difficult	Scafell/Great Gable (p. 381)	5 mi. one way	Difficult
Helm Cragg (p. 379)	4 mi. round-trip	Difficult	Helvellyn (p. 381)	4 mi. one way	Difficult

The Lake District offers some of the best **hiking** in Britain. While there are many trails, be aware that they can be hard to follow at times—even on popular routes. If you plan to go on a long or difficult outing, check with the Park Service, call **weather information** (☎0870 055 0575; 24hr.; YHAs and TICs also post daily forecasts), and leave a plan of your route with your B&B proprietor or hostel warden before setting out. Steep slopes and unreliable weather can quickly reduce visibility to only a few feet. A good map and compass are necessities. The Ordnance Survey Explorer Maps #4-7 (1:25,000; £7) detail the four quadrants of the Lake District, while Landranger Maps #89-91 and 96-98 (1:50,000; £12) chart every hill and bend in the road for those planning especially difficult routes.

The Lakes are also fine **cycling** country. Several long-distance routes (part of the National Cycling Network; ☎01179 290 888) traverse the park. For short routes, pick up *Ordnance Survey One-Day Cycle Rides in Cumbria* (£10). Bike rental is available in many towns. Any cyclist planning an extensive stay should grab the *Ordnance Survey Cycle Tours* (£9), which provides maps of on- and off-trail routes. The circular **Cumbria Cycle Way** tours some of Cumbria's less-traveled areas via a 259 mi. route from Carlisle around the park's outskirts. Pick up *The Cumbria Way Cycle Route* (£4) from TICs for details. Cycling is not permitted on all footpaths in the Lake District. Accessible paths are designated "bridleways" and are marked on any cycle route map. For a comprehensive map of all cycle routes in the Lake District, pick up *Cycling Cumbria Map & Guide* (£2) from TICs or NPICs. For all travelers in the Lakes, beware of the narrow, stone-walled roads off the A591—cars and large buses careen around on the winding lanes.

The Lake District is popular for **rock climbing**. Two good sources for climbing information are Rock and Run, 3-4 Cheapside, Ambleside (☎01539 433 660; open M-Sa 9am-5:30pm, Su 10am-5pm) and the Keswick Indoor Climbing Wall (p. 380).

WINDERMERE AND BOWNESS   ☎015394

The largest tourist center in the Lake District, Windermere and its lakeside sidekick, Bowness-on-Windermere (combined pop. 11,000), are packed with vacationers in July and August, when boats swarm England's largest lake. Together, they form transportation hubs and gateways to the rest of the park.

▐▛ **TRANSPORTATION AND PRACTICAL INFORMATION.** The **train station** and **bus depot** are in Windermere; Bowness is an easy 1½ mi. walk south. From the station, turn left onto Victoria Rd. and stay to the left, following Crescent Rd. through town to New Rd., which becomes Lake Rd. and leads to the pier. **Bus** #599 runs from the station to Bowness (3 per hr., £1.60). For information on getting to Windermere, see p. 371. Try Lakes **Taxis** (☎46 777 or 44 055) for a cab, or **rent bikes** from Country Lanes Cycle Hire at the station. (☎44 544. ½-day £12-14, full-day £17-20. Open Easter-Oct. daily 9am-5pm; Nov.-Easter hours depend on weather.)

The Windermere **Tourist Information Centre,** near the train station, stocks walking guides (from 40p), and books accommodations for free. (☎46 499. Open Easter-Aug. M-Sa 9am-5:30pm, Su 10am-5pm.) The **Bowness Bay NPIC** has a display on the Lake District's topology (p. 372). Both towns have **banks** with **ATMs.** Windermere services include: **luggage storage** at Darryl's Cafe, 14 Church St., just past the TIC (☎42 894; £1.50 per item; open M and Th-Su 8am-6pm); **police,** Lake Rd. (☎0845 330 0247 for the main Cumbria line; ask for Windermere Police Station); **Internet** access at **TriArom,** Birch St. (☎44 639; www.triarom.co.uk; £1 per 10min., £5 per hr.; open M-F 9:30am-5:30pm, Sa 9:30am-5pm); and the **post office,** 21 Crescent Rd. (☎43 245; open M-F 9am-5:30pm, Sa 9am-12:30pm). **Post Code:** LA23 1AA.

▐▟ **ACCOMMODATIONS AND FOOD.** Windermere and Bowness have a number of **B&Bs,** but booking ahead is advisable during the high season. The **YHA hostel** ❷ is 2 mi. north of town (p. 374). In town, **Lake District Backpackers** ❶ is well-suited to independent travelers—the staff make themselves scarce, but they'll give you a comfortable place to sleep. (☎46 374; www.lakedistrictbackpackers.co.uk. Internet access. Dorms £10-12.50. MC/V.) The best values among Windermere's B&Bs include the motorcyclist- and family-friendly **Brendan Chase B&B** ❸, 1-3 College

Rd., with a laid-back atmosphere and large rooms (☎45 638; singles £25; doubles from £40; cash only); the bright **Ashleigh Guest House ❸**, 11 College Rd. (☎42 292; www.ashleighhouse.com; singles £30; doubles £22-32 per person; MC/V); and the homey **Greenriggs ❷**, 8 Upper Oak St. (☎42 265; singles £25; doubles £44-50; cash only). In Bowness, quiet **Laurel Cottage ❸**, St. Martins Pl., is a 400-year-old building off the main road. (☎45 594; www.laurelcottage-bnb.co.uk. Singles £26-29; doubles from £22 per person. MC/V.) Find **camping** at **Park Cliffe ❷**, Birks Rd., 4½ mi. south of Bowness. Take bus #618 from Windermere station. (☎01539 531 344. Open from early Mar. to early Nov. Dorms £18; tents £11-12. MC/V.)

Stock up on supplies in Windermere at Booth's **grocery**, next to the station. (☎46 114. Open M-F 8:30am-8pm, Sa 8:30am-7pm, Su 10am-4pm.) ⬛**The Light House ❷**, at the top of Main Rd., sells light fare throughout the day (sandwiches £4), but the three floors stay open late as a trendy bar and bistro. (☎88 260; www.lighthouse-cafebar.co.uk. Open Apr.-Oct. M-Sa 8:30am-11pm, Su 8:30am-10:30pm, food served until 10pm; Nov.-Mar. daily 8:30am-9pm. MC/V.) **Jackson's ❸**, St. Martins Pl., serves huge portions of modern British cuisine. (☎46 264. 3-course meal £14. Open M-F 6-11pm, Sa-Su 5:30-11pm. MC/V.)

🔷🔺 **SIGHTS AND OUTDOORS.** Sample the natural beauty of Windermere's surroundings on a **lake cruise**. A number of sightseeing boats depart from Bowness Pier. **Windermere Lake Cruises** (☎43 360) is the main operator, with trips north to Waterhead Pier in Ambleside (30min., round-trip £7.50) and south to Lakeside (40min., £7.80). Nonstop sightseeing cruises are also available (45min., £5.70). On all routes, departures are frequent from April to October and reduced for the rest of the year. The **Freedom of the Lake** pass allows unlimited travel for 24hr. from time of purchase (£13.25). A cruise to **Lakeside**, at Windermere's southern tip, lets you visit the freshwater **Aquarium of the Lake** (☎01539 530 153; www.aquarium-ofthelakes.co.uk; open daily 9am-6pm; last admission 5pm; £7.20, concessions £6.20), or take a ride on the 3½ mi. steam-powered **Lakeside and Haverthwaite Railway** (☎01539 531 594; Easter-Oct.; £5). Booths at the Bowness and Ambleside piers sell tickets that combine the lake cruise with one or both of these attractions. Motorboat and **rowboat rentals** are available at Bowness Pier. (☎40 347. Motorboats £14 for 2 people per hr. Rowboats £5 per person per hr.)

Town sights are less remarkable than the lake's offerings, but Jemima Puddle-duck fans both young and old will delight in **The World of Beatrix Potter,** a recreation of scenes from the author's stories. (☎88 444; www.hop-skip-jump.com. Open daily Apr.-Oct. 10am-5:30pm; Nov.-Mar. 10am-4:30pm. £6.) If Peter Rabbit irritates you as much as he did Mr. McGregor, you're better off sticking to the lake. The short climb to **Orrest Head** (1½ mi. round-trip) gives 360° views of the Lake District. It begins on the A591 near the TIC, which has a guide (40p) to the walk.

AMBLESIDE ☎015394

Set in a valley 1 mi. north of Windermere's waters, Ambleside is an attractive village with convenient access to the southern lakes. It's popular with hikers, who are drawn by its location and absurd number of outdoor gear shops. Lake cruises depart from the Waterhead Pier, where you can also rent boats. Walking **trails** extend in all directions. Panoramic views of the Southern Lakes can be had from the top of **Loughrigg** (moderately difficult 7 mi. round-trip). The **Stockghyll Force** waterfall is concealed in a wooded area an easy mile from town. Area TICs have guides to these and other walks.

Ambleside's ⬛**YHA hostel** (p. 372) is near the steamer pier at Waterhead, a pleasant 1 mi. walk from the town center. **Ambleside Backpackers ❷**, Old Lake Rd., offers 72 bunks in a comfortable, clean house. (☎32 340. Self-catering kitchen. Breakfast included. Laundry available. Internet access £1 per 30min. Reception 8:30am-1pm and 4-8:30pm. Dorms £15. MC/V.) B&Bs cluster on **Church Street** and **Compston Road**, while others line the busier **Lake Road** leading in from Windermere. **Linda's B&B and Bunkhouse ❷**, Compston Rd., is a combination hostel-B&B, renting out four private rooms as well as dorm accommodations with optional breakfast. (☎ 32 999. Dorms £12; singles £20, with breakfast £25. Cash only.) At Granny Smith's **grocery**, Market Pl., you will find organic produce and other natural foods. (☎ 33 145. Open M-F 8am-5pm. Cash only.) **Pippin's ❶**, 10 Lake Rd., serves great sandwiches, all-day breakfasts, and pizza—plus it's open late. (☎ 31 338. Meals £3-5. Open M-Th and Su 8:30am-10pm, F-Sa 8:30am-11pm. AmEx/MC/V.) **Lucy's ❸**, on Church St., will pack hikers a picnic lunch. Its conservatory restaurant has a large selection of tempting dishes for special diets and allergies, and its wine bar across the street offers a tasty range of tapas. (☎ 31 191; www.lucysofambleside.co.uk. Entrees £13-15. Open daily 10am-9pm, wine bar 5-11pm. MC/V.) The **Glass House ❸**, Ryndal Rd., serves Mediterranean and modern British cuisine, and gets its name from the eclectic collection of locally blown glass decorating its cool interior. (☎ 32 137. Lunch £6.50-8. Dinner £11-15. Early-bird special 6:30-7:30pm. Open M-F noon-2:30pm and 6:30-9:30pm, Sa noon-5pm and 6:30-10pm, Su noon-5pm and 6:30-9:30pm. Reserve ahead. MC/V.) Around the corner is the **Golden Rule ❷**, Smithy Brow, a friendly pub that taps local beer. (☎ 32 257. Open M-Sa 11am-midnight, Su noon-midnight. Cash only.)

Buses stop on Kelsick Rd. Bus #555 runs within the park to Grasmere, Windermere, and Keswick (every hr.). Bus #505 joins at Hawkshead and Coniston (Apr.-Oct. M-Sa every hr., Su 6 per day). Rent **bikes** from Ghyllside Cycles, The Slack. (☎ 33 592. £12 ½-day, £14 full-day. Open May-Oct. daily 9:30am-5:30pm; Nov.-Apr. M-Tu and Th-Su 9:30am-5:30pm.) The **Tourist Information Centre** is in the Central Building on Market Cross. It offers services identical to those of the TIC in Windermere (p. 375) and doubles as an NPIC. (☎ 32 582. Open daily 9am-5pm.) Tiny Bridge House, off Rydal Rd., shelters a cramped **National Trust Information Centre.** (☎ 32 617. Open Apr.-Oct. M and Th-Su 10am-5pm. Free.) Other services include: **banks** with **ATMs** on Market Pl.; **Internet** access at the **library** on Kelsick Rd., opposite the buses (☎ 32 507; 50p per 15min.; open M and W 10am-5pm, Tu and F 10am-7pm, Sa 10am-1pm); the **police** (☎ 0845 330 0247 for the main Cumbria line; ask for Ambleside Police Station); and the **post office**, Market Pl. (☎ 32 267; open M-F 9am-5:30pm, Sa 9am-12:30pm). **Post Code:** LA22 9BU.

CONISTON
☎ 015394

Less touristed than its neighbors, Coniston retains the rustic feel of the region's past. Fells to the north and **Coniston Water** to the south make it popular with hikers and cyclists. The town is known for its former resident, Victorian artist-writer-critic John Ruskin. The **John Ruskin Museum**, on Yewdale Rd., displays his sketches and photographs, as well as exhibits on the history and geology of Coniston. (☎ 41 164. Open Mar.-Oct. daily 10am-5:30pm; Nov.-Feb. W-Su 10am-3:30pm. Last admission 45min. before close. £4.50.) Ruskin's **gravestone** is in St. Andrew's Churchyard. Pretty **Brantwood,** Ruskin's 250-acre 1872 manor, looks across the lake at Coniston and the Old Man (p. 377); it holds Ruskin's art and prose collections. (☎ 41 396; www.brantwood.org.uk. Open from mid-Mar. to mid-Nov. daily 11am-5:30pm; from mid-Nov. to mid-Mar. W-Su 11am-4:30pm. £5.50, students £4.)

The easiest way to reach Brantwood is by water: the National Trust offers trips on an elegant Victorian **steam yacht.** (☎ 35 599. Apr.-Oct. 5 per day. Round-trip £6.20.) The Coniston Launch also cruises to Brantwood and offers other excursions. (☎ 36 216; www.conistonlaunch.co.uk. Apr.-Nov. 8 per day. North lake cruise £5.20, south lake cruise £7.60.) Hikers can explore the nearby, abandoned **Coppermines** area (4½ mi.) in search of the "American's stope"—an old copper

NORTHWEST ENGLAND

mine shaft named for a Yankee who leapt over it twice successfully and survived a 160 ft. fall the third time. Another popular walk is to **Tarn Hows** (from Coniston 5 mi. round-trip). The feisty, 2633 ft. **Old Man** is just to the north of town (5 mi. round-trip). The TIC has more information on these and other walks in the area.

YHA Holly How ❷ (p. 373) is just north of town. Enjoy honey from the owner's own bees at **Orchard Cottage ❸,** 18 Yewdale Rd. (☎41 319; www.conistonholidays.co.uk. £28 per person. Cash only.) The **Beech Tree Guest House ❸,** Yewdale Rd., has a vegetarian breakfast. (☎41 717. Doubles £44-46, ensuite £56. Cash only.)

Bus #505 travels between Ambleside and Coniston, with some trips originating in Windermere (50min. from Windermere; M-Sa 12 per day, Su 6 per day). Buses stop at the corner of Tilberthwaite and Ruskin Ave. Coniston's **Tourist Information Centre** is on Ruskin Ave. (☎01539 441 533. Open daily 9:30am-5pm.) The town has **no ATMs,** but **banks** are available on Yewdale Rd. The **post office** is also on Yewdale Rd. (☎41 259. Open June-Aug. M-F 9am-12:30pm and 1:30-6pm, Sa 9am-noon; Sept.-May M-F 9am-12:30pm and 1:30-5pm, Sa 9am-noon.) **Post Code:** LA218DU.

HAWKSHEAD   ☎015394

In the village of **Hawkshead,** 4 mi. east of Coniston, you can imagine yourself pulling little Willy Wordsworth's hair and passing him notes at the ◪**Hawkshead Grammar School,** Main St., where the poet studied from 1779 to 1787. See the original desks with inscriptions carved by students dating back as far as the 1500s. (☎36 735. Open Apr.-Oct. M-Sa 10am-5pm, Su 1-5pm. £2.) Also on Hawkshead's main street is the **Beatrix Potter Gallery.** Housed in offices once used by her husband, the gallery displays sketches and watercolors from her beloved children's stories. (☎36 355. Open Apr.-Oct. M-W and Sa-Su 10:30am-4:30pm. Last admission 4pm. £3.60.) Potter lived 2 mi. from Hawkshead on her farm at **Hill Top.** The house, featured in many of her stories, remains exactly as she left it. (☎36 269. Open Apr.-Jul. and Sept.-Oct. M-W and Sa-Su 10:30am-4:30pm; Aug. M-Th and Sa-Su 10:30am-4:30pm. Last admission 4pm. £5.30.) **Tarn Hows,** a pond near a pine grove, is a popular picnic spot. Walk uphill past Hawkshead Grammar School through the gate into the churchyard. Go through the churchyard, through two more gates, and turn right at the fork in the path. The trail to Tarn Hows is signposted from that point.

The nearest accommodation is the ◪**YHA Hawkshead ❷,** 1 mi. south of the village down Newby Bridge Rd. In summer, **bus** #505 stops in Hawkshead on its way between Ambleside and Coniston (M-Sa 12 per day, Su 6 per day). **Mountain Goat** offers a combined boat and bus shuttle to Hill Top from Bowness as well as a bus from Hawkshead. (☎45 164. Apr.-Sept. 8 per day. Round-trip £6, children £4.)

GRASMERE   ☎015394

With a lake and a canonized poet all to itself, the ivy-covered village of Grasmere receives more than its fair share of camera-clicking tourists. Sightseers pour in at midday to visit all things William Wordsworth, but mornings and evenings are peaceful. Guides provide 30min. tours of the early 17th-century **Dove Cottage,** where Wordsworth lived with his wife Mary and his sister Dorothy from 1799 to 1808, and which is almost exactly as he left it. Next door, the outstanding **Wordsworth Museum** includes pages of his handwritten poetry and opinions on his Romantic contemporaries. The cottage and museum are 10min. from the center of Grasmere down Stock Ln. (☎35 544; www.wordsworth.org.uk. Open from mid-Feb. to mid-Jan. daily 9:30am-5pm. Cottage and museum £6.40, students £5. Museum only £5.) **Wordsworth's grave** is in town at St. Oswald's churchyard.

Another 1½ mi. southeast of Grasmere is **Rydal Mount,** the wordsmith's home from 1813 until his death in 1850. The small hut in which he frequently composed verse lies across the garden terrace facing the water. Bus #599 stops here. (☎33

002. Open Mar.-Oct. daily 9:30am-5pm; Nov. and Feb. M and W-Su 10am-4pm. £5, seniors £4, students £3.75, children £2, families £12, YHA members £4. Garden only £2.50.) Hire a **rowboat** and strike out onto the deep green lake from **Faeryland Grasmere,** Red Bank Rd. The boat shop also has a tea garden, offering an idyllic spot to get a pot of tea and gaze across the water at the fells. (Open daily Apr.-Oct. 10am-5:30pm; Nov.-Mar. 10:30am-4:30pm. £6-15 per person; £20 deposit.)

There are two Grasmere **YHA hostel** buildings within a 15min. walk: **Butharlyp Howe ❷** and **Thorney How ❷** (p. 374). ▓**Beck Allans Guest House ❸** is an ivy-covered house centrally located off College St. (☎35 563; www.beckallens.com. £32-40 per person.) Campsites are available on the grounds of **Rydal Hall ❶**, just off the A591 between Ambleside and Grasmere, across the road from Rydal Mount. (☎320 050; www.rydalhall.org. £5.50 per night. 10% prepayment discount.) The bohemian **Jumble Room ❸**, Langdale Rd., serves a number of organic vegetarian and seafood plates. (☎35 188. Open Easter-Oct. W-Su noon-3pm and 6pm until food runs out; Nov.-Easter F-Su noon-3pm and 6pm until food runs out. MC/V.) As if the buttery aroma wafting into the street were not enough to entice you into ▓**Sarah Nelson's Grasmere Gingerbread Shop ❶**, in the Church Cottage, outside St. Oswald's Church, the world-famous gingerbread is a bargain snack at 33p per piece. (☎35 428. www.grasmeregingerbread.co.uk. Open Easter-Sept. M-Sa 9:15am-5:30pm, Su 12:30-5:30pm; Oct.-Easter M-Sa 9:30am-4:30pm, Su 12:30-5:30pm. Cash only.)

Walks starting from Grasmere range from a steep, strenuous scramble (4 mi. round-trip) to the top of **Helm Cragg,** to the gentle 6 mi. **Wordsworth Walk** that circumnavigates the two lakes of the Rothay River, passing the poet's grave. A small **tourist information point** is in the lobby of the Dale Lodge Hotel on Red Bank Rd. (☎35 300. Open daily 10am-5pm.)

KESWICK   ☎017687

Sandwiched between towering Skiddaw peak and the northern edge of Derwentwater, Keswick (KEZ-ick) rivals Windermere as the Lake District's tourist capital. With tranquil charms and a delightful town center, Keswick is a great place to have a pint after a long day's hike.

🖪 **PRACTICAL INFORMATION.** For information on how to get to Keswick, see p. 371. The **NPIC** (p. 372) is in the back entrance of Moot Hall (the clock tower in Market Pl.). Keswick Mountain Bikes, off Main St., in the Southey Hill Industrial Estate, rents

TOP TEN RULES AT HAWKSHEAD GRAMMAR SCHOOL

Here are the harshest rules that William Wordsworth would have endured at Hawkshead:

10. School is to be held in session from 6am until 5pm. Eleven hours? Bet those 6-year-olds' demeanor was delightful by 4pm.

9. School holidays are three weeks at Christmas and three weeks at Easter only. How do they put up with all that school?

8. Only three pints of beer are permitted to be drunk during school hours. Oh. That's how they put up with it.

7. Tobacco is permitted only at lunchtime. It is both fashionable and medicinal. In your face, smoking ban.

6. Missed sermons are punishable by 20 lashes of the rod. Yikes.

5. Any student can be expelled after three missed sermons. They do take church seriously.

4. Greek or Latin must be spoken during all hours. English, Latin—it's all Greek to me.

3. No student may attend taverns. Good thing I'd get all my drinking done during school, then.

2. Girls may not attend Hawkshead Grammar School. With over 100 boys crammed into that tiny building, what girl would want to be locked up in there?

1. Each student is to be issued a penknife, which he is to use to sharpen his writing quill. Or, he could use it to carve 18th-century graffiti into the desk.

bikes. (☎75 202; www.keswickbike.co.uk. £17 per day. Open M-Sa 9am-5:30pm, Su 10am-5:30pm.) Other services include: **banks** with **ATMs** on Main St.; a **launderette,** Main St., at the mini-roundabout (wash £2.50, dry £1.25; open daily 7:30am-7pm); **police,** 8 Bank St. (☎01900 602 422 for the main Cumbria line; ask for Keswick Police Station); **Internet** access at **Java Cafe,** next to the TIC (☎72 568; £1 per 15min., £3 per hr.; open daily 10am-5pm); and the **post office,** 48 Main St. (☎72 269; open M-F 9am-5:30pm, Sa 9am-1pm). **Post Code:** CA12 5JJ.

⚑☐ ACCOMMODATIONS AND FOOD. The **YHA hostels** ☒**Keswick ❷** and ☒**Derwentwater ❷** are in Keswick (p. 373). The area between Station and St. John St. (Ambleside Rd.) and Penrith Rd. abounds with **B&Bs.** The **Whitehouse Guesthouse ❸,** Ambleside Rd., is romantic and peaceful, with huge guest rooms. (☎73 176; www.whitehousekeswick.co.uk. £28 per person. Cash only.) Reside in lakeside splendor at **Berkeley Guest House ❸,** The Heads, whose spacious rooms and modern decor are a wonderful welcome after a long hike. (☎74 222; www.berkeley-keswick.com. Singles £30; doubles from £42.) Away from the lake but still a good bet, **Badgers Wood ❸,** 30 Stanger St., is vegetarian-friendly, with rooms named after trees. Ask Mr. Paylor about the best hiking and walking routes. (☎72 621; www.badgerswood.co.uk. £28 per person. 2-night min stay. Cash only.)

Buy **groceries** at the enormous Co-op on Main St., next to the launderette. (☎72 688. Open M-Sa 7:30am-7pm, Su 10am-5pm.) For some meatless treats, grab sandwiches and wraps (£3-5) at the all-vegetarian **Lakeland Pedlar ❶,** off Market Pl. (☎74 492. Open May-June M-F 10am-4pm, Sa-Su 9am-5pm; July-Sept. M-Th 9am-5pm, F-Sa 9am-9pm; Oct.-Apr. daily 10am-4pm. MC/V.) **Good Taste ❶,** 19 Lake Rd., whips up great sandwiches and salads (£3) for takeaway or to enjoy in their sunny upstairs lounge. Patrons can order a gourmet chef's dinner for only £5 to pick up the next day. (☎775 973. Open M-Sa 8:30am-4:30pm, Su 10am-4:30pm. Cash only.)

Keswick has thriving nightlife. Many traditional pubs line Market Pl. **The Oddfellows Arms,** Market Sq., hosts nightly live music starting at 9:30pm and has a massive beer garden out back. (☎73 809. Open M-Sa 11am-11pm, Su noon-10:30pm.) Trendy **Bar 26,** Lake Rd., also has live music and creative mixed drinks. (☎80 863. Open daily 11am-11pm.) Most bars and pubs close around 11pm, when those looking to dance head to **Loft,** Market Pl., a nightclub that feels like a little slice of London in the lakes. (☎80 834. Cover £3-5, before 11pm free. Open daily 10pm-2am.)

◐☐ SIGHTS AND ENTERTAINMENT. The lapping waves of **Derwentwater** are only a 10min. walk south of the town center along Lake Rd. From here the **Keswick Launch** sends cruises to other points on the lake, has boats for hire at the marina, and lands at the start of a handful of trails around the shore. (☎72 263. 2-person rowboats £9 per hr. 2-person motor boats £23 per hr. Cruises from mid-Mar. to Nov. 6-11 per day; from Dec. to mid-Mar. Sa-Su 5 per day. £7, under 16 £4, families £15.) Answer all those burning questions about pencils at the **Cumberland Pencil Museum,** home to the world's longest colored pencil (26 ft.) and right next door to the original factory. The museum lies just out of the town center along Main St. (☎73 626; www.pencils.co.uk. Open daily 9:30am, last admission 4pm. £3, students £2. Cafe open 9:30am-5pm.) The **Keswick Museum and Art Gallery,** in Fitz Park on Station Rd., has an array of Victorian artifacts. (☎73 263. Open Easter-Oct. Tu-Sa 10am-4pm. Free.) For a dose of culture in the evening, the **Theatre by the Lake,** by the, um, lake, features a year-round program of repertory theater, music, and dance. (☎74 411. Student discounts. Box office open daily 9:30am-8pm.)

☒ HIKING. A standout 4 mi. amble from Keswick crosses slopeside pastures and visits the **Castlerigg Stone Circle,** a Neolithic henge dating back nearly 5000 years. Archaeologists believe it may have been used as a place of worship, astronomical observatory, or trading center. Another short walk hits the beautiful **Friar's Crag,** on the shore of Derwentwater, and **Castlehead,** a viewpoint encompassing the town, lakes, and peaks beyond. Both of these walks have only a few moderately tough moments. The more strenuous **Catbells and Newlands** hike runs 8½ mi. and includes a short passage on the Keswick Launch. Maps and information on these and other walks are available at the NPIC (guides 60p). Climbing enthusiasts can get in a bit of practice before hitting the hills at the **Keswick Indoor Climbing Wall,** a 5min. walk from town along Main St. The staff also leads outdoor tours for groups of five or more, spanning such pursuits as cycling, climbing, and ghyll scrambling. (☎72 000; www.keswickclimbingwall.co.uk. Climbing wall £6, instruction available. Open daily 10am-9pm. Reservations required for outdoor guided tours.)

BORROWDALE   ☎017687

One of Lakeland's most beautiful spots, the valley of Borrowdale winds its way south from the tip of Derwentwater. There are relatively few settlements in the valley, adding to its appeal. **Ashness Bridge,** in the north, is worth a look but is far from the main road. Pick up a guide map to Ashness Bridge at any of the area's hostels or at the TIC for 20p. The tiny village of **Rosthwaite** has a few hotels and B&Bs. Towering over all is **Scafell Pike** (3210 ft.), the highest mountain in England, which, along with nearby and similarly lofty **Scafell** and **Great Gable,** forms an imposing triumvirate with some of the toughest and most rewarding hiking in the lakes. Treks up these peaks begin from **Seatoller,** at the head of the valley. Walks to the summits are very strenuous and should not be taken lightly: Scafell Pike is 4 mi. to the top and a 3100 ft. climb; Great Gable is also 4 mi., although not as steep.

Accommodations are scattered throughout the valley. **YHA Borrowdale ❷** (p. 372) is in the valley itself. Follow Prince Charles's example by taking an incognito weekend at the **Yew Tree Farm ❸,** along a small lane opposite the general store in Rosthwaite. (☎77 675. Breakfast included. Ensuite rooms from £30 per person. Cash only.) Wanderers with deeper pockets might try the elegant **Scafell Hotel ❹,** which also runs a **pub** with passable grub. (☎77 208; www.scafell.co.uk. £49-70 per person. MC/V.) The nearby **Flock-In Tea Room ❶** is a good bet for a bite to eat. (☎77 675. Open M-Tu and Th-Su 10am-5pm.) **Bus** #79 runs from Keswick to Seatoller via Rosthwaite (30min., 10-20 per day).

ULLSWATER   ☎017684

In Ullswater, a new corner of the lake is visible around each rocky outcrop and grassy bank. The main settlements, **Glenridding** and **Patterdale,** are on the southern tip of the water, and either one can be a departure point for the popular climb up **Helvellyn** (3118 ft.). One vertigo-inducing ascent begins in Glenridding and follows four steep miles to the peak. Departing from the Glenridding Pier, the **Ullswater Steamers** cut across the lake with stops at Howtown and Pooley Bridge. (☎82 229; www.ullswater-steamers.co.uk. 19 per day in summer, 4 per day in winter; round-trip from £8.) A less-strenuous route runs along the lake's eastern shore from Glenridding to Howtown, where you can then catch the steamer for a pleasant ride back. Another Ullswater attraction is **Aira Force,** one of the most accessible water-falls in the Lakes, a 20min. walk off the A5091 toward Keswick. The **Glenridding Sailing Centre** rents sailboats, canoes, and kayaks. (☎82 541; www.lakesail.co.uk. Canoes £50 per day; kayaks £35; sailboats £85. Sailing lessons from £25. Open from mid-Mar. to mid-Oct. daily 10am-5pm; from mid-Oct. to mid-Dec. and from mid-Feb. to mid-Mar. F-Su 10:30am-3:30pm.)

Good B&Bs include **Beech House ❷,** on the main road in Glenridding (☎82 037; from £22 per person; MC/V), and **Elm House ❸,** in Pooley Bridge, where homemade marmalade and bread round out a full breakfast. (☎86 334; www.stayullswater.co.uk. Rooms £22-30 per person. Cash only.) **YHA Patterdale ❷** is a basic hostel (p. 374), and Patterdale village has several guest houses.

Public transportation to Ullswater is limited. The only year-round **bus** service is #108 from Penrith, which runs along the lake and connects to Keswick. Sit on the left side for the best views (5 per day, 40min., £3.80). Two more services operate seasonal schedules: #517 from Bowness/Windermere to Glenridding (55min.; Apr.-July Sa-Su 3 per day, Aug. daily) and #208 from Keswick to Patterdale via Aira Force and Glenridding (35min.; June-July Sa-Su 5 per day, Aug. daily). The YHA shuttle (p. 371) goes once daily by request from the southern lakes to Patterdale.

CARLISLE   ☎01228

Cumbria's principal (that is, only) city, Carlisle was once nicknamed "The Key of England" for its strategic position in the Borderlands between England and Scotland. Roman Emperor Hadrian; Mary, Queen of Scots; Robert the Bruce; and Bonnie Prince Charlie have all played lord of the land here. However, the city's true rulers were the violent Border Reiver families, whose gruesome infighting shaped everything from laws to architecture. Today, Carlisle is a stopover for more peaceful border crossings, as well as a good base for exploring Hadrian's Wall (p. 444).

TRANSPORTATION. Carlisle's **train station** is on Botchergate. (Ticket office open M-Sa 4:45am-11:30pm, Su 9am-11:30pm.) **Trains** from Carlisle are frequent and often can be significantly cheaper if you buy your tickets the day before. Trains leave to: Edinburgh (1½hr.; every hr.; £32, £10.30-13.50 with advance booking for any journey leaving after 9:30am); Glasgow (1½hr.; every hr.; £30.50, £10.50-13.50 with advance booking); London (4hr.; every hr.; £82.10, £16.50-31.50 with advance booking); Newcastle (1½hr.; M-Sa every hr., Su 9 per day; £11.10). The **bus station** is on Lonsdale St. (Open M-F 8:30am-6:30pm.) National Express (☎08705 808 080) goes to London (6½hr., 2 per day, £32). Stagecoach in Cumbria bus #555 provides access to the Lake District via Keswick (1¼hr., 3 per day, £5). Hadrian's Wall bus AD122 provides easy summertime access to Hexham and Newcastle (M-Sa 13 per day, Su 7 per day; DayRover ticket £7). **Bike rental** is available at Scotby Cycles, Church St., on the roundabout. (☎546 931. From £15 per day. £20 deposit. Open M-Sa 9am-5:30pm. MC/V.)

ORIENTATION AND PRACTICAL INFORMATION. Carlisle's city center is a pedestrian zone formed by the intersection of **English** and **Scotch Streets.** The **Tourist Information Centre** is in the town center at the Old Town Hall. From the train station, turn left between the large gatehouses, and walk three blocks across Old Town Sq. From the bus station, turn right on Lonsdale St. behind the station, cross Lowther St., and continue straight through to English St. (☎625 600. Open Mar.-Apr. and Sept.-Oct. M-Sa 9:30am-5pm; May-June M-Sa 9:30am-5pm, Su 10:30am-4pm; July-Aug. M-Sa 9:30am-5:30pm, Su 10:30am-4pm; Nov.-Feb. M-Sa 10am-4pm.) Other services include: **banks** on English St.; **police** (☎528 191); **Internet** access at @CyberCafe, 8-10 Devonshire St. (☎512 308; £3 per hr.; open M-Sa 10am-10pm, Su 1-10pm) and the **library,** in the Lanes shopping center, across from the TIC (☎607 310; £2 per hr.; open M-F 9:30am-7pm, Sa 9:30am-4pm, Su noon-4pm); and the **post office,** 20-34 Warwick Rd., with a **bureau de change** (☎512 410; open M-Sa 9am-5:30pm). **Post Code:** CA1 1AB.

ACCOMMODATIONS AND FOOD. While Carlisle has no hostels, **Old Brewery Residences ❷**, Bridge Ln., offers YHA-affiliated accommodations in the university's student housing during their summer vacation in July and August. (☎597 352. Free Wi-Fi. £17.50, under 18 £13.50. MC/V.) Running east out of the city, **Warwick**

Road and its side streets are scattered with a few **B&Bs. Etterby Country House ❸**, north of the town center and next to the River Eden on Etterby Rd., has large, elegantly refurbished rooms that are well worth the 30min. walk. Cross the river, turn left off Scotland St. onto Etterby St., and continue straight ahead until you reach Etterby Rd. on your left. Stagecoach bus #76 (M-Sa every 15min., evenings and Su every hr.) stops at the top of Etterby Rd. and is easy to catch from anywhere in the city. (☎510 472; www.etterbycountryhouse.co.uk. Singles £20-30; doubles £25-30. Cash only.) The welcoming **Cornerways Guest House ❸**, 107 Warwick Rd., is another great option closer to town. (☎521 733; www.cornerwaysbandb.co.uk. Singles £30-35; doubles £50-65. MC/V.) The relaxing **Howard Lodge Guest House ❸**, 90 Warwick Rd., has all rooms ensuite, delivering privacy and proximity to the city center. (☎529 842. Singles £25-30; doubles £40-50. Cash only.)

The fairground interior of **The Market Hall**, off Scotch St., holds fresh fruit, veggies, and baked goods. (Open M-Sa 8am-5pm.) ▨**Teza ❷**, Botchergate, puts a contemporary spin on Indian cuisine, with inexpensive lunch specials like "Naanwiches" (£5) and pricier dinners. (☎525 111; www.teza.co.uk. Open Tu-Su noon-2:30pm and 5:30-10pm. AmEx/MC/V.) Jovial **Casa Romana ❷**, 44 Warwick Rd., has Happy hour specials on pizza, pasta, and risotto (£4-6), and larger meat and fish dishes around £14. (☎591 969. Happy hour daily until 7pm. Open M-Sa noon-2pm and 5:30-10pm. MC/V.)

◸ SIGHTS. The ▨**Tullie House** museum and gallery on Castle St. traces Carlisle's history from Roman times to the modern day with exhibits ranging from art and archaeology through to ecology and fashion. (☎534 781. Open Apr.-June and Sept.-Oct. M-Sa 10am-5pm, Su noon-5pm; July-Aug. M-Sa 10am-5pm, Su 11am-5pm; Nov.-Mar. M-Sa 10am-4pm, Su noon-4pm. £5.20, concessions £3.60.) Built by William II with stones from Hadrian's Wall, **Carlisle Castle** looms in the northwest corner of the city. Hundreds of Scots held in the dungeons after the 1745 Jacobite rebellion stayed alive by slurping water from the trenches of the dark stone walls. Discover these "licking stones" as you learn about forms of torture used on the Scots. Admission grants access to Cumbria's **Regimental Museum,** which pays tribute to more modern warriors. (☎591 922. Open daily Apr.-Sept. 9:30am-5pm; Oct.-Mar. 10am-4pm. £4.20, concessions £3.10. Guided tours Apr.-Sept. 2 per day.)

Despite centuries of warfare, daily services have been held in the **Carlisle Cathedral,** on Castle St., for nearly 900 years. The cathedral is home to exquisite 14th-century stained-glass windows and the **Brougham Triptych,** a beautifully carved Flemish altarpiece. Also noteworthy are the carved wooden **misericords**—seats used by the clergymen so they could rest while standing at prayer. Sir Walter Scott married his sweetheart on Christmas Eve, 1797, in what is now called the Border Regiment Chapel. (☎548 151; www.carlislecathedral.org.uk. Open M-Sa 7:45am-6:15pm, Su 7:45am-5pm. Evensong M-F 5:30pm. Suggested donation £2.)

◪ NIGHTLIFE. The rowdy Botchergate area is lined with pubs and clubs, including the hugely popular **Terminal 1,** just off the main drag behind the Litten Tree and Walkabout. Patrons choose between an ice bar, sports bar, retro club, and Parisian-themed cabaret bar, with packed theme nights every weekend. (☎512 804. Cover £2-5. Open M-W and Su noon-2am, Th noon-3am, F-Sa noon-4am.) On the other side of the town center, **The Brickyard,** 14 Fisher St., is Carlisle's only alternative music venue, keeping the live music scene alive with gigs every weekend and often throughout the week. (☎512 220; www.brick-yard.com. Usually open 5 nights per week 8pm-2am.) Available free in many bars and restaurants, the monthly *By Night* magazine lists upcoming live music and club events (www.bynightmagazine.co.uk).

ISLE OF MAN ☎ 01624

Wherever you go on this small islet in the Irish Sea, you're likely to come across an emblem: three legs joined together like the spokes of a wheel. It's emblazoned on flags flown from buildings, on shopping bags from local grocery stores, and even on the carpet in the ferry terminal. It's the Three Legs of Man, the symbol of Manx pride and independence. Its accompanying motto translates to "Whichever Way You Throw Me, I Stand." This speaks aptly to the predicament of the island over the last few millennia, during which it's been thrown around quite a bit. Vikings conquered the island in the 9th century, and the English and Scottish began to struggle for control in 1266. The English monarchy prevailed and granted dominion over the island to Lord John Stanley in 1405 for a whopping tribute of two falcons per year. Self-government was not restored until 1828.

Today, Man controls its own internal affairs while remaining a crown possession, although it is technically not part of the United Kingdom or the European Union. However limited its version of independence may be, the Tynwald Court, established by the Vikings, is the longest-running Parliament in the world. It is still called to session each year on July 5th, in a ceremony held completely in Manx (a cousin of Irish and Scottish Gaelic) on Tynwald Hill, site of the original Norse governmental structure. Man takes pride in its unique tailless Manx cats and multihorned Manx Loghtan sheep, its Celtic and Viking heritage, and its famed local delicacy—kipper (herring smoked over oak chips). The island might be best known, however, for its T.T. Races, which draw motorcyclists for a fortnight of adrenaline-pumping festivities.

⊠ GETTING THERE

Ronaldsway Airport (☎821 600; www.gov.im/airport) is 10 mi. southwest of Douglas on the coast road. Buses #1, 1C, 2A, and 2 connect to Douglas (25min., 1-3 per hr.), while others stop at points around the island. Manx Airlines has been purchased by British Airways (☎0845 773 3377; www.britishairways.com). **Flights** leave for Birmingham, Glasgow, London Gatwick, Manchester, Liverpool, and others. British European (☎01232 824 354; www.flybe.com), Manx2 (☎0870 242 2226; www.manx2.com), and Euromanx (☎0870 787 7879; www.euromanx.com) also serve the Isle. **Ferries** dock at the **Douglas Sea Terminal.** (Travel shop open M-Sa 6:30am-8pm.) The Isle of Man Steam Packet Company (☎661 661 or 08705 523 523; www.steam-packet.com) runs the only ferries to and from the isle: **Belfast** (2¾hr.; Apr.-Oct. 2 per week, usually W or Th and Su); **Heysham, Lancashire** (3½hr., 2 per day); **Dublin** (3hr.; Jun.-Aug. 2 per week, Sept.-May 1-2 per month); and **Liverpool** (2½hr.; Apr.-Oct. 1-4 per day, Nov.-Mar. 3-4 per week). Fares are highest in summer and on weekends (£15-32, children from £10, round-trip £30-64; standard fares £29, £50 round-trip.) Book online for cheaper fares.

⌐ LOCAL TRANSPORTATION

Despite its profusion of cars, the Isle of Man has an extensive system of public transportation, run by **Isle of Man Transport** (☎662 525; www.iombusandrail.info) in Douglas. The **Travel Shop,** on Lord St. next to the bus station, has free bus maps and schedules. (☎662 525. Open M 8am-12:30pm and 1:30-5:45pm, Tu-F 8am-5:45pm, Sa 8am-12:30pm and 1:30-3:30pm.) The Travel Shop and the Douglas TIC sell **Island Explorer Tickets,** which provide unlimited travel on most Isle of Man Transport buses and trains, as well as on horse trams (1-day £12, 3-day £24, 5-day £35).

Trains: Isle of Man Railways (☎663 366) runs along the east coast from Port Erin to Ramsey (Easter-Oct.; limited service in winter). The 1874 **Steam Railway** runs from Douglas to Port Erin via Castletown (single £5.40; round-trip £9). The 1899 **Electric Railway** runs from Douglas to Ramsey (single £4.80, round-trip £8). **Groudle Glen Railway** is a 2 ft. narrow-gauge railway carrying passengers out to Sea Lion Rocks. The **Snaefell Mountain Railway** runs to Snaefell, the island's highest peak (2036 ft.); trains #1 and 2 are the oldest in the world (single £4.80, round-trip £7.80). Stations marked on the transportation map.

Buses: Frequent buses connect every village. **Douglas** is the hub, with a main station on Lord Street.

Tours: Protours, Summer Hill (☎676 105), buses travelers around for full- and ½-day tours ranging from £11-18, departing from Douglas W and Su at 8:30am. Office on Central Promenade open 45min. before tour departures; telephone booking available M-F 9am-5pm.

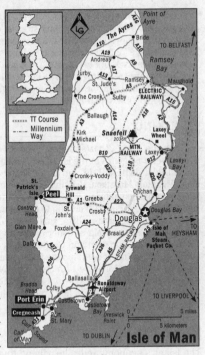

NORTHWEST
ENGLAND

Bicycling: The island's small size makes it easy to navigate by bike. The southern ¾ of the Isle are marked by challenging hills—manageable, but worthy of Man's reputation as professional terrain. TICs provide a map of 1-day cycle trails. For rentals in Douglas, try Eurocycles (☎624 909); in Peel, Pedal Power Cycles (☎842 472).

⚡ PRACTICAL INFORMATION

Manx currency is equivalent in value to British currency, but it's not accepted outside the Isle. If you use an ATM on the island, it will probably give you all of your bills in Manx currency. Notes and coins from England, Scotland, and Northern Ireland can be used in Man. Some Manx shops accept Euros—look for signs. Manx coins are reissued each year with different and often bizarre designs, which can be viewed at the **Treasury office** on Bucks Rd. in Douglas. When preparing to leave the island, you will generally be successful asking for your change in UK tender. **Manx stamps** are also unusual: the eagle-eyed will notice that the Queen's head bears no crown. Post offices and newsstands sell Manx Telecom **phonecards,** and mobile phone users on plans from elsewhere in Britain will likely incur surcharges. The Isle shares Britain's **international dialing code,** ☎44. In an **emergency,** dial ☎999 or 112. It's wise to rely on phone cards and landlines for a short stay, although more long-term visitors should probably invest in a **Manx prepay SIM card,** available at the shop on Victoria St. in Douglas for £15. These allow access to the only official service, **Manx Pronto.**

The island-wide **Story of Mann** is a collection of museums and exhibits focused on the island's heritage, including sites in once-capital Castletown, Peel, Ballasalla, and Ramsey. The town of Laxey celebrates the Laxey Wheel, nicknamed Lady Isabella, a 72 ft. waterwheel (the largest in the world), while Cregneash Folk Village recreates Manx crofting life and the Manx Museum in Douglas covers the island's history. A **Heritage Pass** (£11), available from any of the museums, gives admission to any four of the nine fee-charging sites, which otherwise cost £3.30-5.50. (☎648 000; www.storyofmann.com).

HIKING

In 2004, the first ever **Isle of Man Walking Festival** (☎686 766) brought a five-day walking extravaganza to the island, and it has taken place every June and October since. Diehards trek 31 mi. and climb 8000 ft. between Ramsey and Port Erin in the **Manx Mountain Marathon,** Britain's longest one-day race, in early April. **Raad ny Foillan** (Road of the Gull) is a 95 mi. path around the island marked with blue seagull signs. The spectacular ☒**Port Erin to Castletown Route** (12 mi.) offers the best of the south island's beaches, cliffs, surf, and wildlife. **Bayr ny Skeddan** (The Herring Road), once used by Manx fishermen, covers the less thrilling 14 mi. land route between Peel in the west and Castletown in the east, and is marked by signs with pictures of herring. It overlaps the **Millennium Way,** which runs 28 mi. from Castletown to Ramsey along the 14th-century Royal Highway, ending 1 mi. from Ramsey's Parliament Sq. *Walks on the Isle of Man* (free), available at the TIC, gives a cursory description of 11 walks. Free pamphlets also list dozens of routes. Eleven campsites, listed at the TIC, dot the isle.

❊ EVENTS

The island's economy relies heavily on tourism, so frequent festivals celebrate everything from jazz to angling. TICs stock a calendar of events; ask for *What's On the Isle of Man* or check out www.isleofman.com *or www.visitisleofman.com.* During the two weeks at the end of May and beginning of June, Man turns into a mecca for motorcyclists for the **TT (Tourist Trophy) Races** (www.iomtt.com). The population doubles, 10,000 bikes flood the island, the Steam Packet Co. schedules extra ferries at special rates, and Manx Radio is replaced by "Radio T.T." The races were first held on Man in 1907 because restrictions on vehicle speed were less severe (read: nonexistent) on the island than on mainland Britain. The circuit consists of 38 mi. of hairpin turns through towns and countryside that top racers navigate at speeds over 120 mph.

Southern "100" Motorcycle Races (☎822 546; www.southern100.com) run over three days in mid-July, bringing more bikers to the Isle and giving amateurs a chance to race, in contrast to the professional-only TT. July also sees the annual **Manx National Week,** when new legislation is proclaimed at **Tynwald Fair** (☎685 500). Although this ritual relies on fiercely honored traditions (representatives don wigs and traditional robes), other summer activities are a bit looser in execution. The **World Tin Bath Championships,** a race across the harbor in tin tubs in August, a **Baton Twirling Competition,** also in August, an **International Chess Tournament** in September, and a **Darts Festival** in March invite Manx natives and visitors to revel in idiosyncracy.

DOUGLAS ☎01624

Douglas's broad promenade bordered with pastel-colored rowhouses gives it the feeling of a Victorian resort town. This belies its checkered past as a smuggling hub for nearby England and Scotland. Sprawling along a bay on the eastern side of the island, the town is a useful gateway from which to explore the Isle's more scenic corners. Most travelers tend to return to Douglas each evening to enjoy its energetic nightlife.

⊏ TRANSPORTATION. Ferries arrive at the Sea Terminal, at the southern end of town, where North Quay and the Promenade converge near the bus station. Isle of Man Transport (☎663 366), on Lord St., runs local trains and buses (see **Local Transportation,** p. 384). During the summer, slow but inexpensive horse-drawn **trams** clip-clop down the Promenade between the bus and Electric Railway stations. Stops are posted every 200 yd. (☎663 366. Open daily May-Sept. 9am-6pm.) Motorized **buses** (60p) also run along the Promenade, connecting the bus and Steam Railway stations with the Electric Railway. For **taxis,** call 24hr. A-1 Radio Cabs (☎663 344) or Telecabs (☎629 191). Several **car rental** companies are based in Douglas, including Athol, Peel Rd. (☎822 481), or Mylchreests (☎823 533), which operates at the Sea Terminal. Eurocycles, 8a Victoria Rd., off Broadway, rents **bikes.** (☎624 909. Call ahead in summer. £15 per day. ID deposit. Open M-Sa 9am-5pm.)

■✱🛈 ORIENTATION AND PRACTICAL INFORMATION. Douglas stretches for 2 mi. along the shore, from **Douglas Head** to the **Electric Railway** terminal. Douglas Head is separated from town by the **River Douglas.** Ferry and bus terminals lie just north of the river. The **Promenade** curves from the ferry terminal to the Electric Railway terminal along the beach, dividing the coastline from the shopping district with a line of Victorian rowhouses. Shops and cafes line **The Strand,** a pedestrian thoroughfare that begins near the bus station and runs parallel to the Promenade, turning into Castle St. and ending at a taxi queue near the Gaiety Theatre.

The **Tourist Information Centre,** in the Sea Terminal Building just outside the ferry departure lounge, has transportation timetables and the worthwhile *What's On* guide. (☎686 766; www.visitisleofman.com. Open Easter-Sept. M-Sa 8am-7pm, Su 9am-3pm; Oct.-Easter M-F 9:15am-5:30pm.) Other services include: Lloyds TSB **bank,** 78 Strand St. (☎08457 301 280; open M-F 9:30am-4:30pm, Sa 9:30am-12:30pm); Thomas Cook, 7/8A Strand St. (☎626 288; open M-W and F-Sa 9am-5:30pm, Th 10am-5:30pm); a **launderette,** 24 Broadway (☎621 511; wash £3.50, dry 20p per 3min.; open M, W, and F-Sa 8:30am-5pm, Tu 8:30am-4:30pm, Su 11am-4pm); **police,** Glencrutchery Rd. (☎631 212); **Nobles Isle of Man Hospital,** in Bradden (☎650 000; www.gov.im/dhss/health/nobles); **Internet** access at Feegan's Lounge, 8 Victoria St. (☎619 786; www.feegan.com; £1 per 20min.; open M-Sa 8:30am-6pm), the **library,** 10-12 Victoria St. (☎696 461; 75p per 15min., free for students after 4pm; open M-Tu and Th-Sa 9:15am-5:30pm, W 10am-5:30pm), or in the back of the noisy Leisure Amusement Centre, 68-72 Strand St. (☎676 670; £1 per 30min.; open daily 9am-10pm); Boots **pharmacy,** 14-22 Strand St. (☎616 120; open M-Sa 8:30am-5:30pm, Su 1-4:30pm); and the **post office,** at the corner of Regent St. and The Strand (☎686 141; open M and W-F 9am-5:30pm, Tu 9:30am-5:30pm, Sa 9am-12:30pm). **Post Code:** IM1 2EA.

🛏🍴 ACCOMMODATIONS AND FOOD. Douglas is awash with **B&Bs** and **hotels.** For T.T. weeks, they fill a year in advance and raise their rates. The **Devonian Hotel ❷,** 4 Sherwood Terr., on Broadway, is a Victorian-style townhouse conveniently located just off the Promenade. Proprietors accommodate ferry schedules by serving a continental breakfast for early departures and holding luggage for late ones. (☎674 676; www.thedevonian.co.uk. All rooms have TVs. Singles £25-28; doubles from £44. Cash only.) Just next door, **Athol House Hotel ❸,** 3 Sherwood Terr. on Broadway, features elegant ensuite rooms with pine furniture and TVs. (☎629 356; www.atholhouse.net. From £26. Cash only.) **Grandstand Campsite ❶** is behind the T.T. Races' start and finish line. (☎696 330. Showers £1. Laundry £2. Reception M-

F 9am-5pm. Open from mid-June to Sept., closed the last 2 weeks of Aug. From £9.80 per person.) TICs list 11 other campsites. During the T.T. fortnight, seven makeshift sites open in football fields and public parks.

Grill and chip shops line **Duke, Strand,** and **Castle Streets,** while many of the hotels along the **Promenade** feature more elegant restaurants. The Food For Less **grocery** is on Chester St., behind The Strand (open M-W and Sa 8am-8pm, Th-F 8am-9pm, Su 9am-6pm). The dining rooms in **Copperfield's Olde Tea Shoppe and Restaurant ❸,** 24 Castle St., strive for historical ambience, dividing the menu into sections named after characters from Dickens, as well as Viking Feasts and Edwardian Extravaganzas. The food is classically British, with dishes like roast beef (£7) and jacket potatoes (from £6). (☎613 650. Open in summer M-F 11am-8pm, Sa 11am-6pm; in winter M-Sa 10am-4pm. Tea and cakes unavailable noon-2pm. MC/V, with a 50p charge.) At the **Bay Room Restaurant ❶,** in the Manx Museum, diners enjoy hot lunches amid sculptures from the gallery collection. (☎612 211. Open M-Sa 10am-4:30pm. Cash only.) At **Brendann O'Donnell's ❶,** 16-18 Strand St., Guinness posters and traditional music remind patrons of the Isle's proximity to Ireland. (☎621 566. Open M-Th and Su noon-11pm, F-Sa noon-midnight. Cash only.)

🖼🎵 **SIGHTS AND ENTERTAINMENT.** From the shopping district, signs point to the Chester St. parking garage next to Food For Less; an elevator ride to the 8th-floor roof grants visitors access to a footbridge and the entrance of the **Manx Museum.** The museum covers Man from all angles, from the geological to the historical to, in the **Manx National Gallery of Art,** the artistic. Particularly lively are sections about the island's days as a Victorian holiday getaway, when it was unofficially known as the Isle of Woman due to its attractive seasonal population. The museum also traces some of the less appealing aspects of the island's history, such as the story of Jewish refugees interned on the island during WWII and Man's involvement in the slave trade. Archaeological displays include Celtic artifacts from the Isle's early years. (☎648 000. Open M-Sa 10am-5pm. Free.) Past the Villa Marina Gardens on Harris Promenade sits the **Gaiety Theatre,** designed in 1900 and recently restored to something like its former glory. A 1½hr. tour showcases a Victorian trap door system under the stage. (☎694 555. The box office, open M-Sa 10am-9pm, is located in Villa Marina Reception. Tickets can also be purchased at the TIC. The box office inside the theater opens 1hr. before curtain. Tours Apr.-Sept. Sa 10:15am. Tickets £10-20, concessions available. Tours £6.50, children £3.)

Pubs in Douglas are numerous and boisterous, especially during the TT Races. At **Quids Inn,** on the Promenade, once you insert £1 into the subway-like turnstyle, almost all of your drinks will cost £1-1.50. If you go on weekends, prepare to drink standing up. (☎611 769. Hours vary.) Some of the **clubs** in Douglas are 21+ and some have free entrance until 10 or 11pm with a £2-5 cover thereafter. Relax at **Colours,** on Central Promenade, in the Hilton. A spacious sports bar gives way to live cover bands and dance music as the night goes on. (☎662 662. Open daily noon-3:30am. £5 cover after 10pm). **Paramount City,** Queen's Promenade, has two nightclubs: the **Director's Bar** plays favorites from the 50s to the 90s, while the **Dark Room** pumps chart and dance. (Paramount City ☎622 447. Open Sa 10pm-3:30am.)

◤ **DAYTRIP FROM DOUGLAS**

CREGNEASH

The oldest village on the island, Cregneash is a 1½-4hr. walk from Port Erin. It is known for the open-air **Cregneash Village Folk Museum,** which has preserved (and partially recreated) a Manx crofting town from the late nineteenth century, complete with thatched-roof cottages and demonstrations of blacksmithing and wool dyeing. Visitors pick their way among roosters as they wander between buildings including the **Karran Farm,** where old women work on silk patchwork and show visitors points of interest in the various buildings. *(Bus #1 runs to Cregneash from Douglas (1¼hr.; M-Sa 2 per day, 5 per day return) and Port Erin (20min.; M-Sa 6 per day, 6 per day return). ☎648 000. Open daily Apr.-Oct. 10am-5pm. £3.30, children £1.70.)*

PEEL   ☎01624

Long ago, this "cradle of Manx heritage" played host to the Vikings, whose Nordic pedigree still lives on in Manx blood. The Quayside maintains a rough-and-tumble sailor's edge (and holds a miniature Viking longhouse), while 🏛️**ruins** across the harbor loom against western sunsets. The most prominent relics are the stone towers of **Peel Castle,** which share the skyline with **St. Patrick's Isle** with the stone arches of **St. German's Cathedral** and the excavated tomb of a well-to-do Viking woman nicknamed "The Pagan Lady." The audio tour, included in the admission price, informs visitors about the history and significance of the various ruins. The site is located on a cliff overlooking the village of Peel and can be reached by a pedestrian causeway from the Quay. (Open daily Easter-Oct. 10am-5pm. Last admission 1hr. before close. £3.30, children £1.70.) Across the harbor on the Quay, the comprehensive **House of Mannanan** showcases a panorama of audiovisual displays that usher visitors from a fire-lit Celtic roundhouse to fog-machine-enhanced stone crosses, culminating at a 30 ft. Viking war ship shored on a recreated indoor beach. (☎648 000. Open daily 10am-5pm. Last admission 3:30pm. £5.50, children £2.80.) **Moore's Traditional Curers,** Mill Rd., is supposedly the only kipper factory of its kind left in the world. Informal tours let visitors watch kippering in action and even climb up the interior of one of the smoking chimneys. You can also sample a fresh kipper sandwich in the shop. (☎843 622; www.manxkippers.com. Shop open M-Sa 10am-5pm. Tours Apr.-Oct. M-Sa 3:30pm. £2, children free.) Just down the Quay, the **Leece Museum** exhibits a jumble of relics from Peel's past. Downstairs is the "Black Hole" prison cell, which now only locks up unfortunate wax figures. (☎845 366. Open Oct.-Easter Tu-Sa noon-4pm; Easter-Sept. W-Su 10am-4pm. Free.) Outside of Peel at Ballacraine Farm, **Ballacraine Quad Bike Trails** leads 1½hr. trail rides, including training and refreshments. (☎801 219. £40 per person.)

The **Peel Camping Park ❶**, Derby Rd., has laundry facilities and showers. (☎842 341; www.peelonline.net. TV lounge. Electricity £2. Open Easter-Sept. £5, children £2.50.) Shoprite **grocery,** 13 Michael St., is in the center of town (open M-Sa 8:30am-8pm, Su 10am-6pm). The 🏛️**Harbour Lights Cafe and Tearoom ❷**, Shore Rd. on the Promenade, offers Manx kipper teas—tea, kippers, bread, and teacake. (☎843 543. Kipper tea £7.45; 3-course dinner £28. Open Tu-Su 10:30am-5pm. Dinner F-Sa 7-8:30pm, reservations only. MC/V.) "Often licked but never beaten," 🏛️**Davison's Manx Dairy Ice Cream ❶**, on Shore Rd. next to the tea room, boasts flavors like Turkish delight and butterscotch honeycomb. (☎844 761. One scoop £1.50. Open daily Apr.-Sept. 9am-9pm; Oct.-Mar. 10am-5pm. Cash only.)

Buses (☎662 525) arrive and depart across the street from the Town Hall on Derby Rd., going to Douglas (#4, 4B, 5A, 6, 6B, X5; 35min.; M-Sa 1-2 per hr., Su 11 per day; £2) and Port Erin (#8; 55min., M-Sa 4 per day, £2). The **TIC** is a window in the Town Hall, Derby Rd. (☎842 341. Open M-Th 8:45am-4:45pm, F 8:45am-4:30pm.) The **post office** is on Douglas St. (☎842 282; open M-F 9am-12:30pm and 1:30-5:30pm, Sa 9am-12:30pm). **Post Code:** IM5 1AA.

PORT ERIN   ☎01624

A quiet city set in a spectacular locale, Port Erin has beautiful Victorian buildings that are eclipsed by their stunning surroundings. A number of hikes start from the town of Port Erin itself. One of the nicest is the 30min. trail out to **Bradda Head,** which hugs the bay before giving way to a rocky uphill scramble. At the top of the hill, climbers arrive at **Milner's Tower,** a curious structure designed to look like a key. Views of the sea and nearby Calf of Man, a tiny islet that serves as a nature preserve, compensate for the climb up the dimly-lit spiral staircase. The trail begins at the Bradda Glen gates off the Promenade or from the car park 100 yd. down the road. The **Coronation Footpath,** which begins from the same spots, offers a gentler ascent. Trips to the **Calf of Man** depart daily from Port Erin pier. (☎832 339 or 496 793. Trips depart daily 10:15, 11:30am, and 1:45pm in summer, weather permitting; fewer during low season. £15, children £5. Book ahead.)

    Anchorage Guest House ❸, Athol Park, has superb views of the town. (☎832 355; www.anchorageguesthouse.com. Open Feb.-Nov. Singles £25; ensuite doubles £58. MC/V.) Overlooking the ocean, **Regent Guest House** is a perfect base for hiking Bradda Head. (☎833 454; www.regentguesthouse.co.uk. Singles £25; doubles £54-60). For a quick meal in town, stop by **Shore Cafe ❶,** Shore Rd., which offers sandwiches featuring local ingredients (from £2.50) and freshly baked sweets. An ice cream bar next door satisfies sweet teeth.

    Port Erin is easily accessible as a daytrip from Douglas or a bit more of an expedition from Peel. **Buses** #1, 2, and X2 run to Port Erin from **Douglas** (50min., 2 per hr.) and two per day continue all the way to **Cregneash.** Bus #8 runs from Peel to Port Erin less frequently (50 min., 4 per day). Hiking pamphlets are available from the **Tourist Information Centre,** on Bridson St., down the road from the bus station (☎832 298). The **post office** is at 8 Church Rd. (open M-F 9:30am-12:30pm and 1:30-5:30pm, Sa 9am-12:30pm).

a ruinous state

The British thrive on ruin. The delight in the physical remnants of the past, shared by all classes and passed from generation to generation, is one of those cultural tics which makes Britain truly singular among nations. This desire to commune with times long gone, to wax wistful about the ambitions of ages past brought low by history's pratfalls, is as British as milky tea and cow parsley in country lanes.

It's possible to experience the great British romance of ruins at many of the most celebrated piles of stones. The shell of **Tintern Abbey,** near the River Avon, marks the spot where Wordsworth made introspection a national poetic pastime. But the danger of sampling the obvious sites is, of course, the buzzing business of the present—so many tourist coaches, so much bad ice cream, so many postcards. Better to head to the lesser known and commune with bumblebees and the occasional wandering fellow pilgrim.

Go, for instance, to Northamptonshire to see what's left of **Lyveden New Bield,** the late 16th-century oratory of the Anglo-Catholic Thomas Tresham and a ruin almost as soon as it was constructed. The oratory was supposed to be a place where the Elizabethan gentleman, who tried to be loyal to both his Queen and his Church, could practice his devotions safe from the prying eyes of Protestant authorities. Tresham ran out of money and time to finish the structure, and was jailed for failing to pay the recusancy fines imposed for not subscribing to the official church. The entire building was left exposed to the elements, and visitors must now wade through knee-high meadowland to see the delicate frieze of the stations of the cross that adorns its exterior walls.

However, most of the ruins in Britain are the work of sudden disaster rather than the slow crumblings of time. **Corfe Castle** in Dorset bears the charred scars of Oliver Cromwell's besieging army during the Second Civil War of 1647-1648. And some of the imposing Iron Age "brochs" of **Orkney** and **Shetland** look as brutal as they do because at some point they failed to hold back the oncoming waves of invaders and local rivals. Stunning, sandstone-red **Lindisfarne,** on the Northumbrian shore, was twice ravaged, first by Vikings who sacked the place and slaughtered the monks. The monastery was hit again during the Protestant Reformation, when it was predictably emptied of its community and treasures. Equally sudden was the end of the spectacular **Binham Priory** in southern Norfolk. The enforcers of the Reformation under Henry VIII and Edward VI turned what had been one of the most palatial Benedictine foundations into a sparse parish church. Miraculously, the Reformation's erasure of the painted screen separating the nave from the choir have themselves become ruins, peeling away to reveal some of the most astonishing church paintings that survived from the world of Roman Catholic England.

Some of the most commanding ruins are also the most modern. A little way

"Head to the lesser known and commune with bumblebees and fellow pilgrims."

from the center of Dublin stands Kilmainham Gaol, a working prison until 1924. Now a historical museum, the Gaol reveals the complications of crime and punishment in nationalist Ireland. The exterior is just standard-issue prison. But the interior is a cathedral of incarceration; simultaneously shocking and operatically grand, with its iron staircase and rat-hole cells where ancient pallets and fragments of anonymous rags gather grime. The effect is as powerful as it is challenging, but this is how ruins are supposed to get you. Not with a cheap rush of sentiment, much less a pang of nostalgia, but with the tender inspection of ancient scars, which linger to remind us of the resilience and redeeming vulnerability of the human condition.

Simon Schama is University Professor of Art History at Columbia University. He writes for The New Yorker and was the writer and host of the BBC's History of Britain. His most recent book is Rough Crossings: Britain, the Slaves, and the American Revolution (Ecco, May 2006).

NORTHEAST ENGLAND

Framed by Scotland and the North Sea, the northeast is England's best-kept secret. Although less traveled, this corner of the country has something for everyone, from the notorious nightlife of Newcastle to the idyllic wildlife of Northumberland. Hadrian's Wall marks a history of skirmishes with fierce northern neighbors, and the area's three national parks hold some of the most rugged, remote countryside in England. While the principal urban areas of Yorkshire and Tyne and Wear grew out of the wool and coal industries, today the refurbished city centers welcome visitors with a wealth of art and culture.

HIGHLIGHTS OF NORTHEAST ENGLAND

ADMIRE York and its colossal **Gothic cathedral** (p. 399), which contains the largest medieval glass window in the world.

PARTY in the famed nightclubs of **Newcastle** (p. 430), home to crowded dance floors, lively locals, and legendary brown ale.

INVESTIGATE the remains of **Hadrian's Wall** (p. 444), which once delineated the northernmost border of the Roman Empire.

YORKSHIRE

SHEFFIELD
☎ 0114

While Manchester was clothing the world, Sheffield (pop. 550,000) was setting its table with hand-crafted flatware and stainless steel (invented here). When the 20th-century steel industry moved elsewhere, economic depression set in. Today, Sheffield is attempting an ambitious urban transformation and billing itself as a revitalized artistic, cultural, and commercial center. The industrial metropolis has used a green thumb and a keen eye to fill the streets with trendy bar-cafes, popular nightlife, and bountiful gardens.

🖪🆘 TRANSPORTATION AND PRACTICAL INFORMATION. Sheffield lies on the M1 motorway, about 30 mi. east of Manchester and 25 mi. south of Leeds. Midland Station is on Sheaf St., near Sheaf Sq. **Trains** (☎ 08457 484 950) leave from Sheffield to: Leeds (45min., 4 per hr., £7.50); Lincoln (1½ hr., every hr., £11); London St. Pancras (2hr., 4 per hr., £54.30); Manchester (1hr., 3 per hr., £13); and York (1hr., 3 per hr., £13.30). The major **bus** station in town is the Interchange, between Pond St. and Sheaf St. across from the train station. (☎ 275 4905. Lockers £1-2. Open M-F 8am-5:30pm.) National Express (☎ 08705 808 080) buses travel to: Leeds (40min., every hr., £5), Birmingham (2½hr., 5 per day, £16); London (4hr., 6 per day, £15.50); Nottingham (1½-2hr., 10 per day., £6.40). The **Supertram** covers the city (☎ 272 8282; www.supertram.com; daily pass £2.70).

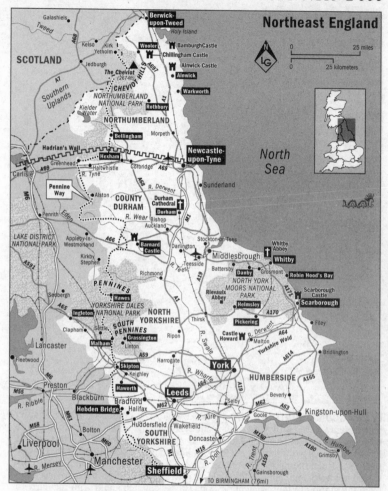

Northeast England

Sheffield's **Tourist Information Centre**, 12-14 Norfolk Row, distributes free detailed maps of the city as well as the handy *Sheffield Visitor Guide*. The TIC unfortunately does not book accommodations for travelers in town, but a booking service is available for £3 by calling ☎0871 7000 121. (☎221 1900; www.sheffieldtourism.co.uk. Open M-Sa 10am-5pm.) Other services in Sheffield include: **banks** and **ATMs** on Pinstone St. and Church St.; **police**, West Bar Green (☎220 2020); Northern General **hospital**, Herries Rd. (☎243 4343); **luggage storage** available at the train station (£2.50 for 24hr.); **Internet** access with free Wi-Fi at **Nylon Bar,** 4 Charter Sq. (☎275 5722; £1.50 per 30min.; open M-Sa noon-10pm), the **Showroom** (p. 394), and at the Central **Library**, Surrey St. (☎273 4712; free; open M 10am-8pm, Tu and Th-Sa 9:30am-5:30pm, W 9:30am-8pm); **post office**, 9 Norfolk Row (☎281 4713; open M-Tu and Th-F 8:30am-5:30pm, W 9am-5:30pm, Sa 8:30am-3pm). **Post Code:** S1 2PA.

Sheffield

🏠 **ACCOMMODATIONS**
York Villa, 3
Gulliver's Guesthouse, 7
Parland's Guesthouse, 6

🍎 **FOOD**
Blue Moon Cafe, 1
Showroom Cafe-Bar, 2

★ **CLUBS**
The Leadmill, 5
Gatecrasher One, 4

ACCOMMODATIONS AND FOOD. Budget accommodations are scarce, and most are a long walk west of the center. If you don't mind the 30min. commute by train, try the **YHA hostel** in **Hathersage ❶** (p. 366). **York Villa ❷**, 63 Norfolk Rd., has small rooms with shared bath. Its location 5min. from the train station can't be beat. (☎272 4566. Singles £17; doubles £28. Cash only.) Most B&B options are converted homes 2-3 mi. outside Sheffield near Ecclessal Rd. South. Local buses run from the station to these neighborhoods (buses #30, 82, and 84 run regularly to Ecclessal Rd. from the city center). For spacious rooms with shared baths try **Gulliver's Guest House ❸**, 167 Ecclessal Rd. South. The matron of the house cooks a delicious breakfast of your choice. (☎262 0729. Singles £25; doubles £44. Cash only.) **Parklands Guest House ❸**, 113 Rustlings Rd., near Endcliffe Park, has small rooms with shared bath and kitchen. Balconies offer an escape from a slightly musty smell. (☎267 0692. Singles £25; doubles £50. Breakfast included. Cash only.)

Sheffield's revitalized city center is full of hip (read: pricey) restaurants and cafes. For cheaper options, take a walk farther west of the city. Wine bars are sandwiched between Indian and Italian restaurants on **Ecclesall Road,** where students from the local universities hang out. Posh eateries with mid-priced menus are located on **Division** and **Devonshire Streets.** The Spar **supermarket** is at the intersection of Division St. and Backfields Alley. (☎275 2900. Open 24hr.) The 🏠**Showroom Cafe-Bar ❷**, 7 Paternoster Row, draws an older local crowd. Lounge on the couch over great burgers or stir-fry (£6.50-12) before watching films next door.

Their "Film and Food" nights (W-Sa 5:30-9pm) offer movie ticket, entree, and wine for £14.50. (☎249 5479; www.showroom.org.uk. M and T student movie tickets £3. Open M-Sa 11am-11pm, Su noon-10:30pm. Food served until 9pm. MC/V.) **Blue Moon Cafe ❶,** 2 St. James St., three blocks up the hill from Castle Sq., after the Cathedral Church of St. Peter and St. Paul, offers a selection of veggie entrees under £6 as well as snacks and desserts (noodles, quesadillas, gluten-free cakes) under £3. (☎276 3443. Open M-Sa 8am-8pm. AmEx/MC/V.)

◨ **SIGHTS.** Although it has an industrial shell, Sheffield is also a garden city with over 200 parks, woodlands, and gardens. The indoor **Winter Garden** has 2500 varieties of plants from around the world. Sheffield's vibrant art scene centers upon the ▨**Millennium Galleries,** Arundel Gate, linked to Tudor Sq. The galleries host national and international touring exhibitions. (☎278 2600. Open M-Sa 10am-5pm, Su 11am-5pm. Free. Special exhibits £4, concessions £2.) The excellent **Ruskin Gallery** was established in 1875 by Victorian critic John Ruskin, who intended to show that "life without industry is guilt, and industry without art is brutality." Today, rotating pieces uphold Ruskin's goal of inspiring the craftsmen (and now visitors) of Sheffield. (☎278 2600; www.sheffieldgalleries.org.uk. Open M-Sa 10am-5pm, Su 11am-5pm. Free. Special exhibits occasionally have an additional charge.) Find works by Picasso and Cézanne in ▨**Graves Gallery,** on Surrey St. above the public library, which also displays post-war British art, Romantic and Impressionist paintings and modern photography. (☎278 2600. Open M-Sa 10am-5pm. Free.) The **Site Gallery,** 1 Brown St., showcases contemporary art and photography. (☎281 2077. Open W-Sa 11am-5:30pm. Free.) At the **Kelham Island Industrial Museum,** Alma St., learn about the city's steel industry and industrial heritage. From the town center, take N. Church St. north and turn right onto West Bar. After a block, turn left and follow Bridge St. as it becomes Alma St. Follow the signs to the museum on the right side of the road. (☎249 8329; www.simt.co.uk. Open M-Th 10am-4pm, Su 11am-4:45pm. Last admission 1hr. before close. £4, concessions £3.)

▨▧ **NIGHTLIFE AND ENTERTAINMENT.** Most clubs are in the southeastern section of the city, around Matilda St. *The Sheffield Guide* has current nightlife listings. For info on Sheffield's gay scene, pick up *Qkultcha* magazine. **The Leadmill,** 6 Leadmill Rd., is a casual hangout with a popular Monday student night. Live music as well indie, pop, and R&B tracks play to packed dance floors. (☎221 2828; www.leadmill.co.uk. Cover £2-5. Open M-F 10pm-2:30am, Sa 10pm-3am.) Dress up at **Gatecrasher One,** 112 Arundel St., for a ritzier evening on the town. The spacious club hosts Sheffield's largest, latest party on Saturdays. (☎428 2726. Cover M and Th £2-3, F £3-5, Sa £10-15 after 10:30pm. Open M and Th-F 10pm-2am, Sa 10pm-6am.) For nightlife without a hangover, visit the **Crucible and Lyceum Theatres** for musicals, plays, and dance shows. Both are in Tudor Sq., with a shared box office on 55 Norfolk St. The complex is the largest center for theater in England outside London. Backstage tours run once a week, usually on the weekends; call for details. (☎249 6000; www.sheffieldtheatres.co.uk. £10-36, same-day tickets £8.)

YORK   ☎01904

With its cobblestoned walkways and busy shopping district, few would guess that York is known as "the most haunted city in the world." Despite—or perhaps because of—its ghostly lore, York remains one of England's most popular destinations. The city's turbulent history is full of sword-bearing Romans, Anglo-Saxons, and Vikings, who used York as a military stronghold. Today, the city's Gothic cathedral, crumbling medieval walls, and countless pubs draw crowds of camera-toting tourists. It may be haunted by the dead, but York is still as lively as ever.

NORTHEAST ENGLAND

⌐ TRANSPORTATION

Trains: York Station, Station Rd. Travel center open M-Sa 8am-7:30pm, Su 9am-7:30pm. Ticket office open M-F 5:30am-10pm, Sa 5:45am-9:40pm, Su 7:30am-9:40pm. Trains (☎08457 484 950) to: **Edinburgh** (2½hr., 2 per hr., £67); **London King's Cross** (2hr., 2 per hr., £74); **Newcastle** (1hr., 4 per hr., £21); **Scarborough** (45min., every hr., £11).

Buses: Stations at 20 Rougier St., Exhibition Sq., the train station, and on Piccadilly. Major bus stop on The Stonebow (Information ☎551 400). National Express (☎08705 808 080) to **Edinburgh** (6hr., 1 per day, £31), **London** (5½hr., 15 per day, £23), and **Manchester** (3hr., 15 per day, £12).

Public Transportation: First York (☎622 992, timetables 551 400) has a ticket office at 20 Rougier St. Open M-F 9am-5pm. Yorkshire Coastliner (☎0113 244 8976 or 01653 692 556; www.coastliner.co.uk) runs buses from the train station to **Castle Howard** (p. 401) and other towns toward the coast. Timetables available at TICs.

Taxis: Station Taxis (☎623 332). 24hr. Wheelchair-accessible service available with advance booking.

Bike Rental: Bob Trotter, 13-15 Lord Mayor's Walk (☎622 868; www.bobtrottercycles.com). From £12 per day. £50 deposit. Open M-W and F-Sa 9am-5:30pm, Th 9:30am-5:30pm, Su 10am-4pm.

✴ ⓘ ORIENTATION AND PRACTICAL INFORMATION

York's streets are winding, short, rarely labeled, and prone to name changes. Fortunately, most attractions lie within the **city walls,** and the towers of the **Minster,** visible from nearly everywhere, provide easy orientation. The **River Ouse** (rhymes with "muse") cuts through the city, curving west to south. The city center lies between the Ouse and the Minster. **Coney Street, Parliament Street,** and **Stonegate** are the main thoroughfares. **The Shambles,** York's quasi-medieval shopping district, lies between Parliament St. and Colliergate.

> **TIP**
> **WHAT'S APUB, DOC?** If someone says "apub" to you as you roam the streets of Yorkshire, they're not necessarily directing you to the nearest pint. "Apub" can mean "hello," "what's up?" or even "bloody hell!"

Tourist Information Centre: Exhibition Sq. (☎550 099; www.visityork.org). Books rooms for £4 plus a 10% deposit. Provides free miniguide with detailed map and sells *Snickelways of York* (£6), a handwritten booklet of walks through York's alleyways. Also sells the York Pass, which covers entry into 28 top attractions for 1 (£21), 2 (£27), or 3 (£34) days. Open Apr.-Oct. M-Sa 9am-6pm, Su 10am-5pm; Nov.-May M-Sa 9am-5pm, Su 10am-4pm. Branch in the train station. Open Easter-Oct. M-Sa 9am-6pm, Su 10am-5pm; Nov.-Easter M-Sa 9am-4pm, Su 10am-4pm. Smaller kiosk on Coppengate St. near Jorvich Viking Centre sells tickets and maps. Hours vary.

Tours: Yorkwalk (☎622 303; www.yorkwalk.co.uk) leads 1½-2hr. guided tours from the Museum Gardens Gate on Museum St. (Feb.-Nov. daily at 10:30am and 2:15pm; Dec.-Jan. Sa-Su only. £5.) The 1¼hr. **Ghost Hunt of York** (☎608 700; www.ghosthunt.co.uk) meets at The Shambles daily at 7:30pm. £5. **City Sightseeing** (☎655 585; www.citysightseeing.com) leads hop-on, hop-off bus tours daily with 22 stops around the city. £9, concessions £7. Several companies along the **River Ouse** near Lendal, Ouse, and Skeldergate Bridges offer 1hr. **boat cruises,** including **YorkBoat,** Lendal Bridge and Kings Staith Landing (☎628 324; www.yorkboat.co.uk). Office open M-F 9am-5:30pm. At least 4 trips per day; call ahead. £8.

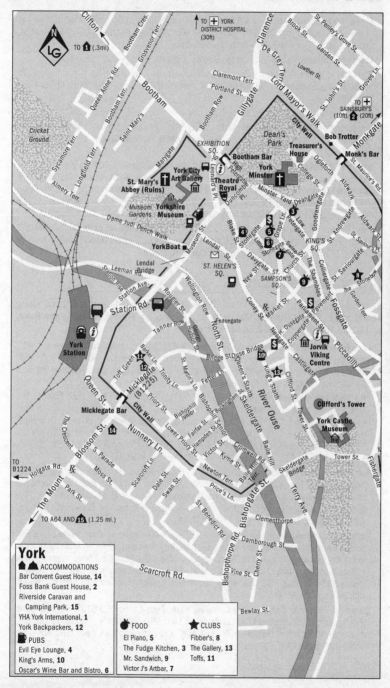

York

ACCOMMODATIONS
Bar Convent Guest House, **14**
Foss Bank Guest House, **2**
Riverside Caravan and
 Camping Park, **15**
YHA York International, **1**
York Backpackers, **12**

PUBS
Evil Eye Lounge, **4**
King's Arms, **10**
Oscar's Wine Bar and Bistro, **6**

FOOD
El Piano, **5**
The Fudge Kitchen, **3**
Mr. Sandwich, **9**
Victor J's Artbar, **7**

CLUBS
Fibber's, **8**
The Gallery, **13**
Toffs, **11**

Financial Services: Banks and **ATMs** abound on Parliament St. and Coney St. Thomas Cook, 4 Nessgate (☎881 400). Open M-Sa 9am-5:30pm. Barclays, 1-3 Parliament St. (☎882 305). Open M-F 9am-5pm, Sa 9am-3pm.

Luggage Storage: At York Station (p. 396). £4 per item. Open daily 8am-8:30pm.

Pharmacy: Boots, 48 Coney St. (☎653 657). Open M-W and F-Sa 8:30am-6pm, Th 8:30am-7pm. **Oliver's,** 59 Blossom St. (☎622 761). Open M-F 9am-5:30pm, Sa 9am-1pm.

Police: Fulford Rd. (☎631 321).

Hospital: York District Hospital (☎631 313), off Wigginton Rd. Take bus #1 or 18 from Exhibition Sq. and ask for the hospital stop. **NIH Walk-in Clinic,** 31 Monkgate St. (☎725 401). Open M-Su 8am-8pm.

Internet Access: Cafe of the Evil Eye, 42 Stonegate (☎640 002). £2 per hr. Wi-Fi access £1 per day. Open M-Th 10am-11pm, F-Sa 10am-late, Su 11am-10:30pm. **York Central Library,** Museum St. (☎655 631), has 25 Internet terminals. £2 per hr. Open M-W and F 9am-8pm, Th 9am-5:30pm, Sa 9am-4pm. **City Screen Cimena,** 12-17 Coney St. (☎612 940). £3 per hour, Wi-Fi £1 per day. Open daily 11am-6pm.

Post Office: 22 Lendal St. (☎0845 722 3344) with a **bureau de change.** Open M and W-Sa 9am-5:30pm, Tu 9:30am-5:30pm. Branch at 4 Colliergate (☎651 398). Open M-F 9am-5:30pm and Sa 9am-4pm. **Post Code:** YO1 8DA.

▐ ACCOMMODATIONS

B&Bs (from £30) are usually located outside the city walls and scattered along **Bootham** and **Clifton Streets, Monkgate** and **Huntington Streets, Bishopthorpe Road,** and in the Mount area down **Blossom Street.**

Foss Bank Guest House, 16 Huntington Rd. (☎635 548). 20min. walk or take bus #12 from the train station and get off on the 1st stop on Huntington Rd. Offers spacious, sun-lit rooms with shower and sink. Wi-Fi access. Mention *Let's Go* when booking for a £1 discount. Singles £29; doubles £60. Cash only. ❸

YHA York International, Water End (☎653 147), Clifton, 2 mi. from train station. The long walk from the train station follows the river path "Dame Judi Dench," which connects to Water End. Caters to school groups but attracts guests of all ages. TV lounge, bar, restaurant, game room, and kitchen. Breakfast included. Bike rental £1.50 per hr., £9.60 per day. Reserve in advance in summer. Dorms £20, under 18 £14.50. Singles £27.50; doubles £52. £3 charge for non-YHA members. MC/V. ❷

Bar Convent Guest House, 17 Blossom St. (☎464 902; www.bar-convent.org.uk). 18-bedroom guest house located in the oldest operational convent in England. Rooms are basic but spotless, and the continental breakfast is filling and delicious. Wi-Fi £1 per hr., £3.50 per day. Laundry, game room, and kitchen. Reception 8am-10pm. Singles £30; doubles £57, ensuite from £70. MC/V. ❸

York Backpackers, 88-90 Micklegate (☎627 720; www.yorkbackpackers.co.uk). Backpackers and tourists alike share this 18th-century mansion. Kitchen, laundry (£3 per load), free secure storage, and TV lounge available. "Dungeon Bar" open every night to guests and more beautiful than its name suggests. Continental breakfast included. Dorms £15; doubles £38. Ask about working in exchange for accommodation. MC/V, with 50p surcharge. ❷

Camping: Riverside Caravan and Camping Park, Ferry Ln. (☎705 812), Bishopthorpe, 2 mi. south of York off the A64. Take bus #11A to Bishopthorpe's Main St. (2 per hr.), or ask to be let off at the campsite. July-Aug. and early Sept. £11 per tent; Apr.-June and mid-Sept. to Oct. £10 per tent. Cash only. ❶

NORTHEAST ENGLAND

🔲🔳 FOOD AND PUBS

Greengrocers have peddled at **Newgate Market** for centuries, between Parliament St. and the Shambles. (Open Apr.-Dec. M-Sa 9am-5pm, Su 9am-4:30pm; Jan.-Mar. M-Sa 9am-5pm.) You can also opt to eat street-side and fill up on sausages (£1.65, £1.80 with cheese), burgers (£2), and fresh lemonade (£2) from stands parked in St. Sampson's Sq. There seem to be more pubs in the center of York than gargoyles on the Minster's east wall. Find cheap eats at the many Indian restaurants just out-side the city gates. **Groceries** are available at Sainsbury's, at the intersection of Foss Bank and Heworth Green. (☎ 643 801. Open M-Sa 8am-8pm, Su 11am-5pm.)

🔲 **Oscar's Wine Bar and Bistro**, 8 Little Stonegate (☎652 002), off Stonegate. Order at the bar and find a seat on the patio (if you can part the crowds) at this local favorite. Huge portions of delicious food like Oscar's special burger (£7.50), lasagna (£7.50), and a spicy bean burger (£6.50). Sandwiches and starters £4. Happy hour M 4-11pm, Tu-F 5-7pm, Su 4-10:30pm. Open M-Sa 11:30am-11pm, Su noon-10:30pm. MC/V. ❷

🔲 **El Piano**, 15 Grape Ln. (☎610 676). Mexican flavors infuse the heart-healthy dishes served up in this laid-back and brightly painted establishment at the corner of the city center. Dishes served in 3 sizes: chica (£3), tapas (£4.25), and ración (£6) are great for nibblers and cheap dates. Catch "cheap chow" M-W 10am-7pm. Smaller dining rooms upstairs are aptly named the "Morrocan Room," adorned with floor pillows, and the bright "Sunshine Room." Open M-Sa 10am-midnight, Su noon-5pm. MC/V. ❷

Evil Eye Lounge, 42 Stonegate (☎464 002). Everything from cocktails to computers at this 3-story restaurant and lounge. Thai and Indonesian dishes are flavorful and afford-able. Over 100 mixed drink selections (£5 each). Wi-Fi £1 per day. Internet £2 per hr. Noodles £5, entrees £6-10. Food served M-F noon-9pm, Sa noon-7pm. Bar open M-Th 10am-11:30pm, F-Sa 10pm-12:30am. MC/V. ❷

Mr. Sandwich, 37 Shambles (☎643 500). Think of all you can buy in England for just £1—yup, not a lot. Thank goodness for Mr. Sandwich, who will make you any one of 47 kinds of sandwiches for £1. Fillings include chicken, roast pork, and mozzarella and fig. Takeaway only. Salads £2. Open M-Sa 8am-5pm, Su 10am-5:30pm. Cash only. ❶

Victor J's Artbar, 1 Finklestreet (541 771). Hidden down an alley off Stonegate. This art-deco bar and bistro serves huge portions of tasty sandwiches (brie, roasted veggies, and pesto ciabatta; £6) and burgers (£5-6) that will please both your belly and your budget. Open M-W 10am-midnight, Th-Sa 10am-1am, Su 11am-6pm. MC/V. ❷

The Fudge Kitchen, 58 Low Petergate (☎645 596). Over 20 flavors of gooey fudge, from Vintage Vanilla, to Banoffee, to Strawberries 'n' Cream (£3-4.50 per slice) are made before your eyes by energetic chefs. Free samples available all day. Open M-Sa 10am-6pm, Su 10am-5:30pm. MC/V. ❶

🔘 SIGHTS

The best introduction to York is a walk along its **medieval walls** (2½ mi.), especially the northeast section and behind the cathedral. The walls are accessible up stair-ways by the gates. Beware the tourist stampede, which only subsides in the early morning and just before the walls close at dusk.

SIGHTS AT YORK MINSTER

🔲**THE CATHEDRAL.** Tourists and pilgrims alike have visited the Minster—the largest Gothic cathedral outside of Italy—for centuries. The cathedral displays an estimated half of all the medieval stained glass in England. The 15th-century Great

East Window, which depicts the beginning and end of the world in more than 100 small scenes, is the world's largest medieval stained-glass window. Look for the statue of Archbishop Lamplugn toward the East Window—he has two right feet. The main chamber of the church is generally mobbed with tourists, but the tombs and stonework are less appreciated and equally impressive. *(Deangate.* ☎*557 216; www.yorkminster.org. Open daily 7am-6:30pm. Evensong M-Sa 5pm, Su 4pm. Free 1hr. guided tours from the entrance when volunteers are available Apr.-Sept. daily 9:30am-3:30pm, Oct.-Mar. 10am-2pm. £5.50, concessions £4.50. Combined ticket with Undercroft £7.50, concessions £5.)*

CHAPTER HOUSE. For something a little less holy, check out the Chapter House's grotesque medieval carvings. Every figure is unique, from mischievous demons to a three-faced woman. Keep an eye out for the tiny Virgin Mary to the right upon entering—so small she went unnoticed by Cromwell's idol-smashing thugs. *(Chapter House open daily 9am-6pm. Free.)*

CENTRAL TOWER. It's a 275-step climb to the top of the tower. Go early—ascents are only allowed during a 5min. period every 30min because the staircase is too narrow for passing traffic. *(Open daily Apr.-Sept. 9:30am-6pm, Oct.-Mar. 10am-4pm. £4.)*

UNDERCROFT, TREASURY, AND CRYPT. In the **undercroft**, learn the story of the Minster's founding and construction and tour the building's huge concrete and steel foundations. The **Roman level** displays remains of Roman legionary headquarters, including the site where Constantine was proclaimed emperor. The **crypt**—not a crypt at all but the altar of the Norman-Saxon church—houses a shrine to **St. William of York** and the 12th-century **Doomstone** upon which the cathedral was built. The **treasury** displays the wealth of the old archbishops, including Yorkshire silver vessels and the Horn of Ulph. Those not paying the entrance fee can sneak a quick peek into the crypt through the gate in the East Wing. *(Open daily Apr.-Sept. 9:30am-5:30pm, Oct.-Mar. 10am-5pm. £4, concessions £3. 45min. audio tour included.)*

OTHER SIGHTS

■**YORK CASTLE MUSEUM.** Who says time travel is impossible? Billed as Britain's premier museum of everyday life, the York Castle Museum does its best to transport visitors back to the days of yore. The comprehensive exhibits are the brainchild of the eccentric Dr. John Kirk, who began collecting household items—Victorian wedding dresses, old-fashioned hard candies, antique vacuum cleaners—during his house calls from the 1890s to the 1920s. The themed exhibitions include **Kirkgate,** an intricately reconstructed Victorian shopping street, and **Half Moon Court,** its Edwardian counterpart. On both streets, visitors can enter the candy store, bar, police station, and others to view period items close up. *(Between Tower St. and Piccadilly.* ☎*687 687. Open daily 9:30am-5pm. £6.50, concessions £5.50)*

JORVIK VIKING CENTRE. As one of the busiest attractions in the city, the center usually has unavoidable lines and hordes of school groups; arrive early or book at least a day ahead in summer. Visitors ride through the York of the 10th century in floating "time cars," past artifacts, painfully accurate smells, and animatronic mannequins. Built atop a major archaeological site, the museum contains unusually well-preserved Viking artifacts. Much of the information presented is based on archaeological evidence from the site. *(Coppergate.* ☎*543 402 for advance bookings; www.vikingjorvik.com. Open daily 10am-5pm. Last admission 1hr. before close. £7.75, concessions £6.60. Pre-booking charge £1 per person.)*

CLIFFORD'S TOWER. Clifford's tower is one of the last remaining pieces of York Castle and a chilling reminder of one of the worst outbreaks of anti-Semitic violence in English history. In 1190, Christian merchants tried to erase their debts to Jewish bankers by annihilating York's Jewish community. On the last Sabbath before Passover, 150 Jews sought refuge in the wooden tower and, faced with the prospect of starvation or butchery, committed suicide by setting the tower on fire. The tower was rebuilt with stone in 1250. *(Tower St. ☎646 940. Open daily Apr.-Sept. 10am-6pm; Oct. 10am-5pm; Nov.-Mar. 10am-4pm. £3, concessions £2.30.)*

YORKSHIRE MUSEUM AND GARDENS. Hidden in 10 gorgeous acres of gardens, the Yorkshire Museum presents Roman, Anglo-Saxon, and Viking artifacts. The highlight is the priceless **Middleham Jewel** (c. 1450), an enormous sapphire set in a gold amulet engraved with the Trinity and the Nativity. In the gardens, children chase pigeons among the ruins of **St. Mary's Abbey,** once the most influential Benedictine monastery in northern England. *(Enter from Museum St. or Marygate. ☎687 687. Open daily 10am-5pm. £5, concessions £4, families £14. Gardens and ruins free.)*

BEST OF THE REST. See more than six centuries of British and European art at the **York City Art Gallery,** in Exhibition Sq. across from the TIC. The gallery shows special exhibitions throughout the year and permanently displays the work of William Etty, York native and pioneer of the English painted nude. *(☎687 687. Open daily 10am-5pm; last admission 4:30pm. Free.)* The **Treasurer's House,** Chapter House St. next to the Minster, holds the collection of antique furnishings amassed by Edwardian connoisseur Frank Green. *(☎624 427. Open Apr.-Oct. M-Th and Sa-Su 11am-4:30pm. £5, children £2.80. Tours of the haunted cellar £2.20. Gardens free.)*

NIGHTLIFE AND FESTIVALS

To discover the best of after-hours York, consult *What's On* and *The Talk,* available at the TIC, for listings of live music, theater, cinema, and exhibitions. Twilight activities take place in **King's Square** and on **Stonegate,** where barbershop quartets share the pavement with jugglers, magicians, and soapboxers. Next to the TIC, the 250-year-old **Theatre Royal,** St. Leonards Pl., offers stage fare. *(☎623 568; www.yorktheatreroyal.co.uk. Box office open M 10am-6pm, Tu-Sa 10am-8pm. £9-18, students and under 25 £5, all matinees £8.)* The always-packed **King's Arms,** King's Staith, has outdoor seating and cheap drinks (bitters £1.50 per pint, lager £1.70 per pint). Be wary in the winter, when the riverside spot earns the nickname "the Pub that Floods." *(☎659 435. Open M-Sa 11am-11pm, Su noon-10:30pm. Cash only.)* One of the only places in York to get your groove on, **The Gallery,** 12 Clifford St., has two hot dance floors and six bars. Be prepared to queue up on popular theme nights. *(☎647 947. Dress smart casual; no sneakers or sportswear on weekends. Cover £3.50-10. Open M-Th and Su 10pm-2am, F-Sa 10pm-3am.)* Break out your glow sticks and head to **Toffs,** 3-5 Toft Green, where three rooms blast house and chart toppers. *(☎620 203. Weekly student nights; discount with student ID. No sneakers or sportswear on weekends. Cover £3.50-8. Open M-Sa 10pm-2am.)* York's main music venue, **Fibber's,** Stonebow House, the Stonebow, has live music nightly. Friday and Saturday become club nights, featuring indie and rock spun by a DJ after live music ends. *(☎651 250; www.fibbers.co.uk. Live music 8-10:30pm. Club cover £5, students £3 before 11:30pm.)* The Minster and local churches host a series of **summer concerts,** including July's **York Early Music Festival.** *(☎658 338; www.ncem.co.uk. Tickets £8-25.)*

DAYTRIP FROM YORK

CASTLE HOWARD

15 mi. northeast of York off A64. Yorkshire Coastliner bus #840 runs to the castle, 842 runs from the castle (40min.; May-Sept. M-Sa 2 per day in each direction, Su 1 per day; round-trip £5.30); 15% off admission with bus ticket (ask for a heritage voucher). Take the morning bus

NORTHEAST ENGLAND

from York to catch the bus back in the afternoon. Bring small bills for the bus. ☎ 01653 648 333; www.castlehoward.co.uk. Open Mar.-Oct. daily 11am-4:30pm; gardens 10am-6:30pm. Last admission 4pm. £9.50, concessions £8.50. Gardens only £7/6.50.

The domed Castle Howard, still inhabited by the Howard family but open to visitors, inspired Evelyn Waugh to write *Brideshead Revisited* and was the setting for the BBC's film adaptation. Roman busts and portraits of Howard ancestors in full regalia clutter the halls. Head to the **chapel** for kaleidoscopic pre-Raphaelite stained glass. More stunning than the castle are its 1000 acres of gardens with fountains, lakes, and roaming peacocks. The **Temple of the Four Winds** offers views of the rolling hills.

PENNINE WAY

The Pennine Way is Britain's first long-distance trail and still challenges diehard hikers. The 268 mi. path begins in Edale, crosses the plateau of Kinder Scout, passes into the Yorkshire Dales at Malham, and reemerges at the peak of Pen-y-ghent. The "Long Green Trail" dreamed up by 20th-century writer Tom Stephenson is now one of Britain's most popular walking routes. Hikers can find solitude among rock-strewn moors as well as lodgings filled with fellow walkers.

⚑ HIKING THE PENNINE WAY

Hikers have completed the Way in as few as ten days (the record is a 2½ day relay), but most spend three weeks on the trail. Brief but rewarding forays on well-traveled walkways leave from major towns. The unusual limestone formations in the Yorkshire Dales and the lonely moor of Kinder Scout are Way-cool highlights. The Pennines do not, however, coddle hikers. Sudden storms can reduce visibility, leave paths swampy, and sink you knee-deep in peat. Even the most hardcore hikers stay away from the Pennines in the winter. Bring a map and compass. Rain gear, warm clothing, and extra food are also essential. (See **Wilderness Safety,** p. 50.) Wainwright's *Pennine Way Companion* (£10), a pocket-sized volume available from bookstores, is a good supplement to Ordnance Survey maps (£6-8), all available at NPICs and TICs. Coverage of the route comes in two National Trail Guides, *Pennine Way North* and *Pennine Way South* (each £12). Information on hikes is also available from *Walk this Way: Pennine Way* (£5). Those wishing to see some of the Way without hoofing the whole thing should pick up bus timetables, available free at NPICs. For £5-10 per bag, the **Pennine Way/Dales Way Baggage Courier** (☎ 01729 830 463 or 07713 118 862) will cart your pack as you hike.

⚑ ACCOMMODATIONS

YHA hostels are spaced within a day's hike (7-29 mi.) of each other. Book online at www.yha.org.uk. Any NPIC or TIC can supply details on trails and alternate accommodations; pick up the free *Yorkshire Dales Official Guide*.

YHA HOSTELS

The following hostels are arranged from south to north, with the distance from the nearest southerly hostel listed. Unless otherwise noted, reception is open from 5pm, and breakfast and evening meals are served. YHA also books rooms through its Northern Region Offices, PO Box 11, Matlock, Derbyshire, DE4.

Edale: (☎ 0870 7705 808) In the Peak District. See p. 366. Dorms £15.20, under 18 £9. ❷

Mankinholes: (☎0870 770 5952). 2 mi. outside Todmorden. 2-, 4-, and 6-person rooms. Curfew 11pm. This 16th-century manor house is now a self-catering hostel. Dorms £14, under 18 £10. MC/V. ❷

Haworth: (☎0870 7705 858). 18 mi. from Mankinholes on Lees Ln. See p. 405. Dorms £14, under 10 £10. ❷

Earby: (☎0870 770 5802), 9-11 Birch Hall Ln., Earby, 12 mi. from Haworth. Self-catering. Open Apr.-Oct. Cottage hostel with garden and waterfall. Dorms £13, under 18 £9.50 MC/V. ❷

Malham: (☎0870 7705 946) 15 mi. from Earby in the Yorkshire Dales. See p. 413. Car park on-site. Dorms £14, under 18 £10. ❷

Hawes: (☎0870 7705 854) 19 mi. from Stainforth in the Yorkshire Dales. See p. 412. Dorms £14, under 18 £10. ❷

Keld: (☎0870 708 868) 9 mi. from Hawes in the Yorkshire Dales. See p. 413. Dorms £7.50. ❶

Langdon Beck: (☎0870 770 5910), Forest-in-Teesdale, 15 mi. from Baldersdale. Great views of the North Pennines. Open year-round; call to confirm. Dorms £12, under 18 £9. MC/V. ❶

Dufton: (☎0870 770 5800), Redstones, Dufton, Appleby, 12 mi. from Langdon Beck. Access to Pennine Way and Cumbria Circle Way. Open daily Apr.-Oct. Dorms £14, under 18 £10. MC/V. ❷

Greenhead: (☎0870 7747 411), 17 mi. from Alston. See p. 445. Good base for Hadrian's Wall heritage site. Dorms £13, under 18 £9.50. ❷

Once Brewed: (☎0870 770 5980), Military Road. 7 mi. east of Greenhead. See p. 445. Dorms £14, under 18 £10. ❷

CAMPING BARNS

In the High Pennines, the YHA operates six camping barns. Amenities—electricity, hot water, heating, showers, and so on—vary from farm to farm. To book, call ☎0870 770 8868 or email campingbarns@yha.org.uk. More information is available on the YHA website (www.yha.org.uk) and in the free *Camping Barns in England*, available at some TICs. **The Holwick Barn ❶**, Low Way Farm, Holwick, owned by Mr. and Mrs. Scott, is 3 mi. north of Middleton-in-Teesdale. Heaters, showers, gas cooking facilities, and hot water are included. Electricity on meter. (☎0870 7708 868. Sleeps 15. £6.50 per person. MC/V.) **The Witton Barn ❶**, Witton Estate, Witton-le-Wear, is just off the Weardale Way. This converted 15th-century castle now includes modern amenities like a swimming pool, public bars, shop and cafeteria. (Sleeps 20. £6.50 per person. MC/V.)

SOUTH PENNINES

Visitors to the South Pennines enjoy brisk country hikes along the dramatic, dandelion-dotted hills known as "the moors." Walks among the abandoned cotton and wool mills always prove breathtaking, especially during the long summer days. The picturesque villages of Hebden Bridge and Haworth offer an eyeful of green, a host of fluffy sheep, and the refreshing feel of domestic country life.

▐ TRANSPORTATION AND ORIENTATION

The proximity of the South Pennines to Leeds and Bradford makes **train** transportation (☎08457 484 950) fairly easy. From **Hebden Bridge,** Arriva's Transpennine

Express runs to Blackpool, Leeds, and Manchester. (☎0870 602 3322. M-Sa 7am-9pm several per hr., Su every hr. Leeds £3.50, Manchester £8.) Get to **Haworth** by taking Metro's Airedale line from Leeds to Keighley (KEETH-lee), 5 mi. north of the town (several per hr., £5.50). From there, travel to Haworth via the Keighley & Worth Valley Railway's steam trains (☎01535 645 214; Sa-Su at least 6 per day, July-Aug. 5-10 per day; single £9, rover ticket £12). Those not rail-inclined can take Metroline (☎603 284) **buses** #663-665 and 720 (15min., every 15-30min., £1.20-1.40). Metroline bus #500 runs between Haworth and Hebden Bridge (30min., 4-5 per day, £1.50.) Bus travel will take you through smaller cities. Travel to Halifax to get to Hebden Bridge and to Keighley to get to Haworth—both cities are convenient destinations from **Leeds** and **Manchester.** Local buses make the 30min. journey from these cities to Hebden Bridge and Haworth. For more information, see below or call Metroline (☎0113 245 7676). TICs have a wide selection of trail guides. The Worth Way traces a 5½ mi. route from Keighley to Oxenhope—ride the steam train or Metroline bus back to your starting point. From Haworth to Hebden Bridge, choose a trail from the TIC's *Two Walks Linking Haworth and Hebden Bridge* (50p), which guide visitors along the paths that inspired the Brontë sisters.

HEBDEN BRIDGE   ☎01422

A historic stone village sandwiched between two hills, Hebden Bridge lies close to the **Pennine Way** and the circular 50 mi. **Calderdale Way.** The small medieval village stitched its way to modest expansion in the booming textile years of the 18th and 19th centuries, and many of the trademark "double-decker" stone houses of this period are still standing. Today, there are still more cobblestones than paved streets, and the canals and mountain forests make for excellent walks and hiking. One of the most popular destinations is National Trust's **Harcastle Crags** (☎844 518). The ravine-crossed wooded valley is known locally as Little Switzerland, 1½ mi. northwest along the A6033; pick up a free guide from the TIC. You can also take day hikes to the villages of **Blackshaw Head, Cragg Vale,** or **Hepstonstall.** Hepstonstall holds the remains of Sylvia Plath and the ruins of the oldest Methodist house of worship in the world. **Brontë Boats Canal Cruising** gives boat trips along the Rochdale Canal. (☎845 557; www.bronteboats.co.uk. 1hr. cruises. Times vary; look for the updated schedule near the TIC. £5.50, concessions £3.50.)

Conveniently located 30min. from Leeds and Manchester, Hebden Bridge makes for a great daytrip. For those staying the night, however, ◧**Mytholm House** ❸, Mytholm Bank, offers bright yellow rooms and welcomes walkers and cyclists. Follow Market Rd. west out of town to Church Ln. Mytholm House is across from the church. (☎847 493; www.mytholmhouse.co.uk. Breakfast included. £22.50-25 per person. Cash only.) Near the center of town, **Angeldale Guest House** ❹, a large Victorian house at the north end of Hangingroyd Ln. (not Hangingroyd Rd. or Grove), has lovely, spacious rooms. (☎847 321; www.angeldale.co.uk. Singles £35-59; doubles and twins £25-32. MC/V.) Purchase **groceries** at **Oasis** ❶, Crown and Carlton St., an environmentally conscious market with fresh fruits and vegetables along with specialty wines and beers. (Open daily 8am-10:30pm.) For award-winning scones (£1.30-1.75) or tea and crumpets (£1), visit the **Watergate Tearooms** ❶, 9 Bridge Gate. (☎842 978; www.tandcakes.com. Open daily 10:30am-4:30pm. MC/V.) Satisfying pizzas and pastas (£5-8) are served at local favorite **Hebden's Pizza & Italian Cuisine** ❷, Hangingroyd Ln., just across the bridge from St. George Sq. (☎843 745. Takeaway also available. Open W-Th 4:30-10pm, F-Sa 5:30-10:30pm, Su 4:30-9:30pm. AmEx/MC/V.)

Hebden Bridge lies halfway along the Manchester-Leeds rail line (see Transportation, p. 403). The town's train station is ½ mi. east of town on Station Road; follow the signs to town. Buses stop at the train station and on New Rd. The Hebden Bridge Visitor & Canal Centre (TIC) offers the popular *Walks Around Hebden*

Bridge (40p) and several other walking guides. (☎843 831; www.hebden-bridge.co.uk. Open M-F 9:30am-5:30pm, Sa-Su 10:30am-5:30pm.) NatWest **bank** is located near the town center off Crown St. **Internet** access is free at the **library,** Cheetham and Hope St. (☎842 151. Open M and Th 9:30am-7:30pm, Tu 9:30am-1pm, W and F 9:30am-5pm, Sa 9:30am-4pm.) The **post office** is on Holme St., off New Rd. (☎842 366. Open M-F 9am-5:30pm, Sa 9am-12:30pm.) **Post Code:** HX7 8AA.

HAWORTH ☎01535

Haworth's (HAH-wuth) raison d'être stands at the top of its hill: the parsonage that overlooks Brontëland. A cobbled main street milks all association with the ill-fated literary siblings, with tearooms and shops lining the climb to the Brontë home. The village currently wants for wandering heroines, but the moors remain. Down a tiny lane behind the village church lies the home where England's most famous literary siblings spent their isolated childhoods. The ◼**Brontë Parsonage** details the lives of Charlotte, Emily, Anne, Branwell, and their grumpy father. The quiet rooms, including the dining room where the sisters penned *Wuthering Heights* and *Jane Eyre*, contain original furnishings and momentos. Displays include the sofa on which Emily died, Charlotte's wedding bonnet, locks of the sisters' hair, and the toy figures that inspired their early stories. (☎642 323; www.bronte.info. Open daily Apr.-Sept. 10am-5pm, Oct.-Mar. 11am-5pm. £5, concessions £3.60.) A footpath behind the church leads uphill toward the pleasant (if untempestuous) **Brontë Falls,** a 2 mi. hike.

Once the home of the doctor who attended Charlotte Brontë's death, **Ashmount ❸,** 5min. from the TIC on Mytholmes Ln., has sweeping views and an original neo-Gothic interior. (☎645 726. Singles £35-45; doubles £50-70; triples £75; families £85. MC/V.) Housed in a Victorian mansion, the elegant **YHA Haworth ❶** (also known as Haworth Youth Hostel) is a 15min. hike from the train station; turn left out of the train station, up Lees Ln., then left on Longlands Dr. It offers a TV lounge, a grand staircase complete with stained glass, and a pleasant garden. (☎642 234. Meals £3-5.25. Open mid-Feb. to Oct. daily; Nov. to mid-Dec. F-Sa. £14, under 18 £10. MC/V.) **Ye Sleeping House ❸,** 8 Main St., has affordable standard rooms and ample breakfasts. (☎645 992; www.yesleepinghouse.co.uk. Rates £18-25 per person. Weekends 2-night min. Cash only.) For **groceries,** try Spar on Station Rd. (☎647 662. Open daily 7:30am-10:30pm.) Inexpensive restaurants line **Mill Hey,** just east of the train station. **Haworth Tandoori ❷,** 14 Mill Hey, a neighborhood favorite, serves a wide selection of curries, *biryanis*, and vegetarian dishes. (☎644 726. 15% takeaway discount. Open M-Sa 5:30pm-midnight, Su 6-11:30pm. MC/V.) **Wharenui ❷,** 27 Main St., offers sandwiches and light fare during the day and cooks up gourmet dishes in the evening in a relaxed, sophisticated atmosphere. (☎644 511; www.wharenui.co.uk. Most entrees £6-12. Open M and Th-Su noon-10pm. MC/V.) One of Haworth's most popular pubs, **The Fleece Inn ❶,** 67 Main St., has a classic pub atmosphere that draws crowds of locals. (☎642 172. Open M-Sa 11am-11pm, Su noon-10:30pm. MC/V.)

The **train station** (☎645 214) only serves the **Keighley and Worth Valley Railway's** private steam trains (see **Transportation,** p. 403). The **Tourist Information Centre,** 2-4 West Ln., at Main St.'s summit, provides the useful *Four Walks from the Centre of Haworth* (40p) and the town's mini-guide (35p), and books beds for a 10% deposit. (☎642 329. Open May-Aug. daily 9:30am-5:30pm; Sept.-Apr. 9:30am-5pm.) **Tours,** including a graveyard tour, are available from **Heart of Haworth Village Walks.** Tickets are also sold at the TIC. (☎642 329; www.bronteguide.com. Tours daily; call ahead. Open Apr.-Dec. £5.50, concessions £3.50.) The **post office,** 98 Main St., is the only place to **exchange currency.** (☎644 589. Open M-F 9am-1pm and 1:30-5:30pm, Sa 9am-12:30pm.) **Post Code:** BD22 8DP.

LEEDS ☎0113

Once the center of England's textile industry, Leeds and its fortunes declined when the world lost its burning desire for fine wool coats. Changing times have turned Leeds from fabric producer to fashion consumer, and now designer shops and chains fill its grand Victorian buildings. Must-see sights are few, but the city that gave us Marks & Spencer still draws crowds.

▶ TRANSPORTATION

Trains: City Station, City Sq. Ticket office open 24hr. Trains (☎08457 484 950) to **London King's Cross** (2½hr., every hr., £33-88), **Manchester** (1½hr., 4 per hr., £13.40), and **York** (30min., 3-4 per hr., £9).

Bus Station on New York St., next to Kirkgate Market. Office open M-W and F 8:30am-5:30pm, Th 9:30am-5:30pm, Sa 9am-4:30pm. **National Express** (☎08705 808 080; www.nationalexpress.com) operates from Leeds to most major cities, including: **Birmingham** (3¼hr., every hr., £22); **Edinburgh** (7½hr., 5 per day, £37); **Glasgow** (6hr., 5 per day, £37); **Liverpool** (2hr., 2 per hr., £10.58); **London** (5hr., every hr., £19); **Manchester** (1hr., 2 per hr., £7.80); **York** (45min.; M-Sa every 30min., Su every hr.; £4.60). **Metroline** (☎245 7676; www.metroline.co.uk) runs local buses to **Bradford** (1hr., every 30min., £1.30) and **Hull** (1¾hr., 7 per day, £4). The city also runs a **free bus** service that circles downtown; pick up a map from the bus station.

Taxis: City Cabs (☎246 9999), **Streamline Taxis** (☎244 3322), **Telecabs** (☎263 7777). All 24hr.

▶ PRACTICAL INFORMATION

Tourist Information Centre: Gateway Yorkshire (☎242 5242, bookings 0800 808 050), in the train station. Open M 10am-5:30pm, Tu-Sa 9am-5:30pm, Su 10am-4pm.

Budget Travel: STA Travel, 88 Vicar Ln. (☎0871 468 0627). Open M-Tu, F 9:30am-6pm, W 10am-6pm, Th 9:30am-8pm, Sa 9:30am-5:30pm.

Financial Services: There's a slew of **banks** on Park Row. Most open roughly M-F 9am-5:30pm, Sa 9am-1:30pm.

Work Opportunities: JobCentre, 12-14 Briggate (☎215 5382). Open M-Tu and Th-F 9am-4pm, W 10am-4pm.

Luggage Storage: At the bus station. £2.

Police: Millgarth St. (☎241 3059), north of the bus station.

Pharmacy: Boots (☎242 1713), in Leeds City Station. Open M-F 6am-midnight, Sa 8am-midnight, Su 9am-midnight. Other locations throughout the city with varying hours.

Internet Access: Leeds Central Library, the Headrow (☎247 8911), across the street from Town Hall. Free. ID required. Often full, but visitors may be able to score access. Open M-W 9am-8pm, Th 9:30am-5:30pm, F 9am-5pm, Sa 10am-5pm, Su noon-4pm. Last session 30min. before close.

Post Office: 116 Albion St. (☎08457 223 344). **Bureau de change.** Open M-Sa 9am-5:30pm. **Post Code:** LS2 8LP.

▶ ACCOMMODATIONS

There are no hostels in Leeds, but some low-cost guest houses provide a full English breakfast, saving you money for an extra pint. To get to Headingly's B&B-rich Cardigan Rd., walk 20min. through Hyde Park or take any bus toward Head-

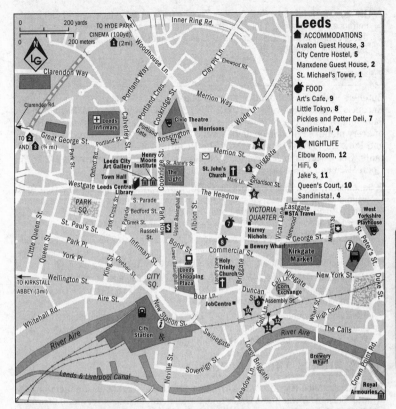

Leeds

♠ ACCOMMODATIONS
Avalon Guest House, 3
City Centre Hostel, 5
Manxdene Guest House, 2
St. Michael's Tower, 1

🍎 FOOD
Art's Cafe, 9
Little Tokyo, 8
Pickles and Potter Deli, 7
Sandinista!, 4

★ NIGHTLIFE
Elbow Room, 12
HiFi, 6
Jake's, 11
Queen's Court, 10
Sandinista!, 4

ingly from Infirmary St., get off at St. Michael's Church (20min.), and walk 5min. down St. Michael's Ln. Posh city hotels offer significant weekend discounts (rates $35-60). Find listings in the TIC's free *Visit Leeds* booklet.

 JUST LIKE HOME. Swing by one of the universities to pick up a list of homes that are willing to act as B&Bs to students. You may have to catch a quick bus to Headingly, but prices can be as low as £12 per night.

The Manxdene Hotel, 154 Woodsley Rd. (☎243 2586), a 15min. walk from the city center. Head east on Great George St., which becomes Clarendon Rd., and turn left on Woodsley Rd. The free bus stops around the corner at Clarendon and Hyde. A warm Kiwi runs this richly hued B&B. TV and coffee pot in each room. Singles £30-50, ensuite £40-60; twins and doubles £40-60. AmEx/MC/V. ❸

St. Michael's Tower Hotel, 5-6 St. Michael's Villa, Cardigan Rd. (☎275 5557). Rooms are small but close to Leeds University student hangouts. Singles £27, ensuite £33; twins and doubles £40-43; ensuite family rooms £20 per person. MC/V. ❸

Avalon Guest House, 132 Woodsley Rd. (☎243 2545; www.avalonguesthouse-leeds.co.uk). Near Manxdene Hotel. Bright blue walls adorn this family-run B&B. Rooms have ensuite sink and small wardrobe. Singles £30-45; doubles and twins £40-55; family rooms £55-75. Call ahead. Some travelers report negotiable prices. MC/V. ❸

City Centre Hotel, 51a New Briggate (☎429 019; www.leedscitycentrehotel.com), entrance on side street. A jolly Frenchwoman runs this cheapest in-town option north of the shopping district. Clean rooms with ensuite bathrooms. Single £35-45; doubles £59; triples £69. MC/V. ❸

▊ FOOD

Butchers and bakers abound at **Kirkgate Market (Leeds Market),** off New York St., Europe's largest indoor market. (☎214 5162. Indoor stalls open M-Tu and Th-Sa 9am-5pm, W 9am-2pm; outdoor stalls close 30min. earlier. Farmers' market 1st Su of every month.) For modish dining, walk along **Greek Street** between East Parade and Park Row. **Vicar Lane,** north of The Headrow, offers less expensive restaurants. Get **groceries** at Morrisons, Woodhouse Ln., Merrion Centre. (☎242 2575. Open M-Tu and Sa 8am-7pm, W-F 8am-8pm, Su 11am-5pm.)

▊ **Sandinista!,** 5/5a Cross Belgrave St. (☎305 0372; www.sandinistaleeds.co.uk). This warm, inviting Cuban oasis features fantastic tapas. Enjoy board games and a special Sunday "recovery" brunch on the patio. Delicious tapas and a la carte meals from £4. Open M-W and Su noon-1am, Th noon-2am, F-Sa noon-3am. MC/V. ❷

Pickles and Potter Deli, 22 Queens Arcade, Victoria Quarter (☎242 7702). An independent deli dishing out 14 filling sandwiches. Build your own with seasonal ingredients from local farmers. Sandwiches from £3.50. Open daily 10am-5pm. MC/V. ❶

Art's Cafe, 42 Calls Ln. (☎243 8243). Small, bustling restaurant with stylish local clientele and original seasonal dishes. Lunch £6-7; dinner £10-15. Open M-F noon-11pm, Sa noon-2am, Su noon-10:30pm. MC/V. ❷

Little Tokyo, 24 Central Rd. (☎439 090). Leeds's favorite Japanese joint offers fabulous sushi as well as vegetarian and cooked options for those who can't go raw. Open M-Th 11am-10pm, F-Sa 11am-11pm. Takeaway available. MC/V. ❷

▊ SIGHTS AND SHOPPING

The ▊**Royal Armouries,** Armouries Dr., has one of the world's best collections of arms and armor. A war buff's Graceland, the museum features every kind of armor imaginable, from a 16th-century "horned helmut" (the museum's trademark) complete with metal beard stubble and spectacles to Mughal elephant armor. Galleries also feature exhibits on civilian weaponry and modern-day handguns. Try your skill on a 16th-century crossbow or a WWI rifle. Don't miss the side building, where you can get up close and personal with horses, birds of prey, and hardworking craftsmen. Demonstrations, including swordplay and an outdoor joust, are held regularly. Call ahead for information on the day's events. On foot, it's best to cross the Millennium footbridge from The Calls and follow the River Aire east until you reach the back of the museum, which is a massive gray stone building. (☎220 1999 or 344 344; www.royalarmouries.org. Open daily 10am-5pm. Free. Special exhibits and joust £2-3.)

Leeds's massive **library** and two **art museums,** clustered adjacent to the Victorian **Town Hall,** form the city's small artistic center. The life-sized chess board and Victorian gardens out front seem straight out of *Alice in Wonderland.* The recently renovated **Leeds City Art Gallery,** The Headrow, features one of the best collections of 20th-century and contemporary British art outside London. (☎247 8248; www.leeds.gov.uk/artgallery. Open M-Tu and Th-Sa 10am-5pm, W 10am-8pm, Su 1-5pm. Free.) The adjacent **Henry Moore Institute,** The Headrow, holds modern sculpture exhibitions in a small gallery. (☎234 3158; www.henry-moore-fdn.co.uk. Open M-Tu and Th-Su 10am-5:30pm, W 10am-9pm. Free.) The ruins of 12th-century **Kirkstall Abbey,** 3 mi. west of the city center on Kirkstall Rd., inspired artist J.M.W.

Turner. The lush greens and lake surrounding the abbey make the perfect setting for a bottle of wine and a picnic. Take bus #33 or 33A and get off when you see the abbey on your left. (☎230 5492. Open daily dawn-dusk. Free.) In town, **St. John's Church**, New Briggate, Mark Ln., is surrounded by a small, gorgeous garden where locals meet for lunch and coffee. The church itself is the oldest in Leeds.

Marks & Spencer started its empire selling goods for a penny in Leeds, and today the city is widely known for its shopping. Housed in old sewing houses, the malls and stores are sights in their own right. The **Victoria Quarter**, a series of arcades off Briggate St., is a marvel of colored glass and steel. It houses the first **Harvey Nichols** department store outside London. The **Corn Xchange**, off Boar Ln., offers a unique alternative to the posh shops throughout the city. Three levels of boutiques from kitsch to couture fill the exchange's gilded chambers, and the main floor holds fairs. (www.cornx.net. Open M-F 10am-5:30pm, Sa 9:30am-6pm, Su 11am-4pm.)

🔊 NIGHTLIFE

With two universities, Leeds wakes up when the sun goes down. Recent grads and young professionals congregate near the city center while eager freshmen shake their jeans and trainers off at the clubs near New Briggate. Clubbers flock to Leeds to partake in neon nights of dance, house, indie-rock, and hip hop. Find up-to-date club listings in the monthly *Absolute Leeds* (£2), available at the TIC.

Sandinista!, 5/5a Cross Belgrave (☎305 0372; www.sandinistaleeds.co.uk). This tapas bar turns into an energetic live music venue at night. With over 30 kinds of rum and an eager, young staff, it's no wonder the small bar is always packed. Try a mojito or coconut caipirinha to get in the mood for dancing. Open M-W and Su noon-1am, Th noon-2am, F-Sa noon-3am.

Elbow Room, 64 Call Ln., 3rd and 4th fl. (☎245 7011; www.elbow-room.co.uk). American-style pool hall with a neon-lit bar. Large plush couches and wooden tables make this a great place to meet with an old friend or make a cute new one. Pool £5-8 per hr. 2-for-1 mixed drinks daily 5-8pm. Cover F-Sa £3-5, free before 9pm. Open M-Th noon-2am, F-Sa noon-3am, Su noon-midnight.

Queen's Court, 167-168 Lower Briggate (☎245 9449; www.queens-court.co.uk). Leeds's premier gay club, housed in a narrow space with an adjoining courtyard. Both fill up quickly for dancing and cheap drinks. M "Pink Pounder," features 2 floors, 2 DJs, all drinks £1. Cover varies, usually around £3. Bar open M-Sa noon-2am, Su noon-midnight. Club open M 9:30pm-2am, Th-Sa 10:30pm-2am. Food served noon-6pm. MC/V.

Jakes, 29 Call Ln. (☎243 1110). This laid-back undergrad bar feels more like your best friend's house party than like a club. Dancers pack the floor when eclectic DJs spin on the weekends. Discounts on beer and whisky of the month. Open M-Sa 5pm-2am.

HiFi, Briggate and Commercial St. (☎242 7353). Basement venue pumps out live jazz, funk, and Latin music. Occasional cover £4. Club nights on weekdays. Pick up a coupon for free entry when you eat lunch at Art's Cafe (p. 408). Open M-Th 10pm-3am, F-Sa 7pm-3am, Su noon-3am.

🎵 ENTERTAINMENT

Hyde Park Picture House, Brudenell Rd. (☎275 2045; www.hydeparkpicturehouse.co.uk), near the Headingly campus. The #56 bus stops directly outside the theater. One-room art house cinema famous for its frequent use in television programs. Daily showings of international and independent films as well as lesser-known mainstream pictures. Su children's film matinee. Tickets £5.50, balcony £6. Times vary; check the website or pick up a monthly guide for details.

West Yorkshire Playhouse, Playhouse Sq., Quarry Hill (☎213 7700; www.wyplay-house.com), across from the bus station. Professional and student productions on 2 stages. M-W under 26 £5. Cafe with Internet access upstairs. Open daily 9am-8pm.

YORKSHIRE DALES NATIONAL PARK

Yorkshire Dales National Park welcomes hikers and history buffs with scattered pastures and one-pub villages. The Dales' valleys, formed by swift rivers and lazy glacial flows, are filled with evidence of earlier inhabitants. Just about everybody left something behind. The Romans abandoned roads and forts. The Bronze and Iron Age tribes blazed "green lanes" and footpaths that remain on the high moorlands. Medieval royalty built castles and 18th-century workers crafted stone walls.

> **NATIONAL PARK COVERAGE.** *Let's Go*'s coverage of Yorkshire Dales National Park includes the towns of **Skipton, Grassington, Malham,** and **Hawes.** The first section provides an overview of transportation, practical information, and general accommodations (such as **YHA hostels**) for the entire park. Local services, B&Bs, and activities are listed within the coverage of the towns.

⎘ TRANSPORTATION

Skipton (p. 413) is the most convenient place to enter the southern tip of the park. **Trains** (☎08457 484 950) run to Bradford (35min., 4 per hr., £4.90), Carlisle (2½hr., every hr., £27), and Leeds (40min., 3 per hr., £6.25). The Settle-Carlisle Railway, run by Northern Rail (☎01729 822 007; www.settle-carlisle.co.uk), meanders through Skipton, Garsdale, and Kirkby Stephen (1¾hr.; 6-7 per day; Day Ranger ticket £20, discount for groups of 10 or more). There is no National Express (☎08705 808 080) office in Skipton, but **buses** run to Leeds (1½hr., 4 per day, £5) and London (6hr., 3 per day, £20) from Skipton's bus station on Keighley St. (KEETH-lee), behind Westland Department Store.

Getting around the Dales without a car can be a challenge. Most local bus and train stations have easy-to-use timetables with reliable schedules. Buses between towns often run only a few times per day, and many only run on Sundays and bank holidays. **Pride of the Dales** (☎01756 753 123) connects Skipton to Grassington (#72; 30min., every hr., round-trip £4.40), sometimes continuing to Kettlewell (#72; 1¼hr., every 2hr., £2.80). **Pennine Bus** (☎01756 749 215) connects Skipton to Malham (#210; 45min.; 2 per day, more frequently on weekends; return £6.70) and Settle (#580; 40min., every hr., £3.90). Other villages are served less regularly. Although **postbuses** run once per day to scheduled towns, they depart very early and stop frequently.

⎙ PRACTICAL INFORMATION

Sampling the Dales requires several days, a pair of sturdy hiking boots, and careful planning. In the south of the park, **Skipton** (p. 413) serves as a transportation hub and provides services not available in the smaller villages. **Grassington** (p. 414) and **Linton,** just north, are scenic bases for exploring southern Wharfedale. **Malham** (p. 415) is a sensible starting point for forays into western Wharfedale and eastern Ribblesdale. To explore Wensleydale and Swaledale in the north, begin from **Hawes** (p. 415) or **Leyburn** (p. 415). In addition to the National Park Information Centres listed below, most towns have TICs.

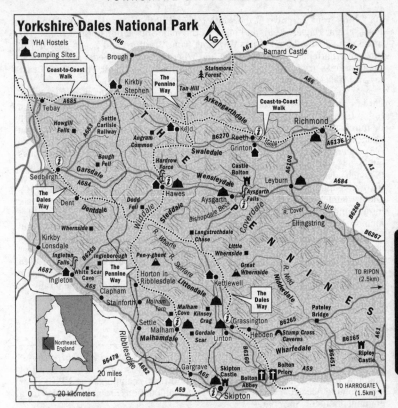

Yorkshire Dales National Park

▲ YHA Hostels
▲ Camping Sites

National Park Information Centres: Pick up the invaluable annual park guides, **The Visitor** and **The Yorkshire Dales Official Guide** (both free), along with maps, walking guides, and the weather forecast. All NPICs book accommodations for a 10% deposit.

Aysgarth Falls: (☎01969 662 910), in Wensleydale, 1 mi. east of the village of Asygarth off A684. Open Apr.-Oct. daily 10am-5pm; Nov.-Mar. F-Su 10am-4pm.

Grassington: Hebden Rd., Wharfedale (☎01756 751 690), in the car park near the village center. Open Apr.-Oct. daily 10am-5pm; Nov.-Mar. F-Su 10am-4pm. 24hr. info terminal outside.

Hawes: Station Yard, Wensleydale (☎01969 667 450), in the Dales Countryside Museum. Open daily 10am-5pm. 24hr. info terminal outside.

Malham: Malhamdale (☎01729 652 380), at the southern end of the village. Open Apr.-Oct. daily 10am-5pm; Nov.-Mar. F-Su 10am-4pm.

Reeth: (☎01748 850 252), in Hudson House on top of Reeth's village green. Open Apr.-Oct. daily 10am-5pm; Nov.-Mar. M-Sa 10am-4pm.

Sedbergh: 72 Main St. (☎01539 620 125). Open Apr.-Oct. daily 10am-5pm; Nov.-Mar. Sa-Su 10am-4pm.

▨ ▧ HIKING AND OUTDOORS

Since buses are infrequent and the scenery is breathtaking, hiking remains the best way to see the Dales. The park's six NPICs can help you prepare for a trek along one of three long-distance footpaths. The challenging 268 mi. **Pennine Way** (p.

402) curls from Gargrave in the south to Tan Hill in the north, passing Malham, Pen-y-ghent, Hawes, Keld, and most of the major attractions of the Dales. The more manageable 80 mi. **Dales Way** runs from Bradford and Leeds past Ilkley, through Wharfedale via Grassington and Whernside, and by Sedbergh on its way to the Lake District; it crosses the Pennine Way near Dodd Fell. The 190 mi. **Coast-to-Coast Walk** stretches from Richmond to Kirkby Stephen.

Arm yourself with a **map and trail guide,** as stone walls and hills start to look similar after a few hours on the path. Prevent runaway cows by leaving gates as you found them. Ordnance Survey maps (£7.50) are available for most paths and can be purchased at any NPIC or outdoors supply store. Outdoor Leisure #2, 30, and Landranger #91 and 98 are good for specific regions; Touring Map and Guide #6 (£5) covers the Dales in general. Harvey also produces a general Yorkshire Dales guide (£4) with more specific coverage of the East, North, South, and West Dales (£7 each). NPICs sell leaflets (£1-3) covering over 30 short routes. YHA produces its own leaflets (50p) on day hikes between hostels. Cyclists can ask at NPICs about rental stores and buy route cards plotting the **Yorkshire Dales Cycleway,** six interconnected 20 mi. routes through the Dales (£2.25). Popular cycle guides include *Harvey's Yorkshire Dales Cycle Way* (£6). Bicycles are forbidden on footpaths, but not on bridleways (trails for horses). Out of breath just thinking about the trek? The **Pennine Way/Dales Way Baggage Courier** will cart your pack for you and deliver it to each night's resting point. (☎01729 830 463, mobile 07713 118 862. £5-10 per bag.) If you prefer some distance between you and nature, ⚑**Cumbria Classic Coaches** runs various trips in 1950s-era double decker buses, generally on Tuesdays, from Kirby Steven to Hawes. (☎01539 623 254; www.cumbriaclassic-coaches.co.uk. £11 per person.)

ACCOMMODATIONS AND CAMPING

The free *Yorkshire Dales Accommodation Guide* (also called *Yorkshire Dales: Official Holiday Guide*) is available at most NPICs and TICs. As in all of England, park officials discourage "wild" (unofficial) camping. The NPICs have more complete lists of camping sites and accommodations around the Dales for a nominal photocopying charge.

YHA HOSTELS
The Yorkshire Dales area hosts seven **YHA hostels.** Hardcore hikers on the Pennine Way will love Hawes, Keld, and Malham. Stainforth, Kettlewell, Dentdale, and Grinton Lodge sit a few miles off the trail. Ingleton, on the western edge of the park, is a good starting point for exploring the Lake District. Those who want to give their feet a rest can get to Kirkby Stephen, north of Hawes, by rail. All YHA facilities fill up weeks ahead, especially in summer, but hostel employees will call other YHAs in search of an empty room.

Grinton: Grinton Lodge (☎08707 705 844), ¾ mi. south on the Reeth-Leyburn road in a former shooting lodge. Kitchen and laundry. Reception 7:30-10am and 5-10pm. Curfew 11:30pm. Open Apr.-Oct. daily; Nov.-Dec. F-Sa; Feb.-Mar. M-Sa. Dorms £14, under 18 £10. MC/V. ❷

Hawes: Lancaster Terr. (☎0870 770 5854), west of Hawes on Ingleton Rd., uphill from town. 54 beds. Curfew 11pm. Open Apr.-Sept. daily; Mar. and Sept.-Oct. Tu-Sa; late Jan.-Feb. and Nov.-Dec. F-Sa. Dorms £14, under 18 £10. MC/V. ❷

Ingleton: Greta Tower (☎0870 770 5880), Sammy Ln., near Market Sq. A renovated Victorian house with 58 beds. Kitchen and laundry. Curfew 11pm. Open Mar.-Sept. and late Dec. daily; Sept.-Oct. M-Sa; Feb. Tu-Sa; from Nov. to mid-Dec. F-Su. Dorms £14, under 18 £10. MC/V. ❷

Keld: Keld Lodge (☎0870 770 5888), Upper Swaledale, west of Keld village. 38 beds. No smoking. Curfew 11pm. Open July-Aug. daily; Apr.-June and Sept.-Oct. Tu-Sa. Dorms £14, under 18 £10. MC/V. ❷

Kettlewell: Whernside House (☎0870 770 5896) in the village center. Easy access to Boton Abbey. 43 beds. Curfew 11pm. Open July-Aug. daily; June and Sept.-Oct. Tu-Sa; Feb.-Mar. and from late Oct. to mid-Sept. W-Sa. Dorms £14, under 18 £10. MC/V. ❷

Kirkby Stephen: Market St. (☎0870 770 5904), on the Coast-to-Coast trail. In a former Methodist Chapel, complete with pews and stained glass. 44 beds. Kitchen and laundry. Lockout 10am-5pm. Curfew 11pm. Open July-Aug. daily; Apr.-June and from mid-Sept. to Oct. M-Sa; Feb.-Mar. and from late Oct. to mid-Sept. W-Sa. Dorms £17, under 18 £13. MC/V. ❷

Malham: John Dower Memorial Hostel (☎0870 770 5946). Well equipped and hiker-friendly. 82 beds. Kitchen and laundry. Reception 7-11am and 5-11pm. Lockout 11am-5pm. Curfew 11pm. Open Feb.-Oct. daily; late Jan. and from Nov. to mid-Dec. Th-Sa. Dorms £14, under 18 £10. MC/V. ❷

DALES BARNS AND CAMPING

Numerous **Dales Barns** dot the park and cost £5-12 per night. Most have showers, kitchens, and central heating. Book weeks ahead and get specific directions along the trails. **Campgrounds** are difficult to reach on foot. Ask TICs for a full list of both.

Skirfare Bridge Dales Barn (☎01756 761 028; www.skirfaredalesbarn.co.uk). 1 mi. from Dales Way between Grassington and Kettlewell. Sleeps 25. £12 per person. Cash only. ❶

Grange Farm Barn, 20 mi. from Skipton (☎01756 760 259). Weekends for parties of 18 only, smaller groups welcome mid-week. Sleeps 18. £8 per person. Cash only. ❶

Hill Top Farm, Malham (☎01729 830 320). A converted 17th-century farmhouse just steps away from Pennine Way and the Limestone formations of Malham Tarn. £8 per person. Cash only. ❶

Craken House Farm, Leyburn (☎01969 622 204), ½ mi. south of town center. £6, rooms £18-20. Camping £4; 2-person tent £7. Sleeps 12. Cash only. ❶

Howarth Farm Camping and Caravan Site, Appletreewick, Skipton (☎01756 720 226). Basic site on a working farm. Discounts for extended stays. £5 per person. Cash only. ❶

Wood Nook, Grassington (☎01756 752 412), off of B6265 from Skipton. Tent and car £8.50 per adult. Electricity £1. MC/V. ❶

Bainbridge Ings Caravan and Camping Site, Hawes (☎01969 667 354; www.bainbridgeings.co.uk), ½ mi. from Hawes on Old Gale Rd. off A684. Open Apr.-Oct. 2-person tent and car £10; each additional person £1. Electricity £1.50. Cash only. ❶

Brompton-on-Swale Caravan and Camping Park, 2 mi. from Richmond (☎01748 824 629). Open Apr.-Oct. 2-person tent £12; each additional person £2.50. MC/V. ❶

Street Head Caravan Park, Aysgarth (☎01969 663 472). £12 per person per tent. Electricity £2. Cash only. ❶

SKIPTON ☎01756

Skipton is most useful as a transportation transfer point or rest stop. Once you've gathered your gear, skip town and strike out for the Dales. Vacant **Skipton Castle,** at the top of High St., is the main attraction and one of the most complete medieval castles in England. The last surviving Royalist bastion in the north, the castle surrendered in 1645 to Cromwell's army after a three-year siege. (☎792 442. Open Mar.-Sept. M-Sa 10am-6pm, Su noon-6pm; Oct.-Feb. M-Sa 10am-4pm, Su noon-4pm. £5.60, concessions £5.)

B&Bs are the best bet for decently priced accommodations in Skipton. Many line **Keighley Road** and **Gargrave Road** and are generally £25-35 per person per night. Although they are plentiful, rooms fill quickly in summer, so plan ahead or prepare to camp. Sleep comfortably in Victorian-themed rooms with canopy beds at **Carlton House ❸**, 46 Keighley Rd. (☎ 700 921. Doubles only £55. MC/V.) The **Dalesgate Lodge ❸**, 69 Gargrave Rd., is a comfortable, convenient option. The full English breakfast will energize you for a long day of hiking. (☎ 790 672. Singles £30-35; doubles £50; Cash only.) Nearby, **Westfield Guest House ❷**, 50 Keighley Rd., has huge beds for low prices. (☎ 790 849. Singles £25; doubles £48-50. Cash only.)

Load up on fresh gooseberries and cheese at the **market** on High St. (open M, W, F-Sa). Duck inside ▧**Bean Loved ❶**, 17 Otley St. for a cup of coffee on an inevitably rainy day. This father-and-son cafe has free Wi-Fi and is worth a stop even in sunny weather. (☎ 791 534. Open daily 8am-6pm. Cash only.) A downtown local favorite, **Bizzie Lizzies ❷**, 36 Swadford St., serves exceptional fish and chips for £5-7. (☎ 701 131. Open daily 11:30am-9pm. Cash only.) **Nosh ❷**, 1 Devonshire Place behind Woolworth's, serves tapas (£3-6) to trendy patrons. (☎ 700 060. Open M and W-Su noon-midnight. MC/V.) Give your arteries a break from heavy English breakfasts at **Healthy Life**, 10 High St., near the church, which stocks soy haggis and more traditional veggie favorites. Upstairs, **Wild Oats Cafe ❶** serves daily vegan and vegetarian specials (£1-5), along with cream tea and sandwiches. (☎ 790 619. Store open M-Sa 9am-5:30pm. Cafe open M-Sa 9:30am-4:30pm. MC/V.)

Skipton's **train station** is located ¼ mi. west of the city center on Broughton Rd. **Buses** stop at the bus station between Swadford St. and Keighley Rd., behind Westland Department Store. You can rent **cars** from Skipton Self Drive, Otley Rd. Garage. (☎ 792 911; www.skiptonselfdriveltd.co.uk. From £29 per day; discounts for longer rentals.) Admire the Dales from the water on a 90min. cruise (£3) with Pennine Cruisers of Skipton, The Boat Shop, 19 Coach St. They also rent **dayboats** on the Leeds and Liverpool Canals. (☎ 795 478. £80-185 per day; from £430 per week.) If you fancy an aerial view, Airborne Adventures sends **hot-air balloons** over the Dales from Skipton and Settle twice daily. (☎ 730 166. £150 per person; 2 person min.) The **Tourist Information Centre**, 35 Coach St., books rooms for a 10% deposit. (☎ 792 809. Open Apr.-Oct. M-Sa 10am-5pm, Su 11am-3pm; Nov.-Mar. M-Sa 10am-4pm.) Other services include: HSBC **bank**, 61 High St. (☎ 0845 740 4404; open M-F 9:30am-4:30pm); **internet** at Skipton Public **Library**, High St. (☎ 792 926; £2.50 per hr.; open M, W, Th 9:30am-7pm, F 9:30am-5pm, Sa 9:30am-4pm); **Station Taxis**, 27 Keighley Rd. (☎ 796 6666 or 700 777; 24hr.); and the **post office**, Westland Department Store, 8 Swadford St. (☎ 792 724; open M-F 9am-5:30pm, Sa 9am-1pm). **Post Code: BD23 1UR.**

WHARFEDALE AND GRASSINGTON ☎ 01756

The valley of Wharfedale, along the River Wharfe, is best explored using cobbled **Grassington** as a base. Spectacular **Kilnsey Crag** lies 3½ mi. from Grassington toward Kettlewell. (Take bus #72 from Grassington to Kilnsey; 10min., 8 per day, £1.30.) The **Stump Cross Caverns**, 5 mi. east of Grassington, are filled with stalagmites and glistening rock curtains. (☎ 752 780. Open Mar.-Oct. daily 10am-6pm; Nov.-Feb. Sa-Su 10am-4pm. Last admission 1hr. before close. £6. Dress warmly.)

Close to the center of Grassington, **Raines Close ❸**, 13 Station Rd., offers spacious rooms with patios or bay windows and spectacular views on the English countryside. (☎ 752 678; www.rainesclose.co.uk. Doubles £58-64. Cash only.) Across the street, **Springroyd House ❸**, 8A Station Rd., offers three clean, if small, rooms. (☎ 752 473. Doubles £56. Cash only.) Pubs and cafes pack Main St., including **Lucy Fold Tea Room ❶**, 1 Garr's Ln., off Main St., whose offerings include omelettes, toasties, and jacket potatoes, all for £2.75-5. (☎752 414. Open W-Su 10:30am-5pm. Cash only.) Stop by **Cobblestone Cafe ❶**, 3 The Square, for a bowl of homemade sticky toffee pudding (£2) and lots of local conversation. (☎752 303. Open daily 10:30am-8pm. Cash only).

Pride of the Dales **bus** #72 leaves Grassington for Skipton at ten minutes to the hour (£2.70). The **NPIC** (p. 411) in the car park on Hebden Rd., stocks the useful *Grassington Footpath Map* (£1.60) and standard park trail guides (£1) and leads occasional guided walks from March to October (£2). Other services include: **outdoor gear** at The Mountaineer, Pletts Barn Centre, at the top of Main St. (☎752 266; open daily 9am-5pm); Barclays **bank,** at the corner of Main St. and Hebden Rd. (☎296 3000; open M-F 9am-3:30pm); and the **post office**, 15 Main St. (☎752 226; open M and W-F 9am-5:30pm, Tu 9:30am-5:30pm, Sa 9am-12:30pm). **Post Code:** BD23 5AD.

MALHAMDALE AND INGLETON   ☎01524

Limestone cliffs and gorges slice the pastoral valley of Malhamdale, creating spectacular natural landscapes within easy walking distance of one another. A 3hr. hike from the **Malham NPIC** (p. 411) passes the stunning, stony swath of **Malham Cove**, a massive limestone cliff, and the placid water of **Malham Tarn.** Two miles from Malham village is the equally impressive **Gordale Scar,** cut by a glacier during the last Ice Age. The **YHA Malham ❷** (p. 413) is a popular hostel with Pennine Way hikers.

Just north of Malham are the high peaks and cliffs of Ingleborough, Pen-y-ghent, and Whernside that form the **Alpes Penninae.** The 24 mi. **Three Peaks Walk,** which connects the Alpes, begins and ends in **Horton in Ribblesdale** at the **Pen-y-ghent Cafe,** a hiker's haunt that also serves as the local TIC. (☎01729 860 333. Open Apr.-Oct. M and W-Su 8am-6pm; Nov.-Mar. W-Su 9am-5pm.) **Ingleton** is near the middle of the trek. The village's **TIC,** in the community center car park, books rooms for a 10% deposit. (☎241 049. Open daily Apr.-Oct. daily 10am-4:30pm.) The 4½ mi. walk through the **Ingleton Waterfalls** is one of the most popular routes. (☎241 930; www.ingletonwaterfallstrail.co.uk. 2½-4hr. £3.50; children £1.50. Open 9am-dusk.) Pick up a leaflet from the TIC or read the Ingleton town trail sign in the town center. The **YHA Ingleton ❷** (p. 412) and several **B&Bs** on Main St. are good budget options. A 1 mi. walk from Ingleton's town center brings you to **Stacksteads Farm ❶**, Tatterthorne Rd., which offers views of the limestone countryside from its 22 beds. (☎241 386. £10. Cash only.)

WENSLEYDALE AND HAWES   ☎01969

That familiar smell in northern Wensleydale is fertile dairyland. Well-preserved **Castle Bolton,** 6 mi. west of Leyburn off the A684, once imprisoned Mary, Queen of Scots. (☎623 981. Open daily Mar.-Nov. 10am-5pm. £5.) Base your forays into the Dales from **Hawes,** which has an **NPIC** (p. 411) in the Dales Countryside Museum that books accommodations for a 10% deposit. Pay 40p at the **Green Dragon Pub** to access the trail to the **Hardrow Force waterfall,** 1 mi. north on the Pennine Way. **B&Bs** (£20-25) line Main St., and the **YHA Hawes ❷** (p. 412) is uphill from town. Pubs, takeaways, and a Barclays **bank** (open M-F 9:30am-3:30pm) are also along Main St. Farther north, **Swaledale** is known for picturesque barns and meadows. Don't miss **Aysgarth Falls** to the east and the natural terrace of the **Shawl of Leyburn.** Aysgarth and Leyburn are served by Pride of the Dales **buses** #156-157 from Hawes to Northallerton (2hr., every hr., £1.40). Aysgarth's **NPIC** is in the car park above the falls (p. 411), and Leyburn has a **TIC** in its city center. (☎623 069. Open Easter-Sept. daily 9:30am-5pm; Oct.-Easter M-Sa 9:30am-4pm.)

NORTH YORK MOORS

The heather-clad expanses and cliff-lined coast of the North York Moors have changed little since they inspired the gothic imaginations of Emily Brontë and Bram Stoker. The region's landscape, from pastoral towns to dramatic coastline, makes the Moors one of Britain's most visually captivating national parks.

▐ TRANSPORTATION

The primary gateways to the North York Moors are York to the south and Middlesbrough to the north. Middlesbrough is a short train ride from Darlington (30min., 2 per hr., £3.40) on the London-Edinburgh rail line. The *Moors Explorer* pamphlet, free at TICs and NPICs, covers bus and rail service in glorious detail—service varies by season and is significantly reduced in winter. Traveline also provides timetables (☎08706 082 608; www.yorkshiretravel.net).

Three **train** lines serve the park. There is frequent service between York and Scarborough (45min., 1-2 per hr., £10.30). The scenic Esk Valley Line runs from Middlesbrough to Whitby via Danby and Grosmont (1½hr., 4 per day, £9.55). The tourist-oriented North Yorkshire Moors Railway (reservations ☎01751 472 508, timetables 01751 473 535) links the north and south, chugging from Pickering to Grosmont, with connections to Whitby (1hr.; 4-9 per day, no service during some low-season times).

Buses run more frequently than trains. Ask the driver for a day or week pass instead of a single ride. Yorkshire Coastliner (☎01653 692 556) bus #840 travels between Leeds, York, Pickering, and Whitby (every hr.), while #843 runs between Leeds, York, and Scarborough (every hr.). Arriva bus #93 journeys between Middlesbrough, Whitby, and Scarborough (every hr.); bus #X56 runs this same route but also offers a stop in Robin Hood's Bay (every hr.). Scarborough District bus #128 covers Scarborough, Pickering, and Helmsley (every hr.). The national park operates the Moorsbus, with seasonal routes through the park; schedules are available at TICs. The Moorsbus runs irregularly; plan ahead. (www.moors.uk.net. Late July-early Sept. daily; Oct.-Apr. Su and holidays only. All-day pass £3.)

Transportation sound confusing? It is. Stop at the local TIC or your hostel/B&B's brochure area to pick up a copy of the free *Moors Explorer* map, which outlines the whole mess in a clear, color-coded format.

▐ ORIENTATION

North York Moors National Park is 30 mi. north of York. Centrally located Pickering is the starting point for the scenic **North Yorkshire Moors Railway**—a relaxing way to take in the views and connect to the park's excellent hikes. Just a short 20min. bus ride toward the park's southwest corner, the tiny market town of **Helmsley** has excellent historic sights and great access to hiking, particularly when the Moorsbus shuttle is operating. The **Esk Valley,** another popular terrain for hikers, cuts across the north of the park and is served by the **Esk Valley Line** railway. The seaside resort town of **Scarborough** is often flooded with summer vacationers looking for traditional boardwalk amusements, while to the north, the fishing village of Whitby greets tourists with plenty of history and local legends. **Robin Hood's Bay,** between Whitby and Scarborough, is a small coastal village. The first part of this section provides an overview of transportation, practical information, and general accommodations (such as YHA hostels) for the entire park. Local services, B&Bs, and activities are listed within the coverage for the individual towns.

NORTHEAST ENGLAND

North York Moors
National Park

▲ YHA Hostels
▲ YHA Camping Barns

5 miles
5 kilometers
0
0

North Sea

Scarborough Castle
Scalby Ness Rocks
W Scarborough
Black Rocks
Yorkshire Wolds Way

A165

Cromer Point

LG

Cloughton

Cleveland Way

Scalby
Forge Valley
Langdale End

R. Derwent
Troutsdale

Harwood Dale

Dalby Forest

A170

Staindale Beck

Thornton-le-Dale
Thornton Beck

A171

Slinnington

Robin Hood's Bay
Boggle Hole
Old Peak/South Check

Ness Point/North Check

Fyling Hall
Fylingthorpe

B1447
B1416

Fylingdales Moor
■ Barn Howe Rigg

Saltergate

Stain Dale

Whitby Abbey
Saltwick Bay

Whitby

Staithes

A174

A171

A174

B1266

Roxby High Moor
Lealholm Moor

R. Esk

Esk Valley Line

Eskdale

Grosmont

Egton High Moor

Goathland

A169

Newton Dale
Newton-on-Rawcliffe

Lockton
Levisham

Newton Dale

North Yorkshire Moors Railway

Pickering Castle
W Pickering

Sinnington

Middlesbrough

A173

A172

A174

Guisborough
Guisborough Woods

Guisborough Moor

Great Ayton

Danby Low Moor

Kildale

CLEVELAND HILLS

Castleton

Danby Castle

R. Esk

Danby

Westerdale

Glaisdale

Glaisdale Rigg

Wheeldale Moor

Pike Hill (TOTOR)

Rosedale Moor

Cropton Forest

Roman Camp ■

Wheeldale
Roman Road

Kirkbymoorside

Hutton-le-Hole

Spaunton Moor

R. Seven

Rosedale

Blakey Ridge

R. Dove

Westerdale Moor

Farndale Moor

Westerdale

Farndale

Cockayne Ridge

Cockayne

Rudland Rigg

Bransdale

Hodge Beck

Kirkdale

Helmsley Castle
W Helmsley

Rievaulx Abbey

Helmsley Moor

B1257

A170

Vale of Pickering

Stokesley

Stockton-on-Tees

Northeast England

CLEVELAND HILLS

Whorlton Moor

Swainby

Osmotherley

A172

Cleveland Way

R. Seph

Snilesworth Moor

Arden Great Moor

Hawnby

Boltby Forest

THE HAMBLETON HILLS

Felixkirk

Thirsk

A19

A167

A61

Sutton Bank

TO YORK (30mi)

A19

NORTHEAST ENGLAND

🛈 PRACTICAL INFORMATION

The *Moors & Coast* visitor guide (50p), available at any TIC or NPIC, is particularly useful, highlighting the region's events and attractions.

National Park Information Centres:

Danby: The Moors Centre (☎01439 772 737; www.moors.uk.net). From the Danby train station, turn left after you pass the gate and right at the crossroads before the Duke of Wellington Inn; the center is ½ mi. ahead on the right. The larger NPIC and an invaluable source. Open Apr.-Oct. daily 10am-5pm; Nov.-Mar. Sa-Su 11am-4pm.

Sutton Bank: (☎01845 597 426), 6 mi. east of Thirsk on the A170. Open Apr.-Oct. daily 10am-5pm; Mar. daily 11am-4pm; Nov.-Feb. Sa-Su 11am-4pm.

Tourist Information Centres:

Goathland: The Village Store and Outdoor Centre (☎01947 896 207). Open Apr.-Sept. daily 10am-6pm; Oct.-Apr. M-W and F-Su 10am-4pm.

Great Ayton: High Green Car Park (☎01642 722 835). Open Easter-Oct. M-Sa 10am-4pm, Su 1-4pm.

Guisborough: Priory Grounds, Church St. (☎01287 633 801). Open Apr.-Sept. Tu-Su 9am-5pm; Oct.-Mar. W-Sa 9am-5pm, Su 9am-4:30pm.

Helmsley: (☎01439 770 173), at the entrance to Helmsley Castle. Open Mar.-Oct. daily 9:30am-5pm; Nov.-Feb. F-Su 10am-4pm.

Pickering: The Ropery (☎01751 473 791; pickering@btconnect.com), down the road from the train station, beside the library. Open Mar.-Oct. M-Sa 9:30am-5pm, Su 9:30am-4pm; Nov.-Feb. M-Sa 9:30am-4pm.

Scarborough: Brunswick Shopping Centre, Westborough (☎01723 383 636). Open M-Sa 9:30am-5:30pm, Su 11am-5pm. Alternate branch at Sandside by South Bay (☎01723 383 636). Open daily Easter-Oct. 9:20am-5:30pm; Nov.-Easter 10am-4:30pm.

Whitby: Station Sq., across Langborne Rd. (☎01723 383 636). Open daily May, June and Sept. 9:30am-5pm; July-Aug. 9:30am-6pm; Oct.-Apr. 10am-12:30pm and 1-4:30pm.

🛏 ACCOMMODATIONS

Local TICs book beds for £2 plus a 10% deposit. **B&Bs, hotels,** and **caravan parks** in or near the national park are listed under the appropriate towns.

YHA HOSTELS

The following YHA hostels provide lodging in the Moors. Reservations are highly recommended throughout the year, especially in summer. Clearly named bus stops are rare; tell drivers where you're headed. Online bookings can be made at www.yha.org.uk.

Lockton: (☎0870 770 5938), Old School, off the Pickering-Whitby Rd. 2 mi. from the North Yorkshire Moors Railway Station at Levisham. 4 mi. north of Pickering; take Coastliner bus #840 toward Whitby. Self-catering kitchen. Awarded "Green Beacon" for eco-friendly renovations. Reception 8-10am and 5-10pm. Curfew 11pm. Book ahead. Dorms £14, under 18 £10. MC/V. ❷

Whitby: (☎01947 602 878), next to Whitby Abbey in the newly restored Abbey House. Immaculate hostel with ensuite family rooms and over 100 beds. Reception 8-11am and 5-11pm. Curfew 11pm. Dorms £18, under 18 £12. MC/V. ❶

Boggle Hole: (☎0870 770 5704), Fylingthorpe. Follow the posted signs on Cleveland Way 1 mi. south from Robin Hood's Bay, either along the cliffs or on the beach at low tide. Large rooms with comfortable mattresses. Breakfast (£4), packed lunch (£4), and dinner (3 courses £8.50) available. Reception 7:30am-10am and 1-11pm. Dorms £14-15.50, under 18 £10. MC/V. ❷

Helmsley: (☎0870 770 5860). From Market Pl. take Bondgate Rd., turn left on Carlton Rd. and left again at Carlton Ln.; hostel is on the left. Breakfast £4; packed lunch from £4.50; dinner £7. Lockout 10am-5pm. Reception 10am-noon, 5pm-10pm. Curfew 11pm. Open Apr.-late Aug. Dorms £14, under 18 £10, under 5 free. MC/V. ❷

Osmotherley: (☎0870 770 5982), Cote Ghyll, Northallerton. Between Stockton and Thirsk, just northeast of Osmotherley. Reception 7am-noon and 5-11pm. Curfew 11:30pm. Open daily early Mar-late Oct. Dorms £14, under 18 £10. MC/V. ❷

Scarborough: (☎0870 770 6022), Burniston Rd. 2 mi. from Scarborough. Take bus #3 from the train station to Scalby Mills Rd., then follow Burniston Rd. away from town and turn a sharp left immediately after crossing a small river into an unmarked drive at the end of the bridge. In a former mill on a river, 15min. from the sea. 48 beds in 4- to 6-bed dorms. Lockout 10am-5pm. Open Mar.-Aug. daily; Sept.-Nov. Tu-Sa. Dorms £16, under 18 £10. MC/V. ❷

CAMPING

YHA operates four **camping barns** (p. 403) in the Moors. Ambitious hikers on the Cleveland Way might want to stay at the barn in **Kildale**, right along the trail (also accessible by the #27 bus). The barn in **Farndale** lies on the Oakhouse farmyard about 2 mi. westward of Lion Inn (M1 or M3 bus). The #26 and #27 buses go to **Westerdale,** on the Broadgate Farm, and the #128 goes to **Sinnington,** on the edge of the park between Pickering and Helmsley. (Reservations ☎0870 770 8868. Barns from £6 per person; families with children under 5 must book the entire barn.)

🏊 🏃 HIKING AND OUTDOORS

Hiking is a popular way to travel the vast tracts of the Moors. Wrapping fully around the national park, the 93 mi. **Cleveland Way** is the central path of the North York Moors and is easily accessible from many youth hostels and campsites. A particularly well-marked and beautiful portion of the Way is the 20 mi. trail between Whitby and Scarborough. The less eager might want to stop in Robin Hood's Bay, 5½ mi. from Whitby, where the path features hills on one side, tranquil sea on the other, and miles of shoreline cliffs ahead. Hardcore hikers might consider tackling the 79 mi. **Wolds Way,** a stunning coastal hike that extends from the Humber Estuary at Hessle to the sandstone cliffs of Filey. The popular **Coast to Coast Walk** (192 mi.) begins in St. Bees and ends in Robin Hood's Bay (at a pub, of course). Excellent day hikes begin at

GOING GREEN

While you're hiking across the North York Moors, you may not think about the effect your travels have on the wild terrain. It's easy to forget that tourism, particularly in busy accommodations like hostels, can drain valuable environmental resources.

Luckily, some of Britain's YHA hostels are taking steps to reduce their impact on the local environment. YHA Lockton and YHA Langdon Beck were recently awarded European Union "Green Beacon" awards for completing eco-friendly renovations that can help guests lead greener lives even after their travels have finished.

Renovations range from recycle bins in rooms to new organic paint on the walls. At YHA Lockton, heat comes from sheep's wool insulation in the walls. In the summer, a grass roof keeps the place cool. Electricity is generated by solar panels, and thermal panels heat water for showers. Both hostels have rain harvesting systems, which collect water to flush the toilets. Not even waste goes to waste: composting toilets collect it to create "humanure."

So far, the YHA has seen huge success with the new additions. Since the renovations, the hostels have cut water consumption by 30% and carbon dioxide emissions by 40%. Other hostels around the country have begun to make similar renovations, joining in the green initiative.

Get more info on Britain's eco-friendly hostels at www.yha.org.uk.

A WEIGHT OFF YOUR SHOULDERS. For hikers tackling the massive Coast to Coast hike, carrying a heavy pack can be exhausting. If your backpack is more pain than gain, head to www.cumbria.com/packhorse and book their baggage transfer service (£6 for a single day or £78.50 for the full trail). Packhorse will pick up your bag in the morning and deliver it safely to your next night's accommodations.

stations on the park's two scenic **railways,** the **Esk Valley Line** (p. 416) and the **North Yorkshire Moors Railway** (p. 424). Trails are not always marked or even visible; hikers should carry a map and compass (see **Wilderness Safety,** p. 50).

Cycling around the Moors is a challenge because of their steepness, but the paths along the plateaus are less strenuous. The **Whitby to Scarborough Coastal Railtrail,** with sea views, refreshment stops, and sections for all skill levels, is especially popular. There are also many well-signed sections of the **National Cycle Network** that pass through the area. (For more info see www.sustrans.org.uk.) You can **rent bikes** at Trailways, Old Railway Station, in Hawsker, 2 mi. south of Whitby on the A171. (☎01947 820 207; www.trailways.info. From £8.50 per day. Open Easter-Nov. daily 10am-6pm; Dec.-Easter call ahead.) TICs and NPICs offer lists of other bike rental stores in the region.

The Moors can be either horribly hot or bitterly cold in the summer. Call the Danby NPIC (☎01439 772 737; p. 418) for the **weather forecast** before setting out. Be aware that conditions can vary dramatically even within the park, and it *is* England—bring rain gear. The National Park Authority produces a number of guides on the Moors such as the *Walks Around* booklet (£1.90), which detail popular short walks. The Ordnance Survey Explorer Maps (£7.50) include guides to the east and west sides of the park. **Disabled travelers** should pick up the *Easy Going North York Moors Guide* (£4.50) or call ☎01439 770 657 for guidance.

SCARBOROUGH ☎01723

Situated on a hilly peninsula separating two long beaches and dominated by a castle-topped crag, Scarborough has been a popular destination since the mid-1600s. Although its seafront amusements can feel old-fashioned, Scarborough is still a major destination for English families, especially in summer. The young and the young at heart enjoy classic boardwalk attractions and traditional fish and chips stalls, all under the watchful gaze of the ever-present seagulls.

▐ TRANSPORTATION. The **train station** is on Westborough, the main shopping street. There are three bus stops in front of the train station. The first two service **regional buses,** while the last services **local buses** only.

▟▐ ORIENTATION AND PRACTICAL INFORMATION. A cliff crowned by Scarborough Castle divides the town into two main areas, **North Bay** and **South Bay,** both fronted by a long stretch of beach. There are two helpful **TICs** in Scarborough (p. 418). Other services include: **banks with ATMs,** along Westborough; **police,** on the corner of Northway and Victoria Rd.; **Internet** access at the public **library** on Vernon Rd. (£1 per hr.); a **launderette,** 48 North Marine Rd. (☎375 763; wash £2-3, dry 20p per 3min.); and the **post office,** 11-15 Aberdeen Walk (open M and Th 8:45am-5:30pm, Tu-W and F 9am-5:30pm, Sa 9am-12:30pm). **Post Code:** YO11 1AB.

▐▐ ACCOMMODATIONS AND FOOD. YHA Scarborough ❷ is 2 mi. from town (p. 419). The cheapest **B&Bs** (£17-20) can be found across from the railway station on West Sq. or along Blenheim Terr., Rutland Terr., and Trafalgar Sq. near North

Bay. **The Whiteley ❸**, 99-101 Queen's Parade, offers attentive service and well-kept ensuite rooms, some overlooking the North Bay. (☎373 514. June-Sept. £24 per person, sea view £26; Oct.-May £22.50. MC/V.) The **Clarence Gardens Hotel ❹** 45 Bleheim Terrace, takes pride in weekly theme nights like Boogie Nights 70s Disco Fridays and is a great deal for families and for groups. (☎374 884; www.clarencegardenshotel.net. Rooms from £40.) Old-fashioned **Parmelia Hotel ❷**, 17 West St., has conveniently located accommodations just south of the town center. (☎361 914. Singles £21.50; doubles £23.50. Cash only.) You haven't experienced the true Scarborough until you've sampled its fish and chips. Many locals swear by **Mother Hubbards ❷**, 43 Westborough, where generous portions of haddock with chips, bread, and tea or coffee are £5. (☎376 109; www.mother-hubbards.co.uk. Open M-Sa 11:30am-6:30pm.) The harbor is lined with dozens of waterside fish and chip stands offering the traditional dish for dirt cheap prices (£1.15-3.50.) Try family-owned **Ruby's Coffee House ❶**, 23 Foreshore Rd., for the self-advertised "best view in Scarborough," as well as warm panini and coffee for under £5. (☎01723 363 734. Open 10am-late.) **Alonzi's Harbour Bar ❶**, 1-3 Sandside, serves fantastic ice cream from a seaside location. Challenge yourself with The Mega (£2.95), an ice-cream cone measuring well over a foot tall. (☎01723 373 662. Open 7:45am-6pm, ice cream served at the bar outside until 9pm.)

◉♫ SIGHTS AND ENTERTAINMENT. Dominating the horizon atop the city's headland, ▦**Scarborough Castle** was built by Henry II in 1158. A longtime strategic stronghold, the site also served as a home to Bronze Age warriors, a Roman signal station, and a Viking fort. History buffs will enjoy the 1hr. audio tour (£1). (☎372 451. Open Apr.-Sept. daily 10am-6pm; Oct. daily 10am-5pm; Nov.-Mar. M and Th-Su 10am-4pm. £4, concessions £2.30.) Just down the hill across Church Ln., the cemetery of the 12th-century **St. Mary's Parish Church** holds the grave of Anne Brontë. (☎500 541. Open May-Sept. M-F 10am-4pm and Su 1-4pm.) The **Stephen Joseph Theatre**, at the corner of Westborough and Northway across from the train station, stages a wide range of productions and shows films. (☎370 541; www.sjt.uk.com. Box office open M-Sa 10am-8pm and before performances.)

WHITBY

☎01947

What do Caedmon, the first English-speaking poet, and Dracula, the first famous vampire, have in common? Both lived (or reputedly lived) in the small fishing village of Whitby, whose cobblestone streets have seen centuries of history, lore, and fish and chips. Here, Lewis Carroll wrote "The Walrus and the Carpenter" while eating oysters. In those times, Whitby was better known for having the highest number of practicing witches in all of England. Although its days of witchcraft have long since died away, residents still take pride in their local legends and traditions, while the breathtaking ruins of Whitby Abbey loom above it all.

▦⁊ ORIENTATION AND PRACTICAL INFORMATION. Whitby populates the west and east banks of the River Esk, with the North Sea bordering the town to the north. The remnants of Whitby Abbey stand atop 199 steps on the east bank of the river. **Trains** and most **buses** stop at **Station Square,** Endeavour Wharf, on the west side of the river. Whitby's **TIC** (p. 418) books rooms for £1 plus a 10% deposit. Other services include: **banks with ATMS** on Baxtergate near the bridge; a **launderette,** 71 Church St. (☎603 957; wash £3-4, dry 20p per 5min.; open M-Tu and Th-Sa 8:30am-5pm); **police,** Spring Hill (☎603 443); **Internet** access at the Coliseum, Victoria Pl., next to the bus station (☎825 000; £2 per hr.); and the **post office,** Langborne Rd., inside the North Eastern Co-op next to the train station (☎600 710; open M-F 8:30am-5:30pm, Sa 9am-3pm). **Post Code:** YO21 1DN.

NORTHEAST-
ENGLAND

ACCOMMODATIONS AND FOOD. Don't be fooled by the haunting exterior of the ▧**YHA Whitby ❶** (p. 418), on a hill next to the abbey—the spotless hostel has incredible views. For those not so keen on climbing the hill's 199 steps to their bed, the **Whitby Backpackers Harbour Grange ❶**, Spital Bridge on the harbor, offers basic but comfortable accommodations, including a self-catering kitchen and a porch with views of the sea. Walk south on Church St. and turn right just after Green Ln. (☎600 817. Linens £1. Curfew 11:30pm. Dorms £14. Cash only.) Many **B&Bs** are on **West Cliff**, along Royal Crescent, Crescent Ave., Abbey Terr., and nearby streets. **Chiltern Guest House ❸**, 13 Normanby Terr., is a clean, well-priced option. (☎604 981. £25. Cash only.)

Whitby has an outdoor **market** on Church St. on Tuesdays and Saturdays, and a farmers' market on Thursdays from May to September. A giant co-op **grocery** is located beside the train station. (☎600 710. Open M-F 8am-10pm, Sa 8am-8pm, Su 10:30am-4:30pm.) Be prepared to queue at ▧**The Magpie Cafe ❷**, 14 Pier Rd., where the fish and chips are renowned throughout England and well worth the wait. (☎602 058. Entrees £7.45-15. Open daily 11:30am-9pm. MC/V.) The "Fast Track Menu" at the **White Horse and Griffin Restaurant ❷**, Church St., offers elegant cuisine for budget prices, with selections such as delicious homemade soup, trademark fisherman's pie, and even chargrilled steak from £4-10. (☎604 857. Fast Track Menu daily noon-3pm and 5-7pm. Reservations recommended for dinner. MC/V.) On the east side of the river, **Sanders Yard Restaurant ❶**, 95 Church St., is a funky cafe tucked away in a courtyard off the road leading up to the abbey, serving excellent soups (£3) as well as more filling options, including a number of vegetarian specials (£5-8). (☎825 010; www.sandersyard.co.uk. Open daily Apr.-Oct. 9am-7pm; Nov.-Mar. 9am-5:30pm.)

SIGHTS AND ENTERTAINMENT. With marvelous views of the bay below, the splendid ruins of ▧**Whitby Abbey** sit atop a wind-blown hill. Bram Stoker was a frequent visitor to Whitby, and the abbey and graveyard are believed to have inspired *Dracula*. The site's nonfictional history began in AD 657 and the present structure dates to the 14th century. The textured stone walls, grass-filled nave, and views of the sea and the town below make this spot a must-see. (☎603 568. Open Apr.-Sept. daily 10am-6pm; Oct. daily 10am-5pm; Nov.-Mar. M and Th-Su 10am-4pm. £4.20, concessions £3.20. Free audio tour.) Next to the Abbey, the medieval **St. Mary's Church** has a triple-decker pulpit and a maze of box pews. (☎603 421. Open daily June-Sept. 10am-4pm; Oct. 10am-3:30pm; Nov.-May 10am-3pm. Donation suggested.) The **Captain Cook Memorial Museum** is at Grape Ln., on the east side of the river. In a house where Cook once lived and worked, the museum contains original letters, drawings, navigational instruments, Captain Cook wax figures, and special exhibits. (☎601 900; www.cookmuseum-whitby.co.uk. Open Apr.-Oct. daily 9:45am-5pm; Mar. Sa-Su 11am-3pm. £3, seniors £2.50, students £2.) If seafaring stories don't pique your interest, visit the **Whitby Museum,** located in Pannett Park. The museum has England's second largest collection of fossils, most found locally. (☎602 908. Open T-Su 9:30am-4:30pm. Adults £3, under 16 £1.)

While Whitby is generally quiet after dark, a few of its bars fill to capacity on Friday and Saturday nights. The retro-modern **Bar 7,** Pier Rd., serves up mixed drinks to a trendy young crowd. (☎605 777. Open daily 11am-11pm.) For a more traditional seaside pub experience, numerous pubs line Church St. on the east side of the river, home to many ghostly legends. **The Black Horse,** Church St., is supposedly the home of the ghost of the spooky Whitby puppeteer, although it is perhaps better known for being the home of some of the best cask ales in town (☎602 536. Open M-Sa 11am-11pm, Su noon-10pm.) The town takes particular pride in its **Folk Festival** (☎708 424; www.folkwhitby.co.uk), which features dance, concerts, and workshops during the last full week in August. The *What's On* brochure at the TIC and the *Whitby Gazette* (published Tu and F) list events around town.

ROBIN HOOD'S BAY   ☎01947

Once known as the smuggler's capital of the Yorkshire coast, picturesque Robin Hood's Bay now attracts a different breed of visitor: hordes of tourists from across Europe flood the tiny Bay each summer. The Bay is divided into the older Bay-town, where maze-like alleys snake between stone cottages, and the Upper Bay. Many of the 19th-century sea captains' villas have B&Bs with sea views. **YHA Boggle Hole ❶** (p. 418), popular with families and walkers on the Cleveland Way, is 1 mi. from town. Cheap and cozy B&B accommodations are also available at **The Old School House ❷,** Fisherhead, although rooms fill up fast and far in advance. (☎880 723; www.old-school-house.co.uk. £17. Call ahead.) At the upper edge of town on the main road, **Candy's Coffee Bar ❶,** Bank Top Rd., is a popular lunch destination known for its homemade cakes (£5), scrumptious sandwiches (£3-5), and unbelievable view of the bay below. (☎880 716. Open daily Mar.-Oct. 9:30am-5pm; Nov.-Feb. 9:30am-4:30pm.) There is a small **information center** on King St., which has free **Internet** access and a dryer (20p). There are **no ATMs** in the bay, so plan ahead. Robin Hood's Bay is an easy daytrip from either Whitby (20min.) or Scarborough (40min.). Arriva bus #X56 stops here en route between the two towns, but travelers making connections should aim to catch an early bus—it often fills up.

PICKERING   ☎01751

The attractive market town of Pickering is best known as an endpoint of the popular **North Yorkshire Moors Railway (NYMR),** although it can also serve as a central base for exploring the national park. Originally built by William the Conqueror to defend against northern invasions, **Pickering Castle** is a classic example of a Norman "motte-and-bailey" castle, originally surrounded by a moat with a keep built on top of a mound. Ruins of this 12th-century keep command excellent views of the countryside. (☎474 989. Open Apr.-Sept. daily 10am-6pm; Oct. M and Th-Su 10am-4pm. £3, concessions £2.30.) The **Parish Church of St. Peter and St. Paul** is a small Norman building with a 15th-century Gothic spire. Its medieval frescoes are in surprisingly good condition. (Open daily dawn-dusk. Suggested donation £1.)

Around the corner from the train station, the **Beck Isle Museum,** on Bridge St., recreates rural village life over the past two centuries and includes a unique and extensive collection of early local photographs. (☎ 473 653; www.beckislemuseum.co.uk. Open daily Mar.-Oct. 10am-5pm. Last entry 4:30pm. £3.50, seniors and students £2.50, children £2, families £8.50.)

Budget accommodations are scarce in Pickering. The nearest hostel is the ■YHA **Old School ❶** in Lockton, the first eco-friendly "green" hostel in Britain (p. 418). Among B&Bs, **Bridge House ❸,** 8 Bridge St., is a pleasant choice close to the train station, with a relaxing garden in the back beside a stream. (☎ 477 234. Singles £35, two or more £28 per person, discounts for 2+ nights.) **Country Crust ❶,** 16a Market Pl. across from the train station, is the perfect place to grab a quick and delicious sandwich (£1.40) to take on your travels. (☎ 477 322. Open M-Sa 10:30am-7pm, Su 11am-6pm.) Across the square, **Tutti ❷,** 3 Market Pl., is a solid choice for Italian dishes. (☎ 470 121. Entrees £4-10. Open M and Th-Su noon-10pm. MC/V.)

Pickering's **Tourist Information Centre** is at The Ropery (p. 418). Other services include: **banks with ATMs** on Market Pl.; **Internet** access at the **library,** next to the TIC (open M-Tu and Th 9:30am-5pm, W 1:30pm-5pm, F 9:30am-7:30pm, Sa 9:30am-4:30pm); and the **post office,** 7 Market Pl., inside Morland's News, with a **bureau de change** (☎ 472 256; open M-F 9am-5:30pm, Sa 9am-1pm). **Post Code:** YO18 7AA.

NORTH YORKSHIRE MOORS RAILWAY. The North Yorkshire Moors Railway (NYMR) is a popular and easy way to access some of the most beautiful terrain in the Moors. The route itself offers spectacular views, and stations along the way offer some good hiking and a closer look. Pick up *Twelve Scenic Walks from the North York Moors Railway* (£2) at any TIC.

Although mainly geared towards tourists, the steam-pulled train is the only railway available in Pickering. Traveling north, the train stops at Levisham, from which you can access the nearby Lockton YHA, and Newton-Dale, the starting point of many backcountry walks (Newton-Dale stop by request only). Goathland has become a popular stop in recent years—the village is featured in the British TV series Heartbeat, and aficionados of the Harry Potter films will recognize the rail station as the setting for Hogsmeade.

(NYMR information ☎ 01751 472 508, timetable 473 535; www.northyorkshiremoorsrailway.com. Apr.-Oct. 4-9 round-trips per day; Nov.-Dec. most weekends; Jan.-Feb. select holidays. Grosmont to Pickering and all-day rover tickets £14, concessions £12.)

HELMSLEY   ☎ 01439

Helmsley centers around its cobbled **Market Place,** site of a Friday market since the 14th century. Built in 1120 to strengthen the Scottish border, **Helmsley Castle** acquired its shattered profile during the Civil War, when Cromwell blew the place in half. (☎ 770 442. Open Apr.-Sept. daily 10am-6pm; Oct.-Mar. M and Th-Su 10am-4pm. £4, concessions £3.) *Secret Garden* readers might appreciate the **walled garden** behind the castle, a hidden floral escape containing over 50 varieties of Yorkshire apple and showcasing orchids in winter. (☎ 771 427; www.helmsleywalledgarden.co.uk. Open daily Apr.-Oct. 10:30am-5pm. £4, concessions £3.) **Duncombe Park,** ¾ mi. south of Market Pl. on Buckingham Sq., is a large park and nature reserve, home to the palatial 18th-century villa of Lord and Lady Feversham. (☎ 770 213; www.duncombepark.com. Gardens open May-Oct. M-Th and Su 11am-5:30pm. Last admission 4:30pm. House open by hourly tour only 12:30-3:30pm. £7.50, concessions £5.50. Gardens only £3.50.) An enjoyable 3½ mi. walk out of town along the beginning of the Cleveland Way leads to the stunning 12th-century **Rievaulx Abbey** (REE-vo). Established by monks from Burgundy, the abbey was an aesthetic masterpiece until Thomas Mannus, first Earl of Rutland, stripped it of its valuables—including the roof. It is now one of the most spectacular ruins in the country. (Open Apr.-Sept. daily 10am-6pm; Oct. M and Th-Su 10am-5pm; Nov.-Mar. M and Th-Su 10am-4pm. £4.50, concessions £3.40.) A steep ½ mi. uphill, the **Rievaulx Terrace & Temples** is a small park above the abbey with 17th-century faux-classical temples at either end. (☎798 340. Open daily Mar.-Sept. 10:30am-6pm; Oct. 10:30am-5pm. Last entry 1hr. before close. £4.)

Helmsley has a comfortable **YHA hostel** (p. 419) and **B&Bs. Carlton Lodge ❸**, Bond-gate, offers cheerful service and a hearty Yorkshire breakfast in an ivy-covered cottage. (☎770 623; www.carlton-lodge.com. £37.50 per person.) **Nice Things Cafe ❶**, 10 Market Pl., serves up tasty toasted sandwiches for £4. (☎771 997. Open M-F 9am-5pm, Sa-Su 9am-5:30pm. Hot food served until 3:30pm.) After lunch, treat yourself to **Chocolaterie ❶**, Market Sq. The Belgian hot chocolate (£2.65) is heav-enly, and the artistically-dipped strawberries are only £2.40 for a box of seven. (☎787 378. Open daily 10am-4pm. www.chocolaterie.co.uk. MC/V.) Numerous **pubs** and **cafes** on Market Pl. present other dining options.

Buses stop on Market Pl., where you'll find most of Helmsley's **banks with ATMs;** the **library,** in the Town Hall, has free **Internet** access (open M 2-5pm and 5:30-7pm, W and F 10am-12:30pm and 2-5pm; Sa 10am-12:30pm). **The Tourist Information Cen-tre** (p. 418), is in Helmsley Castle. Other services include: The **police,** Ashdale Rd., (☎606 0247, open daily 9-10am and 6-7pm); and the **post office,** Bridge St., just off Market Pl. (open M-Tu and Th-F 9am-12:30pm and 1:30-5:30pm, W and Sa 9am-12:30pm). **Post Code:** YO62 5BG.

DANBY AND THE ESK VALLEY   ☎01287

The gorgeous Esk Valley cuts across the northern reaches of North York Moors. Outstanding views can be had without leaving the railcars of the **Esk Valley Line** (p. 416) as they travel between Whitby and Middlesbrough. It's well worth stopping off, however—this is a splendid spot for **hiking,** and marked trails leave from almost every station along the rail route. TICs and NPICs can provide further details and literature, such as *Walks in the Esk Valley* (£1.90). At the small town of **Grosmont,** the Esk Valley Line connects with the **North Yorkshire Moors Railway** (p. 416). Farther west in the valley, rolling hills give way to some of the national park's finest moorland. **The Moors Centre** NPIC (p. 418) is the best place to research possi-ble routes. *Walks from the Moors Centre* (£2) lists excellent nearby walks, among them an easy 30min. jaunt to **Danby Castle,** a roofless jumble of 14th-century stones attached to a working farm. In good weather, the peak of the 981 ft. **Danby Beacon** offers views stretching to the coastline. The village of **Castleton** is one stop beyond Danby, and from here the **Esk Valley Walk** (35 mi.) begins winding its way back to the coast. A lovely walk follows its first 2 mi. and ends in Danby.

COUNTY DURHAM

DURHAM   ☎0191

The commanding presence of England's greatest Norman Romanesque cathedral lends grandeur to the small city of Durham (pop. 90,000). For 800 years, the bish-ops of Durham had absolute authority over the surrounding county, with their own currency, army, and courts. In the 1830s, new rulers—Durham University stu-dents—took over the hilltop city. Today, hordes of tourists and revelers flow through the narrow cobblestone streets, artisans from across Europe vend their wares in the bustling outdoor market, and street musicians serenade dining cou-ples on the banks of the winding River Wear.

▐ TRANSPORTATION

Durham is 20 mi. south of Newcastle on the A167 and 20 mi. north of Darlington. The **train station** is on a steep hill west of town. (☎08457 225 225. Ticket office open M-F 6am-9pm, Sa 6am-8pm, Su 7:30am-9pm.) **Trains** (☎08712 004 950) depart to: Edinburgh (2hr., every hr., £46); London King's Cross (3hr., 2 per hr., £94.30); Newcastle (20min., 4 per hr., £4.80); York (45min., 4 per hr., £19.70). The **bus** station is on North Rd., across Framwellgate Bridge from the city center. National Express (☎08705 808 080) runs to Edinburgh (4hr., 2 per day, £26), Leeds (2½hr., 4 per day, £14.20), and London (6-7hr., 6 per day, £27.50). Arriva buses (www.arriva-bus.co.uk) X1, X21, and X41 run to Eldon Sq. station in Newcastle (1hr., 2 per hr., £5), and serve most local routes. Rent **bikes** at Cycle Force, 29 Claypath. (☎384 0319. £15 per day, £35 deposit. Open M-F 9am-5:30pm, Sa 9am-5pm.)

▐ ORIENTATION AND PRACTICAL INFORMATION

The **River Wear** curls around Durham, crossed by a handful of footbridges. With its cobbled medieval streets, Durham is pedestrian friendly, although travelers burdened with heavy packs may curse its many hills. The **Tourist Information Centre,** 2 Millennium Pl., is on the eastern side of the Millburngate Bridge. (☎384 3720. Open M-Sa 9:30am-5:30pm, Su 11am-4pm.) Other services include: **banks with ATMs** in Market Pl.; **police,** New Elvet (☎386 4222); free **Internet** access at the **library,** Millennium Pl., right across from the TIC (☎386 4003; open M-F 9:30am-7pm, Sa 9am-5pm, Su 10:30am-4:30pm); and the **post office,** 33 Silver St. (☎386 0839; open M and W-Sa 9am-5:30pm, Tu 9:30am-5:30pm). **Post Code:** DH1 3RE.

▐ ACCOMMODATIONS AND FOOD

Durham's accommodations can fill quickly. Reserve ahead (especially during university graduation in late June) or take advantage of the TIC's free in-office booking service (£3 charge if booking by phone). Durham lacks hostels, but the availability of centrally located **dormitory rooms** is a boon for summer travelers. Others merely tour it, but you can pretend to be Lord or Lady of Durham Castle in the ▓**University College** ❸ dorms. The castle also has a small number of luxurious ensuite rooms, including the fabulous Bishop's Suite, a massive two-room affair with 17th-century tapestries on the walls and views of the river. (☎334 4106 or 334 4108; www.durhamcastle.com. Breakfast in the Great Hall included. Singles from £26.50; doubles £47.50; Bishop's Suite £92. MC/V.) Behind Durham Cathedral, **St. Chad's College** ❸, 18 North Bailey, offers YHA-affiliated accommodations during university vacations. (☎334 3358; www.dur.ac.uk/stchads. Reception 9am-6pm. Parking available. YHA members £21, public £25; twins £40; ensuite singles £32; doubles £50.) Some of the few budget **B&Bs** available are **Mrs. Metcalfe's ❷,** 12 The Avenue, near the bus and train stations, (☎384 1020; £20 per person) or **Mrs. M.T. Koltai's ❸,** 10 Gilesgate, a short 10min. walk up the hill from the city's center (☎386 2026; singles £25; doubles £35).

There is a Waitrose **grocery** store in the Gates Shopping Centre beside the Millburngate Bridge. Students congregate over sandwiches and sweet treats (£1-3) in the 16th-century courtyard of **Vennel's ❶,** Saddler St., a cool bohemian alcove up a narrow passage from the street. (Open daily 9:30am-5pm.) The riverside beer garden of the **Chase Lounge Bar ❶** at the Boathouse, Elvet Bridge, is the perfect place to have a drink and a late lunch. (☎386 6210. Sandwiches and wraps £3. Pizzas £5. Free Wi-Fi. Food served daily noon-6pm. Bar open noon-1am.) There are many Italian restaurants scattered around the central city, a number of which offer

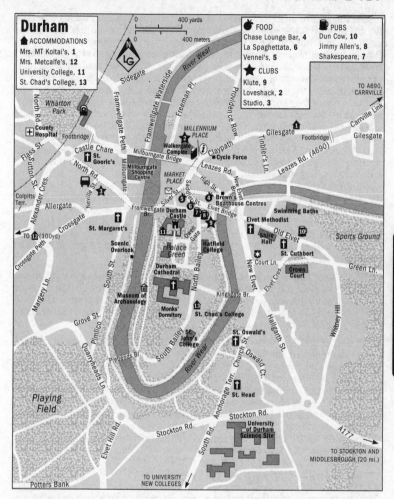

Durham

ACCOMMODATIONS
Mrs. MT Koltai's, **1**
Mrs. Metcalfe's, **12**
University College, **11**
St. Chad's College, **13**

FOOD
Chase Lounge Bar, **4**
La Spaghettata, **6**
Vennel's, **5**

PUBS
Dun Cow, **10**
Jimmy Allen's, **8**
Shakespeare, **7**

CLUBS
Klute, **9**
Loveshack, **2**
Studio, **3**

NORTHEAST ENGLAND

Happy hour deals before 7pm. With cheap pizza and pasta (from £4.50), **La Spaghettata ❶**, 66 Saddler St., is always filled with a raucous and cheerful crowd, possibly due to their specials on 2L bottles of wine. (☎383 9290. Open M-F 5:30-10:30pm; F-Su 11:30am-2pm and 5:30-10:30pm.)

👁 SIGHTS

▧ DURHAM CATHEDRAL. Built between 1093 and 1133 and still largely intact, the extraordinary Durham Cathedral stands, in the words of Sir Walter Scott, as "half church of God, half castle 'gainst the Scot." It is considered the finest Norman cathedral in the world. Explanatory panels guide visitors through the cathedral, although a more detailed pamphlet (£1) is available. The stunning **nave** was the first in England to incorporate pointed arches, and the beautiful **Galilee Chapel** at the end features 12th-century wall paintings. Nearby is the simple tomb of the Venerable Bede, author of the 8th-century *Ecclesiastical History of the English People*, the first history of England. Behind the choir is the **tomb of Saint Cuthbert**, who died in AD 687 and was buried on Holy Island. When 9th-century Danish raiders sent the island's monks packing, the brothers brought along the saint's body as they fled. After the monks had wandered for 120 years, a vision led them to Durham, where they built White Church (later the cathedral) to shelter the saint's shrine. The **Bishop's throne**, next to the choir, has received criticism because it stands nearly 3 in. higher than the Pope's throne at the Vatican. *(Crowning the hill in the middle of the city. ☎386 4266; www.durhamcathedral.co.uk. Open June-Aug. M-Sa 9:30am-8pm, Su 12:30-8pm; Sept.-May M-Sa 9:30am-6pm, Su 12:30-5pm. Tours July-Sept. Suggested donation £4.)* The cathedral's central ■ **tower** reaches 218 ft. and is supported by intricately carved stone pillars. The spectacular view from the top is well worth the dizzying 325-step climb. *(Open from mid-Apr. to Sept. M-Sa 10am-4pm; from Oct. to mid-Apr. M-Sa 10am-3pm, weather permitting. £3, families £8.)* The **Monks' Dormitory** houses pre-Conquest stones and casts of crosses under an enormous 600-year-old timber roof. *(Open Apr.-Sept. M-Sa 10am-3:30pm, Su 12:30-3:15pm. £1.)* Off the cloister lie the **Treasures of St. Cuthbert**, which include saintly relics, holy manuscripts dating back 1300 years, and rings and seals of the Bishops. *(Open M-Sa 10am-4:30pm, Su 2-4:30pm. £2.50, concessions £2.)*

DURHAM CASTLE. Begun in 1072, this fortress was for centuries a key bastion of the county's Prince Bishops (religious royalty). Today, it's a splendid residence for university students and summer travelers. *(Across from the Cathedral. ☎334 3800. Admission by guided tour only. Open Mar.-Sept. daily; Oct.-Feb. M, W, and Sa-Su. Schedule changes daily; call for tour times. £5.)*

BEST OF THE REST. Wandering the horseshoe bend of the River Wear is a pleasant way to spend an afternoon. A scenic walk along the bank between Framwellgate Bridge and Prebends Bridge leads to the **Museum of Archaeology**, which showcases an extensive collection of Roman stone altars alongside finds from the prehistory to the present. *(☎334 1823. Open Apr.-Oct. daily 11am-4pm; Nov.-Mar. M and F-Su 11:30am-3:30pm. £1, students free, concessions 50p.)* **Brown's Boathouse Centres**, Elvet Bridge, rents rowboats. *(☎386 3779. £3 per hr. per person. £10 deposit.)* For a less arduous journey, the center runs a 1hr. cruise on the **Prince Bishop River Cruiser**. *(☎386 9525. July-Sept. daily, Easter-June Sa-Su; times depend on weather and university boating events. £4.50, concessions £4.)*

▥ ▓ NIGHTLIFE AND FESTIVALS

Don't let Durham's stuffy history fool you: come evening a rollicking crowd of students and locals enlivens the scene. Most students start the night at a local pub like **The Dun Cow**, Old Elvet St. (☎386 9219. Open M-Sa 11am-11pm, Su noon-10:30pm) or **The Shakespeare**, Saddler St. (☎384 3261. Open M-Sa 11am-midnight, Su noon-11pm) to sample some of the area's famous cask ale. A little later, warm up your dance moves by hitting a few trendy riverside bars. **Jimmy Allen's**, 19-21 Elvet Bridge, draws students on weeknights with £2 mixed drinks, while an older crowd of local fills its three floors and stylish bar on weekends. (☎357 7574. Open daily 7pm-1am.) The city's new nightclubs heat up after hours. Try **Studio**, 15-17 North Rd., which spins house music on the top floor and R&B below. Monday through Wednesday require a student ID for entrance. (☎384 3900. Open daily until late if university is in session; Th-Su during university holidays. Cover 50p-£3.) If you're feeling particularly frisky, go to the ever-popular **Loveshack**, Walkergate Complex next to the library, where nightly themes, elaborate 70s décor, and specialty drinks such as the Toffee Orgasm and the Brain Haemorrhage draw a libidinous crowd every night. (☎386 4789. Open daily 8pm-2am. Cover M-Th £1-3, no cover F-Sa.) The notorious ▨ **Klute Nightclub,** located beneath Elvet Bridge, was ranked the second worst nightclub in Europe by *FHM* in 1996. When the winning Belgian club later burned down, Klute was catapulted into the number one position. Clubbers form long lines in a filthy alleyway to get inside, where 1980s taped rugby championships play on loop while Barry Manilow croons overhead. In the words of one student, "The bouncers are terrible, the bartenders are evil, the management is always looking for a fight—and there's no better place on earth." (☎386 9589. Open daily 8pm-2am. Cover £1-3.)

The TIC stocks the free pamphlet *What's On*, a great source of information on festivals and local events. Durham holds its **Summer Festival** during the first weekend of July, showcasing folk music, craftsmaking, and other amusements, including a town crier competition. Other major events include the June **Durham Regatta,** England's foremost amateur rowing competition since 1834.

▣ DAYTRIP FROM DURHAM

BEAMISH OPEN AIR MUSEUM. Perhaps the area's most famous attraction outside of Durham, Beamish is a detailed re-creation of 19th- and early 20th-century life in North England, featuring an 1825 replica railway, a manor house, villages with costumed actors, and a tour into a former drift mine. There's quite a lot to see; plan on spending about three hours. Some attractions operate only in high season. *(12 mi. northwest of Durham on the A693. Take Arriva bus X1 or X21 to Chester-le-Street (2 per hr.), then change to Go North East bus X8 or #28, which stop at Beamish Museum Main Gates (2 per hr.). ☎370 4000. Open Apr.-Oct. daily 10am-5pm; Nov.-Mar. Tu-Th and Sa-Su 10am-4pm. Last admission 3pm. Closed late Dec. Spring-fall £16, students £12.50; winter £6.)*

BARNARD CASTLE   ☎01833

Twenty miles southwest of Durham along the River Tees, Barnard Castle—the name of both a peaceful market town and its Norman ruins—is the best base for exploring the castles of Teesdale and the peaks of the North Pennine Hills. Perched above the River Tees, the remains of **Barnard Castle,** including a well-preserved inner keep, sprawl across six acres. (☎638 212. Entrance beside the TIC at the end of Galgate. Open Apr.-Sept. daily 10am-5pm; Oct. daily 10am-4pm; Nov.-Mar. M and Th-Su 10am-4pm. £4, concessions £3.20.) In the 19th century, John and Josephine Bowes built the remarkable ▨**Bowes Museum** along Newgate. It houses the couple's extensive private collection of European decorative arts. Among its many treasures is the largest gathering of Spanish paintings in Britain—El Greco's magnificent *Tears of St. Peter*, among others—as well as a mechanized silver swan (activated every day at 2pm) fancied by Mark Twain. The museum also hosts a regular program of plays and concerts. (☎690 606; www.thebowesmuseum.org.uk. Open daily 11am-5pm. Grounds open 24hr. Tours June-Sept. £7, concessions £6, under 16 free.) For those traveling by car, the **Dickens Drive** is a 25 mi. route that traces the path the author took in 1838 while researching for *Nicholas Nickleby*. Pick up *In the Footsteps of Charles Dickens*, free from the TIC. Overlooking the River Tees, the ruins of 12th-century **Egglestone Abbey** are a pleasant 3 mi. circular walk along the river to the southeast of town. Dales and District Bus #79 from Barnard Castle will also drop you there. (Open daily 10am-6pm. Free.) Northeast of Barnard Castle on the A688, 14th-century **Raby Castle** (RAY-bee) is set in a deer park. If some of the stonework looks familiar, it's probably because Barnard Castle was partially dismantled in the 16th century to provide materials for Raby's completion. Take Arriva bus #75 (20min., every hr.) toward Darlington.

NORTHEAST ENGLAND

(☎660 202; www.rabycastle.com. Castle open July-Aug. M-F and Su 1-5pm; May, June, and Sept. W-Su 1-5pm. Park and gardens open M-F and Su 11am-5:30pm. Last admission 4:30pm. £9, students £8; park and gardens only £4/3.50.)

Barnard Castle has no hostels but is blessed with excellent B&Bs, most of which can be found on tree-lined Galgate. One option is the **Homelands Guest House ❸**, 85 Galgate, which offers airy rooms, bathrobes, and a garden. (☎638 757; www.home-landsguesthouse.co.uk. Singles £30, ensuite £40; doubles £56-65. MC/V.) **Stables Restaurant ❶**, on the lower floor, has sandwiches, jacket potatoes, soups, and other entrees for under £5. (☎690 670. Open M-Sa 9am-4:30pm, Su 10am-3:30pm. Cash only.) The **Hayloft**, 27 Horsemarket, is an eclectic indoor market jammed with antiques, bric-a-brac, and produce. (Open W and F-Sa 10am-5pm.)

To reach Barnard Castle from Durham, take Arriva **bus** #723 to Darlington (1hr., 2 per hr.), and then change to Arriva bus #75 to Barnard Castle (40min., every hr.). A day pass (£5) is valid on both services. Buses start and end on Galgate, at the end of which is the well-stocked **Tourist Information Centre**, Woodleigh, Flatts Rd. which also has **Internet** access. (☎690 909. Internet £1.50 for 30min. Open Apr.-Oct. M-Sa 9:30am-5pm, Su 11am-5pm; Nov.-Mar. M-Sa 11am-4pm.) Other services include: **banks** with **ATMs** on Market Pl.; **police**, Harmire Rd. (☎637 328); and the **post office**, 2 Galgate, with a **bureau de change** (☎638 247; open M-Sa 9am-5:30pm). **Post Code:** DL12 8BE.

TYNE AND WEAR

NEWCASTLE-UPON-TYNE ☎0191

The largest city in the northeast, Newcastle (pop. 278,000), is notorious as one Britain's nightlife capitals. But it's much more than a nightly party—Newcastle is at once a bastion of medieval history, a hotbed of architectural richness spanning from the 12th century to the modern, and a cultural trendsetter in fashion, music, and contemporary art. The one constant in this rapidly changing city is its spirit: Newcastle Geordies are proud of their accent, very proud of their football club, and very, very proud of their brown ale.

◧ TRANSPORTATION

Newcastle lies 1½hr. north of York on the A19 and 1½hr. east of Carlisle on the A69. Edinburgh is 2½hr. north of Newcastle on the A1, which follows the North Sea coast; or the A68, which cuts inland.

Trains: Central Station, Neville St. Sells same-day tickets M-Sa 4:30am-9:20pm, Su 7:10am-10pm; advance tickets M-F 7am-8pm, Sa 7am-7pm, Su 8:40am-8pm. Trains (☎08457 484 950) to: **Carlisle** (1½hr., every hr., £11.80); **Durham** (15min., 4 per hr., £4.80); **Edinburgh** (1½hr., several per hr., £39); **London King's Cross** (3hr.; every 30min.; Saver Pass available M-F for trains leaving after 8:30am, all day Sa-Su £95; book ahead online for further deals); **York** (1hr.; several per hr.; Saver Pass available M-F for trains leaving after 9am, all day Sa-Su £20.40; trains before 9am £23).

Buses: Newcastle has 3 main bus stations.

St. James Station, St. James Blvd., serves National Express (☎08705 808 080) buses to **Edinburgh** (3hr., 4 per day, £15) and **London** (7hr., 4 per day, £26.50).

Haymarket Station, by the Metro stop, and adjunct **Eldon Square Station,** Percy St., are the gateways for local and regional service by Arriva (☎261 1779) and Go Northeast (☎0845 606 0260). Ticket office open M-F 7am-5pm, Sa 9am-4pm.

Central Station, Neville St., is a stop on the **Megabus** line (☎0900 160 0900; www.megabus.com), which offers £1 fares to select cities. No ticket office; call or book ahead online.

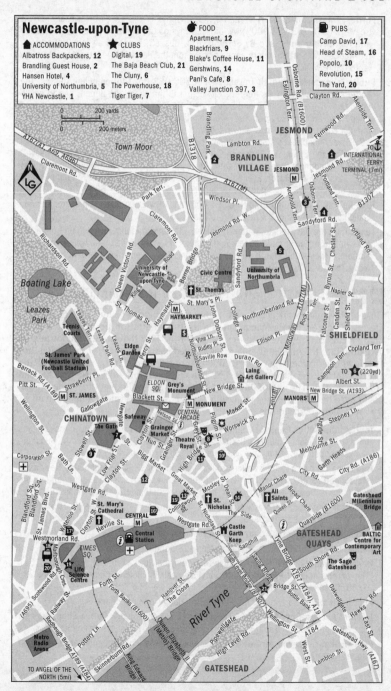

Newcastle-upon-Tyne

ACCOMMODATIONS
Albatross Backpackers, **12**
Brandling Guest House, **2**
Hansen Hotel, **4**
University of Northumbria, **5**
YHA Newcastle, **1**

★ **CLUBS**
Digital, **19**
The Baja Beach Club, **21**
The Cluny, **6**
The Powerhouse, **18**
Tiger Tiger, **7**

🍎 **FOOD**
Apartment, **12**
Blackfriars, **9**
Blake's Coffee House, **11**
Gershwins, **14**
Pani's Cafe, **8**
Valley Junction 397, **3**

🍺 **PUBS**
Camp David, **17**
Head of Steam, **16**
Popolo, **10**
Revolution, **15**
The Yard, **20**

NORTHEAST ENGLAND

Ferries: International Ferry Terminal, Royal Quays, 7 mi. east of Newcastle. DFDS Seaways (☎08705 333 000; www.dfdsseaways.co.uk) offers ferry service to **Norway** and the **Netherlands** (see **By Ferry,** p. 31). Bus #327 serves all ferry departures, leaving Central Station before each sailing. From the Percy Main Metro stop, the quay is a 20min. walk.

Public Transportation: Call Traveline (☎08706 082 608) for complete details. The Metro **subway** system runs from the city center to the coast, the airport, and to neighboring towns like Gateshead and Sunderland. Tickets (£1.30-2.60) must be purchased ahead and are checked onboard. Many stations don't have change machines; bring enough coins. The **DaySaver** allows 1 day of unlimited travel (£3.40). Trains run 6am-12:15am. Local **buses** stop throughout the city, with main terminals at the Haymarket Metro and the Eldon Sq. Shopping Centre. The bright yellow **Quaylink** buses follow 2 routes that connect many of the central city's key attractions. (80p, HourRider £1, Day Pass £1.50). A **DayRover,** available at TICs and Metro and bus offices, offers unlimited travel on all Tyne & Wear public transportation (£5, under 18 £2.50).

Bike Rental: Tyne Bridge Bike Hire (☎277 2441; www.tynebridgebikehire.co.uk) in the Guildhall TIC. £5 per hr., ½-day £10, full day £15.

Taxis: Taxis are easy to find in the city center, although you must pick one up from a taxi rank (found on most main streets and in front of Central Station, as well as both bus stations). They won't stop if you try to flag one down; your best bet is to call ahead. **Noda Taxi** (☎222 1888).

✴? ORIENTATION AND PRACTICAL INFORMATION

Most of Newcastle's attractions are within easy walking distance of each other in the city's center. **Grey's Monument** is a useful orientation point. Dedicated to Charles, Earl of Grey, the man responsible for the 1832 Reform Bill and for mixing bergamot into tea, this 80 ft. pillar was erected as the keystone of the famed **Grey Street,** whose ornate 19th century architecture has earned it the reputation as the most beautiful city street in the UK. The main shopping drag, **Northumberland Street,** is nearby. The city of **Gateshead,** only a 10min. walk over the Swing Bridge, sits across the Tyne (rhymes with "mine") from Newcastle and is home to many of the area's newer attractions.

Tourist Information Centres: Central Arcade, 27 Market St. (☎277 8000). Books rooms for a 10% deposit. Open M-F 9:30am-5:30pm, Sa 9am-5:30pm. Branch at Guildhall, Quayside open M-F 10am-5pm, Sa 9am-5pm, Su 9am-4pm.

Tours: The TIC offers various walking tours June-Sept. for £3. **Citysightseeing Newcastle Gateshead** (☎08716 660 000; www.city-sightseeing.com) operates a popular hop-on, hop-off tour. Departures every ½-1hr. from Central Station (£7, concessions £6).

Financial Services: Barclay's Bank, 141 Northumberland St. (☎0845 755 5555). **ATMs** are on most main streets.

Luggage Storage: At the Central Train Station. £4 per bag.

Police: (☎214 6555), at the corner of Market St. and Pilgrim St.

Hospital: Emergencies: General Hospital, Westgate Rd. (24 hr. hotline ☎233 6161). **Non-emergencies: National Health Services,** walk-in clinic at Central Station (☎233 3760. Open M-F 7am-7pm).

Pharmacies: There are numerous pharmacies along Northumberland St.

Internet Access: Both **TICs** (p. 432). Free for 15min. **Starbuck's Coffee Shop,** Grainger St., Wi-Fi only (£5 for 1st hr.). Also available free at all Newcastle branch **libraries.**

Post Office: 9 Clayton St. (☎281 3882), inside the shopping center entrance. **Post Code:** NE2 4RP.

ACCOMMODATIONS

Inexpensive lodgings are scarce in Newcastle, and weekends in particular fill up well in advance; call ahead. Pickings are slim in the city center, but the city's few **B&Bs**, the local YHA hostel, and numerous overpriced small hotels cluster in residential **Jesmond**, 1 mi. from the city center and serviced by the Metro (last service from city center around 12:15am, depending on the stop).

Albatross Backpackers, 51 Grainger St. (☎233 1330; www.albatrossnewcastle.com). This new addition to Newcastle's budget scene has everything you could want in a city hostel: secure, modern facilities; excellent location 2min. from the train station and adjacent to major nightlife areas; 24hr. reception; Internet access (£1 per 30min.); and even a wine cellar. Don't count on a full night's sleep on weekends, when partiers fill its 171 beds. Dorms £16.50-22.50. MC/V. ❷

YHA Newcastle, 107 Jesmond Rd. (☎08707 705 972). Metro: Jesmond. A 20min. walk from the city center. 52 beds in a comfortable townhouse. Often full; call well in advance. Self-catering kitchen. Internet access £2.50 per 30min. Reception 7am-11pm. Curfew 11pm. Open from mid-Jan. to mid-Dec. Dorms £17.50, under 18 £14. AmEx/MC/V. ❷

University of Northumbria, Sandyford Rd. (☎227 3215; www.unn.ac.uk). Metro: Haymarket. Check in at Claude Gibb Hall. Standard dorm bed-basin-desk combos in close proximity to the city center. Breakfast included. Open from mid-June to Aug. Reception M-Th and Su 7am-midnight, F-Sa 24hr. Singles M-Th and Su from £24.50, F-Sa from £29. MC/V. ❸

Brandling Guest House, 4 Brandling Park (☎281 3175). Metro: Jesmond. Family-run B&B 5min. from the Metro station with spacious and quiet rooms. Singles from £29; doubles from £48. MC/V. ❸

Hansen Hotel, 131 Sandyford Rd. (☎281 0289). Metro: Jesmond. Even the basic rooms of this small hotel, a 15min. walk from the city center, are fully booked on weekends. Internet access in hotel cafe 7am-4:30pm. Singles £25; doubles £46-50. Discounts for groups of 4 or more. AmEx/MC/V. ❸

FOOD

Newcastle has plenty of inexpensive curry, fish and chips, pasta, pizza, and tandoori spots. Chinese eateries form a small Chinatown along **Stowell Street** near St. James Blvd.; all-you-can-eat specials for £6 are common. Many of the restaurants lining **Dean Street** serve cheap lunch and happy hour specials until 7 or 7:30pm. A Safeway **supermarket,** Clayton St., is located in the city center. (☎261 2805. Open M-Sa 8am-7pm, Su 11am-5pm.) The **Grainger Indoor Market** is on Grainger St., near the monument. (Open M and W 8am-5pm, Tu and Th-Su 8am-5:30pm.)

Pani's Cafe, 61 High Bridge St. (☎232 4366; www.paniscafe.com). Italian eatery with a bustling vibe just steps from Grey St. A great place to unwind after a long day of shopping or sightseeing. Dishes £5-10. Open M-Sa 10am-10pm. MC/V. ❷

Apartment, 28 Collingwood St. (☎230 4114; www.apartment-luxebar.com). Newcastle's most stylish club offers reasonable set price menus (2 courses £11, 3 courses £14) in its seductively lit dining room. Open M-Sa for noon-2:30pm and 6-11pm, Su noon-4pm and 6-11pm. ❸

Gershwins, 54 Dean St. (☎261 8100; www.gershwinsrestaurant.co.uk). Cool underground restaurant with overhead star lighting. Serves special theater menus and Continental cuisine (with a few notable exceptions like seared ostrich) for £10-15. Excellent

NORTHEAST ENGLAND

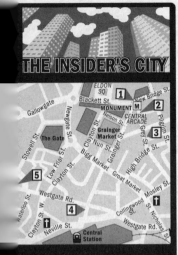

THE INSIDER'S CITY

NEWCASTLE ART WALK

Newcastle is home to one of the largest collections of public art in Europe. Nearly everywhere you look in the city—on the walls of buildings, in sculpture gardens, in architecture, sometimes even on the sidewalk itself—artwork lends individuality to the city's bustling streets. Here are a few highlights of Grainger Town, the historic heart of the city.

1 The 80 ft. pillar of **Grey's Monument** is hard to miss. Modeled after a Romanesque icon column, this statue commemorates Charles Earl Grey (the tea man himself), who wrote the Great Reform Bill and was a prominent voice in the British anti-slavery movement. A spiral staircase leads to the top of the monument, which is occasionally open to viewers.

2 After craning your neck up to see Grey's Monument, take a look down at your feet. Four **head cubes,** each containing a cast of Charles Grey's noggin, are set into the ground. Artist

lunch and early-bird (until 7pm) specials—2 courses and wine for £7. Reservations recommended on theater nights. Open M-F 11:30am-2:30pm and 5:30-11pm, Sa 11:30am-11pm. MC/V. ❸

Blake's Coffee House, 53 Grey St. (☎261 5463). A popular and jazzy central hangout with a range of lunch fare (£4-5) and sandwiches (£2-3). Open M-Sa 7am-6pm, Su 10am-4pm. Cash only. ❶

Valley Junction 397, Archbold Terr. (☎281 6397), in an old train station near the Jesmond Metro terminal. Delicious Bengali-influenced cuisine served in an antique railway car. The Indian lager Kingfisher (£3.25) blends well with *saag paneer* (£6-7). Vegan fare available. Open Tu-Sa noon-2pm and 6-11:30pm, Su 6-11:30pm. MC/V. ❷

Blackfriars Cafe Bar, Friar St. (☎261 5945; www.blackfriarsrestaurant.co.uk). Blackfriars award-winning menu includes mouth-watering selections such as wild mushroom and chestnut pie or seared kingfish. Medieval monastery with stonework fireplaces and beautiful wall tapestries. Entrees £15-20. Early set menu available for lunch daily, or weekday dinners 6-7pm (2 courses £12.50). Open Tu-Sa noon-2:30 and 6pm-late. ❹

👁 SIGHTS

Excellent views of the city are the reward for the dizzying climb up the narrow stairs of the **Castle Garth Keep,** at the foot of St. Nicholas St. The largely intact keep is all that remains of the 12th-century New Castle, which was built on the site of the castle of Robert Curthose, William the Conqueror's illegitimate son. Oddly enough, the "New Castle" for which the city is named is actually the original Curthose structure. (☎232 7938. Open daily Apr.-Sept. 9:30am-5:30pm; Oct.-Mar. 9:30am-4:30pm. £1.50, students 50p.) Just uphill at the corner of Mosley St. is the **Cathedral Church of St. Nicholas,** which tells the story of Newcastle's medieval history in wood, glass, and stone. (Open M-F 7am-6pm, Sa 8am-4pm, Su 7am-noon and 4-7pm. Free.) The **Laing Art Gallery,** New Bridge St., displays a striking array of watercolors, sculptures, and pieces by pre-Raphaelite masters. (☎232 7734. Open M-Sa 10am-5pm, Su 2-5pm. Free.) Recently, Newcastle has spearheaded urban renewal projects showcasing science, technology, and the arts. The **Centre for Life,** Times Sq., on Scotswood Rd. by the train station, is a family-friendly, hands-on science museum with a motion simulator and 3D movies. (☎243 8210; www.life.org.uk. Open M-Sa 10am-6pm, Su 11am-6pm. Last admission 3:30pm. £7.50, concessions £5.95.)

Newcastle is home to one of the largest public art collections in Europe—statues, sculptures, bridge lightings, and even short films can be enjoyed free any time simply by walking down the street. Housed in a renovated warehouse on the Gateshead side of the Tyne, the ⬛BALTIC Centre for Contemporary Art is the largest center for contemporary visual art outside London. Its rotating exhibits keep it on the cutting edge of the art scene. (☎478 1810; www.baltic-mill.com. Open M-Tu and Th-Su 10am-6pm, W 10am-8pm. Free.) Newcastle's **Swing Bridge** is the world's only rotating bridge, swiveling once or twice a day to allow ships to pass (usually morning or midday; check signs at the bridge's end for the week's times). A walk along the Quayside is most beautiful in the evening, when the city's stunning riverside architecture and bridges, like the **Gateshead Millennium Bridge,** are illuminated by colored lights. Also spectacular at night is the nearby **Sage Gateshead** concert hall, a giant expanse of steel and glass that dominates the riverbank. Completed in 2004, the world-class complex of performance halls is home to **Northern Sinfonia,** the orchestra of the Northeast, and **Folkworks,** an agency dedicated to promoting traditional music. It's worth a visit even for those not attending a concert. (☎443 4661; www.thesagegateshead.org. Box office open M-Sa 10am-8pm, Su 10am-6pm. Tours Sa-Su noon and 5:30pm. £6. Tickets from £7. MC/V.) Heading south from Newcastle by rail or road, you can't miss the **Angel of the North,** 4 mi. from the city at the junction of the A1 and A167. Admired by about 33 million people per year, the striking 200-ton steel sculpture is 66 ft. tall and wider than a jumbo jet.

▣ NIGHTLIFE

Newcastle's streets are home to a seemingly insupportable number of bars and clubs. But support them the locals do, with considerable help from a massive influx of weekend partiers from across Britain and Northern Europe. Rowdy Geordies line the notorious **Bigg Market.** Be cautious in this area—stocky footballer Paul "Gazza" Gascoigne was beaten up twice here for deserting Newcastle. Close by is the classier **Diamond Mile,** along Collingwood and Moseley St. These streets are lined with opulent clubs and lounges, most with their own exclusive members' areas. Beside the river, **Quayside** (KEY-side) and Gateshead (across the Tyne) attract a slightly younger crowd, while **The Gate** complex on Newgate has a bit of something for everybody. Newcastle's underground music venues are scattered throughout the city and continue to churn out a countless num-

Simon Watkinson created the cubes after hearing a legend of the Earl's head being knocked off the monument by a bolt of lightning. The cubes are lit by neon-colored lights.

3 At night, a canopy under the portico of the **Theatre Royale** is lit with a variety of colors. The lights can be seen from up and down Grey St., and were meant to provide a modern contrast to the classical facade of the theater.

4 From the theater, a 5min. walk leads to **Man with Potential Selves.** The lifelike bronze sculptures stand, walk, and float along Grainger St. Artist Sean Henry intended the figures to be three alter egos of the same man, representing different ideas of reality.

5 At the end of Grainger St., turn right on Westgate Rd. to reach **Ever Changing,** an inverted cone of polished stainless steel standing at the bottom of Bath Ln. The cone acts as a warped mirror that reflects the continual changes in the surrounding pedestrians, traffic, and sky. It was designed by modern artist Ellis O'Connell.

ber of successful bands. For a less heart-stopping, bass-thumping night out, **Osborne Road,** in Jesmond, 1 mi. north of the city center, is increasingly popular with students and locals for traditional bar-hopping. ⊠ **The Crack** (monthly; free at record stores) is the best source for music and club listings in Newcastle.

PUBS AND BARS

Pubs and bars in Newcastle are generally open Monday to Saturday 11am-11pm and Sunday noon-10:30pm; some are only open in the evenings. Most offer Happy hours until 8pm.

⊠ **Revolution,** Collingwood St. (☎261 5774). A modern mecca of mixed drinks in a sizzling atmosphere. Treat your friends to the specialty raspberry mojito. Impressive decor melds the city's 19th century architecture with massive Roman pillars, flashing lights and pumping bass. Open daily 11am-1am.

The Head of Steam, 2 Neville St. (☎232 4379). Across from Central Station. This venue features a chill upstairs bar and up-and-coming bands in the basement. DJs F-Sa 9pm. Live bands M-Th and Su 8pm. Open M-Sa noon-1am, Su noon-midnight.

Popolo, 82 Pilgrim St. (☎232 8923). Some of the best mixed drinks in Newcastle are served in this stylish hangout. Open M-W 11am-midnight, Th-Sa 11am-1am, Su noon-midnight.

Camp David, 8-10 Westmorland Rd. (☎232 0860). Casual bar that hosts a free BBQ on its rooftop terrace each evening, with great DJs spinning nightly. Open M-W 5pm-12:30am, Th-Sa 5pm-1:30am, Su 1pm-12:30am.

CLUBS

Opening hours and special events vary by season. Most clubs expect sharp streetwear; leave the sneakers at home.

⊠ **The Cluny,** 36 Lime St. (☎230 4474). This hidden indie hotspot is well worth the 20min. walk from the city center. Catch live bands any night of the week, and make sure you keep track of that £4 LP you pick up at the merch table—the band you see here tonight will be big tomorrow. Cover changes nightly. Open daily 11am-late.

Digital, Time Sq. (☎261 9755; www.yourfutureisdigital.com). A state-of-the-art sound system keeps things pumping through dawn. Sa night "Shindig" attracts the area's top DJs. Cover £3-12. Open M-Tu and Th 10:30pm-2:30am, F-Sa 10:30pm-4am.

The Baja Beach Club, Pipewellgate, Gateshead (☎477 6205). Churning out hip hop hits and pop anthems, this club maintains a huge following thanks in large part to its bikini-clad staff. Cover £2-6. Open M and Th-Su 10pm-2am.

Tiger Tiger, The Gate (☎235 7065; www.tigertiger.co.uk). There is always a party to be found at this giant club's 7 bars. Phone ahead on weekends to be added to the guest list and cruise past the queues. M student night, Tu popular salsa night. Cover £4-11. Open M-Sa noon-2am, Su noon-12:30am.

GLBT-FRIENDLY NIGHTLIFE

Newcastle's "Pink Triangle" of gay bars and clubs lies just west of the Centre for Life, along Westmorland Rd., St. James Blvd., and Marlborough Cres. Check out www.newcastlegayscene.co.uk for upcoming events and new openings.

The Powerhouse, Westmorland Rd. (☎261 6824). Large über-popular gay club. Cover £5-10. M-Tu and Su 11pm-3am, F-Sa 11pm-4am.

The Yard, 2 Scotswood Rd. (☎232 2037). A relaxed pub that rejects the clubby atmosphere of its neighbors. Uproarious drag shows M and Su. Karaoke Su 5-11pm. Open M-Th 1pm-1am, F-Sa noon-1am, Su 1pm-12:30am.

🎵 ENTERTAINMENT

The lush, gilt-and-velvet **Theatre Royal,** 100 Grey St., shows over 380 performances per year behind its elaborate Greek temple facade. (☎0870 905 5060; www.theatreroyal.co.uk. Booking office open M-Tu and Th-Sa 9am-8pm, W 10am-8pm.) Concession tickets are half-price on the day of performance when not sold out. The **Royal Shakespeare Company** makes a month-long stop at the Theatre Royal, complementing the top-notch array of operas and musicals with Shakespeare and contemporary plays (usually in the fall; check the box office or TIC for exact dates).

St. James' Park, home of the **Newcastle United Football Club, is** a prominent feature of the city skyline and a testament to how seriously the Geordies take their football. Tickets can be hard to come by and are only available for sale up to two weeks in advance. (☎201 8400, ticket office 261 1571; www.nufc.co.uk.) The **Newcastle Racecourse,** in the enormous High Gosforth Park, holds a number of top horse-racing events each year and makes for a great day at the track. (☎236 2020.) **Kingston Park Stadium,** a 5min. walk from the Kingston Park Metro station, is home to one of Britain's top rugby teams, the **Newcastle Falcons.** (Call ahead for tickets ☎214 558; www.newcastle-falcons.co.uk.)

NORTHUMBERLAND

NORTHUMBERLAND NATIONAL PARK

Northumberland National Park is often foregone by tourists in favor of more famed or central areas. Free from the litter of hurried cities and bustling crowds, this corner of England offers a tranquil getaway full of heathered moorlands and wild coniferous forests. The ruins of Hadrian's Wall and the small towns fiercely fortified against border raiders are the only clue that great civilizations once thrived in this serene area. Now the park is every outdoorsman's dream, with excellent hiking, camping, horseback riding, and cycling.

🚍 TRANSPORTATION

Renting a car is the easiest way to access the park. Public transportation is limited and requires advance planning. **Buses** offer the most extensive services, and although getting to the area by bus is tricky (and getting around the area by bus is even trickier) it is definitely doable with the proper planning. The best transportation hubs are Newcastle, Hexham, Alnwick, and Berwick. **Hexham** is best for accessing Hadrian's Wall, and the AD122 bus connects Hexham with Carlisle, Haltwhistle, Corbridge, and Newcastle. (M-Sa 12 per day during summer months; Su only spring and fall. The AD122 does not run from October-April.) During the winter, your best bet is to take the train. Hexham also has reliable bus service to many towns with great hiking in the southern region: take bus #880 to Bellingham (M-Sa 10 per day, Su 3 per day), and if you want to get out to Kielder, catch the irregular #714 connection in Bellingham (Su only 3 per day). **Alnwick** is a good hub for transportation to the middle of the park, with service to Chillingham and Wooler on buses #470 and #473 (M-Sa 5 per day) and to Warkworth on bus #518 (daily, every hr.). In the north, travel from **Berwick** to Wooler on bus #464 (M-Th 6 per day, F-Sa

8 per day), to Bamburgh on bus #411 (M-F 10 per day, Sa 8 per day, Su 4 per day), and to Holy Island on bus #477 (M-Sa 7 per day, Su 5 per day). **Newcastle** links all of these hubs, with service to Hexham, Haltwhistle, and Carlisle on bus #685 (M-Sa every hr., Su 4 per day), and service to Morpeth, Alnwick, and Berwick on buses #505, #515, and #525 (M-Sa 14 per day, Su 8 per day). If you're stranded on the west side of the park, don't panic: make your way back to **Carlisle,** where frequent buses and trains run back to Hexham or Newcastle.

Although transportation is complicated, fear not: the Experience Northumberland by Bus brochure is free at any bus station, TIC, or NPIC. This handy little booklet demystifies the entire Northumberland bus system with clear maps and organized timetables.

ORIENTATION AND PRACTICAL INFORMATION

The park runs from **Hadrian's Wall** (p. 444) in the south up along the Scottish border as far north as the Cheviot foothills. **Bellingham, Rothbury,** and **Wooler** are small towns near the park's eastern edge that offer accommodations and good access to walking routes. In the southwest just outside the park, Europe's largest manmade lake, **Kielder Water,** appropriately surrounded by England's largest manmade forest, **Kielder Forest,** is a popular destination for hikers and cyclists. The A69 marks the park's southern border while the A68 cuts through the center toward Scotland. The Ministry of Defense operates a **live firing range** in the middle of the park south of the Cheviot Hills—while its well-kept paths make for scenic walking and cycling, they are only open to the public for a month or so each year, usually from mid-April to mid-May. At all other times, walkers should heed the warning signs.

Northumberland National Park operates three **National Park Information Centres (NPICs),** which can recommend hikes and activities and book accommodations. During the warmer months, they offer ranger-led talks and walks. There are also several **Tourist Information Centres** in the area.

National Park Information Centres:

Ingram: Visitor Centre (☎01665 578 890). Open daily Mar.-Oct. 10am-5pm.

Once Brewed: For Hadrian's Wall, see p. 445.

Rothbury: Church St. (☎01669 620 887). Open May-Oct. daily 10am-5pm; Nov.-Apr. Sa-Su 10am-5pm.

Tourist Information Centres:

Bellingham: Main St. (☎01434 220 616). Open from Easter to mid-May and Oct. M-Sa 9:30am-1pm and 2-5pm, Su 1-5pm; mid-May-Sept. M-Sa 9:30am-1pm and 2-5:30pm, Su 1-5pm; Nov.-Easter M-F 1-4pm.

Kielder Forest: Visitor Centre (☎01434 250 209), off the C200 in Kielder Castle. Open Apr.-Oct. daily 10am-5pm; Nov.-Dec. Sa-Su 11am-4pm.

Tower Knowe (Kielder); Visitor Centre (☎01434 240 436), off the C200. Open daily July-Aug. daily 10am-6pm; Apr.-May and Sept.-Oct. 10am-5pm.

Wooler: Cheviot Centre, 12 Padgepool Pl. (☎01668 282 123). Open Easter-Oct. daily 10am-4:30pm; Nov.-Mar. Sa-Su 10am-4:30pm.

HIKING AND OUTDOORS

Northumberland offers some of the best cycling in England, with miles of traffic-less roads, bridleways, and unused railways. A spectacular section of the mammoth 355 mi. **Pennine Cycleway** runs through Northumberland, as do 92 mi. of the Tynemouth-Edinburgh **Coast & Castles Cycle Route.** The **Reivers Cycle Route** crosses Britain and passes through Kielder Water on its way to the border. The National Cycle Network (☎0845 113 0065; www.nationalcyclenetwork.org.uk) has com-

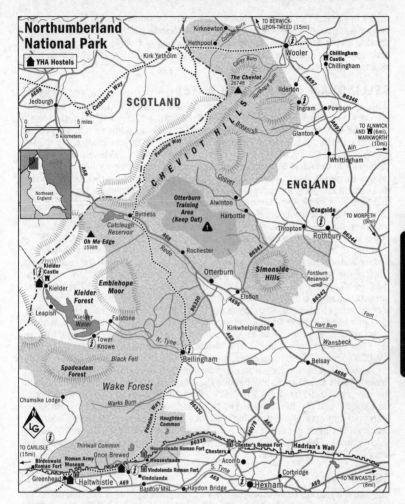

plete information on all long-touring routes, while TICs and NPICs can give information on short daytrips from most of the towns in the Park. Get the free *Cycle Northumbria* brochure at any TIC, or check out www.cyclenorthumbria.org.uk to get details on bike rental shops in the area.

There are also plenty of options for those without wheels. The 268 mi. **Pennine Way** (p. 402) traverses the park, entering at Hadrian's Wall, passing through Bellingham and the Cheviot Hills, and terminating at Kirk Yetholm, Scotland. The slightly shorter, still ambitious 80 mi. **St. Cuthbert's Way** runs through the Cheviot Hills and Wooler on its way between Melrose, Scotland, and Holy Island. Shorter options abound, including walks in the **Simonside Hills,** based out of Rothbury, and the **Cheviot foothills,** based out of Wooler. Ordnance Survey produces two Explorer maps, which together cover the entire park and are available at local NPICs and TICs (£8 each). Many books, including *Walking the Cheviots* (£8), describe walks in depth. The area's isolation makes for beautiful walks, but maps and proper equipment are essential (see **Wilderness Safety,** p. 50). NPICs and TICs can provide hiking suggestions. There are also a number of camping and caravan sites near each town; call the TIC for details. Be prepared to share your tent with swarms of gnats in the warmer months.

BELLINGHAM AND KIELDER WATER
☎01434

With an attractive rural backdrop, modest Bellingham (BELL-in-jum) sits right along the Pennine Way near Hadrian's Wall. Beginning hikers will enjoy the easy 3 mi. round-trip walk to ◪**Hareshaw Linn,** a beautiful waterfall in a rocky gorge that has attracted picnickers since Victorian times. Guides (20p) are available at the **TIC** on Main St. (p. 438). A longer 18 mi. hike goes south to Once Brewed. In town, the 12th-century **Church of St. Cuthbert** was built with a rare stone-vaulted roof so that raiding Border Reivers couldn't burn it down. Right down the street, **Oscar's Bistro ❷**, Lock Up Ln., serves meaty suppers to hungry hikers. Entrees such as deep-fried haddock, filet steak, local lamb cutlets, and Wednesday night curry range from £8-13. (☎220 228; www.oscarsbistro.co.uk. MC/V.) Although there are not many accommodations in Bellingham, all-ensuite **Lyndale Guest House ❸**, West View, offers relaxing decor and a jacuzzi. (☎220 361. Singles £28; doubles £56. MC/V.)

About 10 mi. beyond Bellingham and just outside the park lies **Kielder Water.** The **Kielder Water Ferry Osprey** departs from Tower Knowe and tours the reservoir. It stops at the **Leaplish Waterside Park,** a popular spot for campers, lodgers, and caravans. (☎250 312. 1¼hr. Apr.-Oct. 5 per day. £5.75, concessions £5.) The **Hawkhirst Adventure Camp** (☎250 217) offers a variety of activities, including canoeing, archery, and climbing; availability varies significantly, so call ahead. The reservoir also offers great **trout fishing;** be sure to consult the *Northumbrian Waters Angling Guide,* available at TICs. If you want to stay the night in Kielder, there are a few options, including the **YHA Kielder ❷**, Butteryhaugh, Kielder Village, off the C200, which offers a spacious, modern facility. (☎08707 705 898. Open daily Easter-Oct. Reception 8am-noon and 5-8pm. Dorms £14, under 18 £10. MC/V.) **Reiver's Rest's ❸**, at Leaplish Waterside Park, is perfectly located for jaunts around the lake. (☎250 294. Doubles £37. MC/V.) Pitching a tent is usually the most popular option—call the Bellingham TIC to check availability of Kielder campsites. Plan your trip carefully if traveling without a car, as buses only run to Kielder on Sundays. If you do decide to stay overnight in the area, take a moment to look to the heavens—Kielder has the lowest level of light pollution in England, attracting stargazers from far and wide.

ROTHBURY
☎01669

Rothbury, a market town along the River Coquet, is a popular starting point for excursions into the nearby **Simonside Hills.** Rothbury's **NPIC** (p. 438) gives advice on local trails. Among them, the **Sacred Mountain Walk** (9 mi.) is a great choice for intermediate hikers, rewarding those who complete its three-hour climb with some of the finest views in the park. Another popular choice, the **Rothbury Terraces** (2 mi.), is a good walk for beginning hikers, following an old carriage path and crossing the old Cragside estate grounds. For detailed information on walks, pick up the free *Rothbury and Coquetdale: Northumberland National Park* at the NPIC. One mile north of Rothbury on the B6341 sits ◪**Cragside,** one of the most advanced houses of the 19th century. Built by Lord Armstrong, the house was the first in the world to be lit by hydroelectricity, and today it is home to Lord Armstong's eclectic collection of gadgets. The grounds are large enough for hiking and have an impressive rock garden. Bus #508 (5min., June-Sept. Su 2 per day, 70p) connects Newcastle and Cragside via Rothbury. (☎620 150. Open Apr.-Oct. Estate open 10:30am-7pm. Last admission 5pm. £11.55.) Rothbury is home to a host of cozy B&Bs. Charming **Katerina's Guest House** ❹ offers four-post, quilt-covered beds, homebaked scones, and hosts with a wealth of local knowledge. (☎620 691; www.katerinasguesthouse.co.uk. Singles £40; doubles £56-64. Cash only.) The Co-op, High St., sells **groceries.** (☎620 456. Open daily 8am-10pm.)

WOOLER   ☎01668

The town of Wooler makes a good base for exploring the northern part of the park and the nearby **Cheviot Hills** (CHEE-vee-it). A number of short walks include the popular routes to **Humbleton Hill** and a self-guided trail to the Iron Age **Yeavering Bell** hill fort, where evidence of prehistoric civilization is still visible. The long-distance **St. Cuthbert's Way** also pays Wooler a visit (p. 438). Numerous other hikes leave from Wooler; call the Wooler TIC (p. 438) for suggestions on the walk best suited to your needs and tastes. Six miles southeast of Wooler, ▨**Chillingham Castle** is proud of its reputation as "the most haunted castle in England." English eccentricity is on full display here—the castle is crammed with a variety of bizarre objects collected by current owner Sir Humphry Wakefield. Every room holds something different, from tapestries to taxidermy, sculptures to scepters, and gadgets to ghosts. The gloomy dungeon is so dark that some torture devices are only visible using flash photography. The castle also offers a few self-catering **apartments** ❹. Call for rates (hauntings included at no extra charge). (☎215 359; www.chillingham-castle.com. Open May-Sept. M-F and Su noon-5pm. £6, concessions £5.50.) In a park beside the castle graze sixty-odd **wild cattle,** the only entirely purebred cattle in the world. Originally enclosed in 1235, the cattle have been inbred for over seven centuries. They resemble other cows, but cannot be herded, are potentially dangerous, and even kill one of their own if he or she is touched by human hands. (☎215 250. Open Apr.-Oct. M and W-Sa 10am-noon and 2-5pm, Su 2-5pm; by warden-led 1-1½hr. tours only. £4.50, concessions £3.)

Impeccably groomed hedges greet guests at **Winton House** ❸, 39 Glendale Rd., where ensuite rooms start at £25 per person. (☎281 362. Cash only.) The Co-op, 14-18 High St., sells **groceries.** (☎281 528. Open M-Sa 8am-6pm.) **Internet** access is in the Cheviot Centre, below the **TIC.** (£1 per session. Open M-F 9am-5pm, Sa-Su 10am-4:30pm.)

ALNWICK AND WARKWORTH   ☎01665

About 31 mi. north of Newcastle off the A1, the small town of Alnwick (AHN-ick) is secondary to the magnificent ▨**Alnwick Castle,** home to the Percy family since 1309. The castle's memorable profile may look familiar: its manicured grounds and stately home appeared most recently as Hogwarts in the *Harry Potter* films. Don't miss the ornamented state rooms, which display the family's heirlooms and an impressive art collection. (☎605 847. Open daily Apr.-Oct. 10am-6pm. State rooms 10am-5pm. Last admission 4:30pm. £8.50, concessions £7.50.)

A short walk from the castle leads to the 40-acre ▨**Alnwick Garden.** Far more than your typical English ornamental rose garden (although it has one of those, too), Alnwick has a bamboo maze, a giant treehouse, a carefully gated poison garden, and a cascading fountain. (☎511 350; www.alnwickgarden.com. Open daily Apr.-May and Oct. 10am-6pm; June-Sept. 10am-7pm; Nov.-Mar. 10am-4pm. £6, concessions £5.75, under 16 free.) Although Shakespeare described it as a "worm-eaten hold of ragged stone," today the ruins of 12th-century **Warkworth Castle** make a great stop 7 mi. outside Alnwick. Guarding the mouth of the River Coquet, this Percy fortress was the setting for many scenes of the Bard's *Henry IV.* (☎711 423. Open Apr.-Sept. daily 10am-5pm; Oct. daily 10am-4pm; Nov.-Mar. M and Sa-Su 10am-4pm. £3.40, concessions £2.60. Free audio tour.) A short walk down the river lies the 14th-century **hermitage,** artfully carved right into the Coquet cliffs. Walk down the river from the castle and the staff will ferry you to the opposite bank. (Open Apr.-Sept. W and Su 11am-5pm. £2.40, concessions £1.80.) Many B&Bs line Alnwick's Bondgate St. **The Georgian Guest House ❸** has hotel-like rooms just outside the town walls. (☎602 398. Singles from £25; doubles £59.) **The Eating Room ❶,** 39 Market St., is a great place to design your own gourmet sandwich to take away or eat in. (☎606 601. Sandwiches £1.80-2.20. Open M-Sa 8am-4pm. MC/V.)

The **bus station** is at 10 Clayport St. Buses #505, 515, and 525 connect Alnwick with Berwick (1hr.; M-Sa 8 per day, Su 5 per day) and Newcastle (1¼hr.; M-Sa 14 per day, Su 5 per day). Buses #420, 422, and 518 make hourly trips between Alnwick and Warkworth (25min.). The **Tourist Information Centre** is located at 2 The Shambles, Market Pl. (☎511 333. Open July-Aug. M-Sa 9am-6pm, Su 10am-4pm; Sept.-June M-Sa 9am-5pm, Su 10am-4pm.) Along Bondgate Without (yes, that's a street name), **Barter Books,** housed in a disused Victorian railway station, provides **Internet** access. The secondhand bookshop also has one of the largest used book selections in Britain, including rows upon rows of shelves containing rare first editions. (☎604 888. Internet £2 per 30min. Open daily Easter-Oct. 9am-7pm; Nov.-Easter 9am-5pm.) The **post office** is at 19 Market St. (☎602 141. Open M-F 8:45am-5:30pm, Sa 8:45am-12:30pm.) **Post Code:** NE66 1SS.

BERWICK-UPON-TWEED ☎01289

Just south of the Scottish border, Berwick-upon-Tweed (BARE-ick) has changed hands more often than any town in Britain—13 times between 1296 and 1482 alone. The town's history of strife has helped propagate the local legend that Berwick is still at war with Russia (see **A Really Cold War,** p. 443). Most of the original **Berwick Castle** is buried beneath the train station, although some of the 13th-century fortress still stands beside the river. The best way to see the town is via a walk around the **town wall,** including the Elizabethan **Berwick Ramparts,** which replaced the northern and eastern sections of the original medieval wall. The walk will take you past the **Berwick Barracks,** England's first purpose-built infantry barracks. Before the barracks, soldiers were housed in local taverns or private homes. The barracks also hold the regimental **museum** of the King's Own Scottish Borderers. (At the corner of Parade and Ravensdowne. ☎301 869. Open daily Apr.-Sept. 9:30am-6pm; Oct. 10am-5pm. £3.30, concessions £2.50.)

Berwick Backpackers ❷, 56-58 Bridge St., proves that hostels can feel like homes. Twenty beds in a jumble of rooms around a central courtyard connect to a bright kitchen and common room. Lumpy mattresses are more than made up for with hearty continental breakfasts, free coffee, tea, and Wi-Fi, and a helpful staff. (☎331 481; www.berwickbackpackers.co.uk. Laundry service £5. Reception M-Sa 9am-noon and 4-8pm. Dorms £15; singles £24; doubles and triples £20-25 per person. MC/V.) Stay in former officers' quarters at **Allanah House ❸,** 84 Church St., just around the corner from the Barracks. (☎307 252. Doubles and twins £25-30. Cash only.) Excellent hospitality can also be found on the other bank of the Tweed, at **Maggie's Guest House ❸,** Main Rd., where recently renovated rooms greet guests. (☎307 215. Single £25; double £60; ensuite £70. Cash only.) Stock up on **groceries** at Somerfield, Castlegate. (☎308 911. Open M-Sa 8am-8pm, Su 10am-4pm.)

Just because Berwick lacks a hopping nightlife doesn't mean you can't have a hot night. **Magna Tandoori ❷,** Bridge St., boasts some of the spiciest curry in Northern England. (☎302 736. Entrees £6.45-11; 20% off takeaway. Open daily noon-2pm and 5-11:30pm. MC/V.) At **Foxton's ❸,** 26 Hide Hill, diners can survey exhibitions of local art while they eat. (☎308 448. Entrees £9-12. Open June-Aug. M-Sa 9am-11pm, Su 11am-2pm; Sept.-May M-Sa 9am-11pm. MC/V.) Castlegate is lined with fish and chips shops and sandwich places.

Berwick is a useful transportation hub for both the Northeastern coast and crossings into Scotland. The **train station** has rail service to Edinburgh (45min., 1-2 per hr., £15.30), London King's Cross (4hr., 1-2 per hour, £116), and Newcastle (50min., 1-2 per hour, £16.30). From the train station, it's a 5min. walk down Castlegate to the town center. Most **buses** stop at the train station and on Golden Sq. Bus #505/515/525 travels to and from Newcastle (2¼hr.; M-Sa 7 per day, Su 5 per day; £12.20) via Alnwick (1hr.). The **Tourist Information Centre,** 106 Marygate, books rooms for a 10% deposit. (☎ 330 733. Open June-Sept. M-Sa 10am-6pm, Su 11am-4pm; Oct.-May M-Sa 10am-3pm, Su 11am-3pm.) Get free **Internet** access at the Berwick **Library,** Walkergate. (☎ 334 051. Open M-Tu 10am-5:30pm, W and F 10am-7pm, Sa 9:30am-12:30pm.) Tweed Cycles, 17a Bridge St., provides **bike rental** and good trail advice. (☎ 331 476. £15 per day. Open M-Sa 9am-5:30pm.) The **post office** is on West St. (☎ 307 596. Open M-F 9am-5:30pm, Sa 9am-12:30pm.) **Post Code:** TD15 1BH.

HOLY ISLAND AND BAMBURGH CASTLE ☎ 01289

Ten miles from Berwick-upon-Tweed, windswept **Holy Island** rises just off the coast. At low tide, it is connected to the mainland by a 5 mi. seaweed-strewn causeway, allowing access to the island via bus, car, or adventurous walk. Seven years after Northumberland's King Edwin converted to Christianity in AD 627, the missionary Aidan arrived from the Scottish island of Iona to found England's first monastery. While his wooden structure is long gone, the sandstone ruins of the later **Lindisfarne Priory** still stand in the island's tiny village. (☎ 389 200. Open Apr.-Sept. daily 9:30am-5pm; Oct. daily 9:30am-4pm; Nov.-Jan. M and Sa-Su 10am-2pm; Feb.-Mar. M and Sa-Su 10am-4pm. £3.60, concessions £2.80.) A free view is available from the low hill behind the ruins. **Saint Cuthbert's Isle,** marked by a wooden cross 220 yd. off the coast of the priory, is where the hermit saint took refuge when even the monastery proved too distracting. A mile's walk from the Priory, **Lindisfarne Castle** is a dramatic 16th-century fort that sits atop a hill, with a crowded and less inspiring interior of 19th-century furnishings. (☎ 389 244. Opening times vary with the tide; castle open Mar.-Oct. Tu-Su 4½ hours per day, always including noon-3pm, call ahead for exact times the day before. £5.80) After returning to the village, try the blend of fermented honey and white wine known as **Lindisfarne Mead,** a syrupy-sweet concoction brewed since ancient times. Free samples are available at **Lindisfarne Lim-**

LOCAL LEGEND

A REALLY COLD WAR

Despite the perpetual and divisive intra-Continental conflicts of the 20th century, Europe has unified. Today, Icelanders and Greeks and everyone in between live in economic and political cooperation. Everyone, that is, except for the citizens of Russia and of the small English village of Berwick-upon-Tweed.

Due to an unfortunate accident of semantics, Berwick-upon-Tweed has been at war with Russia for 153 years. In a 1502 treaty, Berwick was described as being "of" the Kingdom of England, rather than "in" it; Berwick received special mention in every ensuing royal proclamation. Nothing came of this inconvenience until 1853, when Queen Victoria signed a declaration of war on Russia, in the name of "Victoria, Queen of Great Britain, Ireland, Berwick-upon-Tweed, and the British Dominions beyond the sea." In the peace treaty ending the war, no mention of Berwick appeared.

Sources vary on what happened next. Some say the matter was cleared up by Tsarist Russia in 1914. Others assert a Soviet official signed a peace treaty in 1966 with the mayor of Berwick, who then said, "please tell the Russian people that they can sleep peacefully in their beds." Either way, no official documents have surfaced that can resolve the debate. Berwick, for its part, appears to have no intention of backing down.

TIDAL TROUBLES. Pay close attention to the tide schedules on Holy Island. Each season, dozens of visitors must be rescued from the water because they try to cross during unsafe times. Even if the causeway looks safe, the tide can rise in a matter of minutes, leaving you in a pretty soggy predicament.

ited, across from the Priory. (☎389 230. Opens 30min. before low tide, closes 30min. after.) Bus #477 runs from Berwick to Holy Island; times change depending on the tide (Aug. daily; Sept.-July W and Sa). **Border Cabs** can drive you over the causeway before the tide sweeps in. (☎389 236. £18.50 to Berwick.) If the waves trap you, the island does have a few beds, but they fill up quickly despite their staggering rates. The comfortable rooms of **The Bungalow ❹**, Chaire Ends, offer views across the fields to the castle. (☎389 308; www.holy-island.info/bungalow. No smoking. Doubles only £70 per night. 2 night min. stay. Book in advance. MC/V.)

Bamburgh Castle, a Northumbrian landmark, commands stunning views of the coastline 25 mi. south of Berwick. The public rooms offer a look at one of the largest armories outside London and the ornate, vaulted ceilings of the **King's Hall** house beautiful works of art. Visitors can also watch archaeologists dig in the castle's northern trenches, where workers have unearthed evidence of thousands of years of continuous human occupation. (☎01668 214 515; www.bamburghcastle.com. Open Apr.-Oct. daily 11am-5pm. Last admission 4:30pm. £6, concessions £5.) Beyond the dunes, the beaches are better suited for brisk walks than tanning, but provide great views of the castle. Reach Bamburgh by **bus** (#411 from Berwick; 45min.; M-Sa 8 per day, Su 4 per day). Holy Island and Bamburgh Castle can be seen in a single day, but tides can make scheduling tight.

HADRIAN'S WALL

In AD 122, Roman Emperor Hadrian ordered the construction of a wall to guard Rome's farthest borders, hoping to prevent those uncouth blue-tattooed barbarians to the north from infiltrating his civilized empire. His order created the most important Roman monument in Britain, stretching 73 mi. from Bowness on the Solway Firth to Wallsend on the River Tyne. The years have not been kind to the emperor's massive undertaking. Most of the stones have been carted off and reused in surrounding structures, and the portions of wall that do remain either stand at half their original height or are buried under a modern highway. However, the wall and the surrounding Roman ruins give travelers a rare insight into the daily lives of Roman soldiers and citizens, with artifacts that date back thousands of years. The best-preserved ruins are along the mid-section of the wall, at the southern edge of Northumberland National Park (p. 437).

◧ **TRANSPORTATION.** Although traveling by **car** is the easiest way to see the wall, the ◪**Hadrian's Wall Bus AD122** (who knew public transportation had a sense of humor?) provides daily reliable service to the ruins. At select times, the bus has a guide on board who gives an informative overview of the wall's sights and their place in Roman England's history. Service runs from Carlisle to Newcastle, stopping at every historical sight, including ruins and museums. Buy the **Hadrian's Wall Bus DayRover Ticket,** available from TICs or bus drivers, to get the most out of your AD122 experience. (Bus runs 2¼hr.; Apr.-Oct. M-Sa 7 per day, Su 8 per day. Guides on board 2 per day. DayRover ticket £7.) Bus #685 runs year-round between Newcastle and Carlisle via Hexham, Haltwhistle, Greenhead, and other wall towns (2hr.; M-Sa every hr., Su 4 per day). **Trains** (☎08457 484 950) run frequently between Carlisle and Newcastle (1½hr., every hr., £10.60), but stations lie at least

1½ mi. from the wall; be prepared to hike to the nearest stones. Trains stop at: Brampton, 2 mi. from Lanercost and 5 mi. from Birdoswald; Haltwhistle, 2 mi. from Cawfields; Bardon Mill, 2 mi. from Vindolanda and 4½ mi. from Housesteads; and Hexham. Make sure to pick up the free and invaluable **Hadrian's Wall Bus AD122 Bus & Rail Timetables** brochure, available from any area TIC or bus.

■🛈 ORIENTATION AND PRACTICAL INFORMATION. Hadrian's Wall runs 73 mi. between Carlisle in the west and Newcastle in the east, spanning Cumbria, Northumberland, and Tyne and Wear. The towns of **Greenhead, Haltwhistle, Once Brewed, Bardon Mill, Haydon Bridge, Hexham** (the hub of Wall transportation), and **Corbridge** lie parallel to the wall from west to east. For general information, call the **Hadrian's Wall Information Line** (☎01434 322 002; www.hadrians-wall.org). Useful information and accommodation bookings are available at the Hexham **Tourist Information Centre,** at the bottom of the hill from the abbey on Hallgate Rd. (p. 446), and the **National Park Information Centre** in Once Brewed, on Military Rd. (☎01434 344 396. Open Apr.-Oct. daily 9:30am-5pm; Nov.-Mar. Sa-Su 10am-3pm.)

🛏 ACCOMMODATIONS. Both Carlisle and Hexham have many **B&Bs** and make good bases for daytrips to the wall. Other towns near the wall, such as Corbridge and Haltwhistle, also have accommodations. Two hostels lie along the Hadrian's Wall Bus route. **YHA Greenhead ❷**, 16 mi. east of Carlisle near the Greenhead bus stop, is in a converted chapel a short walk from the wall. (☎08707 705 842. Breakfast £4. Packed lunch £3.50-4.50. Dinner from £5.50. Reception 8-10am and 5-10pm. Curfew 11pm. Dorms £13, under 18 £9.50. MC/V.) **YHA Once Brewed ❷**, Military Rd., Bardon Mill, is centrally located—the AD122 stops right at its front door ½ mi. from the wall. (☎08707 705 980. Breakfast £4. Packed lunch £3.50-4.50. Dinner from £5.50. Laundry available £1. Internet access £2.50 per 30min. at the pub next door. Reception 8-10am and 2-10pm. Open Feb.-Nov. Dorms £15, under 18 £10. MC/V.) The isolated **Hadrian Lodge ❸** makes a good base for serious walkers. Take a train to Haydon Bridge, then follow the main road uphill 2½ mi. Relax in the spacious rooms and have a pint at the bar and lounge. (☎01434 684 867; www.hadrianlodge.co.uk. Book in advance. Singles £39.50; doubles £59.50. AmEx/MC/V.)

📷 SIGHTS. Heading west from Newcastle or north from Hexham, the cavalry fort of **Chesters** lies beside the wall a ¼ mi. walk west of Chollerford. The well-

GIVING BACK

ROAMIN' RUINS

Vindolanda is a fascinating Roman fort and settlement lying just south of Hadrian's Wall. Recent excavations have uncovered numerous buildings and some of the most unusual and well-preserved artifacts from the Roman world. In the superb site museum, set in charming gardens, you can see Roman boots, shoes, armor, jewelry, and coins.

From April to August each year, the excavations are open to any enthusiastic digger who doesn't mind getting his or her hands dirty. Archaeologists predict that it will take at least another 100 years to unearth all the site's secrets, so they need all the help they can get. The recommended stay is two weeks, but volunteers can work for a week or longer by arrangement.

Excavations take place Monday through Friday and on Sunday. A typical work day involves 4½hr. of digging, with breaks and meals in between. The closest accommodation is at **YHA Once Brewed Hostel,** only 1½ mi. from the site. There are also B&Bs in the nearby towns of Haltwhistle, Bardon Mill, or Haydon Bridge. The program costs £55. Applicants must be at least 16 years old and physically fit.

For more information visit www.vindolanda.com or call Andrew Birley at ☎01434 345 277.

preserved remains of a bath house show just how seriously the Romans took their hygiene—hot saunas and cooling rooms sit alongside a still-intact latrine. (☎ 01434 681 379. Open daily Apr.-Sept. 9:30am-6pm; Oct. 10am-5pm; Nov.-Mar. 10am-4pm. £3.80, concessions £3.) Continuing west, **Housesteads** is a popular site because of its size and location. Set ½ mi. from the road on a ridge overlooking the Northumbrian countryside, the extensive ruins adjoin one of the best-preserved sections of the wall. (☎ 01434 344 363. Open daily Apr.-Sept. 10am-6pm; Oct. 10am-5pm; Nov.-Mar. 10am-4pm. £3.80, concessions £3.) Just 1 mi. southeast of Once Brewed, archaeologists find artifacts daily at the ongoing excavation of ▨**Vindolanda** fort and settlement. Watch them at work Monday through Friday and Sunday, and view their previous finds at the on-site museum. (☎ 01434 344 277; www.vindolanda.com. Open daily Apr.-Sept. 10am-6pm; mid-Feb.-Mar. and from Oct. to mid-Nov. 10am-5pm. £5, concessions £4.10; Joint Saver tickets with Roman Army Museum £6.50/5.50.) Built from stones "borrowed" from the wall, the **Roman Army Museum** sits at Carvoran, 1 mi. northeast of Greenhead, five stops away from Vindolanda on the AD122. It offers insights into the daily life of Rome's most remote soldiers, with interactive exhibits and impressive stockpiles of artifacts. (☎ 01697 747 485. Open daily Apr.-Sept. 10am-6pm; Feb.-Mar. and Oct.-Nov. 10am-5pm. Last admission 30min. before close. £4, concessions £3.50.)

Known to the Romans as "Banna," **Birdoswald Roman Fort**, 15 mi. east of Carlisle, offers views of walls, turrets, and milecastles. The interactive **Visitor's Centre** traces Birdoswald's 2000-year-old history with an audiovisual exhibit. (☎ 01697 747 602. Open daily Apr.-Sept. 10am-5:30pm; Mar. and Oct. 10am-4pm. Museum and wall £3.80, concessions £3.) To the west of Carlisle, on the cliffs of Maryport, the **Senhouse Museum** houses Britain's oldest antiquarian collection, with exhibits on Roman religion and warfare. (☎ 01900 816 168; www.senhousemuseum.co.uk. Open July-Oct. daily 10am-5pm; Apr.-June Tu and Th-Su 10am-5pm; Nov.-Mar. F-Su 10:30am-4pm. £2.50.) Follow the footsteps of the legions on the **Hadrian's Wall National Trail**, an 84 mi., six-day route from coast to coast. The trail also links to over 80 short walks around the wall. Guides and information are available at TICs. Alternatively, the recently opened **Hadrian's Cycleway** provides access to all the wall's main attractions following minor roads and traffic-free cycle paths.

HEXHAM ☎ 04134

The tiny town of Hexham is one of the best bases for exploring Hadrian's Wall. Hexham is only a short drive or train ride west of Newcastle on the A69, taking you through surrounding fields and farmlands. The cobbled town center encircles the impressive **Hexham Abbey**, a site of Christian worship since AD 674. The abbey's main building dates mostly to the 12th century, although the 7th-century crypts are largely intact. (☎ 602 031; www.hexhamabbey.org.uk. Open daily 9:30am-5pm. Suggested donation £3.) Facing the abbey, the well-fortified 14th-century **Moot Hall** bears the marks of Hexham's turbulent struggle against Scottish border reivers. More of the area's dark history can be found in the 14th-century dungeon of the **Hexham Old Gaol**, England's first purpose-built prison (before then, most prisons were converted castles or abbeys with dungeons), behind Market Pl. on Hallgate. (☎ 652 351. Open Feb.-Nov. M-Tu and Sa 10am-4:30pm. Last admission 4pm. £3.50, concessions £3.)

Budget accommodations are scarce in Hexham; call the TIC for availability. The ▨ **West Close House ❸**, at the end of Hextol Terr. off Allendale Rd., treats you like family and offers stunning interior decoration and a garden. (☎ 603 307. From £25 per person. Cash only.) Hungry in Hexham? **Phat Katz Coffee House and Restaurant ❸** has cheap cafe dining during the day (soups, sandwiches, and jacket potatoes for £5), and finer dinner fare like steak and fish at night. (☎ 606 656. Entrees £14-18. Open M-Sa 9:30am-11pm, Su noon-4pm. MC/V for purchases over £10.)

Hexham's **train station** is a 10min. walk from the Abbey and the town center (see **Transportation,** p. 444). The **Tourist Information Centre** stands between the train station and town center, on the edge of a large car park and down Hallgate from the marketplace. (☎ 652 220. Open May-Sept. M-Sa 9am-6pm, Su 10am-5pm; Oct.-Apr. M-Sa 9am-5pm.) Other services include: **banks** with **ATMs,** along Priestpopple Rd.; **police,** Shaftoe Leazes (☎ 604 111); **General Hospital,** Corbridge Rd. (☎ 655 655); free **Internet** access at the **library,** Beaumont St., inside Queens Hall (☎ 652 488; open M and F 9:30am-7pm, Tu-W 9:30am-5pm, Sa 9:30am-12:30pm); **bike** rental at the Bike Shop, 16-17 St. Mary's Chase (☎ 601 032; £15 per day; open M-Sa 10am-5pm; MC/V); and the **post office,** Priestpopple Rd., in Robbs store (☎ 602 001; open M-Tu, Th, and Sa 8:30am-5:30pm, W 9am-5:30pm, F 8:30am-6pm). **Post Code:** NE46 1NA.

NORTHEAST
ENGLAND

WALES (CYMRU)

Known to early Anglo-Saxon settlers as *waleas* (foreigners), but self-identified as *cymry* (compatriots), the people of Wales (pop. 3,000,000) have always had a fraught relationship with their neighbors to the east. Although they share an island with the English, the Welsh assert their national independence—if many had their choice, they would be floating miles away. Wales clings to its Celtic heritage, and the Welsh language endures in conversation, commerce, and literature. When heavy industry became unprofitable after the technology boom in the 1970s, Wales turned its attention to tourism. Travelers today are lured by peaceful towns and imposing castles nestled among miles of beaches, cliffs, and mountains.

TRANSPORTATION

GETTING THERE

Most travelers reach Wales through London. **Flights** to Cardiff International Airport originate within the UK and from a few European destinations. **Aer Arann** flies to Cardiff from Dublin for about £20-40. **Ferries** cross the Irish Sea, shuttling travelers between Ireland and Holyhead, Pembroke, Fishguard, and Swansea (see **By Ferry**, p. 31). Frequent **trains** leave London for Cardiff (2hr., from £11); call **National Rail** (☎08457 484 950; www.nationalrail.co.uk) or **Arriva Wales** (☎08456 061 660; www.arrivatrainswales.co.uk) for schedules and prices. **National Express buses** (☎08705 808 080; www.nationalexpress.com) are a slower, cheaper way to get to Wales: a trip from London to Cardiff takes about three hours and costs £5-25.

GETTING AROUND

BY TRAIN. BritRail (☎866 274 87245; www.britrail.com) passes are accepted on all trains, except narrow-gauge railways, throughout Wales; check their website for more information about a variety of combination passes that allow for travel within Wales, England, and Scotland. Call **Arriva Trains** (☎08456 061 660) for information. **Narrow-gauge railways** tend to be tourist attractions rather than actual means of transportation, but trainspotters can purchase a **Great Little Trains of Wales Discount Card** (£10; ☎01286 870 549; www.greatlittletrainsof-wales.co.uk), which gives a 20% discount on a round-trip journey on each of the nine member rail lines.

BY BUS. The overlapping routes of Wales's numerous bus operators are difficult to navigate. Most are local services; most regions are dominated by one or two companies. **Traveline** has updated bus information for all services (☎08712 002 233; www.traveline-cymru.org.uk); regional carriers, unless noted, use Traveline for ticket booking and customer service. **Cardiff Bus** (www.cardiffbus.com) blankets the area around the capital. **TrawsCambria** runs the main north-south bus routes from Cardiff and Swansea to Aberystwyth, Machynlleth, and Bangor. **Stagecoach** (www.stagecoachbus.com) buses serve routes from Cambridge and Hereford in England; the routes cover the Wye Valley, Abergavenny, and Brecon. **First Cymru** (☎01792 572 255; www.firstgroup.com/ukbus/wales/swwales/home) covers the Gower peninsula and southwest Wales, including Pembrokeshire Coast National Park. **Arriva Cymru** (☎08448 004 411; www.arriva.co.uk) provides service in North

Wales

TO DÚN LAOGHAIRE, DUBLIN (70mi)

TO ROSSLARE (65mi)

TO ROSSLARE (85mi)

TO CORK (220mi)

Isle of Anglesey

Irish Sea

ENGLAND

Liverpool

Birkenhead

Prestatyn

Llandudno

Conwy Bay

Rhyl

Amlwch

Llanaligo

Holyhead

Holy Island

Penmon

Beaumaris

Llanfair P.G.

Conwy

Bangor

Trefriw

Llanrwst

Betws-y-Coed

Ruthin

Chester

M53

R. Mersey

M56

A55

A5025

A5105

A5

A470

A55

A525

Caernarfon Bay

Menai Strait

Caernarfon

Llanberis

Capel Curig

Snowdon Mountain Railway

Mt. Snowdon (3560 ft)

Blaenau Ffestiniog

Ffestiniog Railway

Corwen

Wrexham

Llangollen

A5

A483

A487

A494

Dee

Ceiriog

Oswestry

Tanat

Tre'r Ceiri

Porthmadog

Portmeirion

SNOWDONIA NATIONAL PARK

Lake Bala

Llŷn Peninsula

Llanystumdwy

Criccieth

Pwllheli

Harlech

A497

A499

Aberdaron

Abersoch

Bardsey I.

Barmouth

Doigellau

Lake Vyrnwy

Shrewsbury

Welshpool

A483

Severn

CAMBRIAN MOUNTAINS

Cader Idris (2927ft)

Dovey

Machynlleth

Newtown

A49

Cardigan Bay

Aberdovey

Borth

Aberystwyth

A44

A493

Knighton

Ludlow

Rhayader

Llandrindod Wells

Aberaeron

Tregaron

Teifi

Wye

Aberporth

Lampeter

Builth Wells

Hereford

Cardigan

Llanwrtyd Wells

Hay-on-Wye

A49

PEMBROKESHIRE COAST NATIONAL PARK

Newcastle Emlyn

Llandovery

Brecon

A487

A483

A470

Wye

A438

Fishguard

St. David's

St. Bride's Bay

Llandeilo

BLACK MTS.

BRECON BEACONS NATIONAL PARK

Abergavenny

Monmouth

Carmarthen

A40

A40

Haverfordwest

A4A

Tawe

Merthyr Tydfil

Aberdare

Pontypool

Cwmbran

Tintern

Wye Valley

A449

A40

Chepstow

PEMBROKESHIRE COAST NATIONAL PARK

Pembroke

Tenby

Llanelli

Swansea

Gower Peninsula

Mumbles

Port Talbot

Bridgend

Newport

M4

A470

R. Severn

Carmarthen Bay

Swansea Bay

Cardiff

Barry

Mouth of the Severn

Bristol

Bristol Channel

ENGLAND

WALES

0   20 miles

0   20 kilometers

N

LG

Wales. Regional public transportation guides, available free at Tourist Information Centres (TICs), exist for many areas, but for some you'll have to consult an array of small brochures. The very useful *Wales Bus, Rail, and Tourist Map and Guide* provides information on routes, but not timetables. **Local buses often don't run on Sunday.** Some special tourist buses, however, run *only* on Sundays in summer. Bus schedules and prices change often; check them often and in advance.

BY FOOT, BICYCLE, AND THUMB. Wales has numerous beautiful, well-marked footpaths and cycling trails; the **Offa's Dyke Path** (p. 463) and the **Pembrokeshire Coast Path** (p. 463) are particularly popular. The **Wales Tourist Board** (☎ 08708 300 306; www.visitwales.com) maintains the websites **Walking Wales** (www.walking.visitwales.com) and **Cycling Wales** (www.cycling.visitwales.com), provides links to tour operators and other useful sites, and publishes print guides of the same names. The **Countryside Council for Wales** (☎ 08451 306 229; www.ccw.gov.uk) may also be helpful. *Let's Go* does not recommend **hitchhiking,** but some people choose this form of transportation, especially in the summer and in cases of bungled bus schedules.

LIFE AND TIMES

HISTORY

CELTS AND ROMANS AND NORMANS, OH MY! Thanks to widespread emigration and invasion by its neighbors, Wales has been influenced by an eclectic mix of peoples and cultures since prehistoric times. Stone, Bronze, and Iron Age inhabitants dotted the Welsh landscape with stone villages, earth-covered forts, and *cromlechs* (stone-chambered tombs also known as dolmens). Ruins of these settlements still stand as reminders of Wales's earliest residents. It was the Celts, however, who became the country's most influential settlers and resident rabble-rousers. Celts from northern Europe and the Iberian peninsula immigrated to Wales during the 4th and 3rd centuries BC and established a lively warrior culture. In AD 59, when Romans had invaded much of Britain, the wily Celts resisted occupation and fought against the Romans at the fortress at Segontium (present-day Caernarfon, p. 509), beginning a long Welsh tradition of conflict and struggle for independence. The Celts were so stubborn that the Romans were forced to station nearly half their legions in Britain along the Welsh border.

When the Romans departed from Britannia in the early 5th century AD, they left behind not only towns, amphitheaters, and roads, but also the Latin language and Christianity—both of which became central to the development of Welsh society. For the next 700 years, the Celts (supposedly once ruled by **King Arthur** and his wizard friend **Myrddin,** or **Merlin**) did their best to hold back invasions from Saxons, the Irish, and Vikings. Their best wasn't quite enough in the 8th century, when Anglo-Saxon **King Offa** and his troops pushed what Celts remained in England into Wales and other corners of the island. To make sure they stayed put, Offa built **Offa's Dyke** (p. 463), a 150-mile dirt wall that marked the first official border between England and Wales. Although connected by language and law, the Celtic kingdoms of Wales did not unify until the 13th century, when **Llywelyn ap Gruffydd** became the only Welsh ruler recognized by the English as the Prince of Wales.

THE ENGLISH CONQUEST. Within 50 years of William the Conqueror's invasion of England in 1066, the **Normans** had taken over a quarter of Wales. They built a series of castles and market towns, established the feudal system, and murdered many Welshmen. After the English **Plantagenet Kings** killed Prince Llywelyn ap

WALES

Gruffydd in 1282, **Edward I** dubbed his son the new "Prince of Wales." Two years later, he dubbed the Welsh "English subjects." To keep these perennially unruly subjects in check, Edward constructed a ring of castles at strategic spots throughout Wales. These include magnificent surviving fortresses at **Conwy** (p. 493), **Caernarfon** (p. 509), **Caerphilly** (p. 462), **Harlech** (p. 505), and **Beaumaris** (p. 515).

In the early 15th century, the bold insurgent warfare of **Owain Glyndŵr** (Owen Glendower) temporarily freed Wales from English rule. Reigniting Welsh nationalism, Glyndŵr and his followers captured the castles at Conwy and Harlech, threatened the stronghold of Caernarfon, and convened a national parliament at **Machynlleth**. Glyndŵr fostered the ideal of a unified and independent Wales that has inspired the country ever since—don't make the mistake of calling a Welshman "English." Despite support from Ireland, Scotland, and France, the rebellion soon waned due to poverty, war, the plague, and Glyndŵr's mysterious disappearance into the mountains. With one leader gone, Wales placed its hope in Welshborn **Henry VII,** who emerged victorious from the Wars of the Roses and ascended the English throne in 1485 (p. 70).

Things were looking brighter for Wales in 1536, when the **Act of Union** granted the Welsh the same rights as English citizens and returned the administration of Wales to the locals. But increased equality came at a price: there was a new influx of English language and customs.

CHURCH AND CHARTISTS. The 18th and 19th centuries were a time of revolution, change, and of course, more conflict. The **Methodist revolution** attracted 80% of the population by 1851, introducing **chapel life** to Wales. Chapels housed tight local communities who shared religion, heritage, and language. Chapel life remains one of the most distinctive features of today's Welsh society. Stores in Wales (particularly in the north) still close on Sundays, and the harmonic songs of rabid rugby fans are so close to choir music that attending a match at Millennium Stadium can be akin to a religious experience.

The **Industrial Revolution** swept the Isles in the 19th century, and Wales became one of the most important coal mining centers in the world. New roads, canals, and most importantly, **steam railways,** popped up around the country, and the Welsh population grew from 450,000 to 1.2 million between 1750 and 1851. Especially in the south, rolling hills became mining wastelands, and workers faced dangerous conditions and low pay. When early attempts at unionism failed, the workers turned to violence. The **Chartist Movement,** which demanded political representation for all men, culminated in a deadly uprising in Newport in 1839 and gained small victories for organized labor. Welsh society became characterized by two forces: a strongly leftist political movement and large-scale emigration. Welsh miners and religious groups replanted themselves in America (particularly in Pennsylvania), and in 1865 a group founded **Y Wladfa** (The Colony) in the Patagonia region of Argentina, where Welsh is still spoken today.

The strength of the Liberal Party bolstered the career of **David Lloyd George,** who rose from homegrown ruffian to Britain's Prime Minister (1916-22). **World War I** hit the country hard; over 35,000 Welsh soldiers never returned from battle.

THE LANGUAGE BARRIER. Issues of national language came to the forefront in the latter half of the 20th century. Renewed nationalism and nonviolent protest led to the 1967 **Welsh Language Act,** which established the legitimacy of both Welsh and English in legal courts. The 1988 **Education Reform Act** ensured that all Welsh children would be introduced to the language. Welsh publications, radio stations, and even a Welsh television channel (Sianel Pedwar Cymru, "Channel 4 Wales," or S4C) have emerged and thrived, and the 1993 **Welsh Language Act** stipulated that Welsh and English should be regarded as equal in public business.

Nationalist movements emerged in other political arenas as well. The efforts of **Plaid Cymru,** the Welsh Nationalist Party, were rewarded on September 18, 1997— when the Welsh voted in favor of **devolution** to make Wales a sovereign nation. The referendum squeaked by, with only 50.3% support, but Wales has finally gotten a taste of its long-sought self-governance with the 60-seat **Welsh Assembly**. Still, Wales retains strong bonds with Westminster, sharing its educational and legal system with England.

WALES TODAY

Long home to a distinct culture and people, Wales is beginning to grow into its new role as a more independent political entity. The road has been rocky: the decline of the once-booming coal and steel industries caused poverty and unemployment that has proved stubborn despite efforts to **economic rebuilding.** A recent surge in **tourism** is promising, however, and visitors are discovering a Wales that outshines its conflict-ridden, industrial past. **Cardiff** (p. 455), the Welsh capital since 1955, has reinvented itself as a center of art and culture, and the rest of the country is following suit as it welcomes guests with warmth and revitalized spirit.

CULTURE AND CUSTOMS

Cardiff's cosmopolitan bustle rivals that of other European cities, but the real Wales lies in rural towns and villages, where pleasantries are exchanged across hedges, locals swap gossip at the post office, and a visitor can expect to remain anonymous for about three minutes. Welsh **friendliness** and **hospitality** seem unfailing: long conversations and cheerful attention abound. The **Welsh language** is an important part of everyday life, and travelers can expect to find road signs, pamphlets, and timetables written both in English and Welsh. **Nationalism** runs deep, and the Welsh are fiercely proud of their history and heritage.

Wales has long been a country defined by a tradition of **folk culture.** The country's unique traditions—witnessing an **eisteddfod** (p. 454), listening to a harmonic male choir, or tasting homemade baked goods—are as enlightening as they are enjoyable. Welsh national symbols are the **red dragon, the leek,** and the **daffodil.** The red dragon, an emblem of battle throughout Welsh history, also appears on the Welsh flag over a background of green and white. In honor of Wales's patron saint, **St. David's Day** is celebrated on March 1 and is a perfect opportunity to see the Welsh **national costume**—a long red cloak and tall black hat. **All Hallow's Eve** (Oct. 31) is the start of the Celtic New Year.

LANGUAGE

> Let me not understand you, then; speak it in Welsh.
> —William Shakespeare, *Henry IV*

Although modern *Cymraeg* (Welsh) borrows from English, as a member of the **Celtic family** of languages, it is based on an entirely different grammatical system. Today, more than one quarter of the country speaks Welsh, one eighth as a first language. Welsh-speaking communities are particularly strong in the rural north and west.

Although English suffices nearly everywhere in Wales, some familiarity with the language will help to avoid garbling the names of destinations. Welsh shares with German the deep, guttural **ch** heard in "Bach" or "loch." **Ll**—the unfortunately common and confounding Welsh consonant—is produced by placing your tongue against the top of your mouth as if you were going to say "l" and blowing. If this technique proves baffling, try saying "hl" (hlan-GO-hlen for "Llangollen"). **Dd** is pronounced either "th" as in "there" or "th" as in "think" (hence the county of

Gwynedd is pronounced "Gwyneth"). **C** and **g** are always hard, as in "cat" and "Gosh, this language is complicated." **W** is generally used as a vowel and sounds like the "oo" in either "drool" or "good." **U** is pronounced like the "e" in "he." Tricky **y** changes its sound with its placement in the word, sounding either like the "u" in "ugly" or the "i" in "ignoramus." **F** is spoken as a "v," as in "vertigo," and **ff** sounds exactly like the English "f." Emphasis nearly always falls on the penultimate syllable, and there are (happily) no silent letters.

Most Welsh place names are derived from prominent features of the landscape. *Afon* means "river," *betws* or *llan* "church" or "enclosure," *caer* "fort," *llyn* "lake," *mynydd* "mountain," and *ynys* "island." The Welsh call their land *Cymru* (KUM-ree) and themselves *Cymry* (KUM-ruh; compatriots). Because of the Welsh system of letter mutation, many of these words appear with different initial consonants. For example, *cath* (meaning "it") pronounced "cat" may be seen as gath, chath, or nghath. For more Welsh words, see **Appendix,** p. 720.

THE ARTS

LITERATURE
In Wales, as in other Celtic countries, much of the national literature stems from a vibrant **bardic tradition.** The earliest poetry in Welsh comes from 6th-century northern England, where the **cynfeirdd** (early poets), including the influential poet **Taliesin,** composed oral verse for their patron lords. The 9th–11th centuries brought sagas focusing on pseudo-historical figures, most notably the legend of **King Arthur.** In the 14th century, **Dafydd ap Gwilym** developed the flexible poetic form *cywydd.* Often called the greatest Welsh poet, he turned to love and nature as subjects and influenced the work of later poets such as **Dafydd Nanmor** and **Iolo Goch** well through the 17th century.

In 1588, Bishop William Morgan wrote the **Welsh translation of the Bible,** which helped standardize the language and provided the foundation for literacy throughout Wales. A circle of popular romantic Welsh poets, **Y Beridd Newydd** (the New Poets), including **T. Gwynn Jones** and **W.J. Gruffydd,** wrote in the 19th century, but the romantic mood faded from Welsh literature after the horrors of WWI. Authors of the 20th century wrote about Welsh identity and national ideals in both Welsh and English. One of the best-known Welsh writers is Swansea's **Dylan Thomas,** whose emotionally powerful poetry, as well as popular works like *A Child's Christmas in Wales* and the radio play *Under Milk Wood,* describe his homeland with nostalgia, humor, and occasional bitterness. *Matilda, James and the Giant Peach,* and *Charlie and the Chocolate Factory* were all born in Cardiff, where **Roald Dahl** spun his famous tales of fantasy. Wales's literary heritage is preserved in the **National Library of Wales** in Aberystwyth (p. 490), which receives a copy of every Welsh-language book published in the UK.

MUSIC
The Welsh word **canu** means both "to sing" and "to recite poetry," and indeed music and literature are closely linked in Welsh culture. Although little Welsh music from before the 17th century has survived, traditional medieval music was likely played on instruments like the **harp,** the **pipe** (hornpipe or bagpipe), and the **crwth,** a six-stringed bowed instrument. The rise of chapels in the 18th century led to a lasting tradition of church music. Composers adapted Welsh folk tunes into sacred songs, and the hymns of composers such as **Ann Griffiths** became popular. Wales developed its famed harmonic **choral singing** in the 19th and 20th centuries, and many associate the all-male choir with Welsh culture. Both single-sex and mixed choirs are still an integral part of traditional life, and choral festivals like the **cymanfa ganu** (singing meeting) occur throughout Wales.

WALES

Cardiff's **St. David's Hall** regularly hosts both Welsh and international orchestras. The **Welsh National Opera,** featuring renowned tenor **Bryn Terfel,** has established a worldwide reputation. The most famous classical export is soprano **Charlotte Church,** who earned international attention with her 1998 debut, *Voice of an Angel.* **Tom Jones** and **Shirley Bassey** topped pop charts in the 70s, but **rock music** is the voice of today's youth, expressing satirical but often fiercely nationalist sentiment about life in Wales. Current popular Welsh bands, like the **Lostprophets, Goldie Lookin Chain,** and **Funeral for a Friend,** range from Britpop to hardcore and are gaining recognition on an international scale.

FOOD

Traditional Welsh cooking relies on leeks, potatoes, onions, dairy products, lamb (considered the best in the world), pork, fish, and seaweed. Rich soups and stews like **cawl** are usually accompanied by bread. Wales produces a wide range of dairy products, including **Caerphilly,** a soft white cheese. **Welsh rarebit** (also called "Welsh rabbit") is buttered toast topped with a thick, cheesy, mustard-beer sauce. Most visitors are drawn to the distinctive, tasty **breads and cakes**—buttery, scone-like treats studded with currants and golden raisins and traditionally cooked on a bakestone or griddle. The adventurous may want to sample **laverbread** (a cake-like slab made of seaweed), while the sweet-toothed will love **bara brith** (a fruit and nut bread served with butter) and **teisennau hufen** (fluffy, doughnut-like cakes filled with whipped cream). **Cwrw** (beer) is another Welsh staple. **Brains S.A.** is the major brewer in Wales.

FESTIVALS

The most significant of Welsh festivals is the **eisteddfod** (ice-TETH-vod), a competition of Welsh literature (chiefly poetry), music, and arts and crafts that dates back to the 12th century. Hundreds of local *eisteddfodau* are held each year, generally lasting one to three days. The most important of these is the **Eisteddfod Genedlaethol Cymru** (National Eisteddfod), which takes place annually in the first week of August and usually alternates between North and South Wales (www.eisteddfod.org.uk). The **International Musical Eisteddfod,** held in Llangollen (p. 501) in July and August, draws folk dancers, singers, and choirs from around the world for performances and competitions.

WALES

SOUTH WALES

The mountains and coastlines of South Wales have witnessed count-less episodes of invasion and oppression, from 12th-century English kings to 1980s mining shutdowns. Once reliant upon the coal and shipping industries, South Wales has reinvented itself with cultural centers and peaceful wilderness trails. The scarred mining fields of its central hills, pastoral scenes of its river valleys, and grit and hum of its major ports draw tourists in rapidly increasing numbers. Today, the land manages to maintain both its rural charms and its growing urban savvy, drawing from the best of its English influences and Welsh heritage.

HIGHLIGHTS OF SOUTH WALES

HIKE the Wye Valley for views of **Tintern Abbey** (p. 463) and proceed north to the stark peaks of **Brecon Beacons National Park** (p. 466).

BROWSE the shelves of **Hay-on-Wye**'s literary wonderland, which boasts the largest secondhand bookstore in the world (p. 464).

EXPLORE the rugged coastline of **Pembrokeshire National Park** (p. 478), home to the holiday town of **Tenby** (p. 481) and the majestic **St. David's Cathedral** (p. 484).

CARDIFF (CAERDYDD)   ☎02920

Cardiff calls itself "Europe's Youngest Capital" and seems eager to meet the demands of the title, presenting rich history alongside its metropolitan renaissance. Standing next to traditional monuments are landmarks of a different tenor: a towering new stadium by the river and an array of cosmopolitan dining and entertainment venues. At the same time, local pride, shown in the red dragons on flags and in windows, remains as strong as ever.

▆ TRANSPORTATION

Trains: Central Station, Central Sq., south of the city center, behind the bus station. Ticket office open M-Sa 5:45am-9:30pm, Su 6:45am-9:30pm. Trains (☎08457 484 950; www.nationalrail.com) to: **Bath** (1-1½hr., 1-3 per hr., £14); **Birmingham** (2hr., 2 per hr., £31.80); **Bristol** (45min., 3 per hr., £11); **Edinburgh** (7-7½hr., 3 per day, £100); **London Paddington** (2hr., 2 per hr., £53); **Swansea** (1hr., 2 per hr., £9).

Buses: Central Station, on Wood St. National Express booking office and travel center. Show up at least 15min. before close to book a ticket. Open M-Sa 7am-5:45pm, Su 9am-5:45pm. National Express (☎08705 808 080; www.nationalexpress.com) to: **Birmingham** (2hr., 8 per day, £21); **London** (3½hr., 11 per day, £19.70); **London Gatwick** (5hr., 11 per day, £39.50); **London Heathrow** (3hr., 11 per day, £36); **Manchester** (6hr., 8 per day, £38.20). Avoid confusion by picking up timetables at the bus station and a free *Wales Bus, Rail, and Tourist Map and Guide* at the TIC.

Local Transportation: Cardiff Bus (Bws Caerdydd), St. David's House, Wood St. (☎666 444). Office open M-F 8:30am-5:30pm, Sa 9am-4:30pm. Runs a 4-zone network of green and orange buses in Cardiff and surrounding areas. Stops are often shared with Stagecoach and other carriers. Show up at the stop 5-10min. early; schedules can be unreliable, especially on Su. Service ends M-Sa 11:20pm, Su 11pm. Fares start at £1; reduced fares for seniors and children. Week-long **Multiride Passes** available (£13,

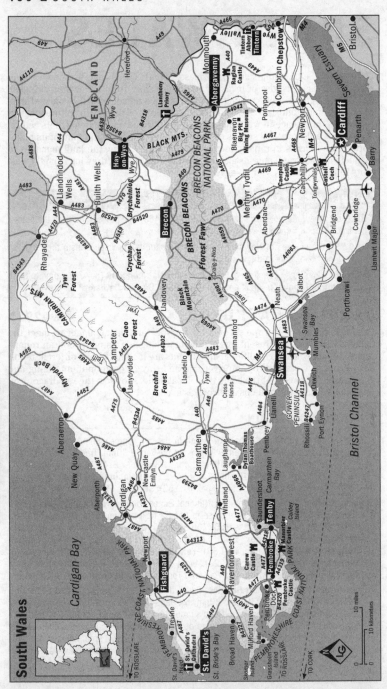

South Wales

ENGLAND

Cardigan Bay

Bristol Channel

Severn Estuary

TO ROSSLARE

TO CORK

SOUTH WALES

children £8). **Day to Go** tickets allow 1 day of unlimited travel in the greater Cardiff area and can be purchased from drivers (£3, children £2, families £7). Pick up the free *Guide to Bus Fares* from the bus station or TIC.

Taxis: Castle (☎344 344). **Dragon** (☎333 333).

⬛ 🛈 ORIENTATION AND PRACTICAL INFORMATION

Cardiff Castle is the historical center of the city, although the shops lining **Queen Street** and **The Hayes** see much of Cardiff's foot traffic. Farther east, the **River Taff** bounds Bute Park Arboretum, separating residential neighborhoods from downtown and flowing into Cardiff Bay. The **Civic Centre,** university, and **National Gallery** are north of the castle. Cardiff's signature "arcades," covered pedestrian shopping lanes south of the castle, provide much of the city's cultural fare.

Tourist Information Centre: The Hayes (☎870 1211 258; www.southernwales.com), in the newly renovated Old Library. Books rooms for £2 plus a 10% deposit. Open M-Sa 9:30am-6pm, Su 10am-4pm. Offers **luggage storage,** £3 per item.

Tours: City Sightseeing Cardiff (☎384 291; www.city-sightseeing.com). Offers a hop-on, hop-off bus tour that departs from Cardiff Castle Apr.-Oct. every 30min. Purchase tickets on board, at the TIC, or online. £8, concessions £6, children £4, families £20. **Cardiff Waterbus** (☎07940 142 409; www.cardiffcats.com). In summer every hr. £5, children £2.50. Vehicles tour Cardiff Bay, starting in Penarth and passing Mermaid Quay.

Financial Services: Banks with **ATMs** line Queen St. and St. Mary St. **American Express,** 3 Queen St. (☎649 301). Open M-Tu and Th-F 9am-5:30pm, W 9:30am-5:30pm, Sa 9am-5pm. **Thomas Cook,** 16 Queen St. (☎422 500). Commission-free currency exchange. Open M-Th and Sa 9am-5:30pm, F 10am-5:30pm, Su 11am-5pm.

Work Opportunities: Signs appear in many windows during the tourist and rugby seasons. **Job Centre Plus,** 64 Charles St. (☎428 400). Open M-Tu and Th-F 9am-5pm, W 10am-5pm. Employers sometimes post notices on the bulletin board at the Cardiff International Backpacker (p. 458).

Volunteer Opportunities: The **Volunteer Centre**, 109 St. Mary's St. (☎227 625), 3rd fl. Listings for volunteer possibilities in and around Cardiff. Open M-F 10am-4pm.

Launderette: Drift In, 104 Salisbury Rd. (☎239 257), northeast of Cardiff Castle. Wash £3.40, dry 20p per 3min. Open M-F 9am-9pm, Sa 9am-6pm, Su 10am-6pm.

Police: King Edward VIII Ave. (☎222 111).

Hospital: University Hospital of Wales, Heath Park, North Cardiff (☎747 747), 3 mi. from the city center.

Pharmacy: Boots, 36 Queens St. (☎231 291). Open M, W, F 8am-6pm, Tu and Sa 8:30am-6pm, Th 8am-8pm, Su 11am-5pm.

Internet Access: The public **library** (☎382 116), on Bute St. just past the rail bridge, offers free access in 30min. slots. Open M-W and F 9am-6pm, Th 9am-7pm, Sa 9am-5:30pm. Sign up in advance. The **TIC** provides access for £1 per 30min. **McDonald's,** 12-14 Queen St. (☎222 604). 4 kiosks. £1 per 30min. Open M and Th-Sa 6:30am-3am, Tu-W and Su 6:30am-midnight. BT public telephones are sometimes accompanied by Internet booths, starting at 10p per min.

Post Office: In the St. David's Centre, on the 1st fl. of Queen's Arcade. Open M-Sa 9am-5:30pm. **Bureau de change.** MoneyGram wiring service. **Post Code:** CF10 2SJ.

🏠 ACCOMMODATIONS

Budget accommodations are tough to find in the city center, but the TIC lists reasonable **B&Bs** (£18-20) on the outskirts. More expensive B&Bs (from £25) lie on **Cathedral Road,** a short ride on bus #32 or a 15min. walk; better bargains await on side streets. Pick up a free accommodations guide at the TIC.

■ **Cardiff International Backpacker,** 98 Neville St. (☎345 577; www.cardiffback-packer.com). From Central Station, go west on Wood St., turn right onto Fitzhamon Embankment just across the river and left onto Despenser St. (not Pl.). Backpacker is a well-known establishment in Cardiff, with a central location and a distinctive purple-and-yellow exterior. Lounge, kitchen, and bar. Happy hour M-Th and Su 7-9pm. Free coffee and toast. Lockers free with £5 deposit. Internet access £1 per 30min. Curfew M-Th and Su 2:30am. Dorms £17.50; singles £24; doubles £38; triples £48. MC/V. ❷

Nos Da, 53-59 Despenser St. (☎388 741; www.nosda.co.uk). A former hotel converted into a hostel by the owners of Cardiff Backpacker, with charming rooms and brand-new common spaces. Dorms and ensuite rooms. Lounge, kitchen, restaurant, and nightclub. Wi-Fi. Dorms M-Th £18.50, F-Sa £20; singles £36/42. MC/V. ❷

YHA Cardiff, 2 Wedal Rd., Roath Park (☎0870 770 5750). Take bus #28 or 29 from Central Station (20min., 4-5 per hr., £1.30) and get off at Wedal Rd. Nearby public gardens offer streamside walks. Breakfast included. Internet access £1 per 15min. Reception 7am-11pm. Check-out 10am. Dorms £19, under 18 £15. MC/V. ❷

Austin's, 11 Coldstream Terr. (☎377 148; www.hotelcardiff.com). On the River Taff opposite Millennium Stadium, 3min. from the castle. An affordable B&B option with basic rooms. Singles £32; doubles £49. AmEx/MC/V. ❸

Annedd Lon, 157 Cathedral Rd. (☎223 349). This comfortable, beautifully decorated house provides a peaceful escape 20min. from the castle. All rooms ensuite. Breakfast included. Singles £40, doubles £55. Reserve ahead. MC/V. ❹

Acorn Camping and Caravanning (☎01446 794 024; www.acorncamping.com), near Rosedew Farm, Ham Ln. South, Llantwit Major. 1hr. by bus X91 from Central Station; 15min. walk from the Ham Ln. stop. Electricity £3. £6.75 for 1 person, £9 for 2; each additional person £3.75. Dogs 50p. AmEx/MC/V. ❶

◼ ▣ FOOD AND PUBS

Pubs, chains, and British fare dominate popular locations like **Mill Lane.** The **Old Brewery Quarter,** at the corner of St. Mary St. and Caroline St., offers mid-range and higher-end restaurants. **Caroline Street** shops are post-club hotspots, selling fish and chips and kebabs past clubs' closing hours (most open M-W until 3am and Th-Sa until 4am). Corner stalls and local bakeries are everywhere, although more expensive restaurants (£10-15) await in the streets immediately south of the castle. Greek, Indian, and kebab takeaways congregate on **Salisbury Street** right near the university.

Europa Cafe, 25 Castle St. (☎667 776), across from the castle, near the river. Stone walls and abstract art combine with worn floors and a leather couch. Upcoming performers and theme nights chalked on the wall. Big mochas (£2.50) and sandwiches (£3.70). Open daily 10am-3:30pm and evenings for special events. Cash only. ❶

Pancake House, Old Brewery Quarter (☎644 954). A glass cube in the middle of the quarter. Specialty crepes at reasonable prices. Try the bacon, avocado, and sour cream (£3.75); the apple and cinnamon (£3); or go with one of the daily specials (£4.15). Newspapers and magazines provided. Open M-Th 10am-10pm, F 10am-11pm, Sa 9am-11pm, Su 9am-10pm. AmEx/MC/V. ❶

Tafarn, 53-59 Despenser St. (☎388 741), in Nos Da. Serves Welsh favorites such as hearty cawl (£5) and Welsh rarebit (£3) in a bright dining room with a patio overlooking the Taff. Wi-Fi. Open daily noon-10pm. MC/V. ❶

The Plan, 28-29 Morgan Arcade (☎398 764). Watch shoppers as you eat organic breakfasts and lunches, including filled baguettes (£4.50), elaborate salads (£6), and specialty coffees. Open M-Sa 8:30am-5pm, Su 11am-4pm. Cash only. ❶

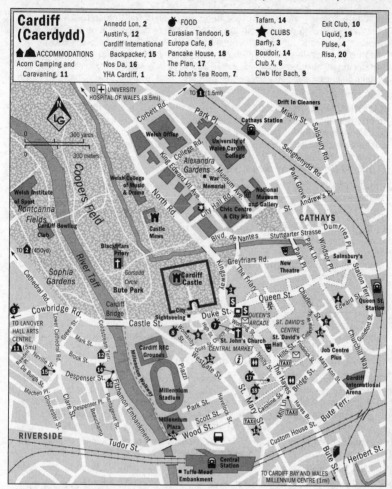

Cardiff (Caerdydd)

Annedd Lon, **2**	Austin's, **12**
Cardiff International Backpacker, **15**	Nos Da, **16**
YHA Cardiff, **1**	

▲▲ ACCOMMODATIONS
Acorn Camping and Caravaning, **11**

🍎 FOOD
Eurasian Tandoori, **5**
Europa Cafe, **8**
Pancake House, **18**
The Plan, **17**
St. John's Tea Room, **7**

Tafarn, **14**

★ CLUBS
Barfly, **3**
Boudoir, **14**
Club X, **6**
Clwb Ifor Bach, **9**

Exit Club, **10**
Liquid, **19**
Pulse, **4**
Risa, **20**

SOUTH WALES

St. John's Tea Room, in St. John's Parish Church, near the TIC. Parish volunteers serve tea, cakes, and sandwiches in a small upper room dominated by 2 arching stained-glass windows. Tea from 60p; scones 50p. Proceeds fund the renovation of the ancient parish building. Wi-Fi. Open W-Sa approx. 9am-3pm. Cash only. ❶

Eurasian Tandoori, 68 Cowbridge Rd. (☎398 748), near Cardiff Backpacker. Indian and Indonesian cuisine a cut above standard. Entrees £5-8. Free delivery for orders over £11. Open M-Th and Su 6pm-12:30am, F-Sa 6pm-2am. AmEx/MC/V. ❷

👁 SIGHTS

🏛**CARDIFF CASTLE.** First a Roman legionary outpost, then a Norman keep, then a medieval stronghold, and finally a Victorian neo-gothic curiosity, Cardiff Castle has seen some drastic changes in its nearly 2000-year existence. The central keep, or "White Tower," was built in 1081 upon the ruins of the Roman fort. The newer great halls were only completed in the late 1800s at the request of the Third Marquess of Bute, who hired the medieval enthusiast William Burges to recreate his vision of the castle's past. Watch for owls during falconry shows and peacocks wandering the grounds. *(Castle St. ☎878 100. Open daily Mar.-Oct. 9:30am-6pm; Nov.-Feb. 9:30am-5pm. Last admission 1hr. before close. Free tours in summer every 20min., in winter every 45min. £7.50, students £6, children and seniors £4.50.)*

NATIONAL MUSEUM AND GALLERY. The gallery holds a number of priceless impressionist works, but the local history displays are more extensive and intriguing. See a room full of Celtic stone crosses, the "world's largest turtle," a stuffed basking shark, and a walk-through exhibit on Wales's turbulent environmental history, from the Big Bang to the present day. *(Cathays Park, next to City Hall. ☎397 951. Open Tu-Su 10am-5pm. Free, donation requested.)*

CIVIC CENTRE. The Centre comprises the white stone City Hall and the National Museum, along with the courts and police building. The structures, built during Cardiff's steel and coal boom, overlook Alexandra Gardens. *(Cathays Park. Free.)*

CARDIFF BAY. The 21st century's answer to the 19th-century Civic Centre, the Bay has been the target of a massive regeneration project over the last two decades. Today, it houses the glass and steel Millennium Centre, the National Assembly Building, and various shopping and dining options. *(Walk ¾ mi. down Lloyd George Ave., or take a bus (every 10min.) from the city center. Free.)*

🎵 NIGHTLIFE

After 11pm, most of Cardiff's downtown pubs stop serving alcohol, and the action migrates to nearby clubs—most located around **St. Mary Street.** Cardiff's dress code is trendy, but not strict. Hail a cab after dark. For nightlife listings, pick up the *Itchy Cardiff* guide ($3.50) or *Buzz* (free) from the TIC.

Clwb Ifor Bach (The Welsh Club), 11 Womanby St. (☎232 199; www.clwb.net). 3 worlds collide in the eclectic Clwb: the ground fl. plays cheesy pop, especially on W student nights; the middle fl. bar has softer music; the top rocks out to live bands or trance. Drink specials every night. Cover is £3-4, higher (up to £10) when popular bands play. Open M-W and Su until 2am, Th-Sa until 3am. Call ahead for opening hours.

Liquid, St. Mary's St. (☎645 464; www.liquidnightclub.co.uk). Cardiff's trendiest new venue. F is casual "Release" theme night. Sa is dressy. Open F-Sa 9:30pm-5am.

Risa, Millennium Plaza (☎377 184; www.cardiff.risa.uk.com), via Wood St. New, chic venue with huge crowds in its 3 fl. complex. Entry level has a bar and lounge area; below is a dance floor. On the top floor is the comedy club Jongleurs, which offers live entertainment, a bar, and a moonbounce. Dress smartly, bouncy castle notwithstanding. W student night, drink promos. F-Sa 21+. Cover starts W £2 and F-Sa £3. Open W noon-2am, Th 7pm-1am, F-Sa noon-2am.

Barfly, The Kingsway (☎667 658), across from Cardiff Castle. At the center of Cardiff's alternative rock scene, Barfly hosts indie bands most nights in its small, underground location. Club nights Th and Sa. Cover £3-7. Open M-Tu and Th 7:30-11:30pm, W and F-Sa 7:30pm-2am, Su 7:30pm-midnight.

Boudoir, 31 Westgate St. (☎399 400). Chandeliers, couches, pink curtains, and low-key music lend burlesque elegance. Open W-Th 5pm-11pm, F-Sa 10pm-3am.

GLBT-FRIENDLY NIGHTLIFE

Cardiff's gay scene revolves around **Charles Street,** where black lights and multi-leveled neon walls give clubbers a thrill.

Pulse, on Churchill Way (☎641 010; www.pulse-cardiff.com). The newest, most popular entry to the city's gay scene. Pulse features an extensive ground fl. bar and stage, which sees live shows 3 times per week, as well as a basement dance club. Cover up to £5. Open M-Tu and Th 5pm-1am, W and Su 5pm-2am, F-Sa 5pm-3am.

Club X, 35 Charles St. (☎400 876; www.club-x-cardiff.co.uk). Mixed gay and straight crowd. Front room with techno and dance music, a back room with live bands and drag nights, and a lower level bar and beer garden. Keeps the latest hours in Cardiff. W student night with no cover. Cover £3-7. Open W 9pm-4am, F-Sa 10pm-6am.

Exit Club, 48 Charles St. (☎640 102). Smaller and less flashy than Club X located just across the street, Exit provides a relaxed bar setting on the lower entrance level and a dance floor with chart-topping hits above. Su night live entertainment or drag shows. Cover £2-3, free before 9:30pm. Open M-Th and Su 8pm-2am, F-Sa 8pm-4am.

♫ ENTERTAINMENT

ARTS
Cardiff is experiencing a renewed interest in Welsh vocal, theatrical, and artistic traditions. The TIC offers free brochures for local events.

Wales Millennium Centre, in Cardiff Bay (☎08700 402 000; www.wmc.org.uk). Built in 2004, the Centre is the crown jewel of the Cardiff arts scene. It hosts a variety of Broadway-style shows, ballets, and traditional music events. Box office open M-F 10am-6pm, Sa-Su 11am-5pm, until 30min. after curtain on performance nights. Tickets from £5. Backstage tours 4 times daily. £5, concessions £4.

New Theatre, Park Pl. (☎878 889; www.newtheatre-cardiff.co.uk), north of Queen St. The former home of the Welsh National Opera. Now hosts musicals, ballets, and comedies. Box office open M-Sa 10am-6pm, until 8pm on performance nights. Tickets £8-50; student standby tickets available M-F after 6pm performance nights £5.

St. David's Hall, The Hayes (☎878 444), opposite the TIC. St. David's hall stands as one of Britain's best-known concert halls. The venue hosts the **BBC National Orchestra of Wales** as well as various bands and comedians throughout the year. Box office open M-Sa 9:30am-5:30pm, until 8pm on performance nights; Su until 1hr. before performances. Tickets £5.50-60; concessions available.

SONGS FOR A SONG

Welsh male choirs began as informal gatherings of mine workers who cleared out their lungs and sang traditional songs together. Today, they're an important part of Welsh national heritage, and the more famous groups perform all over the world. Tickets for these concerts can cost a pretty penny. If you don't want to shell out the pounds, you can get a free listen by attending a rehearsal.

Many of the choirs in Cardiff and throughout Wales hold open rehearsals once or twice per week, hoping to stir up interest and gain recruits. They might be at a pub, church, community center, or even a rugby club. When they have spectators, the choirs frequently end rehearsal of new material early to sing some of the older, well-rehearsed favorites. If they know it, they'll even sing the national anthems of those in attendance. Men may find themselves pressed into singing along, and heavily recruited over a pint afterward.

The Cardiff TIC keeps a list of local voice choirs, along with contact info and rehearsal times. Call ahead to make sure times and places haven't changed. Major choirs include the South Wales Male Choir (www.cmdc.org.uk) and the Cardiff Male Choir (www.cardiffmalechoir.co.uk), although there are several more in the area and throughout the country.

SPORTS

Rugby matches are played at the **Millennium Stadium**, a 73,000-seater with a retractable roof. (☎822 228; www.millenniumstadium.com. Open M-Sa 10am-5pm, Su 10am-4pm. Tours £5.50, concessions £3.50, children £3. Book in advance.) Tours leave from the **Millennium Stadium Shop**, at Entrance 3, Westgate St. (Open M-Sa 10am-5:30pm, Su 10am-4pm.) During the fall rugby season, tickets are available at the shop or from the **Welsh Rugby Union** (☎08700 138 600; www.wru.co.uk).

▓ DAYTRIPS FROM CARDIFF

The fairgrounds and sandy beaches of **Barry Island** attract travelers all year. The beaches are open year-round. Take the train from Cardiff (25min., 3-4 per hr., £3 for same-day return). **Taff Trail** winds from Cardiff Bay through the Taff Valley to Brecon, in the Brecon Beacons National Park (p. 466).

■ **CAERPHILLY CASTLE.** Visitors might find this 30-acre castle easy to navigate, but 13th-century attackers had to contend with a "Chinese Box" system of concentric walls, double parapets, and moats. It is small wonder the castle withstood every assault it faced, although parts of the castle were eventually defeated by the marshy ground—one tower leans 10 degrees from the vertical. The castle was built by an English baron around 1270 to defend against the Welsh. *(Take the train, 20min., M-Sa 2 per hr., £3.30 return, or bus #26. ☎883 143. Open June-Sept. daily 9:30am-6pm; Apr.-May daily 9:30am-5pm; Oct.-Mar. M-Sa 9:30am-4pm, Su 11am-4pm. Last admission 30min. before close. £3.50, concessions £3, families £10. Audio tour £1.)*

MUSEUM OF WELSH LIFE (AMGUEDDFA WERIN CYMRU). Four miles west of Cardiff in **St. Fagan's Park**, this open-air museum occupies more than 100 acres with over 40 buildings—some nearly 500 years old. The Celtic Village and Welsh peasant cottage are full of authentic touches. A highlight is **St. Telio's church**, a 15th-century structure undergoing restoration using traditional techniques. Horse-and-cart rides are available (£1, children 50p), as are crafts workshops. *(Buses #32 and 320 run to the museum from Central Station (20min., 1-2 per hr., £2.60 return). ☎573 500. Open daily 10am-5pm. Free. Guidebook £2, map 30p.)*

LLANDAFF CATHEDRAL. A Celtic cross, one of the oldest Christian relics in Britain, stands outside this 12th-century cathedral. Inside, the ancient arch over the altar contrasts with a controversial 1950s aluminum-plated installation over the nave. St. Dyfrig and St. Teilo are entombed here, and Dante Gabriel Rossetti's triptych *Seed of David* stands in one corner. The ivy-covered ruins of the **Castle of the Bishops of Llandaff** lie nearby. Although its luster has somewhat faded—800 years have seen the cathedral turned into a "hog trough" by Cromwell and gutted by a German bomb—Llandaff's grounds still emanate grace and history. *(Take bus #60 or 62 from Central Station to the Black Lion Pub and walk up High St., or walk down Cathedral Rd., through Llandaff Fields, and straight on the small path behind the rugby club. ☎564 554. Open daily 7:30am-7pm, staffed by helpful volunteers 10am-4pm. Evensong daily 6pm. Free.)*

CASTELL COCH. Lord Bute and architect William Burges rebuilt the ruins of this 13th-century castle in the late 1800s. Their attempt to resurrect a medieval style ultimately looks like something from a fairy tale, with spires, latticed gables, and ornate decorative murals. Unlike other castles near Cardiff, Castell Coch occupies a secluded forest hillside and offers hikers connections to the Taff Trail. *(Take bus #26 or 26a from Central Station to Tongwynlais. 25min., 1-2 per hr. Get off across from the post office, and walk 15min. up Mill St. ☎810 101. Open Apr.-May and Oct. daily 9:30am-5pm; June-Sept. daily 9:30am-6pm; Nov.-Dec. and from mid-Feb. to Mar. M-Sa 9:30am-4pm, Su 11am-4pm. £3.50, concessions £3, families £10. Audio tour £1.)*

WYE VALLEY

The occasional 12th-century fortress marks this once turbulent Welsh-English border territory, but today it's hard to imagine a more peaceful area. Few towns interrupt the flow of the meandering River Wye, but those that do have varied histories as outposts, sheep farms, and trading centers.

▐ TRANSPORTATION

Chepstow provides the easiest entrance to the valley. **Trains** (☎08457 484 950; www.nationalrail.com) run from Chepstow to Cardiff (40min., 1-2 per hr., £6) and Newport (20min., every 2hr., £4.70). National Express (☎08705 808 080; www.nationalexpress.com) **buses** go to Cardiff (50min., 13 per day, £4.60), London (2½hr., 7 per day, £19.20), and Newport (25min., every hr., £3.10). Stagecoach Red and White buses #65 and 69 loop between Chepstow and Monmouth (8-9 per day); bus #69 stops in Tintern. Stagecoach sells 1-day **Network Rider** passes (£5.50, concessions £3.10, families £11) for travel on all Stagecoach Red and White, Phil Anslow, and Cardiff buses. Few buses run on Sunday in the valley. TICs offer the free *Monmouthshire Local Transport Guide* for timetables and *Discover the Wye Valley by Foot and by Bus* (50p) for hikes. Hitchhikers wait on the A466 in the summer; some stand near Tintern Abbey or the Wye Bridge in Monmouth. *Let's Go* does not recommend hitchhiking.

▐ HIKING

The hills near the Wye offer wooded trails, open meadows, and valley views. Two main trails, the Wye Valley Walk and Offa's Dyke Path, follow the river on either side and are accessible from many different points. TICs disperse pamphlets and sell Ordnance Survey maps (1:25,000; £8.50). Campsites are scattered throughout the area; ask at the Chepstow, Tintern, Hereford, and Powys TICs.

Wye Valley Walk (136 mi.), west of the river. Marked by a leaping salmon logo. This walk heads north from Chepstow via Hay-on-Wye to Prestatyn along forested cliffs and farmland, eventually ending in Rhayader. From **Eagle's Nest Lookout**, 3 mi. north of Chepstow, 365 steps descend to the riverbank. At **Symond's Yat Rock**, 15 mi. north of Chepstow, the hills drop away to a panorama of the Wye's horseshoe bends. The Chepstow TIC offers a guide to this 12 mi. hike for 80p. Consult www.wyevalleywalk.org.

Offa's Dyke Path (177 mi.), east of the river. Starts in Sedbury's Cliffs and winds along Offa's Dyke on the Welsh-English border, ending at Prestatyn on the northern coast. Built by Saxon King Offa to keep the Welsh at bay, it is Britain's longest archaeological monument, and some of the earthwork (20 ft. high) still stands. Join at Chepstow, Monmouth, Bisweir, or Redbrook, and follow the yellow arrows and acorn signs. Check trail maps (available at TICs); some paths change grade suddenly. Consult the **Offa's Dyke Association,** (☎01547 528 753) halfway up the trail in Knighton.

Royal Forest of Dean. This 27,000-acre forest lies across the English border. Once the hunting ground of Edward the Confessor and Williams I and II. Contact the **Forest Service,** Bank St. (☎01594 833 057), in Coleford, England, across the river from Monmouth. Open M-Th 8:30am-5pm, F 8:30am-4pm). **Forest of Dean Tour Guides** (☎01594 529 358; www.forestofdeantours.org; £6-20) offers guided tours.

TINTERN   ☎01291

The village of Tintern, 5 mi. north of Chepstow on the A466, is a small grouping of stone houses, shops, and inns on the banks of the Wye. It thrives on the tourism brought by ⊠**Tintern Abbey,** the center of a 12th-century society of Cistercian monks. Doves now roost in the abbey's ancient walls, and visitors crowd the site daily. (☎689 251. Open June-Sept. daily 9:30am-6pm; Apr.-May and Oct. daily 9:30am-5pm; Nov.-Mar. M-Sa 9:30am-4pm, Su 11am-4pm. £3.50, concessions £3, families £10. 45min. audio tour £1, plus £5 deposit. Last admission 30min. before close.) Those interested in Wordsworth's view from "a few miles above" should ask for directions to **Monk's Trail,** a wooded path that winds through the hills across the river. An uphill hike (2 mi.) leads to **Devil's Pulpit,** a huge stone from which Satan is said to have tempted the monks as they worked in the fields.

There are several sights of interest between the abbey and the Old Station on A466. At the **Anchor Tintern** (☎689 207), sample the fruits of a cider mill once used by the monks—supposedly the oldest in existence. **Stella Books,** on Monmouth Rd., in the middle of the village proper, stores over 50,000 volumes behind its unassuming storefront. (☎689 755; www.stellabooks.com. Open daily 9:30am-5:30pm.) **Parva Farm Vineyard,** next to the Wye Valley Hotel on the A466, produces nearly 4000 bottles of wine and honey mead per year. The owners let visitors tour the hillside for £1 and offer free wine tastings. (☎689 636. Open daily 10:30am-6:30pm.)

The nearest **YHA hostel** is ⊠**St. Briavel's Castle ❷,** 4 mi. northeast of Tintern across the English border. Once King John's hunting lodge and later a fortress against the Welsh, this 12th-century castle offers a hostel experience unlike any other. Don't miss the 17th-century graffiti on one dorm wall. From the A466 (bus #69 from Chepstow; ask to be let off at Bigsweir Bridge) or Offa's Dyke, follow signs uphill for a 2 mi. hike from the edge of the estate. On Wednesdays, bus L12 runs from Monmouth to St. Briavel's. (☎01594 530 272. Open Mar.-Oct. F-Sa. Lockout 10am-5pm. Curfew 11:30pm. Dorms £16.50, under 18 £12.50. MC/V.) A few **B&Bs** lie along the A466 in the village. **Campers** can use the **field ❶** next to the old train station (£2 per person). Near St. Briavel's Castle hostel is the **George Inn Pub ❶,** a 16th-century local favorite with low, timber ceilings and subdued lighting straight out of a medieval tale inspired by harvest season. (☎01594 530 228. Open M-Th 11:30am-2:30pm and 6:30-11pm, F 11am-2:30pm and 6:30-11pm, Sa 11:30am-11:30pm, Su noon-2:30pm and 7-11pm. Cash only.) **The Moon and Sixpence ❶,** High St., serves country foods with glorious views of the Wye. (☎689 284. Open daily noon-11pm. Food served noon-2:30pm and 6:30-9:30pm. Cash only.)

Tintern's **Old Station** lies a mile north of the abbey on the A466, but the Wye Valley Path provides a more scenic route. The out-of-service train station holds old railway carriages, one of which houses the **Tourist Information Centre.** The TIC books accommodations for £1. (☎689 566. Open Apr.-Oct. daily 10:30am-5:30pm.)

HAY-ON-WYE (Y GELLI) ☎01497

Hay-on-Wye is a town defined by its 30 bookstores. The little village owes its reputation as the world's foremost "Town of Books" mainly to Richard Booth, founder of Booth's Books, the largest second-hand bookstore in the world. The winding River Wye and 2227 ft. Hay Bluff also impress visitors.

🖪 🗷 TRANSPORTATION AND PRACTICAL INFORMATION. The closest **train station** is in Hereford, England (p. 292). Stagecoach Red and White (☎01633 838 856) **bus** #39 stops at Hay between Hereford and Brecon (to Hereford 1hr., to Brecon 45min.; M-Sa 7 per day). Yeoman's (☎01432 356 202) bus #40 runs the same route (Su 3 per day). The **Tourist Information Centre,** Oxford Rd., in the shopping center, has Internet access (75p per 15min.) and books beds for £2. (☎820 144; www.hay-on-wye.co.uk. Open daily Apr.-Oct. 10am-1pm and 2-5pm; Nov.-Mar. 11am-1pm and 2-4pm.) Other services include: Barclays **bank,** on Broad St. (open M-F 10am-4pm); free **Internet** access at the **library,** Chancery Ln. (☎820 847; open M

10am-1pm, 2-4:30pm, and 5-7pm; Th-F 10am-1pm and 2-5pm, Sa 9:30am-1pm); and the **post office**, 3 High Town (☎820 536; open M, W, F 9am-1pm and 2-5:30pm, Tu 9am-1pm, Th 9am-5:30pm, Sa 9am-12:30pm). **Post Code:** HR3 5AE.

▉▉ ACCOMMODATIONS AND FOOD. B&Bs occupy the center of town. Delightful stays await at ▉**The Bear ❸**, Bear St., a 16th-century coaching inn with low-timbered ceilings and fireplaces, several of which are filled with books. (☎821 302; www.the-bear-hay-on-wye.com. Singles £30; twins £55; doubles £65. MC/V.) **Oxford Cottage ❷**, Oxford Rd., provides sunlit rooms. (☎820 008; www.oxfordcot-tage.co.uk. £22 per person; singles £25-35 depending on the season. Cash only.) **Camp** along the Wye Valley Walk or Offa's Dyke (p. 463); inquire at the TIC.

Get **groceries** at Spar, 26 Castle St. (☎820 582; open M-F 7:30am-10pm, Sa-Su 8am-10pm.) Charlie Hicks Greengrocer is nearby, offering local farm produce (☎822 742; www.charliehicks.com. Open Tu-W and F-Sa 10am-4pm, Th 9:30am-4pm). **The Granary ❷**, Broad St., has extravagant salads (£8), free Wi-Fi, and patio seating. (☎820 790; info@granaryhay.co.uk. Open daily July-Aug. 10am-10pm; Sept.-June 10am-5:30pm. AmEx/MC/V.) **Oscars ❷**, 17 High Town, offers scones and pastries (£1-1.50) as well as lunch staples. (☎821 193. Open daily 10am-4:30pm. MC/V.) Cheaper eats await at **Xtreme Organix ❶**, 10 Castle St., a burger joint that uses local organic meat. (☎821 921. Open M-Tu and Th noon-2pm and 5-10:30pm, F noon-2pm and 5-11pm, Sa 10am-11pm, Su 5-10pm. Cash only.) **Shepherd's Ice Cream Parlour and Coffee Bar ❶**, 9 High Town, sells its signature sheepsmilk ice cream for £1.30. (☎821 898. Open M-Sa 9:30am-5pm, Su 10:30am-5pm. Cash only.)

◐ ▓ SIGHTS AND FESTIVALS. Hay's 13th-century **Norman castle,** scarred by wars, fires, and neglect, no longer houses traditional royalty. Rather, Richard Booth, the "King of Hay," stores just a fraction of his unfathomable number of secondhand books on the first floor. The castle is part of Booth's huge network of stores (many of them **honesty bookshops,** where a paybox sits near outdoor shelves of 30p books), which shaped Hay into a bibliophile's dream. Other independent stores offer equally delightful selections; some shops have specialties, like the Poetry Bookshop or Murder and Mayhem, dedicated to mysteries. To browse Hay's offerings, pick up the TIC's free *Second-hand & Antiquarian Booksellers & Printsellers* map and brochure or search over a million titles at www.haybooks.com. The world-renowned, annual 10-day **literary festival,** in late May and early June, brings

NO WORK, ALL PLAY

HAY DAY

It's the "Woodstock of the mind," according to Bill Clinton. The Guardian Hay Festival, held in late May and early June in Hay-on-Wye, is a celebration of all things literary, packing the town with 80,000 bibliophiles and hundreds of speakers and performers. Street banners all over the city proclaim, "People say that life is the thing, but I prefer reading."

It's a far cry from the original Guardian Hay Festival in 1988, which was not so much a monumental meeting of the minds as a dinner party with some friends and authors. Two decades later, it pulls in Nobel laureates and political, theatrical, and literary dignitaries by the hundreds for 392 events over the course of just 10 days. It has spawned sister festivals in Colombia and Spain. The concurrent Hay Fringe Festival has more informal readings and streetside theatrical productions like "Hay: The Musical!"

Book festival accommodations months in advance and expect queues at restaurants and events. If you don't mind working a bit, sign up as a volunteer. Workers get to see some events for free in exchange for working as many 3-4hr. shifts as they wish.

For more information or to sign up to be a steward, visit the festival website at www.hayfestival.com.

international luminaries (recently Seamus Heaney, Bill Clinton, Terry Gilliam, and Al Gore) to give readings. (www.hayfestival.com. Book accommodations early. Tickets £6-16.) For those interested in less cerebral pursuits, **Paddles & Pedals,** across the Wye via Bridge St. and on the riverbank to the left, rents canoes and kayaks. (☎820 604. Canoes £22.50 per ½-day, £35 per day. Kayaks £15 per ½-day, £25 per day. Book ahead. Free pickup.)

BRECON BEACONS

Brecon Beacons National Park (Parc Cenedlaethol Bannau Brycheiniog) encompasses 520 sq. mi. of varied landscape. The park divides into four regions: the mist-cloaked farms and peaks of Brecon Beacons, a possible location of King Arthur's mountain fortress; the lush woods of Fforest Fawr, with the waterfalls of Ystrad-fellte; the Tolkienesque Black Mountains to the east; and the remote western ridges of Black Mountain (singular), above Upper Swansea Valley. The park, founded in 1957, is almost entirely owned by farmers. Fringe towns make pleasant touring bases, but hostels allow easier access to the inner park.

NATIONAL PARK COVERAGE. Let's Go's coverage of Brecon Beacons National Park includes the towns of **Abergavenny** and **Brecon.** The first section provides an overview of transportation, practical information, and general accommodations (such as **YHA hostels**) for the entire park. Local services, B&Bs, and activities are listed within the coverage for individual towns.

▐ TRANSPORTATION

Getting to the more remote hostels and trails not serviced by public transportation proves a challenge. The **train** line (☎08457 484 950) from London Paddington to South Wales runs via Cardiff to Abergavenny at the park's southeastern corner and to Merthyr Tydfil on the southern edge. The Heart of Wales rail line passes through Llandeilo and Llandovery in the Black Mountain region, eventually terminating in Swansea. National Express (☎08705 808 080) **bus** #509 runs once per day from Brecon, on the northern side of the park, to London (5 hr., £23) and Cardiff (1hr., £3.60). Stagecoach Red and White (☎01685 388 216) buses cross the park en route to Brecon from: Abergavenny (X43; 50min., 6 per day); Hay-on-Wye (#39 or 40; 45min.; M-Sa 8 per day, Su 2 per day); Swansea (#63; 1½hr., 3 per day). Bus B8 runs between Brecon and Abergavenny once on Sundays. The free *Brecon Beacons: A Visitor's Guide,* available at most TICs, details some bus coverage and describes walks accessible by public transportation. For travel on Sundays and bank holidays, use Beacons Buses (☎01873 853 254; www.visitbreconbeacons.com), which caters to tourists and will drop you off almost anywhere. Brecon Cycle Centre (p. 472), among others, rents **mountain bikes.** Some people find it easier to hitch a ride on major roads. *Let's Go* does not recommend hitchhiking.

▐ PRACTICAL INFORMATION

Stop at a **National Park Information Centre (NPIC)** before venturing forth. Free maps are available, but Ordnance Survey Outdoor Leisure Maps #12 and 13 (£7.50) are indispensable for serious exploring and for reaching safety in bad weather. The park staff conducts guided walks between April and November; call ahead.

National Park Information Centres:

Mountain Centre (National Park Visitor Centre in Libanus): (☎01874 623 366; www.breconbeacons.org), in Libanus. Walk or take bus X43 to Libanus (7min., M-Sa 6 per day), 5 mi. from Brecon, then walk 1½ mi. uphill; or take a shuttle to the front door (15min., July-Aug. Su 6 per

Brecon Beacons National Park

ACCOMMODATIONS
YHA Brecon, 3
YHA Danywenallt, 4
YHA Llanddeusant, 1
YHA Llwyn-y-Celyn, 2

SOUTH WALES

ENGLAND

BLACK MOUNTAINS

BRECON BEACONS

Fforest Fawr

BLACK MOUNTAIN

Hay-on-Wye
Capel-y-Ffin
Gospel Pass
Offa's Dyke Path
Llanthony Priory
Honddu R.
Cwmyoy
Craig Mawr
Skirrid Fawr 1596ft
Abergavenny
Blorenge 1833ft
Big Pit Mining Museum
Blaenavon World Heritage Site
Abertillery
Sugar Loaf 1955ft
Pen-cerrig-calch 2301ft
Crickhowell
Pen y Gadair 2624ft
Grwyne Fawr
Waun Fach 2660ft
Iron Age Cairn
Cwmdu
Tretower
Usk and Brecon Canal
Talgarth
Llangynidr
Brynmawr
Ebbw Vale
Llangorse
Llangorse Lake
Tor-y-Foel 1807ft
Talybont Reservoir
Merthyr Tydfil
BRECON MOUNTAIN RAILWAY
Waun Rydd 2502ft
Brecon
Llanfaes
Llanddew
Libanus
Talybont Reservoir
Pen-y-Fan 2907ft
Storey Arms
Fan Fawr 2408ft
Fan y Big
Corn Du
Hirwaun
Aberdare
Pant
Pontsticill
Taf Fechan Reservoir
Sennybridge
Trecastle
Llywel
Roman fort
Iron Age fort
Fan Llia 2071ft
Bronze Age Monument
Fan Nedd 2176ft
Fan Gyhirych 2381ft
Porth-yr-Ogof
Ystradfellte
Sgwd-yr-eira Waterfall
Glyn Neath
Myddfai
Llandovery
HEART OF WALES RAILWAY
Cwm Wysg Reservoir
Fan Brycheiniog 2630ft
Dan-yr-Ogof Showcaves
Craig-y-nos
Abercrave
Llanddeusant
Llangadog
Carreg Cennen Castle
Trapp
Llandeilo
Ammanford
Ystradgynlais

Wales

TO HEREFORD (21mi)
TO CARDIFF (25mi)
TO SWANSEA (10mi)
TO CARMARTHEN (15mi)

5 miles
5 kilometers
0

Wye R.
Honddu R.
Nant Bran R.
Usk River
Cray R.
Tawe R.
Mellte R.
Neath R.
Hepste R.
Amman R.
Sawdde R.

A4348, B4423, A465, B4233, A472, A4042, A4043, B4264, A467, A4046, A4048, A4469, A465, A470, A4059, A4221, A4067, A40, A4215, A4520, B4520, B4560, B4558, A479, A4018, B4560, A438, A483, A482, A4069, A4068, A483, A4109 day) or bus B6 (15min., 2 per day) from Brecon. Open daily July-Aug. 9:30am-6pm; Nov.-Feb. 9:30am-4:30pm; May-June 9:30am-5:30pm; Mar.-Apr. and Sept.-Oct. 9:30am-5pm.

Abergavenny: see p. 470.

Craig-y-nos: (☎01639 730 395), at the Craig-y-nos Country Park. Take Stagecoach Bus #63 (from Brecon 30min., M-Sa 3 per day); ask to be dropped at Craig-y-nos. Open Easter-Sept. M-F 10am-5pm, Sa-Su 10am-5:30pm; Oct.-Easter M-F 10am-4pm, Sa-Su 10am-4:30pm.

Llandovery: Kings Rd. (☎01550 720 693), near Black Mountain. Take Heart of Wales train or bus #280 from Carmarthen. Open Easter-Sept. daily 10am-1pm and 1:45-5:30pm; Oct.-Easter M-Sa 10am-1pm and 1:45-4pm, Su 2-4pm.

ACCOMMODATIONS

The most comprehensive accommodations listing is at www.brecon-beacons.com, which lists guest houses, hostels, cottages, caravans, farms, and campsites.

Campsites ($4-10 per tent) are plentiful, but often difficult to reach without a car. Many offer laundry and grocery facilities, and all have parking and showers. Farmers may let you camp on their land if you ask first and leave the site as you found it. Be prepared to make a donation. The *Stay on a Farm* guide, available at the TIC, lists over 100 such farms across Wales. NPICs in the region also give out *Camping on Farms*, which lists many options in the park.

Scattered across the park are four YHA hostels, including **Ty'n-y-Caeau,** near Brecon (p. 471). The other three are:

Danywenallt (DAN-you-eh-nahlt; ☎0870 770 6136; danywenallt@yha.org.uk), in the Brecon Beacons near Talybont-on-Usk. Take the X43 bus from Brecon or Abergavenny and ask to be let off at the post office in Talybont-on-Usk. From the post office, cross the canal bridge and follow signs for the Talybont Reservoir. Turn left onto the dam wall and then take another left onto the track to Danywenallt. Reception open 8am-noon and 5-10:30pm. Call ahead. Dorms £17.50, under 18 £14. MC/V. ❷

Llanddeusant (HLAN-thew-sont; ☎0870 770 5930; llanddeusant@yha.org.uk), at the foot of Black Mountain near Llangadog village. Take the Trecastle-Llangadog road for 9 mi. off the A40. The nearest bus stop is in Llangadog. Restricted daytime access 10am-5pm. Curfew 11pm. Open from mid-Apr. to Aug.; from Sept. to mid-Apr., call 48hr. ahead. Dorms £11, under 18 £8. MC/V. ❶

Llwyn-y-Celyn (HLEWN-uh-kel-in; ☎0870 770 5936; llwynycelyn@yha.org.uk), 7 mi. south of Brecon, 2 mi. north from Storey Arms car park on the A470. Take Sixty Sixty Bus #43 from Brecon or Merthyr Tydfil (M-Sa every 2hr., Su 3 per day). Close to Pen-y-Fan and the Beacons. Lockout 10am-noon. Curfew 11pm. Reception open 8-10am and 5-10pm. Open Easter-Aug. daily; Sept.-Oct. Tu-Sa; Nov. and Feb.-Easter F-Sa. Book 2-3 weeks ahead. Dorms £14, under 18 £10. MC/V. ❷

HIKING

THE BRECON BEACONS

Llangorse Lake, 8 mi. from Brecon, is the highest natural lake in South Wales and is home to several unusual bird species and a crannog (Iron Age dwelling) on a man-made island. To the south, the Mountain Centre NPIC, outside Libanus (p. 466), houses an exhibit on the lake's history and wildlife. Paths weave through fields of sheep and occasionally stop at sights. The most popular path to the top of **Pen-y-Fan** (pen-uh-VAN; 2907 ft.), the highest mountain in South Wales, begins at **Storey Arms** (a car park and bus stop 5 mi. south of Libanus on the A470) and offers views of **Llyn Cwm Llwch** (HLIN-koom-hlooch), a 2000 ft. glacial pool in the shadow of **Corn Du** (CORN-dee) peak. The easiest route begins behind a car park and public toilets called **Pont ar Daf,** just past Storey Arms on the A470 coming from Brecon. Most

> **WARNING.** Even in summer, winds over 20mph and sudden mists can cause summit temperatures to plummet below freezing. In violent weather, do not take shelter in caves or under isolated trees, which tend to draw lightning. Move to lower altitude and avoid exposed ridges and open areas. A compass is essential; landmarks get lost in mists. In an emergency, call ☎999 and ask for Mountain Rescue. Keep in mind that mobiles do not work in some areas of the park. For more information, see **Wilderness Safety**, p. 50.

other paths are unmarked—consult NPICs for recommendations and directions. Pen-y-Fan has a reputation as the most dangerous mountain in Wales. An arduous ridge path leads from Pen-y-Fan to other peaks in the Beacons.

The touristy **Brecon Mountain Railway,** which departs from Pant Station in Merthyr Tydfil, allows a glimpse of the south side of the Beacons as the narrow-gauge train runs along the Taf Fechan Reservoir north to Pontsticill. (☎01685 722 988; www.breconmountainrailway.com. Mar.-late Oct. 5 per day, 11am-4pm. £9, children £4.75, seniors £8.25. MC/V.)

THE WATERFALL DISTRICT (FOREST FAWR)

Near the southern edge of the park on a limestone outcrop, Forest Fawr erupts with mosses and ferns. The triangle defined by the towns of **Hirwaun, Ystradfellte,** and **Pontneeddfechan** marks the forest boundaries. Rivers tumble through rapids, gorges, and spectacular falls near Ystradfellte, 7 mi. southwest of the Beacons. At **Porth-yr-Ogof** ("Mouth of the Cave"), the River Mellte ducks into a cave at the base of the cliff and emerges as an icy pool. Swimming is ill-advised—the stones are slippery and the pool deepens suddenly. Erosion makes the paths narrow and hard to navigate. Remote but worth the sweat is the **Sgwd yr Eira** waterfall (which means "Fall of Snow," but is also called "Lady's Fall" after one of the 26 daughters of King Brychan) on the River Hepste, ½ mi. from its intersection with the Mellte. You can stand behind thundering water in the hollow of a cliff face and remain dry as a bone. Follow the marked paths to the falls from Gwaun Hepste. Hikers reach the waterfall district from the Beacons by crossing the A470 near the YHA Llwyn-y-Celyn, climbing Craig Cerrig-gleisiad cliff and Fan Frynych peak, and descending along a rocky Roman road. The route crosses a nature reserve and trackless heath.

Between Swansea and Brecon, off the A4067, the **Dan-yr-Ogof Showcaves** are the park's most highly promoted attractions. Although their stalagmites and eerie rock formations are impressive, their "showcave" status has left them commercial and heavily trafficked. One of the biggest draws is the award-winning **Dinosaur Park,** complete with a "fearsome" T-Rex. (☎01639 730 284, 24hr. info 730 801. Open daily Apr.-Oct. 10am-3pm. £10.50, children £6.50.) Ten miles of trails pass **Fforest Fawr** on their way to the caves. A **campsite ❶** is nearby. After turning off the A406 for the Showcaves, turn right at the T-junction. (Camping £5 per person. Caravans £12. Electricity free.) Relax at **Craig-y-nos Country Park,** ½ mi. away. (☎01639 730 395. Open May-Aug. M-F 10am-6pm, Sa-Su 10am-7pm; Mar.-Apr. and Sept.-Oct. M-F 10am-5pm, Sa-Su 10am-6pm; Nov.-Feb. M-F 10am-4pm, Sa-Su 10am-4:30pm. Free.) Stagecoach **bus** #63 (1½hr., 3 per day) stops at the caves and campsite.

THE BLACK MOUNTAINS

Located in the easternmost section of the park, the Black Mountains are a group of ridges offering 80 sq. mi. of solitude. Summits like **Waun Fach** (2660 ft.), the highest point, may seem dull and boggy, but ridge walks offer views unsurpassed in Wales. Ordnance Survey Outdoor Leisure Map #13 (1:25,000; £8) is essential. **Crickhowell,** on the A40 and Roy Brown's Coaches route between Abergavenny and Builth Wells (#82; 25min., 1 every Tu), is one of the best starting points for forays into the area, although hikers staying overnight might want to base themselves in Abergavenny. You can also explore by **bus:** Stagecoach Red and White #39 between Brecon and Hay-on-Wye descends the north side of the Black Mountains. **Gospel Pass,** the park's highest mountain pass, often sees sun above the cloud cover. Nearby, **Offa's Dyke Path** (p. 463) traces the park's eastern boundary. On Sundays and bank holidays from May to September, Offa's Dyke Flyer bus runs from Hay-on-Wye to Llanfihangel Crucorney and stops at access points to the Black Mountains on the way (☎01873 853 254; www.visitbreconbeacons.com; 3 per day).

ABERGAVENNY (Y FENNI)   ☎01873

On the eastern edge of Brecon Beacons National Park, Abergavenny (pop. 10,000) trumpets itself as the "Gateway to Wales." While shop-lined pedestrian areas offer all the charms of Welsh village life, the region's real draw lies outside city limits: Abergavenny is the starting point of countless hikes through the Black Mountains.

TRANSPORTATION. Trains (☎08457 484 950; www.nationalrail.com) run to: Bristol (1hr., 1-2 per hr., £9.20); Cardiff (40min., every hr., £8.50); Hereford (25min., 2 per hr., £6.50); London (2¼hr., every hr., £73); Newport (25min., 1-2 per hr., £5.60). To get to town, turn right at the end of Station Rd. and walk 5min. along Monmouth Rd. The **bus station** is on Monmouth Rd., by the TIC. Stagecoach Red and White (☎01633 838 856) **buses** roll out to Brecon (X43; 1hr., M-Sa 6 per day), Cardiff (X3; 1½hr., every hr.), and Hereford (X4; 1hr., 6 per day).

PRACTICAL INFORMATION. The well-stocked **Tourist Information Centre,** Monmouth Rd., across from the bus station, arranges local theater bookings and reserves beds for £2. (☎857 588; www.abergavenny.co.uk. Open daily Apr.-Oct. 9:30am-5:30pm; Nov.-Mar. 10am-4pm.) It doubles as the **National Park Information Centre,** with helpful maps for hikers. Other services include: **banks** with **ATMs** along Cross St. and High St.; **police,** Tudor St. (☎852 273), between Nevill and Baker St.; the **hospital** (☎732 732), Nevill Hall, on the A40; free **Internet** access at the Public **Library,** Library Sq., Baker St. (☎735 980; open Tu 10am-7pm, W and F 9am-5:30pm, Th 9am-7pm, Sa 9am-1pm); and the **post office,** St. John's Sq., where Tudor St. turns into Castle St., with a **bureau de change** (☎08457 223 344; open M-F 9am-5:30pm, Sa 9am-12:30pm). **Post Code:** NP7 5EB.

ACCOMMODATIONS AND FOOD. B&Bs lie on **Monmouth Road,** past the TIC, and **Hereford Road,** 15min. from town. **Black Sheep Backpackers ❷,** 24 Station Rd., across from the train station, has a colorful basement lounge with a kitchen and full bar. (☎859 125; www.blacksheepbackpackers.com. Large basement dorm £13.50; nicer upper dorms £15; doubles £30. Cash only.)

The **market** in Market Hall on Cross St. has fresh produce and baked goods (open Tu and F-Sa 9am-5pm; largest on Tu), and weekly flea market (W 9am-5pm). **Harry's Carvery ❶,** St. John's St., off High St., has lunch treats and just-sliced meats (£2-3). Try the panini (£3) or the brie and cranberry foccaccia. (☎852 766. Open daily 8:30am-4pm. Cash only.) **The Trading Post ❶,** 14 Nevill St., has dozens of specialty coffees (£1.45) and teas (£1.10). Enjoy a soup and sandwich in the large dining room. (☎855 448. Open M-Sa 9am-5pm. Cash only.) The elegant restaurant at **The Angel Hotel ❹,** 15 Cross St., delivers inventive dishes using local ingredients. (☎857 121. Entrees from £8. Open daily noon-2:30pm and 7-10pm. MC/V.)

SIGHTS AND OUTDOORS. A site of much medieval intrigue, Abergavenny's **castle** is now reduced to a picturesque ruin. A 19th-century hunting lodge on the grounds houses the **Abergavenny Museum,** which displays artifacts from the Iron Age to the 19th century. (☎854 282. Open Mar.-Oct. M-Sa 11am-1pm and 2-5pm, Su 2-5pm; Nov.-Feb. M-Sa 11am-1pm and 2-4pm. Grounds open daily dawn-5pm. Free.) The **Borough Theatre**, Cross St., puts on a variety of shows. (☎850 805. Box office open Tu-Sa 9:30am-5pm. Tickets from $5, concessions available.)

Abergavenny's real attractions are the surrounding hills. Because almost all of the Black Mountain trails are unmarked, it's crucial to get detailed directions and an Ordnance Survey Map ($6.50-7.50) from the NPIC. Three major summits are accessible from Abergavenny by foot, although all require fairly long hikes. **Blorenge** (1833 ft.) is 2½ mi. southwest of town. A path begins off the B4246 or from the TIC, traversing woodlands to the uplands, and ascends the remaining 1500 ft. in 4½ mi. (12 mi., round-trip 6hr.). The trail to the top of **Sugar Loaf** (1955 ft.), 2½ mi. northwest, starts ½ mi. west of town on the A40. Many report that it's easy to hitch a ride to the car park and start hikes from there, although *Let's Go* does not recommend hitchhiking. The path to **Skirrid Fawr** (the "Holy Mountain"; 1595 ft.) lies northeast of town and starts 2 mi. down the B4521. **Pony trekking** can be enjoyable. Try Grange Trekking Centre (☎890 215; $24 per ½-day, $39 per day) and Llanthony Riding and Trekking (☎890 359; $23 per ½-day, $40 per full day).

▶ DAYTRIPS FROM ABERGAVENNY

When traveling to the sights near Abergavenny by bus, a **Network Rider** pass (p. 463) is usually cheaper than round-trip tickets.

BIG PIT NATIONAL MINING MUSEUM FOR WALES. Recently named a World Heritage Site, the hillsides of Blaenavon, 9 mi. southwest of Abergavenny, were a center of the coal-mining and iron-production industries of South Wales. Visitors descend a 300 ft. shaft to experience the cramped conditions under which miners labored. Ex-miners share stories in the subterranean workshops, while above-ground exhibits explain all aspects of coal mining. *(Take bus X3 to Pontypool. 20min., 13 per day. Transfer to bus #30 to Blaenavon. 20min., every 2hr. ☎01495 790 311. Open from mid-Feb. to Nov. daily 9:30am-5pm. Underground tours 10am-3:30pm. Free. Those under 3 ft. 3 in. not admitted underground. Under 16 not admitted without a guardian.)*

LLANTHONY PRIORY. All the megaliths in the Black Mountains are said to point toward ruined, relatively untouristed Llanthony Priory. In the 12th century, founder William de Lacy rebuilt ancient ruins left at this site so that he could live a hermetic life. *(Take Stagecoach Red and White bus X4 (M-Sa 6 per day) or follow the A465 to Llanfihangel Crucorney, where the B4423 begins. Some hitch the last 6 mi. to the priory, but Let's Go does not recommend hitchhiking. Always open. Free.)*

RAGLAN CASTLE. A mere 570 years old, Raglan was the last medieval castle built in Wales. Sir William Thomas constructed it for aesthetic rather than military purposes, but the castle still withstood an English Civil War siege before finally falling to Cromwell's troops in 1646. The remaining ruins comprise a network of open-air towers and crumbling staircases. *(Take bus #83 from Abergavenny or Monmouth. 20min., 6 per day, £4.50. Bus #60 runs from Monmouth or Newport. From Newport 40min., 2 per hr., £3-4.20. From the bus stop in Raglan, follow Castle Rd. to the highway and cross over the pedestrian path to the road up to the castle. ☎01291 690 228. Open June-Sept. daily 9:30am-6pm; Apr.-May and Oct. daily 9:30am-5pm; Nov.-Mar. M-Sa 9:30am-4pm, Su 11am-4pm. Last admission 30min. before close. £3, concessions £2.50, families £8.30.)*

BRECON (ABERHONDDU)   ☎01874

Just north of the mountains, Brecon (pop. 8000) is the best base for exploring the dramatic northern region of Brecon Beacons National Park. Georgian architecture looms over tiny side streets where residents and backpackers sip tea and plan hikes through neighboring forests. A motley crew comes to Brecon in August, when the exceptional Jazz Festival fills every bed and street corner.

SOUTH WALES

⌐ TRANSPORTATION. Buses arrive regularly at the Bulwark in the central square. Ask for schedules at the TIC. National Express (☎08705 808 080; www.nationalexpress.com) bus #509 runs to London (6hr., 1 per day, £23) via Cardiff (1¼hr., 1 per day, £3.60). Stagecoach Red and White (☎01633 838 856) buses run to Abergavenny (X43; 50min., 6 per day) and Swansea (#63; 1½hr., M-Sa 3 per day, £4-5). Buses #39 and 40 go to Hereford via Hay-on-Wye (M-Sa 8 per day); on Sundays, Yeomans (☎01432 356 202) follows the same route (#40; Su 3 per day). Bipedcycles, 10 Ship St., rents **mountain bikes.** (☎07970 972 186 or 622 296. £18 per day. Open M-F 9am-5:30pm, Sa 9am-5pm.) Bikes and Hikes rents bikes and organizes expeditions. (☎610 071. Bike rental £18, activities £25-40 per day.)

⚡ PRACTICAL INFORMATION. The **Tourist Information Centre** is located in the Cattle Market car park; walk through Bethel Sq. off Lion St. (☎622 485. Open M-Sa 9:30am-5:30pm, Su 9:30am-4pm.) Other services include: Barclays **bank,** at the corner of St. Mary's and High St. (☎01633 205 000; open M-F 9am-5pm); a **launderette,** St. Mary's St. (☎07960 979 625; £6-9; open M-Sa 9am-5:30pm); **police,** Lion St. (☎622 331); Boots **pharmacy,** Bethyl Sq. (☎622 917; open M-Sa 9am-4pm); **Internet** access at Brecon Branch **Library,** Ship St. (☎623 346; free; open M and W-F 9:30am-5pm, Tu 9:30am-7pm, Sa 9:30am-1pm) and **Brecon Cyber Cafe,** 10 Lion St. (☎624 942; £1 per 12min., students 60p, max. charge £10; open M-Sa 10am-5pm); and the **post office,** in the Cooperative Pioneer, off Lion St. (☎623 735; open M-F 8:30am-5:30pm, Sa 8:30am-4pm). **Post Code:** LD3 7HY.

⌐ ACCOMMODATIONS. Book in advance for mid-August, when Jazz Festival-goers claim every pillow in town. **Mulberry House ❸,** 3 Priory Hill, offers comfortable, bright rooms across from the cathedral. (☎624 461. £25 per person. Cash only.) **Paris Guest House ❸,** on Watton Rd. near the city center, offers free Wi-Fi and satellite TV. (☎624 205; www.parisguesthouse.co.uk. Singles £27, ensuite £30; doubles £44, ensuite £25.) The nearest **YHA** hostel is **Brecon (Ty'n-y-Caeau) ❶** (tin-uh-KAY-uh), 3 mi. out of town. From the town center, walk down The Watton to the A40-A470 roundabout. Follow the Abergavenny branch of the A40. After the roundabout, take the path to the left of Groesffordd and turn left on the main road. Continue 10-15min., bearing left at the fork; the hostel is on the right. The X43 bus stops in Groesffordd (7 per day), a 1½ mi. walk away. The Victorian house has a TV room and kitchen. (☎665 270. Dorms £14, under 18 £10. MC/V.) **Camp** at **Pencelli Castle Caravan and Camping Park ❶,** 2 mi from Brecon on the Taff Trail (☎665 451; www.pencelli-castle.com. £7.50-8.50 per person, varies by season). During the Jazz Festival, campsites open on farms.

⌐ FOOD. Buy **groceries** at the Cooperative Pioneer, off Lion St. (☎625 257. Open M-Sa 8am-9pm, Su 10am-4pm.) Enjoy traditional pub fare at **The Wellington ❶,** a family-friendly inn across from the bus stop in the town center. In back is a popular pub, and above the courtyard is Brecon's only nightclub, **Blooz.** (☎610 459. Open M-Sa noon-9pm, Su noon-8pm. Nightclub open Th 10pm-12:30am, F-Sa 10pm-1:45am.) **St. Mary's Bakery ❶,** 4 St. Mary St., sells baked goods (35p-£1) and warm pork baps for £2.25. (☎624 311; www.stmarysbakery.co.uk. Open M-F 6:30am-5pm, Sa 7am-2pm. Cash only.) **Pilgrim's Tea Rooms and Restaurant ❶,** attached to the cathedral's Heritage Center, is a small, peaceful cafe run by parishioners. (☎610 610. Open M-Sa 10am-5pm, Su 11am-4pm. Cash only.)

◨ ▦ SIGHTS AND FESTIVALS. Brecon Cathedral holds the standards of the Welsh 24th Regiment and impressive examples of craftsmanship. History is literally carved into the stone columns—see the "mason's marks" that illiterate stoneworkers used to label their work. The **Heritage Centre,** in the cathedral enclave, describes the art of bell-ringing and tells the story of the cathedral. Look for the stone that Brecknock archers used to sharpen their arrows. (Cathedral ☎623 857, heritage center 625 222. Cathedral open M-Sa 9am-5:30pm. Center open Mar.-Dec. M-Sa 10:30am-4:30pm.) The **Brecknock Museum and Art Gallery,** in the Assize Courthouse near the Bulwark, features artifacts from rural Wales such as walking sticks and milk churns. (☎624 121. Open Apr.-Sept. M-F 10am-5pm, Sa 10am-1pm and 2-5pm, Su noon-5pm; Oct.-Mar. M-F 10am-5pm, Sa 10am-1pm and 2-5pm. £1, concessions 50p, children free.) At the **Royal Regiment of Wales Museum Brecon,** The Barracks, military paraphernalia commands all available space. (☎613 310; www.rrw.org.uk. Open Apr.-Sept. M-F 10am-5pm, Sa 10am-4pm; Oct.-Mar. M-F 10am-5pm. Last admission 4:30pm. £3.) For the August **Brecon Jazz Festival** (☎611 622; www.breconjazz.co.uk), the streets are blocked as thousands converge to enjoy jazz and local brews. Other events include **antique fairs** (last Sa of the month) and **crafts fairs** in Market Hall (Easter-Nov. every 3rd Sa of the month).

THE GOWER PENINSULA

The 18 mi. Gower Peninsula is full of unexpected sights. Ancient burial mounds, castles, and churches dot the land, and expansive white beaches border flower-covered limestone cliffs. Mumbles, its largest city, has beaches, nightlife, and a seaside as unassuming as its name.

█ TRANSPORTATION. Buses to the peninsula go primarily to Swansea's Quadrant Station. First Cymru (☎08706 082 608) buses #2 and 2A leave Oystermouth Sq. in Mumbles for Swansea (20min., 4 per hr., £1.75) and Langland Bay and Caswell Bay. Buses #117 and 118 run to Swansea from Oxwich (40min., 2 per day, £3.30) and from Rhossili via Port Eynon (1hr., every hr., £3.30). Bus #14 shuttles to Swansea from Pennard (35min., every hr., £3.30). The **First Cymru Day Saver** is valid through Gower and Swansea (£3.70), while the **Gower & City Rider** allows a week's unlimited travel around the Peninsula (£12.50). A.A. **Taxis** (☎360 600) provides cabs. The Swansea **Bikepath and Promenade** traces the coast from Swansea Bay to Mumbles pier; rent **bikes** in Swansea at Action Bikes, St. David's Square. (☎464 640. Open M-Sa 9am-5:30pm, Su 11am-4pm. £12 per day. ID required.)

█ PRACTICAL INFORMATION. Mumbles, the largest city on Gower, has the most helpful services. The **Tourist Information Centre** shares space with Mumbles Methodist Church on Mumbles Rd. (☎361 302. Open July-Aug. M-Sa 10am-4pm, Su noon-4pm; Sept.-June M-Sa 10am-4pm.) Other services include: Barclays **bank,** 16 Newton Rd. (☎0870 241 281; open M-F 9am-5pm); a **police** station on Newton Rd., near Castle St.; Singleton **hospital,** Sketty Park Ln. (☎205 666); Boots **pharmacy,** across from the TIC on Mumbles Rd. (☎366 195; open M-F 9am-5:30pm, Sa 8:45am-5:30pm); free **Internet** access at Oystermouth **Library,** Dunns Ln., a block from the TIC (☎368 380; photo ID required; open M-Th 9am-6pm, F 9am-8pm, Sa 9am-5pm, Su noon-4pm; advance booking recommended); and the **post office,** 522 Mumbles Rd. (☎366 821; open M-Sa 9am-5:30pm). **Post Code:** SA3 4DH.

█ █ ACCOMMODATIONS AND FOOD. West Gower, including **Oxwich, Port Eynon,** and **Rhossili,** has cheaper accommodations than **Mumbles. B&Bs** in Mumbles charge upwards of £25 for singles and cluster on **Mumbles Road** and in the **South End** area (a 10min. walk from the TIC); singles are hard to find. With large bay windows, the gabled **Coast House ❸,** 708 Mumbles Rd., has views of schooners in the water. (☎368 702. Bath and TV in most rooms. Singles £35; doubles from £55. MC/V.) To camp at **Three Cliffs Bay Caravan Park ❶,** North Hills Farm, Penmaen, take bus #118 from Swansea. (☎371 218. £6 per person. Electricity £1.50. Cash only.)

SOUTH WALES

SPOONING

Years ago, if a rural Welsh farmer wanted to do well with the ladies, he had to learn to lovespoon. Among the illiterate lower classes, carved wooden spoons replaced love letters. These lovespoons acted as emblems of affection and delivered specific messages in their intricate carvings.

Some symbols are fairly straightforward: a horseshoe represents good luck, a twist represents companionship, and a vine represents the couple growing together. A wheel would assure the lady that the man who carved the spoon would work hard for her, and a key would symbolize the couple's shared home. More frisky men could carve small wooden balls trapped in a cage to indicate the number of children he hoped to have with the recipient. Even if a woman accepted the gift, it didn't mean the couple would be spooning forever. Some village women collected many lovespoons before finally selecting a husband.

These symbols were carved out of the large handle of a wooden spoon that ranging from a couple inches to more than a foot long. Examples can be seen in Mumbles's Lovespoon Gallery and other museums of local history throughout Wales. Today, the craft is a commercial one—gift shops and TICs sell the tokens so that you, too, can get a taste of love.

Bus #118 runs from Swansea to Port Eynon, west of Mumbles and home to the ☒YHA Port Eynon ❷. This former lifeboat house on the beach has a clean kitchen and common area. (☎390 706. Reception 8-10am and 5-10pm. Check-in 5pm. Open Easter-Nov. £15, under 18 £11. MC/V.) Tan-y-Bryn ❸ provides cozy B&B accommodations in Port Eynon. (☎391 182. £30 per person, £25 for multiple night stays.) Beachside camping is also possible in Port Eynon at Carreglwyd Camping and Leisure. (☎390 795; www.porteynon.com. Sites £18 for 2 adults during high season.)

In Mumbles, the Somerfield supermarket is at 512 Mumbles Rd. (Open daily 8am-9pm.) Both locations of The Choice is Yours, at 7 Newton Rd. and on Mumbles Rd. near the TIC, sell fresh produce. (☎367 255. Open M-Sa 8:30am-5:30pm. MC/V.) Madisons ❶, 620 Mumbles Rd., is a small cafe with a big view of the bay. (☎368 484. Open daily 8am-5pm. Cash only.) Davies of Mumbles ❶, next to the TIC on Mumbles Rd., offers scones, cakes, and pastries from 40p. (☎366 648. Open in summer daily 8am-5pm; in winter M-Sa 8am-5pm, Su 10am-5pm. Cash only.) On a wooden pier Verdi's ❶, at the southern end of Mumbles Rd., serves expensive bistro cuisine. It also has an ice cream bar, scooping out traditional flavors and more distinctive ones like honeycomb and apple cobbler. (☎369 135. Single scoop £1.25. Open Apr.-Sept. daily 10am-9pm; Oct.-Mar. M-Th 10am-6pm. MC/V.)

🔵🔶 SIGHTS AND BEACHES. High above Mumbles, the ramparts of 13th-century Oystermouth Castle, on Castle Ave. off Newton Rd., offer a bird's eye view of the labyrinthine streets. (☎368 732. Open daily from Apr. to mid-Sept. 11am-5pm. £1, concessions 80p.) Clyne Gardens and Country Park, at Blackpill near Mumbles, is a riot of color in spring. Woodland walking and cycle paths and a mid-1800s castle draw visitors year-round. The #2a, 2b, 3a, 3b, and 37 buses from Swansea stop at Blackpill. (☎401 737; www.swansea.gov.uk/clyneinbloom. Free. Weekly guided walks £1.) The small collection at the Lovespoon Gallery, 492 Mumbles Rd., displays and sells traditional Welsh love tokens. (☎360 132; www.lovespoons.co.uk. Spoons from £3, engraving £6. Open M-Sa 10am-5:30pm. AmEx/MC/V.)

The Gower Peninsula is strewn with gorgeous beaches, some more swimming friendly than others. From Southgate and Pennard, a 30min. walk along the Coast Path brings you to Three Cliffs, a cave-ridden area largely submerged at high tide. Langland Bay, Caswell Bay, Oxwich Bay, and Port Eynon Bay are all popular and clean, with superb views. To reach Langland, walk 45min. along the Bays Footpath that begins around the point of Mumbles Head. Caswell is another 45min., and Oxwich and Port Eynon are several miles beyond; buses #117 and 118 from Swansea will stop there. On the peninsula's western tip, cliffs hug the sweeping curve of ⚑**Rhossili Beach,** whose wide expanse and seclusion make overcrowding unlikely (take bus #118 from Swansea). Within about 2½hr. of low tide, a causeway of jagged black rocks provides access to the seabird haven **Worm's Head,** crags that look like a *wurm* (Welsh for dragon) lumbering out to sea. A kiosk near the head posts safe crossing times, or call ☎306 534 for information on tides. **Llangennith Beach,** north of Rhossili, draws surfers from all over Wales.

🖭🌿 **NIGHTLIFE AND FESTIVALS.** A fishing hole by day, **Mumbles** becomes a watering hole at night. The stretch of **Mumbles Road** at Mumbles Head is lined with pubs, some of them former haunts of Dylan Thomas. In University of Swansea lingo, to hang out on Mumbles Rd. is to "go mumbling," and to start at one end and have a pint at each pub is to "do the Mumbles Mile." Flower's, Usher's, Buckley's, and Felin Foel are local ales. The **Gower Festival** fills the peninsula's churches with string quartets and Bach chorales during the last two weeks of July (booking ☎475 715; tickets £8-12). The *What's On* guide, free at the Mumbles TIC, has details.

SWANSEA (ABERTAWE)   ☎01792

Native son Dylan Thomas got it right when he called Swansea (pop. 230,000) an "ugly, lovely town." The ugly bit is obvious: concrete buildings line urban roads, industrial equipment borders the coast, and box houses cover the hillsides in well-defined grids. Yet Swansea is an active city, with a university, colorful cafes, and free museums. Its maritime quarter is undeniably charming, and a beautiful expanse of sandy beaches extends to the west onto the nearby Gower Peninsula.

▣ **TRANSPORTATION.** At the **train station,** 35 High St., **trains** (☎08457 484 950; www.nationalrail.com) depart to Birmingham (3½hr., 2 per hr., £38), Cardiff (1hr., 1-2 per hr., £9), and London (3hr., every hr., £58). The **Quadrant Bus Station** (☎0870 608 2608) is near the Quadrant Shopping Centre and the TIC. National Express (☎08705 808 080; www.nationalexpress.com) runs **buses** to Birmingham (3½hr., 3 per day, £27), Cardiff (1¼hr., 12 per day, £6.40), and London (4½hr., 5 per day, £22.50). First Cymru (☎08706 082 608) buses cover the Gower Peninsula and southwest Wales; a shuttle runs to Cardiff (1hr., M-Sa 2-4 per hr., £7.50). A **First Cymru DaySaver** ticket (£3.10, concessions £2, families £5) allows unlimited travel for a day in Swansea, and a £1.40 pass gives unlimited travel M-Th after 7pm. The **Swansea Bay Pass,** purchased on the bus, covers a week of travel on the Peninsula (£12.50, concessions £8.40). Stagecoach Buses run to smaller towns, including Brecon (1½hr., 3 per day). Data Cabs (☎474 747 and 545 454) and Yellow Cab (☎644 446) offer **taxi** services.

🛈 **PRACTICAL INFORMATION.** On the north side of the bus station, the **Tourist Information Centre** books rooms for £2 plus a 10% deposit. (☎468 321; www.visitswanseabay.com. Open in summer M-Sa 9:30am-5:30pm, Su 10am-4pm; in winter M-Sa 9:30am-5:30pm.) Other services include: Barclays **bank,** The Kingsway (☎01633 205 000; open M-F 9am-5pm); **American Express,** 28 The Kingsway (☎455 006; open M-F 9am-5pm, Sa 9am-4pm); **police,** Grove Pl. (☎456 999), at the bottom of Mt. Pleasant Hill; Singleton **Hospital,** Sketty Park Ln. (☎205 666); Co-op **pharmacy,** 13 Orchard St. (☎643 527; open M-F 9am-5:30pm, Sa 9am-1pm); free **Internet** access at the Public **Library,** Alexandra Rd. (☎516 750; book ahead; photo ID required; open Tu and Th 9am-6pm, W and F 9am-8pm, Sa 9am-5pm); and the **post office,** on the second floor of WHSmith in the Quadrant Shopping Centre (open M-Sa 9am-5:30pm). **Post Code:** SA1 5LF.

⌘🏠 ACCOMMODATIONS AND FOOD. The closest hostel is the popular **YHA Port Eynon ❶**, an hour out of town by bus (p. 473). Inexpensive **B&Bs** and guest houses line **Oystermouth Road,** along the bay. Frequent buses make downtown access easy. **Ael-y-Bryn House ❷**, 88 Bryn Rd., has bay views and well-furnished rooms with TV and tea. (☎466 707. £26-33.50 per person. MC/V.) **Harlton Guest House ❷**, 89 King Edward Rd., offers small, inexpensive rooms with TV and Wi-Fi. (☎466 938; www.harltonguesthouse.co.uk. £15 per person. MC/V.) In summer, many travelers **camp** at sites along the Gower Peninsula.

Indian and Chinese takeaways line **St. Helen's Road.** Small cafes, bistros, and trendy restaurants dominate **Oxford** and **Wind Streets.** Shoppers convene at the **Swansea Market,** the largest indoor market in Wales, on the side of the Quadrant Shopping Centre opposite the bus station (open M-Sa 8:30am-5:30pm). **Govinda's Vegetarian Restaurant ❶**, 8 Cradock St., is a small, quiet spot just off The Kingway. (☎468 469. Open M-Th and Su noon-3pm, F-Sa noon-6pm. Cash only.) **Mambo ❶**, 46 The Kingsway, serves tasty Caribbean and Mediterranean fare (tapas from £1.50, lunch entrees from £3.50) and becomes a trendy watering hole in the evening. (☎456 620. Open daily noon-late. AmEx/MC/V.) The **Cross Keys ❶**, 12 St. Mary's St., is a sprawling pub with a menu as large as its beer garden and flashy games to occupy the bar-shy. (☎630 921. Open M-Sa 11am-11pm, Su noon-10:30pm. Food served M-Th 11am-8pm, F-Sa 8am-5:30pm, Su noon-6pm. MC/V.)

◪ SIGHTS. The bronze, hollowed eyes of **Dylan Thomas** gaze seaward at the end of Swansea's marina. The late poet, a demi-god of local culture and national litera-ture, inspires many tours, which shepherd tourists along the **Dylan Thomas Uplands Trail** and **City Centre Trail,** past the poet's favorite haunts. Detailed guidebooks to the trails (from £1.50) are available at the **Dylan Thomas Centre,** Somerset Pl., which venerates Thomas and his "craft of sullen art." Visitors can listen as Thomas breathlessly recites five of his poems. Famous portraits hang alongside his notori-ously sizeable bar tabs ($8 in 1953). The center also presents dramatic, cinematic, and literary performances. (☎463 980, box office 463 892. Open daily 10am-4:30pm. Free.) The **Swansea Museum,** Victoria Rd., is the oldest in Wales and fea-tures the most extensive collection of cycling memorabilia in the UK, the Egypt Centre, and the "Cabinet of Curiosities," a celebration of randomness. (☎653 763; www.swanseaheritage.net. Open Tu-Su 10am-5pm. Last admission 4pm. Free.) The collection at the **Glynn Vivian Art Gallery,** Alexandra Rd., reflects the eclectic tastes of its largest donor, Richard Glynn Vivian. Seasonal shows feature local art-ists. (☎516 900; www.glynnviviangallery.org. Open Tu-Su 10am-5pm. Free.) In the **National Waterfront Museum,** near the Swansea Museum, visitors examine the his-tory of Swansea through a series of interactive displays. An exhibit on the world's first passenger railway, which ran from Mumbles to Swansea, is next door. (☎653 763. Open daily 10am-5pm. Free.)

◪♫ NIGHTLIFE AND ENTERTAINMENT. The students of Swansea do not go gentle into weekend nights. Festivities begin at pre-club bars as early as 7pm and rage, rage until 3am. Most clubs see a sharp downturn during summer vacation. Nightlife centers around **The Kingsway,** where swarms of students club-hop on weekend nights. **Time & Envy,** 72 The Kingsway, is the most popular club simply because it can squeeze in the biggest crowd. (☎653 142. F £10, including 6 drinks; Sa £5 after 11pm. Open F 10pm-3am, Sa 10pm-4am.) A couple blocks away, **Sin City** is a new, popular addition to Swansea nightlife. Its two floors blast metal, indie, and pop tunes, with occasional live music. (☎07976 136 194; www.alterna-tiveswansea.com. Club open F 10pm-3am, Sa 10pm-4am. Live bands play through-out the week; call or check website for details. Cover £3-10.) Five miles away, Gower's Mumbles Road (p. 475) gets packed on weekends.

SOUTH WALES

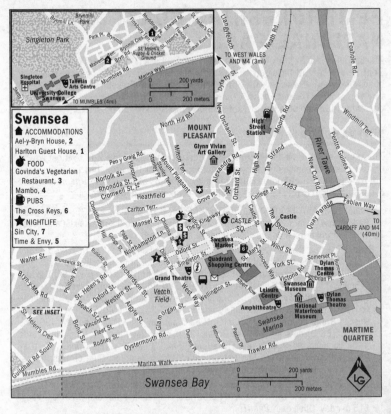

Swansea

♠ ACCOMMODATIONS
Ael-y-Bryn House, 2
Harlton Guest House, 1

🍴 FOOD
Govinda's Vegetarian
Restaurant, 3
Mambo, 4

🍺 PUBS
The Cross Keys, 6

★ NIGHTLIFE
Sin City, 7
Time & Envy, 5

The bimonthly *What's On*, free at the TIC, lists events around town. The **Dylan Thomas Theatre,** located along the marina, stages dramas and musicals. (☎473 238; www.dylanthomastheatre.org.uk. Box office open M-Th 9am-5pm, F 9am-4:30pm. Tickets from £6, concessions from £5.) The **Grand Theatre,** on Singleton St., puts on operas, ballets, concerts, and comedies. (☎475 715; www.swanseagrand.co.uk. Box office open M-Sa 9:30am-6pm, until 8pm on performance days, Su 1hr. before show. Tickets £8.50-35; same-day concessions often available.) The **Taliesin Arts Centre,** University College, hosts films, art shows, and dance performances, and also has a bookstore and cafe on-site. (☎602 060; www.taliesinartscentre.co.uk. Box office open M-F 10am-6pm, Sa noon-3pm and 3:30-6pm, until 8pm on performance days. Brochures available on campus.)

In mid-August, the village of Pontardawe, located 8 mi. north of Swansea, is flooded with folk and rock musicians from all over the world, in town for the annual **Pontardawe International Music Festival** (☎830 200; www.pontardawefestival.com; weekend ticket £50). The **Swansea Festival** (☎411 570, bookings 475 715), held in October of every year, features shows, concerts, and family activities throughout the city. The revelry continues with the **Dylan Thomas Celebration** (☎463 980; www.dylanthomasfestival.com), which includes a variety of readings, shows, and lectures that run from Thomas's birthday all the way through to the date of his death (Oct. 27-Nov. 9).

PEMBROKESHIRE COAST NATIONAL PARK

The 225 sq. mi. of Pembrokeshire Coast National Park (Parc Cenedlaethol Arfordir Penfro) are spread between oceanside stretches and inland pockets. The park spans the wooded Gwaun Valley and Celtic ruins in the Preseli Hills, but the coastline remains its biggest draw. Coves and sea cliffs lure hikers along 186 mi. of coastal trail, while beaches attract sunbathers, kayakers, and surfers.

▐ TRANSPORTATION

The region's best base is **Haverfordwest.** Buses travel from this hub to most towns on the Pembrokeshire coast. Some hitchers frequent the area, but *Let's Go* does not recommend hitchhiking. Bikes are a good means of transportation on one-lane roads, but avoid riding on the coastal path—it is illegal and dangerous.

Trains: (☎08457 484 950) run to **Cardiff** (3hr., 8-10 per day, £16.30) and **London Paddington** (4½hr., 7-9 per day, £67). Also to **Fishguard** on the north coast and **Tenby** and **Pembroke Dock** on the south (change at **Whitland**).

Buses: The free *Pembrokeshire Bus Timetables* and *Pembrokeshire Coastal Bus Services Timetables* are available at local TICs. Richards Brothers (☎02139 613 756) #411 runs from **Haverfordwest** to **Fishguard** (1½hr., 5 per day) via **St. David's** (45min., 11 per day). First Cymru (☎01792 580 580) runs from **Haverfordwest** to **Tenby** via **Pembroke** (#349; 1½hr., M-Sa every hr., Su 5 per day). Silcox Coaches (☎01646 683 143) and Taf Valley Coaches (☎01994 240 908) run from **Haverfordwest** to **Broad Haven** (#311; 20min., M-Sa 5 per day). The Puffin Shuttle #400 runs between **St. David's** and **Milford Haven** (2hr., 3 per day), and the Strumble Shuttle #404 connects **St. David's** and **Fishguard** (1½hr., 3 per day). First Cymru's **FirstDay Pass** (£5) gives unlimited bus transportation within Pembrokeshire on their buses, while the more useful **West Wales Rover Ticket** (£6.30) works all day on any bus.

Bike Rental: St. David's Cycle Hire, with **Voyages of Discovery,** Cross Sq. (☎01437 721 911), opposite Lloyd's Bank in St. David's. Helmets not provided. £10 per ½-day, £15 per day. Open daily 8am-7pm.

Outdoor Equipment: You can find everything from canoes to ponies for rental or guided lessons and trips. Check *Explore Pembrokeshire* or *Coast to Coast,* available at NPICs, for outdoor shop locations. Among the most popular outdoor activity centers is the excellent **TYF Adventure** (see **Crazy, or Coasteering?,** p. 479) in St. David's (☎01437 721 611 or 0800 132 588; www.tyf.com).

▌ PRACTICAL INFORMATION

The **National Park Information Centers (NPICs)** below sell annotated maps (from 40p) of the coastal path. The indispensable trail guide is pricey (£13) but detailed and includes color maps. Ask about guided walks offered by the park. For **weather information,** call any NPIC; in an emergency, contact **rescue rangers** at ☎999 or 112.

National Park Information Centres:

Newport: 2 Bank Cottages, Long St. (☎01239 820 912). Open June-Aug. M-Sa 10am-5:30pm, Su 10am-1:15pm; Apr.-May and Sept.-Oct. M-Sa 10am-5:30pm.

St. David's: The Grove (☎01437 720 392; www.stdavids.co.uk). Doubles as the town TIC. Open Easter-Oct. daily 9:30am-5:30pm; Nov.-Easter M-Sa 10am-4pm. Closed 2 weeks in Jan.

Tourist Information Centres:

Fishguard: see p. 485.

Haverfordwest: 19 Old Bridge (☎01437 763 110), adjacent to the bus stop. Open M-Sa Apr.-Sept. 9:30am-5:30pm; Oct.-Mar. 10am-4pm.

Milford Haven: 94 Charles St. (☎01646 690 866). Open Apr.-Oct. M-Sa 10am-1pm and 1:30-5pm.

Saundersfoot: The Barbecue, Harbour Car Park (☎01834 813 672). Open Apr.-Oct. daily 10am-5:30pm; Nov.-Mar. M and F-Sa 10am-4pm.

Tenby: see p. 481.

ACCOMMODATIONS

Many farmers convert fallow fields into summer **campsites** (about £4 per tent); inquire before pitching. Roads between Tenby, Pembroke, and St. David's are home to plenty of **B&Bs** (£15-30), but they fill quickly in summer, and buses are infrequent. Along the coastal path, the park's **YHA hostels**, listed below, are all within a day's walk of one another. If you plan at least two weeks ahead, you can book these by calling ☎08702 412 314 or visiting www.yha.org.uk.

Broad Haven (☎01437 781 688), on St. Bride's Bay off the B4341. Take bus #311 from Haverfordwest to Broad Haven (20min., 5 per day) or #400 from St. David's (35min., 3 per day) or Milford Haven (1¼hr., 3 per day). 77 beds near the beach. Lockout 10am-1pm. Curfew 11pm. Book in advance. Dorms £19, under 18 £16. MC/V. ❷

Manorbier, Skrinkle Haven (☎01834 871 803; manorbier@yha.org.uk). From the train station, walk past the A4139 to the castle, turn left onto the B4585, right to the army camp, and follow the signs. Modern building near the castle (p. 483). Access to laundry, kitchen, and computer lab with free Internet. Meals available. Lockout 10am-5pm. Curfew 10:30pm. Open daily Mar.-Oct. Dorms £15, under 18 £11. MC/V. ❷

Marloes Sands (☎01646 636 667), near the Dale Peninsula. Take Puffin bus #400 (1¼hr., 3 per day) from St. David's or Milford Haven; ask to be let off at the hostel. Farm buildings with access to a huge beach. Good site for water sports. Lockout 10am-5pm. Curfew 11pm. Open Apr.-Oct. Dorms £9.50, under 18 £7. MC/V. ❶

Pwll Deri (☎08707 706 004), set atop 300 ft. cliffs around Strumble Head near Fishguard. Lockout 10am-5pm. Curfew 11pm. Open from mid-July to Aug. daily; Sept.-Oct. and Apr.-June M and Th-Su. Dorms £11, under 18 £8. MC/V. ❶

St. David's (☎01437 720 345), near St. David's Head. From the A487 (Fishguard Rd.), turn onto the B4583 and follow signs from the golf club. Celtic Coaster bus runs every hr. in summer and drops off 1 mi. from St.

THE BIG SPLURGE

CRAZY, OR COASTEERING?

St. David's may be the birthplace of the Welsh patron saint, but in recent years, it's witnessed a different kind of *naissance:* the rise of a unique adventure sport (or insanity) called **coasteering.**

Picture it—you swim through churning waves to a rocky outcropping at the base of a cliff. You clamber out of the sea, then scale the rock face until you reach a ledge 30 ft. above. You pause and peer into the water far below. The crashing surf obscures the surface, but you know what to do: you draw in a deep breath, brace yourself, and take the plunge.

Inspired by Pembrokeshire's dramatic shoreline, coasteering is a thrilling combination of rock scrambling, cliff diving, and open-water swimming. You'll spend at least 3hr. navigating up and down the coast, so some level of fitness is required. Still, the beginning level trips are far from grueling, so coasteering is a surprisingly accessible sport.

TYF Adventure in St. David's specializes in coasteering and offers courses in three levels, from novice to advanced. A half-day of coasteering is £45 (children under 16 £30). TYF also offers weekend packages, including meals, two nights' stay in the TYF-run B&B, and multiple sessions of coasteering (£200).

Booking office on High St. in St. David's. ☎01347 721 611; www.tyf.com. Open daily 9am-5:30pm, longer in summer.

David's. Converted farm buildings. Men in the cowshed, women in the stables. Self-catering kitchen. Reception before 10am and 5pm-10pm. Open from mid-July to Aug. daily; Sept.-Oct. and from Apr. to mid-July W-Su. Dorms £14, under 18 £11. MC/V. ❷

🚶 🏞 HIKING AND OUTDOORS

For short hikes, stick to accessible **St. David's Peninsula** in the northwest. Otherwise, set out on the 186 mi. **Pembrokeshire Coast Path,** marked with acorn symbols. For general information on the path, call ☎0845 345 7275. Leaflets, available at NPICs and TICs for 50p, describe points of interest and transportation along individual sections of the path. Larger booklets describe four circular walks near towns ($1.50). The coast path begins in the southeast at Amroth and continues west across sandstone through Tenby. **Bosherton's Lily Ponds,** manmade inlets that bloom in early summer, circle around to St. Govan's Head, where steps lead to **St. Govan's Chapel.** The waters of the well are said to heal ills and grant wishes, and supposedly no mortal can count the steps. From here to **Elegug Stacks**—offshore rocks with the largest seabird colonies of the coastline—the path passes natural sea arches and limestone stacks. The famous 80 ft. **Green Bridge** is particularly striking. The stretch from St. Govan's Head to the Stacks (6 mi.) is sometimes used as an artillery range and closed to hikers. Call the **Castemartin Range Office** (☎01646 662 367) or the **Pembroke National Visitor Centre** (☎01646 622 388) for openings or check at the Tenby TIC. For 10 mi. west of the Stacks, the coast is permanently off-limits, and the path veers inland to **Freshwater West,** crossing industrial areas and passing **Stack Fort,** built to defend against the French.

From Freshwater West to **Angle Bay,** the coastline walk covers mild terrain. At Milford Haven, the path is cut by a large channel. From the Dale Peninsula, the path passes by the long beaches of **St. Bride's Bay, Marloes Sands,** and the **Three Chimneys,** columns of stone shaped by erosion. The path curves to **St. David's Head,** the site of many Iron Age hill settlements. Past St. David's at Abereiddi, the sea has re-filled an old slate quarry to create the **Blue Lagoon.** The final stretch of the Coastal Path, between Newport and St. Dogmaels, is strenuous—its total ascent is equal to that of Mt. Snowdon. The free *Explore Pembrokeshire,* available at TICs, gives trail tips and provides bus information. To explore Pembrokeshire by **horseback,** contact Heatherton Riding Centre (near Tenby; ☎01646 651 025; open Easter-Oct.; £13.50 per hr., novice ride £15 per hr.) or Maesgwynne Riding Stables (near Fishguard; ☎01348 872 659; david-llewhelin1@virgin.net; £12 per hr.).

🏝 ISLANDS OFF THE PEMBROKESHIRE COAST

GRASSHOLM AND SKOMER. On Grassholm, the most distant island, 35,000 pairs of gannets raise their young each year. **Dale Sailing Company** sails around, but not to, the island (3hr., M 12:30pm, £25). The boats leave from Martin's Haven on the Dale Peninsula and often encounter Manx shearwaters and storm petrels. (☎0800 028 4090; www.dale-sailing.co.uk.) The company sails more often to Skomer, a marine reserve for auks, seals, and puffins. (Tours Apr.-Oct. Tu-Su; usually 3 per day, call ahead. £8 boat fee, £6 landing fee; children £6, no landing fee.)

RAMSEY ISLAND. Owned by the Royal Society for the Protection of Birds, Ramsey Island hosts many rare seabirds and the largest gray seal colony in Wales off St. David's Peninsula. On the east side of the island lurk ▥**The Bitches,** a rock chain that has brought countless sailors to their doom. Thousand Islands Expeditions, Cross Sq., in St. David's, sails around the island from St. Justinian's lifeboat station. (☎01437 721 686; www.thousandislands.co.uk. 1½hr. Easter-Nov. daily 9am-6pm. £15, children £7.50; more extensive journeys from £20, children £12.) Voyages of Discovery and Ramsey Island Cruises, Cross Sq., in St. David's, runs tours and trips through rock gorges on specially designed rubber craft. (☎0800 854 367. Tours from £22, concessions £18, children £12.)

TENBY (DINBYCH-Y-PYSGOD)   ☎01834

Called "the Welsh Riviera," Tenby is neither a traditional Welsh town nor a polished seaside resort. The city's namesake, Dinbych-y-Pysgod, translates as "the little fort of the fishes." The colorful rows of beachfront guest houses, boutiques, and cafes are popular all year long, but Tenby sees huge crowds in July and August, when multitudes of English holidaymakers pour onto its beaches.

▐ TRANSPORTATION. The unstaffed **train station** is at the bottom of Warren St. Activity Wales, Tudor Sq., offers travel services. (☎844 000. Open M-Sa 9am-5pm.) **Trains** (☎08457 484 950; www.nationalrail.co.uk) depart to: Cardiff (2½hr., 4 per day, £16.30); Carmarthen (45min., 3 per day, £6); Pembroke (30min.; M-Sa 3 per day, Su 2 per day; £3.40); Swansea (1½hr., 3 per day, £9.60). **Buses** leave from the bulwark in front of the car park on Upper Park Rd. First Cymru (☎01792 580 580) goes to Haverfordwest via Pembroke (#349; M-Sa every hr. until 6:05pm, Su 4 per day), or head from Swansea to Carmarthen (X11; M-Sa 2 per hr.) and transfer to Silcox Coaches (☎842 189; www.silcoxcoaches.co.uk) bus #333 (1hr.; M and W-F 1 per day, Tu and Sa 2 per day). A Silcox Coaches office is in the Town Hall Arcade between South Parade and Upper Frog St. National Express (☎08705 808 080) also runs to Swansea (#508; 1½hr., 3 per day, £7). **First Cymru FirstDay Saver** (£5) and **FirstWeek Saver** (£18) allow unlimited weekly travel within Pembrokeshire on First buses, while the **West Wales Rover Ticket** (£6.30) works on all bus lines. **Taxis** congregate near pubs on Friday and Saturday nights; call Tenby's Taxis (☎843 678).

◢▮ ORIENTATION AND PRACTICAL INFORMATION. Tenby sits on a small section of land that juts out from the coast, coming to a point at **Castle Hill.** The town overlooks and is bordered by **North Beach** and **South Beach.** The train station is on **Warren Street,** which approaches the town and becomes **White Lion Street** before it veers north and reaches the cliff promenade above North Beach, **The Norton.** Off White Lion St., **South Parade** and **Upper Frog Street** run parallel through town toward South Beach, separated by the remnants of the **town wall.** Toward Castle Hill, The Norton divides into **Crackwell Street,** which leads to the castle, and **High Street,** which leads to **Tudor Square.** Away from Castle Hill, **The Croft** turns north off The Norton and follows the coastline above North Beach.

The **Tourist Information Centre,** on Upper Park Rd. by the bus station and Somerfield, gives out free accommodations listings. (☎842 404. Bookings £2 plus a 10% deposit. Open June-Aug. daily 9:30am-5pm; Sept.-May M-Sa 10am-4pm.) Other services include: Barclays **bank,** 18 High St. (the **ATM** is on Frog St.; open M-F 9am-4:30pm); Washeteria **launderette,** Lower Frog St. (☎842 484; wash £1.70-2.60, dry 20p per 5min., soap 20p; open daily M-Sa 8:30am-9pm, Su 10am-4pm); **police,** Warren St. (☎0845 330 2000), near the church off White Lion St.; Tenby Cottage **Hospital,** Church Park Rd. (☎842 040), near Trafalgar Rd.; Boots **pharmacy,** High St. (☎842 120; open M-Sa 9am-5:30pm); **Internet** access at Tenby County **Library,** Greenhill Ave. (☎843 934; free; open M and W-F 9:30am-5pm, Tu 9:30am-6pm, Sa 9:30am-12:30pm), or at **Webb Computers,** Warren St. (☎844 101; £1 per 20min.; open M-F 9am-5pm, Sa 9am-4pm); and the **post office,** Warren St., at South Parade (☎843 213; open M-F 8:30am-5:30pm, Sa 8:30am-12:30pm). **Post Code:** SA70 7JR.

▐ ACCOMMODATIONS. On **Warren Street,** outside the town wall near the train station, **B&Bs** (£20-26) line the sidewalks. The side streets of **Greenhill Avenue** and those off the Esplanade, Southcliffe St., and Trafalgar Rd. have almost as many. You can also take a bus to **Saundersfoot** (#352; in summer M-Sa every hr., Su 1-2 per hr.). Overlooking North Beach, bright rooms await in the **Blue Dolphin Hotel ❷**, St. Mary's St. (☎842 590. Rooms £21 per person; ensuite with breakfast £30. MC/V.) Nearby at **Myrtle House Hotel ❸**, St. Mary's St., the welcoming proprietor offers ensuite rooms and a full breakfast. (☎842 508. Rooms £30 per person. MC/V.) **Lyndale ❸**, Warren St., has ensuite rooms that may have you spending more time in bed than on the beach. (☎842 836. Singles May-Sept. £30; Oct.-Apr. £23. Cash only.) Campers head to **Meadow Farm ❶**, at the top of The Croft, overlooking North Beach. (☎844 829. Open Easter-Sept. £6. Free showers. Cash only.)

🍴 **FOOD.** Most of Tenby's restaurants cater to vacationers and charge accordingly. Lunch specials can soften the blow at nicer eateries. Lower Frog St. has several cheap takeaways. **Tenby Market Hall,** between High St. and Upper Frog St., sells deli goods and baked treats. (Open July-Sept. daily 8:30am-5pm; Oct.-June M-Sa 8:30am-5pm.) A Somerfield **supermarket** is located on Upper Park Rd. (Open M-Sa 8am-9pm, Su 10am-4pm.) The sandwich crafters at **The Country Kitchen ❶**, Upper Frog St., have turned the stuffed baguette into a science. (☎843 539. Baguettes from £2.10. Sandwiches from £1.50. Open daily in summer 9:30am-4pm; in winter M-Sa 9:30am-4pm. Cash only.) In an alleyway connecting Bridge St. and St. Julian's St., a jungle of flowers marks **Plantagenet House ❹**, Quay Hill. Diners feast by candlelight on organic Welsh pork with cheddar and chives (£8) or local sea bass (£21) in the hearth of the oldest (10th century) and tallest (39 ft.) medieval Flemish chimney in Wales. Dinners are pricey, but lunch starts at £5. (☎842 350. Starters from £6, entrees from £17. Open Easter-Oct. daily noon-3pm and 6pm-late; Nov.-Easter F-Sa 6pm-late, Su noon-3pm. MC/V.) **The Ceramic Cafe ❷**, St. George's St., has pottery painting activities (from £4.50) in addition to sandwiches and cakes. (☎845 968. Food from £3. Open M-Sa 10am-5pm. MC/V.)

📷📷 **SIGHTS AND BEACHES.** A sun-bleached **Prince Albert the Good** stands atop Castle Hill, overlooking the ruins of the castle and colorful Tenby. On clear days, the views reach across Carmarthen Bay, Rhossili Beach's Worm's Head, and the Devon coast. In a renovated section of the castle, the **Tenby Museum and Art Gallery** has a wax recreation of the Tenby Pirate "Leekie Porridge" and details the ravages of John Paul Jones along the coast. (☎842 809. Open Easter-Nov. daily 10am-5pm; Dec.-Easter M-F 10am-5pm. £3, concessions £2.50, children £1.50.) The three floors of the **Tudor Merchant's House**, on Quay Hill off Bridge St., reveal much about life in a 16th-century Welsh household, with staff in each room to point out highlights. (☎842 279. Open daily Apr.-Oct. M-F and Su 10am-5pm. £2.50, children £1.20, families £6.20.) At night, Tenby's ghouls share the streets with resort revelers. The guided 1½hr. **Walk of Tenby** and **Ghost Walk of Tenby** depart from the Lifeboat Tavern in Tudor Sq. at 8pm. (☎845 841. From mid-June to mid-Sept. daily; from mid-Sept. to mid-May M-Sa. Advance booking required. £4, concessions £3.75, children £3, families £13.)

On sunny days, **North Beach,** below the Croft, and **South Beach,** beyond the Esplanade, swarm with pensioners and toddlers. At the eastern tip of Tenby, **Castle Beach** reaches into caves that lure curious explorers, but more remote beaches offer escape from the oceanside throng. A variety of **boat excursions** leave from the harbor; check the kiosks at Castle Beach (Apr.-Sept. ☎07980 864 509, Oct.-Mar. 07973 280 651) for the "Seal Safari," a 1hr. boat ride to St. Margaret's Island and Cathedral Caves (£12, children £7), or the Sunset Cruise, a 2hr. excursion held only in July and August (£9.50, children £5.50).

➤ DAYTRIPS FROM TENBY

CALDEY ISLAND. Three miles south of Tenby, this largely unspoiled island hosts a diverse community of seabirds, seals, and 20 Cistercian monks, who produce perfume from indigenous lavender in their Italianate monastery. The **chocolate factory,** inspired by the monks' Belgian roots, turns out over 12 tons of sweets per year (bars from £1.10), sold on the island and in a shop in Tenby. *(Caldey Boats sails from Tenby Harbor. ☎844 453; www.caldey-island.co.uk. Cruises 20min. Easter-Oct. 3 per hr. M-Sa 10am-3pm; last round-trip 5pm, weather permitting. Round-trip £10, children £5, seniors £9.)*

DYLAN THOMAS BOATHOUSE. Dylan Thomas spent his last four years in the boat house in **Laugharne** (LAN), about 15 mi. northeast. The boathouse contains original furniture, toys dug up from the garden, and a recreated version of Thomas's writing shed. *(Take First Cymru bus #351 to Pendine. 50min., every 2hr. Transfer to #222, which goes from Pendine to Laugharne. 12min., M-Sa 10 per day. ☎01994 427 420; www.dylanthomasboathouse.com. Open daily May-Oct. 10am-5:30pm; Nov.-Apr. 10:30am-3:30pm. £3.50, concessions £2.75, children £1.75.)*

MANORBIER CASTLE. Gerald of Wales, a noted 12th-century historian of rural life, called Manorbier "the pleasantest spot in Wales." He may have been a little biased (he was born here), but the castle is certainly a contender for that title. It offers stunning views of Manorbier beach and gardens. Life-size wax figures inside the castle attempt to recreate scenes of medieval life and Welsh legend. *(First Cymru bus #349 shuttles between Tenby, Manorbier, Pembroke, and Haverfordwest. M-Sa every hr., in summer Su 3 per day. ☎01834 871 394. Open daily Easter-Sept. 10am-6pm. £3.50, children £1.50, seniors and students £2.50.)* Manorbier has a **YHA hostel ❷** (p. 479) as well as numerous **B&Bs.**

CAREW CASTLE. Handsome Carew Castle, 5 mi. northwest of Tenby, is an odd mixture of Norman fortress and Elizabethan manor. Strong defensive towers give way to large, delicate windows. Check *Coast to Coast,* free at most TICs, for events at the castle. *(Take Silcox bus #361 from Tenby to the castle. 45min., M-Sa 3 per day. ☎01646 651 782. Open daily Mar.-Oct. 10am-5pm. Tours at 2:30pm. Castle and mill £3.50, concessions £2.50, children £1.50, families £8.)*

PEMBROKE (PENFRO)   ☎01646

In a county known as "Little England beyond Wales," Pembroke no longer feels like the military stronghold its Norman occupants designed. Battlements that once formed anti-Cromwell resistance now shade hungry picnickers, and the waters that once served to protect the castle now harbor swans.

▐ TRANSPORTATION. Pembroke's unstaffed **train station** is on Lower Lamphey Rd. at the opposite end of Main St. from the castle. **Trains** (☎08457 484 950) run from Pembroke and Pembroke Dock to Tenby (20min., 7 per day, £3.40), Swansea (2hr.; M-F 6 per day, Sa 7 per day, Su 3 per day; £9.60), and points farther east. In Pembroke, **buses** going east stop outside the Somerfield supermarket; those going north stop at the castle. National Express (☎08705 808 080) goes to Cardiff via Swansea (3¾hr., 3 per day, £14) and London (6¾hr., 2 per day, £26.50). First Cymru (☎01792 580 580) #349 stops in Pembroke and at Pembroke Dock on its route between Tenby (40-50min.; M-Sa every hr., Su 5 per day; £2-3) and Haverfordwest (35-40min.; M-Sa every hr., Su 5 per day).

SOUTH WALES

■ ☎ ORIENTATION AND PRACTICAL INFORMATION. Pembroke Castle lies up the hill on the western end of **Main Street;** the street's other end (at the train station) fans into five roads from a roundabout. Across the river and to the north is **Pembroke Docks.** Downhill from Pembroke's town center, the **Tourist Information Centre,** Commons Rd., has displays on the Pembrokeshire Coastal Path. The staff books accommodations for £2 plus a 10% deposit. (☎ 622 388. Open daily July-Oct. 10am-5:30pm; Easter-June 10am-5pm.) Other services include: Barclays **bank,** 35 Main St. (open M-F 9am-5pm); Pembroke Dock **police,** 4 Water St. (☎ 682 121); the Pembroke Dock **hospital,** Fort Rd. (☎ 682 114); Mendus **pharmacy,** 31 Main St. (☎ 682 370; open M-F 9am-6pm, Sa 9am-1pm); **Internet** access at the Pembroke **library,** 38 Main St. (☎ 682 973; free; open Tu open F 10am-1pm and 2-5pm, W and Sa 10am-1pm, Th 10am-1pm and 2-7pm; book ahead), and at **Dragon Alley,** 63 Main St. (☎ 621 456; £1 per 15min., £3 per hr.; open Tu-Sa 10am-5pm); and the **post office,** 49 Main St. (☎ 682 737; open M-F 9am-5:30pm, Sa 9am-1pm). **Post Code:** SA71 4JT.

☎ ☖ ACCOMMODATIONS AND FOOD. The nearest **YHA hostel** is in Manorbier between Tenby and Pembroke (p. 479). The few **B&Bs** in Pembroke are scattered, although some options are on Main St. Singles are scarce, so book ahead. Mrs. Willis fosters an elegant atmosphere at her bright blue ■**Beech House ❷,** 78 Main St. With crystal chandeliers, you'll be amazed that you aren't spending more. (☎ 683 740. £17.50 per person. Cash only.) **Woodbine ❸,** 84 Main St., pampers with ensuite rooms with TV and flowers. (☎ 686 338. £25 per person. Cash only.)

Stock up at Somerfield **supermarket,** 6-10 Main St. (Open M-Sa 8am-8pm, Su 10am-4pm.) Wisebuys **grocery,** 19 Main St., has an assortment of local jams. (☎ 687 046. Open M-Sa 7am-5:45pm.) **Comfort Zone Bakery ❶,** on Main St., bakes a tempting array of quiches and pastries (£2-3). The Ploughman's lunches and jacket potatoes (both starting at £4) are delicious. (☎ 814 582. Open M-Sa 9:30am-4pm. MC/V.) Across the Northgate St. bridge is **Watermans Arms ❷,** 2 The Green, where locals and tourists alike enjoy quality pub fare on the waterfront patio. (☎ 682 718. Open daily Easter-Oct. noon-11pm; winter hours vary. Food served noon-10pm.)

◖ SIGHTS. Austere ■**Pembroke Castle** shadows Pembroke's Main St. Today, the castle's stone chambers provide hours of exploration. Henry VII, founder of the Tudor dynasty, was born in one of the seven massive towers. The **Great Keep** rises 75 ft., and visitors ascend more than 100 slippery steps to reach its domed top. The underground gloom of **Wogan's Cavern** provided shelter for Stone Age cave-dwellers. (☎ 684 585; www.pembrokecastle.co.uk. Open daily Apr.-Sept. 9:30am-6pm; Mar. and Oct. 10am-5pm; Nov.-Feb. 10am-4pm. £3.50, concessions £2.50, families £10. Tours May-Aug. M-F and Su 4 per day. £1.) Located in a converted Methodist Church, **The Pembroke Antiques Centre,** Wesley Chapel, on Main St., has a motley collection of knick-knacks. (☎ 687 017. Open M-Sa 10am-5pm.)

ST. DAVID'S (TYDDEWI)   ☎ 01437

St. David's is the smallest city in Britain. It is little more than a few streets curled around a central village green, but its impressive cathedral has been a favored destination among pilgrims for almost a millennium. In the Middle Ages, two pilgrimages to St. David's were considered equivalent to one trip to Rome.

◪ ☎ TRANSPORTATION AND PRACTICAL INFORMATION. Pick up the *Pembrokeshire Bus Timetables,* free at any Pembrokeshire TIC. The Richards Brothers (☎ 01239 613 756) Haverfordwest-Fishguard **bus** hugs the coast via St. David's (#411; 50min. from both; M-Sa 5-6 per day to Fishguard, 11 per day to Haverfordwest; Su 1 per day to Fishguard, 4 per day to Haverfordwest). Other buses terminate at St. David's during the week. For a cab, call Tony's **taxis** (☎ 720 931).

The **National Park Information Center** is in Cross Sq. until summer 2008, when it will return to its location on High St. (☎720 392; www.stdavids.co.uk. Open Easter-Oct. daily 9:30am-5:30pm; Nov.-Easter M-Sa 10am-4pm.) Other services include: Barclays **bank,** at High St. and New St. (open M-F 9:30am-4pm); **police,** High St. (☎0845 330 2000); St. David's **pharmacy,** 13-14 Cross Sq. (☎720 243; open M-F 9am-6:30pm, Sa 9am-4:30pm); free **Internet** access at the **library,** in City Hall, on High St. (open Tu and F 10am-1pm and 2-5:30pm); and the **post office,** 13 New St. (☎720 283; open M-F 9am-5:30pm, Sa 9am-1pm). **Post Code:** SA62 6SW.

⌂ ⌂ ACCOMMODATIONS AND FOOD. The **YHA St. David's ❶** (p. 479) lies 2 mi. northwest of town at the foot of a rocky outcrop near St. David's Head. **Pen Albro ❷,** 18 Goat St., offers colorful rooms for a low price in the center of St. David's. (☎721 865. £20 per person.) Beautiful **Alandale ❸,** 43 Nun St., has lovely ensuite rooms and a balcony with cathedral and sea views. (☎720 404. £35 per person.) In the center of town, **The Coach House ❷,** 15 High St., has clean lodgings, all with TV and mostly ensuite. The breakfast menu caters to special dietary needs using local organic items. (☎720 632. £25 per person, children £12.50. £10 deposit. MC/V.)

At **Pebbles Yard Gallery and Espresso Bar ❶,** Cross Sq., a cafe serves generous portions of stuffed pitas, salads, and coffee in a trendy loft. (☎720 122. Open daily 9:30am-5:30pm. Cash only.) Across the street is **Chapel Chocolates ❶,** The Pebbles, whose ice cream became so popular that the cathedral had to prohibit its consumption inside. (☎720 023; www.chapelchocolates.com. Open daily 10am-5:30pm. AmEx/MC/V.) **Cartref ❷,** 23 Cross Sq., serves breakfast from £4, and classic pub fare in the evening. (☎720 422. Open daily Mar.-May 9:30am-2:30pm and 6:30-8:30pm; June-Aug. 9:30am-10pm. MC/V.) A **supermarket,** CK Foodstores, can be found on New St. (☎721 127. Open daily 7am-10pm. MC/V.)

◉ SIGHTS. St. David's Cathedral, perhaps the finest in Wales, stands below the village. It dates from the 6th century, when David and his followers lived ascetic lives in isolation. Construction on the current building started in the late 1100s. Modern-day pilgrims file past the **reliquary** reputed to hold the bones of St. David, patron saint of Wales, and his comrade St. Justinian. The latter was killed on nearby Ramsey Island but, with saintly conscientiousness, carried his own head back to the mainland. In the St. Thomas à Becket **chapel,** a stained-glass window portrays three surly knights jabbing swords at the martyr. (☎720 060; www.stdavidscathedral.org.uk. Open M-Sa 8:30am-6pm, Su 12:45-5:45pm, and for evening services. Suggested donation £3, concessions £2, children £1.) Those with a love for pealing bells are welcome to sit in on a ringer's practice session in the tower. (W and F 7:45-9pm, Su 10:45-11:10am and 5:30-6pm. Suggested donation £1.) The **Bishop's Palace,** a collection of ruins across a stream from the cathedral, was built by Bishop Henry Gower in the 14th century. (☎720 517. Open June-Sept. daily 9:30am-6pm; Oct. and Apr.-May daily 9:30am-5pm; Nov.-Mar. M-Sa 9:30am-4pm, Su 11am-4pm. £3, concessions £2.50, families £8.30.) A mile south of town, near the coast, the walls of **St. Non's Chapel** mark St. David's birthplace. Water from the nearby well, free for the taking, supposedly cures all ills; take Goat St. downhill and follow the signs. Tours run to **Ramsey Island,** off the coast (p. 480).

FISHGUARD ☎01348

Buses run from Fishguard to smaller villages on the Pembrokeshire Coast, making the town a convenient hub for the region. The area offers many scenic walks and short hikes, while longer coastal paths hug the cliffs. Proud of their maritime history, Fishguard's pubs play host to numerous local legends of smugglers' caves and pirate attacks.

SOUTH WALES

TRANSPORTATION. Trains (☎ 08457 484 950) leave Fishguard Harbour for London via Bristol, Newport, Cardiff, Swansea, and Whitland (4½hr., 2 per day, £67). **Buses** stop at Fishguard Sq. Ask at the TIC for a free bus and train timetable. To travel north, take Richards Brothers (☎ 01239 613 756) buses to Cardigan (#412; 45min., M-Sa 13 per day, £3-4) and Aberystwyth (#550 or X50; 2hr., M-Sa 8 per day). Take First Cymru (☎ 01792 580 580) buses to Haverfordwest (#412; 45min., every hr.) and change to #349 for Tenby or Pembroke (#349; 1hr.; M-Sa every hr., Su 5 per day; £2.40). Town bus #410 shuttles between Fishguard Harbour and Fishguard Sq. (5min., 2 per hr., 45p). Merv's **taxis** (☎ 875 129) are on call 24hr.

PRACTICAL INFORMATION. The **Tourist Information Centre,** in the Town Hall in Market Sq., books rooms for £2 plus a 10% deposit. (☎ 873 484. Open Easter-Oct. M-W and F-Sa 9:30am-5pm, Th 9:30am-6:30pm, Su 10am-4pm; Nov.-Easter M-Sa 10am-4pm.) Other services include: Barclays **bank,** across from the TIC (open M-F 9am-5pm); **police,** Brodog Terr. (☎ 0845 330 2000); a **launderette,** Brodog Terr. (☎ 872 140; wash £2.20, dry 80p; open M-Sa 8:30am-5:30pm; last wash 4:30pm); free **Internet** access at the **library** in the Town Hall (☎ 872 694; open M-Tu and F 9:30am-1pm and 2-5pm, W and Sa 9:30am-1pm, Th 9:30am-1pm and 2-6:30pm); Boots **pharmacy,** Market Sq. (☎ 872 856; open M-Sa 9am-5:30pm); and the **post office,** 57 West St. (☎ 873 863; open M-F 9am-5:30pm, Sa 9am-12:30pm). **Post Code:** SA65 9NG.

ACCOMMODATIONS AND FOOD. B&Bs (from £20) are on High St. in Upper Fishguard. **Hamilton Guest House and Backpackers Lodge ❷,** 21-23 Hamilton St., has a book-lined TV lounge, toast-and-tea breakfasts, and a sauna. (☎ 874 797; www.fishguard-backpackers.com. £14. Cash only.) **Avon House ❷,** 76 High St., offers pristine rooms 5min. from the town center. (☎ 874 476; www.avonhouse.co.uk. £20 per person; ensuite £22.50. Cash only.) **Y Pantri ❶,** 31 West St., makes filled baguettes (£1.75) and pasties (£1), although the array of cakes and pastries may prove more tempting. (☎ 872 637. Open M-Sa 9am-5:30pm. Cash only.) **The Taj Mahal ❷,** 22 High St., serves a variety of curries. (☎ 874 593. Entrees from £5. Restaurant open daily 5-11:30pm. Takeaway 5pm-midnight. MC/V.) **The Old Coach House ❷,** High St., has pub food (£4-10) and draws a young crowd. (☎ 875 429. Sa night live music. Open M-F 11am-11pm, Sa 11am-1am, Su noon-10:30pm. Food served noon-2:30pm and 6-9pm. Cover Sa after 10:30pm £2. AmEx/MC/V.)

SIGHTS AND NIGHTLIFE. The **Marine Walk,** a paved path that follows the coastline through woods and along grassy cliffs, is marked by plaques with historical trivia about pirates and cross-dressing rioters. Ramblers can also see **Goodwick Harbor,** where the flagship *Lusitania* stopped on its ill-fated voyage from Liverpool to New York in 1915. **Preseli Venture,** based in nearby Mathry, offers half- and full-day adventures that include sea kayaking, surfing, and awesome coasteering. (☎ 837 709. 18+. £45 per ½-day. All-inclusive weekend £175-195.) During the day, sunbathers dot pebbly **Goodwick Beach.** Inquire at the TIC about hikes into the **Preseli Hills,** ancient grounds full of stone circles and a mysterious standing stone. Weekend nightlife erupts into a lively pub scene. **The Old Coach House** is the place to be, but all the pubs along **High Street** see some action until 11pm. **The Royal Oak,** West St. at Market Sq., is proud of its history—the infamous "last invasion" surrender treaty was signed here in 1797 after some misguided Napoleonic troops ran out of supplies. The pub keeps the original table on display and serves pub food starting at £7. (☎ 872 514. F-Sa Live music. Open M-Sa 11am-midnight, Su noon-10:30pm. Food served noon-2pm and 6-9pm.)

SOUTH WALES

NORTH WALES

North Wales is a land of impressive fortresses. Edward I built an "iron ring" of castles in the 12th century to aid in his campaigns against the Welsh kings, who defended their land in the natural strongholds of Snowdonia. Their patriotism is still evident in signs printed only in Welsh and devotion to local traditions. To escape the crowds swarming the coastal castles, head to Snowdonia National Park, which spans most of northwest Wales. To the west, the Llŷn Peninsula's sandy beaches beckon; to the northwest, the Isle of Anglesey is rich in prehistoric remains; and to the east, quiet villages sit in the Vale of Conwy.

HIGHLIGHTS OF NORTH WALES

SCALE one of many craggy peaks at **Snowdonia National Park** (p. 501), land of high moors, dark pine forests, and deep glacial lakes.

FROLIC in the refreshing streams and unspoiled surroundings of villages like Betws-y-Coed (p. 498) in the **Vale of Conwy.**

ADMIRE Edward I's castles at **Beaumaris** (p. 515), **Caernarfon** (p. 504), **Conwy** (p. 493), and **Harlech** (p. 505).

ABERYSTWYTH   ☎ 01970

Home of the largest university in Wales, Aberystwyth (ah-ber-RIST-with) thrives on youthful vigor. Where 19th-century vacationers once enjoyed the frivolities of resort living, bars now buzz with spirited academics during the school year. In the summer months, the Georgian boardwalk is awash with activity as locals and holidaymakers thread through shopping districts and take in bayside breezes.

▐ TRANSPORTATION

A transport hub for all of Wales, Aberystwyth sits at the end of a rail line running from Birmingham, England.

Train Station: On Alexandra Rd. Office open M-F 6:20am-5:25pm, Sa 6:20am-3:20pm. Trains (☎08457 484 950) to **Machynlleth** (30min.; M-Sa 9 per day, Su 6 per day; £4) and **Shrewsbury** (1¾hr.; M-Sa 7 per day, Su 4-5 per day; £16.60). Machynlleth is the southern terminus of the Cambrian Coaster line, which runs from **Pwllheli.** The **Day Ranger** ticket covers travel on the line (£7, children £3.50, families £13.20). The Vale of Rheidol Railway (☎625 819) goes to Devil's Bridge (p. 491).

Bus Station: On Alexandra Rd., beside the train station. National Express (☎08705 808 080) to **London** (8hr., noon, £28) via **Birmingham** (7hr., 1pm, £22.50). TrawsCambria bus #701 to **Cardiff** via **Swansea** (4hr., 2 per day). Arriva Cymru (☎08706 082 608) to **Bangor** via **Porthmadog** (X32; 3½hr.; M-Sa 5 per day, Su 2 per day), and **Machynlleth** (#32; 45min., M-Sa 7 per day, £2.80). Richard Brothers (☎01239 613 756) to **Cardigan** via **Synod Inn** (#550/X50; 1hr., M-Sa 6 per day). Arriva Cymru/Summerdale Coaches (☎01348 840 270) runs the same route twice on Su. **Day Rover** tickets (£6.30, children £4.20 or £3.15 with paying adult) are valid on most buses in the Ceredigion, Carmarthenshire, and Pembrokeshire areas. The **North and Mid-Wales Rover** is valid on buses and trains on the North Wales main line, the Conwy Valley, and the Cambrian Line (1-day £20, 3-day £30, 7-day £44).

Taxis: Express (☎612 319).

🔢 PRACTICAL INFORMATION

Tourist Information Centre: Lisburn House, Terrace Rd. (☎612 125). Books rooms for £2 plus a 10% deposit. Open July-Aug. daily 10am-6pm; Sept.-June M-Sa 10am-5pm.

Launderette: Wash 'n' Spin 'n' Dry, 16 Bridge St. (☎820 891). Wash £2.20, dry 20p, soap 10p. Bring change. Open M-F and Su 7am-9pm, Sa 8am-9pm. Last wash 8:30pm.

Bank: Barclays, 26 Terrace Rd. (☎653 353). Open M-F 9am-5pm.

Police: Blvd. St. Brieuc (☎0845 330 2000), at the end of Park Ave.

Hospital: Bronglais General Hospital, Caradog Rd. (☎623 131), off Penglais Rd.

Pharmacy: Boots, Terrace Rd. Open M-F 9am-6pm, Sa 9am-5:30pm, Su 10am-4pm.

Internet Access: Library, Corporation St. (☎633 703), at the corner of Baker St. Free. Book ahead. Open M-F 9:30am-8pm, Sa 9:30am-5pm.

Post Office: 8 Great Darkgate St. (☎632 630). **Bureau de change.** Open M and W-F 9am-5:30pm, Tu 9:30am-5:30pm, Sa 9am-12:30pm. **Post Code:** SY23 1DE.

🏠 ACCOMMODATIONS

Aberystwyth's streets overflow with **B&Bs** (from £20) and more upscale seaside **hotels,** especially near the beachfront.

Maes-y-Môr, 25 Bath St. (☎639 270). Cheap option just a block away from the ocean. Rooms have access to a common kitchen. Launderette on ground fl. £2 wash, dryer 20p per 4min., soap 70p. Singles £20. Cash only. ❷

The Cambria, Marine Terr. (☎626 350; www.thecambria.co.uk). Student housing with rooms available July-Aug. Ocean views. Singles £15-25; twins £25-35. Cash only. ❷

Sunnymead B&B, 34 Bridge St. (☎617 273). Cheerful, yellow-trimmed home with hospitality to match. Bright, cozy rooms with TV. £25 per person. MC/V. ❷

YHA Borth (☎871 498; borth@yha.co.uk), 8 mi. north of Aberystwyth, overlooking the ocean. Take the train to Borth, or ride Crosville bus #511 or 512 and ask to stop at the hostel. From the train station, turn right onto the main road and walk 5min. Internet access, kitchen, and laundry. Lockout 10am-5pm. Curfew 11pm. Open daily Mar.-Oct. with 48hr. notice; Nov.-Feb. call ahead. Dorms £12, under 18 £9. MC/V. ❶

Midfield Caravan Park (☎612 542; www.midfieldcaravanpark.co.uk), 1½ mi. from town on the A4120, 200 yd. uphill from the A487 junction. From Alexandra Rd., take any bus to Southgate. Turn left for Devil's Bridge and walk 200 yd. uphill. Lovely site with views of town. £9, 2 people £14; each additional person £2. Electricity £2.50. Cash only. ❶

🍴 FOOD

Pier Street takeaways are cheap, as are beachside shacks and some sit-down restaurants. Spar **market,** 32 Terrace Rd., is open 24hr. A picnic at the castle will save you some money and gives great views.

The Treehouse Cafe, 14 Baker St. (☎615 791; www.treehousewales.co.uk). Feel wholesome when eating your veggie burger (£5.75) or any one of the daily specials (£6 and up)—they're all organic, as are the various fruits and vegetables sold on the ground fl. Cafe open M-Sa 9am-5pm. Food store open M-Th 9am-6pm, F 9am-6:30pm, Sa 9am-5pm. MC/V. ❷

Fresh Ground Cafe, Cambrian Pl. (☎611 472), off Terrace Rd. Trendy but comfortable vibe, with globe lanterns in bright dining rooms. Grab a leather couch and sip a steaming mocha (£1.40). Open daily 10am-11pm. Cash only. ❶

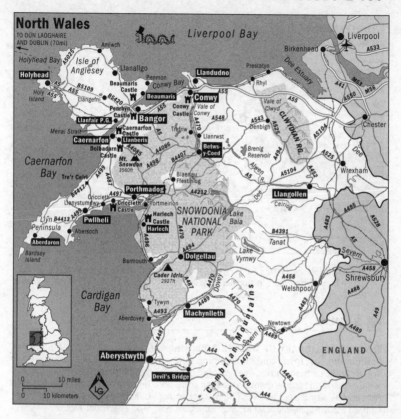

North Wales

Liverpool Bay

TO DÚN LAOGHAIRE AND DUBLIN (70mi)

Holyhead Bay

Amlwch

Llanallgo

Isle of Anglesey

Holyhead

Holy Island

Llangefni

Beaumaris Castle

Penmon

Conwy Bay

Prestatyn

Llandudno

Rhyl

Liverpool

Birkenhead

Beaumaris

Conwy

Vale of Clwyd

Chester

Penrhyn Castle

Llanfair P.G.

Bangor

Conwy Castle

Vale of Conwy

Denbigh

CLWYDIAN RG.

Caernarfon

Caernarfon Castle

Trefriw

Llanrwst

Dolbadarn Castle

Llanberis

Betws-y-Coed

Brenig Reservoir

Wrexham

Caernarfon Bay

Tre'r Ceiri

Mt. Snowdon 3560ft

Blaenau Ffestiniog

Alwen R.

Porthmadog

Criccieth

Criccieth Castle

Portmeirion

SNOWDONIA NATIONAL PARK

Llangollen

Ceiriog

Llanystumdwy

Llŷn Peninsula

Pwllheli

Harlech Castle

Harlech

Lake Bala

Tanat

Severn

Abersoch

Aberdaron

Bardsey Island

Barmouth

Dolgellau

Lake Vyrnwy

Shrewsbury

Cardigan Bay

Cader Idris 2927ft

Welshpool

Tywyn

Aberdovey

Machynlleth

Newtown

ENGLAND

Aberystwyth

Devil's Bridge

0   10 miles
0   10 kilometers

Spartacus, Terrace Rd. (☎627 799). Offers basic panini and baguettes (from £2) and a salad bar in a small seating area. Second location across town on Northgate St. is take-away only. Open M-Sa 8am-6pm, Su 9am-5:30pm. Cash only. ❶

PUBS AND CLUBS

The Academy, St. James Sq. (☎636 852). This converted chapel piles bottles of absinthe (£3.20 per shot) on the organ. Barflies flank the pulpit, watching the 16 ft. screen. M-Th and Su drink specials. Open M-W noon-11pm, Th-F noon-midnight, Sa 11am-midnight, Su noon-11pm. Food served noon-3pm and 6-8:30pm.

Rummer's, Pont Trefechan Bridge (☎625 177). A vine-covered riverside beer garden packed with students. Views of the nearby bridge and hills. W DJ, Th-Sa live music. Happy hour M-Th and Su 7-9:30pm. Open M-Th and Su 7pm-1am, F-Sa 6pm-2am.

Lord Beechings, Alexandra Rd. (☎625 069). Dark wood interior and an enormous array of comfort foods (most under £6). Open M-Sa 11am-11pm, Su noon-10:30pm. Food served W-F and Su noon-3pm, Sa noon-7pm.

Pier Pressure, The Royal Pier, Marine Terr. (☎636 100). Mirrors quake and clubbers shake. Th rocks to 60s-80s tunes. F-Sa "Cheese Factory" pulls a young crowd. Cover Tu and Th-F £4, Sa £6. Th-F £1 drinks. Open Tu and Th-F 10:30pm-3am, Sa 10:30pm-4am.

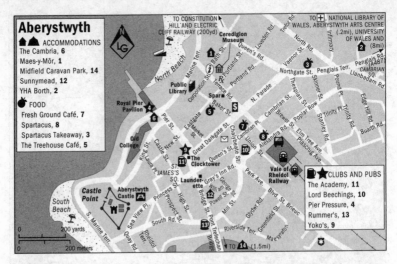

Aberystwyth

▲■ ACCOMMODATIONS
The Cambria, 6
Maes-y-Môr, 1
Midfield Caravan Park, 14
Sunnymead, 12
YHA Borth, 2

🍴 FOOD
Fresh Ground Café, 7
Spartacus, 8
Spartacus Takeaway, 3
The Treehouse Café, 5

🍺★ CLUBS AND PUBS
The Academy, 11
Lord Beechings, 10
Pier Pressure, 4
Rummer's, 13
Yoko's, 9

Yoko's, 12 Pier St. (☎623 963). Young clubbers crowd comfy couches and a steamy dance floor. Crowd thins in summer. Cover after 10:30pm F £4, Sa £5. Open M-W and Su 10pm-3am, Th-Sa 10pm-4am.

🔘 SIGHTS

■**NATIONAL LIBRARY OF WALES.** Occupying a grand classical building overlooking the sea, town, and surrounding cliffs, this library houses almost every Welsh book or manuscript ever printed. The **Gregynog Gallery** features work by local artists and rotates displays ranging from bookbinding to Welsh homelife. (Off Penglais Rd., past the hospital. ☎632 800; www.llgc.org.uk. Reading room open M-F 9:30am-6pm, Sa 9:30am-5pm, free ticket required. Exhibitions open M-Sa 10am-5pm. Free.)

ELECTRIC CLIFF RAILWAY. At the northern end of the promenade, an electric railcar has been creaking up the steep 430 ft. slope of Constitution Hill since 1896. At the top is a frisbee golf course and the world's largest camera obscura. The camera's crisp magnification led some locals to protest on grounds that viewers could peer into their windows. (☎617 642. Runs daily July-Aug. M-W 10am-6pm, Th-Su 10am-9:30pm; from mid-Mar. to June and Sept.-Oct. 10am-5:30pm. 6 per hr. Round-trip £2.75, concessions £2.25, children £1.75. Camera obscura 50p, children free.)

ABERYSTWYTH CASTLE. Castle Point, south of the Old College and the site of one of Edward I's many ruined castles, is an ideal picnic site, with benches and tables scattered around the surrounding park. (Always open. Free.)

OTHER SIGHTS. Located directly above the TIC, the **Ceredigion Museum** fills a grand Edwardian music hall and houses two floors on local history. (☎633 088. Open M-Sa 10am-5pm. Free.) Up Penglais Rd., at the University of Wales, the **Aberystwyth Arts Centre** sponsors drama and films in Welsh and English and has a bookstore, gallery, and cafe. (☎623 232; www.aber.ac.uk/artscentre. Box office open M-Sa 10am-8pm, Su noon-5:30pm. Films every weeknight. Tickets from £3.50; concessions available.) At the end of Pier St., the once-famous Victorian **Royal Pier** is now overrun with an arcade, pizza parlor, pub, and nightclub. (Arcade open daily Mar.-Sept. 10am-11pm; Oct.-Feb. 10am-10pm.)

DAYTRIP FROM ABERYSTWYTH

DEVIL'S BRIDGE

The scenic narrow-rail Vale of Rheidol train runs from Aberystwyth. The area is not accessible by other forms of public transportation. From mid-July to Aug. M-Th 4 per day, F-Su 2 per day; from Easter to mid-July and Sept.-Oct. 2 per day. £13, children £3.

Originally built to serve lead mines, the **Vale of Rheidol Railway** (☎625 819) winds through farmland and gorgeous hills. An hour's ride leads to **Devil's Bridge** (reputedly built by the Evil One himself), which is actually three bridges of varying ages built atop one another. The lowest bridge was probably constructed in the 12th century by monks from the nearby **Strata Florida Abbey.** (☎01974 831 261. Abbey open Apr.-Sept. W-Su 10am-5pm. Last admission 30min. before close. Grounds open daily Apr.-Sept. 10am-5pm; Oct.-Mar. 10am-4pm. £3, concessions £2.50, families £8.30. Oct.-Apr. grounds free, but exhibits closed.) Catch great views of the bridge with a 10min. walk down the turnstile-accessible path to **Jacob's Ladder** and the **Devil's Punchbowl** in the stream. (☎890 233. Jacob's Ladder £2.50, concessions £2, children £1.25. Punchbowl £1.) From there, an easy 30min. walk through the hills affords views of the 300 ft. waterfall and more of the bridge.

MACHYNLLETH   ☎01654

Machynlleth (mach-HUN-hleth) is best known for its brief stint as the capital of Wales. Freedom-fighter Owain Glyndwr set up a parliament here in the 15th century, summoning delegates from across Wales and even signing an alliance with France against the British. Although the rebellion unraveled, the Celtic pride behind it lives on in the museums and street signs of Machynlleth's city center.

▣ TRANSPORTATION. The train station (☎702 887), Doll St., sends **trains** (☎08457 484 950) to: Aberystwyth (30min., 11 per day, £4); Birmingham (2¼hr.; M-F 10 per day, Sa 11 per day, Su 6 per day; £10.50); Shrewsbury (1¼hr.; M-F 10 per day, Sa 11 per day, Su 6 per day; £12.40). The Cambrian Coaster Day Ranger covers routes from Aberystwyth (£7, children £3.50, families £13.50, after 4:30pm £3.70). **Buses** stop by the clock tower. Arriva Cymru (☎08706 082 608) buses #32 and X32 pass through Machynlleth as they shuttle between Aberystwyth and Dolgellau (30min. to both; M-F 8 per day to Aberystwyth, 10 per day to Dolgellau, both Sa 8 per day, Su 2 per day). Buses #28 and 33 provide east-west transportation to and from smaller towns. Rent **bikes** at The Holey Trail Cycle Hire, 31 Maengwyn St. (☎700 411; www.theholeytrail.co.uk. Open in summer M-Sa 10am-6pm, Su 10am-3pm; in low season M-Sa 10am-6pm. £20 per day. ID and deposit required.)

▣ ORIENTATION AND PRACTICAL INFORMATION. Pentrehedyn Street, Penrallt Street, and **Maengwyn Street** converge at the **clock tower.** From the train station, turn left onto Doll St., veer right at the church onto Penrallt St., and continue until you see the tower. The **Tourist Information Centre, located** in the Royal House, Penrallt St., near the clock tower, books rooms for £2 plus a 10% deposit. (☎702 401. Open in summer M-Sa 9:30am-5pm, Su 9:30am-4:30pm; in winter M-Sa 9:30am-5pm, Su 9:30am-4:30pm.) Other services include: Barclays **bank,** on Penrallt St. beneath the clock tower (open M-F 9am-5pm); a **launderette,** New St., around the corner from Spar (wash £2.50, dry 20p; open M-Sa 8:30am-8pm, Su 9am-8pm; last wash 7:15pm); **police,** Doll St. (☎0845 330 2000); the **hospital,** off Maengwyn St. (☎702 266); Rowland's **pharmacy,** 8 Pentrehedyn St., near the tower (☎702 237; open M-W and F 9am-5:30pm, Th 9am-12:30pm, Sa 9am-4:30pm); free **Internet** access at the **library,** Maengwyn St. (☎702 322; open M and F 9:30am-1pm and 2-7pm, Tu-W 9:30am-1pm and 2-5pm, Sa 9:30am-1pm); and the **post office,** 51-53

ON THE MENU

BRAINY BOOZE

If someone lurches into a pub in Wales and demands brains, don't be afraid. In fact, you might consider trying some brains yourself. Don't expect something squishy from a sheep or a cow (although those are on the menu in Wales, too). Brains is the most successful independent brewery in Wales. Several varieties of Brains beers are in nearly every Welsh pub, recognizable by their patriotic red dragon logo.

The Brains name isn't wordplay: the company was formed when Samuel Arthur Brain and his uncle Joseph Benjamin Brain bought the Old Brewery in the center of Cardiff in 1882. Reasonably enough, they decided to name their newly-formed company after the family, and set out to get the Welsh some Brains.

The company has been passed down through the generations, with the same family remaining the, um, brains of the operation. Brains has bought out most of the other major Welsh brewers, and beers like Brains Bitter and Brains Dark have become international favorites. Even the Football Association of Wales has Brains—brew #45 is the official beer of Welsh football. So go ahead and gulp down some Brains. It's guaranteed to be less squishy than it sounds.

Maengwyn St., inside Spar (☎702 323; office open M-Th 8:30am-5:30pm, F 9am-5:30pm, Sa 9am-1pm). **Post Code:** SY20 8AF.

■ ACCOMMODATIONS AND FOOD. Machynlleth has few budget accommodations, but **Reditreks Bunkhouse ❷**, 31 Maengwyn St., next to the Holey Trail Cycle Hire, offers a TV lounge and kitchen. (☎702 184; www.reditreks.co.uk. 16 beds. Shower facilities. Sheets and pillows provided; duvets and covers £3.50 extra. Dorms £15, groups of 8 or more £12.50. Cash only.) Nearby Corris has a bunkhouse and a hostel. Take bus #32 or X32 bus (10min.; M-F 10 per day, Sa 8 per day, Su 2 per day). **Braich Goch Bunkhouse ❷**, across from the bus stop, has a climbing wall, kitchen, and laundry. Bring a sleeping bag or rent one for a small fee. (☎761 229; www.braich-goch.co.uk. Dorms £15.) **Corris Youth Hostel ❷**, on Corris Rd., is housed in an old schoolhouse a 5-10min. walk from the bus stop. Go into town and turn left up the hill after the creek. (☎761 686. Laundry available. Lockout 10am-5pm. Dorms £14, under 18 £12. Cash only.) **B&Bs** in Machynlleth are expensive and hard to find; ask the TIC for an accommodations guide. Campers can seek out riverside **Llwyngwern Farm ❶**, off the A487 next to the Centre for Alternative Technology. (☎702 492. Open Apr.-Sept. 2 people £9.50. Cash only.)

A Spar **supermarket** is at 51-53 Maengwyn St. (Open M-Sa 7am-11pm, Su 7am-10:30pm.) An impressive **market**, which dates from 1291, runs along Maengwyn St., Pentrehedyn St., and Penrallt St. (Open W 9:30am-4pm.) The **◙Quarry Cafe and Shop ❶**, 13 Maengwyn St., part of the Centre for Alternative Technology, serves delicious vegan soups and salads (under £3), as well as a rotating list of daily entrees (from £3.50). The poster-plastered wall of the cafe publicizes festivals and concerts. (☎702 339. Open July-Aug. M-W and F 9am-5pm, Th 9am-2pm, Su 10am-4pm; Sept.-June M-W and F 9am-5pm, Th 9am-2pm. Cash only.) Machynlleth pubs don't offer diverse dining options, but tasty dishes are served beside a massive hearth at the **Skinners Arms ❷**, 14 Penrallt St., near the clock tower. Entrees in the lounge are £5-11; lighter meals are £2-4.50 at the bar. (☎702 354. Open M-Tu noon-11pm, W-Sa 11am-11pm, Su noon-10:30pm. Food served daily noon-2pm and 6-8pm. Cash only.)

◙ SIGHTS. On a former slate quarry 3 mi. north of town along the A487 is the **◙Centre for Alternative Technology.** The staff here has been developing and promoting environmentally sound lifestyles since

1974. Chug up the 200 ft. cliff via a funicular powered by water imbalances. Fascinating outdoor displays teach about wave, wind, and solar power sources. Don't miss the child favorite "Mole Hole," featuring models of various tiny critters, or the "Compost Sampler," which encourages you to touch and smell various types of natural fertilizer. Take Arriva bus #34 (5-10min., M-Sa 11 per day, £2.40) to the entrance, or bus #32 (5min., M-Sa 10 per day, £2.40) to Pantperthog and walk 200 yd. north across the bridge. (☎705 950; www.cat.org.uk. Open daily Apr.-June 10am-5:30pm; July-Aug. 9:30am-6pm; Sept.-Dec. 10am-dusk. Last admission 1hr. before close. Funicular open Apr.-Oct. £8, concessions £7, children £4; Nov.-Dec. £6, concessions £5, children £4. Free audio tour.) Farther up the A487, the passages of another old slate mine lure tourists to **King Arthur's Labyrinth,** a surreal celebration of the Arthurian legend on a subterranean boat tour. To get there from Machynlleth, take bus #32 or 35 toward Dolgellau and ask to get off at the Corris Craft Centre. (☎761 584; www.kingarthurslabyrinth.com. Dress warmly. Open daily Apr.-Oct. 10am-5pm. £5.75, concessions £5.20, children £4.10.) Next to Y Tabernacl on Penrallt St., the **Museum of Modern Art, Wales** features rotating exhibits of contemporary Welsh art. Don't miss the Taliesin mosaics, created by villagers under the guidance of a local artist. On some evenings, the neighboring performance hall fills with music. (☎703 355; www.momawales.org.uk. Open M-Sa 10am-4pm. Free.) The museum and theater are central to the late August **Machynlleth Festival,** which features musical performances and lectures. (☎703 355; www.momawales.org.uk. Tickets £5-15.)

VALE OF CONWY

Much of the Vale of Conwy lies within Snowdonia National Park, but its lush swales, tall conifers, and streams suggest an ecosystem far gentler than Snowdon's desolate peaks. Biking is popular here, and the excellent *Gwydyr Forest Guide* (£2) details 14 walks through the mossy glens and waterfalls.

◪ TRANSPORTATION

The single-track, 27 mi. Conwy Valley line (☎08457 484 950; www.conwyvalleyrailway.co.uk) offers unparalleled views. **Trains** run between Llandudno and Blaenau Ffestiniog, stopping at Llandudno Junction, Llanrwst, and Betws-y-Coed (1hr.; M-Sa 5 per day, Su 3 per day). The **North and Mid-Wales Rover** ticket is good for nearly unlimited bus and train travel as far south as Aberystwyth (4-day train and 8-day bus £45). Most area **buses** stop at Llanrwst; some also at Betws-y-Coed. The main bus along the Conwy River is Arriva Cymru (☎08706 082 608) #19/X19, which runs from Llandudno and Conwy to Llanrwst (M-Sa 1-2 per hr., Su 10 per day). Sherpa bus S2 runs from Llanrwst to Pen-y-Pass via Betws-y-Coed (30min.; M-Sa 7 trips per day, Su 8 per day). Bus #97A connects Betws-y-Coed with Porthmadog (1hr., 3 per day). Routes often change; consult the invaluable *Gwynedd* or *Conwy County* transportation booklets, free at local TICs. Arriva's **Explorer Pass** allows unlimited travel on Arriva buses (1 day £5; 1 week £12.50).

CONWY   ☎01492

Conwy's distinctive town walls, remnants of Edward I's attempt to keep the Welsh out of his 13th-century castle, now enclose a town that is more willing to share its narrow streets, quayside, and eclectic assortment of attractions.

NORTH WALES

◧ TRANSPORTATION

Trains: Conwy Station, off Rosehill St. Trains (☎08457 484 950) stop only by request. The station lies on the North Wales line, between **Holyhead** and **Chester.** Trains stop at nearby **Llandudno Junction,** which connects to the Conwy Valley line. Ticket office open M-Sa 5:30am-6:30pm, Su 11:30am-6:30pm. Not to be confused with Llandudno proper (a resort town 1 mi. north; p. 496), Llandudno Junction is a 20min. walk from Conwy. Turn left after exiting the station, walk under a bridge, and climb the stairs to another bridge across the estuary.

Buses: Buses are the best way to get directly to Conwy, with two main stops on Lancaster Sq. and on Castle St. before the corner of Rosehill St. Arriva Cymru (☎0870 608 2608) buses #5 and 5X stop in Conwy as they climb the northern coast from **Caernarfon** via **Bangor** to **Llandudno** (1¼hr.; M-Sa 2-4 per hr., Su every hr.). Bus #9 leaves Conwy for **Llangefni,** on the Isle of Anglesey, in one direction (1hr., M-Sa every hr.) and **Llandudno** in the other (½hr., M-Sa every hr.). Bus #19 crosses Conwy on its **Llandudno-Llanrwst** journey down the Vale of Conwy (to Llandudno 15min., to Llanrwst 40min.; M-Sa 1-2 per hr., Su 11 per day, continuing on to Llangollen 4 times per day). The free *Conwy Public Transport Information* booklet is available at the TIC.

Taxis: Castle Cars (☎593 398).

▓◪ ORIENTATION AND PRACTICAL INFORMATION

Old Conwy is roughly triangular in shape. The castle is in one corner; **Castle Street,** which becomes **Berry Street,** runs from the castle parallel to the **Quay** and the river beyond it. **High Street** stretches from the Quay's edge to **Lancaster Square,** from which **Rosehill Street** circles back to the castle. In the opposite direction, **Bangor Road** heads north past the wall.

Tourist Information Centre: (☎592 248) in the same building as the castle entrance. Stocks street maps and books beds for £2 plus 10% deposit. Open daily June-Sept. 9:30am-6pm; Oct.-Nov. and May 9:30am-5pm; Dec.-Apr. 9:30am-4pm.

Bank: Barclays, 23 High St. (☎616 616), with an **ATM.** Open M-F 9:30am-4:30pm.

Hospital: (☎860 066) off Maesdu Rd. in Llandudno.

Internet Access: Library, Town Hall, Castle St. (☎596 242). Free. Open M and Th-F 10am-5:30pm, Tu 10am-7pm, Sa 10am-1pm.

Pharmacy: Numark, 24 High St. (☎592 418). Open M-Sa 9am-5:30pm.

Post Office: 7 Lancaster Sq. (☎573 990). Open M-Tu 8:30am-5:30pm, W-F 9am-5:30pm, Sa 9am-1:30pm. **Post Code:** LL32 8HT.

◪ ACCOMMODATIONS

▨ **Swan Cottage,** 18 Berry St. (☎596 840; http://myweb.tiscali.co.uk/swancottage), in a 16th-century building near the center of town. One of few B&Bs within the town walls. Cozy rooms, most ensuite, with timber ceilings and TV. Singles £25, doubles £45. Cash only. ❷

YHA Conwy, Larkhill, Sychnant Pass Rd. (☎593 571), a 10min. uphill hike from the town walls. From Lancaster Sq., head down Bangor Rd., turn left on Mt. Pleasant and right at the top of the hill. The hostel is up a driveway on the left. Self-catering kitchen and TV room. Free lockers. Laundry wash £2, dry £1 per 20min. Internet access 50p per 7min. Bike rental £6.50 per ½-day. Dorms £15.50, under 18 £11. MC/V. ❷

Bryn B&B (☎592 449; www.bryn.org.uk), outside the gates at St. Agnes Rd. and Synchant Pass. Flanked by a colorful garden and the city wall. Ensuite rooms are beautifully decorated, with views of the valley and castle. Singles £40; doubles £60. Cash only. ❹

Glan Heulog, Llanrwst Rd., Woodlands (☎593 845), a 5-10min. walk from the castle. Go under the arch near the visitor center on Rosehill St., down the steps, and across the car park. Turn right and walk 5min. down Llanrwst Rd. Huge manor house with sloping lawns. Ensuite rooms with TV and a large selection of fresh fruit at breakfast. Singles from £35; doubles from £54. MC/V. ❸

Camping: Conwy Touring Park, Trefriw Rd. (☎592 856; www.conwytouringpark.com), Follow Trefriw Rd. (B5106) out of town for 1½ mi. and turn left at the sign. Open Easter-Sept. £4-12 per tent. Electricity £3. MC/V. ❶

❐ FOOD

While the usual assortment of tea rooms and pubs graces Conwy's town center, High St. is lined with a number of classier (and pricier) restaurants. Spar sells inexpensive **groceries.** (Open daily 7am-10pm.)

▨ Pen-y-Bryn Tea Rooms, High St. (☎596 445). Great tea (full Welsh tea £4.50) and rich 16th-century timbered nooks. Assortment of sandwiches from £3.50. Open M-Th and Su 10am-5pm, F-Sa 10am-9pm. Cash only. ❶

Edward's Butchery, 18 High St. (☎592 443; www.edwardsofconwy.co.uk). Well-deserved accolades adorn the huge meat counter. Hearty pies (from £1.15) are the specialty. Open M-Sa 7am-5:30pm. AmEx/MC/V. ❶

Shakespeare Restaurant, High St. (☎582 800), in the Castle Hotel. This award-winning venue uses local foods in daily specials. Decorated with panels of Shakespeare-inspired scenes by Victorian artist John Dawson-Watson, who supposedly used the paintings to pay rent. Entrees are pricey (£17-19), but the starter menu offers fairly large portions (£6-7). Open M-Sa 7-9:30pm, Su 12:30-2:30pm and 7-9pm. MC/V. ❹

Bistro Conwy, Chapel St. (☎596 326), near the wall close to Bangor Rd. Inspired Welsh fare amid dried floral bouquets. Entrees from £12. Open W-Sa 6:30-9pm, Su noon-2:30pm. MC/V. ❹

◎ SIGHTS

▨ CONWY CASTLE. Conwy is possibly the most imposing and magnificent of Edward I's 13th-century fortresses. Parapets joining eight rugged towers sit atop craggy rocks to form a natural defense. An untold number of Normans wasted away in the prison, and Richard II was betrayed in the chapel in 1399. The £1 guided tour is worth it; try to get on "celebrity" guide Neville Hortop's tour—his ferocious approach to history is ultimately more entertaining than unsettling. (☎592 358. Open June-Sept. daily 9:30am-6pm; Apr.-May and Oct. daily 9:30am-5pm; Nov.-Mar. M-Sa 9:30am-4pm, Su 11am-4pm. £4.50, concessions £4, families £14.)

PLAS MAWR. The National Trust has lovingly restored this 16th-century mansion to its days as the home of merchant Robert Wynn, right down to the exquisite furnishings and plasterwork. Don't miss the display on Tudor-era hygiene and its discussion of so-called "pisse prophets." The entrance price includes a free 1hr. audio tour that attempts to psychoanalyze Wynn according to his architectural choices. (☎580 167. Open June-Aug. Tu-Su 9:30am-6pm; Apr.-May and Sept. Tu-Su 9:30am-5pm; Oct. Tu-Su 9:30am-4pm. £4.90, concessions £4.50, families £15. Audio tour free with admission.)

SMALLEST HOUSE. When this nearly 400-year-old house was condemned in 1900, its owner (a strapping 6 ft., 3 in. fisherman) spent years measuring other tiny homes to prove that this one was the smallest in Britain. You can question his taste in housing all you like, but with a frontage measuring 6 ft., you can't question the legitimacy of his claim. There's (obviously) not much to see here beyond the house's two floors and a bewildering display of large brain coral. *(Head down High St. and onto the Quay.* ☎593 484. *Open daily Aug. 10am-9pm; Easter-July and Sept.-Oct. 10am-6pm. Closing times are approximate. £1, children 50p.)*

LLANDUDNO ☎01492

Around 1850, the Mostyn family envisioned the farming village of Llandudno (hlan-DID-no) as a resort town. They constructed a city with wide avenues open to sea and sky, and sure enough, the tourists arrived. Today, Victorian hotels and shores packed with sunbathers prove the family's foresight. The Great Orme, a massive craggy hill on a peninsula, lures many to its slopes for hiking in the summer and tobogganing in the winter.

⊏ TRANSPORTATION. Llandudno is the northern end of several transportation lines. The train station is at the end of Augusta Rd. (Ticket office open July-Aug. M-Sa 8:40am-3:30pm, Su 10:15am-5:45pm; Sept.-June M-Sa 8:40am-3:30pm.) **Trains** (☎08457 484 950) run to Blaenau Ffestiniog via Llanrwst and Betws-y-Coed (1¼hr.; M-Sa 8 per day, Su 2 per day; £5.70). Trains leave Llandudno Junction, 1 mi. south of town, to Bangor (20min., 1-3 per hr., £4.40), Chester (1hr., 1-4 per hr., £12.20), and Holyhead (50min., 19 per day, £9.30). Trains sometimes stop at Llandudno by request. National Express (☎08705 808 080) **buses** stop at Mostyn Broadway daily and go to Chester (1¾hr., £9.20), London (8hr., £27), and Manchester (4¼hr., 2 per day, £12). Arriva Cymru (☎0870 608 2608) buses #5, 5A, and 5X run to Bangor (1hr., 1-4 per hr.), Caernarfon (1½hr., 1-4 per hr.), and Conwy (20min.; M-Sa 2-3 per hr., Su every hr.; £1.60). Bus #19 goes to Llanrwst, passing through Conwy (1hr.; M-Sa 2 per hr., Su 11 per day). Snowdon Sherpa S2 runs to Betws-y-Coed (1hr., 1 per day). Kings Cabs (☎878 156; last cab M-W and Su 1:30am, F-Sa 3-4am) runs **taxis.** Rent **bikes** at West End Cycles, 22 Augusta St., near the train station. (☎876 891. From £7 per day. £25 deposit. Open daily 9am-5:30pm.)

■✦⁊ ORIENTATION AND PRACTICAL INFORMATION. Llandudno is flanked by two **beaches** with pretty boardwalks; the West Shore is less built up than the North, which has Victorian promenades and a long pier. Mostyn St., which follows the shore a block inland from the promenade, is the main drag. Turn left from the train station to find the **Tourist Information Centre,** in a shopping center on Mostyn St. It books rooms for £2 plus a 10% deposit. (☎876 413. Open Easter-Oct. M-Sa 9am-5:30pm, Su 9:30am-4:30pm; Nov.-Easter M-Sa 9am-5pm.) Other services include: Barclays **bank,** at the corner of Mostyn St. and Market St. (open M-F 9:30am-4:30pm, Sa 9:30am-12:30pm); **police,** Oxford Rd. (☎517 171); **General Hospital,** near the Maesdu Golf Course on the West Shore (☎860 066); free **Internet** access at the **library,** upstairs from the TIC on Mostyn St. between Lloyd St. and Trinity Sq. (☎876 826; open M-Tu and F 9am-6pm, W 10am-5pm, Th 9am-7pm, Sa 9:30am-1pm) and at Le Moulin Rouge (p. 497); and the **post office,** 14 Vaughn St., with a **bureau de change** (☎876 125; open M and W-F 9am-5:30pm, Tu 9:30am-5:30pm, Sa 9am-12:30pm). **Post Code:** LL30 1AA.

⌐☐ ACCOMMODATIONS AND FOOD. Lodging is easy to find in Llandudno, although the town becomes crowded in summer. The **▦Llandudno Hostel ❷,** on 14 Charlton St. near the Alice in Wonderland Centre, offers bright, clean dorms near the city center and train station. School groups usually rent the building out M-Th from Apr.-July, so call ahead. (☎877 430. Continental breakfast included. Dorms £16; twins £38, ensuite £42. Cash only.) Budget travelers can also seek out **B&Bs** (£20-25) on **Chapel Street, Deganwy Avenue,** and **St. David's Road. Beach Cove ❷,** 8 Church Walks, offers rooms with TV in an excellent location. (☎879 638. Singles

£22.50; doubles £40, ensuite £48. MC/V.) Nearby **Merrydale Hotel ❷**, 6 Chapel St., has simple, cheery rooms. (☎860 911. £20 per person. Cash only.) **Burleigh House ❸**, 74 Church Walks across from Beach Cove, offers large ensuite rooms close to the beach. (☎875 946. £23-30 per person. Singles cost an extra £10. Cash only.)

Dozens of dining options line main streets, including an enormous ASDA **supermarket** on Conway Rd. (☎860 068. Open M-Sa 8am-10pm, Su 10am-4pm.) The **Fat Cat Cafe-Bar ❶**, 149 Mostyn St., serves non-traditional dishes in its modern, cool-colored rooms along with two-for-one meals weekdays 3-5pm. (☎871 844; www.fatcatcafebar.co.uk. Open daily 10am-11pm. Food served until 10pm. AmEx/MC/V.) Down a set of stairs off an alleyway, **The Cocoa House ❷**, George St., provided the social atmosphere of a pub while serving cocoa instead of alcohol during the temperance movement. These days, it is fully licensed and offers creative lunch specials from £3. (☎876 601. Open M-Sa 10am-4:30pm, food served until 3pm. Cash only.) **Le Moulin Rouge ❶**, 104 Mostyn St., serves crisp panini with fillings like bacon, tomatoes, Stilton, and pears. (☎874 111. Panini £3.10. Free Internet access for 20min. with £3 purchase. Open daily 8am-5:30pm. Cash only.) **Bonjour Café ❷**, on Madoc St., specializes in crepes (from £2.60) and offers many hot drinks in huge mugs. Sip a "cho-rum," a cream-topped hot chocolate infused with rum (£3), as you listen to accordion music. (☎878 930. Open daily approx. 10am-5pm. Cash only.) **The Cottage Loaf ❷**, Market St., serves good pub grub in a tavern-like atmosphere with a beer garden. (☎870 762. Entrees from £6. Open M-Sa 11am-11pm, Su noon-10:30pm. Food served noon-2:30pm. Cash only.)

◪ SIGHTS. Llandudno's pleasant beaches—the Victorian **North Shore** and the quieter **West Shore**—are both outdone by the looming **Great Orme,** a huge nature reserve full of caves, pastures, and some 200 Kashmir goats. At the 679 ft. summit, even gift shops and arcades cannot entirely distract from the flowered hillside. Pick up the free *Walks to the Summit* brochure from the TIC. The **Great Orme Tramway,** which departs from Church Walks, offers a quicker trip. (☎879 306; www.greatormetramway.co.uk. 20min. Apr.-Oct. 3 per hr. 10am-6pm. Single £3.80, children £2.70; round-trip £5/3.50.) Perhaps the most exciting way to reach the summit, however, is on the **Llandudno Cable Cars,** which depart from the Happy Valley Gardens. (☎877 205. 20min. round-trip. Open 10am-5pm, weather permitting. Round-trip £6, children £3.) Halfway up the side of the Great Orme, stop for a tour of the **Bronze Age Copper Mines** and explore narrow underground passages where miners exposed ore veins with rocks and animal bones 4000 years ago. (☎870 447. Open daily Mar.-Oct. 10am-5pm. £5, children £3.50, families £15.)

Near the TIC, the **War Museum's** "Homefront Experience," New St., off Chapel St., has torch-lit corridors and a bomb shelter, introducing visitors to the blackout and blitz of the British home front. (☎871 032. Open Mar.-Oct. M-Sa 10am-4:30pm, Su 11am-3pm. £3.20, seniors £2.60, children £2, families £9.) Alice Liddell, muse to Lewis Carroll, spent her childhood summers in Llandudno, and enterprising citizens have used this connection to justify a fantasy recreation at the **Alice in Wonderland Centre,** 3-4 Trinity Sq. Dramatic readings accompany mechanized characters and stuffed animals in formal attire. (☎860 082; www.wonderland.co.uk. Open Easter-Oct. M-Sa 10am-5pm, Su 10am-4pm; Nov.-Easter M-Sa 10am-5pm. £3.25, children £2.50. Audio tour free with admission.)

Eight miles south of Llandudno, twisting pathways cross the lawns and carp-filled ponds of **Bodnant Gardens.** The upper terraces give way to a river glen down the hill. The gardens are the setting for plays on summer evenings. From Llandudno, take Arriva bus #25 (45min., M-Sa 11 per day) to the gates or the Conwy Valley train (M-Sa 6 per day, Su 3 per day) to the Tal-y-Cafn stop, 2 mi. away. (☎650 460; www.bodnantgarden.co.uk. Open daily from mid-Mar. to early Nov. 10am-5pm. Last admission 4:30pm. £7, children £3.50.)

🔊📺 NIGHTLIFE AND ENTERTAINMENT. Llandudno's two clubs are a 10min. walk from the town center down Mostyn St. **Broadway Boulevard,** Mostyn Broadway next to the North Wales Theatre, is a student-friendly venue with cheap drinks and a solid mix of chart favorites. (☎879 614. No sneakers. Cover £3-6. Open W and F 10pm-2:30am, Sa 10pm-3am. Last admission midnight.) A bit farther down Mostyn Broadway and left on Clarence Rd. is **Washington.** The wine bar on the ground floor draws an older crowd than the more traditional dance club upstairs does. (☎877 974. No sneakers. Cover £3-4. Th "Upfront" gay night. Open Th 9pm-1:30am, F-Sa 9pm-2am; wine bar open M-F and Su 4pm-midnight, Sa noon-midnight.) **Venue Cymru,** the large theater between Mostyn Broadway and the Promenade, hosts plays and concerts. (☎872 000; www.venuecymru.co.uk. Box office open M-Sa 9:30am-8:30pm, Su noon-4pm, 2-8pm on performance days. Tickets £6-47, concessions available.)

BETWS-Y-COED   ☎01690

At the southern tip of the Vale of Conwy and the eastern edge of the Snowdonia mountains, picturesque Betws-y-Coed (BET-oos uh COYD) has evolved from an artist colony into a tourist haven. Its main street is crammed with novelty shops, hotels, and outdoor supply stores, and visitors arrive on coach tours in droves. Yet a small-town feel remains, and the stunning surroundings overcome Betws-y-Coed's commercialization.

🚆 TRANSPORTATION. Trains (☎08457 484 950) stop in Betws-y-Coed on the Conwy Valley line (p. 493). Sherpa **buses** S2 and S97, operated by Arriva Cymru, connects Betws-y-Coed with **Pen-y-Pass,** stopping at some area hostels (20min., M-Sa 1 per hr.) and **Llanrwst** (10min., 1-2 per hr.). S97 continues on to **Porthmadog** (1¼hr., 5 per day). Bus #19 runs to Llandudno (1¼hr., 4 per day) and Llangollen (1hr., 4 per day). On Saturdays, Arriva bus #70 runs to Corwen, Wrecsam, and Llangollen in one direction and Llanrwst and Llandudno in the other. Rent **bicycles** from Beics Betws, up the street behind the post office. (☎710 766; www.bike-wales.co.uk. From £16 per day. Open daily 9:30am-5pm.)

📑🔧 ORIENTATION AND PRACTICAL INFORMATION. The main street is **Holyhead Road** (A5). It runs northwest from the River Conwy, slants past the park at the town center where Station Rd. branches toward the train station, and turns west toward Swallow Falls. Possibly the busiest **Tourist Information Centre** in North Wales (also a Snowdonia NPIC), the Betws TIC is at the Old Stables, between the train station and Holyhead Rd. An energetic staff books rooms for £2 plus a 10% deposit. (☎710 426; www.eryri-npa.gov.uk. Open daily Easter-Oct. 9:30am-5:30pm; Nov.-Easter 9:30am-4:30pm.) From April to September, **guided walks** around Betws are available by appointment; inquire at the TIC. (☎01514 880 052 or 07790 851 333. Walks 6-8 mi., 5-6hr. £5.)

A number of **outdoor stores** line Holyhead Rd. Two Cotswold outlets are among them, one (☎710 710) next to the Royal Oak Hotel, the other (☎710 234) south of town. (Both open M-Tu, Th, and Su 9am-6pm, W 10am-6pm, F-Sa 9am-7pm.) The latter provides **Internet** access for 50p per 15min. (Printing 10p per pg. Cash only.) Other services include: an HSBC **bank** with an **ATM** at the southern edge of Holyhead Rd. near the train station (open M 9:15am-2:30pm, Tu-F 9:15am-1pm); **police** (☎710 222); and the **post office,** with a commission-free **bureau de change,** inside the Londis, at the T-junction of Holyhead and Station Rd. (☎710 565; open M-F 9am-5:30pm, Sa 9am-12:30pm). **Post Code:** LL24 0AA.

⌐⌐ ACCOMMODATIONS AND FOOD. The best deal among Betws's expensive, centrally located accommodations is the **Bunkhouse ❶**, at the Glan Aber Hotel. The price and location make up for the spartan amenities—don't expect anything more than a bed and a bathroom down the hall. (☎ 710 325. Dorms from £13. Bring your own sleeping bag.) Two hostels are located somewhat near town: **YHA Capel Curig ❷** (p. 503) and **YHA Betws-y-Coed ❷**, at the Swallow Falls Complex 2 mi. west of town on the A5. (☎ 710 796; www.swallowfallshotel.co.uk. Kitchen, laundry, and restaurant. Reception 8am-9pm. Call 48hr. ahead. £14.50, under 18 £10. Cash only.) Most **B&Bs** (from £18) cluster along Holyhead Rd. For views of riverside lambs, head to **Glan Llugwy ❸**, on the western edge of town, about 10min. from the park. Walk along Holyhead Rd. toward Swallow Falls, or call the owners for a lift. They provide packed lunches and laundry service on request. (☎ 710 592. Singles £25, £23 for subsequent nights; doubles £50/46. Cash only.) **Bryn Llewelyn ❸** is a bit closer to the town center on Holyhead Rd. (☎ 710 601; www.bryn-llewe-lyn.co.uk. Singles £30; doubles £55. MC/V.) **Riverside Caravan Park ❶** sits behind the train station. (☎ 710 310. Open from mid-Mar. to Oct. £6 per person. Electricity £2. Laundry £3. Refrigerator available. Cash only.)

Spar **market,** at the northern bend of Holyhead Rd., houses a large bakery and sandwich bar. (☎ 710 324. Open daily 8am-10pm.) A small cafe with hand-painted tables, ▧**Caban-y-Pair ❷**, Holyhead Rd., serves affordable comfort food. Most soups and sandwiches cost £3-4. Don't miss the specialty coffee offerings from around the world. (☎ 710 505. Open daily June-Oct. 9am-5:30pm. Food served 9am-4:30pm; Nov.-May 10am-5pm. Cash only.) A knight guards the door at **Three Gables ❷**, Holyhead Rd., keeping watch over the gaudy treasures adorning its walls and the standard English fare adorning its tables. (☎ 710 328. Open Easter-Oct. daily noon-9:30pm; Nov.-Easter F-Su noon-9:30pm. AmEx/MC/V.)

◲ SIGHTS. Betws is well-connected with eight **bridges.** The first bridge was built in 1475. Inigo Jones may have played a role in building the second, which consists of 11 stone arches vaulting from rock to rock. Of particular note is Telford's 1815 cast-iron **Waterloo Bridge,** situated at the village's southern end and named for the battle that cut Napoleon down to size. A miniature **suspension bridge** spans the Conwy, while **Pont-y-Pair Bridge,** "the bridge of the cauldron," crosses the Llugwy to the north. Behind the train station, weathered gravestones surround the humble 14th-century **St. Michael's Church.** Two miles west, signposted off the A5, the waters of the Llugwy froth at **Swallow Falls.** Local lore claims that the soul of an evil 17th-century sheriff is trapped below. (Always open. £1.) Bus S2 between Betws and Snowdon stops at the falls, as do most #97A buses to Porthmadog (4min., 1-3 per hr.). A half-mile farther along the A5, "the Ugly House," **Tŷ Hyll** (tih-hih), lives up to its name, with a rough facade of randomly stacked boulders. Now the house serves as the Snowdonia Society headquarters and has a display and shop area. (☎ 720 287. Open daily Apr.-Sept. 9am-5pm. £1.) Outdoor stores on Holyhead Rd. can arrange excursions into the stunning surroundings. The **National Whitewater Centre,** in nearby Bala, offers river expeditions. (☎ 01678 521 083; www.ukrafting.co.uk. Expeditions £27-295, wetsuit rental £2-5.)

LLANGOLLEN   ☎01978

Set in a hollow in the hills near the English border, Llangollen (hlan-GOTH-hlen) is best known for its annual International Musical Eisteddfod, a festival that has drawn over 400,000 performers and competitors since it began in 1947. The town is also convenient to surrounding natural attractions; hikers head to Horseshoe Pass and whitewater enthusiasts tackle the Dee and its tributaries.

☎⁊ TRANSPORTATION AND PRACTICAL INFORMATION. Despite being a tourist town, Llangollen can be difficult to reach by public transportation. **Trains** (☎ 08457 484 950; www.nationalrail.co.uk) leave from Wrexham, 30min. away, for **Chester** (20min., every hr., £3.30), **London** (4hr., 2 per hr., £61.70), and **Shrewsbury** (40min., every hr., £5.20). A closer train station is Ruabon, from which B&B owners occasionally fetch travelers. To get to Llangollen from Wrexham, take Bryn Melyn (☎ 860 701) bus X5 (30min., M-Sa 4 per hr., £2.60). Direct service from Llangollen is possible on some **buses;** Arriva Cymru (☎ 0870 608 2608) bus #94 goes to Barmouth (2hr.; M-Sa 8 per day, Su 4 per day; £5.20), Dolgellau (1½hr.; M-Sa 8 per day, Su 4 per day; £3.50), and Chester (1¼hr., M-Sa 7 per day). Arriva Cymru's bus #19 runs to Llandudno via Conwy and Betws-y-Coed (2¼hr.; M-Sa 4 per day, Su 3 per day). Lloyd's Coaches (☎ 01654 702 100) runs #694, which stops at Llangollen on the first and third Saturdays of the month.

The **Tourist Information Centre,** on Castle St. in The Chapel, displays local art and books rooms for £2 plus a 10% deposit. (☎ 860 828. Open daily Easter-Oct. 9:30am-5:30pm; Nov.-Easter 9:30am-5pm.) Activity weekends are available from **Pro Adventure,** Old Weaver's Shed, Parade St. (☎ 861 912; www.proadventure.co.uk. Open M 11am-3pm, Tu-F 9:30am-5pm, Sa 9am-5pm. Kayaking £42 per ½-day. Bike rental £18 per day.) Other services include: Barclays **bank,** with an **ATM,** 9 Castle St., opposite the TIC (☎ 202 700; open M-Tu and Th-F 10am-4pm, W 10:30am-4pm); Blue Bay **launderette,** 3 Regent St. (wash £2.50, dry 20p per 5min.; open M-Sa 9am-6pm); **police** (☎ 01492 517 171, ext. 54940); free **Internet** access at the **library,** upstairs from the TIC (☎ 869 600; open M 9:30am-7pm, Tu-W and F 9:30am-5:30pm, Sa 9:30am-12:30pm); and the **post office,** 41 Castle St., with a **bureau de change** (☎ 862 812; open M-F 9am-5:30pm, Sa 9am-12:30pm). **Post Code:** LL20 8RU.

⌐⌐ ACCOMMODATIONS AND FOOD. B&Bs (£20-25) are numerous, especially along **Regent Street. Glasgwm ❸** features cozy rooms and huge breakfasts in a sunlit front room. (☎ 861 97. Singles from £30. Cash only.) The gardens of stately **Oakmere ❹,** Regent St., create relaxing evenings. (☎ 861 126; www.oakmere.llangollen.co.uk. Singles from £45; doubles £60. Cash only.) **Campsites** abound; ask at the TIC, or try **Abbey Farm Caravan Park ❶,** at the Valle Crucis Abbey. (☎ 861 297. £3.50 per person, children £3; cars £2. Electricity £2. Cash only.)

Spar, 26-30 Castle St., in the center of town, sells **groceries.** (☎ 860 275. Open M-Sa 7am-11pm, Su 8am-10:30pm.) Classy cuisine has found a home in pub-like quarters at ⊠**The Corn Mill ❸,** Dee Ln., where the patio hangs low over the River Dee. If the entrees are too expensive (£7.45-15), spend a few pounds on a pint or a sizeable starter (£4-5) and watch the waterwheel spinning outside. (☎ 869 555. Open M-Sa noon-11pm, Su noon-10:30pm. Food served M-Sa noon-9:30pm, Su noon-9pm. AmEx/MC/V.) At **Maxine's Cafe and Books ❶,** 17 Castle St., thumb through thousands of volumes in the warehouse upstairs and grab a meal in the dining room below. (☎ 861 963. Free Wi-Fi. All-day breakfast £4.25. Open daily 9am-5pm. MC/V.) **Ecclestons Bakers and Confectioners ❶,** Castle St., serves cheap and freshly-prepared takeaway pasties, sandwiches, and salads. (☎ 861 005. Open M-Sa 8:30am-4:30pm. Cash only.)

◎ SIGHTS. The ruins of ⊠**Castell Dinas Brân** (Crow Castle) lie on a hilltop above town, "to the winds abandoned and the prying stars," as Wordsworth once mused. On a clear day, the view spans from Snowdonia to the English Midlands, and the grassy mounds of the summit are scattered with crumbling archways and walls. Two main paths lead to the castle: a 40min. gravel trail zig-zags up the side facing Llangollen, while a 1hr. walk from the other side follows a pastoral road. Reach both via an unmarked trail that begins where Wharf and Dinbren Rd. meet, uphill from the canal bridge. When you reach the intersection of dirt roads, continue straight up the hill following the sign for Offa's Dyke Path. Up Hill St. from the town center, **Plas Newydd** is the former *ferme ornée* (estate in miniature) of two noblewomen who fled Ireland in 1778. "Two of the most celebrated virgins in Europe," they appealed to the era's intellectuals. Wellington and Sir Walter Scott visited, as did Wordsworth, who penned a poem in their honor. Today, the women are remembered on souvenir mugs. (☎708 223. Open daily Easter-Oct. 10am-5pm. Last admission 4:15pm. £3.50, concessions £2.50, families £10. Includes audio tour. Gardens open year-round 8am-6pm. Free. Guided tours of the servants' quarters by request.) The ruins of 13th-century **Valle Crucis Abbey** grace a valley 30-45min. from Llangollen along Abbey Rd. Its empty arches frame trees, sky, and a cluster of caravans from the campsite next door. (☎860 326. Open daily Apr.-Sept. 10am-5pm; the rest of the year the abbey is open but unstaffed. £2.50, concessions £2, families £7.) Both the abbey and Castell Dinas Bran have been considered as possible locations of the Holy Grail. Other sights in the area include **Croes Gwenhwyfar** (Guinevere's Cross) and **Eliseg's Pillar**, both ancient stone monuments.

Views of the gently sloping Dee River Valley greet passengers on the **Llangollen Railway**, which stops at a convenient station where Castle St. hits highway A593/A452. (☎860 951; www.llangollen-railway.co.uk. Runs Apr.-Oct. daily 3-7 per day; Nov.-Mar. Sa-Su 3 per day. Times vary; call ahead.)

🌺 **FESTIVALS.** Every summer, the town's population of 3000 swells to 80,000 for the **International Musical Eisteddfod** (ice-TETH-vod). In early July, the hills are alive with the singing and dancing of competitors from 50 countries. Book tickets and rooms far in advance through the **Eisteddfod Box Office,** Royal International Pavilion, Abbey Rd. (☎862 000, bookings 862 001; www.international-eisteddfod.co.uk. Open from mid-Mar. through the festival M-F 10am-5pm. Tickets £8-65. Unreserved seats and admission to grounds sold on performance days. £8, children £5.)

SNOWDONIA NATIONAL PARK

Surrounded by Edward I's 13th-century "iron ring" of castles, Snowdonia is a huge (823 sq. mi.) natural fortress. Known in Welsh as Eryri ("Place of Eagles"), Snowdonia has diverse terrain—green slopes rise above mountain lakes, and the cliff-faces of abandoned slate quarries sit among wooded hills. Rock climbing attracts many to Snowdonia; Sir Edmund Hillary trained here before attempting Everest. Although Snowdonia is largely private—only 0.3% belongs to the National Park Authority—public footpaths accommodate visitors. Snowdonia is also a stronghold of national pride: the native tongue of 65% of its inhabitants is Welsh.

NATIONAL PARK COVERAGE. Let's Go's coverage of Snowdonia National Park includes the towns of **Dolgellau, Harlech, Llanberis, Caernarfon,** and **Bangor.** The first section provides an overview of transportation, practical information, and general accommodations (such as **YHA hostels**) for the entire park. Local services and B&Bs are listed within coverage of individual towns.

▛ TRANSPORTATION

Trains (☎08457 484 950) stop at larger towns, including Bangor and Conwy. The Cambrian Coaster railway stops at Harlech and Dolgellau in the south. The Conwy Valley Line runs across the park from Llandudno through Betws-y-Coed to Blaenau Ffestiniog (1hr.; M-Sa 6 per day, Su 2-3 per day). **Buses** serve the interior. *The Gwynedd Public Transport Maps and Timetables* and *Conwy Public*

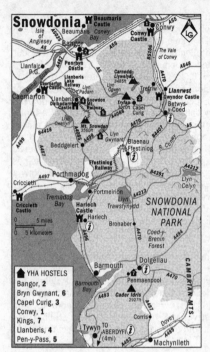

Snowdonia.

Isle of Anglesey

Beaumaris Castle
Conwy Bay
Conwy
Conwy Castle

Bangor

The Vale of Conwy

Llanfair P.G.

Penrhyn Castle

Carnedd Llywelyn 3485ft

Caernarfon

Llanberis Lake Railway

Llyn Ogwen

Trefriw

Llanrwst
Gwydor Castle

Betws-y-Coed

Llanberis
Dolbadarn Castle

Snowdon Mtn. Railway

Tryfan 3010ft
Capel Curig

Llyn Padarn

Mt. Snowdon 3560ft

Llyn Gwynant

Blaenau Ffestiniog

R. Conwy

Llyn Celyn

Beddgelert

Criccieth

Ffestiniog Railway

Portmadog

Llyn Trawsfynydd

SNOWDONIA NATIONAL PARK

Tremadog Bay

Portmeirion

Criccieth Castle

Harlech Castle
Harlech

Bronaber

Coed-y-Brenin Forest

0 5 miles
0 5 kilometers

Barmouth

Dolgellau

Penmaenpool

CAMBRIAN MTS.

▲ YHA HOSTELS
Bangor, 2
Bryn Gwynant, 6
Capel Curig, 3
Conwy, 1
Kings, 7
Llanberis, 4
Pen-y-Pass, 5

Barmouth Bay

Cader Idris 2927ft

Corris

Dovey

Tywyn TO ABERDYFI
(4mi)

Machynlleth

Transport Information booklets, indispensable for travel in the two counties that constitute the park, are both available for free in the region's TICs. Snowdon Sherpa buses maneuver between the park's towns and trailheads with irregular service, and will stop at any safe point in the park on request. A **Gwynedd Red Rover** ticket (£5, children £2.45) buys a day's unlimited travel on all buses in Gwynedd and Anglesey; a **Snowdon Sherpa Day Ticket** secures a day's worth of rides on Sherpa buses (most routes run every 1-2hr.; £4, children £2).

Narrow-gauge railway lines let you enjoy the countryside without a hike, although they tend to be pricey. The **Ffestiniog Railway** (p. 517) weaves from Porthmadog to Blaenau Ffestiniog, where mountain views give way to the raw cliffs of slate quarries. You can travel part of its route to Minffordd, Penrhyn-deudraeth, or Tan-y-bwlch. At Porthmadog, the rail meets the Cambrian Coaster service from Pwllheli to Aberystwyth; at Blaenau Ffestiniog, it connects with the Conwy Valley Line. (☎ 01766 516 000. 3hr.; 4-8 per day; £16, concessions £12.80.) The Snowdon Mountain Railway and the Llanberis Lake Railway make trips from Llanberis (p. 507).

ⓘ PRACTICAL INFORMATION

TICs and National Park Information Centres (NPICs) stock leaflets on walks, drives, and accommodations, as well as Ordnance Survey maps (£6.50-7.50). For details, contact the **Snowdonia National Park Information Headquarters** (☎ 01766 770 274). A booklet published by the Snowdonia National Park Authority, free at TICs across North Wales, is a good source of information on the park. You can also check out www.eryri-npa.gov.uk or www.gwynedd.gov.uk. Snowdonia has five **National Park Information Centres.** The busiest and best stocked is in **Betws-y-Coed** (p. 498). Other large offices are in **Dolgellau** (p. 504) and **Harlech** (p. 505). There are also offices in **Aberdyfi** (Wharf Gardens ☎ 01654 767 321; open daily Apr.-Oct. 9:30am-5:30pm) and **Blaenau Ffestiniog** (Isallt Church St. ☎ 01766 830 360; open daily Apr.-Oct. 9:30am-12:30pm and 1:30-5:30pm).

ⓘ ACCOMMODATIONS

In the mountains, **camping** is permitted as long as you leave no mess, but the Park Service discourages it because of recent erosion. In the valleys, the landowner's consent is required. Public campsites line the roads in summer; check listings below and inquire at NPICs. This section lists **YHA hostels** in Snowdonia; **B&Bs** are listed under individual towns. The seven hostels in the mountain area are some of the best in Wales. All have kitchens, and most offer meals and laundry ($3 wash, 20p per 10min. dry). All have a 10am-5pm lockout and an 11pm curfew. YHA strongly advises booking hostels 48hr. in advance, as many have unpredictable opening dates in winter. Book online at www.yha.org.uk.

Bryn Gwynant (☎08707 705 732), above Llyn Gwynant and along the Penygwryd-Beddgelert Rd. On Su and bank holidays, take Snowdon Sherpa S4 from Caernarfon (40min., 5 per day) or Pen-y-Pass (10min., 9 per day). In summer, Sherpa #97a comes from Porthmadog or Betws-y-Coed (30min. each way; 3 per day). Victorian house in the heart of the park. Kitchen. Open Mar.-Oct. Dorms £12, under 18 £9. MC/V. ❶

Capel Curig (☎08707 705 746). 5 mi. from Betws-y-Coed on the A5. Sherpa buses S2 and S3 stop nearby from Llandudno, Betws-y-Coed, and Pen-y-Pass. At the crossroads of many mountain paths. Favored by climbers and school kids. Spectacular view of Mt. Snowdon across a lake. Kitchen and laundry available. Breakfast included. Open from mid-Feb. to Oct. daily; Nov.-Jan. F-Sa. Dorms £17, under 18 £13.50. MC/V. ❷

Kings (☎08707 705 900), Penmaenpool, 4 mi. from Dolgellau. Arriva bus #28 from Dolgellau (5min; M-Sa 9 per day); the hostel is 1 mi. uphill from the stop. Country house in the Vale Ffestiniog. Kitchen. Open from mid-Apr. to Aug. daily; Sept.-Oct. and Mar.-Apr. F-Sa; Nov.-Mar. open for rent. Dorms £12, under 18 £9. MC/V. ❷

Llanberis (☎08707 705 928), ½ mi. up Capel Goch Rd., follow signs from High St. Views of Llyn Peris, Llyn Padam, and Mt. Snowdon. Kitchen available. Open Apr.-Oct. daily; Nov.-Dec. F-Sa; Jan.-Feb. open for rent; Mar. varied. Fills up with school groups much of July and Aug. Dorms £14, under 18 £10. MC/V. ❷

Pen-y-Pass, Nant Gwynant (☎08707 705 990), 6 mi. from Llanberis and 4 mi. from Nant Peris. Take Sherpa bus S1 from Llanberis (20min.; late May-Sept. every hr.; Oct.-late May M-Sa 6 per day, Su 9 per day). At the head of Llanberis Pass, 1170 ft. above sea level. Doors open onto a track to the Snowdon summit. Outdoors shop sells supplies and rents hiking gear. Kitchen. Dorms £14, under 18 £10. MC/V. ❷

⚠ OUTDOOR ACTIVITIES

Weather on Snowdonia's mountains shifts quickly, unpredictably, and with a vengeance. No matter how beautiful the weather is below, it will be cold and wet on the high mountains. The free *Stay Safe in Snowdonia* is available at NPICs and offers advice and information on hiking and climbing. (See **Wilderness Safety,** p. 50.) Pick up the Ordnance Survey Landranger Map #115 (1:50,000; $6.50), Outdoor Leisure Map #17 (1:25,000; $7.50), and path guides (40p) at TICs and NPICs. Call **Mountaincall Snowdonia** (☎09068 500 449) for the forecast.

Snowdonia National Park Study Centre, Plâs Tan-y-Bwlch, Maentwrog, Blaenau Ffestiniog, conducts two- to seven-day courses on naturalist topics, such as botanical painting. (☎01766 590 324. Courses $140-450, includes accommodations.) **YHA Pen-y-Pass,** Nant Gwynant (p. 503), puts groups in touch with guides for outdoor sports. **Beics Eryri Cycle Tours,** 44 Tyddyn Llwydyn, offers trips from Caernarfon for multi-night forays into the park, supplying maps, bikes, and accommodations. (☎01286 676 637. From $40 per night.) **Dolbadarn Trekking** operates out of Llanberis (p. 507). Ask park rangers about guided **day walks.** The brave can paraglide off peaks with the help of **Snowdon Gliders.** (☎01248 600 330; www.snowdongliders.co.uk. Call ahead.) The less brave can climb indoors at the **Beacon Climbing Centre.** (☎01286 650 045; www.beaconclimbing.com. 1½hr. session $50. Open M-F 11am-10pm, Sa-Su 10am-10pm.) **Llyn Tegid,** Bala, Wales's largest natural lake, has excellent windsurfing. Find other adventures in *The Snowdon Peninsula: North Wales Activities* brochure, available at TICs and NPICs.

DOLGELLAU   ☎01341

Set in a deep river valley, Dolgellau (dohl-GECTH-hlai) is a refuge from the formidable mountains above. Low clouds drift overhead, often shrouding the nearby peaks. The majestic views and extensive paths attract hikers of all skill levels to the town, whose stone and slate houses are hewn from local rock.

⊏ TRANSPORTATION. Buses stop in Eldon Sq. near the TIC, which details all local services in *Gwynedd Public Transport Maps and Timetables*. Arriva (☎0870 608 2608) bus X94 (M-Sa 8 per day, Su 4 per day) heads to Barmouth (20min.) in one direction, and Llangollen (1½hr.) and Wrexham (2hr.) in the other. Buses #32 and X32 pass through Dolgellau on their way to Porthmadog, Caernarfon, and Bangor in one direction (M-Sa 6 per day, Su 2 per day), and Machynlleth (40min.; M-Sa 10 per day, Su 2 per day; £2.80), and Aberystwyth (1¼hr.; M-Sa 8 per day, Su 2 per day) in the other. Bus #28 goes to Machynlleth (1½hr., M-Sa 6 per day). Rent bikes at Dolgellau Cycles, Smithfield Rd. (☎423 332; www.dolgellaucycles.co.uk. £13 per ½-day; £20 per full day. Open daily 9:30am-5pm. MC/V.)

◪ PRACTICAL INFORMATION. The **Tourist Information Centre**, Eldon Sq., by the bus stop, books rooms for £2 plus a 10% deposit. It doubles as a **Snowdonia National Park Information Centre**, with an exhibit on local mountains and trails. (☎422 888. Open July-Aug. daily 9:30am-5:30pm; Easter-May and Sept.-Oct. daily 9:30am-12:30pm and 1:30-5:30pm; Nov.-Easter M and Th-Su 9:30am-12:30pm and 1-4:30pm.) Equip yourself with camping and hiking gear and Ordnance Survey maps (£7-13) at **Cader Idris Outdoor Gear**, Eldon Sq., across from the bus stop. (☎422 195; www.cader-idris.co.uk. Open June-Sept. M-Sa 9am-5:30pm, Su 10am-4pm; Oct.-May M-Sa 9am-5:30pm.) Other services include: HSBC **bank**, Eldon Sq. (☎525 400; open M-F 9:30am-4:30pm); a **launderette**, Smithfield St., across from Aber Cottage Tea Room (wash £2.20-3.40, dry £1; open M and W-Su 9am-7pm; last wash 6:30pm); **police**, Old Barmouth Rd. (☎0845 607 1002); Dolgellau/Barmouth District **Hospital**, off Penbrynglas (☎422 479); Boots **pharmacy**, 3 Eldon Row (☎08450 708 090; open M-Sa 9am-5:30pm); free **Internet** access at the **library**, Bala Rd. (☎422 771; open M-F 9:30am-6pm and Sa 9:30am-noon); and the **post office**, inside Spar at Plas yn Dre St. (☎422 466; open M-F 9am-5:30pm, Sa 9am-12:30pm). **Post Code:** LL40 1AD.

⊓⊓ ACCOMMODATIONS AND FOOD. The **YHA Kings ❶** (p. 503) is 4 mi. away. In Dolgellau itself, lodging is scarce and expensive, starting around £22-25. The refurbished, 350-year-old **Aber Cottage Gallery B&B ❸**, on Smithfield St. near the bridge, has pristine, elegant bedrooms and houses the owner's art gallery and cafe. (☎422 460. Breakfast included; outdoor dining available. Singles £35; doubles £60. Cash only.) Two **B&Bs** with lower rates and views of the Idris range cling to the hills just north of town. **Arosfyr ❷**, Pen y Cefn, is a working farm with bright, airy rooms. From the bus stop, walk past the TIC, cross Smithfield St. bridge, turn left, then right at the school. Follow the steep road until a sign on the right directs you to the house just before the farm sheds. (☎422 355. Singles £22.50. Cash only.) Comfortable **Dwy Olwyn ❸** keeps horses and serves big breakfasts. Cross the Smithfield St. bridge, turn right, then left onto the unmarked road after the Somerfield, and follow the signs 5min. uphill. (☎422 822; www.dwyolwyn.co.uk. Singles £28; doubles £44. Cash only.) **Camping** is available at the deluxe **Tanyfron Caravan and Camping Park ❶**, a 10min. walk south on Arron Rd. onto the A470. (☎422 638. From £11 per tent; car £2 extra. Electricity £2. Free showers. Cash only.) Spar **market** is on Plas yn Dre St. (☎422 200. Open daily 8am-10pm.) The **Aber Cottage Tea Room ❷**, Smithfield St., is part of the B&B and gallery. Patrons unwind in plush chairs and sample gourmet soups (from £3) and pastries. The paintings covering the walls are the owners' own work. (Open Tu-Su 10am-5pm. Cash only.) **Popty'r Dref ❶** bakery and delicatessen, Upper Smithfield St., just off Eldon Sq., tempts customers with pastries, preserves, and cheeses packed to the ceiling. (☎422 507. Pastries 50p-£2. Open M-F 8am-5pm, Sa 8am-4pm. Cash only.) Duck under the low portal at **Y Sospan ❷**, Queen's Sq., behind the TIC, for sandwiches (from £2.50) and minty lamb steak (£10.25). The venue turns from a lunch spot into an upscale bistro and wine bar after 6pm. (☎423 174. Open M-F 9am-9pm, Sa-Su 9am-9:30pm. AmEx/MC/V.)

◯ SIGHTS. The famous **Precipice Walk** (3 mi., 2hr.) follows an easy path revealing views of Mawddach Estuary and the huge Idris range. Once restricted to the well-to-do guests of the nearby Caeynwch estate, the **Torrent Walk** (2½ mi., 1½hr.) circles along an ancient Roman path through woods and past waterfalls. Walks after heavy rains are deluged with gushing torrents. The **Llyn Cau, Cader Idris, and Tal-y-Llyn Walk** (7 mi., 5½hr.) is a strenuous excursion that should only be attempted in good weather. The hard work pays off in views of a glacial lake from 2617 ft. Mynydd Pencoed. At the end, pick up pamphlets (40p) for individual walks, or *Local Walks Around Dolgellau* (£4) at the TIC for 15 hikes for all levels. The entrances to most footpaths are not in the town itself; ask for directions at the TIC.

CADER IDRIS

This dark mountain (2930 ft.) offers stunning terrain and scenic walks that are less crowded than those of Mt. Snowdon. All paths cross privately owned farmland; be courteous and leave all gates as you found them. The 5 mi. pony track from **Llanfihangel y Pennant** is the longest but easiest path to the summit. After a level section, the path climbs through wind-sculpted rocks overlooking the Mawddach estuary and continues over the mountain. The 3 mi. trail from Tŷ Nant is not particularly strenuous and begins at **Tŷ Nant farm,** 3 mi. from Dolgellau. Avoid **Fox's Path,** which ascends Idris from the same place: many accidents occur on its steep slope. The **Minffordd Path** (about 3 mi.) is the shortest and steepest ascent. On its way to the summit, the path crosses through an 8000-year-old oak wood and rises above the lake of **Llyn Cau.** Watch out for the **Cwn Annwn** (Hounds of the Underworld), said to fly around the range's peaks. Allow 5hr. for any of these walks. Booklets (40p) charting each are available at the NPIC. For longer treks, the Ordnance Survey Outdoor Leisure #23 or Landranger #124 map (£6.50-7.50) is essential.

The 9000-acre **Coed-Y-Brenin Forest Park** covers the area around the Mawddach and Eden rivers and is known for its world-class mountain biking trails. The **Temptiwr Cycling Trail** covers 9km and is suitable for intermediate cyclists. The aptly named **Beast Trail** covers 38km of hills that total nearly one vertical kilometer. Difficult hills channel the Addams Family with names like "Morticia" and "Gomez." The forest also has trails reserved for hikers and is best entered 7 mi. north of Dolgellau off the A470, near the Coed-Y-Brenin Visitor Centre. (☎440 666. Open Apr.-Oct. daily 9am-5pm; Nov.-Mar. Sa-Su 10am-5pm.) Rent mountain bikes in the park from Beics Brenin for £40 per day. (☎440 728. Open May-Sept. daily 10am-5pm, Oct.-Nov. and Mar.-Apr. M and Th-Su 10am-5pm or dusk, Dec.-Feb. F-Su 10am-5pm or dusk.) Mountaineers and sportsmen will find the town of Dolgellau (p. 504) and the **Corris Youth Hostel ❷** (p. 492) convenient spots to rest.

HARLECH   ☎01766

From the Welsh "harddlech," meaning "beautiful slope," Harlech's name says it all. The steep ascent from the coast rises above sand dunes and passes the tea rooms and inns of High St. (Stryd Fawr) before leading to Harlech's castle above the sea. From the castle, clear days allow views of mountainous skyline and town lights.

📧 **TRANSPORTATION.** Harlech lies midway on the Cambrian Coaster line. The uphill walk to town from the unstaffed train station is a challenge; follow the signs until you arrive at a sculpture of "Two Kings" from the Mabinogion. **Trains** (08457 484 950) leave for Machynlleth (1¼-1½hr.; M-Sa 7 per day, Su 3 per day; £7.80); Porthmadog (20min.; M-F 9 per day, Sa 7 per day, Su 3 per day; £2.40); Pwllheli (45min.; M-F 9 per day, Sa 7 per day, Su 3 per day; £5.30); and other towns on the Llŷn Peninsula. The **Cambrian Coaster Day Ranger** (£7, children £3.50, families £13.50) allows unlimited travel on the Coaster line for a day. Arriva Cymru (☎0870 608 2608) **bus** #38 links Harlech to southern Barmouth (M-Sa 11 per day £2-3) and northern Blaenau Ffestiniog (M-Sa 9 per day), stopping at the car park on Stryd Fawr and the train station.

🏢🛈 **ORIENTATION AND PRACTICAL INFORMATION.** The castle opens out onto **Twtil.** Slightly uphill is the town's major street, **Stryd Fawr** (often called High St.). Near the castle, the **Tourist Information Centre,** Stryd Fawr, doubles as a **National Park Information Centre.** The staff stocks Ordnance Survey maps (£7-13), and books accommodations for £2 plus a 10% deposit. (☎780 658. Open Easter-Oct. daily 9:30am-12:30pm and 1:30-5:30pm.) Other services include: HSBC **bank,** Stryd Fawr (open M-F 9:30-11:30am); **police** (☎01492 517 171); free **Internet** access at the **library,** up the hill on Stryd Fawr past the Spar (☎780 565; open M and F 3:30-6pm, W 10am-1pm); and the **post office,** Stryd Fawr (☎780 231; open M-Tu and Th-F 9:30am-5:30pm, W 9am-12:30pm, Sa 9am-5pm). **Post Code:** LL46 2YA.

🏠🍴 **ACCOMMODATIONS AND FOOD.** Relax in spacious rooms at ▩**Arundel** ❷, Stryd Fawr, where breakfast is served in a conservatory with views of the ocean and castle. Walk past the TIC and take a right before the Yr Ogof Bistro. The lovable proprietor, Mary Stein, will pick you up from the train station. (☎780 637. Singles £16. Cash only.) The **Byrdir Guest House** ❷, a former hotel on Stryd Fawr near the bus stop, offers a ground floor bar and comfortable rooms with TV. (☎780 316; www.byrdir.com. Singles from £26.50; doubles from £49. Discounts for multiple nights. Cash only.) Spar **market** is near the edge of Stryd Fawr's main drag, right before the road curves. (☎780 592. Open daily 8am-8pm.) **The Weary Walker's Cafe** ❶, on Stryd Fawr near the bus stop, has sandwich options for £2-3. (☎780 751. Open in summer 9:30am-5pm; in low season 10:30am-4pm. Closed Th. Cash only.) The bar at the **Lion Hotel** ❷, off Stryd Fawr above the castle, provides pints in this nearly publess town. Bar snacks are 70p-£4; meals run £7-10. (☎780 731. Open M-F noon-11pm, Sa 11am-11pm, Su noon-10:30pm. Food served until 8:30pm. MC/V.)

🔆 **SIGHTS. Harlech Castle's** walls, once touched by the now receded oceans, seem to spring naturally from their craggy cliff. It was one of the "iron ring" fortresses built by Edward I to watch over spirited Welsh troublemakers. Spiral scaffolding and rounded windows hint at the foreign influences in the castle's design. Welsh rebel Owain Glyndwr had a brief occupancy and parliament here. (☎780 552. Open June-Sept. daily 9:30am-6pm; Apr.-May and Oct. daily 9:30am-5pm; Nov.-Mar. M-Sa 9:30am-4pm, Su 11am-4pm. Last admission 30min. before close. £3.50, concessions £3, families £10. Audio tours £1.) Public **footpaths** run from Harlech's grassy dunes to the forested hilltops above the town; get recommendations and directions at the TIC. **Theatr Ardudwy** (☎780 667; www.theatrardudwy.co.uk), on the A496, hosts a variety of operas, comedies, concerts, and the occasional band of dancing Buddhist monks (tickets £3-20). Sun seekers will appreciate the white sand **beach,** 20min. from town on foot. Walk down the road by the castle, turn right on the A496, and then turn left through the golf course, following the signs.

MOUNT SNOWDON AND VICINITY   ☎01286

By far the most popular destination in the park, **Mount Snowdon** (3560 ft.) is the highest peak in both England and Wales. The Welsh name for the peak, Yr Wyddfa (ur-WITH-va; "burial place"), comes from a legend that Rhita Gawr, a giant cloaked with the beards of the kings he slaughtered, is buried here. Over half a million hikers tread the mountain each year. In fair weather (ha), the steep green slopes and shimmering lakes tucked beneath the mountain's ragged cliffs are stunning. Future hikes were in peril in 1998 when a plot of land that included Snowdon's summit was put up for sale, but celebrated Welsh actor Sir Anthony Hopkins sprang to the rescue, contributing a vast sum to the National Trust to save the pristine peak. Park officers request that hikers stick to the six well-marked trails to avoid damaging Snowdon's ecosystem. The most popular route is the **Llanberis Path** (5 mi.), which begins right outside of Llanberis. It is the longest and easiest of the trails, but other paths, like the **Miner's Track,** offer superior views and cross numerous valleys. The more challenging **Pyg Track** begins in nearby Pen-y-Pass. Start climbing early in the day to avoid crowds. Trains run up to the summit on the **Snowdon Mountain Railway** (p. 507); a mailbox at the top allows you to send postcards with a special stamp. A visitor center at the summit will open in 2008.

Although Mt. Snowdon is the main attraction in the northern part of the park, experienced climbers cart pick-axes and ropes to the **Ogwen Valley.** Climbs to **Devil's Kitchen** (Twll Du), the **Glyders** (Glyder Fawr and Glyder Fach), and **Tryfan** all begin from **Llyn Ogwen.** Tryfan's peak has been immortalized in countless National Park posters. Its elevation has been set at 3010 ft., but nobody's quite sure which of two adjacent rocks (nicknamed Adam and Eve) is the summit. For the most complete experience, some travelers jump through the crags at the top (about 3ft.), a feat performed at their own risk. Climbers should pick up Ordnance Survey maps and get advice on equipment at **Joe Brown's Store** (p. 507). Horseback riding is available at the **Dolbadarn Trekking Centre,** High St., Llanberis. (☎870 277; www.dolbadarnhotel.co.uk. 1hr. £15; 2hr. £25.)

LLANBERIS   ☎01286

Beneath its quiet facade, Llanberis bursts with youthful energy, local pride, and rugged outdoorsmanship. The town's shifting community of climbers, cyclists, and hikers keeps it lively seven days a week (and most nights as well), while its lake and mountains provide numerous forays for outdoor adventurers.

⎁⎘ TRANSPORTATION AND PRACTICAL INFORMATION. Situated on the western edge of the park, Llanberis is a short ride from Caernarfon on the A4086. Catch KMP (☎870 880) **bus** #88 or 9A to Caernarfon (25min.; £1.50, round-trip £2; M-Sa every hr., Su 8 per day). KMP #85 and 86 run frequently to Bangor (35-50min.; M-Sa 1-2 per hr., Su 6 per day).

The **Tourist Information Centre,** 41b High St., gives hiking tips and books beds for £2 plus a 10% deposit. It stocks a number of brochures on hikes in Snowdonia, including pamphlets (40p) on the six routes up Mt. Snowdon. (☎870 765. Open Easter-Oct. daily 9:30am-5pm; Nov.-Easter M and F-Su 11am-4pm.) Pick up hiking gear, maps, coffee, and trail advice at **Joe Brown's Store,** Menai Hall, High St. (☎870 327. Open in summer M-F 9am-5:30pm, Sa 9am-6pm, Su 9am-5pm; in winter M-F and Su 9am-5pm, Sa 9am-5:30pm.) Other services include: HSBC **bank,** 29 High St. (open M and W 9:30am-11:30pm, Tu and Th-F 1:30-3:30pm) and the bankless Barclays **ATM,** at the entrance to Electric Mountain on the A4086; Rowlands **pharmacy,** High St. (☎870 264; open M-F 9am-1pm and 2-5:30pm, Sa 9am-1pm.); **Internet** access at Pete's Eats (p. 508); and the **post office,** 36 High St. (☎870 201; open M-Tu and Th-F 9am-5:30pm, W and Sa 9am-7:30pm). **Post Code:** LL55 4EU.

▐▍ ACCOMMODATIONS AND FOOD. During summer weekends, the town fills fast; plan ahead. The outskirts of Llanberis hold tiny ▨**Snowdon Cottage ❸**. From the bus station, walk up the hill past the railway station. The Cottage is about 200 yd. past the Victoria Hotel, around the bend and on your left. With a castle-view garden, sweet-smelling rooms, an Egyptian-inspired bathroom, and a gracious host, guests may be tempted to ditch the mountains and stay indoors. (☎872 015. £25 per person. Discounts for multiple nights. Cash only.) Plenty of sheep keep hostelers company at the **YHA Llanberis ❷** (p. 503). **Pete's Eats** (p. 508) has basic dorm-style rooms starting at £12; twins are £30. Camp at **Llwyn Celyn Bach,** a farm adjacent to the YHA Llanberis on Capel Goch Rd. (☎07796 420 179. Kitchen, laundry, and showers. £3-4 per night. Cash only.) On weekends, the **Heights Hotel ❷**, 74 High St., draws locals to its two ground-floor bars, glass-walled "conservatory" (smoking lounge), and pool room. (☎871 179. Singles £35; doubles £55; 3- to 6-person rooms £25 per person. AmEx/MC/V.) Enjoy mostly ensuite rooms and fluffy towels at the grand **Plas Coch Guest House ❸**, High St. (☎872 122; www.plascoch.co.uk. Singles from £30; doubles £56-68. Cash only.)

Spar **market** is at the corner of High St. and Capel Goch Rd. (Open M-Sa 7am-11pm, Su 7am-10:30pm.) Lively ▨**Pete's Eats ❶**, 40 High St., opposite the TIC, is the place to refuel with a vegetarian walnut cheeseburger (£2.50) or chili (£5.40) with a mug of tea (£85p) among an eclectic crowd of high chair-bound tots and grungy hikers. (☎870 117. Internet access 5p per min. Open daily July-Aug. 8am-9pm; Nov.-June 8am-8pm. MC/V.) **Snowdon Honey Farm ❶**, High St., sells a huge selection of its own meads, Celtic wines, and honey, as well as sandwiches, cakes, and ice cream. The owners dish out samples. (☎870 218. Open daily 7am-6pm. Cash only.)

◪ SIGHTS. Most attractions lie near the fork where the A4086 meets High St. Part self-promotion, part journey to the center of the earth, **Electric Mountain** takes visitors on an underground tour of the Dinorwig power station. Located deep in a mountain formerly quarried for slate, the station occupies the largest manmade cavern in Europe—St. Paul's Cathedral could fit inside. (☎870 636. Open June-Aug. daily 9:30am-5:30pm; Feb.-May and Sept.-Dec. daily 10:30am-4:30pm. Advance bookings only. £7, concessions £3.50, families £19.50.) The immensely popular but pricey **Snowdon Mountain Railway** has been letting visitors "climb" Snowdon's summit since 1896, winding along tracks from its base station on the A4086. The 2½hr. round-trip loop allows 30min. at the peak, but one-way tickets are available. (☎08704 580 033; www.snowdonrailway.co.uk. Runs daily from Mar. to early Nov. 9am-5pm; Mar.-May trains stop halfway up. Weather permitting. £11, concessions £8, children £7; round-trip £15/12/11.)

In nearby **Parc Padarn,** accessed by a footpath next to the bus stop on the A4086, the **Welsh Slate Museum** explores the history of mining with a 3D film, recreated miners' dwellings, and live displays of slate splitting and finishing. Don't miss the largest waterwheel in mainland Britain. (☎870 630; www.nmgw.ac.uk. Open Easter-Oct. daily 10am-5pm; Nov.-Easter M-F and Su 10am-4pm. Last admission 1hr. before close. Free.) A short walk takes you to the **Quarry Hospital Visitor Centre.** This old hospital, built by the owner of the mines to deal with health issues "privately," now houses morbid artifacts from the days before anti-germ procedures, including sinister medical instruments and a morgue with slate tables. (☎870 892. Open from Apr. to early Sept. daily 11am-5pm. £1.) The park is also home to the **Llanberis Lake Railway,** which runs from Gilfach Ddu station at Llanberis through the woods along the lake. (☎870 549; www.lake-railway.co.uk. 40min. round-trip. Open Apr.-May and Sept.-Oct. M-F and Su; June-Aug. daily. Open other months intermittently; call ahead. £6.50, children £4.50.) The **Woodland and Wildlife Centre,** at the halfway point, is a nice picnic spot. Follow the road into the park until a footbridge to the right leads to **Dolbadarn Castle,** where Prince Llywelyn of North Wales is said to have imprisoned his traitorous brother for 23 years. Only a single, ragged tower remains. The area affords views of the **Lady of Snowdon,** a rock formation that supposedly resembles Elizabeth II. (Free.) For views of the waterfall **Ceunant Mawr,** follow the marked footpath from Victoria Terr. by the Victoria Hotel (¾ mi.).

CAERNARFON   ☎01286

Occupied since pre-Roman times and once the center of English government in northern Wales, Caernarfon has witnessed countless struggles for regional political control. It was originally built for English settlers, but during a 1294 tax revolt, the Welsh managed to break in, sack the town, and massacre its English inhabitants. Caernarfon is now the traditional place for the crowning of Princes of Wales, most recently Charles in 1969. Although its streets are lined with modern shops and cafes, Caernarfon embraces its traditional Welsh character; visitors can hear the town's own dialect used in its streets and pubs.

▐ TRANSPORTATION. The nearest **train** station is in Bangor (p. 511), but numerous **buses** pass through Caernarfon on their way north. The central stop is on Penllyn in the city center. Arriva Cymru (☎0870 608 2608) buses #5 and 5X run to Conwy and Llandudno via Bangor (to Llandudno 1¾hr.; M-Sa 4 per hr., Su every hr.). Express Motors (☎881 108) bus #1 goes to Porthmadog (45-60min., M-Sa every hr., £2.60), as does Arriva bus #32 (M-Sa 6 per day, Su 2 per day). Clynnog & Trefor (☎660 208) and Berwyn (☎660 315) run bus #12 to Pwllheli (45min.; M-Sa every hr., Su 3 per day). KMP (☎870 880) buses #9A and 9B run to Llanberis (25min.; M-Sa 1-2 per hr., Su every hr. until 6:50pm). Arriva's TrawsCambria bus #701 runs daily to Cardiff (7½hr.). National Express (☎08705 808 080) bus #545 runs to London via Chester (9hr., daily, £28) or with a change in Birmingham (9½hr., daily, £28). A **Gwynedd Red Rover ticket** provides unlimited bus travel in the county for one day (£5, children £2.45). *Gwynedd Public Transport Maps and Timetables* gives info on bus and train routes. Castle Sq. shelters a **taxi** stand, or try Tacsi Aindows (☎677 391).

▐▐ ORIENTATION AND PRACTICAL INFORMATION. The heart of Caernarfon lies within and just outside the town walls. From the castle entrance, the TIC is across **Castle Ditch Road,** which runs past **Castle Square** in one direction and down to the Promenade in the other. **Castle Street** intersects Castle Ditch Rd. at the castle entrance and leads to **High Street. Bridge Street** runs north from Castle Square and turns into the busy **Bangor Street.**

The **Tourist Information Centre,** Castle St., facing the castle entrance, stocks the free *Visitor's Guide to Caernarfon* and books accommodations for £2 plus a 10% deposit. (☎672 232. Open Apr.-Oct. daily 9:30am-4:30pm; Nov.-Mar. M-Sa 9:30am-4:30pm.) Get **camping supplies** at 14th Peak, 9 Palace St. (☎675 124. 10% student discount. Open M-Sa 9am-5:30pm, Su 1-4pm.) Other services include: **banks** with **ATMs** in Castle Sq. and down Bridge St.; a **launderette,** on Skinner St., off Bridge St. (☎678 395; open M-Th 9am-6pm, F-Sa 9am-5:30pm, Su 11am-5:30pm; last wash 1hr. before close; £5); **police,** Maesincla Ln. (☎673 333, ext. 5242); free **Internet** access at the **library,** at the corner of Bangor St. and Lon Pafiliwn (☎675 944; open M-Tu and Th-F 10am-7pm, W 10am-1pm, Sa 9am-1pm) or at the Dylan Thomas Internet Cafe, 4 Bangor St. (☎678 777; Internet access and Wi-Fi £3 per hr.; open M-Sa 9am-6pm; cash only); a **pharmacy,** 1A Castle Sq. (☎672 352; open M-Sa 8:30am-6:30pm, Su 11:30am-2pm); and the **post office** with a **bureau de change,** Castle Sq. (☎08457 223 344; open M-F 9am-5:30pm, Sa 9am-12:30pm). **Post Code:** LL55 2ND.

ACCOMMODATIONS. Rooms abound, but cheap ones don't. **B&Bs** (£23-25) line **Church Street** inside the old town wall. Cheaper options can be found on **St. David's Road**, a 10min. walk from the castle and uphill off the Bangor St. roundabout. **Totter's Hostel ❷**, 2 High St. provides spacious, light dorms. The basement has a kitchen, a hand-crafted banquet table, and medieval stone arches. (☎672 963; www.totters.co.uk. Dorms £14. MC/V.) **Tegfan ❸**, 4 Church St., offers an excellent location and clean rooms with TV. (☎673 703. £22 per person. Cash only.) At **Bryn Hyfryd ❸**, St. David's Rd., travelers can sink into flowery bedspreads. One room has a sun deck, another coast views, and all are ensuite. (☎673 840. Singles £27.50; doubles £55; family rooms £70. Cash only.) **Marianfa ❸**, St. David's Rd., has a variety of spacious ensuite rooms with views of the Isle of Anglesey. Ask about group motorbike and sightseeing packages. (☎674 815; www.ukworld.net/marianfa. £25-30 per person, depending on the season. Cash only.) **Camp** at **Cadnant Valley ❶**, Cwm Cadnant Rd. (☎673 196; www.cwmcadnantvalley.co.uk. Showers and laundry. Tents £4, with car £9, plus £2.25 per person. Discounts in low seasons. MC/V.)

FOOD AND PUBS. A Morrison's **supermarket** sits on North Road (A487). Take Bangor St. past the roundabout. (Open M-Th 8:30am-10pm, F 8am-10pm, Sa 8am-8pm, Su 10am-4pm.) Spar, 29-31 Castle Sq. stocks a much smaller selection closer to the center of town. (☎676 805. Open M-Sa 7am-11pm, Su 7am-10:30pm.) On Saturdays and some Mondays, a **market** takes over Castle Sq. (Open 9am-4pm.) **Hole-in-the-Wall Street** is a narrow alleyway known for its dense collection of eateries. **Stones Bistro ❸**, 4 Hole-in-the-Wall St., near Eastgate, has candlelit tables and local art adorning its walls. Welsh lamb (£14.50) is served with your choice of mint, honey, yogurt, pepper, or tomato-garlic sauce. (☎671 152. Open Tu-Sa 6-11pm, Su noon-3pm. Reservations strongly recommended. AmEx/MC/V.) Relax within the stone walls of **Bwyty Oyof Y Odraig's (The Dragon's Cave) ❸**, 26 Hole-in-the-Wall St., which serves innovative Welsh fare. A variety of meat, vegetarian, and fish options, such as salmon and spinach in pastry (£11.50), await in the cozy dining room. (☎677 322. Open M and W-Su 6pm-late. MC/V.) The stout wooden doors of the **Anglesey Arms ❶** open onto the Promenade just below the castle. Relax outdoors with a pint as the sun dips into the shimmering Menai. (☎672 158. F live entertainment. Open M-Sa 11am-11pm, Su noon-10:30pm. MC/V.) Young crowds flock to **Cofi Roc**, on Castle Sq., for tribute bands every Friday. (☎673 100; www.cofiroc.com. Open M-Th 9am-4pm, F-Sa 9am-2am, Su 9am-midnight. F and Sa cover £4, after 10pm £5. MC/V.)

SIGHTS AND ENTERTAINMENT. Built by Edward I to resemble Roman battlements, **Caernarfon Castle** has been called by one resentful Welshman a "magnificent badge of our subjection." Its eagle-crowned turrets, colorful stones, and polygonal towers cost Edward the equivalent of the Crown's annual budget and nearly 17% of his skilled labor force. Its walls withstood a rebel siege in 1404 with only 28 defenders. Summer sees a variety of performances, including scenes from the Welsh epic Mabinogion. Wisecracking docents run tours every hour for £2, and a free 20min. video recounts the castle's history. The **regimental museum** of the Royal Welsh Fusiliers, inside the castle, is huge and worthwhile. Medals, uniforms, and helmets accompany rich historical exhibits. Don't miss the "Goat Major," responsible for taking care of the regiment's goat mascot, whose gilded horns and headplate have inspired generations of Fusiliers. (☎677 617. Open June-Sept. daily 9:30am-6pm; Apr.-May and Oct. daily 9:30am-5pm; Nov.-Mar. M-Sa 9:30am-4pm, Su 11am-4pm. £5, concessions £4.50, families £15.) Most of Caernarfon's 13th-century **town wall** survives, and a stretch between Church St. and Northgate St. is open for climbing during the same hours as the castle. The remains of a

Celtic settlement scatter atop **Twt Hill,** alongside the Bangor St. roundabout. The jutting peak offers an excellent overlook above the town and castle. For views of Menai Strait and its surroundings, call **Menai Strait Pleasure Cruises** (☎672 772), which runs 40min. tours from May to October (cruises run 11:30am-4:30pm, weather and tides permitting; £5, children £3.50). Hilltop **Segontium Roman Fort** was once the center for military activity in North Wales. Plundered by the builders of Caernarfon Castle, the fort is now reduced to its foundations. The adjoining museum houses a display of Roman artifacts found in the area, plus models of the fort in its various stages. From Castle Sq., follow signs uphill along Ffordd Cwstenin. (☎675 625; www.segontium.org.uk. Museum open Tu-Su 12:30-4pm. Grounds open daily 10am-4:30pm. Free.) Six miles south of Caernarfon, **Parc Glynllifon** is bordered by the remains of a log fence built to "keep the peasants out and the pheasants in," but visitors are now welcome to wander through the lawns and exotic trees. Take bus #12 (15min., every hr., £1.70 round-trip) south from Caernarfon to the Parc Glynllifon stop. (☎830 222. Open daily 10am-6pm. £3, children and seniors £1.50, families £8.) The new arts complex **Y Galeri,** on Victoria Dock, shows films, hosts speakers and musicians, and has a gallery for local artists. (☎685 222; www.galericaernarfon.com. Tickets free-£20, concessions available.) The town's biggest nightclub is **K2,** St. Helen's Rd., off Castle St. below Cofi Roc, downstairs next to the post office. (☎673 100. No sneakers. Cover Sa £5, after 10pm £6. Open Sa 10pm-2am.) A local crowd flocks to **Medi,** Palace St., a diverse venue with a bar, disco, and lounge on three floors. (☎674 383. No sportswear. Cover Sa 11:30pm-12:30am £2. Open F-Sa 9am-2am, Su 9am-11pm. MC/V.)

BANGOR   ☎01248

Once a stronghold of Welsh princes, Bangor is now a lively university town and the most convenient base from which to explore the coast and nearby Isle of Anglesey. Dozens of shops line Bangor's town center, and term-time students cram its pubs at all hours.

⊏ TRANSPORTATION. Bangor is the transportation hub for the Isle of Anglesey to the west and Snowdonia to the southeast. The **train station** is on Holyhead Rd., at the end of Deiniol Rd. (Ticket office open in summer M-Sa 5:30am-6:30pm, Su 7:15am-6:30pm; in winter M-Sa 5:30am-6:30pm, Su 9am-6:30pm.) **Trains** (☎08457 484 950) go to Chester (1¼hr., 1-2 per hr., £14.10), Holyhead (30min.; M-Sa 15 per day, Su 10 per day; £6.30), and Llandudno Junction (20min.; M-Sa 1-2 per hr., Su 10 per day; £4.40). The **bus station** is on Garth Rd., downhill from the town clock. Arriva Cymru (☎08706 082 608) bus #4 runs to Holyhead via Llangefni and Llanfair P.G. (1-1½hr., M-Sa 1-2 per hr., £3.60). On Sunday, #44 makes the trip six times. Buses #53, 57, and 58 go to Beaumaris (30min.; M-Sa 1-3 per hr., Su 8 per day; £2.60). Arriva buses #5 and 5X journey to Conwy (40min.; M-Sa 2-3 per hr., Su every hr.; £1.80) and Llandudno (1hr., £2). Transfer at Caernarfon for the Llŷn Peninsula, including Porthmadog. National Express (☎08705 808 080) buses come from London (8½hr., 1 per day, £28). For **taxis,** call Ace Taxi (☎351 324).

◢◪ ORIENTATION AND PRACTICAL INFORMATION. Bangor's age-old street plan and unmarked roads can be confusing. The central corridor is bounded by **Deiniol Road** (Ffordd Deiniol) and **High Street** (Stryd Fawr), which run parallel to each other. **Garth Road** (Ffordd Garth) starts from the town clock on High St. and goes past the bus station, merging with Deiniol Rd. **Holyhead Road** begins its ascent at the train station. The **University of Wales at Bangor** straddles both sides of **College Road.** The free map from the TIC lists most streets in Welsh.

The **Tourist Information Centre,** Town Hall, Deiniol Rd., by the bus station, books rooms for £2 plus a 10% deposit. (☎352 786. Open May-Sept. M-F 9:30am-4pm.) Other services include: **banks** with **ATMs** on High St. near the clocktower; **police** (☎370 333), behind the Town Hall on Deiniol Rd.; the **hospital** (☎384 384), Penthosgarnedd; a **pharmacy,** 276 High St. (☎362 822; open M-Sa 9am-5:30pm); free **Internet** access at the **library,** across from the TIC (☎353 479; open M-Tu and Th-F 9:30am-7pm, W and Sa 9:30am-1pm); and the **post office,** 60 Deiniol Rd., with a **bureau de change** (☎377 301; open M-F 9am-5:30pm, Sa 9am-12:30pm). **Post Code:** LL57 1AA.

📷🍴 **ACCOMMODATIONS AND FOOD.** Finding a room in Bangor during graduation festivities (the 2nd week of July) is difficult; book months ahead. The ⬛**YHA Bangor ❷,** Tan-y-Bryn, is ½ mi. from the town center. Follow High St. to the water and turn right onto the A5122 (Beach Rd.), then right at the sign. Buses #5 and 5X, 9, 66, 67, 77, and 78 (to Llandudno or Bethesda; every 10-15min.) pass the hostel; ask to be let off. This 19th-century country estate on the former grounds of Penrhyn Castle once housed Vivien Leigh and Sir Laurence Olivier. (☎353 516. Kitchen and lounge with foosball. Laundry £3 per wash, dry 20p per 10min. Open Apr.-Sept. daily; Oct. and Mar. Tu-Sa; Nov. and Jan.-Feb. F-Sa. Dorms £14, under 18 £10. MC/V.) The best **B&B** options (from £17) in Bangor occupy the townhouses on **Garth Road** and its extensions. **Mrs. S. Roberts ❷,** 32 Glynne Rd., between Garth Rd. and High St., has a colorful garden, an affectionate cat, and 13 choices for breakfast. (☎352 113. Singles £17. Cash only.) Comfortable **Dilfan ❸** is a 5-10min. walk from the TIC, across from the swimming pool on Garth Rd. (☎353 030. Singles £30; doubles £50. Cash only.) **The University of Wales at Bangor ❷,** Victoria Dr., offers dorm accommodations from June to mid-September. (☎382 558. Ensuite rooms. No children under 11. Singles £18.75, with breakfast £24.25. Advance booking only. MC/V.) Camp at **Dinas Farm Touring Farm ❶,** 3 mi. from Bangor on the banks of the River Ogwen. Follow the A5 past Penrhyn Castle and turn left off the A5122. (☎364 227. Open Apr.-Oct. £5 per person. Electricity £2. Cash only.)

High Street has a surprisingly varied selection of bakeries, pubs, and eateries. The closest **supermarket** is Aldi, on Garth Rd. by the bus station. (Open M-F 9am-7pm, Sa 8:30am-7pm, Su 10am-4pm.) Vegetarian-friendly **Herbs ❷,** 162 High St., has a salad bar (£3.25), cheap lunches (from £3), and a multicultural menu in a dining room decorated with mosaics and potted plants. (☎351 249; www.herbsrestaurant.co.uk. Open M-Th 10am-3pm, F-Sa 10am-9pm. AmEx/MC/V.) **Gerrards ❶,** 251 High St., near the clock tower, has bakery fare and monthly specials (such as two lunches for £6) in a spacious, old-fashioned venue. Don't miss the caramel fudge. (☎371 351. Open M-Sa 9am-5pm. Sandwiches served until 4:30pm. Cash only.) Choose between Asian-inspired "East" or solidly British "West" on the menu at the mellow **Java Restaurant ❷,** up an alley off of High St., near Abbey St. Specials include a burger with salad, chips, and a pint for £7. (☎361 652. Open M-Tu 10am-6pm, W-Sa 10am-10pm. Hot food served 10am-3pm and 6-9pm. MC/V.)

🎥🎵 **SIGHTS AND ENTERTAINMENT.** George Hay Dawkins-Pennant's 19th-century ⬛**Penrhyn Castle** is the pinnacle of the short-lived neo-Norman school, which attempted to recreate Edward I's castle-building style. The intricate main staircase is full of carved faces and took over 10 years to complete. The house is also home to the second-largest art collection in Wales, after the National Gallery, including a Rembrandt over the dining room fireplace. Its slate-baron owner was on a mission to prove that the material has numerous uses—elaborate slate dressers, a slate billiard table, and even a slate canopy bed can be found inside. Walk up High St. toward the bay, then turn right on the A5122 and go north 1 mi., or catch bus #5 or 5X from town to the grounds entrance (10min.; M-Sa 2 per hr., Su every hr.; 60p). The castle is another mile farther. (☎353 084. Castle open July-Aug. M and W-Su 11am-5pm; late Mar.-June and Sept.-Oct. M and W-Su noon-5pm. Grounds open daily July-Aug. 10am-5pm; late Mar.-June and Sept.-Oct. 11am-5pm. Last admission 30min. before close. £8, children £4, families £20.)

The site of **St. Deiniol's Cathedral**, Gwynedd Rd., off High St., has been the ecclesiastical center of this corner of Wales for 1400 years, and the building has been there for over 700. Today, it sits humbly amid the commercial district. (☎353 983. Open M-F 9am-4:30pm, Sa 9am-1pm, Su for services.) The **Bangor Museum and Art Gallery**, also on Gwynedd Rd., houses an authentic man-trap—a leg-breaking contraption used as an anti-poaching device by sneaky landowners—and a collection of regional crafts and artifacts, with local art on the first floor. (☎353 368. Open Tu-F 12:30-4:30pm, Sa 10:30am-4:30pm. Free.) Watch tides ebb and flow at the long, onion-domed Victorian **pier** at the end of Garth Rd. The modern **Theatr Gwynedd**, Deiniol Rd., at the base of the hill, houses a thriving troupe that performs in Welsh and English. (☎351 708. Box office open M-F 9:30am-5pm, Sa 10am-5pm, and until 8pm on performance nights. Tickets £5-26; concessions available.) Bangor's students keep clubs buoyant during the term, and many pubs along **High Street** pump up the volume on weekends. Dance your way to happiness (or buy it in liquid form) at **The Octagon**, Dean St., off High St. Dress up on theme nights to bypass the cover. (☎354 977. Cover £2-6. Open W and F 9:30pm-2am, Sa 9:30pm-3am.) At cover-free **Joop's**, 358-360 High St., a young, low-key crowd parties. (☎372 040. Open F-Sa 9pm-2am.)

ISLE OF ANGLESEY (YNYS MÔN)

Anglesey's old name, Môn mam Cymru (Anglesey, mother of Wales), indicates roots embedded deep in old Celtic culture. Although you won't find spectacular castles or cathedrals, druidic burial sites and tiny chapels dot farmlands whose granaries have long supported Wales. Anglesey's sense of Welsh heritage is hardly confined to history: three out of five islanders speak Welsh as a first language.

⌐ TRANSPORTATION

Apart from its major towns, Anglesey can be difficult to explore without a car—buses connect much of the island, but routes are sporadic. Bangor, on the mainland, is the best hub. **Trains** (☎08457 484 950) run on the North Wales line from Holyhead to Bangor (30min.; M-F 1-2 per hr., Su 13 per day; £6.30); some stop at Llanfair P.G. The main **bus** company is Arriva Cymru (☎0870 608 2608), whose buses make the trip out to most of the island's major towns from the Menai and Britannia bridges. Smaller bus companies fill the gaps. Buses are reliable, albeit bumpy. Arriva bus #4 travels north from Bangor to Holyhead via Llanfair P.G. and Llangefni (1½hr., M-Sa 2 per hr., £3.60). On Sundays, #44 follows a similar route (6 per day). Buses #53, 57, and 58 hug the southeast coast from Bangor to Beaumaris (30min.; M-Sa 2 per hr., Su 8 per day; £2.60); some continue to Penmon (40min.; M-Sa 12 per day, Su 4 per day). Bus #62 goes to Amlwch, on the northern coast, from Bangor (1hr.; M-Sa 1-2 per hr., Su 5 per day; £1.75). Bus #42 from Bangor curves along the southwest coast to Aberffraw before continuing north to Llangefni (to Aberffraw 50min., to Llangefni 1¼hr.; M-Sa 9 per day, Su 3 per day). Lewis y Llan (☎01407 832 181) bus #61 travels from Amlwch to Holyhead (50min.; M-Sa 7 per day, Su 4 per day). Bus #32 shuttles north from Llangefni to Amlwch (40min.; M-Sa 8 per day, Su 4 per day). The **Gwynedd Red Rover** ticket (£5, children £2.45) covers a day's travel in Anglesey and Gwynedd. Pick up the free *Isle of Anglesey Public Transport Timetable* at TICs.

NORTH WALES

⊙ SIGHTS

Burial chambers, cairns, and other prehistoric remains are scattered in Holyhead and along the eastern and western coasts. Most ancient monuments now lie on farmers' fields, so a map detailing exactly how to reach them is helpful. TICs sell Ordnance Survey Landranger Map #114 (1:50,000; £6) and the more detailed Explorer #262 and 263, each of which covers half of the island (1:25,000; £7). The *Guide to Ancient Monuments* (£3) details the history of various prehistoric relics, while the pamphlet *Rural Cycling on Anglesey* is a must for bikers (free at TICs). Bus drivers will drop you off as close to sights as possible if you let them know what you want to see.

PLAS NEWYDD. The 19th-century country home of the Marquess of Anglesey, 2 mi. south of Llanfair P.G., is filled with ornate decor. The 58 ft. Rex Whistler *trompe l'oeil* mural in the dining room is a whimsical Mediterranean cityscape (with images of Wales, the painter, and the Marquess's family sneakily slipped in) and is the largest painted canvas in Britain. Don't miss the painter's trick: the mountains and footprints seem to move as you walk across the dining room. *(Take bus #42 from Bangor to the house (30min.; M-Sa 11 per day, Su 6 per day), or catch #4 to Llanfair P.G. (25min., M-Sa 2 per hr.) and walk carefully along the occasionally treacherous A4080. ☎01248 714 795. House open Apr.-Oct. M-W and Sa-Su noon-5pm. Garden open M-W and Sa-Su 11am-5:30pm. Last admission 4:30pm. £6.60, children £3.30. Garden only £4.60/2.30.)*

BRYN CELLI DDU. The most famous of Anglesey's remains, Bryn Celli Ddu (brin kay-HLEE thee; "The Mound in the Dark Grove") is a burial chamber dating from the Neolithic period. Excavators reconstructed most of the chamber and mound in 1928. The original 5000-year-old construction was at least three times larger. Bring a flashlight to view the wall etchings inside. The spiral rock outside of the chamber is a reproduction—the original is at the National Gallery in Cardiff. *(Bangor-Holyhead bus #4 stops at Llandaniel (M-Sa 14 per day); continue walking for 200 yd. toward Holyhead until a sign directs you left, down the A4080. Site is signposted 1 mi. down the road. Bus #42 will stop close by; tell the driver you're going to Bryn Celli Ddu. Free.)*

PENMON PRIORY. The late medieval priory of Penmon houses two ruined buildings and Europe's largest dovecote (a cylinder of nesting holes for pigeons). From the parking lot, a path leads to 6th-century **St. Seiriol's Well,** reputed to have healing qualities. *(Take Arriva Cymru bus #57 or 58 from Bangor or Beaumaris to Penmon (from Bangor 40min., from Beaumaris 20min.; M-Sa 11 per day, Su 5 per day) and follow the sign to Penmon Point. The priory is a 25min. walk on the same road. Free.)*

LLANFAIRPWLL...   ☎01248

Llanfairpwllgwyngyllgogerychwyrndrobwllllantysiliogogogoch (don't try to impress the locals with this: HLAN-vair-poohl-gwin-gihl-go-ger-uch-wern-dro-bwihl-hlan-tu-sil-eyo-go-go-goch) prides itself on having the longest name of any village in the world (58 letters). The full name is on any sign that will fit it, and a pronunciation guide hangs in the train station. Give or take a controversial adjective, the name translates to: "Saint Mary's Church in the hollow of white hazel near the rapid whirlpool and the Church of Saint Tysillio near the red cave." Sights in both New Zealand and Thailand claim longer titles—at 92 and 163 letters, respectively—although these names (one of them packed with extensive reference to "the man with the big knees...known as land eater") bear signs of publicity-seeking embellishment. For more information on this otherwise nondescript village's claim to fame, visit the **Tourist Information Centre,** which conveniently adjoins a network of shops selling heaps of commemorative trinkets. *(☎713 177. Books accommodations for £2* plus a 10% deposit. Open Apr.-Oct. M-Sa 9:30am-5:30pm, Su 10am-5pm; Nov.-Mar. M-Sa 9:30am-5pm, Su 10am-5pm.) Mercifully, the town is known locally as "Llan-fairpwll" or "Llanfair P.G." The #4 bus comes through Llanfair P.G. on its route between Bangor and Holyhead (M-Sa 1-2 per hr., Su every hr.).

BEAUMARIS   ☎01248

Four miles northeast of the Menai Bridge lies the tiny town of Beaumaris. It's a lively, colorful, tourist-fueled place, mostly built alongside the last and largest of Edward I's castles. ▨Beaumaris Castle sits in marshland just off the Menai's shore. It was to be the finest of Edward I's "iron ring" castles and, although unfinished, is still regarded as one of the best castle designs in Britain. (☎810 361. Open June-Sept. daily 9:30am-6pm; Apr.-May and Oct. daily 9:30am-5pm; Nov.-Mar. M-Sa 9:30am-4pm, Su 11am-4pm. Last admission 30min. before close. £3.50, concessions £3, families £10.) Beaumaris Gaol, on Bunkers Hill, presents a fascinating and chill-ing view of incarceration in Victorian Anglesey. Individual cells feature histories of past occupants and hold grim relics, including a system of ropes that allowed female inmates to rock their babies from the working rooms below. Out back, vis-itors can see one of Britain's only remaining treadwheels, which demanded hours of grueling labor from inmates to supply the prison with water. (☎810 921. Open daily Easter-Sept. 10:30am-5pm. Last admission 4:30pm. £3.50, concessions £2.75, families £12.) Its sister museum is the Old Courthouse, which lacks the morbid fas-cination of the gaol but provides insight into the workings of the courts over the last several centuries, including the days when juries were locked in a room with no toilet to encourage a speedy verdict. (Open Easter-Sept. daily 10:30am-5pm. £3, concessions £2.25, family £10.) Inexpensive catamaran cruises (1¼hr.) down the Menai Strait and around Puffin Island leave from the Starida booth on the pier. (☎07860 811 988. Weather permitting; call ahead. £6, children £4.50, families £18.)

The closest hostel is the YHA Bangor ❷ (p. 512). Few of the town's B&Bs offer sin-gles; consider sleeping in Bangor or Caernarfon. Summers are extremely busy. Camping is best at Kingsbridge Caravan Park ❶, 1½ mi. from town, toward Llan-goed. At the end of Beaumaris's main street, follow the road past the castle to the crossroads, turn left toward Llanfaes, and continue 400 yd. Arriva buses #57 and 58 from Bangor will stop nearby if you ask. (☎490 636. Open Mar.-Oct. £4-5, chil-dren £1.50-2. Electricity £2. Cash only.) Buy groceries at Spar, 11 Castle St. (Open M-Su 7am-11pm.) Tea shops cluster around the castle. One of the nicest is Beau's Tea Shop ❶, 30 Castle St., where stained-glass lamps cast an amber glow. (☎811 010. Open M-Sa 10am-4:30pm, Su 11am-4:30pm. Cash only.) Sarah's Delicatessen ❶, 11 Church St., sells gourmet fare and local cheeses. (☎811 534. Open M-Th 9am-5pm and F-Sa 9am-5:30pm. MC/V.) Buses stop on Castle St. The Tourist Information Cen-tre, located in Town Hall, on Castle St., provides a free town map and accommoda-tions listings. (☎810 040. Open Easter-Oct. M-Th and Sa 10am-4:45pm.) An HSBC bank is also on Castle St. (Open M-F 1pm-3:30pm.) The post office is at 10 Church St. (☎810 320. Open M-Tu and Th-F 9am-5:30pm, W and Sa 9am-12:30pm.) Post Code: LL58 8AB.

HOLYHEAD (CAERGYBI)   ☎01407

An unremarkable town attached to Anglesey by a causeway and a bridge, Holy-head is primarily known as a port for ferries headed to Ireland. Irish Ferries (☎08705 171 717) and Stena Line (☎08705 421 170) run ferries and catamarans (double-hulled boats) to Dublin and its suburb, Dún Laoghaire. Foot passengers check in at the terminal adjoining the train station; cars proceed along the asphalt. Arrive 30min. early and remember your passport. (See By Ferry, p. 31.)

NORTH WALES

Trains leave Holyhead every hour (Su every 2hr.) for Bangor (30min., £6.30), Chester (1½hr., £17.10), and London (4½-6hr.; 2 weeks in advance £15.50, same day £68.40). Arriva Cymru (☎0870 608 2608) **bus** #4 comes runs to Bangor via Llanfair P.G. and Llangefni (1½hr., M-Sa 2 per hr., £3.60); on Sundays #44 journeys to Bangor, sometimes stopping in Ysbyty Gwynedd (1½hr., 8 per day). Eurolines/Bus Éireann #861/871 goes to London (7½hr., 2 per day, £29-34) via Birmingham (4hr.) and #880 runs to Leeds (6hr., daily, £39) through Manchester (4¾hr.) and Liverpool (2½hr.) For a **taxi**, call Alphacab (☎765 000). For information regarding budget accommodations in Holyhead, food options, and sights, see the **Tourist Information Centre**, accessible through Terminal One of the train and ferry station. (☎762 622. Sells ferry tickets and books rooms for a £2 plus 10% deposit. Open daily 8:30am-6pm.) Other services include: **banks** on Market St.; **police** (☎762 323) at the top of Stanley St. by the library; free **Internet** access at the **library**, Newry Fields (☎762 917; open M 10am-5pm, Tu and Th-F 10am-7pm, W 10am-1pm, Sa 9:30am-12:30pm); and the **post office**, 13a Stryd Boston, with a **bureau de change** (☎08457 223 344; open M-F 9am-5:30pm, Sa 9am-12:30pm). **Post Code:** LL65 1BP.

LLŶN PENINSULA

The pastoral scenes and cliffs of the Llŷn Peninsula are the stuff of fairy tales. They have humbled visitors since the Middle Ages, when pilgrims crossed the peninsula on their way to Bardsey Island. The Coastal villages have become a source of contention, as locals are alarmed by the influx of English vacationers. It's easy to understand why the Llŷn has become a holiday haven. The golden beaches fill with weekenders—Hell's Mouth is famous for surfing, and Black Sands, near Porthmadog, is a favorite for everything else.

▐ TRANSPORTATION

The northern end of the Cambrian Coaster (☎08457 489 450) **train** line runs through Porthmadog to Pwllheli. Trains from Porthmadog and Pwllheli to Aberystwyth or Birmingham require a change at Machynlleth (2hr.; M-Sa 8 per day, Su 3 per day). The **Cambrian Coaster Day Ranger** offers unlimited travel along the line (£7 per day, children £3.50).

National Express (☎08705 808 080) **bus** #545 runs from Pwllheli to London via Bangor, Birmingham, Caernarfon, and Porthmadog (10-10½hr., 1 per day, £28.) Bus #380 goes to Newcastle via Manchester, Liverpool, and Bangor (12-14hr., 1 per day, £49.50.) TrawsCambria bus #701 stops in Porthmadog once per day and goes to Aberystwyth (2hr.), Cardiff (7hr.), and Swansea (6hr.). In the other direction, it travels from Porthmadog to Bangor (1hr.). Express Motors (☎01286 881 108) bus #1 stops in Porthmadog on its route between Blaenau Ffestiniog (30min.; in summer M-Sa every hr., Su 5 per day; rest of the year M-Sa every hr.) and Caernarfon (1hr.), continuing to Bangor (1-1¼hr.; M-Sa 6 per day, Su 3 per day). Berwyn (☎01286 660 315) and Clynnog & Trefor (☎01286 660 208) run bus #12 between Pwllheli and Caernarfon (45min.; M-Sa every hr., Su 3 per day).

Several bus companies, primarily Arriva Cymru (☎0870 608 2608), serve most spots on the peninsula for about £2. Check schedules in the *Gwynedd Public Transport Maps and Timetables*, available from TICs and on buses. Arriva and Caelloi (☎01758 612 719) run bus #3 from Porthmadog to Pwllheli (30-40min.; M-Sa 1-2 per hr., Su 6 per day). Leaving from Pwllheli, buses #8, 17, 17B, and 18 weave around the western tip of the peninsula. A **Gwynedd Red Rover ticket** secures a day of bus travel throughout the peninsula (£5, children £2.45).

PORTHMADOG   ☎01766

Porthmadog (port-MA-dock) is a busy travel hub. Its principal attraction is the ▇Ffestiniog Railway, a narrow-gauge line that departs from Harbour Station on High St. The train is only three seats wide, but it offers spectacular views and a bumpy 13½ mi. ride into Snowdonia. (☎516 000; www.festrail.co.uk. Round-trip 3hr. June-Aug. 2-8 per day; Apr.-May and Sept.-Oct. 2-6 per day; Nov.-Mar. call for timetables. £17, concessions £15.30.) At the Llechwedd Slate Caverns, outside of Blaenau Ffestiniog, visitors can venture into the leftovers of the Welsh slate mining industry. The Deep Mine Tour, with a Victorian ghost for a guide, offers Britain's steepest passenger railway and views of an underground lake. The Miner's Tramway Tour guides visitors through cathedral-like caves and mining demonstrations. Bus #142 connects the slate mines to the Blaenau Ffestiniog station (5min.) and coordinates with trains (round-trip 5 per day). The mines are just off the A70, 10 mi. south of Betws-y-Coed. (☎830 306; www.llechwedd-slate-caverns.co.uk. Open daily from 10am. Last tours leave Mar.-Sept. at 5:15pm; Oct.-Feb. 4:15pm. Book ahead. Tours £9.25, concessions £7.75, children £7. Both tours £14.75/12.50/11.25.)

At the other end of Porthmadog, across from the train station, the modest Welsh Highland Railway (along with Russell, its dogged 1906 locomotive) was once the longest narrow-gauge line in Wales, the track runs to Pen-y-Mount. (☎513 402; www.whr.co.uk. Round-trip 40min. Timetables available at Tremadog Rd. Station; call for exact schedules. Easter-Sept. 6 per day; Oct. and Feb. 5 per day. £5.50, seniors £4.50, children £3, families £15. Tickets valid all day.) For an adrenaline rush, try flying a Hovercraft over land or water with Llŷn Hovercrafts, just outside of Abersoch. (☎01758 713 527; www.tanrallt.com. £45 per 30min. Open daily Easter to Sept. 10am-5pm; in winter by arrangement.)

The best places to stay in town are located 10-15min. down High St. (past the railway station, where it becomes Church St.) in neighboring Tremadog. National Express #545 and 380 and local bus Arriva #3 stop in Tremadog. The first house on the right on Church St., best known as Lawrence of Arabia's birthplace, now houses the colorful ▇Snowdon Lodge ❷, with a TV, fireplace, and kitchen. The owners offer expert hiking advice. (☎515 354; www.snowdonlodge.co.uk. Breakfast included. Laundry £2. Dorms £15. Twins and doubles £35-38; family room £65. AmEx/MC/V.) At the popular ▇Jessie's ❶, 75 High St., choose from a huge range of cheap sandwiches and baked goods. (☎512 814. Open M-Sa 9am-5pm, Su 10am-4pm. Cash only.) Tudor Bakery ❶, 92 High Street, sells tasty pasties and sandwiches (£2 for takeaway), as well as freshly baked *bana brith*, a Welsh bread. (☎770 258. Open daily 8:30am-5pm. Cash only). The Australia ❶, 31-33 High St., has good food (£3-7) and a wide-screen TV. (☎510 930. Happy hour M-Th 5-9pm. Open M-Sa 11am-11:30pm, Su noon-10:30pm. Food served M-F noon-3pm and 6-8:30pm, Sa-Su noon-3pm. MC/V.)

From the train station, a right turn on High St. leads to town. Buses stop on High St. and outside the park. Dukes Taxis (☎514 799) is reliable. The Tourist Information Centre, High St., by the harbor, books rooms for £2 plus a 10% deposit. (☎512 981. Open daily Easter-Oct. 9:30am-5:30pm; Nov.-Easter 10am-5pm.) Other services include: Barclays bank, 79 High St. (☎0845 600 0651; open M-F 9:30am-4:30pm); free Internet access at the library, Chapel St. (☎514 091; open M-Tu and Th-F 10am-12:30pm and 2-6pm, W and Sa 10am-12:30pm); Madog launderette, 34 Snowdon St. (☎512 121; wash £3, dry £1.20; open M-Su 8am-7pm; last wash 6:30pm); Rowland pharmacy, 68 High St. (☎513 921; open M-F 9am-5:30pm, Sa 9am-12:30pm); and the post office, at the corner of High St. and Bank Pl., with a bureau de change (☎512 010; open M-F 9am-5:30pm, Sa 9am-12:30pm). Post Code: LL49 9AD.

NORTH WALES

PWLLHELI   ☎01758

The Cambrian Coaster rail line terminates at Pwllheli (poohl-THEL-ly), 8 mi. west of Criccieth, but there are many buses to aid transportation from this convenient hub. While antique shops and touristy stores dominate the main stretches, farther away are two **beaches:** Abererch Beach, with windsurfers and a shallow grade that attracts families, and lesser known South Beach.

Bank Place Guest House ❷, 29 High St., is convenient and all rooms have TV. (☎612 103. £25 per person. Cash only.) Area **camping** is good. Try **Hendre Caravan Park ❶,** 1½ mi. down the road to Nefyn at Efailnewydd. (☎613 416. Laundry and showers. Open Mar.-Oct. From £8 per tent. Cash only.) Get pastries and produce at the open-air **market** in front of the bus station (open W 9am-5pm). The Spar **supermarket** is on Y Maes Sq. (☎612 993; open daily 8am-10pm). **Jane's Sandwich Bar ❶,** 55 High St. serves inexpensive sandwiches (from £1.85), soups (£1) and pastries. (☎614 464. Open M-Sa 7am-2:30pm, Su 8am-2pm. Cash only.) **Bella Notte Ristorante ❷,** High St., serves Italian fare in a small, candlelit room. (☎614 441. Pastas and pizzas £6-9. 3-course meal £10, includes dessert. Open 5-10pm daily.)

The **train** station is in Station Sq. The **bus** station is on Ffordd-y-Cob. Call **999 Taxi** at ☎740 999. The **Tourist Information Centre,** Station Sq., books rooms for £2 plus a 10% deposit. (☎613 000. Open Apr.-Oct. daily 9am-4:30pm; Nov.-Mar. M-W and F-Sa 10am-4pm.) Other services include: HSBC **bank,** 48 High St. (☎632 700; open M-F 9am-4:30pm); **police** (☎701 177) on Ala Rd.; free **Internet** access at the **library,** in Neuadd Dwyfor (the Town Hall, Stryd Penlan; ☎612 089; open M 2-7pm; Tu, Th, Sa 10am-1pm; W and F 10am-1pm and 2-7pm); and the **post office,** New St. (☎612 658; open M-F 9am-5:30pm, Sa 9am-12:30pm). **Post Code:** LL53 5HL.

ABERDARON   ☎01758

Once the next-to-last stop on the holy Ynys Enlli (Bardsey Island) pilgrimage, the tiny village of Aberdaron sits on the tip of Llŷn Peninsula. In a quiet inlet bounded by steep green hills, Aberdaron has managed to retain some of the small-town serenity that other Llŷn towns have lost. Right next to the ocean, the **Church of Saint Hywyn** has held fast against the tides and winds since medieval times. The 20th century witnessed the construction of a sturdy seawall and the arrival of celebrity vicar-turned-poet **R.S. Thomas,** whose experiences working with his rural congregation feature prominently in his works. (Open daily in summer 10am-5pm; Aug. 10am-6pm; in winter 10am-4pm. Free.) **St. Mary's Well,** 1½ mi. west of town, is close to the ocean, but its water supposedly stays fresh even when flooded by high tide. About 5 mi. away lies the beach at **Porth Oer,** where footfall causes the "whistling sands" to live up to their name (bus #8B stops near the beach once per day). Long a religious site—its first monastery was allegedly built in the 6th century— **Bardsey,** the "Island of Twenty Thousand Saints," was once so holy that three pilgrimages there equaled one to Rome. Because so many holy men made the pilgrimage late in life, the "twenty thousand" in its name refers to the number of pilgrims buried there. Visitors can admire the ruins of the old abbey and observe hundreds of migratory birds. (☎760 667. Trust open daily Easter-Sept. 1-5pm. Ferries depart from Pwllheli and Porth Meudwy, toward the tip of the peninsula from Aberdaron. From Porth Meudwy, the trip takes 15-20min., allowing 3½hr. visits; frequency depends on weather and demand. £25, children £15. From Pwllheli £30, children £18. Longer stays in the island's "crogloft" cottages are available.) A **National Trust information point** occupies the Coast Guard hut overlooking Bardsey at the Uwchmynydd headland. Aberdaron houses a **Bardsey Island Trust Booking Office,** at which visitors can buy tickets and get information about the island (☎1758 730 740; www.bardsey.org).

NORTH WALES

For accommodations in Aberdaron, follow the sign pointing toward Whistling Sands, or simply head up the hill behind the bus stop to the lovely **Bryn Mor ❷**, where elegant rooms have sea views and TV. (☎760 344. £27. Cash only.) A small Spar provides **groceries.** (☎760 234. Open Apr.-Sept. M-Sa 8am-9pm, Su 8:30am-9pm; Oct.-Mar. daily 8am-5:30pm.) Food has been served since 1300 in the small building now occupied by **Y Gegin Fawr ❶** (The Big Kitchen). Enjoy a "Pilgrim's Lunch" of cheese, fruit, and bread (£5.50) on the creekside patio or in the tea room. (☎760 359. Open daily July-Aug. 10am-6pm; Easter-June and Sept.-Oct. 10am-5:30pm. Cash only.) **Bus** #17 runs from Pwllheli (40min., M-Sa 9 per day); #17B follows a coastal route and takes 5min. longer (2 per day). The **post office** is inside the Spar market. (Open M-Tu and Th-F 9am-12:30pm and 1:30-5:30pm, W and Sa 9am-noon.) **Post Code:** LL53 8BE.

SCOTLAND

Half the size of England with only a tenth the population, Scotland possesses open spaces and wild natural splendor unrivaled by its neighbor to the south. The craggy Highlands, beaches of the western coast, and mists of the Hebrides are awe-inspiring, while the farmland to the south and tiny fishing villages to the east convey a more subtle beauty. The Scots revel in a distinct culture ranging from the fevered nightlife of Glasgow and the festival atmosphere of Edinburgh to the isolated communities of the Orkney and Shetland Islands. The Scots defended their independence for hundreds of years before reluctantly joining England to create Great Britain in 1707, and only regained a separate parliament in 1999. The mock kilts and bagpipes of the big cities can grow tiresome: discover Scotland's true colors by venturing off the beaten path to find Gaelic-speaking B&B owners, peat-cutting crofters, or fishermen setting out in skiffs at dawn.

TRANSPORTATION

GETTING THERE

Reaching Scotland from outside Britain is often easiest and cheapest through London, where the **Scottish Tourist Board,** 19 Cockspur St., SW1 Y5BL (☎020 7930 2812; www.visitscotland.com), has brochures and reserves train, bus, and plane tickets.

BY PLANE. The cheapest fares between England and Scotland are available from no-frills airlines. **easyJet** (☎0871 244 2366; www.easyjet.com) flies to Edinburgh and Glasgow from London Gatwick, Luton, and Stansted. The fares are web-only; book in advance and fly for as little as £5. **Ryanair** (☎08712 460 000; www.ryanair.com) flies to Edinburgh and to Glasgow Prestwick (1hr. from the city) from Dublin and London. **British Airways** (☎08708 509 850; www.ba.com) sells round-trip tickets between England and Scotland from £85. British Midland (☎08706 070 555; www.flybmi.com) offers round-trip fares from London to Glasgow and Edinburgh from £90. Book as far in advance as possible for the best fares.

BY TRAIN AND BUS. From London, **GNER** runs **trains** (☎08457 225 225; www.gner.co.uk) to Edinburgh and Glasgow, which take 4½-6hr. Fares vary depending on when you buy (£27-£100). A pricier option is the **Caledonian Sleeper,** run by **First Scotrail** (☎08456 015 929; www.firstgroup.com/scotrail), which leaves London Euston near midnight and gets to Edinburgh at 7am (fares range from £20-140). Although **buses** from London to Glasgow and Edinburgh can take from 8-12hr., it may be much cheaper than rail travel. **National Express** (☎08705 808 080; www.nationalexpress.com) connects England and Scotland.

GETTING AROUND

BY TRAIN AND BUS. In the Lowlands (south of Stirling and north of the Borders), trains and buses run many routes frequently. In the Highlands, Scotrail and GNER **trains** run a few routes. Many stations are unstaffed—buy tickets on board. **Buses** tend to be the best and cheapest way to travel. **Scottish Citylink** (☎08705 505 050; www.citylink.co.uk) runs most intercity routes; **Traveline Scotland** has the best information on all routes and services (☎0871 200 2233; www.travelinescotland.com). Bus service is infrequent in the northwest Highlands and stops on Sun-

Scotland

days almost everywhere. **Postbuses** (Royal Mail customer service ☎ 08457 740 740) pick up passengers and mail once or twice a day in the most remote parts of the country, typically charging £2-5 (and sometimes nothing). Many travelers find that they can be a reliable way to get around the Highlands.

The **Freedom of Scotland Travelpass** allows unlimited train travel and transportation on most **Caledonian MacBrayne** ("CalMac") ferries. Purchase the pass *before* traveling to Britain at any BritRail distributor (see **By Train,** p. 32).

BY BUS TOUR. A thriving industry of tour companies is eager to whisk travelers into the Highlands. ▓HAGGIS (☎ 0131 558 3738; www.haggisadventures.com) and **MacBackpackers** (☎ 01315 589 900; www.macbackpackers.com) cater to the young and adventurous, with a number of tours departing from Edinburgh. Both run hop-on, hop-off excursions that let you travel Scotland at your own pace (usually under three months). HAGGiS is geared toward set tours with specific itineraries, run by witty local guides; the company guarantees accommodation at a few favorite stopping points. MacBackpackers guarantees accommodation at any of the social **Scotland's Top Hostels** in Edinburgh, Fort William, Skye, Oban, and Inverness (see **Bus Tours,** p. 35). **Celtic Adventures** (☎ 01312 253 330; www.thecelticadventures.com) covers Scotland and Ireland in a variety of four- to 12-day tours, with one-way, round-trip, and hop-on, hop-off options.

BY CAR. Driving affords travelers access to Scotland's remote corners without the fear of being stranded by complicated bus services. As in the rest of Britain, driving in Scotland is on the left, seatbelts are required at all times, the minimum age to drive with a foreign license is 17, and the legal minimum age to rent is 21. In rural areas, roads are often single-track, and vehicles may have to slow to a crawl to negotiate oncoming traffic. Often one car must pull into a passing place (shoulder turn-off) to enable another to pass. Drivers should also use caution on rural roads, which are often traversed by livestock. Sure, highland cows are cute, but not once they've gone through your windshield.

BY BICYCLE. Scotland's biking terrain is scenic and challenging. You can usually rent bikes, even in very small towns, and transport them by ferry for little or no charge. Fife and regions south of Edinburgh and Glasgow offer gentle country lanes. Orkney, Shetland, and the Western Isles are negotiable by bicycle, although cyclists should be aware of strong winds and wet roads in the region . In the Highlands, touring by bike is more difficult. Most major roads have only one lane, and locals drive at high speeds. Transporting a bike by public transportation in the Highlands can be challenging. Many trains can carry four or fewer bikes, so reservations are essential.

BY THUMB. Hitchhikers report that drivers tend to be most receptive (and often downright friendly) in the least-traveled areas. Far to the northwest and in the Western Isles, the Sabbath is strictly observed, making it difficult or impossible to get a ride on Sundays. *Let's Go* does not recommend hitchhiking.

BY FOOT. Two long-distance footpaths, established under the Countryside Act of 1967, traverse Scotland. The **West Highland Way** begins just north of Glasgow in Milngavie and continues 95 mi. north along Loch Lomond, through Glen Coe to Fort William and Ben Nevis. The **Southern Upland Way** runs 212 mi. from Portpatrick on the southwest coast to Cockburnspath on the east coast, snaking through Galloway Forest Park and the Borders. Most Tourist Information Centres (TICs) distribute simple maps of the ways and a list of accommodations along the routes. For information on these paths, write or call the **Scottish Tourist Board,** 23 Ravelston Terr., Edinburgh EH4 3EU (☎ 0131 332 2433; www.visitscotland.com) or visit www.walkscotland.com. Detailed guidebooks are available at most bookstores.

Mountain ranges, like the Cuillins, the Cairngorms, and Glen Coe, have hostels that are bases for hillwalking or biking. Walk along mainland Britain's highest **cliffs** at Cape Wrath or ramble across the **moors** of the Outer Hebrides. One of the most attractive aspects of hiking in Scotland is that you can often pick your own route. The wilds do pose certain dangers: stone markers can be unreliable, and expanses of open heather can be disorienting. Heavy mists are always a possibility, and blizzards occur even in July. Never go up into the mountains without proper equipment (see **Wilderness Safety,** p. 50). Many trails cross privately owned land. Be respectful and ask permission from the landowner. Leave a copy of your route and timetable at a hostel or rescue station, and if you're out between mid-August and mid-October, be sure to ask about areas in which deer hunters might be at work. For info on walking and mountaineering in Scotland, consult Poucher's *The Scottish Peaks* (£13), the Scottish Mountaineering Club's *The Munros* (£20), or the introductory Tourist Board booklet, *Walk Scotland.*

LIFE AND TIMES

HISTORY

EARLY TIMES. Little is known about the early inhabitants of Scotland, but their no-nonsense toughness warded off the Romans and scared **Emperor Hadrian** into hiding behind his 73 mi. long wall (p. 444). Later invaders were more successful, however, and by AD 600 four groups inhabited the Scottish mainland: the native **Picts,** the Celtic **Scots,** and the Germanic **Angles** and **Saxons.** In AD 843, the Scots decisively defeated the Picts and formed the beginnings of a consolidated kingdom. United against the threat of horn-helmeted **Vikings,** various groups gathered under King **Duncan,** and the **House of Dunkeld** or **Canmore** reigned over Scotland for 200 years. In the early 12th century, Scotland grew under the popular, pious King **David I** (1124-53), who built castles, abbeys, and cathedrals all over the Lowlands. Subsequent Scottish monarchs found their independence threatened by an increasingly powerful England. During the 13th century, the nation maintained a tenuous peace punctuated with occasional fighting as Scottish kings struggled to contend with civil revolts and Scandinavian attacks.

WARRING WITH ENGLAND. In 1286, King **Alexander III** died without an heir, and the resulting contest over the Scottish crown fueled the territorial ambitions of **Edward I** of England. Edward quickly seized most of Scotland, beginning a long history of English oppression. His not-so-gentle governing hand earned him the nickname "Hammer of the Scots." The **Wars of Independence** bred figures like William Wallace (yes, the *Braveheart* guy), but it was **Robert the Bruce** who emerged as Scotland's leader after a slew of assassinations. Robert led the Scots to victory over Edward II's forces at **Bannockburn** (p. 592) in 1314, and won Scotland its independence.

The reigns of **James IV** (1488-1513) and **James V** (1513-42) saw the arrival of both the **Renaissance** and the **Reformation** (p. 70). Following the death of James V, the infant **Mary, Queen of Scots** (1542-67), ascended the throne and was promptly shipped off to France. Lacking a strong ruler during her absence, Scotland was vulnerable to the revolts of the Reformation as Protestantism became more prevalent. In 1560, the **Scottish Parliament** denied the Pope's authority in Scotland and established the Presbyterian Church as Scotland's new official church.

In 1561, after the death of her husband, Catholic Mary returned to Scotland. Unpopular with Scottish nobles and Protestants, Mary's rule fanned the flames of discontent, and civil war resulted in her forced abdication and imprisonment in 1567. She escaped her Scottish captors and made it across the border only to face more shackles thanks to her cousin Elizabeth I. As Mary languished in an English prison, her son **James VI** was crowned king of Scotland. Nine years later, with Catholic Spain a rising threat, Queen Elizabeth made a tentative alliance with the nominally Protestant James, which didn't stop her from executing his mother in 1587.

UNION WITH ENGLAND. When Elizabeth died without an heir in 1603, James VI was crowned **James I,** uniting Scotland and England. James ruled from London, and his half-hearted attempts to reconcile the Scots to British rule were tartly resisted. Scottish Presbyterians supported Parliamentary forces against James's successor **Charles I** during the **English Civil War** (p. 71), but when the Parliamentarians executed Charles, the Scots shifted alliances and named the deceased king's son King **Charles II.** Oliver Cromwell defeated him, but in a conciliatory gesture gave Scotland representation in the English Parliament. The victory of Protestant William of Orange over James II in the **Glorious Revolution** (p. 71) convinced Scotland's Presbyterian leaders that its interests were safer with the Anglicans than with longtime Catholic ally France. The Scottish Parliament was subsumed by England in the 1707 **Act of Union,** satisfying Scottish traders with interests in English trade.

THE JACOBITE REBELLION. Scottish supporters of James II (called **Jacobites**) attempted a series of unsuccessful anti-union uprisings, after which they launched the **"Forty-Five"**—the 1745 rebellion that captured the imaginations of Scots and Romantics everywhere. James's grandson Charles (or **Bonnie Prince Charlie**) landed in Scotland, where he succeeded in mustering unseasoned troops from various Scottish clans. He rallied the troops in **Glenfinnan** (p. 630) and marched to Edinburgh, where he prepared a rebellion. Despite the Jacobite victories at Stirling and Falkirk in 1746, desertions and the uncertainty of French aid undermined the rebellion. While Charles, disguised as a serving maid, eventually escaped back to France, his Highland army fell heroically on the battlefield of **Culloden** (p. 623). The English subsequently enacted a new round of oppressive measures: they forbade hereditary **tartans** and **bagpipes,** discouraged the speaking of **Gaelic,** and forcibly eradicated much of traditional Scottish culture.

ENLIGHTENMENT AND THE CLEARANCES. Despite Jacobite agitation and reactionary English counter-measures, the 18th century proved to be one of the most prosperous in Scotland's history. As agriculture, industry, and trading boomed, a vibrant intellectual environment and close links to Continental **Enlightenment** thought produced such luminaries as **Adam Smith, David Hume,** and **Thomas Carlyle.**

Although political reforms did much to improve social conditions in the 19th century, economic problems proved disastrous. The Highlands in particular were affected by a rapidly growing population, limited arable land, archaic farming methods, and the demands of greedy landlords. The resulting poverty led to mass **emigration,** mostly to North America, and the infamous **Highland Clearances.** Between 1810 and 1820, the Sutherland Clearances, undertaken by the Marquis of Stafford, forcibly relocated thousands of poor farmers to small landholdings called **crofts** to make way for expanded sheep ranching. Resistance to the relocations was met with violence—homes were burned and countless people were killed. Other clearances occurred throughout the Highlands, in some cases evicting entire villages and shipping their people overseas. The **Industrial Revolution** led to growth in Glasgow and the rest of southern Scotland and contributed to increasingly poor living conditions for new industrial laborers. The situation worsened in the mid-19th century when the **Highland Potato Famine** caused widespread starvation, death, and continuing emigration from the Highlands.

THE 20TH CENTURY. Scotland, like the rest of Britain, lost countless young men in WWI and suffered the ensuing economic downturn. In the 1930s, the **Depression** hit Scotland as hard, if not harder, than the rest of the world. The **Home Rule** (or

SCOTLAND

Devolution) movement, begun in 1886 and put on hold during WWI, continued the push for a separate parliament in Edinburgh. The **Scottish National Party (SNP)** was founded in 1934 on the strength of nationalist sentiments. On Christmas of 1950, four young agitators broke into Westminster Abbey and liberated the **Stone of Scone** (or "Stone of Destiny," a block of sandstone historically used as a seat in the coronation of the Scottish monarchy), which had been removed from Scotland by Edward I. The discovery of North Sea oil gave Scotland an economic boost and incited a new breed of nationalism embodied by the SNP's 1974 political slogan, "It's Scotland's Oil!" Polls in the 70s indicated that as much as three-quarters of Scotland's population favored devolution, but the crucial **1979 referendum** failed to win the required 40% proportion of the electorate.

After the World Wars, Labour governments nurtured Scotland's **industrial boom,** nationalizing many industries. **Thatcherism,** however, removed many of the publicly funded projects sustaining industries in the north of Britain, and Scotland's workforce was reduced by 20%. The country faced economic troubles similar to, if not more intense than, that of the industrial meccas of Northern England.

SCOTLAND TODAY

Stands Scotland where it did?
 —William Shakespeare, *Macbeth*

CURRENT POLITICS. September 1997 brought a victory for the proponents of home rule when Scottish voters supported **devolution** by an overwhelming three-to-one margin. The first elections for the new **Scottish Parliament** occurred in 1999, inaugurating a Labour-Liberal Democrat coalition and the SNP in the position of primary opposition. Although Scotland has a new Parliament house at **Holyrood,** Edinburgh (p. 540), it still holds seats in the United Kingdom's House of Commons. The precise nature of Scotland's constitutional relationship with England remains disputed, as Scottish politicians debate whether to seek incremental or immediate independence from Parliament. The mention of "Bannockburn" still stirs nationalist feeling among Scots, and the last party supporting union with England has been purged from the Scottish Parliament. However, many Scottish politicians remain more closely tied to London than to their own constituents.

WHAT'S HAPPENIN'. Out of the post-industrial ruins, Glasgow began a cultural revitalization in the late 80s that continues today. **Edinburgh,** long a magnet for cultural events, has recently seen its 61-year-old **International Festival** (and attendant events like **The Fringe,** p. 528) make headlines around the world—today, over 15% of revelers come from overseas. Edinburgh's festivals peak during August but fuel the economy year-round, generating thousands of jobs and millions of pounds.

Cultural tourism draws droves of heritage-seekers and Celtic devotees to the country each summer. Although industrial trades still comprise Scotland's largest workforce, tourism employs more people than any other field in holiday spots like the Highlands and islands. On July 5, 1996, **Dolly** the sheep—the first mammal to be cloned from an adult cell—was "born" in the labs of the Roslin Institute, conceived by Dr. Ian Wilmut. Scotland also produces a large portion of the superconductors in the UK, earning central Scotland the nickname "Silicon Glen." Leading the trend among the countries of the UK, the Scottish government implemented a **smoking ban** in enclosed public places in March 2006 despite substantial opposition from Scottish citizens. The rest of Britain followed Scotland's lead in July 2007.

CULTURE AND CUSTOMS

The cold, drizzling skies of Scotland loom over some of the warmest people on earth. The Scottish reputation for openness and good nature is well-founded. Life

SCOTLAND

is generally slower outside the densely populated belt running between Glasgow and Edinburgh, and etiquette is somewhat less important here than in London's urban sprawl. But this is no reason to forget your manners. **Hospitality** and **conversation** are highly valued, and most Scots will welcome you with geniality and pride (unless you call them English). In parts of the Highlands, **nationalism** runs deep and strong. Here, using the technically correct "British" will win you no friends. **Religion** and **football**, and the religion of football, are topics best left untouched if you're not prepared to defend yourself—verbally and otherwise. Even the sweetest little old lady can turn out to be a hot-blooded football fanatic.

A WORD ABOUT KILTS. Although it's unlikely you'll see very many during your travels, the kilt is not a purely romanticized, Hollywood concept. Criminalized as Highland garb after the Jacobite rebellion, kilts were revived during the mid-19th-century nostalgia for Highland culture. **Tartan** plaids originally denoted the geographic base of the weaver. Today, few Scots still wear their family tartan, although many do own one for use at formal gatherings and sporting events.

 KILT IT UP. You don't have to be Scottish to wear a kilt. Renting a kilt costs upwards of £45, or £50 for the whole nine yards, including kilt, hose (socks), flashes for the hose (worn facing outwards), Ghillie Brogues (shoes), sgian dubh (ceremonial dagger, usually false, that tucks into the right sock with only the handle showing), Bonnie Prince Charlie jacket (a tuxedo-like top), waistcoat (vest), and the important sporran, worn across the front and serving as your only pocket. What goes underneath is up to you.

LANGUAGE

While settlers in southern Scotland transported their native tongues—Gaelic from Ireland, Norse from Scandinavia, and an early form of English (Inglis) from northern England—no record of the original **Pictish** language remains. By the 11th century, **Scottish Gaelic** (pronounced GAL-ick; Irish Gaelic is GAYL-ick), had become the official language of Scottish law. As the political power of southern Scotland increased, Gaelic speakers migrated to the Highlands. **Inglis**, a dialect of English now called Scots, became the language of the Lowlands and the monarchy.

While a number of post-1700 Scottish literati, most notably **Robert Burns** and the contemporary poet **Hugh MacDiarmid**, have composed in Scots, union with Britain and the political and cultural power of England led to the rise of the English language in Scotland. Today, standard English is spoken throughout Scotland, but the Scots influence is still strong. In the Highlands, for example, "ch" becomes a soft "h," as in the German "ch" sound. Modern Scottish Gaelic, a linguistic cousin of modern Irish, is spoken by approximately 60,000 people in Scotland, particularly in the western islands. Recent attempts to revive Gaelic have led to its introduction in the classroom and even on street signs in the Hebrides, ensuring that some form of the language will continue to exist in Scotland for years to come. (For a glossary of Scottish Gaelic and Scots words and phrases, see **Appendix**, p. 720.)

THE ARTS

LITERATURE. In a nation where stories have long been recounted by fireside, **oral literature** is as much a part of literary tradition as novels. Unfortunately, most medieval Scottish manuscripts were lost in raids on monastic centers of learning, effectively erasing pre-14th-century records. **John Barbour** is the best-known writer in Early Scots. His famous work, *The Bruce* (c. 1375), preceded Chaucer and favorably chronicled the life of Robert I in an attempt to strengthen national unity.

In 1760, **James Macpherson** published the works of **"Ossian,"** supposedly an ancient Scottish bard who rivaled Homer. Macpherson was widely discredited, however, when he refused to produce the original manuscripts. **James Boswell** (1740-95), the biographer of Samuel Johnson (p. 78), composed Scots verse as well as journals detailing his travels with the good Doctor. "Scotland's National Bard," **Robert Burns** (1759-96), ignored pressure from the south to write in English, instead composing in his native Scots. New Year's Eve revelers owe their anthem to him, although most mouth "Auld Lang Syne" (Old Long Time) without knowing what it means. **Sir Walter Scott** (1771-1832) was among the first Scottish authors to achieve international accolades for his work. *Ivanhoe* is one of the best-known, if sappiest, novels of all time. Scott was also quite nostalgic, and his historic novels (such as *Waverley*) may have single-handedly sparked the 19th-century revival of Highlands culture. **Robert Louis Stevenson** (1850-94) is most famous for his tales of high adventure, including *Treasure Island* and *Kidnapped*, which still fuel children's imaginations. His *Strange Case of Dr. Jekyll and Mr. Hyde* is nominally set in London, but some recognize Edinburgh's streets in Stevenson's Gothic descriptions. Scotland's authorial sons also include **Sir Arthur Conan Doyle** (1859-1930), whose *Sherlock Holmes* series is beloved by would-be gumshoes across the world, and **J. M. Barrie** (1860-1937), inventor of Peter Pan.

Scotland's literary present is as vibrant as its past. A series of 20th-century poets—most notably **Hugh MacDiarmid** and **Edwin Morgan**—have returned to the language of Burns, fueling a renaissance of Scottish Gaelic, particularly the Lowlands ("Lallands") dialect. **Neil Gunn** (1891-1973) wrote short stories and novels about Highland history and culture. More recent novelists include **Alasdair Gray, Tom Leonard,** and **James Kelman,** who won 1995's Booker Prize for his controversial, sharp-edged novel *How Late It Was, How Late*. **Irvine Welsh's** *Trainspotting*, the 1993 novel about Edinburgh heroin addicts that was adapted into a 1996 film, has been both condemned as immoral and hailed as the chronicle of a new generation.

ART. Scottish visual art reflects the beauty of the nation's countryside and people. Eighteenth and 19th-century portraitists like **Allan Ramsay** and **Sir Henry Raeburn,** and genre painter **David Wilkie** are recognized figures in the world of art, while **James Guthrie** and others from the **Glasgow School** reveal the influence of Impressionism in their works. As a participant in both the Arts and Crafts movement and the Art Nouveau scene, Glaswegian artist and architect **Charles Rennie Mackintosh** (1868-1928) boosted Scotland's artistic prestige with his elegant designs.

MUSIC. The Gaelic music of western Scotland has its roots in the traditional music of Irish settlers. As in Ireland, **ceilidhs** (KAY-lees)—spirited gatherings of music and dance—bring jigs, reels, and Gaelic songs to halls and pubs. Evidence suggests the *clarsach*, a Celtic harp, was the primary medium for musical expression until the 16th century, when the Highlander **bagpipes** (one of the oldest musical instruments in the world) and the violin introduced new creative possibilities. **Ballads**—narrative songs often performed unaccompanied—are significant to Scottish musical heritage. The folk tradition is evident in the Scottish pop music, including native Scots **The Proclaimers,** folk-rockers **Belle and Sebastian,** and Britpop entries **Texas** and **Travis.** Glasgow has been a thriving exporter of talent since the 80s, generating bands like **Simple Minds** and **Tears for Fears.** Today, Glaswegians are most proud of their stylish guitar rock revival band **Franz Ferdinand.**

FOOD AND DRINK

B&B regulars will encounter a **Scottish breakfast,** consisting of beans, fried eggs, potato cakes, fried tomato, and a rasher of bacon. In general, Scottish cuisine greatly resembles English food. Although buttery **shortbread** will please everyone, only adventurous travelers are likely to sample more traditional dishes, which include **Scotch eggs** (boiled eggs wrapped in a sausage meat mixture, breaded, and fried) and the infamous **haggis,** the national dish made from sheep stomach. Those courageous enough to try it will be rewarded with a zesty, if mushy, delicacy. Sugar-lovers will seek out Scotland's sweetest specialty, the **fried Mars bar.** While the fad may be over, many chip shops will still make you the crispy, gooey treat.

If the food is not for you, Scotland's **whisky** (spelled without the "e") may well be. Remember: all Scotch is whiskey, but not all whiskey is whisky. Scotch whisky is either "single malt" (from a single distillery), or "blended" (a mixture of several different brands). The malts are excellent and distinctive, with flavors and strengths varied enough to accommodate novices and lifelong devotees alike. Raise a glass yourself at the **distilleries** in Pitlochry (p. 587), the Speyside area (p. 618), or on the Isle of Islay (p. 598). Due to heavy taxes on alcohol sold in Britain, scotch may be cheaper at home or from duty-free stores than it is in Scotland. The Scots know how to party: they have the highest alcohol consumption rate in Britain, and, no surprise, are more generous with their licensing laws than England and Wales—drinks are served later and pubs are open longer (often until midnight or later).

SPORTING AND MERRYMAKING

The Scottish are passionate about **football**, and the intensity of devotion in Glasgow in particular rivals that of their English neighbors. Scottish **rugby** takes a close second to football, with three professional teams drawing crowds in the thousands. **Golf,** the "tyrannizing game" that continues to dominate St. Andrews (p. 576), was first invented in 15th-century Scotland. The over 400 golf courses in Scotland testify to the persistent influence of this sport. Traditional Scottish or **Highland games** originated from competitions under English military oppression, when participants could use only common objects such as hammers, rounded stones, and tree trunks to compete. Although **"tossing the caber"** may look easy, it actually requires a good deal of talent and practice to chuck an 18 ft., 150 lb. pine trunk. Weekend clan gatherings, bagpipe competitions, and Highland games occur frequently in Scotland, especially in summer; check for events at TICs and in local newspapers. In addition, the Scottish Tourist Board publishes the annual *Scotland Events*, which details happenings across Scotland.

Each year, a slew of festivals celebrate Scotland's distinctive history and culture. June and July's **Common Ridings** in the Borders (p. 548) and the raucous **Up Helly Aa** in Shetland on the last Tuesday in January (p. 667) are among the best known. Scotland is also famous for its New Year's Eve celebration, known as **Hogmanay.** The party goes on all over the country, taking over the streets in Edinburgh and Glasgow (check www.hogmanay.net for events and locations). The granddaddy of all events is the **Edinburgh International Festival** (Aug. 8-31 in 2008 and Aug. 14-Sept. 6 in 2009; ☎0131 473 2099; www.eif.co.uk), one of the largest in the world. The concentration of musical and theatrical events in the space of three weeks is dizzying, and Edinburgh's cafes and shops stay open all hours as pipers roam the streets. Be sure to catch the **Fringe Festival** (Aug. 3-25 in 2008; ☎0131 226 0026; www.edfringe.com), the much less costly sibling of the International Festival. There are literally hundreds of performances every day, including drama, comedy acts, and jazz concerts. Travelers planning to go to Scotland in August should plan well ahead and be sure to swing by Edinburgh.

SOUTHERN
SCOTLAND

Southern Scotland offers a rich past and a vibrant present. In the Borders region, castles and ruined abbeys chronicle Scotland's struggles with England. Nearly 80% of Scots cluster in the metropolitan areas of Edinburgh and Glasgow. Scotland's capital and the fountainhead of the Enlightenment, Edinburgh is a exceptionally beautiful city that draws enormous crowds each summer and during its festivals. Glasgow hosts formidable art collections and a kinetic, student-fed nightlife.

HIGHLIGHTS OF SOUTHERN SCOTLAND

CATCH a play (or 19) at the world's biggest arts festival—the simultaneous **Edinburgh International and Fringe**—held every August (p. 546).

PONDER the past at the four **Border Abbeys** (p. 548), a ring of medieval ruins with a bloody history set among quiet villages and hills.

INDULGE at **Gourmet Glasgow,** a 2-week festival in August when over 50 restaurants and bars offer free tastings (p. 575).

EDINBURGH   ☎0131

A city of elegant stone set between rolling hills and ancient volcanoes, Edinburgh (ED-in-bur-ra; pop. 500,000) is the pride of Scotland. Since King David I granted it burgh (town) status in 1130, it has been a hotbed for forward-thinking artists and intellectuals. Today, world-class universities craft the next generation of Edinburgh's thinkers, while new clubs and lively pubs emerge from beneath the city's medieval spires. In August, Edinburgh becomes a mecca for the arts, drawing talent and crowds from around the globe to its International and Fringe Festivals.

▲ INTERCITY TRANSPORTATION

Edinburgh lies 45 mi. east of Glasgow and 405 mi. northwest of London on Scotland's east coast, on the southern bank of the Firth of Forth.

Flights: Edinburgh International Airport (☎0870 040 0007), 7 mi. west of the city. Lothian **Airlink** (☎555 6363) shuttles between the airport and Waverley Bridge (25min.; every 10-15min., after midnight every hr.; £3, children £2; round-trip £5/3).

Trains: Waverley Station, between Princes St., Market St., and Waverley Bridge. Free bike storage beside Platform 1. Ticket office open M-Sa 4:45am-12:30am, Su 7am-12:30am. Trains (☎08457 484 950) to: **Aberdeen** (2½hr.; M-Sa every hr., Su 8 per day; £33.20); **Glasgow** (1hr., 4 per hr., £9.70); **Inverness** (3½hr., every 2hr., £32); **London King's Cross** (4¾hr., every hr., £103); **Stirling** (50min., 2 per hr., £6.10).

Buses: The modern **Edinburgh Bus Station** is on the eastern side of St. Andrew Sq. Open daily 6am-midnight. Ticket office open daily 8am-8pm. **National Express** (☎08705 808 080) to **London** (10hr., 4 per day, £29). **Scottish Citylink** (☎08705 505 050) to **Aberdeen** (4hr., every hr., £17.20), **Glasgow** (1hr.; M-Sa 4 per hr., Su 2

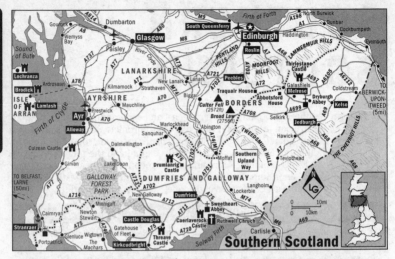

Southern Scotland

per hr.; £4.10), and **Inverness** (4½hr., 8-10 per day, £17.20). A bus-ferry route via Stranraer goes to **Belfast** (2 per day, £20) and **Dublin, Ireland** (1 per day, £26.50). Edinburgh is also serviced by Megabus; for cheapest fares book ahead online at www.megabus.com or call ☎0900 160 0900, lines open 7am-10pm.

◈ ORIENTATION

Edinburgh is a glorious walking city. The city center is divided into two halves, **Old Town** and **New Town,** connected by three bridges: **North Bridge, Waverly Bridge,** and **The Mound.** The bridges cross over **Waverley Station,** which lies directly between Old Town and New Town. The **Royal Mile** and **Edinburgh Castle** are in Old Town and are the center of most tourist activities, while New Town has upscale shopping. When reading maps, remember that Edinburgh is a multi-dimensional city—many streets that appear to intersect are actually on differ-ent levels. Two miles northeast of New Town, **Leith** is the city's seaport on the Firth of Forth.

▤ LOCAL TRANSPORTATION

Public Transportation: Although walking is usually the fastest and easiest way around the city center, Edinburgh has a comprehensive bus system. **Lothian** (☎555 6363; www.lothianbuses.com) provides most buses. Exact change required (£1 flat fare, chil-dren 60p). Buy a 1-day **Daysaver** ticket (£2.30, children £2) from any driver or in the **Lothian Travelshops** (☎555 6363) on Waverley Bridge, Hanover St., and Shandwick Pl. Open M-Sa 8:15am-6pm. **Night buses** cover selected routes after midnight (£2). **First Edinburgh** (☎0870 872 7271) also operates buses locally. **Traveline** (☎0870 608 2608; www.traveline.co.uk) has information on local public transportation.

Taxis: Stands located at all stations and on almost every corner on Princes St. **City Cabs** (☎228 1211). **Central Radio Taxis** (☎229 2468). **Central Taxis Edinburgh** (☎229 2468; www.taxis-edinburgh.co.uk).

Car Rental: The TIC has a list of rental agencies, from £25 per day. **Thrifty,** 42 Haymar-ket Terr. (☎337 1319). **Avis,** 100 Dalry Rd. (☎337 6363).

Bike Rental: Biketrax, 11 Lochrin Pl. (☎228 6633; www.biketrax.co.uk). Mountain bikes £12 per ½-day, £16 per full day. Open M-Sa 9:30am-5:30pm, Su noon-5pm. **Edinburgh Cycle Hire,** 29 Blackfriars St. (☎556 5560), off High St. Organizes cycle tours. Mountain bikes £10-15 per day, £50-70 per week. Open daily 10am-6pm.

ⓩ PRACTICAL INFORMATION

TOURIST AND FINANCIAL SERVICES

Tourist Information Centre: Waverley Market, 3 Princes St. (☎0845 22 55 121), north of Waverley Station. Helpful and often mobbed, the mother of all Scottish TICs books rooms for £3 plus a 10% deposit; sells bus, museum, tour, and theater tickets; and has free maps and pamphlets. **Bureau de change.** Open July-Aug. M-Sa 9am-8pm, Su 10am-8pm; May-June and Sept. M-Sa 9am-7pm, Su 10am-7pm; Apr. and Oct. M-Sa 9am-6pm, Su 10am-6pm; Nov.-Mar. M-Sa 9am-5pm, Su 10am-5pm.

Budget Travel: STA Travel, 27 Forrest Rd. and 72 Nicholson St. (both ☎226 7747). Open M-W and F 10am-6pm, Th 10am-7pm, Sa 10am-5pm.

Financial Services: Banks are everywhere. **American Express,** 69 George St. (☎718 2505, or 08706 001 600). Open M-Tu and Th-F 9am-5:30pm, W 9:30am-5:30pm, Sa 9am-7pm.

Work Opportunities: In summer, young travelers are employed by festival organizers to help manage offices, set up, etc. Hostel notice boards often help employment agencies seeking temporary workers. **Temp Agency** (☎478 5151); **Wesser and Partner** (☎01438 356 222, www.wesser.co.uk); **Kelly Services** (☎220 2626).

LOCAL SERVICES

Luggage Storage: At the Waverley train station or the bus station. £5 per item per day.

Camping Supplies: Millets the Outdoor Store, 12 Fredrich St. (☎558 7777). All the essentials, but no rentals. Open M-Sa 9am-7pm, Su 11am-6pm.

GLBT Resources: Edinburgh Lesbian, Gay, and Bisexual Centre, 58a-60 Broughton St. (☎478 7069), inside the Sala Cafe-Bar, or visit Gay Edinburgh at www.visitscotland.com. See also **GLBT Nightlife,** p. 544.

Disabled Services: Contact the TIC prior to travelling for a free *Accessible Scotland* guide, or check www.edinburgh.org and www.capability-scotland.org.uk for info on access to restaurants and sights. **Shopmobility,** The Mound (☎225 9559), by the National Gallery, lends motorized wheelchairs for free. Open Tu-Sa 10am-3:45pm.

Public Showers: In the "Superloo" at the train station. Shower, toilet, and towel £3. Toilet 20p. Open daily 4am-12:45am.

EMERGENCY AND COMMUNICATIONS

Police: Headquarters at Fettes Ave. (☎311 3901; www.lbp.police.uk). Other stations at 14 St. Leonard's St. (☎662 5000), Torphichen Pl. (☎229 2323), and 188 High St. (☎226 6966). Blue **police information boxes** are scattered throughout the city center, with tourist information and an emergency assistance button.

Hospitals: Royal Infirmary of Edinburgh, 51 Little France Cir. (☎536 1000, emergencies 536 6000). **Royal Hospital for Sick Children,** 9 Sciennes Rd. (☎536 0000).

Pharmacy: Boots, 48 Shandwick Pl. (☎225 6757), and 101-103 Princes St. (☎225 8331). Open M-F 8:30am-6pm, Sa 9am-6pm.

Internet Access: Free at the **Central Library** (☎242 8000), on George IV Bridge. Open M-Th 10am-8pm, F 10am-5pm, Sa 9am-1pm. Signs to Internet cafes are on every sec-

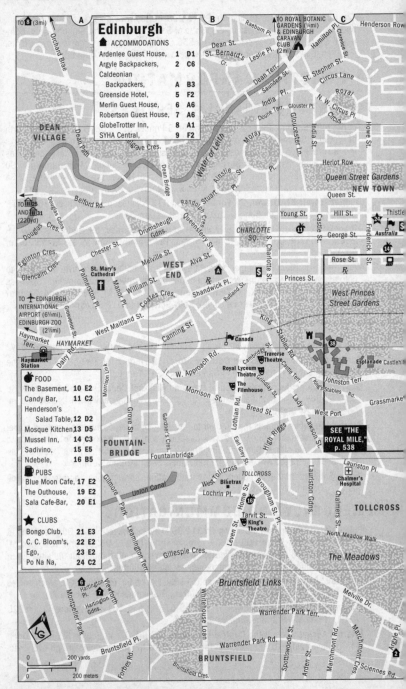

Edinburgh

⌂ ACCOMMODATIONS

Ardenlee Guest House,	**1** D1
Argyle Backpackers,	**2** C6
Caldeonian	
Backpackers,	**A** B3
Greenside Hotel,	**5** F2
Merlin Guest House,	**6** A6
Robertson Guest House,	**7** A6
GlobeTrotter Inn,	**8** A1
SYHA Central,	**9** F2

🍎 FOOD

The Basement,	**10** E2
Candy Bar,	**11** C2
Henderson's	
Salad Table,	**12** D2
Mosque Kitchen	**13** D5
Mussel Inn,	**14** C3
Sadivino,	**15** E5
Ndebele,	**16** B5

🍺 PUBS

Blue Moon Cafe,	**17** E2
The Outhouse,	**19** E2
Sala Cafe-Bar,	**20** E1

★ CLUBS

Bongo Club,	**21** E3
C. C. Bloom's,	**22** E2
Ego,	**23** E2
Po Na Na,	**24** C2

SEE "THE ROYAL MILE," p. 538

SOUTHERN SCOTLAND

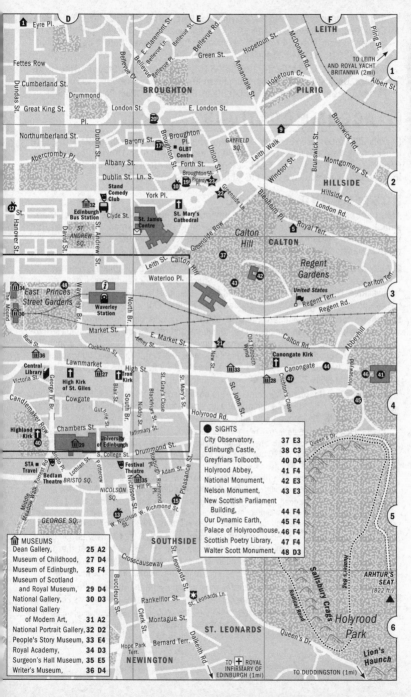

SIGHTS

City Observatory,	**37 E3**
Edinburgh Castle,	**38 C3**
Greyfriars Tolbooth,	**40 D4**
Holyrood Abbey,	**41 F4**
National Monument,	**42 E3**
Nelson Monument,	**43 E3**
New Scottish Parliament	
Building,	**44 F4**
Our Dynamic Earth,	**45 F4**
Palace of Holyroodhouse,	**46 F4**
Scottish Poetry Library,	**47 F4**
Walter Scott Monument,	**48 D3**

MUSEUMS

Dean Gallery,	**25 A2**
Museum of Childhood,	**27 D4**
Museum of Edinburgh,	**28 F4**
Museum of Scotland	
and Royal Museum,	**29 D4**
National Gallery,	**30 D3**
National Gallery	
of Modern Art,	**31 A2**
National Portrait Gallery,	**32 D2**
People's Story Museum,	**33 E4**
Royal Academy,	**34 D3**
Surgeon's Hall Museum,	**35 E5**
Writer's Museum,	**36 D4**

ond corner along the Royal Mile. **easyInternet Cafe,** 58 Rose St. (☎220 3577), inside Caffe Nero, has hundreds of terminals in the New Town. £1 per 30min. Open M-Sa 7am-10pm, Su 9am-10pm. A few free terminals are in the **Bongo Club Cafe,** 6 New St. (☎558 7604). Open M-F 11am-late, Sa 12:30pm-late.

Post Office: St. James Centre (☎556 9546), beside the Bus Station. **Bureau de change.** Open M-Sa 9am-5:30pm. Branch at 46 St. Mary's St. (☎556 6351). Open M-Tu and Th-F 9am-12:30pm and 1:30-5:30pm, Sa 9am-noon. **Post Code:** EH1 3SR.

ACCOMMODATIONS

Hostels and hotels are the only options in the city center, while **B&Bs** and **guest houses** appear on the edges of town. Book ahead in summer. During Festival time (from late July to early Sept.) and New Year's, prices often rise significantly. Many locals let their apartments; the TIC's booking service works magic.

HOSTELS AND CAMPING

This backpacker's paradise offers a bevy of convenient hostels, many of them smack-dab in the middle of town. Hostels range from the small and cozy to the huge and party-oriented. Expect cliques of long-term residents. Several also offer more expensive private rooms with varying amenities.

▨ **Budget Backpackers,** 37-39 Cowgate (☎226 2351; www.budgetbackpackers.co.uk). The most modern of the inner-city hostels. Spacious 2- to 12-bed rooms; female dorms available. Free city tour daily; pub crawl M-Sa. Breakfast £2. Key card access. Lockers free. Internet 15p per 30min. Reception 24hr. Rooms £9-24. 18+. MC/V. ●

▨ **Globetrotter Inn,** 46 Marine Dr. (☎336 1030; www.globetrotterinns.com). 15min. bus ride from Waverley train station and Edinburgh International Airport. Large grounds next to the Firth of Forth. An hourly shuttle service runs to and from the city, although a shop, TV room, gym, hot tub, and 24hr. bar make it tempting to stay put. Curtained bunks offer privacy. Light breakfast included. Key card access. Lockers free. Dorms £9.50-19. Ensuite doubles and twins £23. MC/V. ●

Scotland's Top Hostels (www.scotlands-top-hostels.com). This chain's 3 Edinburgh hostels all have a fun, relaxed environment with similar facilities. Also runs MacBackpacker tours in the city and around Scotland.

 Castle Rock Hostel, 15 Johnston Terr. (☎225 9666). Just steps from the castle, with a party atmosphere and a top-notch cinema room. Nightly movies. Ask about their haircut offer: £10 with a free shot of vodka. 220 beds in 8- to 16-bed dorms. Dorms £13-15; doubles and triples £15-17. AmEx/MC/V. ●

 Royal Mile Backpackers, 105 High St. (☎557 6120). The smallest of the chain's hostels. Well-kept and cozy, with a community feel. Free Wi-Fi. 8-bed dorms £13-15. AmEx/MC/V. ●

 High St. Hostel, 8 Blackfriars St. (☎557 3984). Ideally located just off the Royal Mile. Laid-back party environment and 16th-century architecture. Pub crawls, movie nights, and pool competitions. Free Wi-Fi. 4- to 18-bed rooms; co-ed available. Dorms £13-15. AmEx/MC/V. ●

Edinburgh Backpackers, 65 Cockburn (CO-burn) St. (☎220 1717; www.hoppo.com). Energetic hostel with common areas, pool table, and TV. 15% discount at the downstairs cafe. 96 beds in 8- to 16-bed coed dorms. Laundry and Internet access. Reception 24hr. Check-out 10am. Dorms £14-18.50; private rooms from £45. MC/V. ●

SYHA Hostels (www.syha.org.uk). Not the most popular with the young and the restless, but clean, safe, and some of the few child-friendly hostel options in the city's center.

 Central, 9 Haddington Pl. (☎0870 155 3255), on Leith Walk. Brand new, with modern ensuite rooms, bar, and bistro. Laundry and Internet access £1 each. Single, double, and family rooms, in addition to 4- to 8-bed dorms. Dorms £15-24, under 18 £13-23. MC/V. ●

International and Metro. SYHA turns two University of Edinburgh dorms into hostels during the university's summer vacation in July and Aug. **International,** Kincard's Ct., Guthrie St. (☎0871 330 8519) and **Metro,** Robertson's Close, Cowgate (☎0871 330 8517). Plain, spacious single rooms. Self-catering kitchens on each fl. Laundry. Rooms £13-24. MC/V. ❷

Argyle Backpackers, 14 Argyle Pl. (☎667 9991; www.argyle-backpackers.co.uk). Take bus #41 from The Mound to Warrender Park Rd. 3 renovated townhouses with a back-yard and free coffee. A B&B-like alternative to louder city hostels. Private rooms, many with TV, along with 4- to 10-bed dorms. Lockable dorms. Internet access £1.50 per hr. Reception 9am-10pm. Dorms £12-14; doubles and twins £37; triples £45. MC/V. ❶

St. Christopher's Inn, 9-13 Market St. (☎226 1446; www.st-christophers.co.uk), across from Waverley Station. A cramped, friendly outpost of a chain. Attracts a large party crowd, probably due to the downstairs bar offering varying discounts to guests. Breakfast included. Laundry and Internet access. Dorms £10.50-22.50. MC/V. ❶

Caledonian Backpackers, 3 Queensferry St. (☎476 7224; www.caledonianbackpackers.com), at the west end of Princes St. Make friends from around the world and join in the cacophony of snoring in the 38-bed dorm. Backpackers' bar stays open late with Tu open mic and live music F-Sa. 284 beds in 4- to 38-bed dorms. 2 kitchens. Lockers. Laundry and Internet access. Dorms £8-16; private rooms from £36. MC/V. ❷

Camping: Edinburgh Caravan Club Site, Marine Dr. (☎312 6874), by the Forth. Take bus #8A from North Bridge. Clean and family-friendly. Electricity, showers, hot water, laundry, and shop. £4-5.30 per person, pitch £4.50-7.50. Cash only. ❶

HOTELS

Most of the independent city center hotels have stratospheric prices. At the affordable end are budget **chain hotels**—lacking in character, but comfortable.

Greenside Hotel, 9 Royal Terr. (☎557 0022). A refurbished Georgian building with views of the Firth from its top floors. Breakfast included. Free Wi-Fi. Singles £40-90. AmEx/MC/V. ❸

Grassmarket Hotel, 94 Grassmarket (☎220 2299), formerly Premier Lodge. In the heart of Old Town. Singles £46-72. MC/V. ❸

B&BS AND GUEST HOUSES

B&Bs cluster in three colonies, all of which you can walk to or reach by bus from the city center. Try Gilmore Pl., Viewforth Terr., or Huntington Gardens in the **Bruntsfield** district, south from the west end of Princes St. (bus #11, 16, or 17 west/southbound); Dalkeith Rd. and Minto St. in **Newington,** south from the east end of Princes St. (bus #7, 31, or 37, among others); or **Pilrig,** northeast from the east end of Princes St. (bus #11 east/northbound). See www.visitscotland.com/listings/Edinburgh-Guest-Houses.html for a thorough list, or call the TIC for availability.

🏆 **Ardenlee Guest House,** 9 Eyre Pl. (☎556 2838; www.ardenlee.co.uk). Take bus #23 or 27 from Hanover St. northbound to the corner of Dundas St. and Eyre Pl. Near the beautiful Royal Botanic Gardens. Comfortable beds complete with teddy bears. £25-45 per person, prices vary with season. MC/V. ❸

Merlin Guest House, 14 Hartington Pl. (☎229 3864), just over 1 mi. southwest of the Royal Mile. An easy walk to the castle and other attractions, or you can take Bus #10 or 27 from Princes St. Clean, well-priced rooms. £18-24 per person. Cash only. ❷

Robertson Guest House, 5 Hartington Gardens (☎229 2652; www.robertson-guest-house.com). Bus #10 or 27 from Princes St. Quiet and welcoming, with a relaxing garden patio. £29-60 per person. MC/V. ❸

🔾 FOOD

Edinburgh features a wide range of cuisines and restaurants. If it's traditional fare you're after, find everything from pub haggis to creative "modern Scottish" at the city's top restaurants. For food on the cheap, many **pubs** offer student and hosteler discounts in the early evening, while fast-food joints are scattered across New Town. Takeaway shops on **South Clerk and Leith Streets** and **Lothian Road** have affordable Chinese and Indian fare. For **groceries,** try **Sainsbury's,** 9-10 St. Andrew Sq. (☎225 8400. Open M-Sa 7am-10pm, Su 10am-8pm.)

OLD TOWN

🔳 **The City Cafe,** 19 Blair St. (☎220 0125), right off the Royal Mile behind Tron Kirk. This perennially popular Edinburgh institution is a cafe by day and a flashy pre-club spot by night. Try the herbed chicken and avocado melt (£6). Streetside seating and incredible milkshakes. Happy hour daily 5-8pm. Open daily 11am-1am (3am during festival). Food served M-Th until 11pm, F-Su until 10pm. MC/V. ❷

🔳 **The Mosque Kitchen,** 50 Potterrow. Tucked away in the courtyard of Edinburgh's modern central mosque, a jumble of mismatched chairs and long tables make up an outdoor cafeteria. Popular with students. Their heaping plates of curry (£3) are hard to beat. Open M-Th and Sa-Su noon-7pm, F noon-1pm and 1:45-7pm. Cash only. ❶

Ndebele, 57 Home St., Tolcross (☎221 1141; www.ndebele.co.uk), ¾ mi. south from the west end of Princes St. Grab an ostrich and mango sandwich (£2.60) and chocolate chili cheesecake (£2), then head to the Meadows for a picnic. Extensive collection of South African wines, beers, and brandies. Open M-Sa 9am-6pm, Su noon-5pm. MC/V. ❶

The Elephant House, 21 George IV Bridge (☎220 5355). Harry Potter and Dumbledore were born here on scribbled napkins. A perfect place to chill, chat, and read a newspaper. Exotic teas and coffees and the best shortbread in the universe. Great views of the castle. Live music Th 8pm. Happy hour daily 8-9pm. Open daily 8am-11pm. MC/V. ❶

Sadivino, 52 West Richmond St. (☎667 7719). A friendly sidewalk cafe that fills up quickly at lunchtime. Best of all, everything from panini to more substantial Italian fare is under £4. Open M-F 11am-6pm, Sa noon-6pm. Cash only. ❶

The Outsider, George IV Bridge (☎226 3131). A stylish restaurant without the usual high price tag or attitude. Chunky kebabs (£9) are great for sharing, or look down the menu to the excellent seafood section (£9-15). Su brunch is a laid-back affair with live DJ sets. Reservations recommended; request a window table for a spectacular view of the castle lit up at night. Open daily noon-11pm. MC/V. ❷

NEW TOWN

The Basement, 10a-12a Broughton St. (☎557 0097; www.thebasement.org.uk). The menu changes daily, with plenty of vegetarian options. Draws a lively mix of locals to its candlelit cavern for Sa-Su Mexican and W Thai nights. Energetic vibe with a dynamic waitstaff. Entrees £6-9.50. Reservations recommended. Food served daily noon-10:30pm. Bar open until 1am. AmEx/MC/V. ❷

Henderson's Salad Table, 94 Hanover St. (☎225 2131). The founding member of Edinburgh's vegetarian scene, Henderson's has been dishing up seriously good salads (£4) for as long as anyone can remember. At night the wine bar gets going, offering a range of organic and vegan wines, beers, and spirits. Open daily 7:30am-10:30pm. MC/V. ❶

Candy Bar, 113-115 George St. (☎225 9179). A world away from the tartan plaid of the Royal Mile, this popular bar serves up a great value menu of burgers, noodles, and salads. Excellent sharing platters (£4 per person). Steer clear of the tempting 14-page drink menu outside of Happy hour (5-8pm) if you want to leave with your budget intact. Open daily noon-9pm. Bar open until 1am. AmEx/MC/V. ❷

Mussel Inn, 61-65 Rose St. (☎225 5979; www.mussel-inn.com). Muscle in for superior local shellfish. Gourmet entrees all under £10. Open M-Th noon-3pm and 6-10pm, F-Sa noon-10pm, Su 12:30-10pm. MC/V. ❷

⊙ SIGHTS

TOURS

Edinburgh is best explored by foot, but Lothian buses run several hop-on, hop-off open-top bus tours around the major sights, beginning at Waverley Bridge. **City Sightseeing Edinburgh** is popular; others include the **Majestic Tour** to New Haven and the Royal Yacht Britannia, vintage **MacTours,** and **Edinburgh Tours.** (General tour bus information ☎220 0770; www.edinburghtour.com. All tours run Apr.-Oct. every 20-30min. £9, concessions £8, children £3, families £20. Tickets can be used for reduced admission at many attractions.) A 24hr. Edinburgh **Grand Tour** ticket (£12, concessions £10) combines all four.

While a great array of tour companies in Edinburgh tout themselves as "the original" or "the scariest," the most worthwhile of the bunch is ▓**McEwan's Edinburgh Literary Pub Tour.** Led by professional actors, this 2hr., booze-filled crash course in Scottish literature meets outside the Beehive Inn on Grassmarket. (☎226 6665; www.edinburghliterarypubtour.co.uk. June-Sept. daily 7:30pm; Mar.-May and Oct. Th-Su 7:30pm; Nov.-Feb. F 7:30pm. £8, students and unemployed £6. Discount for online booking.) The popular **City of the Dead Tour,** convening nightly outside St. Giles' Cathedral, promises a one-on-one encounter with the MacKenzie Poltergeist. (☎225 9044; www.blackhart.uk.com. Daily Easter-Halloween 8:30, 9:15, and 10pm; Halloween-Easter 7:30 and 8:30pm. £8.50, concessions £6.50.) **Mercat Tours,** leaving from Mercat Cross, enter Edinburgh's spooky underground vaults, relying upon long ghost stories rather than staged frights. (☎225 5445; www.mercattours.com. £6.50-7.50, families £16-19.)

THE OLD TOWN AND THE ROYAL MILE

Edinburgh's medieval center, the **Royal Mile,** is the heart of **Old Town** and home to many attractions—it's an energetic traveler's playground. The Mile gets its name from the royal edifices on either end: **Edinburgh Castle** on top of the hill at the west end and the **Palace of Holyrood** anchoring the bottom of the hill at the east end. The top of the Mile is known as **Castle Hill.** Continuing east downhill from the castle, the street becomes **Lawnmarket,** then **High Street,** then **Canongate,** and finally ends at **Holyrood.** Each segment is packed with attractions and cheesy souvenir shops.

CASTLE HILL AND LAWNMARKET

▓**EDINBURGH CASTLE.** Looming over the city center atop a dormant volcano, Edinburgh Castle dominates the skyline. Its oldest surviving building is tiny, 12th-century **St. Margaret's Chapel,** built by King David I in memory of his mother. The castle compound developed over the course of centuries; the most recent additions date to the 1920s. The central **Palace,** begun in the 1430s, was home to Stuart kings and queens and contains the room where Mary, Queen of Scots, gave birth to James VI. It also houses the **Scottish Crown Jewels,** which are older than those in London. The storied (although visually unspectacular) Stone of Scone, more commonly known as the **Stone of Destiny** (p. 524) is also on permanent display. Other sections of the sprawling compound, like the Scottish National War Memorial, the National War Museum of Scotland, and the 15th-century monster cannon Mons Meg, definitely merit a visit, despite the uphill climb. The **One O'Clock Gun** fires Monday to Saturday—you can guess the time. Buy tickets online to skip the queues at the gate. (☎225 9846; www.historic-scotland.gov.uk. Open daily Apr.-Oct. 9:30am-

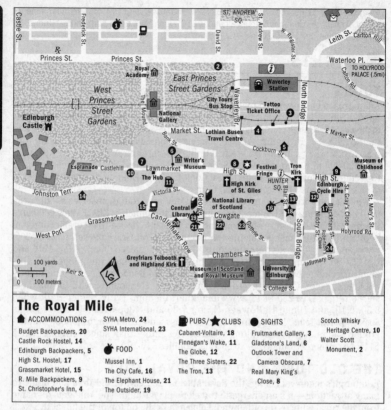

The Royal Mile

ACCOMMODATIONS
Budget Backpackers, **20**
Castle Rock Hostel, **14**
Edinburgh Backpackers, **5**
High St. Hostel, **17**
Grassmarket Hotel, **15**
R. Mile Backpackers, **9**
St. Christopher's Inn, **4**

SYHA Metro, **24**
SYHA International, **23**

FOOD
Mussel Inn, **1**
The City Cafe, **16**
The Elephant House, **21**
The Outsider, **19**

PUBS/★CLUBS
Cabaret-Voltaire, **18**
Finnegan's Wake, **11**
The Globe, **12**
The Three Sisters, **22**
The Tron, **13**

SIGHTS
Fruitmarket Gallery, **3**
Gladstone's Land, **6**
Outlook Tower and
Camera Obscura, **7**
Real Mary King's
Close, **8**

Scotch Whisky
Heritage Centre, **10**
Walter Scott
Monument, **2**

6pm; Nov.-Mar. 9:30am-5pm. Last admission 45min. before close. Free guided tours of the castle depart regularly from the entrance. £11, concessions £9, children £5.50, under 5 free. Excellent audio tour £3, concessions £2, children £1.)

■ **THE SCOTCH WHISKY EXPERIENCE.** Learn about the "history and mystery" of Scotland's most famous export at the Scotch Whisky Heritage Centre, located right next to the castle. The 50min. tour takes you on a barrel ride through animatronic displays and lots of free samples—it's like Disney, but drunk. (350 Castle Hill. ☎ 220 0441. Open daily June-Sept. 9:45am-5:30pm; Oct.-May 10am-5pm. Tours every 15min. £9, concessions £7, children £4.75, families £20.)

■ **CAMERA OBSCURA AND WORLD OF ILLUSIONS.** Climb Outlook Tower to see the 150-year-old camera obscura, which captures moving color images of the street below. The museum's dazzling exhibits use lights, mirrors, lenses, and other 19th-century technology to create illusions that still manage to amaze and confound visitors. (☎ 226 3707. Open daily July-Aug. 9:30am-7:30pm; Apr.-June and Sept.-Oct. 9:30am-6pm; Nov.-Mar. 10am-5pm. Last camera presentation 1hr. before close. £7, concessions £5.50, children £4.50.)

REAL MARY KING'S CLOSE. Under the souvenir shops and cafes of the Royal Mile lies a long-abandoned underground neighborhood. Accessed just off the Mile via Warriston's Close, the narrow alley of Mary King's Close was sealed off when the Royal Exchange was built in 1753. Today, tours of the street and its dark dwellings allow a fascinating glimpse into the lives of its 16th- and 19th-century residents. (☎08702 430 160; www.realmarykingsclose.com. Open Apr.-Oct. daily 10am-9pm; Nov.-Mar. M-F and Su 10am-4pm, Sa 10am-9pm. 1hr. tours every 20min. Book ahead. £8, concessions £7, children £6.)

GLADSTONE'S LAND. Staffed with knowledgeable guides, the oldest surviving house on the Royal Mile (completed in 1620) has been carefully preserved, with hand-painted ceilings and a fine collection of 17th-century Dutch art. (477b Lawnmarket. ☎226 5856. Open daily July-Aug. 10am-7pm; Apr.-June and Sept.-Oct. 10am-5pm. Last admission 30min. before close. £5, concessions £4, families £14. Braille guidebook available.)

WRITER'S MUSEUM. Inspirational quotations are etched in the pavement of this tribute to literary personae, just off the Royal Mile down Lady Stair's Close. The museum contains memorabilia and manuscripts from three of Scotland's greatest wordsmiths: Robert Burns, Sir Walter Scott, and Robert Louis Stevenson. (Lawnmarket. ☎529 4901. Open M-Sa 10am-5pm; during Festival also Su 2-5pm. Free.)

PRINCES STREET GARDENS. The gardens are in the city center, with fantastic views of Old Town and the castle. The lush park stands on the site of now-drained Nor'Loch, where Edinburghers used to drown accused witches. The Loch has been replaced with an impeccably manicured lawn, stone fountains, winding avenues with benches, and enough trees to provide shade from the Scottish "sun." (Open daily. Hours vary, usually closes at dusk.)

HIGH STREET

High Street marks the middle of the Royal Mile with *kirks* (churches) and monuments. Watch for sandwich board signs advertising ghost or underground tours—many convene throughout the day and night along the High Street section.

HIGH KIRK OF ST. GILES. This *kirk* is Scotland's principal church, sometimes known as **St. Giles's Cathedral.** From its pulpit, Protestant reformer John Knox delivered the sermons that drove the Catholic Mary, Queen of Scots, into exile. Stained-glass windows illuminate the structure, whose crown spire is one of Edinburgh's hallmarks. The 20th-century **Thistle Chapel** honors the Most Ancient and Most Noble Order of the Thistle, Scotland's prestigious chivalric order. St. Giles is flanked on the east by the stone **Mercat Cross,** marking the site of the medieval market ("mercat"), and on the west by the **Heart of Midlothian,** inlaid in the pavement. According to legend, spitting on the Heart protects you from being hanged in the square. It appears as though many visitors are under the impression that they get extra protection if they spit their gum on the Heart. The cathedral hosts free concerts throughout the year. (Where Lawnmarket becomes High St. ☎225 9442; www.stgilescathedral.org.uk. Open daily M-Sa 9am-5pm, Su 1-5pm. Suggested donation £1.)

TRON KIRK. A block downhill from St. Giles rises the high-steepled Tron Kirk, built to deal with the overflow of 16th-century religious zealots from St. Giles. Today, it houses the **Old Town Information Centre,** inside the kirk beside an open archaeological dig, and is the focus of Edinburgh's Hogmanay celebrations. (☎225 8408. Open daily Apr.-Oct. 11am-7pm; Nov.-Mar. noon-5pm; extended Festival hours. Free.)

CANONGATE

Canongate, the steep hill that constitutes the last segment of the Royal Mile, was once a separate burgh and part of an Augustinian abbey. Now it is home to cafes and shops that are quieter than their High Street counterparts.

CANONGATE KIRK. Royals used to worship in this 17th-century chapel. Adam Smith, founder of modern economics, lies in the slope to the left of the entrance. Down the hill from his grave, find the joint effort of three literary Roberts: Robert Louis Stevenson commemorated a monument erected here by Robert Burns in memory of Robert Fergusson. (*Open from Apr. to mid-Sept. M-F 9am-7pm, Sa 9am-5pm, Su 1-5pm; from mid-Sept. to Mar. M-Sa 9am-5pm, Su 1-5pm. Free.*)

SCOTTISH POETRY LIBRARY. In an award-winning piece of modern architecture, the library has a fine collection of Scottish and international poetry. (*5 Crichton's Close. ☎557 2876; www.spl.org.uk. Open M-F 11am-6pm, Sa 1-5pm. Free.*)

HOLYROOD

The lower end of the Royal Mile is occupied mostly by the huge palace and park.

PALACE OF HOLYROODHOUSE. This Stuart palace at the base of the Royal Mile remains Queen Elizabeth II's official Scottish residence. As a result, only parts of the ornate interior are open to the public. Once home to Mary, Queen of Scots, whose bedchamber is on display, the palace is every bit a royal residence. Dozens of portraits inside the **Great Gallery** chronicle its proud history. On the palace grounds lie the ruins of **Holyrood Abbey,** built by King David I in 1128 and ransacked during the Reformation. Most of the ruins date from the 13th century, but only a single doorway remains from the original construction. Located in a recently renovated 17th-century schoolhouse near the palace entrance is the **Queen's Gallery,** which displays exhibits from the royal art collection. (*At the bottom of the Royal Mile. ☎556 5100. Open Apr.-Sept. daily 9:30am-6pm; Nov.-Mar. M-Sa 9:30am-4:30pm. Last admission 1hr. before close. No admission while royals are in residence (often June-July). Palace £9.50, students and seniors £8.50, children £5.50, families £24.50, under 5 free. Queen's Gallery £5.50/5/3.50/13.50. Joint £13/11.50/7.50/33.50. Audio tour free.*)

HOLYROOD SCOTTISH PARLIAMENT BUILDING. After years of controversy and massive budget overdraws, the new Scottish Parliament Building is functional and open to visitors. Built from steel, oak, and stone, the building is an attempt to bring cosmopolitan craziness back to the natural. Architect Enric Miralles was influenced by the surrounding landscapes, the paintings of Charles Rennie Mackintosh, and boats on the seashore. (*☎348 5200; www.scottish.parliament.uk. Open Apr.-Oct. M and F 10am-6pm, Tu-Th 9am-7pm, Sa-Su 10am-4pm; Nov.-Mar. M, F, and Sa-Su 10am-4pm, Tu-Th 9am-7pm. Hours may vary; call ahead. Guided tours on non-business days £3.50, concessions £1.75, children under 6 free. Free tickets to the parliamentary sessions; book in advance.*)

HOLYROOD PARK. A true city oasis, Holyrood Park is filled with hills, moorland, and lochs. At 823 ft., ⬛**Arthur's Seat,** the park's highest point, affords stunning views of the city and Highlands. Considered a holy place by the Picts, Arthur's Seat is probably derived from "Ard-na-Saigheid," Gaelic for "the height of the flight of arrows." Traces of forts and Bronze Age terraces dot the surrounding hillside. From the Palace of Holyroodhouse, the walk to the summit takes about 45min. **Queen's Drive** circles the park and intersects with Holyrood Rd. by the palace.

ELSEWHERE IN THE OLD TOWN

Believe it or not, there is more to Old Town than the Royal Mile.

GREYFRIARS TOLBOOTH AND HIGHLAND KIRK. Off George IV Bridge, the 17th-century kirk rests in a churchyard that, while lovely, is estimated to contain 250,000 bodies and has long been considered haunted. A few centuries ago, the infamous body-snatchers Burke and Hare dug up corpses here before resorting to murder in order to keep the Edinburgh Medical School's anatomy laboratories well-supplied. A more endearing claim to fame is the loyal pooch Greyfriars Bobby, whose much-photographed statue sits at the southwestern corner of

George IV Bridge in front of the churchyard's gates. *(Beyond the gates, atop Candle-makers Row. ☎ 225 1900. English services daily 11am, Gaelic services Su 12:30pm. Open for touring Apr.-Oct. M-F 10:30am-4:30pm, Sa 10:30am-2:30pm; Nov.-Mar. Th 1:30-3:30pm. Free.)*

NATIONAL LIBRARY OF SCOTLAND. The library rotates exhibitions from its archives, which include a Gutenberg Bible, the last letter of Mary, Queen of Scots, and the only surviving original copy of *The Wallace*, an epic poem. *(George IV Bridge. ☎ 226 4531. Open M-F 9:30am-8:30pm, Sa 9:30am-1pm, Su 2-5pm. Free.)*

THE NEW TOWN

Don't be fooled by the name—Edinburgh's New Town, a masterpiece of Georgian design, has very few buildings that are "newer" than 1900. James Craig, an unknown 23-year-old architect, won the city-planning contest in 1767. His rectangular grid of three parallel streets (**Queen, George,** and **Princes**) linking two large squares (**Charlotte** and **St. Andrew**) reflects the Scottish Enlightenment belief in order. Queen and Princes St., the outer streets, were built up on only one side to allow views of the Firth of Forth and the Old Town. Princes St., Edinburgh's main shopping drag, is also home to the venerable **Jenner's,** the Harrods of Scotland. *(☎ 225 2442. Open M-Sa 9am-6pm, Su 11am-5pm. AmEx/MC/V.)*

WALTER SCOTT MONUMENT. Statues of Sir Walter and his dog preside inside the spire of this Gothic "steeple without a church." Climb 287 narrow, winding steps past carved figures of Scott's most famous characters to reach the top. An eagle's-eye view of Princes St., the castle, and the surrounding city awaits. The journey to the top is not recommended for those who suffer from claustrophobia or vertigo. *(Princes St. between The Mound and Waverley Bridge. ☎ 529 4098. Open Apr.-Sept. M-Sa 9am-6pm, Su 10am-6pm; Oct.-Mar. M-Sa 9am-3pm, Su 10am-3pm. £2.50.)*

CALTON HILL. This hill at the eastern end of New Town provides views of the city and the Firth of Forth. Climb 143 steps inside the **Nelson Monument,** built in 1807 in memory of the admiral and the Battle of Trafalgar. *(☎ 556 2716. Open Apr.-Sept. M 1-6pm, Tu-Sa 10am-6pm; Oct.-Mar. M-Sa 10am-3pm. £2.50.)* The hilltop is also home to the old **City Observatory** (1818) and the **National Monument** (1822), affectionately known as "Edinburgh's Disgrace." The structure, a poor man's Parthenon designed to commemorate those killed in the Napoleonic Wars, was scrapped when civic coffers ran dry after a mere 12 columns were built. For all its faults, it does offer beautiful views of the sunrise between its columns from Waverley Bridge.

BEYOND THE CITY CENTER

LEITH AND THE BRITANNIA. Two miles northeast of the city center, the neighborhood of **Leith** has undergone a dramatic revival. Its abandoned warehouses have been replaced (or at least supplemented) by upscale flats, restaurants, and bars. The **Royal Yacht Britannia,** used by the royal family from 1953 to 1997 (when the government decided it was too expensive and decommissioned it), sailed around the world on state visits and royal holidays. Visitors can listen to a free audio tour of the entire flagship, which remains exactly as it was when decommissioned, and visit the royal apartments. Even the Queen's bedroom, off-limits at every other royal residence, is open to visitors. Other highlights include the officers' mess and the engine room. *(Entrance on the Ocean Terminal's 3rd fl. Take bus #22 from Princes St. or #35 from the Royal Mile to Ocean Terminal. £1. ☎ 555 5566; www.royalyachtbritannia.co.uk. Open daily Mar.-Oct. 9:30am-4pm; Nov.-Feb. 10am-4:30pm. £9, seniors £7, students and children £5, families £25.)*

CRAIGMILLAR CASTLE. This 15th-century castle stands 3½ mi. southeast of central Edinburgh. Mary, Queen of Scots, fled here after the murder of her secretary at

Holyroodhouse. While she was here, plans emerged for the murder of her second husband, Lord Darnley. *(Take bus #2, 14, or 32 from Princes St. to the corner of Old Dalkeith Rd. and Craigmillar Castle Rd., then walk 10min. up the castle road. ☎661 4445. Open daily Apr.-Sept. 9:30am-5:30pm; Oct.-Mar. 9:30am-4:30pm. £4, seniors £3, children £2.)*

EDINBURGH ZOO. At long last, your search for the world's largest penguin pool has come to an end. You'll find it 2½ mi. west of the city center, along with exhibits featuring some 1000 other animals. *(Take bus #12, 26, or 31 westbound from Princes St. ☎334 9171. Open daily Apr.-Sept. 9am-6pm; Oct. and Mar. 9am-5pm; Nov.-Feb. 9am-4:30pm. £10, children and seniors £7.)*

ROYAL BOTANIC GARDENS. Edinburgh's herbaceous oasis has plants from around the world. Guided tours wander across lush grounds and greenhouses crammed with orchids, tree ferns, and towering palms. *(Inverleith Row. Take bus #23 or 27 from Hanover St. ☎552 7171. Open daily Apr.-Sept. 10am-7pm; Mar. and Oct. 10am-6pm; Nov.-Feb. 10am-4pm. Free. Glasshouses £4, concessions £3, children £1, families £8.)*

🏛 MUSEUMS AND GALLERIES

NATIONAL GALLERIES OF SCOTLAND

Edinburgh's four major galleries are an elite group, all connected by a free shuttle that runs every 45min. (☎624 6200; www.nationalgalleries.org. All open daily 10am-5pm; during Festival 10am-6pm. All free.)

◼ NATIONAL GALLERY OF SCOTLAND. Housed in a grand 19th-century building designed by William Playfair, this gallery has a superb collection of works by Renaissance, Romantic, and Impressionist masters, including Raphael, Titian, Gauguin, Degas, and Monet. Don't miss the octagonal room, which displays Poussin's entire *Seven Sacraments*. The basement houses a selection of Scottish art. *(On The Mound between the halves of the Princes St. Gardens.)* The next-door ◼ **Royal Academy** hosts exhibits from the National Gallery and runs a high-profile show each summer. *(At the corner of The Mound and Princes St. Special late night Th until 7pm.)*

SCOTTISH NATIONAL PORTRAIT GALLERY. The gallery displays the stern faces of the famous men and women who have shaped Scotland's history. Military, political, and intellectual figures are all represented, including the definitive portraits of wordsmith Robert Louis Stevenson, renegade Bonnie Prince Charlie, and royal troublemaker Mary, Queen of Scots. *(1 Queen St., north of St. Andrew Sq.)*

SCOTTISH NATIONAL GALLERY OF MODERN ART. In the west end of town, this permanent collection includes works by Braque, Matisse, and Picasso. The newly completed landscaping in front of the museum, a bizarre spiral of grass set into a pond, represents the concept of chaos theory with dirt and greenery. *(75 Belford Rd. Take the free shuttle, bus #13 from George St., or walk along the Water of Leith Walkway.)*

DEAN GALLERY. Across the road from the Gallery of Modern Art, the newest addition to the National Galleries is dedicated to Surrealist and Dada art. The gallery owes much of its fine collection to the sculptor Eduardo Paolozzi, whose towering, three-story statue, *Vulcan*, stands at the main entrance. *(73 Belford Rd., across from the Gallery of Modern Art. Special exhibits £3.50.)*

OTHER MUSEUMS AND GALLERIES

MUSEUM OF SCOTLAND AND ROYAL MUSEUM. The superbly designed ◼ **Museum of Scotland** traces the whole of Scottish history through an impressive collection of treasured objects and decorative art. Highlights include the working Corliss Steam Engine and the Maiden, Edinburgh's guillotine, used on High St.

around 1565. The rooftop terrace provides a 360° view. Gallery tours and audio tours in various languages are free. The ▨ **Royal Museum** has rotating exhibits on natural history, European art, contemporary Scottish art, and ancient Egypt, to name a few. The **Millennium Clock,** a towering, ghoulish display of figures representing human suffering in the 20th century, chimes three times daily. Free tours, from useful intros to 1hr. circuits of the highlights, leave from the Main Hall's totem pole in the Royal Museum and the Museum of Scotland's Hawthornden Court. *(Chambers St. ☎247 4422; www.nms.ac.uk. Both open daily 10am-5pm. Free.)*

OUR DYNAMIC EARTH. This glitzy, high-tech lesson in geology is part amusement park, part science experiment, appealing mainly to children. Look for the white, tent-like structure next to Holyroodhouse. *(Holyrood Rd. ☎550 7800; www.dynamicearth.co.uk. Open July-Aug. daily 10am-6pm; Apr.-June and Sept.-Oct. daily 10am-5pm; Nov.-Mar. W-Su 10am-5pm. Last entry 1½hr. before closing. £8.45, concessions £7, children £5.75.)*

OTHER MUSEUMS. The **Museum of Childhood** displays an array of antique and contemporary childhood toys, from 19th-century dollhouses to 1990s Teletubbies. *(42 High St. ☎529 4142. Open M-Sa 10am-5pm, Su noon-5pm. Free.)* **Canongate Tolbooth** (c. 1591), with a beautiful clock face above the Royal Mile, once served as a prison and gallows for "elite" criminals. Now it houses the **People's Story Museum,** an eye-opening look at the life of Edinburgh's working classes. *(163 Canongate. ☎529 4057. Open M-Sa 10am-5pm; during festival also Su 10am-5pm. Free.)* The **Surgeon's Hall Museum,** in the majestic Royal College of Surgeons, has displays on the history of surgery and dentistry. Don't venture into the pathology rooms if you've just had lunch. *(Nicholson St. ☎527 1649; www.edinburgh.surgeonshall.museum. Open from mid-July to mid-Sept. daily 10am-4pm; from mid-Sept. to mid-July M-F noon-4pm. £5, concessions £3.)*

▨ NIGHTLIFE

PUBS

Pubs on the **Royal Mile** tend to attract a mixed crowd of old and young, tourists and locals. Students and backpackers gather in force each night in the Old Town. Casual pub-goers groove to live music on **Grassmarket, Candlemaker Row,** and **Victoria Street.** The New Town also has its share of worthy watering holes, some historical, and most strung along **Rose Street,** parallel to Princes St. Gay-friendly **Broughton Street** is increasingly popular for nightlife, although its pubs are more trendy than traditional. Wherever you are, you'll usually hear last call sometime between 11pm and 1am, or 3am during the Festival.

TOURIST TO PURIST. Don't order your Scotch on the rocks if you want to avoid looking like a tourist. Scotch Whisky should be drunk neat, with no ice. Locals may mix with a splash of water—real pros ask for mineral water from the region in which the whisky was distilled.

▨ **The Tron,** 9 Hunter Sq. (☎226 0931), behind Tron Kirk. Friendly student bar. Downstairs is a mix of alcoves and pool tables. Frequent live music. Burger and a pint £4.50. W night £1 pints. Open M-Sa noon-1am, Su 12:30pm-1am; during Festival 8:30am-3am. Food served noon-9pm.

▨ **The Outhouse,** 12a Broughton St. (☎557 6668). Hidden up an alleyway off Broughton St. and well worth the hunt. More stylish than your average pub but just as cheap, with one of the best beer gardens in the city. Open daily 11am-1am.

The Globe, 13 Niddry St. (☎557 4670). This hole in the wall is recommended up and down the Royal Mile by sports fans and karaoke enthusiasts. DJs and quiz nights. Open M-F 4pm-1am, Sa noon-1am, Su 12:30pm-1am; during Festival until 3am.

The Three Sisters, 139 Cowgate (☎622 6801). Loads of space for dancing, drinking, and lounging. Attracts a young crowd to its 3 bars (Irish, Gothic, and American). Beer garden sees close to 1000 people pass through on Sa nights. Open daily 9am-1am. Food served M-F 9am-9pm, Sa-Su 9am-8pm.

Finnegan's Wake, 9b Victoria St. (☎226 3816). Drink the Irish way at this traditional pub. Several stouts on tap, road signs from Cork, and live music nightly at 10pm. Gaelic football and hurling on a big screen during the summer. Open daily 1pm-1am.

Jolly Judge, 7 James Ct. (☎226 2669). Hidden just off the Royal Mile, with a cozy atmosphere. 17th-century painted ceiling. M quiz night, Th live music, both 9pm. Open M and Th-Sa noon-midnight, Tu-W noon-11pm, Su 12:30-11pm. Food served noon-2pm.

CLUBS

Edinburgh may be best known for its pubs, but the club scene is none too shabby. It is, however, in constant flux, with club nights switching between venues and bringing in very different clientele from one night to the next. Consult *The List* (£2.20), a comprehensive guide to events, available from any local newsstand, for the night's hotspot. Clubs cluster around the city's historically disreputable **Cowgate,** just downhill from and parallel to the Royal Mile; most close at 3am (5am during the Festival). Smart street-wear is necessary for clubbing in Edinburgh.

▨ **Cabaret-Voltaire,** 36-38 Blair St. (☎220 6176, www.thecabaretvoltaire.com). Playing everything from jazz to breakbeat, this innovative club knows how to throw a party. Cavernous interior packs a loyal crowd. M cheap drinks; W huge "We are Electric." Cover up to £12. Open daily 7pm-3am.

Bongo Club, 6 New St. (☎558 7604), off Canongate. Particularly noted for its hip hop and the immensely popular "Messenger" (reggae; 1 Sa per month) and "Headspin" (funk and dance; 1 Sa per month) nights. Cover up to £7. Cafe with free Internet access during the day. Open Su-W 10am-noon, Th-Sa 10am-3am.

Po Na Na, 43b Frederick St. (☎226 2224), beneath Cafe Rouge. Go down the steps to a yellow cartoon image of a man in a fez. Moroccan-themed, with parachute ceilings, red velvet couches, and an eclectic blend of R&B, hip hop, disco, and funk. Cover £2.50-6. Open M, Th, and Su 11pm-3am, F-Sa 10:30pm-3am; during Festival until 5am. Call ahead to get on the guest list for discounted entry and drink specials.

GLBT NIGHTLIFE

The Broughton St. area of the New Town (better known as the Broughton Triangle) is the center of Edinburgh's gay community. Lesbian club nights, such as the long-running **Velvet,** and the younger **Fur Burger,** are held monthly—check *The List* for venues and times.

▨ **Sala Cafe-Bar,** 60 Broughton St. (☎478 7069). Live music and an eclectic menu. Tapas from £2.60. Open Tu-Th 4pm-midnight, F 12:30pm-1am, Sa 11am-1am, Su 11am-11pm. Food served until 9:30pm T-Th, 10:30pm F-Sa, 9pm Su. Cash only.

C.C. Bloom's, 23-24 Greenside Pl. (☎556 9331), on Leith St. No cover and a new up-and-coming DJ each night. Su Cabaret from 3pm, karaoke from 10pm. Open M-W and F-Su 3pm-3am, Th 8pm-3am.

Blue Moon Cafe, 36 Broughton St. (☎557 0911), at the corner of Barony St. A popular pub serving food to a mixed gay and straight crowd. Food served M-F 11am-10pm, Sa-Su 10am-10pm. Bar open M-F 11am-11pm, Sa 10am-11pm, Su noon-11pm.

Ego, 14 Picardy Pl. (☎478 7434; www.clubego.co.uk). Not strictly a gay club, but hosts several gay nights, including Vibe (Tu) and Blaze (2 F per month). Cover £3-10. Open M-W and Su 10pm-1am, Th-Sa 11pm-3am; check *The List* for gay night dates.

♪ ENTERTAINMENT

For all the latest listings, check out *The List* (£2.20), available at newsstands.

THEATER AND FILM

▩ The Stand Comedy Club, 5 York Pl. (☎558 7272; www.thestand.co.uk). Hilariously unhinged acts every night and all day Su. Special 17-shows-per-day program for the Fringe Festival. Call ahead. Tickets £1-10.

Festival Theatre, 13-29 Nicholson St. (☎529 6000; www.eft.co.uk). Stages predominantly ballet and opera, turning entirely to the Festival in August. Box office open M-Sa 10am-6pm and before performances. Tickets £5-55.

King's Theatre, 2 Leven St. (☎529 6000; www.eft.co.uk). Promotes musicals, opera, and the occasional pantomime. Box office open 1hr. before show and between matinee and evening performances. Tickets also available through the Festival Theatre.

Royal Lyceum Theatre, 30 Grindlay St. (☎248 4848; www.lyceum.org.uk). The finest in Scottish and English theater, with many international productions. Box office open M-Sa 10am-6pm; until 8pm on performance nights. Tickets £8-20, students ½-price.

Traverse Theatre, 10 Cambridge St. (☎228 1404; www.traverse.co.uk). Presents almost exclusively new drama and experimental theater with lots of local Scottish work. Box office open daily 10am-6pm. Tickets £5, concessions £3.50.

Bedlam Theatre, 11b Bristo Pl. (☎225 9873). A university theater with excellent student productions, ranging from comedy and drama to F night improv, all in a converted church. A Fringe Festival hot spot. Box office open M-Sa 10am-6pm. Tickets £4-5.

The Filmhouse, 88 Lothian Rd. (☎228 2688). European and arthouse films, though Hollywood fare appears as well. Tickets £3.50-5.50. For mainstream cinema, try **Odeon,** 7 Clerk St. (☎667 0971), or **UGC Fountainpark,** Dundee St., Fountainbridge (bus #1, 28, 34, and 35; ☎0870 902 0417).

LIVE MUSIC

Thanks to an abundance of university students who never let books get in the way of a good night out, Edinburgh's live music scene is vibrant and diverse. Excellent impromptu and professional folk sessions take place at pubs (p. 543), and many university houses sponsor live shows—look for flyers near Bristol Sq. *The List* (£2.20) has comprehensive listings. **Ripping Records,** 91 South Bridge (☎226 7010), sells tickets to rock, reggae, and pop performances.

Henry's Cellar, 8a Morrison St. (☎538 7385; www.henrysjazz.co.uk), downstairs off Lothian Rd. Hosts both local and international jazz and alternative musicians in a laidback atmosphere. Cover varies, usually around £5. Open daily 8pm-3am.

Whistle Binkie's, 4-6 South Bridge (☎557 5114). A subterranean pub with 2 live shows every night, open to bands of any genre. Gets busy late. Open daily until 3am.

The Royal Oak, 1 Infirmary St. (☎557 2976). Classic pub setting with live traditional and folk music every night. Tickets £1-3. Open M-F 10am-2am, Sa 11am-2am, Su 12:30pm-2am. Live music from 7pm.

❀ FESTIVALS

Edinburgh has special events year-round, but the real show is in August. Prices rise, pubs and restaurants stay open later than late (some simply don't close), and street performers have the run of the place. What's commonly referred to as "the Festival" actually includes a number of independently organized events. For more information and links to each festival, check out www.edinburghfestivals.co.uk.

IN RECENT NEWS

YOU'VE GOT GRAIL

The folks at Rosslyn Chapel may wish Dan Brown's novel *The Da Vinci Code* hadn't sold quite so many copies. Rosslyn was featured in the novel as a possible resting place for the Holy Grail, and its number of visitors has since increased from 40,000 per year to 175,000 in 2006.

This huge influx has created challenges for the small chapel. A new entrance has to be built. The parking lot and visitor center have to be expanded. Cameras, disguised as carvings of angels, were installed to protect against the greedy fingers of grail hunters. Curators estimate that renovations will cost about £13 million.

The chapel itself seems to be taking the hordes of visitors relatively well—for now. Rosslyn is made of soft sandstone, which will start to erode if the flow of visitors remains so high. "We might be the only attraction in existence that actually wants to get people to *stop* coming," joked Rosslyn Interpretation and Events Manager Simon Beattie.

Has the chapel seen any grail sleuthing? "We had one man try to steal the cross from the front of the chapel," Beattie says. "He didn't have a bag or anything, he just tried to walk the front with it, but it's rather large. Needless to say, we caught him." Beware, souvenir hunters: the angels are watching.

Renovation begins in July 2008. Check www.rosslyn-chapel.com for closures and details.

■ EDINBURGH INTERNATIONAL FESTIVAL. Begun in 1947, the **Edinburgh International Festival** attracts the top performers from all over the globe, mainly in the realms of classical music, ballet, opera, and drama. The most popular single event is the festival's grand finale: a spectacular **Fireworks Concert** with pyrotechnics choreographed to orchestral music. Most tickets go on sale in early April, and a full program is published by then. Tickets to the biggest events sell out well in advance, but all hope is not lost—at least 50 tickets for major events are held and sold on the day of the performance at the venue. Throughout the festival, visitors can buy tickets at **The Hub** or at the door 1hr. prior to showtime. Selected shows are half-price on the day of performance. *(Aug. 8-Aug. 31, 2008. Bookings can be made by post, phone, web, or in person at The Hub, Edinburgh's Festival Centre, Castlehill, Edinburgh EH1 2NE. ☎473 2000 or 473 2001; www.eif.co.uk. Open M-Sa from early Apr.; daily from late July. Tickets £7-58, students and children ½-price; £5 tickets held at the door for sale 1hr. before curtain.)*

■ EDINBURGH FESTIVAL FRINGE. Longer and more informal than the International Festival, the Fringe is the world's biggest arts festival, showcasing everything from Shakespeare to coconut-juggling dwarves. It began in 1947, when eight theater companies arrived to Edinburgh uninvited and had to book "fringe" venues to perform. Today, the Fringe draws more visitors to Edinburgh than any other event. Anyone who can afford the small registration fee can perform; this orgy of eccentricity attracts a multitude of good and not-so-good acts and guarantees a wild month. Head to the **Half Price Hut** bright and early to grab tickets for that day's shows at 50% off. *The Fringe* editorial, published in late spring, has a full listing of festivities (available free in just about every doorway of the city). *(Aug. 3-25, 2008. ☎226 0000; www.edfringe.com. Tickets available online, by phone, in person, or by post at The Fringe Office, 180 High St., Edinburgh EH1 1QS. Open M-F 10am-5pm; during Festival daily 10am-9pm. Tickets up to £25. Half Price Hut open 11am-9pm.)*

■ HOGMANAY. The long, dark winter can't stop the party. Having long marked the turn of the calendar and the return of the sun, Hogmanay is Scotland's traditional New Year's Eve celebration, a nation-wide party with pagan roots. Official events in Edinburgh include concerts, torchlight processions, and a street party that packs the Royal Mile and bursts into a rousing rendition of "Auld Lang Syne" at midnight. New Year's Day sees a number of options to shake that hangover, from a triathlon to a mid-winter dip in the Forth. Many events are free, though some require

THE GRAND FINALE FOR POCKET CHANGE. The closing fire-works ceremony of the Edinburgh International Festival (see left), accompanied by the Scottish Chamber Orchestra, is not to be missed. Tickets to watch the concert in Princes Street Gardens are notoriously hard to come by. While you can see the fireworks from pretty much anywhere in the city, the best spot is **Inverleith Park**, by the Botanic Gardens. In addition to unobstructed views of the lit sky, a big-screen TV and giant speakers are set up to broadcast the concert live—and it's all free.

tickets to limit numbers. (☎529 3914; www.edinburghshogmanay.org. The Hub (p. 546) also provides ticket information. Tickets and program available from October.)

OTHER SUMMER FESTIVALS. The following festivities are just a few of the events that take place during the five-week period surrounding the Festival in August. The **Military Tattoo** is a magnificent spectacle of military bands, bagpipes, and drums performed at the gates of the castle. (Aug. 1-23, 2008. Tattoo Ticket Sale Office, 33-34 Market St., Edinburgh EH1 1QB. ☎08707 555 118; www.edintattoo.co.uk. Book well in advance—they sell out as early as Feb. A small number of ½-price preview tickets go on sale in early Aug. Tickets £13-36.) One highlight of the **Jazz and Blues Festival** is the free **Jazz on a Summer's Day** in Ross Theatre. (☎467 5200; www.edinburghjazzfestival.co.uk. Late July-early Aug. Program available in June; bookings by phone, or at The Hub. Tickets £5-25.50.) Charlotte Sq. Gardens hosts the **International Book Festival**, Europe's largest book celebration, in August. (☎0845 373 5888; www.edbookfest.co.uk. Program available starting in mid-June. Tickets £5-10; some free events.) The **International Film Festival** occurs during the last two weeks of August. (Film Festival, The Filmhouse, 88 Lothian Rd. ☎228 4051; www.edfilmfest.org.uk. Box office sells tickets in late July.)

⚑ DAYTRIPS FROM EDINBURGH

SOUTH QUEENSFERRY. Eight miles west of Edinburgh and easily accessible by the #43 bus, the town of South Queensferry lies at the narrowest part of the Firth of Forth, where two bridges—the **Forth Road Bridge** and the **Forth Rail Bridge**—cross the waterway. From Hawes Pier, under Forth Rail Bridge, the **Maid of the Forth** ferries visitors to Inchcolm Island. Float by colonies of seals to **Inchcolm Abbey**, the best-preserved 12th-century abbey in Scotland. (Ferry ☎331 5000; www.maidofthe-forth.co.uk. Runs from mid-July to early Sept. daily; Apr.-June and Oct. Sa-Su. Round-trip ticket includes abbey admission. £13, concessions £11, children £4.70.) Two miles west of South Queensferry stands **Hopetoun House** and its 150 acres of sprawling land, including a wooded deer park. Begun around 1700 and designed by Sir William Bruce (who is also responsible for Holyroodhouse), it offers views of the Forth and is the setting for many British television shows. (No public transportation runs to Hopetoun; take a taxi from South Queensferry. ☎331 2451; www.hopetounhouse.com. Open daily from mid-Apr. to late Sept. 10am-5:30pm. Last admission 4:30pm. £8, concessions £7, children £4.25.)

ROSLIN. The ▧**Rosslyn Chapel**, in the village of Roslin, 7 mi. south of Edinburgh, is one of the many British sites claiming to harbor the Holy Grail. The stone carvings filled with occult symbols raised eyebrows in 15th-century Scotland, and the chapel found new popularity after its mention in Dan Brown's *The Da Vinci Code*. Thousands of recreational Grail hunters flock to its intricate walls. Outside the chapel, footpaths lead to the ruined Roslin Castle in Roslin Glen. (From Edinburgh, take bus #15A from St. Andrew Sq. (40min.) ☎440 2159; www.rosslynchapel.com. Open M-Sa 9:30am-6pm, Su noon-4:45pm. £7, concessions £6, children free.)

THE BORDERS

From Roman occupation through Jacobean rebellion, the Borders were caught in a violent tug-of-war between Scotland and England. Present-day Borderers, however, suffer no crisis of identity. Grooms wear tartan kilts at their weddings and the blue and white cross of St. Andrew reigns over the Union Jack. The Scottish land is dotted with fortified houses and ruined abbeys in Dryburgh, Jedburgh, Kelso, and Melrose. These grim reminders of warfare contrast with the gentle countryside, which inspired the poetry of Sir Walter Scott.

▐ TRANSPORTATION

There are no trains in the Borders, but **buses** are frequent. Galashiels, or "Gala," has few visitor attractions of its own, but is a travel hub for the surrounding towns. (Bus station open M-F 9am-5pm.) First (☎01896 752 237) runs most of the longer routes across the region, while Munro's (☎01835 862 253) operates many local services. TICs and Traveline (☎08706 082 608) have schedules. Bus #60 (M-F 10 per day, Sa-Su 8 per day) goes from Berwick to Galashiels (1¾hr.) via Melrose (1½hr.). Bus #62 goes from Melrose to Edinburgh via Galashiels and Peebles (2¼hr.; M-Sa 2 per hr., Su every hr.). To get to Edinburgh from Jedburgh, take bus #51/67 (2hr.; M-Sa every hr., Su 6 per day). Bus #52/68 runs to Edinburgh from Kelso (2hr.; M-Sa every hr., Su 6 per day). National Express #383 (1 per day) heads from Edinburgh to Newcastle via Galashiels, Melrose, and Jedburgh. Bus #95/X95 (8 per day) travels from Carlisle to Edinburgh (3½hr.) via Galashiels (1¼hr.). Bus #68/71 goes to Jedburgh from Galashiels (1½hr.) via Melrose (15min.).

▐ ACCOMMODATIONS

TICs can help you book a bed for £3 plus a 10% deposit. For advance bookings call Scottish Borders Customer Service Centre (☎08706 080 404). The following **SYHA hostels** in the Borders are strategically dispersed—a fourth is in **Melrose** (p. 549). All have a 10:30am-5pm lockout and are only open from April to September.

Broadmeadows (☎08700 041 107), 5 mi. west of Selkirk off the A708 and 1¼ mi. south of the Southern Upland Way. The first SYHA hostel (opened 1931), close to the Tweedsmuir Hills. 20 comfortable beds in small dorms. Dorms £13.50, under 18 £10.50. Cash only. ❷

Coldingham Sands (☎08700 041 111), a 20min. walk from Coldingham at St. Abbs Head, 5min. from the ocean. 36 beds. Dorms £12.50-13, under 18 £9.25. MC/V. ❶

Kirk Yetholm (☎08700 041 132), at the junction of the B6352 and B6401, near Kelso. 7 buses per day run from Kelso. Located at the end of the Pennine Way. Popular with hikers and cyclists. 20 beds. Dorms £12.50, under 18 £9. Cash only. ❶

▐ ▐ HIKING AND OUTDOOR ACTIVITIES

Hikers of all levels enjoy the Borders for late afternoon strolls in the hills or journeys through the wilderness. The valley of the **River Tweed** offers many beautiful stretches for a day's trek. At the river's source in the west, the **Tweedsmuirs** provide difficult terrain. In the north, the **Moorfoots** and **Lammermuir** hills are well-suited to the country rambler. Two long-distance paths cross the Borders. Marked by thistle in a hexagonal symbol, the challenging **Southern Upland Way** winds through the region for 82 mi., passing near Galashiels and Melrose on its route to the sea. **Saint Cuthbert's Way** runs 62 mi. from Melrose to Holy Island on the English coast and is marked by crosses. The Borders are covered extensively by Ordnance Survey Landranger (#72-75, 79, 80; £6.50) and Explorer (#330, 331, 336-340, 346; £7.50) maps, which are essential. Upon arriving in the Borders, grab a free copy of the superb *Walking the Scottish Borders* at any TIC, which details 30 day-long walks, or look for *Short Walks on the Eastern Section of the Upland Way* (£2.50). The Borders also cater to on- and off-trail **bikers.** Excellent **mountain biking** can be found near Peebles on trails at Glentress and Innerleithen, part of the award-winning 7stanes project (www.7stanes.gov.uk). A number of well-marked trails cross the region, including the **Tweed Cycleway,** a 90 mi. route that hugs the Tweed River from Biggar to Berwick, and the **Four Abbeys Cycle Route,** which connects the abbeys at Melrose, Dryburgh, Jedburgh, and Kelso. The 250 mi. **Borderloop** offers more strenuous trails. *Cycling in the Scottish Borders* (free at TICs) outlines these routes and 20 shorter trails, lists local cycle shops, and dispenses good advice. The *Scottish Borders* series also offers guides to golfing and fishing.

MELROSE   ☎01896

Melrose is the prettiest of the region's towns, and most of its visitors come for its abbey. The town is within convenient reach of **Dryburgh Abbey** and **Abbotsford,** Sir Walter Scott's country home (p. 550). A stop on the **Four Abbeys Cycle Route,** Melrose is also the start of **Saint Cuthbert's Way** and lies near both the **Southern Upland Way** and **Tweed Cycleway,** making it the best base camp for outdoor activities in the Borders. The fascinating ▨**Melrose Abbey** dates to the 12th century, although it was later reconstructed in the Gothic style after a particularly harsh pillaging by the English. Search the grounds for the tombstone marking Robert the Bruce's embalmed heart. The abbey's famed gargoyles include a bagpipe-playing pig and a warrior kitten. The **Abbey Museum** displays objects unearthed from the abbey grounds and regional Roman forts. It also details Sir Walter Scott's life, death, and poetic dishonesty. (☎822 562. Open daily Apr.-Sept. 9:30am-5:30pm; Oct.-Mar. 9:30am-4:30pm. Last admission 30min. before close. £4.50, seniors £3.50, children £2.) A Roman fort once spanned the three volcanic summits of the **Eildon Hills,** which tower above the town. (Guided walks leave from the tiny Trimontium museum on Market Sq. July-Aug. Tu and Th 1:30pm; Apr.-June and Sept.-Oct. Th 1:30pm. £3.) Legend has it that King Arthur and his knights lie asleep in a cavern beneath the hills—if they're not in Wales, Glastonbury, or anywhere else that makes similar claims. The bare peaks afford fabulous views of the town. The easy **Eildon Hills Walk** (4 mi.) leaves from the abbey and is marked on the town map available from the TIC. Close to the town center, ▨**SYHA Melrose ❶,** off High Rd., is housed in a huge estate with views of the abbey, which is lit at night and makes a haunting spectacle as it looms behind the trees. From Market Pl., follow the footpath between Anderson fishmonger and the Ship Inn. Bear right going through the car park. (☎822 521. Self catering. Laundry £4. Internet access £1 per 20min. Reception 7am-11pm. Curfew 11:30pm. Dorms £13.25-14, under 18 £11. MC/V.) **Braidwood B&B ❸,** Buccleuch St., strikes a good balance between cost and comfort. (☎822 488; www.braidwoodmelrose.co.uk. No smoking. Ensuite rooms start at £27 per person. Cash only.) **Caravan Club Park ❶,** off High St., provides clean facilities within easy walking distance of the town center. (☎822 969. £7.50. MC/V.) Walter's, Market Sq., sells basic **groceries** (open M-Sa 7am-10pm, Su 8am-10pm).

  Buses to Melrose stop in Market Sq. Active Sports, Annay Rd., beside the River Tweed, **rents bikes** and leads river trips. (☎822 452. Take the road going out of town past the Abbey and bear left at the fork, heading toward the footbridge over the river. Bikes £17 per day; 24hr. rental. Call ahead. Open daily 9:30am-9:30pm.) The **Tourist Information Centre** is across from the abbey on Abbey St. (☎08706 080 404. Open July-Aug. M-Sa 9:30am-5pm, Su 10am-4pm; June and Sept. M-Sa 9:30am-5pm, Su 10am-2pm; Apr.-May M-Sa 10am-5pm, Su 10am-2pm; Oct. M-Sa 10am-4pm,

Su 10am-2pm; Nov.-Mar. M-Sa 10am-2pm.) Get free **Internet** access at the **Melrose Library,** Market Sq. (☎823 052. Open M and W 10am-1pm and 2:30-5pm, F 2:30-5pm and 5:30-7pm.) The **post office** is on Buccleuch St. (☎822 040. Open M-F 9am-1pm and 2-5:30pm, Sa 9am-noon.) **Post Code:** TD6 9LE.

DAYTRIPS FROM MELROSE

■**DRYBURGH ABBEY.** The grounds of Dryburgh Abbey host extensive ruins, views of the Tweed Valley, and the grave of Sir Walter Scott. Built in 1150, the abbey was inhabited by Premonstratensian monks for nearly two centuries. When Edward II began removing his English troops from Scotland in 1322, the abbey's monks rang their bells in premature celebration. Angry soldiers retraced their steps and set the abbey on fire. *(From Melrose take bus #67 or 68 (10min., frequent) to St. Boswell's, turn left from the bus station, then follow St. Cuthbert's Way along the River Tweed, eventually crossing a metal footbridge to reach the abbey. 30min. By car, take Scott's View, north of Dryburgh on the B635. The Four Abbeys Cycle Route connects Melrose and Dryburgh. ☎01835 822 381. Open Apr.-Sept. daily 9:30am-6:30pm; Oct.-Mar. M-Sa 9:30am-4:30pm, Su 2-4:30pm. Last admission 30min. before close. £4, concessions £3, children £1.60.)*

ABBOTSFORD. It's easy to picture Sir Walter Scott toiling away in the dark, romantic interior of this mock-Gothic estate 2 mi. west of Melrose. The libraries were the birthplace of most of Scott's Waverley novels, while the bedrooms were the place of his death in 1832. The house has 9000 rare books, a collection of weapons, Rob Roy's gun, a lock of Bonnie Prince Charlie's hair, and a piece of the gown worn by Mary, Queen of Scots at her execution. The gardens extend toward the river. *(Frequent buses between Galashiels and Melrose stop nearby. Ask the driver to let you off at the first Tweedbank stop, walk back to the roundabout, and follow the sign to the house, which is ¼ mi. down B6360. ☎752 043; www.scottsabbotsford.co.uk. Open Mar.-May and Oct. M-Sa 9:30am-5pm, Su 2-5pm; June-Sept. daily 9:30am-5pm. £6, students £3, children £2.75.)*

THIRLESTANE CASTLE. The ancient seat of the Duke of Lauderdale, Thirlestane Castle stands 10 mi. north of Melrose on the A68, near Lauder. The defensive walls in the panelled room and library are 13 ft. thick. The beautiful restoration belies the castle's bloody history—jealous nobles hanged a host of King James III's supporters here in 1482. *(From Melrose or Galashiels, take bus #61 toward Lauder and ask to be let off at the castle. ☎01578 722 430; www.thirlestanecastle.co.uk. Open Easter-Sept. M, W, Th, and Su 10:30am-4pm. Last admission 3pm. £5.50. Grounds only £2.)*

PEEBLES   ☎01721

Peebles lies along the River Tweed 18 mi. west of Galashiels. The **Tweed Cycleway** and many other bike trails pass through town and connect to the other Border towns. One excellent short walk departs from the Kingsmeadow car park and follows a 5 mi. circular route down and back along the River Tweed. **Neidpath Castle** is about 20min. into the walk on the town center side of the river. The 11 ft. thick walls were breached only once in their long history. Today, visitors can explore its many preserved levels and admire the view from the top. Inside, batiks, artwork created by dripping wax on cloth, depict the life of Mary, Queen of Scots. (☎720 333. Open May-Sept. W-Sa 11am-6pm, Su 1-5pm. £3, concessions £2.50, children £1.) Learn about the region's history in the free **Tweeddale Museum and Gallery,** in the Chambers Institute on High St. (☎724 820. Open Apr.-Oct. M-F 10am-noon and 2-5pm, Sa 10am-1pm and 2-4pm; Nov.-Mar. M-F 10am-noon and 2-5pm.)

Get a great night's rest in the spacious rooms of the inviting ■**Rowanbrae** ❸, 103 Northgate. (☎721 630. No smoking. Rooms from £24 per person. Cash only.) At the Victorian **Viewfield** ❸, 1 Rosetta Rd., you can spend the evening relaxing in the garden. (☎721 232. Singles from £22; doubles from £38. Cash only.) Campers will feel at home at the **Rosetta Caravan Park ❶**, Rosetta Rd., 10min. from town. (☎720 770; www.rosettacaravanpark.com. Open Apr.-Oct. £7.50 per person, children 50p. Cash only.) Grab your **groceries** at Somerfield, Northgate. (☎722 626 518. Open M-Sa 8:30am-8pm, Su 9am-6pm.) The **Sunflower Restaurant ❸**, 4 Bridgegate, prepares modern Mediterranean cuisine (entrees £12-14), including excellent vegetarian options. Try the smoked chicken and fig salad (£7) for a gourmet lunch. (☎722 420; www.thesunflower.net. Open M-W and Su 10-11:30am and noon-3pm; Th-Sa 10-11:30am, noon-3pm, and 6-9pm. MC/V.)

The **Tourist Information Centre**, 23 High St., books rooms in town for £3 plus a 10% deposit. (☎08706 080 404. Open June-Sept. M-Sa 9am-6pm, Su 10am-4:30pm; Apr.-May M-Sa 9am-5pm, Su 11am-4pm; Oct. M-Sa 9:30am-5pm, Su 11am-4pm; Nov.-Dec. M-Sa 9:15am-5pm, Su 11am-3pm; Jan.-Mar. M-Sa 9:30am-4pm.) Other services include: **banks** along High St.; free **Internet** access at the **library**, High St. (open M, W, F 9:30am-5pm, Tu and Th 9:30am-7pm, Sa 9am-12:30pm); and the **post office**, 14 Eastgate (☎720 119; open M-F 9am-5:30pm, Sa 9am-12:30pm). **Post Code:** EH45 8AA.

🔽 **DAYTRIP FROM PEEBLES: TRAQUAIR HOUSE.** Twelfth-century 🔷**Traquair House** (trar-KWEER), the oldest inhabited house in Scotland, stands 6 mi. east of Peebles and about 1 mi. south of the A72. The interior is a maze of low-ceilinged rooms and spiral staircases, but it's no challenge compared to the famed hedge labyrinth outside. Celebrate finding your way out of either maze with a free sample of Traquair Ale, from the house's own 300-year-old brewery, and try dinner at the 1745 Cottage Restaurant downstairs. *(From Peebles, take bus #62 toward Galashiels to Innerleithen, and walk 1½ mi. There is also a scenic back road running 7 mi. from Peebles to the house; biking is a good option. For a taxi, call Alba Taxis ☎01896 831 333. Traquair House ☎01896 830 323; www.traquair.co.uk. Open June-Aug. daily 10:30am-5pm; Apr.-May and Sept. daily noon-5pm; Oct. daily 11am-4pm; Nov. Sa-Su 11am-3pm. £6.30, children £3.40.)*

JEDBURGH ☎01835

In Jedburgh (known to locals as "Jethart"), 13 mi. south of Melrose, King David I founded **Jedburgh Abbey.** Although pillaging Englishmen were successful in sacking the abbey on numerous occasions, much of the magnificent 12th-century structure still stands. Climb the spiral staircase at the end of the

GRUESOME GLOSSARY

Border towns like Carlisle and Hexham bore centuries of feuding between the English and Scottish. All that pillaging, burning, and killing left its mark on the region, especially its language. Here's a guide to help you learn Border Reiver lingo, and to see how much of today's criminal jargon comes from this bad blood.

1. Reive: to forcibly steal.

2. Reiver: a raider, robber, or bandit. The bad guys.

3. Bereaved: to be reived of a loved one, either by death or by kidnap for ransom to the Reivers.

4. Blackmail: tribute paid by Border residents so that the Reivers wouldn't raid their homes. Usually paid in goods or labor, as opposed to "white mail," which was paid in silver.

5. Jeddart Justice: hang first, trial later.

6. Trod: to follow someone.

7. Hot Trod: the lawful trailing of Reivers. A hot pursuit with flaming torches.

8. Pele Tower: a fortified stone house, found in every town in the Borders.

9. Fray: to frighten or alarm. Reivers would fray the wives of other Reivers when they knew the men were out at a pub.

10. Gear: goods stolen during a Border raid.

nave and admire the views from the top. (☎ 863 925. Open daily Apr.-Sept. 9:30am-5:30pm; Oct.-Mar. 9:30am-4:30pm. Last admission 30min. before close. £4.50, concessions £3.50, children £2. Free audio tour.) For the best free view of the abbey, walk along Abbey Close, off Castlegate. The **Mary, Queen of Scots House,** down Smiths Wynd on Queen St., tells the story of the queen's life through paintings, tapestries, and artifacts. The house itself is a rare example of a 16th-century structure fortified against border conflict. (☎ 863 331. Open Mar.-Nov. M-Sa 10am-5pm, Su 11am-4:30pm. £3, concessions £2, children free.) The 19th-century **Jedburgh Castle Jail and Museum** looms atop a hill on Castlegate. The jail was built on the site of the original Jethart Castle, which was destroyed in 1409. (☎ 864 750. Open Mar.-Oct. M-Sa 10am-4:30pm, Su 1-4pm. Last admission 30min. before close. £2, concessions £1.50, children free. Free audio tour.) Walkers may enjoy the circular route leaving from the TIC, which temporarily follows **Dere Street,** an old Roman road, before tracing Jed Water back to town (roughly 5 mi.). Cyclists can join the **Four Abbeys Cycle Route** in town or pedal out to the **Borderloop.** Both routes offer views of all the historic sights you could ever wish to see from behind bars—handle bars, that is.

B&Bs are scattered throughout town. Family-friendly **Meadhon House ❸**, 48 Castlegate, has a secluded garden and a room with a view of the abbey. (☎ 862 504; www.meadhon.com. Singles £36; doubles £26.50 per person. Cash only.) **Craigowen Guest House ❷**, 30 High St., is a cheap option in the town center. (☎ 862 000. £20 per person. Cash only.) Fun-loving campers can head to **Jedwater Caravan Park ❶** for clean facilities and a recreational atmosphere, complete with a game room and trampoline. The site also offers access to fishing, hiking, and other outdoor pursuits. (4 mi. south of the town center off the A68; watch for signs. ☎ 840 219; www.jedwater.co.uk. Showers, laundry, hair dryers. Open Mar.-Oct. 2-person site including car £12. Cash only.) For **groceries,** try Co-op Superstore, at the corner of Jeweller's Wynd and High St. (☎ 862 944. Open M-Sa 8am-10pm, Su 9am-6pm.) At **Simply Scottish ❷**, 6-8 High St., enjoy meaty Scottish fare and vegetarian options. Specials go for £7-10, and a fine three-course dinner is a steal at £12. (☎ 864 696. Open M-Th 10am-8:30pm, F-Sa 10am-9pm, Su 11am-9pm.)

Buses stop on Canongate, near the abbey and next to the **TIC.** The TIC sells National Express tickets, books rooms for £3 plus a 10% deposit, and has a commission-free **bureau de change.** (☎ 08706 080 404. Open July-Aug. M-Sa 9am-6:30pm, Su 10am-6pm; June and Sept. M-Sa 9am-6pm, Su 10am-5pm; Oct. M-Sa 9:15am-5pm, Su 10am-5pm; Nov.-Mar. M-Sa 9:15am-4:45pm.) Free **Internet** access is available at the **library,** Castlegate (open M-Tu and Th-F 9:30-11:30am), and just next door at The Forrester's Arms (open daily 11am-11pm). The **post office** is at 37 High St. (☎ 862 268; open M-F 9am-5:30pm, Sa 9am-12:30pm). **Post Code:** TD8 6DG.

KELSO   ☎ 01573

Described by Sir Walter Scott as "the most beautiful if not the most romantic town in Scotland," Kelso sits at the meeting of the Tweed and Teviot Rivers, near the English border. One mile from the town center along the Tweed, the Duke and Duchess of Roxburgh reside in the palatial ■**Floors Castle.** The largest inhabited castle in Scotland, Floors has vast grounds, stately rooms, and a window for each day of the year—really. James II met his end while inspecting a cannon in the yard, and Queen Victoria once took her afternoon tea in the gardens. (☎ 223 333. Open Easter-Oct. daily 10am-5pm. Last admission 4:30pm. £6.50, students £5.50, children £3.25, families £16. Grounds only £3.) Little remains of the once grand **Kelso Abbey,** near Market Sq., another victim of English invasion. Impressive even in its reduced state, the abbey is still worth a visit. (Open Apr.-Sept. daily 9:30am-6:30pm; Oct.-Mar. M-W and Sa-Su 9:30am-4:30pm. Free.) A farther option available to those with their own transportation is **Mellerstain House,** one of Scotland's finest

Georgian homes, 6 mi. northwest of Kelso on the A6089. Begun in 1725 by William Adam and completed by his son Robert, the house is noted for its art collection. (☎410 225; www.mellerstain.com. Open May-Sept. M, W-F, and Su 12:30-5pm, gardens 11:30am-5:30pm. House and gardens £6, children free. Grounds only £3.50.) Serious walkers can try the 13 mi. section of the **Borders Abbeys Way,** which runs alongside the River Teviot and links Kelso to Jedburgh. Cyclists can pedal onto the **Four Abbeys Cycle Route** and the **Borderloop** from Kelso (p. 552).

The **SYHA Kirk Yetholm** ❶ (p. 548) is 6 mi. southeast of Kelso. Guests of ▨**Craignethan House** ❸, Jedburgh Rd., are rewarded for their hillside climb with panoramic views from their rooms and with Mrs. MacDonald's nightly baking. From the market square, walk along Bridge St. past the Abbey and over the river. Cut across the park and continue up the hill, taking a right on Jedburgh Rd. across from the gas station. Buses from Jedburgh also stop right outside. (☎224 8181. £25 per person. Cash only.) Closer to town, the spacious **Bellevue Guest House** ❹, Bowmont St., makes a great base for touring the city. (☎224 588. Singles £35; doubles £58. MC/V.) Restock at Somerfield **grocery,** Roxburgh St. (☎225 641. Open M-Sa 8am-8pm, Su 9am-6pm.) If you're hungry for a good steak, **Oscar's** ❷, 35-37 Horsemarket, can satisfy your craving. Lively music and an early bird menu (entrees £10 until 7pm) are the best deal in town. (☎224 008. Open daily 5-10pm.)

Buses stop on Woodmarket. The **Tourist Information Centre,** Market Sq., books rooms for £3 plus a 10% deposit. (☎08706 080 404. Open July-Aug. M-Sa 9:30am-5pm, Su 10am-2pm; Apr.-June and Sept.-Oct. M-Sa 10am-5pm, Su 10am-2pm; Nov.-Mar. M-Sa 10am-4pm.) Get free **Internet** access at the **library,** Bowmont St. (Open M and F 10am-1pm and 2-5pm; Tu and Th 10am-1pm, 2-5pm, and 5:30-7pm; W 10am-1pm; Sa 9:30am-12:30pm.) The **police** are located on Coalmarket (☎223 434). The **post office** is at 13 Woodmarket. (☎224 795. Open M-F 9am-5:30pm, Sa 9am-12:30pm.) **Post Code:** TD5 7AT.

DUMFRIES AND GALLOWAY

Although Dumfries and Galloway see less tourism than other parts of the country, this corner of Scotland has historic attractions and beautiful landscapes. J.M. Barrie created *Peter Pan*'s Neverland while watching schoolboys play in the region's famous gardens, and most of the area's sights are devoted to local heroes like Robert the Bruce and Robert Burns. Wise visitors head for the country, where mountains, forest, and 200 mi. of coastline supply rewarding scenery.

▐ TRANSPORTATION

Trains serve Dumfries and Stranraer. Although **buses** reach other towns, service is infrequent. TICs carry timetables for all areas of the region; call Traveline (☎0870 608 2608) for schedule information. A **Day Discoverer Ticket,** available on buses, allows unlimited travel in Dumfries and Galloway (£5, children £2, families £10).

▐ ACCOMMODATIONS

B&Bs and **hotels** are listed in individual towns. Of the region's two **SYHA hostels,** only Minnigaff is easily reached by public transport.

Kendoon (☎08700 041 130). Bus #520 can stop on the A713 opposite the hostel. Ask the driver to let you off at Kendoon. Small, rustic hostel near Loch Doon and the Southern Upland Way. Open Apr.-Sept. Dorms £12.50, under 18 £9.50. Cash only. ●

Minnigaff, Minigaff village (☎01671 402 211), across the bridge, ½ mi. from Newton Stewart. Accessible by bus from Dumfries, Stranraer, and Kirkcudbright. Popular with hikers and anglers, with an ideal location and knowledgeable staff. 36 beds. Open Apr.-Sept. Dorms £12.50, under 18 £9.50. MC/V. ●

HIKING AND OUTDOORS

The best of Dumfries and Galloway lies outdoors, and with some 1300 mi. of marked trails, there is something for everyone. **Merrick** (2765 ft.) in the **Galloway Hills** and **White Coomb** (2696 ft.) in the **Moffat Hills** provide a challenge for seasoned hikers, along with the region's main draw—the **Southern Upland Way.** Beginning in Portpatrick on the coast of the Irish Sea and snaking 212 mi. across Scotland, this tough long-distance route cuts through Dumfries and Galloway, passing near the region's two SYHA hostels. The official *Southern Upland Way* guide (£16) breaks the route into 15 sections and includes a complete Ordnance Survey map (1:50,000) of its course. In the west, the **Galloway Forest Park** is Britain's largest at over 300 sq. mi., although its excellent walking, cycling, and horseback riding trails can be difficult to reach without a car. The park has three visitor centers: **Clatteringshaws** (☎01644 420 285), 6 mi. west of New Galloway; **Glen Trool** (☎01671 402 420), 12 mi. north of Newton Stewart; and **Kirroughtree** (☎01671 402 165), 3 mi. east of Newton Stewart. (All open daily Apr.-June 10:30am-5pm; July-Aug. 10am-5:30pm; Oct. 10:30am-4:30pm.) Guides from the *Walks In and Around* series sell for £1 and detail day outings and afternoon walks, or pick up the free *Twelve Walks in Dumfries and Galloway.* Along the coasts and inland, the region is popular with serious birdwatchers, particularly around the **Mull of Galloway,** Scotland's southernmost coast—its sea cliffs are home to thousands of marine birds. **Mountain bikers** will be in heaven in six award-winning trail parks, part of the 7stanes project. See www.7stanes.gov.uk for further details, including **bike rental** near the trails. Touring **cyclists** will find *Cycling in Dumfries and Galloway* (free at TICs) useful. The #7 and 74 **National Cycle Routes** cross Dumfries and Galloway. The **KM Cycle Trail** runs from Drumlanrig down to Dumfries.

DUMFRIES ☎01387

Dumfries (DUM-freez; pop. 37,000) boasts little but the tales of two Roberts. Robert the Bruce proclaimed himself King of Scotland after stabbing Red Comyn at Greyfriars in 1306. A few centuries later, Robert Burns immortalized the town's local women in verse—hopefully he included the mothers of his 13 mostly illegitimate children. The beloved writer made Dumfries his home from 1791 until his death in 1796, and the town devotes many (many) a site to him.

TRANSPORTATION AND PRACTICAL INFORMATION. The **train station** is on Station Rd. (☎255 115. Open M-Sa 6:35am-7:30pm, Su 10:30am-7:55pm.) Trains (☎08457 484 950) depart to: Carlisle (40min., every hr., £7.60); Glasgow Central (1¾hr.; M-Sa 8 per day, Su 2 per day; £11.40); London Euston (change in Carlisle; 5¼hr., 10 per day, £115); Stranraer via Ayr (3hr., 3 per day, £27.40). Buses arrive and depart along Whitesands, and #974 runs to Glasgow (2hr.; M-Sa 3 per day, Su 2 per day; £6.50). Bus #100 travels to Edinburgh (2¾hr.; M-Sa 3 per day, Su 2 per day; £6.50) via Penicuik (2¼hr.), while #500/X75 connects Dumfries to Carlisle (1hr., 2 per day, £2.40) and Stranraer (2¼hr., 8 per day, £5).

The **Tourist Information Centre,** 64 Whitesands Rd., books beds for £3 plus a 10% deposit and sells National Express tickets. (☎253 862. Open July-Aug. M-Sa 9am-6pm, Su 11am-4:30pm; Easter-June M-Sa 9:30am-5pm, Su and bank holidays noon-4:30pm; Sept. M-Sa 9am-5:30pm, Su 11am-4:30pm; Oct. M-Sa 9:30am-5pm, Su 11am-4pm; Nov. M-Sa 9am-5pm; Dec.-Easter M-F 9:30am-5pm, Sa 9:30am-4pm.) Other services include: **banks** along High St.; free **Internet** access at Ewart **Library,** Catherine St. (☎253 820; open M-W and F 9:15am-7:30pm, Th and Sa 9:15am-5pm); **police** on Loreburn St. (☎250 484); and the **post office,** 73 Whitesands (☎269 058; open M 8am-5:30pm, Tu 9:30am-5.30pm, W-Sa 9am-5:30pm). **Post Code:** DG1 1AA.

⌐▢ ACCOMMODATIONS AND FOOD. A number of **B&Bs** line Lover's Walk, steps from the train station, including welcoming **Torbay Lodge ❸,** 31 Lover's Walk. (☎253 922; www.torbaylodge.co.uk. From £25 per person. MC/V.) Find **groceries** at **Morrisons** on Brooms Rd. (☎266 952. Open M-W 8:30am-8pm, Th-F 8:30am-10pm, Sa 8am-8pm, Su 9am-8pm.) The tasty Italian dishes at **Fabrizio's ❷,** 95 Queensberry, are a highlight in an otherwise dull dining scene. (☎255 752. Open daily 5:30pm-11pm. MC/V.) Top off a Burns-filled day with a pint at **The Globe Inn,** 56 High St., one of the poet's favorite haunts. (☎252 335; www.globeinndumfries.co.uk. Open M-W 10am-11pm, Th 10am-midnight, F-Sa 10am-1am, Su 11:30am-midnight. Food served M-Th and Su 10am-3pm, F-Sa 10am-3pm and 7-9pm.)

◙ SIGHTS. Robert Burns fans, rejoice! Every sight in town pays homage to Dumfries's favorite son. Pick up a free copy of *Dumfries: A Burns Trail* at the TIC for an easy-to-follow Burns walking tour. Across the river, the **Robert Burns Centre,** Mill Rd., attempts to explain the phenomena that surround Scotland's national poet. Next door is a theater that shows an audio-visual presentation on Burns's life. (☎264 808. Open Apr.-Sept. M-Sa 10am-8pm, Su 2-5pm; Oct.-Mar. Tu-Sa 10am-1pm and 2-5pm. Museum free; audio-visual presentation £1.50, concessions 75p.) Visit **Burns House,** Burns St., where Burns scratched his autograph into the upstairs study windows. Memorabilia on display includes a snuff box made with wood from the bed where the poet died at the young age of 37. (☎255 297. Open Apr.-Sept. M-Sa 10am-5pm, Su 2-5pm; Oct.-Mar. Tu-Sa 10am-1pm and 2-5pm. Free.) Complete your pilgrimage at the **Burns Mausoleum** in St. Michael's Kirkyard, where a marble Burns leans on a plow and gazes at the attractive muse hovering overhead. (Guided tours available through the Robert Burns House; ask for times.) On the top floor of the **Dumfries Museum,** Rotchell Rd., check out the town through the lens of Britain's oldest camera obscura. (☎253 374; www.dumgal.gov.uk. Open Apr.-Sept. M-Sa 10am-5pm, Su 2-5pm; Oct.-Mar. Tu-Sa 10am-1pm and 2-5pm. Museum free. Camera obscura £2, concessions £1.) To escape the Burns-fest, try a relaxing walk through **The Crichton,** a parkland 1 mi. south of Dumfries town center, which has huge rock gardens and an arboretum. (Follow posted signs from the town center. Grounds accessible 24hr. Free.)

▶ DAYTRIPS FROM DUMFRIES

▨ CAERLAVEROCK CASTLE. Eight miles southeast of Dumfries, on the B725 just beyond Glencaple, Caerlaverock Castle (car-LAV-rick) is one of Scotland's finest medieval ruins. Although no one is sure whether this strategic marvel was built for Scottish defense or English offense, it was seized by England's Edward I in 1300 and passed around like a hot kipper thereafter. Beyond the castle is a path that runs down to the shore of the Solway Firth (10min.), past the ruins of an earlier castle. The mountains of the Lake District rise up in the distance beyond the firth, which at low tide is nothing but sand for 20 mi. *(Stagecoach Western Bus #371 runs to* *the castle from the Loreburn Shopping Centre, off Irish St. in Dumfries (20min.; M-Sa 12 per day, Su 2 per day; round-trip £3). ☎770 244. Open daily Apr.-Sept. 9:30am-6:30pm; Oct.-Mar. 9:30am-4:30pm. Last admission 30min. before close. £4.50, concessions £3.50, children £2.)*

■ **DRUMLANRIG CASTLE.** Eighteen miles north of Dumfries off the A76, Drumlanrig Castle is the home of the Duke of Buccleuch. Surrounded by formal gardens and a large country park, the castle's noted art collection includes works by Rembrandt and Da Vinci. Take a time out in the classy cafe, or browse the many shops and galleries in the converted stableyard. *(☎01848 331 555; www.buccleuch.com. Castle open by guided tour May-Aug. daily 11am-4pm. Grounds open Easter-Sept. daily 11am-5pm. £7, concessions £6, children £4; grounds only £4/3.50/3.)*

SWEETHEART ABBEY. This abbey, 8 mi. south of Dumfries along the A710, was founded in the late 13th century by Lady Devorguilla Balliol in memory of her husband, John. She was later buried here with John's embalmed heart clutched to her breast. The line between romantic and creepy is very thin. Now a well-preserved ruin, the abbey still has high arches and a large central spire that stand in testament to their love. *(Take MacEwan's bus #372 to New Abbey from Dumfries. 20min.; M-Sa 1-2 every 2hr., Su 2 per day. ☎850 397. Open Apr.-Sept. daily 9:30am-6:30pm; Oct.-Mar. M-W and Sa-Su 9:30am-4:30pm. £2.50, concessions 90p.)*

RUTHWELL CHURCH. Nine miles from Dumfries, the church holds the 7th-century **Ruthwell Cross,** whose stone bears carvings of vine, scrolls, and beasts. The Anglo-Saxon poem (and Scotland's oldest surviving fragment of written English) "The Dream of the Rood" crowds its margins. *(Take Stagecoach bus #79 to Annan via Clarencefield (30min.; M-Sa every hr., Su every 2hr.) and get off at Ruthwell. ☎870 249. Free.)*

CASTLE DOUGLAS ☎01556

Between Dumfries and Kirkcudbright, Castle Douglas resembles most other towns in Scotland's southwest, with its grey stone storefronts and windows lined with flowering pots. One mile west, however, the 60-acre **Threave Garden** deserves a visit, with native and exotic blooms pruned by students of the nearby School of Gardening. Buses #501 and 502 (10min., every hr.) between Kirkcudbright and Castle Douglas pass the garden turnoff; ask the driver to stop, then walk 15min. (☎502 575. Garden open daily 9:30am-sunset. Walled garden and greenhouses open daily 9:30am-5pm. £6, concessions £5.) The **Threave Estate Walk** (2½-7½ mi.) meanders through the countryside. Leaving from the garden car park, it leads hikers to good bird-watching spots as well as the scenic ruins of 14th-century **Threave Castle.** A stronghold of the Earls of Douglas and built by Archibald the Grim, this massive tower-castle sits on an island in the River Dee. The Kirkcudbright bus can drop you off at the roundabout on the A75. From there, follow the signs for 1½ mi. along a one-lane road and then a marked footpath. Once at the river, ring the ship's bell and a boatman will appear to ferry you across to the castle. (Open Apr.-Sept. daily 9:30am-6:30pm; last boat 5:30pm. £3.50, concessions £2.50, children £1.50.)

The best-priced accommodation in town is at **The Craig ❸,** 44 Abercromby Rd., with spacious rooms near the golf course. (☎504 840. No smoking. Singles £23-30; doubles and twins £46-54. Cash only.) Castle Douglas proclaims itself Galloway's "Food Town" thanks to the number of cafes and delis that line **King Street.** Beneath an art gallery, ■ **Designs ❷** serves sandwiches on homebaked ciabatta and has great specials from noon-3pm. (☎504 552. Open 9:30am-5pm. MC/V.) For **groceries,** the Co-op Superstore is on Cotton St. (Open M-Sa 8am-10pm, Su 9am-6pm.) **Buses** #501 and 502 zip from **Dumfries** to **Kirkcudbright** via Castle Douglas (from Dumfries 40min., from Kirkcudbright 20min.; 2 per hr.; £3.50). **Banks** with **ATMs** can be found on King St. For local lodgings, ask at the **Tourist Information Centre.** (☎502 611. £3 fee. Open July-Aug. M-Sa 9:30am-6pm, Su 10am-4pm; Apr.-June M-Sa 10am-5pm, Su 11am-4pm; Sept. M-Sa 10am-4pm, Su 11am-4pm; Oct. M-Sa 10am-4pm.) The **post office** is at 100 King St. (☎502 577. Open M-F 9am-5:30pm, Sa 9am-4:30pm.)

KIRKCUDBRIGHT   ☎01557

Situated at the mouth of the River Dee, Kirkcudbright (ker-COO-bree) is a quiet town with colorful homes and, unlike nearby towns, sights that have nothing to do with Robert Burns. In the 1880s, the town attracted a group of artists known as the Glasgow Boys, and Kirkcudbright still fancies itself an artists' colony.

⊟⊠ TRANSPORTATION AND PRACTICAL INFORMATION. Buses #501 and 502 travel to Dumfries via Castle Douglas (every hr., £3.50), and bus #431 travels to Gatehouse of Fleet (20min.; M-Sa 12 per day, Su 6 per day). The **Tourist Information Centre,** Harbour Sq., books rooms for £3. (☎330 494. Open July-Aug. M-Sa 9:30am-6pm, Su 10am-5pm; Feb.-June and Sept.-Nov. M-Sa 10am-5pm, Su 11am-4pm.) Other services include: Shirley's **launderette,** 20 St. Cuthbert St. (☎332 047; laundry £5; open M-F 9am-4pm, Sa 9am-1pm); free **Internet** access at the **library,** High St. (☎331 240; open M 2-7:30pm, Tu and F 10am-7:30pm, W noon-7:30pm, Th and Sa 10am-5pm); and the **post office,** 5 St. Cuthbert's Pl. (☎330 578; open M-F 9am-5:30pm, Sa 9am-12:30pm). **Post Code:** DG6 4DH.

⊓⊡ ACCOMMODATIONS AND FOOD. 1 Gordon Place ❸, High St., is a cozy but cheap option right in the middle of the "action" on historic High St. (☎330 472. Singles from £25. Cash only.) Family-run **Castle Restaurant ❸,** 5 Castle St., has a variety of options including fish, vegetarian fare, and plates piled high with meat. (☎330 569; www.thecastlerestaurant.net. Open daily 11:30am-2:30pm and 6:30-9pm. MC/V.) Get **groceries** at Somerfield, 52 St. Cuthbert St., at Millburn St. (☎330 516. Open M-Sa 8:30am-6pm, Su 10am-5pm.)

◪ SIGHTS. Surprisingly, **▨ Broughton House and Garden,** 12 High St., the former home of E.A. Hornel, doesn't hold many of the artist's greatest works. But the house itself, with a studio, gallery, and library, shows the results of Hornel's years of collecting and eye for design. (☎330 437. House and garden open July-Aug. daily noon-5pm; Apr.-June and Sept. M and Th-Su noon-5pm. Garden also open Feb.-March daily 11am-4pm. £8, concessions £5, families £20.) The **Tollbooth Art Centre,** High St., explains the artist migration to Kircudbright in the 1880s and displays the work of local artists. (☎331 556. Open July-Aug. M-Sa 10am-5pm, Su 2-5pm; May-June and Sept. M-Sa 11am-5pm, Su 2-5pm; Oct. M-Sa 11am-4pm, Su 2-5pm; Nov.-Dec. M-Sa 11am-4pm. Free.) **MacLellan's Castle,** a 16th-century tower house, dominates the town on Castle St. Sneak into the "Laird's Lug," a secret chamber behind a fireplace from which the lord could eavesdrop on conversations in the Great Hall. (☎331 856. Open Apr.-Sept. daily 9:30am-1pm and 2-6:30pm. £3.20, concessions £2.50, children £1.50.) One fine **walk** in the area departs from the TIC and runs along the coastal headland to **Torrs Point** (8½ mi. round-trip). Pick up a guide (20p) from the TIC before you head out.

STRANRAER AND THE RHINS OF GALLOWAY   ☎01776

Scottish Gaelic for "the fat nose," an Sron Reamhar, or Stranraer (stran-RAHR), and the hammerhead peninsula known as "the Rhins" hang off the southwestern tip of Scotland. It's a short ride over to Northern Ireland, so Stranraer plays host to many tourists taking daytrips to Belfast or staying the night before catching the morning ferry. Locals have a unique accent, and as most early residents came from Ireland, they are often referred to as the Galloway Irish.

SOUTHERN SCOTLAND

☎☑ TRANSPORTATION AND PRACTICAL INFORMATION. The **train station**, by the ferry pier, is open daily 9:30am-3pm and 4-6:30pm. **Trains** (☎08457 484 950) depart to Ayr (1½hr.; M-Sa 7 per day, Su 2 per day; £11.70) and Glasgow (2½hr.; M-Sa 4-7 per day, Su 3 per day; £17). **Buses** leave from Port Rodie in Stranraer to Ayr (#358; 1½hr., 2 per day, £4.50) and Dumfries (#500/X75; 2hr.; M-Sa 10 per day, Su 3 per day; £4.50). National Express (☎08705 808 080) runs to Carlisle (2½hr., £15), London (10hr., 1 per day, £39), and Manchester (6hr., 2 per day, £28). Buses #358, 367, and 411 serve Portpatrick from Stranraer (25min.; M-Sa 16 per day, Su 3 per day; £2.35). **Ferries** travel from Northern Ireland across the North Channel. Stena Line (☎08705 707 070; www.stenaline.co.uk) sails between Belfast and Stranraer (1¾hr.-3¼hr.; 5-7 per day; £14-24, concessions £10-19, children £7-12). Five miles up the coast at Cairnyan, P&O Ferries (☎08702 424 777; www.poirishsea.com) provide access to Larne (1-1¾hr.; 5-8 per day; £17-26, concessions £13-22). Discounts are available when booking sea passage with a connecting bus or train.

The **Tourist Information Centre**, 28 Harbour St., sells bus and ferry tickets and books rooms for £3 plus a 10% deposit. (☎702 595. Open July-Aug. M-Sa 9:30am-5pm, Su noon-4pm; Sept.-June M-Sa 10am-4pm.) Other services in town include: **banks** with **ATMs** throughout the town; Boots **pharmacy**, across from the castle (☎707 224; open M-Sa 9:30am-5pm); free **Internet** access at the Stranraer **Library**, 2-10 N. Strand St. (☎707 400; open M-F 9:15am-7:30pm, Sa 9:15am-1pm and 2-5pm); and the **post office,** in Tesco on Charlotte St. (☎702 587; open M-F 7am-6pm, Sa 7am-5pm), reachable by **bus** #407 (20min.; M-Sa 10 per day, Su 3 per day). **Post Code:** DG9 7EF.

☐ ACCOMMODATIONS. There are a number of hotels and B&Bs in Stranraer and Portpatrick, with a scattering of other options across the Rhins. Feel like a part of the family at the ◪**Balyett B&B ❸,** Cairnyarn Rd., possibly the most welcoming B&B in Scotland. The seaside farm has ensuite rooms and runs a small 5-bed **hostel ❶** in a caravan. Call ahead and the owner will pick you up from the ferry, bus, or train station. (☎703 395. Breakfast included. B&B £25 per person; hostel £15 per person. MC/V.) **Lakeview Guest House ❸,** 19 Agnew Crescent, near the town center, has seafront accommodations run by a friendly young couple. (☎703 472; www.lakeviewguesthouse.co.uk. £25 per person. MC/V.) Catch a plate of fresh fish at one of the waterfront fish shops on Charlotte St., or pick up **groceries** at Tesco, on Charlotte St. near the ferry terminal. (Open M-Sa 7am-8pm, Su 10am-6pm.)

◪ SIGHTS. Stranraer provides ferry access to Northern Ireland—and that's about it. Four miles east of Stranraer on the A75, the ◪ **Castle Kennedy Gardens** include 75 acres of lovely landscaping between a pair of lochs and castles. Tree-lined walks offer great picnic spots. From Stranraer, buses (#430, 416, and 500) pass the castles; ask the driver to let you off and walk 1mi. from the main road. (☎702 024. Open Apr.-Sept. daily 10am-5pm. £4, concessions £3, children £1.) Back in town, the tiny **Castle of St. John,** George St., is a 1510 edifice with great views. Its rooftop was once the exercise yard of the town prison. (☎705 088. Open from Easter to mid-Sept. M-Sa 10am-1pm and 2-5pm. Free.)

If you've come this far west, it's worth traveling to the small seaside town of **Portpatrick,** where pastel houses look across to Northern Ireland. The coast-to-coast Southern Upland Way (p. 548) begins here, and there's also a coastal path leading back to Stranraer. Another path runs along the cliffs to the ruins of ◪**Dunskey Castle,** an empty shell sitting high above the pounding surf. At the **Mull of Galloway,** the southernmost point in Scotland, a lighthouse and thousands of sea birds teeter atop cliffs. Live cameras in the visitor center allow for non-disruptive observation. On a clear day, Northern Ireland and the Isle of Man are visible.

AYRSHIRE

AYR
☎01292

The pleasant seaside town of Ayr (AIR; pop. 50,000) is little more than a base for exploring surrounding Ayrshire. Racing fans head to Scotland's top horse track, which hosts the **Scottish Grand National** in April and the **Ayr Gold Cup** in September. (☎264 179. Call for race dates. Tickets £10-25.) The world's only remaining ocean paddle steamer, the **Waverley,** departs from the south side of Ayr's harbor during July and August, touring many of the nearby islands, including the Isle of Arran. (☎0845 130 4647; www.waverleyexcursions.co.uk. Cruises July-Aug. M-W. £16-27.)

Among the many **B&Bs** near the beach, **Eglinton Guest House ❸,** 23 Eglinton Terr., certainly isn't the flashiest, but it is the cheapest. (☎264 623. £22 per person. Cash only.) **Craggallan Guest House ❹,** 8 Queens Terr., has a pool table and access to the Ayrshire golf courses. (☎264 998; www.craggallan.com. Singles from £30; doubles or twins from £56; triples £60-65. AmEx/MC/V.) Across from the train station on Castlehill Rd., Morrison's **supermarket** has everything you need. (☎283 906. Open M-W 8:30am-8pm, Th-F 8:30am-9pm, Sa 8am-8pm, Su 9am-5pm.) Fresh seafood practically swims onto your plate at **Waterside Restaurant ❸,** South Harbour St., near the new bridge. (☎280 212. Entrees £8-15. 2 courses £12.50 until 6:45pm. Open M-Th and Su noon-2:45pm and 5-9:45pm, F-Sa noon-2:45pm and 5-10:30pm.)

Ayr's **train station** is a 10min. walk from the town center at the crossroads of Station Rd., Holmston Rd., and Castle Hill Rd. (Open M-Sa 5:30am-11:10pm, Su 8:30am-11:10pm.) Trains (☎08457 484 950) run to Glasgow (1hr., 2 per hr., £6.20) and Stranraer (1½hr.; M-Sa 4 per day, Su 3 per day; £11.70). The **bus station** is on Fullerton St. off Sandgate. It sends Stagecoach Western (☎613 500) buses to Glasgow (1hr., every 30min., £3.15) and Stranraer (1¼hr.; M-Sa every 2hr., Su 4 per day; £6.20). The **Tourist Information Centre** is at 22 Sandgate. (☎0845 225 512. Open July-Aug. M-Sa 9am-6pm, Su 10am-5pm; Sept. M-Sa 9am-5pm, Su 11am-4pm; Oct.-June M-Sa 9am-5pm. Other services include: **banks** on High St.; free **Internet** access at the Carnegie **Library,** 12 Main St. (☎286 385; open M-F 10am-7:30pm, Sa 10am-5pm); **bike rental** at AMG Cycles, 55 Dalblair Rd. (☎287 580; £12.50 per day, £35 per week; open M-Sa 9:30am-5:15pm); and the **post office,** 65 Sandgate, with a **bureau de change** (☎0845 601 122; open M-Sa 9am-5:30pm). **Post Code:** KA7 1AA.

⚡ DAYTRIP FROM AYR

CULZEAN CASTLE AND COUNTRY PARK. Twelve miles south of Ayr along the A719, romantic Culzean (cul-LANE) Castle commands panoramic views of the Ayrshire coast from its clifftop setting. According to legend, one of the cliff's caves holds the Phantom Piper, who plays to his lost flock when the moon is full. Much of the castle was designed by renowned architect Robert Adam. The people of Scotland gave the building's top floor to Dwight Eisenhower for use during his stays in the country—with a presidential budget you can rent his digs for the night (£375, other castle accommodations from £225; MC/V). Popular during the summer, the castle is surrounded by a 560-acre country park that includes one of the nation's finest walled gardens, a swan pond, and miles of wooded walkways. At the entrance to the castle and country park, close to the bus stop, the **Glenside Culzean Caravan and Camping Park ❷** provides a great place to pitch your tent, with fresh sea air and views of the Isle of Arran. (☎01655 760 627. Showers and laundry. Call ahead if arriving late. Open from mid-Mar. to Oct. 2 non-members with car

£14.70-19.20. MC/V.) *(From Ayr take bus #60. 30min., 2 per hr. to the Culzean stop. The castle is signposted about 1 mi. from the main road. ☎ 08701 181 945; www.culzeancastle.net. Castle open Apr.-Oct. daily 10:30am-5pm; last admission 4pm. Park open year-round 9:30am-sunset. £12, concessions £8, families £30. Park only £8/5/20.)*

ISLE OF ARRAN ☎ 01770

The glorious Isle of Arran (AH-ren; pop. 4750) justifiably bills itself as "Scotland in Miniature." Gentle lowland hills, majestic highland peaks, and dense forests crowd into an island less than 20 mi. long. The crags of Goatfell and the Caisteal range dominate the north. Near the western coast, prehistoric stone circles rise out of boggy grass. Linked by reliable transportation, the eastern coastline winds south from Brodick Castle past Holy Island into meadows and white beaches.

◤ TRANSPORTATION

Transportation between the mainland and Arran is available from CalMac **ferry** (☎ 08705 650 000), which runs crossings between Brodick and Ardrossan (55min.; M-Sa 5-6 per day, Su 4 per day; £5.20, bikes £1.20). There's also a summer ferry service between Lochranza and Claonaig on the Kintyre Peninsula (30min.; from mid-Apr. to mid-Oct. 8-9 per day; £4.65, bikes £1.20). The island has a very reliable **local bus** service operated by Stagecoach Western (☎ 302 000; office at Brodick pier). A connection to and from every part of the island meets each Ardrossan-Brodick ferry, and frequent buses also meet the Lochranza ferry (fares up to £2.35). The *Arran Area Transport Guide*, distributed free at the TIC and on the ferry, contains transportation information and all bus schedules for the island. Additional services are run by the Royal Mail **postbus** (☎ 302 507). Available on board, the Rural Rover Ticket grants a full day of travel on Stagecoach and postbus services (£4.20, children £2). From April to October, Stagecoach offers half- and full-day **island tours** departing from Brodick pier (full-day £8, ½-day £5). **Car rental** is available at the Brodick pier (☎ 302 121; from £25).

◪ ▮ ORIENTATION AND PRACTICAL INFORMATION

The A841 completes a 56 mi. circuit around the Isle of Arran. Ferries from Ardrossan arrive at **Brodick**, on the eastern shore; those from Claonaig arrive at **Lochranza**, in the north. The villages of **Lamlash** and **Whiting Bay** line the picturesque southeastern coast. **Blackwaterfoot** is the largest town on the sparsely populated western shore. Home to green hills, deep valleys, and pine forests, the interior of the island is practically uninhabited. Brodick has the widest range of services, including Arran's only **Tourist Information Centre**, across from the ferry pier. It books B&Bs for £3 plus a 10% deposit. (☎ 303 774. Open June-Sept. M-Sa 9am-7:30pm, Su 10am-5pm; Oct.-May M-Th 9am-5pm, F 9am-7.30pm, Sa 10am-5pm.) From May to September, a tourist information desk on the Ardrossan-Brodick ferry answers questions. The island's **police** station (☎ 302 574) is located on Shore Rd. in Lamlash.

▨ ▧ HIKING AND OUTDOORS

Despite Arran's proximity to Glasgow, much of its wilderness in the north and southwest remains untouched. Ordnance Survey Landranger #69 (£7) and Explorer #361 (£8) maps cover the island in extraordinary detail. Among the available literature, the Forestry Commission produces the small, popular *A Guide to the Forest Walks of The Isle of Arran* (£1) and the more comprehensive *Walking*

> **DON'T GET SHOT.** Deer-hunting season on Arran runs from August to February (peak Aug.-Sept.), when hunting parties trek through estates in the northern part of the island. To avoid unfortunate run-ins with hunter or hunted, pick up the free leaflet from the TIC (available starting in late July) for a list of areas to avoid each day, or call **Hillphones** (☎01770 302 363).

on The Isle of Arran (£11), available at bookstores. The TIC has free leaflets for all area walks. Highlights include the path up ✦**Goatfell,** Arran's highest peak (2866 ft.). Beginning on the road between Brodick and Brodick Castle, this hike passes forests, heather, and mountain streams before the final rocky ascent into the clouds (7 mi. round-trip). The route takes around 5hr. and only becomes challenging in the last 300 ft. The view from the cold, windy peak (on a clear day, all the way to Ireland) is worth the final scramble. **Glen Rosa** offers some great scenery without the mountain climb. The terrain remains mostly flat as the walk follows the glen into the heart of Arran's peaks. From Brodick, head about a mile north, turn left onto "The String" road toward Blackwaterfoot, then take the first right. Another fine walk is the 8 mi. **Cock of Arran** route, which departs from Lochranza and circles the northern tip of the island, passing the ruins of **Lochranza Castle** and running along miles of beach, on which basking sharks are common. Well-marked shorter walks depart from Whiting Bay and north of Blackwaterfoot.

   Biking on the hilly island is a rewarding challenge. Pedaling all or part of the 57 mi. circuit ringing the island affords splendid views, and traffic is light in most stretches, except at the height of summer. Adrenaline junkies will want to try one of the off-road routes that leave from Brodick and Whiting Bay, listed in the free *Mountain Biking and Cycling* brochure available in bike shops and at the TIC. Located 300 yd. from Brodick pier along Shore Rd., Arran Adventure has expedition leaders who tackle everything from rock climbing to gorge walking and offer mountain **bike rental.** (☎302 244; www.arranadventure.com. Bikes £15 per day, £45 per week; includes safety equipment. Open Apr.-Sept. daily 9am-5:30pm.) For bike rental elsewhere on Arran, try Blackwaterfoot Garage, in Blackwaterfoot. (☎860 277. £8 per day, £20 per week. Open M-F and Su 8:30am-5:30pm, Sa 9am-5pm.)

BRODICK   ☎01770

North of town, the **Brodick Castle and Country Park** overlooks the harbor, with a backdrop of rugged mountains and a small sweep of beach. Built on the site of an old Viking fort, the castle resembles a Victorian manor and contains a collection of paintings and deer-hunting trophies. Giant rhododendrons bloom in the garden. If you can't manage a visit, look on the back of a Scottish £20 note. (30min. walk from Brodick ferry, or take bus #324 or 327. ☎302 202. Castle open daily Easter-Sept. 11am-4:30pm; Oct. 11am-3:30pm. Garden open daily 9:30am-sunset. Castle and gardens £10, concessions £7, families £25. Gardens only £5/4/14.)

   As the hub of island transportation, Brodick has many options if you're looking to spend the night. Upscale and close to the ferry is ✦**Dunvegan House ❸,** Shore Rd., where you can enjoy beach views from the elegant dining room. (☎302 811; www.dunveganhouse.co.uk. No smoking. Dinner £18. No singles. £30 per person. Cash only.) Another option is sandstone **Carrick Lodge ❸,** 5min. uphill from the ferry pier. (☎302 550. £29 per person. MC/V.) **Glen Rosa Farm ❶,** just over 2 mi. north of Brodick pier, provides basic **camping** facilities and a lush valley. (☎302 380. Toilets and cold water. £3.50 per person. Cash only.) Brodick's Co-op, across from the ferry, is the only **supermarket** on the island. (☎302 515. Open M-Sa 8am-10pm, Su 9am-7pm.) A number of bars and inexpensive restaurants line Shore Rd.

Brodick's **Shore Road** has almost all services on the island, including the only **banks** and **ATMs.** Free **Internet** access can be found at the Arran **Library,** Shore Rd. (Open Tu 10am-5pm, Th and F 10am-7:30pm, Sa 10am-1pm.) The **post office** is set back from Shore Rd. on Mayish Rd. (☎303 578. Open June-Aug. M-F 9am-5:30pm, Sa 9am-12:45pm; Sept.-May M-F 9am-5pm, Sa 9am-12:45pm.) **Post Code:** KA27 8AA.

WHITING BAY AND LAMLASH

The popular sailing center of **Lamlash Bay** is dominated by the sacred site of **Holy Island.** Home to St. Molaise in the 6th century, the island is cared for today by a group of Tibetan Buddhist monks, whose rock carvings and gardens share the hills with herds of wild ponies. The island also has a number of walking paths, including one up **Mulloch Mor** (1030 ft.), the highest point on the island, with splendid views of Arran's mountains and the bright blue sea below. The southern end of the island is closed off to the public as a cloistered private space for 12 women completing a three-year, three-month Tibetan Buddhist retreat. Holy Island requests that you respect their spiritual study by avoiding this area; pick up the free Holy Island leaflet that maps out acceptable walking routes from the TIC. A regular **ferry** (☎600 349) departs Lamlash for Holy Island (15min.; May-Sept. 8 per day, depending on tides; round-trip £9), although arrangements must be made in winter. Farther south, **Whiting Bay** is a sleepy seaside village stretched along the A841. From a trailhead toward the southern end of town, two easy walks lead to the **Glenashdale Falls** (1 mi.) and the megalithic stone structures at **Giant's Graves.**

In Lamlash, a small co-op sells **groceries** along the A841 (open M-Sa 8am-10pm, Su 10am-6pm). Just past where the A841 veers from the coast toward Brodick, the **Shore B&B ❸,** Shore Rd., has Scandinavian-style lodgings with fantastic views of Holy Island. (☎600 764. Doubles £60. MC/V.) Several hotels also serve food. 🅂**The Coffee Pot ❶,** toward the southern end of Whiting Bay on the coastal road, is a picturesque spot for afternoon tea (£1-2) or a bowl of scrumptious homemade soup. (☎700 382. Open daily 10am-5pm. Food served until 4pm. Cash only.)

LOCHRANZA

Northern Arran is a land of green hills, bare peaks, and rocky coast. Sheep roam the streets and the remains of a 13th-century **castle** in peaceful Lochranza. (Always open. Free.) The whisky produced in the **Isle of Arran Distillery,** on the road to Brodick, is less peaty than other malts and is thus more palatable to the uninitiated. (☎830 264; www.arranwhisky.com. Open Mar.-Oct. daily 10am-6pm; Nov.-Feb. reduced hours; call for details. Tours start 30min. past the hr., 10:30am-4:30pm, and include a wee dram. £3.50, concessions £2.50, under 12 free.) One mile down the coast, the fishing village of **Catacol Bay** harbors the **Twelve Apostles,** a dozen connected white houses that differ only in the shapes of their windows. A number of the northern peaks, including **Caisteal Abhail** (2817 ft.), are within a day's walk.

Toward the southern end on the main road to Brodick, the quiet 🅂**SYHA Lochranza ❶** has 64 beds and a fence to keep the sheep out. For 10p, you can get a leaflet of hiking routes that leave from the hostel. (☎08700 041 140. Laundry and Internet access. Lockout 10:30am-5pm. Curfew 11:30pm. Open Mar.-Oct. Dorms £12.50-13.50, under 18 £9.50. MC/V.) Housed in a century-old former church across from the castle, the **Castlekirk B&B ❸** has high ceilings and a lounge with stained-glass windows. (☎830 202; www.castlekirkarran.co.uk. No smoking. Prices start at £22.50 per person. Cash only.) Campers can pitch at the **Lochranza Golf Course Caravan and Camping Site ❶,** also home to the only shop in the village. (☎830 273. Toilets, showers, and laundry. Open Apr.-Oct. £4 per person, from £2.60 per tent. Cash only.) The restaurant at the **Isle of Arran Distillery ❷** features a daily menu of local produce, from traditional cullen skink (£7) to sirloin steak flavored with

Arran Malt. (Open Mar.-Oct. daily 10am-6pm; Nov.-Feb. F-Su 10am-4pm. MC/V.) In the evening, the **Lochranza Hotel ❷**, along the ferry pier, serves typical pub grub. (☎830 223. Open daily 11am-9pm. Cash only.) For a cheap, ready-to-go alternative, stop by **The Sandwich Station ❶**, across from the pier and to the right. Call in advance for picnic lunches. (☎07917 671913. Open M-Tu and Th-Su 8am-5pm. Cash only.) There are **no banks or ATMs** in Lochranza. **Post Code:** KA27 8HJ.

WESTERN ARRAN

The western shore of Arran harbors a handful of tiny settlements separated by miles of coastline. The **Machrie Moor Stone Circle,** a mysterious Bronze Age arrangement of standing stones and boulders, lies at the end of an easy 3 mi. walk. According to legend, the standing stone with the hole in it was where the mythical giant Fingal tethered his giant dog, Bran. Follow the farm path 1 mi. south of Machrie village along the A841. Another mile south, the trail leading to the **King's Cave** (3 mi.) begins in a Forestry Commission car park. Passing along coastal cliffs, the walk terminates at the caves where Robert the Bruce learned a lesson in perserverance from a spider, who inspired him to return to the mainland and claim the throne. It is another 2½ mi. south to **Blackwaterfoot,** where you can reconnect with island transportation and find a few places to eat and sleep.

GLASGOW   ☎0141

Glasgow (pop. 560,000), once a dreary industrial shipyard, has transformed into a destination city for the young and hip. Fueled by a large student population, the West End's chic pubs and restaurants complement the sweaty after-hours party scene in the city center. Glasgow University's classic Gothic architecture stands across the River Clyde from the futuristic multi-million dollar Science Centre, representing an ever-changing vision of Scotland's biggest city. In the summer months, Glasgow buzzes with festivals full of cutting-edge art, performances, and music (yes, bagpipes too).

✈ INTERCITY TRANSPORTATION

Glasgow lies along the River Clyde, 40 mi. west of Edinburgh. The M8 motorway links the two cities. Glasgow marks the northern end of the M74, which runs to England.

Flights: Glasgow is served by 2 international airports.

> **Glasgow International Airport (GLA;** ☎08700 400 0008; www.baa.co.uk/glasgow), 8 mi. west in Abbotsinch. Scotland's major airport, served by **KLM, British Airways,** and local airlines. Scottish Citylink (www.citylink.co.uk) bus #905 runs from the airport to downtown Buchanan Station. Hop on or off at any point along the route. (25min.; 5:40am-6pm every 10min., 6pm-midnight every 15-30min.; £3.50 single fare, £5.30 round-trip.)

> **Prestwick International Airport (PIK;** ☎08712 230 700; www.gpia.co.uk), 32 mi. southwest of the city center. **Ryanair** flies to England and other countries in Europe. Trains from PIK to Central Station (30min.; M-Sa 6am-11pm, Su 8am-11pm every 30min.; £5.20, with Ryanair printout £2.60). Express bus #X99 runs from the terminal to Buchanan St. (50min., every hr., £7).

Trains: Bus #88 connects Glasgow's 2 main stations, but it's only a 5-10min. walk between them. Book in advance online (www.nationalrail.co.uk) for discounts.

> **Central Station,** Gordon St. U: St. Enoch. Toilets 20p; shower with soap and towel £2. Open daily 5:30am-midnight. Ticket office open M-Sa 6am-9:30pm, Su 7:10am-11pm. Trains to: **Ardrossan** (1hr., 10-12 per day, £4.80); **Carlisle** (1½hr., every hr., £27); **Dumfries** (1¾hr.; M-Sa 7 per day, Su 2 per day; £10.30); **London King's Cross** (6hr., every hr., £90.60); **Manchester** (4hr., every hr., £40); **Stranraer Harbor** (2½hr.; M-Sa 8 per day, Su 3 per day; £16.30).

Queen Street Station, George Sq. (☎0845 748 4950). U: Buchanan St. Serves trains from the north and east. Toilets 20p. Lockers £3-5 per day. Open M-Sa 5:10am-11:55pm, Su 7:10am-11:55pm; travel center M-Sa 6:15am-9:45pm, Su 7am-10pm. Trains to: **Aberdeen** (2½hr.; M-Sa every hr., Su 7 per day; £34); **Edinburgh** (50min., 4 per hr., £8.20); **Fort William** (3¾hr., 2-4 per day, £19.50); **Inverness** (3¼hr.; M-Sa 7 per day, Su 4 per day; £34).

Buses: Buchanan Station, Killermont St. (☎331 3708), 2 blocks north of Queen St. Station. National Express and Scottish Citylink buses. Toilets 20p. Luggage storage £3-5. Open M-Sa 9am-5pm; ticket office daily 7am-9:30pm; lockers daily 6:30am-10:30pm. Scottish Citylink (☎08705 505 050) to: **Aberdeen** (4hr., every hr., £18); **Edinburgh** (1¼hr., every 15min., £4.20); **Perth** (1½hr., every hr., £7); **Inverness** (3½-4½hr., every hr., £18); **Oban** (3hr., 5 per day, £13.55). National Express (☎08705 808 080) travels to **London** (8½hr., 3 per day, £18).

✳ ORIENTATION

George Square is the center of town; the train and bus stations and TIC are all within three blocks. Sections of **Sauchiehall** (Sackie-HALL), **Argyle,** and **Buchanan Streets** are lined with stores and open only to pedestrians, forming an L-shaped outdoor shopping district in the center of the city. The vibrant, upscale **West End** revolves around **Byres Road** and **Glasgow University,** 1 mi. northwest of George Sq. The city extends south of the **River Clyde** toward Pollok Country Park and southeast toward the Science Centre.

DRIVING CULTURE. When driving in Glasgow, beware unmarked one-way streets. Often, one-way signs don't crop up until after you need them.

▐ LOCAL TRANSPORTATION

Travel Center: Strathclyde Passenger Transport (SPT) Authority, St. Enoch's Sq. (☎0870 608 2608; www.spt.co.uk), just 2 blocks from Central Station. U: St. Enoch. Offers travel advice, passes, and Underground maps. Open M-Th 8:30am-4:45pm, F 8:30am-4pm.

Public Transportation: Glasgow's transportation system includes suburban rail, private local bus services, and the small, circular **Underground (U)** subway line, a.k.a. the "Clockwork Orange" (☎0845 748 4950; www.spt.co.uk). U trains run every 4-8min. M-Sa 6:30am-11pm, Su 11am-5:30pm. Prices vary depending on final stop. New "Nightrider" bus service (every 20min., F-Su midnight-6:30am, £2) at marked bus stops near U stations. Several stations provide locker facilities, secure bike facilities, and park and ride service. **Underground Journey** and **Season Tickets** are a good deal; bring a photo ID to the office at St. Enoch station (10 trips £8, children £4; 20 trips £15/7.50; 7 days £9/4.50; 28 days £28/14). The **Discovery Ticket** (£1.90) for 1 day of unlimited travel is valid on the Underground M-Sa after 9:30am and Su all day. The **Traveline** service (☎08706 082 608; www.traveline.org.uk) helps travelers coordinate bus, train, and ferry trips in Scotland.

Taxis: Airport Taxi Services (☎848 4900) provides 24hr. service from Glasgow International Airport. Wheelchair-accessible services available. **Glasgow Taxis LTD** (☎429 2900). 1-3hr. tours.

Bike Rental: Plenty of bikers brave Glasgow's busy streets. There are bike paths on both sides of the River Clyde and through Glasgow Green and Kelvingrove Park. **Bike Booty Wheels,** 1103 Argyle St. (☎0777 278 4049), rents bikes from £5 per day.

Glasgow

BR = See Byres Road Map (p. 570)

ACCOMMODATIONS

Alamo Guest House,	1 A1
Blue Sky Hostel,	BR
Bunkum Backpackers,	BR
Euro Hostel Glasgow,	2 E4
Liberty House,	3 E3
McLays Guest House,	4 C2
Merchant Lodge,	5 F3
Smith's Hotel,	6 A2
SYHA Glasgow,	7 B3
University of Strathclyde,	BR
University of Glasgow,	BR

MUSEUMS

Gallery of Modern Art,	8 E3
Hunterian Museum and Art Gallery,	BR
Kelvingrove Art Gallery and Museum,	BR
McLellan Galleries,	9 D2
Provand's Lordship,	10 G3
St. Mungo Museum,	11 G3

FOOD

Big Slope Restaurant,	12 B2
Firebird,	13 A2
Grassroots Cafe,	14 C1
Kings Cafe,	15 C2
Mao,	16 F4
Stravaigin,	BR
Two Fat Ladies,	BR
Wee Curry Shop,	17 D2
Wee Curry Shop,	BR
Willow Tea Rooms,	18 D2

PUBS

The 13th Note,	19 F4
Babbity Bowster,	20 F3
Bar Soba,	21 E3
Brel,	BR
Mojama,	22 D2
Nice'n'Sleazy,	23 C2
Uisge Beatha,	BR

★ **CLUBS**

Bennets,	24 F3
The Buff Club,	25 D2
Cathouse,	26 E3
The Cube,	27 E3
The Garage,	28 C2
The Polo Lounge,	29 F3
Subclub,	30 E4

● **SIGHTS AND SERVICES**

Buchanan Galleries,	31 E2
Centre for Contemporary Arts,	32 D2
City Chambers,	33 F3
City Hall/Ticket Centre,	34 F3
Glasgow LGBT Centre,	35 F4
Glasgow School of Art,	36 D2
Glasgow Film Theatre,	37 D2
Market Square,	38 F3
Princes Sq. Shopping Centre,	39 E3
Royal Concert Hall,	40 E2
St. Enoch Shopping Ctr.	41 E3
Somerfield Supermarket,	42 E4
Thomas Cook,	43 E3
Tron Theatre,	44 F4
STA Travel,	45 F3

SEE "BYRES ROAD," p. 573

500 yards
500 meters

🛂 PRACTICAL INFORMATION

TOURIST, FINANCIAL, AND LOCAL SERVICES

Tourist Information Centre: Visit Scotland, 11 George Sq. (☎204 4400; www.visitscotland.com), off George Sq. south of Queen St. Station, northeast of Central Station. U: Buchanan St. Books accommodations for £3 plus a 10% deposit, sells CalMac ferry tickets, and arranges car rentals. Contains a bookshop, a Western Union, a **bureau de change,** and a wide selection of maps. Pick up the free *Essential Guide to Glasgow*, *Essential Guide to Scotland*, or any of 14 regional accommodation guides. Open July-Aug. M-Sa 9am-8pm, Su 10am-6pm; June and Sept. M-Sa 9am-7pm, Su 10am-6pm; Oct.-May M-Sa 9am-6pm, occasional Su around Easter and Christmas. MC/V.

Tours: City Sightseeing (☎204 0444; www.citysightseeingglasgow.co.uk). Tours on big red buses allow unlimited hop-on, hop-off access. Look for the bus stop signs or get on in George Sq. Handicap-accessible. Book online for discounts. (£9, concession £7.) Phoning the **Glasgow City Rangers** (☎287 5064) ahead of time can get you free Glasgow green tours as well as tours of the Necropolis. Through **Glasgow City Walk** (☎946 4542), members of the Scottish Tour Guides Association will provide groups with excellent tours and copious historical information (£40 per group).

Budget Travel: STA Travel, 122 George St. (☎552 6505). Branch at 84 Byres Rd. (☎338 6000). Student and budget travel arrangements. Open M-Th 9:30am-5:30pm, F-Sa 10:30am-5:30pm.

Financial Services: Banks are plentiful. **Thomas Cook,** 15-17 Gordon St. (☎201 7200), just beyond Central Station. Open M-Sa 8:30am-5:30pm, Su 10am-4pm. **American Express,** 115 Hope St. (☎0870 600 1060). Open M-Tu and Th-F 8:30am-5:30pm, W 9:30am-5:30pm, Sa 9am-noon. **ATMs** are on many corners.

Work/Volunteer Opportunities: Tourists descend upon Glasgow during the summer. If you are fluent in 2 European languages, you can apply to Glasgow's TIC for a seasonal position. Other work in Scotland can be found by visiting www.s1jobs.com. Also try the Glasgow **Central Job Centre,** 50-58 Jamaica St. (☎085 6060 234; www.jobcentreplus.gov.uk). Glasgow's **Volunteer Centre,** 84 Miller St. 4th fl. (☎226 3431; www.volunteerglasgow.org). Provides useful volunteer listings and contact information.

GLBT Services: Glasgow LGBT Centre, 84 Bell St. (☎552 4958; www.glgbt.org.uk). The first center of its kind in Scotland, with support groups, get-togethers, and information on gay and lesbian clubs, bars, and activities. Brand new onsite coffee shop is open to all, providing a safe and open space for conversation and community. F and Sa karaoke. Open daily 11am-midnight.

Launderette: Bank Street Laundry, 39-41 Bank St. (☎339 8953). U: Kelvin Bridge. Wash £2, dry 20p per 5min. Open M-F 9am-7:30pm, Sa-Su 9am-5pm.

EMERGENCY AND COMMUNICATIONS

Police: 173 Pitt St. (☎532 2000).

Hospital: Glasgow Royal Infirmary, 84-106 Castle St. (☎211 4000).

Pharmacy: Boots, 200 Sauchiehall St. (☎332 1925). Open M-W and F-Sa 8am-6pm, Th 8am-7pm, Su 8:30am-5:30pm.

Internet Access: Mitchell Library, North St. (☎287 2999; www.mitchelllibrary.org). Register for a temporary membership at the front desk. Free. Open M-Th 9am-8pm, F-Sa 9am-5pm. **Gallery of Modern Art,** Royal Exchange Sq. (☎229 1996). Free. **Sip and Surf,** 521 Great Western Road (339 4449). Free Wi-Fi with drink purchase. Open daily 7am-7pm. **EasyInternet Cafe,** 57-61 St. Vincent St. (☎222 2365), adjoining Caffe Nero. £1 per 30min. Open daily 7am-10:45pm.

Post Office: 47 St. Vincent St. (☎08457 223 344). **Bureau de change.** Open M-F 8:30am-5:45pm, Sa 9am-5:30pm. Branches at Hope St. and Bothwell St.

Post Code: G2 5QX.

ACCOMMODATIONS

Glasgow has hostels, B&Bs, and hotels to suit any budget. The best places fill up in the summer; book well ahead. Those on a tight budget need not worry—hostels run only £12-14 per night. Many of Glasgow's B&Bs are scattered on **Argyle Street** in the university area or near **Renfrew Street.** The major universities offer summer housing, and plenty of apartments offer summer or student discounts.

HOSTELS

SYHA Glasgow, 7-8 Park Terr. (☎332 3004 or 0870 004 1119). U: St. George's Cross. Take bus #44 from Central Station, ask for the 1st stop on Woodlands Rd., and follow the signs around a loop to Park Terr. Overlooks Kelvingrove Park from a quiet street in the heart of the West End. Once the residence of a nobleman, later an upscale hotel, now the best hostel in town. Low-key atmosphere with children and families to balance a steady stream of twenty-somethings. Coffeehouse in the basement offers Internet £1 per hr. and an array of light eats. All rooms (4-8 beds) ensuite. Bike shed, kitchen, and TV and game rooms. Laundry available. Dorms June-Sept. £16, under 18 £12; Oct.-May prices vary, starting at £12. MC/V. ❶

Euro Hostel Glasgow (☎222 2828; www.euro-hostels.co.uk), at the corner of Clyde St. and Jamaica St., near Central Station. U: St. Enoch. Screams "student friendly" but caters to everyone from ruddy backpackers to families on holiday. Located near some of Glasgow's hippest clubs, the hostel itself feels like a destination, satisfying a late-night crowd with its own bar and big-screen TVs. Rooms are quiet and clean. Breakfast included. Laundry £2. Free Wi-Fi. Computer access £1 per 15min. Wheelchair-accessible. 14-person dorms £15; singles £40. MC/V. ❷

Bunkum Backpackers, 26 Hillhead St. (☎581 4481; www.bunkumglasgow.co.uk), up the hill from Glasgow University and the West End. U: Hillhead. Half-hidden on a small residential street, Bunkum has charm to spare. The busy kitchen and common areas fill with travelers in the know who have discovered a home away from home in this refurbished Victorian house. Lockers £10 deposit. Laundry £2.50. Free parking. Dorms £12; twins £16. Sept.-Apr. £60 per week. MC/V. ❷

Blue Sky Hostel, 3 Bank St. (☎337 7000; www.blueskyhostel.com), U: Kelvingrove. Offers crowded but clean facilities for the lowest price in town. Free continental breakfast. TVs in common area. Ensuite bathrooms. Dorms £11; private rooms, £38. ❶

UNIVERSITY DORMS

University of Glasgow, 73 Great George St. (☎330 4116, bookings 330 2766; www.cvso.co.uk). Off Hillhead St. in the Queen Margaret Bldg. Summer housing at several dorms. Office open daily 9am-5pm. Cairncross House, 20 Kelvinhaugh Pl., has self-catering rooms off Argyle St. near Kelvingrove Park. Tea, coffee, soap, towels, and linens provided. Singles from £16.25; doubles from £31. MC/V. ❷

University of Strathclyde, Office of Sales and Marketing, 50 Richmond St. (☎553 4148; www.rescat.strath.ac.uk). On the hill, between Cathedral St. and George St. Dorm-style rooms and apartments available in summer. Furnished rooms. 1 kitchen per fl., laundry, and towels. Mail and telephone message service. Book well in advance. Open from mid-June to mid-Sept. Singles £23, with breakfast £24.60-34.60. MC/V. ❸

Liberty House, 59 Miller St. (☎248 9949; libertystudents.com). Dorm-style rooms for students, on Queen St. near the shopping district. Rooms include desk, shelves, ensuite bathroom, and communal kitchen. Very secure facility and a value option for long-term stays. Open June-Sept. Singles £20, £100 per wk. MC/V. ❸

B&BS

▨ **Alamo Guest House,** 46 Gray St. (☎339 2395; www.alamoguesthouse.com). On a quiet street with access to the West End and Sauchiehall St. A family feel and a surplus of helpful services make this luxurious Victorian house the absolute best deal in Glasgow. Newly refurbished rooms include elegant baths and large windows overlooking Kelvingrove Park. Pet the cat, chat with the owners, and enjoy the fresh continental breakfast. DVD players in each room for use with house collection of over 200 movies and free temporary local gym membership. Free Wi-Fi. Pets allowed by arrangement. Book far ahead. Singles from £26; doubles from £24 per person. MC/V. ❸

McLays Guest House, 264-276 Renfrew St. (☎332 4796; www.mclays.com). With 3 elegant dining rooms, satellite TV, and phones in each room, this posh B&B looks and feels like a hotel. Modern rooms in an old house create an air of trendy dignity. Full Scottish breakfast included. Most rooms ensuite. Singles from £28, ensuite £36; doubles £48/56; family (1 double bed, 2 singles) £70/80. Internet £2 per 30min. Book ahead, especially for singles. AmEx/MC/V. ❸

Merchant Lodge, 52 Virginia St. (☎552 2424; www.the-merchant-lodge.sagenet.co.uk). Calm location among the hubbub in the city center. The building still boasts the original stone spiral staircase from its days as a tobacco store in the 1800s. Courteous staff and quiet lounges allow for privacy and relaxation. All rooms ensuite. Full Scottish breakfast included. Singles £40; doubles £62; triples £80; quads £90. AmEx/MC/V. ❹

Smith's Hotel, 963 Sauchiehall St. (☎339 7674; www.smiths-hotel.com), 1 block east of Kelvingrove Park in the West End. Near the pub-packed action of upper Sauchiehall, Smith's provides a welcome respite from the city's racket. Book in advance for long-term budget rooms. Breakfast included. Singles £26, ensuite £36; doubles £40/52; triples ensuite only £69. MC/V. ❸

◘ FOOD

Glasgow is often called the curry capital of Britain, and for good reason. The city's West End brims with kebab and curry joints, and fusion cuisine is all the rage. In the past few years, the organic food and fair trade movements have begun to change the focus of many of Glasgow's restaurants toward more inventive vegetarian and organic menu options. **Byres Road** and the trendy **Ashton Lane** thrive with cafes, bars, and bistros. **Groceries** are available at Sainsbury's, 236-240 Buchanan Galleries (☎332 1480; www.sainsburys.co.uk; open M-Sa 7am-10pm, Su 7am-9pm).

▨ **Willow Tea Rooms,** 217 Sauchiehall St. (☎332 0521; www.willowtearooms.co.uk). U: Cowcaddens, upstairs from Henderson Jewellers. Light streams through the windows of this 3-story ode to architect Charles Rennie Mackintosh. A Glasgow landmark, the building's facade was designed by Mackintosh himself, and the cozy upstairs features handsome chairs in the classic "Glasgow style." Sample over 20 teas (£2 per pot) or indulge in 3-course high tea (£10.50). Salads and sandwiches £4-7. Open M-Sa 9am-5pm, Su 11am-4:45pm. MC/V. Branch at 97 Buchanan St. U: Buchanan St. ❷

▨ **Grassroots Cafe,** 97 St. George's Rd. (☎333 0534). U: St. George's Cross. Bold colors, creative organic dishes, and an open kitchen make this the hottest vegetarian restaurant in town. Thai-inspired seasonings draw the adventurous. Try the curried fries with a trio of dipping sauces (£7.50). A mecca for Glasgow veggie culture, with Green Party offices upstairs. Open daily 10am-9:45pm. AmEx/MC/V. ❷

Wee Curry Shop, 7 Buccleuch St. (☎353 0777). U: Cowcaddens. The best bang for your buck in a town full of *pakora* and *puri*. Small size allows for personal attention and culinary surprises. 2-course lunch £4.75. Entrees £5.80-10. Seats 25; reservations are a must. Open M-Sa noon-2:30pm and 5:30-10:30pm. Cash only. Branch at 23 Ashton Ln. (☎357 5280). U: Hillhead. MC/V. ❶

Kings Cafe, 71 Elmbank St. (☎332 3247). On a small alleyway off Sauchiehall St. This tiny diner offers authentically cheap, greasy, and satisfying meals and snacks for the Scottish palate. Family-owned, offering everything from haggis to pizza. Try the home-made lentil soup (£1.40) or fill up on a stuffed roll for just £1. Fried Mars Bars and Irn Bru round out the experience and the stomach. Takeaway available. Most items £1-3. Open 7am-11pm. Cash only. ❶

Firebird, 1321 Argyle St. (☎334 0594). U: Kelvinhall. A staple for veteran pubbers in the area, Firebird treats a diverse crowd to daily specials and locally famous pizzas (£9.50). Try the new Portuguese fish stew (£11) and enjoy the orange walls and good company. Free Wi-Fi. DJ F-Sa night. Open M-Th 11:30am-midnight, F-Sa 10am-1am, Su 12:30pm-midnight. MC/V. ❸

Stravaigin, 28 Gibson St. (☎334 2665; www.stravaigin.com). U: Kelvinbridge. The mantra "think globally, eat locally" inspires dishes of fresh seafood, game, and produce. Creatively lit upstairs and more formal downstairs serve the same menu of Thai- and Indian-inspired dishes. Known for their take on traditional haggis (£9). Entrees £14-26. Now open for breakfast M-F 9:30am-noon, Sa-Su 11am-4pm. For dinner, open Tu-Th and Su 5-11pm, F-Sa noon-2:30pm and 5-11pm. Branch: **Stravaigin 2,** 8 Ruthaven Ln. (☎334 7165), off Byres Rd. U: Hillhead. Less pricey. AmEx/MC/V. ❹

Big Slope, 36 Kelvingrove St. (☎564 5201). U: Kelvingrove. Fast becoming one of the West End's more celebrated restaurants, Big Slope's underground bar and booths are a great place for a relaxing meal. Ample outdoor tables. Specialty pizzas and moderately priced meats (steak and chips, £8) along with the unique breakfast-in-a-pint (£3.50) make it worth a look. Open M-Su 9am-2pm and 5pm-midnight. AmEx/MC/V. ❷

Mao, 84 Brunswick St. (☎564 5161; www.cafemao.com). U: St. Enoch. With Andy Warhol-esque portraits of Mao in the window and a soundtrack of relaxing jazz music, this Asian fusion restaurant and bar provides tasty dishes like crispy roast pumpkin spring rolls (£6). Open M-Sa noon-11pm, Su 12:20-10pm. AmEx/MC/V. ❷

Two Fat Ladies, 88 Dumbarton Rd. (☎339 1944; www.twofatladies.org). An open kitchen and bronze facade welcome epicures to this small, well-known restaurant in the West End. Serves gourmet seafood in a casual atmosphere. The delicious Two Fat's fish platter (£16) changes daily, but leave room for desserts like the signature Trio of Crème Brûlée (£5). Lunch M-Su noon-3pm, dinner M-Su 5:30-10pm. ❹

◎ SIGHTS

Glasgow is a paradise for the budget traveler. Many of the best sights are part of the **Glasgow Museums** network, whose free collections are scattered across the city. Don't shy away from trekking a mile or two out of town for gorgeous city views and attractions. *The List* (£2.50, www.list.co.uk), available from newsstands, is an essential review of current exhibitions, galleries, music, and nightlife.

THE CITY CENTER

▨**GLASGOW CATHEDRAL AND NECROPOLIS.** Glasgow Cathedral is a humbling example of 13th-century Gothic architecture. Descend the stairs to visit the tomb of St. Mungo, patron saint of Glasgow. Statues of Glasgow leaders and reformers stand among gravestones in the outdoor courtyard. (*Castle St.* ☎552 6891. *Open Apr.-Sept. M-Sa 9:30am-6pm, Su 1-5pm; Oct.-Mar. M-Sa 9:30am-4pm, Su 1-4pm. Organ recitals and*

TIMELINE OF TERROR

In the summer of 2007, Britain became the target of multiple terrorist events that raised the nation's security alert to its highest level. Here is a timeline of the attempted attacks as they unfolded:

June 29: Car bombs in two Mercedes are discovered near central London's Tiger Tiger club. Both are disarmed.

June 30: A Jeep is set on fire and driven through a plate glass window at Glasgow International Airport. Two men are arrested at the scene.

July 1: Two more suspects are arrested in Scotland. Police search homes throughout Britain in an attempt to recover clues about the attempted attacks.

July 2: A man attempting to board a plane in Australia is arrested in connection to the attempted bombings. The authorities find links between several foreign-born UK doctors and the attacks.

July 3: A total of eight suspects arrested. All but one have connections to Britain's National Health Service.

August 3: A passenger of the Glasgow Jeep is confirmed dead by hospital officials. The suspect's death is the attack's only fatality.

Thankfully, the potential damage of the attacks was largely avoided, as neither of the attempts were successfully completed. At press time, the suspects are awaiting preliminary hearings in late 2007.

concerts July-Aug. Tu 7:30pm, £7. Free personal tours.) A statue of reformer John Knox looks over the **Necropolis,** where tombstones, statues, and obelisks lie aslant. Climb up the hill for a view of the city. (Behind the Cathedral over the Bridge of Sighs. Open 24hr. Free.)

GEORGE SQUARE. This grand, red-paved landmark has always been the physical, cultural, commercial, and historical center of Glasgow. Filled with couples, tourists, and pigeon feeders, the square is frequently the site of city-wide displays and events. Although named for George III, the square's 80 ft. central column features a statue of Sir Walter Scott, Scottish novelist and poet. The **City Chambers,** on the east side of George Sq., house an elaborate Italian Renaissance interior with mosaic floors and marble columns and staircases. (☎287 4017. Free 1hr. tours M-F 10:30am and 2:30pm.) The eclectic **Gallery of Modern Art (GoMA),** Queens St., south of George Sq., displays cutting-edge—but occasionally underwhelming—installations inside a building that was once the Royal Exchange. (☎229 1996. Open M-W and Sa 10am-5pm, Th 10am-8pm, F and Su 11am-5pm. Free.)

ST. MUNGO MUSEUM OF RELIGIOUS LIFE AND ART. Home to Britain's first Japanese Zen garden, the museum houses artifacts and info about hundreds of religions and cultural traditions. The third floor survey's Scotland's religious history. (2 Castle St. ☎553 2557. Open M-Th and Sa 10am-5pm, F and Su 11am-5pm. Free.)

CENTRE FOR CONTEMPORARY ARTS (CCA). Three free galleries, a theater, artists' residences, a cafe, and a cinema make up this avant-garde mecca, which houses the prestigious Beck's Futures prize (the UK's top prize for contemporary visual art) every June and July. Exhibits are increasingly focused on computer art, and student shows display the work of Glasgow's up-and-coming artists. (350 Sauchiehall St. ☎352 4900; www.cca-glasgow.com. Open Tu-W 11am-11pm, Th 11am-midnight, F 11am-1am, Sa 10am-1am. Free galleries. Performances begin at 8pm. Film prices vary.)

OTHER CENTRAL SIGHTS. Duck down low to enter the small rooms of **Provand's Lordship,** the oldest house in Glasgow. Mannequins of monks in musty red robes seem creepy at first, but at least they don't move or speak. Antique furnishings and a 3rd floor dedicated to Scottish cartoons and photos round out this eclectic walk through Glasgow's past. (3-7 Castle St. ☎552 8819. Open M-Th and Sa 10am-5pm, F and Su 11am-5pm. Free.) The **People's Palace** on Glasgow Green provides a thorough walk through Glasgow's history, with rotating exhibits that tend to focus on current sections of the city and the people who live there. In the adjacent "winter gardens," visitors relax in a greenhouse and chat in the cafe. (☎271 2951. *Open M-Th and Sa 10am-5pm, F and Su 11am-5pm. Free.)*

THE WEST END

KELVINGROVE PARK, MUSEUM, AND ART GALLERY.
Along the River Kelvin, **Kelvingrove Park** provides green space for walkers and bikers, along with fountains and statues of obscure but influential Glaswegians. The park also houses recreational tennis courts, a skate park, playground, and lawn bowling green. Don't be surprised to hear bagpipes played by shirtless, bearded college students. City-sponsored festivals often fill the park with more official traditional music. Spires of the **Kelvingrove Art Gallery and Museum** rise from the park's southwest corner. The museum features everything from tastefully taxidermied animals to a large re-creation of the homes designed by Charles Rennie Mackintosh. (☎276 9599; www.glasgowmuseums.com. Argyle St. U: Kelvinhall. Bus #6, 16, 18, 42, 62, 64. *Open M-Th and Sa 10am-5pm, F and Su 11am-5pm. Free.)* Across the street from the Kelvingrove Museum, the **Museum of Transport,** 1 Bunhouse Rd., is full of interactive and kid-friendly exhibits tracing the history of getting around in Scotland. (☎287 2720. U: Kelvinhall. *Open M-Th and Sa 10am-5pm, F and Su 11am-5pm. Free.)*

UNIVERSITY OF GLASGOW.
The central spire of the neo-Gothic university towers over University Ave. Stately archways lead to the different wings of campus from a series of central quads. Pick up *Welcome to the University of Glasgow*, free at the TIC, or stop by the **Visitor Centre** for a free map and self-guided tour. (☎330 5511. U: Hillhead. *Open M-Sa 9:30am-5pm. Free tours and tower access F 2pm.)* Up the red-carpeted staircase is the **Hunterian Museum,** the oldest museum in Scotland. The newly renovated halls house the university's Blackstone chair, where all students had to sit for oral examinations while timed by an hourglass suspended overhead. Other attractions include the foot bones of famous Scotsmen, an ancient elephant skeleton, and £1 million turned into pulp. Call for information about bicentennial celebrations throughout 2007-2008. (☎330 4221; www.hunterian.gla.ac.uk. *Open M-Sa 9:30am-5pm. Free.)* Across University St. on Hillhead St., the **◙Hunterian Art Gallery** displays 19th-century Scottish art, the world's largest Whistler collection, and a variety of Rembrandts and Pissarros. Next door are the reconstructed rooms of the **Mackintosh House.** (☎330 5431. *Open M-Sa 9:30am-5pm; closed during exam period. Gallery free. House £2.50, students free; W after 2pm free.)*

FROM THE ROAD

GLASGOW WAS ATTACKED? WHERE WAS I?

On June 30, 2007, I woke up to rain on the Isle of Arran, 30 mi. west of Glasgow. I was disappointed. I had been planning on taking an all-day hike, but the heavy rain drowned my fleeting athleticism. When the rain stopped, I took a walk to photograph the sunset over Lochranza Bay. The next day, I left the isles and made my way toward Ayr. The train was crowded. Asking a fellow passenger, I learned travelers were being shuttled to Prestwick International Airport from Glasgow Airport, 30 mi. away. "Oh," I replied, and went back to my reading, not thinking anything more of it. You can imagine my surprise when, three days later, I found an email from my editors letting me know about a terrorist attack in Glasgow on June 30. I had to read the email twice to make sure it wasn't a hoax. I was 20 minutes away from Glasgow. How had I not heard about this? I felt ignorant for missing this attack that had happened right under my nose. But then I realized that there was something reassuring in the normalcy of my days after June 30. Despite a violent attempt to disrupt peace, life in Scotland went—and goes—on. Farmers still feed pigs in the hills, fishermen still launch tiny boats from isle ports, and pubbers still toast their enduring spirit with stiff shots of good Scotch whisky.

—Annie Austin

BOTANIC GARDENS. Creatively landscaped gardens cover the stretch of the River Kelvin along Byres Rd. On sunny days, it feels as though all of Glasgow comes here before heading to the beer gardens on nearby Ashton Ln. Look for the wall of carnivorous plants as well as the Scottish national collection of tree ferns, orchids, and begonias in the **Main Range** hothouse. Wander around the herb, rose, and uncommon vegetable gardens outside. The newly renovated **Kibble Palace** is a gleaming glass structure containing an international collection of temperate plants. *(730 Great Western Rd. and Byres Rd. ☎334 2422. U: Hillhead. Gardens open daily 7:30am-sunset. Kibble Palace and Main Range open daily Apr.-early Oct. 10am-4:45pm; late Oct.-Mar. 10am-4:15pm. Tours available by reservation. Free.)*

SOUTH OF THE CLYDE

POLLOK COUNTRY PARK AND BURRELL COLLECTION. The **Pollok Country Park** is a beautifully integrated expanse of darkened forest paths, art galleries, grazing highland cattle, and lots of native Scottish flora. The famous **Burrell Collection** can be found in a glass building in the middle of the park. Once the private stash of ship magnate William Burrell, the collection includes paintings by Cézanne and Degas, Egyptian and Buddhist sculptures, medieval armor and tapestries, Persian textiles, and fine china. *(☎287 2550. Open M-Th and Sa 10am-5pm, F and Su 11am-5pm. Tours daily 11am and 2pm. Free.)* Also in the park is the less spectacular **Pollok House,** a Victorian mansion with a small collection, including pieces by El Greco, Goya, and William Blake. *(☎616 6410. Take bus #45, 47, 48, or 57 from Jamaica St. 15min., £1.20. Open daily 10am-5pm. £5, students £3.75; Nov.-Mar. free.)*

GLASGOW SCIENCE CENTRE. Like a glittering eye on the river, the UK's only titanium-clad exterior is covered in glass panes overlooking the Clyde. The three buildings require three tickets. The first houses Scotland's only **IMAX theater.** *(Open daily 10am-6pm.)* The second contains hundreds of interactive exhibits. *(Open Tu-Su 10am-5pm.)* Lastly, the 417 ft. **Glasgow Tower** is the only building in the world that rotates 360° from the ground up. Climb the 523 steps to the top or follow the crowd to the lift. Offering the very best views of Glasgow, the building is a cone whose weight rests on a base of just a few centimeters. *(50 Pacific Quay. ☎420 5010; www.gsc.org.uk. U: Cessnock, accessible by Bells Bridge. Open M-Th and Su noon-6pm, F-Sa noon-8pm. Each building £7, concessions £5; any 2 buildings £10/8.)*

☐ SHOPPING

THE BARROWS. A cross between a farmers' market and a flea market, "The Barrows" is an escape from the high prices of big-name stores in Glasgow. Located at the intersection of Argyle and Trungate St. (under the sign marked "Barrowland"), The Barrows offers a dizzying array of commodities at bargain prices. Open Sa-Su 10am-5pm. —*Katie Rieser*

You'll pass kilted mannequins and Charles Rennie Mackintosh jewelry for blocks on end as you make your way up **Sauchiehall Street** and down **Buchanan Street.** The two streets form a pedestrian-only zone and provide excellent shopping. Shops stay open late on Thursdays, but close early on the weekends. The three main indoor shopping centers are **Princes Square,** 48 Buchanan St., a high-end shopping mall; **St. Enoch Centre,** 55 St. Enoch Sq.; and the **Buchanan Galleries** at the north end of Buchanan St. The West End's Byres Rd. is full of boutiques, often with a focus on fair trade and organic products.

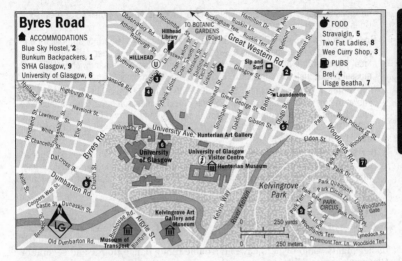

Byres Road

▲ ACCOMMODATIONS
Blue Sky Hostel, 2
Bunkum Backpackers, 1
SYHA Glasgow, 9
University of Glasgow, 6

🍎 FOOD
Stravaigin, 5
Two Fat Ladies, 8
Wee Curry Shop, 3

🍺 PUBS
Brel, 4
Uisge Beatha, 7

☒ NIGHTLIFE

Glaswegians have a reputation for partying hard. Three universities and the highest student-to-resident ratio in Britain guarantee a kinetic after-hours vibe. *The List* (www.list.co.uk, £2.50), available from newsstands, has detailed nightlife and entertainment listings, while *The Gig* (www.gigguide.co.uk, free) highlights what's happening in the live music scene.

PUBS

You'll never find yourself far from a frothy pint in this city of beer gardens. Students from the University of Glasgow schmooze with twenty-somethings on **Ashton Lane** and **Byres Road.** In the East End, the University of Strathclyde and the Glasgow School of Art are well supplied by the more lively **Buchanan Street.**

🍺 **Babbity Bowster,** 16-18 Blackfriars St. (☎552 5055). U: Queen St. An authentic Glaswegian experience: few kilts and little Gaelic music, but you are likely to hear the sound of a pint hitting the bar and a jubilant patron asking for another. Small patio on a quiet street. Offerings range from the unique cauliflower and mung bean moussaka (£7.25) to the traditional fish soup (£4.25). Food served until 10pm. Open M-Sa 11am-midnight, Su 10am-midnight. MC/V.

🍺 **Uisge Beatha,** 232 Woodlands Rd. (☎564 1596). U: Kelvinbridge. *Uisge Beatha* (ISHker VAH-ha) is Gaelic for "water of life" (whiskey), and this pub has over 100 malts (from £2.50). The dark interior and traditional decor adds an authentic feel without seeming cheesy. Th Irish tunes after 8pm; Su live Scottish music. Happy hour daily 4-7pm. Open M-Sa noon-midnight, Su 12:30pm-midnight. Light snacks served noon-5pm.

The 13th Note, 50-60 King St. (☎553 1638; www.13thnote.net). U: St. Enoch. A reasonably priced all-organic, all-vegetarian menu (veggie haggis £5.40) and excellent local music ranging from electro-hardcore to folk (starts daily 9pm). Relaxed atmosphere. Open daily noon-midnight. Food served noon-10pm.

Mojama, 426 Sauchiehall St. (☎332 4760). Charing Cross rail. Bright fuchsia walls scare away the timid, but Mojama's ultra-cheap drinks (most drinks £1.50 all night) draw an ultra-hip crowd, including many students from nearby Glasgow School of Art.

Inexpensive, basic burgers, and simple dishes. Order at the bar. 1 dish £3, 2 dishes £5. Open daily noon-midnight.

Brel, Ashton Ln. (☎342 4966; www.brelbarrestaurant.com). Named for an obscure Belgian folk singer, Brel specializes in exotic but delicious Belgian beer and undiscovered local bands. Outdoor seating. The restaurant menu also offers sandwiches (£5) and mussel pots (small £5, large £10). Entrees £7-11. Open daily 10am-midnight.

Nice'n'Sleazy, 421 Sauchiehall St. (☎333 0900). Charing Cross rail. Sleazy's, as it is known to hipster Glaswegians, is one of many local venues that features up-and-coming local bands at its cavernous underground stage nearly every night. More nice than sleazy, this colorful hotbed of funk and punk serves food and alcohol upstairs. Open daily 11:30am-11:45pm.

Bar Soba, 11 Mitchell Ln. (☎204 2404; www.barsoba.co.uk). U: Queen St. Tucked down an alleyway off Buchanon St. Perfect for quiet conversation over drinks. Exotic, Thai-inspired dishes like prawn with pumpkin (£9) complement an impressive beer and wine list. Open M-Sa 11am-midnight, Su noon-midnight.

CLUBS

With loads of options for picky clubbers and giant venues to house everyone else, Glasgow parties hard every night of the week. Even Monday tends to be one of the busier nights. Club owners have no trouble filling dance floors, and several of Glasgow's more well-known venues have been consistently expanding.

> **TIP** **HARDCORE.** Although most clubs are open until 3am, Glasgow authorities maintain the authority to order large and potentially disruptive groups in public to disperse after 2am.

 The Buff Club, 142 Bath Ln. (☎248 1777; www.thebuffclub.com), behind Bath St. The after-hours club in Glasgow. A wee club and hard to find, but packed every night of the week. 2 dance floors and attached pub. Floral wallpaper, disco balls, and enthusiastic crowd. Music ranges from indie to 80s trash and funky house music. Tu guest DJ. Cover M-Th and Su £3, F-Sa £6. Open M-Th and Su 11pm-3am, F-Sa 10:30pm-3am.

The Polo Lounge, 84 Wilson St. (☎553 1221). Behind gold colored curtains, Glasgow's largest gay and lesbian club heats up early. 80s music and mainstream pop in a space that feels both elite and fun. Cover £5. Chill out with a martini in the adjoining cocktail bar, **Moda,** 62 Virginia St. Both open M-Th 5pm-1am, F-Sa 5pm-3am.

The Cube, 34 Queen St. (☎226 8990; www.cubeglasgow.co.uk). Home to some of the longest queues in Glasgow. The tiny window in the front door holds intrigue and, often, the face of the bouncer. Ultra-cool, with padded leather walls and a heavily misted dance floor. M-Tu gay and lesbian, W R&B, Th student night. F-Sa dress smart. M-Tu cover £3; W £5, concessions £3; Th £3 before midnight, £2 after; F cover £5, concessions £3; Sa £8/6. Open daily 11pm-3am.

Cathouse, 15 Union St. (☎248 6606; www.glasgowcathouse.co.uk). Grunge, goth, and indie please a younger crowd in this 3 fl. club. Under-18 rockers can headbang downstairs in the Voodoo Room. Tu rock 'n' roll night and all drinks £1.50. Cover £2-5, students £1-3. Open Th-Su 11pm-3am.

Subclub, 22 Jamaica St. (☎248 4600; www.subclub.co.uk). The smooth, silver exterior is impossibly cool. Mostly hired out at night by different promoters—check the website for some of Glasgow's more cutting-edge bands. Sa-Su cover £6-7. Open Sa-Su 11:30pm-3am. Other nights vary; look for local advertising.

Bennets, 90 Glassford St. (☎552 5761; www.bennets.co.uk). Bennets is a staple of the gay and lesbian cruising scene. Music varies by room, and decor is simple but rarely noticed by the energetic crowd. Cover varies. Girls Only Night 1st F of the month. Open Tu and Th-Su 11:30pm-3am.

The Garage, 490 Sauchiehall St. (☎332 1120). Look for the yellow truck hanging over the door. One of Glasgow's biggest clubs, The Garage is expanding, already helping over 3000 frenetic dancers get their fill on weekend nights. Flashing neon signs stud the staircases and several dance floors host a variety of music. Upstairs **Attic** plays indie with an occasional DJ. VIP lounge has after parties and the occasional celebrity. Cover £2-6; frequent student discounts. Open M-F and Su 11pm-3am, Sa 10:30pm-3am.

ENTERTAINMENT AND FESTIVALS

The city's dynamic student population ensures countless film, food, and music events from October to April. **Ticket Centre,** City Hall, Candleriggs, has information on plays, films, and concerts taking place at Glasgow's dozen-odd theaters. (☎287 5511. Open M-Sa 9:30am-9pm.) Theaters include: **Theatre Royal,** Hope St. (☎332 9000); the **Tron Theatre,** 63 Trongate (☎552 4267); and the **Citizens' Theatre,** 119 Gorbals St. (☎429 0022). The **Cottier Theatre,** 935 Hyndland St. (☎357 3868), hosts a variety of theatrical events, from avant-garde to opera. **The Glasgow ABC,** 300 Sauchiehall St., hosts bands and events throughout the year in a building that housed Glasgow's first cinema (☎0870 4000 818). The **Royal Concert Hall,** Sauchiehall St., is a frequent venue for the Royal Scottish National Orchestra. (☎353 8000. Box office open M-Sa 10am-6pm.) The **Glasgow Film Theatre,** 12 Rose St., screens both mainstream and sleeper hits and hosts the traveling London Lesbian and Gay Film Festival in September. (☎332 8128; www.gft.org.uk. Box office open M-Sa noon-9pm, Su 30min. before first film. £5, concessions £4; matinees £4.50/3.50.)

GLASGOW SHOWS FOR POCKET CHANGE. Ask about "preview" performance nights (day before opening) at theater box offices. At the **Citizens' Theatre,** these tickets sell for £2, available only on the day of the preview from the box office itself. Students can get these tickets for free the same way.

The year kicks off with a month-long Scottish *ceilidh* (dance party) at the **Celtic Connections** (www.celticconnections.com) festival in January. The fun continues with the three-year-old **Glasgow Film Festival** (www.glasgowfilmfestival.org.uk) in the middle of February. If the city already seems saturated with art, it gets completely drunk on it for one weekend in early April with the **Glasgow Art Fair** (www.glasgowartfair.com). Summer is the real festival season, bringing tourists from around the globe. During the **West End Festival** (www.westendfestival.co.uk) in June, the city comes alive with longer bar hours and guest musicians. The **Glasgow International Jazz Festival** (☎552 3552; www.jazzfest.co.uk), in late June, draws international jazz greats. The **Glasgow River Festival,** in mid-July, celebrates the nautical history of the city with music and activities on the Clyde. **Bard in the Botanics** (www.glasgowrep.org), "Shakespeare in the Park," takes place in the West End Botanic Gardens during June and July. Take advantage of the fine dining during **Gourmet Glasgow** (www.gourmetglasgow.com), when for two weeks in August over 50 restaurants and bars offer fixed-price meals and free tastings. Pick up *Gourmet Glasgow,* free at the TIC. On the 2nd Saturday of August, over 100 bagpipe bands compete on the Glasgow Green for the **World Pipe Championships** (☎221 5414). One weekend in early September brings **Whisky Live** (www.whiskylive.com), an extravaganza surrounding the much-vaunted national drink.

CENTRAL
SCOTLAND

Less rugged than the Highlands to the north and more subdued than the cities to the south, central Scotland has draws all its own. The eastern shoulder, curving from Fife to the Highland Boundary Fault along the North Sea, has centuries-old communities and historical landmarks. To the west, the landscape flattens from snow-covered peaks into the plains of the Central Lowlands. Escape Celts and kilts in the remote Inner Hebrides, where palm trees, stucco homes, and sandy beaches offer a relaxing change from the mainland.

HIGHLIGHTS OF CENTRAL SCOTLAND

ADMIRE the 5½ ft. sword of William Wallace and one of Britain's grandest castles in **Stirling,** the historic royal seat of Scotland (p. 591).

RELAX on the bonnie, bonnie banks of **Loch Lomond** before exploring **the Trossachs,** Scotland's 1st national park (p. 592).

DRINK famous **Islay** whisky at one of the island's many distilleries (p. 598).

ST. ANDREWS   ☎ 01334

St. Andrews is the unquestioned homeland of golf. The game's rules were formally established here in 1764, and its courses draw giddy amateurs from around the world as well as pros seeking British Open acclaim. Although plaid pants and shiny golf shoes are common around town, St. Andrews is full of attractions for those whose idea of the game is limited to putters and windmills. The town is home to Scotland's oldest university, a number of medieval sights, and the highest concentration of pubs in the UK.

TRANSPORTATION

Drivers can take the A917, (Fife Coastal Tourist Route), or the faster M90 to A91 to Edinburgh. All **trains** (☎08457 484 950) stop 5 mi. away in **Leuchars** (LU-cars). Most trains from Leuchars travel to Edinburgh (about 3 per hr.) or Perth (1hr., every hr., £8.70), a transfer point for trains to Aberdeen, Inverness, and London. From Leuchars, buses #94, 96, and 99 run to St. Andrews (5 per hr. 6am-10:30pm, £1.85). The **bus station** (☎474 238) is on City Rd. Scottish Citylink (☎01383 621 249) **bus** X60 runs to Edinburgh (2hr., M-Sa 1-2 per hr., £7); the X24 runs to Glasgow (2½hr., M-Sa every hr., £7). Buses run reduced service in the evenings and on Sundays. Call Traveline (☎08706 082 608) for info.

ORIENTATION AND PRACTICAL INFORMATION

The three main streets—**North Street, Market Street,** and **South Street**—run nearly parallel to each other, terminating by the cathedral at the town's east end.

Central Scotland

North Sea

Atlantic Ocean

Firth of Forth

Edinburgh

Glasgow

Perth

Dundee

Stirling

Fort William

Oban

Loch Lomond and The Trossachs National Park

West Highland Way

Grampian Hills

Mull of Kintyre

Arran

Islay

Jura

Mull

Coll

Tiree

TOP TEN LIST

TOP TEN WAYS TO CLOG YOUR ARTERIES

Scotland is famous for its fried foods. Here are the greasiest options:

10. Deep Fried Cheeseburger: Patty and cheese are deep fried, then placed on the bun and enjoyed as usual.

9. Deep Fried Sausage: Tastes a bit like a corn dog, looks a bit like—well, never mind.

8. Deep Fried Haggis: The traditional Scottish favorite. Improved upon? Opinions differ.

7. Deep Fried Steak: This is no filet mignon. Think deep fried burger, minus the bun.

6. Deep Fried Skittles: How do they not lose the Skittles through the holes in the bottom of the fryer? More importantly, who was the first person who thought, "Hey, these Skittles are good. You know what would make them even better? Dousing them in a pan of hot lard."

5. Deep Fried Pizza: With your choice of toppings.

4. Deep Fried Black Pudding: The only way to improve upon a sausage made from pig's blood is to throw it in a deep fat fryer.

3. Deep Fried White Pudding: Like black pudding, but white.

2. Deep Fried Mars Bar:

1. Deep Fried Hospitality: Many chip shops will deep fry anything you want, if you bring it to the shop and ask nicely. Be creative!

Tourist Information Centre: 70 Market St. (☎472 021). Ask for the free *St. Andrews Town Map and Guide*, and the extremely useful *Essential Guide to Fife*. Books accommodations for £3 plus a 10% deposit. **Bureau de change.** Open Apr.-June M-Sa 9:30am-5:30pm, Su 11am-4pm; July-Sept. M-Sa 9:30am-7pm, Su 9:30am-5pm; Oct.-Mar. M-Sa 9:30am-5pm.

Financial Services: Royal Bank of Scotland, 113-115 South St. (☎472 181). **Bureau de change.** Open M-Tu and Th-F 9:15am-4:45pm, W 10am-4:45pm.

Launderette: Caremore Laundry Services, 14b Woodburn Terr. (☎475 150), outside of town. £5 per load. Open M-Sa 9am-7pm, Su 9am-5pm. Last wash 1½hr. before close.

Police: 100 North St. (☎418 700).

Hospital: St. Andrews Memorial, Abbey Walk (☎472 327), southeast of town. 24hr. medical attention also available at the **Health Centre,** Pipeland Rd. (☎476 840).

Internet Access: St. Andrews Library, Church Sq. (☎412 685). Free, with free library membership. Open M and F-Su 9:30am-5pm, Tu and Th 9:30am-7pm. Also **Costa Coffee,** 83 Market St. £1 per 20min. Open M-Sa 8am-6pm, Su 10am-5:30pm.

Post Office: 127 South St. (☎08457 223 344). **Bureau de change.** Open M-F 9am-5:30pm, Sa 9am-12:30pm. **Post Code:** KY16 9UL.

ACCOMMODATIONS

St. Andrews makes a plausible daytrip from Edinburgh, and is also an ideal base for visiting the Fife Seaside. The town has only one year-round hostel, but is packed with **B&Bs** (most from £30); over 20 separate establishments line **Murray Park** and **Murray Place** alone. Prices are often lower during term time, from October to May.

St. Andrews Tourist Hostel, St. Mary's Pl. (☎479 911), above the Grill House restaurant. From the bus station, turn right on City Rd., then left on St. Mary's Pl. Colorful, spacious hostel for a comfortable place to stay between rounds. In the center. Laundry £2. Internet £1 per hr. Reception in summer 8am-11pm; winter 8am-3pm and 6-10pm. Dorms £12-16. MC/V. ❶

SYHA St. Andrews, Buchanan Gardens (☎476 726), in the David Russell Apartments. From City Rd., turn right onto Argyle St., continue on Hepburn Gardens, and take the right fork at Buchanan Gardens. New hostel in university housing. Hotel-style rooms suit the high prices. Open from mid-July to Sept. Singles £25; doubles £38. MC/V. ❸

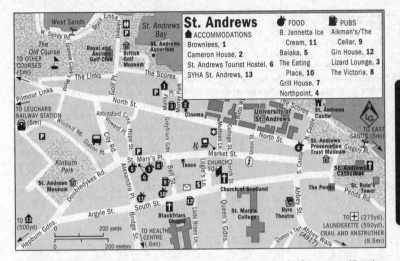

St. Andrews

FOOD

ACCOMMODATIONS
Brownlees, **1**
Cameron House, **2**
St. Andrews Tourist Hostel, **6**
SYHA St. Andrews, **13**

FOOD
B. Jannetta Ice
Cream, **11**
Balaka, **5**
The Eating
Place, **10**
Grill House, **7**
Northpoint, **4**

PUBS
Aikman's/The
Cellar, **9**
Gin House, **12**
Lizard Lounge, **3**
The Victoria, **8**

CENTRAL SCOTLAND

Brownlees, 7 Murray Pl. (☎473 868; www.brownlees.co.uk). A 19th-century Victorian house. Huge beds and TV. Plaid. Full Scottish breakfast included. Singles £34-38; doubles from £50. MC/V. ❸

Cameron House, 11 Murray Park (☎472 306). Soft crimson-hued decor and golf enthusiast owners. Walk out the front door for a sweeping view of the ocean. Singles £30-38. MC/V. ❸

🍴 FOOD

Although St. Andrews is famed for its pubs, bakeries and cafes are just as common. With a variety of high-end cuisine and plenty of late-night takeaways, you won't go hungry. Tesco **supermarket** is at 138-140 Market St. (☎413 600. Open M-Sa 7:30am-midnight, Su 10am-10pm.)

🏅**Northpoint,** 24 North St. (☎473 997). The ultimate student cafe. Hardwood tables and a steady stream of intellectual conversation complement soups (from £2.35) and sandwiches (from £4). Try the baked brie, cranberry chutney, and caramelized onion (£4.75). Happy hour 8am-10am, when all hot beverages are £1. MC/V. ❷

🏅**B. Jannetta Ice Cream,** 32 South St. (☎473 285). 52 flavors of ice cream, frozen yogurt, and sorbet made from local ingredients. Tourists shoulder up alongside hungry locals. Outdoor seating available. Open M-Sa 9am-5pm, Su 10am-5pm. MC/V. ❶

Balaka, 3 Alexandra Pl. (☎474 825), on the lower level. Celebrities and royalty, including the King of Malaysia, make pilgrimages to this house of incredible South Asian cuisine. Romantic tables and fantastic chicken *tikka masala* (£11). Open M-Th noon-3pm and 5pm-1am, F-Sa noon-1am, Su 5pm-1am. AmEx/MC/V. ❸

The Eating Place, 177-179 South St. (☎475 671). Scottish pancakes (under £5)—smaller and less sweet than your average flapjack—served up all day in this diner. Large portions. Open M 9:30am-5pm, Tu-Sa 9:30am-9pm, Su 11am-5pm. MC/V. ❷

Grill House Restaurant, St. Mary's Pl. (☎470 500), between Alexandra Pl. and Bell St. Conveniently situated downstairs from the St. Andrews Tourist Hostel. Cheerful and bright, with a large Mexican-inspired menu. Take advantage of the 2-course *prix-fixe* meal (£5). AmEx/MC/V. ❸

CENTRAL SCOTLAND

▮ PUBS

After a long day of golf, it's the 19th hole that's most important, and St. Andrews has plenty of options to choose from. Get a lesson in whisky while you tap your feet to live Scottish music at **Aikman's/The Cellar Bar,** 32 Bell St. Techno beats pound upstairs, while the basement fills with beer and good company. (☎477 425; www.aikmans.co.uk, www.cellarbar.co.uk. Open M-Sa 11am-1am, Su noon-1am.) The sleek, wooden door of the **Gin House,** 116 South St., next to the Blackfriars ruin, opens up to posh martinis in a club with comfy couches and a huge flat-screen TV. On "Scottish Sundays" the bar serves haggis, neeps, and tatties (£6.25), with major discounts on local whisky. (☎473 473; www.ginhouse.co.uk. Entrees £5-9. Open M-W and Su 10am-midnight, Th-Sa 10am-1am.) **The Victoria Cafe,** 1 St. Mary's Pl., has leather chairs, live music, and drink specials. (☎476 964. Entrees £4-8. Free Wi-Fi until 5pm. Open M-W and Su 9am-midnight, Th-Sa 9am-1am.) The **Lizard Lounge,** 127 North St., in the basement of the Oak Rooms Bar, is a good place to down a pint (2.80) and sink into the over-sized furniture. (☎473 387. Live music Th and Su night. Open M-Tu 6pm-midnight, W-Su 6pm-1am.)

◉ ▮ SIGHTS AND OUTDOOR ACTIVITIES

GOLF. If you love golf, play golf, or think that you might ever want to play golf, this is your town. It was such a popular pastime in St. Andrews that Scotland's rulers outlawed the sport three times just to get people off the links. At the northwest edge of town, the **Old Course** stretches along the **West Sands,** a beach as well-manicured as the greens. Mary, Queen of Scots, supposedly played here just days after her husband was murdered. Nonmembers must present a handicap certificate or letter of introduction from a golf club. Book at least a year or two in advance, enter your name into a near-impossible lottery by 2pm the day before you hope to play, or get in line before dawn by the caddie master's hut as a single. Tee times are easier to obtain at the less-revered but still excellent **New, Jubilee, Eden,** and **Strathyrum** courses. The budget option is the nine-hole **Balgove Course.** (☎466 666; www.standrews.org.uk, also try www.fifegolf.com for the most up-to-date information. Old Course Apr.-Oct. £80-120 per round; Nov.-Mar. £59. New, Jubilee, Eden, and Strathyrum courses £16-57 per round. Balgove course £10 per round. Club rental £20-30 per day.)

ST. ANDREWS CATHEDRAL. The haunting, romantic ruin of what was Scotland's largest building is still the heart and soul of St. Andrews, especially since its stones make up most of the facades along South St. The old cemetery has overtaken the inside, so the ruins now enclose a field of graves. The stones are beautiful in dim light, so come at dawn or dusk if you aren't interested in the museum. The square **St. Rule's Tower** still stands above the site where the Greek monk St. Rule buried the relics of St. Andrew. Climb the steep stairs in the tower for spectacular views of the sea and countryside. The **St. Andrews Cathedral Museum** houses ancient Pictish carvings and modern tombs. (☎472 563. Open daily Apr.-Sept. 9:30am-5:45pm; Oct.-Mar. 9:30am-3:45pm. Cathedral free. Museum and tower £4. Joint ticket with castle £6.)

ST. ANDREWS CASTLE. The castle features siege tunnels (not for the claustrophobic) and bottle-shaped dungeons (not for anyone). The walls were designed to keep out religious heretics, who nevertheless stormed the castle in 1546. For stellar views, descend the path south of the castle fence, where seagulls nests in the crags. (Be careful after dark. On the water at the end of North Castle St. ☎477 196. Open daily Apr.-Sept. 9:30am-6:30pm; Oct.-Mar. 9:30am-4:30pm. £5, children £2, concessions £4. Joint ticket with cathedral museum £6/2.70/4.50. Tours offered daily at 11:30am and 3:30pm.)

BRITISH GOLF MUSEUM. A huge display of golf gear punctuated with historical artifacts and mannequins, this collection holds some of the earliest spoons (clubs) and feathers (balls). Modern tributes include the sweat-stained hat that Tiger Woods wore while winning his first British Open. *(Bruce Embankment. ☎460 046. Open Apr.-Oct. M-Sa 9:30am-5:30pm, Su 10am-5pm; Nov.-Mar. M-Sa 10am-4pm. £5.25, concessions £4.25. Combined museum ticket and tour of Old Course £5.)*

UNIVERSITY OF ST. ANDREWS. Founded in 1410, Scotland's oldest university maintains a well-heeled student body (including recent alumnus Prince William) and a strong liberal arts program. Tours include tales of the school's many traditions, from polar bear swims to commencement quirks. Meander into placid quads through the entrances on North St., including **St. Mary's,** where a thorn tree planted in 1563 by Mary, Queen of Scots, still grows. *(Between North St. and The Scores. Buy tickets from the Admissions Reception, Butts Wynd, beside St. Salvator's Chapel Tower on North St. ☎462 245. 1hr. tours from mid-June to Aug. M-F 11am and 2:30pm. £5.50, concessions £4.50, children £2, under 12 free.)*

OTHER SIGHTS AND ACTIVITIES. The **St. Andrews Museum** keeps its focus off golf and on fairly obscure medieval history. *(Kinburn Park, down Doubledykes Rd. ☎412 690. Open daily Apr.-Sept. 10am-5pm; Oct.-Mar. 10:30am-4:30pm. Free.)* An olde chemist's shoppe and painful-looking dentistry tools are among artifacts in the tiny **St. Andrews Preservation Trust Museum.** *(North St. ☎477 629. Open daily June-Sept. 2-5pm. Donations welcome.)* The **St. Andrews Aquarium** houses over 100 species of wildlife and overlooks the ocean where their relatives swim free. *(The Scores. ☎474 786. Open in summer daily 10am-6pm; call for winter hours. Seal feeding 11:30am and 3pm. £6.20, concessions £5.)* From Shakespeare to off-Broadway hits, **Byre Theatre** puts on plays year-round. *(Abbey St. ☎475 000; www.byretheatre.com. Ticket prices vary, usually £12.50, concessions £8.50. Student discounts available.)* For beachgoers, the immaculate **West** and **East Sands** on either side of town are perfect for a long stroll. *(Free.)*

■ DAYTRIP FROM ST. ANDREWS: FIFE SEASIDE

"A fringe of gold on a beggar's mantle" is how James II of Scotland described these burghs, built among the sheltered bays of the Kingdom of Fife. The tidy gardens and gabled roofs of the fishing villages in the East Neuk (East Corner) stretch from Edinburgh to St. Andrews. The coastal road A917 **(Fife Coastal Tourist Route)** links the small villages, each with its own harbor attractions. Non-drivers need not worry: take a bumpy ride on the double-decker Stagecoach #95 from St. Andrews to Leven for the full coastline experience. The **Fife Coastal Walk** runs along the shore and allows for walking, hiking, and biking within and between towns.

CRAIL. The oldest of Fife's villages, Crail developed around a 12th-century castle and presents a maze of streets and stone cottages. Crail's **Tourist Information Centre,** 62-64 Marketgate, adjoins a small local history museum. *(☎01333 450 869. Open Apr.-Sept. M-Sa 10am-1pm and 2-5pm, Su 2-5pm.)* Guided walks leave from the museum. *(1½-2hr.; July-Aug. Su 2:30pm; £2, children £1.)* Visit **Crail Pottery,** 75 Nethergate, for ceramics handmade by a family of master potters, displayed in their 17th-century cottage. *(☎01333 451 212. Open M-F 9am-5pm, Sa-Su 10am-5pm.)* The **Crail Festival,** during the last two weeks of July, brings concerts, colorful parades, and craft shows.

ANSTRUTHER. The largest of the seaside towns, Anstruther lies 5 mi. west of Crail on the A917 and 9 mi. southeast of St. Andrews on the B9131. The excellent **Scottish Fisheries Museum,** Shore St., uses artifacts to tell the multi-layered story of fishing and smuggling in Fife. *(☎01333 310 628. Open Apr.-Sept. M-Sa 10am-5:30pm, Su 11am-5pm; Oct.-Mar. M-Sa 10am-4:30pm, Su noon-4:30pm. Last admission 45min. before close. £5, concessions £4.)* Six miles off the coast, the stunning mile-long **Isle of May**

Nature Reserve is home to a large population of puffins, kittiwakes, razorbills, guillemots, shags, seals, and sometimes, dolphins and whales. Inland from the towering cliffs stand the ruins of Scotland's first lighthouse and the haunted 12th-century **St. Adrian's Chapel,** named after a monk murdered here by the Danes in AD 875. From June to August, weather and tide permitting, the *May Princess* sails from Anstruther to the Isle. *(☎01333 310 103; www.isleofmayferry.com. 5hr. round-trip, including time ashore. May-Sept. £16, concessions £14, children £8. Cash only.)* Call ahead for times, or check with Anstruther's **Tourist Information Centre,** beside the museum. *(☎01333 311 073. Open Apr.-Nov. M-Sa 10am-5pm, Su 11am-4pm.)* On the way back from the bay and lighthouse, the **Anstruther Fish Bar and Restaurant ❷,** 44-46 Shore St., has repeatedly won the award for Scotland's best fish and chips (£6.30, takeaway £4.10). Watch out for the crafty seagulls who will conspire to steal your food. *(☎01333 310 518. Open daily 11:30am-10pm. MC/V.)*

SECRET BUNKER. In the 1950s, the British government built a subterranean shelter halfway between Anstruther and St. Andrews (off the A917) to house British leaders during a nuclear war. Over 20,000 sq. ft. of strategy rooms, sensory equipment, and weapons-launching systems lie 100 ft. below a Scottish farmhouse. Locals claimed knowledge of the bunker long before the "secret" broke in 1993. Take **bus** #61 Anstruther-St. Andrews, ask to get off near the Bunker, walk 1 mi. east on B940, then follow a winding road for ½ mi. *(☎01333 310 301. Open Apr.-Oct. daily 10am-5pm. £7.50, concessions £6. Group discounts available. Free Internet access.)*

ELIE. On sunny summer days, every person in Elie is either wearing a bathing suit, eating ice cream, riding a bike, or managing all three at once. Elie's sweeping beachfront is an ideal spot for water sports, walks, and (chilly) swims. The town boasts an ancient **granary** on its rebuilt 15th-century pier. The picturesque **Ruby Bay,** named for the garnets occasionally found on its red-tinted sands, is a great place to turn yourself into a floating ice cube. It's worth the short walk to the 18th-century **Lady's Tower,** where Lady Janet Anstruther built a stone changing room on the cliffs and sent a bell-ringing servant to warn villagers to keep away when she was swimming, lest some commoner see her in her scivvies. **Elie Watersports,** down Stenton Row, at the end of The Toft, gives instruction on water sports. *(☎01333 330 962; www.eliewatersports.com. Bikes £8 per ½-day, £12 per day, £35 per week. Wetsuits £10 per day. Windsurfers, canoes, dinghies, and paddleboats £14-20 per hr.; windsurfing and sailing lessons from £20 per hr. Waterskiing £18; water tube ride £7, banana boat rides £6.)* South St. is home to the oldest houses in Elie, including the **Castle** (from the 16th century). While on The Toft, check out the **Ship Inn ❷,** a classic seaside bar with light fish and chips (£8.50) and rustic outdoor seating. *(☎01333 330 246. Entrees £7-10. Open M-Th 11am-midnight, F-Sa 11am-1am, Su 12:30pm-midnight. Food served M-Sa noon-2:30pm, Su 12:30-3pm. Garden open Apr.-Aug. Su 12:30-3pm. MC/V.)* If St. Andrews (p. 576) is all booked up, golf at **Elie Sports Club.** *(☎01333 330 955. From £7 per round.)*

PERTH ☎01738

Scotland's capital until 1452, today Perth is a transportation and shopping hub with a residential feel. Providing access to nearby historical and natural sights, Perth offers tourists pleasant city walks and hikes in Kinnoull Hill Wood.

◤ TRANSPORTATION. The **train station** is on Leonard St. (open M-Sa 6:45am-8:30pm, Su 8:15am-8:25pm). **Trains** (☎08457 484 950) to: Aberdeen (1¾hr., every hr., £25.50); Edinburgh (1hr., 7 per day, £11.60); Glasgow (1hr., every hr., £11.60); Inverness (2½hr., 7 per day, £19.50). The **bus station** is a block away on Leonard St. Ticket office open M-F 7:45am-5:30pm, Sa 8am-1:30pm. Scottish Citylink (☎08705 505 050) **buses** go to: Aberdeen (2hr., 8 per day, £15.70); Dundee (35min., every hr.,

£5); Edinburgh (1½hr., every hr., £7.70); Glasgow (1½hr., every hr., £8); Inverness (2½hr., every 2hr., £14); Pitlochry (40min., every 2hr., £7). For more information, call Traveline. (☎08706 082 608. Open M-Su 8am-8pm.)

⁊ PRACTICAL INFORMATION. The **Tourist Information Centre,** Lower City Mills, books local rooms for £3 plus a 10% deposit. From either station, turn right on Leonard St., bear right onto County Pl., and take a left on Old High St. (☎450 600; www.perthshire.co.uk. Open July-Aug. M-Sa 9:30am-6:30pm, Su 10am-5pm; Nov.-Mar. M-F 9am-5pm, Sa 9:30am-4:30pm; Apr.-June and Sept.-Oct. M-Sa 9:30am-5pm, Su 11am-4pm.) Other services include: numerous **banks;** Fair City **launderette,** 44 N. Methven St. (☎631 653; wash £3, dry £1.60 per 30min.; open M-F 9am-6pm, Sa 9am-5pm); **police,** Barrack St. (☎621 141); **Perth Royal Infirmary,** Taymount Terr. (☎623 311); Superdrug **pharmacy,** 100 High St. (☎639 746; open M-Sa 8:30am-5:30pm, Su 1:30-4:30pm); **Internet** access at **Gig@Bytes,** 5 St. Paul's Sq. (☎451 580; £1.50 per 15min.; open M-Sa 10am-6:30pm), and free at the **library,** York Pl., with free membership (☎444 949; open M, W, F 9:30am-5pm, Tu and Th 9:30am-8pm, Sa 9:30am-4pm); and the **post office,** 109 South St., with a **bureau de change** (☎624 413; open M and W-Sa 9am-5:30pm, Tu 9:30am-5:30pm). **Post Code:** PH2 8AF.

⌂🞕 ACCOMMODATIONS AND FOOD. Perth has slim pickings for the budget traveler. Plenty of **B&Bs** line **Glasgow Road,** a 10min. walk from the city center, and **Pitcullen Crescent,** across the river. ◪**Hazeldene Guest House ❸** is chock full of amenities including Wi-Fi and flat-screen TV. (☎623 550; www.hazeldeneguest-house.com. Singles, doubles, and family room from £25 per person. MC/V.) **Dunal-lan House ❹,** 10 Pitcullen Crescent, has ensuite rooms with TV and white, lacy decor. (☎622 551; www.dunallan.co.uk. Free Wi-Fi. Singles, doubles, and twins from £35 per person. AmEx/MC/V.) Just up the road, **Pitcullen Guest House ❸,** 17 Pitcullen Crescent, is a more modern accommodation with a quiet garden. (☎626 506. Singles £20-35. MC/V.) Those on a tighter budget can **camp** at **Scone Camping and Caravanning ❶,** 4 mi. from the city center, next to the racetrack. Head to Scone Palace and then follow signs for the racetrack or take bus #58 to Old Scone. The site has great facilities, including laundry and table tennis, and quiet areas to pitch a tent away from the caravans. (☎552 323. Tents £3.80-5.40. MC/V.)

An enormous Morrison's **supermarket** is located on Caledonian Rd. (☎442 422. Open M-W 8:30am-8pm, Th-F 8:30am-9pm, Sa 8am-8pm, Su 9am-8pm.) Restaurants crowd the city's main streets. High-end establishments are easily visible, and more affordably priced sandwich shops and takeaway spots cluster on side streets. **Scar-amouche ❶,** 103 South St., is worn-in and homey, serving up cheap, ample portions. Great for an afternoon pint, or stay into the evening for dancing. (☎637 479. Open M-Th 11am-11pm, F 11am-11:45pm, Sa 11am-12:30am, Su 12:30-11pm. Food served noon-8pm. MC/V.) Tucked behind the vintage facade of Perth Theatre, **Red-rooms ❷,** 185 High St., combines a warm atmosphere and a theater-going crowd. The breakfasts (black pudding omelette £3.75) are quite good. (☎472 707; www.redrooms.co.uk. Entrees around £7. Open M-Sa 10am-9:30pm, Su noon-9:30pm. MC/V.) Grab a hot panini and two salads for £3-6 at the family-owned **Caffe Canto ❶,** 64 George St., by the Perth Museum. (☎451 938. Open M-W and Su 8:30am-5:30pm, Th-Sa 8:30am-8pm. MC/V.)

🞕🞕 SIGHTS AND OUTDOOR ACTIVITIES. Try on 17th-century clothing at the **Perth Museum and Art Gallery,** at the intersection of Tay St. and Perth Bridge. The old, stately museum chronicles city life and hosts exhibits by local artists. Visitors are invited to try the medieval toilet seat. (☎632 488. Open M-Sa 10am-5pm. Free.) In 1559, John Knox delivered a fiery sermon from the pulpit of **St. John's Kirk,** on St. John's Pl., sparking the Scottish Reformation. (☎638 482. Open for Su services 9:30

and 11am. Open to visitors 10am-4pm.) The **Fergusson Gallery,** in the Old Perth Water Works, at the corner of Marshall Pl. and Tay St., displays the paintings and sketches of local artist J.D. Fergusson. (☎441 944. Open M-Sa 10am-5pm. Free.) The **Perth Theatre,** 185 High St., hosts shows and concerts year-round. (☎0845 612 6320. Box office open M-Sa 10am-5pm; on performance nights 10am-8pm.) The 16th-century home of the Earls of Kinnoull, **Balhousie Castle,** off Hay St., north of the city, now functions as a regimental headquarters and houses the **Black Watch Regimental Museum.** The museum traces the history of Scottish military involvement in several wars and includes many memorials to former officers. (☎01313 310 8530. Open May-Sept. M-Sa 10am-4:30pm; Oct.-Apr. M-F 10am-3:30pm. Free.)

A 20min. walk across the **Perth Bridge** leads to **Kinnoull Hill Woodland Park** and its four nature walks, all of which finish at a magnificent summit with views of the countryside and river. Beginners can try the **Tower Walk,** while experienced hikers might choose the **Nature Walk,** which winds through the thick of the forest. The Kinnoull Hill bus runs up the hill from South St. (every hr., £1). Across the **Queen's Bridge,** near the Fergusson Gallery, the 1 mi. **Perth Sculpture Trail** begins in the Rodney Gardens and surveys 24 pieces of modern art along the river. **Bell's Cherrybank Gardens** provide a beautifully sculpted place to stroll amid 900 types of heather. Take bus #7 from South St. (every 20min.) or walk 20min. uphill along Glasgow Rd. (☎472 818; www.thecalyx.co.uk. Hours change seasonally; call ahead. Open Mar.-Oct. M-Sa 10am-5pm, Su noon-5pm; Nov.-Dec. M-Sa 10am-4pm, Su noon-4pm. £3.75, concessions £3.40, children £2.50, under 12 free.)

◼ DAYTRIPS FROM PERTH

▨**SCONE PALACE.** Scone (SKOON), 3 mi. northeast of Perth on the A93, is still occupied by the Earl of Mansfield and his family. The regal halls are lined with an impressive collection of china, portraits, ivories, and furniture, as well as the Earl of Mansfield's spectacular orchids. Find the unique holographic portrait of Queen Elizabeth II amid the descriptions of the nation's rulers. Macbeth, Robert the Bruce, and Charles II were crowned on the humble **Stone of Scone.** Peacocks roam the grounds, which include the challenging **Murray Star Maze,** with a fountain at its center. The attached cafe makes a mean scone for £1.75. *(Directly off the A94. Take bus #58 or 3 from South St. (every hr., £1) and tell the driver where you're going.* ☎*01738 552 300; www.scone-palace.co.uk. Open daily Apr.-Oct. 9:30am-5pm. £7.50, concessions £6.20, under 16 £4.20. Grounds only £4/3.65/2.75.)*

DUNKELD AND BIRNAM ☎01350

The medieval towns of Dunkeld (dun-KELD) and Birnam are separated by a small bridge over the River Tay. The region is known for the towering forests that line the river, and both towns boast famous past residents, from history's supervillain Wolf of Badenoch to the cuddly Beatrix Potter. Enjoy a pint at some of the most musical pubs in Scotland or explore the woods on one of a dozen local walks.

◪ **TRANSPORTATION.** The unstaffed **train station** in Birnam is on the Edinburgh-Inverness line. **Trains** (☎08457 484 950) run to: Edinburgh (2hr., 7 per day, £11.60); Glasgow (1½hr., 7 per day, £11.60); Inverness (1½hr., 8 per day, £19.50); Perth (15min., 7 per day, £5.50). Scottish Citylink **buses** (☎08705 505 050) leave the Birnam House Hotel to: Edinburgh (1½hr., 3 per day, £10.80); Glasgow (2hr., 3 per day, £10.80); Inverness (2½hr., 3 per day, £12.70); Perth (20min., 3 per day, £5.80); Pitlochry (20min., 3 per day, £5.50). Grab the essential *Highland Perthshire and Stanley Area Local Public Transportation Guide,* free from any TIC, or call Traveline (☎08706 082 608).

⁊ PRACTICAL INFORMATION. Nearly all public transportation arrives in Birnam (a popular Victorian vacation spot), but most tourist amenities are in more historic Dunkeld. The Dunkeld **Tourist Information Centre,** by the fountain in the town center, 1½ mi. from the train station, books beds for £3 plus a 10% deposit. (☎727 688. Open Apr.-June and Sept. M-Sa 9:30am-5pm, Su 11am-4pm; July-Aug. M-Sa 9:30am-6:30pm, Su 10am-5pm; Nov.-Mar. M and Th-Sa 9:30am-4:30pm, Su 10am-4pm.) Other services include: a **Bank** of Scotland, High St. (☎727 759; open M-F 9am-12:30pm and 1:30-5pm); Davidson's Chemists **pharmacy,** 1 Bridge St. (open M-F 9am-1pm and 2-5:30pm, Sa 9am-1pm and 2-5pm); free **Internet** access at the Birnam **Library,** Station Rd. (☎727 971; reserve a slot; open M 6am-8pm, W 2-4pm and 6-8pm, F-Sa 10am-noon); the **post office,** Bridge St. (☎727 257. Open M-W and F 9am-1pm and 2-5:30pm, Th 9am-1pm, Sa 9am-12:30pm.) **Post Code:** PH8 0AH.

⌂♥ ACCOMMODATIONS AND FOOD. The town hostel owners throw a mean *ceilidh*, but quiet **B&Bs** are easy to find throughout the two towns—the TIC has a handy list outside its office. The cozy ◙**Wester Caputh Hostel ❷** has a nice countryside location, a garden with roses and raspberries, and instruments adorning the walls. From Dunkeld, head east on the A984, turn right after the church in Caputh and right on the next block; the hostel is in the second group of buildings. (☎01738 710 449. Dorms £13. Bikes £6-10 per day. Cash only.) **Taybank Hotel ❸,** once owned by legendary folk musician Dougie Maclean of "Caledonia" fame, is by the Dunkeld Bridge and offers stylishly rustic rooms and music-themed decor. (☎727 340; www.taybank.com. Singles from £22.50; doubles from £45. MC/V.)

The Co-op **supermarket,** 15 Bridge St., is in Dunkeld. (☎727 321. Open M-Sa 8am-10pm, Su 9am-6pm.) Don't miss out on a "session" (a wee dram of something local and a song) at the **Taybank Hotel pub ❷,** where they serve "stovies" (potatoes mashed with meat or veggies; £4.35) and host casual gatherings of musicians. (☎727 340. Open M-Th 11am-11pm, F-Sa 11am-11:45pm, Su noon-11pm. MC/V.) For lunch, head to the modern **Palmerston's Coffee House and Bistro ❶,** 20 Atholl St., for freshly prepared contemporary Scottish cuisine like a baguette with venison and salad (£4.25), or have your tea with a freshly made scone for £1.30. (☎727 231. Open M-Sa 10am-5pm, Su 11am-5pm. Cash only.)

◙⚠ SIGHTS AND OUTDOORS. Carefully maintained 18th-century houses line the way to the towns' main attraction, ◙**Dunkeld Cathedral,** High St., just steps from the TIC. A peaceful spot on the grand banks of the River Tay, the cathedral still holds services and events. Its oldest sections are postcard-worthy ruins. The Wolf of Badenoch, known for his chess game with the devil and various bad deeds, rests inside the cathedral. (Open Apr.-Sept. M-Sa 9:30am-6:30pm, Su 2-6:30pm; Oct.-Mar. M-Sa 9:30am-4pm, Su 2-4pm. Free.) Beatrix Potter spent most of her childhood holidays in Birnam; at the **Beatrix Potter Garden** at the **Birnam Institute,** Station Rd., wander among the whimsical sculptures of Potter's most beloved characters. (☎727 674; www.birnaminstitute.com. Open daily 10am-4pm. Free.)

Pick up *Dunkeld & Birnam Walks* (50p) at the TIC for a guide to the many area rambles. Paths lead north from Birnam to the great **Birnam Oak,** the sole remnant of the Birnam Wood made famous by *Macbeth*. The roaring waterfalls of the ◙**Hermitage** tumble 1½ mi. away in a gorge in the middle of the ancient forest. A well-marked 1 mi. path passes through designated photo-ops. The **Birnam Hill Walk** ascends 1000 ft. and rewards dedicated climbers with vast views. Birdwatchers will enjoy the **Loch of the Lowes,** a wildlife reserve east of Dunkeld and just south of the A923 (20min. on a path from the TIC). Since 1969, the Loch has served as a summer home for ospreys who fly all the way from Gambia. (☎727 337; www.swt.org.uk. Open daily from mid-July to mid-Aug. 10am-6pm; from Apr. to mid-July and from mid-Aug. to Oct. 10am-5pm.) To **fish,** obtain a license (£3-5) from the Spar Shop, 2-3 Murthly Terr. (☎727 395. Open M-F 6:30am-8pm, Sa 7am-8pm, Su 7:30am-6pm.) Trout season lasts from mid-March to mid-October.

🢒 DAYTRIP FROM DUNKELD AND BIRNAM: THE CATERAN TRAIL. Highland Perthshire, northeast of Dunkeld and Birnam, is home to the spectacular Cateran Trail, a 64 mi. hike that heads north parallel to the A924 before looping past cairns and ruins to end at Blairgowrie. The route approximates the "Cateran Brands" trail of medieval cattle rustlers and is well-marked, although visitors are strongly encouraged to pick up Ordnance Explorer Maps #381 and 387 before setting off (available at TICs; £7.50). Five of the six trails are for beginners, and each ends in a town with several B&Bs. *(Takes approx. 4-5 days. For more information, visit www.pkct.org/caterantrail or call the Blairgowie Tourist Information Centre ☎01250 872 960.)*

KILLIN AND LOCH TAY ☎01567

The pristine Loch Tay lies southwest of Pitlochry and acts as the eastern gateway to Trossachs National Park. The Loch is bookended by the towns of Aberfeldy to the north and Killin to the south, with the A827 winding from end to end. Although difficult to reach without a car, Loch Tay provides a welcome relief from more heavily touristed areas. Killin is the best base for exploring the loch.

🢒 TRANSPORTATION. Public transportation around Loch Tay is challenging. Pick up a copy of *Highland Perthshire and Stanley Area Buses* from the Aberfeldy TIC and inquire about services that are currently running. One **postbus** per day circles Loch Tay, passing through Killin and Aberfeldy (#213; 3hr.). Other postbuses travel from Crianlarich (#973; 45min., 1 per day) and Tyndrum (#97; 45min., 1 per day). Postbuses do not run on Sunday, and coverage can be variable. Scottish Citylink bus #973 runs to Crianlarich (¼hr., M and F-Su 2 per day, £4).

🢒 PRACTICAL INFORMATION. The **Tourist Information Centre,** by the Falls of Douchart on Main St., offers information on countless local walks. (☎820 254. Open daily.) Aberfeldy also has a TIC. (☎01887 820 276. Open July-Aug. M-Sa 9:30am-6:30pm, Su 10am-4pm; Sept.-June M-Sa 10am-4pm.) Other services in Killin include: a **Bank** of Scotland (☎01877 302 000; open M-F 10am-12:30pm and 1:30-4pm); Grant's **launderette** (☎820 235; wash £2, dry 20p per 5min.; open M-Sa 9am-10pm, Su 11am-10pm); **police** on Main St. (☎820 222); **Internet** access at the Killin **Library,** Main St. (☎820 571; 30min. free, then £1 per hr.; open M 10am-1pm and 2-5pm, Tu and F 10am-1pm and 3-7pm, W 2-5pm); and the **post office** (open M-Tu and Th-F 8:30am-5pm, W 8:30am-2pm, Sa 8:30am-1pm). **Post Code:** FK21 8UH.

🢒 ACCOMMODATIONS AND FOOD. A mile from town, the **SYHA Killin ❶** is a quiet hostel in a Victorian townhouse with especially comfortable bunks. (☎820 546. Laundry £2. Internet £1 per 20min. Open Mar.-Oct. Dorms £12-13, under 18 £9. AmEx/MC/V.) Pick up **groceries** at the Co-op, Main St. (☎820 255. Open M-Sa 8am-10pm, Su 8am-8pm.) Grab homemade food from the **Coach House ❷,** Lochay Rd., down the A827 from the SYHA hostel. With local music, a small beer garden, and a bar dog, this pub provides a lively night for locals and visitors alike. (☎820 349. Open M-Th and Su 11am-8pm, F-Sa 11am-1am. MC/V.) The warm, fragrant **Shutters Restaurant ❷,** Main St. serves a homemade farmhouse breakfast all day long for £6 and has delicious soups for £1.80. (☎820 314. Open daily 10am-8pm. MC/V.)

🢒 SIGHTS AND ENTERTAINMENT. About 5 mi. past Aberfeldy on the southern shore of Loch Tay (A827) resides the **Scottish Crannog Centre,** which offers a look into the water-based dwellings and life as it was 2600 years ago. Tunic-clad guides explain why Iron Age Scots may have worn hair gel and enjoyed cheese toasties. After the tour, visitors have the chance to use Iron Age tools. (☎01887 830 583; www.crannog.co.uk. 1hr. tour, every hr. Open from mid-Mar. to Oct. daily 10am-5:30pm, last tour leaves 4:15pm; Nov. W 10am-4pm. £5, concessions £4.25. The center suggests booking ahead; inquire about group discounts.) In Killin, visit the two-room **Breadalbane Folklore Centre**, Main St., above the TIC in a mill built before written records. There, discover the legends that surround St. Fillan and view his famous healing stones. (Open daily June-Sept. 10am-6pm; Oct. and Mar.-May 10am-5pm. £2.50, concessions £1.65.) A free 2hr. hike starts from behind the schoolyard on Main St. and travels past the **Falls of Dochart**, leading to a sheep's-eye view of the loch. Encircling Loch Tay on the A87 and A827 by foot or car makes an excellent daytrip. Just outside town, follow signs to the **Moirlanich Long-house** and explore the preserved mid-19th-century home and the surrounding meadow. (☎820 988. Open May-Sept. W and Su 2-5pm; £3, concessions £2.) Heading north on the western shore of the lake, a spectacular single-track road takes you off the A827 for a scenic route up the side of mighty **Ben Lawers** to its **Visitor Centre**. The center offers information about hiking the Ben Lawers, weather conditions, and a small audio-visual display. (☎820 397. Open daily Easter-Sept. 10:30am-5pm. £2, concessions £1.) The tiny village of **Fortingall,** on the northern end of Loch Tay, is the supposed birthplace of Pontius Pilate. It is also home to a 5000-year-old yew tree, the oldest living organism in Europe. At **Dewar's World of Whisky,** ½ mi. north of Aberfeldy on the A827, take a guided tour through the distillery, which includes an interactive, audio-guided whisky exhibit and a recreated blender's lab. (☎01887 822 010; www.dewarsworldofwhisky.com. Open Apr.-Oct. M-Sa 10am-6pm, Su noon-4pm; Nov.-Mar. M-Sa 10am-4pm. £5, concessions £4.) Beginning just north of Killin, the 60 mi. **Lowland Highland Trail** leads ambitious cyclers over the famous **Highland Boundary Fault** to the south and passes through the area's varied landscapes. Pick up a trail map at the TIC in Killin (☎820 254).

PITLOCHRY ☎01796

The small, Victorian town of Pitlochry, the "gateway to the Highlands," sits at the intersection of the lowlands and the mountains. More than just a travel hub, it offers two distilleries, several famous pubs, and boundless hospitality.

⧉ TRANSPORTATION. Trains (☎08457 484 950) leave from near the town center to: Edinburgh (2hr., 7 per day, £20.80); Glasgow (1¾hr., 7 per day, £23); Inverness (1¾hr., 9 per day, £16.60); Perth (30min., 9 per day, £10). Scottish Citylink **buses** (☎08705 505 050) leave from outside the Fishers Hotel on Atholl Rd. to: Edinburgh (2hr., 10 per day, £11); Glasgow (2½hr., 5 per day, £11); Inverness (2hr., 5 per day, £11.10); Perth (40min., every hr., £7). From Perth, Pitlochry is accessible by local buses; call Traveline (☎08706 082 608) for information. Call ahead to **rent bikes** at Escape Route, 3 Atholl Rd. (☎473 859. £10 per ½-day, £18 per day. Open M-Sa 9am-5:30pm, Su 10am-5pm.) Pitlochry Backpackers (p. 588) also rents at a lower rate.

⃞ PRACTICAL INFORMATION. The Tourist Information Centre, 22 Atholl Rd., stocks *Pitlochry Walks* (50p), an essential map for hikers, and has a **bureau de change.** (☎472 751. Open July-Aug. M-Sa 9am-7pm, Su 9:30am-6pm; Nov.-Mar. M-F 9am-5pm, Sa 10am-4pm; Sept., Oct. and Apr.-June M-Sa 9am-6pm, Su 9:30am-4:30pm.) Other services include: a Royal **Bank** of Scotland, 84 Atholl Rd. (☎472 771; open M-Tu and Th-F 9:15am-12:30pm and 1:30-4:45pm, W 10am-12:30pm and 1:30-4:45pm); a **launderette,** 3 West Moulin Rd. (☎474 044; wash £3, dry £2; open M-W and F 8:30am-5pm, Th and Sa 9am-5pm); Lloyds **pharmacy,** 122-124 Atholl Rd. (☎472 414; open M-F 9am-5:30pm, Sa 9am-5pm); **Internet** access at the **Computer**

Services Centre, 67 Atholl Rd. (☎473 711; £2.75 per hr. or 5p per min.; open M-F 9am-5:30pm, Sa 9am-12:30pm); and a **post office,** 92 Atholl Rd. (open M-F 9am-12:30pm and 1-5:30pm, Sa 9am-12:30pm). **Post Code:** PH16 5BL.

▐▌▐▌ ACCOMMODATIONS AND FOOD. ▓Pitlochry Backpackers ❶, 134 Atholl Rd., in the center of town, has hand-written tips for exploring the area lining the walls. The staff keeps things lively. Rooms are big, and bike rentals are cheap at £6 per half-day. (☎470 044. Curfew M-Th and Su 1am, F-Sa 2am. Open Apr.-Oct. Dorms £12-13.50; twins £28-33; doubles £32-37. AmEx/MC/V.) Across from the TIC, **Atholl Villa ❸,** 29 Atholl Rd., provides ensuite rooms along with free parking and spacious family areas. (☎473 820. Singles £25-55; doubles £45-65. MC/V.) Orange bedspreads spice up **SYHA Pitlochry ❷,** at Knockard and Well Brae Rd., on a hill with great views of town. From the train station, turn right on Atholl Rd. and left onto Bonnethill Rd., from which the hostel is signposted. (☎472 308. Laundry £2. Internet access £1 per 20min. Reception 7am-11pm. Curfew 11:45pm. Dorms from £13, under 18 from £9.50. AmEx/MC/V.) Two miles past town on Atholl Rd., camp at **Faskally Caravan Park ❶.** (☎472 007; www.faskally.co.uk. Open from mid-Mar. to Oct. £6.80-7.50 per person. Charge for electricity, sauna, pool, and hot tub. MC/V.)

On West Moulin Rd., the Pitlochry Co-op provides **groceries.** (☎474 088. Open daily 8am-10pm.) The 300-year-old **Moulin Inn ❷,** Moulin Sq., in the wee village of Moulin just north of Pitlochry, consistently wins brewing awards. Try the signature "Braveheart Ale" (souvenir bottles available) and chow with the locals on the pub fare, including veggie options. (☎472 196. Entrees £6-12. Open M-Th and Su noon-11pm, F-Sa noon-midnight. Food served until 9:30pm. Free brewery tours M-F noon-3pm.) For Mediterranean food, head to the romantic, upscale **Fern Cottage Restaurant and Tea Room ❸,** Ferry Rd., just off Atholl Rd. The *moussaka* (£10.50) and whole stuffed vegetables (£9-13) are especially tasty. (☎473 840. Open daily 10:30am-9pm. MC/V.) End the night at **McKays ❷,** 138 Atholl Rd., the large pub next door to Pitlochry Backpackers. Long benches at large tables are great for groups. Entrees about £9. (☎473 888; www.mckayshotel.co.uk. Open M 9am-11pm, Tu-W 9am-12:30am, Th 9am-1am, F-Sa 9am-1:30am, Su 9am-midnight. MC/V.)

◨▐▌ SIGHTS AND OUTDOORS. Pitlochry stands on the cusp of the Cairngorms and serves as an entrance point to the endless miles of trails in the area. For local jaunts, **hikers** should arm themselves with *Pitlochry Walks* (50p), available at the TIC. For a quick walk around town, take the path over the suspension footbridge or the road behind the train station to the **Pitlochry Dam and Salmon Ladder.** Cross over the dam to the observation chamber, where fish struggle ceaselessly against the current as an electronic fish counter keeps tally. (☎473 152. Open July-Aug. daily 10am-5:30pm; Apr.-June and Sept.-Oct. M-F 10am-5:30pm. Observation chamber and dam free. Visitor Centre £3, concessions £2.) **Fishing permits** (£3-5 per day; from £20 for salmon fishing) are available at the TIC.

If **whisky** is the water of life, Pitlochry just might live forever. At the polished **Blair Athol Distillery,** ½ mi. from the TIC down the main road, kilted guides lead tours of the leading contributor of the famous **Bell's Blend.** (☎482 003. Open Easter-May M-Sa 9:30am-5pm; June-Sept. M-Sa 9:30am-5pm, Su noon-5pm; Oct.-Easter M-F 10am-4pm. Tours 11am, 1, and 3pm. £4, includes dram and discount voucher. MC/V.) Just 3 mi. away on a pristine lawn, **Edradour,** Scotland's smallest distillery, produces only 40 bottles per day and uses methods that seem like ancient history compared to larger distilleries. Enjoy the folksy video and tour and try a handmade sample. Edradour is a 2½ mi. walk from Pitlochry, past Moulin along the A924. (☎472 095; www.edradour.co.uk. Open Apr.-Oct. M-Sa 9:30am-6pm, Su noon-5pm; Nov.-Dec. M-Sa 9:30am-5pm, Su noon-5pm; Jan.-Mar. M-Sa 10am-4pm, Su noon-4pm. Distilling ends at 3pm. Free.)

⛶ ENTERTAINMENT. The **Pitlochry Festival Theatre,** over the Aldour Bridge, hosts traveling theater productions from larger cities at affordable prices. (☎484 626; www.pitlochry.org.uk. Ticket prices vary; concessions available.) In the recreation fields southwest of town, near Tummel Crescent, **Highland Nights** features local pipe bands and traditional folk dancing. (May-Sept. M 8pm. Tickets available at the gate. £5, concessions £3.50, children £1.) Pick up the free *What's On in Perthshire* at the TIC for other entertainment ideas.

▶ DAYTRIPS FROM PITLOCHRY

▨ BLAIR CASTLE. Emerge from the forest to discover the gleaming Blair Castle, whose white turrets burst from the wooded landscape 7 mi. north of Pitlochry on the A9. The long-time residence of the Dukes of Atholl, its 30 furnished rooms are some of the most elegant and well-preserved in Scotland, brimming with paintings and weapons used by Atholl's army, the only private army in Britain. The grounds regularly host international equestrian trials, featuring some of the world's most talented riders. *(Take the train to Blair Atholl and walk 10min., or hop on bus #87 from the West End Car Park in Pitlochry. ☎481 207; www.blair-castle.co.uk. Open Apr.-Oct. daily 9:30am-4:30pm. £7. Grounds only £2.20.)*

BEN-Y-VRACKIE. The 2757 ft. **Ben-y-Vrackie** provides views that stretch to Edinburgh on a clear day. Turn left onto the road directly behind the Moulin Inn and follow the curve until you reach a fork. At the fork, the Dane's Stone, a solitary standing stone, will be in the field right in front of you. Take the right-hand road to Ben-y-Vrackie. The left-hand road leads to **Craigower Hill** for a western view from Loch Tommel and Loch Rannoch to the Glencoe Mountains.

PASS OF KILLIECRANKIE. A few miles north of Pitlochry, right off the A9, the valley of the River Garry narrows into a deep gorge. Stop at the **National Trust Visitors Centre** down the path to learn more about the unique wildflowers that line the walk. In 1689, a Jacobite army slaughtered William III's troops here in an attempt to reinstall James VII of Scotland to the English throne. One soldier, Donald MacBean, preferring to risk the steep fall than to surrender, successfully vaulted 18 ft. across **Soldier's Leap.** The area is also home to an array of wildlife, from the buzzard to the great tit. *(Elizabeth Yule bus #87 runs from the West End Car Park to the pass in summer. ☎473 233. Open Apr.-Oct. daily 10am-5:30pm.)*

STIRLING ☎01786

Located between Edinburgh and Glasgow at the narrowest point of the Firth of Forth, Stirling controlled the flow of goods in and out of Scotland for centuries. As a result of this economic power, it has been the site of many political struggles. At the 1297 Battle of Stirling Bridge, William Wallace overpowered the English army. Despite modern development, this former royal capital hasn't forgotten its heroes: Stirling swarms with *Braveheart* fans searching for the Scotland of old.

⎕ TRANSPORTATION

The **train station** is in the town center on Goosecroft Rd. (☎08457 484 950. Travel Centre open M-F 6am-9pm, Sa 6am-8pm, Su 8:50am-10pm.) Trains run to: Aberdeen (2hr.; M-Sa every hr., Su 6 per day; £35); Edinburgh (50min., 2 per hr., £6.20); Glasgow (40min.; M-Sa 2-3 per hr., Su every hr., £6); Inverness (3hr.; M-Sa 4 per day, Su 3 per day; £53.70); London King's Cross (5½hr., 1 per day, £123.50). The **bus station** is also on Goosecroft Rd. (☎446 474. Ticket office open M-Sa 9am-5pm. Station

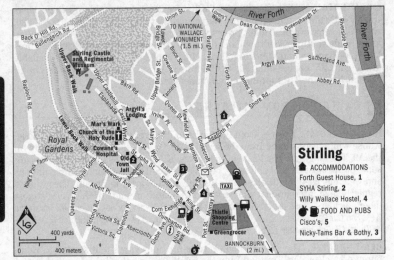

Stirling

▲ ACCOMMODATIONS
Forth Guest House, **1**
SYHA Stirling, **2**
Willy Wallace Hostel, **4**

🍴🍺 FOOD AND PUBS
Cisco's, **5**
Nicky-Tams Bar & Bothy, **3**

open M-Sa 6:45am-10pm, Su 10:15am-5:45pm.) Scottish Citylink (☎0870 505 050) **buses** run to Fort William (2¾hr., 1 per day, £15.70), Glasgow (40min., 1 per hr., £4.30), and Inverness via Perth (3¾hr., 4-6 per day, £15.30). First (☎01324 613 777) bus #38 runs to Edinburgh (1¼hr., every hr., £4.30).

🛈 PRACTICAL INFORMATION

The **Tourist Information Centre** is at 41 Dumbarton Rd. (☎475 019. Open July-Aug. M-Sa 9am-7pm, Su 9:30am-6pm; mid-June and early Sept. M-Sa 9am-6pm; from Apr. to early June M-Sa 9am-5pm; from mid-Sept. to mid-Oct. M-Sa 9:30am-5pm; from mid-Oct. to Mar. M-F 10am-5pm, Sa 10am-4pm.) City Sightseeing Stirling runs a hop-on, hop-off **tour** that departs directly from the train station, traveling on to Bannockburn, Stirling Castle, the Wallace Monument, and Stirling University. (☎446 611. £7.50, concessions £5, children £3.) Other services include: **banks** with **ATMs** on nearly every street, free **Internet** access at the **library,** Corn Exchange (☎432 107; open M, W, F 9:30am-5:30pm; Tu and Th 9:30am-7pm; Sa 9:30am-5pm); **police,** Randolphfield (☎456 000); a **launderette,** 9 Barnsdale Rd. (☎473 540; open M-F 8:15am-7pm, Sa 9am-6pm, Su 10am-5pm) and the **post office,** 84-86 Murray Pl. (☎465 392; open M-F 9am-5:30pm, Sa 9am-12:30pm), with a **bureau de change. Post Code:** FK8 2BP.

🛏🍴 ACCOMMODATIONS AND FOOD

At the bright, colorful 🏨 **Willy Wallace Hostel ❶,** 77 Murray Pl., in the center of town, a party atmosphere prevails in high-ceilinged rooms. (☎446 773. 54 beds. 1 all-female dorm. No lockable dorms, no lockers. Self-catering kitchen, laundry, and Internet access. Dorms £14. MC/V.) The **SYHA Stirling ❷,** St. John St., halfway up the hill to the castle, occupies an old Separatist Church and offers a quiet stay in small rooms. (☎473 442. 126 beds in 2- to 6-bed dorms. Self-catering kitchen, laundry, and Internet access. Curfew 2am. Dorms £15, under 18 £10.25-12. MC/V.) Near the station, **Forth Guest House ❸,** 23 Forth Pl., is a Georgian house with meticulously decorated ensuite rooms. (☎471 020. Rooms from £24 per person. MC/V.)

Tucked down an alleyway, the Greengrocer **market,** 81 Port St., has fresh fruits and veggies. (☎479 159. Open M-Sa 9am-5:30pm.) Find every sandwich combination under the sun (£1.25-3.75) as well as milkshakes and delicious homebaked cakes (50p-£1.50) at ▨ **Cisco's ❶,** 70 Port St. (☎445 900. Open M-Sa 10am-4pm. MC/V.) **Nicky-Tams Bar & Bothy ❶,** 29 Baker St., is a laid-back nighttime hangout with live music on Wednesdays and most weekends. (☎472 194; www.nickytams.co.uk. Th DJs, Su quiz night. Open M-Th and Su 11am-midnight, F-Sa 11am-1am. MC/V.)

◉ SIGHTS

▨**STIRLING CASTLE.** From atop a dormant volcano surrounded by the scenic Ochil Hills, Stirling Castle has superb views of the Forth Valley and prim gardens that belie its turbulent history. The castle's regal gargoyles presided over the 14th-century Wars of Independence, a 15th-century royal murder, and the 16th-century coronation of Mary, Queen of Scots. Beneath the cannons pointed at Stirling Bridge lie the 16th-century **great kitchens,** where visitors can walk among the recreated chaos of cooks preparing game for a royal banquet. Near the kitchens, the **North Gate,** built in 1381, is the oldest part of the sprawling complex. Beyond the central courtyard, make your way into **Douglas Garden,** named for the Earl of Douglas, who was murdered in 1452 by James II before his body was dumped here. Free 30min. **guided tours** leave twice per hour from inside the castle gates. *(☎450 000. Open daily Apr.-Oct. 9:30am-6pm; Nov.-Mar. 9:30am-5pm. Last admission 45min. before close. £9, concessions £7. Audio tour £2, concessions £1.50, children £1.)* The castle also contains the **Regimental Museum of the Argyll and Sutherland Highlanders,** which follows the regiments based at Stirling Castle. *(Open daily Easter -Sept. 9:30am-5pm; Oct.-Easter 10am-4:15pm. Last admission 15min. before close. Free.)* Many consider **Argyll's Lodging,** the 17th-century Earl's mansion below the castle, to be the most important surviving Renaissance mansion in Scotland. It has been impressively restored, with the original staircases and fireplaces intact. *(Open daily Apr.-Oct. 9:30am-6pm; Nov.-Mar. 9:30am-5pm. £4, concessions £3, children £1.60. Free with castle admission.)*

THE NATIONAL WALLACE MONUMENT. This 19th-century tower offers incredible views to those determined enough to climb its 246-step, wind-whipped spiral staircase. Halfway up, catch your breath and admire William Wallace's actual 5½ ft. sword. One can't help but wonder how he lugged that thing around all the time. *(Hillfoots Rd. 1½ mi. from Stirling proper. Sightseeing Stirling runs here, as do local buses #62 and 63 from Murray Pl. ☎472 140; www.nationalwallacemonument.com. Open daily July-Aug. 9:30am-6pm; June 10am-6pm; Sept. 9:30am-5pm; Mar.-May and Oct. 10am-5pm; Nov.-Feb. 10:30am-4pm. £6.70, concessions £5, children £4, families £17.)*

THE OLD TOWN. On Mar's Walk, **Castle Wynd,** an elaborate Renaissance facade, is all that was completed of a 16th-century townhouse before its wealthy patron died. Next door is the **Church of the Holy Rude,** which held the coronation of James VI and shook under the fire and brimstone of John Knox (p. 523). Check out the stained-glass windows and the organ, each considered among the finest in the UK. *(Open daily May-Sept. 11am-4pm. Su service July-Dec. 10am; Jan.-June 11:30am. Organ recitals May-Sept. W 1pm. Donations appreciated.)* Down the driveway lies 17th-century **Cowane's Hospital,** built as an almshouse for members of the merchant guild. *(Open M-Sa 9am-5pm, Su 1-5pm. Free.)* The ▨ **Old Town Jail,** St. John St., features reenactments of 19th-century prison life. The roof has an exhibit on prisons today and views of the Forth Valley. *(☎450 050. Open daily June-Sept. 9am-6pm; Apr.-May 9:30am-5:30pm; Oct. 9:30am-5pm; Nov.-Mar 10am-4pm. £6, students £4.50, families £15.70.)* Stirling's **town walls** are some of the best-preserved in Scotland; follow them along the **Back Walk.**

BANNOCKBURN. Two miles south of Stirling at **Bannockburn,** a statue of Robert the Bruce overlooks the field where his men defeated the English in 1314, initiating 393 years of Scottish independence. "Bannockburn" still inspires Scottish nationalist sentiment to this day. In mid-September, the site fills with falcons and archers for the annual reenactment of the Battle of Bannockburn. *(☎812 664. Heritage Centre and Shop open daily Mar.-Oct. 10:30am-4pm.)*

⚡ DAYTRIP FROM STIRLING

DOUNE CASTLE. Above a bend in the River Teith is the 14th-century fortress Doune Castle. Many of the castle's original rooms are entirely intact, most notably the great hall and the kitchen, with a fireplace large enough to roast a cow. Today, scholars of medieval architecture share the castle with Monty Python fans—many scenes from *Monty Python and the Holy Grail* were filmed here, including the ▧ **Knights of Ni.** The ticket desk provides coconut shells for reenactors. *(From Stirling, First bus #59 stops in Doune on its way to Callander (25min., every hr.). The castle is a 5min. walk from town; ask the bus driver for directions. ☎01786 841 742. Open daily Apr.-Sept. 9:30am-6:30pm; Oct.-Mar. 9:30am-4:30pm. £3.70, concessions £2.50, children £1.50)*

THE TROSSACHS   ☎01877

The lush tranquility of the Lowlands meets the rugged beauty of the Highlands in the Trossachs, Scotland's first national park. The most accessible tract of Scotland's wilderness, the mountains and lochs are popular for their moderate hikes and unbeatable beauty. Here you will find cycle routes winding through dense forest, the glassy serenity of Loch Lomond, and Scotland's most manageable peaks.

▤ TRANSPORTATION. Accessing the Trossachs is easiest from **Stirling.** First (☎01324 613 777) **bus** connects the region's main towns, running buses #59 and M59 between Stirling and Callander (45min., 12 per day, £3) and bus #11 between Stirling and Aberfoyle (45min., 4 per day, £2.50). Scottish Citylink runs a bus to Edinburgh and Callander via Stirling (1¾hr., 1 per day, £9.60). Bus service between Aberfoyle and Glasgow requires a change at Balfron. During the summer, the useful **Trossachs Trundler** (☎01786 442 707) loops between Callander, Aberfoyle, and the Trossachs Pier at Loch Katrine. One daily trip begins in Stirling and is the only public transportation that connects the Trossachs towns. (July-Sept. M-Th 4 per day; Day Rover £5, concessions £4, children £1.75; with travel from Stirling £8/6/2.50). **Postbuses** reach some remote areas of the region; find timetables at TICs or call the **Stirling Council Public Transport Helpline** (☎01786 442 707).

 TRAVELING THE TROSSACHS. Public transportation can be nearly impossible in the Trossachs, with ever-changing bus schedules and seasonal closings. Even the word "seasonal" is subjective—some summer routes don't begin until mid-July. Plan your route carefully and ask the TIC which buses are running during your visit.

▥ OUTDOOR ACTIVITIES. Get the scenic layout of the area by taking a drive or a ride on the Trossachs Trundler down the **Trossachs Trail.** Really just the A821, the road offers fantastic views of the majestic Loch Katrine, the setting of Sir Walter Scott's *The Lady of the Lake.* The popular **Steamship Sir Walter Scott** cruises Loch Katrine from Trossachs Pier, stopping at Stronachlachar on the northwest bank in the mornings. (☎376 316. Apr.-Oct. M-Tu and Th-Su 11am, 1:45, and 3:15pm; W 1:45 and 3:15pm. 45min. tour £6.50, children £4.50; 1hr. tour £7.50, children £5.50.) At

Loch Lomond and The Trossachs National Park

ACCOMMODATIONS
Lomond Woods Holiday Park, **6**
Station Cottages, **7**
SYHA Inveraray, **1**
SYHA Loch Lomond, **5**
SYHA Rowardennan, **3**
Trossachs Backpackers, **2**
Trossachs Holiday Park, **4**
Forest Areas

the pier, rent **bikes** from **Katrinewheelz.** (☎376 316. ₤15 per day, ₤10 per ½-day.) For a good daytrip, take the ferry to Stronachlachar and then walk or ride back along the 14 mi. wooded shore road to the pier. Above the loch hulks **Ben A'an** (1187 ft.), a reasonable 2 mi. ascent beginning from a car park lot 1 mi. down the A821.

Set beside the quiet River Teith, the town of **Callander** makes a good base for exploring the Trossachs and lies close to outdoor attractions. Dominating the horizon, **Ben Ledi** (2883 ft.) is a manageable trek. A 6 mi. trail up the mountain begins just north of town along the A84. A number of walks depart from Callander itself: **The Crags** (6½ mi.) heads up through the woods to the ridge above town, while the popular walk to **Bracklinn Falls** (5 mi.) wanders along a picturesque glen. In Callander, cyclists can join **The Lowland Highland Trail**, a lovely stretch running north to Strathyre along an old railway line. Passing through forest and beside Loch Lubnaig, a sidetrack from the route runs to **Balquhidder,** where Rob Roy, Scotland's legendary patriot, and his family are buried. The renegade's surname, MacGregor, was outlawed in Scotland, but his grave is marked by a stone reading, "MacGregor Despite Them." Callander's **Rob Roy and Trossachs Visitor Centre,** Main St., is a combined TIC and exhibit on the 17th-century local hero. Pick up Ordnance Survey maps, Explorer #378 (₤7.50), or Landranger #57 (₤6.50). Walkers will find the *Callander Walks and Fort Trails* pamphlet (₤2) useful, and cyclists can consult *Rides Around The Trossachs*. (☎330 342. Open daily June-Sept. 10am-6pm; Mar.-May and Oct. 10am-5pm; Nov.-Feb. 11am-4pm. Exhibit ₤3.60, concessions and children £2.40, families £9.60.) Rent **bikes** at **Cycle Hire Callander**, Ancaster Sq., beside the TIC. (☎331 052. £10 per day, £7 per ½-day. Open daily 9am-6pm. MC/V.)

Aberfoyle is another springboard into the surrounding wilderness. The **Queen Elizabeth Forest Park**, established in 1953 to celebrate her coronation, covers a vast stretch of territory from the shore of Loch Lomond to the slopes of the Strathyre Mountains, with Aberfoyle at its center. For more information on trails, visit the **Trossachs Discovery Centre**, a TIC in town. (☎382 352. Open July-Aug. daily 9:30am-6pm; Apr.-June and Sept.-Oct. daily 10am-5pm; Nov.-Mar. Sa-Su 10am-5pm.) A walk from town leads to the top of **Doon Hill** (2 mi.), where the ghost of Reverend Robert Kirk is supposedly trapped in an ancient pine. After publishing *The Commonwealth* in 1661 and exposing the world of elves and pixies, legend says the good reverend was spirited away and entrapped in the giant pine tree on top on Doon Hill, clad in nothing but his knickers.

⌂⬚ ACCOMMODATIONS AND FOOD. For lodgings and hiking, the star of the region is ▨**Trossachs Backpackers ❷**, Invertrossachs Rd. A TV lounge, barbecue, kitchen, and cycle hire await visitors, making it worth the 1½ mi. walk from Callander's town center. (Hostel ☎331 200, bike hire 331 100. 32 beds in 2- to 8-bed rooms. Breakfast included. Laundry. Bikes £13 per day, £8 per ½-day. Dorms £15. MC/V.) In Callander's center, **White Shutters B&B ❷**, 6 South Church St., is just steps from the main road. There are no ensuite rooms, but the owners make a delicious hot breakfast. (☎330 442. £18 per person, £17 for more than one night. Cash only.) In Aberfoyle, keep an eye out for deer and foxes near **Corrie Glen B&B ❹**, Manse Rd., where the modern decor and bright colors almost make you forget that you're out in the wild. (☎382 427. Open Mar.-Nov. Singles from £30; doubles from £25 per person. Cash only.) Limited **camping** is available at the well-equipped **Trossachs Holiday Park ❶**, 2 mi. south of Aberfoyle on the A81, with a game room and TV lounge that are nicer than those at most hostels. (☎382 614; www.trossachsholidays.co.uk. Toilets, showers, laundry, and bike rental. Open Mar.-Oct. £10-16. AmEx/MC/V.) Co-op **grocery** stores and **banks** with **ATMs** are easily found in both Callander and Aberfoyle, as well as a number of bakeries and eateries whose delicious aromas fill the towns' centers. **Munchy's Restaurant ❷**, Main St., Callander, has wholesome, home-cooked vittles like haddock and chips. (☎331 090. Open in summer M and W-Sa 10:30am-7pm, Su noon-7pm. Cash only.)

LOCH LOMOND AND BALLOCH   ☎01389

Immortalized by the famous ballad, Loch Lomond and its surrounding wilderness continue to awe visitors. Britain's largest lake is dotted by 38 islands, and its proximity to Glasgow makes it the perfect destination for a daytrip. The bonnie banks get crowded, especially during summer, when daytrippers pour into the area's largest town. A short walk from the southern tip of the lake, Balloch sits beside the River Leven and is a good transportation hub.

◨⬚ TRANSPORTATION AND PRACTICAL INFORMATION. The Balloch **train station** is on Balloch Rd., across the street from the TIC. **Trains** (☎08457 484 950) depart to Glasgow Queen St. Monday through Saturday, and to Glasgow Central on Sunday (45min., 2 per hr., £3.80). Scottish Citylink (☎08705 505 050) runs frequent **buses** between Glasgow and Balloch (45min., 7 per day, £4.30), leaving about 1 mi. from the town center, north of the Balloch roundabout. These buses continue along the loch's western shore to Luss and Tarbet. First runs #204, 205, and 215 from Glassford St. between Glasgow and Balloch Town Center (1½hr., frequent, £3.80). To reach the eastern side of the loch, take bus #309 from Balloch to Balmaha (25min., 7 per day, £1.80). Bus #305 heads for Luss (15min., 9 per day,

₤1.50). Macfarlane's **mailboat** takes passengers between the lake's four inhabited islands, leaving Balmaha at 11:30am (10:50am in winter) with a 1hr. lunch stop on Inchmurrin (2½hr; July-Aug. M and W-Sa; May-June and Sept. M, Th, and Sa; Oct.-Apr. M and Th; weather permitting; ₤8, children ₤4). Balloch's **Tourist Information Centre,** Balloch Rd., is in the Old Station Building, across the street from the end of the platform, and has a **bureau de change.** (☎753 533. Open daily July-Aug. 9:30am-6pm; May 10am-5pm; June 9:30am-5:30pm; Sept. 10am-5:30pm.) The larger **National Park Gateway Centre** sits 1 mi. to the north at the Loch Lomond Shores complex. (☎722 199. Open daily Apr.-Sept. 9:30am-6:30pm; Oct.-Mar. 10am-5pm.)

█ ACCOMMODATIONS. Hostels don't get much grander than **█SYHA Loch Lomond ❷,** a turreted 19th-century tobacco baron's mansion 2 mi. north of Balloch on the A85. Adventure-seekers can ask for the haunted room. Citylink buses to Oban and Cambelltown stop right outside, as do buses #305 and 306 from Balloch—just be sure to tell the driver where to let you off. From the train station, turn left and follow the main road ¾ mi. to the second roundabout. Turn right, continue 1½ mi. and turn left at the sign for the hostel; it's a short walk up the hill. (☎850 226. Self-catering and far from a grocer; be sure to bring food with you. Laundry and Internet access. Open Mar.-Oct. Dorms ₤15, under 18 ₤11. MC/V.) On Loch Lomond's eastern shore, the **SYHA Rowardennan ❶,** the first hostel along the West Highland Way, overlooks the lake and is convenient for exploring the region. From Balloch, take the bus to Balmaha and walk 8 mi. along the well-marked path. (☎0870 004 1148. 75 beds. Laundry and basic groceries. Curfew 11:30pm. Open Apr.-Oct. Dorms ₤12-13.50, under 18 ₤9-9.50.) **B&Bs** congregate on Balloch Rd., close to the train station and TIC. Across from the train station, **Station Cottages ❸,** Balloch Rd., provides a peaceful and luxurious environment. (☎750 759. ₤30 per person. MC/V.) The **Lomond Woods Holiday Park ❶,** Old Luss Rd., up Balloch Rd. from the TIC, is a convenient place to park your caravan. Self-catering holiday homes are also available for rent and are popular with groups. (☎755 000. Laundry, pool table, and table tennis. July-Aug. ₤20; Sept.-June. ₤15-17. Home rental prices vary with season from ₤30-82. MC/V.)

█▲ HIKING AND OUTDOOR ACTIVITIES. Stock up on supplies and information at the TIC or Gateway Centre. Ordnance Survey Explorer maps #347 and 364 (₤7.50) chart the south and north of the loch, respectively, while Landranger map #56 (₤6.50) gives a broader view of the entire region. The **West Highland Way** runs 95 mi. from Milngavie to Fort William and skirts Loch Lomond's eastern shore, allowing for long walks. *The West Highland Way* official guide (₤15) includes maps for each section of the route. Rising above all, **Ben Lomond** (3195 ft.) is the southernmost of Scotland's 284 Munros (peaks over 3000 ft.). A popular walk departs from the 19th-century **Balloch Castle and Country Park,** across the River Leven from the train station, where you will find both a visitors center and park ranger station. (Castle closed to the public.) Outside of **Balmaha,** the strenuous 5 mi. hike up **Conic Hill** rewards hikers with magnificent views of the loch. Visitors can arrange a short boat ride with MacFarlanes mailboat (☎01360 870 214) from Balmaha to the island of **Inchcailloch,** where a 1½ mi. walk surrounds a nature preserve. The **Glasgow-Loch Lomond Cycleway** runs 20 mi. from the city to the lake along mostly traffic-free paths. At Balloch, where the route ends, **National Cycle Route #7** heads east to the Trossachs; the smaller **West Loch Lomond Cycle Path** follows the lake to the west.

Loch Lomond Shores is the region's lakeside visitor complex, full of eateries and gift shops designed to ensure that tourists leave with empty wallets. Its centerpiece, **Drumkinnon Tower,** is home to the new **Loch Lomond Aquarium.** (☎721 500. Open daily 10am-5pm. ₤8, students ₤7, children ₤5.50.) Across from the Shores, rent bikes or paddle boats from **Can You Experience,** which also offers guided paddling and cycling tours. (☎602 576; www.canyouexperience.com. Bikes £15 per day, £10 for 4hr. Canoes £15 per hr., £10 per 30min. MC/V only.) **Sweeney's Cruises** provide one of the best introductions to the area with 1-2hr. tours, departing from the Balloch TIC on the River Leven and from Loch Lomond Shores in the summer. (☎752 376; www.sweeneyscruises.com. Every hr. 10:30am-4:30pm. 1hr. tour £5.50, children £3, families £19.50. 2hr. tours daily 1 and 3pm. £12, children £6, families £32. Evening tours daily 7:30pm. £9.50, children £5, families £26.) Avert your eyes (or don't) from the nudist colony on one of the islands.

INVERARAY   ☎01499

In the 18th century, the Duke of Argyll tore down and rebuilt the town of Inveraray to make room for his very own lakefront castle. The resulting village retains a regal air, although Loch Fyne is the main attraction. Today, palatial **Inveraray Castle** is still home to the Duke and Duchess of Argyll. The third Duke of Argyll built the castle as a sign of a more peaceful era in Scottish history, although it still bristles with an array of weapons. (☎302 203. Open June-Sept. M-Sa 10am-5:45pm, Su 1-5:45pm; Apr.-May and Oct. M-Sa 10am-1pm and 2-5:45pm, Su 1-5:45pm; last admission 5pm. £6.30, concessions £5.20, children £4.10, families £17. Grounds free.) *Five Walks in Inveraray Estate* (£1), available from the TIC or castle, details short walks (1-2½ mi.) that leave from the castle car park, touring the forest and the top of **Dun na Cuaiche.** The morbid **Inveraray Jail** welcomes visitors with a "Torture, Death, and Damnation" exhibit. Guests can try the Whipping Table, sit in on a 19th-century court scene, or try to stop the wax figures from branding (melting) each other with hot irons. (☎302 381. Open daily Apr.-Oct. 9:30am-6pm; Nov.-Mar. 10am-5pm. Last admission 1hr. before close. £6.25, concessions £4.15, children £3.15, families £17.20.) A receipt from the jail also saves visitors 20% on entry to the buoyant **Inveraray Maritime Museum,** inside the schooner *Arctic Penguin* on the pier. Visitors can read Valentines that sailors carved out of shells and whales' teeth for their honeys back home, or learn about the *Penguin's* history as one of the last iron sailing ships. (☎302 213; www.inveraraypier.com. Open daily 10am-6pm. £3.80, concessions £2.80, children £2.20, families £11.)

Relax in the privacy of 2- to 4-bed dorms in the small, basic **SYHA Inveraray ❷,** on the northern edge of town on Dalmally Rd. Take a left through the arch next to the Inveraray Woollen Mill onto Oban Rd. (☎08700 041 125. Self-catering kitchen. Lockout 11am-5pm. Curfew 11:30pm. Open Apr.-Sept. Dorms £13, under 18 £9. MC/V.) The **Creag Dhubh ❸,** a 7min. walk south along Newton Rd. away from town, has views of the loch and a luxurious lounge. (☎302 430. Singles from £35; doubles £27-30 per person. Cash only.) Cafes, tearooms, and a **grocery store** line Main St.

Scottish Citylink **buses** (☎08705 505 050) connect Inveraray with Glasgow (1¾hr., 6 per day, £8) and Oban (1hr., 3 per day, £7). The **Tourist Information Centre,** Front St., has **Internet** access (£1 for 15min.) and books accommodations for £3 plus a 10% deposit. (☎302 063. Open July-Aug. daily 9am-6pm; early Apr. M-Sa 10am-5pm, Su noon-5pm; from late Apr. to June M-Sa 9am-5pm, Su 11am-5pm; Sept.-Oct. daily 10am-5pm; Nov.-Mar. daily 10am-3pm.) The **police** are on the A89 (☎302 222) and the **post office** is on Main St. South. (☎302 062. Open M-Tu and Th-F 9am-1pm and 2-5:30pm, W 9am-1pm, Sa 9am-12:30pm.) **Post Code:** PA32 8UD.

OBAN   ☎01631

The saltiest ferry port on Scotland's west coast, Oban (OH-ben; pop. 8500) welcomes thousands of visitors bound for the Inner Hebrides every summer, making the colorful town a fine base for exploring the islands and Argyll countryside.

C TRANSPORTATION. The **train station** (☎08457 484 950) is on Railway Pier. **Trains** run from Oban to Glasgow Queen St. (3hr., 3 per day, £17). Scottish Citylink **buses** (☎08705 505 050) leave from the train station to Fort William (1½hr., M-Sa 4 per day, £8.20) and Glasgow (3hr.; M-Sa 6 per day, Su 5 per day; £13.40).

Caledonian MacBrayne **ferries** sail from Railway Pier to the Inner Hebrides and the southern Outer Hebrides. Pick up an *Explorer* timetable at the ferry terminal or TIC. Ferries go to: Craignure, Mull (45min.; M-Sa 7 per day, Su 5 per day; extra sailings July-Aug.; £4.15); Lismore (50min., M-Sa 2-4 per day, £3); Colonsay (2½hr., M and W-Su 1 per day, £11.50); Tiree (3¾hr., 1 per day, £13) via Coll (2¾hr.); South Uist (7hr., 4 per week, £20.30) via Barra (5hr.). Passengers with a car should book ahead. Ferry services are reduced in winter. (☎566 688, reservations 08705 650 000. Terminal open M 6am-6pm, Tu and Th 6:45am-6pm, W 4:45am-8pm, F 4:45am-10:30pm, Sa 5:45am-8pm, Su 7:45am-6pm.)

From Oban, several operators offer **day tours** to the isles of Mull, Iona, and Staffa. From April to October, **Bowman's Tours,** across from Railway Pier, runs daily to Mull and Iona and adds Staffa for a bit more money. (☎812 313. Mull and Iona £31.40, children £17; including Staffa £44/23.)

⚎ ☷ ORIENTATION AND PRACTICAL INFORMATION. Corran Esplanade runs along the coast north of town, **Gallanach Road** along the coast to the south. Fronting the harbor, **George Street** is the heart of Oban. A block inland, **Argyll Square** defies geometry and is actually a roundabout. The **Tourist Information Centre,** Argyll Sq., inhabits the vaulted interior of an old church and books beds for £3 plus a 10% deposit. (☎563 059. Open late June-Aug. M-Sa 9am-7pm, Su 9am-7pm; from late Apr. to mid-June M-Sa 9am-5:30pm, Su 10am-5pm; Sept.-Oct. M-Sa 9am-5:30pm, Su 10am-4pm; Nov.-Mar. M-F 9:30am-5pm, Sa 10am-5pm, Su noon-5pm.) **Internet** access is available in the Oban **Library,** Albany St. (free; open M and W 10am-1pm and 2-7pm, Th 10am-1pm and 2-6pm, F 10am-1pm and 2pm-5pm, Sa 10am-1pm), and at the TIC (£1 per 12min.). Boots **pharmacy,** 34-38 George St., is on the north harbor (open M-Sa 8:45am-5:30pm). Rent **bikes** at **Evobikes,** 29 Lochside St., across from the Tesco. (☎566 996. £15 per day, £10 per ½-day. Open Feb.-Oct. M-Sa 9am-5:30pm; Nov.-Mar. M-Tu and Th-Sa 9am-5pm.) There are **post offices** in Tesco, Lochside St. (☎510 450; open M-Sa 8am-6pm, Su 10am-1pm) and on Corran Esplanade across town (open M-F 9am-5:30pm, Sa 9am-1pm). **Post Code:** PA34 4HP.

☖ ACCOMMODATIONS. The waterfront ◪SYHA Oban ❶, Corran Esplanade, lies ¾ mi. north of the train station, just past St. Columba's Cathedral. Enjoy spacious dorms and sea views from bay windows, but beware of the strict no-alcohol policy. (☎562 025. 128 beds in 6- to 10-bed dorms plus 42 beds in 4-bed ensuite rooms. Laundry and Internet access. Reception until 11:30pm. Curfew 2am. Handicapped-accessible. Dorms £13-15, under 18 £9-13; private rooms from £30. MC/V.) A party atmosphere pervades ◪Oban Backpackers ❶, 21 Breadalbane St., part of the Scotland's Top Backpackers chain and often filled with enthusiastic (read: drunk) MacBackpackers groups. You'll still sleep soundly in the blissfully soft beds. Take George St. away from Railway Pier and bear right at the first fork; the hostel is on the right. (☎562 107. 48 beds in 6- to 12-bed single-sex dorms. Self-catering kitchen. Breakfast £2. No lockable dorms, no lockers. Safe at reception. Laundry £2.50. Internet access 80p per 30min. Curfew M-Th and Su 12:30am, F-Sa 2am. 18+. Dorms £12.50. AmEx/MC/V.) **Corran House ❷,** 1-2 Victoria Crescent, sits near the water north of the train station, affiliated with (and located on top of) Markie Dan's Ale House. (☎566 040. 36 beds in 2- to 6-bed dorms and 11 private rooms with TV. Self-catering kitchen. Donation expected for breakfast. No lockable dorms, no lockers. Laundry £5. Dorms £14-16; private rooms £25-35. MC/V.) B&Bs abound in the hills near the pier—call the TIC for the cheapest available option.

■☑ FOOD AND PUBS. Pick up **groceries** at Tesco, Lochside St. (open M-Sa 8am-10pm, Su 9am-6pm). Abundant fish and chips shops line the pier area, proving that seafood is what Oban does best. Splurge on fine food and finer wine at **Ee'Usk ❸**, on the North Pier, Oban's best seafood restaurant. (☎565 666. Open daily noon-3pm and 6-10pm. MC/V.) **O'Donnell's Irish Pub ❶**, Breadalbane St., across the street from Oban Backpackers, draws a young backpacking crowd to its underground digs with live music, karaoke, and quiz nights. (☎566 159. Open M-W 4pm-1am, Th 4pm-2am, F and Su 2pm-2am, Sa noon-2am; reduced low season hours.) **Markie Dan's ❶**, Victoria Crescent, off Corran Esplanade under Corran House, has live music, drink specials, and a jovial bar staff. (☎564 448. Open daily 11am-1am.)

◙ SIGHTS. If your feet are hurting from a long day of wandering the pier, a stop at the renowned **■Oban Distillery** will cure all your aches and pains with a free sample of the local malt whisky following a 45min. tour. (☎572 004. Open July-Sept. M-F 9:30am-7:30pm, Sa 9:30am-5pm, Su noon-5pm; Apr.-June and Oct. M-Sa 9:30am-5pm; Mar. and Nov. M-F 10am-5pm; Dec.-Feb. call ahead. Tours every 15min. in summer, less frequent in low season; call ahead for reservations. £5.) The Colosseum-esque structure dominating the skyline is **McCaig's Tower.** Commissioned at the end of the 19th century by John Stuart McCaig, it was intended as an art gallery, but construction was abandoned when McCaig died. Take the steep stairway at the end of Argyll St., then turn left along Ardconnel Rd. and right up Laurel St. (Always open. Free.) North of town, the ivy-covered ruins of 7th-century **Dunollie Castle,** Oban's oldest building, sit atop a cliff. From town, walk 20min. north along the water until you've curved around the castle, then take the overgrown path up the hill. (Perfect for hide-and-seek. Always open. Free.)

▧ DAYTRIPS FROM OBAN

KERRERA. Across the bay from Oban is the beautiful, nearly deserted isle of Kerrera (CARE-er-uh), where a no-car policy (the only motor vehicles are owned by the 30 residents) guarantees a peaceful habitat for seals and eagles. Ringed by a network of gravel roads, Kerrera makes for great walking and mountain biking. From the ferry landing, turn left and follow the road for 2½ mi. to the southern tip of Kerrera, where tiny **Gylen Castle** stands atop the cliffs in an isolated spot overlooking the sea. Enjoy a hearty meal made with home-grown veggies or spend the night in the cozy **■Kerrera Bunkhouse and Tea Garden ❶**, 2 mi. from the pier near the castle. Plans are in the works for a creative studio with facilities for photography, painting, video, writing, and music. (☎570 223. Tea Garden open Easter-Oct. W-Su 10:30am-4:30pm. 7 beds. Self-catering kitchen with free tea and coffee. Dorms £12. Cash only.) A **ferry** crosses to Kerrera from a pier 2 mi. south of Oban along Gallanach Rd. Turn the board to the black side to signal that you wish to cross. The ferryman also dispenses helpful maps of the island. (☎563 665. In summer daily 2 per hr. 10:30am-12:30pm and 2-6pm, also M-Sa 8:45am; in winter 5-6 per day, but call ahead. Round-trip £4, children £2; bikes 50p.)

ISLE OF ISLAY   ☎01496

Although it may be known to many as "Whisky Island," the Isle of Islay (EYE-luh) has more to offer than its famed "liquid sunshine." Birdwatchers, walkers, and cyclists are greeted by sweeps of empty coastline and woodland paths. The island's eight distilleries are home to some of the world's finest single malts.

⌐ TRANSPORTATION

CalMac **ferries** (☎302 209) leave from **Kennacraig Ferry Terminal,** 7 mi. south of Tarbert on the mainland Kintyre Peninsula, and sail to Port Askaig and Port Ellen (Port Askaig 2hr.; Port Ellen 2¼hr.; 1-4 per day; £8.40). To reach Kennacraig, take Scottish Citylink **bus** #926 (☎08705 505 050) running between Glasgow and Campbeltown (Glasgow to Kennacraig 3½hr.; M-Sa 4 per day, Su 1-2 per day). Travelers going to Arran can catch bus #448 from Kennacraig to the Claonaig ferry landing (15min., M-Sa 3 per day, £2.60) or call a taxi (☎01880 820 220; approx. £15). On Wednesdays in summer, a ferry leaves Oban, stops on Colonsay, and continues to Port Askaig (4hr., £12). The comprehensive *Islay and Jura Area Transport Guide,* available at TICs, has more on these services and island bus timetables. Islay Coaches (☎840 273) operates a few daily buses between Islay towns. Bus #451 connects Port Ellen and Port Askaig via Bowmore (M-Sa 5-6 per day); bus #450 and **postbus** #196 (☎01246 546 329) run from Port Ellen to Port Charlotte via Bowmore (M-Sa 5-6 per day). Many bus times apply to schooldays only, so read schedules carefully. **Hitchhikers** may find more success here than on the mainland, although rides may be sparse off the main roads. *Let's Go* does not recommend hitchhiking. British Airways Express **planes** (☎08705 444 000) fly from Glasgow Airport to the Islay Airport, located between Port Ellen and Bowmore (45 min., 1-3 per day, £40). For **taxis,** contact Carol's Cabs (☎302 155, mobile 0777 578 2155; www.carols-cabs.co.uk), which provides 24hr. service and **island tours.**

PORT ELLEN

Port Ellen lacks the usual bustle of a ferry town. Its white houses and empty streets are quieter than the island's other main villages, but it serves as a base for many walks and bicycle journeys. To the west, the windswept coast **Oa** (OH-uh) drops dramatically into the sea. A 1½ mi. walk along the Oa road leads to the solar-powered **Carraig Fhada lighthouse,** one of the few square lighthouses in Scotland. Beyond the lighthouse lies crescent-shaped **Traigh Bhan,** a favorite beach of many locals who frequent its "singing sands" in the summer heat. A longer trek (about 6 mi.) will bring you to the end of the peninsula and a massive **American Monument,** built to commemorate two ships that were sunk off this point in 1918. Heading east along the A846, you will find three of Islay's finest distilleries: ▨**Laphroaig** (2 mi.; ☎302 418; tours M-F, call ahead; visitors center open M-F 9am-7pm), **Lagavulin** (3 mi.; ☎302 730; guided tours M-F 9:30, 11:15am, and 2:30pm), and **Ardbeg** (4 mi.; ☎302 244; tours June-Aug. M-F 10:30, 11:30am, 2:30, and 3:50pm; Sept.-May M-F 11:30am and 2:30pm). They're easy to get to by bus, but traveling between them is best done by bike (unless you've been enjoying too many whisky samples). Behind Lagavulin, the grass-covered rubble of 16th-century **Dunyvaig Castle** looms beside the sea. Just past Ardbeg you will come across the **Loch an t-Sailein,** known as "Seal Bay" for its breeding colonies. Another 3 mi. east along the A846 from Ardbeg, 12th-century **Kildalton Chapel** holds the ▨**Kildalton High Cross,** a carved Celtic blue stone thought to date from the mid-8th century.

In town, Mr. and Mrs. Hedley's ▨**Trout Fly Guest House ❸,** 8 Charlotte St., has tartan carpets and rooms across from the ferry. (☎302 204. No smoking. £27 per person. Cash only.) On the eastern coast, the **Kintra Farmhouse B&B ❸** stands on a working farm. (☎300 090. From £25 per person. Cash only.) Kintra also welcomes **camping ❶** in the dunes at the southern end of the **Big Strand** (p. 600), where beachside fires are permitted. (Toilet and showers. Open Apr.-Sept. £14 for 2 people, including tent.) To reach Kintra from Port Ellen, take the Mull of Oa road 1 mi., then follow the right fork for 2¼ mi. In Port Ellen, Frederick Crescent rings the harbor and has a Co-op for **groceries.** (☎302 446. Open M-Sa 8am-8pm, Su 12:30-7pm.) The **Mactaggart Community Cyber Cafe ❶,** 30 Mansfield Pl., offers diner-style

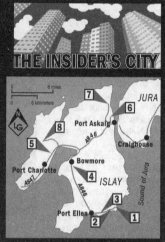

THE WHISKY TRAIL

Islay is renowned for its malt whis-
kys and boasts eight distilleries.
The island's malts are known for
their peaty flavor, which is not surprising given that half of Islay is a
peat bog. The island's clean environment and fresh water supply
are ideal for a flourishing whisky
trail. What gives each malt its distinctive flavor? Water supply, air
quality, temperature, the barley—
even the shape of the pot-still
(distilling structure). Pick up *The
Islay and Jura Whisky Trail,* free at
TICs, or use our guide:

1 Ardbeg: (☎302 244), on the
southeast coast, 4 mi. from
Port Ellen. The peatiest of the
island's malts. Ardbeg is rapidly emerging as one of Islay's
best. Tours M-Sa. £2.

2 Lagavulin: (☎302 400), 3 mi.
from Port Ellen. Check out the
massive washbacks that overflow with foam during the fer-
menting process. Tours M-F. £4.

meals (cheeseburger and fries £3.20), satellite TV,
and a pool table. (☎302 693. Internet access £1 per
30min. Pool 30p per 30min. Open daily noon-7pm.
Food served until 6:30pm.) **Bike rental** is available
from Port Ellen Playing Fields, at the edge of town on
B846. (☎302 349 or 07831 246 911. £7 per day, £4 per
½-day. Open May-Sept. daily noon-4pm and 6-9pm.)
There is a **bank** in town, but no **ATM.**

BOWMORE

Located 10 mi. from both Port Ellen and Port Askaig,
Bowmore maintains charm even though it is Islay's
largest town. It is arranged in a grid centering on
Main Street, with the 18th-century **Bowmore Round
Church** at the top. The church was built perfectly circular to keep Satan from hiding in corners. (Open
daily 9am-6pm. Free.) Across from the TIC, the **Bowmore Distillery,** School St., is the island's oldest. (☎810
671; www.bowmore.com. Open July-Sept. daily 9am-
5pm; Easter-June M-Sa 9am-5pm; from mid-Sept. to
Easter M-F 9am-5pm, Sa 9am-noon. Tours M-F 10,
11am, 2, and 3pm, and Sa 10am. £2, under 18 free.)
The **Big Strand,** 7 mi. of white-sand beach with waves
perfect for **bodysurfing** (if you can stand the cold),
lines the coast between Bowmore and Port Ellen.

Among a flock of similarly priced B&Bs, the
friendly proprietors of the **Lambeth Guest House ❸,**
Jamieson St., offer decent lodgings supplemented by
good conversation. (☎810 597. No singles. From £22
per person. AmEx/MC/V.) A small Co-op sells **groceries** on Main St. (☎810 201. Open M-Sa 8am-8pm, Su
12:30-7pm.) The **Harbour Inn Restaurant ❺** serves
excellent local seafood. (3 courses £25. Food served
daily noon-2pm and 6-9pm; bar open M-Sa 11am-1am,
Su noon-1am. MC/V.)

Islay's **Tourist Information Centre,** Main St., books
accommodations for £3 plus a 10% deposit. Ordnance
Survey Explorer #352 and 353 (£8) and Landranger
#60 (£7) maps cover Islay. *The Isles of Islay, Jura
and Colonsay Walks* (£2) details hikes. (☎810 254.
Open July-Aug. M-Sa 9:30am-5:30pm, Su 2-5pm; May-
June M-Sa 9:30am-5pm, Su 2-5pm; Apr. M-Sa 10am-
5pm; Sept.-Oct. M-Sa 10am-4pm; Nov.-Mar. M-F
10am-4pm.) Other services include: two **banks** with
ATMs; a launderette and **swimming pool** in the Mactaggart Leisure Centre, School St. (☎810 767; wash
£3.75, dry £1.75 for 15min.; swimming £2.70, children
£1.70; open Tu 12:30-9:30pm, W 11am-9:30pm, Th-F
12:30-9pm, Sa 10:30am-5:30pm, Su 10:30am-5:30pm);
Internet access at the **Servicepoint** on Jamieson St.
(☎301 301; open M-F 9am-5pm); and the **post office,**
Main St. (☎810 366; open M-W and F 9am-5:30pm, Th
9am-1pm, Sa 9am-12:30pm), which also rents **bikes**
(£10 per day). **Post Code:** PA43 7JH.

ISLE OF JURA ☎01496

Separated from Islay by a narrow strait, the Isle of Jura (Deer Island) has grown more wild and isolated during the past century. A census in 1841 found 2299 people; today, less than 200 call the island home. Living in scattered houses along a single-track road on the eastern shore, these hardy folk are outnumbered by deer 30 to one. Jura was remote enough to satisfy novelist George Orwell, who escaped to Jura while penning *1984*. The entire western coast and center of the island is uninhabited, offering true wilderness for explorers. Its great **hiking** country includes a series of tough ascents up the three **Paps of Jura** (all over 2400 ft.), scaled by runners in the annual Jura Fells Race in May. The land surrounding **Loch Tarbet** is harsh but beautiful. At the island's northern tip, the **Corryvreckan Whirlpool**—the second largest in the world—churns violently. Ordnance Survey Explorer #353 (£8) and Landranger #361 and 61 maps cover the island and *Jura: A Guide for Walkers* (£3.50) details various hikes. More conservative walkers will enjoy the rare plant species that inhabit the **Jura House Walled Garden.**

Although the distance between Islay and Jura is short, do not attempt the swim, as tidal currents are powerful. The Jura **Ferry** (☎840 681) takes cars and passengers across the Sound of Islay from Port Askaig to Feolin (5min.; in summer M-Sa 13-16 per day, Su 6 per day; in winter times more limited; £2.70). During the summer and on weekdays during the school year, the Jura **Bus Service** meets the ferry by request (☎820 314 or 820 221).

CRAIGHOUSE. Jura's only village is a tiny, one-road settlement 10 mi. north of the ferry landing. At the center of Craighouse, the **Isle of Jura Distillery** employs 5% of the island's population and offers tours by appointment. (☎820 385. Shop open Easter-Oct. M-F 10am-4pm.) Nearby, a small, unstaffed **information center** has walking and wildlife guides. More detailed information and free **Internet** access can be found a 5min. walk down the street from the distillery, headed away from the ferry, at the **Jura Service Point** (☎820 161; open M-F 10am-1pm). Craighouse is home to one hotel and a couple of B&Bs. The only restaurant in Craighouse is in the **Jura Hotel ❷**, where bar lunches (noon-2pm) and evening meals (7-9pm) average £5-12. The hotel also offers **camping ❶** on its front lawn. (☎820 243; www.jurahotel.co.uk. Camping free. Laundry, showers, and toilets available for a fee. Hotel from £35 per person. AmEx/MC/V.) Jura has **no banks,** but the hotel will give

3 **Laphroaig** (la-FROYG): (☎302 418), 2 mi. from Port Ellen. In Gaelic its name means "beautiful hollow by the broad bay." Considered by many to be Islay's finest malt. Tours M-F 2 per day. Often closed July-Aug. Call ahead. £2-4. Info Center M-F 9am-5pm.

4 **Bowmore:** (☎810 441), in town. The oldest of Islay's distilleries in full operation (est. 1779) and one of the last to malt its own barley. Tours M-F 4 per day, Sa 1-4 per day. £4.

5 **Bruichladdich** (brook-LAD-dee): (☎850 190), 2 mi. from Port Charlotte. A smoother malt, produced with 19th-century equipment. The only one on Islay that bottles its own product. Tours M-F 3 per day, Sa 2 per day. £4.

6 **Caol Ila** (cool-EE-la): (☎302 760), 1 mi. from Port Askaig. Fine views across the sound and a complimentary swig. Tours Apr.-Sept. by appointment. £4.

7 **Bunnahabhain** (bun-na-HAV-en): (☎840 646). Home to the "Black Bottle," containing all seven of Islay's malts. Tours M-F 3 per day. Free.

8 **Kilchoman:** (☎850 011) Islay's newest distillery is at Rockside Farm, 4 mi. from Port Charlotte. But don't expect a dram on your tour—bottles won't be out until 2011. Tours daily 2 per day. £2.

cash back on purchases. There's also a van run by the Royal Bank of Scotland that functions as a **bank on wheels** and is in town from about 1-3pm on Wednesdays. Across from the distillery, Jura Stores sells **groceries** and houses a **post office.** (☎820 231. Store open M-Th 9am-1pm and 2-5pm, F-Sa 9am-1pm and 2-4:30pm. Post office open M-Tu and Th-F 9am-12:30pm, W 9-9:30am, Sa 9am-1pm and 2-4:30pm.) **Post Code:** PA60 7XS.

ISLE OF MULL

Never thought you'd see palm trees in Scotland? Welcome to Mull, the largest (pop. a whopping 2800) and most accessible of the Inner Hebrides. Towering mountains, remote glens, and pristine coastline reward explorers who venture beyond the well-trodden routes. Much of Mull's Gaelic heritage has yielded to the pressure of English settlers, who now comprise over two-thirds of the population, but life-long locals keep tradition alive.

▐ TRANSPORTATION

CalMac (Craignure Office ☎01680 812 343) runs a **ferry** to Oban from Craignure (45min.; M-Sa 6 per day, Su 5 per day; more in July-Aug.; £4.10). Smaller ferries run from Lochaline on the Morvern Peninsula, north of Mull, to Fishnish, on the east coast 6 mi. northwest of Craignure (15min.; M-Sa 13-14 per day, Su 9 per day; £2.80), and from Kilchoan on the Ardnamurchan peninsula to Tobermory (35min.; M-Sa 7 per day; June-Aug. also Su 5 per day; £4). Winter schedules are reduced. **Day tours** run to Mull, Iona, Staffa, and the Treshnish Isles from Oban (p. 596). Pick up a copy of the Explorer CalMac timetable for comprehensive listings.

Check the sometimes erratic **bus** times to avoid stranding yourself. Bowman Coaches (☎01680 812 313) operates the main routes. Bus #496 meets the Oban ferry at Craignure and goes to Fionnphort (1¼hr.; M-F 4 per day, Sa 3 per day, Su 1 per day; round-trip £10). Bus #495 runs between Craignure and Tobermory via Fishnish (50min.; M-F 6 per day, Sa 4 per day, Su 3-4 per day; round-trip £7.30). R.N. Carmichael (☎01688 302 220) #494 links Tobermory and Calgary (45min.; M-F 4 per day, Sa 2 per day; round-trip £3.80). TICs stock copies of the comprehensive (but confusing) *Mull and Iona Area Transport Guide.*

▟ ORIENTATION

Mull's main hubs, **Tobermory** (northwest tip), **Craignure** (east tip), and **Fionnphort** (FINN-a-furt; southwest tip), form a triangle bounded by the A849 and A848. A left turn off the **Craignure Pier** leads 35 mi. along the southern arm of the island to Fionnphort. There, the ferry leaves for **Iona**, a tiny island to the southwest.

▟ ▟ HIKING AND OUTDOOR ACTIVITIES

The Isle of Mull features a range of terrain for hikers, from headland treks to sea-to-summit ascents to gentle forest strolls. The coastline has some of the most scenic paths, and paths inland run over mountains and deep glens. Ordnance Survey Landranger Maps #47-49 (£6) cover Mull, while *Walking in North Mull* and *Walking in South Mull and Iona* (£4 each) highlight individual trails. From Tobermory, a 2 mi. walk departs from the Royal Lifeboat Station at the end of Main St. and follows the shore to a **lighthouse.** Outside of Craignure, the **Dun da Ghaoithe Ridge** walk begins just past the entrance to Torosay Castle on the A849. This 11 mi. route ascends 2513 ft., follows a ridge with views over the Sound of Mull, and finishes on the A848 on the bus route. Popular climbs up

Ben More (3169 ft.) and Ben Buie (2352 ft.) start from the sea. You can also take the bus along the road to ⬛Calgary Bay, where stretches of white-sand beach and rocky headland border the water. The council permits free short-term camping in the bay, which has toilets but no drinking water. In Tobermory, Tackle and Books, 10 Main St., runs 3hr. fishing trips suited to experienced anglers and first-timers alike. (☎302 336. Trips Apr.-Oct. 2-5pm. Call in advance to arrange a sailing. £18, children £15. Store open M-Sa 9am-5:30pm, Su 11am-4pm.) Tobermory is also home base for wildlife tours. The boats of Sea Life Surveys, on Main St. by the bus stop, head out in search of whales, seals, and basking sharks. (☎01688 302 916; www.sealifesurveys.com. 3-6 trips per day. Call ahead. £12-60, children £6-35.)

CRAIGNURE
☎01680

Craignure, Mull's main ferry port, is a tiny town with one main street. From the pier, turn left and take the first left again to reach Mull Rail, where you can ride a vintage narrow-gauge toy of a train that will make you feel like a giant. (☎812 494; www.mullrail.co.uk. Runs from mid-Mar. to mid-Oct. 4-11 per day. Round-trip £4.50, children £3, families £13. MC/V.) The train rolls 1 mi. south to Torosay Castle. Most people visit for the gardens, but the house itself encourages visitors to take a seat and browse the family's scrapbooks. A 1 mi. walk leads from Craignure to the house; take the footpath that veers off the main road past the police station. (☎812 421. Open Apr.-Oct. daily 10:30am-5pm. Gardens open Apr.-Oct. daily 9am-7pm. £6, concessions £5.50, children £3.20, families £17. Gardens only £5/4/2.80/15.) Farther along the coast, spectacular ⬛Duart Castle, a 700-year-old stronghold 4 mi. from Craignure, remains the seat of the MacLean clan chief. It is the most widely photographed attraction on Mull, with its ancient keep and dungeons still intact. The bus runs to the end of Duart Rd., 2 mi. from the castle. (☎812 309; www.duartcastle.com. Open May-Oct. daily 10:30am-5:30pm; Apr. M-Th and Su 11am-4pm. £5.50, concessions £5, children £3, families £13.) The Duart Castle Coach meets the ferry from Oban. (May-Oct. £9 for coach and castle.)

Every tent has stunning sea views at ⬛Shieling Holidays Campsite ❶, a short walk to the left of the ferry terminal. Super-clean toilet and shower facilities, a TV lounge, and a variety of permanent tents with gas cookers provide hostel-like accommodations. (☎812 496; www.shielingholidays.co.uk. Open from late Mar. to Oct. Tent sites from £12.50, with car from £14.50; bed in permanent tent £10. Bedding £2. MC/V.) Aon a'Dha ❷, 1-2 Kirk Terr., ½ mi. from the ferry, has beds at bargain prices. (☎812 318. Breakfast £3. £15 per person. Cash only.)

Across from the ferry, the Tourist Information Centre books rooms for £3 plus a 10% deposit. (☎812 377. Open July-Aug. M-F 8:30am-7pm, Sa-Su 10am-6:30pm; Apr.-June and Sept.-Oct. M-F 8:30am-5:15pm, Sa-Su 10:30am-5:30pm; Nov.-Mar. M-Sa 9am-5pm, Su 10:30am-noon and 3:30-5pm.) The adjoining CalMac ferry office is Mull's largest. (☎08705 650 000. Open from 1hr. prior to the first ferry until the last ferry leaves.) Rent bikes at Kells Gallery and Craft Shop, near the TIC. (☎812 580. £12 per day, £6 per ½-day. Open daily 9am-7pm.) Although the closest bank is in Tobermory, get cash back at Spar on the main street, which also has a post office. (☎812 301. Store open M 7:30am-7pm, Tu-Sa 8am-7pm, Su 10am-7pm. Post office open M-W and F 9am-1pm and 2-5pm, Th and Sa 9am-1pm.) Post Code: PA65 6AY.

TOBERMORY
☎01688

Bright buildings surround a leisurely fishing harbor in Mull's largest town. Just across from the bus stop is the Tobermory Distillery, which conducts 30min. tours and offers samples of the "water of life." (☎302 645. Open M-F 10am-5pm. Tours every hr. 11am-4pm. £3, seniors £2. Reservations recommended.) Farther along Main St., the tiny Mull Museum chronicles the island's history with local artifacts.

(Open Easter-Oct. M-F 10am-4pm, Sa 10am-1pm. £1, children 20p.) During the last weekend of April, Tobermory hosts the **Mull Music Festival,** and the first week of July brings the **Mendelssohn Festival** with concerts in churches and castles. Much of the composer's work was inspired by the Hebridean Isles. The **Mull Highland Games** feature caber-tossing, hammer-throwing, and bagpipes (3rd Th of July).

The pink-painted **SYHA Tobermory ❶,** on the far end of Main St. from the bus stop, has bright rooms with bonnie sea views. (☎302 481. 39 beds. Internet 5p per min. Open April-Oct. Dorms £12.50, under 18 £9. MC/V.) Cheaper **B&Bs** line Breadalbane St. above the bay. **Failte Guest House ❸** is one option on waterfront Main St., spoiling visitors with comfortable ensuite rooms and great breakfasts. (☎302 495. From £25 per person. MC/V.) The Co-op **supermarket,** Main St., sits opposite Fisherman's Pier. (☎302 004. Open M-Sa 8am-8pm, Su 12:30-7pm.) Grab fish and chips (£3.50) from the stall on **Fisherman's Pier ❶.** (Open in summer M-Sa 12:30-9pm.) The **Island Bakery and Delicatessen ❶,** 26 Main St., offers sandwiches, pizzas, and an impressive array of local cheeses. (☎302 225. Open Apr.-Oct. M-W 9am-5:30pm, Th-Sa 9am-7:30pm, Su noon-4pm; Nov.-Mar. M-Sa 9am-5:30pm. Cash only.)

Tobermory's **Tourist Information Centre,** on the pier near the bus stop, sells tour tickets and books rooms for £3 plus a 10% deposit. (☎302 182. Open late Apr.-June M-F 9am-5pm, Sa-Su 11am-5pm; early Apr. M-F 9am-5pm, Sa-Su noon-5pm; July-Aug. M-Sa 9am-6pm, Su 10am-5pm; Sept.-Oct. M-Sa 9am-5pm, Su noon-5pm.) Other services include: a **CalMac** office next to the TIC (☎302 517; open M-F 9am-5:30pm, Sa 9am-1pm and 2-4pm); **bike rental** at Archibald Brown & Son, 21 Main St. (☎302 020; £10 per ½-day, £15 per day; open M-Sa 8:45am-1pm and 2-5:30pm); Clydesdale **bank,** Main St., the only bank and **ATM** on the island (open M-Tu and Th-F 9:15am-4:45pm, W 9:45am-4:45pm); **Internet** access with printer- and webcam-equipped computers at **Posh Nosh Cafe/Restaurant,** on Main St. next to the Co-op (☎302 499; £1.50 for 30min., 75p for each subsequent 15min.; open daily 10am-10pm); and the **post office,** 36 Main St. (open M-Tu and Th-F 9am-1pm and 2-5:30pm, Sa 9am-1pm). **Post Code:** PA75 6NT.

IONA, STAFFA, AND TRESHNISH ISLES

The isolation and rugged beauty offered by these tiny islands off Mull's west coast make them worth the effort it takes to get there. Of the three, **Iona,** birthplace of Christianity in Scotland, is the only one that is still inhabited. **Staffa** rises from the sea 8 mi. north of Iona—its towering basalt columns are natural masterpieces. The **Treshnish Isles** teem with rare birds and other wildlife.

Iona is the only island accessible by public ferry; the other two must be seen by tour. CalMac **ferries** (Fionnphort office ☎01681 700 559) sail between Iona and Fionnphort (5min., frequent, round-trip £3.75). **Tours** of Staffa and the Treshnish Isles, although organized, are usually self-directed. During the summer, **Gordon Grant Tours** (☎01681 700 338; www.staffatours.com) send boats from Fionnphort to Staffa (2½hr., £17) and the Treshnish Isles (5½hr., £37). **The Kirkpatricks** (☎01681 700 358) offer daily cruises to Staffa from Fionnphort and Iona (3hr.; from Iona 9:45am and 1:45pm; from Fionnphort 10am and 2pm; £18, children £8). **Turus Mara** operates tours that leave from the town of Ulva Ferry on Mull. (☎08000 858 786. Staffa and Iona £27.50, children £14. Staffa and Treshnish Isles £35/17.) Day tours also operate from Oban (p. 596).

IONA   ☎01681

The isle of Iona (pop. 150) beckons travelers with white-sand beaches, brilliant blue waters, and rugged hills. For nearly two centuries after Irish St. Columba landed on this island in AD 563, Iona was one of Europe's cradles of Christianity. A 13th-century **nunnery,** one of the better-preserved medieval convents in Britain, faces visitors as soon as they step off the ferry. Signs lead from the nunnery to the **Iona Heritage Centre,** which traces the history of the island from St. Columba through WWII. (☎ 700 576. Open Easter-Oct. M-Sa 10:30am-4:30pm. £2, concessions £1.50.) The centerpiece of the island is **Iona Abbey,** a 13th-century structure on the site of St. Columba's original monastery. Follow signs from the pier to the abbey. (☎ 700 512. Open daily Apr.-Sept. 9:30am-6:30pm; Oct.-Mar. 9:30am-4:30pm. Services daily 9am, 2, and 9pm; Su 10:30am and 9pm. £4.50, concessions £3, children £2.20.) Next to the abbey, **St. Columba's Shrine** contained relics of St. Columba until they were brought back to Ireland in the 10th century for protection from Viking raids. Tiny 12th-century **St. Oran's Chapel** is the oldest ecclesiastical building on the isle. The burial ground supposedly holds 48 kings, including Macbeth. Question: if a sheep falls in Iona and nobody shears it, does it make a sound?

On the isle's north end, the isolated ⬛**Iona Hostel ❷,** on a working croft 1½ mi. from the pier along the road past the abbey, seeks to reunite its guests with nature. There is no TV, radio, or Internet, but postcard-perfect beaches nearby are ideal for contemplative walks. (☎ 700 781; www.ionahostel.co.uk. 21 beds in 2- to 6-bed dorms. Dorms £17.50, children £12. Cash only.) The island has scattered **B&Bs** by the pier; call the Tobermory TIC to book ahead, as the small number of rooms fill up fast. Get your **groceries** at Spar, uphill from the ferry. (☎ 700 321. Open Apr.-Oct. M-Sa 9am-5:30pm, Su noon-5pm; Nov.-Mar. M-Sa 10am-1pm and 2-4pm.) The **Argyll Hotel ❸** serves fine cuisine with ingredients straight from the organic garden outside. (☎ 703 334; www.argyllhoteliona.co.uk. Entrees £8.50-£12.50. Food served 12:30-2pm, 3-5pm, and 7-8pm. MC/V.)

Left of the pier, Finlay Ross rents **bikes** and runs a **launderette.** (☎ 700 357. Bikes £4.50 per ½-day, £8 per day. £10 deposit. Laundry £5. Open M-Sa 10am-5:15pm, Su 11am-4:30pm.) The **post office** is near the pier. (☎ 700 515. Open M-Tu and Th-F 9am-1pm and 2-5pm, Sa 9am-12:30pm.) **Post Code:** PA76 6SJ.

STAFFA. Sixty million years ago, lava was cooled by the sea and formed the hexagonal basalt columns that have made Staffa famous. Ringed by treacherous cliffs, the 80 acres of soil that blanket the stone were inhabited by a handful of hardy folk as recently as the late 18th century. All that remain today are the ruins of a building erected in 1820 and a colony of puffins. At low tide, enter ⬛**Fingal's Cave** and marvel at its natural basalt cathedral. When rough seas roar into the cavern, the noise echoes off the walls. The pounding waves inspired one of Felix Mendelssohn's most famous works, the *Hebrides Overture.*

TRESHNISH ISLES. The Treshnish Isles are a paradise for all kinds of wildlife, especially birds. Unthreatened by humans, the animals tolerate up-close examination on these isolated islands, which require a bit of rock scrambling to explore. Along the cliffs of Lunga, birds perch on one of the only remnants of human habitation, a 13th-century **chapel.** Legend holds that monks from Iona buried their library on one of the Treshnish Isles to save it from pillage during the Reformation. Many have tried digging for it, so far without luck.

HIGHLANDS AND ISLANDS

Misty and remote, the untamed wilds of the Scottish Highlands have long been the stuff of legend and fantasy. These sheep-dotted moors, sliced by the narrow lochs of the Great Glen and framed by stoic granite mountain ranges, have endured for thousands of years. Once home to kilted clans, the Highlands' current residents include some of Scotland's last Gaelic-speaking Scots, artisans, and crofters. Raging winds and ocean currents can be forbidding, but the land's unparalleled beauty draws thousands of visitors every year.

HIGHLIGHTS OF THE HIGHLANDS AND ISLANDS

CLIMB Ben Nevis, the highest mountain in the Britain, whose 4406 ft. peak hides behind a layer of clouds. On a clear day, you can see all the way to Ireland (p. 628).

DISCOVER an unparalleled wealth of ancient ruins set amid sheep, sky, and ocean in the **Orkney and Shetland Islands** (p. 657).

TREK through the mighty **Cuillin Mountains** and misty waters of the **Isle of Skye** (p. 632).

▶ TRANSPORTATION IN THE HIGHLANDS AND ISLANDS

Although it's possible to travel through the Highlands in the summer months, advance planning is essential, as bus and train schedules seem to shift with the winds. In winter, treacherous weather conditions and many fewer buses and trains make travel even more difficult. The essential *Public Transport Travel Guides* (£1), available at TICs, are region-specific and up-to-date. **Trains** (☎08457 484 950) travel to major destinations and shipping areas, and Scottish Citylink **buses** (☎08705 505 050) often connect train travelers to smaller towns. Citylink offers an **Explorer Pass** (3 consecutive days £35, 5 days in 10 £59, 8 days in 16 £79), which includes 50% off on CalMac ferries. The Royal Mail operates a postbus service (www.postbus.royalmail.com) that is often the best way to access remote areas in summer months. **Driving** in the Highlands is more convenient but involves navigating single-lane roads, icy winter conditions, and sheep with a death wish (see **By Car,** p. 35). Most **ferries,** especially on the west coast, are operated by Caledonian MacBrayne (CalMac; ☎08705 650 000; www.calmac.co.uk). Peruse the website for the combination ticket (the "Island Hopscotch" pass) that best suits your trip.

NORTHEAST SCOTLAND

ABERDEEN   ☎01224

On sunny days, Aberdeen's (pop. 210,000) stark grey buildings have a towering, elegant appeal. In poor weather, the uniform architecture of the "Granite City" can be downright discouraging. A healthy student population along with a number of city parks and museums all add color to a city that has struggled to define itself away from its industrial and shipping roots.

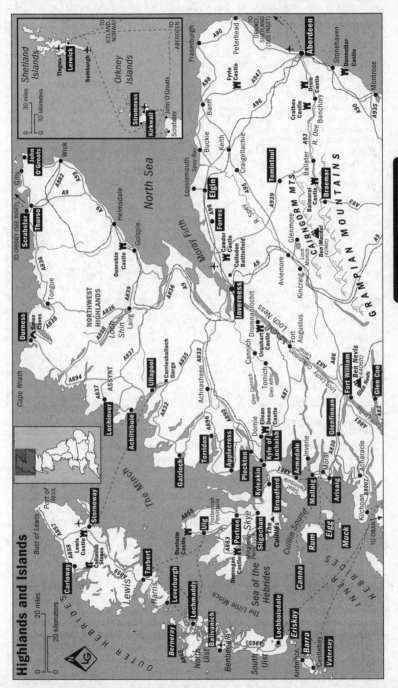

HIGHLANDS
AND ISLANDS

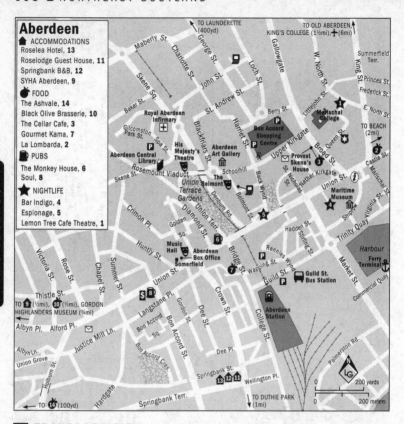

Aberdeen

ACCOMMODATIONS
Roselea Hotel, 13
Roselodge Guest House, 11
Springbank B&B, 12
SYHA Aberdeen, 9

FOOD
The Ashvale, 14
Black Olive Brasserie, 10
The Cellar Cafe, 3
Gourmet Kama, 7
La Lombarda, 2

PUBS
The Monkey House, 6
Soul, 8

NIGHTLIFE
Bar Indigo, 4
Espionage, 5
Lemon Tree Cafe Theatre, 1

TRANSPORTATION

Flights: Aberdeen Airport (☎08700 400 006; www.aberdeenairport.com). Stagecoach Bluebird #10, 307, and 737 run to the airport from the bus station (every hr., 7:20am-7:20pm, £1.30) and First (☎650 065) #27 runs from Guild St. (every hr. until 7:20pm, £1.45). British Airways (☎08457 733 377) flies to **London** (11 per day, £30-105).

Trains: Station on Guild St. Ticket office open M-F 6:30am-7:30pm, Sa 7am-7pm, Su 8:45am-7:30pm. Trains (☎08457 484 950; www.firstscotrail.com) to: **Edinburgh** (2½hr., every hr., £36.40); **Glasgow** (2½hr., every hr., £36.40); **Inverness** (2¼hr., every 1½hr., £22.40); **London King's Cross** (7½hr., 3 per day, £132).

Buses: Station on Guild St. (☎212 266). Ticket office open M-F 8:30am-6pm, Sa 8:30am-5pm. National Express (☎08705 808 080) to **London** (2 per day, £19). Mega-bus (☎09001 600 900) to **London** (2 per day, £19). Scottish Citylink (☎08705 505 050) to **Edinburgh** and **Glasgow** (both 4hr., every hr., £20.70). Stagecoach Bluebird (☎212 266) #10 to **Inverness** (4hr., every hr., £8.10).

Ferries: Aberdeen Ferry Terminal, Jamieson's Quay (☎08456 000 449; www.northlink-ferries.co.uk). Turn left at the traffic light off Market St. onto Commercial Quay. Open Tu, Th, and Sa-Su 7am-5pm; M, W, F 7am-7pm. Northlink Ferries run to **Kirkwall, Orkney** (6hr.; Tu, Th, and Sa-Su 5pm; round-trip from £24.30) and **Lerwick, Shetland** (12-14hr.; M, W, F, and Su 7pm; Tu, Th, and Sa 5pm; round-trip from £39.30).

Local Transportation: First Aberdeen, 47 Union St. (☎650 065), runs public **buses.** Office open M-Sa 8:45am-5:30pm. Unlimited day travel £3.50.

Car Rental: Major car rental companies have offices at the airport and in town. **Arnold Clark Car Hire** (☎249 159; www.arnoldclarke.com) is one of the cheapest. 23+. Open M-F 8am-8pm, Sa 8am-5pm, Su 9am-5pm. From £19 per day, £99 per week.

Taxis: Com Cabs (☎353 535).

🛈 PRACTICAL INFORMATION

Tourist Information Centre: 23 Union St. (☎288 828; www.agtb.org). From the bus station, turn right on Guild St., then left on Market St.; take the 2nd right on Union St. Books rooms for £3 plus a 10% deposit. Open July-Aug. M-Sa 9am-6:30pm, Su 10am-4pm; Nov.-Mar. 9am-4:30pm; Apr.-June, and Sept.- Oct. M-Sa 9am-5:30pm.

Tours: Grampian Coaches (☎650 024; www.firstgroup.com) runs various day tours to nearby castles, Royal Deeside, the Whisky Trail, Loch Ness, and beyond. June-Sept. £15-20, concessions £11-14.

Financial Services: Banks are ubiquitous. **Thomas Cook,** 335-337 Union St. (☎807 000). Open M-W and F-Sa 9am-5:30pm, Th 10am-5:30pm.

Beyond Tourism: Volunteer Service Aberdeen, 38 Castle St. (☎212 021; www.vsa.org.uk or www.volunteerscotland.org). Open M-Th 9:15am-12:30pm and 1:30-4:15pm, F 10am-12:30pm and 1:30-4:15pm.

Launderette: A1, 555 George St. (☎621 211). Full service £9.50. Open daily 8am-6pm.

Police: Queen St. (☎08456 005 700).

Hospital: Aberdeen Royal Infirmary, on Foresterhill Rd. (☎681 818).

Pharmacy: Boots, Bon Accord Shopping Centre (☎626 080). Open M-W and F-Sa 8:30am-6pm, Th 8:30am-8pm, Su 10:30am-5:30pm.

Internet Access: Free in the Media Centre of the **Aberdeen Central Library,** on Rosemount Viaduct (☎652 532). Open M-Th 9am-7pm, F-Sa 9am-5pm. The city has many cafes offering Internet access, including **The Hub,** 22 John St. (☎658 844). £1.50 per 30min. Open M-F 8am-5pm, Sa-Su 11am-5pm. **Books and Beans,** 22 Belmont St. (☎646 438). £3 per hr. Open M-Sa 10am-5pm, Su 11am-4pm.

Post Office: 489 Union St. **Bureau de change.** Open M-F 9am-5:30pm, Sa 9am-12:30pm. **Post Code:** AB11 6AZ.

🏠 ACCOMMODATIONS

With only one hostel convenient to the city, Aberdeen few budget accommodations. **B&Bs** pepper **Bon Accord** and **Springbank Terrace,** near the train station. From the bus and train stations, turn south from Guild St. on College St., then west on Wellington Pl., which melds into Springbank Terr. Generally, the farther away from Union St., the cheaper the accommodation.

THE REAL DEAL. The weekend is the best time for a stopover in Aberdeen. During the week, oil rig workers fill up hotel and B&B rooms, driving up prices. When the workers leave the city, many rates are slashed significantly.

SYHA Aberdeen, 8 Queens Rd. (☎646 988). A long walk on Union St. and Albyn Pl. or a short ride on bus #14, 15, or 27. In an old stone house, with a large dining room. Free parking. Breakfast £2.60. Laundry. Internet access £1 per 20min. Reception 7am-11pm. Curfew 2am. Seasonal dorms £12-15, under 18 £7.75-12. AmEx/MC/V. ❶

Roselodge Guest House, 3 Springbank Terr. (☎586 794). Vegetarian breakfasts and small rooms with a few housecats. Singles £28-35; doubles £45-50. Cash only. ❸

Springbank B&B, 6 Springbank Terr. (☎592 048). Family-owned B&B with comfortable furniture and dim, tidy rooms. Singles £30-35; doubles £40-45. Cash only. ❸

Roselea Hotel, 12 Springbank Terr. (☎583 060; www.roseleahotel.demon.co.uk). Family-owned with large roses outside. Singles from £28; doubles from £39. MC/V. ❸

🞄 FOOD

Save money at Somerfield **supermarket,** 204 Union St. (☎645 583. Open M-W and Sa 8am-8pm, Th-F 8am-9pm, Su 10am-7pm.) **Union Street** and its branches feature dozens of restaurants offering international cuisine.

▨ **The Ashvale,** 42-48 Great Western Rd. (☎596 981). The award-winning Ashvale serves up the best fish and chips around (£6.65). The adventurous can try the deep-fried 9 in. pizza (£2.45). Open daily 11:45am-1am. MC/V. ❷

La Lombarda, 2-8 King St. (☎640 916), by the TIC. A romantically lit Italian restaurant in the pedestrian-only district. Extensive menu of pasta, pizza, and risotto (£8-9); meat and fish (£11-17); and lunch entrees (£5). Outdoor seating available. Open M-Th and Su 10am-2pm and 5-9:30pm, F-Sa 10am-2pm and 5-10pm. AmEx/MC/V. ❷

Black Olive Brasserie, 32 Queens Rd. (☎208 877), up the street from the SYHA Hostel, away from town. Modern food served in a crisply decorated, glass-enclosed sun room. Starters like the asparagus and parmesan tart (£5) make excellent snacks. Entrees £6-12. Open M-Sa 10am-10pm; summers also Su 11am-6:30pm. AmEx/MC/V. ❷

The Cellar Cafe, Provost Skene's House (☎01224 522 743). After touring the reconstructed rooms in the house, enjoy the cafe fare in the fortified basement. Tall windows keep it pleasant. Lunch £4, muffins 95p. Open M-Sa 10am-4:45pm. MC/V. ❶

Gourmet Kama, 20 Bridge St. (☎575 754; www.gourmetkama.co.uk). Hole-in-the-wall serving delectable fare straight from Delhi. Sit-down and takeaway. Entrees £7-10. Open daily noon-midnight. MC/V. ❷

🎵🞄 ENTERTAINMENT AND NIGHTLIFE

Seagulls aren't the only things to listen to in Aberdeen; the city sways to the rhythms of performers seven nights a week. Find out about the latest events from **Aberdeen Box Office,** next to the Music Hall. (☎641 122; www.boxofficeaberdeen.com. Open M-Sa 9:30am-6pm.) The **Music Hall,** on Union St. (www.musichallaberdeen.com), features pop bands, musicals, and orchestra recitals; **His Majesty's Theatre,** Rosemount Viaduct (www.hmtheatre.com), has a more classical focus; and the **Aberdeen Arts Centre,** 33 King St. (www.aberdeenartscentre.org.uk), stages avant-garde and traditional plays. Catch independent flicks at **The Belmont Picture House,** 49 Belmont St. (☎343 536; tickets £3.70-6.10).

Lemon Tree Cafe Theatre, 5 West-North St. (☎642 230; www.lemontree.org), near Queen St. Small venue serving homemade food and drink in front of its main stage. Tickets £9-12, concessions £6-8. Hours vary depending on event; check website or pick up a copy of *The Lemon Tree Magazine* for the latest showtimes. Box office open M 11am-6pm, Tu-Sa 10am-6pm, Su noon-4pm.

Soul, 333 Union St. (☎211 150). Trendy pub/club combo in an old cathedral. Stained-glass windows and a DJ in the pulpit create an ironic environment. In the pub, try the Irn Bru sorbet (£4). Free Wi-Fi. Turns into club at 10pm. Entrees £5-8. Open M-Th and Su 10am-midnight, F-Sa 10am-1am. Food served noon-9:30pm. MC/V.

Espionage, 120 Union St. (☎561 006; www.espionage007.co.uk). Great theme nights that are often Bond focused, with large dance spaces and occasional live music. Martinis (shaken or stirred) are available (£5), and beer flows faster than a chase scene (£2). No cover. Open M-Th and Su 007pm-2am, F-Sa 007pm-3am.

HIGHLANDS AND ISLANDS

The Monkey House, 1 Union Terr. (☎251 120). Kid-friendly restaurant that transitions into an upscale club at 10pm. Burgers and fish entrees make it crowded with Union St. shopping hordes. Entrees £8-13. Open M-Th and Su noon-midnight, F-Sa noon-1am. Food served M-F noon-8:30pm, Sa-Su noon-9:30pm. MC/V.

Bar Indigo (Oh Henry's), 20 Adelphi Ln. (☎586 949), off Union St. by the TIC. Gay-friendly club overlooking the harbor. Draws crowds for hyper dance nights F-Sa. F-Sa cover £3. Open M-Th 5pm-2am, F-Sa 5pm-3am, Su 8pm-2am.

◉ SIGHTS

The columned ■**Aberdeen Art Gallery,** on Schoolhill, features traveling exhibits and stately rooms with a focus on Scottish contemporary art. (☎523 700. Open M-Sa 10am-5pm, Su 2-5pm. Free.) Great for families, the **Maritime Museum** has interactive exhibits and a huge collection of navigation tools and instruments in a sleek facility on Shiprow. The museum provides a comprehensive history of Aberdeen's long affair with the sea, from whaling to drilling for oil. (☎337 700. Open M-Sa 10am-5pm, Su noon-3pm. Free.) Just up Broad St., tour the castle-like **Provost Skene's House,** 45 Guestrow, whose rooms have been decorated to recall its 17th-century roots. (☎641 086. Open M-Sa 10am-5pm, Su 1-4pm. Free.) Across the street, inside **Marischal College,** the **Marischal Museum** chronicles northeast Scotland's history and has an impressive collection of gold artifacts from Egypt. (☎274 301. Open M-F 10am-5pm, Su 2-5pm. Free.)

Old Aberdeen and **King's College,** a short bus ride (#1, 2, 5, or 15) from the city center or a long walk along King St., have stately Gothic buildings. For a complete tour, pick up the Old Aberdeen Trail guide at the TIC. Stop at the **Chapel** to see the 16th-century "misery seats"—students were forced to sit on the un-orthopedic chairs for hours. (☎272 137. Open daily 9am-4:30pm. Tours July-Aug. Su 2-5pm. Free.) The **Cruikshank Botanic Gardens,** St. Machar Dr., are a well-documented collection of plants managed by the University of Aberdeen. (☎493 288. Open May-Sept. M-F 9am-4:30pm, Sa-Su 2-5pm; Oct.-Apr. M-F 9am-4:30pm. Free.)

At the other end of town lies flowering **Duthie Park** (DA-thee), by the River Dee at Polmuir Rd. and Riverside Dr. and accessible by bus #16 and 17. The expanse sports an extensive rose garden and the **Winter Gardens Hothouse,** home to enormous bougainvillea, hibiscus, and thistle. (☎585 310. Hothouse open daily May-Aug. 9:30am-7:30pm; Apr. and Sept.-Oct. 9:30am-5:30pm; Nov.-Mar. 9:30am-4:30pm. Free.) The newly refurbished **Gordon Highlanders Museum,** Viewfield Rd., follows the exploits of the heroic 18th-century British regiment through interactive displays and a short film. Walk down Queens Rd. or take bus #14 or 15 from Union St. (☎311 200; www.gordonhighlanders.com. Open Apr.-Oct. Tu-Sa 10:30am-4:30pm, Su 12:30-4:30pm; Nov. and Feb.-Mar. Th-Sa 10am-4pm. £3.50, concessions £2.50.) Aberdeen's beach is often crowded in the summer and leads to an amusement park, a central promenade, and a golf course.

▶ DAYTRIPS FROM ABERDEEN: THE GRAMPIAN COAST AND ROYAL DEESIDE

■**DUNNOTTAR CASTLE.** The misty lawn surrounding Dunnottar Castle (dun-AHT-ur) drops off into an elegant waterfall, framing the cliffside ruins. One of Scotland's best-defended castles, Dunnottar was built in the 14th century and was the site of many bloody battles. Here, Presbyterians were imprisoned in the Reformation, the crown jewels of Scotland were stolen during Cromwell's reign, and **William Wallace** burned an English garrison. (*Trains 20min., 1-2 per hr. and Bluebird Northern buses #107 and 117 1hr., 2 per hr. connect Aberdeen to Stonehaven. 30min. walk south* *from town; follow signs. ☎01569 762 173. Open Easter-Oct. M-Sa 9am-6pm, Su 2-5pm; Nov.-Easter M-F 9am-dusk. £4, children £1.)*

FYVIE CASTLE. Northwest on the A947, 25 mi. from Aberdeen, 13th-century Fyvie Castle is as picturesque as any postcard and has found its way onto many. The castle is plagued by a ghost called the "Green Lady" who taps visitors on the shoulder (and appears in about 10 other Scottish castles). The grounds include fruit and vegetable gardens along with the requisite sculpted gardens. Wander through the rooms and marvel at the castle's collection of paintings, particularly the Raeburns. *(Stagecoach Bluebird ☎01224 212 266 #305 runs from Aberdeen 1hr., every hr. ☎01651 891 266. Open July-Aug. daily 11am-5pm; Easter-June Sa-Su noon-5pm; Sept. Sa-Su noon-5pm. Last admission 4:15pm. Grounds open daily 9:30am-dusk. £8, concessions £5, families £20.)*

DRUM CASTLE. The oldest of the preserved castles in Scotland, Drum was continuously occupied from 1323 to 1975. Although the castle is less dramatic than some of its peers, the large rose garden and grounds make for a lovely walk, while the castle rooms contain their share of impressive art and preserved knick-knacks. Located 8 mi. west of Aberdeen on the A93. *(☎01330 811 204. Open daily July-Aug. 10am-5:30pm; Apr.-June and Sept. M, W-Th, Sa-Su 12:30-5pm. Grounds open daily 9:30am-dusk. £8, concessions £5, families £20. Grounds and garden only £2.50/2/5.)*

CRATHES CASTLE. Fourteen miles west of Aberdeen on the A93, Crathes Castle sits overlooking award-winning gardens. A fine example of a 16th-century manor, Crathes has the **Horn of Leys,** supposedly given as a gift from Robert the Bruce in 1323, among its treasures. Another "Green Lady" allegedly haunts this castle. *(☎01330 844 525. Castle open daily Apr.-Sept. 10:30am-5:30pm; Oct. 10am-4:30pm. Last admission 45min. before close. Garden open daily 9am-sunset. Castle £8, concessions £5. Castle and garden £10, concessions £7, families £25.)*

BRAEMAR ☎01339

Sixty miles west of Aberdeen on the A93, Braemar serves as an excellent base for seeing the Royal Deeside and trekking into the Cairngorms.

⌑ TRANSPORTATION. The only way into and out of Braemar by public transportation is the Stagecoach (☎08706 082 608) **bus** from Aberdeen (#201; 2¼hr., 6-7 per day, £11), which stops at Crathie for Balmoral 15min. away. Heather Hopper buses (operated by the Highland Council) #501 and 502 stop in Braemar en route to Pitlochry. Check with the TIC for specific times and prices. Drivers can reach Braemar from Perth or Aberdeen on the A93.

⏶ PRACTICAL INFORMATION. Rent **bikes** from the Mountain Sports Shop, Invercauld Rd., at the town's eastern edge. (☎741 242. Bikes £10 per ½-day, £15 per day, skis £16. Open daily 9am-6pm.) The **Tourist Information Centre,** on Mar Rd., at the Mews, books accommodations and provides information about local hikes and walks. (☎741 600. Open daily July-Aug. 9am-6pm; Mar.-June and Sept. daily 10am-5pm; Nov.-Feb. M-Sa 10:30am-4:30pm, Su 1-4pm.) The **post office** can be found in the Alldays Co-op, across from the TIC. (☎741 201. Open M-W and F 9am-noon and 1-5:30pm, Th 9am-1pm.) **Post Code:** AB35 5YL.

⌑⌑ ACCOMMODATIONS AND FOOD. The rugged **Rucksacks Bunkhouse ❶,** 15 Mar Rd., behind the TIC, is welcoming and warm, with cozy bunks and a large kitchen. (☎741 517. Laundry £2. Internet access £1 per hr. Dorms £10; bunks £7. Cash only.) The 64-bed **SYHA Braemar ❷,** 21 Glenshee Rd., is located in a sheltered stand of trees. The large stone house has a large common room and standard bunks. (☎741 659. Reception 7:30-10:30am and 5-11pm. Dorms £13, under 18 £9.

AmEx/MC/V.) Attached to the Braemar Hotel, the **Braemar Lodge Bunkhouse ❶,** 6 Glenshee Rd., offers a comfortable wooden bunkhouse with a huge breakfast (£7.50). Located just up from SYHA on the southern side of town. (☎741 627. Dorms £11. Cash only.) **SYHA Inverey ❶,** Linn of Dee Rd. 4 mi. from Braemar, offers almost no amenities but is located in a gorgeous field at the foot Ben Macdui. The daily **postbus** stops at the hostel before swinging by the Linn. (☎01339 741 969. No showers. Open May-Oct. Dorms £12, under 18 £9. AmEx/MC/V.)

Braemar has several tea shops and plenty of packaged haggis in its many gift stores. Grab groceries at the Alldays Co-op **supermarket** (☎741 201; open M-Sa 8am-7pm, Su 8:30am-7pm; MC/V), or enjoy the locally renowned burgers (£4.20) at **The Hungry Highlander ❶,** on 14 Invercauld Rd. (☎741 556. Open Tu-Th and Su 10am-8:30pm, F-Sa 10am-9:45pm.)

 SIGHTS AND HIKING. On the first Saturday in September, the town hosts the ▧**Braemar Gathering,** part of the Highland Games. In this 900-year-old tradition, buff Highland athletes compete in events like caber-tossing, pipers entertain, and Her Majesty's military forces have a tug of war. (☎741 095; www.braemargathering.org. Seats £13-15; field admission £7. Book seats in advance.)

> **TIP** **NTS MEMBERSHIP.** If you are visiting many sights in Scotland, consider becoming a member of the National Trust for Scotland. **NTS membership** for those under 25 costs £15 and grants free admission at any National Trust sight; it's also a good deal for the normal membership cost of £37. The 3-, 7-, or 14-day **Discovery Tickets** are a bargain. (☎0131 243 9555; www.nts.org.uk).

The area around Braemar has hikes for all skill levels, centering around the frothy **Linn of Dee.** The area's best-known hike traverses the steep **Ben Macdui** and should be attempted only by the fit and well-prepared (21 mi., 3100 ft). Begin at the car park at the Linn of Dee and follow the signs, although eventually a map is needed for the steepest part of the climb. For a more leisurely day, try the 2hr. round-trip **Derry Lodge Walk** around the river. This walk also begins at the Linn of Dee and passes through the forests around the Cairngorms. Signposts often stop short of the end of hikes: don't be caught without a map (Ordnance Survey #43; £6.50; ask for other applicable maps at the TIC). To get to the Linn, drive 10min. west of Braemar on the Linn of Dee Rd. or catch the daily **postbus** from the Braemar post office between 1:30 and 2:30pm; check at the TIC for exact schedules. Otherwise, walk or bike the scenic 7 mi. alongside the Linn of Dee Rd.

▶ DAYTRIP FROM BRAEMAR: BALMORAL CASTLE

An hour west along the A93 from Braemar, **Balmoral Castle and Estate** rests on the southern side of the River Dee. As a current palace used by the royal family, Balmoral is a popular tourist destination. Travel into the estate via the waiting tractor and enjoy a 1hr. tour of the grounds. Inside the palace, only the ballroom and exhibition are open to the public. *(Stagecoach bus #201. ☎01339 742 534; www.balmoralcastle.com. Open daily Apr.-July 10am-5pm. £7, under 16 £1, seniors £5.)*

CAIRNGORM MOUNTAINS ☎01479

Cairngorm National Park is Britain's largest, and its mountains tower well above the treeline, providing one of Europe's sweetest ski spots and views stretching as far as Ben Hope, 96 mi. to the north. Temperatures on the mountains dip low even in the warmest months, providing challenging hikes for seasoned climbers and chilly walks for casual view-seekers.

┏ TRANSPORTATION

The largest town in the Cairngorms, **Aviemore** is located on the main Inverness-Edinburgh rail and bus lines. The **train station** is on Grampian Rd., just south of the TIC. (☎01780 784 404. Open M-F 8am-9:25pm, Sa 8am-2:40pm, Su 10am-5:35pm.) **Trains** serve Edinburgh and Glasgow (both 2hr., 8-9 per day, ₤35.70) and Inverness (45min., ₤8.70). Southbound **buses** stop at the shopping center north of the train station, while northbound buses stop at the Cairngorm Hotel. Scottish Citylink (☎08705 505 050) runs every hour to Edinburgh (3hr., ₤17), Glasgow (3½hr., ₤17), and Inverness (40min., ₤6.40). **Kincraig,** 6 mi. south of Aviemore on the A9, is accessible by Scottish Citylink #957 from Perth (2 per day). For updates and detailed information, call Traveline (☎08706 082 608).

The principal path into Glenmore Forest Park, the Ski Road, begins south of Aviemore (on B970) and heads eastward. The road passes the sandy beaches of **Loch Morlich** before carrying on to **Glenmore** and ending at the base of **Cairn Gorm.** From Aviemore's train station, Highland Country bus #31 travels the same route (every hr.). The Cairngorm Service Station, on Aviemore's Main St., rents **cars.** (☎810 596. ₤36-42 per day, ₤190-210 per week. Open M-F 8:30am-5pm.) For **bike rental,** head to Bothy Bikes, Grampian Rd. (☎810 111. ₤10 per ½-day, ₤15 per day. Open daily 9am-5pm. MC/V.) Ellis Brigham, two doors down from the TIC on Grampian Rd., **rents skis** during the winter and climbing equipment during the summer. (☎810 175. Open daily 9am-6pm.) The Glenmore Shop and Cafe, opposite the SYHA Cairngorm in Glenmore, rents bikes, skis, snowboards, and mountainboards. (☎861 253. Bikes ₤9 per ½-day, ₤15 per day. Open daily 9am-5pm.)

◆ ▶ ORIENTATION AND PRACTICAL INFORMATION

Britain's busiest ski village in winter, **Aviemore** stays busy in summer, when tourists come to hike, bike, sail, surf, and swim. The areas surrounding Aviemore provide endless opportunities for outdoor activities. **Glenmore** offers an up-close view of the range, and **Kincraig,** to the south, sustains visitors with a welcome breath of non-touristed air on the tranquil shores of **Loch Insh.** Smaller towns like **Boat-of-Garten** or **Grantown** are also packed with places to stay, often at lower rates.

The **Aviemore and Spey Valley Tourist Information Centre,** on Grampian Rd., sells bus tickets, exchanges currency, and books B&Bs for ₤3 plus a 10% deposit. (☎810 363. Open from July to mid-Sept. M-Sa 9am-6pm, Su 10am-5pm; from mid-Sept. to June M-Sa 9am-5pm, Su 10am-5pm.) The **Rothiemurchus Estate Visitors Centre,** near Inverdruie, 1 mi. east on the Ski Rd. from Aviemore, provides information on tours and activities in the area. (☎812 345. Open daily 9:30am-5:30pm.) **Glenmore Forest Park Visitors Centre,** at the end of the Ski Rd. in Glenmore, offers maps and advice on walks west of the mountains. (☎861 220. Open daily 9am-5pm.) Other services in Aviemore include: a **Bank** of Scotland, on Grampian Rd., across from Tesco (☎887 000; open M-Tu and Th-F 9am-5pm, W 9:30am-5pm); **police,** Grampian Rd. (☎810 222); free **Internet** access at Aviemore **Library,** Grampian Rd., behind the bank (☎811 113; 1hr. slots. Open Tu 2-5pm and 6-8pm; W 10am-12:30pm, 2-5pm, and 6-8pm; F 10am-12:30pm and 2-5pm); and the **post office,** Grampian Rd. (☎811 056; open M-F 9am-5:30pm, Sa 9am-12:30pm.) **Post Code:** PH22 1RH.

┏ ACCOMMODATIONS

▨ **Lazy Duck Hostel** (☎821 642; www.lazyduck.co.uk), in Nethy Bridge. Catch Highland Country bus #34 or 15 from Aviemore (20min., 6-9 per day) and look for the small lawn signs in town. Tiny, comfortable cottage. 6-8 beds, wood burning stove, sauna, and resident white horse. Free Internet access. Call ahead. Dorms £10. MC/V online only. ❶

Slochd Mhor Lodge (SLOKT-moor; ☎841 666; www.slochd.co.uk). From Carrbridge, turn left off the A9 to Slochd Mhor; owners pick up guests from Carrbridge or Aviemore. Gorgeous wooden lodge perfect for getting away from it all. Handicap-accessible. Bike and ski rentals and lessons. Dorms from £14; twins from £16. Cash preferred. ❷

Carrbridge Bunkhouse (☎01429 841 250; www.carrbridge-bunkhouse.co.uk), 20min. walk from Carrbridge village; ask at Aviemore for the Highland Country bus. Lawn is littered with sculptures carved in the Scottish Chainsaw Carving Championships (held annually in Carrbridge). Chickens roam (fresh eggs from £1), and 2 wood-burning stoves keep the 3-tiered bunks toasty in winter. Sauna £4. Dorms £9.50. Cash only. ❶

Fraoch Lodge (☎831 331; www.scotmountain.co.uk), on Deshar Rd. in Boat-of-Garten, 6 mi. northeast of Aviemore on the A95. Ask at the Aviemore bus station to be let off in Boat-of-Garten. Social owners and exceptional meals (breakfast £2; packed lunch £4; 2-course dinner £10). Owner leads area hikes in summer and larger winter mountaineering expeditions. Family rooms and twins from £18 per person. Cash only. ❶

Ardenbeg Bunkhouse (☎872 824; www.ardenbeg.co.uk). Take the A9 to Grantown on Spey and turn left before the 1st traffic light; at the end of the road, turn right. First building on the left. Accessible by Highland Country bus from Aviemore. Owners offer outdoor instruction and equipment for guests. Laundry £1.50. Free Wi-Fi. Alpine-style bunks £12.50; bring your own sheet liner or rent one for £1. MC/V. ❶

Insh Hall Lodge (☎01540 651 272; www.lochinsh.com), 1 mi. downhill from Kincraig on Loch Insh; take Highland Country bus #35 or 38 from Aviemore (15min., 3 per weekday). From water sports with instructors in summer to ski school in winter, Insh Hall is like a lakeside camp. Rooms are simple and piney. Daily wildlife tours (£8). Free use of water sport equipment with 2-night stay. Singles from £24. MC/V. ❷

Aviemore Bunkhouse, Dalfaber Rd. (☎811 181), near the town center. New and conveniently located, offering storage lockers, wooden bunks, and an adjoining pub. Dorms £16; doubles £20. Cash only. ❷

SYHA Aviemore, 25 Grampian Rd. (☎810 345), south of the TIC. The ranch-style hostel has the usual SYHA amenities. 106 beds, 4-8 per room. Curfew 2am. Internet £1 per 20min. Dorms £12-13, under 18 £11. AmEx/MC/V. ❶

SYHA Cairngorm Lodge (☎861 238), Glenmore. Catch Highland Country Bus #34 or 36 from the Cairngorm Hotel opposite the rail station and ask to be dropped off. Loch Morlich beach across the road. 7 mi. from Aviemore, 2 mi. from Cairn Gorm ski area. Beautiful mountain backdrop. Doubles, dorms, and family rooms available. Optional 2-course dinner (£6.75). £13-15 per person, under 18 £9. AmEx/MC/V. ❷

Glenmore Forest Camping and Caravan Park (☎861 271), opposite the SYHA Cairngorm Lodge. At the base of the peaks with ample space and good facilities. Open Dec.-Oct. £6.50-7.50 per person. MC/V. ❶

Rothiemurchus Camp and Caravan Park (☎812 800), 1½ mi. south of Aviemore on Ski Rd. Lacks Glenmore's view but is cheaper and closer to town. £5 per person. MC/V. ❶

⬛ FOOD

Aviemore's **Grampian Road** is lined with pubs and cafes to suit any budget. For **groceries,** the local Tesco is north of the train station. (☎08456 779 017. Open M-Sa 8am-10pm, Su 9am-6pm.) **Royal Tandoori ❶,** 43 Grampian Rd. offers a 10% discount on takeaway. The lunch specials (3 courses for £5) provide a fresh, filling taste of Bangladesh. (☎811 199. Open daily noon-2pm and 5-11:30pm. MC/V.) The modern **Cafe Mambo ❷,** 12-13 Grampian Rd., is a pub with delicious burgers (£7-8.50) and soothing hot chocolate for £2. (☎811 670. Open daily noon-1am. Free Wi-Fi with a coffee order. Food served M-Th and Su until 8:30pm, F-Sa until 7:30pm. MC/V.)

🗻 🎿 HIKING AND SKIING

The Cairngorms have Scotland's highest concentration of ski resorts. Outdoor enthusiasts and snowbunnies converge at **CairnGorm Mountain** (on the mountain **Cairn Gorm**) for skiing in winter and views in summer. On the **funicular railway,** sit facing down the mountain for great views on the ride up to **Ptarmigan Centre,** Britain's highest train station (3600 ft.). Catch the peak of **Ben Nevis** to the west from the observation deck. Due to conservation concerns, railway-riders may not set foot outside the station. The only way to explore the peak is to hike from the bottom. The hike (3hr. round-trip) is not difficult on the main paths. (Highland County Bus #31 from Aviemore. ☎861 261; www.cairngormmountain.com. Trains every 15-30min. Ticket office opens 9:30am. Trains 10am-4:30pm. Funicular £8.50.)

> ❗ **SAFETY PRECAUTIONS.** Although the Cairngorms rise only 4000 ft., the region can have the weather patterns of the Arctic tundra. Many trails are not posted or blazed, and trekkers must rely on a map, compass, and good navigational skills. Make sure to use an **Ordnance Survey map** (Landranger #35 and 36), available at the TIC. Leave a description of your intended route with the police or at the mountain station, and learn the locations of the shelters (known as bothies) along your trail. For more information, see **Wilderness Safety,** p. 50.

To reach the peak of **Ben Macdui,** Britain's second highest at 4296 ft., take the **Northern Corries Path** from the car park to its terminus, and navigate the unmarked route using the Ordnance Survey Landranger Map (£7). The famous mountain should only be attempted by the well-prepared (7hr. round-trip). The strenuous but shorter **Windy Ridge Trail** (3-4hr. round-trip) reaches the top of Cairn Gorm. Before setting out, consult the helpful **Cairngorm Rangers** about trail and weather conditions and fill out a route plan sheet. The office is next to the Cairn Gorm Mountain car park. (☎861 703. Open daily 9am-5pm, weather permitting.)

The Cairngorm Rangers also host free **guided hikes.** For forest walks, **Glenmore Visitors Centre** has several trails; the most popular is the easy-going 3hr. **Ryovan Trek** through the woods and along **Green Lochen.** Closer to Aviemore, the renowned **Lairig Ghru** trail (p. 631) heads south through 20 mi. of lush valley to Braemar. Be ready for an all-day trek on unmarked paths. **Loch an Eilein** sports paths that circle the lake through the woods, with gorgeous views of the castle at its center.

For **skiers,** a day ticket with a railpass at Cairngorm costs £26 (concessions £20). Several companies run ski schools and rent equipment; pick up a copy of *Ski Scotland* at the Aviemore TIC for details. Three miles west of the funicular, the interactive **Cairngorm Reindeer Centre** is home to dozens of the majestic creatures—the only remaining herd in Britain. Visit them in the pen attached to the center, or take the trek to the hillside at 11am or 2:30pm to hand-feed the free-rangers. (☎861 228. Open daily 10am-5pm. Paddock viewing £2, concessions £1.50; trek to the herd £8, concessions £4, families £20.) At **Working Sheepdogs** on Leault farm, just south of Kincraig on the A95, watch one of the only remaining Cairngorm shepherds command eight enthusiastic dogs at once. (☎01540 651 310. Demonstrations at 4pm and often at other times, depending on demand. Reservations welcome. Admission £4.) The 269 acres of **Highland Wildlife Park,** in Kincraig, provide lots of kid-friendly opportunities to see local wildlife. (☎01540 651 270; www.kincraig.com/wildlife. Open daily June-Aug. 10am-7pm; Apr.-May and Sept.-Oct. 10am-6pm; Nov.-Mar. 10am-4pm. Last admission 2hr. before close. £8.50, seniors £7.50, concessions £6, families £29.) The **Carrbridge Pony Trekking Centre,** off Station Rd. in Carrbridge, offers a wonderful way to see the area on horseback, with treks for all ages and levels. (☎01479 841 602. 1hr. treks at 4:30pm, £15; 2hr. treks at 10am and 2pm, £30. Call ahead for reservations and seasonal prices.)

ELGIN
☎ 01343

A visit to Elgin (el-GHIN; pop. 20,000) provides a look at a prototypical Highland town. Located between Aberdeen and Inverness on the A96, the ruins of **Elgin Cathedral**, nicknamed the "Lantern of the North," warrant a stopover. Once the largest Scottish church, the cathedral was burned twice in its 800-year history, reducing it to a scattered graveyard and two 90 ft. towers. (☎547 171. Open Apr.-Sept. daily 9:30am-6:30pm; Oct.-Mar. M-W and Sa-Su 9:30am-4:30pm. £4.50, children £2.25.) Next door, all 104 plants mentioned in the Good Book thrive in the **Biblical Garden.** (Open daily May-Sept. 10am-7:30pm. Free.) The **Elgin Museum,** 1 High St., boasts a fossil collection and Roman coins. (☎543 675; www.elginmuseum.org.uk. Open Apr.-Oct. M-F 10am-5pm, Sa 11am-4pm. £3, concessions £1.50.)

With lots of B&Bs catering to the Whisky Trail crowd, Elgin has few options for the budget traveler. North of High St., **Richmond Bed & Breakfast ❸,** 48 Moss St., offers vegetarian breakfast options, ensuite rooms, and garden-side seating. (☎542 561. Singles £30-35; doubles £50. Cash only.) Next to the Elgin Bowling Club, the high ceilings of the **Auchmillan Guest House ❸,** 12 Reidhaven St., give its rooms a regal feel. (☎549 077. Singles £35; doubles £50. MC/V.) Camp at **Riverside Caravan Park ❶,** West Rd. (☎542 813. Open Apr.-Oct.; closed when ground is wet. £5 per person. Cash only.) Pick up **groceries** at Marks & Spencer Simply Food, 221-223 High St. (☎559 319. Open M-F 9am-8pm, Sa 9am-7pm, Su 10am-6pm. AmEx/MC/V.) **Thunderton House Pub ❶,** off High St., offers bargain lunches (£4). Locals come in droves for quiz night on Sundays. (☎554 921. Open M-Th and Su 10am-11pm, F-Sa 10pm-1am. MC/V.) **Scribbles ❶,** 154 High St., fills with a Saturday crowd who know how delicious its pizzas (£6) are. (☎542 835. Open M-Sa 10am-10pm, Su noon-10pm. MC/V.) **Quismat ❷,** 202-204 High St., features a mix of Sottish favorites along with Tandoori cuisine. (☎541 461. Entrees £8-13. Open M-Th noon-2pm and 5-11:30pm, F-Sa noon-2pm and 5-11:30pm, Su 5-11:30pm. AmEx/MC/V.)

The **train station** is 5min. south of the city center, at the end of South Guildry St. (Ticket office open M-Sa 6:15am-9:30pm, Su 10:30am-5:30pm.) Trains (☎08457 484 950; www.firstscotrail.com) run to Aberdeen (1½hr., 10 per day, £12.40) and Inverness (45min., 11 per day, £8.20). **Buses** stop behind High St. and the St. Giles Centre. Stagecoach Bluebird (☎01343 544 222) buses #10 and 305 leave the **bus station,** on Alexandra Rd., across from the Town Hall, to Aberdeen (2¼hr., every hr., £8.10) and Inverness (1¼hr., 2 per hr., £8.10). Call Traveline (☎08706 082 208) for complete schedules and information. Rent **bikes** at Bike and Bowl, 7 High St. (☎549 656. Open M-Sa 9am-5pm. £10 per day.) The **Tourist Information Centre,** 17 High St., leads ghost walks around the town on Thursday nights at 8pm (☎076 926; www.whiskydrama.co.uk; £6) and books accommodations for £3 plus a 10% deposit. (☎542 666. Open July-Sept. M-Sa 9am-6pm, Su 11am-4pm; Mar. and May-June M-Sa 10am-5pm, Su 11am-3pm; Apr. and Oct. M-Sa 10am-5pm; Nov.-Feb. M-Sa 10am-4pm.) Other services include: **banks** and **ATMs** on High St.; free **Internet** access at Elgin **Library** in Cooper Park (☎562 600; open M-F 10am-8pm, Sa 10am-4pm); and the **post office,** 99 Batchen St. (☎546 466; open M-F 8:30am-6pm, Sa 8:30am-4pm). **Post Code:** IV30 1BH.

SIGHTS NEAR ELGIN

FORRES. Immortalized in Shakespeare's *Macbeth* as the location of Cawdor Castle, today, Forres boasts award-winning garden sculptures that make the town itself a floral exhibit. On the east end of town is the **Sueno's Stone,** which is the largest carved Pictish cross-slab in all of Europe. *(Stagecoach Bluebird #10 and 305 make the 30min. bus trip to Forres, located halfway between Elgin and Inverness on the A96. 2 per hr., £2.40.)*

HIGHLANDS AND ISLANDS

⊠THE MALT WHISKY TRAIL. Enticing smells hang in the air above the eight distilleries on the world-famous Malt Whisky Trail in the Speyside area. *(Stagecoach Bluebird bus #10 covers Keith, Elgin, and Forres. Always tell the driver where you want to go. Day Rover ticket £11.)* The trail begins at the **Strathisla Distillery** in Keith, the oldest in the Highlands, offering guided tours and two different drams to willing tasters. *(5min. walk from the bus and train stations in Keith. ☎01542 783 044; www.chivas.com. Open from mid-Mar. to Nov. M-Sa 9:30am-4pm, Su noon-4pm. £5. No charge—and no drinking—for those under 18.)* Follow the marked trail along the A941 south to **Glenfiddich,** whose well-known whisky is doled out on the free "Original Tour" of the facility. If you have deeper pockets and a discerning nose, opt for the Connoisseurs' Tour (£20), which offers a tutored nosing of at least five of Glenfiddich's offerings. *(17 mi. south of Elgin. Take Stagecoach Bluebird bus #336 from Elgin to the distillery. 40min., every hr. ☎01340 820 373; www.glenfiddich.com. Open from Jan. to mid-Dec. M-F 9:30am-4:30pm; from Easter to mid-Oct. M-Sa 9:30am-4:30pm, Su noon-4:30pm.)* Stagecoach bus #336 to Glenfiddich (glen-FID-ick) will stop on request at the **Speyside Cooperage,** which repairs over 100,000 casks every year and displays the process. *(¼ mi. south of Craigellachie on the A941. ☎01340 871 108; www.speysidecooperage.co.uk. Open M-F 9:30am-4:30pm. Last admission 4pm. £3.10, concessions £2.50.)*

TOMINTOUL AND THE SPEYSIDE WAY. Tomintoul, the self-proclaimed highest point in the Highlands, stands 1150 ft. above sea level and serves as a beautiful stopping point for area hikers. The challenging **Speyside Way,** an 84 mi. trail along the river from Buckie at Spey Bay to Aviemore in the Cairngorms, veers into Tomintoul, resulting in a few of the more rugged backpackers milling through town. *(Speyside Way Ranger Service ☎01340 881 266. Consult the free, indispensable Speyside Way Long Distance Route pamphlet and Land Ordnance maps (£7-8) at the Tomintoul or Elgin TIC.)* The famous **Glenlivet Distillery,** Ballindalloch, is located 10 mi. north of Tomintoul on a rustic moor. You can sample the whisky and malted barley. *(Whisky-flavored ice cream £1. ☎01542 783 220; www.theglenlivet.com. Open Apr.-Oct. M-Sa 10am-4pm, Su 12:30-4pm. Free.)* Located in the town's former schoolhouse, **SYHA Tomintoul ❷,** Main St., has a large kitchen and comfortable beds. *(☎08700 041 152. Open Mar.-Oct. £13, under 18 £9. AmEx/MC/V.)* **Camp** on the Glenlivet Estate, ½ mile from the TIC, where Main St. ends, or anywhere sheep aren't grazing. *(Glenlivet Estate Ranger Service ☎01807 580 283. Free. Toilets available a short walk from the campsite into the town center.)* Tomintoul is difficult to reach without a car or mountain bike. Roberts (☎544 222) **buses** run to Keith and Dufftown *(#362; Tu and Sa 1 per day)* and Elgin *(#363; Th 1 per day, £4).* The **Tourist Information Centre,** in The Square, finds accommodations and offers a guide to trails. *(☎01807 580 285. Open July-Aug. M-F 9am-5:30pm, Sa 9am-1pm and 2-5:30pm, Su 1-5pm; Apr.-June and Sept.-Oct. M-Sa 9:30am-1pm and 2-5pm.)*

THE GREAT GLEN

INVERNESS   ☎01463

As the only city in the Highlands, Inverness retains an appealing mix of Highland hospitality and urban hustle. Split by the sparkling River Ness, the city serves as a departure point for exploring more remote areas, and its amenities and location near Loch Ness ensure a constant stream of tourists in summer. Visitors to Inverness benefit from cheap accommodations, a smattering of local food venues, and proximity to some of Scotland's most famous castles and attractions.

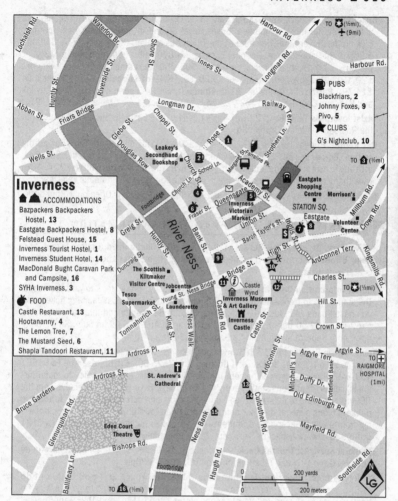

PUBS
Blackfriars, **2**
Johnny Foxes, **9**
Pivo, **5**
★ **CLUBS**
G's Nightclub, **10**

Inverness

♠ ▲ ACCOMMODATIONS
Bazpackers Backpackers
Hostel, **13**
Eastgate Backpackers Hostel, **8**
Felstead Guest House, **15**
Inverness Tourist Hostel, **1**
Inverness Student Hotel, **14**
MacDonald Bught Caravan Park
and Campsite, **16**
SYHA Inverness, **3**
🍴 FOOD
Castle Restaurant, **13**
Hootananny, **4**
The Lemon Tree, **7**
The Mustard Seed, **6**
Shapla Tandoori Restaurant, **11**

HIGHLANDS
AND ISLANDS

⊏ TRANSPORTATION

Flights: Inverness Airport (☎01667 464 000; www.hial.co.uk), 9 mi. east of the city and accessible by bus (M-Sa every hr.). British Airways (☎08457 733 377; www.brit-ishairways.com) flies to **Dublin, Edinburgh, Glasgow, London, Orkney,** and **Shetland.** EasyJet (☎08706 000 000; www.easyjet.co.uk) flies to London and Dublin.

Train Station: On Academy St., in Station Sq. Travel center open M-F 6:30am-8:30pm, Sa 6:30am-6:30pm, Su 9:15am-8:30pm. Luggage storage £3. Trains (☎08457 484 950) to: **Aberdeen** (2½hr., 10 per day, £22.40); **Edinburgh** (3½hr., 8 per day, £36.40); **Glasgow** (3½hr., 8 per day, £36.40); **Kyle of Lochalsh** (2½hr., 4 per day, £16.50); **London** (8-11hr., 1 per day, £133); **Thurso** (3½hr., 3 per day, £14.60).

Buses: Farraline Park Bus Station (☎233 371), off Academy St. Scottish Omnibuses sells tickets for most companies. Buses travel around Inverness throughout the day; pick up the Travel Times brochure at the TIC or bus station. Office open M-Sa 8:30am-5:30pm, Su 9am-5:30pm. National Express (☎08705 808 080) to: **London** (13hr., 1 per day, £39). Scottish Citylink (☎08705 505 050) to: **Edinburgh** (4½hr., every hr., £20.19); **Glasgow** (4hr., every hr., £20.19); **Kyle of Lochalsh** (2hr., 2 per day, £14.79); **Perth** (3hr., every hr., £15); **Thurso** (3½hr., 4-5 per day, £15). Both Citylink and Rapsons Coaches (☎01463 222 244) to **Ullapool** (1½hr., M-Sa 2 per day, £9).

Taxis: Inverness Taxis (☎222 900). Taxis queue by the Eastgate Shopping Centre or at the Railroad Station in Station Sq.

Car Rental: Budget (☎713 333; www.albacarhire.com) is on Railway Terr., behind the station. **Europcar** (☎235 525; www.northernvehiclehire.co.uk) has a Telfer St. office, although rates may be slightly higher. **Thrifty,** 33 Harbour Rd. (☎224 466; www.thrifty.co.uk) has delivery service to airport and a fleet of automatic vehicles.

Bike Rental: Barney's, 35 Castle St. (☎232 249). £10 per day. Open daily 9am-dusk.

✳ 🔢 ORIENTATION AND PRACTICAL INFORMATION

The **River Ness** divides Inverness. On the east bank, **Castle Road, Church Street,** and **Academy Street** are connected by pedestrian-only **High Street** and hold most attractions and restaurants.

Tourist Information Centre: Castle Wynd (☎234 353), up the steps toward the castle. The staff helps track Nessie by bus, boat, and brochure. Books CalMac ferry tickets and non-hostel beds (£3 plus a 10% deposit). **Bureau de change** and Internet access (£1 per 20min., £2.50 per hr.). Open from mid-June to Aug. M-Sa 9am-6pm, Su 9:30am-4pm; from Sept. to mid-June M-Sa 9am-5pm, Su 10am-4pm.

Tours: Puffin Express (☎717 181; www.puffinexpress.co.uk) runs daily summer minibus tours to John O'Groats and several Scottish Isles (£25-60). **CitySightseeing** (☎01667 459 849; www.city-sightseeing.com.) buses allow hop-on, hop-off service to major historical sights (depart bus station every hr.). **Inverness Taxis** (☎222 900) leave from the TIC and give tours to nearby sights. Numerous tours hit **Loch Ness** (p. 623). **MacBackpackers** offers a stellar day tour of Inverness geared toward twenty-somethings, departing from the MacBackpackers Student Hotel (p. 621) about once per week. (☎0131 558 9900; www.macbackpackers.com. Office open daily 9am-6pm. £15.)

Financial Services: Thomas Cook, 9-13 Inglis St. (☎08701 111 111), has a **bureau de change.** Open M-W and F-Sa 9am-5:30pm, Th 10am-5:30pm.

Work/Volunteer Opportunities: Inverness JobCentre, Young St. (☎888 200 or 888 100) places temporary workers. In summer, the best bet for jobs is to go knocking on hostel, restaurant, and tourist attraction doors. Open M-Tu, and Th-F 9am-5pm, W 10am-5pm. **Volunteering Highland,** 1 Millburn Rd. (☎711 393), across from Morrisons, places volunteers in and around Inverness; call in advance for an appointment.

Launderette: New City, 17 Young St. (☎242 507). Wash £3, dry £1 per 15min. Open Apr.-Sept. M-F 8am-8pm, Sa 8am-6pm, Su 10am-4pm; Oct.-Mar. M-F 8am-6pm, Sa 8am-6pm, Su 10am-4pm. Internet £1 per 20min. Last wash 1hr. before close.

Police: Burnett Rd. (☎715 555).

Hospital: Raigmore Hospital, Old Perth Rd. (☎704 000).

Pharmacy: Super Drug, 12-22 High St. (☎232 587). Open M-Sa 8:30am-5:30pm, Su noon-4pm.

Internet Access: Library, Farraline Park (☎236 463), north of the bus station. Free. Photo ID required. Call ahead or be prepared to wait. Open M and F 9am-7:30pm, Tu and Th 9am-6:30pm, W 10am-5pm, Sa 9am-5pm. **Mailboxes, Etc.,** 24 Station Rd. (☎234 700). £2 per 15min., £3 per 30min., £5 per hr.

Post Office: 14-16 Queensgate (☎243 574). Open M and W-Sa 9am-5:30pm, Tu 9:30am-5:30pm. **Post Code:** IV1 1AA.

ACCOMMODATIONS

■ **Inverness Student Hotel,** 8 Culduthel Rd. (☎236 556). Riverside hangout playing loud music with cozy, quiet rooms. Part of the MacBackpacker's company. Breakfast £2. Laundry service £2.50. Internet access £80p per 30min. Dorms £12-13.50. MC/V. ❶

■ **Bazpackers Backpackers Hotel,** 4 Culduthel Rd. (☎717 663). Gothic building with a working fireplace, the homey Bazpackers has a laid-back vibe, just a few minutes walk from the city center. Open from mid-June to Sept. Dorms £13; doubles £32. MC/V. ❷

Inverness Tourist Hostel (Backpackers Hostel), 34 Rose St. (☎241 962), in the alley-way behind the bus station. Newly renovated hostel offering satellite TV and leather couches. Dorms £11-14. MC/V. ❶

Eastgate Backpackers Hostel, 38 Eastgate (☎718 756; www.eastgatebackpackers.com), in the pedestrian Eastgate Precinct. 38 beds. Urban hostel with a social crowd and murals on the walls. Dorms £10-13; twins £27-32. MC/V. ❶

SYHA Inverness, Victoria Dr. (☎231 771). From the station, turn left on Academy St., go up Millburn Rd., and turn right on Victoria Dr. Industrial facilities, hotel-style hallways, and large numbers of guests create an impersonal feel. Comfortable beds, free parking, and great security compensate. Laundry wash £2, dry 20p per 15min. Internet £1 per 20min. Curfew 2am. Dorms £12-15, under 18 £9-10.50. AmEx/MC/V. ❶

Felstead Guest House, 18 Ness Bank (☎231 634; www.jafsoft.com/felstead/felstead.html). 1 mi. south of the city center. Round windows overlook the river and blossoming yard at this B&B. £32-44 per person. MC/V. ❹

MacDonald Bught Caravan Park and Campsite, Bught Ln. (☎236 920). By the River Ness; easy to access from the A82. Well-kept campsite full of amenities. Laundry wash £3, dry £3. Internet £1 per 30min. Open Apr.-Sept. £6 per 1- or 2-person tent, £3 per additional person. MC/V. ❶

FOOD

Inverness is full of international food options and some of the best traditional cuisine the Highlands has to offer. Buy **groceries** from Morrison's, 15 Millburn Rd., near the train station; follow Academy St. east and then north. (☎250 260. Open M and Sa 8:30am-8pm, Tu-W 8:30am-9pm, Th-F 8:30am-10pm, Su 9am-7pm.)

■ **The Mustard Seed,** 16 Fraser St. (☎220 220; www.themustardseedrestaurant.co.uk). One of the most popular restaurants in town. Elegant entrees like sea bass with saffron sauce (£9) and creative uses of its namesake condiment. Early evening menu includes 2 courses and wine for £12. Excellent river views complete a splurge-worthy evening. Entrees from £9. 2-course lunch £6. Open noon-3pm and 5:30-10pm. AmEx/MC/V. ❸

■ **Hootananny,** 67 Church St. (☎233 651; www.hootananny.com). A feisty, wood-studded bar combining authentic Scottish song and dance with a mouth-watering Thai restaurant downstairs (entrees £5-6). Upstairs Mad Hatter Club. Downstairs open daily noon-1am. Mad Hatter open W-Th 8pm-1am, F-Sa 8pm-3am. MC/V. ❶

The Lemon Tree, 18 Inglis St. (☎241 114), north of High St. Contagiously cheerful staff and delicious homemade food. Try the popular Thai soup (£2.25) or cakes made fresh daily (£2). Open M-Sa 8:30am-5:30pm. Cash only. ❶

Shapla Tandoori Restaurant, 2 Castle Rd. (☎241 919). Climb the mirror-lined stairs to reach the dining room overlooking the river. Generous portions at fair prices. Splitting 1 course is plenty for 2. 3-course lunch £5. Open daily noon-11pm. AmEx/MC/V. ❷

Castle Restaurant, 41 Castle St. (☎230 925). Packed with families chowing on home-cooked American food. Great macaroni and cheese (£5.25) and a bustling diner backdrop. Entrees £5-9. Open M-Sa 9am-8:15pm. Cash only. ❷

🍺🍴 NIGHTLIFE AND PUBS

The bar and club scene blends together in Inverness, where the party begins and ends on the early side. An odd law states that all patrons must be inside a bar or club by midnight if they want to stay later, forcing full capacity earlier in the evening. The city's pubs are full of select local whiskies, and it's almost too easy to find that good, old-fashioned Scottish pint.

Blackfriars, 93-95 Academy St. (☎233 881). Feel like a lad or lass at this foot-stomping bar. Scottish beer, Scotch whisky, Scottish food, Scottish music, and Scottish Scottishness. A diverse mix of visitors and locals. Open W-Th 11am-midnight, F 11am-1am, Sa 11am-12:30am, Su 12:30pm-midnight. Food served noon-3pm and 5-9pm.

G's Nightclub, 21 Castle St. (☎233 322). The most talked-about club in Inverness, G's is the party standard, with live music and long lines. Cover Th-Sa £3-6. Open W-Th 9:30pm-2am, F-Su 9:30pm-3am.

Pivo, 38-40 Academy St. (☎713 307). Solid, upscale burgers and, later on, a cutting-edge bar scene with leather lounge areas and steel tables. Entrees £6-7. Open M-F 11:30am-midnight, Su noon-midnight.

Johnny Foxes, 26 Bank St. (☎236 577). Irish bar and lively backpacker hangout. Ample outdoor seating. Entrees £6-8. M-Sa live music. Su karaoke. Open M-Th 11am-1am, W-Sa 11am-2am, Su 12:30pm-2am. Food served noon-3pm. MC/V.

👁 SIGHTS

The pink sandstone **Inverness Castle** and its meticulously-landscaped grounds dominate the city's skyline—its monumental facade is worth seeing. Although it was built in the 12th century and used as a fortress for the vindictive Mary, Queen of Scots, the castle now serves as the city's courthouse. Down the hill, the newly opened **Inverness Museum and Art Gallery,** in Castle Wynd, has a large collection of works of both local and national importance, with a view of the castle from the window. (☎237 114. Open M-Sa 9am-5pm. Free.) The tall shelves of **Leakey's Secondhand Bookshop,** at the northern end of Church St. in Greyfriars Hall, hold over 100,000 volumes. Enjoy a cup of tea with your new old read at the cushy balcony cafe. (☎239 947. Open M-Sa 10am-5:30pm; cafe open M-Sa 10am-4:30pm. MC/V.) The **Scottish Kiltmaker Visitor Centre,** 4-9 Huntly St., has designed kilts for movies such as *Braveheart* and *Rob Roy*. Tour the museum, which features hunky mannequins in kilts, a video musical medley of kilts in the media, and kilt-makers live in action. (☎222 781. Open from mid-May to Sept. M-Sa 9am-9pm, Su 10am-5pm; from Oct. to mid-May M-Sa 9am-5pm. £2, concessions £1.) Get a jolt at the **Whisky Shop,** which features over 1000 types of whisky and offers free tastings. (☎710 525. Open July-Aug. M-Sa 9am-10pm; Sept.-June M-Sa 9am-5:30pm.)

🎵🎭 ENTERTAINMENT AND FESTIVALS

Inverness Dolphin Cruises offer a chance to see dolphins and is a sure-fire way to enjoy Inverness by sea. Sightings are especially common 3hr. before high tide (tidal information available at TIC). Boats leave from the Shore St. quay, downstream from the city center. (☎717 900. 1½hr. Mar.-Oct. 6 per day. £12.50, students £10.) In late July, enjoy the endless kilts and Highland machismo at the **Inverness Highland Games**. (☎724 262; www.invernesshighlandgames.com; tickets from £2). At Ft. George, the **Inverness Tattoo Festival** is an epic military salute to Scotland and its history. (☎242 915; www.invernesshighlandtattoo.co.uk. £15.) In August, the **Marymas Fair** (☎715 760) begins with a horse and carriage parade and recreates medieval life with craft stalls and performances.

▶ DAYTRIPS FROM INVERNESS

The Highland Country **Tourist Trail Day Rover** ticket (☎222 244; £6) is great for those who wish to see multiple sights. It allows one day of unlimited bus travel between Inverness, Culloden Battlefield, Cawdor Castle, and other sights. Buses leave from the Inverness bus station or Queensgate. Car rental is a pricier option (p. 620).

■**DUNROBIN CASTLE.** Dunrobin is one of the few castles to still be occupied (part time) by its original owners, the Sutherland family. A tour of the castle provides a look at numerous additions as well as plenty of rumors about mysteries and ghosts in its walls. The castle gardens are an exhibit to themselves, modeled after those at Versailles. The twice daily **Falconry Display** draws crowds for the opportunity to have birds of prey fly close overhead. *(300 yd. north of Dunrobin station, 1½ mi. north of Golspie. Train from Inverness 2hr., 2 per day, return £14. Castle ☎01408 633 177; www.highlandescape.com. Open Apr.-June and from Sept. to mid-Oct. M-Sa 10:30am-4:30pm, Su noon-4:30pm; July-Aug. M-Sa 10:30am-5:30pm, Su noon-5:30pm. Last admission 30min. before close. £7, students £6.)*

MONIACK WINERIES. 7 mi. west of Inverness on the A862, Moniack Wineries creates six signature wines made with local flowers and plants. In an area known for its spirits and notoriously lacking in grapes, the winery itself is a rarity. A 20min. tour explains country wine and jam production culminating in an unlimited tasting of the sweet, juicy wines. *(☎831 283. Open M-Sa Apr.-Dec. 10am-5pm; Jan.-Mar. 11am-4pm. £2.)*

CULLODEN BATTLEFIELD. The large field sits just east of Inverness on the B9006. Wander around the barren heath where Bonnie Prince Charlie, charismatic but no genius in battle, lost 1200 men in 40min. Grave stones commemorate the losses suffered by several major clans in the last battle to be fought on Scottish ground. A scenic 1½ mi. south, a grove hides the stone circles of the Bronze Age **Cairns of Clava**. *(Highland Country bus #7 15min., every hr., round-trip £2.40. Visitors center ☎790 607. Open daily Apr.-May and Sept.-Oct. 9:30am-5pm; June-Aug. 9am-6pm; Feb.-Mar. and Nov.-Dec. 11am-4pm. Fields free. Centre £4. Guided tour £4.)*

CAWDOR CASTLE. The fairytale-like castle sits on grounds alongside a mini-golf course, putting green, restaurant, and 5 mi. of hiking trails. Made famous by its role in Shakespeare's *Macbeth*, the castle's drawbridge and garden maze enhance its billing as Scotland's most romantic castle. It has been the residence of the Thane of Cawdor's descendants since the 15th century and is still inhabited for much of the year. *(Between Inverness and Nairn on the B9090, off the A96. Highland Country bus #12, 30min., M-Sa every hr., round-trip £5; departs from the post office at Queensgate. ☎01667 404 401; www.cawdorcastle.com. Open daily May-Oct. 10am-5pm. Last admission 5pm. £7, concessions £6. Golf £9 per round.)*

LOCH NESS   ☎01456

The **Loch Ness Monster** has captivated the world for hundreds of years, and even with a 24hr. webcam trained on the loch (www.lochness.co.uk), thousands of tourists make the trip each year to be awed by its mysteries. In AD 565, St. Columba repelled a savage sea monster as it attacked a monk; whether a prehistoric leftover, giant sea snake, or product of an overactive imagination, the monster and its lair remain a mystery. The loch is 700 ft. deep just 70 ft. from its edge, and theories about giant sturgeons satisfy some scientists, but no one has definitively determined how vast the loch really is or what life exists at its bottom. The easiest way to see the loch is with one of the dime-a-dozen tour groups. **Jacobite Cruises,** Tomnahurich Bridge, Glenurquhart Rd., offers a variety of bus and boat trips. (☎01463 233 999; www.jacobite.co.uk. £9-20, includes castle admission.) Many **boat cruises** leave Drumnadrochit or Inverness and tour Loch Ness for £9-20, including **Castle Cruises Loch Ness** (located in the Art Gallery; ☎450 695) and **Loch Ness Cruises** (located in the Original Loch Ness Visitor Centre; ☎450 395), whose boats are equipped with underwater cameras.

In tiny **Drumnadrochit,** 13 mi. south of Inverness, two visitors centers develop the Nessie legend. The **Original Loch Ness Visitors Centre** offers current footage of the loch and recent sightings. It also has a *Braveheart* center, focusing on Robert the Bruce's famous battle at Bannockburn. (☎450 342. Open daily 9am-9pm. £5, students £4.25.) The **Official Loch Ness Exhibition Centre,** with its 40min. visual display (available in 17 languages), uses science to dispel the hoaxes. The dramatic sound effects create a spooky, live-action version of a sixth-grade text book. Both centers have monstrous gift shops. (☎450 573; www.loch-ness-scotland.com. Open daily July-Aug. 9am-8pm; June and Sept. 9am-6pm; Oct. 9:30am-5:30pm; Nov.-Easter 10am-3:30pm. £6.) **Urquhart Castle** (URK-hart) was one of the largest castles in Scotland before it was blown up in 1692 to prevent Jacobite occupation. A video boils down 1000 years of history into a 10min. viewing, culminating in an unveiling of a panoramic castle view. Tours from Inverness stop at the ruins. (☎450 551. Open Apr.-Sept. daily 9:30am-6:30pm; Oct.-Mar. M-Sa 9:30am-4:30pm. £6.50, concessions £5.) The **Abriachan Wood paths** (www.wildaboutswoods.org.uk), off A82, provide a view of the loch and a hidden picnic spot. The **Great Glen Cycle Route** passes the loch on its way to Fort William. The River Foyers empties into the loch in a series of waterfalls 18 mi. down.

Within walking distance of Loch Ness, the homey **Loch Ness Backpackers Lodge ❷,** Coiltie Farm House, East Lewiston, has a lively outdoor courtyard with a house band, frequent bonfires, and parties. Continue along the A82 from Drumnadrochit just south to Lewiston, turn left at the sign beyond the gas station, and look for the white building with a gigantic Nessie mural. The lodge provides an entire wall of maps to get you to pubs and vistas, including to the 100 ft. **Divach Falls,** a 1hr. walk from the hostel. (☎450 807; www.lochness-backpackers.com. Continental breakfast £2. Internet access £1; Wi-Fi. Dorms £13; doubles £30.) The more remote **SYHA Loch Ness ❷** stands alone on the loch's western shore, 7½ mi. south of the castle. (☎0870 004 1138. Laundry £2. Internet access £1 per 20min. Reserve in advance July-Aug. Open Apr.-Oct. Dorms from £13, under 18 from £9.) Both hostels lie on the Scottish Citylink bus routes between Inverness and Fort William (#919 and 917; every 2hr., £5 from Inverness). **Fiddler's ❷,** the Village Green, opposite the Drumnadrochit TIC, has patio seating, a huge selection of whisky lining the walls (£3-6), and entrees (£8-15) one step above the usual pub fare. Try the boozy ice cream for £4.50. (☎450 678. Open daily 8am-9pm. MC/V.)

Scottish Citylink **buses** from Inverness to the Isle of Skye (#917; 3-5hr., 3 per day); stop at Drumnadrochit, Urquhart Castle, and Fort William (#919; 2hr., 6 per day; £9). The Drumnadrochit **Tourist Information Centre,** located on the main road, offers its own take on the loch's mysteries and has travel specifics. (☎459 050. Open June-Sept. M-Sa 9am-6pm, Su 10am-4pm; Oct.-Apr. M-Sa 10am-1:30pm.)

FORT WILLIAM AND BEN NEVIS ☎01397

In 1654, General Monck founded the town of Fort William among Britain's highest peaks to keep out "savage clans and roving barbarians." But the town's location on the banks of Loch Linnhe caused his plan to backfire; today thousands of Highlands-bound hikers invade Fort William. Despite the tourists, the town makes an excellent base for exploring impressive wilderness, including Ben Nevis.

� TRANSPORTATION

The **train station** is just beyond the north end of High St. Walk under the overpass to the right of the supermarket. **Trains** (☎08457 484 950) come from Glasgow Queen St. (3¾hr.; M-Sa 3 per day, Su 2 per day; £19.50) and Mallaig (1½hr.; M-Sa 4 per day, Su 1-3 per day; £8.10). Many opt for the incredible ◪**West Coast Railway** (☎01463 239 026; www.westcoastrailway.co.uk) Jacobite Steam train, which travels to Mallaig through some of the Highland's most pristine wilderness, including vistas used in the *Harry Potter* films. (Runs June-Oct. M-F; July-Aug. M-F and Su. Departs Fort William at 10:20am and Mallaig at 2:10pm. £20, round-trip £27.) The Caledonian sleeper train runs to London Euston (12hr., 1 per day, £99). **Buses** arrive next to the Morrison's by the train station. Scottish Citylink (☎08705 505 050; www.citylink.co.uk) travels to: Edinburgh (4hr., 3 per day, £21); Glasgow (3hr., 4 per day, £14.70); Inverness (2hr., 7-8 per day, £9.20); Kyle of Lochalsh (2hr., 3 per day, £13.30); Oban (1½hr., M-Sa 2-4 per day, £8.40). Scottish Citylink/Shiel sends a bus from Mallaig (1½hr., M-F 1 per day, £5). Book at least 48hr. in advance for significantly reduced fares.

Locally, Highland Country Buses (☎702 373) travel around Fort William and the surrounding area. From June to September, #42 departs from the bus station and heads to the SYHA Glen Nevis and the Ben Nevis trailhead (10min.; M-Sa 7 per day, Su 4 per day; £1.30). An unnamed shuttle runs between the Glen Nevis town center and Lower Falls (£1.30). Bus #45 runs to Corpach from the car park behind the post office (15min.; M-Sa 3 per hr., Su every hr.; £1). **Taxis** queue outside the Tesco on High St.; try Al's Tours & Taxi (☎700 700). Rent **bicycles** at Offbeat Bikes, 117 High St. (☎704 008. £10 per half-day, £15 per day. Open daily 9am-5:30pm. MC/V.)

▮▮ ORIENTATION AND PRACTICAL INFORMATION

From the bus and train stations, an underpass leads to **High Street,** Fort William's main pedestrian avenue. The hectic **Tourist Information Centre,** Cameron Sq., books accommodations for a £3 charge plus a 10% deposit. (☎703 781. Open July-Aug. M-Sa 9am-7pm, Su 9:30am-5pm; Sept.-Oct. and Apr.-June M-Sa 9am-6pm, Su 10am-4pm; Nov.-Mar. M-Sa 9am-5pm.) Fort William keeps its droves of hikers well outfitted with numerous **outdoors shops;** try Nevisport, Airds Crossing, at the north end of High St. (☎704 921. Hiking boots £3.50 per day plus deposit. Ski, boot, and pole rental £15-25 per day. Open daily 9am-5:30pm and occasionally until 10pm on weekends in the high season. MC/V.) Other services include: **banks** on High St.; **police** and the Lochaber Mountain Rescue Post, High St. (☎702 361); Belford **hospital,** Belford Rd. (☎702 481); Boots **pharmacy,** High St. (☎01463 715 555; open M-F 9am-6pm, Sa 9am-5:30pm); **Internet** access at One World, 123 High St. (☎702 673; £3 per hr.; open daily 9:30am-9pm; cash only) and the Fort William **library,** High St., across from Nevisport (open M and Th 10am-8pm, Tu and F 10am-6pm, W and Sa 10am-1pm); and the **post office,** 5 High St., with a **bureau de change** (☎702 827; open M-F 9am-5:30pm, Sa 9am-12:30pm). **Post Code:** PH33 6AR.

ACCOMMODATIONS

Take care to reserve cheap accommodations early on weekends, especially on rainy days when sensitive backpackers run for cover. Fort William's B&Bs might outnumber their local residents, but "no vacancy" signs are a common sight in the summer months. Follow the A82 into **Glen Nevis** for accommodations closer to the mountain trails and farther from the "city lights" of Fort William.

> **TIP** **GET A ROOM.** If it starts to rain in Scotland during your stay, get on the phone and start calling accommodations as soon as possible. Rain drives tenting backpackers indoors, causing every accommodation around base camps like Fort William and Inverness to fill up at record speed.

Fort William Backpackers, 6 Alma Rd. (☎700 711; www.scotlands-top-hostels.com). From the train station, turn left on Belford Rd., right on Alma Rd. just before the Leisure Center, and bear left at the split. Rugged, welcoming atmosphere and facilities geared toward hikers. Watch the sun setting over Loch Linnhe from the back deck. 38 beds in 6- to 8-bed co-ed dorms; single-sex arrangements available. Self-catering kitchen. Breakfast £2. Laundry £2.50. Internet access £1 per 20min. Bike rental £12 per day. Curfew 2am. Reception closed 1:30-4pm. Dorms £12.50-13.50. AmEx/MC/V. ❶

Calluna, Connochie Rd. (☎700 451; www.fortwilliamholiday.co.uk), past the West End Roundabout, off Lundavara Rd.; call for a lift. Flower gardens surround this self-catering, spacious lodge. The owner, a local guide, rents equipment (£5 per day), leads expeditions, and gives lessons. 22 beds in 2- to 4-bed rooms. Drying rooms. Dorms £12-14. Internet £1 per 15min. Laundry £3. MC/V. ❶

Farr Cottage Lodge (☎772 315; www.farrcottage.com), on the A830 in Corpach. Take Highland Country bus #45 from Fort William. A licensed bar and affordable food service make Farr Cottage worth the 10min. drive. The perfect place to plan an outdoor adventure. Full or continental breakfast (£2.50-5), bagged lunches for climbers (£3.50), and hot dinner by request (£5). Laundry service £4. Internet £5 per hr. Dorms £13; private rooms from £17 per person. MC/V. ❶

Achintee Farm B&B and Hostel, Achintee Farm (☎702 240; www.achinteefarm.com), across the river from the Glen Nevis Visitor Centre, 2 mi. from town on the Glen Nevis Rd. Walk across the footbridge or call for a lift. Ideal for exploring Glen Nevis, with large, comfortable rooms and a self-catering kitchen. 14 beds in 2- to 5-bed dorms. No lockers. Laundry available. Dorms £12-14; private rooms £30 per person. MC/V. ❶

SYHA Glen Nevis (☎702 336), 3 mi. from town on the Glen Nevis Rd. Walk or take Highland Country Bus #42. Backpackers' hub with ideal location—the front door opens onto the trail to Ben Nevis. 88 beds in 6- to 8-bed single-sex dorms. Self-catering kitchen. Laundry available. Wi-Fi and Internet access £1 per 20min. Curfew 2am. Dorms £14, under 18 £11.50. MC/V. ❶

Distillery House, North Rd. (☎700 103). From the train station, turn left on Belford Rd. and continue to the roundabout. Whisky barrel tables stand in the lobby. Set of large white houses less than a mile from the famous distillery. Relax with complimentary whisky and shortbread provided in the lounge. The fully equipped cottages are ideal for a longer stay. No smoking. Singles £38-45; doubles £76-90; self-catering cottages £45 per week. AmEx/MC/V. ❹

Bank Street Lodge, Bank St. (☎700 070; www.bankstreetlodge.co.uk), just off High St. opposite the post office, above the Stables Restaurant. Comfortable wooden bunks with kitchen and TV lounge. 43 beds in 5- to 7-bed dorms. Laundry £3 wash and dry. Dorms £14; doubles £45-55. AmEx/MC/V. ❶

Glen Nevis Caravan and Camping Park (☎702 191), 2½ mi. from town on the Glen Nevis Rd. Ben Nevis towers nearby, but your view is likely to include trailer-owning neighbors. Toilets, showers, electricity, and laundry. Reservations July-Aug. Open from mid-Mar. to Oct. £5.40-9 per tent plus £1.60-2.50 per person. MC/V. ❶

🔦🍺 FOOD AND PUBS

High Street offers classic Scottish food in addition to a smorgasbord of international fare with questionable authenticity but plenty of character. At the north end of High St., Tesco sells **groceries**. (☎902 400. Open M-Sa 8am-9pm, Su 9:30am-6pm.)

🍺 **Maryburgh Inn,** 26 High St. Follow the sounds of merriment down an underground alleyway. "Discovered" when a townsperson fell through the floor of a shop and into a well, the Maryburgh has become a new kind of town drinking fountain. Now, a colored light fountain bursts from the floor where the well used to be, and the bar hosts karaoke Th-Sa nights. Open M-W and Su, 9am-midnight, F-Sa 9am-1am.

Nevis Bakery, 49 High St. (☎704 101). The lowest prices in town, award-winning Scotch pies served cold or heated (£1.50), and packed lunches (£3) perfect for a day on the mountain. Open M-F 8am-5pm, Sa 8am-4pm. Cash only. ❶

Crannog Seafood Restaurant (☎705 589), on the pier. Fresh fish practically flop into the dining room, which is fashioned out of Fort William pier. Try the Scottish Cheese Board with traditional "Brammle" whisky £7.50. Entrees £10-17. Open daily noon-2:30pm and 6pm-late. MC/V. ❸

Everest Indian Restaurant, 141b High St. (☎700 919). Escape the crowds down a small alleyway at this hole-in-the-wall restaurant overlooking the loch. Light, buttery naan, plenty of vegetarian options, and attentive servers. Entrees £6-11. Open daily noon-2pm and 5:30-11pm. MC/V. ❷

Grog & Gruel, 66 High St. (☎705 078). The lively and always packed Grog has an odd mix of Cajun and Tex-Mex along with the requisite haggis. Kelp Seaweed Ale (£1.50) is made from fresh ingredients straight from the loch. Entrees £8-13. Food served at the bar noon-9pm, in the restaurant 5-9:30pm. Open daily noon-10pm. MC/V. ❷

⊙ SIGHTS

The size of the natural environment is Fort William's main attraction. For the shopaholic, pedestrian-only **High Street** teems with tourists searching for that perfect swatch of Scottish plaid. 🚂**The Jacobite,** a.k.a. the *Harry Potter* train, is a vintage steam-powered locomotive that travels 42 mi. to Mallaig as part of the scenic **West Highland Railway.** (☎01463 239 026. Runs June and Sept.-Oct. M-F; July-Aug. M-F and Su. Departs Fort William at 10:20am. £20, round-trip £27.) **The West Highland Museum,** most famous for its Jacobite college, houses paintings and artifacts from the area in an old house next to the visitor center. (☎702 169; www.westhighlandmuseum.org.uk. Open M-Sa 10am-5pm. Adults £3, children 50p.) Two miles outside of town, on the A82 to Inverness, the **Ben Nevis Distillery** leads tours that include free samples and discounts on select whisky. (☎700 200. Open July-Aug. M-F 9am-5pm, Sa 10am-4pm, Su noon-4pm; Easter-June and Sept. M-F 9am-5pm, Sa 10am-4pm; Oct.-Easter M-F 9am-5pm. Last tour 1hr. before close. £4.) Hop aboard **Crannog Cruises** to scope out a local seal colony. Boat trips along Loch Linnhe leave from the town pier. (☎700 714; www.crannog.net. 1½hr. cruises depart from Mar. to mid-May 11am and 2pm; from mid-May to mid-Sept. 10am, noon, 2, 4pm. £8. MC/V.) In nearby Corpach, **Treasures of the Earth** has an unexpectedly large collection of gems on display, including local stones and fossils. A hanging pteranodon and a cartoon mural of a T-Rex add kitsch. Tours available for larger groups. (☎772 283. Open daily July-Sept. 9:30am-7pm; Feb.-June 10am-5pm. £4.)

▐▚ ▟ HIKING AND OUTDOORS

GLEN NEVIS AND BEN NEVIS. South of Fort William, Glen Nevis serves as a jumping-off point for outdoor enthusiasts. By far the biggest draw to the region is Britain's tallest mountain, Ben Nevis (4406 ft.), which is a challenging but manageable hike. The 10 mi. ascent typically takes between six and eight hours round-trip. The record, set in 1984 during the annual Ben Nevis Race (www.bennevis-race.co.uk), is an incomprehensible 85min. up and back. For the most beautiful views, pause at Lochan Mull, a stunningly clear lake about halfway up. For those not planning on tackling Ben Nevis, venturing into the glen provides spectacular views of mountains, gorges, rivers, and waterfalls. The drive up the glacial valley brings you to some fine day hikes. At the end of Glen Nevis Rd., a popular 3 mi. walk heads to Nevis Gorge and Steall Falls. Head to the Glen Nevis Visitor Centre to stock up on info, get the latest weather report, and acquire a nifty ecological history of the area. (☎705 922. Open daily Easter-Oct. 9am-5pm.) Walkers will find the Pathfinder Guide #7 (£11) useful. Ordnance Survey Explorer #392 (£8) and Landranger #41 (£8) maps cover the entire area with a focus on Ben Nevis.

AONACH MOR AND THE NEVIS RANGE SKI AREA. Seven miles northeast of Fort William, along the A82 and on the slopes of Aonach Mor (4006 ft.), the Nevis Range is Scotland's highest ski area. Journey beyond the clouds, up 2150 ft., on the resort's gondola. (☎705 825. Open July-Aug. daily 9:30am-6pm; from Sept. to mid-Nov. and from mid-Dec. to June daily 10am-5pm. Weather permitting. Round-trip £8.25.) Highland Country buses #41 and 42 travel to Aonach Mor from Fort William's bus station (15min.; M-Sa 8 per day, Su 4 per day). Nevis Range hosts the World Cup in downhill mountain bike racing in September on its famous 2100 ft. downhill track. Pick up a mountain bike racing kit from **OffBeat Bikes** at the Nevis Range. (☎704 008; www.offbeatbikes.co.uk. £25, includes bike, helmet, body armor, and ticket for Nevis Range track.)

OTHER ACTIVITIES. The **West Highland Way** completes its 95 mi. track in Fort William. Hikers or cyclists hungry for more can venture another 60-odd miles along the **Great Glen Way,** which runs north to Inverness Castle. The 75p *Cycling in the Forest—The Great Glen* pamphlet breaks the route into 11 manageable sections and includes maps. Numerous adventure sports are offered around Fort William, from canyoning, abseiling (rapelling), and kayaking around the unreal **Inchree Falls** to river rafting and hang-gliding in the glen. **Rock Hopper Sea Kayaking** offers gear rental and lessons and leads trips. (☎0773 983 4344; rockhopperscotland.co.uk. Activities from £35. Open daily.) ▐**Vertical Descents** (☎01855 821 593; www.verti-caldescents.com) provides gear and guides to outfit a variety of adventure sports.

GLEN COE   ☎01855

The Glen Coe valley seems to rise from nowhere to enfold the unsuspecting traveler in jaw-dropping mountains on all sides. The bloody massacre of the Mac-Donald clan in 1692 did much to shape the tiny villages dwarfed by their natural surroundings. Today, Glen Coe offers outdoor adventure to suit all types and temperaments as well as a hefty dose of highland merriment and music.

▐▟ TRANSPORTATION AND PRACTICAL INFORMATION. The Glen Coe valley comprises the villages of Glencoe and Ballachulish, which rest near the edge of

Loch Leven, at the mouth of the River Coe. The A82 runs the length of the valley. Food and accommodations lie on a parallel road that winds from Ballachulish through Glencoe. Scottish Citylink (☎08705 505 050) **buses** travel from Fort William to Glasgow (4 per day, £4.50) and provide direct access to the valley. Highland Country bus #44 serves Glencoe village from Fort William (35min., M-Sa 9 per day). Buses for Glen Coe stop at Glencoe village. Some travelers find that buses will pick them up anywhere if they motion with their arms in a place where the bus can pull over safely.

South of Glencoe Village, you'll find the **Tourist Information Centre** (☎811 866; open daily Apr.-Sept. 9am-6pm; Oct.-Mar. M-Sa 9am-5pm, Su 10am-5pm) just off the A82 in Ballachulish. Just off A82, 1 mi. southeast of Glencoe village, ⊠**Glen Coe Visitor Centre** provides succinct, detailed information on a dozen mountain trails. To walk from the village to the center and avoid the highway, take the Woodland Trail, a short hike that passes by the ruins of one of the massacre homesteads. The center also features extensive displays on the history and topography of the area along with practical weather and gear information for climbers and backpackers. The adjacent cafe provides simple soups and sandwiches. (☎811 307. Open Apr.-Aug. daily 9:30am-5:30pm; Sept.-Oct. daily 10am-5pm; Nov.-Feb. M and F-Su 10am-4pm; Mar. daily 10am-4pm. Exhibit £5, concessions £4.) The Spar **market** (☎811 367; open in summer daily 9am-9pm; reduced winter hours) and the **post office** (open M-Tu and Th-F 9am-1:30pm) can both be found along the parallel road, just beyond the TIC. **Post Code:** PH49 4HS.

◪◩ ACCOMMODATIONS AND FOOD. Many of Glen Coe's accommodations are situated along or just off a minor riverside road that runs 4 mi. up the valley to Glencoe village, roughly parallel to the A82. Turn right on this road to access the **SYHA Glencoe ❶**, 1½ mi. southeast of Glencoe village. (☎811 219. 60 beds in 6- to 8-bed dorms. Self-catering kitchen, laundry and drying room, and Internet (£1 per 20min). Book in advance. Curfew M-Th and Su 11:45pm, F-Sa 12:30am. Dorms £12-14, under 18 £9.50-10.50. AmEx/MC/V.) The **Glencoe Independent Hostel ❶**, halfway between Glencoe Village and the A82, provides creative accommodations in the midst of renovations. (☎811 906. 2-person log cabin £16, 8-person dorms £12, 16-person barn bunkhouse £9.50.) With a front lawn at the base of a mountain, the family-run **Clachaig Inn ❹** provides comfortable B&B lodging with spectacular views of nearby summits. From A82, turn right onto the riverside road and the Inn is less than a mile on the left. (☎811 252; www.glencoescotland.com. £38-42 per person. Self-catering cottages June-Aug. £545 per week; Sept.-May £400 per week. Dogs allowed by prior arrangement. MC/V.) Glencoe Village is full of B&Bs, most of which tend to fill quickly in the summer. The **Glen Coe Caravan and Camping Site ❶**, next to the visitor center, is well maintained, secure, and a good hiking base. (☎811 397. Toilets, showers, laundry, and cooking shelters. Open Apr.-Oct. £4.20-6.40 per person. Cash only.) Beside the River Coe, the **Red Squirrel Campsite ❶**, 1¾ mi. along the riverside road off A82, just beyond The Clachaig Inn, offers flat campsites and views of both sides of the valley. (☎811 256; www.redsquirrelcampsite.com. £7 per person. Showers 50p. Cash only.) The Clachaig Inn is the place to go for food and entertainment. The dimly lit, social restaurant serves Scottish fare such as steak pie and venison burgers (£6-10). Most of the meat comes from local game. The Inn also provides packed lunches (from £4.45). The lively **public bar ❷**, a traditional trail's-end pub, serves 15 beers on tap and hosts live local music on weekends. Look for special package deals in October and May for Glencoe's two beer festivals. (☎811 252. Open M-Th and Su 11am-11pm, F 11am-midnight, Sa 11am-11:30pm. Food served noon-9pm. MC/V.) In the village, the **Frying Scotsman** travels to Glencoe when you need him, serving mobile fish and chips at the Crossroads. (M 8-9pm, Tu 7:30-8:30pm, Th 6-7:10pm, F 7:30-8:30pm. Cash only.)

🅗🅡 **HIKING AND OUTDOORS.** Glen Coe offers some of Scotland's most striking outdoor experiences for visitors of all ability levels. Walkers stroll the floor of the valley, climbers head for the cliffs, and skiers race down the slopes and ice-climbers ascend frozen waterfalls. Although it pales in comparison to the surrounding scenery, **The Ice Factor** mountaineering center, 5 mi. away off B863 Kinlochleven, features the UK's largest indoor ice wall as well as hiking and climbing lessons. (☎831 100; www.ice-factor.co.uk. Open M and F-Su 9am-7pm, Tu-Th 9am-10pm.) Many of the trailheads lie several miles beyond Glencoe. With the right timing, you can use the Scottish Citylink **buses** that travel up the A82. For a small fee, most area hostels will shuttle hikers to the trailheads. Always bring a map; Landranger #41 (£7), Pathfinder Guide #7 (£11), and Short Walks #30 (£6) detail the area. Short but challenging daytrips abound. At the Glencoe Lachon Hiking Area just through Glencoe village, the 45min. Woodland Walk provides an easy introduction to the area. Pick up a trout fishing pass at Scorrybreac Guest House just beyond, and fish on the Lachan trail, which runs about 1 mi. around the lake. In the upper valley, the **Two Passes** route (9 mi.) climbs some 2100 ft., passing through two U-shaped glacial scars. For serious backpackers, the **Three Sisters,** Glen Coe's signature triumvirate of peaks along the **Aonach Eagach Ridge,** takes hikers along narrow paths with 2000 ft. drops on either side. Over the Pass of Glen Coe just off the A82, find ski fields and the **Glen Coe Ski Centre Chairlift.** During the winter, daily lift passes (£20-25) are available. (☎851 226. Open June-Aug. 9:30am-4pm, weather permitting. £6.) When the weather behaves, **Glencoe Cruises and Fishing Trips** (☎811 658) scuttle across Loch Leven, leaving from the pier in **Ballachulish. Glencoe Safaris** travel from the visitor center into the wilderness with guides who discuss Glencoe's wildlife and the famous McDonald massacre. (☎811 307. Apr., July-Aug., and Oct. Wildlife Tour at dusk, Massacre Tour at 10:15am.)

ROAD TO THE ISLES

The A830 travels from Fort William to Mallaig, following the historic Road to the Isles route (Rathad Iarainn nan Eilean). The winding drive to the coast captures the many landscapes of Scotland—rocky mountains, shady forests, and shallow lochs. Still single-lane in parts, the road often requires as much attention as the scenery. The 🅦**West Highland Railway** (originating in Glasgow; p. 625) runs alongside the road, providing sublime views at a fast clip (3-4 per day, £8.10). In summer, **"The Jacobite"** steam train (p. 627) runs from Fort William to Mallaig (via Glenfinnan and the 21-arch viaduct) in the morning and back in the afternoon. (June and Sept.-Oct. M-F; July-Aug. M-F and Su. Departs Fort William at 10:20am and Mallaig at 2:10pm. £20.50, round-trip £28.) Buses make the same trip (1½hr.; July-Sept. M-Sa 1 per day, Oct.-June M-F 1 per day; £4.25).

GLENFINNAN. The road runs westward from Fort William along Loch Eil, arriving after 12 mi. at Glenfinnan, on **Loch Shiel.** Trains often stop on trestle-bridged **Glenfinnan Viaduct.** A towering monument recalls Bonnie Prince Charlie's row up Loch Shiel to rally the clans around the **Stewart Standard** (see **The Jacobite Rebellion,** p. 524). For a panoramic view of the loch and the viaduct, visitors can climb a spiral staircase and stand atop the monument next to the statue of the Young Pretender. Purchase tickets in the **Visitor Center** (£3). Look for gliding golden eagles as you drift on 2hr. **Loch Shiel Cruises** as far as **Acharacle,** at the loch's far shore. Trips depart from the Glenfinnan House Hotel. (☎01687 470 322; www.highland-cruises.co.uk. £12-18. AmEx/MC/V.)

🅗**Glenfinnan Sleeping Car** ❶, a red railway-car-turned-hostel at the train station, provides unique, if cramped, lodgings. There are two bunks in each of four compartments. (☎01397 722 295. Food served from 8:30am. Linens £2. Dorms £10. Cash only.) Take a self-guided tour of the adjacent historical train station for just 50p. For a twilight loch view, opt for pub grub at the **Glenfinnan House Hotel ❷.** (☎01397 722 235. Open M-Sa 11am-midnight, Su noon-midnight. Food served noon-9pm. AmEx/MC/V.) The **Visitor Centre** has pamphlets on local history, which you can read with a slice of homemade carrot cake (£1.80) in the **cafe ❷.** (☎01397 722 250. Open daily Apr.-June and Sept.-Oct. 10am-5pm; July-Aug. 9:30am-5:30pm.) By **train,** Glenfinnan is 30min. from Fort William (£4.20) and 50min. from Mallaig (£5.30); by Scottish Citylink **bus,** the trips are both 30min. (£4.20).

ARISAIG AND LOCH MORAR. The road meets the west coast at the sprawling settlement of Arisaig. A popular spot for caravans and camping, Arisaig has patches of rocky beach with striking views of the outer islands. Stop at the volunteer-run **Land, Sea and Island Centre,** 7 New Buildings, for tide tables and other outdoor information as well as exhibits about area wildlife. (☎01687 450 263. Open M-F 10am-4pm, Sa-Su 1-4pm.) Compact white beaches with hidden coves are 3 mi. south of town on the A830; from the Camusdarach campsite, follow the signposted path. A winding 5½ mi. walk west of the town center follows the banks of **Loch Morar,** Britain's deepest freshwater loch (1017 ft.), home to Morag, Nessie's cousin. Three miles north on the A830 from Arisaig, the placid **Camusdarach campsite ❶,** as well groomed as the golf course around the corner, overlooks the beach. (☎01687 450 221. £10 per tent. Laundry £1. Showers free with £5 key deposit. Cash only.) The Spar on Main St. is the only **supermarket** between Fort William and Mallaig; inside is an **ATM** (open M-Sa 8:30am-8pm, Su 9:30am-7pm). Dine on homemade pastries (from £1.50) as you surf the Internet at the **Rhu Cafe ❶** in Arisaig. (☎01687 450 707. Internet £1 per hr. Open daily 10am-6pm. AmEx/MC/V.) Down the street from the Rhu and the Spar is the **post office.** (☎08457 450 375. Open M-F 9am-5:30pm, Tu and Sa 9am-1pm.) Arisaig Marine Ltd. operates regular **day cruises** from Arisaig to Rum, Eigg, and Muck from £17. (☎01687 450 224; www.arisaig.co.uk. Departs daily 11am.)

MALLAIG   ☎01687

The scenic A830 ends in Mallaig (MAL-egg). The port provides pretty views of the inner isles but not a whole lot to do. Fishermen and travelers fill the streets on weekends, waiting to depart for their next destination and feasting on the town's ample seafood offerings in the meantime.

Family-owned **Sheena's Backpackers Lodge ❶,** on the right after the station, above the Tea Garden restaurant, provides rooms filled with plants and flowers. Book ahead. (☎462 764. Dorms £13. Cash only.) Check out the view of the harbor from the bright **Moorings Guest House ❸,** East Bay (☎462 225. £20-25 per person. Cash only.) Closest to the pier, the **Marine Hotel ❸,** Station Rd., fills its bar with rowdy locals at night and has slightly shabby but comfortable accommodations. (☎462 217. £40 per person. MC/V.) **Groceries** can be found at the Co-op, in the center of town. (☎462 240. Open M-Sa 8am-10pm, Su 9am-9pm. MC/V.) The **Fishmarket Restaurant ❷** serves up the best fish in town, with views of the ocean they came from. Large starters and soups begin at £2.30. (☎462 299. Open daily noon-2:30pm and 6-9pm. Entrees £8-17. MC/V.) The **Tea Garden ❸** at Sheena's Backpackers serves fresh vegetables and upscale seafood with great views of the hanging garden and harbor. (Entrees £9-15. Cash only.) The **Fisherman's Mission ❶** is a muted cafeteria with rich, inexpensive food popular with fishermen on week-long breaks from the sea. Grab a homemade sugar-filled donut (£1.60) and enjoy the big-screen TV and fishermen's stories. (☎462 086. Open M-F 8:30am-10pm, Sa 8:30am-noon. Food served M-F 8:30am-1:45pm and 5:30-10pm, Sa 8:30am-noon. Cash only.)

GIVING BACK

A RUM DEAL

The Isle of Rum is a land of craggy mountains, hidden waterfalls, deserted stretches of sandy beach, and some of the most intimate volunteer opportunities in Scotland. The **Scottish Natural Heritage (SNH)** owns the island and oversees a variety of upkeep projects. These projects are open to public volunteers, who can arrange work and job training with the island manager.

Despite Rum's remarkably small size, tasks are varied. Volunteers can survey the local bird and otter populations, garden, round up the island's cattle herd, care for farm animals, repair fences, plant trees, and work with Rum's herd of 19 domesticated horses. Four days of service will earn you an entire week's worth of free accommodation. If you're lucky, your bed could even be in **Kinloch Castle** (p. 639).

Volunteering on Rum is especially enjoyable because of the welcoming island community and the varied nature of the jobs. While regular traveling can expose many aspects of a country, working to care for some part of it can show you a different side—one that is infinitely more satisfying. On Rum, it will also earn you a free bed with time to explore one of Scotland's most beautiful islands, blissfully out of reach of the tourist horde.

Island Manager ☎ 01687 462 026. More info at www.snh.org.uk.

CalMac **ferries** (☎ 08705 650 000; www.calmac.co.uk) sail from Mallaig to Armadale, Skye (May-Sept. daily 8 per day; Oct.-Apr. M-Sa 8 per day; £3.40, 5-day round-trip £5.80; car £18.40/31.50) and to the Small Isles. **Cycles2U** (☎ 450 291) transports bikes in a van to Mallaig and surrounding areas; call for delivery (£16 per day). North of the pier, the Water's Edge **Tourist Information Centre** has a free telephone for booking accommodations. (☎ 07876 518 042; www.thewatersedgetic.co.uk. Open M-Sa 10:15am-3:45pm.) Other services include: a **Bank** of Scotland by the train station (☎ 462 265; open M-Tu and Th-F 9:15am-1pm and 2-4:45pm, W 9:30am-1pm and 2-4:45pm); a **library** in the Mallaig Community Centre, across the tracks from the Heritage Centre (☎ 460 097; free; open M 1-5pm, Tu 10:30am-2pm, W 9:30am-1:30pm, Th 5-8pm, Sa 10am-noon); and the **post office**, located in the Spar up the hill from the tourist office. (☎ 462 419. Post office open M-F 9am-5pm, Sa 9am-12:30pm. Spar open M-Sa 8am-10pm, Su 9:30am-9pm.) **Post Code:** PH41 4PU.

THE INNER HEBRIDES

ISLE OF SKYE

Mountains extend into the clouds on the Isle of Skye, whose hills, peninsulas, and seaside walks hold many secrets for the savvy tourist. Small towns pepper the island, providing glimpses into Highland culture and Gaelic traditions. Because visitors tend to stick to major roads, many of Skye's landscapes lay virtually undisturbed—a far cry from the island's revived castles and their summer crowds.

◪ GETTING THERE

The tradition of ferries that carried passengers "over the sea to Skye" ended with the construction of the Skye Bridge, which links Kyleakin to the mainland's Kyle of Lochalsh. Pedestrians can take either the bridge's 1½ mi. **footpath** or the **shuttle bus** (every hr., 70p). **Trains** (☎ 08457 484 950) run from Kyle to Inverness (2½hr.; M-Sa 4 per day, Su 2 per day; £15.20). Scottish Citylink **buses** #915 and 917 travel daily to Fort William (2hr., 3 per day, £13.30), Glasgow (6hr., 3 per day, £22), and Inverness (2hr., 3 per day, £12). From the Outer Hebrides, CalMac **ferries** (☎ 08705 650

000) sail from Uig to Tarbert, Harris, and Lochmaddy, North Uist (1½hr.; M-Sa 1-2 per day; £9.80, 5-day round-trip £16.75; cars £47/80). Ferries also run from Armadale in southwest Skye to Mallaig on the mainland (30min.; June-Aug. daily 8-9 per day, Sept.-May M-Sa 8-9 per day; £3.40, 5-day round-trip £5.80; cars £18.40/31.50). From Aros or Portree, take an On the Wing guided bus tour through Skye (☎01478 613 649; www.aros.co.uk).

▐ LOCAL TRANSPORTATION

To avoid headaches, pick up the handy *Public Transport Map: The Highlands, Orkney, Shetland and Western Isles* at any TIC. On Sunday, buses run only to meet the Rassay and Armadale ferries (June-Aug.). Prices listed below are often estimates—fares can change rapidly and often depend on the driver of the bus.

Buses: Highland Country buses traverse Skye. They are not necessarily timed to coordinate travel with other means of transportation or even other buses. The most reliable service is Scottish Citylink. Buses #915 and 916 travel from **Kyleakin** to **Broadford** to **Portree** on the A87. The **Skye Rover** ticket offers unlimited bus travel on Skye and can be purchased on any local bus (1-day £6, 3-day £15).

Bike Rental: Cycling is common and enjoyable on Skye, but be prepared for steep hills, nonexistent shoulders, and rain. Most buses will not carry bikes. Rent bikes in Broadford at **Fairwinds Cycle Hire** (☎01471 822 270; £8 per day, £10 deposit for overnight rental); in Portree, **Island Cycles** (☎01478 613 121; £14 per day, discounts for longer rentals). Reserve ahead, especially in summer.

Car Rental: Kyle Taxi Company (☎01599 534 323) has a low delivery fee. 23+. £35-42 per day.

Tours: The **National Trust of Scotland** (☎01599 511 231) has 3hr. guided walks (£5) through the countryside and longer trips to the Three Sisters and the Falls of Glomach. Advance booking required. For the eager and intrepid, the stellar ▮**MacBackpackers Skye Trekker Tour** (☎01599 534 510; www.macbackpackers.com), which departs from the hostel in Kyleakin, and offers a 1-day tour emphasizing the mythology and history of the island (£18; weekly departure Sa 7:30am).

♪ ▒ ENTERTAINMENT AND FESTIVALS

Cultural life on Skye is vibrant, engaging tourists and locals alike. Snag a copy of the monthly newspaper, *The Visitor*, for a list of special events, or consult the TIC. The **Skye Music Festival** draws bands and fans from across the UK on the last weekend in May. The 2008 festival will be held on May 23-24 (www.skyemusicfestival.co.uk; day ticket £50). In mid-July, **Feis an Eilein** (☎01471 844 207; www.skyefestival.com), on the Sleat Peninsula, is a 10-day celebration of Gaelic culture, featuring concerts, *ceilidhs*, workshops, and films. Additional revelry can be found at the **Highland Games** (☎01478 612 540; www.skye-highland-games.com), a day of bagpipes and merriment in Portree on the first Wednesday in August, and **Highland Ceilidh**, with *ceilidhs* (p. 527) in Portree, Broadford, and Dunvegan. (☎01470 542 228. June M and W; July-Aug. M-W.)

KYLE AND KYLEAKIN   ☎01599

Kyle of Lochalsh ("Kyle" for short) and Kyleakin (Ky-LAACK-in) bookend the Skye Bridge, both serving as hubs for tired backpackers headed to and from the island. Kyle's upscale accommodations and restaurants cater to a different crowd than Kyleakin's buzzing backpacker nightlife.

🔁 TRANSPORTATION AND PRACTICAL INFORMATION. The Kyle **train station** is near the pier; the **bus stop** is just to the west. Highland Country buses meet incoming trains and go to Kyleakin (every 30min., 15p). The Kyle **Tourist Information Centre**, by the pier, has a phone for booking accommodations (open May-Oct. M-F 9:30am-5pm, Sa-Su 10am-4pm). Other services include a **Bank** of Scotland, Main St. (☎534 220; open M-Tu and Th-F 9am-5pm, W 9:30am-5pm), **Internet** access at the Kyle **Library** (☎534 146; open Tu 12:30-3:30pm and 4:30-8pm; free), and a **post office** (☎534 246; open M-F 9am-5:30pm, Sa 9am-12:30pm). **Post Code:** IV40 8AA.

🔦 ACCOMMODATIONS. In Kyle of Lochalsh, **Cu'chulainn's Backpackers Hostel ❶**, Station Rd., offers standard hostel bunks with easy access to the pub and restaurant that shares its name. (☎534 492. Laundry £2.50. Internet £2 per hr. Key deposit £5. Dorms £9-12.50. Cash only.) Follow the sign to the **Kyle Hotel ❹**, Main St., which has plaid bedspreads and views of the main drag. (☎534 204; www.oxfordhotelsandinns.com. Singles £40-52; doubles £80-120. AmEx/MC/V.)

Kyleakin serves as the hostel hub of the area. The laid-back staff and humorous themed rooms at **🔲Skye Backpackers ❶** create a social starting point for any trip to Skye. (☎534 510; www.scotlands-top-hostels.com. Laundry £2.50. Internet access 80p per 30min. Curfew M-Th and Su 12:30am, F-Sa 1:30am. Dorms £11-13.50. AmEx/MC/V.) **Dun-Caan Hostel ❶** is a 200-year-old, renovated cottage overlooking the bay. The surrounding gardens make for lovely views no matter the room. (☎534 087; www.skyerover.co.uk. Bike rental £10 per day. Dorms £12. MC/V.) In the white building on the village green, **SYHA Kyleakin ❷** has a larger, institutional feel offset by a knowledgeable staff providing info about area hikes. (☎534 585. Laundry £2. Internet access £1 per 20min. Dorms £12-14, under 18 £9.50-11. AmEx/MC/V.) Two doors down from SYHA, **Saucy Mary's ❸** operates a small hostel and B&B adjacent to the most rowdy bar in town. (☎534 845. Wi-Fi and optional breakfast £2.50. Dorms £13. B&B rooms from £20. AmEx/MC/V.)

🍴 FOOD AND PUBS. In Kyle, grab **groceries** at the Co-op, up the hill to the west of the Kyle bus station. (☎530 190. Open M-Sa 8am-10pm, Su 10am-6pm.) **Cu'chulainn's ❶** offers upscale local seafood and great vegetarian options in its flowering beer garden. (☎534 492. Open M-Sa 11am-12:45am. Food served 11am-8pm. MC/V.) By the pier, **Hector's ❶** serves homemade ice cream and sweets. (☎534 248. Open M-Sa noon-10pm, Su noon-9pm.)

In the more lively Kyleakin, **Saucy Mary's,** named after a Norse seductress, packs in pints, crowds, and occasional live music. (Open M-Th 5pm-midnight, F 5pm-1am, Sa 5-11:30pm, Su 5-11pm.) The large **King Haakon Bar,** at the east end of the village green, serves delicious seafood in a room ripe for dancing. (☎534 164. Open M-Th 12:30pm-midnight, F 12:30pm-1am, Sa 12:30pm-12:30am, Su 12:30-11:30pm. 18+ after 8:30pm. Food served 12:30-8:30pm. MC/V.)

🔳 SIGHTS. The child-oriented **Bright Water Visitor Centre,** on the pier in Kyleakin, contains tactile exhibits on local wildlife. (☎530 040. Open Apr.-Oct. M-F 10am-4pm. Free.) The center runs 1½hr. walking tours to **Eilean Ban,** the island under the Skye Bridge. Departure times vary and are limited, so call ahead. (M-F 1 per day; £6, concessions £5.) The colorful boats in **Kyleakin Harbor** make for a calm walk around the pier, especially at sunset. Across the harbor, scramble up the hill to reach the small ruins of **Castle Maol.** Look for tiles that mark the way and the foreboding "Beware the Tides" stone. Heed its warning—the ruins are accessible only when the tide is out. According to legend, Norwegian princess "Saucy Mary" built the original castle and stretched a chain across the water, charging a toll to ships. She supposedly flashed those who paid the toll—hence her spicy moniker. (Always open. Free.) In Kyle, the **Seaprobe Atlantis** is a glass-bottomed boat that allows for close-up views of the ocean, which teems with sealife. (☎ 0800 980 4846; www.seaprobeatlantis.com. £12.50 for a 1hr. trip.)

SLEAT PENINSULA AND ARMADALE   ☎ 01471

Two miles south of Broadford, the A851 leaves the clouds behind, revealing lush green gardens and glimmering sea views. Seventeen winding miles later it reaches the scattered town of Armadale. Follow the sprawling nature paths through the **Armadale Castle Gardens** near the ruins of the former MacDonald stronghold. **Museum of the Isles** provides an articulate and beautifully displayed look at 1500 years of Scottish history. The adjacent study center is one of the best places in Scotland for **genealogical research.** (☎ 844 305; www.clandonald.com. Open daily Apr.-Oct. 9:30am-5:30pm. Last admission 5pm. Research is an additional £7 per ½-day. Gardens and museum £5, concessions £3.80, families £14.) In the building that used to keep the MacDonalds' horses, ▨**Stables Cafe ❶** makes exceptional homemade soups (from £2) and overlooks the gardens. (☎ 844 305; M-Su 9:30am-5pm.) The **Sleat Peninsula** juxtaposes views of nearby islands Rum, Muck, and Eigg with those of heavily forrested areas and the Cuillins. A short footpath beginning at the shore of Loch Eishort (west off the A851) leads to little-known **Dunscaith Castle** ruins (1 mile). A longer hike (3-3½hr. round-trip) reaches Skye's southernmost tip, the **Point of Sleat**, with a lighthouse and views of the Cuillins to the north. The trailhead begins at the end of the A851, south of **Ardvasar** at the **Aird of Sleat.** An hour's walk rewards with awesome views of **Rum** from the inlet of **Acairseid an Rubha.**

> **TIP**
>
> **LOST IN TRANSLATION.** North of Armadale at Ostaig, the famous Gaelic college Sabhal Mòr Ostaig offers language courses for a few hours or a week, many of which cater to tourists. (☎ 888 000; www.smo.uhi.ac.uk. Courses £140 for single week. MC/V.)

The owner of **Flora MacDonald Hostel ❶**, 3 mi. north of Armadale, will pick you up at the Armadale ferry and bring you to his rustic lodge, which is surrounded by Eriskay ponies. (☎ 844 272 or 844 440. Kitchen and TV. Dorms £11. Cash only.) The **SYHA Armadale ❶** is located just south of the castle gardens and has a pristine view of the water. (☎ 844 260. Lockout 10:30am-5pm. Curfew 11:30pm. Open Apr.-Sept. Dorms £12, under 18 £9. AmEx/MC/V.) **Ferries** run from Armadale to Mallaig (10 per day; single £3.40, 5-day round-trip £5.80, cars £18.40/31.50). Highland Country **buses** run between Armadale and Broadford (4-6 per day, £3).

CENTRAL SKYE   ☎ 01478

The dominant Cuillin Hills (COO-leen) are the highest peaks in the Hebrides and can be seen from all over Skye as well as from many of the smaller isles. The Kyleakin-Portree road winds its way through the Red Cuillins, which beckon to hikers through the misty clouds. Tiny Sligachan (SLIG-a-chan), at the junction of A87 to Portree and the A863 to Dunvegan, serves as an excellent base for exploring the hills. The famous trail through Glen Sligachan (p. 636) begins in Sligachan.

 ACCOMMODATIONS AND FOOD. A five-minute walk from the bus station, the **Sligachan Bunkhouse ❶** is a red cabin in the woods—perfect for a quiet night. (☎ 650 204. Linens £2. Dorms £10. MC/V.) The **Sligachan Hotel ❹** has rooms with soft beds for weary hikers. (☎ 650 204. Singles £40-50; doubles £60-80. MC/V.) The **Sligachan Campsite ❶** is just across the road. (Open May-Sept. £4. Cash only.) Several miles south of Sligachan on Loch Brittle, the wooden **SYHA Glenbrittle ❶**

stands against the wind. Down a single-lane track lined with evergreens, the town of Glenbrittle can be reached by Highland Country bus #53 from Portree, which runs twice per day. (☎640 278. Open Apr.-Sept. Dorms £11-11.50, under 18 £8.75-9.75. MC/V.) The **Glenbrittle Campsite ❶** is at the foot of the Black Cuillins and overlooks the loch. (☎640 404. Open Apr.-Oct. Reception 8am-7pm. £4.50. MC/V.) The Sligachan Hotel's **Seumas' Bar ❷** is the only pub around, offering a broad selection of beers and malts. (Live music F-Sa. Open daily 8am-11:30pm. MC/V.)

◪ ◪ **HIKING AND OUTDOORS.** The Cuillin Hills are great for experienced hikers but risky for beginners. TICs, campsites, and hostels are well stocked with maps and books for walks throughout the region (see **Wilderness Safety,** p. 50). For a list of current guided walks, pick up a copy of *Ranger Guided Walks and Events* from a TIC. The pitted peat of the Cuillins is always drenched and summer temperatures dip low—expect wet, frigid feet. A short, scenic path follows the stream from Sligachan to the head of **Loch Sligachan.** After crossing the old bridge, fork right off the main path and walk upstream along the right-hand bank. The narrow, boggy path leads past pools and waterfalls, in some places tracing the top of a small cliff (3 mi. round-trip). The 2537 ft. **Glamaig** proves a steep, challenging 3½hr. hike. A smaller trail branches off after 1 mi. and leads up the ridge.

The daunting **Sgurr nan Gillean,** to the southwest of Glamaig, provides an all-day hike into the clouds, towering 3167 ft. above a tiny lake. For more level terrain, take the 8 mi. walk down **Glen Sligachan** through the heart of the Cuillins to the beach of **Camasunary,** with views of the isles of Rum and Muck. From Camasunary, you can hike 5 mi. along the coast to **Elgol.** From there, a sailing trip to **Loch Coriusk** with **Bella Jane Boat Trips** grants a different view of Skye and the surrounding isles. (☎01471 866 244. Runs Apr.-Oct. M-Sa; call for reservations 7:30-10am. Round-trip £20-30. MC/V.) Elgol is 14 mi. southwest of Broadford on the B8083; Highland Country Buses #50 and 52 travel to Broadford and Portree (M-Sa 4 per day, Su 2 per day). Scottish Citylink buses #916 and 917 also travel between Kyle and Portree via Broadford and Sligachan (M-Sa 6 per day, Su 4 per day.) Eight miles from Sligachan, the staff of **Cuillin Trail Riding** offers guided horseback rides for all ability levels. (☎07789 714 106; www.cuillintrailriding.co.uk. Open M-Sa dawn-dusk.)

THE MINGINISH PENINSULA   ☎01478

The Minginish Peninsula is the road less traveled on Skye, but the serene seaside towns are full of lovely ocean views and places to stay. On the road to Talisker, the expansive **Talisker Distillery** sits on Loch Harport and offers straightforward tours of its processes. The 45min. distillery tour is bland, but the whisky isn't: Skye's only malt packs a fiery finish. (☎614 308. Open Apr.-Oct. M-Sa 9:30am-4:30pm; Nov.-Mar. M-F 2-4:30pm. £5.) Four miles past Sligachan toward Dunvegan, **The Old Inn ❶** has pirate-themed rooms overlooking the water and a giant kitchen and common area. (☎640 205; www.carbost.f9.co.uk. Laundry £4.50. Dorms £12, ensuite £13. MC/V.) Up the road, the stylish **Taigh Ailean's ❸** plaid furniture creates a homey atmosphere for its B&B crowd. The attached pub serves some of the best ale in the area. (☎640 271. £25-40 per person. MC/V.) The **Skyewalker Independent Hostel ❶**, Fiskavaig Rd., Portnalong, has average accommodations and operates the best (and only) **cafe ❶** on the peninsula. (☎08000 277 059. Dorms £8.50; doubles £18; tents £3. MC/V.) **Croft Bunkhouse ❶** sits in a sunny field and fills its narrow common area with guests year-round. (☎640 254. Dorms and bothies £8.50. Camping available in adjacent field. MC/V.) Highland Country **buses** #53 and 54 travel to Portree and Sligachan (M-F 4 per day, Sa 1-2 per day), stopping at Carbost and the Talisker Distillery and continuing to Portnalong. The **post office** is in the hostel (open M and W-Th 9-11am). **Post Code:** IV47 8SL.

PORTREE   ☎01478

Most visitors to Skye end up in Portree at one point or another. It's the island's largest town and best transportation hub, with colorful buildings and harbor crowds that create a center for cultural life. The bright green **Portree Independent Hostel ❶**, in the center of town, has plenty of amenities including a well-stocked kitchen. (☎613 737. Dorms £12-13. MC/V.) Right as you enter Portree, the **Easdale B&B ❸**, Bridge Rd., is hidden up a stone pathway, behind a garden complete with old iron farm tools and garden gnomes. (☎613 244. £20-25 per person. Cash only.) For higher-end lodgings, the **Portree Hotel ❹**, Somerled Sq., has occupied its castle-like building in the square since 1865. (☎612 511. £35-55 per person. MC/V.)

The Somerfield **supermarket** is on Bank St. (☎612 855. Open M-Sa 8:30am-8pm, Su 10am-5pm.) Stock up on fusion cuisine from all over the world at ⚑**Cafe Arriba ❷**, on Quay Brae. (☎611 830. Entrees £4-8. Open daily 7am-10pm. MC/V.) Vegetarian options and warm bread make the **Granary ❶**, Somerled Sq., a snacker's heaven. (☎612 873. Open Apr.-Oct. daily 9am-4:30pm; Nov.-Mar. M-Sa 9am-5pm. MC/V.) Feast on delicate entrees at **Bosville Hotel ❷**, Bank St. (☎612 846. Entrees £8-16. 2 courses £28, 3 courses £37. Open daily noon-10pm. AmEx/MC/V.) The **Caledonian Hotel pub**, upstairs on Wentworth St., is removed from the buzz of the main square. On weekends, it's the place to be for dancing. (☎612 641. Live music F-Su. Open M-F 2pm-1am, Sa 12:30pm-12:30am, Su 12:30-11:30pm.) The **Isles Inn**, Somerled Sq., is a refurbished croft house that featuring frequent live music and a large selection of ales. (☎612 129. Open M-Sa 11am-midnight, Su 12:30-11:30pm. MC/V.)

Scottish Citylink and Highland Country **buses** travel from Somerled Sq. to Kyle and Kyleakin (M-Sa 8-10 per day, Su 5 per day). To reach the **Tourist Information Centre,** Bayfield Rd., from the square, face the Bank of Scotland, turn left down the lane, and left again onto Bridge Rd. The staff books lodgings for a £3 plus a 10% deposit. (☎612 137. Open July-Aug. M-Sa 9am-6pm, Su 10am-4pm; Sept.-Oct. and Apr.-June M-F 9am-5pm, Su 10am-4pm; Nov.-Mar. M-Sa 9am-4pm.) Other services include: a Royal **Bank** of Scotland, Bank St. (☎612 822; open M-Tu and Th-F 9:15am-4:45pm, W 10am-4:45pm); a **launderette,** underneath the Independent Hostel (☎613 737; open M-Sa 9am-9pm); **Internet** access at the TIC (£2.50 per hr.) or up the street at the **library** (☎612 697; free, but book ahead; open M and W 1-8pm, Th-F 10am-5pm, Sa 10am-1pm); and the **post office,** Wentworth St. (☎612 533; open M-Sa 9am-5:30pm). **Post Code:** IV51 9DB.

▶️ DAYTRIPS FROM PORTREE: TROTTERNISH PENINSULA, DUNTULM CASTLE, AND DUNVEGAN CASTLE.

Many cliffs, waterfalls, and ancient standing stones on Trotternish remain seemingly untouched. A steep hike *(1hr. round-trip)* leads to the **Old Man of Storr,** a 165 ft. basalt stone at the top of the highest peak in Trotternish (2358 ft.), located north of Portree on the A855. Begin from the car park to attempt this ascent. North of Staffin, a footpath leads through the **Quirang** rocks, known as some of the most striking geological formations in the world *(3hr. round-trip).* Nearby **Staffin Bay** abounds with Jurassic fossils and pottery remains from more recent settlers. South of Staffin, **Kilt Rock** has "pleated" lava columns above a rocky base crumbling into the sea. Climb to the top of nearby **Mealt Falls** (300 ft.) for the best view of the formation. The challenging 12 mi. hike along the **Trotternish Ridge** encompasses many of the sights on the peninsula. Begin at the Old Man of Storr car park and follow the signs to Staffin. On a bluff 5 mi. north of Staffin, the **Dun Flodigarry Hostel ❶** has a huge, colorful kitchen and overlooks the cliffs and ocean. Check out the fossils gathered by recent guests in buckets by the door. Take the Staffin bus from Portree and ask to be let off. *(☎01470 552 212. Internet access £1 per 30min. Dorms £12.50. Camping £6 per person. Cash only.)*

At the northern tip of the peninsula, **Duntulm Castle** ruins stand at the edge of the sea, creating a powerful image of the former stronghold of the MacDonald clan. According to legend, the house was cursed when a nurse dropped the chief's child from a window. *(Be careful of the edge. Always open. Free.)* Near Duntulm at Kilmuir, iron tools dot the yard of the **Skye Museum of Island Life,** a preserved crofter village of 18th-century black houses. *(☎01470 552 206. Open Easter-Oct. M-Sa 9:30am-5:30pm. £2.)* Down the road from the museum is the **Kilvaxter Iron Age Farmstead and Souter-rain,** which dates back to 300 BC. Crawl down the narrow tunnel at your own risk.

Off the A850, **Dunvegan Castle** is the longest inhabited Scottish castle, occupied since the 13th century. Elegantly restored rooms, a vast number of sculptured gardens, and a video about the MacLeod clan await visitors. Arrive early or late in the day to avoid hordes of summer tourists. For a free view of the castle and grounds, try the **Two Churches walk,** a few miles north of Dunvegan on the A850. Highland Country bus #56 *(M-Sa 2 per day)* runs from Portree to the castle. *(☎01470 521 206; www.dunvegancastle.com. Open daily from mid-Mar. to Oct. 10am-5:30pm; from Nov. to mid-Mar. 11am-4pm. £7, concessions £6. Gardens only £5/3.50. From Portree, Highland Country buses run to the various sights. M-Sa 3-8 per day.)*

UIG   ☎01470

Serving as little more than a sleepy stepping stone for island travelers, Uig (OO-ig) has a calm harbor and accommodations that make for a solid night of rest. The **SYHA Uig ❶,** a 30min. walk from the ferry dock, has rooms capable of keeping out the pervasive early summer light. Turn left on the winding road from the ferry dock. *(☎542 211. Internet £1 per 20min.; Wi-Fi £3. Reception closed 10am-5pm. Curfew midnight. Open Apr.-Oct. Dorms from £12, under 18 from £9. AmEx/MC/V.)* Navigate colorful yard decor to reach **Orasay B&B ❷,** next to the pier, where all rooms are ensuite. *(☎542 316. £22.50-25 per person. Cash only.)* **The Pub at the Pier ❷** is the town's lounge and bar, with classic food offerings (burger £3.30, entrees £9-14) and the occasional local band. *(☎542 212. Open M-F 11am-1am, Sa 11am-12:30am, Su 12:30-11pm. Food served 11:30am-4:45pm and 6-9pm. MC/V.)* CalMac runs a **ferry** connecting Uig to Tarbert, Lewis and to Lochmaddy, North Uist (1½hr.; M-Sa 1-2 per day; £9.80, 5-day round-trip £16.75; with car £47/80). While waiting for a ferry, stop by the **Isle of Skye Brewery,** next to the pier. Employees give brief tours when they're not busy brewing. *(☎542 477. Open M-F 10am-6pm, Su 12:30-4:30pm. £2. Advance booking requested.)* Highland Country **buses** #57A and 57D and Scottish Citylink buses also run to Portree (M-Sa 4-5 per day, Su 3 per day; £3).

THE SMALL ISLES   01687

The small isles of Rum, Eigg, Muck and Canna make stunning daytrips from the mainland. They offer everything from tours of a working Highland farm to Celtic music festivals to 2000 ft. mountain hikes. Small communities of islanders provide tons of information about their beloved homes, but set aside plenty of time to explore and discover the islands' remote beauty on your own.

▐▘ GETTING THERE

CalMac **ferries** (☎462 403) sail from Mallaig to Rum (£8.35, 5-day round-trip £14.55), Eigg (£5.65/10), Muck (£8.55/15.15), and Canna (£10.55/25.50); call for schedules. Ferries require that cars have governmental permission to board, but many find that having a car registered in Scotland will suffice. They are timed to connect with trains from Glasgow and Fort William and charge £2.20 per bicycle. Arisaig Marine Ltd. (☎450 224) sails on the MV *Shearwater* at 11am from Arisaig (p. 631) to Rum (June-Aug. Tu, Th, and Sa-Su; Easter-June and Sept. Tu and Th;

FERRY ANNOYING. Don't assume that ferries to the Small Isles will return to pick you up after your visit. Schedules vary and many assume an overnight excursion on the isle. Come prepared with schedule information and, if needed, camping gear.

round-trip £22, under 16 £11, under 12 £8), Eigg (M-W and F-Su; £16, under 16 £11, under 12 £8), and Muck (M, W, F; £17).

RUM. Rum's miles of pristine trails and uneven coastline make for gorgeous hiking and camping. The largest of the four isles, Rum is owned by the Scottish National Trust, whose staff help protect and preserve the island's elusive Manx shearwaters, Red Deer, and sea eagles. At the ferry landing, pick up a self-guided tour of the **Loch Scresort Trail** (2hr. round-trip), a straightforward path that runs along the coast and allows for the occasional seal sighting. To the left of the trail lies the sprawling red stone ⛶**Kinloch Castle** (☎462 037). Built in 1897 as the plaything of George Bullough, a former owner of the isle, the castle's rooms are cluttered with animal skins and imported tapestries. Scottish National Heritage staff lead daily tours timed with the arrival of the CalMac ferries (M 1:15pm, Tu-Th and Sa 2pm, F 2:30pm. £5.) The adjacent **Community Hall Tea Shop** offers snacks (from £1.50). With ferries arriving in the middle of the day, a night spent on Rum leaves time for plenty of exploring. Spend the night in the **Kinloch Castle Hostel ❷**, whose rooms overlook the lake. The castle's fresh, organic meals are worth the splurge. (☎462 037. Open Mar.-Oct. Laundry £2. Kitchen. Breakfast £5, packed lunch £5, 3-course dinner £13.50. Advance booking required. £14 per person; B&B £30 per person. MC/V.) For information on camping or using either of the two bothies on Rum, contact the Island Manager, Scottish Natural Heritage, Isle of Rum, PH43 4RR (☎462 026; tent or bothy by donation; showers available at the hostel for £2). In the morning, take the rugged **Ridgewalk trail** up over 2000 ft. to the island's highest point and enjoy one of the most stunning views in the region.

EIGG. With a population of 78, Eigg is home to the largest and youngest community of the small isles, and the parties at the island's pub are the place to be for hip travelers from the mainland. The only island owned by the community that lives there, Eigg has seen its share of land squabbles in the past few years. The curious **Sgurr of Eigg** (1290 ft.), a massive lava cliff that juts up from the center of the island, makes Eigg easily recognizable. Ranger John Chester offers guided historical and wildlife walks. (☎482 477. £3. Call in advance to schedule a tour.) A minibus meets each ferry for a trip to the **Singing Sands** (round-trip £4). For **bicycles**, look for the shed just north of the grocery store. (☎482 432. £8 per ½-day, £12 per day.) **Glebe Barn ❶** offers cozy beds with a wood-burning stove and views of Rum and Muck. The hostel is located 1 mi. from the pier. (☎482 417. Open Apr.-Oct. Dorms £10-12. Book ahead. Cash only.) For B&Bs, the best value is **Laig Farm Guest House ❸**, nestled in a private valley with a nearby beach. The guest house is 4 mi. from the pier, along the same road as the hostel. (☎482 412. £35 per person; includes dinner and breakfast. Cash only.) For a **taxi,** call ☎482 494.

MUCK. Three generations of the McEwen family have lived and farmed on Muck over the past 100 years. The small island (2 mi. long) is a sprawling farm with cows sleeping on the beach, horses roaming the hills, and sheep lining up to be sheared in early summer. Visit the **Tea Room and Restaurant ❶** for savory leek and potato soup (£2) or the signature lamb burger for just £2.50. (☎462 362. Open daily 11am-5pm or call ahead to book a dinner.) The adjoining **craft shop** features beautiful, handmade wool items (from £3). Take a tractor tour of the isle for £1 or venture down to the beach and explore beds of iridescent seaweed. Stay at the refinished

Port Mor Guest House ❹ (☎462 365; full board £37; cash only) or the cozy **Isle of Muck Bunkhouse ❶.** (☎462 042. £10.50. Linens £1. Cash only.)

CANNA. On Wednesdays and Saturdays, the CalMac **ferry** gives travelers time to spend a few hours on the isle of Canna (Gaelic for "porpoise"), home to 14 residents. Walk the harbor road to find two chapels and the **Harbor View Tearoom ❶,** which has scrumptious pastries. (☎462 465. Open M-Sa 11am-2pm and 6-11pm; book your dinner choice before 5pm. AmEx/MC/V.) When the tide is out, ambitious powerwalkers can access the ruins of **St. Columba's Chapel,** a 7th-century nunnery. The SNH also runs **Kate's Cottage ❷,** a simple converted cottage with views of Rum and the Cuillins. (☎462 466. Singles £20. Cash only.)

THE OUTER HEBRIDES

With cairns, standing stones, and the remnants of generations displayed against a landscape of exposed rock, the ancient past comes to life in the Outer Hebrides. Steeped in tradition, you're more likely to get an earful of Gaelic here than anywhere else in Scotland. On the Calvinist islands of Lewis, Harris, and North Uist, most establishments close and public transportation ceases on Sundays (although one or two places may assist lost souls with a pint), while to the south, on Benbecula, South Uist, and Barra, tight-shuttered Sabbatarianism gives way to pictures of the Pope. The extreme seclusion and quiet of the islands make the Western Isles one of Scotland's most undisturbed, unforgettable realms.

█ TRANSPORTATION

CalMac (☎08705 650 000) has a near-monopoly on passenger and car **ferries** along major routes. It runs from Ullapool to Stornoway, Lewis (2¾hr.; 2-3 per day; £15, 5-day round-trip £26; car £73/125); from Uig, Skye to Lochmaddy, North Uist (1¾hr.; 1-2 per day; £9.80, 5-day round-trip £16.75; car £47/80); and to Tarbert, Harris (1½hr.; 1-2 per day; £9.80, 5-day round-trip £16.75; car £47/80) and from Oban to Castlebay, Barra and Lochboisdale, South Uist (6½hr.; 1 per day; £21.55, 5-day round-trip £37; car £79/134). Call ahead if you wish to take a car.

In the archipelago, ferries brave rough sounds, and infrequent buses cross causeways connecting the islands. TICs carry the invaluable, free *Discover Scotland's Islands with Caledonian MacBrayne, Lewis and Harris Bus Timetables,* and *Uist and Barra Bus Timetables.* **Cycling** is popular, although windy hills and sudden rains often wipe out novice riders. Traffic is light, but hitchhikers report frequent lifts on all the islands. *Let's Go* does not recommend hitchhiking. Inexpensive **car rental** (from £25 per day) is available. Road signs are in Gaelic first and English second, if at all. Although many names are similar in English, TICs often carry translation keys, and *Let's Go* lists Gaelic equivalents after English place names where appropriate.

█ ACCOMMODATIONS

Mobility on the islands is limited by infrequent ferries and inconsistent ferry schedules. If you plan to stay overnight near a ferry terminal, try to book a bed ahead. Area TICs book **B&Bs** for £3 plus a 10% deposit. **Camping** is allowed on public land in the Hebrides, but freezing winds and sodden ground often make it a miserable experience. Lewis's remote **SYHA Kershader ❶,** Ravenspoint, Kershader, South Lochs, is a standard small hostel, with a shop next door in the community center. (☎01851 880 236. Laundry £2. Dorms £9.75, under 18 £8.75. MC/V.)

The Outer Hebrides are home to the unique ▨Gatliff Hebridean Trust Hostels ❶ (www.gatliff.org.uk), four 19th-century thatched croft houses turned into very simple year-round hostels. The hostels accept no advance bookings but very seldom turn travelers away. Aside from basic facilities, all provide cooking equipment, range tops, cutlery, crockery, and hot water. Blankets and pillows are provided, but the hostels only have coal fires; you'll want a warm sleeping bag. Hostels cost £9 per person (under 18 £6) and **camping** is £5. (Cash only.)

Berneray (Bhearnaraigh): Off North Uist. Frequent buses W19 and W17 shuttle between the hostel, the Otternish pier (where ferries arrive from Harris), the Lochmaddy pier on North Uist, and the Sollas Co-op food store (30min., M-Sa 6-9 per day, £1). A beautifully thatched and whitewashed building overlooking a picture-perfect beach.

Garenin (Na Gearranan): Lewis, 1½ mi. north of Carloway. Unsurpassed surroundings. Buses on the W2 "West Side Circular" route from Stornoway (M-Sa 10-11 per day) go to Carloway, if not Garenin village itself. Free taxi service meets some buses at Carloway.

Howmore (Tobha Mòr): South Uist, about 1hr. north of Lochboisdale by foot. W17 buses from Lochboisdale to Lochmaddy stop at the Howmore Garage (M-Sa 5-8 per day, £1); from there, follow the sign 1 mi. west from the A865. Overlooks a ruined chapel; near the rubble that was once Ormiclate Castle.

Rhenigidale (Reinigeadal): North Harris. Take the free minibus from the car park next to the Tarbert TIC (☎01859 502 221; M-Sa 2 per day; call ahead). The bus will take your pack if you want to attempt the tough 6 mi. hike along the eastern coast. From Tarbert, take the road toward Kyles Scalpay for 2 mi. and follow the signposted path left to Rhenigidale. The path ascends 850 ft. before zig-zagging down steeply (3hr. round-trip). By car, follow the turn-off to Maaruig (Maraig) from the A859, 13 mi. north of Tarbert.

LEWIS (LEODHAS)

The sloping moors of Lewis make for great walking and biking, and its historical artifacts are among the most celebrated in Scotland. Stornoway, Lewis's capital city, offers a splash of world culture, while many people in surrounding communities preserve a commitment to sustainable farming and traditional craftsmanship.

STORNOWAY (STEORNOBHAIGH)   ☎01851

The urban feel of Stornoway comes as a shock after any exploration of the remote Outer Hebrides. Parks and museums make the town well worth the visit, and lively traditional music flows through its pubs on weekends.

▤▨ **TRANSPORTATION AND PRACTICAL INFORMATION.** CalMac **ferries** sail to Ullapool (2¾hr.; M-Sa 2-3 per day; £15, 5-day round-trip £26; car £73/125). **Buses** operated by Western Isles depart from the Beach St. station; pick up a free *Lewis and Harris Bus and Ferry Services Timetable*. (☎704 327. Luggage storage 20p-£1. Station open M-Sa 8am-5:45pm.) Destinations include Callanish (Calanais; 1hr., M-Sa 4-6 per day), Port of Ness (Nis; 1hr., M-Sa 6-8 per day), and Tarbert (An Tairbeart; M-Sa 3-7 per day, £4.15). **Car rental** is cheaper here than on the mainland. Try Lewis Car Rentals, 52 Bayhead St. (☎703 760. £25-45 per day. 21+. Open M-Sa 9am-6pm. AmEx/MC/V.) Rent **bikes** at Alex Dan's Cycle Centre, 67 Kenneth St. (☎704 025. £11.50 per day. Open M-Sa 9am-6pm. MC/V.)

The **Tourist Information Centre** is on 26 Cromwell St. From the ferry terminal, turn left onto South Beach and right on Cromwell St. (☎703 088. Open Apr.-Oct. M-F 9am-6pm and 8-9pm; Nov.-Mar. M-F 9am-5pm.) From April to October, **Stornoway Trust** (☎702 002) organizes free **walks** through the town and countryside. Lewis

THE LOCAL STORY

THE SCREEN MACHINE

For islanders who rarely leave the Outer Hebrides, a good film is hard to come by. Newspapers arrive on doorsteps, mail is delivered by ferry each day, and televisions light up many houses at night. However, silver-screen movies are a rare occurrence on the isles, which contain 50% of Scotland's land mass but only 0.6% of the UK's population.

In the mid-1990s, the Highland Arts Council set out to design a way to bring movies to the isles. The solution? The Screen Machine. Housed in a large blue truck that island-hops on ferries, the Screen Machine unfolds like a pop-up book to reveal a portable, 80-seat theater, complete with a concessions stand and red carpet lining the metal stairs.

The Screen Machine takes about six weeks to comb the Outer Hebrides, screening two Hollywood blockbusters for islanders hungry for pop culture. The summer of 2007 also marked the Screen Machine's first island film festival, held on Eriskay and featuring films whose plot or scenery highlighted life on the isles.

For more information, visit www.the-booth.co.uk and www.hi-arts.co.uk, or call ☎01463 720 890 for show times. Most films cost £5.50.

also has a **JobCentre Plus**, 13-15 Francis St. (☎763 100. Open M-Tu and Th-F 9am-5pm, W 10am-5pm.) Other services include: a **Bank** of Scotland, across from the TIC (☎705 252; open M-Tu and Th-F 9am-5pm, W 9:30am-5pm); a **pharmacy**, 29-31 Cromwell St. (☎703 131; M-Tu and Th-Sa 9am-6pm, W 9am-5pm); free **Internet** access at the Stornoway **Library** (☎708 631; open M-W and Sa 10am-5pm, Th-F 10am-6pm); and the **post office**, 16 Francis St. (open M-F 9am-5:30pm, Sa 9am-12:30pm). **Post Code:** HS1 2AA.

Γ̃ Ꮯ̃ ACCOMMODATIONS AND FOOD. Hands down the best place to stay in Stornoway, the immaculate ◼Heb Hostel ❶, 25 Kenneth St., offers exceptional facilities, including a beautiful fireplace. (☎709 889. Internet £1 per 30min. £15 per person. Cash only.) **Mr. and Mrs. Hill ❸**, Robertson Rd., open their home to travelers who seek a quiet space removed from the hustle and bustle of the main square. Exiting the bus station, turn right and follow James St. up the hill; turn left on Matheson Rd. and right on Robertson. (☎706 553. £25 per person. Cash only.) The **Laxdale Bunkhouse ❶**, off Bayhead Rd., sleeps 16 in four small, modern rooms on the Laxdale Holiday Park campgrounds, 1½ mi. from downtown. (☎706 966; www.laxdaleholidaypark.com. Bunks £11-12; tents £5 plus £2 per person. Cash only.) The **Stornoway Backpackers Hostel ❶**, 47 Keith St., offers basic metal-frame beds near the town center. (☎703 628; www.stornoway-hostel.co.uk. Reception daily 1-2pm and 8-9pm. Dorms from £10. Cash only.)

Cheap chow is plentiful in takeaway-heavy Stornoway. Stock up on **groceries** at the Co-op on Cromwell St. (☎702 703. Open M-Sa 8am-8pm.) Feast on classic dishes in the green-curtained glow of the ◼Thai Cafe ❷, 27 Church St., which serves inexpensive, mouth-watering entrees (£4-6) by candlelight. (☎701 811. Open M-Sa noon-2:30pm and 5-11pm. MC/V.) The **library cafe ❶**, attached to the library on Cromwell St., satisfies large lunchtime crowds with its home-made soups and sandwiches, starting at £2. (☎708 632. Open M-Sa 10am-4pm).

◩ SIGHTS. The **An Lanntair Arts Centre**, on Kenneth St., has a year-round program of visual and performing arts, a plush bar and restaurant, and an evening film series. (☎703 307; www.lanntair.com. Open M-Sa 10am-11pm. Free; film series prices vary.) The **Museum nan Eilean**, Francis St., has fascinating exhibits on 9000 years of Hebridean history. (☎709 266; www.cne-siar.gov.uk. Open Apr.-Sept. M-Sa 10am-5:30pm; Oct.-Mar. Tu-F 10am-5pm, Sa 10am-1pm. Free.) The woods surrounding the mock Tudor **Lewis Castle** provide shaded walks along the water. The castle itself was built in the 19th century and stands overlooking the town, adjacent to the golf course. The entrance is on Cromwell St., but you can admire it from across the water on N. Beach St. Turn left after the footbridge from New St.

NIGHTLIFE AND FESTIVALS. Stornoway livens up unexpectedly on weekend nights. **Pubs** and **clubs** crowd the area between Point St., Castle St., and the two waterfronts. Formerly a center that offered alternatives to alcohol, **McNeill's** has returned to its roots as a classic pub that serves a solid pint. (☎703 330. W live music. Open M-W 11am-11pm, Th-Sa 11am-1am. Cash only.) **The Clachan Bar** features live music and a traditional pub atmosphere for unwinding after a long day. (☎703 653. M-W and Su 11am-11:30pm, Th and Sa 11am-12:30am, F 11am-1:30am. Cash only.) There's no better place to watch a big-time sporting event than on the screen at the popular **Crown Inn,** N. Beach St. (☎703 181. Open M-W 11am-11pm, Th-F 11am-1am, Sa 11am-11:30pm.) **The Heb,** Point St., has a large dance floor where islanders really let loose. (No phone. Open F 10pm-3am, Sa 7pm-1am.) The **Hebridean Celtic Festival** (☎621 234) in mid-July draws top musical talent from Scotland and all over the world. The main acts sell out far in advance.

DAYTRIPS ON LEWIS

Travel up the **west coast** of Lewis for a glimpse of thousands of years of the island's history preserved in ruins, museums, and reconstructed houses. The W2 bus operates on a circuit beginning at the Stornoway bus station (M-Sa 4-6 per day). **Galson Motors** (☎840 269) offers a day pass on this route (£6), or a round-trip ticket to see one, two, or three of the sights from May to October (£4-5). Alternatively, travel with **Out and About Tours.** (☎612 288. ½-day £67, full day £102.) **Albannach Guided Tours** offers personalized excursions. (☎830 433. From £10 per hr. per person.)

CALLANISH STONES (CALANAIS). The gargantuan Callanish Stones, 14 mi. west of Stornoway on the A858, are second only to Stonehenge in grandeur and are less overrun with tourists. Some archaeologists believe that prehistoric peoples used Callanish and two nearby circles to track the movements of the heavens. The Visitor Centre has a comprehensive exhibit and a short video. (☎621 422. Open Apr.-Sept. M-Sa 10am-6pm; Oct.-Mar. W-Sa 10am-4pm. Stones free; exhibit and film £1.85, concessions £1.35.) Nibble scones at the newly renovated **Callanish Tea House ❶,** the only privately owned black house on the island. (☎621 373; www.callanishblackhouse.com. Open M-Sa 9am-6pm. Cash only.) A mile south of Callanish, the W3 bus makes its way across the bridge to the stark-white beaches of the island of Great Bernera. Travel underground to tour the excavated Bostadh Iron Age House. (Open June-Aug. M-F noon-4pm. £2, concessions £1.)

CARLOWAY BROCH (DÙN CHARLABHAIGH). Five miles north of Callanish along the A858 lies the crofting settlement of **Carloway** (Charlabhaigh), dominated by the Iron Age **Carloway Broch.** Dating from the first century BC, this double-walled stone tower would have been home to a powerful community leader and is one of the largest remaining brochs. The visitor center provides a marginally interactive tour revealing what life would have been like in a broch. (☎643 338. Visitor Centre open Apr.-Sept. M-Sa 10am-5pm. Broch always open. Free.)

GEARRANNAN BLACK HOUSE VILLAGE AND ARNOL BLACK HOUSE. Up the road in Carloway proper is a restored community of traditional black houses that were occupied as recently as the 1960s. These houses had no chimneys, and fires constantly burned in the center of the stone floor. The smoke helped hold the roof together. A local weaver works in the houses and tells the history of the community. Three-hour guided historical walks leave from the settlement. (☎643 416.

Open M-Sa 9:30am-5:30pm. £2.50. Guided walks £2.50; call for hours.) Farther north on the A858, in Arnol beyond Shawbost, lies a restored crofter's cottage known as the Arnol Black House. Walk along the beach near the black house to find pieces of pottery from surrounding communities. *(☎710 395. Open Apr.-Sept. M-Sa 9:30am-6:30pm; Oct.-Mar. M-Sa 9:30am-4:30pm. Last admission 30min. before close. £4.50.)*

BUTT OF LEWIS. Besides being the butt of terrible puns, the Butt of Lewis has an enormous natural stone arch that stands where the Atlantic crashes into the cliffs with deafening ferocity. Legend has it that the Vikings attached a chain to the arch and tried to pull the Hebrides back to Norway with them, causing the islands to split apart into the formation they have today. To the north you'll pass the village of Galson and the quiet **Galson Farm Guesthouse and Bunkhouse ❶,** whose sturdy wooden beds make for sound sleeping. Be sure to call ahead. *(Butt of Lewis always open. Free. Galston Farm ☎850 492; www.galsonfarm.freeserve.co.uk. Bunks £11. MC/V.)*

DALMORE BEACH AND SURF SPOTS. Several beaches on Lewis and Harris are quickly becoming known as world-class (if chilly) surf spots. In Lewis, competitors flock to **Dalmore Beach,** near the town of Dalbeg, as well as to the beaches of **Valtos** and **Europie,** farther down the western coast. Amateur archaeologists and shell hunters search for Neolithic artifacts and the pink shells fabled to be mermaid fingernails. With its riptide currents, the **Port of Ness** is a dangerous place to surf—only the experienced should head there. **Hebridean Surf Holidays,** on the corner of Keith and Francis St. in Stornoway, offers all-inclusive surfing lessons, rents equipment, and shuttles surfers to the beach. *(☎07939 194 880; www.lewissurf-ftrek.com. Lessons from £35 per day; board and ride to beach from £20.)* The W2 **bus** route (M-Sa 6-10 per day) runs past Dalbeg and Dalmor Beach, while W4 buses (M-Sa 2-4 per day) from Stornoway pass other spectacular surf spots farther down the coast. The W1 bus (M-F 8-9 per day, Sa 6 per day) travels along the northwest coast to the Butt and the Port of Ness.

HARRIS (NA HEARADH)

Harris shares an island with Lewis, but the two regions are different worlds—when the ruling MacLeod clan split, so did the isle. The deserted flatlands of Lewis in the north stand in stark contrast to the rugged peaks of Harris. Tufts of grass dispersed between slabs of rock give the landscape an eerie, moon-like appearance. Toward the west coast, the Forest of Harris (in fact a treeless, heather-splotched mountain range) descends onto brilliant crescents of white sand bordered by cerulean waters and *machair* (sea meadows). The A859, or "Golden Road" (named for the king's ransom spent blasting it from the rock), winds to Harris's southern tip—it's a trip for seasoned cyclists or bus travelers ready for a bumpy ride. Roads branch from Tarbert to the small fishing community Scalpay (Scalpaigh), connected to Harris by a causeway.

TARBERT (AN TAIRBEART)   ☎01859

As the largest town on Harris, Tarbert serves both as a ferry port for traveling to the Isle of Skye and as a good base for a series of walks and hikes around Harris. The **Harris Walkway** runs north from Clisham to Scaladal, passing through Tarbert in the middle. The tallest peaks lie in the **Forest of Harris,** whose main entrances are off the B887 to Huishinish Point, at Glen Meavaig, and farther west at 19th-century **Amhuinnsuidhe Castle,** 15 mi. from Tarbert. The infrequent summertime W12 bus from Tarbert serves these points (3 per day). If you don't have much time, use one of the unmarked eastern trails to hike up **Gillaval** (1554 ft.; at least 1hr.) or take a

ROCK THE TWEED. Buying tweed in larger towns and shops ensures a high-quality product from a Highland source. Look for the Harris Tweed authenticity patch to verify that your item was made by a crofter on Harris.

coastal stroll from Taobh Tuath to Horgabost. Ordnance Survey maps for these areas are available in the TIC. Tarbert itself has few attractions, but it is a good place to buy swatches and teddy bears made of the world-famous Harris tweed. **Rent bicycles** from Paula Williams. (☎520 319. £10-12 per day.)

The homey **Drinishader Hostel ❶** is located 6 mi. from Tarbert. Get there by going south on the A859 and following signs to Drinnishader. (☎511 255. Dorms from £9. Cash only.) If you're stuck in Tarbert for the night, the sparsely decorated **Rockview Bunkhouse ❶** is less than a 5min. walk from the pier on Main St. It's run by two postal clerks—you can check in at the post office. (☎502 211. Dorms £10. MC/V.) Up the road from the ferry terminal, the **Harris Hotel ❹** sits among sculptured gardens and proudly sports J.M. Barrie's graffiti on its dining room window. (☎502 154. £35-65 per person, with dinner £68-88. MC/V.) A.D. Munro **market,** Main St., serves Tarbert as grocer, butcher, and baker. (☎502 016. Open M-Sa 7:30am-6pm. MC/V.) Nestled behind fragrant flowering bushes, the **Firstfruits Tearoom ❶,** across from the TIC, pours hot drinks in a homey setting. (☎502 439. Open Apr.-Sept. 10am-4:30pm. Evening meals served from 7-9pm. Cash only.) The **Harris Hotel Restaurant and Bar ❹** serves entrees (£14-18) in the main building's upscale dining room for residents and non-residents alike. (☎502 154. Bar open M-Sa 11am-11pm, Su 12:30-2:30pm and 6:30-10:30pm. MC/V.)

Ferries sail from Tarbert to Uig, Skye (M-Tu, Th, and Sa 2 per day; W and F 1 per day; £9.80, 5-day round-trip £16.75). Check with CalMac (☎502 444) at the pier in Tarbert for timetables. Hebridean Transport runs **buses** (☎01851 705 050) from Leverburgh and Stornoway (bus W10; 1hr., M-Sa 3-7 per day, £4.15). The **Tourist Information Centre** is on Pier Rd., and Tarbert's only **ATM** is located at the back of the building. (☎502 011. Open from Apr. to mid-Oct. M-Sa 9am-5pm; Tu, Th, and Sa 7:30-8:30pm; from mid-Oct. to Mar. for ferry arrivals.) A **Bank** of Scotland is uphill from the pier. (☎502 453. Open M-Tu and Th-F 10am-12:30pm and 1:30-4pm, W 11:15am-12:30pm and 1:30-4pm.) Free **Internet** access is available in the public **library** in Sir E. Scott School, a cream-colored building 10min. along the A859 to Stornoway. (☎502 926. Open M 9:30am-6pm, Tu and Th-F 9:30am-4:20pm, W 9:30am-4:20pm and 6-7:45pm; Sa 10am-12:30pm.) The **post office** is on Main St. (☎502 211. Open M-Tu and Th-F 9am-1pm and 2-5:30pm, W 9am-1pm, Sa 9am-12:30pm.) **Post Code:** HS3 3DB.

RODEL AND LEVERBURGH ☎01859

Rodel (Roghadal), at Harris's southern tip, is the site of **St. Clement's Church,** which houses three MacLeod tombs from the 16th century. Climb the wooden ladders to the top of the church for sweeping views of the isle. Three miles up the road is **Leverburgh,** a small port. Colorful anchors and coiled rope decorate the lawn of the ▨ **Am Bothan Bunkhouse ❷,** a funky, comfortable hostel in town ¼ mi. from the Leverburgh pier. Ask the owner about taking a ride in his boat. (☎520 251; www.ambothan.com. Dorms £15. Camping £10. MC/V.) The straightforward **Anchorage Restaurant ❷** serves classic seafood dishes on Leverburgh's pier. Enjoy a casual dinner (entrees £7-12) or a full breakfast for £4.50. (☎520 225. Open M-Sa 11am-8pm. AmEx/MC/V.) CalMac (☎01876 500 337) **ferries** sail to Leverburgh from Ardmaree, Berneray (M-Sa 3-4 per day; £5.60, 5-day round-trip £9.50). **Buses** W10 and W13 run from Tarbert (1hr., M-Sa 3-7 per day, £4.15).

HIGHLANDS AND ISLANDS

THE UISTS (UIBHIST)

The sky seems to grow larger above the flat, windswept Uists (YOO-ists). Sheep graze roadside and lochs dot the landscape over the 125 mi. chain of islands whose blazing wildflowers light up the land in summer. The Uists are home to two towns: Lochboisdale on South Uist and Lochmaddy on North Uist. Each packs its own Highland culture and hospitality. The small island of Benbecula, which has the Uists' sole airport, is the stepping stone between the two larger isles.

⌐ TRANSPORTATION

CalMac **ferries** (☎08705 650 000; www.calmac.co.uk) travel from Lochmaddy to Uig, Skye (1¾hr.; 1-2 per day; £9.80, 5-day round-trip £16.75; car £47/80). Ferries travel from Berneray to Leverburgh, Harris (1¼hr.; M-Sa 3-4 per day; £5.60, 5-day round-trip £9.50; with car £25.50/43.50) and from Lochboisdale to Oban (7hr.; Tu, Th, and Sa-Su 1 per day; £21.55, 5-day round-trip £37; car £79/134). The island council also runs the tiny Sound of Barra Ferry (☎08151 701 702) from Eriskay to Barra (1hr.; 4-5 per day; £6, 5-day round-trip £10.20; car £17.70/30.50). **Airplanes** operated by British Airways (☎08457 799 977; www.britishairways.com) travel from Benbecula to Barra (1 per day, from £30).

Pick up the latest bus schedule from the TIC. **Bus** W17 runs along the main road from Lochmaddy to the airport in Balivanich and Lochboisdale (M-Sa 5-6 per day, £3.20). Buses W17 and W19 meet at least one ferry per day in Ardmaree for departures to Harris; W17 and W29 go to Eriskay in the south for connections to Barra (5-9 per day). Most buses stop running by 7pm; book accommodations close to the ferry dock if arriving late. For **car rental,** call MacLennan's Self Drive Hire, Balivanich, Benbecula. (☎01870 602 191. From £25 per day. 21+. Open M-F 9am-5:30pm, Sa 9am-noon. AmEx/MC/V.) **Rothan Cycles,** in Howmore, rents and repairs bicycles. (☎01870 620 283; www.rothan.com. £8 for the first day, £6 thereafter. Call ahead.) Closer to Lochmaddy, rent bikes at **Langass Lodge**. (☎01876 580 285; www.langasslodge.co.uk. £10 per day.)

✱ ORIENTATION AND PRACTICAL INFORMATION

The Uists lie south of the Isle of Lewis, separated from the Isle of Skye and the Scottish mainland by the Sea of the Hebrides. The small island of Benbecula separates North Uist and South Uist.

There are **Tourist Information Centres** on the piers at Lochboisdale (☎01878 700 286; open Apr.-Oct. M-Sa 9am-1pm and 2-5pm) and Lochmaddy (☎01876 500 321; open Apr.-Oct. M-F 9am-5pm, Sa 9:30am-5:30pm), which book accommodations and stay open late for ferry arrivals. There are three **banks** on the Uists: in Lochboisdale, a Royal Bank of Scotland (☎01878 700 399; open M-Tu and Th-F 9:15am-4:45pm, W 10am-4:45pm), in Benbecula, a Bank of Scotland (☎01870 602 044; open M-Tu and Th-F 9am-5pm, W 9:30am-5pm), and in Lochmaddy a Bank of Scotland (☎01876 500 323; open M-Tu and Th-F 9:30am-12:30pm and 1:30-4:30pm). Benbecula has the Uists' sole **launderette,** Uist Laundry, by Balivanich Airport. (☎01870 602 876. Wash £4, dry £2; kilts £9. Open M-F 8:30am-4:30pm, Sa 9am-1pm.) **Internet** access is available at Nunton Steadings teashop and the information center in Benbecula (£1.50 per 30min.; free Wi-Fi with cafe order) or at the **Claddach Kirkibost Centre,** just north of Clachan, North Uist on the A865 (☎01876 580 390; open M-F 9:30am-5pm). The Cafe Taigh Chearsabhagh houses the Lochmaddy **post office.** Balivanich in Benbecula also has a post office, across from the bank (open M-Tu and Th-F 9am-5pm, W 9am-3pm, Sa 9am-12:30pm). **Post Codes:** HS6 5BD (Lochmaddy) and HS8 5SS (Lochboisdale).

ACCOMMODATIONS

B&Bs are scattered throughout the Uists; the TICs can help find vacancies upon arrival. In Lochboisdale, **Bay View ❷,** just up the street from the ferry terminal, offers comfortable beds and lives up to its name with views of the water. (☎01878 700 329. From £20 per person. Cash only.) Also near the ferry terminal, the **Lochboisdale Hotel ❹** is family owned and serves as a good base for island activities. (☎01878 700 332. From £50. MC/V.) Bring a sleeping bag to stay at the **Howmore ❶** hostel in South Uist, north of Lochboisdale. (☎08701 553 255. £9.) **The Angler's Retreat ❸,** at the northern tip of South Uist, offers a family environment and discounts on fly fishing tackle. (☎01870 610 325; www.anglersretreat.net. £25. Cash only.) Find the **Gatliff Hebridean Trust Hostel ❷,** a very basic accommodation, up the road in **Berneray** (p. 641). The only hostel near Lochmaddy is the **Uist Outdoor Centre ❶,** which offers overnight expeditions and courses in rock climbing, canoeing, and water sports from £25 per half-day. Follow signposts west from the pier for 1 mi. (☎01876 500 480. Bring a sleeping bag and book ahead. Linens £2. Dorms £10. MC/V.) **The Old Courthouse ❸,** in Lochmaddy, has stone walls and arched doorways. (☎01876 500 358. £22 per person, with breakfast £27-30. Cash only.) For the best accommodation splurge on the islands, try the exceptionally modern red and yellow **Tigh Dearagh Hotel ❺,** in Lochmaddy, recently reopened with state of the art facilities. The exercise room, sauna, steam room, restaurant, and pub are all open to the public for £5. (☎01876 500 700; www.tighdearghotel.co.uk. Breakfast included. Free Wi-Fi. Doubles £60-£139. AmEx/MC/V.) You can **camp** almost anywhere on the Uists, but ask the crofters first.

FOOD AND PUBS

For **groceries** on the islands, there are Co-ops in: Daliburgh (Dalabrog) on South Uist (☎01878 700 326; open M-Sa 8am-8pm, Su 12:30-6pm; AmEx/MC/V); Creagorry at the bottom of Benbecula (☎01870 602 231; open M-Tu and Sa 8am-8pm, W-F 8am-9pm, Su 12:30-6pm; AmEx/MC/V); and Sollas (Solas) on North Uist (☎01876 560 210; open M-W and Sa 8:30am-6pm, Th-F 8:30am-7pm; AmEx/MC/V). On Eriskay, the **Am Politician ❷** pays homage to the famous wreck of the whisky-filled SS *Politician* and serves delicious pub food. (☎01878 720 246. Open M-Sa 11am-midnight, Su 12:30pm-1am. MC/V.) **The Lochboisdale Hotel ❹,** a short walk from the ferry port, offers fresh seafood in a simple dining room. (☎01878 700 332; www.lochboisdale.com. Food served noon-2:30pm

IN RECENT NEWS

HEDGEHOG FUND

If you see a hedgehog on the Uists, don't let it out of sight until you get your £20. Since 2003 these prickly island denizens have been much sought after, and not because they make good winter coats. Hedgehogs were introduced to the Uists in the 1970s as a means of controlling garden slugs and other pests. Without natural predators, their population quickly exploded, and they began preying on the eggs of waders, a type of bird protected by the Royal Society for the Protection of Birds (RSPB).

The RSPB spearheaded the Uist Wader Project, designed to rid the Uists of hedgehogs by lethal injection—costing them a remarkable £1,283.78 per successful hedgehog execution in 2006. Naturally, this sparked the formation of another group, the Uist Hedgehog Rescue, currently moving hedgehogs from Uist to the mainland. Uist Hedgehog Rescue consists of many different animal rights groups, the most notable being St. Tiggywinkles (of Beatrix Potter fame) Animal Hospital. Battling between RSPB and the hedgehog-rescuers has raised the price for live hogs to £20—there are even rumors of canny islanders importing hedgehogs from the mainland in order to cash in on the bounty.

So, don't hedge your bets: find a hedgehog and check out www.sttiggywinkles.org.uk for more info.

and 5-9pm. MC/V.) Off the main road in Benbecula, follow the signs to **Stepping Stone ❸,** an upscale restaurant with a large selection of local meat and fish. (☎01870 603 377. Entrees £10-16. Open M-F 9am-9pm, Sa 11am-9pm, Su noon-8pm. MC/V.) Across the street from the Lochmaddy Hotel, the **Cafe Taigh Chearsabhagh ❶** sells baked goods, soup, and sandwiches for £1.50-4. (☎01876 500 450. Open M-Sa 10am-5pm. Cash only.) For elegant twists on classic Scottish dishes, try **Langass Lodge ❹,** halfway between Clachan and Lochmaddy. (☎01876 580 285. 2-course dinner £24, 3-course £29. Lunch daily noon-2:30pm; dinner daily 7-9:30pm. MC/V.) The pub grub (£6-12) at **Lochmaddy Hotel ❷** hits the spot for ferry crowds. (☎01876 500 331. Open M-Th 11am-11pm, F 11am-1am, Sa 11am-11:30pm, Su 12:30pm-11pm. AmEx/MC/V.)

👁 SIGHTS

In Lochboisdale, the **Museum and Craft Shop** features exhibits by local artists as well as a history of the area. Attached are a cafe with homemade soups (£2.50) and a craft center. (Open M-Sa 10am-5pm. Craft center open M-Sa 11am-4pm. £2.) The vibrant ⊠**Taigh Chearsabhagh** (tie KEAR-sa-vah) **Museum and Arts Centre** in Lochmaddy is home to exhibits of contemporary Scottish artwork. (☎01876 500 293. Open daily 10am-5pm. Donation suggested.) The path behind the museum leads to displays of public art, like a mackerel mosaic. Just up the road is the **Hut of the Shadow,** a camera obscura set in a cairn-like structure. The image of the bay is reflected onto the wall of the faux-primitive hut. A series of walks takes visitors through wildlife sanctuaries and ancient burial grounds. **Loch Druidibeg** on South Uist is a remote nature reserve that provides regular sightings of golden eagles and peregrine falcons. Cairns, war memorials, old croft houses, and other historic sites proudly stand across the flat land. Walk along the beach in Benbecula before heading north to experience the **RSPB Balranald Reserve** on western North Uist, north of Bayhead and signposted from the A867. The warden offers guided walks to see the hundreds of species of birds that land there. (☎01876 560 287. M-Sa 3-4 per day. Walks £3-4.) On the northwest coast, the **North Uist Riding School** provides a chance to see the land on horseback. (☎07786 817 577. £20.)

SMALLER ISLANDS

ERISKAY (EIRIOSGAIGH). Off the southern tip of South Uist, Eriskay connects to the larger island by a causeway. Buses W17 and W29 run from Lochboisdale (45min., 10 per day). It is also the departure point of the ferry to Barra (40min., 5 per day). Eriskay residents tell the story of the SS *Politician,* a ship that crashed on the island in 1941 while carrying 260,000 bottles of whisky bound for America. Islanders "helped" salvage the drink and enjoyed it for years to come. Inspired by the story, filmmakers adapted it into the movie *Whisky Galore!* in 1949. The island's rare feral ponies roam wild over machair plains covered with wildflowers.

BERNERAY (BEÀRNARAIGH). Connected to North Uist's north coast by a causeway, the tiny island of Berneray is speckled with pristine beaches and restored thatched black houses. Stay at the simple ⊠**Gatliff Trust Hostel ❶,** which overlooks the ocean opposite the ferry terminal. No reservations required. (www.gatliff.org.uk. Dorms £8. Cash only.) **Camping** is available next to the hostel by the beach. Trails to the beach leave from the road behind the welcoming **Burnside Croft ❸.** (☎01876 540 235; www.burnsidecroft.fsnet.co.uk. Open Feb.-Nov. Singles from £27. Cash only.) Berneray is the **ferryport** for Harris arrivals; frequent **buses** W17 and W19 run from Lochmaddy (30min., M-Sa 6-9 per day, £1).

BARRA (BARRAIGH)   ☎ 01871

The southern outpost of the Western Isles, Barra is the Hebrides in a nutshell. Most of Barra's 1200 residents speak some Gaelic, and the island's castle ruins, craft shops, and community centers keep a strong sense of culture and history. Walks on Barra are filled with the colors of the over 1000 species of wild flowers, the stark white sands of the beach, and close-up views of grazing sheep and cattle.

TRANSPORTATION. CalMac **ferries** (☎08705 650 000) sail from Castlebay (Bagh A Chaisteil) to Eriskay (40min.; M-Sa 4 per day, Su 2 per day; £6, 5-day round-trip £10; car £17.50/30), Lochboisdale (1¾hr.; Tu, Th, and Su 1 per day; £6, 5-day round-trip £10.20; car £35/59), and Oban (5-6hr.; 1 per day; £16.40, 5-day round-trip £30; car £66/113). Castlebay Ferry office is open daily 9am-2pm. Times change frequently; call the TIC or CalMac. An **airplane** operated by British Airways (☎08457 799 977) lands on the beach once daily from Glasgow (from £30).

See all of Barra in a day by **bicycle**. To rent from Cycle Hire, drop by the long wooden shed on the main road. (☎810 438. From £10 per day. Discounts for longer rentals. Open daily by appointment) You can also hop on and off **bus** W32 as it zooms around the circular island road (☎810 262; £2.50. 1½hr. circuit, M-Sa 1-2 per hr.). **Car** rental is available from MacMillen Self Drive. (☎890 366. £25-30 per day. Discounts for longer rentals. Ask about pick-up by local bus service. Cash only.) If you tire of land, try a guided **sea-kayaking tour** with Chris Denehy. (☎810 443. £15 per evening, £25 per ½-day, £35 per day.)

ORIENTATION AND PRACTICAL INFORMATION. The A888 rings the island, passing through **Castlebay**, Barra's only town. The airport is located on the opposite side of the island from Castlebay. The **Tourist Information Centre** is around the bend to the east of the pier. They'll find you a B&B for £3 plus a 10% deposit, but book ahead—a wedding, festival, or positive weather forecast can fill every bed on the island. (☎701 818; www.isleofbarra.com. Open Easter-Oct. M-Sa 9am-5pm, Su noon-4pm. Remains open for late ferries.) Barra has one **ATM**, at the Royal **Bank** of Scotland across from the TIC. (☎810 281. Open M-Tu and Th-F 9:15am-12:30pm and 1:30-4:45pm, W 10am-12:30pm and 1:30-4:45pm.) **Internet** access is available at the Castlebay School **Library**, 10min. west of the Castlebay Hotel. (☎810 124. Open M and W 9am-1pm and 2-4:30pm; Tu and Th 9am-1pm, 2-4:30pm, and 6-8pm; F 9am-1pm and 2-3:30pm; Sa 10am-12:30pm.) The **post office** is next to the bank. (☎810 312. Open M-W and F 9am-1pm and 2-5:30pm, Th 9am-1pm, Sa 9am-12:30pm.) **Post Code:** HS9 5XD.

ACCOMMODATIONS AND FOOD. The excellent ◼**Dunard Hostel ❶**, up the hill from the pier, has multicolored rooms, views of the pier, and large common spaces. (☎810 443. Dorms £11-15. Cash only.) Five miles from Castlebay on Barra's east side, **The Northbay House B&B ❸** occupies an old schoolhouse and has plush living rooms, full Scottish breakfast, and a view of the quiet Loch Na Obe (☎890 255; www.barraholidays.co.uk. From £30 per person. Cash or traveler's checks.) The **Heathbank Hotel ❹**, to the north of Castlebay, has modern facilities including satellite TVs and shiny ensuite bathrooms. (☎890 266; www.barraho-tel.co.uk. Singles £48-55, doubles £76-86. MC/V.) Close to the pier, the **Craigard Hotel's ❸** light-filled rooms have gorgeous views of the ocean. The hotel also features a restaurant and a lively pub. (☎810 200. Singles £55; doubles £80. MC/V.) **Camp** near the 24hr. bathrooms at Eoligarry Jetty at the island's northern tip (free).

Below the Craigard Hotel is the Co-op **grocery** store. (☎810 308. Open M-W and Sa 8:30am-6pm, Th-F 8:30am-7pm, Su 12:30-6pm. AmEx/MC/V.) In good weather, ◼**Hebridean Toffee Shop ❶**, just below the ferry dock, serves homemade sand-

wiches and soups (from £2.50) on the deck along with delectable toffee made on site. (☎810 898. Open daily 10am-5pm. MC/V.) **Cafe Kisimul ❸**, Main St., across from the pier, has become a local favorite with its mix of Italian and Indian food, oceanfront location, and candle-lit dining room. (☎810 645. Entrees from £10. Open M-Sa 10am-late. Cash only.) Barra's most high-end fare can be found at the **Castlebay Hotel Restaurant ❸**, uphill from the harbor, where local ingredients make seafood specials stand out. (☎810 223; www.castlebay-hotel.co.uk. Bar open 11am-midnight. Food served 5:30-8:30pm. MC/V.)

◪ SIGHTS. Stone ruins, standing sculptures, and ancient graves share the island with thousands of species of birds—many that have migrated from as far as North America. To see the whole island, follow the one-lane A888, which makes a 14 mi. circle around the 1260 ft. slopes of **Ben Heavel**, Barra's highest peak. Pick up the *What to See and Do on the Isle of Barra* pamphlet at the TIC for maps and details about many walks around the island. **◪Kisimul Castle,** a medieval bastion of the Clan MacNeil, rests in solitude in the middle of Castle Bay. Take a motorboat from the pier in front of the TIC to the castle gate. (☎810 313. Open Apr.-Oct. M-Sa 9:30am-6:30pm. Weather permitting. £4, concessions £3.) The **"Dualchas" Barra Heritage and Cultural Centre,** near the school, features exhibits exploring Highland and Gaelic culture. (☎810 413. Open Mar.-Sept. M-F 11am-4pm, Sa 10am-1pm. £2, concessions £1.50.) The road west from Castlebay passes **Ben Tangasdale,** the island's highest point, before arcing north to a long, white beach at **Halaman Bay.** Continue north to **Seal Bay** and listen for the calls of hundreds of seals from off-shore reefs. The most remote **golf course** in Britain provides nine challenging holes complete with farm animals and high winds. (£10 per day, payable in the honesty box on the shed.) Near the island's northern tip in **Eoligarry** is **Cille Bharra Cemetery,** with its rare gravestone containing both Nordic and Celtic epitaphs. For an unbeatable vantage point of the entire island, try the Barra-Benbecula **Sightseer Flight.** (☎890 283. M-F 1 per day, times depend on tides. Book on day of flight only. £30. MC/V.)

◪ DAYTRIP FROM BARRA: VATERSAY AND MINGULAY. A short causeway connects Barra to **Vatersay** (Bhatarsaigh; pop. 70), the southernmost inhabited isle in the Outer Hebrides. The island is surrounded by virtually untouched white beaches. At the entrance to the isle, a monument commemorates the *Annie Jane*, which crashed into a Vatersay beach in 1853. Informal **campgrounds** are located next to the public hall (£4 donation; toilet facilities). **Bus** W33 runs to Vatersay from the Castlebay post office by the pier (£2, M-Sa 4-5 per day). Bird-watchers should visit the mysterious deserted island of **Mingulay** to the south. Call Donald MacLeod at Barra Fishing Charters to inquire about **boat trips** from Castlebay in summer. (☎ 890 384. Fishing trips also available. By arrangement only. £20 for 3hr.)

NORTHWEST HIGHLANDS

Removed from the tourist hordes that pass through the islands, the Northwest Highlands remain largely unexplored. The scree-covered Torridon Mountains challenge the most seasoned climbers, while harbor towns preserve the fishing and farming lifestyles that have fueled their existence for thousands of years. Easiest to tour by foot or car, the Northwest Highlands push the limits of civilization with awe-inspiring beauty.

▐ TRANSPORTATION

Without a car, traversing the northwest coast is tricky in summer and nearly impossible in winter. Inverness is the area's main transportation hub. Scotrail (☎ 08457 484 950) runs **trains** from Inverness to Kyle of Lochalsh (2½hr., 4 per day, £15.20) and Thurso (4hr., 3 per day, £13.50). Scottish Citylink (☎ 08705 505 050) and Rapson **buses** travel from Inverness to Kyle (2½hr., 6 per day, £12.60), Thurso (3½hr., 5 per day, £13), and Ullapool (1½hr., M-Sa 2-4 per day, £8.20). From April to October, the **Northern Explorer Ticket,** available at bus stations, provides unlimited travel between Inverness and Thurso (3 consecutive days £35; 5 of 10 £59; 8 of 16 £79). **Postbuses** are another option; consult the public transportation guide. The narrow roads are full of fast-moving locals and more tentative visitors.

PLOCKTON   ☎ 01599

The colorful fishing village of Plockton tempts visitors to come the 6 mi. north from Kyle of Lochalsh with its clean streets, calm harbor, and smattering of palm trees. Keep your eyes peeled for seals, otters, and porpoises in the cove. **Calum's Seal Trips,** at the Main Pier or on the pontoon next to the car park, facilitates natural encounters; the office on the waterfront also rents canoes, rowboats, and paddleboats at £5-15 per hr. (☎ 544 306. 1hr. tours daily Easter-Oct. at 10am, noon, 2, and 4pm. £6. Free if no seal sightings. MC/V.) For a longer adventure, meet in Plockton for ranger-guided **kayak tours** and lessons led by the National Trust for Scotland (☎ 0844 493 2231; www.nts.co.uk. From £40. MC/V.) Opposite the train station, the **Station Bunkhouse ❶** is a comfortable hostel with plenty of windows and soft furniture. (☎ 544 235. Dorms £12. Cash only.) The owners also run a B&B, **Nessun Dorma ❷,** next door to the bunkhouse. (Singles from £20. Cash only.) Grab exceptionally fresh grub at **Off the Rails ❸,** a seafood restaurant in the train station. (☎ 544 423. Entrees from £10. Open M-Sa 6:30-9pm.) **Craig Highland Farm,** 2 mi. from Stromferry outside Plockton, is a glorified Highland petting zoo with a range of activities for families (☎ 544 205. Open daily 10am-dusk. £1.50.) Scotrail runs **trains** from Inverness and Kyle (3-4 per day, £1.70). Plockton is also served by the Kyle-Plockton-Ardnarff **postbus** (#119; 1-3 per day).

APPLECROSS   ☎ 01520

A tiny village with big views, Applecross is worth the death-defying car ride it takes to get there. Take the single-lane **Bealach na Ba (Cattle) Pass,** famous for being Britain's highest road (2054 ft.) and impassible in winter. At the top of the mountain, a car park allows a break from driving stress and a look at the astounding Lochs that pepper the mountain. The circuitous **coastal route** is a less terrifying option. A 9500-year-old dwelling in Sand and a **Viking lime kiln** in Keppoch, along with other prehistoric and natural wonders, are described in the free *Applecross Scenic Walks* available from the information center. **Mountain and Sea Guides** offers kayaking and trekking trips. (☎ 744 394; www.applecross.uk.com. 2hr. session £20, ½-day £30; discounts for longer excursions.)

In Applecross, turn right at the red barn to discover the ⬛**Applecross Flower Tunnel Cafe ❶,** a greenhouse where flowers hang low over the tables. Baristas make thick lattes and serve up slices of the unspeakably stupendous toffee banana pie. (☎ 744 268. Open daily 10am-5pm. AmEx/MC/V.) **Camping ❶** is available in the grassy field next to the cafe. (£6 per person, children free. AmEx/MC/V.) Stop by the **Applecross Inn ❷,** down the hill on the waterfront, for low-key fine dining and the best seafood in town. The upstairs **B&B ❸** has small, sunny rooms with panoramic ocean views. (☎ 744 262. Restaurant-bar open 10am-midnight. Singles £35; doubles £80. MC/V.) From Applecross, the Inverbain/Kenmore walking path is a 3-4hr. trek through surrounding hills and woodlands (15km). Applecross is served by **postbus** #92 from Torridon and Shieldaig (1 per day, departs Torridon 10:45am). The nearest **train** station is 17 mi. away in Strathcarron.

TORRIDON
☎ 01445

The teensy village of Torridon (pop. 230) lies between **Loch Torridon** and the Torridon Hills, serving as a base for lodging and information about the surrounding peaks and archaeological sites. The exhibits at the **Torridon Countryside Centre,** at the crossroads in Torridon, 100 yd. east of the hostel, provide highly specific information about area flora and fauna. (☎ 791 221. Open daily Easter-Sept. 10am-5pm.) Walk to the nearby **Red Deer Museum** and park to catch a glimpse of one of Scotland's most studied species. East of the Countryside Centre, the daunting **Liathach peak** (3456 ft.) provides a day hike for the adventurous. On the coast of Loch Torridon, an open-air church recalls the splitting of the Church of Scotland in 1843.

At the base of the Liathach, the **SYHA Torridon ❷** feels like a large athletic center and is the site of Torridon Mountain rescue. (☎ 791 284. Open Mar.-Oct. Dorms from £12, under 18 from £9. AmEx/MC/V.) The rangers allow **camping** between their office and the SYHA. The small general store, 300 yd. west along the road, is your only bet for **groceries.** (☎ 791 400. Open M-Sa 9:30am-5:30pm, Su 9:30-11:30am and 3-5:30pm.) From Inverness, **trains** (☎ 08457 484 950) run to Achnasheen (1¼hr.; M-Sa 4 per day, Su 2 per day; £9.70). There, **postbus** #92 (12:10pm) connects to Torridon. Buses do not meet every train; some shuttle **buses** connect with the Inverness train at Strathcarron (Lochcarron Garage bus; 1hr., M-Sa 10:40pm, £3).

GAIRLOCH
☎ 01445

The coastal settlements surrounding Loch Gairloch stretch from the southern Red Point to the stately Rua Reidh lighthouse 12 mi. north of Strath. Grey mountains tower over small clusters of houses and shops, providing shaded walks and more challenging climbs. Six miles north along the coastal road, get lost in the expansive ⬛**Inverewe Gardens,** a collection of plants and flowers from different regions of the world, sustained in a tropical microclimate heated by the passing jetstream. Free guided walks are available from mid-April to mid-September. Westerbus runs from Gairloch to the gardens at least twice per day during the week (£1); check the timetable at the TIC first. (☎ 781 200. Garden open daily from mid-Mar. to Oct. 9:30am-9pm; from Nov. to mid-Mar. 9:30am-4pm. £8, concessions £5.) Horseback riders can ride or get lessons at the **Gairloch Trekking Centre,** just south of the pier. (☎ 712 652. £7.50 per 30min. lessons available.) The pleasantly cluttered **Gairloch**

Heritage Museum chronicles the past few centuries of life in the Gairloch area with tools and handwritten signs. (☎712 287. Open Mar.-Sept. M-Sa 10am-5pm; Oct. 10am-1pm; call ahead in winter. £3.)

Twelve miles north on the winding coastal road, ▧**Rua Reidh Lighthouse ❶** (ROO-ah RAY) towers over the sea with soft blue rooms and comforters in the hostel on the lower level. Dinner is open to all, by prior arrangement. From Gairloch, take the road signposted to Melvaig. (☎771 263; www.ruareidh.co.uk. Dorms £10; private rooms £28-38. MC/V.) **SYHA Carn Dearg ❶**, 2 mi. northwest of town on the B8021, stores binoculars in common spaces for birdwatching. Get off the Gairloch bus at the village of **Strath** and walk toward the sea from there. (☎712 219. Reception 7-10:30am and 5-11:30pm. Curfew 11pm. Open from mid-May to Sept. Dorms £12-13.50, under 18 £9-10. AmEx/MC/V.) Just ½ mi. west of the hostel, campers can pitch a tent at the beachside **Sands Holiday Centre ❶** (☎712 152; www.sandsholidaycentre.co.uk; £8-12 per tent). Follow your ears to the live music at the **Old Inn ❹**, at the south end of Gairloch. A quiet stream adds a background bubble to the lively crowd on the back patio. (☎712 006. Food served noon-10pm. Singles £32-45; doubles £45-89. MC/V.) In Strath village on B8021, the fresh aroma of the **Mountain Coffee Company ❶** seeps into the street. (☎712 316. Open daily 9:30am-5:45pm. MC/V.) **Cafe Blueprint ❷** serves fancy local fare across the street. (☎712 397; www.blueprintgairloch.com. Entrees £6-9. Open daily 10am-4pm and 6:30-9pm. MC/V.)

For a £3 charge plus a 10% deposit, the **Tourist Information Centre** books B&Bs in Gairloch and Dundonnell, just east of the Ardessie Gorge. (Reservations ☎712 130; local information ☎712 071. Open June-Aug. M-F 9:30am-5:30pm, Sa 10am-6pm, Su 11am-3pm; Sept.-Oct. and Easter-June M-Sa 10am-5pm; Nov.-Easter M-Sa 10am-4pm.) Buy **groceries** at Somerfield, on the A832 just south of its intersection with the B8021. (☎712 242. Open M-F 7:30am-9pm, Sa 8am-9pm.) There is **Internet** access (£1 per 30min.) at **Wordworks,** above the Harbour Centre on Pier Rd. (☎712 712; £1 per 30min.), and a **post office** in Strath's center (☎08457 223 344; open M-W and F 9am-1pm and 2-5:30pm). **Post Code:** IV21 2BZ.

ULLAPOOL   ☎01854

Ullapool stands as a center of transportation and activity in the middle of the Highlands. Its summer stream of ferry-riding tourists enhance business at its several restaurants and cafes, while its proximity to some of the most wild places of Scotland make it a favored stopping place for more rough-and-tumble hikers. Although many come to Ullapool for a rest from hiking, a local, well-trod walk up **Ullapool Hill** offers great views of the area without too much effort. Follow the signs from North Rd., near the school. The SYHA hostel (p. 653) provides free leaflets detailing longer walks that traverse **Scots Pine** and the **Inverpolly Nature Reserve.** Situated in a former parliamentary church, the **Ullapool Museum,** W. Argyle St., has an impressive collection of artifacts and maps detailing the history of the area. (☎612 987. Open Apr.-Oct. M-Sa 10am-5pm; Nov.-Mar. by arrangement. £3, concessions £2, children 50p.) Explore the **Summer Isles** (p. 654) on a powerboat trip with **Seascape Expeditions** (☎633 708; £23), or opt for a longer trip aboard the **Summer Queen** (☎612 472; www.summerqueen.co.uk).

The bright common spaces of the **SYHA Ullapool ❶**, Shore St., overlook the harbor in the front and a small garden out back. (☎612 254. Laundry £2. Internet £1 per 20min. Curfew M-W and Su midnight, Th-Sa 12:30am. Dorms £12-13.50, under 18 £9-10. AmEx/MC/V.) The social **Scotpackers West House ❷**, W. Argyle St., has an open kitchen, a computer room, and a hipster feel. (☎613 126; www.scotpackershostels.co.uk. Internet access £1 per 30min. Dorms £14. MC/V.) For more privacy, try the affiliated **Crofton House ❸** (☎613 126. Includes breakfast. Doubles £40. MC/V.) **Camping** is available at Broomfield Holiday Grounds, a large field on W. Argyle St. (£7). Somerfield, Seaforth Rd., supplies **groceries** (☎613 291; open M-Sa 8:30am-

8pm, Su 9am-6pm). Costcutter, across from the post office, has a smaller selection (☎612 261; open M-W 7am-8pm, Th-Sa 8am-10pm, Su 8am-8pm). For fresh seafood, **⬛The Seaforth ❷** makes award-winning fish and chips ($4.75) in a diner-style kitchen. (☎612 122; www.theseaforth.com. Entrees $5-13. Open M-F 9am-1am, Sa 9am-midnight, Su noon-midnight. MC/V.) A hotel, cafe, bar, bookstore, and gallery, **The Ceilidh Place ❸**, 14 W. Argyle St., has flowers and vines covering its stark white building. (☎612 103; www.theceilidhplace.com. Entrees $9-18. Rooms from $48. Open daily 8:30am-9pm. AmEx/MC/V.) The fragrant **Jasmine Tandoori ❶**, West Ln., is Ullapool's best take on Indian food, offering a three-course lunch for $7. (☎613 331. Entrees $7-11. Open daily noon-2pm and 5-11pm. MC/V.)

Except for the 1am arrivals, **ferries** from Stornoway, Lewis (M-F 2-3 per day; $15, 5-day round-trip $26; with car $73/125) are met by Scottish Citylink and Rapsons Coaches **buses** (☎01463 222 244). Buses run to Inverness (1½hr., 2 per day, $7.70), including one with an attachment for bicycles (☎01349 883 585; 1¾hr., 1 per day, $8.50). The **Tourist Information Centre** is on Argyle St. (☎612 486. Open July-Aug. M-Sa 9am-6pm, Su 10am-5pm; Apr.-June and Sept.-Oct. M-Sa 9am-5pm, Su 10am-4pm; Nov.-Mar. M-Sa 10am-4pm.) An **ATM** can be found at the **Bank** of Scotland on W. Argyle St. (☎08457 801 801. Open M-Tu and Th-F 9am-12:30pm and 1:30-5pm; W 9:30am-12:30pm and 1:30-5pm.) Access free **Wi-Fi** above Northwest Outdoors, W. Argyle St., in the coffeeshop (open M-Sa 9:30am-4:30pm). The **post office** is on W. Argyle St. (☎612 228. Open M-Tu and Th-F 9am-1pm and 2-5:30pm, W 9am-1pm.) **Post Code:** IV26 2TY.

SIGHTS NEAR ULLAPOOL

⬛CORRIESHALLOCH GORGE. On the A835, 12 mi. south of Ullapool, the River Broom cascades 150 ft. down the **Falls of Measach** into a deep, dramatic gorge. Turn right on the footpath across from the bus stop and follow the path to the jutting overlook for gorgeous views. A suspension bridge allows the brave to sway in the breeze overlooking the 40m drop to the icy water. The gorge has been intermittently closed for repairs to the bridge; check at a TIC. It is easily accessible by any Ullapool-Inverness **bus;** check that a return exists before you set out.

ACHILTIBUIE. The foliage thickens on the way to Achiltibuie (Ah-KILL-ta-booee), a coastal town 14 mi. northwest of Ullapool. Ferns and mosses line the hillsides, which provide plenty of walks inland when the beach strolls grow tiresome. Off the coast, the remote **Summer Isles** are home to seals and puffins. In town, the **Hydroponicum** touts itself as the "garden of the future" and grows a variety of edible plants using rocks instead of soil. (☎622 202. Tours every hr. Open daily from mid-Apr. to Sept. 11am-4pm. $5.50, concessions $4.50.) At the **Achiltibuie Smokehouse**, 4 mi. northwest in Altandhu, fishmongers walk visitors through the slitting, slicing, and smoking of the fish. (☎622 353. Open M-Sa 9:30am-5pm. Free.)

While Achiltibuie's sights are eclectic, there are few places to eat or stay in town. Three miles out of town, park at the car park, hike down a short path, and cross the bridge over a gushing stream to reach the **SYHA Achininver ❶**, ¼ mi. from the beach. The dorm has few amenities, but its skylights and the stunning natural setting compensate. (☎613 701. Open from mid-May to Sept. Dorms $12, under 18 $9. AmEx/MC/V.) The ingredients at the quiet **Lily Pond Cafe ❷** are straight from the Hydroponicum's garden. (Open daily from mid-Apr. to Sept. 11am-4pm. MC/V.)

Tour Achiltibuie from Ullapool (p. 653) or take touring ship MV *Hectoria* from **Badentarbet Pier,** at the western end of Achiltibuie. (☎01854 622 200. 3½hr. tours Apr.-Oct. M-Sa 10:30am and 2:15pm. $15. 7hr. tours Apr.-Oct. M-Sa 10:30am. $20.) Spa Coaches runs **buses** from Ullapool (M-F 2 per day, Sa 1 per day; $4). If driving, take the A835 north 10 mi. from Ullapool, then go west along the signposted single-track road, following it 15 mi. to the coast. On the main road in town, Achiltibuie

Store sells **groceries.** (☎622 496. Open M-Sa 9am-5:30pm. MC/V.) The **post office** is 50 yd. down the road. (☎622 200. Open M-W and F 9am-noon and 1-5:30pm, Th 9am-1pm, Sa 9am-12:30pm.) **Post Code:** IV26 2YG.

LOCHINVER AND ASSYNT   ☎01571

Thirty miles up the northwest coast, Lochinver punches an odd, industrial hole into an idyllic landscape. However, it serves as a great stopping point for exploring the remote treasures of nearby Assynt and the Culag woods. Ten miles south of Lochinver on the A837, the mysterious **bone caves** are ripe for exploring and contain animal and human remains from thousands of years ago. From Lochinver, trails (8-10hr.) climb the **Suilven** and **Canisp** mountains. While lengthy, these treks are accessible to walkers of all levels. Going south from the Visitor Centre, the second left leads to **Glencanisp Lodge,** where a footpath, famed for wildlife sightings, skirts the River Inver (2hr. round-trip). The **Culag Wood Walk** (1hr. round-trip) starts west of the field near the pier and features occasional heron sightings. From the SYHA hostel (see below), a **nature trail** passes the ruined mill of **Alt-na-Bradhan** before reaching the striking rock formation at **Clachtoll** (2-3hr. round-trip). The Ranger Service (☎844 654) offers free **guided walks** once per week in summer. For excellent, privately guided walks, **Caledonia Hilltreks** leads hikes around the area (☎01224 326 925; www.caledoniahilltreks.com). Assynt Angling Group (☎844 076) can recommend **fishing** hotspots, and the TIC provides permits (£5 per day).

There are a number of decent B&Bs in town. The affordable **Ardglas Guest House ❸,** across the stone bridge, is a comfortable place to rest for the night. (☎844 257. Singles from £21.) **Hostels** are difficult to access without a car but can be great starting points for all manner of fishing and hiking trips. The bare-bones **SYHA Achmelvich ❶,** Recharn, is 3 mi. west of town on a wooded footpath or 20min. by the 11:15am postbus. (☎844 480. Reception 7-10:30am and 5-11pm. Open Apr.-Sept. Dorms £12, under 18 £9. AmEx/MC/V.) The nearby **Achmelvich campsite ❶** sits along a windy beach with frigid water. (☎844 393. Tent £7.) Another 13 mi. inland on the A837 from Ullapool, the dramatic ruins of **Ardvreck Castle** are located 1 mi. from the massive ▓**Inchnadamph Lodge ❶,** Assynt Field Centre. The social lodge offers everything from Internet access to frozen foods for sale at the reception desk. Ullapool-Lochinver buses stop upon request. (☎822 218; www.inch-lodge.co.uk. Breakfast included. Laundry £1.50. Internet £1 per 30min. Handicap-accessible. Dorms £15; doubles £40. MC/V.)

The only public transportation that enters this forbidding countryside is the KSM Motors **bus,** which runs once or twice per day from Ullapool (£3.50). Check with the TIC for times. Postbus #123 trundles in from the Lairg train station (M-Sa 12:45pm). The **Assynt Visitor Centre,** on the waterfront in Lochinver, serves as a TIC. (☎844 330. Open June-Sept. M-Sa 10am-5pm, Su 10am-4pm; Easter-May and Oct. M-Sa 10am-5pm.) A Royal **Bank** of Scotland is at the west end of town, just before the pier. (☎844 215. Open M-Tu and Th-F 9:15am-12:30pm and 1:30-4:45pm, W 10am-12:30pm and 1:20-4:45pm.) The Spar **supermarket** is on the far end of the same street. (☎844 207. Open M-Sa 8am-6:30pm.) The **post office** is just down the road from the Spar. (☎844 201. Open M, W and F 8:30am-1pm and 2-5pm, Tu 8:30am-1pm, Sa 8:30am-12:30pm.) **Post Code:** IV27 4JY.

DURNESS   ☎01971

Durness caters to surfers with its big waves and small-town vibes. The ▓**Smoo Caves** draw tourists in for a look at the deep holes in the limestone, rumored to have been used in smuggling operations and murder cover-ups. Take a tour and float via rubber dinghy past the interior waterfall. (☎511 704; 20min. tours depart from cave entrance Apr.-Sept. daily 10am-5pm. £3.) Stop in Blairmore on the northwestern coast to walk the 4 mi. path to **Sandwood Bay,** a pristine bit of coast

HIGHLANDS
AND ISLANDS

home to rare ferns. **Cape Wrath's** cliffs, 12 mi. west of Durness, are the tallest on mainland Britian. From the Cape Wrath Hotel (1½ mi. west of the town center), a ferry crosses to Kyle of Durness (☎511 376; 3-4 per day, round-trip £4.50), where it's met by a minibus that completes the trip to Cape Wrath (☎511 287; round-trip £7.50). Ferries and buses operate on demand May-Sept. from 9:30am. The Cape may be closed for Royal Air Force training; call the TIC to check.

In the center of town, relax on the porch of the ■**Lazycrofter Bunkhouse ❶** before turning in for the night. (☎511 202; www.durnesshostel.com. Dorms £11. Check in at Mackay's Hotel next door.) The two-building complex of **SYHA Durness ❶**, 1 mi. north of town along the A838, features a coal-burning stove, outdoor picnic tables, a barbecue, and a small garden. (☎511 244. Reception 7-10:30am and 5-11pm. Open Apr.-Sept. Dorms £12, under 18 £9. AmEx/MC/V.) Next to the visitor center, the **Sango Sands Camping Site ❶** is basically beachside. (☎511 726. Reception 9-9:30am and 6-6:30pm. Tent £4.75. Cash only.) Stock up on organic food, rent surfing equipment, and hang out with the owners of the incense-filled ■**Lotus Leaf.** (☎165 034. Open M-Tu and Th-Su approximately 9am-6pm. Surfboards from £13 per day.)

To reach Durness, Easteross Coaches roll in from Lairg at 3pm (M-Sa 1-2 per day). Tim Dearman buses also come from Inverness (5hr., 1 per day, round-trip £21) and Ullapool (3hr., 1 per day, round-trip £18.50). The **Tourist Information Centre** books B&Bs for £3 plus a 10% deposit. (☎511 368. Open daily Apr.-Oct. 10am-5pm; Nov.-Mar. 10am-1:30pm.) The **post office** is up the road in the Spar store. (☎511 209. Store open M-F 8am-5:30pm, Sa 9am-5:30pm. The store's staff can open the post office if it appears closed.) **Post Code:** IV27 4QF.

THURSO AND SCRABSTER   ☎01847

A big fish in a very small pond, Thurso (pop. 10,000) is considered a veritable metropolis by the crofters and fishermen of Scotland's desolate north coast. A hub of the northern Highlands, Thurso offers little in the way of cultural sights but has plenty of amenities that cater to travelers on their way to nearby destinations. On the east side of town, **castle ruins** sparkle against the ocean where one of the best **surf spots** in the world awaits enthusiasts willing to brave the icy waters. Rent wetsuits (£10 per day) and surfboards (£10 per day) from **Tempest Surf,** Thurso Harbor, on the waterfront. (☎892 500. Open daily 10am-6pm. MC/V.) Scrabster, 2½ mi. east, is no more than an Orkney ferry port (p. 657).

■**Sandra's Backpackers Hostel ❶**, upstairs at 26 Princes St., is centrally located with 30 bunks in ensuite dorms with TVs. The owners provide lifts to Scrabster for noon ferry connections. (☎894 575; www.sandras-backpackers.ukf.net. Continental breakfast included. Facilities for the disabled available. Bike rental from £6 per day. Free Internet access. Dorms £11.50; private rooms £30. Cash only.) **Thurso Youth Club Hostel ❶** is a short walk out of town in a converted mill. From the train station, walk east down Lover's Ln., turn north on Janet St., cross the river, and follow the park path to the right. (☎892 964. Continental breakfast included. Open July-Aug. Dorms £9. Cash only.) **Sandra's Snack Bar and Takeaway ❶**, beneath the hostel, is filled with locals looking for a quick bite and is happy to serve a hearty breakfast to backpackers from the hostel. (☎894 575. Open M-F 10am-11pm, Sa 10am-midnight, Su 12:30-10:30pm. 10% discount for hostelers. Cash only.) For fancy but affordable dining, try the newly refurbished **Red Pepper Restaurant and Bar ❷** at 16 Princes St. Locals get dressed up to enjoy the crab salad (£6) and ambience. (☎892 771. Open daily 10:30am-9pm.) In Scrabster, grab morning eats at **The Fisherman's Mission ❶**. (☎892 402. Open M-Sa 7:30am-5pm. Breakfast from £2.50.) Various hotel bars have open mic nights and live music. On Wednesdays, the **Commercial (Comm) Bar,** 1 Princes St., fills with local bands playing traditional folk music. (☎893 366. Open M-Th 11am-midnight, F-Sa 11am-1am, Su noon-11pm.) On Trail St., Friday and Saturday live music shows and Wednesday open mics draw crowds to the **New Market Bar.** (☎ 895 803. Open M-Th 11am-midnight, F-Sa 12:30pm-11:45pm, Su 12:30pm-11:45pm.)

The Thurso town service **bus** #78 travels between Thurso and Scrabster (M-F 5 per day, Sa and Su 3 per day). First Scotrail travels to Inverness (M-Sa 3 per day, Su 2 per day). Highland County bus #80 runs to John O'Groats (M-F 5 per day, Sa 3 per day). Schedules change frequently; check in at the TIC or call ☎ 0871 200 2233 for more information. A **Tourist Information Centre,** Riverside Rd., treats Thurso's sights with casual indifference but its visitors with warmth. (☎ 08452 255 121. Open June-Aug. M-Sa 10am-5pm and Su 10am-4pm; Apr.-May and Sept.-Oct. M-Sa 10am-5pm.) There is a **launderette** on Grove Ln. (Open M-F 9am-6pm, Sa 10am-5:30pm.) Thurso also offers a **Bank** of Scotland on Trail St. with an **ATM** (open M-Sa 9:30am-5pm) and a **post office** inside the Coop **market** on Grove Ln. (☎ 893 117; open M-Sa 9:30am-5pm). **Post Code:** KW14.

JOHN O'GROATS   ☎ 01955

Named for the first man to arrange ferries to the islands (Jan de Groot, a Dutchman), John O'Groats is proud of its position as mainland Britain's northernmost town. The surrounding islands are the real destination. While in town, have a professional photographer take a photo of you at the personalizable **Land's End Sign** by the ferry dock (from £7.) **Wildlife Cruises,** run by John O'Groats Ferries, cruise the waters of Pentland Firth, home to kittiwakes and great black backs. (☎ 611 353; www.jogferry.com. Runs daily June-Aug. 2:30pm. 1½hr. tours £15. MC/V.) **Dunnet Head,** halfway from John O'Groats to Thurso, is the northernmost point on the Isle, but the Geo of Sclaites at **Duncansby Head,** 2 mi. east of town, has a better view overlooking the Pentland Firth toward Orkney and is home to a large variety of rare seabirds. If stuck on the mainland, make your way 2½ mi. west to Canisbay and the quaint **SYHA John O'Groats ❶.** (☎ 08700 041 129. Reception 7-10am and 5-10pm. Curfew 11:30pm. Open Easter-Oct. Dorms from £12, under 18 £9. AmEx/MC/V.) To reach town from the **Wick train station,** take Highland Country **bus** #77 (40min., 4-5 per day), which also runs to Thurso (1hr.; M-F 9 per day, Sa 3 per day) and passes the hostel. From May to August, John O'Groats Ferries's Orkney Bus runs from Inverness (daily 2:20pm, June-Aug. 7:30am and 2:20pm; £15). The **Tourist Information Centre,** County Rd., by the pier, helps plan escapes to surrounding areas and can arrange accommodations if you miss a ferry. (☎ 611 373. Open daily June-Aug. 9am-6pm; Apr.-May and Sept.-Oct. 10am-5pm.)

ORKNEY ISLANDS   ☎ 01856

The remote Orkney Islands are a mix of beaches, docile farmland, and archaeological wonders. In Orkney, sheep feast on seaweed, seagulls roost in hay fields, and soccer pitches are carved from cow pastures. Here, Nordic traditions have battled Celtic customs for centuries, creating a distinct Orcadian dialect and vocabulary. From the fishing boats at the capital city of Kirkwall to miraculous sunsets on the virtually abandoned far northern isles, Orkney's wild beauty is not soon forgotten.

◀ GETTING THERE

Ferries are the main mode of transportation between Orkney and mainland Scotland. The affordable Pentland Ferry (☎ 01856 831 226; www.pentlandferries.co.uk) runs from Gills Bay, west of John O'Groats on the A836 (1hr.; 3-4 per day; £12, children £6, cars £28; MC/V). Ferries land at St. Margaret's Hope on Orkney. **Orkney Coaches** runs a bus service to Kirkwall (M-Sa 4 per day). John O'Groats Ferries (☎ 01955 611 353; www.jogferry.co.uk) travel from John O'Groats to Burwick,

WATCH YOUR MOUTH. For locals, the terms "Orkneys" and "Shetlands" hold a strong taboo. To avoid ruffling any feathers, use "Orkney" and "Shetland" when referring to the islands as a group. For example: "I took a ferry to Orkney, where I met the love of my life. We will be honeymooning in the Shetland Islands, which I sometimes also refer to as 'Shetland,' since I am savvy."

Orkney, where a free bus plays rousing accordion tunes as it takes passengers to Kirkwall (ferry 40min., bus 35min.; June-July 4 per day; May 2 per day; Sept. 2 per day; round-trip £24-28). **Puffin Express Tours** offers a one-day trip from Inverness to Orkney for only £27, which includes visits to many of the island's prehistoric sights. (☎01463 717 181; www.puffinexpress.co.uk/orkney. Mar.-Oct. Th; May-Sept. Su; May-Oct. Tu. Departs Inverness TIC 9:15am and returns 8pm.) John O'Groats Ferries also offers several **ferry-tour packages.** Their Maxi Day Tour makes stops at major sights and includes a 2hr. break in Kirkwall (9am-7:45pm, last boarding 8:50am; £38; book ahead). The Highlights Day Tour hits the same sights but stops in Kirkwall for only 20min. (10:30am-6pm; £35). Northlink Ferries (☎08456 000 449) offers trips from Scrabster to Stromness on the plush *Hamna-voe* with an ensuite B&B on board the ship (1½hr.; M-F 3 per day, Sa-Su 2 per day; round-trip £25.40-29.60). A bus departs from the Thurso rail station for Scrabster before each crossing. Northlink also sails from Aberdeen to Kirkwall (6-8hr.; Tu, Th and Sa-Su departs Aberdeen 5pm; round-trip from £24.30).

▐ LOCAL TRANSPORTATION

Orkney Coaches (☎01856 870 555; www.rapsons.co.uk) runs **buses** between Kirkwall bus station and Stromness Pier Head (30min., M-Sa every hr., £2.20). The staff at Orkney **Ferries** (☎01856 872 044; www.orkneyferries.co.uk), based on Shore St. at the Kirkwall harbor, can help travelers island-hop. Some ferries are foot-passenger only, all ferries offer student discounts, and schedules are likely to change; call ahead. Ferries (£6.40-12.80, concessions £3.20-6.40, cars £19.20-28.50) depart from Kirkwall to: Eday (1¼hr.); Sanday (1½hr.); Shapinsay (25min.); Stronsay (1½hr.); Westray and Papa Westray (1½hr.). Ferries also depart Tingwall to Rousay, Egilsay, and Wyre (30-60min.). Ferries leave Houton (20min. west of Kirkwall on the A964) to Flotta (45min.) and Lyness in the south of Hoy (20-45min.). A passenger-only ferry runs from Stromness to Moaness in the north of Hoy (15min.).

Car rental is by far the most convenient way of getting around Orkney. Try W.R. Tullock, Castle St., Kirkwall Airport. (☎876 262. 21+. From £32 per day.) Orkney Car Hire, Junction Rd., Kirkwall (☎872 866; www.orkneycarhire.co.uk; 21+; from £28 per day) and Stromness Car Hire, John St., Kirkwall (☎850 973; 21+; from £28 per day, £159 per week) also rent cars. **Biking** is an alternative, although fast-changing weather conditions make rain gear essential. Rent wheels in Kirkwall from Cycle Orkney, Tankerness Ln., off Broad St. (☎875 777; www.bobbyscycles.co.uk; £10 per day, £6 per ½-day; open M-Sa 9am-5:30pm, closed W noon-1pm) or in Stromness at Orkney Cycle Hire, 54 Dundas St. (☎850 255. Helmet and map included. From £6 per day. Open daily 8:30am-9pm.)

KIRKWALL ☎01856

The buzzing center of Orkney swells with people during the long summer days as cars and shoppers meander through town, making plans to see the islands, peeking in store windows, and enjoying Orkney's famously rich ice cream. Every school child in Kirkwall learns to play a musical instrument, and the community's love of music doesn't stop there. In late June, Kirkwall is flooded with musicians

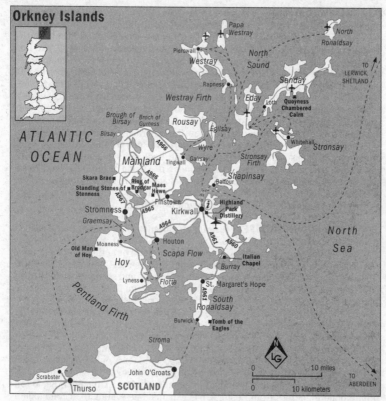

Orkney Islands

Papa Westray
North Ronaldsay
Pierowall
Westray
North Sound
Rapness
Sanday
TO LERWICK, SHETLAND
Westray Firth
Eday
Loth
Quoyness Chambered Cairn
ATLANTIC OCEAN
Brough of Birsay
Broch of Gurness
Rousay
Egilsay
Whitehall
Birsay
Wyre
Stronsay
Mainland
Tingwall
Gairsay
Stronsay Firth
Skara Brae
Ring of Brodgar
Maes Howe
Shapinsay
Standing Stones of Stenness
Balfour
Finstown
Highland Park Distillery
Stromness
Kirkwall
North Sea
Graemsay
Houton
Moaness
Old Man of Hoy
Scapa Flow
Italian Chapel
Hoy
Burray
Lyness
Flotta
St. Margaret's Hope
Pentland Firth
South Ronaldsay
Burwick
Tomb of the Eagles
Stroma
N
John O'Groats
0   10 miles
Scrabster
SCOTLAND
0   10 kilometers
Thurso
TO ABERDEEN

from all over the world, from folk singers to the BBC Philharmonic, for the **St. Magnus Festival** (St. Magnus Festival Office, 60 Victoria St.; ☎871 445; www.stmagnus-festival.com). With ferries headed for the smaller isles virtually every hour, Kirkwall makes the perfect starting place for exploring the wilds of Orkney.

⌖ PRACTICAL INFORMATION. The Kirkwall **Tourist Information Centre,** 6 Broad St., books B&Bs for £3 plus a 10% deposit. (☎872 856. Open June-Sept. daily 8:30am-8pm; Oct.-May M-F 9am-5pm, Sa 10am-4pm, Su 10am-4pm.) Guidebooks are also available at **The Orcadian Bookshop** on Albert St. (☎878 888). Inter-island ferry bookings can be obtained at Orkney Ferries, Shore St. (☎872 044; www.orkneyferries.co.uk.) Other services include: a **Bank** of Scotland, 56 Albert St. (☎682 000; open M-Tu and Th-F 9am-5pm, W 9:30am-5pm); Kelvinator **launderette,** 47 Albert St. (☎872 982; open M-F 8:30am-5:30pm, Sa 9am-5pm; wash £3.50, dry 25p per min.; soap 20p); **police,** Great Western Rd. (☎872 241); Boots **pharmacy,** 49-51 Albert St. (☎872 097; open M-Sa 9am-5:30pm); **Internet** access at **Support Training Limited,** 2 W Tankerness Ln. (☎873 582; £1 per 10min., £5 per hr.; open M-F 8:30am-7pm, Sa 10am-5pm) or free next door at the public **library** (☎873 166; 1hr. per day; open M-Th 9am-7pm, F-Sa 9am-5pm); **Volunteer Center Kirkwall,** 12 Bridge St. (☎872 897; www.orkneycommunities.co.uk/vc; open M-F 9am-5pm); and the **post office,** 15 Junction Rd. (☎874 249; open M-Tu and Th-F 9am-5pm, W 9am-4pm, Sa 9:30am-12:30pm). **Post Code:** KW15 1AA.

▐ ACCOMMODATIONS. A number of hostels, B&Bs, and croft houses can be found in the Tourist Board's annual publication, available around town and at the TIC. Keep in mind that sometimes the best budget accommodations are in the most remote areas. Ten cozy beds fill up quickly in the **Peedie Hostel ❶**, 1 Ayre Rd., across from the pier. All rooms have a TV, but there is no common room. (☎875 477. Book far in advance. Dorms £10.) Kirkwall's dimly lit **SYHA hostel ❶** is on Old Skapa Rd. Follow Junction St. south for 1 mi. and turn right on Wellington St.; follow the signs to the hostel. The large common room is often lively at night. (☎872 243. Reception 8-10:30am and 3:30pm-12:30am. Curfew 12:30am. Open Apr.-Oct. Dorms £12-13, under 18 £10.) At **Mr. and Mrs. Flett's B&B ❷**, Cromwell Rd., stay at the top of a ship's staircase and get to know the fishermen who often stay there on weekends. (☎873 160. £18-20 per person.) **West End Hotel ❹**, Main St., sits just out of the way of pedestrian traffic, providing soft beds in its ensuite rooms. (☎872 368. Breakfast included. Singles £46; doubles £76.) **Camp** at the refinished **Pickaquoy Centre Caravan & Camping Site ❶**, on Pickaquoy Rd. just south of the A965. (☎879 900. £7.50 per caravan, £4-7.20 per tent.) You can pitch a tent almost anywhere on the islands, but always ask the landowner first.

▐▐ FOOD AND NIGHTLIFE. Stock up on **groceries** before a trip to the islands at Somerfield, on the corner of Broad St. and Great Western Rd. (☎228 876; open M-W and Sa 8am-8pm, Th and F 8am-9pm, Su 9am-6pm) or at the Co-op next door (☎873 056; open M-F 9am-5pm, Sa 9am-7:30pm, Su 9am-6pm). **Trenabies Cafe ❶**, 16 Albert St., imports ice cream from Shetland (from £2), and serves extremely fresh cafe fare. (☎874 336. Sandwiches £4-5. Open M-F 8:30am-5:30pm, Sa 9am-5:30pm, Su noon-4pm. MC/V.) Across the street, the **Peppermill Deli's ❶** homemade soup is a steal at £1. Browse for the freshest locally grown veggies and meats. (☎878 878. Open M-F 9am-6pm, Sa 9am-5:30pm. MC/V.) An American flag and the front end of a Ford Mustang hang on the walls of **Buster's Diner ❶**, 1 Mounthoolie Pl., which cooks up pizza and burgers for less than £5. (☎876 717. Open May-Sept. T-Th noon-2pm and 4:30-9pm, F-Sa noon-midnight, Su 4:30-9pm. Cash only.) At **Indian Gaidu ❷**, 37 Junction St., grab tasty classic dishes and takeaway late into the night. (☎875 575. Entrees from £8. Open daily 5pm-midnight. MC/V.) **The Bothy Bar ❶**, on Mounthoolie Pl. across from Buster's, has expanded its seating to accommodate the crowds of locals and travelers who come to dance and drink the night away. (☎876 000. Su night live folk music. Open M-W 11am-midnight, Th-Sa 11am-1am, Su noon-midnight. Food served 5-9:30pm.) Cut a rug at **Fusion**, Kirkwall's only nightclub. (☎853 359; www.fusionclub.co.uk. Cover £2. Open Th 10pm-1:30am, F-Sa 10pm-2:30am, last entrance 11:45pm. Cash only.)

▐ SIGHTS. Nicknamed "The Light in the North" and famous for the red and yellow sandstone bands that line its walls, **St. Magnus Cathedral** is the town's central landmark. The cathedral was created to honor Earl Magnus, who was killed at the direction of his cousin, Haakon Paulson. Travel to the back of the church to view the tomb of John Rae, the famous Orcadian Arctic explorer. (Open Apr.-Sept. M-Sa 9am-6pm, Su 1-6pm; Oct.-Mar. M-Sa 9am-1pm and 2-5pm. Free.) Across Palace Rd. from the cathedral, the **Bishop's and Earl's Palaces** once housed the Bishop of Orkney and his enemy, the wicked Earl Patrick Stewart. The houses were joined when the earl was executed for treason. The beautiful palace gardens and lawn are perfect for picnics or waiting for the bus. (☎871 918. Both open daily Apr.-Sept. 9:30am-6:30pm. £3.50, concessions £1.75. Ticket for all 6 Historic Scotland Orkney sights £15, concessions £11.50, children £6.) For a thorough history lesson, check out the **Orkney Museum**, Broad St., in the center of town, across from the chapel. (☎873 191. Open Apr.-Sept. M-Sa 10:30am-5pm, Su 2-5pm; Oct.-Mar. M-Sa 10:30am-12:30pm and 1:30-5pm. Free.) The 200-year-old **Highland Park Distillery**, a 20min.

walk to the south of town on Holm Rd., is the world's northernmost Scotch whisky distillery and the largest of the three distilleries on Orkney. Originally the sight of an illicit smuggling operation, the distillery now offers samples of its acclaimed single malts, a tour, and a goofy informational video. Walk to the southern end of Broad St., turn west on Clay Loan, then south on Bignold Park Rd. and take the right fork on Holm Rd. (☎874 619; www.highlandpark.co.uk. Open Apr. and Sept.-Oct. M-F 10am-5pm; May-Aug. M-Sa 10am-5pm, Su noon-5pm; Nov.-Mar. M-F 1-5pm. Tours every 30min.; last tour 4pm. £5, concessions £4.)

STROMNESS   ☎01856

The Vikings originally named Stromness "Hamnavoe," meaning "The Haven Inside the Bay," and the town is rich in maritime history. Cars clank down the narrow stone streets past historic buildings, giving Stromness a distinct charm complete with beautiful bay views. The **Pier Arts Centre,** Victoria St., houses the work of contemporary Scottish artists and a brilliant collection of 20th-century British artists, including Hepworth and Wallis, all in a sparkling new facility. (☎850 209; www.pierartscentre.com. Open Tu-Sa 10:30am-12:30pm and 1:30-5pm. Free.) The **Stromness Museum,** 54 Alfred St., was founded in 1837 and has built an impressive collection of boating artifacts and stuffed Orkney birds. (☎850 025. Open Apr.-Sept. daily 10am-5pm; Oct.-Mar. M-Sa 11am-3:30pm. £3, concessions £2.)

The simple **Brown's Hostel ❷,** 45-47 Victoria St., offers small single and double rooms for a bargain, along with free Wi-Fi. (☎850 661; www.hostel-scotland.com. All beds £12. Cash only.) **The Orca Hotel ❸,** tucked into an alleyway at 76 Victoria St., offers B&B-style service in the middle of town and keeps an unpretentious restaurant, **Bistro 76 ❸,** below. Enjoy the fresh catch of the day amid romantic nautical decor. (Hotel ☎850 447; www.orcahotel.com. £20-25 per person, MC/V. Restaurant ☎851 308. Entrees £8-13. Open M-Sa 7-10pm. Cash only.) A bastion of Stromness history, the century-old **Stromness Hotel ❹,** at the Pier Head on Victoria St., has a collection of 100 malt whiskies, which it serves in its two bars and restaurant. (☎850 298; www.stromnesshotel.com. May-Sept. £48 per person; Apr. £41; Oct.-Mar. £29. MC/V.) One mile south of town on Victoria St., the **Point of Ness Caravan and Camping Site ❶** sits on a lawn overlooking the placid bay. (☎851 235. Open from May to mid-Sept. £7.50 per caravan, £4-7.20 per tent. Showers 20p. Laundry wash £1, dry 40p. Cash only.) Across from the pier, the animated **Julia's Cafe & Bistro ❶,** 20 Ferry Rd., has baked goods, vegetarian options (£5-8), and a sweeping view of Stromness ferry arrivals. (☎850 904. Open Apr.-Sept. M-W 9am-5pm, Th-Sa 9am-5pm and 6:30-9:30pm; Oct.-Mar. daily 9am-5pm. MC/V.)

The **Northlink Ferry** runs the *Hamnavoe* from Scrabster to Stromness (p. 661). Almost everything you'll need (and almost everything in town) is on **Victoria Street,** which parallels the harbor. Cheap **bike** rental is available from £6 per day at Orkney Cycle Hire, 54 Dundas St. (☎850 225. Includes free maps and helmets.) The **Tourist Information Centre,** in an 18th-century warehouse on the pier, provides free maps. (☎850 716. Open May-Sept. daily 9am-5pm; Oct.-Apr. M-Sa 9:30am-3:30pm.) The **Bank** of Scotland, 99 Victoria St., has an **ATM.** (☎0847 801 801. Open M-Tu and F 9:45am-12:30pm and 1:30-4:45pm, W 10:45am-12:30pm and 1:30-4:45pm.) Find free **Internet** access at the **library,** 2 Hellihole Rd. (☎850 907. Open M-Th 2-7pm, F 2-5pm, Sa 10am-5pm.) The **post office** is at 37 Victoria St. (☎850 225. Open M-F 9am-1pm and 2-5:15pm, Sa 9am-12:30pm.) **Post Code:** KY16 3BS.

▶ DAYTRIPS ON THE ORKNEY MAINLAND

The Orkney mainland is bursting with Iron and Stone Age treasures that have gradually come to light, representing over 5000 years of archaeological history. As excavating sites on the isles continues, artifacts and stone formations add to scientists' understanding of these ancient societies. In addition to the service bus #98 that runs between Kirkwall and Stromness (£3.40 round-trip), multiple tour buses service the four main archaeological sites between Kirkwall and Stromness.

SKARA BRAE. Five thousand years ago, Skara Brae was a Stone Age village; today it is an archaeological marvel, representing the most well-preserved and oldest Neolithic village in the world. Sand covered the village until 1850, when a storm revealed the first remnants of nine houses, a workshop, and covered town roads. Travel around the village on a small, grassy path. The **Skail House,** home of the unsuspecting gentleman who "discovered" Skara Brae in his backyard, provides a look at Orkney during the more accessible 18th and 19th centuries. *(19 mi. northwest of Kirkwall on the B9056; take the A965 from Kirkwall to Stromness and turn right at the sign after Maes Howe. Continue along the road until the signs for Skara Brae or Skail House.* ☎841 815. Open Apr.-Sept. daily 9:30am-6:30pm; Oct.-Mar. M-Sa 9am-4:30pm, Su 9:30am-4pm. Last admission 45min. before close. £6.50, concessions £5.)*

RING OF BRODGAR. Six miles east of Skara Brae and 5 mi. northeast of Stromness on the B9055 stands a group giant stones arranged in a perfect circle. Thought to have been built in 2500 BC, the Ring of Brodgar may once have witnessed gatherings of local chieftains or burial ceremonies. In a year, the stones witness more sunlight than almost any other spot on the island, revealing the builders' deep understanding of solar and lunar patterns. The 60 stones (only 27 of which still stand) draw large crowds in the middle of the day; arrive early in the morning for a more private viewing. *(Always open. Free.)*

STANDING STONES OF STENNESS. One mile east of the Ring on the B9055, the bern-enclosed Standing Stones of Stenness have been reduced over time to a humble few. The oldest remaining archaeological artifacts on the island, the stones were probably once used with the Brodgar stones in the same ceremonies. By 1760, only four of the original 12 stones remained—locals angered by the monument's pagan origins likely knocked down the others. *(Always open. Free.)* After a visit to the standing stones, visit the tiny **Gerry's Ice Cream** in Stenness. Featuring stone-themed treats and ice cream made on Orkney, the parlor is a little-known spot. *(Open daily about 9am-5pm.)*

MAES HOWE TOMB. Between Kirkwall and Stromness on the A965, this tomb may have held the bones of the area's earliest settlers (from 2700 BC). Walk onto the hill to see the rune carvings on the stones, created by the plundering Vikings in the mid-12th century. The largest collection of runic inscriptions in the world, linguists cracked the runic alphabet here, translating the profound statements: "This was carved by the greatest rune carver" and "Ingigerth is the most exquisite of women." *(☎761 606; www.maeshowe.co.uk. Open Apr.-Sept. daily 9:30am-6pm; Oct.-Mar. M-Sa 9:30am-4:30pm, Su 1:30-4:30pm. Last tour 1hr. before close. £4. Call ahead.)*

BROCH OF GURNESS. Off the A966, on the north coast of the Evie section of Mainland, this broch is the site of a preserved Iron Age village, fortuitously unearthed by the ultimate Orcadian Renaissance man, Robert Rendall, in 1929. The reconstructed Pictish and Viking settlements are worth a stop on the way between towns. *(☎751 414. Open daily Apr.-Sept. 9:30am-12:30pm and 1:30-6pm. £4.50.)*

CHURCHILL BARRIERS AND SCAPA FLOW. At the end of WWII, German Admiral von Reuter ordered all 74 of his ships to be scuttled rather than remain in British hands. The ships sank at **Scapa Flow,** the bay south of Houton on Mainland. To the delight of scuba divers worldwide, seven of the wrecks remain. **Scapa Scuba,** in the red Lifeboat House on Dundas St., Stromness, offers non-certified "try-a-dive" lessons, equipment, and a dive to the wrecks. They also offer more involved tours for experienced divers. *(☎851 218. £60 per ½-day.)* If you don't want to get wet, **Rov-**

ing **Eye Enterprises** does the marine work for you via a roaming underwater camera. The boat leaves from Houton Pier and stops on Hoy. (☎811 360; www.orknet.co.uk/rov. Tours daily 12:30pm. £28, children £14.) In 1939, German U-boats entered the straits leading to the Scapa Flow naval anchorage during an exceptionally high tide, sinking a warship, killing 800 seamen, and escaping unscathed. The next year, Prime Minister Churchill erected barriers to seal the seas from attack. The POWs who built the barriers used over a quarter-million tons of rock. The barrier's **causeways** now link Mainland to the smaller southeast islands (p. 665).

ORKNEY CRAFT TRAIL AND ARTISTS STUDIO TRAIL. Founded in the 1990s, the Orkney Craft Industry Association, a group of local artists, weavers, jewelers, woodworkers, and other artisans designed a route connecting their workshops (usually also their homes). The stops include shops with varying prices and styles, from **Hoxa Tapestry Gallery** in St. Margaret's Hope (☎831 395) to **Orkney Stained Glass,** on Shapinsay (☎771 276). Brown signs (sometimes faded to orange) direct drivers to hidden hamlets of tradition and creativity. Pick up the *Craft Trail* brochure in the TIC or visit www.orkneydesignercrafts.com.

SMALLER ISLANDS ☎01856

The smaller islands, most accessible by car or ferry from Kirkwall or Stromness, have individual character and are full of historical and natural sights. Take particular care when traveling; with erratic ferry schedules dependent upon tides, you could end up sleeping with the seals and birds. Make sure to tell someone where you're going and to bring warm clothing and rain gear with you.

 ISLAND FLIGHTS FOR POCKET CHANGE. Spending the night on one of Orkney's smaller islands can cut the cost of your plane ticket by more than half. For example, if you spend the night on North Ronaldsay, the price of a round-trip Loganair flight drops from the normal price of £30 to £12 because the government wants to support the local tourism trade. The discount will factor automatically into the price of round-trip tickets during booking.

HOY. Hoy, the second-largest of the Orkney Islands (57 sq. mi.), gets its name from the Norse word "Haey," meaning "high island." Hoy is spectacularly hilly in the north and west, while the south and east are lower and more fertile. Its most famous landmark, the ◪**Old Man of Hoy,** is a 450 ft. sea stack of sandstone off the west coast of the island. Hikers can take the steep footpath from the partially abandoned crofting village of Rackwick, 2 mi. away (3hr. round-trip). The **North Hoy Bird Reserve** offers respite for guillemots and a host of other species. Puffins roost during breeding season, from late June to early July. The **SYHA Hoy ❶,** near the pier, and the eight beds of the simple **SYHA Rackwick ❶,** at the start of the path toward the Old Man, offer a place to sleep. Visitors must bring a sleeping bag. (☎873 535. Hoy open from May to mid-Sept. Rackwick open from mid-Mar. to mid-Sept. Hoy dorms £12, under 18 £9.25; Rackwick dorms £9.45, under 18 £8.30.) If you plan to stay overnight on Hoy, bring adequate provisions.

SHAPINSAY. Only 25min. from Kirkwall, with frequent ferry services, Shapinsay is the most accessible of the outer isles. **Ward Hill,** the island's highest point at 210 ft., slopes gently above the island's flat ground. From its "peak" on a rare clear day, you can see almost all the islands. An excellent example of the Victorian Baronial style, 19th-century **Balfour Castle,** near the ferry dock on the southwestern side of the isle, was once home to the influential lairds of Balfour and is now a posh guest house. Guided tours of the castle depart from Kirkwall pier and include the ferry ride and tea. (☎711 282, tours 872 856; www.balfourcastle.com. Tours May-Sept. Su 2:15pm. £18. Rooms from £100.) **Burroughston Broch,** an Iron Age shelter, lies 5 mi. north of the ferry pier. There are no hostels on Shapinsay, but the award-winning **Girnigoe B&B ❹,** near the beach, has two rooms in a converted farmhouse. (☎711 256; www.girnigoe.net. Twins and doubles from £50. Cash only.)

ROUSAY. Many argue that Orkney's finest archaeological sights lie not on Mainland, but on Rousay. The **Midhowe Broch** and **Cairn** has Stone, Bronze, and Iron Age remnants. The **Knowe of Yarso Cairn** stands on a cliff overlooking Eynhallow Sound, and the **Westness Walk** winds past sites from the Neolithic, Pictish, Viking, and medieval eras. Above the ferry terminal, a visitors center has an exhibition on the points of interest in Rousay and nearby Egilsay and Wyre. Stay at the **Rousay Hostel ❶** on Trumland Farm near the pier; turn left from the ferry port and walk 5min. down the main road. (☎01856 821 252. Linens £2. Dorms £10-12. Cash only.)

STRONSAY. Seven miles long, this island is a collection of bays and beaches. Along the east coast, between Lamb Ness and Odiness, is the stunning **Vat of Kirbister,** an opening ("gloup") spanned by a dramatic natural stone arch. There are Pictish settlements and an Iron Age fort on the southeastern bay. Stay at **Stronsay Fishmart ❷,** a former herring boning station in Whitehall Village, which also has a cafe. (☎616 386. £14. Cash only.)

EDAY. Home to tales of captured pirates and tombs of the ancients, Eday's peat-covered hills remain home to a handful of crofters and hundreds of species of birds. One of the quieter, smaller islands, Eday contains chambered tombs like the **Vinquoy** and **Huntersquoy Cairns,** the towering **Stone of Setter,** and, on the Calf of Eday, the remnants of an Iron Age roundhouse. The newly renovated **SYHA Hostel ❷** is located on the main north-south road, 4 mi. from the pier. (☎01857 622 206. Laundry £2. Open Mar.-Oct. Dorms £12, under 18 £7. Camping £2. Cash only.)

SANDAY. Home to the elusive Sanday Vole and the vast beaches that give the island its name, Sanday offers more than just one day of island exploration; plan to stay overnight. The island is 87 mi. long, and beachside and inland walks traverse the isle. Bernie meets ferries in his large red **bus** and drops passengers wherever they want to go; call for a pickup (☎600 284). Rangers also meet ferry arrivals on select "Sanday Sundays" for island tours. Check the Kirkwall TIC for details. Seal pups can be seen swimming at Otterswick in June, and gray seals are born on the beaches in November. On the south side of the island, turn south off the main road and follow the signs to the **Quoyness Chambered Cairn.** The cairn, accessible by foot via a spectacular beachside walk, is worth the 40min. trip. It held the remains of at least 15 people and dates back to 2900 BC. Take the torch by the door and crawl into the well-preserved rooms. The **Orkney Angora Craft Shop,** in Upper Breckan, features incredibly soft wool from Angora rabbits. Ask the owner for a tour of the workshop. (☎600 421; www.orkneyangora.co.uk. Open daily 1:30-5:30pm or by arrangement.) At ◧**Ayre's Rock Hostel and Campsite ❶,** about 7 mi. from the ferry on the main road, find a spotless bunkhouse with two double rooms, a family room, a kitchen, and sunsets over the ocean. (☎600 410. Internet access 50p per hr. Dorms from £12. Cash only.)

WESTRAY. Just west of Papa Westray, (mama) Westray features ruined **Noltland Castle,** the **Knowe O'Burristae Broch,** ancient rubble, and magnificent cliffs. Legend holds that the windowless castle, marked by over 60 gun holes, is linked underground to the **Gentlemen's Cave,** which hid supporters of Bonnie Prince Charlie. The castle's first owner, Gilbert Balfour, was implicated in two royal assassination plots, the second of which got him executed. Bird-watchers rejoice on **Noup Head**

Reserve and on the opposite end of the island, where thousands of puffins congregate. You'll feel like one of the family at ⬛The Barn ❶, Chalmersquoy, at the southern end of Pierowall village, in a wonderfully converted stone barn. (☎01857 677 214; www.thebarnwestray.com. ₤13, children ₤8.80. Cash only.) ⬛Bis Geos Hostel ❶, 2 mi. west of Pierowall, is a fabulous croft ruin-turned-hostel, complete with Internet access (₤1 per 30min.), heated floors, and a gorgeous room overlooking the cliffs. (☎01857 677 420; www.bisgeos.co.uk. Open Apr.-Oct. Dorms ₤11. Cash only.)

PAPA WESTRAY. "Papay" is home to a mere 75 or so Orcadians and is best suited to those seeking birds and solitude. This northern "isle of the priests" once supported an early Christian Pictish settlement. Fly from Kirkwall (Loganair ☎872 494; M-F 3 per day, Sa 2 per day, Su 1 per day; ₤15); if the plane stops at Westray, you get a certificate for world's shortest commercial flight. On the west coast, the **Knap of Howar** marks the location of the oldest standing house in northern Europe (c. 3500 BC), built centuries before the pyramids of Egypt. The **Bird Sanctuary** at North Hill has Arctic terns and other rare Northern birds; schedule a tour at the Co-op. Two miles north of the pier and ½ mi. south of the airstrip, **Beltane House ❶** is attached to the community Co-op. Hostelers enjoy ensuite dorms, while B&B guests get a lovely sitting room. All have access to the only liquor-licensed place on the island—a ⬛closet full of booze. (☎644 267 reaches house, Co-op, and tour guide bookings. Dorms ₤10, children ₤8; B&B ₤25 per person. MC/V.)

NORTH RONALDSAY. Due to the warm Gulf Stream, this northernmost Orkney is an average of 10°F warmer than its latitudinal neighbors. North Ronaldsay offers archaeological wonders, like the **Broch of Burrian,** an unusual standing stone with a hole through it, and two weathered lighthouses. The lighthouse keeper gives excellent tours (☎07703 112 224; ₤4, children ₤2). The island's famous ⬛seaweed-eating sheep graze on the beaches, producing coveted wool. Viciously protective nesting birds are all over—take a cue from them and stay at the solar- and wind-powered **North Ronaldsay Bird Observatory Hostel ❶.** (☎01857 633 200. Internet access free. Call ahead for a ride from the airport. Dorms ₤12, full board ₤27. Cash only.)

SOUTHEAST ISLANDS. Accessible by road from Mainland, this string of islands, including Lamb Holm, Burray, and South Ronaldsay, is quiet and full of wonderful craft shops and an organic farm hostel. On Lamb Holm, the **Italian Chapel** is all that remains of Camp 60, a WWII prison that held hundreds of Italian POWs, who used food cans for sacred lighting and transformed their bare cement hut into a beautiful house of worship that is still in use today. (Open daily Apr.-Sept. 9am-10pm; Oct.-Mar. 9am-4:30pm. Occasionally closed F afternoons, the traditional time for Orkney weddings. Services 1st Su of the month. Free.) During the summer, **buses** chug over the Churchill Barriers from Kirkwall to the pier at St. Margaret's Hope (3-4 per day), on the larger isle of South Ronaldsay.

A fantastic eight-bed hostel and organic farm, **Wheems Bothy ❶,** stands on the blustery promontory of South Ronaldsay. Fresh produce is available. Call ahead for pickup. (☎831 535. Open Apr.-Oct. Dorms ₤6.50. Camping ₤2-3 per person.) The greatest treasure to be found on South Ronaldsay, however, is the family-run ⬛Tomb of the Eagles. Farther south, outside of St. Margaret's Hope in Isbister, lies the farm of the Simison family. They own and operate a fantastic visitors center, where you can handle 5000-year-old artifacts, including marvelously intact human skulls and eagle talons. A quarter of a mile from the visitors center is a Bronze Age burnt mound, a stone dwelling with a plumbing system, the dramatic sea cliffs, and the spectacular Stone Age tomb after which the property is named. (☎831 339; www.tomboftheeagles.co.uk. Open daily Apr.-Oct. 9:30am-6pm; Nov.-Mar. 10am-noon or by appointment. ₤5.50, concessions ₤4.50, children ₤2-3.)

SHETLAND ISLANDS   ☎ 01595

Closer to Norway than to mainland Britain, Shetland's people and landscapes have a rich dual heritage. The islands' peat-covered hills give them a rougher appeal than beach-studded Orkney, and famously friendly Shetland ponies roam the land. Best suited for the traveler with plenty of time to explore, the islands are full of hidden craft shops, cafes, and a number of archaeological marvels.

✈ GETTING THERE

Air travel is the fastest, most expensive way to Shetland. Flights are usually cheaper if you stay over a Saturday night. British Airways (☎ 08457 733 377) flies from: Aberdeen (1hr.; M-F 3 per day, Sa-Su 2 per day; £80-110); Edinburgh (1½hr., 1 per day, £181-250); Glasgow (2½hr.; M-F 2 per day, Sa-Su 1 per day; £96-200); Inverness (1½hr., 1 per day, round-trip £124-294); Kirkwall, Orkney (35min., 1 per day, round-trip £80-170). **Travel agents** Shetland Travelscope (☎ 696 644) and John Leask & Son (☎ 693 162; www.leaskstravel.co.uk) purchase tickets and organize trips. All flights land at **Sumburgh Airport,** on the southern tip of Shetland's Mainland, which also has a visitors center with Internet access, Wi-Fi (£1 per 20min.), and a knowledgeable staff. The airport is 25 mi. (and a hefty £30-35 taxi ride) from Lerwick, the islands' capital and largest town. John Leask & Son buses make the journey to Lerwick (1hr.; M-Sa 5 per day, Su 3 per day; £2.20), and an alternative express bus meets midday flights (½hr., 2-3 per day, £5). Buses arrive at the **Viking Bus Station** (☎ 694 100), 5min. from the city center on Commercial Rd.

Ferries are the other means of travel to Shetland. Although cheaper, they take far longer than flights. Most ferries arrive at **Holmsgarth Terminal,** a 20min. walk northwest of Lerwick's town center, or the smaller **Victoria Pier,** across from the TIC. Northlink Ferries (☎ 08456 000 449; www.northlinkferries.co.uk) arrive from Aberdeen (12-14hr.; M, W, F 7pm; Tu, Th, Sa-Su 5pm; £22-32) and Kirkwall, Orkney (7¾hr.; Tu, Th, Sa-Su 11:45pm; £13.50-19.20). Arrive 30min. in advance. P&O Smyril Line (☎ 690 845; www.smyril-line.com) runs in summer from Lerwick to Bergen, Norway (12hr., M 11:30pm, £77.50) and to Iceland (30hr.; W 2am; £150, with car from £184) via the Faroe Islands (13hr., £77.50). Call ahead for prices and times from mid-September to April.

▐ LOCAL TRANSPORTATION

Infrequent public transportation makes getting around Shetland difficult without a car. **Car rental** companies include John Leask & Son (☎ 693 162; £31-42 per day), the more extensive Bolts Car Hire, 26 North Rd. (☎ 693 636, airport branch 01950 460 777; www.boltscarhire.co.uk; 21+; £35-49 per day), and Grantfield Garage, 44 North Rd. (☎ 692 709; www.grantfieldgarage.co.uk; 23+; £24-30 per day).

Travel between the islands is heavily subsidized. **Ferries** sail to the larger islands nearly every hour and to the smaller islands at least once per day; no trip costs more than £5. Shetland's main **bus** provider is John Leask & Son (☎ 693 162). Whites Coaches (☎ 809 443) handles the North Mainland services. The TIC stocks the vital Shetland Transport Timetable (£1) with bus, ferry, and plane schedules. Eric Brown's Cycle Hire, on the second floor of Grantfield Garage, offers **bike rentals.** (☎ 692 709. £7.50 per day, £45 per week. Helmets £1. Open M-W 8am-9pm, Th-Sa 8am-10pm, Su 11am-9pm.) Winds and hills can make biking difficult.

Tour companies offer convenient ways of seeing Shetland. Puffins are a dime a dozen on ▪Seabirds-and-Seals, a 3hr. tour, which consistently yields close encounters with seals and features an underwater camera that reveals Shetland's submerged kelp forest. Tea and coffee are served on board. Trips depart from Victoria

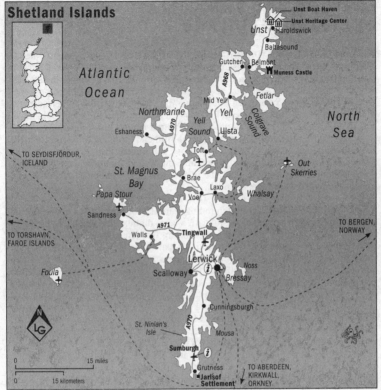

Shetland Islands

Atlantic Ocean

North Sea

Unst Boat Haven
Unst Heritage Center
Unst
Haroldswick
Baltasound
Gutcher
Belmont
Muness Castle
Mid Yell
Fetlar
Northmarine
Yell
Yell
Sound
Colgrave Sound
Eshaness
Ulsta
Toft
Out Skerries
St. Magnus Bay
Brae
Laxo
Papa Stour
Voe
Whalsay
Sandness
TO SEYDISFJÖRDUR, ICELAND
A970
A971
Walls
Tingwall
TO BERGEN, NORWAY
TO TORSHAVN, FAROE ISLANDS
Foula
Lerwick
Noss
Scalloway
Bressay
Cunningsburgh
St. Ninian's Isle
A970
Mousa
Sumburgh
Grutness
Jarlsof
Settlement
TO ABERDEEN, KIRKWALL, ORKNEY

N

0   15 miles
0   15 kilometers

Pier, Lerwick. (☎693 434; www.seabirds-and-seals.com. Daily May-Aug. 9:30am and 2pm. £35.) Walking tours include the **Shetland Ranger Service's** guided treks across the islands, which are great for bird-watching (☎01957 711 528 or 0195 694 688; May-Aug. £2.50), **Geo Tours's** day-long geology and landscape expeditions (☎859 218; www.shetlandgeotours.com), and the folklore-oriented **Island Trails** with locals Elma Johnson and Douglas Sinclair. (☎01950 422 408. May-Sept. 2hr. tour £10-15, children £4.) For the more adventurous, Tom Smith leads introductory (£20), half-day (£35), and full day (£60) **kayaking trips** around the islands. (☎01595 859 647; www.seakyakshetland.co.uk.)

❈ FESTIVALS

Shetland's endless daylight in summer and endless darkness in winter make for long summer festivals and fiery winter ones. The **Shetland Folk Festival** (☎741 000; www.sffs.shetland.co.uk), at the end of April, celebrates Shetland's music scene and lures fiddlers from around the world, while the **Shetland Fiddle and Accordion Festival** takes place in Lerwick in mid-October. Enjoy live music and a lamb burger at the **Flavour of Shetland** on Victoria Pier in mid-July. The annual **Up Helly Aa Festival** (www.uphellyaa.com), held in Lerwick (p. 668) on the last Tuesday in January, celebrates the Viking influence on the islands and is Europe's largest fire festival.

LERWICK AND THE SHETLAND MAINLAND

■■■ ORIENTATION AND PRACTICAL INFORMATION. On the eastern coast of Mainland, Lerwick sits on the island's central artery, the A970. The **Tourist Information Centre,** Market Cross, books beds for £3 plus a 10% deposit. (☎693 434; www.visitshetland.com. Internet access £1 per 30min, Wi-Fi available. Open Apr.-Oct. M-F 8am-6pm, Sa-Su 8am-4pm; Nov.-Mar. M-F 9am-5pm.) Other services include: the Royal **Bank** of Scotland, 81 Commercial St. (☎694 520; open M and W-F 9:15am-4:45pm, Tu 10am-4:45pm); free **Internet** access in the Learning Centre adjacent to the Shetland **Library,** on Lower Hillhead (☎693 868; open M and Th 9:30am-8pm, Tu-W and F-Sa 9:30am-5pm); **Job Centre** Plus, Commercial Rd. (☎08456 072 026; open M-Tu and Th-F 9am-5pm, W 10am-5pm); and the **post office,** 46-50 Commercial St. (☎08457 223 344; open M and W-F 9am-5pm, Tu 9:30am-5pm, Sa 9am-12:30pm). **Post Code:** ZE1 0EH.

▐ ACCOMMODATIONS. The community-run █SYHA Lerwick ❷, at King Harald and Union St., is an expansive hostel with a large dining room, excellent facilities, a popular cafe, and gardens. The four rotating wardens love to talk about Shetland. (☎692 114. Laundry £2. Reception 9-9:30am, 4-4:30pm, and 9:45-10:15pm; at other times, go to the Community Centre across the street. Curfew 11:45pm. Open Apr.-Sept. Dorms £15.50, under 18 £13. AmEx/MC/V.) At the **Glen Orchy Guest House** ❹, 20 Knab Rd., dine on homemade Thai cuisine and enjoy lovely aqua-colored rooms with views of Lerwick. Rooms include a TV, complimentary fresh fruit, and full Scottish breakfast. (☎692 031. Free Wi-Fi. Handicap-accessible. Meals available with advance reservation; dinner £18. Singles £47-50; doubles £74-80. MC/V.) There are three **campgrounds** on Mainland, but you can pitch almost anywhere with the landowner's permission. **Clickimin Caravan and Camp Site** ❶ is close to the Lerwick ferry terminal. Turn left on Holmsgarth Rd. (A970), go through the roundabout, and merge onto North Lochside; it's on the right. (☎741 000. Showers, pool, bar, and cafe. Reception 8:30am-10pm. Open May-Sept. Pitches £6.70-9.40. MC/V.)

▐▐ FOOD AND PUBS. Stock up on **groceries** at Somerfield, South Rd., or at the Co-op, Holmsgarth Rd., one block from the ferry station. (Somerfield ☎692 426. Co-op ☎693 419. Both open M-W and Sa 8am-8pm, Th-F 8am-9pm, Su 9am-6pm.) **Osla's Cafe** ❶, 88 Commercial St., specializes in pancakes, pizzas, and pastas. (☎696 005. Entrees £6-9. Open M-Sa 9am-10pm, Su noon-8pm.) On the Esplanade, the two-story **Peerie Shop Cafe** ❶ has outdoor seating and serves fresh sandwiches, baked goods, organic cider, and a sinful hot chocolate (£1.25, with rum £3). The shop next door sells funky woollens. (☎692 817. Open M-Sa 9am-6pm.) **Raba** ❸, 26 Commercial St., offers traditional Indian cuisine and atmosphere. (☎695 554. All-you-can-eat Su buffet £8.50; 3-course business lunch £6. Open M-Sa noon-2pm and 5pm-midnight, Su noon-midnight.) For hostelers, the city's most convenient food awaits at the simple **Isleburgh Community Centre Cafe** ❶, on the first floor of the hostel, and at the **Blue Rock Cafe** ❶, next door at the Community Centre. (Both ☎692 114. Isleburgh Community Centre Cafe open M-Sa 8am-2:30pm, Su 8-11am. Blue Rock Cafe open M-Sa 9:45am-9pm, Su noon-4pm and 6:30-9pm.)

The Lounge, 4 Mounthooly St., is the busiest pub. Although the downstairs area is small, it fills with Shetland fiddle music and dancing on Wednesday and Thursday nights in summer. (☎692 231. Open M-Sa 11am-1am.) **Captain Flint's,** in Market Cross, stays busy well into the night and has great harbor views. (☎692 249. Happy hour F 5-7pm. Open M-Sa 8am-1am, Su 12:30pm-1am. Food served M-Sa noon-

2:15pm, Su 12:30-2:15pm.) Rack 'em up on the pool tables and chat with the Shetland natives at **Thule Bar** (THOO-lee) near Victoria Pier. (☎692 508. Open M-Sa 11am-1am, Su 12:30pm-1am.)

◉ SIGHTS. Lerwick is a souvenir shopper's paradise. Take home some famous ⬛Shetland wool, which can be found in all forms, from freshly sheared to mittens and handbags, in stores throughout town. Observe a local weaver at work and buy local wares at the **Spider's Web**, 41 Commercial St., across from the Queen's Hotel. (☎695 246. Open M-Sa 9am-5pm.) Weather permitting, you can cruise around the bay on the ⬛**Dim Riv**, a full-scale replica of a Viking longship. (☎07970 864 189. Open June-Aug.; call ahead for times, usually M 7pm. Book in advance. £5.) The newly opened **Shetland Museum**, Hay's Dock, contains all kinds of geographic and historical information on the isles, as well as sheep's wool displays and plenty of rotating exhibits, all in an old Böd with a modern addition. (☎695 057. Open M-W, F, and Sa 10am-5pm, Th 10am-7pm, Su noon-5pm. Free.) The **Islesburgh Exhibition**, in the Islesburgh Community Centre, features traditional music, dance, crafts, and a replica of a 1920s croft house. (☎692 114. Open Jun.-Sept. M and W 7-9:30pm. £4, concessions £2.) For a great view of Lerwick and the ferry boats rocking in the water, climb the giant pentagonal **Fort Charlotte**, just off Commercial St. at the north end of town, which offers the best views of Lerwick and its harbor. (Open daily 9am-10pm. Free.) The **Knab**, a small, impressive promontory at the end of Knab Rd., is a short coastal walk from **Clickimin Broch**, 1 mi. west of city center. The broch was built in a stronghold from 400 BC and stands in the middle of a loch. Climb to the grassy top for a great view. (Always open. Free.) Don't miss the **Up-Helly-Aa Exhibition** in the **Galley Shed**, Saint Sunniva St., Lerwick, where costumes and elaborate party regalia from the last 50 years are on display. (Open from mid-May to mid-Sept. Tu 2-4pm and 7-9pm, F 7-9pm, Sa 2-4pm. £3, concessions £1.)

▶ DAYTRIPS ON THE SHETLAND MAINLAND

Mainland Shetland's windy hills offer many sights and culinary treasures. En route north or south of Lerwick, detour west to the tiny town of Walls to visit **The Baker's Rest Tearoom ❶** for perhaps the most delectable shortbread (£1.20) in the world. (☎809 308; www.wallsbakery.co.uk. Open M-Sa 9am-5pm.) Outside Lerwick, the best budget accommodations come in the form of **Böds ❶** (Old Norse for "barns"; www.camping-bods.com). In various states of repair, these converted fishing cottages now serve as "camping barns." Bring a sleeping bag, camping stove, cooking utensils, and coins for electricity (when available). Böds are available from April to September. All Böds cost £6-8 per night and must be booked in advance through the Lerwick TIC or the Shetland Amenity Trust (☎694 688).

SCALLOWAY. Scalloway, 7 mi. west of Lerwick, offers an authentic taste of the fishing industry in Shetland. Crumbling **Scalloway Castle** looms large over the harbor and was once home to tyrannical Earl Patrick Stewart. Get the key from the Scalloway Hotel. (☎880 444. Castle open daily 9am-5pm. Free.) Popular ⬛**Da Haaf Restaurant ❶**, located within the North Atlantic Fisheries College, serves the best fish—fried, baked, or grilled—on the island. The Shetland salmon is £7.20. Call ahead to reserve a table. (☎880 747. Open M-F 12:30-2pm and 5-8pm. MC/V.) John Leask & Son sends **buses** from Lerwick (☎693 162; M-Sa 10 per day, round-trip £2.60).

JARLSHOF AND SOUTH MAINLAND. At the southern tip of Mainland, southwest of Sumburgh Airport, **Jarlshof** is one of Europe's most impressive archaeological sites. In 1896, a storm uncovered stone walls and artifacts, some over 4000 years old. (☎01950 460 112. Open daily Apr.-Sept. 9:30am-6:30pm. Last admission 6pm.

£3.30.) A mile up the road, the **Old Scatness Broch** is the site of ongoing excavation. Remains were discovered in 1975 during airport construction; since, then an entire Iron Age village and over 20,000 artifacts have surfaced. Guided tours include re-enactments of life in the broch and info on the ongoing excavation. (☎694 688. *Open from July to mid-Aug. M-Th 10am-5pm, Sa-Su 10:30am-5:30pm. £4, children £3, conces-sions £3.*) On nearby **Sumburgh Head,** gulls, guillemots, and puffins rear their young on steep cliff walls. Four miles north of the airport at Voe, the ◧**Croft House Museum,** signposted off of A970, is a restored working croft house, barn, watermill, and byre from the 19th century. (☎01595 695 057. *Open daily May-Sept. 10am-1pm and 2-5pm. Free.*) Next door to Old Scatness, **Betty Mouat's Böd** has hot water and show-ers. All South Mainland sights can be reached by the Leask **bus** that runs to Sum-burgh Airport from Lerwick (☎693 162; 5 per day).

NORTHMAVINE. A drive north across Mavis Grind, a 100 yd. wide isthmus, reveals the stark cliffs and jutting rocks of Northmavine, the northeastern tip of the Shetland mainland. Begin at the **Eshaness Lighthouse** and walk with the sea at your left to the majestic **cliffs of Eshaness,** which provide shelter for rare sea birds and are a great place to spot seals. To the east of the lighthouse, the **Dore Holm nat-ural arch** is one of the most impressive in the world. Explore the rocky shore with only the sheep for company. ◧**Da Böd Cafe ❷,** on the waterfront in Hillswick, serves outstanding organic vegetarian food in front of a peat fire and donates all proceeds to the seal and otter sanctuary. Ring the big brass bell for service and pay what you think you owe in the donation box by the door. (☎01806 503 348. *Menu changes daily. Open May Sa-Su 11am-late; June-Sept. Tu-Su 11am-late.*) The **Tangwick Haa Museum** offers free tea and coffee and has CDs of Shetland natives recalling their lives on the island (☎01806 503 389; *open May-Sept. daily 11am-5pm. Free.*) Stay at **Johnnie Notions Böd,** in Hamnavoe.

SMALLER ISLANDS

BRESSAY AND NOSS. Hike to the summit of the conical **Ward of Bressay,** locally called "Da Wart" (742 ft.), for an open view of the sea. From Bressay's east coast, 3 mi. past the Lerwick ferry port (follow the "To Noss" signs), dinghies go to the isle of Noss. Stand at the "Wait Here" sign and wave to flag one down. Great skuas and arctic terns dive-bomb visitors at the bird sanctuary—wave a hat or stick over your head to ward them off. The best views of Bressay, Noss, and the bird sanctu-ary are from the ocean. Stay at **Bressay Lighthouse Böd.** Ferries (☎980 317; 7min.; every hr.; £3, cars £7) sail from Lerwick to Bressay. (National Nature Reserve ☎693 345. Open June-Sept. Tu-W and F-Su 10am-5pm. Round-trip £3.20, conces-sions £2.60. Noss open Tu-W and F-Su 10am-5pm. Overnight stays forbidden.)

MOUSA. The tiny, uninhabited island of Mousa, just off the east coast of Main-land, is famous for its 6000 pairs of the miniscule nocturnal storm petrels. It also holds the world's best preserved Iron Age broch, a 50 ft. drystone fortress that has endured 1000 years of Arctic storms. Catch a Sumburgh-bound Leask bus in Ler-wick and ask the driver to let you off at the Setter Junction for Sandsayre (£5 round-trip); it's a 15min. walk from there to the ferry. (☎01950 431 367. Ferry departs Apr.-May and Sept. M-Th and Sa 2pm, F and Su 12:30 and 2pm; June-Aug. M, W-F, and Su 12:30 and 2pm, Tu and Sa 2pm. £9.30.) The tour service Trips to Mousa also provides, well, trips to Mousa, departing from Sandwick. (☎01950 431 367; www.mousaboattrips.co.uk. Call ahead for schedules. £10, concessions £9.)

YELL. The soft peat of Yell (ahhh!) adds spring to walks on the island, but for most it passes in a blur on the way to the Unst ferry. Aptly named Otterswick, on the southeastern side of the island, is the best place to spot otters, which can sometimes wander up to the road; watch out if you're driving. In the center of the isle, the haunted ruins of the Windhouse date back 5000 years. Next door, the **Windhouse Lodge Böd** provides shelter from the wind and a place to stay the night. At the ferry terminal, the ◨**Wind Dog Cafe** features folklore posters, stuffed animals by the piano, and well-made food. Try the Crofter's lunch of ham, cheese, homemade oatcakes, and a pickle (£3) for a literal taste of Highland life. (☎ 01957 744 321. Internet access £1 per 30min. Open M-F 9am-5pm, Sa-Su 10am-5pm. Cash only.) Killer whales are occasionally spotted in Bluemull Sound between Yell and Unst. Ferries run from Toft, Mainland to Ulsta, Yell (20min.; 1-2 per hr.; £3.20, cars £7.60).

ST. NINIAN'S ISLE. Off the southwest coast of Mainland, an unusual **tombolo**—a beach surrounded on both sides by the sea—links St. Ninian's Isle to Mainland, just outside of **Bigton.** Inhabited from the Iron Age to the 18th century and the site of an early monastery, the isle is now home to a ruined church, rabbits, and sheep. It achieved brief fame in 1958 when a hoard of silver was discovered. In order to visit St. Ninian's in a day—necessary, since there are no accommodations—take the noon Sumburgh-bound bus from Lerwick to Bigton, and the 2pm bus back from Bigton to Lerwick, allowing 1¼hr. to explore the island.

UNST. Unst (www.unst.org), the northernmost inhabited region in Britain, is home to impressive bird life, quirky museums and shops, and walks that lead to the end of the earth and back again. At the ◨**Hermaness National Nature Reserve,** puffins and gannets nest by the thousands on the inner faces of giant cliffs. Beginning at the **Visitors Centre,** a 3½hr. loop around the top of the isle travels past insect-eating plants. Follow the path to the north and touch the tip of Britian, gazing at spectacular views of the **Muckle Flugga Lighthouse** and the ocean. At the center of the isle off the A968 is the roofless **Muness Castle,** built in the late 16th century and often raided by pirates. Grab a key and torch from the nearby cottage to explore the dark rooms. (Open all year. Free.) In South Quoys, stop by the exceptional ◨**Foords Chocolates and Tearoom ❶** for a taste of some of Britian's finest handmade chocolates in the unlikeliest of locations. Ask for a tour of the two-room shop and grab homemade cake (£2) in the tea room. (☎ 01957 711 882; www.foordschocolates.com. Open M-Sa 9am-5pm.) To get to Unst, take a **ferry** from Gutcher to Belmont (10min.; 1-2 per hr.; £3 per person, £7 per car).

NO WORK, ALL PLAY

UP HELLY AA

It has been nearly a millennium since the Vikings set sail in their sleek longships to conquer the Shetland Isles, but the wild Norsemen of Lerwick still party like it's 999. In the endless darkness of the last Tuesday of January, a thousand or so revelers bearing shields and torches bedeck themselves in the garb of their Nordic ancestors—animal skins, armor, and horned helmets. The *guizers,* or revelers, elect a Shetlander to be the presiding Guizer Jarl (Earl), who organizes the event. On the morning of Up Helly Aa, a proclamation known as the "Bill," which contains the year's best gossip and local humor, is nailed to the Market Cross in the center of Lerwick. That night the guizers march through the streets bearing a meticulously reconstructed 30 ft. Viking longship. The ship's life is short. The guizers attack it with burning torches to welcome the springtime daylight, singing a rousing rendition of the traditional song "The Norseman's Home."

The blazing pyre signals just the beginning of the festivities. The procession dashes off to the first of a dozen halls where the guizer squads perform with song and dance until dawn. The next day is a public holiday in Lerwick, and the streets are deserted while the town recovers from the previous night's merriment.

(Visitors welcome; call the Lerwick TIC ☎ 01595 693 434; www.shetland-tourism.co.uk.)

A Leask **bus** leaves Lerwick daily at 7:50am, 2:30pm (M-F), and 3:45pm (Th-F) and connects with ferries to Haroldswick on Unst (2¼hr., £4.80). The Baltasound **post office** (open M-Tu and F 9am-1pm and 2-5:30pm, W 9am-1pm and 2-4:30pm, Th and Sa 9am-1pm) features Britain's northernmost **Post Code:** ZE2 9DP.

OTHER ISLANDS. Shetland's outer islands are perfect for the traveler looking to leave civilization and head out into remote landscapes. Plan to stay overnight, as ferry schedules can be erratic and ferries do not operate in inclement weather. **Planes** depart for the islands from Tingwall on Mainland, but **ferries** are cheaper. Many run from Walls, Vidlin, and Laxo on Mainland, which can be reached by bus from Lerwick (generally under 1hr.; consult the *Shetland Transport Timetable*).

Whalsay ("whale island" in Norse; pop. 1000) is the center of Shetland's fishing industry. The prosperous isle is accessible by bus and ferry from Lerwick and is home to coastal walks and Stone Age relics. **Symbister House,** an impressive example of Georgian architecture, bankrupted its owners. Ferries depart Laxo every hr. (30min.; £3.20, cars £7.60). The **Out Skerries** settlement supports 80 hardy fishermen. Stay at **The Grieve House Böd** (former home of poet Christopher Grieve, alias Hugh MacDiarmid). Planes (☎840 246; M and W-Th 1-2 per day, £20) arrive from Tingwall, while ferries come from Lerwick and Vidlin (Vidlin 1½hr., 10 per week; Lerwick 2½hr., 2 per week; £3.20, cars £7.60).

Papa Stour's (pop. 24) coastline features sea-flooded cliff arches and used to house a colony of "lepers" on the southwest side of the isle. As it turns out, the poor folk simply suffered from terrible malnutrition and vitamin deficiencies. Backpackers can camp or head to **Hurdiback ❶.** (☎873 229. May-Sept. £10, under 16 £8.50. Cash only.) To get to Papa Stour, fly (Tu only, £17.50) from Tingwall or sail (☎810 460; 8 per week; £2.80, cars £3.80; book ahead) from West Burrafirth.

Far to the west, rugged **Foula** is home to 35 humans, 2000 sheep, and the highest sheer cliff in Britain (1220 ft.). Barely Scottish, the inhabitants of Foula had their own monarch until the late 17th century, spoke the now-extinct Nordic language of Norn until 1926, and still celebrate Christmas and Easter according to the now-defunct Julian calendar. From May to September, ferries (☎753 254) travel from Walls (Tu, Th, Sa; £2.80, cars £7) and Scalloway (every other Th; £2.80, cars £12.40), while planes (☎840 246) fly from Tingwall (1¼hr., 5-6 per week, £25).

NORTHERN
IRELAND

The calm tenor of everyday life in Northern Ireland has long been over-shadowed by headlines about riots and bombs. While the violence has subdued and the Irish Republican Army (IRA) and Ulster Volunteer Force (UVF) have agreed to total disarmament, the divisions in civil society continue. Protestants and Catholics usually live in separate neighborhoods, attend separate schools, patronize different stores and pubs, and even play different sports. The 1998 Good Friday Agreement, designed by leaders of Northern Ireland, Great Britain, and the Republic of Ireland to end the Troubles, began a slow march to peace. All sides have renewed their efforts to make their country as peaceful as it is beautiful.

NORTHERN IRELAND HIGHLIGHTS

BEHOLD ballet at Belfast's historical **Grand Opera House** (p. 682).

EXPLORE the geological wonder of the **Giant's Causeway** in Co. Antrim (p. 692).

GET TIPSY at the **Bushmills Distillery,** the oldest licensed whiskey producer in the world (p. 693).

MONEY. Legal tender in Northern Ireland is the pound sterling. Northern Ireland has its own bank notes, which are identical in value to English and Scottish notes of the same denominations but are not accepted outside Northern Ireland. Both English and Scottish notes, however, are accepted. Euros are generally not accepted, except in some border towns.

SAFETY AND SECURITY. Although sectarian violence is at an all-time low since the height of the Troubles, some neighborhoods and towns still experience unrest during sensitive political times. It's best to remain alert and cautious while traveling in Northern Ireland, especially during **Marching Season,** which reaches its peak July 4-12. August 12, when the **Apprentice Boys** march in Derry/Londonderry, is also a testy period. Despite these concerns, Northern Ireland has one of the lowest tourist-related crime rates in the world. Unattended luggage is always considered suspicious and is often confiscated. It is generally unsafe to hitch a ride in Northern Ireland. *Let's Go* does not recommend hitchhiking.

The **phone code** for every town in Northern Ireland is **028.**

HISTORY AND POLITICS

Since the partition of 1920, the people of Northern Ireland have retained their individual cultural and political identities, even at the cost of lasting peace. Many continue to defend the lines that define their differences, whether ideological divisions across the chambers of Parliament or actual streets marking the end of one culture and the beginning of the next. Generally speaking, the 950,000 Protestants are **Unionists,** who want the six counties of Northern Ireland to remain in the UK; the 650,000 Catholics tend to identify with the Republic of Ireland, not Britain,

Northern Ireland

and many are **Nationalists,** who wish the six counties to be part of the Republic. The more extreme (generally working-class) members of either side are known respectively as **Loyalists** and **Republicans.** These groups have historically defended their turf with rocks and gas bombs.

A DIVIDED ISLAND. In the 12th century, the English took control of Ireland, and King Henry VIII declared himself King of Ireland in 1541. Irish uprisings encouraged King James I to begin a series of plantations in six of the nine counties of **Ulster** (a British name for Northern Ireland) in the 17th century. Two of the main events currently commemorated by Protestants in Northern Ireland took place during this early period: in 1688 the gates of Derry were shut against the troops of the Catholic James II (commemorated each August by the **Apprentice Boys of Derry**), and in 1690 William III defeated James II at the **Battle of the Boyne** (commemorated in July by the Orange Order). The **Orange Order** (named after the uniforms of Protestant William III's army) formed in County Armagh in 1795 and provided explosive opposition to the first **Home Rule Bill** in 1886. After the **Easter Rising** in the Republic in 1916, the 1920 **Government of Ireland Act** split Ireland into two self-governing units: 28 counties in the south and six counties in northeast Ireland, soon to be Northern Ireland. In 1949 the Republic was officially established, and the **Ireland Act** recognized Northern Ireland's right to autonomy; violence (barring the occasional border skirmish) diminished. Between 1956 and 1962, the IRA launched attacks on the border, but this ended due to lack of support.

THE TROUBLES. In 1966, Protestant Unionists founded the **Ulster Volunteer Force (UVF),** which was declared illegal. The UVF and the IRA actively bombed each other (and civilians) throughout 1966. In response, the religiously mixed **Northern Ireland Civil Rights Association (NICRA)** sponsored a march in Derry/Londonderry in 1968. The march became a bloody mess, eventually broken up by the **Royal Ulster Constabulary (RUC)** with several water cannons. Violent rioting during parades became so common that police stopped entering parts of some cities, particularly Derry/Londonderry, where the slogan **"Free Derry"** became famous. The IRA later split in two; the more violent and extreme faction, the **Provisional IRA (or Provos),** took over with less ideology and more guns.

On January 30, 1972, British troops fired into a peaceful crowd of protesters in Derry/Londonderry. **Bloody Sunday,** and the ensuing reluctance of the British government to investigate, increased Catholic outrage. In 1978, Nationalist prisoners in the **Maze Prison** began a campaign for political prisoner status, going on a **hunger strike** in 1981. Republican leader **Bobby Sands** was elected to Parliament while imprisoned and leading the strike. He died at age 26 after 66 days of fasting; he remains one of the conflict's most powerful symbols. Bombings and factioning continued on both sides throughout the 80s and 90s. The IRA attained an estimated 30 tons of arms, used in Northern Ireland and England. In 1991, the **Brooke Initiative** led to the first multiparty talks in Northern Ireland in over a decade.

1994 CEASEFIRE. On August 31, 1994, the IRA announced a "complete cessation of military activities." The **Combined Loyalist Military Command,** speaking on behalf of all Loyalist paramilitary organizations, offered "to the loved ones of all innocent victims...abject and true remorse" as they announced their ceasefire. The peace held for over a year. The ceasefire ended in 1996, when the IRA bombed an office building in London's Docklands. The stalled peace talks, chaired by US Senator **George Mitchell,** were planned but fell apart when a blast in a Manchester shopping district injured more than 200 people. In May 1997, the Labour party swept British elections. **Tony Blair** became Prime Minister, and the government ended its ban on talks with **Sinn Féin** (the political party of the IRA). Hopes for a renewed ceasefire were dashed when the UVF bombed the car of a prominent Republican. In retaliation, the IRA shot two members of the RUC.

GOOD FRIDAY AGREEMENT. After long negotiations between politicians and paramilitaries from Northern Ireland, the Republic of Ireland, and Britain, during which Blair blocked a door to prevent participants from walking out, the delegates approved a draft of the 1998 Northern Ireland Peace Agreement—better known as the **Good Friday Agreement.** The pact emphasized that change in Northern Ireland could come only with majority will and the recognition of "birthright," allowing citizens of Northern Ireland to adopt British, Irish, or dual citizenship.

On May 22, 1998, in the first island-wide vote since 1918, residents of Northern Ireland and the Republic voted the agreement into law; 71% of Northern Ireland and 94% of the Republic voted to reform Northern Ireland's government. As per the agreement, the main body, a 108-member **Northern Ireland Assembly,** assigns committee posts and chairs proportionately to the parties' representation and is headed by a First Minister. The second strand of the new government, a **North-South Ministerial Council,** serves as a cross-border authority. The final strand, the **British-Irish Council,** controls governance across the isles.

But shortly after these leaps forward, Marching Season began. The July 4 **Drumcree parade** was forbidden from marching down war-torn Garvaghy Road, spurring a stand-off between Republican and Loyalist paramilitaries. On the night of July 11, three young boys died in a firebombing of a Catholic home. The attack was universally condemned, and the **Drumcree Standoff** lost support. On August 15, a bombing in **Omagh,** intended to undermine the Good Friday Agreement, left 29 dead and 382 injured; a splinter group called the **Real IRA** claimed responsibility.

CURRENT EVENTS. At midnight on May 29, 2000, Britain restored a power-sharing Northern Irish government (as outlined in the Good Friday Agreement) after the IRA promised to begin disarming. In 2001, the RUC became **Police Service of Northern Ireland.** Sinn Féin has a plurality (as voted in November, 2003), but the Assembly remains suspended. On July 28, 2005, the IRA ordered a formal paramilitary disarmament, announcing that it would pursue its political ends only through peaceful means. The **Bloody Sunday Inquiry** records testimonies from British military and IRA figures. All sides are now making efforts to reconcile the past. In May 2007, the UVF finally responded to the IRA's disarmament by unofficially renouncing violence. The Assembly has since been re-opened, and Ian Paisley and Martin McGuinness (of Sinn Féin) occupy the First and Deputy First Minister posts. While they often fail to communicate, there is hope that the joint government will lead to lasting peace.

BELFAST (BÉAL FEIRSTE)

The second-largest city on the island, Belfast (pop. 270,000) is the focus of Northern Ireland's cultural, commercial, and political activity. Queen's University testifies to the city's rich academic history—luminaries such as Nobel Laureate Seamus Heaney and Lord Kelvin (of chemistry fame) once roamed the halls of Queen's, and Samuel Beckett taught the young men of Campbell College. The Belfast pub scene ranks among the best in the world, combining the historical appeal of old-fashioned watering holes with more modern bars and clubs. While Belfast has suffered from the stigma of its violent past, it has rebuilt itself and now surprises most visitors with its neighborly, urbane feel. This is true for most of the city, with the exception of the still divided West Belfast area, home to separate communities of Protestants and Catholics.

■ INTERCITY TRANSPORTATION

Flights: Belfast is served by 2 airports.

Belfast International Airport (☎9442 2448; www.belfastairport.com) in Aldergrove. **Aer Lingus** (☎0845 084 4444); **British Airways** (☎0845 850 9850); **British European** (Flybe; ☎0870 567 6676); **BMI** (☎0870 607 0555); **Continental** (☎0845 607 6760); and **Easyjet** (☎0870 600 0000; www.easyjet.com) operate from here. **Translink Bus 300** has 24hr. service from the airport to Europa bus station in the city center (M-F every 10min. 7:20am-6:15pm, every 15-40min. otherwise; Sa every 20min. 7:20am-6:40pm, at least once per hr. otherwise; Su every 30min. 8:45am-6:15pm, at least once per hr. otherwise; call ☎9066 6630 or visit www.translink.co.uk for full timetables). £6, round-trip £9 if you return within 1 month. **Taxis** (☎9448 4353) get you there for £25-30.

Belfast City Airport (☎9093 9093; www.belfastcityairport.com), at the harbor, holds **British European.** To get from City Airport to Europa bus station, take **Translink Bus 600** (M-F every 20min. 9:45am-10:05pm, at least every 30min. otherwise; Sa every 20min. 8:05am-6:05pm, at least every 30min. otherwise 6am-9:50pm; Su at least every 45min. 7:30am-9:50pm).

Trains: For train and bus info, contact **Translink.** (☎9066 6630; www.translink.co.uk. Inquiries daily 7am-8pm.) Trains leave Belfast's **Central Station,** E. Bridge St. to **Derry/Londonderry** (2hr.; M-F 10 per day, Sa 9 per day, Su 5 per day; £10) and **Dublin** (2hr.; M-Sa 8 per day, Su 5 per day; £24). The **Metro** buses are free with rail tickets.

Buses: Europa Bus Terminal, off Great Victoria St., behind the Europa Hotel (☎9066 6630; ticket office open M-Sa 7:30am-6:30pm, Su 12:30-5:30pm). Buses to **Derry/Londonderry** (1¾hr.; M-F 34 per day, Sa 20 per day, Su 11 per day; £9) and **Dublin**

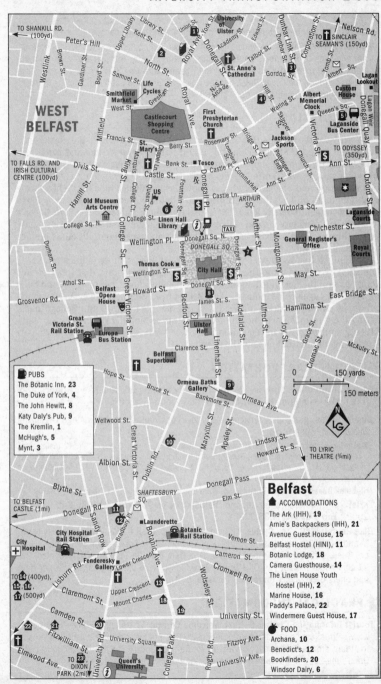

NORTHERN IRELAND

PUBS

The Botanic Inn, **23**
The Duke of York, **4**
The John Hewitt, **8**
Katy Daly's Pub, **9**
The Kremlin, **1**
McHugh's, **5**
Mynt, **3**

Belfast

ACCOMMODATIONS

The Ark (IHH) **19**
Arnie's Backpackers (IHH), **21**
Avenue Guest House, **15**
Belfast Hostel (HINI), **11**
Botanic Lodge, **18**
Camera Guesthouse, **14**
The Linen House Youth
  Hostel (IHH), **2**
Marine House, **16**
Paddy's Palace, **22**
Windermere Guest House, **17**

FOOD

Archana, **10**
Benedict's, **12**
Bookfinders, **20**
Windsor Dairy, **6**

(3hr.; M-Sa 17 per day, Su at 11pm, leaving from Glengall St. rather than Europa; £9.65). The Centrelink bus connects the station with the city center.

Ferries: Norfolk Ferries (www.norfolkline-ferries.co.uk) operates out of the SeaCat terminal and runs to **Liverpool, England** (8hr., starting at £59 with car and £20 without). Book online to avoid a £10 booking fee.) **Stena Line** (☎0870 570 7070; www.stenaline.com), up the Lagan River, has the quickest service to Scotland, docking in **Stranraer** (1¾hr.; fares seasonal, book online).

■ ORIENTATION

Buses arrive at the Europa Bus Station on **Great Victoria Street.** To the northeast is **City Hall** in **Donegall Square.** Donegall Pl. turns into **Royal Avenue** and runs from Donegall Sq. through the shopping area. To the east, in **Cornmarket,** pubs in narrow **entries** (small alleyways) offer an escape. The stretch of Great Victoria St. between the bus station and Shaftesbury Sq. is known as the **Golden Mile** for its high-brow establishments and Victorian architecture. **Botanic Avenue** and **Bradbury Place** (which becomes **University Road**) extend south from Shaftesbury Sq. into **Queen's University** turf. The city center, Golden Mile, and the university are relatively safe areas. Although locals advise caution in the east and west, central Belfast is safer for tourists than most European cities.

Westlink Motorway divides working-class **West Belfast,** more politically volatile than the city center, from the rest of Belfast. The Protestant district stretches along Shankill Rd., just north of the Catholic neighborhood, centered around Falls Rd. The **River Lagan** splits industrial **East Belfast** from Belfast proper. The shipyards and docks extend north on both sides of the river as it grows into **Belfast Lough.** During the week, the area north of City Hall is essentially deserted after 6pm. Although muggings are infrequent in Belfast, it's wise to use taxis after dark, particularly near clubs and pubs in the northeast.

▐ LOCAL TRANSPORTATION

Transportation cards and tickets are available at the pink kiosks in Donegall Sq. W. (open M-F 8am-6pm, Sa 9am-5:20pm) and around the city.

Buses: Belfast has 2 bus services. Many local bus routes connect through Laganside Bus Station, Queen's Sq.

Metro bus service (☎9066 6630; www.translink.co.uk) gather in Donegall Sq. 12 main routes cover Belfast. Ulsterbus "blue buses" cover the suburbs. Day passes £3. Travel within the city center £1 (£1.30 beyond), under 16 £0.50. 5-journey £5.25-7.25/3.40-4.50, depending on which zones of the city will be visited.

Nightlink Buses travel from Donegall Sq. W. to towns outside Belfast. Sa 1 and 2am. £3.50.

Taxis: 24hr. metered cabs abound. **Value Cabs** (☎9080 9080); **City Cab** (☎9024 2000); **Fon a Cab** (☎9033 3333).

Bike Rental: McConvey Cycles, 183 Ormeau Rd. (☎9033 0322; www.mcconvey.com). M and F-Su £20; otherwise £10 per day, £40 per week. Locks supplied. Panniers £15 per week. £50 deposit. Open M-W and F-Sa 9am-6pm, Th 9am-8pm. **Life Cycles,** 36-37 Smithfield Market (☎9043 9959; www.lifecycles.co.uk) rents bikes (£9 per day) and offers **bicycle city tours** (see **Tours,** p. 679).

▐ PRACTICAL INFORMATION

Tourist Information Centre: Belfast Welcome Centre, 47 Donegall Pl. (☎9024 6609; www.gotobelfast.com). Offers comprehensive free booklet on Belfast and info on surrounding areas. Books reservations in Northern Ireland (£2) and the Republic (£3). Open June-Sept. M-Sa 9am-7pm, Su noon-5pm; Oct.-May M-Sa 9am-5pm.

Financial Services: ATMs at: **Bank of Ireland,** 54 Donegall Pl. (☎9023 4334); **First Trust,** 92 Ann St. (☎9032 5599); **Northern Bank,** 14 Donegall Sq. W. (☎9024 5277); **Ulster Bank,** Donegall Sq. E. (☎9027 6000). Most banks open M-F 9am-4:30pm.

Launderette: Globe Drycleaners & Launderers, 37-39 Botanic Ave. (☎9024 3956). £6.75. Open M-F 8am-9pm, Sa 8am-6pm, Su noon-6pm.

Police: 6-18 Donegall Pass and 65 Knock Rd. (☎9065 0222).

Hospitals: Belfast City Hospital, 91 Lisburn Rd. (☎9032 9241). From Shaftesbury Sq., follow Bradbury Pl. and take a right at the fork. **Royal Victoria Hospital,** 12 Grosvenor Rd. (☎9024 0503). From Donegall Sq., take Howard St. west to Grosvenor Rd.

Internet Access: Belfast Central Library, 122 Royal Ave. (☎9050 9150). Open M and Th 9am-8pm, Tu-W and F 9am-5:30pm, Sa 9am-1pm. £1.50 per 30min. for nonmembers. **Belfast Welcome Centre,** 47 Donegall Pl., is the most central. £1.25 per 15min., students £1 per hr. Open M-Sa 9:30am-7pm, Su noon-5pm.

Post Office: Central Post Office, on the corner of High St. and Bridge St. (☎08457 223 344). Open M-Sa 10am-5:30pm. **Post Code:** BT2 7FD.

TOURS

BLACK CAB TOURS. Black Cab tours provide commentary on the murals and sights on both sides of the Peace Line. Most drivers have been personally affected by the Troubles, but they make pains to avoid bias. Many hostels book tours with their favored **black cab** operators, usually for £8. **The Original Belfast Black Taxi Tours** give impassioned yet even-handed commentary, and one of the five Protestant and five Catholic drivers will answer any question. (*☎0800 032 2003 or ☎077 5165 5359 for Laurence, one of the owners. 1½hr. tour from £8 per person.*) Walter of **Backpackers Black Taxi Tours** (*☎077 2106 7752*) is the original of the bunch. Now in his 11th year, he still covers all the bases with his insight and wry humor.

BAILEYS HISTORICAL PUB TOURS OF BELFAST. A departure from recreational pubbing, this tour is really a primer in Pint Studies. The tour guides visitors through seven or more of Belfast's oldest and best pubs with a little sightseeing and city history served up on the side. (*☎9268 3665; www.belfastpubtours.com. 2hr. tour departs from Crown Dining Rooms, above the Crown Liquor Saloon, May-Oct. Th 7pm, Sa 4pm. £6, £5 for groups of 10 or more; excludes drinks, although a complimentary tumbler of Bailey's Irish Cream is included.*)

BIKE TOURS. In addition to bike rental, **Life Cycles** (see **Bike Rental,** p. 678) and **Irish Cycle Tours,** 27 Belvoir View Pk. (*☎667 128 733; www.irishcycletours.com*), offer tours of Belfast for £15 per day.

BUS TOURS. Mini-Coach (*☎9031 5333*) conducts tours of Belfast (*1hr.; departs M-F noon; £8, children £4*) and the Giant's Causeway (*M-Sa 9:40am-7pm, Su 9am-5:45pm; £15/10*). Tours depart from the Belfast International Youth Hostel. Tickets available at Belfast Welcome Centre.

ACCOMMODATIONS

Despite fluctuating tourism and rising rents, Belfast boasts a solid lineup of hostels for travelers. Almost all are near Queen's University, close to the city's pubs and restaurants, and a short walk or bus to the city center. This area is by far the best place to stay in Belfast. If you are hindered by baggage, catch **Citybus** #69, 70, 71, 83, 84, or 86 from Donegall Sq. to areas in the south. Walking to the area takes 10-20min. from bus or train stations. Reservations are necessary during the summer, when hostels and B&Bs often fill to capacity.

HOSTELS

Arnie's Backpackers (IHH), 63 Fitzwilliam St. (☎9024 2867). Look for a cutout sign of a sky-gazing backpacker. Arnie, the hostel's jovial owner, may greet you with a cup of tea. Bunked beds in bright, clean rooms. Library of travel info includes bus and train timetables. Kitchen often has a little stack of free, donated food. If you're looking to find work, check out the bulletin board in the entryway. 8-bed dorms £9; 4-bed £11. ❶

The Belfast Palace (Paddy's Palace), 68 Lisburn Rd. (☎9033 3367; www.paddyspalace.com), use the entrance at 70 Fitzwilliam St. Sociable new hostel offers free Internet access (daily 8am-10:30pm), satellite TV, videos in the lounge, and free breakfast with tea and coffee. Kitchen and laundry facilities. Book ahead in summer. Reception M-Th and Su 8am-8pm, F-Sa 8am-10pm. Dorms from £9.50-16.50. ❶

The Ark (IHH), 44 University St. (☎9032 9626). 10min. walk from Europa bus station. Spacious dorms and a busy, stocked kitchen with free tea and coffee. Staff provides info on finding work. Books tours of Belfast (£8) and Giant's Causeway (£16). Internet access £1 per 20min. Weekend luggage storage. Laundry £5. Curfew 2am. Book ahead on bank holidays and in the summer. Co-ed 4- to 6-bed dorms £11; doubles £36; long-term housing from £60 per wk. ❶

Belfast Hostel (HINI), 22 Donegall Rd. (☎9031 5435; www.hini.org.uk), off Shaftesbury Sq. Modern rooms and the Causeway Cafe. Groups in the large common room can get loud. Books tours of Belfast and Giant's Causeway. Cafe open daily 8-11am. Full breakfast £4. Wheelchair-accessible. Internet access 5p per min. on house computers, and Wi-Fi £3 per hr. or £10 per 4hr. 24hr. reception. Laundry £3. M-Th and Su 4- to 6-bed dorms £8.50, F-Sa £9.50; ensuite upgrade £1. Triples £42/45. MC/V. ❶

The Linen House Youth Hostel (IHH), 18-20 Kent St. (☎9058 6444; www.belfasthostel.com), bordering West Belfast. Converted 19th-century linen factory now packs 130 bunks into bare rooms. 24hr. secure parking £4 per day. Posts employment opportunities. Internet £1 per 30min. Luggage storage £0.50. Towels £0.50. Laundry £4. 18- to 20-bed all-female dorms £7.30, co-ed £6.50; 10- to 12-bed dorms £9; 6- to 8-bed dorms £10; 4-bed dorms 12; M-Th and Su singles £20, F-Sa £25; M-Th and Su doubles £15, F-Sa £18. Longer stays: singles £40-45 per week; doubles £35 per week; triples £30 per week; £150 deposit. ❶

BED AND BREAKFASTS

B&Bs cluster south of Queen's University between **Malone** and **Lisburn Roads.**

Windermere Guest House, 60 Wellington Park (☎9066 2693; www.windermereguesthouse.co.uk). Relatively cheap for a B&B. Leather couches provide comfy seating in the living room. Singles £28, with bath £40; doubles £52/55. Cash only. ❸

Camera Guesthouse, 44 Wellington Park (☎9066 0026; malonedrumm@hotmail.com). Quiet, pristine Victorian house is tough to beat. Breakfasts offer wide selection of organic foods and herbal teas that cater to specific dietary concerns. Singles £34, with bath £48; doubles £56/62. MC/V 3% commission; AmEx. ❹

Avenue Guest House, 23 Eglantine Ave. (☎9066 5904; www.avenueguesthouse.com). Four large, airy rooms equipped with TV and Wi-Fi. Comfortable living room has free DVDs and books. £25 per person. ❸

Botanic Lodge, 87 Botanic Ave. (☎9032 7682), corner of Mt. Charles Ave. Larger B&B in the heart of the Queen's University area, surrounded by restaurants. All rooms with sink and TV. Singles £30; doubles £45, with bath £50. MC/V 5% surcharge. ❸

Marine House, 30 Eglantine Ave. (☎9066 2828). Mansion with high ceilings and wonderful housekeeping, all rooms renovated in 2003. Esteemed 3-star guest house. All rooms with TV, bath, and phones. Singles £45; doubles £60; triples £65. ❹

FOOD

Dublin Rd., Botanic Ave., and the Golden Mile around **Shaftesbury Square,** have the highest concentration of restaurants. The huge Tesco **Supermarket,** 2 Royal Ave., in an old bank building, has better prices than most of the city's convenience stores. (☎9032 3270. Open M-W and Sa 8am-7pm, Th 8am-9pm, F 8am-8pm, Su 1-5pm.)

The Other Place, 79 Botanic Ave. (☎9020 7200). Bustling eatery serves fried breakfasts (until 5pm, from £3; M-F 8-11am special 99p fry), hearty specials, and ethnic entrees. Try the "bang bang chicken," with spicy soy, sweet chili, and crunchy peanut sauce. M steak (£7), Tu and Th tapas (£5-10), W wraps (£5). Open daily 8am-10pm. ❷

Bookfinders, 47 University Rd. (☎9032 8269). One block from the University, on the corner of Camden St. and University Rd. Cluttered bookshelves and mismatched dishes. Occasional poetry readings. Art gallery upstairs features student work. Soup and bread £2.50; sandwiches £2.20. Open M-Sa 10am-5:30pm. ❶

Benedict's, 7-21 Bradbury Pl. (☎9059 1999; www.benedictshotel.co.uk). Swanky hotel restaurant providing an upscale break from sandwiches and pizza. "Beat the Clock" meal deal offers fine meals daily 5-7:30pm for £7.50-10. Curried chicken, seafood, and vegetarian options. Lunches £7.50-12. Dinners £12-16. Open M-Sa noon-2:30pm and 5:30-10:30pm, Su noon-3:30pm and 5:30-9pm. ❸

Archana, 53 Dublin Rd. (☎9032 3713; www.archana.info). Cozy curry house. Dishes made with chicken, lamb, or vegetables. Features Handi dishes, complete with personal candlelit stove. Downstairs *Thali* lunch £2.50, dinner £7-9; upstairs from £5/8. Takeaway available. Lunch M-Sa 11am-2pm; dinner M-Sa 5-11pm, Su 5-10pm. MC/V. ❸

Windsor Dairy, 4 College St. (☎9032 7157). Family-run bakery doles out piles of pastries (under £1), pies, and satisfying daily specials (£2-3). Come early before locals gobble up the best batches. Open M-Sa 7:30am-10:30pm. ❶

⬡ SIGHTS

BELFAST CITY HALL. The most dramatic and impressive piece of architecture in Belfast is also its administrative and geographic center. Dominating the grassy square that serves as the locus of downtown Belfast, its green copper dome is visible from nearly any point in the city. Inside, a grand staircase ascends to the second floor, where portraits of the city's Lord Mayors line the halls. The City Council's oak-paneled chambers, used only once per month, are deceptively austere, considering the Council's reputation for rowdy meetings (fists have been known to fly). The interior of City Hall is only accessible by guided tour. *(☎9027 0456. 1hr. tours M-F 11am, 2, 3pm; Sa 2 and 3pm. Tour times may vary; no tours on Bank and Public Holidays. Tours may be cancelled for a period of time starting July 2007, when the Hall begins renovations. Free. Gift shop open 9:30am-4pm.)*

QUEEN'S UNIVERSITY BELFAST. Charles Lanyon designed the beautiful Tudor Gothic brick campus in 1849, modeling it after Magdalen College, Oxford. The **Visitors Centre,** in the Lanyon Room to the left of the main entrance, offers Queen's-related exhibits and merchandise, as well as a free pamphlet detailing a walking tour of the grounds. Upstairs, the **Naughton Gallery** displays rotating exhibits of contemporary art. *(University Rd. Visitors Centre ☎9033 5252; www.qub.ac.uk/vcentre. Wheelchair-accessible. May-Sept. open M-Sa 10am-4pm with tour Sa noon; Oct.-Mar. open M-F 10am-4pm, tours by request. Gallery open M-Sa 11am-4pm. Free.)*

ODYSSEY. The posterchild of Belfast's riverfront revival, this attraction packs five distinct sights into one entertainment center. *(2 Queen's Quay. ☎9045 1055;*

NORTHERN IRELAND

THE CATHOLIC MURALS

The murals of West Belfast are a powerful testament to the volatile past and fierce loyalties of the divided neighborhoods. Many of the most famous Catholic murals are on Falls Rd., an area that saw some of the worst of the Troubles.

1 Mural illustrating protestors during the **Hunger Strikes of 1981,** in which they fasted for the right to be considered political prisoners.

2 Portrayal of **Bobby Sands,** the first hunger-striker to die, is located on the side of the Sinn Féin Office, Sevastopol St. Sands was elected as a member of the British Parliament under a "political prisoner" ticket during this time and is remembered as the North's most famous martyr.

3 Formerly operating as Northern Ireland's National **RUC Headquarters,** the most bombed of any police station in England, the Republic, or the North. Its fortified, barbed wire facade is on Springfield St.

www.theodyssey.co.uk.) The **Odyssey Arena,** with 10,000 seats, is the largest indoor arena in Ireland. When the Belfast Giants ice hockey team isn't on the ice, big-name performers heat up the stage. *(Performance box office ☎9073 9074; www.odysseyarena.com. Hockey ☎9059 1111; www.belfastgiants.com.)* The **W5 Discovery Centre** (short for "whowhatwherewhenwhy?") is a playground for curious minds and hyperactive schoolchildren. Design your own racecar and roller-coaster, waltz up the musical stairs, or operate a replica of the Harland & Wolff cranes in a model of Port Belfast. *(☎9046 7700; www.w5online.co.uk. Workshops run throughout the summer. Wheelchair-accessible. Open M-Sa 10am-6pm; closes at 5pm when school is in session, Su noon-6pm; last admission 1hr. before closing. £6.50, children £4.50. Family discounts available.)* The **Sherbidan IMAX Cinema** plays both 2D and 3D films on its enormous 62 by 82 ft. screen, while **Warner Village Cinemas** shows Hollywood blockbusters on its own 14 screens. *(IMAX ☎9046 7014; www.belfastimax.com. £5; M-Th students £4.50, children £4. Multiplex ☎9073 9234. £6/4/3.80. M-F before 5pm £4.50.)* The **Pavilion** contains shops, bars, and restaurants—including that tourist mecca, the **Hard Rock Cafe.** *(Hard Rock Cafe ☎9076 6990. Open M-Sa noon-1am, Su noon-midnight.)*

GRAND OPERA HOUSE. The opera house was cyclically bombed by the IRA, restored to its original splendor at enormous cost, and then bombed again. Visitors today enjoy the calm in high fashion, while tours offer a look behind the ornate facade and include a complimentary coffee and danish at their cafe, Luciano's. *(☎9024 1919; www.goh.co.uk. Office open M-F 8:30am-9pm. Tours begin across the street at the office W-Sa 11am. Times may vary, so call ahead. £3, seniors/students/children £2.)*

BELFAST CASTLE. Built in 1870 by the Third Marquis of Donegall, the castle sits atop **Cave Hill,** long the seat of Ulster rulers, and offers the best panoramas of the Belfast port—on a clear day views extend as far as Scotland and the Isle of Man. The ancient King Matudan had his McArt's Fort here, where the more modern United Irishmen plotted rebellion in 1795, although these days it sees more weddings than skirmishes. Marked trails lead north from the fort to five **caves** in the area, which historians postulate are ancient mines. Only the lowest is accessible to tourists. For those on foot, the small path to the right of the gate makes for a far shorter and prettier walk than the road. *(☎9077 6925; www.belfastcastle.co.uk. Open M-Sa 9am-10pm, Su 9am-5:30pm. Free.)*

ST. ANNE'S CATHEDRAL. This Church of Ireland cathedral was begun in 1899, but to keep from disturbing regular worship, it was built around a smaller church already on the site. Upon completion of the new exterior, builders extracted the earlier church brick by brick. Each of the cathedral's 10 interior pillars names one of Belfast's professional fields: Science, Industry, Healing, Agriculture, Music, Theology, Shipbuilding, Freemasonry, Art, and Womanhood. In an enclave called the **Chapel of Unity**, visitors pray for understanding among Christians of all denominations. *(Donegall St., a few blocks from the city center. Open M-Sa 10am-4pm, Su before and after services at 10, 11am, 3:30pm.)*

SINCLAIR SEAMEN'S CHURCH. Designed to accommodate the hordes of sinning sailors landing in Belfast port, this quirky church does things its own way—the minister delivers his sermons from a pulpit carved in the shape of a ship's prow, collections are taken in miniature lifeboats, and the choir uses an organ from a Guinness barge with port and starboard lights. *(Corporation St., down from the SeaCat terminal. ☎9071 5997. Open W 2-5pm; Su service at 11:30am and 7pm.)*

SIR THOMAS AND LADY DIXON PARK. The most stunning of the parks, visitors find it sitting pretty on Upper Malone Rd. 20,000 rose bushes of every variety imaginable bloom here each year. The gardens were founded in 1836 and include stud China roses, imported between 1792 and 1824. *(Open M-Sa 7:30am-dusk, Su 9am-dusk.)*

BELFAST ZOO. Set in the hills alongside Cave Hill Forest Park, the zoo's best attribute is its natural setting—catching sight of a lumbering elephant against the backdrop of Belfast lough can be a surreal experience. The recommended route highlights the standard lineup of tigers, giraffes, camels, zebras, and the acrobatic spider monkey. *(4 mi. north of the city on Antrim Rd. Take Metro bus #1. ☎9077 6277. Open daily Apr.-Sept. 10am-7pm; Oct.-Mar. 10am-4pm. Last admission 1hr. prior to closing. Apr.-Sept. £7.80, children £4.10; Oct.-Mar. £6.30/ 3.20. Seniors, children under 4, and disabled free.)*

WEST BELFAST AND THE MURALS

West Belfast has historically been at the heart of political tensions in the North. The Troubles reached their peak in the 1970s; the particularly violent year of 1972 saw 1000 bomb explosions and over 400 murders. While there have not been any large-scale outbreaks of violence in recent years, tensions remain high. The Catholic area (centered on **Falls Road**) and the Protestant neighborhood (centered on the **Shankill**) are separated by the **peace line,** a grim, gray wall with a number of gates that close at nightfall.

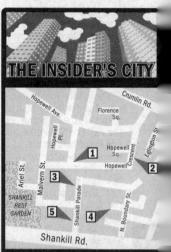

THE INSIDER'S CITY

THE PROTESTANT MURALS

The Protestant murals, in the Shankill area of West Belfast, tend to be overtly militant. Most are found near Hopewell St. and Hopewell Cr., to the north of Shankill Rd., or down Shankill Parade, and are accessed by traveling south from Crumlin Rd.

1 Painting of a **Loyalist martyr,** killed in prison in 1997.

2 A collage of Loyalist militant groups including the **Ulster Volunteer Force** (**UVF**), the **Ulster Defense Union** (**UDU**), and the **Ulster Defense Association** (**UDA**). Presiding over the whole mural is the portrait of a menacing **Ulster Freedom Fighter** (**UFF**).

3 Mural of the **Battle of the Boyne,** commemorating William of Orange's 1690 victory over James II.

4 The **Marksman's** gun seems to follow you as you pass by.

5 Portrait of the infamous **Top Gun,** a man responsible for the deaths of many high-ranking Republicans.

Along the wall, abandoned buildings and barricaded homes testify to a tumultuous history and an uneasy future. One bit of the peace line, near **Lanark Way,** connecting the Falls and Springfield roads, contains peace paintings and signatures—left mostly by tourists—promoting hope for a brighter future. West Belfast is not a tourist site in the traditional sense, although the walls and houses along the streets display political **murals** which speak to Belfast's religious and political divide. These murals are the city's most popular attraction.

Those traveling to these sectarian neighborhoods often take **black taxis,** community shuttles that whisk residents to the city center, transporting passengers along their set routes. Some black taxis and **black cabs** can also be booked for tours of the Falls or Shankill (p. 679). *Let's Go* offers two **neighborhood maps** (see **Catholic and Protestant Murals,** at right and left) of the Catholic and Protestant artistic representations of the past, allowing individuals to explore the murals for themselves.

It's best to visit the Falls and Shankill during the day, when the neighborhoods are full of locals and, more importantly, the murals are visible. Do not visit the area during Marching Season (the weeks around July 12) when the parades are underscored by mutual antagonism that can lead to violence (see **History and Politics,** p. 673). As the area around the peace line remains politically charged, travelers should be wary of visiting outside of daylight hours. Travelers are advised not to wander from one neighborhood to the other, but to return to the city center between visits to Shankill and the Falls.

New murals in the Falls and Shankill are constantly produced, so the descriptions below and the neighborhood maps describe only a fraction of what is there. Before taking a camera, ask about the current political climate. Taking pictures is not advised during Marching Season. However, photography is acceptable on black cab tours, as drivers have agreements with the communities.

THE FALLS. This Catholic and Republican neighborhood is larger than Shankill, following Castle St. west from the city center. As Castle St. continues across A12/ Westlink, it becomes **Divis Street.** A high-rise apartment building marks **Divis Tower,** an ill-fated housing development built by optimistic social planners in the 1960s. The project soon became an IRA stronghold and saw some of the worst of Belfast's Troubles in the 1970s. The British Army still occupies the top floors.

Continuing west, Divis St. turns into **Falls Road.** The **Sinn Féin** office is easily spotted: one side of it is covered with an enormous portrait of Bobby Sands (see **The Troubles,** p. 675) and an advertisement for the Sinn Féin newspaper, *An Pho-blacht.* Continuing down Falls Rd. reveals a number of murals, most of which are on side streets. In the past both the Falls and the Shankill contained many representations of paramilitaries (the IRA in the Falls, UVF and UDA in the Shankill) with armed men in balaclavas; this and commemorative murals were the main subjects in the past, but both communities have focused on historical and cultural representations for the newest murals, even replacing many older works. The newest Falls murals recall Celtic myths and legends, and depict The Great Hunger, the phrase Northern Catholics use to refer to the Famine. Earlier militant murals still exist including a few that depict the Republican armed struggle.

Falls Rd. soon splits into **Andersonstown Road** and **Glen Road,** one of the few urban areas with a predominately Irish-speaking population. On the left are the Celtic crosses of **Milltown Cemetery,** the resting place of many fallen Republicans. Inside the entrance, a memorial to Republican casualties is bordered by a low, green fence on the right; the grave of Bobby Sands lies here. Nearby, **Bombay Street** was the first street to be burned down during the Troubles. Another mile along Andersontown Rd. lies a housing project that was formerly a wealthy Catholic neighborhood—and more murals. The Springfield Rd. Police Service of Northern Ireland station, previously named the RUC station, was the **most attacked police** station in Ireland and the UK. It was recently demolished. The **Andersonstown Barracks,** at the corner of Glen and Andersonstown Rd., are still heavily fortified.

SHANKILL. The Shankill Rd. begins at the Westlink and turns into Woodvale Rd. as it crosses Cambrai St. The Woodvale Rd. intersects Crumlin Rd. at the Ardoyne roundabout and can be taken back into the city center. The Shankill Memorial Garden honors 10 people who died in a bomb attack on Fizzel's Fish Shop in October 1993; the garden is on the Shankill Rd., facing Berlin St. On the Shankill Rd., farther toward the city center, is a mural of James Buchanan, the 15th President of the United States (1857-1861), who was a descendant of Ulster Scots (known in the US as the "Scots-Irish"). Other cultural murals depict the 50th Jubilee of the coronation of Queen Elizabeth in 1952 and the death of the Queen Mother in 2002. These are at the beginning of the Shankill near the Rex Bar. Historical murals include a memorial to the UVF who fought at the Battle of the Somme in 1916 during WWI (see **A Divided Island,** p. 674), also near the Rex Bar. In the Shankill Estate, some murals represent Cromwell suppressing the 1741 Rebellion against the Protestant plantation owners. The densely decorated **Orange Hall** sits on the left at Brookmount St. McClean's Wallpaper; on the right was where Fizzel's Fish Shop stood before being demolished. Through the estate, Crumlin Rd. heads back to the city center, passing an army base, the courthouse, and the jail.

SANDY ROW AND NEWTOWNARDS ROAD. This area's Protestant population is growing steadily, partly due to the redevelopment of the Sandy Row area, and also because many working-class residents are leaving the Shankill. This stretch is a turn off Donegall Rd. at Shaftesbury Sq. An orange arch topped with King William once marked its start. Nearby murals show the Red Hand of Ulster, a bulldog, and William crossing the Boyne. East Belfast is a secure, growing Protestant enclave. Murals line Newtownards Rd. One depicts the economic importance of the shipyard to the city's history. On the Ballymacart road, which runs parallel to Newtownards Rd., is a mural of local son C.S. Lewis's *The Lion, the Witch, and the Wardrobe.*

▐◧ ▐◪ NIGHTLIFE AND PUBS

Pubs in Belfast are the place to experience the city's *craic* and meet its colorful characters. Pubs were targets for sectarian violence at the height of the Troubles, so most are new or restored, although many retain their historic charm. Those in the city center and university area are now relatively safe. *Bushmills Irish Pub Guide,* by Sybil Taylor, relates the history of Belfast pubs (£7; available at local bookstores). For a full list of entertainment options, grab a free copy of *The Big List* or *Fate,* available in tourist centers, hostels, and certain restaurants and pubs.

▧ **The Duke of York,** 7-11 Commercial Ct. (☎9024 1062). Old boxing venue turned Communist printing press, rebuilt after it was bombed by IRA in the 60s; now home to the city's largest selection of Irish whiskeys. Kitchen serves sandwiches and toasties daily until 2:30pm. Th trad at 10pm, F acoustic guitar, Sa disco with £5 cover. 18+. Open M 11:30am-11pm, Tu-F 11:30am-1am, Su 11:30am-2am.

▧ **Katy Daly's Pub,** 17 Ormeau Ave. (☎9032 5942; www.the-limelight.co.uk). Go straight behind City Hall toward Queen's and make a left on Ormeau Ave. High-ceilinged, wood-paneled, antique pub is a true stalwart of the Belfast music scene. M nights get mocked, grossed out, and roiled up over alternative quiz show, **"Not for the Easily Offended."** Tu adjacent club **Limelight** and next door bar join up to form the 3-room disco **Shag,** 3 DJs and several drink specials for £3 cover. Th singer-songwriter nights. Sa Limelight again partners up to form the White Album inspired 2-room disco **"Helter Skelter,"** playing only 60s tunes until 2am. Local bands W; singer/songwriters Th-Sa. Su night is Club "No Dancing"—figure out what to do over a quiet drink. Lunch served M-F noon-2:30pm. Bar open M-Sa until 1am, Su until midnight.

🏠 **The Botanic Inn,** 23 Malone Rd. (☎9050 9740). Standing in as the unofficial student union, the hugely popular "Bot" is packed nightly. M singer-songwriter night, Tu quiz night, W "Pinch of Snuff" trad session, and various rock gigs Th-F. Upstairs disco features a DJ W-Sa (£5 cover), Su the DJ moves downstairs (no cover). 20+. Kitchen serves pub grub daily noon-8pm. Open M-Sa 11:30am-1am, Su noon-midnight.

The John Hewitt, 51 Lower Donegall St. (☎9023 3768; www.thejohnhewitt.com), around the corner from the Duke. Named after the late Ulster poet and run by the Unemployment Resource Centre. Half the profits go to the Centre, so drink up. M singer-songwriter open mic, Tu-W and Sa trad, Th live bands, F jazz; music starts around 9:30pm. W features "The Half Stoned Cowboys." 1st F of each month brings in Hooker ("rock music for grown ups"); other F nights get The Panama Jazz Band, which plays New Orleans-style jazz. Su nights at 9pm, the fiddles and the banjos come out for The Bluegrass Session. 18+. Open M-F 11:30am-1am, Sa noon-1am, Su 6pm-1am.

McHugh's, 29-31 Queen's Sq. (☎9050 9999; www.mchughsbar.com), across from the Custom House, sells local Belfast Ale. Sleek wrought-iron banisters, a colorful collection of contemporary art, and a chess set featuring caricatures of political figures add to the allure of this historic pub, open since 1711. Restaurant open M-Sa 5-10pm, Su noon-9pm. Th-F and Su live music. Sa DJ Radio K gets the party started for a £5 cover. Open M and Su noon-midnight, Tu-Sa noon-1am.

Mynt, 2-16 Dunbar St. (☎9023 4520; www.myntbelfast.com). Latest offspring of the Parliament and Kube, this spacious club remains a bastion of the Belfast gay scene. Casual cafebar in front leads to 2 floors of clubbing. Last Sa of each month, famed DJ group **Federation** heats up the party. Open M-Tu noon-1am, W-F and Su noon-3am, and a crazy late Sa noon-6am. F separate gay and lesbian parties for £5 cover. Sa karaoke downstairs and DJ upstairs. Cover: W £3, F and Su £5, Sa £6-10.

The Kremlin, 96 Donegall St. (☎9031 6061; www.kremlin-belfast.com). Look for the statue of Lenin. A young crowd sips and flirts in the downstairs Tsar Bar before spilling onto the dance floor around 10:30pm. Free Internet upstairs. Doors close at 1am. Tight security. Cover varies, but free Su. Open Tu 9pm-2:30am, Th-Su 9pm-3am.

🎵 ARTS AND ENTERTAINMENT

Belfast's many cultural events and performances are covered in the monthly *Arts Council Artslink*, free at the tourist office, while the bi-monthly *Arts Listings* covers arts and entertainment throughout Northern Ireland. Listings appear daily in the *Belfast Telegraph* (which also has a Friday Arts supplement) and in Thursday's issue of the *Irish News*. For summer events, check *What About?*, *The Big List*, and *Fate*, which all have concert listings. The **Crescent Arts Centre,** 2 University Rd., supplies some general arts info, but mostly broadcasts specific news about its own exhibits and concerts, which take place September through May. (☎9024 2338. Classes £40-48, children £24-32. Open M-Sa 10am-10pm.) **Fenderesky Gallery,** 2 University Rd., inside the Crescent Arts building, hosts contemporary shows and sells the work of local artists. (☎9023 5245. Open Tu-Sa 11:30am-5pm.) The **Old Museum Arts Centre,** 7 College Sq. N., is Belfast's largest venue for contemporary artwork. (☎9023 5053; www.oldmuseumartscentre.org. Open M-Sa 9:30am-5:30pm.) A small gallery hosts rotating exhibits, but its focus is on performance art. Pick up a booklet detailing upcoming workshops and a variety of dance, theater, and music performances. (Tickets ☎9023 3332. Most tickets £6-9, students and seniors £3.) July and August are slow months for arts; around July 12, the whole city shuts down for Marching Season. The **Grand Opera House,** 4 Great Victoria St., presents opera, ballet, musicals, and drama. (☎9024 0411; www.goh.co.uk.) Tickets for most shows can be purchased either by phone until 9pm or in person at the box office. (☎9024 1919, 24hr. info line ☎9024 9129. Tickets £9-27. Open M-F 8:30am-9pm.) **The Lyric Theatre,**

55 Ridgeway St., which counts Liam Neeson amongst its esteemed alums, presents a mix of classical and contemporary plays with an emphasis on Irish productions. (☎9038 1081; www.lyrictheatre.co.uk. Box office open M-Sa 10am-7pm. Tickets M-W £14, concessions £11; Th-Sa £17.) **Waterfront Hall,** 2 Lanyon Pl., is one of Belfast's newest concert centers, hosting a variety of performances throughout the year. Its concourse features visual arts exhibitions. (☎9033 4400; www.waterfront.co.uk. Student discounts usually available.) The **Ulster Orchestra** plays concerts at Waterfront Hall and Ulster Hall. (☎9066 8798; www.ulster-orchestra.org.uk. Tickets £8-24.)

Take a cab to the **Odyssey Arena** to catch the **Coors Belfast Giants** battle it out on the ice with county competitors (☎9059 1111; www.belfastgiants.com). **Football** (soccer) fanatics catch a game at the **Windsor Park** pitch, located on Donegall Ave. (☎9024 4198). **Gaelic Footballers** run to Andersonstown, West Belfast, to enjoy Sunday afternoon matches. (Contact the Gaelic Athletic Association at ☎9038 3815; www.gaa.ie.) Belfast is crazy about **horse racing;** see the action down at the Maze (☎9262 1256; www.downroyal.com) in Lisburn. Located just 10 mi. from Belfast, the racecourse has a dozen events throughout the year, including the **Mirror May Day** fixture and the **Ulster Harp Derby** in June. **Ulster Rugby,** recent winners of the European Cup, play at **Ravenhill Stadium** (☎9049 3222).

▒ DAYTRIP FROM BELFAST: ULSTER FOLK MUSEUM

The Museum stretches across 170 acres in the town of Holywood. Take the Bangor road (A2) 7 mi. east of Belfast. Buses and trains stop here on the way to Bangor. ☎9042 8428; www.uftm.org.uk. Open July-Sept. M-Sa 10am-6pm, Su 11am-6pm; Mar.-June M-F 10am-5pm, Sa 10am-6pm, Su 11am-6pm; Oct.-Feb. M-F 10am-4pm, Sa 10am-5pm (Nov.-Jan. the Rural Area closes Sa at 4pm), Su 11am-5pm. Folk Museum £5.50, students, seniors, and ages 5-18 £3.50, families £15.50 for 2 adults and 3 children and £11 for 1 adult and 3 children, disabled free. Transport Museum has the same prices, except disabled. Combined admission £7, ages 5-18 £4, 2 adults with 3 children £19, 1 adult with 3 children £13, seniors and students £4. Group discounts and season passes available.

Established by an Act of Parliament in 1958, the ▣**Folk Museum** aims to preserve the way of life of Ulster's farmers, weavers, and craftspeople. The Museum contains over 30 buildings from the past three centuries divided into a town and rural area, the latter containing cottages from all nine Ulster counties, including the usually overlooked Monaghan, Cavan, and Donegal in the Republic. All but two of the buildings are transplanted originals. They have been artfully integrated into a landscape befitting their rural origins; the size of the property and the natural surroundings provide full immersion in the lost-in-time wonderland, creating a remarkable air of authenticity. Unobtrusive attendants in period costume stand nearby to answer questions. In Ballydugan Weaver's House, John the Weaver, a fourth-generation practitioner of his craft, operates the only working linen loom in Ireland. A fully functional printer's press still runs on Main St. Along with a cornmill and a sawmill from Fermanagh, the town is currently in the process of recreating a silent film house from Co. Down. The museum hosts special events, including trad sessions, dance performances and workshops, storytelling festivals, and textile exhibitions. Call ahead for details. Go on a sunny day and leave time to wander.

ANTRIM AND DERRY

The A2 coastal road connects the scenic attractions of Counties Antrim and Derry, providing an easily accessible journey for visitors. North of Belfast, industrial Larne gives way to lovely seaside villages. The breathtaking scenery of the nine Glens of Antrim sweeps visitors north toward the Giant's Causeway, which spills its geological honeycomb into the ocean off the northern coast. This mid-section of the coast road is a cyclist's paradise. Seaside novelties replace natural wonders with the carnival lights of Portrush and Portstewart, and the road finally terminates at Derry/Londonderry, the North's second-largest city.

DERRY/LONDONDERRY

Modern Derry/Londonderry is trying to cast off the legacy of its political Troubles with much success. Although the landscape was razed by years of bombings, recent years have been relatively peaceful. Today's rebuilt city is beautiful and intimate with a cosmopolitan vibe.

> Originally christened *Diore*, meaning "oak grove," the city's name was anglicized to Derry and finally to Londonderry. The city's label remains a source of contention, as the minority Protestant population uses the official title while many Republicans and informal Protestants refer to the city as Derry. Even in the city center, some signs refer to Derry or Londonderry without any consistency.

■ TRANSPORTATION

Flights: Eglinton/Derry Airport, Eglinton (☎ 7181 0784). 4 mi. from Derry. Flights to **Dublin, Glasgow, London-Stansted,** and **Manchester.** The **AIRporter** runs buses from Quayside Shopping Centre to Belfast International and Belfast City airports. (☎ 7126 9996; www.airporter.co.uk. M-F 13 per day 6am-6pm; Sa-Su 6 per day. £15, under 16 £7.50, seniors free; families £35, couples £25, groups of 3 or more £12 per person.)

Trains: Duke St., Waterside (☎ 7134 2228), on the east bank. A free **Rail-Link bus** connects the bus station to the train station. Call the rail or bus station to find the corresponding bus; the Rail-Link runs during all connecting times. Trains from Derry go east to: **Belfast** via **Castlerock, Coleraine, Ballymoney, Ballymena,** and **Lisburn** (2hr.; M-Sa 9 per day, Su 4 per day; £9.80, children £5). Connections may be made from Coleraine to **Portrush** (Derry to Portrush £8, children £4). Bus and train combo passes £14 per day, families £17.50 per day.

Buses: Most stop at the Ulsterbus depot (☎ 0128 9066 6630) on Foyle St., between the walled city and the river. Open daily 7am-10pm. **Ulsterbus** (☎ 7126 2261) serves all destinations in the North and a few in the Republic. (ROI routes are in €, since they are operated by Bus Éireann. Both companies offer ½-fare for children on all routes.) #212 and #273 to **Belfast** (1½-3hr.; at least 1 every 30min. M-F 5:30am-5pm, Sa 8am-1pm; at least every hr. M-F 5am-8pm, Sa 7am-8pm; Su 10 per day; £8.70)

■ PRACTICAL INFORMATION

Tourist Office: 44 Foyle St. (☎ 7126 7284; www.derryvisitor.com), inside the Derry Visitor and Convention Bureau. Be sure to ask for the free and useful *Derry Visitor's Guide* and *Derry Visitor's Map.* 24hr. computerized info kiosk. Books accommodations (£2 plus 10% deposit) and **exchanges currency.** Runs guided walking tours of the city. **Bord Fáilte** (☎ 7136 9501) keeps a desk here, too. Both desks open Mar.-June and Oct. M-F 9am-5pm, Sa 10am-5pm; July-Sept. and Nov.-Feb. M-F 9am-5pm.

Banks: Bank of Ireland, Shipquay St. (☎ 7126 4992). Open M-Tu and Th-F 9:30am-4:30pm, W 10am-4:30pm. **Northern Bank,** Guildhall Sq. (☎ 7126 5333). Open M-W and F 9:30am-3:30pm, Th 9:30am-5pm, Sa 9:30am-12:30pm. All have 24hr. **ATMs.**

Police: Strand Rd. (☎ 7136 7337).

Pharmacy: Gordon's Chemist, 3a-b Strand Rd. (☎7126 4502). Open M-Sa 9am-5:30pm, F 9am-8pm. **O'Hara's Pharmacy,** 43 Great James St. (☎7126 2695). Open M-Sa 9:15am-6:15pm, Su 9:30am-5:30pm.

Hospital: Altnagelvin Hospital, Glenshane Rd. (☎7134 5171). Cross the bridge to the Waterside and follow the signs.

Internet Access: Central Library, 35 Foyle St. (☎7127 2300). £3 per hr. Open M and Th 8:30am-8pm, Tu-W 8:30am-5:30pm, Sa 9:15am-5pm. Snack bar open M-F noon-4pm. Same rates at **Waterside Library,** 23 Glendermot Rd. (☎7134 2963). Open M and W 9:15am-7:30pm, Tu and Th 9:15am-5:30pm, Sa 9:15am-1pm.

Post Office: 3 Custom House St. (☎7136 2563). Open M-F 9am-5:30pm, Sa 9am-12:30pm. Another is at the Diamond, inside the city walls. Unless addressed to 3 Custom House St., *Poste Restante* letters will go to the **Postal Sorting Office** (☎7136 2577), on the corner of Great James and Little James St. **Post Code:** BT48.

TOURS

FREE DERRY TOURS. General tours cover the city walls, the Fountain area, and the Bogside, introducing visitors to the city's conflicts by candid Republican locals. Special-interest tours can be arranged. *(Contact Ruiari ☎7136 6931 or 077 9328 5972; www.freederry.net. Departs daily at 10am and 2pm from The Museum of Free Derry on Rossville St.; other tours by arrangement. Book ahead. From £4.)*

THE DERRY VISITOR AND CONVENTION BUREAU GUIDED TOURS. Most walks circle the top of the city walls, descending to visit various sights. The Derry Visitor and Convention Bureau Guided Walking Tours leave from the tourist office and take visitors around the city walls, including a brief tour of St. Columb's Cathedral. Other tours follow narratives ranging from the 1689 Siege to Emigration. *(☎7126 7284; www.derryvisitor.com. July-Aug. M-F 11:15am and 3:15pm; Sept.-June M-F 2:30pm. 1½hr. tours. £6/€9; students and seniors £5/€7; children under 16 £4/€6.)*

CITY TOURS. Acclaimed City Tours urges the curious to lace their walking shoes and pound the pavement for about 2hr. It is possible to arrange tours through the Sperrins or literary tours throughout Northern Ireland. *(11 Carlisle Rd. ☎7127 1996; www.irishtourguides.com. Depart daily at 10am, noon, 2pm. Book ahead. From £4.)*

ACCOMMODATIONS

Derry City Independent Hostel, 44 Great James St. (☎7137 7989 or 7128 0280). With so much imagination and expense invested in the decor of the 2 buildings, it's little wonder so many hostelers flock to fill Steve and Kylie's 70 beds year after year. Steve greets the crowds with a rundown of Derry's offerings and inspires a laid-back, sociable vibe. With free breakfast, free Internet access, and all-you-can-eat barbecues for £2.50, who could resist the offer to stay a 5th night for free? Dorms £10; doubles £28. ●

The Saddler's House, 36 Great James St. (☎7126 9691; www.thesaddlershouse.com). Knowledgeable owners welcome guests into their lovely Victorian home. Same family runs the more upscale **Merchant's House,** Queen St., an award-winning, restored Georgian townhouse with a gorgeous lounge, elegantly decorated rooms, and fluffy beds. Free Internet access. Ask for the elegant "blue room" (#4 Merchant's House). Singles £25-35; doubles £45-50. ●

Paddy's Palace, 1 Woodlie Terr. (☎7130 9051; www.paddyspalace.com). Although a bit rough around the edges from the regular busloads of tour groups that come by, this relatively new hostel offers a cheap bed near the city center. Pool table in lounge. Free Internet access. Cereal breakfast included. Laundry £5. 6-bed dorms £12, Aug. £15. ●

Abbey B&B, 4 Abbey St. (☎7127 9000 or 077 2527 7864; www.abbeyaccommodation.com). Close to the city center and in the heart of the Bogside neighborhood near the murals. Greets visitors with coffee and spacious peach rooms. Free Internet access. Singles £30; doubles £48. Discounts for families. MC/V. ❸

🍴 FOOD

Groceries are available at Tesco, in the Quayside Shopping Centre, along Strand Rd. (☎7137 4400. Open M-Th 9am-9pm, F 8:30am-9pm, Sa 8:30am-8pm, Su 1-6pm.) Iceland, in the Foyleside Shopping Centre, is another option. (☎7137 7650. Open M-Tu 9am-6pm, W-F 9am-9pm, Sa 9am-7pm, Su 1-6pm.)

Danano, 2-4 Lower Clarendon St. (☎7126 9034). Watch chefs shove tasty pizzas and confused lobsters into the only wood-burning oven in Northern Ireland at this modern Italian eatery. Adjoining takeaway offers pizzas (£6.40-8.40), pastas, and salads for slightly less; call ahead if you're in a hurry. M-Tu 2 pizzas for price of 1 at the takeaway window next door. Open daily 5-11pm. ❸

Exchange, Queens Quay (☎7127 3990), down Great James St. toward the River Foyle, right at the Derry City Hotel. Trendy eatery with private booths. Lunch specials £6-7. Dinner £10-15. Open for lunch M-Sa noon-2:30pm; dinner M-Sa 5:30-10pm, Su 4-9pm. ❹

Ice Wharf/Lloyd's No. 1 Bar, 22-24 Strand Rd., across from The Strand nightclub. Part of the Wetherspoon's pub chain. 2 meals for £6 all day, a £6 "curry club" Th 5-10pm, and a £6 carvery roast Su noon-3pm. Breakfast £2.10 before noon. Open M-W and Su 10am-midnight, Th-Sa 10am-1am. ❷

Spice, 162 Spencer Rd. (☎7134 4875), on the east bank. Cross Craigavon Bridge and continue as it turns into Spencer. Seabass with tomato and coriander salsa £16. Appetizers £3-6.50; entrees £11-15. Separate vegetarian and vegan menu has £4 appetizers and £10 entrees. Open M noon-2:30pm and 5:30-10pm, Tu-F 12:30-2:30pm and 5:30-10pm, Sa 5-10:30pm, Su 5-9pm. ❸

The Sandwich Co., The Diamond (☎7137 2500), 61 Strand Rd., (☎7126 6771), and 33 Spencer Rd., Waterside (☎7131 3171). Trio of eateries lets customers design their own from a selection of breads and fillings. Eat at the Strand location to avoid downtown lunch-break queues. Sandwiches £2.60-4. Open M-F 8am-5pm, Sa 9am-5pm. ❶

👁 SIGHTS

🏛**THE CITY WALLS.** Derry's city walls, 18 ft. high and 20 ft. thick, were erected between 1614 and 1619. The mile-long periphery has never been breached, hence the Protestant nickname "the Maiden City." However, such resilience did not save the city from danger; during the **Siege of 1689,** 600 mortar bombs sent from the nearby hills by fleeing English King James II and his brigade of Catholic Frenchmen went over what they could not go through, decimating the 30,000 Protestants crowded inside. Seven **cannons**—donated by Queen Elizabeth I and the London Guilds who "acquired" the city during the Ulster Plantation—stand along the northeast wall between Magazine and Shipquay Gates. A plaque marks the water level in the days when the Foyle ran along the walls (it now flows 300 ft. away). The 1½ mi. walk around the city walls leads past most of Derry's best-known sights, including the raised portion of the stone wall past New Gate that shields **St. Columb's Cathedral,** the symbolic focus of the city's Protestant defenders. The same area also affords a perfect view of the red-, white-, and blue-painted Unionist **Fountain** neighborhood. Stuck in the center of the southwest wall, **Bishop's Gate** received an ornate face-lift in 1789, commemorating the victory of Protestant William of Orange 100 years earlier. The southwest corner supports **Roaring Meg,** a massive cannon donated by London fishmongers in 1642 and used in the 1689 siege. This corner affords a sprawling view of the **Bogside** neighborhood and a look at some of the murals, which are best accessed from **Butcher's Gate.** Just south of Butcher's Gate, the **Memorial Hall** is the traditional clubhouse of the Apprentice Boys, famous for closing the city gates in 1689.

THE MUSEUM OF FREE DERRY. Covering the Catholic civil rights struggle in Northern Ireland up until Bloody Sunday, the museum tells an eye-opening story, which includes civil rights marches, the Battle of the Bogside, internment, Free Derry, and of course Bloody Sunday. They also serve as the replacement for the old Bloody Sunday Centre. The Free Derry tours depart from here (see **Tours,** p. 689). The museum is located across Rossville St. from the Bloody Sunday monument. *(55 Glenfada Pk. ☎ 7136 0880; www.museumoffreederry.org. Open M-F 9:30am-4:30pm; Mar.-Sept. M-F 9:30am-4:30pm, Sa 1-4pm; June-Sept. M-F 9:30am-4:30pm, Sa-Su 1-4pm. £3/ €4.50, students, seniors, and children £1.50/€2.25.)*

ST. COLUMB'S CATHEDRAL. Named after St. Columcille, whose monastery was the foundation on which Derry was built, the cathedral was constructed between 1628 and 1633 and was the first Protestant cathedral in Britain or Ireland (all older ones were confiscated Catholic cathedrals). The original wooden steeple burnt down after being struck by lightning, while the second (a leaden and rounded replacement) was smelted into bullets and cannonballs during the Great Siege of 1689. The same fate did not befall the cathedral itself, as it was designed to double as a fort with six-inch-thick walls and a walkway for musketeers to shoot from the spire. The porch still holds the mortar shell that delivered the terms of surrender directly to the courtyard. The roughly hewn stone interior holds an exquisite Killybegs altar carpet, an extravagant bishop's chair dating from 1630, and 214 hand-carved Derry-oak pews, of which no two are the same. A small museum in the **chapter house** displays the original locks, along with keys of the four main city gates and other relics. The tombstones lying flat on the ground in the **graveyard** outside were leveled during the siege to protect the graves from Jacobite cannonballs. The small **Mound of Martyrs,** in the back left corner toward the walls, contains the 5000 dead previously buried in the cellars of the nearby houses, transplanted here during the city's redesigning efforts. *(London St., off Bishop St. in the southwest corner of the city. ☎ 7126 7313; www.stcolumbscathedral.org. Open M-Sa Easter.-Oct. 9am-5pm; Nov.-Mar. 9am-4pm. Tours 30-60min. £2. Services M-F 10:30am, Su 8, 11am, 4pm.)*

🎦 🎵 PUBS AND CLUBS

Most pubs line Waterloo St. and the Strand, although new ones are popping up within the city walls. Trad and rock are available almost any night of the week, generally starting around 11pm, and pubs stay lively until the 1am closing time.

🎦 **Peadar O'Donnell's,** 53 Waterloo St. (☎ 7137 2318). Named for the Donegal socialist who organized the Irish Transport and General Workers Union. Celtic and Orangeman paraphernalia hang beside chalkboards of drink specials. Nightlife hub for tourists and locals. Live music 11pm. W and Sa trad 7-9pm, sometimes Su 10pm. Open M-Sa 11:30am-1am (last call at 1am; doors close at 2am), Su 12:30pm-midnight.

The Gweedore, 59-61 Waterloo St. (☎ 7126 3513). Back door has connected to Peadar's since Famine times. Peadar's little brother handles overflow and caters to a slightly younger crowd with rock, bluegrass, and funk bands nightly. Tu-Su live music. Open M-Th 4:30pm-1am, F-Su 4:30pm-2am.

Sandino's Cafe Bar, 1 Water St., next to the bus station (☎ 7130 9297; www.sandinos.com). Named after Nicaraguan guerilla leader Augusto Sandino, this left-wing watering hole is plastered with pictures of Che and Fidel. Venue for poetry readings, local up-and-coming bands, and international music artists. Locals say this is also the best cup of coffee in town. F live bands. Tu and Sa DJs. Su afternoon trad. Open M-Sa 11:30am-1am, Su 1pm-midnight. Upstairs venue opens at 10pm.

Bound for Boston, 27-31 Waterloo St. (☎7127 1315). Young crowd relaxes in spray-painted booths with TV by day and rocks out to alternative bands by night. Upstairs, pool sharks and their prey watch sports at **Club Q.** Tu and Th-Sa live music. Su karaoke. 3-level terraced beer garden. Open M-Sa 1pm-1am, Su 12:15pm-1am.

The Strand Bar, 31-35 Strand Rd. (☎7126 0494). 4 floors of young partiers. F DJs spin dance faves from Top 40 to electronica. Downstairs has live music or Tu and Th-Sa DJs. Top fl. is the scandalous **Buddha.** W karaoke, Su R&B. Open daily noon-1am. Nightclub open Th-Sa 10pm-1:30am. Cover £5.

◪ DAYTRIPS FROM DERRY

THE GIANT'S CAUSEWAY. Geologists believe that the unique rock formations found at ◪**Giant's Causeway** were created some 60 million years ago by lava out-pourings that left curiously shaped cracks in their wake. Although locals have different ideas, everyone agrees that the Causeway is an awesome sight to behold. Comprising over 40,000 symmetrical hexagonal basalt columns, it resembles a descending staircase leading from the cliffs to the ocean's floor. Several other formations stand within the Causeway: **the Giant's Organ, the Wishing Chair, the Granny, the Camel,** and **the Giant's Boot.** Advertised as the 8th natural wonder of the world, the Giant's Causeway is Northern Ireland's most famous natural sight, so don't be surprised if 2000 others pick the same day to visit. Visit early in the morning or after the center closes to avoid crowds.

Once travelers reach the Visitors Centre, they have two trail options: the more popular low road, which directly swoops down to the Causeway (20min.), or the more rewarding high road, which takes visitors 4½ mi. up a sea cliff to the romantic Iron Age ruins of Dunseverick Castle. Bus #172 and the #252 "Antrim Coaster" stop in front of the castle, from which it's 4½ mi. farther to Ballintoy. The trail is well-marked and easy to follow, but you can also consult the free map available at the Visitors Centre. The center also offers a 12min. film about the legend of Finn McCool and posits on the geological explanation for the formations. (The Causeway is always open and free to pedestrians. Ulsterbus #172 to Portrush, the #252 Antrim Coaster, the "Causeway Rambler," and the Bushmills Bus drop visitors at Giant's Causeway Visitors Centre, in the shop next to the car park. The Causeway Coaster minibus runs to the columns. ☎9066 6630; www.translink.co.uk. 2min.; every 15min.; £1, round-trip £2, children 50p/£1. Centre info ☎2073 1855; www.northantrim.com. Open daily July-Aug. 10am-6pm; Sept.-June 10am-5pm. Movie 10am-5pm every 15min.; £1, child £0.50. Parking £5. To avoid the fee, park at nearby Heritage Railway Centre's free car park, a 2min. walk away, or behind the Causeway Hotel.)

DUNLUCE CASTLE. On top of a craggy sea cliff, the remarkably intact ruins of this 16th-century fortress seem to merge seamlessly with their rocky foundation. Indeed, the castle is built so close to the cliff's edge that the kitchen once fell into the sea during a grand banquet, resulting in the arrest of the host and the relocation of the lady of the house (who despised the sound of the sea) to an inland residence. Built as the seat of the MacDonnell family, the castle was considered unbreachable by any army, and it can only be accessed across a small bridge, which was originally a narrow, rocky pass. The east wall has cannons from the *Girona,* a Spanish Armada vessel that sunk nearby. Beneath the castle, a covert **sea cave** offered a quick escape route toward Rathlin Island or Scotland; climbing down can be slippery, but adventurers are rewarded with a different perspective of the castle's cliffside location. While a small fee is required to get up close and personal with the castle, the most spectacular views are afforded by stopping along the A2 coming from Bushmills. From mid-June until mid-September, a free "living history" exhibit shows the castle as it would have been before it was ruined. *(The castle is located along A2, between Bushmills and Portrush; served by the Causeway Rambler bus. ☎ 7032 5400 or 9066 6630; www.translink.co.uk; daily 10:15am-5pm. Open daily Oct.-Mar. 10am-5pm, last admission 4:30pm; Apr.-Sept. 10am-6pm, last admission 5:30pm. £2, children under 16 and seniors £1, children under 4 free.)*

BUSHMILLS DISTILLERY. Ardently Protestant Bushmills has been home to the Old Bushmills Distillery, creator of Bushmills Irish Whiskey, since 1608, when a nod from King James I established it as the oldest licensed whiskey producer in the world. Travelers have been stopping at the distillery since ancient days, when it lay on the route to Tara from castles Dunluce and Dunseverick. In those days, the whiskey's strength was determined by gunpowder's ability to ignite when doused with the fiery liquid. When the plant is operating, the tour shows the various stages involved in the production of Irish whiskey, which is distilled three times rather than the paltry two involved in making Scotch. During the three weeks in July when production stops for maintenance, the far less interesting experience is redeemed only by the free sample at its end.

The sleepy town of Bushmills caters to visitors who decide they can't move on (or move at all, for that matter) after visiting the distillery. The brand-new **Mill Rest Youth Hostel (HI) ❶,** 49 Main St. just up the road from the Diamond, away from the distillery, is a blended whiskey of a hostel—the spacious common room and spotless, lofted rooms are of single malt quality, but the lack of character reminds you that you're still drinking the cheaper stuff. Check back in 12 years to see if it's aged well. (☎ 2073 1222; www.hini.org.uk. Reception closed daily 11am-5pm. Coin-operated **Internet** access 5p per min. Laundry £4. July-Aug. dorms £15; singles £35; doubles £41. Sept.-June £14/22/41. HINI £1 discount per night.) Down the street, the **Hip Chip ❶,** 82 Main St., will line your stomach for whiskey-drinking with a £5 fish supper. *(☎ 2073 1717. Open M-Th 11:30am-11pm, F-Sa 11:30am-11:30pm, Su 1-11pm. The distillery and Bushmills are at the intersection of A2 and B17, 3 mi. east of Portrush and 2 mi. west of the Causeway; served by the Causeway Rambler bus ☎ 7032 5400 or 9066 6630; www.translink.co.uk; daily 10:15am-5pm; and the Bushmills open-top bus #9, which connects Coleraine to the Giant's Causeway, 5 per day. The Giant's Causeway and Bushmills's Railway connect the two. ☎ 2073 2594; www.giantscausewayrailway.org. Runs Mar.-Dec. irregularly; June-Sept. daily 11:15am-4:30pm, every 15min. and 30min. after the hr. £5, children £3.50. Distillery ☎ 2073 1521; www.whiskeytours.ie. Open Apr.-Oct. M-Sa 9:30am-5:30pm, Su noon-5:30pm, last tour 4pm; Nov.-Mar. daily 10am-4:30pm, tours M-F 10:30, 11:30am, 1:30, 2:30, 3:30pm; Sa-Su 1:30, 2:30, 3:30pm. £5, students and seniors £4.)*

CAUSEWAY COAST: CUSHENDUN TO BALLYCASTLE

The coastline between Cushendun and Ballycastle is one of the most famous stretches in Ireland. Although motorists and other travelers seeking a speedy trip between the two towns opt for the wide A2, this road seems tame compared with its coastal counterpart, the scenic (read: occasionally terrifying) **Torr Road.** This narrow coastal road affords incomparable views and sheer cliffs but also demands tricky maneuvers around steep corners and tight squeezes with oncoming traffic. The most famous vista is **Torr Head,** the site of many ancient forts and the closest point on the Isle to the Scottish coast, 12 mi. away. Past Torr Head is **Murlough Bay,** protected by the National Trust, where a stunning landscape hides the remains of the medieval church **Drumnakill,** once a pagan holy site. A small gravel car park above the bay leads to the north and east vistas. The east vista is accessible by car and thus more crowded than the pedestrian-only north vista. The road then bumps on to **Fair Head,** 7 mi. north of Cushendun and 3 mi. east of Ballycastle. This rocky, heather-covered headland winds past several lakes, including **Lough na Cranagh;** in its middle sits a *crannog,* an island built by Bronze Age Celts as a fortified dwelling for elite chieftains. **Bikes** should be left at the hostel: the area is steep and rainy, and it's only a 1½hr. hike from Ballycastle.

The more direct A2, the official bus route, does have its advantages—the road passes its own set of attractions and is more manageable for cyclists, with only one long climb and an even longer descent from boggy plain. Sparse traffic makes hitching impossible. A few miles northeast of Cushendun, a high hollow contains a vanishing lake called **Loughareema** (or **Faery Lough**), which during the summer can appear and disappear into the bog in less than a day. When it's full, the lake teems with fish. When it empties, the fish take refuge in caverns beneath the limestone. Locals claim that the lough is still haunted by the ghosts of Colonel McNeill and his horses after the coachmen misjudged the shifting water levels and drowned. Farther along, part of the plain was drained and planted with evergreens. The result is the secluded **Ballypatrick Forest,** with a scenic drive and pleasant, pine-scented walks. Before Ballycastle town, and roughly 1 mi. into the woods, **Ballycastle Forest** contains the eminently climbable 1695 ft. **Knocklayde Mountain.**

GLENS OF ANTRIM

During the Ice Age, glaciers plowed through the coastline northeast of Antrim, leaving nine deep scars in the mountains. Over the years, water collected in these valleys, nourishing trees, ferns, and other flora not usually found in Ireland. The A2 coastal road connects the mouths of these glens and provides entry to roads inland. Still relatively unspoiled and much less touristed than the northern coast, the nine glens are rich in their own lore and distinct character. While the road offers stunning coastal vistas, the mountains and waterfalls are best explored on daytrips inland from the coastal villages of Glenarm, Waterfoot, and Cushendall.

Most visitors travel the glens by car, but two **Ulsterbus** routes serve the area year-round (Belfast ☎9032 0011; Larne ☎2827 2345). Bus #150 runs between **Ballymena** and **Cushendun** (M-F 5 per day, Sa 4 per day; £4.50) with intermediate stops at **Waterfoot** and **Cushendall** (M-F 4 per day, Sa 3 per day; £5.50). The **Antrim Coaster** (#252) runs year-round, stopping at every town on the road from **Belfast** to **Coleraine** (M-F and Su 2 per day, one of which runs only Belfast to Larne; £4 to Larne and £9 to Belfast). **Cycling** the glens is fabulous. The **Ardclinis Activity Centre** in Cushendall **rents bikes** (p. 694). The coastal road from Ballygally to Cushendun is both scenic and relatively flat. Once the road passes Cushendun, however, it becomes hilly enough to make even motorists groan. Crossroads are reportedly the best places to find a lift, although *Let's Go* never recommends hitchhiking.

CUSHENDALL (BUN ABHANN DALLA)

Cushendall is nicknamed the capital of the Glens, thanks to its natural wonders. The four streets in the town center house a variety of goods, services, and pubs unavailable anywhere else in the region. The town's proximity to Glenaan, Glenariff, Glenballyeomon, Glencorp, and Glendun reinforce its importance as a commercial center. Unfortunately, the closing of its hostel means that budget travelers are diverted to the camping barn outside of town.

█ ⊿ TRANSPORTATION AND PRACTICAL INFORMATION. Ulsterbus (☎9033 3000) stops at the Mill St. tourist office where current bus times are posted. Bus #162 has limited service from **Belfast** (£6.50) via **Larne** and **Cushendall** (£7), then north to **Cushendun** (M-F 3 per day, the first of which doesn't go up to Cushendun).

Bus #252 (a.k.a. the **Antrim Coaster**) goes coastal from **Belfast** to **Coleraine**, stopping in Cushendall and most everywhere else. (M-F and Su 1 per day between Belfast and Coleraine £9, 1 per day between Belfast and Larne £4.) Bus #150, from **Belfast** via **Ballymena**, stops in **Glenariff** (a.k.a. Waterfoot; M-F 5 per day, Sa 3 per day; £4.50). **Ardclinis Activity Centre**, in back of the house at 11 High St., **rents bikes** and provides advice and equipment for hill-walking, canoeing, cycling, rafting, and other outdoor pursuits. They also lead "coasteering" trips which involve jumping, climbing, swimming, and negotiating the coastline by any means necessary. (☎2177 1340; www.ardclinis.com. Mountain bikes £10 per day; deposit £50. Wetsuits £5 per day. Coasteering from £180 for trips of around 10 people.)

The busiest section of Cushendall is its crossroads. From the center of town, **Mill Street** turns into **Chapel Road** and heads northwest toward Ballycastle; **Shore Road** extends south toward Glenarm and Larne. On the north side of town, **High Street** leads uphill from **Bridge Road,** a section of the **Coast Road** (an extension of the A2) that continues toward the sea at Waterfoot. The **tourist office** hands out info at 25 Mill St., near the bus stop at the northern (Cushendun) end of town. (☎2177 1180. Open from mid-June to mid-Sept. M-F 10am-5pm, Sa 10am-1pm; Oct.-May Tu-Su 10am-1pm.) The **library** across from the tourist office offers **Internet** access for £1.50 per 30min. (☎2177 1297. Open Tu 2-8pm, Th and Sa 10am-1pm and 2-5pm). **Cushendall Development Office,** behind the tourist office, has Internet access. (☎2177 1378. £2 per 30min., £3.50 per hr.; students and seniors £1.50/2.50. Open M-Th 9am-1pm and 2-5pm, F 9am-1pm and 2-3pm, although Fridays often don't recover from the lunch break.) **O'Neill's,** 25 Mill St., sells fishing and hiking gear. (☎2177 2009. Open July-Aug. M-Sa 9:30am-6pm, Su 12:30-4pm; Sept.-June M-Sa 9:30am-6pm, Tu close at 1pm). **Northern Bank,** 5 Shore Rd., has a 24hr. **ATM.** (☎2177 1243. Open M 9:30am-12:30pm and 1:30-5pm, Tu-F 10am-12:30pm and 1:30-3:30pm.) **Numark Pharmacist** is on 8 Mill St. (☎2177 1523. Open M-Sa 9am-6pm.) The **post office** is inside the Spar Market, on Coast Rd. (☎2177 1201. Open M and W-F 9am-1pm and 2-5pm, Tu and Sa 9am-12:30pm.) **Postal Code:** BT44.

ACCOMMODATIONS. Ballyeamon Camping Barn ❶, 6 mi. south of town on B14 at 127 Ballyeamon Rd., is Cushendall's last bastion of budget travel. The barn has views of Glenariff Forest Park, and owner Liz is a professional storyteller happy to regale visitors with ghost stories and fairy tales. It's far from town but near the Moyle Way and well worth the trip. The Cushendall-Cargan bus will stop across the field. (☎2175 8451 or 2175 8699; www.taleteam.demon.co.uk. Internet access £1 per 30min. Dorms £10. Call for pickup.) A bevy of B&Bs surround Cushendall, but the majority are just south of town. Overlooking the sea and surrounded by grazing cows, **Glendale ❸,** 46 Coast Rd., has huge rooms and colorful company. Tea, coffee, candy, and biscuits are in each room. (☎2177 1495. Internet access available. Singles £25; doubles £40. MC/V.) **Mountain View ❸,** 1 Kilnadore Rd., a few minutes walk out of town toward Glenariff and a right onto Kilnadore just after the police station, has four smallish but comfortable rooms with bath. (☎2177 1246. Singles £25; doubles £40.) The **Central B&B ❸,** right in the middle of town at 7 Bridge St., is your most convenient choice. (☎2177 1730. All rooms with bath. Singles £25; doubles £50.) The town's caravan parks aren't particularly suited to tents, but campers in need can find a bit of earth. Strong winds can make camping rugged at **Cushendall Caravan Park ❶,** 62 Coast Rd. (☎2177 1699. Free showers. Laundry £1.50. 2-person tent £8.30; family tent £12.40; caravans £16.55 with electricity.)

FOOD AND PUBS. Spar, 2 Coast Rd., past Bridge Rd., sells **groceries.** (☎2177 1763. Open daily 7am-10pm.) **Arthur's ❶,** 6 Shore Rd., is a family-run cafe that serves simple, fresh sandwiches and full breakfasts from £2.75. (☎2177 1627. Panini £3.85-4.45. Open daily 9am-5pm.) Renowned throughout the Glens for its big portions of delicious fish and meat dishes ($5.30-8), **Harry's Restaurant ❸**, 10-12 Mill St., serves upscale pub grub ($4-8) by day and big dinners (entrees $8-13) by night. (☎2177 2022. Kitchen open daily noon-9:30pm; dinner served 6-9:30pm.) One of the Isle's best pubs for Irish music, ◪**Joe McCollam's (Johnny Joe's)**, 23 Mill St., packs in crowds for ballads, fiddle-playing, and slurred limerick recitals. (☎2177 1876. Weekend live music. Opens between 3 and 7pm; last call at midnight, drinkers get booted out at 1:30am.) **An Camán** ("hurling bat"), 5 Bridge St. at the foot of the bridge, is marked on one side of the building by a giant mural of a hurler (but don't be confused by the much larger mural next to the library). Needless to say, they like their hurling, and the game room in the back draws the town's younger crowd. (☎2177 1293. W and F-Su Live music or disco. Open daily 11:30am-1:30am.)

◪ **SIGHTS.** The sandstone **Curfew Tower** in the center of town, on the corner of Mill St. and High St., was built in 1817 by the eccentric, slightly paranoid Francis Turley. This Cushendall landlord made a fortune in China. When he returned to Ireland he built a tower based on a Chinese design. He added openings for pouring boiling oil onto nonexistent attackers in a mad attempt to protect his riches. The bell on the tower was co-opted by the British forces during the Irish Revolution (see **History and Politics,** p. 674) and sounded at the designated curfew, at which time Catholics were confined indoors under watch from on high—hence the tower's name. Today, the structure is privately owned and closed to the public. The extensive remnants of **Layde Church,** a medieval friary, lie along Layde Rd. When it was established in 1306, the church was valued at 20 shillings for tax purposes. Its ruins are noteworthy for their extensive burial sites, which have raised the ground by about a meter, evident in the low portals and windows. The graveyard includes **Cross Na Nagan,** an unusual pagan holestone used for marriage ceremonies and later Christianized into a Celtic cross. Sloping down toward the cliffside, the site also offers spectacular seaviews of Scotland and the pretty **seaside walks** that begin at its car park. (Always open. Free.) **Tieveragh Hill,** ½ mi. up High St., is known locally as Faery Hill, inspired by the otherworldly "little people" who supposedly reside in the area. Although it would make a fine patch of farmland, locals have honored the "wee folk" and let the hedgerows grow. The summit of similarly supernatural **Lurigethan Hill,** more commonly "Lurig Mountain," flattens out 1153 ft. over town. During the **Heart of the Glens** festival, locals have clocked records of 26min. (men) and 38min. (women) racing up the hill for the Lurig Run. The less eager amble up in about 45min. The festival is a 10-day affair that starts the 2nd week of August and ends in a giant block party. During the 2nd week of June, ramblers put on their hiking boots for the new **Glens Walking Festival,** when the *Walk the Glens* groups lead a series of free Glens treks. **Oisín's Grave** (OH-shans) is a few miles away on the lower slopes of **Tievebulliagh Mountain.** Actually a neolithic burial cairn dating from around 4000 BC, it is linked by tradition with the Ulster warrior-bard Oisín, who was supposedly buried here around AD 300. The A2 leads north from Cushendall toward Ballymoney and the lower slopes of Tievebulliagh, where a sign points to the grave. The steep walk up the southern slope of **Glenaan** rewards travelers with views of the lush valley. The **Walk the Glens** group leads occasional (usually monthly) walks around the area for a nominal fee. (Contact the development office for more info ☎2177 1378.)

CUSHENDUN (COIS ABHAINN DUINE)

In 1954, the National Trust bought the minuscule seaside village of Cushendun, 5 mi. north of Cushendall on A2, to preserve its unusual whitewashed, black-shuttered buildings. Along with its Cornish architecture, the town also harbors some natural structures of note—murky **caves** carved into the red seacliffs can be explored along the beach. The less intrepid will enjoy a relaxing meander around the **historic monuments** in town and in nearby **Glendun,** a preserved village and another fine example of Cornish architecture. The **Maud Cottages** lining the main street were built by Lord Cushendun for his wife in 1925. Tourist information signs in town remind visitors not to mistake them for almshouses. During the second week of July, Cushendun swarms with sports fans for the annual **Sports Week.** In the fields northwest of town (toward Ballycastle), various games are played all week; the highlight is the big hurling match that takes place on the last day.

Buses pause on the coast road at Cushendun's Mace **grocery shop,** which also features a **post office** and an **ATM,** on their way to **Waterfoot** via **Cushendall.** (#162; M-F 10 per day, Sa 5 per day, Su 3 per day. Mace open daily 7am-8pm.) Guests at 🖳**Drumkeerin,** 201a Torr Rd., signposted west of town off the A2, may choose between the immaculate **B&B ❸** and the **camping barn ❶.** The barn has unisex dormitory rooms with foam mattresses and a common room with TV and table tennis. Each B&B room boasts a gorgeous view of Cushendun and the coast. Mary was named Landlady of the Year for the whole of the UK in 2002; it's no wonder—she makes her own bread and jams, and offers eggs from her hens. Joe leads hill walks and historical tours. (☎2176 1554; www.drumkeeringuesthouse.com. Camping barn £12. B&B singles with bath £35; doubles £55.) **Cushendun Caravan Site ❶,** 14 Glendun Rd., 50 yd. from the end of the beach, is usually pretty packed and will soon open a game room with TV and a DVD player. (☎2176 1254. No kitchen. Laundry £1. Open Easter-Sept. 2-person tent £8.30, family-size tent £12.40, caravan with electricity £16.55.) The town's most popular attraction is also its only real pub: **Mary McBride's,** 2 Main St., used to be in the *Guinness Book of World Records* as the smallest bar in Europe. The original wee bar has been expanded to create a lounge for viewing sports matches. Cushendun's characters leave the bar only when musicians start a session in the lounge. (☎2176 1511. Summer Sa-Su music, usually trad or country. Bar food £6.50-7.50. Kitchen open daily 12:30-8:30pm. Bar open daily noon-1am.) **Cushendun Tea Rooms ❷,** across the street, serves typical cafe fare while patrons relax on a green lawn. (☎2176 1506. Burgers and sandwiches £2.50; entrees £5-9. Open Apr.-Sept. daily 10am-6pm.)

NEWTOWNARDS

At the head of the Strangford Lough lies Newtownards, Ards borough's capital city. This relatively quiet town falls in the shadows of the iconic Scrabo Tower, provides a wealth of information on its southern neighbors, and serves as a convenient base for further exploration of the Ards Penninsula.

▛ TRANSPORTATION

Buses: 33 Regent St. (☎9181 23910; www.translink.co.uk), next to the tourist office. To **Belfast** (35min.; M-F every 10-30min. 6:15am-9:35pm, Sa at least 1 every hr. 7am-9pm, Su at least 1 every 1½hr. 8am-9pm; £2.30); to **Bangor** (M-F every 15-30min. 6:45am-6pm and every hr. until 10pm, Sa every 30min. 8:15am-6pm and every hr. until 10pm, Su every 2hr. 9:30am-9:30pm; £2); and **Ards Peninsula** towns, including **Portaferry** (50min.; M-F 15 per day, Sa 10 per day, Su 5 per day; £4.50). A bus to **Comber, Downpatrick, Killyleagh,** and **Newcastle** runs July-Aug. M-F at 10:10am, noon, and 2:55pm (returns at 12:15, 2:30, 4:45pm); £7.70 round-trip. All buses stop at Gibsons Ln. between Regent St. and Mill St. The station can hold baggage.

Taxis: Call **Ards Cabs,** 5 Gibsons Ln. (☎9181 1617); **A&G,** Lower Mary St. (☎9181 0360); or the wheelchair-accessible **Rosevale Taxis,** Unit 11 North St. (☎9181 1440 or 9182 1111). Taxis also operate from the bus station at Regent St.

NORTHERN IRELAND

✦🛈 ORIENTATION AND PRACTICAL INFORMATION

Conway Square is home to the town hall and a small pedestrian area. Running north to south on either side of the square are **Church Street,** which becomes **Regent Street** and then **Frances Street** as it progresses southeast to Donaghadee, and **Mill Street,** which becomes **High Street.** Between the two main streets toward the tourist office is **Gibsons Lane,** where all buses stop and leave.

Tourist Office: 31 Regent St. (☎9182 6846; www.ards-council.gov.uk). Books accommodations for a £2 plus a 10% deposit. Stays open year-round and has ample information on all destinations in Northern Ireland. The office is also home to the **Ards Crafts** store, which sells the work of local artisans. Open July-Aug. M-Th 9am-5:15pm, F-Sa 9am-5:30pm; Sept.-June M-Sa 9am-5pm.

Banks: Bank of Ireland, 12 Conway Sq. (☎9181 4200). Open M-Tu and Th-F 9:30am-4:30pm, W 10am-4:30pm. **Northern Bank,** 35 High St. (☎9181 2220). Open M 10am-5pm, Tu-W and F 10am-3:30pm, Th 9:30am-3:30pm, Sa 9:30am-12:30pm. **Ulster Bank,** 22 Frances St. (☎9182 7840). Open M-Tu and Th-F 9:30am-4:30pm, W 10am-4:30pm. All have 24hr. **ATMs.**

Pharmacy: Boots, 12-14 Regent St. (☎9181 3359). Open M-Sa 9am-6pm.

Work Opportunities: Contact **Grafton Recruitment,** 13 High St. (☎9182 6353).

Police: John St. (☎9181 8080).

Hospital: Ards Community Hospital, Church St. (☎9181 2661), treats minor injuries. Open daily 9am-5pm. Emergencies and children under 4 go to **Ulster Hospital,** Upper Newtownards Rd. in **Dondonald** (☎9048 4511).

Internet Access: The **Newtownards Library,** on Regent St. in Queen's Hall (☎9181 4732), a few doors from the tourist office, provides Internet access at £1.50 per 30min. Open M-W 10am-8pm, Th 10am-5pm, F 9:30am-5pm, Sa 10am-4pm.

Post Office: 8 Frances St. (☎084 5722 3344). Open M-F 9am-5:30pm (Tu 9:30am), Sa 9:30am-12:30pm. Also has a **bureau de change.** There is another office in the **Asda** supermarket at **Ards Shopping Center** (☎9182 0203). Open M-F 9am-5:30pm, Sa 9am-1pm. **Post Code:** BT23.

▛ ACCOMMODATIONS

Despite its centrality and accessibility to the rest of the Ards, Newtownards itself does not have a developed accommodations market. There is only one hotel in town, but a 5-10min. taxi or car ride outside the city yields a variety of B&Bs.

Strangford Arms Hotel, 92 Church St. (☎9181 4141; www.strangfordhotel.co.uk). Finally a legitimate reason to indulge, as the town's only hotel just happens to be a 3-star oasis in a land of B&Bs. Singles £79; doubles £99. AmEx/MC/V. ❺

Woodview B&B, 8 Ballywalter Rd. (☎4278 8242; www.kingdomsofdown/woodview), in Greyabbey. Follow signs for Ballywalter; after passing the abbey, the easily missed driveway is on the left where the church wall ends. Peaceful B&B surrounded by farmland. Kind Mrs. Carson welcomes visitors to her home with a cup of tea and biscuits with homemade jam. Singles £25; doubles £44. Discount for stays of 3+ nights. ❸

Rockhaven B&B, 79 Mountain Rd. (☎9182 3987; www.kingdomsofdown.com/rockhaven). Secluded modern home with interesting world art and 2 comfortable rooms just a short drive toward Crawfordsburn (A2). Pass the Leisure Centre and the subsequent traffic light; then make a right on Mountain Rd. Rockhaven is ½ mi. on the right. Parking available. Free Wi-Fi and laundry. Singles £35; doubles £60. ❹

☘✚ FOOD AND PUBS

For **groceries,** visit Tesco (☎9181 5290; open M-F 8:30am-9pm, Sa 8:30am-8pm, Su 1-6pm) or Asda (☎9181 5577; open M-Sa 8am-10pm, Su 1-6pm), in the **Ards Shopping Centre** off Church St. after the Strangford Arms Hotel. Bakeries and fruit stands line Regent St. between Frances St. and the tourist office and Conway Sq.

Cafe Mocha, 23 High St. (☎9181 2616). Tranquil (and delicious) haven amid town square's bustle. Breakfasts £3-5; sandwiches £2.50-3.65; lunches £3.50-6.50. Open M-Th 8am-4:30pm, F-Sa 8am-10pm, Su 9am-3pm. ❶

Regency Restaurant, 5A Regent St. (☎9181 4347). Family-oriented bakery and restaurant features grill options from £6-8.50 and sandwiches (£2) for takeaway. Try the "Ulster Fry" breakfast special—sausage, bacon, eggs, and bread (8:30-10:45am £2, after 10:45am £5). Open M-F 7:30am-5pm, Sa 7:30am-6:30pm. ❶

The Blue Room, 12 Frances St. (☎9182 1217). Focaccia, bagels, croissants, and wraps with a variety of fillings round out the sandwich roster. All-day breakfast features 4 sizes of fried dishes, including the "Bellybuster" (£5.50). Lunches around £5. Open M-Sa 8:30am-4:30pm. ❷

◉ ⚑ SIGHTS AND OUTDOOR ACTIVITIES

Newtownards is the closest hub to the **Scrabo Tower and Country Park,** 203A Scrabo Rd., one of Northern Ireland's favorite postcard subjects. To take your own pictures, head north out of Newtownards taking Blair Maine Rd. from the Newtownards Shopping Centre roundabout, then make a right at Scrabo Rd. and the second left on that road. The bus to Comber also stops at the tower upon request (single £1, all-day ticket £1.70). The 200 ft. tower was erected in 1857 as a memorial to Charles William Steward, Third Marquee of Londonderry (1778-1854), in commemoration of the struggles his tenants faced during the Great Famine. Although Charles Lanyon's elaborate plan for the tower was never realized due to lack of funding, it is one of Northern Ireland's most recognizable landmarks. Visitors enjoy exhibits on the tower's history and the park, as well as an audio/visual presentation. Those who brave the steep spiral staircase leading to the top are rewarded with fantastic 360° views. The adjoining park's quarries supplied the stone for **Greyabbey,** down the road (p. 700), and the Albert Memorial Clock in Belfast. Ramblers are welcome in **Killyneater Wood,** home to many tree-lined walks. (☎9181 1491; www.ehsni.gov.uk. Open Easter-Sept. daily 10:30am-6pm. Free.)

Six miles from Newtownards (12 mi. from Belfast), the Wildfowl and Wetlands Trust maintains **Castle Espie,** 78 Ballydrain Rd., a wetlands preserve that protects endangered birds and has the largest population of ducks, geese, and swans in Ireland. From Newtownards, take C2 toward Comber, then A22 toward Killyleagh. Take the first left at Ballydrain Rd. An emphasis on conservation and environmental education govern the site's woodland walks, children's activities, sustainable garden, and art gallery. Activity is especially high in fall and winter when migrating flocks from the Arctic seek refuge in Northern Ireland's comparatively temperate climate. The visitors center has free maps and wildlife information. (☎9187 4146; www.wwt.org.uk. Open Mar.-June and Sept.-Oct. M-F 10:30am-5pm, Sa-Su 11am-5:30pm; Nov.-Feb. M-F 11am-4pm, Sa-Su 11am-5:30pm; July-Aug. M-F 10:30am-5:30pm, Sa-Su 11am-5:30pm. £5, Gift Aid 5.50; students, seniors, and unemployed £3.80/4.15, children £2.50/2.75, children under 4 free.) At **The Ark Open Farm,** 296 Bangor Rd., about 1 mi. from Newtownards, right off A21, visitors are encouraged to return to their agrarian roots. Milk a cow named Kathy, feed red deer, pet a llama, or ride a pony. The working farm specializes in caring for over 80 rare species of domestic animals, including White Bud cows, which are believed to have been brought to Britain by the Romans. (☎9182 0445; www.thearkopenfarm.com. Open Apr.-Oct. M-Sa 10am-6pm, Su 2-6pm; Nov.-Mar. M-Sa 10am-5pm, Su 2-5pm. £4, ages 3-18, seniors, and students £3.20, under 3 free.) Fishermen look to the **Movilla Trout Fishery** to practice a little catch and release. Fly fishers cast their lines on Movilla Lake, 4 mi. down Donaghadee Rd. (B172) from Newtownards, on Movilla Rd.; make a right after Movilla H.S., and after 2 mi. the fishery will be signposted. (☎9181 3334. 1 fish £16, 2 fish £19; catch and release £12. Open daily 9am-dusk.) Note that a rod license is necessary and can be purchased at **Country Sports,** across from the bus station at 48 Regent St. (☎9181 3403). For indoor sports, head to the **Ards Leisure Centre** on William St. From Regent St., heading away from town hall, make a right on William St. and walk ¼ mi. to the compound. Go for a swim, play some badminton or ping pong (£1.65/1.10), or opt for one of their fitness classes (£4-6); afterwards, grab a bit at the **cafe ❶.** (☎9181 2837; www.leisureards.org.uk. Pool £1.60; children, students, and seniors £1.10. Open M-F 9:30am-8:30pm, Sa 9:30am-4:30pm, Su 1-4:30pm.) After your workout, take a trip to **Movieland,** Blair Mayne Rd. South, to negate all that exercise with an enormous bucket of popcorn. The movie theater is in the same parking lot as the shopping center; take Mill St. out of town to reach it. (☎9182 0000. Matinees £4, children £3.30; evening shows £5, students and children £4.)

DV Diving, 138 Mount Steward Rd., leads dives in Belfast and Strangford loughs and around the peninsula. Leave Newtownards on Portaferry Rd. (E4) and pass Ards Sailing Club after 3½ mi., then make a left onto Mount Steward Rd.; it is 2 mi. down on the left. Certified instructors provide equipment and offer diving qualification courses. (☎Bangor office ☎9146 4671, dive center ☎9186 1686; www.dvdiving.co.uk. £20 per dive; £40 full-equipment hire. 1½hr. introductory lessons £25. 5- to 7-day courses with equipment £225-295.) Land and lough lovers alike delight in the double-whammy bike and kayak rental offered at **Mike the Bike,** 53 Francis St. (☎9181 1311. Bikes £12 per day; kayaks £15 per day. Open daily 9:30am-5:30pm) For an aeronautical thrill, look into **flight lessons** or **helicopter hire** from the **Ards Airport.** Ards Tourist Information organizes occasional tours from Easter through September, ranging from historical guided walking tours of Newtownards to a folklore-themed jaunt. Contact the Tourist Board for schedules.

Festivals are common throughout the peninsula. In August, **The Creative Peninsula** showcases artists and craftsmen's work at the **Ards Arts Gallery** in the Newtownards Town Hall. (☎9182 3131; arts@ards-council.gov.uk. Open M-Th 10am-5pm, F-Sa 10am-4pm. Contact either the Gallery or the tourist office for additional info.) For four days around mid-October, the **Ards International Guitar Festival** fills local cafes, bars, and halls with six-string sounds ranging from folk to flamenco. Late September presents the Ards-wide **Festival of the Peninsula,** when musicians, dramatists, dancers, and other performers come from Donegal, Scotland, and all over Ireland to entertain visitors (contact the tourist office for more info).

GREYABBEY

A few miles down from Mount Stewart through the tiny town of **Greyabbey** lies its famous ruined Cistercian abbey. Founded in AD 1193 by Affreca, wife of Norman conqueror John de Courcey, who also built Inchabbey near Downpatrick, the abbey was the first fully Gothic building in Ireland. The abbey is located a few blocks from the town's crossroads at the bend in the road on Church St. The beautiful ruins have an adjoining cemetery and a medieval 🌿**Physic Garden,** where healing plants were cultivated to cure such common monastic ailments as flatulence, melancholy, and lunacy. Visitors can touch and taste the plants, and often take some home as well. A medieval vegetable garden grows "elephant garlic," kale, and white carrots, which seasoned monks' meals before their orange counterparts came into existence in 1500. (#10 bus from Belfast's Oxford St. Bus Station to Portaferry goes via Greyabbey. ☎9054 4278. Open Apr.-Oct. M-Sa 9am-6pm, Su 1-6pm; Oct.-Mar. for groups by appointment. Free.) Abandon the ascetic life and have a pint or generous meal in the yellow **Wildflower Inn ❷**, 1-3 Main St. (☎4278 8260. Entrees £8-9; M-F and Su 5-7pm, Sa noon-7pm 2 for £10. 4-course Su lunch 12:30-8pm £10. Kitchen open M-Th 12:30am-3pm and 5-8:30pm, F noon-3pm and 5-9pm, Sa noon-9pm, Su noon-8pm.) Across the street, **Pebbles Coffee Shop ❶**, 12 Main St., has coffee, baked goods, sandwiches, and an adjoining craft shop. (☎4278 8031. Meals around £6. Open Tu-F 10am-5pm, Sa 9am-5pm, Su 2-5pm. MC/V.)

PORTAFERRY (PORT AN PHEIRE)

Portaferry lies on the southern tip of the Ards Peninsula and peers at Strangford town across the waters of Strangford Lough. Tourists stop in this seaside town to relax, explore the southern Ards, and enjoy Northern Ireland's largest aquarium.

TRANSPORTATION. To reach Strangford Lough from the bus stop, follow **Ferry Street** or **Castle Street** downhill for about 100m. **Ulsterbuses** from Belfast drop off visitors at **the Square** in the center of town. (1½hr.; M-F 15 per day, Sa 10 per day, Su 5 per day; £5.) **Ferries** leave Portaferry's waterfront at 15 and 45min. past the hour for a 10min. chug to Strangford, returning every 30min. (☎4488 1637. M-F 7:45am-10:45pm, Sa 8:15am-11:15pm, Su 9:45am-10:45pm. £1.10, children 50p, seniors free; return £2/1/8.50. Car and driver £5.30.)

ORIENTATION AND PRACTICAL INFORMATION. To reach the **tourist office** from the bus stop, take **Castle Street** downhill. The tourist office is on the corner of Castle St. and **the Strand,** the shoreline's official name, in front of **Portaferry Castle.** Beyond the usual brochures, accommodations bookings (£2 plus 10% deposit), and a **bureau de change,** it also has a 12min. video on the medieval "tower houses" of Co. Down, precursors of the grand estates. (☎4272 9882. Open July-Aug. M-Sa 10am-5:30pm, Su 1-6pm; Easter-June and Sept. M-Sa 10am-5pm, Su 2-6pm.) Get **Internet** access at the **library,** 45 High St., at the end of the block on the right. (☎4272 8194. £1.50 per 30min. Open M and W 2-8pm, F 10am-1pm and 2-5pm, Sa 10am-1pm.) **Portaferry Pharmacy,** 39 High St. (☎4272 8226), is on the north side of town. (Open M and F 9am-6pm, Tu, Th, Sa 9am-5:30pm, W 9am-5:45pm; closed 1-2pm.) Near the bus station is **Northern Bank** and its 24hr. **ATM,** 1 The Square (☎4272 8208; open M 10am-5pm, Tu-W and F 10am-3:30pm, Th 9:30am-3:30pm; closed daily 12:30-1:30pm), and the **post office,** 28 The Square (☎4272 8201; open M-W and F 9am-1pm and 2-5:30pm, Th 9am-1pm, Sa 9am-12:30pm). **Postal Code:** BT22.

ACCOMMODATIONS. A peaceful stay awaits residents of the **Portaferry Barholm Youth Hostel ❷**, 11 the Strand, across from the ferry dock. Offering both hotel- and hostel-style accommodations, Barholm is a cut above standard hostels and is ideally located right on Strangford Lough, with a conservatory dining room and excellent views. (☎4272 9598. Weekend reservations are necessary. Wheelchair-accessible. Weekend tea room open daily noon-5pm; sandwiches £2.20. For groups: breakfast, lunch, and 3-course dinner £16 per day. Laundry £3. Dorms £13; singles £15; ensuite doubles from £35.) The digs at **Fiddler's Green B&B ❸**, located above the pub on Church St., are unbeatable. Hardwood floors, private baths, and airy rooms with matching bedsheets and curtains add a touch of class. Call ahead as it fills up on weekends. (☎4272 8393, bookings ☎078 1603 0058; info@fiddlersgreenportaferry.com. Free Wi-Fi. Singles £22-35.)

NORTHERN IRELAND

◪◩ FOOD AND PUBS. Numerous fresh fruit and veggie **markets** and convenience stores are scattered around High St. and The Square. For opening hours, you can't beat Spar, 16 The Square. (☎4272 8957. Open daily 6:30am-9pm.) Every Saturday from Easter through September, Market House in The Square welcomes a **country market** (9:30am-noon). For a quick and greasy bite, **Ferry Grill ❶**, 3 High St. across from Spar, stays open late on weekends and serves burgers and fries or fish and chips. (☎4272 8568. Food under £3. Open M-Th noon-2pm and 4:30-8pm, F noon-9:30pm, Sa noon-2pm and 4:30-9:30pm, Su 4:30-9pm.) **White Satin ❷**, 2-8 Castle St., before Exploris and Portaferry Castle, serves Chinese food. Try the two-course weekend lunch deal (F-Su noon-5pm; £6.50). Entrees include a wide selection of duck and squid dishes. (☎4272 9000. Most entrees £7-9. Open M-Th 5-11pm, F-Su noon-11pm.) **Deli-licious ❶**, 1a Castle St. (☎4272 9911), has a warm interior despite the copious amounts of ice cream (from £3). It rounds out the menu with its hot breakfasts for £3 and lunches for £3-5. (Open daily 9am-3pm; July-Aug. open until 5pm; open 8am-8pm during Gala Week.) At night, everyone stumbles to ◪**Fiddler's Green**, 10-14 Church St., where publican Frank and his sons lead rowdy sing-alongs on weekends. As the wall proclaims: "There are no strangers here. Just friends who have not yet met." (☎4272 8393. F-Su live folk, trad, rock, or pop. Open daily 11:30pm-1:30am.) Across the street, locals gather for booze and billiards at **The Milestone**, 1-3 Church St. (☎4272 9629. £5 deposit for billiards. Open daily 11:30am-12:30am.) **M.E. Dumigan's**, 9-11 Ferry St., is up from the waterfront. This pub is so small, you'll have no choice but to rub shoulders with the local crowd. (Open M-Sa 11:30am-11pm, Su 12:30-10pm.)

◪ SIGHTS. Portaferry's pride and joy is ◪**Exploris,** Northern Ireland's only public aquarium and one of the UK's best. Near the pier, beneath the crumbling **Portaferry Castle,** Exploris holds first-rate exhibits on local marine ecology. The journey begins in the shallow waters of Strangford Lough, proceeds through the Narrows, and ends in the depths of the Irish Sea, where one of Europe's largest tanks houses sharks and other large fish. Touch-tanks and interactive displays keep kids educated and engaged. The aquarium is renowned for its **seal sanctuary,** which focuses its efforts on the rehabilitation of injured or orphaned seals along the coastline. Very young injured seals are kept in pens where they are carefully monitored. As they heal they are free to play in the open-air sanctuary before being released back into the wild. October through December is the best time for seal sightings; check out Ballyquinton Point and Cloughy Rocks or ask at the aquarium for the best spots. (☎4272 8062; www.exploris.org.uk. Open Apr.-Aug. M-F 10am-6pm, Sa 11am-6pm, Su noon-6pm; Sept.-Mar. open until 5pm. £7; children, students and seniors £4, families £20, under 4 free.) July brings the massive **Gala Week** of boat races, crowds, performers, drink, and general revelry (www.portaferrygala.com). A lineup of events is available from the tourist office; alternatively, contact Caroline Mageean ☎077 4216 7917.

DUBLIN
(BAILE ÁTHA CLIATH)

Not as cosmopolitan or as large, but just as eclectic as New York or London, Dublin cultivates a culture so magnetic that weekending suburbanites and international hipsters flock to its hotel mattresses. The capital on the rise supports innovative theatrical and musical enclaves but never forgets its artists of the past—nearly every street boasts a literary landmark, statue, birthplace, or favorite pub. Watering holes remain centers of neighborhood communities. Gangs of tourists have danced their way into Temple Bar, but the nightlife hub remains as lively as ever. New late-night hotspots glimmer farther south along Great Georges St., while the area around Grafton St. continues to flourish under an oligarchy of designer fashion. Despite murmurs that the capital has contracted big-city crime and poverty, its cultural and pub-happy attractions retain Irish charm. At the same time, Dublin exudes an air of urban sophistication, making it a deservedly popular destination just a stone's throw from the UK.

IRELAND	❶	❷	❸	❹	❺
ACCOMMODATIONS	under €20	€21-30	€36-45	€46-60	over €60
FOOD	under €10	€11-20	€21-30	€31-40	over €40

PHONE CODES	Country code: 353. **Dublin City Code**: 01. From outside Ireland, dial int'l prefix + 353 + city code (drop the 1st zero); Dublin's code would be 1 + local number. If calling within Dublin, dial 01 + local number.

✈ INTERCITY TRANSPORTATION

Flights: Dublin Airport (DUB; ☎814 1111; www.dublinairport.com). Dublin **buses** #41, 41B, and 41C run from the airport to Eden Quay in the city center (40-45min., every 10min., €1.75). **Airlink shuttle** (☎703 3092) runs nonstop to Busáras Central Bus Station and O'Connell St. (20-25min., every 10-20min. 5:45am-11:30pm, €6), and to Heuston Station (50min., €6). A **taxi** to the city center costs roughly €20-25.

Trains: The **Irish Rail Travel Centre**, 35 Lower Abbey St. (info ☎836 6222; www.irishrail.ie), sells train tickets. Open M-F 9am-5pm.

Connolly Station, Amiens St. (☎703 2358), north of the Liffey and close to Busáras. Bus #20b heads south of the river and #130 goes to the city center, while the DART runs to Tara Station on the south quay. Trains to: **Belfast** (2hr.; M-Sa 8 per day, Su 5 per day; €50), **Sligo** (3hr., 3-4 per day, €34), and **Wexford** and **Rosslare** (3hr., 2 per day, €25).

Heuston Station (☎703 3299), south of Victoria Quay and west of the city center (a 25min. walk from Trinity College). Buses #78 and 79 run to the city center. Trains to: **Cork** (3hr., 6 per day, €67); **Galway** (2¾hr., 7 per day, €42); **Limerick** (2½hr., 9 per day, €55); **Waterford** (2½hr., 4-5 per day, €30).

Pearse Station, Pearse St. (☎828 6000). Ticketing open M-Sa 7:30am-11:50pm, Su 9am-9:50pm. Receives southbound trains from Connolly Station.

Buses: Intercity buses to Dublin arrive at **Busáras Central Bus Station,** Store St. (☎836 6111), next to Connolly Station. Info available at the **Dublin Bus Office,** 59 Upper

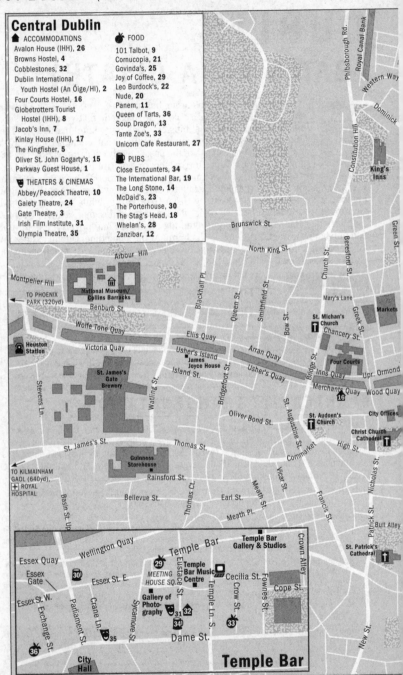

Central Dublin

🏠 ACCOMMODATIONS
Avalon House (IHH), **26**
Browns Hostel, **4**
Cobblestones, **32**
Dublin International
  Youth Hostel (An Óige/HI), **2**
Four Courts Hostel, **16**
Globetrotters Tourist
  Hostel (IHH), **8**
Jacob's Inn, **7**
Kinlay House (IHH), **17**
The Kingfisher, **5**
Oliver St. John Gogarty's, **15**
Parkway Guest House, **1**

🎭 THEATERS & CINEMAS
Abbey/Peacock Theatre, **10**
Gaiety Theatre, **24**
Gate Theatre, **3**
Irish Film Institute, **31**
Olympia Theatre, **35**

🍴 FOOD
101 Talbot, **9**
Cornucopia, **21**
Govinda's, **25**
Joy of Coffee, **29**
Leo Burdock's, **22**
Nude, **20**
Panem, **11**
Queen of Tarts, **36**
Soup Dragon, **13**
Tante Zoe's, **33**
Unicorn Cafe Restaurant, **27**

🍺 PUBS
Close Encounters, **34**
The International Bar, **19**
The Long Stone, **14**
McDaid's, **23**
The Porterhouse, **30**
The Stag's Head, **18**
Whelan's, **28**
Zanzibar, **12**

DUBLIN

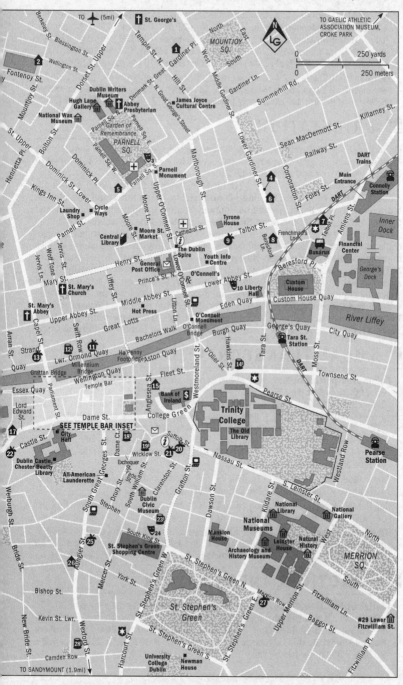

O'Connell St. (☎873 4222; www.dublinbus.ie). Buses to: **Belfast** (3hr., 6-7 per day, €20); **Derry/Londonderry** (4¼hr., 4-5 per day, €27.50); **Donegal** (4¼hr., 4-5 per day, €12.50); **Galway** (3½hr., 15 per day, €8.50); **Limerick** (3½hr., 13 per day, €20.50); **Rosslare** (3hr., 13 per day, €20.50); **Sligo** (4hr., 4-6 per day, €26.50); **Tralee** (6hr., 6 per day, €33.60); **Wexford** (2¾hr.; M-Sa 13 per day, Su 10 per day; €11.50).

Ferries: Irish Ferries, 2-4 Merrion Row, off St. Stephen's Green. (☎661 0511; www.irishferries.com.) Open M-F 9am-5pm, Sa 9am-1pm. **Stena Line** ferries arrive from Holyhead at the **Dún Laoghaire** ferry terminal (☎204 7777; www.stenaline.com).

⚓ ORIENTATION

Dublin is compact. Street names are posted high up on the sides of buildings at most intersections, never on street-level signs. The essential *Dublin Visitor Map* is available for free at the Dublin Bus Office.

The **Liffey River** forms a natural boundary between Dublin's North and South Sides. Heuston Station and the more famous sights, posh stores, and upscale restaurants are on the **South Side,** while Connolly Station, the majority of hostels, and the bus station are on the **North Side.** The North Side is less expensive than the more touristed South Side, but it also has a reputation for being rougher, especially after dark. The streets running alongside the Liffey are called **quays** (KEYS); the name of the quay changes with each bridge. **O'Connell Street,** three blocks west of the Busáras Central Bus Station, is the primary link between northern and southern Dublin. On the North Side, **Henry** and **Mary Streets** constitute a pedestrian shopping zone, intersecting with O'Connell St. two blocks from the Liffey at the **General Post Office.** On the South Side, a block from the river, **Fleet Street** becomes **Temple Bar,** an area full of music centers and galleries. **Dame Street** runs parallel to Temple Bar and leads east to **Trinity College,** the center of Dublin's cultural activity.

▣ LOCAL TRANSPORTATION

Public Transportation: Info on local bus service available at **Dublin Bus Office,** 59 Upper O'Connell St. (☎873 4222; www.dublinbus.ie). Open M 8:30am-5:30pm, Tu-F 9am-5:30pm, Sa 9am-2pm, Su 9:30am-2pm. **Rambler** passes offer unlimited rides for a day (€6) or a week (€21). Dublin Bus runs the **NiteLink** service to the suburbs (M-Th 12:30 and 2am, F-Sa every 20min. 12:30-4:30am; €4-6; passes not valid). The **Luas** (☎461 4910 or Customer Care Freefone 1800 300 604; www.luas.ie; free phone line open M-F 7am-7pm, Sa 10am-2pm), Dublin's Light Rail Transit System, is the city's newest form of mass transit.

Taxis: Blue Cabs (☎802 2222), **ABC** (☎285 5444), and **City Metro Cabs** (☎872 7272) have wheelchair-accessible cabs (call ahead). Available 24hr.

Car Rental: Alamo, Dublin Airport (☎844 4162; www.alamo.com). Economy €47 per day, €160-200 per wk. Ages 24-74.

Bike Rental: Cycle Ways, 185-6 Parnell St. (☎873 4748). Rents quality hybrid or mountain bikes. €20 per day, €80 per wk. with €200 deposit. Open M-W and F-Sa 9:30am-6pm, Th 9:30am-8pm, Su 11am-5pm.

▣ PRACTICAL INFORMATION

Tourist Office: Main Office, Suffolk St. (☎6697 92083; international ☎0800 039 7000; www.visitdublin.com). Near Trinity College in a converted church. Open M-Sa 9am-5:30pm, Su 10:30am-3pm; July-Aug. hours extended M-Sa 9am-7pm. **Northern Ireland Tourist Board,** 16 Nassau St. (☎679 1977 or 1850 230 230). Open M-F 9:15am-5:30pm, Sa 10am-5pm.

Banks: Bank of Ireland, AIB, and **TSB** branches with **bureaux de change** and 24hr. **ATMs** cluster on Lower O'Connell St., Grafton St., and near Suffolk and Dame St. Bureaux de change also in the General Post Office and in the tourist office main branch, and scattered about the city. Most banks open M-W and F 10am-4pm, Th 10am-5pm.

Luggage Storage: Connolly Station. Small lockers €4, large lockers €6. Open daily 7am-10pm. **Busáras.** Lockers €5/7/10. Open 24hr.

Laundry: All-American Launderette, 40 South Great Georges St. (☎677 2779). Self-service €6.50; full-service €9.50. Open M-Sa 8:30am-7pm, Su 10am-6pm.

Police *(Garda):* Dublin Metro Headquarters, Harcourt Terr. (☎666 9500); Store St. Station (☎666 8000); Fitzgibbon St. Station (☎666 8400); Pearse St. Station (☎666 9000). **Police Confidential Report Line:** ☎800 666 111.

Pharmacy: O'Connell's, 56 Lower O'Connell St. (☎873 0427). Convenient to city bus routes. Open M-F 7:30am-10pm, Sa 8am-10pm, Su 10am-10pm. Other branches scattered about the city, including locations on Grafton St. and Westmoreland St.

Hospital: St. James's Hospital, James St. (☎410 3000). Bus #123. **Mater Misericordiae Hospital,** Eccles St. (☎803 2000). Buses #3, 10, 11, 16, 22. **Beaumont Hospital,** Beaumont Rd. (☎809 3000). Buses #103, 104, 27b, 42a, 51a.

Internet Access: The Internet Exchange, with branches at Cecilia St. (☎670 3000) and Fownes St. in Temple Bar (☎635 1680). €3 per hr. Cecilia location open M-F 8am-2am, Sa-Su 10am-2am; Fownes open M-Th and Su 9am-12:30am, F-Sa 10am-1am.

Post Office: General Post Office (GPO), O'Connell St. (☎705 7000). *Poste Restante* pickup at the **Poste Restante** window (see **Mail,** p. 44). Open M-Sa 8am-8pm. Smaller post offices, including one on Suffolk St. across from the tourist office, are typically open M-Tu and Th-F 9am-6pm, W 9:30am-6pm.

Post Code: Dublin is the only place in the Republic that uses post codes. The city is organized into regions numbered 1-18, 20, 22, and 24; even-numbered codes are for areas south of the Liffey, while odd-numbered ones are for the north. The numbers radiate out from the city center: North City Centre is 1, South City Centre is 2.

⌂ ACCOMMODATIONS

Because Dublin is an incredibly popular destination, it is necessary to book accommodations at least one week in advance, particularly around Easter weekend, bank holiday weekends, sporting weekends, St. Patrick's Day, New Year's, and June through August. The tourist office books local accommodations for a fee of €4, but they only deal in Fáilte Ireland-approved B&Bs and hostels. Approved accommodations aren't necessarily better than unapproved ones, although they tend to be a bit cleaner. Phoenix Park may tempt the desperate, but camping there is a terrible idea, not to mention illegal—if the *Garda* or park rangers don't deter you, the threat of thieves should. If the following accommodations are full, consult Dublin Tourism's annual *Sleep! Guide* (€2.50), or ask hostel staff for referrals.

HOSTELS

▨ **Four Courts Hostel,** 15-17 Merchants Quay (☎672 5862). On the south bank of the river. Bus #748 from the airport stops next door. 250-bed hostel with pristine, well-lit rooms and hardwood floors. Quiet lounge and a combination TV/game room provide plenty of space to wind down. Continental breakfast included. In-room lockers. Laundry €7. 8- to 16-bed dorms €15-20; 4- to 6-bed €24-27; doubles €62-70; triples €90. ❶

▨ **Globetrotters Tourist Hostel (IHH),** 46-7 Lower Gardiner St. (☎878 8808; www.globe-trottersdublin.com or www.townhouseofdublin.com). Trendy pop art, tropical fish, a lush courtyard, and all-you-can-eat Irish breakfast make this Georgian mansion more like a posh B&B than a hostel. Private rooms with TV in adjacent **townhouse.** Free Internet access. Free luggage storage. Towels €1 with €6 deposit. Dorms €24-29; singles €70; triples €132; quads €140. ❷

■ **Abbey Court Hostel,** 29 Bachelor's Walk (☎878 0700; www.abbey-court.com). Corner of O'Connell St. and Bachelor's Walk near bridge. Hostel boasts clean, narrow rooms overlooking the Liffey. Hidden apartments each have lounge, TV, and lush courtyard. Internet access €1 per 15min., €2 per 40min. Continental breakfast at NYStyle cafe next door included. Free luggage storage; security box €1. Full-service laundry €8. 12-bed dorms €19-22; 6-bed €24-27; 4-bed €27-30; doubles €78-88. Long-term rate €119 per week includes breakfast. Apartments from €30 per person per night. ❷

Barnacles Temple Bar House, 19 Temple Ln. (☎671 6277). Patrons can nearly jump into bed from Temple Bar pubs, including the actual Temple Bar, next door. Spacious, sky-lit lounge with open fire and TV, and a colorfully tiled kitchen. All rooms ensuite. Continental breakfast included. Free luggage storage. Laundry €6.50, dry only €3.50. Internet access €1 per 15min. 11-bed dorms €15.50-18.50; 6-bed €21-25.50; quads €25.50-28.50; doubles €68-82. ❶

Dublin International Youth Hostel (An Óige/HI), 61 Mountjoy St. (☎830 4555; www.irelandyha.org). Huge, rambling hostel housed in a converted convent and 18th-century school. Complimentary breakfast served in the former chapel. Wheelchair-accessible. Bureau de change. In-room storage; luggage storage at reception €1.25 per day. Towels €1. Laundry €5. Internet access €1 for 15min., €2 for 40min. HI €2 discount per person per night. Dorms €19-22; doubles €48-52; triples €72-78; quads €86-100. Ask at the desk about **work opportunities.** ❷

Browns Hostel, 89-90 Lower Gardiner St. (☎855 0034; www.brownshostelireland.com). Long-term residents cook and play pool in the cavernous wine cellar turned kitchen and lounge. Closet and A/C in every room, TV in most. Locker-room-like showers in the basement. Skylights in the Shannon room. Breakfast included. Next-door cafe (same owners) serves €5 pizza to hostelers. Internet €5 per hr. Lockers €1. Blankets €2. Towels €1-1.50. 20-bed dorms €15; 10- to 14-bed €20; 4- to 6-bed €25. €100 per week. ❶

Kinlay House (IHH), 2-12 Lord Edward St. (☎679 6644). Great location a few blocks from Temple Bar. If you don't a get a room with a view of the Christ Church Cathedral, at least you can watch the plasma TV. Free Internet access. Continental breakfast included. Lockers €1 with €5 deposit. Laundry €8. 16- to 24-bed dorms €17-20; 4- to 6-bed €24-29; singles €44-56; doubles €29-33; triples €27-33. ❶

Avalon House (IHH), 55 Aungier St. (☎475 0001; www.avalon-house.ie). Performers get free accommodation if they spend 1hr. teaching other guests. Foosball, ping-pong, air hockey, and video games also save hostelers from boredom and emptying their wallets in the city. Wheelchair-accessible with elevator. Free Internet access. Light continental breakfast included. Lockers and smaller lockboxes €1 each. Laundry €5. Large dorms €14-20; 4- to 6-bed dorms €24-27; singles €30-39; doubles €66-74. ❶

Cobblestones, 29 Eustace St. (☎677 8154 or 677 5422), in the middle of Temple Bar. Snug rooms with large windows, nice showers, and a fantastic location. Book before Feb. and watch the St. Patrick's Day parade from the patio roof. Continental breakfast included. Free Wi-Fi. Dorms €19-22; doubles €55-60. Discounts available mid-week, for stays 1 week or longer, and for groups. ❶

BED AND BREAKFASTS

B&Bs with a green shamrock sign out front are registered and approved by Bord Fáilte. On the North Side, B&Bs cluster along Upper and Lower Gardiner St., on Sheriff St., and near Parnell Sq. All prices include a full Irish breakfast.

▣ **Parkway Guest House,** 5 Gardiner Pl. (☎874 0469; www.parkway-guesthouse.com). Sports fans bond with the proprietor, a former hurling star, while those less athletically inclined still appreciate his great eye for interior design, great advice, and all-star breakfasts. Singles €40; doubles €60-70, €65-80 with bath.❸

Charles Stewart B&B, 5-6 Parnell Sq. E. (☎878 0350; www.charlesstewart.com). Birthplace of the infamous author Oliver St. John Gogarty, this home has a great location in the oasis of Parnell Sq. Its proximity to the Dublin Writer's Museum adds to the literary feel. Irish breakfast included. Singles €57-63; doubles €69-99; triples €120. ❹

The Kingfisher, 166 Parnell St. (☎872 8732; www.kingfisherdublin.com). Inn, restaurant, and cafe in one. Bathrooms clean enough to sleep in, but the rooms are more comfortable. Irish breakfast included. Restaurant offers cheap takeaway. Free Wi-Fi in cafe. TV/VCR in each room; kitchenettes in some. €35-45 per person; with 4-course dinner from €65 per person. Discounts for stays longer than 5 days. ❸

Marian B&B, 21 Upper Gardiner St. (☎874 4129; marianbb@gofree.indigo.ie). Fine rooms near Mountjoy St. Irish breakfast included. Singles €40; doubles €70. ❸

Oliver St. John Gogarty's Temple Bar B&B, 18-21 Anglesea St. (☎671 1822; www.gogartys.ie). Bright, clean dorms in an old, well-maintained building above a popular pub of the same name. Great location for Temple Bar enthusiasts. Elevator access. Laundry €5. 8- to 10-bed dorms €18-25; 4 to 6-bed €20-35; doubles €30-45. Self-catering quad €200-250; 6-person €210-300. ❶

CAMPING

Most official campsites are far away from the city center. Camping in **Phoenix Park** is both illegal and unsafe.

North Beach Caravan and Camping Park (☎843 7131; www.northbeach.ie), in Rush. Accessible by bus #33 from Lower Abbey St. (45min., 25 per day) and suburban rail. Quiet, beachside location outside the urban jumble. Kitchen for washing dishes. Showers €2. Electricity €3. Open Apr.-Sept. €9 per adult, €5 per child. ❶

Camac Valley Tourist Caravan and Camping Park, Naas Rd. (☎464 0644; www.camacvalley.com), in Clondalkin near Corkagh Park. Take bus #69 (45min. from city center) and ask to be let off at Camac. Wheelchair-accessible. Showers €1. Laundry €4.50. €9-10 per person; €22 per 2 people with car; €24 per caravan. ❶

◖ FOOD

Dublin's many **open-air markets** sell fresh food at relatively cheap prices. Vendors deal in fruit, fresh strawberries, flowers, and fish from their pushcarts. The later in the week, the livelier the market. Bustling Moore St. Market, between Henry St. and Parnell St., is a great place to get fresh veggies. (Open M-Sa 10am-5pm.) The Thomas Street Market, along the continuation of Dame St., is a calmer alternative. (Generally open Th-Sa 11am-5pm, although some stalls are open during the week; drop by to check.) Produce can be found every day along **Wexford Sreet.** The best value for **supermarkets** around Dublin is in the Dunnes Stores chain, with full branches at St. Stephen's Green (☎478 0188; open M and F 8:30am-8pm, Tu-W and Sa 8:30am-7pm, Th 8:30am-9pm, Su 10am-7pm), the ILAC Centre off Henry St., and N. Earl St. off O'Connell; a small convenience version is on Georges St.

▣ **Queen of Tarts,** Dame St. (☎670 7499), across from City Hall. Pastries, light meals, and coffee. Scones (raspberry, raisin, chocolate, or plain), flaky and baked to perfection; €3. Breakfast €3-8. Sandwiches €7. Open M-F 7:30am-7pm, Sa-Su 9am-7pm. ❶

Market Bar, Fade St. (☎613 9094; www.tapas.ie). Right off S. Great Georges after Lower Stephen St. Huge sausage factory given a classy makeover; now serves tapas in heaping portions. Small tapas €7.50; large tapas €11. Kitchen open M-W noon-9:30pm, Th noon-10pm, F-Sa noon-10:30pm, Su 3-9:30pm. ❶

Unicorn Café Restaurant, 12B Merrion Ct. (☎676 2182; www.unicornrestaurant.com). Left off Merrion Row, behind Unicorn Food Store and Café. Legendary Italian restaurant serves classic dishes with panache. Lunch €16-30; dinner €19-32. Open M-Th 12:30-3:30pm and 6-11pm, F-Sa 12:30-3:30pm and 6-11:30pm. **Unicorn Food Store and Café ❷,** Merrion Row (☎678 8588), offers food from the same kitchen, at a fraction of the price, for sit-down or takeaway. St. Stephen's Green, down the block, is perfect for a picnic. Panini €7.50; pasta €7.50-9. Open daily 8am-7pm. ❸

Cornucopia, 19 Wicklow St. (☎677 7583). If there's space, sit down in this cozy spot for a delicious meal (€11-12) or a cheaper salad smorgasbord (€3-8 for choice of 2, 4, or 6 salads). Open M-W and F-Sa 8:30am-8pm, Th 8:30am-9pm, Su noon-7pm. ❷

101 Talbot, 101 Talbot St. (☎874 5011), between Marlborough and Gardiner St., 1 flight up through the red doors. Excellent Mediterranean food catered to Abbey Theatre-goers. Large windows look onto Talbot St. Menu changes frequently. Book ahead. Entrees €14-20. Early-bird 5-8pm €21. Open Tu-Sa 5-11pm. ❷

Tante Zoe's, 1 Crow St. (☎679 4407), across from the back entrance of the Foggy Dew pub. Cajun-Creole food in a casual setting. Mellow instrumental music may whisper "elevator," but the food shouts "delicious." Gumbos €7; entrees €18-28. 2-course lunch €15. Open M-Sa noon-4pm and 5:30pm-midnight, Su 1-10pm. ❸

The Mermaid Cafe, 69-70 Dame St. (☎670 8236; www.mermaid.ie), near S. Great Georges St. Chunky wooden tables and beads hanging in the door frame. Unusual entrees like aubergine Schnitzel (€23-28). Outstanding Su brunch. Menu changes frequently. Open M-Sa 12:30-2:30pm and 6-11pm, Su 12:30-3:30pm and 6-9pm. ❸

Leo Burdock's, 2 Werburgh St. (☎454 0306), behind The Lord Edward Pub across from Christ Church Cathedral. Additional location on Lower Liffey St. Fish and chips served the right way, in brown paper. A nightly pilgrimage for many Dubliners. Takeaway only. Fish €4-6.75; chips €2.65. Open daily noon-midnight. ❶

Fagan's, Lower Drumcondra Rd. (☎836 9491), just before Botanic Ave. Relaxed atmosphere in attractive indoor and outdoor setting combines with gorgeous food to produce a friendly pub. Worthy of a trek from the city and a must-stop for anyone staying in the north. Carvery €11; entrees €10-15. Kitchen open daily 12:30-3pm and 4-9pm. ❷

◎ SIGHTS

TRINITY COLLEGE. Behind ancient walls sprawls Trinity's expanse of stone buildings, cobblestone walks, and grassy-green grounds. The British built Trinity in 1592 as a Protestant seminary that would "civilize the Irish and cure them of Popery." The college became part of the path on which members of the Anglo-Irish elite trod on their way to high positions and has educated such luminaries as Jonathan Swift, Robert Emmett, Thomas Moore, Oscar Wilde, and Samuel Beckett. The Catholic Jacobites who briefly held Dublin in 1689 used the campus as a barracks and a prison. Bullet holes from the 1916 Easter Rebellion still mar the stone entrance. The Catholic Church deemed it a cardinal sin to attend Trinity until the 1960s; when the Church lifted the ban, the size of the student body tripled. Today, it's a celebrated center of learning, located steps away from the teeming center of a cosmopolitan capital, and an unmissable stop on the tourist trail. *(Between Westmoreland and Grafton St., South Dublin. Main entrance fronts the traffic circle now called College Green. Pearse St. runs along the north edge of the college, Nassau St. the south. ☎608 1724; www.tcd.ie. Grounds always open. Free.)*

DISTANCE: 3.5km
DURATION: 8hr.
WHEN TO GO: Begin at 8am.

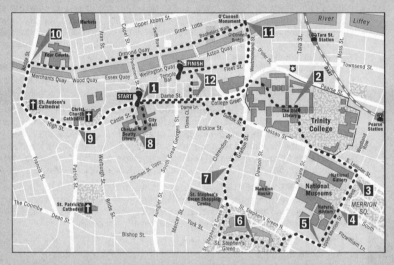

DUBLIN WALKING TOUR

1. QUEEN OF TARTS CAFE. Begin the day with a delicious scone (p. 709).

2. TRINITY COLLEGE. The Old Library, one of the many stately edifices of Dublin's most famous university, holds the **Book of Kells** (p. 710).

3. NATIONAL GALLERY. This gallery has a major collection of international works, from paintings by Picasso and Goya to a wing dedicated to the Yeats family (p. 712).

4. NATURAL HISTORY MUSEUM. A marvel of taxidermy and preservation; everything from beetles to bears are jam-packed into three floors of flora and fauna (p. 712).

5. UNICORN FOOD STORE. This Italian bistro is a great place to grab some lunch. Bring some pasta or a sandwich with you to St. Stephen's Green (p. 710).

6. ST. STEPHEN'S GREEN. Linger over a picnic and enjoy the streams, trees, and flowers in Dublin's answer to Central Park (p. 715).

7. GRAFTON STREET. Try to catch some of the street performers or window-shop on Dublin's trendiest shopping avenue (p. 703).

8. CHESTER BEATTY LIBRARY. Walk through the grounds of Dublin Castle to reach this library of treasures, and gawk over the ancient illuminated texts (p. 712).

9. CHRIST CHURCH CATHEDRAL. Dublin's oldest structure is also supposedly the burial place of Strongbow (p. 713).

10. O'CONNELL STREET. Stop briefly to admire the O'Connell Monument (p. 714).

11. PUB STOP. Because no day in Dublin is complete without a pint, seek out Temple Bar Pub's daily trad session at 4:50pm (p. 716). Alternatively, drink with the locals at The Stag's Head, Dame St. (p. 716).

THE NATIONAL GALLERY. This collection of over 2500 canvases, only 800 of which are on display, contains a comprehensive mix of internationally and locally renowned artists. Paintings by Brueghel, Goya, Carravaggio, Vermeer, and Rembrandt can be seen in the European exhibits, while a major part of the collection is dedicated to the Irish tradition. The works of **Jack Yeats,** brother of poet W.B., and Ireland's most celebrated artist of the 20th century, are of particular interest. Portraits of Lady Gregory, James Joyce, and George Bernard Shaw complete the display. The new **Millennium Wing** houses a 20th-Century Irish Art exhibit, a Yeats archive which celebrates the combined talents of father John B. and his four children, and computer stations that give "virtual tours" of the museum. Summertime brings concerts, lectures, and art classes; inquire at the front desk for schedules. *(Merrion Sq. W. ☎ 661 5133; www.nationalgallery.ie. Open M-W and F-Sa 9:30am-5:30pm, Th 9:30am-8:30pm, Su noon-5:30pm. Free guided tours Sa 3pm, Su 2, 3, 4pm; July also daily 3pm. Admission free. Temporary exhibits €10, students and seniors €6.)*

THE NATIONAL MUSEUM OF ARCHAEOLOGY AND HISTORY. Dublin's largest museum has incredible artifacts spanning the last two millennia. One room gleams with the **Tara Brooch,** the **Ardagh Hoard,** and other Celtic goldwork. Another section is devoted to the Republic's founding years and flaunts the bloody vest of nationalist hero **James Connolly.** *(Kildare St., next to Leinster House. ☎ 677 7444; www.museum.ie. Open Tu-Sa 10am-5pm, Su 2-5pm. Guided tours €2; call for times. Museum free.)*

TEMPLE BAR MUSIC CENTRE. After renovations in 2007, the center promises to bring back its terrific musical events virtually every night of the week. It also houses its own pub and cafe. *(Curved St. ☎ 670 9202; www.tbmc.ie. Music nightly 7:30pm, club 11pm. Cover varies according to act; check with box office for details.)*

■ **CHESTER BEATTY LIBRARY.** Honorary Irish citizen Alfred Chester Beatty was an American mining magnate who amassed a beautiful collection of Asian and Middle Eastern art, sacred scriptures, and illustrated texts. He donated this collection to Ireland upon his death, and a new library behind Dublin Castle houses his abundance of cultural artifacts. It's no wonder that the library won the title of European Museum of the Year in 2002. This collection of truly fascinating objects, from intricate Chinese snuff bottles to some of the earliest fragments of the Biblical Gospels, are arranged on the first floor by region of the world. The second floor contains Beatty's extensive collection of texts from nearly every major world religion. On the roof, a specially designed garden incorporates surfaces of plant life and stones to create a serene space suspended above the urban landscape. *(Behind Dublin Castle. ☎ 407 0750; www.cbl.ie. 45min. tours W 1pm, Su 3 and 4pm. Open May-Sept. M-F 10am-5pm, Sa 11am-5pm, Su 1-5pm; Oct.-Apr. Tu-F 10am-5pm, Sa 11am-5pm, Su 1-5pm. Closed Jan. 1, Good Friday, Dec. 24-26, and M bank holidays. Free.)*

DUBLINIA. This three-story interactive exhibition, which culls its name from one of the ancient Latin terms for the city, is housed on the site of the medieval parish of St. Michael the Archangel. Figures come to life as visitors are ushered through Dublin's medieval history from AD 1170 to 1540. A highlight is the re-creation of a 13th-century Dublin Fair, where you can don period clothes, play games, and catch a glimpse into the archaic world of medieval medicine. *(Across from Christ Church Cathedral. ☎ 679 4611; www.dublinia.ie. Open Apr.-Sept. daily 10am-5pm; Oct.-Mar. M-F 11am-4pm, Sa-Su 10am-4pm. Last admission 45min. before closing. €6.25, students and seniors €5.25, children €3.75. Combined admission with Christ Church Cathedral €9.50.)*

DUBLIN CASTLE. Norman King John built the castle in 1204 on top of the Viking settlement *Dubh Linn* ("black pool"); more recently, a series of structures from the 18th and 19th centuries has covered the site, culminating in an uninspired 20th-century office complex. But for the 700 years after its construction, Dublin Castle was the seat of British rule in Ireland, and its state apartments, which are open to the public for tours, are still used for state functions, and since 1938, every Irish president has been inaugurated here. For the best view of the castle—and a nice picnic—head to the Irish-knot lawn in the back of the complex, next to the Chester Beatty Library. Next door, the intricate inner dome of Dublin City Hall (designed as the Royal Exchange in 1779) shelters statues of national heroes like Daniel O'Connell. *(Dame St., at the intersection of Parliament and Castle St. ☎677 7129; www.dublincastle.ie. State Apartments open M-F 10am-4:45pm, Sa-Su and holidays 2-4:45pm; closed during official functions. €4.50, students and seniors €3.50, children €2. Grounds free.)*

CHRIST CHURCH CATHEDRAL. Built in the name of the universal Church, Irish cathedrals were forced to convert to the Church of Ireland in the 16th century. Sitric Silkenbeard, King of the Dublin Norsemen, built a wooden church on this site around 1038, and the Anglo-Norman Strongbow rebuilt it in stone in 1169. Further additions were made in the following century and again in the 1870s. Stained glass sparkles above the raised crypts, one of which supposedly belongs to Strongbow. In merrier times, the cavernous crypt held shops and drinking houses, but nowadays cobwebs hang from the ceiling, fragments of ancient pillars lie about like bleached bones, and in every corner a looming stone memorial serves as an eerie reminder of the human history captured within its walls. The entrance fee includes admission to the "Treasure of Christ Church," a rotating exhibit that displays the church's hoard of medieval manuscripts, gleaming gold vessels, and funereal busts. *(At the end of Dame St., uphill and across from the Castle. A 10min. walk from O'Connell Bride, or take bus #50 from Eden Quay or 78A from Aston Quay. ☎677 8099. Open daily 9:45am-5pm except during services. €5, students and seniors €2.50.)*

ST. PATRICK'S CATHEDRAL. This church dates back to the 12th century, although Sir Benjamin Guinness remodeled much of the building in 1864. At 100m long, it's Ireland's largest cathedral. Richard Boyle, father of scientist Robert, has a memorial here, and the writer Jonathan Swift spent his last years as Dean of St. Patrick's; his grave is marked on the floor of the south nave. *(From Christ Church, Nicholas St. runs south and downhill, eventually becoming Patrick St. Take bus #49, 49A, 50, 54A, 56A, 65, 65B, 77, or 77A from Eden Quay. ☎475 4817; www.stpatrickscathedral.ie. Open Mar.-Oct. daily 9am-6pm; Nov.-Feb. Sa 9am-5pm, Su 10am-3pm. Church closed to tours Su for 2hr. services beginning at 10:30am and 2:30pm, although visitors are welcome to attend. €5, students and seniors €4.)* **Marsh's Library,** beside the cathedral, is Ireland's oldest public library. A peek inside reveals elegant wire alcoves, a collection of early maps, and exhibits of its holdings. *(☎454 3511. Open M and W-F 10am-1pm and 2-5pm, Sa 10:30am-1pm. €2.50, students and seniors €1.50.)*

GUINNESS STOREHOUSE. The abundance of stout-stamped paper bags hanging from the arms of tourists are a good indication of Ireland's number one tourist attraction. Most can't resist the chance to discover the ins and outs of the famed black magic. Forward-looking Arthur Guinness ensured that his original 1759 brewery would become the success that it is today by signing a 9000-year lease, which is dramatically set into the floor of the massive reception hall. Seven floors of glass and suspended metal catwalks coax you through the production and legacy of Ireland's most famous brew. The self-guided tour ends with a complimentary pint in the top floor's Gravity Bar, a modern, light-filled space that commands a stunning panoramic view of the city. A massive empty pint glass that could hold the equivalent of 14.3 million pints forms the central column of the complex, rising from reception up to the bar's floor. *(St. James's Gate. From Christ Church Cathedral, follow High St. west through its name changes—Cornmarket, Thomas, and James. Or, take bus #51B or 78A from Aston Quay or #123 from O'Connell St. ☎408 4800; www.guinness-storehouse.com. Open daily July-Aug. 9:30am-8pm; Sept.-June 9am-5pm. €14, students over 18 and seniors €9.50, students under 18 €7.50, ages 6-12 €5, under 6 free.)*

KILMAINHAM GAOL. Almost all the rebels who fought in Ireland's struggle for independence between 1792 and 1921 spent time here, and the jail's last occupant was **Éamon de Valera,** the former leader of Éire. Built on raised land outside of the city, its open-barred windows left prisoners exposed to the elements with the belief that the air would dispel disease. The prison's dark history echoes through its frigid, eerie passages. The ghastly, compelling stories of the prisoners are dealt out in two doses, first in the comprehensive museum that sets the gaol in the context of its socio-political history, and then in a 1hr. tour of the dank chambers that ends in the haunting wasteland of an execution yard. *(Inchicore Rd. Take bus #51b, 51c, 78a, or 79 from Aston Quay.* ☎ *453 5984. Open Apr.-Sept. daily 9:30am-5pm; Oct.-Mar. M-F 9:30am-4pm, Su 10am-5pm. Tours every 30min. €5.30, seniors €3.50, students €2.10. Small museum, separate from tour, is free of charge.)*

O'CONNELL STREET. This shopping thoroughfare starts at the Liffey and leads to **Parnell Square.** At 45m, it was once the widest street in Europe. In its pre-Joycean heyday, it was known as Sackville St., but its name was changed in honor of "The Liberator" Joseph Parnell. The central traffic islands contain monuments to Irish leaders such as James Larkin—who organized the heroic Dublin general strike of 1913—O'Connell, and Parnell. **O'Connell's statue** faces the Liffey and O'Connell Bridge; the winged women aren't angels but Winged Victories, although one has a bullet hole from 1916 in a rather inglorious place. **Parnell's statue** points toward nearby Parnell Mooney's pub, while the engraved words at his feet proclaim: "Thus far and no further." In front of the General Post Office stands the recently erected 120m **Dublin Spire.** Originally planned as a Millennium Spire, it wasn't actually completed until early 2003. The spire and the recently planted trees lining the lower part of the street are the first steps to restoring it to its former glory. Visitors won't see is **Nelson's Pillar,** a freestanding column that recalled Trafalgar and stood outside the General Post Office for 150 years; in 1966 the IRA commemorated the 50th anniversary of the Easter Rising by blowing the Admiral out of the water.

THE DUBLIN WRITERS MUSEUM. Sure to delight wordsmiths, this enthralling museum documents Dublin's rich literary heritage and the famous figures who played a part. Manuscripts, rare editions, and memorabilia of giants like Swift, Shaw, Wilde, Yeats, Beckett, Behan, Kavanagh, and O'Casey share space with caricatures and paintings. Don't miss the Gallery of Writers upstairs, an ornate, bust-lined room that harbors one of the most personal items of the collection: James Joyce's piano. Also worth checking out is the one-man performance titled "The Writers Entertain," about some of Ireland's most famous literary figures. *(18 Parnell Sq. N.* ☎ *872 2077; www.visitdublin.com. Open June-Aug. M-F 10am-6pm, Sa 10am-5pm, Su 11am-5pm; Sept.-May M-Sa 10am-5pm, Su 11am-5pm. €6.50, students and seniors €5.50. Combined ticket with the Shaw birthplace €11, students and seniors €9. Performance daily 1:10-2pm; €11-13 includes tour.)* The **Irish Writers Centre,** adjacent to the museum, is the hub of Ireland's living community of writers, providing today's aspiring writers with frequent fiction and poetry readings. It is not a museum, but it does provide information about Dublin's literary happenings. *(19 Parnell Sq. N.* ☎ *872 1302; www.writerscentre.ie. Open M-F 10am-5:30pm.)*

JAMES JOYCE CULTURAL CENTRE. Mock-ups reveal reams of insight into Joyce's life, love, and labor, while intriguing items like the original door to his home at 7 Eccles St., a map tracing Stephen Daedalus's and Leopold Bloom's relative movements, and a 1921 *Ulysses* schema pique literary interest. If in town on June 16th, don't miss the center's Bloomsday festivities, when the halls come alive with reenactments and guided tours. *(35 N. Great Georges St., up Marlborough St. and past Parnell Sq.* ☎ *878 8547; www.jamesjoyce.ie. Open Sept.-June M-Sa 9:30am-5pm, Su 12:30-5pm; July-Aug. M-Sa 9:30am-5pm, Su 11am-5pm. Guided tour daily 2pm; €10, students and seniors €9. Admission to the center €5, students and seniors €4.)*

ST. STEPHEN'S GREEN. This nine-hectare park was a private estate until the Guinness clan bequeathed it to the city. Today, the grounds are teeming with public life. Artificial lakes and hills, carefully manicured gardens, and couples nuzzling in gazebos all make you feel like you've died and gone to Wicklow. After the bustle of Grafton St. and the rowdiness of pub life, St. Stephen's Green is a welcome return to the elements. *(Kildare, Dawson, and Grafton St. all lead to the park.* ☎ *475 7826. Open M-Sa 8am-dusk, Su 10am-dusk.)*

THE CUSTOM HOUSE. Dublin's greatest architectural triumph, the Custom House was designed and built in the 1780s by London-born **James Gandon,** who gave up the chance to be Russia's state architect so that he could settle in Dublin. The Roman and Venetian columns and domes give the cityscape a taste of what the city's 18th-century Anglo-Irish brahmins wanted Dublin to become. There's a small exhibit of the building's design and creation on display inside, but its facade is by far more interesting. Carved heads along the frieze represent the rivers of Ireland; the sole woman is the Liffey. *(East of O'Connell St. at Custom House Quay, where Gardiner St. meets the river.* ☎ *888 2538. Visitors Centre open from mid-Mar. to Nov. M-F 10am-12:30pm, Sa-Su 2-5pm; Nov. to mid-Mar. W-F 10am-12:30pm, Su 2-5pm. €1, students free.)*

ST. MICHAN'S CHURCH. This modest church, dating back to 1095, is noteworthy for its ancient, creepy limestone vaults, which may have inspired Bram Stoker's *Dracula.* Everything in here is real, from the mummified corpses dating back as many as 800 years to the grisly execution order of two 1798 rebels. Touch the hand of the Cavalier, the oldest mummy on display, and you're rumored to be blessed with good luck—not to mention centuries-old dust and a big case of the willies. *(Church St.* ☎ *872 4154. Open Mar. 18-Oct. M-F 10am-12:45pm and 2-4:30pm, Sa 10am-12:45pm; Nov.-Mar. 16 M-F 12:30-3:30pm, Sa 10am-12:45pm. Crypt tours €3.50, students and seniors €3, under 16 €2.50. Church of Ireland services Su 10am.)*

OLD JAMESON DISTILLERY. Learn how science, grain, and tradition come together to form liquid gold—whiskey, that is. The tour walks visitors through the creation of the drink, although the stuff is really distilled in Co. Clare. Not to disappoint those hankering for a taste after all that talking, the tour ends at the bar with a free drink (soft drinks for the uninitiated). Volunteer in the beginning to get the chance to taste-test a tray of six different whiskeys from around the world. *(Bow St. From O'Connell St., turn onto Henry St. and continue straight as the street dwindles to Mary St., then Mary Ln.; the warehouse is on a cobblestone street on the left. Buses #68, 69, and 79 run from city center to Merchant's Quay.* ☎ *807 2355. Tours daily 9:30am-5:30pm, typically every 45min. €9.75, students and seniors €8, children €6.)*

PHOENIX PARK AND DUBLIN ZOO. Europe's largest enclosed public park is most famous for the "Phoenix Park murders" of 1882. The Invincibles, a Republican splinter group, stabbed Lord Cavendish, Chief Secretary of Ireland and his trusty Under Secretary a mere 180m from the **Phoenix Column.** Complications ensued when a Unionist journalist forged a series of letters linking Parnell to the murderers. The column itself, which is capped with a phoenix rising from flames, is something of an inside joke—the park's name actually comes from the Irish *Fionn Uísce,* meaning "clean water." The 714 hectares also harbor the **President's Residence** *(Áras an Uachtarain),* the US Ambassador's residence, cricket pitches, polo grounds, and lots of red deer. To view all the sights without all the hikes, see the friendly owners of **Phoenix Park Bike Hire,** located at the Conyngham Rd. entrance. *(*☎ *086 265 6258. Bikes €5 per hr., €15 per ½-day, €20 per day; tandem €10/ 25/40.)* Even though the park is also home to one of the *Garda*'s largest headquarters, the park is still not safe to travel in at night, especially alone. *(Take bus #10 from O'Connell St. or #25 or 26 from Middle Abbey St. west along the river.)* The most notable attraction within its grounds is **Dublin Zoo,** one of the world's oldest and

Europe's largest. It contains 700 critters and the world's biggest egg. For an urban zoo, the habitats are large and the animals tend to move around—the elephants even swim. (*Bus #10 from O'Connell St.; #25 or 26 from Wellington Quay.* ☎ *474 8900. Open M-Sa 9:30am-6pm, Su 10:30am-6pm. Last admission 5pm. Zoo closes at dusk in winter. €14, students and seniors €11.50, children €9.50.*)

🎵 PUBLIN

James Joyce proposed that a "good puzzle would be to cross Dublin without passing a pub." When a local radio station once offered £100 to the first person to solve the puzzle, the winner explained that any route worked—you'd just have to stop in each one along the way. Dublin's pubs come in all shapes, sizes, and specialties. This is the place to hear trad, Irish rock, and country western in abundance. Ask around or check the publications *In Dublin, Hot Press,* or *Event Guide* for music listings. Normal **pub hours** in Ireland end at 11:30pm Sunday through Wednesday and 12:30am Thursday through Saturday. The laws that dictate these hours are changing—patrons often get about a half-hour after "closing" to finish off their drinks. An increasing number of pubs have **late permits** that allow them to remain open until at least 2am; drink prices tend to rise around midnight to cover the permit's cost (or so they claim). Bars that post their closing time as "late" mean after midnight and, sometimes, after what is legally mandated. **ID-checking** almost always happens at the door rather than at the bar. Note that a growing number of bars are blurring the distinction between pub and club by hosting live music and staying open late into the night on weekdays.

🎵 **The Stag's Head,** 1 Dame Ct. (☎ 679 3701). Atmospheric Victorian pub with stained glass, round marble-topped tables, and evidence of deer decapitation front and center above the bar. Student crowd dons everything from T-shirts to tuxes. Excellent pub grub. Entrees €7.50-11. Kitchen open M-F noon-3:30pm and 5-7pm, Sa noon-2:30pm. Bar open M-Th 10:30am-11:30pm, F-Sa 10:30am-12:30am.

🎵 **The Porterhouse,** 16-18 Parliament St. (☎ 671 5715). Way, way more than 99 bottles of beer on the wall, including 10 self-brewed porters, stouts, and ales. Tough choices, but the Porterhouse Red is a must. 3½ spacious floors fill nightly with great crowd for trad, blues, and rock. Open M-W 11:30am-11:30pm, Th 11:30am-2am, F-Sa 11:30am-2:30am, Su 11:30am-1:30am.

Zanzibar (☎ 878 7212), at the Ha'penny Bridge. Dances between club and pub with explosive results. Unique private rooms on the balcony, one overlooking the Liffey. M-Th and Su €5 mixed drinks before midnight. Tu-Su DJ plays R&B, blues, and chart-toppers. Cover after 11pm F €5, Sa €7. Kitchen open until 10pm. Open M-Th 5pm-2:30am, F 4pm-2:30am, Sa 2pm-2:30am, Su 2pm-1:30am.

Whelan's, 25 Wexford St. (☎ 478 0766; www.whelanslive.com). Pub hosts big-name trad, rock, and everything in between in attached music venue. Live music nightly starting at 8:30pm (doors open at 8pm). Th DJs' Fear and Loathing night. Cover €7-15. Open for lunch (€8-12) 12:30-2pm. Open M-W until 2am and Th-Sa until 3am.

The Long Stone, 10-11 Townsend St. (☎ 671 8102). Multi-level maze of comfortable booths. Frequent live bands. W and Sa 8-10pm live music. Kitchen open M-F 5-8pm, Sa 4-8pm. Open M-Th noon-11:30pm, F-Sa noon-12:30am, Su 4pm-12:30am.

McDaid's, 3 Harry St. (☎ 679 4395), across from Anne St. Once the center of the Irish literary scene in the 50s. Today, the gregarious crowd spills out onto the street in nice weather. Open M-W 10:30am-11:30pm, Th-Sa 10:30am-12:30am, Su 12:30-11pm.

The International Bar, 23 Wicklow St. (☎ 677 9250), on the corner of S. William St. Great place to meet kindred wandering spirits. Downstairs lounge hosts excellent M improv comedy; Tu jazz; W-Su stand-up; Su house music. Arrive early to comedy nights for a seat. W-F cover €10, students €8. Open M-W 10:30am-11:30pm, Th-Sa 10:30am-12:30am, Su 12:30-11pm.

▓ CLUBLIN

As a rule, clubs open at 10 or 10:30pm but don't heat up until the pubs empty around 12:30am. Clubbing is an expensive end to the evening, since covers run €5-20 and pints can surpass €5. To save some money, find a club with an expensive cover but cheap drink prices and stay all night. **Concessions** provide discounts with varying restrictions. The Stag's Head (see **Publin,** p. 716) offers them around 11pm, but any nightclub attached to a pub distributes them in its home bar. A handful of smaller clubs on **Harcourt** and **Camden Streets** are basic but fun. Most clubs close between 1:30 and 3am, but a few have been known to stay open until daybreak. To get home after 11:30pm, when Dublin Bus stops running, take the **NiteLink bus** (M-W 12:30am and 2am, Th-Sa every 20min. from 12:30am to 4:30am; €4), which runs designated routes from the corner of Westmoreland and College St. to Dublin's suburbs. **Taxi** stands are sprinkled throughout the city, the most central being in front of Trinity, at the top of Grafton St. Be prepared to wait 30-45min. on weekend nights. For the most up-to-date information on clubs, check the *Event Guide.*

▓ **The PoD,** 35 Harcourt St. (☎478 0225; www.pod.ie), corner of Hatch St., in an old train station. Stylishly futuristic, orange interior. Serious about its music. Upstairs is **The Red Box** (☎478 0225), a huge, separate club with brain-crushing music and a crowd at the bar so deep it seems designed to winnow out the weak. Mellow train-station-turned-bar **Crawdaddy** hosts musical gigs, including some world stars. Cover €10-20; Th students €5; can rise fast when big-name DJs perform. Open until 3am on weekends.

▓ **Spirit,** 57 Middle Abbey St. (☎877 9999). Huge, popular club with a daunting queue on weekends. Each of the 4 fl. has its own name and musical vibe. "Mind" (basement level): the rock room, with music to match. "Soul" (ground fl.): main bar, with R&B, blindingly colorful lights and a medium-sized dance floor. "Body" (first floor): huge dance floor, and a giant egg-shaped fortress in the middle for the DJs to hatch pounding house music. The top floor, "Virtue," may be the coolest of all, but it's only for VIPs and clubbers with invisibility cloaks. Cover €10-20. Su gay night. Th €5 for students. Open Th-Su 10:30pm-3:30am. Occasional club nights during the week; call for details.

The Dragon, S. Great Georges St. (☎478 1590), a few doors down from The George. Opened in May 2005 as Dublin's newest gay club, although everyone is welcome. It's packed to its trendy rafters on weekend nights. Quieter lounge area in front gives way to a DJ spinning house by the dance floor in back. Massive sculpture of Hercules wrestling a snake floats above the crowd. 18+. Open M 5pm-2:30am, Tu-W 5-11:30pm, Th-Sa 5pm-2:30am, Su 5-11pm.

The Village, 26 Wexford St. (☎475 8555). Posh ground-floor bar. Occasional live music below a popular upstairs weekend club. Th-Sa bands play 7-10:30pm (about €20), then DJs spin chill-out, jungle, and house downstairs. Tickets for live bands available next door. Club F €7, Sa €9. Bar open until 1:30am; club open Th-Sa until 3am.

Traffic, 54 Middle Abbey St. (☎873 4038; www.traffic54.net). Nightly DJ spins hip hop, house, or techno for a young crowd from his throne at the end of the long bar. Flanking TVs flash images to accompany the music. M-Th and Su 2 cocktails for the price of 1; F-Sa they may seem like 1 for the price of 2. Rush-hour traffic jam awaits anyone venturing into the dark downstairs on weekends. 21+. Cover after 11pm Th €6, F-Sa €8-10. Open M-W 3-11:30pm, Th-Sa 3pm-2:30am, Su 3pm-midnight.

Club M, Blooms Hotel (☎671 5622), on Cope St. in Temple Bar. One of Dublin's largest clubs attracts a mixed crowd with multiple levels and bars. 18+ pushes the conversation closer to gym class than career moves. Cover M-Th €5, F-Sa €12-15. Free tickets often distributed in Temple Bar. Open M-Th 11pm-2:30am, F-Sa 10pm-2:30am.

The Mezz (The Hub), 21-25 Eustace St. (☎670 7655). Live bands rock nightly right inside the entrance of this low-ceilinged, atmospheric club—try not to knock over a drum set as you make your way toward the bar. Quiet pub by day transforms into a loud live-music cauldron at night. No cover. It shares the building with **The Hub,** which, as one of the only 18+ clubs in Temple Bar, attracts the younger crowd. Cover at The Hub €5-10. Open daily until 2:30am.

🎵 ENTERTAINMENT

Whether you seek poetry, punk, or something in between, Dublin is ready to entertain. The free *Event Guide* is available at music stores and hotels throughout the city. It comes out every other Friday and has decent listings. The glossier *In Dublin* (free at Tower Records) comes out every two weeks with feature articles and listings for music, theater, art exhibitions, comedy shows, clubs, museums, and movie theaters. *Events of the Week*—a much smaller free booklet—is jammed with ads but also has some good info. Hostel staffers are often reliable, if biased, sources of information. Go to www.visitdublin.com for the latest hotspots.

Abbey Theatre, 26 Lower Abbey St. (☎878 7222; www.abbeytheatre.ie). Founded by W.B. Yeats and Lady Gregory in 1904 to promote the Irish cultural revival and modernist theater, a combination that didn't go over well with audiences. The Abbey's 1907 premiere of J. M. Synge's *Playboy of the Western World* led to storms of protest. Today, the Abbey (and Synge) has gained respectability. Ireland's National Theatre is on the cutting edge of international drama. Tickets €15-30; Sa 2:30pm matinee €18, students and seniors with ID €14. Box office open M-Sa 10:30am-7pm.

Peacock Theatre, 26 Lower Abbey St. (☎878 7222). The Abbey's experimental downstairs studio theater. Evening shows, plus occasional lunchtime plays, concerts, and poetry. Doors open M-Sa at 7:30pm. Tickets €10-17; Sa 2:45pm matinees €12.50. Available at Abbey box office.

Gate Theatre, 1 Cavendish Row (☎874 4045; www.gate-theatre.ie). Contemporary Irish and classic international dramas in intimate, elegant setting. Wheelchair-accessible. Box office open M-Sa 10am-7:30pm. Tickets €16-30; M-Th student ticket at curtain €16 with ID, subject to availability.

🎪 FESTIVALS

Failte Ireland's annual *Calendar of Events* (€1.30) offers info on events throughout Ireland, including Dublin's many festivals, antique and craft fairs, flower marts, horse shows, and the like. The biweekly *Events Guide* or *weekly indublin* (free in stores) are also good sources.

BLOOMSDAY. James Joyce's Dublin comes alive each year on June 16, the date of protagonist Leopold Bloom's 18hr. journey in the famed *Ulysses.* Festivities are held all week leading up to the big day and culminate on the 16th with a slate of events ranging from reenactments to concerts to guided tours of many of the Dublin spots mentioned in the book. The James Joyce Cultural Centre (p. 714) sponsors a reenactment of the funeral and wake, a lunch at Davy Byrne's, and a Guinness breakfast, among other activities. *(Call ☎ 280 9265 for info.)*

THE DUBLIN FILM FESTIVAL. Nearly two weeks of Irish and international movies are screened at all of the major cinematic venues throughout the city, including UGC, the Savoy, and the Screen, with a panoply of seminars in tow. *(From early to mid-Mar. ☎ 661 6216; www.dubliniff.com.)*

GAZE: THE DUBLIN INTERNATIONAL LESBIAN AND GAY FILM FESTIVAL. Over 15 years celebrating GLBT on the big screen, the festival hosts a weeks worth of screenings at the IFI, which showcases the best in gay and lesbian film. *(First week in August. www.gaze.ie. Tickets €8-20.)*

STREET PERFORMANCE WORLD CHAMPIONSHIP. Buskers battle it out on the street for the world title while onlookers search their pockets for spare coins. The competition lasts three days and is free. *(Mid-June. ☎ 639 4850; www.spwc.ie.)*

APPENDIX

CLIMATE

Avg. Temp. (lo/hi), Precipitation	January			April			July			October		
	°C	°F	mm	°C	°F	mm	°C	°F	mm	°C	°F	mm
London	2/7	36/45	79	4/12	39/54	53	11/22	52/72	46	6/15	43/59	74
Cardiff	2/7	36/45	91	4/12	39/54	56	12/20	54/68	74	8/14	46/57	97
Edinburgh	1/6	34/43	57	3/11	37/52	41	10/18	50/65	56	6/13	43/55	66
Belfast	1/7	34/45	87	3/12	37/54	53	11/18	52/65	64	7/13	45/55	89

2008 BANK HOLIDAYS

Government agencies, post offices, and banks are closed on the following days. Businesses, if not closed, may have shorter hours. Transportation in rural areas grinds to a halt, and congestion in urban areas worsens significantly. Holiday destinations are usually open.

DATE	HOLIDAY	AREAS
Jan. 1	New Year's Day	UK
Jan. 2	2nd January	Scotland
Mar. 17	St. Patrick's Day (Celebration Day)	Northern Ireland
Mar. 21	Good Friday	UK
Mar. 24	Easter Monday	UK except Scotland
May 5	May Day Bank Holiday	UK
May 26	Spring Bank Holiday	UK
July 14	Battle of the Boyne (Orangemen's Day)	Northern Ireland
Aug. 4	Summer Bank Holiday	Scotland
Aug. 25	Summer Bank Holiday	UK except Scotland
Dec. 1	St. Andrew's Day	Scotland
Dec. 25	Christmas Day	UK
Dec. 26	Boxing Day/St. Stephen's Day	UK

MEASUREMENTS

Britain uses the metric system, although its longtime conversion to the metric system is still in progress—road signs indicate distances in miles. Gallons in the US and those across the Atlantic are not identical: one US gallon equals 0.83 Imperial gallons. Pub aficionados will note that an Imperial pint (20 oz.) is larger than its US counterpart (16 oz.). Below is a list of Imperial units and their metric equivalents.

MEASUREMENT CONVERSIONS	
1 inch (in.) = 25.4mm	1 millimeter (mm) = 0.039 in.
1 foot (ft.) = 0.30m	1 meter (m) = 3.28 ft.
1 yard (yd.) = 0.914m	1 meter (m) = 1.09 yd.

MEASUREMENT CONVERSIONS

1 mile (mi.) = 1.6109km	1 kilometer (km) = 0.62 mi.
1 ounce (oz.) = 28.35g	1 gram (g) = 0.035 oz.
1 pound (lb.) = 0.454kg	1 kilogram (kg) = 2.205 lb.
1 fluid ounce (fl. oz.) = 29.57mL	1 milliliter (mL) = 0.034 fl. oz.
1 UK gallon (gal.) = 4.546L	1 liter (L) = 0.264 gal.
1 square mile (sq. mi.) = 2.59km²	1 square kilometer (km²) = 0.386 sq. mi.

LANGUAGE

The widespread use of English has given rise to countless variations and slang terms. Below is a list of British words that travelers are most likely to encounter.

BRITISH ENGLISH	AMERICAN ENGLISH	BRITISH ENGLISH	AMERICAN ENGLISH
aubergine	eggplant	give a bollocking to	shout at
bap	a soft bun	grotty	grungy
barmy	insane, erratic	high street	main street
bed-sit, or bed sitter	studio apartment	hire	rental, to rent
beer mat	coaster	holiday	vacation
biro	ballpoint pen	hoover	vacuum cleaner
biscuit	a cookie or cracker	ice-lolly	popsicle
bonnet	car hood	interval	intermission
boot	car trunk	in a street	"on" a street
braces	suspenders	jam	jelly
brilliant, brill	awesome, cool	jelly	Jell-O
camp/campy	effeminate	jumper	sweater
caravan	trailer, mobile home	kip	sleep, nap
car park	parking lot	kit	sports team uniform
cheeky	mischievous	knackered	tired, worn out
cheerio	goodbye	knickers	underwear
cheers	thank you	lavatory, lav	restroom
chemist/chemist's	pharmacist/pharmacy	lay-by	roadside turnout
chips	french fries	legless	intoxicated
chuffed	pleased	lemonade	lemon soda
coach	intercity bus	let	to rent
concession	discount on admission	lift	elevator
courgette	zucchini	loo	restroom
crisps	potato chips	lorry	truck
dear	expensive	mashed	extremely intoxicated
dicey, dodgy	sketchy	mate	pal
the dog's bollocks	the best	minger	an ugly person
dual carriageway	divided highway	motorway	highway
dustbin	trash can	naff	unfashionable
ensuite	with attached bathroom	nosh	food
fag	cigarette	pants	underwear
fanny	vagina	petrol	gasoline
first floor	second floor	pissed	drunk
fortnight	two weeks	plaster	Band-Aid

BRITISH ENGLISH	AMERICAN ENGLISH	BRITISH ENGLISH	AMERICAN ENGLISH
full stop	period (punctuation)	prat	stupid person
get knocked up	get woken up	geezer	adult male
pull	to hit on, seduce	sweet(s)	candy
public school	private school	swish	swanky
punter	average person	take the piss out of	to make fun of
queue up, queue	to line up	toilet	restroom
quid	pound (in money)	torch	flashlight
roundabout	rotary road intersection	tosser	term of abuse; see prat
rubber	eraser, condom	trainers	sneakers
self-catering	with kitchen facilities	trousers	pants
self-drive	car rental	twat	idiot, vagina
serviette	napkin	vest	undershirt
a shag, to shag	sex, to have sex	waistcoat (weskit)	men's vest
single carriageway	non-divided highway	wanker	masturbator; see prat
sod it	forget it	way out	exit
snogging	making out	W.C. (water closet)	toilet, restroom
pudding	dessert	zed	the letter Z

BRITISH PRONUNCIATION

Berkeley	BARK-lee	Magdalen	MAUD-lin
Berkshire	BARK-sher	Norwich	NOR-ich
Birmingham	BIRM-ing-um	Salisbury	SAULS-bree
Derby	DAR-bee	Shrewsbury	SHROWS-bree
Dulwich	DULL-idge	Southwark	SUTH-uk
Edinburgh	ED-in-bur-ra	Thames	TEMS
Gloucester	GLOS-ter	Woolwich	WOOL-ich
Greenwich	GREN-ich	Worcester	WOO-ster
Hertfordshire	HART-ford-sher	gaol	JAIL
Grosvenor	GROV-nor	quay	KEY
Leicester	LES-ter	scones	SKONS

WELSH WORDS AND PHRASES

Consult **Language**, p. 452, for the basic rules of Welsh pronunciation. Listed below are a number of words and phrases you may encounter on the road. Note that the pronunciation of these words may vary depending on regional dialect.

WORD/PHRASE	PRONUNCIATION	MEANING
allan	ahl-LAN	exit
ar agor	ahr AG-or	open
ar gau	ahr GUY	closed
bore da	boh-re DAH	good morning, hello
cariad	CARRY-ad	darling
croeso	CROY-so	welcome
Cymorth!	CUH-morth!	Help!
diolch	dee-OLCH	thank you
dw i'n dy garu di	doo een duh GARee dee	I love you
dwn i ddim	dun ee thim	I don't know
dwr	doorr	water

WORD/PHRASE	PRONUNCIATION	MEANING
dydd da	DEETH dah	good day
Fy eny yw	vu E-noo you	My name is...
Ga i peint o cwrw?	gah-ee PAINT oh coo-roo?	Can I have a pint of beer?
gwerin	GUEH-rin	men
hwyl/hwyl fawr	huh-will/huh-will vour	goodbye
ia	eeah	yes
iawn	eeawn	well, fine
lechyd da	YE-chid dah	cheers
llwybr cyhoeddus	hlooee-BIR cuh-HOY-this	public footpath
merched	mehrch-ED	women
na, nage	nah, nah-GE	no
nos da	nos dah	good night
noswaith dda	nos-WAYTHE tha	good evening
os gwelwch yn dda	ohs gwell–OOCH uhn tha	please
perygl	pehr-UHGL	danger
preifat	PRAY-vat	private
safle'r bws	savlehr boos	bus stop
siaradwch yn araf	sha-RA-dooch un arav	speak more slowly
stryd Fawr	streed VOUR	High street

IRISH WORDS AND PHRASES

You may come across the following words and phrases in your travels in Northern Ireland. Spelling conventions almost never match English pronunciations: "mh" sounds like "v," and "dh" sounds like a soft "g."

WORD/PHRASE	PRONUNCIATION	MEANING
an Lár	on lahr	city center
Conas tá tú?	CUNN-us thaw too?	How are you?
Dia dhuit	JEE-a dich	Good day, hello
dia's Muire dhuit	JEE-as MWUR-a dich	reply to "good day"
Éire	AIR-uh	Ireland; official name of the Republic of Ireland
fáilte	FAWLT-cha	welcome
go raibh maith agat	guh roh moh UG-ut	thank you
ní hea	nee hah	no (literally, "it is not")
oíche mhaith dhuit	EE-ha woh ditch	good night
Oifig an Phoist	UFF-ig un fwisht	Post Office
sea	shah	yes
sláinte	SLAWN-che	cheers, to your health
slán agat	slawn UG-ut	goodbye
sraid	shrawd	street
Tá mé are meisce.	taw may air mesh-keh	I am very drunk.
Tá tu go halainn.	taw two guh haul-inn	You are beautiful.

SCOTTISH GAELIC WORDS AND PHRASES

Consult **Language**, p. 526, for information on Scottish Gaelic. Listed below are a number of words and phrases you may encounter on the road.

WORD/PHRASE	PRONUNCIATION	MEANING
allt	ALT	stream
An toir thu dhomh pòg?	Un TUH-r oo ghawnh pawk?	Will you give me a kiss?

WORD/PHRASE	PRONUNCIATION	MEANING
baile	BAL-eh	town
beinn	BEN	mountain
Ciamar a tha sibh?	KI-mer a HA shiv?	How are you?
De an t-ainm a th'oirbh?	JAY an TEN-im a HO-riv?	What's your name?
Failte gu...	FAL-chuh goo	Welcome to...
gleann	GLAY-ahn	valley
Gle mhath	GLAY va	very well
Gabh mo leisgeul	GAV mo LESH-kul	excuse me
Is mise...	ISH MISH-uh	My name is...
Latha ma	LA-huh MA	good day
ionad	EE-nud	place, visitor center
Madainn mhath	MA-ting VA	good morning
Oidhche mhath	a-HOY-chuh VA	good night
rathad	RAH-hud	road
Slàinte mhòr agad!	SLAHN-tchuh! VORR AH-kut!	Cheers! Good health to you!
sraid	SRAHJ	street
Tapadh leibh	TA-pa LEEV	Thank you
Tha gaol agam ort.	Hah GEUL AH-kum orsht.	I love you.
Tha gu math	HA gu MA	I'm fine

SCOTS WORDS AND PHRASES

Consult **Language,** p. 526, for more info on Scots, a distinct dialect of English. Listed below are a few of the many Scots words and phrases used in standard Scottish English and their pronunciation, if applicable.

WORD/PHRASE	MEANING	WORD/PHRASE	MEANING
aye	yes	kirk	church
ben	mountain	lad	man, boy
blether, or guid blether	talk idly, chat (good BLA-ther)	lass	woman, girl
breeks	pants	nae	no (NAY)
bonnie	beautiful	nicht	night
brae	hill near water (BRAY)	sassenach	Lowlander (SAS-uh-nach)
braw	bright, strong, great	strath	broad valley
burn	stream	tatty	potato
cannae	cannot (CAN-eye)	thane	minor noble
eejit	idiot	tipple	a drink
gye	very	weegie	Glaswegian (WEE-gee)

INDEX

A

Abbey Road 125
abbeys
  Anglesey 325
  Bath 196
  Battle 157
  Buckland 225
  Dryburgh 550
  Egglestone 429
  Glastonbury 207
  Greyabbey 699, 700
  Hexham 446
  Holyrood 540
  Inchcolm 547
  Iona 605
  Jedburgh 551
  Kelso 552
  Kirkstall 408
  Lewes Priory 167
  Lindisfarne Priory 443
  Llanthony Priory 471
  Melrose 549
  Newstead 311
  Penmon Priory 514
  St. Augustine's 148
  St. Edmund 337
  St. Mary's 401
  Shrewsbury 305
  Strata Florida 491
  Sweetheart 556
  Tewkesbury 285
  Tintern 464
  Valle Crucis 501
  Westminster 110
  Whitby 422
Abbotsford 550
Aberdaron 518
Aberdeen 606
Aberfoyle 594
Abergavenny 470
Aberystwyth 487
accommodation types 45
Achiltibuie 654
Achnasheen 652
aerogrammes 44
AIDS. See sexually transmitted
  infections.
airplane travel
  courier 29
  fares 27
  standby 30
airports
  Aberdeen 608
  Ards 700
  Belfast City 676

Belfast International 676
Dublin 703
Edinburgh International 529
Eglinton/Derry 688
Gatwick 89
Glasgow 563
Heathrow 89
Inverness 619
Luton 89
Man, Isle of 384
Manchester 353
Prestwick 563
Stansted 89
Sumburgh 666
Uists 646
Alfriston 160
Alnwick 441
Alum Bay 179
Amberley 161
Ambleside 372, 376
American Express. See credit
  cards.
An Óige 47
Anglesey, Isle of 513
Anstruther (Fife) 581
Antrim 687
Aonach Mor 628
Applecross 651
Apsley House 119
Arisaig 631
Armadale 635
Arnol 643
Arran, Isle of 560
Arundel 168
Ashbourne 365
Ashburton 223
Assynt 655
ATM cards 17
au pair work 65
Audley End 325
Austen, Jane 78, 110, 179,
  182, 184, 192, 196
Avebury 69, 192
Ayr 559
Ayrshire 559–560
Aysgarth Falls 411

B

Bakewell 365, 369
Balloch 594
Ballycastle 693
Balquhidder 593
Bangor 511
bank holidays 87, 720
Bank of England Museum 128

Banksy 82
Bannockburn 592
Barbican Hall 133
Bardon Mill 445
Bardsey Island 518
Barnard Castle. See castles.
Barra 649
Bath 69, 192
Battle 157
battles
  Agincourt 70
  Bannockburn 523, 592
  Boyne 674
  Britain 73
  Culloden 524, 623
  Hastings 70, 156, 157
  Killiecrankie 589
beaches
  Abererch 518
  Big Strand 600
  Bournemouth 210
  Camasunary 636
  Dalmore 644
  Falmouth 242
  Fistral 239
  Goodwick 486
  Gower Peninsula 474
  Llandudno 497
  Newquay 239
  Padstow 237
  Pembrokeshire Coast 480
  Pleasure (Blackpool) 362
  Porth Oer 518
  Portsmouth 231
  Rhossili 475
  St. Ives 250
  Tenby 482
  Thurso 656
  Torquay 227
Bealach na Ba (Cattle) Pass 651
Beamish Open Air Museum 429
The Beatles 82, 131, 349, 353
Beaumaris 515
Becket, St. Thomas à 145, 148,
  182, 268, 485
beer 77
Belfast 676
Bellingham 440
Ben Macdui 616
Ben Nevis 625
Ben-y-Vrackie 589
Berneray 641, 648
Berwick-upon-Tweed 442
Betws-y-Coed 498
Beyond Tourism 58–67
Big Pit National Mining Museum.

See Blaenavon.
biking. See cycling.
Birmingham 297
Birnam 584
Bishop's Palace 205
Black Death 70
Black Mountains 469
Blackmoor Gate 220
Blackpool 359
Blaenavon 471
Blair, Tony. See Prime Ministers.
Blaneau Ffestiniog 501
Blenheim Palace 274
Bloody Sunday 675
Bloomsbury Group 79, 151
Boat-of-Garten 614
Bodmin 233
Bodmin Moor 232
Boggle Hole 418
Bonnie Prince Charlie 71, 382,
   524, 542, 550, 623, 630,
   664
The Borders 548
Borrowdale 372, 381
Boscastle 235
Bournemouth 209
Bourton-on-the-Water 289
Bovey Tracey 223
Bowmore 600
Bowness 375
Bowness Bay 372
Braemar 612
Brecon 471
Brecon Beacons. See National
   Parks.
Bressay 670
Brighton 161
Bristol 198
British Broadcasting Corporation
   (BBC) 85
British Council 62, 64
British Library 115
British Museum 127
BritRail Passes 33
Broad Haven 479
Broadmeadows 548
Broadway 290
Brockhole 372
Brodick 561
Brontë sisters 78, 405, 421
Brown, "Capability" 274, 296,
   307
Brown, Gordon. See Prime
   Ministers.
Brundell 336
Buckfastleigh 223
BUNAC 66
Burghley House 307
Buriton 161
Burns, Robert 526, 527, 540,
   554, 555

Burpham 161
Bury St. Edmunds 337
buses 34
Bushmills 693
Butt of Lewis 644
Buxton 365, 368
Byron, Lord 79, 311, 322

C

Cabinet War Rooms 131
Cader Idris 505
Caernarfon 509
Cairngorm Mountains. See
   National Parks.
Cairnyan 558
Caldey Island 483
Caledonian MacBrayne
   (CalMac) 38, 522
Calf of Man 390
Callanish Stones 643
Cambridge 317
Cambridgeshire 317–328
Camelot 232
campers 52
camping 51
Canna, Isle of 640
Cannel Tunnel (Chunnel) 31
Canterbury 69, 145
Canterbury Cathedral. See
   cathedrals.
Cardiff 455
Cardiff Castle. See castles.
Carlisle 382, 445
Carloway 643
Carroll, Lewis 80, 268, 421,
   497
cars
   assistance 38
   driving in the UK 37
   driving permits 36
   insurance 36
   rental 35
Castle Douglas (Dumfries) 556
Castlebay 649
castles
   Abergavenny 470
   Aberystwyth 490
   Alnwick 441
   Amhuinnsuidhe 644
   Arundel 169
   Balfour 663
   Balhousie 584
   Balmoral 613
   Bamburgh 444
   Barnard 429
   Beaumaris 515
   Belfast 682
   Berkeley 292
   Berwick 442
   of the Bishops of Llandaff 462

Blair 589
Bolton 415
Brodick 561
Caerlaverock 555
Caernarfon 70, 510
Caerphilly 462
Canterbury 150
Cardiff 459
Carew 483
Carisbrooke 179
Carlisle 383
Cawdor 623
Chillingham 441
Coch 462
Colchester 338
Conwy 495
Corfe 210
Cornet 255
Craigmillar 541
Crathes 612
Culzean 559
Danby 425
Deal 156
Dinas Bran (Crow) 500
Dolbadarn 509
Doune 592
Dover 154
Drogo 225
Drum 612
Drumlanrig 556
Duart 603
Dublin 712
Dunluce 692
Dunnottar 611
Dunollie 598
Dunrobin 623
Dunskey 558
Dunster 221
Duntulm 637
Dunvegan 637
Dunyveg 599
Durham 428
Edinburgh 537
Floors 552
Fyvie 612
Gylen 598
Harlech 506
Hastings 156
Helmsley 424
Howard 401
Inveraray 596
Inverness 622
Kinloch 639
Kisimul 650
Leeds 151
Lewes 167
Lewis 642
Lincoln 315
Lindisfarne 443
Lochranza 562

MacLellan 557
Maiden 213
Manorbier 483
Maol 634
Mont Orgueil 254
Muness 671
Neidpath 550
Newcastle 434
Noltland 664
Norwich 334
Nottingham 310
Oxford 270
Oystermouth 474
Peel 389
Pembroke 484
Pendennis 242
Penrhyn 512
Peveril 368
Pickering 423
Portaferry 702
Raby 429
Raglan 471
Rising 330
St. Andrews 580
St. Mawes 242
St. Michael's Mount 247
Scalloway 669
Scarborough 421
Scone Palace 584
Shrewsbury 305
Skipton 413
Southsea 176
Stirling 591
Sudeley 289
Thirlestane 550
Threave 556
Tintagel 234
Torosay 603
Urquhart 624
Walmer 156
Warkworth 441
Warwick 295
Winchester 183
Windsor 261
Wolvesey 183
York 400
castles (glossary) 80
Castleton 365, 367
cathedrals
Arundel 169
Brecon 472
Bristol 203
Canterbury 148
Carlisle 383
Chester 344
Chichester 171
Christ Church 713
Christ Church (Oxford) 268
Dunkeld 585
Durham 427

Elgin 617
Ely 327
Exeter 216
Glasgow 569
Hereford 293
Lincoln 315
Liverpool 349
Llandaff 462
Metropolitan (Liverpool) 350
Newcastle 434
Norwich 334
St. Alban's 259
St. Andrews 580
St. Anne's 682
St. Bride's 118
St. Clement Danes 118
St. Columb's 691
St. David's 485
St. Deiniol's 513
St. Edmundsbury 337
St. Giles 539
St. Magnus 660
St. Martin-in-the-Fields 121
St. Patrick's 713
St. Paul's 111
Salisbury 190
Southwark 120
Wells 205
Westminster 122
Winchester 182
Worcester 281
York Minster 399
cathedrals (glossary) 80
Causeway Coast 693
ceilidhs 527
cell phones. See telephones.
Celts 69, 450
Centers for Disease Control
   (CDC) 24
Central Scotland 576–605
Central Skye 635
Cerne Abbas 212
Channel Islands 252
Channel Tunnel (Chunnel) 152
Charles, Prince of Wales 75,
   126, 330, 509
Chatsworth House 370
Chaucer, Geoffrey 78, 110,
   145, 169
Chawton 184
Cheddar 205
Chedworth 291
Cheltenham 281
Chester 339
Cheviot Hills 441
Chichester 169
Chipping Campden 291
Churchill, Winston. See Prime
   Ministers.
Cirencester 291

Cirrus 17
Cley-next-the-Sea 331
climate 720
Clovelly 231
Cockermouth 372
Cocking 161
Colchester 338
Coldingham 548
colleges and universities
   Cambridge 63, 321
   Edinburgh 63, 535
   Eton College 261
   Glasgow 63, 567, 571
   Leeds 63
   London School of Economics 63
   Oxford 63, 262
   Queen's University (Belfast) 63,
      681
   Sabhal Mor Ostaig 635
   St. Andrews 63, 581
   Stirling 590
   Strathclyde 567
   Trinity College 710
   Ulster 63
   Univ. College London 63, 115
Colsterworth 308
Coniston 373, 377
consulates 10
Conwy 493
Corbridge 445
Cornwall 232–251
Corrieshalloch Gorge 654
The Cotswolds 286
Coventry 296
Cowes 177
Craighouse 601
Craignure 603
Craig-y-nos 468
Crail (Fife) 581
Craven Arms 306
credit cards 17
Cregneash 388
cricket 86, 125
Crickhowell 469
Cromer 330, 336
Cromwell, Oliver 71, 182, 270,
   327, 424, 524
crown jewels. See Tower of
   London.
Cuillin Hills 635
Culloden 623
Cumbria 371–383
currency exchange 15
Cushendall 694
Cushendun 693, 696
customs 15
cycling
   Arran 561
   Borderloop 549
   Camel Trail 236
   Coast & Castles 438

Cumbria Cycle Way 375
Dartmoor 225
Dumfries and Galloway 554
Four Abbeys 549
Great Glen Cycle Route 624
Hadrian's Cycleway 446
Isle of Man 385
Lake District 375
Loch Lomond 595
North York Moors 420
Peak District 366
Pennine Cycleway 438
Reivers Cycle Route 438
Saints' Way 236
Snowdonia 503, 505
South Downs Way 158
Swansea Bikepath 473
Tarka Trail 220, 224
Tweed Cycleway 549
Wight 179
Yorkshire Dales 412

D

Danby 418, 425
Dartmoor National Park. See National Parks.
Darwin, Charles 304, 322
Deal 155
debit cards 17
Derry. See Londonderry.
Derwentwater 373
Devil's Bridge 491
Devon 214–232
Diana, Princess of Wales 75, 119
Dickens, Charles 78, 429
dietary concerns 56
  halal foods 56
  kosher foods 56
  vegetarian and vegan foods 56
disabled travelers 54
Discover Britain 1–4
diseases
  food- and water-borne 25
  insect-borne 25
  other 26
distilleries 528
  Ardbeg 599
  Ardberg 600
  Arran 562
  Ben Nevis 627
  Blair Athol 588
  Bowmore 600, 601
  Bruichladdich 601
  Bunnahabhainn 601
  Bushmills 693
  Caol Ila 601
  Dewar's 587
  Edradour 588
  Glenfiddich 618

Glenlivet 618
Highland Park 660
Jura 601
Lagavulin 599, 600
Laphroaig 599, 601
Oban 598
Old Jameson 715
Strathisla 618
Talisker 636
Tobermory 603
Dolgellau 504
Dorchester 211
Dorset Coast 209
Douglas 386
Dover 152
Drake, Sir Francis 225, 230, 323
driving permits. See cars.
drugs 20
Drumnadrochit 624
Dublin 703–719
  accommodations 707
  entertainment 718
  festivals 718
  food 709
  intercity transportation 703
  local transportation 706
  nightlife 717
  orientation 706
  practical information 706
  pubs 716
  sights 710
Dufton 403
Dumfries 554
Dumfries and Galloway 553–559
Dunkeld 584
Dunster 221
Durham 425
Durness 655
duty. See customs.

E

Earby 403
East Anglia 316–338
Eastbourne 160
Eastwood 312
ecotourism 52
Edale 365, 402
Eday 664
Eden Project 243
Edinburgh 529
Eigg, Isle of 639
eisteddfod 454
Elgin 617
Elgol 636
Elie 582
Eliot, T.S. 79
Elizabeth I. See queens.

Elizabeth II. See queens.
Ely 326
email. See Internet.
embassies 10
emergency medical services 26
England 69–87
  art 80
  culture and customs 77
  festivals 87
  film 84
  food 76
  history 69
  literature 78
  music 82
  sports 85
English breakfast 76
English Civil War 71, 268, 310, 524
entrance requirements 10
Eriskay 648
Esk Valley 416, 425
Essentials 10–57
Eton 260
Eurail Pass 34
euro 15, 15
European Economic Area (EEA) 65
European Union 12, 15
Excalibur 185, 233
exchange rates. See currency exchange.
Exeter 214
Exmoor National Park. See National Parks.
Eyam 366

F

Fairholmes 365
Falmouth 240
farming abroad 66
Federal Express 45
Felixstowe 317
ferries 31, 38
festivals
  Arundel 169
  Balloon Fiesta (Bristol) 204
  Bath 198
  Battle of Flowers 256
  Beatles Convention 351
  Birmingham Jazz 301
  Bloomsday 718
  Bournemouth 211
  Braemar Gathering 613
  Brecon Jazz 473
  Brighton 167
  Brighton Pride 167
  Bristol 203
  Bury 337
  Cambridge 325
  Cambridge Shakespeare 324

Canterbury 151
Capital of Culture (Liverpool) 351
Cheltenham 284
Chester 345
Chichester Festivities 171
Cotswold Olympic Games 291
Crail 581
Creative Peninsula 700
Cycling (Wight) 179
Durham Regatta 429
Dylan Thomas 477
Edinburgh Fringe 528, 546
Edinburgh International 528, 546
Edinburgh Jazz 547
Eights Week 273
Eisteddfod (Llangollen) 501
English Surf Championships 240
Exeter 217
Flower Show (Shrewsbury) 306
Gaze 719
Glasgow Jazz 575
Glastonbury 208
Golowan 248
Gourmet Glasgow 575
Gower 475
Guy Fawks Night Carnival 208
Hat Fair 184
Hay 465
Heart of the Glens 696
Hebridean Celtic 643
Highland Ceilidh 633
Highland Games 604, 623, 633
Highland Nights 589
Hogmanay 528, 546
Homelands Music Festival 183
Illuminations 362
King's Lynn 329
Lady Godiva 296
Lincoln Early Music 315
Machynlleth 493
Isle of Man 386
Manchester 359
May Week (Cambridge) 324
Mendelssohn 604
Mull Music 604
National Eisteddfod 454
National Fireworks Championship 231
Norfolk and Norwich 336
Oxford 273
Oyster (Falmouth) 243
Plymouth Navy Days 231
Robin Hood 312
Run to the Sun 240
Salisbury International Arts 191
Sheep Racing 256
Shetland 667

Shrewsbury Art 306
Speed (Goodwood) 172
Sports Week 697
Stamford Shakespeare 307
Stour Music 151
Stratford 279
Swansea 477
Tennerfest 254
Up Helly Aa 528, 667, 671
Walking (Wight) 179
West End (Glasgow) 575
Whitby Folk 423
York Early Music 401
Fforest Fawr 469
Fife Seaside 581
Fishbourne (Isle of Wight) 172
Fishbourne Roman Palace 171
Fishguard 485
Foot and Mouth Disease. See diseases.
football 85
  Belfast 687
  Everton 350
  Liverpool 350
  Manchester United 86, 358
  Newcastle United 437
Forres 617
Fort William 625
Fortingall 587
Foula 672

G

Gaelic (Irish) 723
Gaelic (Scottish) 526, 723
Gairloch 652
Galashiels 548
Garenin 641
Gatwick. See airports.
Gearrannan Village 643
Giant's Causeway 692
Glasgow 563
Glastonbury 206
GLBT travelers 54
Glen Coe 628
Glenfinnan 524, 630
Glenmore 614
Glenridding 381
Glens of Antrim 694–697
Globe Theatre. See Shakespeare's Globe Theatre.
Goathland 418
golf 528
  Barra 650
  British Golf Museum 581
  Elie 582
  Old Course, St. Andrews 580
Good Friday Agreement 74, 673, 675
Goodwood 172
Gower Peninsula 473

grail. See Holy Grail.
Grampian Coast 611
Grantchester 325
Grantham 307
Grantown 614
Grasmere 374, 378
Grassholm Island 480
Grassington 410, 414
Great Ayton 418
The Great Glen 618–630
Great Langdale Valley 377
Great Yarmouth 336
Green Park 122
Greenhead 403, 445
Greyabbey 700
Grinton 412
Guernsey 254
Guildhall 116
Guisborough 418

H

Haddon Hall 370
Hadrian 382, 444, 523
Hadrian's Wall 382, 444
haggis 528
halal foods. See dietary concerns.
Haltwhistle 445
Hampshire 172–184
Hampstead Heath 124
Hampton Court Palace 144
Hardy, Thomas 211, 212
Harlech 505
Harris, Isle of 644
Harrods 137
Harry Potter 80, 268, 424, 441, 536, 625, 627
Harwich 317
Hastings 156
Hatfield House 259
Hathersage 366
Haverfordwest 478
Hawes 403, 410, 415
Hawkshead 374, 378
Haworth 403, 405
Haydon Bridge 445
Hay-on-Wye 464
Haytor 222
health 24
Heart of England 257–293
Heathrow. See airports.
Hebden Bridge 404
Helmsley 416, 424
Helvellyn 381
Henry VIII. See kings.
Hepstonstall 404
Hereford 292
Herm 256
Hexham 446
High Kirk of St. Giles. See

cathedrals.
Highland Games 528
Highlands and Islands
606–672
hiking equipment 51
hiking trails. See walking trails.
hitchhiking 39
Holland Park 119
Holmes, Sherlock 225
Holy Grail 185, 547
Holy Island 443
Holyhead 515
Holyroodhouse 540
Home Office 65
horseracing 87
Horton in Ribblesdale 415
Hostelling International. See
  Youth Hostels Association
  (YHA).
Houghton Hall 330
Houses of Parliament 114
Howmore 641
Hoy 663
Hunstanton 330
Hyde Park 118

I

identification 13
Ilfracombe 221
immunizations 23
Imperial War Museum 129
Industrial Revolution 72, 451
Ingleton 412, 415
Ingram 438
Inner Hebrides 632–640
insurance 23, 36
International Driving Permit (IDP)
  36
Internet 39
Inveraray 596
Inverness 618
Iona, Isle of 604
Irish Republican Army (IRA) 74,
  675
Ironbridge 301
Islay, Isle of 598

J

Jacobite Rebellion 383, 524,
  526, 589, 630
Jarlshof 669
Jedburgh 551
Jersey 252
John O'Groats 657
Joyce, James 79, 714, 716,
  718
Jura, Isle of 601
Jurassic Coast 210

K

Keats, John 183
Keld 403, 413
Kelso 552
Kendoon 554
Kensington Gardens 118
Kensington Palace 119
Kent 145–156
Kerrera 598
Keswick 372, 379
Kettlewell 413
Kew Gardens. See Royal
  Botanical Gardens, Kew.
Kewick 374
Kielder Water 440
Killin 586
kilts 526
Kincraig 614
Kinder Scout 366
King's College Chapel
  (Cambridge) 321
King's Lynn 328
kings
  Alexander III 523
  Alfred the Great 69, 179, 183,
    269
  Arthur 183, 185, 208, 232,
    234, 450, 453, 466, 493,
    549
  Charles I 179, 261, 268, 310,
    524
  Charles II 71, 179, 524, 584
  David I 523, 540, 551
  Edgar 196
  Edward I 70, 451, 487, 515,
    523, 555
  Edward II 85, 330, 550
  Æthelbert of Kent 69, 149
  George III 261, 281, 570
  George IV 161, 164
  Harold II 70, 156, 157
  Henry I 334
  Henry II 70, 145, 262
  Henry V 70, 172
  Henry VI 70, 261, 321
  Henry VII 451, 484
  Henry VIII 70, 148, 156, 167,
    175, 176, 183, 240, 242,
    261, 289, 322
  James I 693
  James I (James IV) 523, 524
  James II 71, 524, 552, 690
  James V 523
  John 70, 281, 292, 337
  Macbeth 584
  Offa of Mercia 450
  Richard II 70, 495
  Robert the Bruce 382, 523,
    549, 554, 563, 584, 592
  William III (William of Orange)

  71, 524, 690
  William the Conqueror 69, 145,
    156, 157, 179, 183, 184,
    214, 261, 270, 450
Kingston 161
Kirk Yetholm 548
Kirkby Stephen 413
Kirkcudbright 557
Kirkwall 658
kosher foods. See dietary
  concerns.
Kyle of Lochalsh 633
Kyleakin 633

L

Labour Party 72
Lairig Ghru 616
Lake District National Park. See
  National Parks.
Lamb Holm 665
Lamlash 562
Land's End 251
Langdon Beck 403
Laugharne 483
Lavenham 337
Leeds 72, 406
Legoland 262
Leith 541
Lennon, John 352
Lerwick 668
Leuchars 576
Leverburgh 645
Lewes 161, 167
Lewis, C.S. 80, 262, 271, 323
Lewis, Isle of 641
Leyburn 410
Libanus 466
Linby 311
Lincoln 312
Linton 410
Littleton Down 161
Liverpool 345
Lizard Peninsula 244
Llanberis 507
Llandovery 468
Llandudno 496
Llanfair P.G. 514
Llangadog 468
Llangollen 499
Llwyn-y-Celyn 468
Llyn Peninsula 516
Llywelyn ap Gruffydd 450
Loch Lomond and The
  Trossachs. See National Parks.
Lochinver 655
Lochranza 562
lochs
  an Eilein 616
  an t-Sailein 599
  Coriusk 636

Fyne 596
Insh 614
Linnhe 625
Lomond 594
Morar 631
Morlich 614
Ness 623
Rannoch 589
Shiel 630
Sligachan 636
Tarbet 601
Tay 586
Tommel 589
Torridon 652
Lockton 418
London 88–144
    accommodations 98
    entertainment 132
    food 103
    intercity transportation 89
    local transportation 95
    museums and galleries 126
    nightlife 139
    orientation 92
    practical information 97
    shopping 137
    sights 109
    theater 135
London Eye 121
London Zoo. See zoos.
Londonderry 688
Long Melford 338
Looe 231
Luton. See airports.
Lyme Regis 213
Lyndhurst 184
Lynton 220

M

Macbeth 585, 623
MacGregor, Rob Roy 550, 593
Machynlleth 451, 491
Mad Cow Disease. See
    diseases.
Madame Tussaud's 120
Magna Carta 70, 190, 292, 337
Maidstone 151
mail 44
Malhamdale 403, 410, 415
Mallaig 631
Malt Whisky Trail 618
Man, Isle of 384
Manchester 72, 353
Mankinholes 403
Manorbier 479
Marching Season 673, 675,
    684
Marks & Spencer 409
Marloes Sands 479
Mary, Queen of Scots. See

queens.
MasterCard. See credit cards.
Matlock 365
Matlock Bath 365
May Week. See festivals.
medical assistance 24
Melrose 549
metric system 720
The Midlands 294–315
Milford Haven 479
Milton, John 78, 285, 322
Minack Theatre 248
Minehead 220
Minginish Peninsula 636
Mingulay 651
Minigaff 554
minority travelers 55
Monty Python 85, 324, 592
Monument 116
Moreton-in-Marsh 290
Mount Snowdon. See Snowdon.
Mousa 670
Muck, Isle of 639
Mull of Galloway 558
Mull, Isle of 602
Mumbles 473
Museum of London 128

N

National Express 34
National Gallery (Dublin) 712
National Gallery (London) 126
National Gallery (Scotland) 542
National Health Service (NHS)
    26
National Parks
    Brecon Beacons 466
    Cairngorm Mountains 613
    Dartmoor 221
    Exmoor 217
    Lake District 371
    Loch Lomond and the Trossachs
        592
    Norfolk Broads 336
    North York Moors 416
    Northumberland 437
    Peak District 362
    Pembrokeshire Coast 478
    Snowdonia 501
    South Downs Way 157
    Yorkshire Dales 410
National Portrait Gallery
    (London) 127
National Theatre 136
Nelson, (Admiral Lord) Horatio
    175, 541
New Forest 184
Newbridge 223
Newcastle-upon-Tyne 430
Newport (Isle of Wight) 177

Newport (Wales) 478
Newquay 237
Newton, Sir Isaac 71, 307, 322
Newtownards 697
Norfolk 328–336
Norfolk Broads National Park.
    See National Parks.
North Ronaldsay 665
North Wales 487–519
North York Moors. See National
    Parks.
Northeast England 392–
    447
Northeast Scotland 606–618
Northern Ireland 673–702
Northern Norfolk Coast 330
Northmavine 670
Northumberland 437–444
Northumberland National Park.
    See National Parks.
Northwest England 339–
    390
Northwest Highlands 651–657
Norwich 331
Noss 670
Nottingham 308

O

Oban 596
Okehampton 223
Old Sarum 192
Once Brewed 403, 445
Orkney Craft Trail 663
Orkney Islands 657
Orwell, George 79, 601
Osborne House 179
Osmotherley 419
Ostaig 635
Out Skerries 672
outdoors 49
Outer Hebrides 640–651
Oxenholme 371
Oxford 262
Oxwich 473

P

Padstow 235
Papa Stour 672
Papa Westray 665
Parliament
    Cardiff 452
    Early English 70
    Great Britain 114
    Isle of Man 384
    London 74
    Scottish 523, 525, 540
Parracombe 220
Pass of Killiecrankie 589
passports 12

Patterdale 374, 381
Peak District National Park. See National Parks.
Peebles 550
Peel 389
Pembroke 483
Pembrokeshire Coast National Park. See National Parks.
Pennine Way. See walking trails.
Penrith 382
Penwith Peninsula 250
Pen-y-Fan 468
Penzance 244
Perth 582
Petworth House 169
phones. See telephones.
Photographers' Gallery 130
Pickering 423
Picts 523
Pitlochry 587
Plockton 651
Plymouth 227
police 20
polo 87
Polperro 231
Porlock 220
Port Ellen 599
Port Erin 389
Port Eynon 473
Portaferry 701
Porthcurno 248
Porthmadog 517
Portree 637
Portsmouth 172
postal service. See mail.
Postbridge 223
postbuses 522
poste restante 45
Potter, Beatrix 376, 378, 585
Prime Meridian 125
Prime Ministers
  Blair, Tony 73, 75, 124, 675
  Brown, Gordon 75, 124
  Churchill, Winston 73, 156, 274, 662
  George, David Lloyd 451
  Thatcher, Margaret 73, 307
  Walpole, Robert 330
Prince Charles. See Charles, Prince of Wales.
Princess Diana. See Diana, Princess of Wales.
Princetown 223
priories. See abbeys.
pubs 77
punting 324
Pwll Deri 479
Pwllheli 518
Pyecombe 161

Q

queens
  Boudicca 338
  Elizabeth I 70, 260, 269, 524, 690
  Elizabeth II 75, 171, 261, 509, 540, 685
  Mary, Queen of Scots 71, 110, 70, 260, 261, 368, 382, 523, 541, 550, 552, 580, 581, 591
  Victoria 72, 164, 176, 179, 261
quidditch 87

R

rabies. See diseases.
railways
  Brecon Mountain 469
  Electric Cliff 490
  Esk Valley Line 416, 425
  Ffestiniog 502, 517
  Llanberis Lake 508
  Llangollen 501
  Mull 603
  narrow-gauge 448
  North Yorkshire Moors 416, 424
  Snowdon Mountain 507, 508
  Vale of Rheidol 491
  Volk's 165
  Welsh Highland 517
  West Coast 625
  West Highland 627, 630
Ramsey Island 480, 485
Ranworth 336
Ravenstor 366
Red Cross 24
Reeth 411
Regent's Park 119
renting a car. See cars.
Rhenigidale 641
Rhins of Galloway 557
Rhossili 473
Ring of Brodgar 662
Road to the Isles 630
Rob Roy. See MacGregor, Rob Roy.
Robin Hood 311
Robin Hood's Bay 416, 423
Rodel 645
Rodmell 161
Roslin 547
Rosslyn. See Roslin.
Rosthwaite 381
Rothbury 440
Rousay 664
Royal Academy of Arts 130

Royal Botanical Gardens, Kew 143
Royal Courts of Justice 118
Royal Deeside 611
Royal Mail 45
Royal Shakespeare Company 84, 279, 437
rugby 86
Rum, Isle of 639
RVs. See campers.
Ryde 172, 177

S

safety 20, 22, 673
Saffron Walden 325
St. Albans 69, 257
St. Andrews 576
St. David's 484
St. Helier 253
St. Ives 248
St. James's Palace 122
St. Just 251
St. Martin-in-the-Fields. See cathedrals.
St. Mawes 242
St. Ninian's Isle 671
St. Paul's Cathedral. See cathedrals.
St. Paul's Church 121
St. Peter Port 255
Salisbury 187
Sanday 664
Sandown 177
Sandringham 330
Sandy Row 685
Sark 256
Saundersfoot 479
Scafell Pike 381
Scalloway 669
Scalpay 644
Scapa Flow 662
Scarborough 416, 420
Science Museum (London) 129
Scone Palace 584
Scotland 520–528
  culture and customs 525
  food 527
  history 523
  literature 526
  music 527
  sports 528
  transportation 520
Scots (language) 526
Scott, Sir Walter 383, 427, 501, 527, 539, 541, 548, 550, 570
Scottish Citylink 34, 520
Scottish Tourist Board 520, 522
Scottish Youth Hostels

Association (SYHA) 47
Scrabster 656
Seatoller 381
Sedbergh 411
self defense 23
Sennen Cove 251
Seven Years' War 71
sexually transmitted infections
  26
Shakespeare, William 69, 110,
  155, 274, 441, 452
Shakespeare's Globe Theatre
  120, 136
Shankill 685
Shanklin 177
Shapinsay 663
Sheffield 392
Sheringham 330
Sherwood Forest 312
Shetland Islands 666
Shrewsbury 303
Sinn Féin 74, 675, 684
Sinnington 419
Sissinghurst Castle Garden 151
Skara Brae 662
Skipton 410, 413
Skomer Island 480
Skye, Isle of 632
The Slaughters 290
Sleat Peninsula 635
Slimbridge 292
Small Isles (Hebrides) 638
Mt. Snowdon 507
Snowdonia National Park. See
  National Parks.
Soho 122
solo travelers 53
Somerset and Avon 192–214
South Downs Way. See National
  Parks.
South England 145–184
South Pennines 403
South Queensferry 547
South Ronaldsay 665
South Wales 455–486
Southease 160
Southern Scotland 529–
  575
Southsea 174
Southwark Cathedral. See
  cathedrals.
Southwest England 185–
  256
St. James's Park 122
Staffa 604, 605
Staffin 637
Stamford 306
Stansted. See airports.
Stenness 662
Stirling 589
STIs. See sexually transmitted

infections.
Stone of Destiny. See Stone of
  Scone.
Stone of Scone 525, 537, 584
Stonehenge 69, 190, 191
Stornoway 641
Stourhead 191
Stow-on-the-Wold 290
Stranraer 557
Stratford-upon-Avon 274
Strath 653
Stromness 661
Stronsay 664
Strumpshaw 336
student visas 65
study abroad 61
Sudbury 337
Suffolk and Essex 337–338
Summer Isles 654
Sussex 156–??
Sutton Bank 418
Swaledale 415
Swansea 475

T

Tarbert 644
Tate Gallery
  Britain (London) 128
  Liverpool 349
  Modern (London) 126
  St. Ives 249
Tavistock 223
taxes 19
teaching abroad 64
telephones 41
  cell phones 43
  GSM 44
  pay-as-you-go 44
  top-up cards 44
Telford 302
The Temple 117
Tenby 481
tennis 86
Tennyson, Alfred Lord 79, 179,
  322
Tewkesbury 285
Thatcher, Margaret. See Prime
  Ministers.
The Falls 684
Thomas Cook 16
Thomas, Dylan 453, 476, 483
Thurso 656
Tintagel 234
Tintern 463
Tintern Abbey. See abbeys.
tipping 18
Tobermory 603
Tolkien, J.R.R. 80, 269, 271
Tomintoul 618
Torquay 226

Torridon 652
Totland Bay 178
Tourist Offices 11
Tower Bridge 116
Tower Knowe 438
Tower of London 110
Trafalgar Square 121
trains 32
Traquair House 551
travel agencies 28
traveler's checks 16
Traveline 32, 448, 520
Tremadog 517
Treshnish Isles 604, 605
Trossachs. See National Parks.
Trotternish Peninsula 637
TT Races (Isle of Man) 87, 386
Tube. See Underground.
Tyne and Wear 430–437

U

Uig 638
The Uists 646
Ullapool 653
Ullswater 372, 381
Ulster 674
Ulster Folk Museum 687
Ulsterbus 35
Underground 96
universities. See colleges and
  universities.
Unst 671
Upper Beeding 161

V

vaccinations. See
  immunizations.
Vale of Conwy 493
value added tax (VAT) 15, 19
Vatersay 650
vegetarian and vegan travelers.
  See dietary concerns.
Ventnor 177
Victoria and Albert Museum 127
Victoria. See queens.
Visa. See credit cards.
visas 13, 62, 65
VisitBritain 11
volunteering 58

W

Wales 448–454
  art 453
  culture and customs 452
  festivals 454
  food 454
  history 450
  language 452

literature 453
music 453
transportation 448
Wales Tourist Board 450
walking tours
Millennium Mile 112–113
walking trails
Abergavenny 471
Ben Nevis 628
Brecon Beacons 468
The Cairngorms 616
Calderdale Way 404
Cateran 586
Coast to Coast 412, 419
Cock of Arran 561
Cotswolds 289
Dales Way 412
Dartmoor Way 224
Devon Coast to Coast 225
Forty Acre Lane 161
Glen Coe 630
Goatfell 561
Great Glen Way 628
Hadrian's Wall National Trail 446
Isle of Man 386
Kinnoull Hill Woodland Park 584
Lake District 374
Land's End-John O'Groats 232
Mull 602
North York Moors 419
Offa's Dyke Path 450, 463
Peddar's Way 317, 330
Pembrokeshire Coast Path 450, 480
Pennine Way 366, 402, 411, 439
Royal Forest of Dean 463
St. Cuthbert's Way 439, 548
Saints' Way 236
Severn Way 289
South Downs Way 157
South West Coast Path 187
Southern Upland Way 522, 548, 554
Speyside Way 618
Tarka Trail 220, 224
The Trossachs 593
West Highland Way 522, 628

Wordsworth Walk 379
Worth Way 404
Wye Valley Walk 463
Wallace, William 523, 589, 591, 611
War of the Roses 70, 259, 285
Warkworth 441
Warwick 294
Warwick Castle. See castles.
Weald and Downland Open Air Museum 171
weather. See climate.
Wellington Arch 119
Wellington, Duke of 119, 156
Wells 204
Wells-next-the-Sea 330
Welsh (language) 722
Wensleydale 415
Wessex 212
Western Arran 563
Western Union 18
Westminster Abbey. See abbeys.
Westminster Cathedral. See cathedrals.
Westray 664
Whalsay 672
Wharfedale 414
whisky 528, 600
See also distilleries.
Whitby 421
Whitehall 122
Whiting Bay 562
Wight, Isle of 172, 176
Wilde, Oscar 269, 710, 714
William the Conqueror. See kings.
William, Prince of Wales 76
Wilmington 160
Wilton House 192
Wiltshire 187–192
Wimbledon 86, 126
Winchcombe 289
Winchester 179
Winchester Cathedral. See cathedrals.
Windermere 374, 375
Windsor 260
Windsor Castle. See castles.
wiring money 18

women travelers 53
Wookey Hole 206
Wooler 441
Woolf, Virginia 79, 161, 167, 248
Woolsthorpe Manor 308
Worcester 279
Wordsworth, William 79, 378, 464, 501
work permits 13, 65
working abroad 63
Wren, Christopher 81, 111, 116, 117, 118, 119, 125, 144, 171, 269, 270, 315, 323
Wroxham 336
Wye Valley 292, 463

Y

Yarmouth 177
Yell 670
York 395
York Minster. See cathedrals.
Yorkshire 392–425
Yorkshire Dales. See National Parks.
Youlgreave 366
Youth Hostels Association (YHA) 47
Yr Wyddfa. See Snowdon.
Ystradfellte 469

Z

Zennor 250
zoos
Belfast 683
Chester 344
Dublin 715
Edinburgh 542
London

MAP INDEX

Aberdeen 608
Aberystwyth 490
Bath 193
Belfast 677
Birmingham 298
Brecon Beacons National
  Park 467
Brighton 163
Bristol 199
Britain xiv-xv
  Chapters xvi
Cambridge 319
Canterbury 149
Cardiff 459
Central Scotland 577
Cheltenham 282
Chester 343
The Cotswolds 287
Dartmoor National Park 222
Dover 153
Dublin 704-705
Durham 427
East Anglia 316
Edinburgh 532-533
  Royal Mile 538
Exeter 215
Exmoor National Park 219
Falmouth 241

Glasgow 565
  Byres Road 573
Heart of England 258
Highlands and Islands 607
Inverness 619
Isle of Man 385
Lake District National
  Park 373
Leeds 407
Lincoln 313
Liverpool 347
Loch Lomond and The Tros-
  sachs National Park 593
London 90-91
  West End 123
  Westminster 124
Manchester 355
The Midlands 295
Newcastle-upon-Tyne 431
North Wales 489
North York Moors National
  Park 417
Northeast England 393
Northern Ireland 674
Northumberland National
  Park 439
Northwest England 340
Norwich 333

Nottingham 309
Orkney Islands 659
Oxford 264-265
  Pub Crawl 272
Peak District National Park 363
Penzance 245
Plymouth 228
Portsmouth 173
Salisbury 188
Scotland 521
Sheffield 394
Shetland Islands 667
Snowdonia 502
South Downs Way 158-159
South England 146
South Wales 456
Southern Scotland 530
Southwest England 186
St. Andrews 579
Stirling 590
Stratford-upon-Avon 275
Swansea 477
Wales 449
Winchester 181
York 397
Yorkshire Dales National
  Park 411

MAP LEGEND

Symbol	Description	Symbol	Description	Symbol	Description
✈	Airport	🏨	Hotel/Hostel	▲ 0-3280 ft. ▲ 3280-6560 ft. ▲ >6560 ft.	Mountain
✚	Hospital	🚌	Bus Station	▲	Camping
✪	Police	🚉	Train Station	🍴	Restaurant
✉	Post Office	⊖	London Tube Station	★	Nightlife/Clubs
ⓘ	Tourist Information Centre	U M	Subway Station		Nightlife/Pubs
🄸	National Park Information Centre	TAXI	Taxi Stand		Theatre
$	Bank	⚲	Beach	🏛	Museum
℞	Pharmacy	🕆	Church/Cathedral		Mountain Pass
▪	Site or Point of Interest	⊓	Gate/Entrance		Observatory
⚑	Embassy or Consulate		Ship/Submarine	∫	Waterfall
📖	Library		Wildlife Reserve	∧	Cave
💻	Internet Cafe		Surfing	🗼	Lighthouse
P	Parking	⚑	Stone Monument		Pedestrian Zone
⚓	Ferry Route/Landing		Castle		Stairs

Mountain Range
Contour Lines
Tunnel
Footpaths/Trails
Railroads
Park
Beach
Water
Buildings
City Walls

The Let's Go compass always points N O R T H.